# Collins *Gem*

# French
# Dictionary

# Collins *Gem*

# French Dictionary

French ▶ English   English ▶ French

**DICTIONNAIRES LE ROBERT**

## Collins Gem
*An Imprint of HarperCollinsPublishers*

**seventh edition 2003**

© William Collins Sons & Co. Ltd. 1979, 1988
© HarperCollins Publishers 1993, 1997, 2000, 2001, 2003

HarperCollins Publishers
Westerhill Road, Bishopbriggs, Glasgow G64 2QT
Great Britain

**www.collinsdictionaries.com**

Collins Gem® and Bank of English® are registered
trademarks of HarperCollins Publishers Limited

ISBN 0-00-715594-8

*contributors*
Jean-François Allain, Sabine Citron
Catherine Love, Joyce Littlejohn
John Podbielski

*based on the first edition by*
**Pierre-Henri Cousin**
Renée Birks, Elizabeth Campbell, Hélène Lewis
Claude Nimmo, Phillipe Patry
Lorna Sinclair Knight

Dictionnaires Le Robert
27, rue de la Glacière, 75013 Paris

ISBN 2-85036-891-1
Dépôt légal janvier 2003
Achevé d'imprimer novembre 2002

A catalogue record for this book is
available from the British Library

Typeset by Morton Word Processing Ltd, Scarborough
Printed and bound in Great Britain by Charles Letts & Company Ltd

# TABLE DES MATIÈRES

# CONTENTS

## les marques déposées

## Note on trademarks

# INTRODUCTION

Nous sommes très heureux que vous ayez décidé d'acheter ce dictionnaire et espérons que vous aimerez l'utiliser et que vous en tirerez profit au lycée, à la maison, en vacances ou au travail.

Cette introduction a pour but de vous donner quelques conseils sur la meilleure façon d'utiliser au mieux votre dictionnaire, en vous référant non seulement à son importante nomenclature mais aussi aux informations contenues dans chaque entrée. Ceci vous aidera à lire et à comprendre, mais aussi à communiquer et à vous exprimer en anglais contemporain.

Le dictionnaire commence par la liste des abréviations utilisées dans le texte et par la transcription des sons par des symboles phonétiques. À la fin vous trouverez des tables de verbes français ainsi que la liste des verbes irréguliers en anglais, suivis d'une section finale sur les nombres et sur les expressions de temps.

## COMMENT UTILISER VOTRE DICTIONNAIRE

Ce dictionnaire offre une masse d'informations et use de divers formes et tailles de caractères, symboles, abréviations, parenthèses et crochets. Les conventions et symboles utilisés sont expliqués dans les sections qui suivent.

### Entrées

Les mots que vous cherchez dans le dictionnaire (les 'entrées') sont classés par ordre alphabétique. Ils sont imprimés en **caractères gras** pour pouvoir être repérés rapidement. Les deux entrées figurant en haut de page indiquent le premier et le dernier mot qui apparaissent sur la page en question.

Les informations sur l'usage ou sur la forme de certaines entrées sont données entre parenthèses, après la transcription phonétique. Ces indications apparaissent sous forme abrégée et en italiques (ex (*fam*), (*COMM*)).

Dans les cas appropriés, les mots apparentés aux entrées sont regroupés sous la même entrée (**ronger, rongeur; accept,**

**acceptance**) et apparaissent en caractères gras, légèrement plus petits que ceux de l'entrée.

Les expressions courantes dans lesquelles apparaît l'entrée sont indiquées par des caractères romains gras différents (ex **avoir du retard**).

## Transcription phonétique

La transcription phonétique de chaque entrée (indiquant sa prononciation) est indiquée entre crochets immédiatement après l'entrée (ex **fumer** [fyme]; **knead** [ni:d]). Une liste de ces symboles figure à la page xiv.

## Traductions

Les traductions des entrées apparaissent en caractères ordinaires et, lorsque plusieurs sens ou usages coexistent, ces traductions sont séparées par un point-virgule. Vous trouverez souvent entre parenthèses d'autres mots en italiques qui précèdent les traductions. Ces mots fournissent souvent certains des contextes dans lesquels l'entrée est susceptible d'être utilisée (ex **rough** (*voice*) ou (*weather*)) ou offrent des synonymes (ex **rough** (*violent*)).

## 'Mots-clés'

Une importance particulière est accordée à certains mots français et anglais qui sont considérés comme des "mots-clés" dans chacune des langues. Cela peut être dû à leur utilisation très fréquente ou au fait qu'ils ont divers types d'usages (ex **vouloir plus**; **get, that**). Une combinaison de losanges et de chiffres vous aident à distinguer différentes catégories grammaticales et différents sens. D'autres renseignements utiles apparaissent en italiques et entre parenthèses dans la langue de l'utilisateur.

## Données grammaticales

Les catégories grammaticales sont données sous forme abrégée et en italiques après la transcription phonétique des entrées (ex *vt, adv, conj*).

Les genres des noms français sont indiqués de la manière suivante: *nm* pour un nom masculin et *nf* pour un nom féminin. Le féminin et le pluriel irréguliers de certains noms sont également indiqués (**directeur, -trice; cheval, -aux**).

masculin et le féminin des adjectif sont indiqués lorsque ces ~~eux~~ ux formes sont différentes (ex **noir, e**). Lorsque l'adjectif a un ~~minin~~ ninin ou un pluriel irrégulier, ces formes sont clairement indiquées (ex **net, nette**). Les pluriels irréguliers des noms, et les formes irréguliers des verbes anglais sont indiqués entre parenthèses, ~~ant~~ avant la catégorie grammaticale (ex **man** ... (*pl* **men**) *n*; **give** (*pt* ~~ve~~ **give**, *pp* **given**) *vt*).

# INTRODUCTION

We are delighted you have decided to buy this dictionary a
hope you will enjoy and benefit from using it at school, at hom
on holiday or at work.

This introduction gives you a few tips on how to get the most o
of your dictionary — not simply from its comprehensive wordli
but also from the information provided in each entry. This w
help you to read and understand modern French, as well
communicate and express yourself in the language.

The dictionary begins by listing the abbreviations used in the te
and illustrating the sounds shown by the phonetic symbols. Ye
will find French verb tables and English irregular verbs at th
back, followed by a final section on numbers and time expre
sions.

## USING YOUR DICTIONARY

A wealth of information is presented in the dictionary, usi
various typefaces, sizes of type, symbols, abbreviations and brac
ets. The conventions and symbols used are explained in th
following sections.

### Headwords

The words you look up in a dictionary — "headwords" — a
listed alphabetically. They are printed in **bold type** for rap
identification. The two headwords appearing at the top of ea
page indicate the first and last word dealt with on the page
question.

Information about the usage or form of certain headwords
given in brackets after the phonetic spelling. This usually appe
in abbreviated form and in italics (e.g. (fam), (COMM)).

Where appropriate, words related to headwords are grouped
the same entry (**ronger, rongeur; accept, acceptance**) in a sligh
smaller bold type than the headword.

Common expressions in which the headword appears are show
in a different bold roman type (e.g. **avoir du retard**).

## onetic spellings

e phonetic spelling of each headword (indicating its pronuncia-
n) is given in square brackets immediately after the headword
g. **fumer** [fyme]; **knead** [ni:d]). A list of these symbols is given
page xiv.

## anslations

eadword translations are given in ordinary type and, where
ore than one meaning or usage exists, these are separated by a
mi-colon. You will often find other words in italics in brackets
fore the translations. These offer suggested contexts in which
e headword might appear (e.g. **rough** (*voice*) or (*weather*)) or
ovide synonyms (e.g. **rough** (*violent*)).

## ey" words

ecial status is given to certain French and English words which
e considered as "key" words in each language. They may, for
ample, occur very frequently or have several types of usage (e.g.
uloir, plus; get, that). A combination of lozenges and numbers
lps you to distinguish different parts of speech and different
eanings. Further helpful information is provided in brackets and
italics in the relevant language for the user.

## rammatical information

arts of speech are given in abbreviated form in italics after the
onetic spellings of headwords (e.g. *vt, adv, conj*).

enders of French nouns are indicated as follows: *nm* for a
asculine and *nf* for a feminine noun. Feminine and irregular
ural forms of nouns are also shown (**directeur, -trice; cheval,
ux**).

djectives are given in both masculine and feminine forms where
ese forms are different (e.g. **noir, e**). Clear information is
ovided where adjectives have an irregular feminine or plural
rm (e.g. **net, nette**).

# ABRÉVIATIONS

# ABBREVIATIONS

| | | |
|---|---|---|
| abréviation | ab(b)r | abbreviation |
| adjectif, locution adjective | adj | adjective, adjectival phrase |
| adverbe, locution adverbiale | adv | adverb, adverbial phrase |
| administration | ADMIN | administration |
| agriculture | AGR | agriculture |
| anatomie | ANAT | anatomy |
| architecture | ARCHIT | architecture |
| article défini | art déf | definite article |
| article indéfini | art indéf | indefinite article |
| l'automobile | AUT(O) | the motor car and motoring |
| aviation, voyages aériens | AVIAT | flying, air travel |
| biologie | BIO(L) | biology |
| botanique | BOT | botany |
| anglais de Grande-Bretagne | BRIT | British English |
| chimie | CHEM | chemistry |
| commerce, finance, banque | COMM | commerce, finance, banking |
| comparatif | compar | comparative |
| informatique | COMPUT | computing |
| conjonction | conj | conjunction |
| construction | CONSTR | building |
| nom utilisé comme adjectif | cpd | compound element |
| cuisine, art culinaire | CULIN | cookery |
| article défini | def art | definite article |
| déterminant: article; adjectif démonstratif ou indéfini etc | dét | determiner: article, demonstrative etc |
| diminutif | dimin | diminutive |
| économie | ECON | economics |
| électricité, électronique | ELEC | electricity, electronics |
| exclamation, interjection | excl | exclamation, interjection |
| féminin | f | feminine |
| langue familière (! emploi vulgaire) | fam (!) | colloquial usage (! particularly offensive) |
| emploi figuré | fig | figurative use |
| (verbe anglais) dont la particule est inséparable du verbe | fus | (phrasal verb) where the particle cannot be separated from main verb |
| généralement | gén, gen | generally |
| géographie, géologie | GEO | geography, geology |
| géométrie | GEOM | geometry |
| impersonnel | impers | impersonal |
| article indéfini | indef art | indefinite article |
| langue familière (! emploi vulgaire) | inf(!) | colloquial usage (! particularly offensive) |
| infinitif | infin | infinitive |
| informatique | INFORM | computing |
| invariable | inv | invariable |
| irrégulier | irrég, irreg | irregular |

# ABRÉVIATIONS

# ABBREVIATIONS

| | | |
|---|---|---|
| domaine juridique | **JUR** | law |
| grammaire, linguistique | **LING** | grammar, linguistics |
| masculin | **m** | masculine |
| mathématiques, algèbre | **MATH** | mathematics, calculus |
| médecine | **MÉD MED** | medical term, medicine |
| masculin ou féminin, suivant le sexe | **m/f** | masculine or feminine depending on sex |
| domaine militaire, armée | **MIL** | military matters |
| musique | **MUS** | music |
| nom | **n** | noun |
| navigation, nautisme | **NAVIG, NAUT** | sailing, navigation |
| adjectif ou nom numérique | **num** | numeral adjective or noun |
| | **o.s.** | oneself |
| péjoratif | **péj, pej** | derogatory, pejorative |
| photographie | **PHOT(O)** | photography |
| physiologie | **PHYSIOL** | physiology |
| pluriel | **pl** | plural |
| politique | **POL** | politics |
| participe passé | **pp** | past participle |
| préposition | **prép, prep** | preposition |
| pronom | **pron** | pronoun |
| psychologie, psychiatrie | **PSYCH** | psychology, psychiatry |
| temps du passé | **pt** | past tense |
| quelque chose | **qch** | |
| quelqu'un | **qn** | |
| religions, domaine ecclésiastique | **REL** | religions, church service |
| | **sb** | somebody |
| enseignement, système scolaire et universitaire | **SCOL** | schooling, schools and universities |
| singulier | **sg** | singular |
| | **sth** | something |
| subjonctif | **sub** | subjunctive |
| sujet (grammatical) | **su(b)j** | (grammatical) subject |
| superlatif | **superl** | superlative |
| techniques, technologie | **TECH** | technical term, technology |
| télécommunications | **TEL** | telecommunications |
| télévision | **TV** | television |
| typographie | **TYP(O)** | typography, printing |
| anglais des USA | **US** | American English |
| verbe (auxiliaire) | **vb (aux)** | (auxiliary) verb |
| verbe intransitif | **vi** | intransitive verb |
| verbe transitif | **vt** | transitive verb |
| zoologie | **ZOOL** | zoology |
| marque déposée | **®** | registered trademark |
| indique une équivalence culturelle | **≈** | introduces a cultural equivalent |

xiii

# TRANSCRIPTION PHONÉTIQUE

## CONSONNES

NB. **p, b, t, d, k, g** sont suivis d'une aspiration en anglais.

## CONSONANTS

NB. **p, b, t, d, k, g** are not aspirated in French.

| | | |
|---|---|---|
| *poupée* | p | *puppy* |
| *bombe* | b | *baby* |
| *tente thermal* | t | *tent* |
| *dinde* | d | *daddy* |
| *coq qui képi* | k | *cork kiss chord* |
| *gag bague* | g | *gag guess* |
| *sale ce nation* | s | *so rice kiss* |
| *zéro rose* | z | *cousin buzz* |
| *tache chat* | ʃ | *sheep sugar* |
| *gilet juge* | ʒ | *pleasure beige* |
| | tʃ | *church* |
| | dʒ | *judge general* |
| *fer phare* | f | *farm raffle* |
| *valve* | v | *very rev* |
| | θ | *thin maths* |
| | ð | *that other* |
| *lent salle* | l | *little ball* |
| *rare rentrer* | ʀ | |
| | r | *rat rare* |
| *maman femme* | m | *mummy comb* |
| *non nonne* | n | *no ran* |
| *agneau vigne* | ɲ | |
| | ŋ | *singing bank* |
| *hop!* | h | *hat reheat* |
| *yeux paille pied* | j | *yet* |
| *nouer oui* | w | *wall bewail* |
| *huile lui* | ɥ | |
| | x | *loch* |

## DIVERS

pour l'anglais: le r final se prononce en liaison devant une voyelle

pour l'anglais: précède la syllabe accentuée

## MISCELLANEOUS

ʳ   in French wordlist: no liaison

ˈ   in French transcription: no liaison

xiv

# PHONETIC TRANSCRIPTION

## VOYELLES

NB. La mise en équivalence de certains sons n'indique qu'une ressemblance approximative.

| | |
|---|---|
| ici vie lyre | i i: |
| | ɪ |
| jouer été | e |
| lait jouet merci | ɛ |
| plat amour | a æ |
| bas pâte | ɑ ɑ: |
| | ʌ |
| le premier | ə |
| beurre peur | œ |
| peu deux | ø ə: |
| or homme | ɔ |
| mot eau gauche | o ɔ: |
| genou roue | u |
| | u: |
| rue urne | y |

## VOWELS

NB. The pairing of some vowel sounds only indicates approximate equivalence.

| | |
|---|---|
| heel bead | |
| hit pity | |
| | |
| set tent | |
| bat apple | |
| after car calm | |
| fun cousin | |
| over above | |
| urn fern work | |
| wash pot | |
| born cork | |
| full soot | |
| boon lewd | |

## DIPHTONGUES

| | |
|---|---|
| | ɪə |
| | ɛə |
| | eɪ |
| | aɪ |
| | au |
| | əu |
| | ɔɪ |
| | uə |

## DIPHTHONGS

| | |
|---|---|
| beer tier | |
| tear fair there | |
| date plaice day | |
| life buy cry | |
| owl foul now | |
| low no | |
| boil boy oily | |
| poor tour | |

## NASALES

| | |
|---|---|
| matin plein | ɛ̃ |
| brun | œ̃ |
| sang an dans | ɑ̃ |
| non pont | ɔ̃ |

## NASAL VOWELS

# FRANÇAIS – ANGLAIS
# FRENCH – ENGLISH

## A, a

[a] *vb voir* **avoir**

MOT-CLÉ

**à** [a] (*à + le* = **au**, *à + les* = **aux**) *prép* **1** (*endroit, situation*) at, in; **être à Paris/au Portugal** to be in Paris/Portugal; **être à la maison/à l'école** to be at home/at school; **à la campagne** in the country; **c'est à 10 km/à 20 minutes (d'ici)** it's 10 km/20 minutes away

**2** (*direction*) to; **aller à Paris/au Portugal** to go to Paris/Portugal; **aller à la maison/à l'école** to go home/to school; **à la campagne** to the country

**3** (*temps*): **à 3 heures/minuit** at 3 o'clock/midnight; **au printemps/mois de juin** in the spring/the month of June

**4** (*attribution, appartenance*): **le livre est à Paul/à lui/à nous** this book is Paul's/his/ours; **donner qch à qn** to give sth to sb

**5** (*moyen*) with; **se chauffer au gaz** to have gas heating; **à bicyclette** on ou by bicycle; **à la main/machine** by hand/machine

**6** (*provenance*) from; **boire à la bouteille** to drink from the bottle

**7** (*caractérisation, manière*): **l'homme aux yeux bleus** the man with the blue eyes; **à la russe** the Russian way

**8** (*but, destination*): **tasse à café** coffee cup; **maison à vendre** house for sale

**9** (*rapport, évaluation, distribution*): **100 km/unités à l'heure** 100 km/units per an hour; **payé à l'heure** paid by the hour; **cinq à six** five to six

**abaisser** [abese] *vt* to lower, bring down; (*manette*) to pull down; **s'~** *vi* to go down; (*fig*) to demean o.s.

**abandon** [abɑ̃dɔ̃] *nm* abandoning; giving up; withdrawal; **être à l'~** to be in a state of neglect

**abandonner** [abɑ̃dɔne] *vt* (*personne*) to abandon; (*projet, activité*) to abandon, give up; (*SPORT*) to retire ou withdraw from; (*céder*) to surrender; **s'~ à** (*paresse, plaisirs*) to give o.s. up to

**abasourdir** [abazurdir] *vt* to stun, stagger

**abat-jour** [abaʒur] *nm inv* lampshade

**abats** [aba] *nmpl* (*de bœuf, porc*) offal *sg*; (*de volaille*) giblets

**abattement** [abatmɑ̃] *nm*: **~ fiscal** ≈ tax allowance

**abattoir** [abatwar] *nm* slaughterhouse

**abattre** [abatr] *vt* (*arbre*) to cut down, fell; (*mur, maison*) to pull down; (*avion, personne*) to shoot down; (*animal*) to shoot, kill; (*fig*) to wear out, tire out; to demoralize; **s'~** *vi* to crash down; **ne pas se laisser ~** to keep one's spirits up, not to let things get one down; **s'~ sur** to beat down on; (*fig*) to rain down on

**abbaye** [abei] *nf* abbey

**abbé** [abe] *nm* priest; (*d'une abbaye*) abbot

**abcès** [apsɛ] *nm* abscess

**abdiquer** [abdike] *vi* to abdicate

**abdominaux** [abdomino] *nmpl*: **faire des ~** to do exercises for one's abdominals, do one's abdominals

**abeille** [abɛj] *nf* bee

**aberrant, e** [aberɑ̃, ɑ̃t] *adj* absurd

**aberration** [aberasjɔ̃] *nf* aberration

**abêtir** [abetir] *vt* to make morons of (*ou* a moron of)

**abîme** [abim] *nm* abyss, gulf

**abîmer** [abime] *vt* to spoil, damage; **s'~** *vi* to get spoilt *ou* damaged

**ablation** [ablasjɔ̃] *nf* removal

**aboiement** [abwamɑ̃] *nm* bark, barking

**abois** [abwa] *nmpl*: **aux ~** at bay

**abolir** [abɔliʀ] *vt* to abolish

**abominable** [abɔminabl] *adj* abominable

**abondance** [abɔ̃dɑ̃s] *nf* abundance

**abondant, e** [abɔ̃dɑ̃, ɑ̃t] *adj* plentiful, abundant, copious; **abonder** *vi* to abound, be plentiful; **abonder dans le sens de qn** to concur with sb

**abonné, e** [abɔne] *nm/f* subscriber; season ticket holder

**abonnement** [abɔnmɑ̃] *nm* subscription; (*transports, concerts*) season ticket

**abonner** [abɔne] *vt*: **s'~ à** to subscribe to, take out a subscription to

**abord** [abɔʀ] *nm*: **au premier ~** at first sight, initially; **~s** *nmpl* (*environs*) surroundings; **d'~** first

**abordable** [abɔʀdabl] *adj* (*prix*) reasonable; (*personne*) approachable

**aborder** [abɔʀde] *vi* to land ♦ *vt* (*sujet, difficulté*) to tackle; (*personne*) to approach; (*rivage etc*) to reach

**aboutir** [abutiʀ] *vi* (*négociations etc*) to succeed; **~ à** to end up at; **n'~ à rien** to come to nothing

**aboyer** [abwaje] *vi* to bark

**abréger** [abʀeʒe] *vt* to shorten

**abreuver** [abʀœve]: **s'~** *vi* to drink; **abreuvoir** *nm* watering place

**abréviation** [abʀevjasjɔ̃] *nf* abbreviation

**abri** [abʀi] *nm* shelter; **être à l'~** to be under cover; **se mettre à l'~** to shelter

**abricot** [abʀiko] *nm* apricot

**abriter** [abʀite] *vt* to shelter; **s'~** *vt* to shelter, take cover

**abrupt, e** [abʀypt] *adj* sheer, steep; (*ton*) abrupt

**abruti, e** [abʀyti] *adj* stunned, dazed ♦

*nm/f* (*fam*) idiot, moron; **~ de travail** overworked

**absence** [apsɑ̃s] *nf* absence; (*MÉD*) blackout; **avoir des ~s** to have mental blanks

**absent, e** [apsɑ̃, ɑ̃t] *adj* absent ♦ *nm* absentee; **absenter: s'absenter** *vi* to take time off work; (*sortir*) to leave, go out

**absolu, e** [apsɔly] *adj* absolute; **absolument** *adv* absolutely

**absorbant, e** [apsɔʀbɑ̃, ɑ̃t] *adj* absorbent

**absorber** [apsɔʀbe] *vt* to absorb; (*gén MÉD: manger, boire*) to take

**abstenir** [apstəniʀ] *vb*: **s'~ de qch/de faire** to refrain from sth/from doing

**abstraction** [apstʀaksjɔ̃] *nf* abstraction

**abstrait, e** [apstʀɛ, ɛt] *adj* abstract

**absurde** [apsyʀd] *adj* absurd

**abus** [aby] *nm* abuse; **~ de confiance** breach of trust; **abuser** *vi* to go too far, overstep the mark; **abuser de** (*duper*) to take advantage of; **abusif, -ive** *adj* exorbitant; (*punition*) excessive

**acabit** [akabi] *nm*: **de cet ~** of that type

**académie** [akademi] *nf* academy; (*SCOL: circonscription*) ≈ regional education authority

Académie française

*The Académie française was founded by Cardinal Richelieu in 1635 during the reign of Louis XIII. It consists of forty elected scholars and writers who are known as "les Quarante" or "les Immortels". One of the Académie's functions is to regulate the development of the French language and its recommendations are frequently the subject of lively public debate. It has produced several editions of its famous dictionary and awards specific literary prizes.*

**acajou** [akaʒu] *nm* mahogany

**acariâtre** [akaʁjɑtʁ] *adj* cantankerous

**accablant, e** [akɑblɑ̃, ɑ̃t] *adj* (*chaleur*) oppressive; (*témoignage, preuve*) overwhelming

**accablement** [akɑbləmɑ̃] *nm* despondency

**accabler** [akɑble] *vt* to overwhelm, overcome; ~ **qn d'injures** to heap ou shower abuse on sb

**accalmie** [akalmi] *nf* lull

**accaparer** [akapaʁe] *vt* to monopolize; (*suj: travail etc*) to take up (all) the time *ou* attention of

**accéder** [aksede]: ~ **à** *vt* (*lieu*) to reach; (*accorder: requête*) to grant, accede to

**accélérateur** [akseleʁatœʁ] *nm* accelerator

**accélération** [akseleʁasjɔ̃] *nf* acceleration

**accélérer** [akseleʁe] *vt* to speed up ♦ *vi* to accelerate

**accent** [aksɑ̃] *nm* accent; (*PHONÉTIQUE, fig*) stress; **mettre l'~ sur** (*fig*) to stress; ~ **aigu/grave/circonflexe** acute/grave/circumflex accent; **accentuer** [aksɑ̃tɥe] *vt* (*LING*) to accent; (*fig*) to accentuate, emphasize; **s'accentuer** *vi* to become more marked *ou* pronounced

**acceptation** [aksɛptasjɔ̃] *nf* acceptance

**accepter** [aksɛpte] *vt* to accept; ~ **de faire** to agree to do

**accès** [aksɛ] *nm* (*à un lieu*) access; (*MÉD: de toux*) fit; (*: de fièvre*) bout; **d'~ facile** easily accessible; **facile d'~** easy to get to; ~ **de colère** fit of anger; **accessible** *adj* accessible; (*livre, sujet*): **accessible à qn** within the reach of sb

**accessoire** [aksɛswaʁ] *adj* secondary; incidental ♦ *nm* accessory; (*THÉÂTRE*) prop

**accident** [aksidɑ̃] *nm* accident; **par ~** by chance; ~ **de la route** road accident; ~ **du travail** industrial injury *ou* accident; **accidenté, e** *adj* damaged; injured; (*relief, terrain*) uneven; hilly; **accidentel, le** *adj* accidental

**acclamations** [aklamasjɔ̃] *nfpl* cheers

**acclamer** [aklame] *vt* to cheer, acclaim

**acclimater** [aklimate]: **s'~** *vi* (*personne*) to adapt (o.s.)

**accolade** [akɔlad] *nf* (*amicale*) embrace; (*signe*) brace

**accommodant, e** [akɔmɔdɑ̃, ɑ̃t] *adj* accommodating, easy-going

**accommoder** [akɔmɔde] *vt* (*CULIN*) to prepare; **s'~ de** *vt* to put up with; (*se contenter de*) to make do with

**accompagnateur, -trice** [akɔ̃paɲatœʁ, tʁis] *nm/f* (*MUS*) accompanist; (*de voyage: guide*) guide; (*de voyage organisé*) courier

**accompagner** [akɔ̃paɲe] *vt* to accompany, be *ou* come *ou* go with; (*MUS*) to accompany

**accompli, e** [akɔ̃pli] *adj* accomplished

**accomplir** [akɔ̃pliʁ] *vt* (*tâche, projet*) to carry out; (*souhait*) to fulfil; **s'~** *vi* to be fulfilled

**accord** [akɔʁ] *nm* agreement; (*entre du styles, tons etc*) harmony; (*MUS*) chord; **d'~!** OK!; **se mettre d'~** to come to an agreement; **être d'~ (pour faire qch)** to agree (to do sth)

**accordéon** [akɔʁdeɔ̃] *nm* (*MUS*) accordion

**accorder** [akɔʁde] *vt* (*faveur, délai*) to grant; (*harmoniser*) to match; (*MUS*) to tune; **s'~** *vt* to get on together; to agree

**accoster** [akɔste] *vt* (*NAVIG*) to draw alongside ♦ *vi* to berth

**accotement** [akɔtmɑ̃] *nm* verge (*BRIT*), shoulder

**accouchement** [akuʃmɑ̃] *nm* delivery, (child)birth; labour

**accoucher** [akuʃe] *vi* to give birth, have a baby; ~ **d'un garçon** to give birth to a boy; **accoucheur** *nm*: (**médecin**) **accoucheur** obstetrician

**accouder** [akude]: **s'~** *vi* to rest one's elbows on/against; **accoudoir** *nm* armrest

**accoupler** [akuple] *vt* to couple; (*pour*

**accourir**

la reproduction) to mate; **s'~** vt to mate

**accourir** [akuʀiʀ] vi to rush ou run up

**accoutrement** [akutʀəmã] (péj) nm (tenue) outfit

**accoutumance** [akutymãs] nf (gén) adaptation; (MÉD) addiction

**accoutumé, e** [akutyme] adj (habituel) customary, usual

**accoutumer** [akutyme] vt: **s'~ à** to get accustomed ou used to

**accréditer** [akʀedite] vt (nouvelle) to substantiate

**accroc** [akʀo] nm (déchirure) tear; (fig) hitch, snag

**accrochage** [akʀɔʃaʒ] nm (AUTO) collision; (dispute) clash, brush

**accrocher** [akʀɔʃe] vt (fig) to catch, attract; **s'~** (se disputer) to have a clash ou brush; **~ qch à** (suspendre) to hang sth (up) on; (attacher: remorque) to hitch sth (up) to; **~ qch** (à) (déchirer) to catch sth (on); **~ un passant** (heurter) to hit a pedestrian; **s'~ à** (rester pris à) to catch on; (agripper, fig) to hang on ou cling to

**accroissement** [akʀwasmã] nm increase

**accroître** [akʀwatʀ] **s'~** vi to increase

**accroupir** [akʀupiʀ] **s'~** vi to squat, crouch (down)

**accru, e** [akʀy] pp de **accroître**

**accueil** [akœj] nm welcome; **comité d'~** reception committee; **accueillir** vt to welcome; (aller chercher) to meet, collect

**acculer** [akyle] vt: **~ qn à** ou **contre** to drive sb back against

**accumuler** [akymyle] vt to accumulate, amass; **s'~** vi to accumulate; to pile up

**accusation** [akyzasjɔ̃] nf (gén) accusation; (JUR) charge; (partie): **l'~** the prosecution

**accusé, e** [akyze] nm/f accused; defendant; **~ de réception** acknowledgement of receipt

**accuser** [akyze] vt to accuse; (fig) to

---

emphasize, bring out; to show; **~ qn de** to accuse sb of; (JUR) to charge sb with; **~ réception de** to acknowledge receipt of

**acerbe** [asɛʀb] adj caustic, acid

**acéré, e** [aseʀe] adj sharp

**acharné, e** [aʃaʀne] adj (efforts) relentless; (lutte, adversaire) fierce, bitter

**acharner** [aʃaʀne] vb: **s'~ contre** to set o.s. against; (suj: malchance) to dog; **s'~ à faire** to try doggedly to do; (persister) to persist in doing

**achat** [aʃa] nm purchase; **faire des ~s** to do some shopping; **faire l'~ de qch** to purchase sth

**acheminer** [aʃ(ə)mine] vt (courrier) to forward, dispatch; **s'~ vers** to head for

**acheter** [aʃ(ə)te] vt to buy, purchase; (soudoyer) to buy; **~ qch à** (marchand) to buy ou purchase sth from; (ami etc: offrir) to buy sth for; **acheteur, -euse** nm/f buyer; shopper; (COMM) buyer

**achever** [aʃ(ə)ve] vt to complete, finish (blessé) to finish off; **s'~** vi to end

**acide** [asid] adj sour, sharp; (CHIMIE) acid(ic) ♦ nm (CHIMIE) acid; **acidulé, e** adj slightly acid

**acier** [asje] nm steel; **aciérie** nf steel works sg

**acné** [akne] nf acne

**acolyte** [akɔlit] (péj) nm associate

**acompte** [akɔ̃t] nm deposit

**à-côté** [akote] nm side-issue; (argent) extra

**à-coup** [aku] nm: **par ~~s** by fits and starts

**acoustique** [akustik] nf (d'une salle) acoustics pl

**acquéreur** [akeʀœʀ] nm buyer, purchaser

**acquérir** [akeʀiʀ] vt to acquire

**acquis, e** [aki, iz] pp de **acquérir** ♦ nm (accumulated) experience; **son acquis nous est ~e** we can count on her help

**acquit** [aki] vb voir **acquérir** ♦ nm (quittance) receipt; **par ~ de conscience** to set one's mind at rest

**acquitter** [akite] vt (JUR) to acquit; (facture) to pay, settle; **s'~ de** vt (devoir) to discharge; (promesse) to fulfil

**âcre** [akʀ] adj acrid, pungent

**acrobate** [akʀɔbat] nm/f acrobat; **acrobatie** nf acrobatics sg

**acte** [akt] nm act, action; (THÉÂTRE) act; **prendre ~ de** to note, take note of; **faire ~ de candidature** to apply; **faire ~ de présence** to put in an appearance; **~ de naissance** birth certificate

**acteur** [aktœʀ] nm actor

**actif, -ive** [aktif, iv] adj active ♦ nm (COMM) assets pl; (fig): **avoir à son ~** to have to one's credit; **population active** working population

**action** [aksjɔ̃] nf (gén) action; (COMM) share; **une bonne ~** a good deed; **actionnaire** nm/f shareholder; **actionner** vt (mécanisme) to activate; (machine) to operate

**activer** [aktive] vt to speed up; **s'~** vi to bustle about; to hurry up

**activité** [aktivite] nf activity; **en ~** (volcan) active; (fonctionnaire) in active life

**actrice** [aktʀis] nf actress

**actualiser** [aktɥalize] vt to bring up to date

**actualité** [aktɥalite] nf (d'un problème) topicality; (événements): **l'~** current events; **les ~s** nfpl (CINÉMA, TV) the news; **d'~** topical

**actuel, le** [aktɥɛl] adj (présent) present; (d'actualité) topical; **à l'heure ~le** at the present time; **actuellement** adv at present, at the present time

**acuité** [akɥite] nf acuteness

**acuponcteur** [akypɔ̃ktœʀ] nm acupuncturist

**acuponcture** [akypɔ̃ktyʀ] nf acupuncture

**adaptateur** [adaptatœʀ] nm (ÉLEC) adapter

**adapter** [adapte] vt to adapt; **s'~ (à)** (suj: personne) to adapt (to); **~ qch à** (approprier) to adapt sth to (fit); **~ qch sur/dans/à** (fixer) to fit sth on/into/to

**additif** [aditif] nm additive

**addition** [adisjɔ̃] nf addition; (au café) bill; **additionner** vt to add (up)

**adepte** [adɛpt] nm/f follower

**adéquat, e** [adekwa(t), at] adj appropriate, suitable

**adhérent, e** [adeʀɑ̃, ɑ̃t] nm/f member

**adhérer** [adeʀe]: **~ à** vt (coller) to adhere ou stick to; (se rallier à) to join; **adhésif, -ive** adj adhesive, sticky; **ruban adhésif** sticky ou adhesive tape; **adhésion** nf joining; (fait d'être membre) membership; (accord) support

**adieu, x** [adjø] excl goodbye ♦ nm farewell

**adjectif** [adʒɛktif] nm adjective

**adjoindre** [adʒwɛ̃dʀ] vt: **~ qch à** to attach sth to; (ajouter) to add sth to; **s'~** vt (collaborateur etc) to take on, appoint; **adjoint, e** nm/f assistant; **adjoint au maire** deputy mayor; **directeur adjoint** assistant manager

**adjudant** [adʒydɑ̃] nm (MIL) warrant officer

**adjuger** [adʒyʒe] vt (prix, récompense) to award; (lors d'une vente) to auction (off); **s'~** vt to take for o.s.

**adjurer** [adʒyʀe] vt: **~ qn de faire** to implore ou beg sb to do

**admettre** [admɛtʀ] vt (laisser entrer) to admit; (candidat: SCOL) to pass; (tolérer) to allow, accept; (reconnaître) to admit, acknowledge

**administrateur, -trice** [administʀatœʀ, tʀis] nm/f (COMM) director; (ADMIN) administrator

**administration** [administʀasjɔ̃] nf administration; **l'A~** ≈ the Civil Service

**administrer** [administʀe] vt (firme) to manage, run; (biens, remède, sacrement etc) to administer

**admirable** [admiʀabl] adj admirable, wonderful

**admirateur, -trice** [admiʀatœʀ, tʀis] nm/f admirer

**admiration** [admiʀasjɔ̃] nf admiration

**admirer** [admiʀe] vt to admire

**admis, e** [admi, iz] *pp de* **admettre**

**admissible** [admisibl] *adj* (*candidat*) eligible; (*comportement*) admissible, acceptable

**admission** [admisjɔ̃] *nf* admission; acknowledgement; **demande d'~** application for membership

**ADN** *sigle m* (= *acide désoxyribonucléique*) DNA

**adolescence** [adɔlesɑ̃s] *nf* adolescence

**adolescent, e** [adɔlesɑ̃, ɑ̃t] *nm/f* adolescent, teenager

**adonner** [adɔne]: **s'~ à** *vt* (*sport*) to devote o.s. to; (*boisson*) to give o.s. over to

**adopter** [adɔpte] *vt* to adopt; **adoptif, -ive** *adj* (*parents*) adoptive; (*fils, patrie*) adopted

**adorable** [adɔrabl] *adj* delightful, adorable

**adorer** [adɔre] *vt* to adore; (*REL*) to worship

**adosser** [adose] *vt*: **~ qch à** *ou* **contre** to stand sth against; **s'~ à** *ou* **contre** to lean with one's back against

**adoucir** [adusir] *vt* (*goût, température*) to make milder; (*avec du sucre*) to sweeten; (*peau, voix*) to soften; (*caractère*) to mellow

**adresse** [adrɛs] *nf* (*domicile*) address; (*dextérité*) skill, dexterity

**adresser** [adrese] *vt* (*lettre: expédier*) to send; (: *écrire l'adresse sur*) to address; (*injure, compliments*) to address; **s'~ à** (*parler à*) to speak to, address; (*s'informer auprès de*) to go and see; (: *bureau*) to enquire at; (*suj: livre, conseil*) to be aimed at; **~ la parole à** to speak to, address

**adroit, e** [adrwa, wat] *adj* skilful, skilled

**adulte** [adylt] *nm/f* adult, grown-up ♦ *adj* (*chien, arbre*) fully-grown, mature; (*attitude*) adult, grown-up

**adultère** [adyltɛr] *nm* (*acte*) adultery

**advenir** [advenir] *vi* to happen

**adverbe** [adverb] *nm* adverb

**adversaire** [adverser] *nm/f* (*SPORT, gén*) opponent, adversary

**adverse** [advers] *adj* opposing

**aération** [aerasjɔ̃] *nf* airing; (*circulation de l'air*) ventilation

**aérer** [aere] *vt* to air; (*fig*) to lighten; **s'~** *vi* to get some (fresh) air

**aérien, ne** [aerjɛ̃, jɛn] *adj* (*AVIAT*) air *cpd*, aerial; (*câble, métro*) overhead; (*fig*) light; **compagnie ~ne** airline

**aéro...** [aero] *préfixe*: **aérobic** *nm* aerobic; **aérogare** *nf* airport (buildings); (*en ville*) air terminal; **aéroglisseur** *nm* hovercraft; **Aéronavale** *nf* ≈ Fleet Air Arm (*BRIT*); ≈ Naval Air Force (*US*); **aérophagie** *nf* (*MÉD*) wind, aerophagia (*MÉD*); **aéroport** *nm* airport; **aéroporté, e** *adj* airborne, airlifted; **aérosol** *nm* aerosol

**affable** [afabl] *adj* affable

**affaiblir** [afeblir]: **s'~** *vi* to weaken

**affaire** [afɛr] *nf* (*problème, question*) matter; (*criminelle, judiciaire*) case; (*scandaleuse etc*) affair; (*entreprise*) business; (*marché, transaction*) deal; business *no pl*; (*occasion intéressante*) bargain; **~s** *nfpl* (*intérêts publics et privés*) affairs; (*activité commerciale*) business *sg*; (*effets personnels*) things, belongings; **ce sont mes ~s** (*cela me concerne*) that's my business; **ça fera l'~** that will do (nicely); **se tirer d'~** to sort it *ou* things out for o.s.; **avoir ~ à** (*être en contact*) to be dealing with; **les A~s étrangères** Foreign Affairs; **affairer: s'affairer** *vi* to busy o.s., bustle about

**affaisser** [afese]: **s'~** *vi* (*terrain, immeuble*) to subside, sink; (*personne*) to collapse

**affaler** [afale] *vb*: **s'~ (dans/sur)** to collapse *ou* slump (into/onto)

**affamé, e** [afame] *adj* starving

**affectation** [afɛktasjɔ̃] *nf* (*nomination*) appointment; (*manque de naturel*) affectation

**affecter** [afɛkte] *vt* to affect; **~ qch à** to allocate *ou* allot sth to; **~ qn à** to appoint sb to; (diplomate) to post sb to

**affectif, -ive** [afɛktif, iv] adj emotional

**affection** [afɛksjɔ̃] nf affection; (mal) ailment; **affectionner** vt to be fond of; to like

**affectueux, -euse** adj affectionate

**affermir** [afɛRmiR] vt to consolidate, strengthen; (muscles) to tone up

**affichage** [afiʃaʒ] nm billposting; (électronique) display

**affiche** [afiʃ] nf poster, (officielle) notice, (THÉÂTRE) bill

**afficher** [afiʃe] vt (affiche) to put up; (réunion) to put up a notice about; (électroniquement) to display; (fig) to exhibit, display; **"défense d'~"** "stick no bills"

**affilée** [afile]: **d'~** adv at a stretch

**affiler** [afile] vt to sharpen

**affilier** [afilje]: **s'~ à** vt (club, société) to join

**affiner** [afine] vt to refine

**affirmatif, -ive** [afiRmatif, iv] adj affirmative

**affirmation** [afiRmasjɔ̃] nf assertion

**affirmer** [afiRme] vt to assert

**affligé, e** [afliʒe] adj distressed, grieved; **~ de** (maladie, tare) afflicted with

**affliger** [afliʒe] vt (peiner) to distress, grieve

**affluence** [aflyɑ̃s] nf crowds pl; **heures d'~** rush hours; **jours d'~** busiest days

**affluent** [aflyɑ̃] nm tributary

**affluer** [aflye] vi (secours, biens) to flood in, pour in; (sang) to rush, flow

**affolant, e** [afɔlɑ̃, ɑ̃t] adj frightening

**affolement** [afɔlmɑ̃] nm panic

**affoler** [afɔle] vt to throw into a panic; **s'~** vi to panic

**affranchir** [afRɑ̃ʃiR] vt to put a stamp ou stamps on; (à la machine) to frank (BRIT), meter (US); (fig) to free, liberate; **affranchissement** nm postage

**affréter** [afRete] vt to charter

**affreux, -euse** [afRø, øz] adj dreadful, awful

**affront** [afRɔ̃] nm affront; **affronte-**

**ment** nm clash, confrontation

**affronter** [afRɔ̃te] vt to confront, face

**affubler** [afyble] (péj) vt: **~ qn de** to rig ou deck sb out in

**affût** [afy] nm: **à l'~ (de)** (gibier) lying in wait (for); (fig) on the look-out (for)

**affûter** [afyte] vt to sharpen, grind

**afin** [afɛ̃]: **~ que** conj so that, in order that; **~ de faire** in order to do, so as to do

**africain, e** [afRikɛ̃, ɛn] adj, nm/f African

**Afrique** [afRik] nf: **l'~** Africa; **l'~ du Sud** South Africa

**agacer** [agase] vt to irritate

**âge** [aʒ] nm age; **quel ~ as-tu?** how old are you?; **prendre de l'~** to be getting on (in years); **âgé, e** adj old, elderly; **âgé de 10 ans** 10 years old

**agence** [aʒɑ̃s] nf agency, office; (succursale) branch; **~ de voyages** travel agency; **~ immobilière** estate agency (BRIT) ou real estate (US) agent's (office)

**agencer** [aʒɑ̃se] vt to put together; (local) to arrange, lay out

**agenda** [aʒɛ̃da] nm diary

**agenouiller** [aʒ(ə)nuje]: **s'~** vi to kneel (down)

**agent, e** [aʒɑ̃, ɑ̃t] nm/f (aussi: **~(e) de police**) policeman (policewoman); (ADMIN) official, officer; **~ d'assurances** insurance broker

**agglomération** [aglɔmeRasjɔ̃] nf town; built-up area; **l'~ parisienne** the urban area of Paris

**aggloméré** [aglɔmeRe] nm (bois) chipboard

**aggraver** [agRave]: **s'~** vi to worsen

**agile** [aʒil] adj agile, nimble

**agir** [aʒiR] vi to act; **il s'agit de** (ça traite de) it is about; (il est important de) it's a matter ou question of

**agitation** [aʒitasjɔ̃] nf (hustle and) bustle; (trouble) agitation, excitement; (politique) unrest, agitation

**agité, e** [aʒite] adj fidgety, restless; (troublé) agitated, perturbed; (mer) rough

**agiter** [aʒite] vt (bouteille, chiffon) to

shake; (bras) to wave; (préoccuper, exciter) to perturb; s'~ vi (enfant) to fidget

**agneau, x** [aɲo] nm lamb

**agonie** [agɔni] nf mortal agony, death pangs pl; (fig) death throes pl

**agrafe** [agraf] nf (de vêtement) hook, fastener; (de bureau) staple; **agrafer** vt to fasten; to staple; **agrafeuse** nf stapler

**agrandir** [agrɑ̃dir] vt to enlarge; **s'~** vi (ville, famille) to grow, expand; (trou, écart) to get bigger; **agrandissement** nm (PHOTO) enlargement

**agréable** [agreabl] adj pleasant, nice

**agréé, e** [agree] adj: **concessionnaire ~** registered dealer

**agréer** [agree] vt (requête) to accept; **~ à** to please, suit; **veuillez ~ ...** (formule épistolaire) yours faithfully

**agrégation** [agregasjɔ̃] nf highest teaching diploma in France; **agrégé, e** nm/f holder of the agrégation

**agrément** [agremɑ̃] nm (accord) consent, approval; **agrémenter** vt to embellish, adorn

**agresser** [agrese] vt to attack; **agresseur** nm aggressor, attacker; (POL, MIL) aggressor; **agressif, -ive** adj aggressive

**agricole** [agrikɔl] adj agricultural; **agriculteur** nm farmer; **agriculture** nf agriculture, farming

**agripper** [agripe] vt to grab, clutch; **s'~ à** to cling to (on) to, clutch, grip

**agroalimentaire** [agroalimɑ̃ter] nm farm-produce industry

**agrumes** [agrym] nmpl citrus fruit(s)

**aguerrir** [agerir] vt to harden

**aguets** [age] nmpl: **être aux ~** to be on the look out

**aguicher** [agiʃe] vt to entice

**ahuri, e** [ayri] adj (stupéfait) flabbergasted

**ai** [e] vb voir **avoir**

**aide** [ed] nm/f assistant; carer ♦ nf assistance, help; (secours financier) aid; **à l'~ de** (avec) with the help ou aid of; **ap-**

peler (qn) à l'~ to call for help (from sb); **~ familiale** home help, mother's help; **~ judiciaire** ♦ nf legal aid; **~ sociale** ♦ nf (assistance) state aid; **aide-éducateur, -trice** nm/f classroom assistant; **aide-mémoire** nm inv memoranda pages pl; (key facts) handbook; **aide-soignant, e** nm/f auxiliary nurse

**aider** [ede] vt to help, make use of **s'~ de** (se servir de) to use, make use of

**aie** etc [ε] vb voir **avoir**

**aïe** [aj] excl ouch!

**aïeul, e** [ajœl] nm/f grandparent, grandfather(-mother)

**aïeux** [ajø] nmpl grandparents; (ancêtres) forebears, forefathers

**aigle** [egl] nm eagle

**aigre** [εgr] adj sour, sharp; (fig) sharp, cutting; **aigre-doux, -ce** adj (sauce) sweet and sour; **aigreur** nf sourness, sharpness; **aigreurs d'estomac** heartburn sg; **aigrir** vt (personne) to embitter; (caractère) to sour

**aigu, ë** [egy] adj (objet, douleur) sharp; (son, voix) high-pitched, shrill; (note) high(-pitched)

**aiguille** [eguij] nf needle; (de montre) hand; **~ à tricoter** knitting needle

**aiguiller** [egyije] vt (orienter) to direct; **aiguilleur du ciel** nm air-traffic controller

**aiguillon** [egyijɔ̃] nm (d'abeille) sting; **aiguillonner** vt to spur ou goad on

**aiguiser** [egize] vt to sharpen; (fig) to stimulate; (: sens) to excite

**ail** [aj, o] nm garlic

**aile** [εl] nf wing; **aileron** nm (de requin) fin; **ailier** nm winger

**aille** etc [aj] vb voir **aller**

**ailleurs** [ajœr] adv elsewhere, somewhere else; **partout/nulle part ~** everywhere/nowhere else; **d'~** (du reste) moreover, besides; **par ~** (d'autre part) moreover, furthermore

**aimable** [εmabl] adj kind, nice

**aimant** [εmɑ̃] nm magnet

**aimer** [eme] vt to love; (d'amitié, affec-

...tion, par goût) to like; (souhait): j'~ais ... I would like ...; bien ~ qn/qch to like sb/sth; j'~ais mieux faire I'd much rather do

**aine** [ɛn] nf groin

**aîné, e** [ene] adj elder, older; (le plus âgé) eldest, oldest ♦ nm/f elder child; ou one, eldest boy ou son/girl ou daughter

**ainsi** [ɛsi] adv (de cette façon) like this, in this way, thus; (ce faisant) thus ♦ conj (aussi) as well as; ~ que (comme) (just) as; (et aussi) as well as; pour ~ dire so to speak; et ~ de suite and so on

**aïoli** [ajɔli] nm garlic mayonnaise

**air** [ɛʀ] nm (gén); (mélodie) tune; (expression) look, air; prendre l'~ to get some (fresh) air; (avion) to take off; avoir l'~ (sembler) to seem; avoir l'~ de to look like; avoir l'~ de faire to look as though one is doing, appear to be doing; en l'~ (promesses) empty

**aisance** [ɛzɑs] nf ease; (richesse) affluence

**aise** [ɛz] nf comfort; être à l'~ ou à son ~ to be comfortable; (pas embarrassé) to be at ease; (financièrement) to be comfortably off; se mettre à l'~ to make o.s. comfortable; être mal à l'~ to be uncomfortable; (gêné) to be ill at ease; en faire à son ~ to do as one likes; aisé, e adj easy; (assez riche) well-to-do, well-off

**aisselle** [ɛsɛl] nf armpit

**ait** [ɛ] vb voir avoir

**ajonc** [aʒɔ] nm gorse no pl

**ajourner** [aʒuʀne] vt (réunion) to adjourn; (décision) to defer, postpone

**ajouter** [aʒute] vt to add

**ajusté, e** [aʒyste] adj: bien ~ (robe etc) close-fitting

**ajuster** [aʒyste] vt (régler) to adjust; (vêtement) to alter; (coup de fusil) to aim; (cible) to aim at; (TECH, gén: adapter): ~ qch à to fit sth to

**alarme** [alaʀm] nf alarm; donner l'~ to give ou raise the alarm; **alarmer** vt

to alarm; **s'alarmer** vi to become alarmed; **alarmiste** adj, nm/f alarmist

**album** [albɔm] nm album

**albumine** [albymin] nf albumin; avoir de l'~ to suffer from albuminuria

**alcool** [alkɔl] nm: l'~ alcohol; un ~ a spirit, a brandy; bière sans ~ non-alcoholic ou alcohol-free beer; ~ à brûler methylated spirit (BRIT), wood alcohol (US); ~ à 90° surgical spirit; **alcoolique** adj, nm/f alcoholic; **alcoolisé, e** adj alcoholic; une boisson non alcoolisée a soft drink; **alcoolisme** nm alcoholism; **alcootest** ® nm Breathalyser ®; (test) breath-test

**aléas** [alea] nmpl hazards; **aléatoire** adj uncertain; (INFORM) random

**alentour** [alɑtuʀ] adv around, round about; ~s nmpl (environs) surroundings; aux ~s de in the vicinity ou neighbourhood of, round about; (temps) round about

**alerte** [alɛʀt] adj agile, nimble; brisk, lively ♦ nf alert; warning; ~ à la bombe bomb scare; **alerter** vt to alert

**algèbre** [alʒɛbʀ] nf algebra

**Alger** [alʒe] n Algiers

**Algérie** [alʒeʀi] nf: l'~ Algeria; **algérien, ne** adj Algerian ♦ nm/f: **Algérien, ne** Algerian

**algue** [alg] nf (gén) seaweed no pl; (BOT) alga

**alibi** [alibi] nm alibi

**aliéné, e** [aljene] nm/f insane person, lunatic (péj)

**aligner** [aline] vt to align, line up; (idées, chiffres) to string together; (adapter): ~ qch sur to bring sth into alignment with; s'~ (soldats etc) to line up; s'~ sur (POL) to align o.s. on

**aliment** [alimɑ] nm food; **alimentaire** adj: denrées alimentaires foodstuffs; **alimentation** nf (commerce) food trade; (magasin) grocery store; (régime) diet; (en eau etc, de moteur) supplying; (INFORM) feed; **alimenter** vt to feed; (TECH): **alimenter (en)** to supply (with);

to feed (with); *(fig)* to sustain, keep going

**alinéa** [alinea] *nm* paragraph

**aliter** [alite]: **s'~** *vi* to take to one's bed

**allaiter** [alete] *vt* to (breast-)feed, nurse; *(suj: animal)* to suckle

**allant** [alɑ̃] *nm* drive, go

**alléchant, e** [aleʃɑ̃, ɑ̃t] *adj (odeur)* mouth-watering; *(offre)* enticing

**allécher** [aleʃe] *vt*: **~ qn** to make sb's mouth water; to tempt *ou* entice sb

**allée** [ale] *nf (de jardin)* path; *(en ville)* avenue, drive; **~s et venues** comings and goings

**allégé, e** [aleʒe] *adj (yaourt etc)* low-fat

**alléger** [aleʒe] *vt (voiture)* to make lighter; *(chargement)* to lighten; *(souffrance)* to alleviate, soothe

**allègre** [a(l)lɛgʀ] *adj* lively, cheerful

**alléguer** [a(l)lege] *vt* to put forward (as proof *ou* an excuse)

**Allemagne** [almaɲ] *nf*: **l'~** Germany; **allemand, e** *adj* German ♦ *nm/f*: **Allemand, e** German ♦ *nm (LING)* German

**aller** [ale] *nm (trajet)* outward journey; *(billet: aussi:* **~ simple)** single *(BRIT) ou* one-way *(US)* ticket ♦ *vi (gén)* to go; **~ à** *(convenir)* to suit; *(suj: forme, pointure etc)* to fit; **~ (bien) avec** *(couleurs, style etc)* to go (well) with; **je vais y ~/me fâcher** I'm going to go/to get angry; **~ voir** to go and see, go to see; **allez!** come on!; **allons!** come now!; **comment allez-vous?** how are you?; **comment ça va?** how are you?; *(affaires etc)* how are things?; **il va bien/mal** he's well/not well, he's fine/ill; **ça va bien/mal** *(affaires etc)* it's going well/not going well; **~ mieux** to be better; **s'en ~** *(partir)* to be off, go, leave; *(disparaître)* to go away; **~ retour** return journey *(BRIT)*, round trip; *(billet)* return (ticket) *(BRIT)*, round trip ticket *(US)*

**allergique** [alɛʀʒik] *adj*: **~ à** allergic to

**alliage** [aljaʒ] *nm* alloy

**alliance** [aljɑ̃s] *nf (MIL, POL)* alliance; *(bague)* wedding ring

**allier** [alje] *vt (POL, gén)* to ally; *(fig)* to combine; **s'~** to become allies; to combine

**allô** [alo] *excl* hullo, hallo

**allocation** [alɔkasjɔ̃] *nf* allowance; **(de) chômage** unemployment benefit; **~s familiales** ≈ child benefit

**allocution** [a(l)lɔkysjɔ̃] *nf* short speech

**allonger** [alɔ̃ʒe] *vt* to lengthen, make longer; *(étendre: bras, jambe)* to stretch (out); **s'~** *vi* to get longer; *(se coucher)* to lie down, stretch out; **~ le pas** to hasten one's step(s)

**allouer** [alwe] *vt* to allocate, allot

**allumage** [alymaʒ] *nm (AUTO)* ignition

**allume-cigare** [alymsigaʀ] *nm inv* cigar lighter

**allumer** [alyme] *vt (lampe, phare, radio)* to put *ou* switch on; *(pièce)* to put *ou* switch the light(s) on in; *(feu)* to light; **s'~** *vi (lumière, lampe)* to come *ou* go on

**allumette** [alymɛt] *nf* match

**allure** [alyʀ] *nf (vitesse)* speed, pace; *(démarche)* walk; *(aspect, air)* look; **avoir de l'~** to have style; **à toute ~** at top speed

**allusion** [a(l)lyzjɔ̃] *nf* allusion; *(sousentendu)* hint; **faire ~ à** to allude *ou* refer to; to hint at

---

MOT-CLÉ

**alors** [alɔʀ] *adv* **1** *(à ce moment-là)* then, at that time; **il habitait alors Paris** he lived in Paris at that time
**2** *(par conséquent)* then; **tu as fini, alors je m'en vais** have you finished, I'm going then; **et alors?** so what?
**alors que** *conj* **1** *(au moment où)* when, as; **il est arrivé alors que je partais** he arrived as I was leaving
**2** *(pendant que)* while, when; **alors qu'il était à Paris, il a visité ...** while *ou* when he was in Paris, he visited ...
**3** *(tandis que)* whereas, while; **alors**

que son frère travaillait dur, lui se
reposait he would rest while his
brother was working hard, HE would rest

**alouette** [alwɛt] *nf* (sky)lark

**alourdir** [aluʀdiʀ] *vt* to weigh down,
make heavy

**aloyau** [alwajo] *nm* sirloin

**Alpes** [alp] *nfpl*: les ~ the Alps

**alphabet** [alfabɛ] *nm* alphabet; (*livre*)
ABC (book); **alphabétique** *adj* alphabetical; **alphabétiser** *vt* to teach to
read and write; (*pays*) to eliminate illiteracy in

**alpinisme** [alpinism] *nm* mountaineering, climbing; **alpiniste** *nm/f* mountaineer, climber

**Alsace** [alzas] *nf* Alsace; **alsacien, ne**
*adj* Alsatian ♦ *nm/f*: **Alsacien, ne** Alsatian

**altérer** [alteʀe] *vt* (*vérité*) to distort; **s'~**
*vi* to deteriorate

**alternateur** [altɛʀnatœʀ] *nm* alternator

**alternatif, -ive** [altɛʀnatif, iv] *adj* alternating; **alternative** *nf* (*choix*) alternative; **alternativement** *adv* alternately; **alterner** *vi* to alternate

**Altesse** [altɛs] *nf* Highness

**altitude** [altityd] *nf* altitude, height

**alto** [alto] *nm* (*instrument*) viola

**aluminium** [alyminjɔm] *nm* aluminium
(*BRIT*), aluminum (*US*)

**amabilité** [amabilite] *nf* kindness

**amadouer** [amadwe] *vt* to mollify,
soothe

**amaigrir** [amegʀiʀ] *vt* to make
thin(ner); **amaigrissant, e** *adj* (*régime*) slimming

**amalgame** [amalgam] (*péj*) *nm*
(*strange*) mixture

**amande** [amɑ̃d] *nf* (*de l'amandier*) almond; **amandier** *nm* almond (tree)

**amant** [amɑ̃] *nm* lover

**amarrer** [amaʀe] *vt* (*NAVIG*) to moor;
(*gén*) to make fast

**amas** [ama] *nm* heap, pile; **amasser** *vt*

to amass; **s'amasser** *vi* (*foule*) to
gather

**amateur** [amatœʀ] *nm* amateur; **en ~**
(*péj*) amateurishly; **~ de musique/
sport** *etc* music/sport *etc* lover

**amazone** [amazon] *nf*: **en ~** side-
saddle

**ambassade** [ɑ̃basad] *nf* embassy; **l'~
de France** the French Embassy; **ambassadeur, -drice** *nm/f* ambassador
(-dress)

**ambiance** [ɑ̃bjɑ̃s] *nf* atmosphere

**ambiant, e** [ɑ̃bjɑ̃, jɑ̃t] *adj* (*air, milieu*)
surrounding; (*température*) ambient

**ambigu, ë** [ɑ̃bigy] *adj* ambiguous

**ambitieux, -euse** [ɑ̃bisjø, jøz] *adj* ambitious

**ambition** [ɑ̃bisjɔ̃] *nf* ambition

**ambulance** [ɑ̃bylɑ̃s] *nf* ambulance;
**ambulancier, -ière** *nm/f* ambulance
man(-woman) (*BRIT*), paramedic (*US*)

**ambulant, e** [ɑ̃bylɑ̃, ɑ̃t] *adj* travelling,
itinerant

**âme** [ɑm] *nf* soul

**amélioration** [ameljɔʀasjɔ̃] *nf* improvement

**améliorer** [ameljɔʀe] *vt* to improve;
**s'~** *vi* to improve, get better

**aménager** [amenaʒe] *vt* (*agencer,
transformer*) to fit out; to lay out;
(: *quartier, territoire*) to develop; (*installer*) to fix up, put in; **ferme aménagée**
converted farmhouse

**amende** [amɑ̃d] *nf* fine; **faire ~ honorable** to make amends

**amener** [am(ə)ne] *vt* to bring; (*causer*)
to bring about; **s'~** *vi* to show up
(*fam*), turn up

**amenuiser** [amənɥize]: **s'~** *vi*
(*chances*) to grow slimmer, lessen

**amer, amère** [ameʀ] *adj* bitter

**américain, e** [ameʀikɛ̃, ɛn] *adj* American ♦ *nm/f*: **A~, e** American

**Amérique** [ameʀik] *nf*: **l'~** America;
**l'~ centrale/latine** Central/Latin America; **l'~ du Nord/du Sud** North/South
America

**amertume** [amɛʀtym] *nf* bitterness

**ameublement** [amœbləmã] *nm* furnishing; (*meubles*) furniture

**ameuter** [amøte] *vt* (*peuple*) to rouse

**ami, e** [ami] *nm/f* friend; (*amant/maîtresse*) boyfriend/girlfriend ♦ *adj*: **pays/groupe ~** friendly country/group

**amiable** [amjabl]: **à l'~** *adv* (JUR) out of court; (*gén*) amicably

**amiante** [amjãt] *nm* asbestos

**amical, e, -aux** [amikal, o] *adj* friendly; **amicalement** *adv* in a friendly way; (*formule épistolaire*) regards

**amidon** [amidɔ̃] *nm* starch

**amincir** [amɛ̃siʀ] *vt*: **~ qn** to make sb thinner ou slimmer; (*suj: vêtement*) to make sb look slimmer

**amincissant, e** [amɛ̃sisã, ãt] *adj*: **régime ~** (slimming) diet; **crème ~e** slimming cream

**amiral, -aux** [amiʀal, o] *nm* admiral

**amitié** [amitje] *nf* friendship; **prendre en ~** to befriend; **~s, Christèle** best wishes, Christèle; **présenter ses ~s à qn** to send sb one's best wishes

**ammoniaque** [amɔnjak] *nf* ammonia (water)

**amnistie** [amnisti] *nf* amnesty

**amoindrir** [amwɛ̃dʀiʀ] *vt* to reduce

**amollir** [amɔliʀ] *vt* to soften

**amonceler** [amɔ̃s(ə)le] *vt* to pile ou heap up; **s'~** *vi* to pile ou heap up; (*fig*) to accumulate

**amont** [amɔ̃]: **en ~** *adv* upstream

**amorce** [amɔʀs] *nf* (*sur un hameçon*) bait; (*explosif*) cap; primer; priming; (*fig: début*) beginning(s), start; **amorcer** *vt* to start

**amorphe** [amɔʀf] *adj* passive, lifeless

**amortir** [amɔʀtiʀ] *vt* (*atténuer: choc*) to absorb, cushion; (*bruit, douleur*) to deaden; (COMM: *dette*) to pay off; **~ un achat** to make a purchase pay for itself; **amortisseur** *nm* shock absorber

**amour** [amuʀ] *nm* love; **faire l'~** to make love; **amouracher: s'amouracher de** (*péj*) *vt* to become infatuated with; **amoureux, -euse** *adj* (*regard, tempérament*) amorous; (*vie, problèmes*) love *cpd*; (*personne*): **amoureux (de qn)** in love (with sb) ♦ *nmpl* courting couple(s); **amour-propre** *nm* self-esteem, pride

**amovible** [amɔvibl] *adj* removable, detachable

**ampère** [ɑ̃pɛʀ] *nm* amp(ere)

**amphithéâtre** [ɑ̃fiteɑtʀ] *nm* amphitheatre; (*d'université*) lecture hall ou theatre

**ample** [ɑ̃pl] *adj* (*vêtement*) roomy, ample; (*gestes, mouvement*) broad, (*ressources*) ample; **amplement** *adv* **c'est amplement suffisant** that's more than enough; **ampleur** *nf* (*de dégâts, problème*) extent

**amplificateur** [ɑ̃plifikatœʀ] *nm* amplifier

**amplifier** [ɑ̃plifje] *vt* (*fig*) to expand increase

**ampoule** [ɑ̃pul] *nf* (*électrique*) bulb; (*de médicament*) phial; (*aux mains, pieds*) blister; **ampoulé, e** (*péj*) *adj* pompous bombastic

**amputer** [ɑ̃pyte] *vt* (MÉD) to amputate (*fig*) to cut ou reduce drastically

**amusant, e** [amyzã, ãt] *adj* (*divertissant, spirituel*) entertaining, amusing (*comique*) funny, amusing

**amuse-gueule** [amyzgœl] *nm inv* appetizer, snack

**amusement** [amyzmã] *nm* (*divertissement*) amusement; (*jeu etc*) pastime, diversion

**amuser** [amyze] *vt* (*divertir*) to entertain, amuse; (*égayer, faire rire*) to amuse; **s'~** *vi* (*jouer*) to play; (*se divertir*) to enjoy o.s., have fun; (*fig*) to mess around

**amygdale** [amidal] *nf* tonsil

**an** [ɑ̃] *nm* year; **avoir quinze ~s** to be fifteen (years old); **le jour de l'~, le premier de l'~, le nouvel ~** New

Year's Day

**analogique** [analɔʒik] adj (INFORM, montre) analog

**analogue** [analɔg] adj: ~ (à) analogous (to), similar (to)

**analphabète** [analfabɛt] nm/f illiterate

**analyse** [analiz] nf analysis; (MÉD) test; **analyser** vt to analyse; to test

**ananas** [anana(s)] nm pineapple

**anarchie** [anaʀʃi] nf anarchy

**anatomie** [anatɔmi] nf anatomy

**ancêtre** [ɑ̃sɛtʀ] nm/f ancestor

**anchois** [ɑ̃ʃwa] nm anchovy

**ancien, ne** [ɑ̃sjɛ̃, jɛn] adj old; (de jadis, de l'antiquité) ancient; (précédent, ex-) former, old; (par l'expérience) senior ♦ nm/f (dans une tribu) elder; ~ **combattant** nm war veteran; **ancienneté** [ɑ̃sjɛnte] nf (ADMIN) (length of) service; (privilèges obtenus) seniority

**ancre** [ɑ̃kʀ] nf anchor; **jeter/lever l'~** to cast/weigh anchor; **ancrer** vt (CONSTR: câble etc) to anchor; (fig) to fix firmly

**Andorre** [ɑ̃dɔʀ] nf Andorra

**andouille** [ɑ̃duj] nf (CULIN) sausage made of chitterlings; (fam) clot, nit

**âne** [ɑn] nm donkey, ass; (péj) dunce

**anéantir** [aneɑ̃tiʀ] vt to annihilate, wipe out; (fig) to obliterate, destroy

**anémie** [anemi] nf anaemia; **anémique** adj anaemic

**ânerie** [ɑnʀi] nf stupidity; (parole etc) stupid ou idiotic comment etc

**anesthésie** [anɛstezi] nf anaesthesia; **faire une ~ locale/générale à qn** to give sb a local/general anaesthetic

**ange** [ɑ̃ʒ] nm angel; **être aux ~s** to be over the moon

**angélus** [ɑ̃ʒelys] nm angelus; (cloches) evening bells pl

**angine** [ɑ̃ʒin] nf throat infection; **~ de poitrine** angina

**anglais, e** [ɑ̃glɛ, ɛz] adj English ♦ nm/f: **A~, e** Englishman(-woman) ♦ nm (LING) English; **les A~** the English; **filer à l'~e**

to take French leave

**angle** [ɑ̃gl] nm angle; (coin) corner; ~ **droit** right angle

**Angleterre** [ɑ̃glətɛʀ] nf: **l'~** England

**anglo...** [ɑ̃glɔ] préfixe Anglo-, anglo(-); **anglophone** adj English-speaking

**angoisse** [ɑ̃gwas] nf anguish, distress; **angoissé, e** adj (personne) distressed; **angoisser** vt to harrow, cause anguish to ♦ vi to worry, fret

**anguille** [ɑ̃gij] nf eel

**anicroche** [anikʀɔʃ] nf hitch, snag

**animal, e, -aux** [animal, o] adj, nm animal

**animateur, -trice** [animatœʀ, tʀis] nm/f (de télévision) host; (de groupe) leader, organizer

**animation** [animasjɔ̃] nf (voir animé) busyness; liveliness; (CINÉMA: technique) animation; **~s culturelles** cultural activities

**animé, e** [anime] adj (lieu) busy, lively; (conversation, réunion) lively, animated

**animer** [anime] vt (ville, soirée) to liven up; (mener) to lead; **s'~** vi to liven up

**anis** [ani(s)] nm (CULIN) aniseed; (BOT) anise

**ankyloser** [ɑ̃kiloze]: **s'~** vi to get stiff

**anneau, x** [ano] nm (de rideau, bague) ring; (de chaîne) link

**année** [ane] nf year

**annexe** [anɛks] adj (problème) related; (document) appended; (salle) adjoining ♦ nf (bâtiment) annex(e); (jointe à une lettre) enclosure

**anniversaire** [anivɛʀsɛʀ] nm birthday; (d'un événement, bâtiment) anniversary

**annonce** [anɔ̃s] nf announcement; (signe, indice) sign; (aussi: ~ **publicitaire**) advertisement; **les petites ~s** the classified advertisements, the small ads

**annoncer** [anɔ̃se] vt to announce; (être le signe de) to herald; **s'~ bien/difficile** to look promising/difficult; **annonceur, -euse** nm/f (publicitaire) advertiser; (TV, RADIO: speaker) announcer

**annuaire** [anɥɛʀ] nm yearbook, annual; **~ téléphonique** (telephone) directory, phone book

**annuel, le** [anɥɛl] adj annual, yearly

**annuité** [anɥite] nf annual instalment

**annulation** [anylasjɔ̃] nf cancellation

**annuler** [anyle] vt (rendez-vous, voyage) to cancel, call off; (jugement) to quash (BRIT), repeal (US); (MATH, PHYSIQUE) to cancel out

**anodin, e** [anɔdɛ̃, in] adj (blessure) harmless; (détail) insignificant, trivial

**anonymat** [anɔnima] nm anonymity

**anonyme** [anɔnim] adj anonymous; (fig) impersonal

**ANPE** sigle f (= Agence nationale pour l'emploi) national employment agency

**anorak** [anɔʀak] nm anorak

**anormal, e, -aux** [anɔʀmal, o] adj abnormal

**anse** [ɑ̃s] nf (de panier, tasse) handle

**antan** [ɑ̃tɑ̃]: **d'~** adj of long ago

**antarctique** [ɑ̃taʀktik] adj Antarctic ♦ nm: **l'A~** the Antarctic

**antécédents** [ɑ̃tesedɑ̃] nmpl (MÉD etc) past history sg

**antenne** [ɑ̃tɛn] nf (de radio) aerial; (d'insecte) antenna, feeler; (poste avancé) outpost; (succursale) subbranch; **passer à l'~** to go on the air

**antérieur, e** [ɑ̃teʀjœʀ] adj (d'avant) previous, earlier; (de devant) front

**anti...** [ɑ̃ti] préfixe anti...; **antialcoolique** adj anti-alcohol; **antiatomique** adj: **abri antiatomique** fallout shelter; **antibiotique** nm antibiotic; **antibogue** adj debugging ♦ nm debugging device; **antibrouillard** adj: **phare antibrouillard** fog lamp (BRIT) ou light (US)

**anticipation** [ɑ̃tisipasjɔ̃] nf: **livre/film d'~** science fiction book/film

**anticipé, e** [ɑ̃tisipe] adj: **avec mes remerciements ~s** thanking you in advance ou anticipation

**anticiper** [ɑ̃tisipe] vt (événement, coup) to anticipate, foresee

**anti...: anticonceptionnel, le** adj contraceptive; **anticorps** nm antibody; **antidote** nm antidote; **antigel** nm antifreeze; **antihistaminique** nm antihistamine

**antillais, e** [ɑ̃tije, ɛz] adj West Indian, Caribbean ♦ nm/f: **A~, e** West Indian, Caribbean

**Antilles** [ɑ̃tij] nfpl: **les ~** the West Indies

**antilope** [ɑ̃tilɔp] nf antelope

**anti...: antimite(s)** adj, nm: **(produit) antimite(s)** mothproofer; moth repellent; **antimondialisation** nf antiglobalization; **antipathique** adj unpleasant, disagreeable; **antipelliculaire** adj anti-dandruff

**antipodes** [ɑ̃tipɔd] nmpl (fig): **être aux ~ de** to be the opposite extreme of

**antiquaire** [ɑ̃tikɛʀ] nm/f antique dealer

**antique** [ɑ̃tik] adj antique; (très vieux) ancient, antiquated; **antiquité** nf (objet) antique; **l'Antiquité** Antiquity; **magasin d'antiquités** antique shop

**anti...: antirabique** adj rabies cpd; **antirouille** adj inv anti-rust cpd; **antisémite** adj anti-Semitic; **antiseptique** adj, nm antiseptic; **antivol** adj, nm: **(dispositif) antivol** anti-theft device

**antre** [ɑ̃tʀ] nm den, lair

**anxiété** [ɑ̃ksjete] nf anxiety

**anxieux, -euse** [ɑ̃ksjø, jøz] adj anxious, worried

**AOC** sigle f (= appellation d'origine contrôlée) label guaranteeing the quality of wine

> **AOC**
>
> AOC is the highest French wine classification. It indicates that the wine meets strict requirements concerning the vineyard of origin, the type of vine grown, the method of production, and the volume of alcohol present.

**août** [u(t)] nm August

**apaiser** [apeze] vt (colère, douleur) to soothe; (personne) to calm (down) pacify; **s'~** vi (tempête, bruit) to die down, subside; (personne) to calm down

**apanage** [apanaʒ] nm: **être l'~ de** to be the privilege ou prerogative of

**aparté** [aparte] nm (entretien) private conversation; **en ~** in an aside

**apathique** [apatik] adj apathetic

**apatride** [apatrid] nm/f stateless person

**apercevoir** [apɛrsəvwar] vt to see; **s'~ de** vt to notice; **s'~ que** to notice that

**aperçu** [apɛrsy] nm (vue d'ensemble) general survey

**apéritif** [aperitif] nm (boisson) aperitif; (réunion) drinks pl

**à-peu-près** [apøpʀɛ] (péj) nm inv vague approximation

**apeuré, e** [apœre] adj frightened, scared

**aphte** [aft] nm mouth ulcer

**apiculture** [apikyltyr] nf beekeeping, apiculture

**apitoyer** [apitwaje] vt to move to pity; **s'~ (sur)** to feel pity (for)

**aplanir** [aplanir] vt to level; (fig) to smooth away, iron out

**aplatir** [aplatir] vt to flatten; **s'~** vi to become flatter; (écrasé) to be flattened; **s'~ devant qn** (fig: s'humilier) to crawl to sb

**aplomb** [aplɔ̃] nm (équilibre) balance, equilibrium; (fig) self-assurance; nerve; **d'~** steady

**apogée** [apɔʒe] nm (fig) peak, apogee

**apologie** [apɔlɔʒi] nf vindication, praise

**a posteriori** [aposterjori] adv after the event

**apostrophe** [apostrof] nf (signe) apostrophe

**apostropher** [apostrofe] vt (interpeller) to shout at, address sharply

**apothéose** [apoteoz] nf pinnacle of achievement; (MUS) grand finale

**apôtre** [apotr] nm apostle

**apparaître** [aparɛtr] vi to appear

**apparat** [apara] nm: **tenue d'~** cere-

monial dress

**appareil** [aparɛj] nm (outil, machine) piece of apparatus, device; (électrique, ménager) appliance; (aéro)plane, aircraft inv; (téléphonique) phone; (dentier) brace (BRIT), braces (US); **"qui est à l'~?"** "who's speaking?"; **dans le plus simple ~** in one's birthday suit; **appareiller** vi (NAVIG) to cast off, get under way ♦ vt (assortir) to match up; **appareil(-photo)** nm camera

**apparemment** [aparamɑ̃] adv apparently

**apparence** [aparɑ̃s] nf appearance; **en ~** apparently

**apparent, e** [aparɑ̃, ɑ̃t] adj visible; (évident) obvious; (superficiel) apparent

**apparenté, e** [aparɑ̃te] adj: **~ à** related to; (fig) similar to

**apparition** [aparisjɔ̃] nf appearance; (surnaturelle) apparition

**appartement** [apartəmɑ̃] nm flat (BRIT), apartment (US)

**appartenir** [apartənir]: **~ à** vt to belong to; **il lui appartient de** it is his duty to

**apparu, e** [apary] pp de **apparaître**

**appât** [apa] nm (PÊCHE) bait; (fig) lure, bait; **appâter** vt to lure

**appauvrir** [apovrir] vt to impoverish

**appel** [apɛl] nm call; (nominal) roll call; (: SCOL) register; (MIL: recrutement) callup; **faire ~ à** (invoquer) to appeal to; (avoir recours à) to call on; (nécessiter) to call for, require; **faire ~** (JUR) to appeal; **faire l'~** to call the roll; to call the register; **sans ~** (fig) final, irrevocable; **~ d'offres** (COMM) invitation to tender; **faire un ~ de phares** to flash one's headlights; **~ (téléphonique)** (tele)phone call

**appelé** [ap(ə)le] nm (MIL) conscript

**appeler** [ap(ə)le] vt to call; (faire venir: médecin etc) to call, send for; **s'~** vi: **elle s'appelle Gabrielle** her name is Gabrielle, she's called Gabrielle;

**comment ça s'appelle?** what is it called?; **être appelé à** (*fig*) to be destined to

**appendice** [apɛ̃dis] *nm* appendix; **appendicite** *nf* appendicitis

**appentis** [apɑ̃ti] *nm* lean-to

**appesantir** [apəzɑ̃tiʀ]: **s'~** *vi* to grow heavier; **s'~ sur** (*fig*) to dwell on

**appétissant, e** [apetisɑ̃, ɑ̃t] *adj* appetizing, mouth-watering

**appétit** [apeti] *nm* appetite; **bon ~!** enjoy your meal!

**applaudir** [aplodiʀ] *vt* to applaud ♦ *vi* to applaud, clap; **applaudissements** *nmpl* applause *sg*, clapping *sg*

**application** [aplikasjɔ̃] *nf* application

**applique** [aplik] *nf* wall lamp

**appliquer** [aplike] *vt* to apply; (*loi*) to enforce; **s'~** *vi* (*élève etc*) to apply o.s.; **s'~ à** to apply to

**appoint** [apwɛ̃] *nm* (*extra*) contribution *ou* help; **chauffage d'~** extra heating

**appointements** [apwɛ̃tmɑ̃] *nmpl* salary *sg*

**apport** [apɔʀ] *nm* (*approvisionnement*) supply; (*contribution*) contribution

**apporter** [apɔʀte] *vt* to bring

**apposer** [apoze] *vt* (*signature*) to affix

**appréciable** [apʀesjabl] *adj* appreciable

**apprécier** [apʀesje] *vt* to appreciate; (*évaluer*) to estimate, assess

**appréhender** [apʀeɑ̃de] *vt* (*craindre*) to dread; (*arrêter*) to apprehend; **appréhension** *nf* apprehension, anxiety

**apprendre** [apʀɑ̃dʀ] *vt* to learn; (*événement, résultats*) to learn of, hear of; **~ qch à qn** (*informer*) to tell sb (of) sth; (*enseigner*) to teach sb sth; **~ à faire qch** to learn to do sth; **~ à qn à faire qch** to teach sb to do sth; **apprenti, e** *nm/f* apprentice; **apprentissage** *nm* learning; (*COMM, SCOL: période*) apprenticeship

**apprêté, e** [apʀete] *adj* (*fig*) affected

**apprêter** [apʀete] *vt*: **s'~ à faire qch** to get ready to do sth

**appris, e** [apʀi, iz] *pp de* **apprendre**

**apprivoiser** [apʀivwaze] *vt* to tame

**approbation** [apʀɔbasjɔ̃] *nf* approval

**approchant, e** [apʀɔʃɑ̃, ɑ̃t] *adj* similar; **quelque chose d'~** something like that

**approche** [apʀɔʃ] *nf* approach

**approcher** [apʀɔʃe] *vi* to approach, come near ♦ *vt* to approach; (*rapprocher*): **~ qch (de qch)** to bring *ou* put sth near (to sth); **s'~ de** to approach, go *ou* come near to; **~ de** (*lieu, but*) to draw near to; (*quantité, moment*) to approach

**approfondir** [apʀɔfɔ̃diʀ] *vt* to deepen; (*question*) to go further into

**approprié, e** [apʀɔpʀije] *adj*: **~ (à)** appropriate (to), suited to

**approprier** [apʀɔpʀije]: **s'~** *vt* to appropriate, take over

**approuver** [apʀuve] *vt* to agree with; (*trouver louable*) to approve of

**approvisionner** [apʀɔvizjɔne] *vt* to supply; (*compte bancaire*) to pay funds into; **s'~ en** to stock up with

**approximatif, -ive** [apʀɔksimatif, iv] *adj* approximate, rough; (*termes*) vague

**appt** *abr* = **appartement**

**appui** [apɥi] *nm* support; **prendre ~ sur** to lean on; (*objet*) to rest on; **l'~ de la fenêtre** the windowsill, the window ledge; **appui(e)-tête** *nm inv* headrest

**appuyer** [apɥije] *vt* (*poser*): **~ qch sur/contre** to lean *ou* rest sth on/ against; (*soutenir: personne, demande*) to support, back (up) ♦ *vi*: **~ sur** (*bouton, frein*) to press, push; (*mot, détail*) to stress, emphasize; **s'~ sur** to lean on; (*fig: compter sur*) to rely on

**âpre** [ɑpʀ] *adj* acrid, pungent; **~ au gain** grasping

**après** [apʀɛ] *prép* + *adv* afterwards; **2 heures ~** 2 hours later; **~ qu'il est** *ou* **soit parti** after he left; **~ avoir fait** after having done; **d'~** (*selon*) according to; **~ coup** after the event, afterwards; **~ tout** (au fond) after all; **et (puis) ~?** so what?; **après-demain** adv the day after tomorrow; **après-guerre** nm post-war years pl; **après-midi** nm ou nf inv afternoon; **après-rasage** nm inv aftershave; **après-shampooing** nm inv conditioner; **après-ski** nm inv snow boot

**à-propos** [aprɔpo] nm (d'une remarque) aptness; **faire preuve d'~~** to show presence of mind

**apte** [apt] adj capable; (MIL) fit

**aquarelle** [akwarɛl] nf watercolour

**aquarium** [akwarjɔm] nm aquarium

**arabe** [arab] adj Arabic; (désert, cheval) Arabian; (nation, peuple) Arab ♦ nm/f: **A~** Arab ♦ nm (LING) Arabic

**Arabie** [arabi] nf: **l'~ (Saoudite)** Saudi Arabia

**arachide** [araʃid] nf (plante) groundnut (plant); (graine) peanut, groundnut

**araignée** [arɛɲe] nf spider

**arbitraire** [arbitrɛr] adj arbitrary

**arbitre** [arbitr] nm (SPORT) referee; (: TENNIS, CRICKET) umpire; (fig) arbiter, judge; (JUR) arbitrator; **arbitrer** vt to referee; to umpire; to arbitrate

**arborer** [arbɔre] vt to bear, display

**arbre** [arbr] nm tree; (TECH) shaft; **~ généalogique** family tree

**arbuste** [arbyst] nm small shrub

**arc** [ark] nm (arme) bow; (GÉOM) arc; (ARCHIT) arch; **en ~ de cercle** semi-circular

**arcade** [arkad] nf arch(way); **~s** nfpl (série) arcade sg, arches

**arcanes** [arkan] nmpl mysteries

**arc-boutant** [arkbutɑ̃] nm flying buttress

**arceau, x** [arso] nm (métallique etc) hoop

**arc-en-ciel** [arkɑ̃sjɛl] nm rainbow

**arche** [arʃ] nf arch; **~ de Noé** Noah's Ark

**archéologie** [arkeɔlɔʒi] nf arch(a)eology; **archéologue** nm/f arch(a)eologist

**archet** [arʃɛ] nm bow

**archevêque** [arʃəvɛk] nm archbishop

**archi...** [arʃi] (fam) préfixe tremendously; **archicomble** (fam) adj chock-a-block; **archiconnu, e** (fam) adj enormously well-known

**archipel** [arʃipɛl] nm archipelago

**architecte** [arʃitɛkt] nm architect

**architecture** [arʃitɛktyr] nf architecture

**archives** [arʃiv] nfpl (collection) archives

**arctique** [arktik] adj Arctic ♦ nm: **l'A~** the Arctic

**ardemment** [ardamɑ̃] adv ardently, fervently

**ardent, e** [ardɑ̃, ɑ̃t] adj (soleil) blazing; (amour) ardent, passionate; (prière) fervent

**ardeur** [ardœr] nf ardour (BRIT), ardor (US); (du soleil) heat

**ardoise** [ardwaz] nf slate

**ardu, e** [ardy] adj (travail) arduous; (problème) difficult

**arène** [arɛn] nf arena; **~s** nfpl (amphithéâtre) bull-ring sg

**arête** [arɛt] nf (de poisson) bone; (d'une montagne) ridge

**argent** [arʒɑ̃] nm (métal) silver; (monnaie) money; **~ de poche** pocket money; **~ liquide** ready money, (ready) cash; **argenté, e** adj (couleur) silver, silvery; **en métal argenté** silver-plated; **argenterie** nf silverware

**argentin, e** [arʒɑ̃tɛ̃, in] adj Argentinian, Argentine

**Argentine** [arʒɑ̃tin] nf: **l'~** Argentina, the Argentine

**argile** [arʒil] nf clay

**argot** [argo] nm slang; **argotique** adj slang cpd; (très familier) slangy

**argument** [argymɑ̃] nm argument

**argumentaire** [argymɑ̃tɛr] nm sales leaflet

**argumenter** [argymɑ̃te] vi to argue

**argus** [argys] nm guide to second-hand car etc prices

**aride** [aʀid] *adj* arid

**aristocratie** [aʀistɔkʀasi] *nf* aristocracy; **aristocratique** *adj* aristocratic

**arithmétique** [aʀitmetik] *adj* arithmetic(al) ♦ *nf* arithmetic

**armateur** [aʀmatœʀ] *nm* shipowner

**armature** [aʀmatyʀ] *nf* framework; (de tente etc) frame; **soutien-gorge à/ sans ~** underwired/unwired bra

**arme** [aʀm] *nf* weapon; ~s *nfpl* (~ment) weapons, arms; (blason) (coat of) arms; **~ à feu** firearm

**armée** [aʀme] *nf* army; **~ de l'air** Air Force; **~ de terre** army

**armement** [aʀməmɑ̃] *nm* (matériel) arms *pl*, weapons *pl*

**armer** [aʀme] *vt* to arm; (arme à feu) to cock; (appareil-photo) to wind on; **~ qch de** to reinforce sth with; **s'~ de** to arm o.s. with

**armistice** [aʀmistis] *nm* armistice; **l'A~** ≈ Remembrance (BRIT) ou Veterans (US) Day

**armoire** [aʀmwaʀ] *nf* (tall) cupboard; (penderie) wardrobe (BRIT), closet (US)

**armoiries** [aʀmwaʀi] *nfpl* coat *sg* of arms

**armure** [aʀmyʀ] *nf* armour *no pl*, suit of armour; **armurier** *nm* gunsmith

**arnaque** [aʀnak] (fam) *nf* swindling; **c'est de l'~** it's a rip-off; **arnaquer** (fam) *vt* to swindle

**aromates** [aʀɔmat] *nmpl* seasoning *sg*, herbs (and spices)

**aromathérapie** [aʀɔmateʀapi] *nf* aromatherapy

**aromatisé, e** [aʀɔmatize] *adj* flavoured

**arôme** [aʀom] *nm* aroma

**arpenter** [aʀpɑ̃te] *vt* (salle, couloir) to pace up and down

**arpenteur** [aʀpɑ̃tœʀ] *nm* surveyor

**arqué, e** [aʀke] *adj* arched; (jambes) bandy

**arrache-pied** [aʀaʃpje]: **d'~~** *adv* relentlessly

**arracher** [aʀaʃe] *vt* to pull out; (page etc) to tear off, tear out; (légumes,

herbe) to pull up; (bras etc) to tear off; **s'~** *vt* (article recherché) to fight over; **~ qch à qn** to snatch sth from sb; (fig) to wring sth out of sb

**arraisonner** [aʀɛzɔne] *vt* (bateau) to board and search

**arrangeant, e** [aʀɑ̃ʒɑ̃, ɑ̃t] *adj* accommodating, obliging

**arrangement** [aʀɑ̃ʒmɑ̃] *nm* arrangement, arrangement

**arranger** [aʀɑ̃ʒe] *vt* (gén) to arrange; (réparer) to fix, put right; (régler: différend) to settle, sort out; (convenir à) to suit, be convenient for; **s'~** *vi* (se mettre d'accord) to come to an agreement; **je vais m'~** I'll manage; **ça va s'~** it'll sort itself out

**arrestation** [aʀɛstasjɔ̃] *nf* arrest

**arrêt** [aʀɛ] *nm* stopping; (de bus etc) stop; (JUR) judgment, decision; à l'~ stationary; **tomber en ~ devant** to stop short in front of; **sans ~** (sans interruption) non-stop; (très fréquemment) continually; **~ de travail** stoppage (of work); **~ maladie** sick leave

**arrêté** [aʀete] *nm* order, decree

**arrêter** [aʀete] *vt* to stop; (chauffage etc) to turn off, switch off; (fixer: date etc) to appoint, decide on; (criminel, suspect) to arrest; **s'~** *vi* to stop; **~ de faire** to stop doing

**arrhes** [aʀ] *nfpl* deposit *sg*

**arrière** [aʀjɛʀ] *nm* back; (SPORT) fullback ♦ *adj inv*: **siège/roue ~** back ou rear seat/wheel; à l'~ behind, at the back; **en ~** behind; (regarder) back, behind; (tomber, aller) backwards; **arriéré, e** *adj* (péj) backward ♦ *nm* (d'argent) arrears *pl*; **arrière-goût** *nm* aftertaste; **arrière-grand-mère** *nf* great-grandmother; **arrière-grand-père** *nm* great-grandfather; **arrière-pays** *nm inv* hinterland; **arrière-pensée** *nf* ulterior motive; mental reservation; **arrière-plan** *nm* background; **arrière-saison** *nf* late autumn; **arrière-train** *nm* hindquarters *pl*

**arrimer** [aRime] vt to secure; (cargaison) to stow

**arrivage** [aRivaʒ] nm consignment

**arrivée** [aRive] nf arrival; (ligne ~) finish

**arriver** [aRive] vi to arrive; (survenir) to happen, occur; **il arrive à Paris à 8h** he gets to ou arrives in Paris at 8; **~ à** (atteindre) to reach; **~ à faire qch** to succeed in doing sth; **en ~ à** (finir par) to come to; **il arrive que** it happens that; **il lui arrive de faire** he sometimes does; **arriviste** nmf go-getter

**arrobase** [aRɔbaz] nf(INFORM) @, 'at' sign

**arrogance** [aRɔgɑ̃s] nf arrogance

**arrogant, e** [aRɔgɑ̃, ɑ̃t] adj arrogant

**arrondir** [aRɔ̃diR] vt (forme, objet) to round; (somme) to round off

**arrondissement** [aRɔ̃dismɑ̃] nm (ADMIN) ≈ district

**arroser** [aRoze] vt to water; (victoire) to celebrate (over a drink); (CULIN) to baste; **arrosoir** nm watering can

**arsenal, -aux** [aRsənal, o] nm (NAVIG) naval dockyard; (MIL) arsenal; (fig) gear

**art** [aR] nm art

**artère** [aRtɛR] nf (ANAT) artery; (rue) main road

**arthrite** [aRtRit] nf arthritis

**artichaut** [aRtiʃo] nm artichoke

**article** [aRtikl] nm article; (COMM) item, article; **à l'~ de la mort** at the point of death; **~s de luxe** luxury goods

**articulation** [aRtikylasjɔ̃] nf articulation; (ANAT) joint

**articuler** [aRtikyle] vt to articulate

**artifice** [aRtifis] nm device, trick

**artificiel, le** [aRtifisjɛl] adj artificial

**artisan** [aRtizɑ̃] nm artisan, (self-employed) craftsman; **artisanal, e, -aux** adj of ou made by craftsmen; (cottage) cottage industry cpd; **de fabrication artisanale** home-made; **artisanat** nm arts and crafts pl

**artiste** [aRtist] nmf artist; (de variétés) entertainer; (musicien etc) performer; **artistique** adj artistic

**as¹** [a] vb voir **avoir**

**as²** [ɑs] nm ace

**ascendance** [asɑ̃dɑ̃s] nf (origine) ancestry

**ascendant, e** [asɑ̃dɑ̃, ɑ̃t] adj upward ♦ nm influence

**ascenseur** [asɑ̃sœR] nm lift (BRIT), elevator (US)

**ascension** [asɑ̃sjɔ̃] nf ascent; (de montagne) climb; **l'A~** (REL) the Ascension

Ascension

La fête de l'Ascension is a French public holiday, usually in May. As it falls on a Thursday, many people take Friday off work and enjoy a long weekend; see also faire le **pont**.

**aseptisé, e** (péj) adj sanitized

**aseptiser** [asɛptize] vt (ustensile) to sterilize; (plaie) to disinfect

**asiatique** [azjatik] adj Asiatic, Asian ♦ nmf: **A~** Asian

**Asie** [azi] nf: **l'~** Asia

**asile** [azil] nm (refuge) refuge, sanctuary; (POL): **droit d'~** (political) asylum; **~ (de vieillards)** old people's home

**aspect** [aspɛ] nm appearance, look; (fig) aspect, side; **à l'~ de** at the sight of

**asperge** [aspɛRʒ] nf asparagus no pl

**asperger** [aspɛRʒe] vt to spray, sprinkle

**aspérité** [aspeRite] nf bump, protruding bit (of rock etc)

**asphalte** [asfalt] nm asphalt

**asphyxier** [asfiksje] vt to suffocate, asphyxiate; (fig) to stifle

**aspirateur** [aspiRatœR] nm vacuum cleaner; **passer l'~** to vacuum

**aspirer** [aspiRe] vt (air) to inhale; (liquide) to suck (up); (suj: appareil) to suck up; **~ à** to aspire to

**aspirine** [aspiRin] nf aspirin

**assagir** [asaʒiR]: **s'~** vi to quieten down, settle down

**assaillir** [asajiR] vt to assail, attack

**assainir** [aseniR] vt (logements) to clean

up; *(eau, air)* to purify

**assaisonnement** [asezɔnmɑ̃] *nm* seasoning

**assaisonner** [asezɔne] *vt* to season

**assassin** [asasɛ̃] *nm* murderer; assassin

**assassiner** [asasine] *vt* to murder; *(esp POL)* to assassinate

**assaut** [aso] *nm* assault, attack; **prendre d'~** to storm, assault; **donner l'~** to attack

**assécher** [aseʃe] *vt* to drain

**assemblage** [asɑ̃blaʒ] *nm (action)* assembling; *(de couleurs, choses)* collection

**assemblée** [asɑ̃ble] *nf (réunion)* meeting; *(assistance)* gathering; *(POL)* assembly

**assembler** [asɑ̃ble] *vt (joindre, monter)* to assemble, put together; *(amasser)* to gather (together), collect (together); **s'~** *vi* to gather

**assener, asséner** [asene] *vt*: **~ un coup à qn** to deal sb a blow

**assentiment** [asɑ̃timɑ̃] *nm* assent, consent

**asseoir** [aswar] *vt (malade, bébé)* to sit up; *(personne debout)* to sit down; *(autorité, réputation)* to establish; **s'~** to sit (o.s.) down

**assermenté, e** [asɛrmɑ̃te] *adj* sworn, on oath

**asservir** [asɛrvir] *vt* to subjugate, enslave

**assez** [ase] *adv (suffisamment)* enough, sufficiently; *(passablement)* rather, quite, fairly; **~ de pain/livres** enough *ou* sufficient bread/books; **vous en avez ~?** have you got enough?; **j'en ai ~!** I've had enough!

**assidu, e** [asidy] *adj (appliqué)* assiduous, painstaking; *(ponctuel)* regular

**assied** *etc* [asje] *vb voir* **asseoir**

**assiéger** [asjeʒe] *vt* to besiege

**assiérai** *etc* [asjere] *vb voir* **asseoir**

**assiette** [asjɛt] *nf* plate; *(contenu)* plate(ful); **il n'est pas dans son ~** he's not feeling quite himself; **~ à des-**

**sert** dessert plate; **~ anglaise** assorted cold meats; **~ creuse** (soup) dish, soup plate; **~ plate** (dinner) plate

**assigner** [asiɲe] *vt*: **~ qch à** *(poste, part, travail)* to assign sth to

**assimiler** [asimile] *vt* to assimilate, absorb; *(comparer)*: **~ qch/qn à** to liken *ou* compare sth/sb to

**assis, e** [asi, iz] *pp de* **asseoir ♦** *adj* sitting (down), seated; **assise** *nf (fig)* basis, foundation; **assises** *nfpl (JUR)* assizes

**assistance** [asistɑ̃s] *nf (public)* audience; *(aide)* assistance; **enfant de l'Assistance** child in care

**assistant, e** [asistɑ̃, ɑ̃t] *nm/f* assistant; *(d'université)* probationary lecturer; **~(e) social(e)** social worker

**assisté, e** [asiste] *adj (AUTO)* power assisted; **~ par ordinateur** computer assisted

**assister** [asiste] *vt (aider)* to assist; **~** *(scène, événement)* to witness; *(conférence, séminaire)* to attend, be at; *(spectacle, match)* to be at, see

**association** [asɔsjasjɔ̃] *nf* association

**associé, e** [asɔsje] *nm/f (COMM)* partner

**associer** [asɔsje] *vt* to associate; **s'~** to join together; **s'~ à qn pour faire** to join (forces) with sb to do; **s'~** *(couleurs, qualités)* to be combined with; *(opinions, joie de qn)* to share in; **~ qn à** *(profits)* to give sb a share of; *(affaire)* to make sb a partner in; *(joie, triomphe)* to include sb in; **~ qch** *(allier à)* to combine sth with

**assoiffé, e** [aswafe] *adj* thirsty

**assombrir** [asɔ̃brir] *vt* to darken; *(fig)* to fill with gloom

**assommer** [asɔme] *vt (étourdir, abrutir)* to knock out, stun

**Assomption** [asɔ̃psjɔ̃] *nf*: **l'~** the Assumption

---

Assomption

La fête de l'Assomption on Augus

15 is a French national holiday. Traditionally, large numbers of holiday-makers set out on this date, frequently causing chaos on the roads; see also faire le **pont**.

**assorti, e** [asɔʀti] adj matched, matching; (varié) assorted; ~ **à** matching; **assortiment** nm assortment, selection

**assortir** [asɔʀtiʀ] vt to match; ~ **qch à** to match sth with; ~ **qch de** to accompany sth with

**assoupi, e** [asupi] adj dozing, sleeping

**assoupir** [asupiʀ]: **s'~** vi to doze off

**assouplir** [asupliʀ] vt to make supple; (fig) to relax; **assouplissant** s (fabric) softener

**assourdir** [asuʀdiʀ] vt (bruit) to deaden, muffle; (suj: bruit) to deafen

**assouvir** [asuviʀ] vt to satisfy, appease

**assujettir** [asyʒetiʀ] vt to subject

**assumer** [asyme] vt (fonction, emploi) to assume, take on

**assurance** [asyʀɑ̃s] nf (certitude) assurance; (confiance en soi) (self-)confidence; (contrat) insurance (policy); (secteur commercial) insurance; ~ **maladie** health insurance; ~ **tous risques** (AUTO) comprehensive insurance; ~**s sociales** ≈ National Insurance (BRIT), ≈ Social Security (US); **assurance-vie** nf life assurance ou insurance

**assuré, e** [asyʀe] adj (certain: réussite, échec) certain, sure; (air) assured; (pas) steady ♦ nm/f insured (person); **assurément** adv assuredly, most certainly

**assurer** [asyʀe] vt (FIN) to insure; (victoire etc) to ensure; (frontières, pouvoir) to make secure; (service) to provide, operate; **s'~ (contre)** (COMM) to insure o.s. (against); **s'~ de/que** (vérifier) to make sure of/that; **s'~ (de)** (aide de qn) to secure; ~ **à qn que** to assure sb that; ~ **qn de** to assure sb of; **assureur** nm insurer

**asthmatique** [asmatik] adj, nm/f asthmatic

**asthme** [asm] nm asthma

**asticot** [astiko] nm maggot

**astiquer** [astike] vt to polish, shine

**astre** [astʀ] nm star

**astreignant, e** [astʀeɲɑ̃, ɑ̃t] adj demanding

**astreindre** [astʀɛ̃dʀ] vt: ~ **qn à faire** to compel ou force sb to do; **s'~ à faire** to force o.s. to do

**astrologie** [astʀɔlɔʒi] nf astrology

**astronaute** [astʀonot] nm/f astronaut

**astronomie** [astʀɔnɔmi] nf astronomy

**astuce** [astys] nf shrewdness, astuteness; (truc) trick, clever way; **astucieux, -euse** adj clever

**atelier** [atəlje] nm workshop; (de peintre) studio

**athée** [ate] adj atheistic ♦ nm/f atheist

**Athènes** [atɛn] n Athens

**athlète** [atlɛt] nm/f (SPORT) athlete; **athlétisme** nm athletics sg

**atlantique** [atlɑ̃tik] adj Atlantic ♦ nm: **l'(océan) A~** the Atlantic (Ocean)

**atlas** [atlas] nm atlas

**atmosphère** [atmɔsfɛʀ] nf atmosphere

**atome** [atom] nm atom; **atomique** adj atomic, nuclear

**atomiseur** [atɔmizœʀ] nm atomizer

**atout** [atu] nm trump; (fig) asset

**âtre** [ɑtʀ] nm hearth

**atroce** [atʀɔs] adj atrocious

**attabler** [atable]: **s'~** vi to sit down at (the) table

**attachant, e** [ataʃɑ̃, ɑ̃t] adj engaging, lovable, likeable

**attache** [ataʃ] nf clip, fastener; (fig) tie

**attacher** [ataʃe] vt to tie up; (étiquette) to attach, tie on; (ceinture) to fasten ♦ vi (poêle, riz) to stick; **s'~ à** (par affection) to become attached to; **s'~ à faire** to endeavour to do; ~ **qch à** to tie up ou attach sth to

**attaque** [atak] nf attack; (cérébrale) stroke; (d'épilepsie) fit; ~ **à main armée** armed attack

**attaquer** [atake] vt to attack; (en jus-

*tice*) to bring an action against, sue ♦ *vt* to attack; **s'~ à** ♦ *vt* (*personne*) to attack; (*problème*) to tackle

**attardé, e** [ataʀde] *adj* (*enfant*) backward; (*passants*) late

**attarder** [ataʀde]: **s'~** *vi* to linger

**atteindre** [atɛ̃dʀ] *vt* (*reach*) (*blesser*) to hit; (*émouvoir*) to affect; **atteint, e** *adj* (MÉD): **être atteint de** to be suffering from; **atteinte** *nf*: **hors d'atteinte** out of reach; **porter atteinte à** to strike a blow at

**atteler** [at(ə)le] *vt* (*cheval, bœufs*) to hitch up; **s'~ à** (*travail*) to buckle down to

**attelle** [atɛl] *nf* splint

**attenant, e** [at(ə)nɑ̃, ɑ̃t] *adj*: **~ (à)** adjoining

**attendant** [atɑ̃dɑ̃] *adv*: **en ~** meanwhile, in the meantime

**attendre** [atɑ̃dʀ] *vt* (*gén*) to wait for; (*être destiné ou réservé à*) to await, be in store for ♦ *vi* to wait; **s'~ à** (**ce que**) to expect (that); **~ un enfant** to be expecting a baby; **~ de faire/d'être** to wait until one does/is; **attendez qu'il vienne** wait until he comes; **~ qch de** to expect sth of

**attendrir** [atɑ̃dʀiʀ] *vt* to move to pity; (*viande*) to tenderize; **attendrissant, e** *adj* moving, touching

**attendu, e** [atɑ̃dy] *adj* (*visiteur*) expected; (*événement*) long-awaited; **~ que** considering that, since

**attentat** [atɑ̃ta] *nm* assassination attempt; **~ à la bombe** bomb attack; **~ à la pudeur** indecent assault *no pl*

**attente** [atɑ̃t] *nf* wait; (*espérance*) expectation

**attenter** [atɑ̃te]: **~ à** *vt* (*liberté*) to violate; **~ à la vie de qn** to make an attempt on sb's life

**attentif, -ive** [atɑ̃tif, iv] *adj* (*auditeur*) attentive; (*examen*) careful; **~ à** careful to

**attention** [atɑ̃sjɔ̃] *nf* attention; (*prévenance*) attention, thoughtfulness *no pl*;

**à l'~ de** for the attention of; **faire ~ (à)** to be careful (of); **faire ~ (à ce) que** to be *ou* make sure that; **~! carefull**, watch out!; **attentionné, e** *adj* thoughtful, considerate

**atténuer** [atenɥe] *vt* (*douleur*) to alleviate, ease; (*couleurs*) to soften

**atterrer** [ateʀe] *vt* to dismay, appal

**atterrir** [ateʀiʀ] *vi* to land; **atterrissage** *nm* landing

**attestation** [atɛstasjɔ̃] *nf* certificate

**attester** [atɛste] *vt* to testify to

**attirail** [atiʀaj] (*fam*) *nm* gear; (*péj*) paraphernalia

**attirant, e** [atiʀɑ̃, ɑ̃t] *adj* attractive, appealing

**attirer** [atiʀe] *vt* to attract; (*appâter*) to lure, entice; **~ qn dans un coin** to draw sb into a corner; **~ l'attention de qn** to attract sb's attention; **~ l'attention de qn sur** to draw sb's attention to; **s'~ des ennuis** to bring trouble upon o.s., get into trouble

**attiser** [atize] *vt* (*feu*) to poke (up)

**attitré, e** [atitʀe] *adj* (*habituel*) regular, usual; (*agréé*) accredited

**attitude** [atityd] *nf* attitude; (*position du corps*) bearing

**attouchements** [atuʃmɑ̃] *nmpl* (*sexuels*) fondling *sg*

**attraction** [atʀaksjɔ̃] *nf* (*gén*) attraction; (*de cabaret, cirque*) number

**attrait** [atʀɛ] *nm* appeal, attraction

**attrape-nigaud** [atʀapnigo] (*fam*) *nm* con

**attraper** [atʀape] *vt* (*gén*) to catch; (*habitude, amende*) to get, pick up; (*fam: duper*) to con; **se faire ~** (*fam*) to be told off

**attrayant, e** [atʀɛjɑ̃, ɑ̃t] *adj* attractive

**attribuer** [atʀibɥe] *vt* (*prix*) to award; (*rôle, tâche*) to allocate, assign; (*imputer*): **~ qch à** to attribute sth to; **s'~** (*s'approprier*) to claim for o.s.; **attribut** *nm* attribute

**attrister** [atʀiste] *vt* to sadden

**attroupement** [atʀupmɑ̃] *nm* crowd

**attrouper** [atʀupe]: **s'~** vi to gather

**au** [o] prép +dét = **à +le**

**aubaine** [oben] nf godsend

**aube** [ob] nf dawn, daybreak; **à l'~** at dawn ou daybreak

**aubépine** [obepin] nf hawthorn

**auberge** [obeʀʒ] nf inn; **~ de jeunesse** youth hostel

**aubergine** [obeʀʒin] nf aubergine

**aubergiste** [obeʀʒist] nm/f inn-keeper, hotel-keeper

**aucun, e** [okœ̃, yn] dét no, tournure négative +any; (positif) any + pron sone, tournure négative +any; any(one); **sans ~ doute** without any doubt; **plus qu'~ autre** more than any other; **~ des deux** neither of the two; **~ d'entre eux** none of them; **aucunement** adv in no way, not in the least

**audace** [odas] nf daring, boldness; audacity; **audacieux, -euse** adj daring, bold

**au-delà** [od(ə)la] adv beyond ♦ nm: **l'~~** the hereafter; **~~ de** beyond

**au-dessous** [odsu] adv underneath; below; **~~ de** under(neath), below; (limite, somme etc) below, under; (dignité, condition) below

**au-dessus** [odsy] adv above; **~~ de** above

**au-devant** [od(ə)vɑ̃]: **~~ de** prép: **aller ~~ de** (personne, danger) to go (out) and meet; (souhaits de qn) to anticipate

**audience** [odjɑ̃s] nf audience; (JUR: séance) hearing

**audimat** ® [odimat] nm (taux d'écoute) ratings pl

**audio-visuel, le** [odjovizɥɛl] adj audio-visual

**auditeur, -trice** [oditœʀ, tʀis] nm/f listener

**audition** [odisjɔ̃] nf (ouïe, écoute) hearing; (JUR: de témoins) examination; (MUS, THÉÂTRE: épreuve) audition

**auditoire** [oditwaʀ] nm audience

**auge** [oʒ] nf trough

**augmentation** [ɔgmɑ̃tasjɔ̃] nf increase; **~ (de salaire)** rise (in salary) (BRIT), (pay) raise (US)

**augmenter** [ɔgmɑ̃te] vt (gén) to increase; (salaire, prix) to increase, raise, put up; (employé) to increase the salary of ♦ vi to increase

**augure** [ogyʀ] nm: **de bon/mauvais ~** of good/ill omen; **augurer** vt: **augurer bien de** to augur well for

**aujourd'hui** [oʒuʀdɥi] adv today

**aumône** [omon] nf inv alms sg; **aumônier** nm chaplain

**auparavant** [opaʀavɑ̃] adv before(hand)

**auprès** [opʀɛ]: **~ de** prép next to, close to; (recourir, s'adresser) to; (en comparaison de) compared with

**auquel** [okɛl] prép +pron = **à +lequel**

**aurai** etc [ɔʀe] vb voir **avoir**

**auréole** [ɔʀeɔl] nf halo; (tache) ring

**aurons** etc [ɔʀɔ̃] vb voir **avoir**

**aurore** [ɔʀɔʀ] nf dawn, daybreak

**ausculter** [ɔskylte] vt to sound (the chest of)

**aussi** [osi] adv (également) also, too; (de comparaison) as ♦ conj therefore, consequently; **~ fort que** as strong as; **moi ~** me too

**aussitôt** [osito] adv straight away, immediately; **~ que** as soon as

**austère** [ɔstɛʀ] adj austere

**austral, e** [ɔstʀal] adj southern

**Australie** [ɔstʀali] nf: **l'~** Australia; **australien, ne** adj Australian ♦ nm/f: **Australien, ne** Australian

**autant** [otɑ̃] adv so much; (comparatif): **~ (que)** as much (as); (nombre): as many (as); **~ (de)** so much (ou many); as much (ou many); **~ partir** we (ou you etc) may as well leave; **~ dire que** ... one might as well say that ...; **pour ~** for all that; **d'~ plus/mieux (que)** all the more/the better (since)

**autel** [otɛl] nm altar

**auteur** [otœʀ] nm author

**authenticité** [otɑ̃tisite] nf authenticity

**authentique** [otɑ̃tik] adj authentic,

genuine

**auto** [oto] *nf* car

**auto...: autobiographie** *nf* autobiography; **autobronzant** *nm* self-tanning cream (or lotion etc); **autobus** *nm* bus; **autocar** *nm* coach

**autochtone** [ɔtɔktɔn] *nm/f* native

**auto...: autocollant, e** *adj* self-adhesive; (*enveloppe*) self-seal ♦ *nm* sticker; **auto-couchettes** *adj*: **train auto-couchettes** car sleeper train; **autocuiseur** *nm* pressure cooker; **autodéfense** *nf* self-defence; **autodidacte** *nm/f* self-taught person; **auto-école** *nf* driving school; **autographe** *nm* autograph

**automate** [ɔtɔmat] *nm* (*machine*) (automatic) machine

**automatique** [ɔtɔmatik] *adj* automatic ♦ *nm*: **l'~** direct dialling; **automatiquement** *adv* automatically; **automatiser** *vt* to automate

**automne** [ɔtɔn] *nm* autumn (BRIT), fall (US)

**automobile** [ɔtɔmɔbil] *adj* motor *cpd* ♦ *nf* (motor) car; **automobiliste** *nm/f* motorist

**autonome** [ɔtɔnɔm] *adj* autonomous; **autonomie** *nf* autonomy

**autopsie** [ɔtɔpsi] *nf* post-mortem (examination), autopsy

**autoradio** [otoradjo] *nm* car radio

**autorisation** [ɔtɔrizasjɔ̃] *nf* permission, authorization; (*papiers*) permit

**autorisé, e** [ɔtɔrize] *adj* (*opinion, sources*) authoritative

**autoriser** [ɔtɔrize] *vt* to give permission for, authorize; (*fig*) to allow (of)

**autoritaire** [ɔtɔritɛr] *adj* authoritarian

**autorité** [ɔtɔrite] *nf* authority; **faire ~** to be authoritative

**autoroute** [otorut] *nf* motorway (BRIT), highway (US)

**auto-stop** [otostɔp] *nm*: **faire de l'~~** to hitch-hike; **prendre qn en ~~** to give sb a lift; **auto-stoppeur, -euse** *nm/f* hitch-hiker

**autour** [otur] *adv* around; **~ de** around; **tout ~** all around

---

MOT-CLÉ

**autre** [otr] *adj* 1 (*différent*) other, different; **je préférerais un autre verre** I'd prefer another *ou* a different glass

2 (*supplémentaire*) other; **je voudrais un autre verre d'eau** I'd like another glass of water

3: **autre chose** something else; **autre part** somewhere else; **d'autre part** on the other hand

♦ *pron*: **un autre** another (one); **nous/vous autres** us/you; **d'autres** others; **l'autre** the other (one); **les autres** the others; (*autrui*) others; **l'un et l'autre** both of them; **se détester l'un l'autre/les uns les autres** to hate each other *ou* one another; **d'une semaine à l'autre** from one week to the next; (*incessamment*) any week now; **entre autres** among other things

---

**autrefois** [otrəfwa] *adv* in the past

**autrement** [otrəmɑ̃] *adv* differently (*d'une manière différente*) in another way; (*sinon*) otherwise; **~ dit** in other words

**Autriche** [otriʃ] *nf*: **l'~** Austria; **autrichien, ne** *adj* Austrian ♦ *nm/f*: **Autrichien, ne** Austrian

**autruche** [otryʃ] *nf* ostrich

**autrui** [otrɥi] *pron* others

**auvent** [ovɑ̃] *nm* canopy

**aux** [o] *prép* +*dét* = **à les**

**auxiliaire** [oksiljɛr] *adj, nm/f* auxiliary

**auxquelles** [okɛl] *prép* +*pron* = **à +les quelles**

**auxquels** [okɛl] *prép* +*pron* = **à +les quels**

**avachi, e** [avaʃi] *adj* limp, flabby

**aval** [aval] *nm*: **en ~** downstream downriver

**avalanche** [avalɑ̃ʃ] *nf* avalanche

**avaler** [avale] *vt* to swallow

**ance** [avɑ̃s] nf (de troupes etc) advance; progress; (d'argent) advance; (sur un concurrent) lead; **~s** nfpl (amoureuses) advances; (**être) en ~** (to be) early; (sur un programme) (to be) ahead of schedule; **à l'~, d'~** in advance

**ancé, e** [avɑ̃se] adj advanced; (travail) well on, well under way

**ancement** [avɑ̃smɑ̃] nm (professionnel) promotion

**ancer** [avɑ̃se] vi to move forward, advance; (projet, travail) to make progress; (montre, réveil) to be fast; to gain ♦ vt to move forward, advance; (argent) to advance; (montre, pendule) to put forward; **s'~** vi to move forward, advance; (fig) to commit o.s.

**ant** [avɑ̃] prép, adv before ♦ adj inv: **siège/roue ~** front seat/wheel ♦ nm (d'un véhicule, bâtiment) front; (SPORT: joueur) forward; **qu'il (ne) fasse/de faire** before he does/doing; **~ tout** above all; **à l'~** (dans un véhicule) in (the) front; **en ~** forward(s); **en ~ de** in front of

**antage** [avɑ̃taʒ] nm advantage; **~s sociaux** fringe benefits; **avantager** vt (favoriser) to favour; (embellir) to flatter; **avantageux, -euse** adj (prix) attractive

**ant...: avant-bras** nm inv forearm; **avantcoureur** adj inv: **signe avant-coureur** advance indication ou sign; **avant-dernier, -ière** adj, nm/f next to last, last but one; **avant-goût** nm foretaste; **avant-guerre** nm pre-war years; **avant-hier** adv the day before yesterday; **avant-première** nf (de film) preview; **avant-projet** nm (preliminary) draft; **avant-propos** nm foreword; **avant-veille** nf: **l'avant-veille** two days before

**are** [avar] adj miserly, avaricious ♦ nm/f miser; **~ de** (compliments etc) sparing of

**arié, e** [avarje] adj (aliment) rotting

**aries** [avari] nfpl (NAVIG) damage sg

**avec** [avɛk] prép with; (à l'égard de) to(wards), with; **et ~ ça?** (dans magasin) anything else?

**avenant, e** [av(ə)nɑ̃, ɑ̃t] adj pleasant; **à l'~** in keeping

**avènement** [avɛnmɑ̃] nm (d'un changement) advent, coming

**avenir** [avniʀ] nm future; **à l'~** in future; **politicien d'~** politician with prospects ou a future

**aventure** [avɑ̃tyʀ] nf adventure; (amoureuse) affair; **aventurer: s'aventurer** vi to venture; **aventureux, -euse** adj adventurous, venturesome; (projet) risky, chancy

**avenue** [avny] nf avenue

**avérer** [aveʀe]: **s'~** vb +attrib to prove (to be)

**averse** [avɛʀs] nf shower

**averti, e** [avɛʀti] adj (well-)informed

**avertir** [avɛʀtiʀ] vt: **~ qn (de qch/que)** to warn sb (of sth/that); (renseigner) to inform sb (of sth/that); **avertissement** nm warning; **avertisseur** nm horn, siren

**aveu, x** [avø] nm confession

**aveugle** [avœgl] adj blind ♦ nm/f blind man/woman; **aveuglément** adv blindly; **aveugler** vt to blind

**aviateur, -trice** [avjatœʀ, tʀis] nm/f aviator, pilot

**aviation** [avjasjɔ̃] nf aviation; (sport) flying; (MIL) air force

**avide** [avid] adj eager; (péj) greedy, grasping

**avilir** [aviliʀ] vt to debase

**avion** [avjɔ̃] nm (aero)plane (BRIT), (air)plane (US); **aller (quelque part) en ~** to go (somewhere) by plane, fly (somewhere); **par ~** by airmail; **~ à réaction** jet (plane)

**aviron** [aviʀɔ̃] nm oar; (sport): **l'~** rowing

**avis** [avi] nm opinion; (notification) notice; **à mon ~** in my opinion; **changer d'~** to change one's mind; **jusqu'à nouvel ~** until further notice

**avisé, e** [avize] *adj* sensible, wise; **bien/mal ~ de** well-/ill-advised to

**aviser** [avize] *vt* (*informer*): **~ qn de/que** to advise *ou* inform sb of/that ♦ *vi* to think about things, assess the situation; **nous ~ons sur place** we'll work something out once we're there; **s'~ de qch/que** to become suddenly aware of sth/that; **s'~ de faire** to take it into one's head to do

**avocat, e** [avɔka, at] (JUR) barrister (BRIT), lawyer ♦ *nm* (CULIN) avocado (pear); **~ de la défense** counsel for the defence; **~ général** assistant public prosecutor

**avoine** [avwan] *nf* oats *pl*

---

**MOT-CLÉ**

**avoir** [avwaR] *nm* assets *pl*, resources *pl*; (COMM) credit

♦ *vt* **1** (*posséder*) to have; **elle a 2 enfants/une belle maison** she has (got) 2 children/a lovely house; **il a les yeux bleus** he has (got) blue eyes

**2** (*âge, dimensions*) to be; **il a 3 ans** he is 3 (years old); **le mur a 3 mètres de haut** the wall is 3 metres high; *voir aussi* **faim; peur** *etc*

**3** (*fam: duper*) to do, have; **on vous a eu!** you've been done *ou* had!

**4: en avoir contre qn** to have a grudge against sb; **en avoir assez** to be fed up; **j'en ai pour une demi-heure** it'll take me half an hour

♦ *vb aux* **1** to have; **avoir mangé/dormi** to have eaten/slept

**2** (*avoir +à +infinitif*): **avoir à faire qch** to have to do sth; **vous n'avez qu'à lui demander** you only have to ask him

♦ *vb impers* **1: il y a** (*+ singulier*) there is; (*+ pluriel*) there are; **qu'y-a-t-il?**, **qu'est-ce qu'il y a?** what's the matter?, what is it?; **il doit y avoir une explication** there must be an explanation; **il n'y a qu'à ...** we (*ou* you *etc*) will just have to ...

**2** (*temporel*): **il y a 10 ans** 10 yea ago; **il y a 10 ans/longtemps que le sais** I've known it for 10 year long time; **il y a 10 ans qu'il est ar vé** it's 10 years since he arrived

**avoisiner** [avwazine] *vt* to be near close to; (*fig*) to border *ou* verge on

**avortement** [avɔRtəmã] *nm* abortio

**avorter** [avɔRte] *vi* (MÉD) to have abortion; (*fig*) to fail

**avoué, e** [avwe] *adj* avowed ♦ *nm* (JU ≈ solicitor

**avouer** [avwe] *vt* (*crime, défaut*) to co fess (to); **~ avoir fait/que** to admit confess to having done/that

**avril** [avRil] *nm* April

---

**poisson d'avril**

The traditional prank on April 1 in France is to stick a cut-out paper fis known as a **poisson d'avril**, to someone's back without being caugh

---

**axe** [aks] *nm* axis; (*de roue etc*) ax (*fig*) main line; **axer** *vt*: **axer qch** a to centre sth on

**ayons** *etc* [ej5] *vb voir* **avoir**

**azote** [azɔt] *nm* nitrogen

## B, b

**baba** [baba] *nm*: **~ au rhum** r baba

**babines** [babin] *nfpl* chops

**babiole** [babjɔl] *nf* (*bibelot*) trinket; ( *tille*) trifle

**bâbord** [babɔR] *nm*: **à ~** to port, the port side

**baby-foot** [babifut] *nm* table footbal

**baby-sitting** [babisitiŋ] *nm*: **faire ~~** to baby-sit

**bac** [bak] *abr m* = **baccalauréat** (*récipient*) tub

**baccalauréat** [bakalɔRea] *nm* hi school diploma

n France the **baccalauréat** or **bac** is the school-leaving certificate taken at lycée at the age of seventeen or eighteen, enabling entry to university. Different subject combinations are available from the broad subject range studied.

**âche** [baʃ] nf tarpaulin

**chelier, -ière** [baʃəlje, jɛʀ] nm/f holder of the baccalauréat

**cler** [bakle] vt to botch (up)

**daud, e** [bado, od] nm/f idle onlooker, stroller

**digeonner** [badiʒɔne] vt (barbouiller) to daub

**diner** [badine] vi: ~ **avec qch** to eat sth lightly

**ffe** [baf] (fam) nf slap, clout

**fouer** [bafwe] vt to deride, ridicule

**fouiller** [bafuje] vi, vt to stammer

**frer** [bafʀe] (fam) vi to guzzle

**gages** [bagaʒ] nmpl luggage sg; ~ **à main** hand-luggage

**garre** [bagaʀ] nf fight, brawl; **bagarrer: se bagarrer** vi to have a fight ou scuffle, fight

**gatelle** [bagatɛl] nf trifle

**gne** [baɲ] nm penal colony

**gnole** [baɲɔl] (fam) nf car

**gout** [bagu] nm: **avoir du ~** to have the gift of the gab

**gue** [bag] nf ring; ~ **de fiançailles** engagement ring

**guette** [bagɛt] nf stick; (cuisine chinoise) chopstick; (de chef d'orchestre) baton; (pain) stick of (French) bread; ~ **magique** magic wand

**ie** [bɛ] nf (GÉO) bay; (fruit) berry; ~ (vitrée) picture window

**gnade** [baɲad] nf bathing; "~ interdite" "no bathing"

**igner** [baɲe] vt (bébé) to bath; **se ~** to have a swim, go swimming ou

bathing; **baignoire** nf bath(tub)

**bail** [baj, bo] (pl baux) nm lease

**bâillement** [bajmɑ̃] nm yawn

**bâiller** [baje] vi to yawn; (être ouvert) to gape; **bâillonner** vt to gag

**bain** [bɛ̃] nm bath; **prendre un ~** to have a bath; **se mettre dans le ~** (fig) to get into it ou things; ~ **de soleil**: **prendre un ~ de soleil** to sunbathe; **~s de mer** sea bathing sg; **bain-marie** nm: **faire chauffer au bain-marie** (boîte etc) to immerse in boiling water

**baiser** [beze] nm kiss ♦ vt (main, front) to kiss; (fam!) to screw (!)

**baisse** [bɛs] nf fall, drop; **être en ~** to be falling, be declining

**baisser** [bese] vt to lower; (radio, chauffage) to turn down ♦ vi to fall, drop, go down; (vue, santé) to fail, dwindle; **se ~** vi to bend down

**bal** [bal] nm dance; (grande soirée) ball; ~ **costumé** fancy-dress ball

**balade** [balad] (fam) nf (à pied) walk, stroll; (en voiture) drive; **balader** (fam): **se balader** vi to go for a walk ou stroll; to go for a drive; **baladeur** nm personal stereo, Walkman ®

**balafre** [balafʀ] nf (cicatrice) scar

**balai** [bale] nm broom, brush; **balaibrosse** nm (long-handled) scrubbing brush

**balance** [balɑ̃s] nf scales pl; (signe): **la B~** Libra

**balancer** [balɑ̃se] vt to swing; (fam: lancer) to fling, chuck; (: jeter) to chuck out; ~ vi to swing, rock; **se ~** (fam) not to care about; **balançoire** nf swing; (sur pivot) seesaw

**balayer** [baleje] vt (feuilles etc) to sweep up, brush up; (pièce) to sweep; (objections) to sweep aside; (suj: radar) to scan; **balayeur, -euse** nm/f roadsweeper

**balbutier** [balbysje] vi, vt to stammer

**balcon** [balkɔ̃] nm balcony; (THÉÂTRE) dress circle

**baleine** [balɛn] *nf* whale

**balise** [baliz] *nf* (NAVIG) beacon; (marker) buoy; (AVIAT) runway light, beacon; (AUTO, SKI) sign, marker; **baliser** *vt* to mark out (with lights *etc*)

**balivernes** [balivɛrn] *nfpl* nonsense *sg*

**ballant, e** [balɑ̃, ɑ̃t] *adj* dangling

**balle** [bal] *nf* (de fusil) bullet; (de sport) ball; (fam: franc) franc

**ballerine** [bal(ə)rin] *nf* (danseuse) ballet dancer; (chaussure) ballet shoe

**ballet** [balɛ] *nm* ballet

**ballon** [balɔ̃] *nm* (de sport) ball; (jouet, AVIAT) balloon; **~ de football** football

**ballot** [balo] *nm* bundle; (péj) nitwit

**ballottage** [balɔtaʒ] *nm* (POL) second ballot

**ballotter** [balɔte] *vt:* **être ballotté** to be thrown about

**balnéaire** [balneɛr] *adj* seaside *cpd;* **station ~** seaside resort

**balourd, e** [balur, urd] *adj* clumsy

**balustrade** [balystrad] *nf* railings *pl*, handrail

**bambin** [bɑ̃bɛ̃] *nm* little child

**bambou** [bɑ̃bu] *nm* bamboo

**ban** [bɑ̃] *nm:* **mettre au ~ de** to outlaw from; **~s** *nmpl* (de mariage) banns

**banal, e** [banal] *adj* banal, commonplace; (péj) trite; **banalité** *nf* banality

**banane** [banan] *nf* banana; (sac) waist-bag, bum-bag

**banc** [bɑ̃] *nm* seat, bench; (de poissons) shoal; **~ d'essai** (fig) testing ground

**bancaire** [bɑ̃kɛr] *adj* banking; (chèque, carte) bank *cpd*

**bancal, e** [bɑ̃kal] *adj* wobbly

**bandage** [bɑ̃daʒ] *nm* bandage

**bande** [bɑ̃d] *nf* (de tissu *etc*) strip; (MÉD) bandage; (motif) stripe; (magnétique *etc*) tape; (groupe) band; (: péj) bunch; **faire ~ à part** to keep to o.s.; **~ dessinée** comic strip; **~ sonore** sound track

---

**bande dessinée**

The **bande dessinée** or **BD** enjoys a huge following in France amongst adults as well as children. An international show takes place at Angoulême in January every year. Astérix, Tintin, Lucky Luke and Gaston Lagaffe are among the most famous cartoon characters.

---

**bandeau, x** [bɑ̃do] *nm* headband; (sur les yeux) blindfold

**bander** [bɑ̃de] *vt* (blessure) to bandage; **~ les yeux à qn** to blindfold sb

**banderole** [bɑ̃drɔl] *nf* banner, streamer

**bandit** [bɑ̃di] *nm* bandit; **banditisme** *nm* violent crime, armed robberies *pl*

**bandoulière** [bɑ̃duljɛr] *nf:* **en ~** (slung *ou* worn) across the shoulder

**banlieue** [bɑ̃ljø] *nf* suburbs *pl;* **lignes/quartiers de ~** suburban lines/areas; **trains de ~** commuter trains

**banlieusard, e** [bɑ̃ljøzar] *nm/f* (suburban) commuter

**bannière** [banjɛr] *nf* banner

**bannir** [banir] *vt* to banish

**banque** [bɑ̃k] *nf* bank; (activités) banking; **~ d'affaires** merchant bank; **banqueroute** *nf* bankruptcy

**banquet** [bɑ̃kɛ] *nm* dinner; (d'apparat) banquet

**banquette** [bɑ̃kɛt] *nf* seat

**banquier** [bɑ̃kje] *nm* banker

**banquise** [bɑ̃kiz] *nf* ice field

**baptême** [batɛm] *nm* christening; baptism; **~ de l'air** first flight

**baptiser** [batize] *vt* to baptize, christen

**baquet** [bakɛ] *nm* tub, bucket

**bar** [bar] *nm* bar

**baraque** [barak] *nf* shed; (fam) house; **baraqué, e** (fam) *adj* well-built, hefty; **baraquements** *nmpl* (provisoires) huts

**baratin** [baratɛ̃] (fam) *nm* smooth talk, patter; **baratiner** *vt* to chat up

**barbare** [barbar] *adj* barbaric; **barbarie** *nf* barbarity

**barbe** [barb] *nf* beard; **la ~!** (fam)

damn it!; **quelle ~!** (fam) what a drag
u borel!; **à la ~ de qn** under sb's nose;
**~ à papa** candy-floss (BRIT), cotton candy (US)

**arbelé** [barbəle] adj, nm: **(fil de fer) ~**
barbed wire no pl

**arber** [barbe] (fam) vt to bore stiff

**arbiturique** [barbityrik] nm barbitu-
ate

**arboter** [barbote] vi (enfant) to pad-
not

**arbouiller** [barbuje] vt to daub;
**avoir l'estomac barbouillé** to feel
queasy

**arbu, e** [barby] adj bearded

**arda** [barda] (fam) nm kit, gear

**arder** [barde] (fam) vi: **ça va ~**
sparks will fly, things are going to get
not

**arème** [barɛm] nm (SCOL) scale; (table
de référence) table

**aril** [baril] nm barrel; (poudre) keg

**ariolé, e** [barjɔle] adj gaudily-
coloured

**aromètre** [barɔmɛtr] nm barometer

**aron, ne** [barɔ̃] nm/f baron(ess)

**aroque** [barɔk] adj (ART) baroque;
(fig) weird

**arque** [bark] nf small boat

**arquette** [barkɛt] nf (pour repas) tray;
(pour fruits) punnet

**arrage** [baraʒ] nm dam; (sur route)
roadblock, barricade

**arre** [bar] nf bar; (NAVIG) helm; (écrite)
line, stroke

**arreau, x** [baro] nm bar; (JUR): **le ~**
the Bar

**arrer** [bare] vt (route etc) to block;
(mot) to cross out; (chèque) to cross
(BRIT); (NAVIG) to steer; **se ~** (fam) vi to
clear off

**arrette** [barɛt] nf (pour cheveux) (hair)
slide (BRIT) ou clip (US)

**arricader** [barikade]: **se ~** vi to barricade o.s.

**arrière** [barjɛr] nf fence; (obstacle)
barrier; (porte) gate

**barrique** [barik] nf barrel, cask

**bar-tabac** [bartaba] nm bar (which sells
tobacco and stamps)

**bas, basse** [ba, bas] adj low ♦ nm bottom, lower part; (vêtement) stocking ♦
adv low; (parler) softly; **au ~ mot** at the
lowest estimate; **en ~** down below;
(d'une liste, d'un mur etc) at/to the bottom; (dans une maison) downstairs; **en
~ de** at the bottom of; **un enfant en ~
âge** a young child; **à ~ ...!** down with
...!; **~ morceaux** nmpl (viande) cheap
cuts

**basané, e** [bazane] adj tanned

**bas-côté** [bakote] nm (de route) verge
(BRIT), shoulder (US)

**bascule** [baskyl] nf: **(jeu de) ~** seesaw; **(balance à) ~** scales pl; **fauteuil
à ~** rocking chair

**basculer** [baskyle] vi to fall over, topple (over); (benne) to tip up ♦ vt (gén:
nu) to tip out; (benne) to tip up

**base** [baz] nf base; (POL) rank and file;
(fondement, principe) basis; **de ~** basic;
**à ~ de café** etc coffee etc -based; **~ de
données** database; **baser** vt to base;
**se baser sur** vt (preuves) to base one's
argument on

**bas-fond** [baf5] nm (NAVIG) shallow; **~
~s** nmpl (fig) dregs

**basilic** [bazilik] nm (CULIN) basil

**basket** [basket] nm trainer (BRIT), sneak-
er (US); (aussi: **~-ball**) basketball

**basque** [bask] adj, nm/f Basque

**basse** [bas] adj voir **bas** ♦ nf (MUS) bass;
**basse-cour** nf farmyard

**bassin** [basɛ̃] nm (pièce d'eau) pond,
pool; (de fontaine, GÉO) basin; (ANAT)
pelvis; (portuaire) dock

**bassine** [basin] nf (ustensile) basin;
(contenu) bowl(ful)

**basson** [bas5] nm bassoon

**bas-ventre** [bavɑ̃tr] nm (lower part of
the) stomach

**bat** [ba] vb voir **battre**

**bataille** [bataj] nf (MIL) battle; (rixe)
fight; **batailler** vi to fight

**bâtard, e** [batar, ard] nm/f illegitimate child, bastard (pej)

**bateau, x** [bato] nm boat; ship; **bateau-mouche** nm passenger pleasure boat (on the Seine)

**bâti, e** [bati] adj: **bien ~** well-built

**batifoler** [batifɔle] vi to frolic about

**bâtiment** [batimã] nm building; (NAVIG) ship, vessel; (industrie) building trade

**bâtir** [batir] vt to build

**bâtisse** [batis] nf building

**bâton** [batɔ̃] nm stick; **à ~s rompus** informally

**bats** [ba] vb voir **battre**

**battage** [bataʒ] nm (publicité) (hard) plugging

**battant, e** [batɑ̃, ɑ̃t] nm: **porte à double ~** double door

**battement** [batmã] nm (de cœur) beat; (intervalle) interval; **10 minutes de ~** 10 minutes to spare

**batterie** [batri] nf (MIL, ÉLEC) battery; (MUS) drums pl, drum kit; **~ de cuisine** pots and pans pl, kitchen utensils pl

**batteur** [batœr] nm (MUS) drummer; (appareil) whisk

**battre** [batr] vt to beat; (blé) to thresh; (passer au peigne fin) to scour; (cartes) to shuffle ♦ vi (cœur) to beat; (volets etc) to bang, rattle; **se ~** vi to fight; **~ la mesure** to beat time; **~ son plein** to be at its height, be going full swing; **~ des mains** to clap one's hands

**battue** [baty] nf (chasse) beat; (policière etc) search, hunt

**baume** [bom] nm balm

**baux** [bo] nmpl de **bail**

**bavard, e** [bavar, ard] adj (very) talkative; gossipy; **bavarder** vi to chatter; (commérer) to gossip; (divulguer un secret) to blab

**bave** [bav] nf dribble; (de chien etc) slobber; (d'escargot) slime; **baver** vi to dribble; (chien) to slobber; **en baver** (fam) to have a hard time (of it); **baveux, -euse** (omelette) runny; **ba-**

**voir** nm bib

**bavure** [bavyr] nf smudge; (fig) hitc (policière etc) blunder

**bayer** [baje] vi: **~ aux corneilles** 1 stand gaping

**bazar** [bazar] nm general store; (far jumble; **bazarder** (fam) vt to chuc out

**BCBG** sigle adj (= bon chic bon genr preppy, smart and trendy

**BCE** sigle f (= Banque centrale europ enne) ECB

**BD** sigle f = **bande dessinée**

**bd** abr = **boulevard**

**béant, e** [beã, ãt] adj gaping

**béat, e** [bea, at] adj: **~ d'admiratio** struck dumb with admiration; **béatit** **de** nf bliss

**beau (bel), belle** [bo, bɛl] (m beaux) adj beautiful, lovely; (homm handsome; (femme) beautiful ♦ adv: **fait beau** the weather's fine; **un ~jou** one (fine) day; **de plus belle** mo than ever, even more; **on a ~essaye** however hard we try; **bel et bien** we and truly

*MOT-CLÉ*

**beaucoup** [boku] adv 1 a lot; **il bo beaucoup** he drinks a lot; **il ne bo pas beaucoup** he doesn't drink muc ou a lot

2 (suivi de plus, trop etc) much, a lo far; **il est beaucoup plus grand** he much ou a lot ou far taller

3: **beaucoup de** (nombre) many, a lo of; (quantité) a lot of; **beaucoup d'étudiants/de touristes** a lot of c many students/tourists; **beaucoup d courage** a lot of courage; **il n'a pa beaucoup d'argent** he hasn't go much ou a lot of money

4: **de beaucoup** by far

**beau...: beau-fils** nm son-in-law; (re mariage) stepson; **beau-frère** nm brother-in-law; **beau-père** nm father-

n-law; (remariage) stepfather
beauté [bote] nf beauty; **de toute** ~
beautiful; **finir qch en** ~ to complete
sth brilliantly
beaux-arts [bozar] nmpl fine arts
beaux-parents [boparɑ̃] nmpl wife's/
husband's family, in-laws
bébé [bebe] nm baby
bec [bɛk] nm beak, bill; (de théière)
spout; (de casserole) lip; (fam) mouth; ~
de gaz (street) gaslamp
bec-de-lièvre [bɛkdəljɛvʀ] nm harelip
bêche [bɛʃ] nf spade; bêcher vt to dig
bécoter [bekɔte]: se ~ vi to smooch
becqueter [bɛkte] (fam) vt to eat
bedaine [bədɛn] nf paunch
bedonnant, e [bədɔnɑ̃, ɑ̃t] adj pot-
bellied
bée [be] adj: bouche ~ gaping
beffroi [befʀwa] nm belfry
bégayer [begeje] vt, vi to stammer
bègue [bɛg] nm/f: être ~ to have a
stammer
beige [bɛʒ] adj beige
beignet [bɛɲɛ] nm fritter
bel [bɛl] adj voir beau
bêler [bele] vi to bleat
belette [bəlɛt] nf weasel
belge [bɛlʒ] adj Belgian ♦ nm/f: B~ Belgian
Belgique [bɛlʒik] nf: la ~ Belgium
bélier [belje] nm ram; (signe): le B~
Aries
belle [bɛl] adj voir beau ♦ nf (SPORT) de-
cider; **belle-fille** nf daughter-in-law;
(remariage) stepdaughter; **belle-mère**
nf mother-in-law; stepmother; **belle-
sœur** nf sister-in-law
belliqueux, -euse [belikø, øz] adj aggressive, warlike
belvédère [belvedɛʀ] nm panoramic
viewpoint (or small building there)
bémol [bemɔl] nm (MUS) flat
bénédiction [benediksjɔ̃] nf blessing
bénéfice [benefis] nm (COMM) profit;
(avantage) benefit; **bénéficier: bénéfi-**

cier de vt to enjoy; (situation) to
benefit by ou from; **bénéfique** adj
beneficial
bénévole [benevɔl] adj voluntary, unpaid
bénin, -igne [benɛ̃, iɲ] adj minor,
mild; (tumeur) benign
bénir [beniʀ] vt to bless; **bénit, e** adj
consecrated; **eau bénite** holy water
benjamin, e [bɛ̃ʒamɛ̃, in] nm/f youngest child
benne [bɛn] nf skip; (de téléphérique)
(cable) car; ~ **basculante** tipper (BRIT),
dump truck (US)
BEP sigle m (= brevet d'études professionnelles) technical school certificate
béquille [bekij] nf crutch; (de bicyclette)
stand
berceau, x [bɛʀso] nm cradle, crib
bercer [bɛʀse] vt to rock, cradle; (suj:
musique etc) to lull; ~ **qn de** (promesses
etc) to delude sb with; **berceuse** nf
lullaby
béret (basque) [bere (bask(ə))] nm beret
berge [bɛʀʒ] nf bank
berger, -ère [bɛʀʒe, ɛʀ] nm/f
shepherd(-ess); ~ **allemand** alsatian
(BRIT), German shepherd
berlingot [bɛʀlɛ̃go] nm (bonbon) boiled
sweet, humbug (BRIT)
berlue [bɛʀly] nf: **j'ai la** ~ I must be
seeing things
berner [bɛʀne] vt to fool
besogne [bəzɔɲ] nf work no pl, job
besoin [bəzwɛ̃] nm need; **avoir** ~ **de**
qch/faire qch to need sth/to do sth;
**au** ~ if need be; **le** ~ (pauvreté) need,
want; **être dans le** ~ to be in need ou
want; **faire ses** ~s to relieve o.s.
bestiaux [bɛstjo] nmpl cattle
bestiole [bɛstjɔl] nf (tiny) creature
bétail [betaj] nm livestock, cattle pl
bête [bɛt] nf animal; (bestiole) insect,
creature ♦ adj stupid, silly; **il cherche
la petite** ~ he's being pernickety ou
overfussy; ~ **noire** pet hate

**bêtement** [bɛtmɑ̃] *adv* stupidly

**bêtise** [betiz] *nf* stupidity; (*action*) stupid thing (to say ou do)

**béton** [betɔ̃] *nm* concrete; (**en**) ~ (*alibi, argument*) cast iron; ~ **armé** reinforced concrete; **bétonnière** *nf* cement mixer

**betterave** [betʀav] *nf* beetroot (*BRIT*), beet (*US*); ~ **sucrière** sugar beet

**beugler** [bøgle] *vi* to low; (*radio etc*) to blare ♦ *vt* (*chanson*) to bawl out

**Beur** [bœʀ] *nm/f* person of North African origin living in France

**beurre** [bœʀ] *nm* butter; **beurrer** *vt* to butter; **beurrier** *nm* butter dish

**beuverie** [bøvʀi] *nf* drinking session

**bévue** [bevy] *nf* blunder

**Beyrouth** [beʀut] *n* Beirut

**bi...** [bi] *préfixe* bi..., two-

**biais** [bjɛ] *nm* (*moyen*) device, expedient; (*aspect*) angle; **en** ~, **de** ~ (*obliquement*) at an angle; **par le** ~ **de** by means of; **biaiser** *vi* (*fig*) to sidestep the issue

**bibelot** [biblo] *nm* trinket, curio

**biberon** [bibʀɔ̃] *nm* (*feeding*) bottle; **nourrir au** ~ to bottle-feed

**bible** [bibl] *nf* bible

**biblio...** [biblio] *préfixe*: **bibliobus** *nm* mobile library van; **bibliographie** *nf* bibliography; **bibliothécaire** *nm/f* librarian; **bibliothèque** *nf* library; (*meuble*) bookcase

**bic** ® [bik] *nm* Biro ®

**bicarbonate** [bikaʀbɔnat] *nm*: ~ **(de soude)** bicarbonate of soda

**biceps** [bisɛps] *nm* biceps

**biche** [biʃ] *nf* doe

**bichonner** [biʃɔne] *vt* to pamper

**bicolore** [bikɔlɔʀ] *adj* two-coloured

**bicoque** [bikɔk] (*péj*) *nf* shack

**bicyclette** [bisiklɛt] *nf* bicycle

**bide** [bid] (*fam*) *nm* (*ventre*) belly; (*THÉÂTRE*) flop

**bidet** [bidɛ] *nm* bidet

**bidon** [bidɔ̃] *nm* can ♦ *adj inv* (*fam*) phoney

**bidonville** [bidɔ̃vil] *nm* shanty town

**bidule** [bidyl] (*fam*) *nm* thingumajig

MOT-CLÉ

**bien** [bjɛ̃] *nm* 1 (*avantage, profit*): **fair du bien à qn** to do sb good; **dire du bien de** to speak well of; **c'est pou son bien** it's for his own good

2 (*possession, patrimoine*) possession property; **son bien le plus précieu** his most treasured possession; **avoir d bien** to have property; **biens (d consommation** *etc*) (consumer *et* goods

3 (*moral*): **le bien**: good; **distinguer bien du mal** to tell good from evil

♦ *adv* 1 (*de façon satisfaisante*) well **elle travaille/mange bien** she work eats well; **croyant bien faire, je/il ...** thinking I/he was doing the right thing I/he ...; **c'est bien fait!** it serves hir (*ou her etc*) right!

2 (*valeur intensive*) quite; **bien jeun** quite young; **bien assez** quite enough **bien mieux** (very) much better; **j'es père bien y aller** I do hope to go; **j veux bien le faire** (*concession*) I'r quite willing to do it; **il faut bien l faire** it has to be done

3: **bien du temps/des gens** quite time/a number of people

♦ *adj inv* 1 (*en bonne forme, à l'aise*): **j me sens bien** I feel fine; **je ne m sens pas bien** I don't feel well; **on es bien dans ce fauteuil** this chair is ver comfortable

2 (*joli, beau*) good-looking; **tu es bie dans cette robe** you look good in thi dress

3 (*satisfaisant*) good; **elle est bien cette maison/secrétaire** it's a goo house/she's a good secretary

4 (*moralement*) right; (: *personne* good, nice; (*respectable*) respectable **ce n'est pas bien de ...** it's not righ to ...; **elle est bien, cette femm** she's a nice woman, she's a good sor **des gens biens** respectable people

_(en bons termes):_ **être bien avec qn** to be on good terms with sb

_préfixe:_ **bien-aimé** _adj, nm/f_ beloved; **bien-être** _nm_ well-being; **bienfaisance** _nf_ charity; **bienfaisant, e** _adj (chose)_ beneficial; **bienfait** _nm_ act of generosity, benefaction; _(de la science etc)_ benefit; **bienfaiteur, -trice** _nm/f_ benefactor/benefactress; **bien-fondé** _nm_ soundness; **bien-fonds** _nm_ property; **bienheureux, -euse** _adj_ happy; _(REL)_ blessed, blest; **bien que** _conj_ (al)though; **bien sûr** _adv_ certainly

---

**enséant, e** [bjēseã, ãt] _adj_ seemly

**entôt** [bjēto] _adv_ soon; **à ~** see you soon

**enveillant, e** [bjēvεjã, ãt] _adj_ kindly

**envenu, e** [bjēvny] _adj_ welcome; **envenue** _nf:_ **souhaiter la bienvenue à** to welcome; **bienvenue à** welcome to

**ère** [bjεR] _nf (boisson)_ beer; _(cercueil)_ bier; **~ (à la) pression** draught beer; **~ blonde** lager; **~ brune** brown ale

**fer** [bife] _vt_ to cross out

**teck** [biftεk] _nm_ steak

**urquer** [bifyRke] _vi (route)_ to fork; _(véhicule)_ to turn off

**garré, e** [bigare] _adj_ multicoloured; _(disparate)_ motley

**orneau, x** [bigoRno] _nm_ winkle

**uot, e** [bigo, ɔt] _(pej) adj_ bigoted

**oudi** [bigudi] _nm_ curler

**ou, x** [biʒu] _nm_ jewel; **bijouterie** _nf_ jeweller's (shop); **bijoutier, -ière** _nm/f_ jeweller

**ini** [bikini] _nm_ bikini

**an** [bilã] _nm (fig)_ (net) outcome; _(de victimes)_ toll; _(COMM)_ balance sheet(s); **un ~ de santé** a (medical) checkup; **faire le ~ de** to assess, review; **déposer son ~** to file a bankruptcy statement

**e** [bil] _nf_ bile; **se faire de la ~** _(fam)_ to worry o.s. sick

**bilieux, -euse** [biljø, øz] _adj_ bilious; _(fig: colérique)_ testy

**bilingue** [bilēg] _adj_ bilingual

**billard** [bijaR] _nm (jeu)_ billiards _sg; (table)_ billiard table; **~ américain** pool

**bille** [bij] _nf (gén)_ ball; _(du jeu de ~s)_ marble

**billet** [bijε] _nm (aussi:_ **~ de banque)** (bank)note; _(de cinéma, de bus etc)_ ticket; _(courte lettre)_ note; **~ Bige** cheap rail ticket for under-26s; **billetterie** _nf_ ticket office; _(distributeur)_ ticket machine; _(BANQUE)_ cash dispenser

**billion** [biljɔ̃] _nm_ billion _(BRIT)_, trillion _(US)_

**billot** [bijo] _nm_ block

**bimensuel, le** [bimãsɥεl] _adj_ bimonthly

**binette** [binεt] _nf_ hoe

**bio...** [bjo] _préfixe_ bio...; **biochimie** _nf_ biochemistry; **biodiversité** _nf_ biodiversity; **bioéthique** _nf_ bioethics _sg;_ **biographie** _nf_ biography; **biologie** _nf_ biology; **biologique** _adj_ biological; _(produits, aliments)_ organic; **biologiste** _nm/f_ biologist; **bioterroriste** _nm/f_ bioterrorist

**Birmanie** [biRmani] _nf_ Burma

**bis** [bis] _adv:_ **12 ~** 12a _ou_ A **♦** _excl, nm_ encore

**bisannuel, le** [bizanɥεl] _adj_ biennial

**biscornu, e** [biskɔRny] _adj_ twisted

**biscotte** [biskɔt] _nf_ toasted bread _(sold in packets)_

**biscuit** [biskɥi] _nm_ biscuit; **~ de savoie** sponge cake

**bise** [biz] _nf (fam: baiser)_ kiss; _(vent)_ North wind; **grosses ~s (de)** _(sur lettre)_ love and kisses (from)

**bisou** [bizu] _(fam) nm_ kiss

**bissextile** [bisεkstil] _adj:_ **année ~** leap year

**bistro(t)** [bistRo] _nm_ bistro, café

**bitume** [bitym] _nm_ asphalt

**bizarre** [bizaR] _adj_ strange, odd

**blafard, e** [blafaR, aRd] _adj_ wan

**blague** [blag] _nf (propos)_ joke; _(farce)_

trick; **sans ~!** no kidding!; **blaguer** vi to joke

**blaireau, x** [blɛʀo] nm (ZOOL) badger; (brosse) shaving brush

**blairer** [blɛʀe] (fam) vt: **je ne peux pas le ~** I can't bear ou stand him

**blâme** [blam] nm blame; (sanction) reprimand; **blâmer** vt to blame

**blanc, blanche** [blɑ̃, blɑ̃ʃ] adj white; (non imprimé) blank ♦ nm/f white, white man(-woman) ♦ nm (couleur) white; (espace non écrit) blank; (aussi: ~ **d'œuf**) (egg-)white; (aussi: ~ **de poulet**) breast, white meat; (aussi: **vin ~**) white wine; ~ **cassé** off-white; **chèque en ~** blank cheque; **à ~** (chauffer) white-hot; (tirer, charger) with blanks; **blanche** nf (MUS) minim (BRIT), half-note (US); **blancheur** nf whiteness

**blanchir** [blɑ̃ʃiʀ] vt (gén) to whiten; (linge) to launder; (CULIN) to blanch; (fig: disculper) to clear ♦ vi to grow white; (cheveux) to go white; **blanchisserie** nf laundry

**blason** [blazɔ̃] nm coat of arms

**blasphème** [blasfɛm] nm blasphemy

**blazer** [blazɛʀ] nm blazer

**blé** [ble] nm wheat; ~ **noir** buckwheat

**bled** [blɛd] (péj) nm hole

**blême** [blɛm] adj pale

**blessant, e** [blesɑ̃, ɑ̃t] adj (offensant) hurtful

**blessé, e** [blese] adj injured ♦ nm/f injured person, casualty

**blesser** [blese] vt to injure; (délibérément) to wound; (suj: souliers) to hurt; se ~ to injure o.s.; **se ~ au pied** to injure one's foot; **blessure** nf (accidentelle) injury; (intentionnelle) wound

**bleu, e** [blø] adj blue; (bifteck) very rare ♦ nm (couleur) blue; (contusion) bruise; (vêtement: aussi: ~**s**) overalls pl; ~ **marine** navy blue; **bleuet** nm cornflower; **bleuté, e** adj blue-shaded

**blinder** [blɛ̃de] vt to armour; (fig) to harden

**bloc** [blɔk] nm (de pierre etc) block; (de papier à lettres) pad; (ensemble) group; **serré à ~** tightened right down; **en ~** as a whole; ~ **opératoire** operating ou theatre block; ~ **sanitaire** toilet block; **blocage** nm (des prix) freezing; (PSYCH) hang-up; **bloc-notes** nm note pad

**blocus** [blɔkys] nm blockade

**blond, e** [blɔ̃, blɔ̃d] adj fair, blond; (sable, blés) golden; ~ **cendré** ash blond; **blonde** nf (femme) blonde; (bière) lager; (cigarette) Virginia cigarette

**bloquer** [blɔke] vt (passage) to block; (pièce mobile) to jam; (crédits, compte) to freeze; **se ~** to jam; (PSYCH) to have a mental block

**blottir** [blɔtiʀ]: **se ~** vi to huddle up

**blouse** [bluz] nf overall

**blouson** [bluzɔ̃] nm blouson jacket; ~ **noir** (fig) ≈ rocker

**blue-jean** [bludʒin] nm (pair of) jeans

**bluff** [blœf] nm bluff; **bluffer** vi to bluff

**bobard** [bɔbaʀ] (fam) nm tall story

**bobine** [bɔbin] nf reel; (ÉLEC) coil

**bocal, -aux** [bɔkal, o] nm jar

**bock** [bɔk] nm glass of beer

**body** [bɔdi] nm body(suit); (SPORT) leotard

**bœuf** [bœf] nm ox; (CULIN) beef

**bof!** [bɔf] (fam) excl don't care!; (pas terrible) nothing special

**bogue** [bɔg] nm: **le ~ de l'an 2000** the millennium bug

**bohème** [bɔɛm] adj happy-go-lucky, unconventional; **bohémien, ne** nm/f gipsy

**boire** [bwaʀ] vt to drink; (s'imprégner de) to soak up; ~ **un coup** (fam) to have a drink

**bois** [bwa] nm wood; **de ~, en ~** wooden; **boisé, e** adj woody, wooded

**boisson** [bwasɔ̃] nf drink

**boîte** [bwat] nf box; (fam: entreprise) firm; **aliments en ~** canned ou tinned (BRIT) foods; ~ **aux lettres** letter box

**allumettes** box of matches; (vide) **atchbox**; **~ (de conserve)** can ou tin (ut) (of food); **~ de nuit** night club; **~ x**; **~ vocale** (TEL) voice mail

**ter** [bwate] vi to limp; (fig: raisonnent) to be shaky

**ive** etc [bwav] vb voir **boire**

**e** [bɔl] nm bowl; **un ~ d'air** a breath f fresh air; **j'en ai ras le ~** (fam) I'm d up with this; **avoir du ~** (fam) to lucky

**lide** [bɔlid] nm racing car; **comme n ~** at top speed, like a rocket

**mbardement** [bɔ̃baʀdəmɑ̃] nm mbing

**mbarder** [bɔ̃baʀde] vt to bomb; **~ n de** (cailloux, lettres) to bombard sb th

**mbe** [bɔ̃b] nf bomb; (atomiseur) erosol) spray; **bombé, e** adj (forme) unded; **bomber** vt: **bomber le tor** to swell out one's chest

**OT-CLÉ**

**n, bonne** [bɔ̃, bɔn] adj 1 (agréable, tisfaisant) good; **un bon repas/ staurant** a good meal/restaurant; **re bon en maths** to be good at aths

**(charitable): être bon (envers)** to be od (to)

**(correct)** right; **le bon numéro/ oment** the right number/moment

**(souhaits): bon anniversaire** happy thday; **bon voyage** have a good p; **bonne chance** good luck; **bonne nnée** happy New Year; **bonne nuit** od night

**(approprié, apte): bon à/pour** fit for/ to

**bon enfant** adj inv accommodating, sy-going; **bonne femme** (péj) woan; **de bonne heure** early; **bon maré** adj inv cheap ♦ adv cheap; **bon** ot of witticism; **bon sens** common

sense; **bon vivant** jovial chap; **bonnes œuvres** charitable works, charities
♦ nm **1** (billet) voucher; (cadeau) **bon cadeau)** gift voucher; **bon d'essence** petrol coupon; **bon du Trésor** Treasury bond
**2: avoir du bon** to have its good points; **pour de bon** for good
♦ adv: **il fait bon** it's ou the weather is fine; **sentir bon** to smell good; **tenir bon** to stand firm
♦ excl good!; **ah bon?** really?; voir aussi **bonne**

**bonbon** [bɔ̃bɔ̃] nm (boiled) sweet

**bonbonne** [bɔ̃bɔn] nf demijohn

**bond** [bɔ̃] nm leap; **faire un ~** to leap in the air

**bondé, e** [bɔ̃de] adj packed (full)

**bondir** [bɔ̃diʀ] vi to leap

**bonheur** [bɔnœʀ] nm happiness; **porter ~ (à qn)** to bring (sb) luck; **au petit ~** haphazardly; **par ~** fortunately

**bonhomie** [bɔnɔmi] nf goodnaturedness

**bonhomme** [bɔnɔm] (pl **bonshommes**) nm fellow; **~ de neige** snowman

**bonifier** [bɔnifje] vt to improve

**boniment** [bɔnimɑ̃] nm patter no pl

**bonjour** [bɔ̃ʒuʀ] excl, nm hello; (selon l'heure) good morning/afternoon; **c'est simple comme ~!** it's easy as pie!

**bonne** [bɔn] adj voir **bon** ♦ nf (domestique) maid; **bonnement** adv: **tout bonnement** quite simply

**bonnet** [bɔnɛ] nm hat; (de soutiengorge) cup; **~ de bain** bathing cap

**bonshommes** [bɔ̃zɔm] nmpl de **bonhomme**

**bonsoir** [bɔ̃swaʀ] excl good evening

**bonté** [bɔ̃te] nf kindness no pl

**bonus** [bɔnys] nm no-claims bonus

**bord** [bɔʀ] nm (de table, verre, falaise) edge; (de rivière, lac) bank; (de route) side; **(monter) à ~** to (go) on board;

jeter par-dessus ~ to throw overboard; **le commandant de/les hommes du ~** the ship's master/crew; **au ~ de la mer** at the seaside; **être au ~ des larmes** to be on the verge of tears

**bordeaux** [bɔʀdo] *nm* Bordeaux (wine) ♦ *adj inv* maroon

**bordel** [bɔʀdɛl] *nm* brothel; (*fam!*) bloody mess (!)

**bordelais, e** [bɔʀdəlɛ, ɛz] *adj* of ou from Bordeaux

**border** [bɔʀde] *vt* (*être le long de*) to line; (*qn dans son lit*) to tuck up; (*garnir*): **~ qch de** to edge sth with

**bordereau, x** [bɔʀdəʀo] *nm* (*formulaire*) slip

**bordure** [bɔʀdyʀ] *nf* border; **en ~ de** on the edge of

**borgne** [bɔʀɲ] *adj* one-eyed

**borne** [bɔʀn] *nf* boundary stone; (*aussi*: **~ kilométrique**) kilometre-marker; ≈ milestone; **~s** *nfpl* (*fig*) limits; **dépasser les ~s** to go too far

**borné, e** [bɔʀne] *adj* (*personne*) narrow-minded

**borner** [bɔʀne] *vt*: **se ~ à faire** (*se contenter de*) to content o.s. with doing; (*se limiter à*) to limit o.s. to doing

**bosquet** [bɔskɛ] *nm* grove

**bosse** [bɔs] *nf* (*de terrain etc*) bump; (*enflure*) lump; (*du bossu, du chameau*) hump; **avoir la ~ des maths** (*fam*) to have a gift for maths *etc*; **il a roulé sa ~** (*fam*) he's been around

**bosser** [bɔse] *vi* (*fam*) (*travailler*) to work; (*travailler dur*) to slave (away)

**bossu, e** [bɔsy] *nm/f* hunchback

**botanique** [bɔtanik] *nf* botany ♦ *adj* botanic(al)

**botte** [bɔt] *nf* (*soulier*) (high) boot; (*gerbe*): **~ de paille** bundle of straw; **~ de radis** bunch of radishes; **~s de caoutchouc** wellington boots; **botter** *vt*: **ça me botte** (*fam*) I fancy that

**bottin** [bɔtɛ̃] *nm* directory

**bottine** [bɔtin] *nf* ankle boot

**bouc** [buk] *nm* goat; (*barbe*) goatee; **~ émissaire** scapegoat

**boucan** [bukɑ̃] *(fam) nm* din, racket

**bouche** [buʃ] *nf* mouth; **rester ~ b** to stand open-mouthed; **le ~ à ~** kiss of life; **~ d'égout** manhole; **~ d'** **cendie** fire hydrant; **~ de métro** mé entrance

**bouché, e** [buʃe] *adj* (*temps, ciel*) over cast; **c'est ~** there's no future in it

**bouchée** [buʃe] *nf* mouthful; **~s à la** **reine** chicken vol-au-vents

**boucher, -ère** [buʃe] *nm/f* butcher ♦ *(trou)* to fill up; (*obstruer*) to block up; **se ~** *vi* (*tuyau etc*) to block up, get blocked up; **j'ai le nez bouché** my nose is blocked; **se ~ le nez** to hold one's nose; **boucherie** *nf* butch (*shop*); (*fig*) slaughter

**bouche-trou** [buʃtʀu] *nm* (*fig*) st gap

**bouchon** [buʃɔ̃] *nm* stopper; (*de tu* top; (*en liège*) cork; (*fig*: *embouteilla* holdup; (*PÊCHE*) float

**boucle** [bukl] *nf* (*forme, figure*) loo (*objet*) buckle; (*de cheveux*) curl **d'oreille** earring

**bouclé, e** [bukle] *adj* (*cheveux*) curly

**boucler** [bukle] *vt* (*fermer: ceinture* to fasten; (*terminer*) to finish off; (*enfermer*) to shut away; (*quartier*) seal off ♦ *vi* to curl

**bouclier** [buklije] *nm* shield

**bouddhiste** [budist] *nm/f* Buddhist

**bouder** [bude] *vi* to sulk ♦ *vt* to s away from

**boudin** [budɛ̃] *nm*: **~ (noir)** black pu ding; **~ blanc** white pudding

**boue** [bu] *nf* mud

**bouée** [bwe] *nf* buoy; **~ (de sauve** ge) lifebuoy

**boueux, -euse** [bwø, øz] *adj* mudd

**bouffe** [buf] (*fam*) *nf* grub (*Brit*), chow

**bouffée** [bufe] *nf* (*de cigarette*) puff; **une ~ d'air pur** a breath of fresh air

**bouffer** [bufe] (*fam*) *vi* to eat

**bouffi, e** [bufi] *adj* swollen

**ougeoir** [buʒwaʀ] nm candlestick

**ougeotte** [buʒɔt] nf: **avoir la ~** (fam) to have the fidgets

**ouger** [buʒe] vi to move; (dent etc) to be loose; (s'activer) to get moving ♦ vt to move; **les prix/les couleurs n'ont pas bougé** prices/colours haven't changed

**ougie** [buʒi] nf candle; (AUTO) (spark(ing) plug

**ougon, ne** [buʒɔ̃, ɔn] adj grumpy

**ougonner** [buɡɔne] vi, vt to grumble

**ouillabaisse** [bujabɛs] nf type of fish soup

**ouillant, e** [bujɑ̃, ɑ̃t] adj (qui bout) boiling; (très chaud) boiling (hot)

**ouillie** [buji] nf (de bébé) cereal; **en ~** (fig) crushed

**ouillir** [bujiʀ] vi, vt to boil; **~ d'impatience** to seethe with impatience

**ouilloire** [bujwaʀ] nf kettle

**ouillon** [bujɔ̃] nm (CULIN) stock no pl; **~ de culture** culture medium

**ouillonner** [bujɔne] vi to bubble; (fig: idées) to bubble up

**ouillotte** [bujɔt] nf hot-water bottle

**oulanger, ère** [bulɑ̃ʒe, ɛʀ] nm/f baker; **boulangerie** nf bakery; **boulangerie-pâtisserie** nf baker's and confectioner's (shop)

**oule** [bul] nf (gén) ball; **~s** nfpl (jeu) bowls; **se mettre en ~** (fig: fam) to fly off the handle, to blow one's top; **jouer aux ~s** to play bowls; **~ de neige** snowball

**ouleau, x** [bulo] nm (silver) birch

**ouledogue** [buldɔg] nm bulldog

**oulet** [bulɛ] nm (aussi: **~ de canon**) cannonball

**oulette** [bulɛt] nf (de viande) meatball

**oulevard** [bulvaʀ] nm boulevard

**ouleversant, e** [bulvɛʀsɑ̃, ɑ̃t] adj deeply moving

**ouleversement** [bulvɛʀsəmɑ̃] nm upheaval

**ouleverser** [bulvɛʀse] vt (émouvoir) to overwhelm; (causer du chagrin) to distress; (pays, vie) to disrupt; (papiers, objets) to turn upside down

**boulon** [bulɔ̃] nm bolt

**boulot, te** [bulo, ɔt] adj plump, tubby ♦ nm (fam: travail) work

**boum** [bum] nm bang ♦ nf (fam) party

**bouquet** [bukɛ] nm (de fleurs) bunch (of flowers), bouquet; (de persil etc) bunch; **c'est le ~!** (fam) that takes the biscuit!

**bouquin** [bukɛ̃] (fam) nm book; **bouquiner** (fam) vi to read; **bouquiniste** nm/f bookseller

**bourbeux, -euse** [buʀbø, øz] adj muddy

**bourbier** [buʀbje] nm (quag)mire

**bourde** [buʀd] (fam) nf (erreur) howler; (gaffe) blunder

**bourdon** [buʀdɔ̃] nm bumblebee; **bourdonner** vi to buzz

**bourg** [buʀ] nm small market town

**bourgeois, e** [buʀʒwa, waz] (péj) adj ≃ (upper) middle class; **bourgeoisie** nf ≃ upper middle classes pl

**bourgeon** [buʀʒɔ̃] nm bud

**Bourgogne** [buʀgɔɲ] nf: **la ~** Burgundy ♦ nm: **b~** burgundy (wine)

**bourguignon, ne** [buʀgiɲɔ̃, ɔn] adj of ou from Burgundy, Burgundian

**bourlinguer** [buʀlɛ̃ge] (fam) vi to knock about a lot, get around a lot

**bourrade** [buʀad] nf shove, thump

**bourrage** [buʀaʒ] nm: **~ de crâne** brainwashing; (SCOL) cramming

**bourrasque** [buʀask] nf squall

**bourratif, -ive** [buʀatif, iv] (fam) adj filling, stodgy (péj)

**bourré, e** [buʀe] adj (fam: ivre) plastered, tanked up (BRIT); (rempli): **~ de** crammed full of

**bourreau, x** [buʀo] nm executioner; (fig) torturer; **~ de travail** workaholic

**bourrelet** [buʀlɛ] nm fold ou roll (of flesh)

**bourrer** [buʀe] vt (pipe) to fill; (poêle) to pack; (valise) to cram (full)

**bourrique** [buʀik] nf (âne) ass

**bourru, e** [buʀy] adj surly, gruff

**bourse** [burs] nf (subvention) grant; (porte-monnaie) purse; **la B~** the Stock Exchange

**boursier, -ière** [bursje, jɛr] nm/f (étudiant) grant holder

**boursoufler** [bursufle]: **se ~** vi to swell (up)

**bous** [bu] vb voir **bouillir**

**bousculade** [buskylad] nf (hâte) rush; (cohue) crush; **bousculer** vt (heurter) to knock into; (fig) to push, rush

**bouse** [buz] nf dung no pl

**bousiller** [buzije] (fam) vt (appareil) to wreck

**boussole** [busɔl] nf compass

**bout** [bu] vb voir **bouillir** ♦ nm bit; (d'un bâton etc) tip; (d'une ficelle, table, rue, période) end; **au ~** de at the end of, after; **pousser qn à ~** to push sb to the limit; **venir à ~ de** to manage to finish

**boutade** [butad] nf quip, sally

**boute-en-train** [butɑ̃trɛ̃] nm inv (fig) live wire

**bouteille** [butɛj] nf bottle; (de gaz butane) cylinder

**boutique** [butik] nf shop

**bouton** [butɔ̃] nm button; (sur la peau) spot; (BOT) bud; **~ d'or** buttercup; **boutonner** vt to button up; **boutonnière** nf buttonhole; **bouton-pression** nm press stud

**bouture** [butyr] nf cutting

**bovins** [bɔvɛ̃] nmpl cattle pl

**bowling** [bulin] nm (tenpin) bowling; (salle) bowling alley

**box** [bɔks] nm (d'écurie) loose-box; (JUR): **~ des accusés** dock

**boxe** [bɔks] nf boxing; **boxeur** nm boxer

**boyaux** [bwajo] nmpl (viscères) entrails, guts

**BP** abr = **boîte postale**

**bracelet** [braslɛ] nm bracelet

**braconnier** [brakɔnje] nm poacher

**brader** [brade] vt to sell off; **braderie** nf cut-price shop/stall

**braguette** [bragɛt] nf fly ou flies (BRIT), zipper (US)

**brailler** [braje] vi to bawl, yell

**braire** [brɛr] vi to bray

**braise** [brɛz] nf embers pl

**brancard** [brɑ̃kar] nm (civière) stretcher; **brancardier** nm stretcher bearer

**branchages** [brɑ̃ʃaʒ] nmpl boughs

**branche** [brɑ̃ʃ] nf branch

**branché, e** [brɑ̃ʃe] (fam) adj trendy

**brancher** [brɑ̃ʃe] vt to connect (up); (en mettant la prise) to plug in

**brandir** [brɑ̃dir] vt to brandish

**branle** [brɑ̃l] nm: **mettre en ~** to set in motion; **branle-bas** nm inv commotion

**braquer** [brake] vi (AUTO) to turn (the wheel) ♦ vt (revolver etc): **~ qch sur** to aim sth at, point sth at; (mettre en colère): **~ qn** to put sb's back up

**bras** [brɑ] nm arm; **~ dessus, ~ dessous** arm in arm; **se retrouver avec qch sur les ~** (fam) to be landed with sth; **~ droit** (fig) right hand man; **~ de fer** arm wrestling

**brasier** [brazje] nm blaze, inferno

**bras-le-corps** [bralkɔr] adv: **à ~** (a)round the waist

**brassard** [brasar] nm armband

**brasse** [bras] nf (nage) breast-stroke

**brassée** [brase] nf armful

**brasser** [brase] vt to mix; **~ l'argent/les affaires** to handle a lot of money/business

**brasserie** [brasri] nf (restaurant) café, restaurant; (usine) brewery

**brave** [brav] adj (courageux) brave; (bon, gentil) good, kind

**braver** [brave] vt to defy

**bravo** [bravo] excl bravo ♦ nm cheer

**bravoure** [bravur] nf bravery

**break** [brɛk] nm (AUTO) estate car

**brebis** [brəbi] nf ewe; **~ galeuse** black sheep

**brèche** [brɛʃ] nf breach, gap; **être sur la ~** (fig) to be always ne go

edouille [brəduj] adj empty-handed

edouiller [brəduje] vi, vt to mumble, ammer

ef, brève [brɛf, ɛv] adj short, brief ♦ lv in short; **d'un ton ~** sharply, urtly; **en ~** in short, in brief

ésil [brezil] nm Brazil; **brésilien, -ne** dj Brazilian ♦ nm/f: **Brésilien, ne** Brazilian

etagne [brətan] nf Brittany

etelle [brətɛl] nf (de vêtement, de ac) strap; (d'autoroute) slip road (BRIT), ntrance/exit ramp (US); **~s** nfpl (pour antalon) braces (BRIT), suspenders (US)

eton, ne [brətɔ̃, ɔn] adj Breton ♦ m/f: **B~, ne** Breton

euvage [brœvaʒ] nm beverage, rink

ève [brɛv] adj voir bref

evet [brəvɛ] nm diploma, certificate; (d'invention) patent; **breveté, e** adj atented

bes [brib] nfpl (de conversation) atches; **par ~** piecemeal

colage [brikɔlaʒ] nm: **le ~** do-it-ourself

cole [brikɔl] nf (babiole) trifle

coler [brikɔle] vi (petits travaux) to DIY jobs; (passe-temps) to potter out ♦ vt (réparer) to fix up; **brico-ur, -euse** nm/f handyman(-woman), Y enthusiast

de [brid] nf bridle; **tenir en ~ to** eep a tight rein on sb

dé, e [bride] adj: **yeux ~s** slit eyes

dge [bridʒ] nm (CARTES) bridge

èvement [brijɛvmɑ̃] adv briefly

gade [brigad] nf (POLICE) squad; IL) brigade; **brigadier** nm sergeant

gandage [brigɑ̃daʒ] nm robbery

guer [brige] vt to aspire to

llamment [brijamɑ̃] adv brilliantly

llant, e [brijɑ̃, ɑ̃t] adj (remarquable) ght; (luisant) shiny, shining

ller [brije] vi to shine

mer [brime] vt to bully

brin [brɛ̃] nm (de laine, ficelle etc) strand; (fig): **un ~ de** a bit of; **~ d'herbe** blade of grass; **~ de muguet** sprig of lily of the valley

brindille [brɛ̃dij] nf twig

brio [brijo] nm: **avec ~** with panache

brioche [brijɔʃ] nf brioche (bun); (fam: ventre) paunch

brique [brik] nf brick; (de lait) carton

briquer [brike] vt to polish up

briquet [brikɛ] nm (cigarette) lighter

brise [briz] nf breeze

briser [brize] vt to break; **se ~** vi to break

britannique [britanik] adj British ♦ nm/f: **B~** British person, Briton; **les B~s** the British

brocante [brɔkɑ̃t] nf junk, second-hand goods pl; **brocanteur, -euse** nm/f junkshop owner; junk dealer

broche [brɔʃ] nf brooch; (CULIN) spit; (MÉD) pin; **à la ~** spit-roasted

broché, e [brɔʃe] adj (livre) paper-backed

brochet [brɔʃɛ] nm pike inv

brochette [brɔʃɛt] nf (ustensile) skewer; (plat) kebab

brochure [brɔʃyr] nf pamphlet, brochure, booklet

broder [brɔde] vt to embroider ♦ vi to embroider the facts; **broderie** nf embroidery

broncher [brɔ̃ʃe] vi: **sans ~** without flinching, without turning a hair

bronches [brɔ̃ʃ] nfpl bronchial tubes; **bronchite** nf bronchitis

bronze [brɔ̃z] nm bronze

bronzer [brɔ̃ze] vi to get a tan; **se ~** to sunbathe

brosse [brɔs] nf brush; **coiffé en ~** with a crewcut; **~ à cheveux** hairbrush; **~ à dents** toothbrush; **~ à habits** clothesbrush; **brosser** vt (nettoyer) to brush; (fig: tableau etc) to paint; **se brosser les dents** to brush one's teeth

brouette [bruɛt] nf wheelbarrow

brouhaha [bruaa] nm hubbub

**brouillard** [brujar] nm fog

**brouille** [bruj] nf quarrel

**brouiller** [bruje] vt (œufs, message) to scramble; (idées) to mix up; (rendre trouble) to cloud; (désunir: amis) to set at odds; **se ~** vi (vue) to cloud over; (gens) to fall out

**brouillon, ne** [brujɔ̃, ɔn] adj (sans soin) untidy; (qui manque d'organisation) disorganized ♦ nm draft; (papier) ~ rough paper

**broussailles** [brusaj] nfpl undergrowth sg; **broussailleux, -euse** adj bushy

**brousse** [brus] nf: la ~ the bush

**brouter** [brute] vi to graze

**broutille** [brutij] nf trifle

**broyer** [brwaje] vt to crush; ~ du noir to be down in the dumps

**bru** [bry] nf daughter-in-law

**brugnon** [bryɲɔ̃] nm (BOT) nectarine

**bruiner** [bruine] vb impers: **il bruine** it's drizzling, there's a drizzle

**bruire** [bruir] vi (feuilles) to rustle

**bruit** [brui] nm: **un ~** a noise, a sound; (fig: rumeur) a rumour; **le ~** noise; **sans ~** without a sound, noiselessly; ~ **de fond** background noise; **bruitage** nm sound effects pl.

**brûlant, e** [brylɑ̃, ɑ̃t] adj burning; (liquide) boiling (hot)

**brûlé, e** [bryle] adj (fig: démasqué) blown ♦ nm: **odeur de** ~ smell of burning

**brûle-pourpoint** [brylpurpwɛ̃]: **à ~~** adv point-blank

**brûler** [bryle] vt to burn; (suj: eau bouillante) to scald; (consommer: électricité, essence) to use; (feu rouge, signal) to go through ♦ vi to burn; (jeu): **tu brûles** you're getting hot!; **se ~** to burn o.s. (s'ébouillanter) to scald o.s.

**brûlure** [brylyr] nf (lésion) burn; ~**s d'estomac** heartburn sg

**brume** [brym] nf mist; **brumisateur** nm atomizer

**brun, e** [brœ̃, bryn] adj (gén, bière)

brown; (cheveux, tabac) dark; **elle e ~e** she's got dark hair

**brunch** [brœntʃ] nm brunch

**brunir** [brynir] vi to get a tan

**brushing** [brœʃiŋ] nm blow-dry

**brusque** [brysk] adj abrupt; **brusqu** vt to rush

**brut, e** [bryt] adj (minerai, soie) ra (diamant) rough; (COMM) gross; (pét le) ~ crude (oil)

**brutal, e, -aux** [brytal, o] adj brut handle

**brutaliser** vt to handle roughly, ma handle

**Bruxelles** [brysɛl] n Brussels

**bruyamment** [bruijamɑ̃] adv noisily

**bruyant, e** [bruijɑ̃, ɑ̃t] adj noisy

**bruyère** [bruijɛr] nf heather

**BTS** sigle m (= brevet de technicien sup ieur) vocational training certificate taken the end of a higher education course

**bu, e** [by] pp de **boire**

**buccal, e, -aux** [bykal, o] adj: p voie ~e orally

**bûche** [byʃ] nf log; **prendre une** (fig) to come a cropper; ~ **de No** Yule log

**bûcher** [byʃe] nm (funéraire) pyre; (su plice) stake ♦ vi (fam) to swot (BR slave (away) ♦ vt (fam) to swot (BRIT), slave away at; **bûcheron** woodcutter; **bûcheur, -euse** (fam) hard-working

**budget** [bydʒɛ] nm budget

**buée** [bue] nf (sur une vitre) mist

**buffet** [byfɛ] nm (meuble) sideboa (de réception) buffet; ~ **(de gare)** tion) buffet, snack bar

**buffle** [byfl] nm buffalo

**buis** [bui] nm box tree; (b box(wood)

**buisson** [buisɔ̃] nm bush

**buissonnière** [buisɔnjɛr] adj: fa l'école ~ to skip school

**bulbe** [bylb] nm (BOT, ANAT) bulb

**Bulgarie** [bylgari] nf Bulgaria

**bulle** [byl] nf bubble

**bulletin** [byltɛ̃] nm (communiqué, j

*al*) bulletin; (SCOL) report; **~ d'infor-**
**ations** news bulletin; **~ de salaire**
ay-slip; **~ (de vote)** ballot paper; **~**
**étéorologique** weather report

**reau, x** [byʀo] nm (meuble) desk;
(*pièce, service*) office; **~ de change** (for-
*gn*) exchange office ou bureau; **~ de**
**oste** post office; **~ de tabac** tobac-
onist's (shop); **~ de vote** polling sta-
on; **bureaucratie** [byʀokʀasi] nf
ureaucracy

**rin** [byʀɛ̃] nm cold chisel; (ART) burin
**lesque** [byʀlɛsk] adj ridiculous; (LIT-
 RATURE) burlesque

**s¹** [by] vb voir **boire**
**s²** [bys] nm bus

**squé, e** [byske] adj (nez) hook(ed)
**ste** [byst] nm (torse) chest; (seins)
ust

**¹** [by] vb voir **boire**
**²** [by(t)] nm (cible) target; (fig) goal,
m; (FOOTBALL etc) goal; **de ~ en blanc**
int-blank; **avoir pour ~ de faire** to
m to do; **dans le ~ de** with the in-
ntion of

**ane** [bytan] nm (camping) butane;
*gaz domestique*) Calor gas ®
**té, e** [byte] adj stubborn, obstinate
**ter** [byte] vi: **~ contre (cogner)** to
mp into; (*trébucher*) to stumble
ainst; **se ~** vi to get obstinate, dig in
e's heels; **~ contre une difficulté**
g) to hit a snag
**tin** [bytɛ̃] nm booty, spoils pl; (d'un
e) loot
**iner** [bytine] vi (abeilles) to gather
ctar
**tte** [byt] nf mound, hillock; **être en**
à to be exposed to
**vais** etc [byve] vb voir **boire**
**vard** [byvaʀ] nm blotter
**vette** [byvet] nf bar
**veur, -euse** [byvœʀ, øz] nm/f drink-

# C, c

**c'** [s] dét voir **ce**
**CA** sigle m = **chiffre d'affaires**
**ça** [sa] pron (pour désigner) this; (: plus
loin) that; (comme sujet indéfini) it;
**comment ~ va?** how are you?; **~ va?**
(*d'accord*) OK?, all right?; **où ~?**
where's that?; **pourquoi ~?** why's
that?; **qui ~?** who's that?; **~ alors!** well
really!; **~ fait 10 ans (que)** it's 10 years
(since); **c'est ~** that's right; **~ y est**
that's it

**çà** [sa] adv: **et là** here and there
**cabane** [kaban] nf hut, cabin
**cabaret** [kabaʀɛ] nm night club
**cabas** [kaba] nm shopping bag
**cabillaud** [kabijo] nm cod inv
**cabine** [kabin] nf (de bateau) cabin; (de
piscine etc) cubicle; (de camion, train)
cab; (d'avion) cockpit; **~ d'essayage**
fitting room; **~ (téléphonique)** call ou
(tele)phone box
**cabinet** [kabinɛ] nm (petite pièce) closet; (de médecin) surgery (BRIT), office
(US); (de notaire etc) office; (: clientèle)
practice; (POL) Cabinet; **~s** nmpl (w.-c.)
toilet sg; **~ d'affaires** business consul-
tancy; **~ de toilette** toilet
**câble** [kabl] nm cable
**cabosser** [kabose] vt to dent
**cabrer** [kabʀe]: **se ~** vi (cheval) to rear
up
**cabriole** [kabʀijɔl] nf: **faire des ~s** to
caper about
**cacahuète** [kakaɥɛt] nf peanut
**cacao** [kakao] nm cocoa
**cache** [kaʃ] nm mask, card (for mask-
ing)
**cache-cache** [kaʃkaʃ] nm: **jouer à ~~**
to play hide-and-seek
**cachemire** [kaʃmir] nm cashmere
**cache-nez** [kaʃne] nm inv scarf, muffler
**cacher** [kaʃe] vt to hide, conceal; **se ~**
vi (volontairement) to hide; (être caché)

to be hidden *ou* concealed; **~ qch à qn** to hide *ou* conceal sth from sb

**cachet** [kaʃɛ] *nm* (*comprimé*) tablet; (*de la poste*) postmark; (*rétribution*) fee; (*fig*) style, character; **cacheter** *vt* to seal

**cachette** [kaʃɛt] *nf* hiding place; **en ~** on the sly, secretly

**cachot** [kaʃo] *nm* dungeon

**cachotterie** [kaʃɔtʀi] *nf*: **faire des ~s** to be secretive

**cactus** [kaktys] *nm* cactus

**cadavre** [kadɑvʀ] *nm* corpse, (dead) body

**Caddie** ®, **caddy** [kadi] *nm* (supermarket) trolley

**cadeau, x** [kado] *nm* present; gift; **faire un ~ à qn** to give sb a present *ou* gift; **faire ~ de qch à qn** to make a present of sth to sb, give sb sth as a present

**cadenas** [kadnɑ] *nm* padlock

**cadence** [kadɑ̃s] *nf* (*tempo*) rhythm; (*de travail etc*) rate; **en ~** rhythmically

**cadet, te** [kadɛ, ɛt] *adj* younger; (*le plus jeune*) youngest ♦ *nm/f* youngest child *ou* one

**cadran** [kadʀɑ̃] *nm* dial; **~ solaire** sundial

**cadre** [kadʀ] *nm* frame; (*environnement*) surroundings *pl* ♦ *nm/f* (ADMIN) managerial employee, executive; **dans le ~ de** (*fig*) within the framework *ou* context of

**cadrer** [kadʀe] *vi*: **~ avec** to tally *ou* correspond with ♦ *vt* to centre

**cafard** [kafaʀ] *nm* cockroach; **avoir le ~** (*fam*) to be down in the dumps

**café** [kafe] *nm* coffee; (*bistro*) café ♦ *adj inv* coffee(-coloured); **~ au lait** white coffee; **~ noir** black coffee; **~ tabac** *ou* bacconist's *ou* newsagent's serving coffee and spirits; **cafetière** *nf* (*pot*) coffee-pot

**cafouiller** [kafuje] (*fam*) *vi* to get into a shambles

**cage** [kaʒ] *nf* cage; **~ d'escalier** (stair)well; **~ thoracique** rib cage

**cageot** [kaʒo] *nm* crate

**cagibi** [kaʒibi] (*fam*) *nm* (*débarras*) box room

**cagnotte** [kaɲɔt] *nf* kitty

**cagoule** [kagul] *nf* (*passe-montag* balaclava

**cahier** [kaje] *nm* notebook; **~ brouillons** roughbook, jotter; **~ d'exercices** exercise book

**cahot** [kao] *nm* jolt, bump

**caïd** [kaid] *nm* big chief, boss

**caille** [kaj] *nf* quail

**cailler** [kaje] *vi* (*lait*) to curdle; **ça cai** (*fam*) it's freezing; **caillot** [kajo] *nm* (*bloc* clot

**caillou, x** [kaju] *nm* (little) stone; **ca louteux, -euse** *adj* (*route*) stony

**Caire** [kɛʀ] *nm*: **le ~** Cairo

**caisse** [kɛs] *nf* box; (*tiroir où l'on met recette*) till; (*où l'on paye*) cash de (BRIT), check-out; (*de banque*) cashie desk; **~ d'épargne** savings bank; **~ retraite** pension fund; **~ enregistre** se cash register; **caissier, -ière** *n* cashier

**cajoler** [kaʒɔle] *vt* (*câliner*) to cudd (*amadouer*) to wheedle, coax

**cake** [kɛk] *nm* fruit cake

**calandre** [kalɑ̃dʀ] *nf* radiator grill

**calanque** [kalɑ̃k] *nf* rocky inlet

**calcaire** [kalkɛʀ] *nm* limestone ♦ (*eau*) hard; (GÉO) limestone *cpd*

**calciné, e** [kalsine] *adj* burnt to ashe

**calcul** [kalkyl] *nm* calculation; le (SCOL) arithmetic; **~ (biliai** (gall)stone; **calculatrice** *nf* calcula

**calculer** [kalkyle] *vt* to calculate, work out; **c** **culette** *nf* pocket calculator

**cale** [kal] *nf* (*de bateau*) hold; (*en bc* wedge; **~ sèche** dry dock

**calé, e** [kale] (*fam*) *adj* clever, bright

**caleçon** [kalsɔ̃] *nm* (*d'homme*) shorts; (*de femme*) leggings

**calembour** [kalɑ̃buʀ] *nm* pun

**calendrier** [kalɑ̃dʀije] *nm* calend (*fig*) timetable

**calepin** [kalpɛ̃] *nm* notebook

**er** [kale] vt to wedge ♦ vi (moteur, véhicule) to stall

**feutrer** [kalføtʀe] vt to (make) draughtproof; **se ~** vi to make o.s. snug and comfortable

**ibre** [kalibʀ] nm calibre

**fourchon** [kalifuʀʃɔ̃]: **à ~** adv astride

**in, e** [kalɛ̃, in] adj cuddly, cuddle-some; (regard, voix) tender; **câliner** vt to cuddle

**mant** [kalmɑ̃] nm tranquillizer, seda-; (pour la douleur) painkiller

**me** [kalm] adj calm, quiet ♦ nm calm(ness), quietness; **calmer** vt (douleur, inquiétude) to soothe; **se ~** vi (down); (douleur, inquiétude) to calm own

**omnie** [kalɔmni] nf slander; (écrite) el; **calomnier** vt to slander; to libel

**orie** [kalɔʀi] nf calorie

**otte** [kalɔt] nf (coiffure) skullcap; m: (gifle) slap; **~ glaciaire** (GÉO) ice-

**quer** [kalke] vt to trace; (fig) to copy actly

**vaire** [kalvɛʀ] nm (croix) wayside oss, calvary; (souffrances) suffering

**vitie** [kalvisi] nf baldness

**narade** [kamaʀad] nm/f friend, pal; ηl) comrade; **camaraderie** nf friend-p

**nbouis** [kɑ̃bwi] nm dirty oil ou ease

**nbrer** [kɑ̃bʀe]: **se ~** vi to arch one's ck

**nbriolage** [kɑ̃bʀijɔlaʒ] nm burglary; **nbrioler** vt to burgle (BRIT), burglar-(US); **cambrioleur, -euse** nm/f bur-ar

**nelote** [kamlɔt] (fam) nf rubbish, ish, junk

**néra** [kameʀa] nf (CINÉMA, TV) cam-; (d'amateur) cine-camera

**néscope** ® [kameskɔp] nm cam-der ®

**nion** [kamjɔ̃] nm lorry (BRIT), truck;

**de dépannage** breakdown (BRIT) ou tow (US) truck; **camion-citerne** nm tanker; **camionnette** nf (small) van; **camionneur** nm (chauffeur) lorry (BRIT) ou truck driver; (entrepreneur) haulage contractor (BRIT), trucker (US)

**camisole** [kamizɔl] nf: **~ (de force)** straitjacket

**camomille** [kamɔmij] nf camomile; (boisson) camomile tea

**camoufler** [kamufle] vt to camouflage; (fig) to conceal, cover up

**camp** [kɑ̃] nm camp; (fig) side; **~ de vacances** children's holiday camp (BRIT), summer camp (US)

**campagnard, e** [kɑ̃paɲaʀ, aʀd] adj country cpd

**campagne** [kɑ̃paɲ] nf country, coun-tryside; (MIL, POL, COMM) campaign; **à la ~** in the country

**camper** [kɑ̃pe] vi to camp ♦ vt to sketch; **se ~ devant** to plant o.s. in front of; **campeur, -euse** nm/f camper

**camping** [kɑ̃piŋ] nm camping; (terrain de) **~** campsite, camping site; **faire du ~** to go camping; **camping-car** nm camper, motorhome (US); **camping-gaz** ® nm inv camp(ing) stove

**Canada** [kanada] nm: **le ~** Canada; **canadien, ne** adj Canadian ♦ nm/f: **C~, ne** Canadian; **canadienne** nf (veste) fur-lined jacket

**canaille** [kanaj] (péj) nf scoundrel

**canal, -aux** [kanal, o] nm canal; (natu-rel) channel; **canalisation** nf (tuyau) pipe; **canaliser** vt to canalize; (fig) to channel

**canapé** [kanape] nm settee, sofa

**canard** [kanaʀ] nm duck; (fam: journal) rag

**canari** [kanaʀi] nm canary

**cancans** [kɑ̃kɑ̃] nmpl (malicious) gossip sg

**cancer** [kɑ̃seʀ] nm cancer; (signe): **le C~** Cancer; **~ de la peau** skin cancer

**cancre** [kɑ̃kʀ] nm dunce

**candeur** [kɑ̃dœʀ] nf ingenuousness,

guilelessness

**candidat, e** [kɑ̃dida, at] nm/f candidate; (à un poste) applicant, candidate; **candidature** nf (POL) candidature; (à poste) application; **poser sa candidature à un poste** to apply for a job

**candide** [kɑ̃did] adj ingenuous, guileless

**cane** [kan] nf (female) duck

**caneton** [kantɔ̃] nm duckling

**canette** [kanɛt] nf (de bière) (flip-top) bottle

**canevas** [kanva] nm (COUTURE) canvas

**caniche** [kaniʃ] nm poodle

**canicule** [kanikyl] nf scorching heat

**canif** [kanif] nm penknife, pocket knife

**canine** [kanin] nf canine (tooth)

**caniveau, x** [kanivo] nm gutter

**canne** [kan] nf (walking) stick; **~ à pêche** fishing rod; **~ à sucre** sugar cane

**cannelle** [kanɛl] nf cinnamon

**canoë** [kanɔe] nm canoe; (sport) canoeing

**canon** [kanɔ̃] nm (arme) gun; (HISTOIRE) cannon; (d'une arme: tube) barrel; (fig: norme) model; (MUS) canon

**canot** [kano] nm ding(h)y; **~ de sauvetage** lifeboat; **~ pneumatique** inflatable ding(h)y; **canotier** nm boater

**cantatrice** [kɑ̃tatris] nf (opera) singer

**cantine** [kɑ̃tin] nf canteen

**cantique** [kɑ̃tik] nm hymn

**canton** [kɑ̃tɔ̃] nm district consisting of several communes; (en Suisse) canton

**cantonade** [kɑ̃tɔnad]: **à la ~** adv to everyone in general

**cantonner** [kɑ̃tɔne]: **se ~ à** vt to confine o.s. to

**cantonnier** [kɑ̃tɔnje] nm roadmender

**canular** [kanylaʀ] nm hoax

**caoutchouc** [kautʃu] nm rubber

**cap** [kap] nm (GÉO) cape; (promontoire) headland; (fig: tournant) watershed; (NAVIG): **changer de ~** to change course; **mettre le ~ sur** to head ou steer for

**CAP** sigle m (= Certificat d'aptitude p[...] fessionnelle) vocational training certific[...] taken at secondary school

**capable** [kapabl] adj able, capable, **de qch/faire** capable of sth/doing

**capacité** [kapasite] nf (compéten[...] ability; (JUR, contenance) capacity

**cape** [kap] nf cape, cloak; **rire sous [...]** to laugh up one's sleeve

**CAPES** [kapɛs] sigle m (= Certifi[...] d'aptitude pédagogique à l'enseignem[...] secondaire) teaching diploma

**capillaire** [kapilɛʀ] adj (soins, loti[...] hair cpd; (vaisseau etc) capillary

**capitaine** [kapitɛn] nm captain

**capital, e, -aux** [kapital, o] adj (œuvre) major; (question, rôle) fun[...] mental ♦ nm capital; (fig) stock; **d'u[...] importance ~e** of capital importan[...] voir aussi **capitaux**; (fig): **~ (social)** auth[...] ized capital; **capitale** nf (ville) capital; (lettre) capital (letter); **capitalisme** capitalism; **capitaliste** adj, nm/f ca[...] talist; **capitaux** nmpl (fonds) capital s[...]

**capitonné, e** [kapitɔne] adj padded

**caporal, -aux** [kapɔral, o] nm lar[...] corporal

**capot** [kapo] nm (AUTO) bonnet (BR[...] hood (US)

**capote** [kapɔt] nf (de voiture) hood (BRIT), top (US); (fam) condom

**capoter** [kapɔte] vi (négociations) founder

**câpre** [kɑpʀ] nf caper

**caprice** [kapʀis] nm whim, caprice; **[...] re des ~s** to make a fuss; **capricie[...] -euse** adj (fantasque) capricious, wh[...] sical; (enfant) awkward

**Capricorne** [kapʀikɔʀn] nm: **le ~ C[...]** pricorn

**capsule** [kapsyl] nf (de bouteille) cap; (BOT etc, spatiale) capsule

**capter** [kapte] vt (ondes radio) to p[...] up; (fig) to win, capture

**captivant, e** [kaptivɑ̃, ɑ̃t] adj captiv[...] ing

**captivité** [kaptivite] nf captivity

**turer** [kaptyʁe] *vt* to capture

**uche** [kapyʃ] *nf* hood

**uchon** [kapyʃɔ̃] *nm* hood; (*de stylo*) **o**, top

**ucine** [kapysin] *nf* (BOT) nasturtium

**uet** [kake] *nm*: **rabattre le ~ à qn** *m*) to bring sb down a peg or two

**ueter** [kakte] *vi* to cackle

**abine** [kaʁabin] *nf* rifle

**ctère** [kaʁaktɛʁ] *nm* (*gén*) charac-
**e**; **avoir bon/mauvais ~** to be
od-/ill-natured; **en ~s gras** in bold
**e**; **en petits ~s** in small print; **~s**
**imprimerie** (block) capitals; **carac-
riel, le** *adj* (*traits*) of) character; (*en-
*t*) emotionally disturbed

**ctérisé, e** [kaʁakteʁize] *adj* sheer,
**wnright**

**ctériser** [kaʁakteʁize] *vt* to be
**aracteristic of**

**ctéristique** [kaʁakteʁistik] *adj*, *nf*
**aracteristic**

**afe** [kaʁaf] *nf* (*pour eau, vin ordi-
re*) carafe

**aïbe** [kaʁaib] *adj* Caribbean ♦ *n*: **les**
**s** the Caribbean (Islands)

**ambolage** [kaʁɑ̃bɔlaʒ] *nm* multiple
**ash**, pileup

**amel** [kaʁamɛl] *nm* (*bonbon*) cara-
**el**, toffee; (*substance*) caramel

**apace** [kaʁapas] *nf* shell

**avane** [kaʁavan] *nf* caravan; **cara-
ning** *nm* caravanning

**bone** [kaʁbɔn] *nm* carbon; (*double*)
**bon** (copy); **carbonique** *adj*: **gaz**
**rbonique** carbon dioxide; **neige**
**bonique** dry ice; **carbonisé, e** *adj*
**arred**

**burant** [kaʁbyʁɑ̃] *nm* (motor) fuel
**burateur** [kaʁbyʁatœʁ] *nm* carbu-
**tor**

**can** [kaʁkɑ̃] *nm* (*fig*) yoke, shackles

**casse** [kaʁkas] *nf* carcass; (*de véhi-
e etc*) shell

**diaque** [kaʁdjak] *adj* cardiac, heart

*cpd* ♦ *nm/f* heart patient; **être ~** to
have heart trouble

**cardigan** [kaʁdigɑ̃] *nm* cardigan

**cardiologue** [kaʁdjɔlɔg] *nm/f* cardiolo-
gist, heart specialist

**carême** [kaʁɛm] *nm*: **le C~** Lent

**carence** [kaʁɑ̃s] *nf* (*manque*) deficiency

**caresse** [kaʁɛs] *nf* caress

**caresser** [kaʁese] *vt* to caress; (*animal*)
to stroke

**cargaison** [kaʁgɛzɔ̃] *nf* cargo, freight

**cargo** [kaʁgo] *nm* cargo boat, freighter

**caricature** [kaʁikatyʁ] *nf* caricature

**carie** [kaʁi] *nf*: **la ~ (dentaire)** tooth
decay; **une ~** a bad tooth

**carillon** [kaʁijɔ̃] *nm* (*air, de pendule*)
chimes *pl*

**caritatif, -ive** [kaʁitatif, iv] *adj*: **organisation caritative** charity

**carnassier, -ière** [kaʁnasje, jɛʁ] *adj*
carnivorous

**carnaval** [kaʁnaval] *nm* carnival

**carnet** [kaʁnɛ] *nm* (*calepin*) notebook;
(*de tickets, timbres etc*) book; **~ de
chèques** cheque book; **~ de notes**
school report

**carotte** [kaʁɔt] *nf* carrot

**carpette** [kaʁpɛt] *nf* rug

**carré, e** [kaʁe] *adj* square; (*fig: franc*)
straightforward ♦ *nm* (MATH) square;
**mètre/kilomètre ~** square metre/
kilometre

**carreau, x** [kaʁo] *nm* (*par terre*) (floor)
tile; (*au mur*) (wall) tile; (*de fenêtre*)
(window) pane; (*motif*) check, square;
(CARTES: *couleur*) diamonds *pl*; **tissu à
~x** checked fabric

**carrefour** [kaʁfuʁ] *nm* crossroads *sg*

**carrelage** [kaʁlaʒ] *nm* (*sol*) (tiled) floor

**carrelet** [kaʁlɛ] *nm* (*poisson*) plaice

**carrément** [kaʁemɑ̃] *adv* (*franchement*)
straight out, bluntly; (*sans hésiter*)
straight; (*intensif*) completely; **c'est ~
impossible** it's completely impossible

**carrière** [kaʁjɛʁ] *nf* (*métier*) career; (*de
roches*) quarry; **militaire de ~** professional soldier

**carrossable** [karɔsabl] *adj* suitable for (motor) vehicles

**carrosse** [karɔs] *nm* (horse-drawn) coach

**carrosserie** [karɔsʀi] *nf* body, coachwork *no pl*

**carrure** [karyʀ] *nf* build; (*fig*) stature, calibre

**cartable** [kartabl] *nm* satchel, (school)bag

**carte** [kart] *nf* (*de géographie*) map; (*marine, du ciel*) chart; (*d'abonnement, à jouer*) card; (*au restaurant*) menu; (*aussi*: ~ **de visite**) (visiting) card; **à la** ~ (*au restaurant*) à la carte; **donner** ~ **blanche à qn** to give sb a free rein; ~ **bancaire** cash card; ~ **de crédit** credit card; ~ **de fidélité** loyalty card; ~ **d'identité** identity card; ~ **de séjour** residence permit; ~ **grise** (*AUTO*) (car) registration book, logbook; ~ **postale** postcard; ~ **routière** road map; ~ **téléphonique** phonecard

**carter** [kartɛʀ] *nm* sump

**carton** [kartɔ̃] *nm* (*matériau*) cardboard; (*boîte*) (cardboard) box; **faire un** ~ (*fam*) to score a hit; ~ (*à dessin*) portfolio; **carton-pâte** *nm* pasteboard

**cartouche** [kartuʃ] *nf* cartridge; (*de cigarettes*) carton

**cas** [ka] *nm* case; **ne faire aucun** ~ **de** to take no notice of; **en aucun** ~ on no account; **au** ~ **où** in case; **en** ~ **de** in case of, in the event of; **en** ~ **de besoin** if need be; **en tout** ~ in any case, at any rate

**casanier, -ière** [kazanje, jɛʀ] *adj* stay-at-home

**cascade** [kaskad] *nf* waterfall, cascade; (*fig*) stream, torrent; **cascadeur, -euse** *nm/f* stuntman(-girl)

**case** [kaz] *nf* (*hutte*) hut; (*compartiment*) compartment; (*sur un formulaire, de mots croisés etc*) box

**caser** [kaze] (*fam*) *vt* (*placer*) to put (away); (*loger*) to put up; **se** ~ *vi* (*se marier*) to settle down; (*trouver un em-*

ploi) to find a (steady) job

**caserne** [kazɛʀn] *nf* barracks *pl*

**cash** [kaʃ] *adv*: **payer** ~ to pay cash down

**casier** [kazje] *nm* (*pour courrier*) pigeon-hole; (*compartiment*) compartment; (*à clef*) locker; ~ **judiciaire** police record

**casino** [kazino] *nm* casino

**casque** [kask] *nm* helmet; (*chez le coiffeur*) (hair-)drier; (*pour audition*) (head)phones *pl*, headset

**casquette** [kaskɛt] *nf* cap

**cassant, e** [kasɑ̃, ɑ̃t] *adj* brittle; (*ton*) curt, abrupt

**cassation** [kasasjɔ̃] *nf*: **cour de** ~ final court of appeal

**casse** [kas] (*fam*) *nf* (*pour voiture*) to put to scrap; (*dégâts*): **il y en a de la** ~ there were a lot of breakages; **casse-cou** *adj inv* daredevil, reckless; **casse-croûte** *nm inv* snack; **casse-noix** *nm inv* nutcrackers *pl*; **casse-pieds** (*fam*) *adj inv*: **il est** ~ **casse-pieds** he's a pain in the neck

**casser** [kase] *vt* to break; (*JUR*) to quash; **se** ~ *vi* to break; ~ **les pieds à qn** (*fam*: *irriter*) to get on sb's nerves; **se** ~ **la tête** (*fam*) to go to a lot of trouble

**casserole** [kasʀɔl] *nf* saucepan

**casse-tête** [kastɛt] *nm inv* (*difficulté*) headache (*fig*)

**cassette** [kasɛt] *nf* (*bande magnétique*) cassette; (*coffret*) casket

**casseur** [kasœʀ] *nm* hooligan

**cassis** [kasis] *nm* blackcurrant

**cassoulet** [kasule] *nm* bean and sausage hot-pot

**cassure** [kasyʀ] *nf* break, crack

**castor** [kastɔʀ] *nm* beaver

**castrer** [kastre] *vt* (*mâle*) to castrate (: *cheval*) to geld; (*femelle*) to spay

**catalogue** [katalɔg] *nm* catalogue

**cataloguer** [katalɔge] *vt* to catalogue, to list; (*péj*) to put a label on

**catalyseur** [katalizœʀ] *nm* catalyst; **talytique** *adj*: **pot catalytique** catalytic convertor

**astrophe** [katastʀɔf] *nf* catastrophe, disaster; **catastrophé, e** (*fam*) stunned

**chisme** [katejism] *nm* catechism

**égorie** [kategɔʀi] *nf* category; **catégorique** *adj* categorical

**hédrale** [katedʀal] *nf* cathedral

**holique** [katɔlik] *adj*, *nm/f* (Roman) Catholic; **pas très** ~ a bit shady ou dodgy

**mini** [katimini]: **en ~** *adv* on the quiet

**chemar** [koʃmaʀ] *nm* nightmare

**se** [koz] *nf* cause; (*JUR*) lawsuit, case; **~ de** because of, owing to; **pour ~ de** on account of; **(et) pour ~** and for (very) good reason; **être en ~** (*intérêt*) to be at stake; **remettre en ~** to challenge; **causer** *vt* to cause ♦ *vi* to chat, talk; **causerie** (*conférence*) talk; **causette** *nf*: **faire la causette** to have a chat

**tion** [kosjɔ̃] *nf* guarantee, security; (*JUR*) bail (bond); (*fig*) backing, support; **libéré sous ~** released on bail; **cautionner** *vt* (*répondre de*) to guarantee; (*soutenir*) to support

**alcade** [kavalkad] *nf* (*fig*) stampede

**alier, -ière** [kavalje, jɛʀ] *adj* (*désinvolte*) offhand ♦ *nm/f* rider; (*au bal*) partner ♦ *nm* (*ÉCHECS*) knight

**re** [kav] *nf* cellar

**eau, x** [kavo] *nm* vault

**verne** [kavɛʀn] *nf* cave

**P** *sigle m* = **compte chèques postaux**

*sigle m* (= *compact disc*) CD

**-ROM** [sederɔm] *sigle m* CD-ROM

**n** *abr* (= *Communauté Européenne*)

**cette** [sə, set] (*devant nm* **cet** + *voyelle ou h aspiré*; *pl* **ces**) *dét* (*proximité*) this; these *pl*; (*non-proximité*) that; those *pl*;

**cette maison(-ci/là)** this/that house; **cette nuit** (*qui vient*) tonight; (*passée*) last night

♦ *pron* 1: **c'est** it's *ou* it is; **c'est un peintre** he's *ou* he is a painter; **ce sont des peintres** they're *ou* they are painters; **c'est le facteur** (*à la porte*) it's the postman; **qui est-ce?** who is it?; (*en désignant*) who is he/she?; **qu'est-ce?** who is he/she?

2: **ce qui, ce que** what; (*chose qui*): **il est bête, ce qui me chagrine** he's stupid, which saddens me; **tout ce qui bouge** everything that *ou* which moves; **tout ce que je sais** all I know; **ce dont j'ai parlé** what I talked about; **ce que c'est grand!** it's so big!; *voir aussi* **-ci**; **est-ce que**; **n'est-ce pas**; **c'est-à-dire**

**ceci** [səsi] *pron* this

**cécité** [sesite] *nf* blindness

**céder** [sede] *vt* (*donner*) to give up ♦ *vi* (*chaise, barrage*) to give way; (*personne*) to give in; **~ à** to yield to, give in to

**CEDEX** [sedeks] *sigle m* (= *courrier d'entreprise à distribution exceptionnelle*) *postal service for bulk users*

**cédille** [sedij] *nf* cedilla

**cèdre** [sedʀ] *nm* cedar

**CEI** *abr m* (= *Communauté des États Indépendants*) CIS

**ceinture** [sɛ̃tyʀ] *nf* belt; (*taille*) waist; **~ de sécurité** safety *ou* seat belt

**cela** [s(ə)la] *pron* that; (*comme sujet indéfini*) it; **quand/où ~?** when/where (was that)?

**célèbre** [selebʀ] *adj* famous; **célébrer** *vt* to celebrate

**céleri** [selʀi] *nm*: **~(-rave)** celeriac; **~ (en branche)** celery

**célibat** [seliba] *nm* (*homme*) bachelorhood; (*femme*) spinsterhood; (*prêtre*) celibacy; **célibataire** *adj* single, unmarried ♦ *nm* bachelor ♦ *nf* unmarried woman

**celle(s)** [sɛl] *pron voir* **celui**

**cellier** [selje] *nm* storeroom (*for wine*)

**cellule** [selyl] *nf* (*gén*) cell

**cellulite** [selylit] *nf* excess fat, cellulite

---

*MOT-CLÉ*

---

**celui, celle** [səlɥi, sɛl] (*mpl* **ceux**, *fpl* **celles**) *pron* 1: **celui-ci/là, celle-ci/là** this one/that one; **ceux-ci, celles-ci** these (ones); **ceux-là, celles-là** those (ones); **celui de mon frère** my brother's; **celui du salon/du dessus** the one in (*ou* from) the lounge/below 2: **celui qui bouge** the one which *ou* that moves; (*personne*) the one who moves; **celui que je vois** the one (which *ou* that) I see; the one (whom) I see; **celui dont je parle** the one I'm talking about 3 (*valeur indéfinie*): **celui qui veut** whoever wants

---

**cendre** [sɑ̃dʀ] *nf* ash; **~s** *nfpl* (*d'un défunt*) ashes; **sous la ~** (*CULIN*) in (the) embers; **cendrier** *nm* ashtray

**cène** [sɛn] *nf*: **la ~** (Holy) Communion

**censé, e** [sɑ̃se] *adj*: **être ~ faire** to be supposed to do

**censeur** [sɑ̃sœʀ] *nm* (*SCOL*) deputy-head (*BRIT*), vice-principal (*US*)

**censure** [sɑ̃syʀ] *nf* censorship; **censurer** *vt* (*CINÉMA, PRESSE*) to censor; (*POL*) to censure

**cent** [sɑ̃] *num* a hundred, one hundred ♦ *nm* (*US, Canada etc*) cent; (*partie de l'euro*) cent; **centaine** *nf*: **une centaine (de)** about a hundred, a hundred or so; **des centaines (de)** hundreds (of); **centenaire** *adj* hundred-year-old ♦ *nm* (*anniversaire*) centenary; **centième** *num* hundredth; **centigrade** *nm* centigrade; **centilitre** *nm* centilitre; **centime** *nm* centime; **centime d'euro** cent; **centimètre** *nm* centimetre; (*ruban*) tape measure, measuring tape

**central, e, -aux** [sɑ̃tʀal, o] *adj* central ♦ *nm*: **~ téléphonique** (telephone)

---

exchange; **centrale** *nf* power statio.; **centre** [sɑ̃tʀ] *nm* centre; **~ commer** shopping centre; **~ d'appels** centre; **~ de loisirs** leisure cen **centre-ville** *nm* town centre, do town (area) (*US*)

**centuple** [sɑ̃typl] *nm*: **le ~ de qc** hundred times sth; **au ~** a hundr fold

**cep** [sɛp] *nm* (vine) stock

**cèpe** [sɛp] *nm* (edible) boletus

**cependant** [s(ə)pɑ̃dɑ̃] *adv* however

**céramique** [seramik] *nf* ceramics sg.

**cercle** [sɛʀkl] *nm* circle

**cercueil** [sɛʀkœj] *nm* coffin

**céréale** [seʀeal] *nf* cereal; **~s** *nfpl* bre fast cereal

**cérémonie** [seʀemɔni] *nf* ceremony

**cerf** [sɛʀ] *nm* stag

**cerfeuil** [sɛʀfœj] *nm* chervil

**cerf-volant** [sɛʀvɔlɑ̃] *nm* kite

**cerise** [s(ə)ʀiz] *nf* cherry; **cerisier** cherry (tree)

**cerne** [sɛʀn] *nm*: **avoir des ~s** to h. shadows *ou* dark rings under one's e.

**cerner** [sɛʀne] *vt* (*MIL etc*) to surrou (*fig: problème*) to delimit, define

**certain, e** [sɛʀtɛ̃, ɛn] *adj* certain ♦ **d'un ~ âge** past one's prir not so young; **un ~ temps** (qu some time; **~s** ♦ *pron* some; **cert ment** *adv* (*probablement*) most pr ably *ou* likely; (*bien sûr*) certainly, course

**certes** [sɛʀt] *adv* (*sans doute*) admi tedly; (*bien sûr*) of course

**certificat** [sɛʀtifika] *nm* certificate

**certifier** [sɛʀtifje] *vt*: **~ qch à qn** to sure sb of sth; **copie certifiée conf** me certified copy of the original

**certitude** [sɛʀtityd] *nf* certainty

**cerveau, x** [sɛʀvo] *nm* brain

**cervelas** [sɛʀvəla] *nm* saveloy

**cervelle** [sɛʀvɛl] *nf* (*ANAT*) brain; (*CUL* brains

**ces** [se] *dét voir* **ce**

**CES** *sigle m* (= Collège d'enseignem

*secondaire*) ≈ (junior) secondary school (*BRIT*)

**:esse** [sɛs]: **sans ~** *adv* (*tout le temps*) continually, constantly; (*sans interruption*) continuously; **il n'a eu de ~ que** he did not rest until; **cesser** *vt* to stop ♦ *vi* to stop, cease; **cesser de faire** to stop doing; **cessez-le-feu** *nm inv* ceasefire

**'est-à-dire** [sɛtadiʀ] *adv* that is (to say)

**et, cette** [sɛt] *dét voir* **ce**

**eux** [sø] *pron voir* **celui**

**CFC** *abr* (= *chlorofluorocarbon*) CFC

**CFDT** *sigle f* (= *Confédération française démocratique du travail*) French trade union

**CGT** *sigle f* (= *Confédération générale du travail*) French trade union

**hacun, e** [ʃakœ̃, yn] *pron* each; (*indéfini*) everyone, everybody

**hagrin** [ʃagʀɛ̃] *nm* grief, sorrow; **avoir du ~** to be grieved; **chagriner** *vt* to grieve

**hahut** [ʃay] *nm* uproar; **chahuter** *vt* to rag, bait ♦ *vi* to make an uproar

**haine** [ʃɛn] *nf* chain; (*RADIO, TV:* stations) channel; **~s** (*AUTO*) (snow) chains; **travail à la ~** production line work; **~** (**de montage**) production ou assembly line; **~ de montagnes** mountain range; **~** (**hi-fi**) hi-fi system; **~ laser CD player**; **~** (**stéréo**) stereo (system); **chaînette** *nf* (small) chain

**hair** [ʃɛʀ] *nf* flesh; **avoir la ~ de poule** to have goosepimples *ou* gooseflesh; **bien en ~** plump, well-padded; **en et en os** in the flesh; **~ à saucisse** sausage meat

**haire** [ʃɛʀ] *nf* (*d'église*) pulpit; (*d'université*) chair

**haise** [ʃɛz] *nf* chair; **~ longue** deckchair

**hâle** [ʃɑl] *nm* shawl

**haleur** [ʃalœʀ] *nf* heat; (*fig: accueil*) warmth; **chaleureux, -euse** *adj* warm

**haloupe** [ʃalup] *nf* launch; (*de sauve-*

*tage*) lifeboat

**chalumeau, x** [ʃalymo] *nm* blowlamp, blowtorch

**chalutier** [ʃalytje] *nm* trawler

**chamailler** [ʃamaje]: **se ~** *vi* to squabble, bicker

**chambouler** [ʃɑ̃bule] (*fam*) *vt* to disrupt, turn upside down

**chambre** [ʃɑ̃bʀ] *nf* bedroom; (*POL, COMM*) chamber; **faire ~ à part** to sleep in separate rooms; **~ à air** (*de pneu*) (inner) tube; **~ à coucher** bedroom; **~ à un lit/deux lits** (*à l'hôtel*) single-/twin-bedded room; **~ d'amis** spare *ou* guest room; **~ noire** (*PHOTO*) dark room; **chambrer** *vt* (*vin*) to bring to room temperature

**chameau, x** [ʃamo] *nm* camel

**chamois** [ʃamwa] *nm* chamois

**champ** [ʃɑ̃] *nm* field; **~ de bataille** battlefield; **~ de courses** racecourse; **~ de tir** rifle range

**champagne** [ʃɑ̃paɲ] *nm* champagne

**champêtre** [ʃɑ̃pɛtʀ] *adj* country *cpd*, rural

**champignon** [ʃɑ̃piɲɔ̃] *nm* mushroom; (*terme générique*) fungus; **~ de Paris** button mushroom

**champion, ne** [ʃɑ̃pjɔ̃, jɔn] *adj, nm/f* champion; **championnat** *nm* championship

**chance** [ʃɑ̃s] *nf*: **la ~** luck; **~s** *nfpl* (*probabilités*) chances; **avoir de la ~** to be lucky; **il a des ~s de réussir** he's got a good chance of passing

**chanceler** [ʃɑ̃s(ə)le] *vi* to totter

**chancelier** [ʃɑ̃səlje] *nm* (*allemand*) chancellor

**chanceux, -euse** [ʃɑ̃sø, øz] *adj* lucky

**chandail** [ʃɑ̃daj] *nm* (thick) sweater

**Chandeleur** [ʃɑ̃dlœʀ] *nf*: **la ~** Candlemas

**chandelier** [ʃɑ̃dalje] *nm* candlestick

**chandelle** [ʃɑ̃dɛl] *nf* (tallow) candle; **dîner aux ~s** candlelight dinner

**change** [ʃɑ̃ʒ] *nm* (*devises*) exchange

**changement** [ʃɑ̃ʒmɑ̃] *nm* change; **~**

de vitesses gears pl

**changer** [ʃɑ̃ʒe] vt (modifier) to change, alter; (remplacer, COMM) to change ♦ vi to change, alter; **se ~** vi to change (o.s.); **~ de** (remplacer: adresse, nom, voiture etc) to change one's; (échanger: place, train etc) to change; **~ d'avis** to change one's mind; **~ de vitesse** to change gear

**chanson** [ʃɑ̃sɔ̃] nf song

**chant** [ʃɑ̃] nm song; (art vocal) singing; (d'église) hymn

**chantage** [ʃɑ̃taʒ] nm blackmail; **faire du ~** to use blackmail

**chanter** [ʃɑ̃te] vt, vi to sing; **si cela lui chante** (fam) if he feels like it; **chanteur, -euse** nm/f singer

**chantier** [ʃɑ̃tje] nm (building site); (sur une route) roadworks pl; **mettre en ~** to put in hand; **~ naval** shipyard

**chantilly** [ʃɑ̃tiji] nf voir **crème**

**chantonner** [ʃɑ̃tɔne] vi, vt to sing to oneself, hum

**chanvre** [ʃɑ̃vʀ] nm hemp

**chaparder** [ʃapaʀde] (fam) vt to pinch

**chapeau, x** [ʃapo] nm hat; **~!** well done!

**chapelet** [ʃaplɛ] nm (REL) rosary

**chapelle** [ʃapɛl] nf chapel

**chapelure** [ʃaplyʀ] nf (dried) breadcrumbs pl

**chapiteau, x** [ʃapito] nm (de cirque) marquee, big top

**chapitre** [ʃapitʀ] nm chapter

**chaque** [ʃak] dét each, every; (indéfini) every

**char** [ʃaʀ] nm (MIL): **~ (d'assaut)** tank; **~ à voile** sand yacht

**charabia** [ʃaʀabja] (péj) nm gibberish

**charade** [ʃaʀad] nf riddle; (mimée) charade

**charbon** [ʃaʀbɔ̃] nm coal; **~ de bois** charcoal

**charcuterie** [ʃaʀkytʀi] nf (magasin) pork butcher's shop and delicatessen; (produits) cooked pork meats pl; **charcutier, -ière** nm/f pork butcher

**chardon** [ʃaʀdɔ̃] nm thistle

**charge** [ʃaʀʒ] nf (fardeau) load, burden; (explosif, ÉLEC, MIL, JUR) charge; (rôle, mission) responsibility; **~s** nfpl (du loyer) service charges; **à la ~ de** (dépendant de) dependent upon; (aux frais de) chargeable to; **prendre en ~** to take charge of; (suj: véhicule) to take on; (dépenses) to take care of; **~s sociales** social security contributions

**chargé, e** [ʃaʀʒe] adj (emploi du temps, journée) full, heavy

**chargement** [ʃaʀʒəmɑ̃] nm (objets) load

**charger** [ʃaʀʒe] vt (voiture, fusil, caméra) to load; (batterie) to charge ♦ vi (MIL etc) to charge; **se ~ de** vt to see to; **~ qn de (faire) qch** to put sb in charge of (doing) sth

**chariot** [ʃaʀjo] nm trolley; (charrette) waggon

**charité** [ʃaʀite] nf charity

**charmant, e** [ʃaʀmɑ̃, ɑ̃t] adj charming

**charme** [ʃaʀm] nm charm; **charmer** to charm

**charnel, le** [ʃaʀnɛl] adj carnal

**charnière** [ʃaʀnjɛʀ] nf hinge; (fig) turning-point

**charnu, e** [ʃaʀny] adj fleshy

**charpente** [ʃaʀpɑ̃t] nf frame(work); **charpentier** nm carpenter

**charpie** [ʃaʀpi] nf: **en ~** (fig) in shreds ou ribbons

**charrette** [ʃaʀɛt] nf cart

**charrier** [ʃaʀje] vt (entraîner: fleuve) to carry (along); (transporter) to cart, carry

**charrue** [ʃaʀy] nf plough (BRIT), plow (US)

**charter** [ʃaʀtɛʀ] nm (vol) charter flight

**chasse** [ʃas] nf hunting; (au fusil) shooting; (poursuite) chase; (aussi: **~ d'eau**) flush; **~ gardée** private hunting grounds pl; **prendre en ~** to give chase to; **tirer la ~ (d'eau)** to flush the toilet, pull the chain; **~ à courre** hunting; **chasse-neige** nm inv snowplough (BRIT), snowplow (US); **chasser** vt to hunt; (expulser) to chase away ou out, drive away ou out; **chasseur, -euse** nm/f hunter ♦ nm (avion) fighter

**châssis** [ʃasi] nm (AUTO) chassis; (cadre) frame

**chat** [ʃa] nm cat

**châtaigne** [ʃatɛɲ] nf chestnut; **châtaignier** [ʃatɛɲje] nm chestnut (tree)

**châtain** [ʃatɛ̃] adj inv (cheveux) chestnut (brown); (personne) chestnut-haired

**château, x** [ʃato] nm (forteresse) castle; (résidence royale) palace; (manoir) mansion; ~ **d'eau** water tower; ~ **fort** stronghold, fortified castle

**châtier** [ʃatje] vt to punish; **châtiment** nm punishment

**chaton** [ʃatɔ̃] nm (ZOOL) kitten

**chatouiller** [ʃatuje] vt to tickle; **chatouilleux, -euse** adj ticklish; (fig) touchy, over-sensitive

**chatoyer** [ʃatwaje] vi to shimmer

**châtrer** [ʃatʀe] vt (mâle) to castrate; (: cheval) to geld; (femelle) to spay

**chatte** [ʃat] nf (she-)cat

**chaud, e** [ʃo, ʃod] adj (gén) warm; (très ~) hot; **il fait** ~ it's warm; it's hot; **avoir** ~ to be warm; to be hot; **ça me tient** ~ it keeps me warm; **rester au** ~ to stay in the warm

**chaudière** [ʃodjɛʀ] nf boiler

**chaudron** [ʃodʀɔ̃] nm cauldron

**chauffage** [ʃofaʒ] nm heating; ~ **central** central heating

**chauffard** [ʃofaʀ] nm (péj) reckless driver

**chauffe-eau** [ʃofo] nm inv water-heater

**chauffer** [ʃofe] vt to heat ♦ vi to heat up, warm up; (trop: ~ moteur) to overheat; **se** ~ vi (au soleil) to warm o.s

**chauffeur** [ʃofœʀ] nm driver; (privé) chauffeur

**chaume** [ʃom] nm (du toit) thatch; **chaumière** nf (thatched) cottage

**chaussée** [ʃose] nf road(way)

**chausse-pied** [ʃospje] nm shoe-horn

**chausser** [ʃose] vt (bottes, skis) to put on; (enfant) to put shoes on; ~ **du 38/**

**42** to take size 38/42

**chaussette** [ʃosɛt] nf sock

**chausson** [ʃosɔ̃] nm slipper; (de bébé) bootee; ~ **(aux pommes)** (apple) turn-over

**chaussure** [ʃosyʀ] nf shoe; ~**s à talon** high-heeled shoes; ~**s de marche** walking shoes/boots; ~**s de ski** ski boots

**chauve** [ʃov] adj bald; **chauve-souris** nf bat

**chauvin, e** [ʃovɛ̃, in] adj chauvinistic

**chaux** [ʃo] nf lime; **blanchi à la** ~ whitewashed

**chavirer** [ʃaviʀe] vi to capsize

**chef** [ʃɛf] nm head, leader; (de cuisine) chef; ~ **d'accusation** charge; ~ **d'entreprise** company head; ~ **d'état** head of state; ~ **de famille** head of the family; ~ **de gare** station master; ~ **d'orchestre** conductor; ~ **de service** department head; **chef-d'œuvre** nm masterpiece; **chef-lieu** nm county town

**chemin** [ʃ(ə)mɛ̃] nm path; (itinéraire, direction, trajet) way; **en** ~ on the way; ~ **de fer** railway (BRIT), railroad (US); **par** ~ **de fer** by rail

**cheminée** [ʃ(ə)mine] nf chimney; (à l'intérieur) chimney piece, fireplace; (de bateau) funnel

**cheminement** [ʃ(ə)minmɑ̃] nm progress

**cheminot** [ʃ(ə)mino] nm railwayman

**chemise** [ʃ(ə)miz] nf shirt; (dossier) folder; ~ **de nuit** nightdress

**chemisier** [ʃ(ə)mizje, jɛʀ] nm blouse

**chenal, -aux** [ʃənal, o] nm channel

**chêne** [ʃɛn] nm oak (tree); (bois) oak

**chenil** [ʃ(ə)nil] nm kennels pl

**chenille** [ʃ(ə)nij] nf (ZOOL) caterpillar

**chèque** [ʃɛk] nm cheque (BRIT), check (US); ~ **sans provision** bad cheque; ~ **de voyage** traveller's cheque; **chéquier** [ʃekje] nm cheque book

**cher, -ère** [ʃɛʀ] adj (aimé) dear; (coûteux) expensive, dear ♦ adv: **ça**

coûte ~ it's expensive

**chercher** [ʃɛʀʃe] vt to look for; (gloire etc) to seek; **aller** ~ to go for, go and fetch; ~ **à faire** to try to do; **chercheur, -euse** nm/f researcher, research worker

**chère** [ʃɛʀ] adj voir **cher**

**chéri, e** [ʃeʀi] adj beloved, dear; **(mon)** ~ darling

**chérir** [ʃeʀiʀ] vt to cherish

**cherté** [ʃɛʀte] nf: **la ~ de la vie** the high cost of living

**chétif, -ive** [ʃetif, iv] adj (enfant) puny

**cheval, -aux** [ʃ(ə)val, o] nm horse; (AUTO): ~ **(vapeur)** horsepower no pl; **faire du** ~ to ride; **à** ~ on horseback; **à** ~ **sur** astride; (fig) overlapping; ~ **de course** racehorse

**chevalet** [ʃ(ə)valɛ] nm easel

**chevalier** [ʃ(ə)valje] nm knight

**chevalière** [ʃ(ə)valjɛʀ] nf signet ring

**chevalin, e** [ʃ(ə)valɛ̃, in] adj: **boucherie ~e** horse-meat butcher's

**chevaucher** [ʃ(ə)voʃe] vi (aussi: **se ~**) to overlap (each other) ♦ vt to be astride, straddle

**chevaux** [ʃvo] nmpl de **cheval**

**chevelu, e** [ʃəv(ə)ly] (péj) adj long-haired

**chevelure** [ʃəv(ə)lyʀ] nf hair no pl

**chevet** [ʃ(ə)vɛ] nm: **au ~ de qn** at sb's bedside; **lampe de** ~ bedside lamp

**cheveu, x** [ʃ(ə)vø] nm hair; ~**x** (chevelure) hair sg; **avoir les ~x courts** to have short hair

**cheville** [ʃ(ə)vij] nf (ANAT) ankle; (de bois) peg; (pour une vis) plug

**chèvre** [ʃɛvʀ] nf (she-)goat

**chevreau, x** [ʃavʀo] nm kid

**chèvrefeuille** [ʃɛvʀəfœj] nm honeysuckle

**chevreuil** [ʃavʀœj] nm roe deer inv; (CULIN) venison

**chevronné, e** [ʃavʀɔne] adj seasoned

---MOT-CLÉ---

**chez** [ʃe] prép **1** (à la demeure de) at;

(: direction) to; **chez qn** at/to sb's house ou place; **chez moi** at home (: direction) home

**2** (+profession) at; (: direction) to; **chez le boulanger/dentiste** at ou to the baker's/dentist's

**3** (dans le caractère, l'œuvre de) in: **chez les renards/Racine** in foxes Racine

**chez-soi** [ʃeswa] nm inv home

**chic** [ʃik] adj inv chic, smart; (fam: gé néreux) nice, decent ♦ nm stylishness; **(alors)!** (fam) great!; **avoir le ~ de** to have the knack of

**chicane** [ʃikan] nf (querelle) squabble

**chicaner** vi (ergoter): **chicaner sur** to quibble about

**chiche** [ʃiʃ] adj niggardly, mean ♦ exc (à un défi) you're on!

**chichis** [ʃiʃi] (fam) nmpl fuss sg

**chicorée** [ʃikɔʀe] nf (café) chicory; (sa lade) endive

**chien** [ʃjɛ̃] nm dog; ~ **de garde** guar dog; **chien-loup** nm wolfhound

**chiendent** [ʃjɛ̃dã] nm couch grass

**chienne** [ʃjɛn] nf dog, bitch

**chier** [ʃje] (fam!) vi to crap (!)

**chiffon** [ʃifɔ̃] nm (piece of) rag; **chif fonner** vt to crumple; (fam: tracasse to concern

**chiffre** [ʃifʀ] nm (représentant u nombre) figure, numeral; (montant, to tal) total, sum; **en ~s ronds** in roun figures; ~ **d'affaires** turnover; **chiffre** vt (dépense) to put a figure to, asses (message) to (en)code, cipher; **se chif frer à** to add up to, amount to

**chignon** [ʃiɲɔ̃] nm chignon, bun

**Chili** [ʃili] nm: **le ~** Chile; **chilien, n** adj Chilean ♦ nm/f: **Chilien, ne** Chilear

**chimie** [ʃimi] nf chemistry; **chimiqu** adj chemical; **produits chimique** chemicals

**chimpanzé** [ʃɛ̃pãze] nm chimpanzee

**Chine** [ʃin] nf: **la ~** China; **chinois,** adj Chinese ♦ nm/f: **Chinois, e** Chinese

♦ nm (LING) Chinese

**chiot** [ʃjo] nm pup(py)

**chiper** [ʃipe] (fam) vt to pinch

**chipoter** [ʃipɔte] (fam) vi (ergoter) to quibble

**chips** [ʃips] nfpl crisps (BRIT), (potato) chips (US)

**chiquenaude** [ʃiknod] nf flick, flip

**chirurgical, e, -aux** [ʃiryrʒikal, o] adj surgical

**chirurgie** [ʃiryrʒi] nf surgery; ~ esthétique plastic surgery; **chirurgien, ne** nm/f surgeon

**chlore** [klɔr] nm chlorine

**choc** [ʃɔk] nm (heurt) impact, shock; (collision) crash; (moral) shock; (affrontement) clash

**chocolat** [ʃɔkɔla] nm chocolate; ~ au lait milk chocolate; ~ (chaud) hot chocolate

**chœur** [kœr] nm (chorale) choir; (OPÉRA, THÉÂTRE) chorus; en ~ in chorus

**choisir** [ʃwazir] vt to choose, select

**choix** [ʃwa] nm choice, selection; avoir le ~ to have the choice; premier ~ (COMM) class one; de ~ choice, selected; au ~ as you wish

**chômage** [ʃomaʒ] nm unemployment; mettre au ~ to make redundant, put out of work; être au ~ to be unemployed ou out of work; **chômeur, -euse** nm/f unemployed person

**chope** [ʃɔp] nf tankard

**choper** [ʃɔpe] (fam) vt (objet, maladie) to catch

**choquer** [ʃɔke] vt (offenser) to shock; (deuil) to shake

**chorale** [kɔral] nf choir

**choriste** [kɔrist] nm/f choir member; (OPÉRA) chorus member

**chose** [ʃoz] nf thing; c'est peu de ~ it's nothing (really)

**chou, x** [ʃu] nm cabbage; mon petit ~ (my) sweetheart; ~ à la crème choux bun; ~x de Bruxelles Brussels sprouts; **chouchou, te** (fam) nm/f darling; (SCOL) teacher's pet; **choucroute** nf

sauerkraut

**chouette** [ʃwet] nf owl ♦ adj (fam) great, smashing

**chou-fleur** [ʃuflœr] nm cauliflower

**choyer** [ʃwaje] vt (dorloter) to cherish; (: excessivement) to pamper

**chrétien, ne** [kretjɛ̃, jɛn] adj, nm/f Christian

**Christ** [krist] nm: le ~ Christ; **christianisme** nm Christianity

**chrome** [krom] nm chromium; **chromé, e** adj chromium-plated

**chronique** [krɔnik] adj chronic ♦ nf (de journal) column, page; (historique) chronicle; (RADIO, TV): la ~ sportive the sports review

**chronologique** [krɔnɔlɔʒik] adj chronological

**chronomètre** [krɔnɔmɛtr] nm stopwatch; **chronométrer** vt to time

**chrysanthème** [krizɑ̃tɛm] nm chrysanthemum

**chuchotement** [ʃyʃɔtmɑ̃] nm whisper

**chuchoter** [ʃyʃɔte] vt, vi to whisper

**chut** [ʃyt] excl sh!

**chute** [ʃyt] nf fall; (déchet) scrap; faire une ~ (de 10 m) to fall (10 m); ~ (d'eau) waterfall; la ~ des cheveux hair loss; ~ libre free fall; ~s de pluie/neige rain/snowfalls

**Chypre** [ʃipr] nm/f Cyprus

**-ci** [si] adv (voir par ♦ dét: ce garçon-~/-là this/that boy; ces femmes-~/-là these/those women

**cible** [sibl] nf target

**ciboulette** [sibulɛt] nf (small) chive

**cicatrice** [sikatris] nf scar; **cicatriser** vt to heal

**ci-contre** [sikɔ̃tr] adv opposite

**ci-dessous** [sidəsu] adv below

**ci-dessus** [sidəsy] adv above

**cidre** [sidr] nm cider

**Cie** abr (= compagnie) Co.

**ciel** [sjɛl] nm sky; (REL) heaven; **cieux** nmpl (REL) heaven sg; à ~ ouvert openair; (mine) open-cast

**cierge** [sjɛrʒ] nm candle

**cieux** [sjø] nmpl de **ciel**

**cigale** [sigal] nf cicada

**cigare** [sigaʀ] nm cigar

**cigarette** [sigaʀɛt] nf cigarette

**ci-gît** [siʒi] adv +vb here lies

**cigogne** [sigɔɲ] nf stork

**ci-inclus, e** [siɛ̃kly, yz] adj, adv enclosed

**ci-joint, e** [siʒwɛ̃, ɛ̃t] adj, adv enclosed

**cil** [sil] nm (eye)lash

**cime** [sim] nf top; (montagne) peak

**ciment** [simɑ̃] nm cement

**cimetière** [simtjɛʀ] nm cemetery; (d'église) churchyard

**cinéaste** [sineast] nm/f film-maker

**cinéma** [sinema] nm cinema; **cinématographique** [sinematɔgʀafik] adj film cpd, cinema cpd

**cinglant, e** [sɛ̃glɑ̃, ɑ̃t] adj (remarque) biting

**cinglé, e** [sɛ̃gle] (fam) adj crazy

**cinq** [sɛ̃k] num five; **cinquantaine** [sɛ̃kɑ̃tɛn] nf: **une cinquantaine (de)** about fifty; **avoir la cinquantaine** (âge) to be around fifty; **cinquante** num fifty; **cinquantenaire** adj, nm/f fifty-year-old; **cinquième** num fifth

**cintre** [sɛ̃tʀ] nm coat-hanger

**cintré, e** [sɛ̃tʀe] adj (chemise) fitted

**cirage** [siʀaʒ] nm (shoe) polish

**circonflexe** [siʀkɔ̃flɛks] adj: **accent ~** circumflex accent

**circonscription** [siʀkɔ̃skʀipsjɔ̃] nf district; **~ électorale** (d'un député) constituency

**circonscrire** [siʀkɔ̃skʀiʀ] vt (sujet) to define, delimit; (incendie) to contain

**circonstance** [siʀkɔ̃stɑ̃s] nf circumstance; (occasion) occasion; **~s atténuantes** mitigating circumstances

**circuit** [siʀkɥi] nm (ÉLEC, TECH) circuit; (trajet) tour, (round) trip

**circulaire** [siʀkylɛʀ] adj, nf circular

**circulation** [siʀkylasjɔ̃] nf circulation; (AUTO): **la ~** (the) traffic

**circuler** [siʀkyle] vi (sang, devises) to circulate; (véhicules) to drive (along); (passants) to walk along; (train, bus) to

run; **faire ~** (nouvelle) to spread (about), circulate; (badauds) to move on

**cire** [siʀ] nf wax; **ciré** nm oilskin; **cirer** vt to wax, polish

**cirque** [siʀk] nm circus; (fig) chaos, bedlam; **quel ~!** what a carry-on!

**cisaille(s)** [sizaj] nf(pl) (gardening) shears pl

**ciseau, x** [sizo] nm: **~ (à bois)** chisel; **~x** nmpl (paire de ~x) (pair of) scissors

**ciseler** [siz(ə)le] vt to chisel, carve

**citadin, e** [sitadɛ̃, in] nm/f city dweller

**citation** [sitasjɔ̃] nf (d'auteur) quotation; (JUR) summons sg

**cité** [site] nf town; (plus grande) city; **~ universitaire** students' residences pl

**citer** [site] vt (un auteur) to quote (from); (nommer) to name; (JUR) to summon

**citerne** [sitɛʀn] nf tank

**citoyen, ne** [sitwajɛ̃, jɛn] nm/f citizen

**citron** [sitʀɔ̃] nm lemon; **~ vert** lime; **citronnade** nf still lemonade

**citrouille** [sitʀuj] nf pumpkin

**civet** [sivɛ] nm: **~ de lapin** rabbit stew

**civière** [sivjɛʀ] nf stretcher

**civil, e** [sivil] adj (mariage, poli) civil; (non militaire) civilian; **en ~** in civilian clothes; **dans le ~** in civilian life

**civilisation** [sivilizasjɔ̃] nf civilization

**clair, e** [klɛʀ] adj light; (pièce) light, bright; (eau, son, fig) clear ♦ adv: **voir ~** to see clearly; **tirer qch au ~** to clear sth up, clarify sth; **mettre au ~** (notes etc) to tidy up; **~ de lune** ♦ nm moonlight; **clairement** adv clearly

**clairière** [klɛʀjɛʀ] nf clearing

**clairon** [klɛʀɔ̃] nm bugle; **claironner** (fig) to trumpet, shout from the rooftops

**clairsemé, e** [klɛʀsəme] adj sparse

**clairvoyant, e** [klɛʀvwajɑ̃, ɑ̃t] adj perceptive, clear-sighted

**clandestin, e** [klɑ̃dɛstɛ̃, in] adj clandestine, secret; (mouvement) underground; (travailleur) illegal; **passager ~**

stowaway
**clapier** [klapje] *nm* (rabbit) hutch
**clapoter** [klapɔte] *vi* to lap
**claque** [klak] *nf* (gifle) slap; **claquer** *vi*
(porte) to bang, slam; (fam: mourir) to
snuff it ♦ *vt* (porte) to slam, bang;
(doigts) to snap; (fam: dépenser) to
blow; **il claquait des dents** his teeth
were chattering; **être claqué** (fam) to
be dead tired; **se claquer un muscle**
to pull ou strain a muscle; **claquettes**
*nfpl* tap-dancing *sg*; (chaussures) flip-
flops
**clarinette** [klarinet] *nf* clarinet
**clarté** [klarte] *nf* (luminosité) brightness; (d'un son, de l'eau) clearness;
(d'une explication) clarity
**classe** [klas] *nf* class; (SCOL: local)
class(room); (: leçon, élèves) class; **aller
en ~** to go to school; **classement**
(rang: SCOL) place; (: SPORT) placing;
(liste: SCOL) class list (in order of merit);
(: SPORT) placings *pl*
**classer** [klase] *vt* (idées, livres) to classi-
fy; (papiers) to file; (candidat, concurrent) to grade; (JUR: affaire) to close; **se
~ premier/dernier** to come first/last;
(SPORT) to finish first/last; **classeur** [klu]
(cahier) file
**classique** [klasik] *adj* classical; (sobre:
coupe etc) classic(al); (habituel) standard, classic
**clause** [kloz] *nf* clause
**clavecin** [klav(ə)sɛ̃] *nm* harpsichord
**clavicule** [klavikyl] *nf* collarbone
**clavier** [klavje] *nm* keyboard
**clé** [kle] *nf* key; (MUS) clef; (de mécanicien) spanner (BRIT), wrench (US); **prix
~s en main** (d'une voiture) on-the-road
price; **~ anglaise** (monkey) wrench; **~
de contact** ignition key
**clef** [kle] *nf* = **clé**
**clément, e** [klemã, ãt] *adj* (temps)
mild; (indulgent) lenient
**clerc** [klɛr] *nm*: **~ de notaire** solicitor's
clerk
**clergé** [klɛrʒe] *nm* clergy

**cliché** [kliʃe] *nm* (fig) cliché; (négatif)
negative; (photo) print
**client, e** [klijã, klijãt] *nm/f* (acheteur)
customer, client; (d'hôtel) guest, patron; (du docteur) patient; (de l'avocat)
client; **clientèle** *nf* (du magasin) cus-
tomers *pl*, clientèle; (du docteur, de
l'avocat) practice
**cligner** [kliɲe] *vi*: **~ des yeux** to blink
(one's eyes); **~ de l'œil** to wink; **clignotant** *nm* (AUTO) indicator; **clignoter** *vi* (étoiles etc) to twinkle; (lumière)
to flicker
**climat** [klima] *nm* climate
**climatisation** [klimatizasjɔ̃] *nf* air conditioning; **climatisé, e** *adj* air-
conditioned
**clin d'œil** [klɛ̃dœj] *nm* wink; **en un ~**
in a flash
**clinique** [klinik] *nf* private hospital
**clinquant, e** [klɛ̃kã, ãt] *adj* flashy
**clip** [klip] *nm* (boucle d'oreille) clip-on;
(vidéo) ♦ (pop) video
**cliqueter** [klik(ə)te] *vi* (ferraille) to jangle; (clés) to jingle
**clochard, e** [klɔʃar, ard] *nm/f* tramp
**cloche** [klɔʃ] *nf* (d'église) bell; (fam)
clot; **cloche-pied: à ~ pied** *adv*
on one leg, hopping (along); **clocher**
*nm* church tower; (en pointe) steeple ♦
*vi* (fam) to be ou go wrong; **de clocher**
(péj) parochial
**cloison** [klwazɔ̃] *nf* partition (wall)
**cloître** [klwatr] *nm* cloister; **cloîtrer** *vt*:
**se cloîtrer** to shut o.s. up *ou* away
**cloque** [klɔk] *nf* blister
**clore** [klɔr] *vt* to close; **clos, e** *adj* voir
**maison; huis**
**clôture** [klotyr] *nf* closure; (barrière)
enclosure; **clôturer** *vt* (terrain) to enclose; (débats) to close
**clou** [klu] *nm* nail; **~s** *nmpl* (passage
~té) pedestrian crossing; **pneus à ~s**
studded tyres; **le ~ du spectacle** the
highlight of the show; **~ de girofle**
clove; **clouer** *vt* to nail down ou
down; **clouer le bec à qn** (fam) to shut sb up

**clown** [klun] *nm* clown

**club** [klœb] *nm* club

**CMU** *sigle f* (= couverture maladie universelle) *system of free health care for those on low incomes*

**CNRS** *sigle m* (= Centre nationale de la recherche scientifique) ≃ SERC (BRIT), ≃ NSF (US)

**coaguler** [kɔagyle] *vt, vi* (*aussi*: **se ~**: *sang*) to coagulate

**coasser** [kɔase] *vi* to croak

**cobaye** [kɔbaj] *nm* guinea-pig

**coca** [kɔka] *nm* Coke ®

**cocaïne** [kɔkain] *nf* cocaine

**cocasse** [kɔkas] *adj* comical, funny

**coccinelle** [kɔksinɛl] *nf* ladybird (BRIT), ladybug (US)

**cocher** [kɔʃe] *vt* to tick off

**cochère** [kɔʃɛr] *adj f*: **porte ~** carriage entrance

**cochon, ne** [kɔʃɔ̃, ɔn] *nm* pig ♦ *adj* (*fam*) dirty, smutty; **~ d'Inde** guinea pig; **cochonnerie** (*fam*) *nf* (*saleté*) filth; (*marchandise*) rubbish, trash

**cocktail** [kɔktɛl] *nm* cocktail; (*réception*) cocktail party

**coco** [kɔko] *nm voir* **noix**

**cocorico** [kɔkɔriko] *excl, nm* cock-a-doodle-do

**cocotier** [kɔkɔtje] *nm* coconut palm

**cocotte** [kɔkɔt] *nf* (*en fonte*) casserole; **~ (minute)** pressure cooker; **ma ~** (*fam*) sweetie (pie)

**cocu** [kɔky] (*fam*) *nm* cuckold

**code** [kɔd] *nm* code ♦ *adj*: **phares ~** dipped lights; **se mettre en ~(s)** to dip one's (head)lights; **~ à barres** bar code; **~ civil** Common Law; **~ de la route** highway code; **~ pénal** penal code; **~ postal** (*numéro*) post (BRIT) ou zip (US) code

**cœur** [kœr] *nm* heart; (CARTES: *couleur*) hearts *pl*; (: *carte*) heart; **avoir bon ~** to be kind-hearted; **avoir mal au ~** to feel sick; **par ~** by heart; **de bon ~** willingly; **cela lui tient à ~** that's (very) close to his heart

**coffre** [kɔfr] *nm* (*meuble*) chest; (*d'auto*) boot (BRIT), trunk (US); **coffre(-fort)** *nm* safe; **coffret** *nm* casket

**cognac** [kɔɲak] *nm* brandy, cognac

**cogner** [kɔɲe] *vi* to knock; **se ~ la tête** to bang one's head

**cohérent, e** [kɔerɑ̃, ɑ̃t] *adj* coherent, consistent

**cohorte** [kɔɔrt] *nf* troop

**cohue** [kɔy] *nf* crowd

**coi, coite** [kwa, kwat] *adj*: **rester ~** to remain silent

**coiffe** [kwaf] *nf* headdress

**coiffé, e** [kwafe] *adj*: **bien/mal ~** with tidy/untidy hair

**coiffer** [kwafe] *vt* (*fig: surmonter*) to cover, top; **se ~** *vi* to do one's hair; **~ qn** to do sb's hair; **coiffeur, -euse** *nm/f* hairdresser; **coiffeuse** *nf* (*table*) dressing table; **coiffure** *nf* (*cheveux*) hairstyle, hairdo; (*art*): **la coiffure** hair dressing

**coin** [kwɛ̃] *nm* corner; (*pour ~cer*) wedge; **l'épicerie du ~** the local grocer; **dans le ~** (*aux alentours*) in the area, around about; (*habiter*) locally; **je ne suis pas du ~** I'm not from here; **au ~ du feu** by the fireside; **regard er ~** sideways glance

**coincé, e** [kwɛse] *adj* stuck, jammed; (*fig: inhibé*) inhibited, hung up (*fam*)

**coincer** [kwɛse] *vt* to jam; (*fam: attraper*) to pinch

**coïncidence** [kɔɛ̃sidɑ̃s] *nf* coincidence

**coïncider** [kɔɛ̃side] *vi* to coincide

**coing** [kwɛ̃] *nm* quince

**col** [kɔl] *nm* (*de chemise*) collar; (*encolure, cou*) neck; (*de montagne*) pass; **~ de l'utérus** cervix; **~ roulé** polo neck

**colère** [kɔlɛr] *nf* anger; **une ~** a fit of anger; **(se mettre) en ~** to (get) angry; **coléreux, -euse** *adj*, **colérique** *adj* quick-tempered, irascible

**colifichet** [kɔlifiʃɛ] *nm* trinket

**colimaçon** [kɔlimasɔ̃] *nm*: **escalier e**

~ spiral staircase

**:olin** [kɔlɛ̃] nm hake

**olique** [kɔlik] nf diarrhoea

**olis** [kɔli] nm parcel

**ollaborateur, -trice** [kɔ(l)labɔʀatœʀ, tʀis] nm/f (aussi POL) collaborator; (d'une revue) contributor

**ollaborer** [kɔ(l)labɔʀe] vi to collaborate; ~ à to collaborate on; (revue) to contribute to

**ollant, e** [kɔlɑ̃, ɑ̃t] adj sticky; (robe etc) clinging, skintight; (péj) clinging ♦ nm (bas) tights pl; (de danseur) leotard

**ollation** [kɔlasjɔ̃] nf light meal

**olle** [kɔl] nf glue; (à papiers peints) (wallpaper) paste; (fam: devinette) teaser, riddle; (SCOL: fam) detention

**ollecte** [kɔlɛkt] nf collection; **collectif, -ive** adj collective; (visite, billet) group cpd

**ollection** [kɔlɛksjɔ̃] nf collection; (ÉDITION) series; **collectionner** vt to collect; **collectionneur, -euse** nm/f collector

**ollectivité** [kɔlɛktivite] nf group; ~s **locales** (ADMIN) local authorities

**ollège** [kɔlɛʒ] nm (école) (secondary) school; (assemblée) body; **collégien** nm schoolboy; **collégienne** nf schoolgirl

---
**collège**

The collège is a state secondary school for children aged between eleven and fifteen. Pupils follow a nationally prescribed curriculum consisting of a common core and various options. Before leaving the collège, pupils are assessed by examination and course work for their brevet des collèges.

---

**ollègue** [kɔ(l)lɛg] nm/f colleague

**oller** [kɔle] vt (papier, timbre) to stick (on); (affiche) to stick up; (enveloppe) to stick down; (morceaux) to stick ou glue together; (fam: mettre, fourrer) to stick, shove; (SCOL: fam) to keep in ♦ vi (être collant) to be sticky; (adhérer) to stick; ~ à to stick to; **être collé à un examen** (fam) to fail an exam

**collet** [kɔlɛ] nm (piège) snare, noose; (cou): **prendre qn au ~** to grab sb by the throat

**collier** [kɔlje] nm (bijou) necklace; (de chien, TECH) collar

**collimateur** [kɔlimatœʀ] nm: **avoir qn/qch dans le ~** (fig) to have sb/sth in one's sights; **être dans le ~ de qn** to be in sb's sights

**colline** [kɔlin] nf hill

**collision** [kɔlizjɔ̃] nf collision, crash; **entrer en ~ (avec)** to collide (with)

**colloque** [kɔ(l)lɔk] nm symposium

**collyre** [kɔliʀ] nm eye drops

**colmater** [kɔlmate] vt (fuite) to seal off; (brèche) to plug, fill in

**colombe** [kɔlɔ̃b] nf dove

**Colombie** [kɔlɔ̃bi] nf: **la ~** Colombia

**colon** [kɔlɔ̃] nm settler

**colonie** [kɔlɔni] nf colony; ~ **(de vacances)** holiday camp (for children)

**colonne** [kɔlɔn] nf column; **se mettre en ~ par deux** to get into twos; ~ **(vertébrale)** spine, spinal column

**colorant** [kɔlɔʀɑ̃, ɑ̃t] nm colouring

**colorer** [kɔlɔʀe] vt to colour

**colorier** [kɔlɔʀje] vt to colour (in)

**coloris** [kɔlɔʀi] nm colour, shade

**colporter** [kɔlpɔʀte] vt to hawk, peddle

**colza** [kɔlza] nm rape(seed)

**coma** [kɔma] nm coma; **être dans le ~** to be in a coma

**combat** [kɔ̃ba] nm fight, fighting no pl; ~ **de boxe** boxing match; **combattant** nm: **ancien combattant** war veteran; **combattre** vt to fight; (épidémie, ignorance) to combat, fight against

**combien** [kɔ̃bjɛ̃] adv (quantité) how much; (nombre) how many; ~ **de** (quantité) how much; (nombre) how many; ~ **de temps** how long; ~ **ça coûte/pèse?** how much does it cost/

**combinaison** [kɔ̃binɛz3] *nf* combination; (*astuce*) scheme; (*de femme*) slip; (*de plongée*) wetsuit; (*bleu de travail*) boiler suit (BRIT), coveralls *pl* (US)

**combine** [kɔ̃bin] *nf* trick; (*péj*) scheme, fiddle (BRIT)

**combiné** [kɔ̃bine] *nm* (*aussi:* ~ **téléphonique**) receiver

**combiner** [kɔ̃bine] *vt* (*grouper*) to combine; (*plan, horaire*) to work out, devise

**comble** [kɔ̃bl] *adj* (*salle*) packed (full) ♦ *nm* (*du bonheur, plaisir*) height; ~s *nmpl* (CONSTR) attic *sg*, loft *sg*; **c'est le ~!** that beats everything!

**combler** [kɔ̃ble] *vt* (*trou*) to fill in; (*besoin, lacune*) to fill; (*déficit*) to make good; (*satisfaire*) to fulfil

**combustible** [kɔ̃bystibl] *nm* fuel

**comédie** [kɔmedi] *nf* comedy; (*fig*) playacting *no pl*; **faire la** ~ (*fam*) to make a fuss; ~ **musicale** musical; **comédien, ne** *nm/f* actor(-tress)

*Founded in 1680 by Louis XIV, the* **Comédie française** *is the French national theatre. Subsidized by the state, the company performs mainly in the Palais Royal in Paris and stages mainly classical French plays.*

**comestible** [kɔmestibl] *adj* edible

**comique** [kɔmik] *adj* (*drôle*) comical; (THÉÂTRE) comic ♦ *nm* (*artiste*) comic, comedian

**comité** [kɔmite] *nm* committee; ~ **d'entreprise** works council

**commande** [kɔmɑ̃d] *nf* (COMM) order; ~s *nfpl* (AVIAT *etc*) controls; **sur** ~ to order; (REL) commandment; **commander** *vt* (COMM) to order; (*diriger, ordonner*) to

command; **commander à qn de faire** to command *ou* order sb to do

**commando** [kɔmɑ̃do] *nm* commando (squad)

**comme** [kɔm] *prép* **1** (*comparaison*) like; **tout comme son père** just like his father; **fort comme un bœuf** as strong as an ox; **joli comme tout** ever so pretty

**2** (*manière*) like; **faites-le comme ça** do it this way, do it this way; **comme ci, comme ça** so-so, middling

**3** (*en tant que*) as a; **donner comme prix** to give as a prize; **travailler comme secrétaire** to work as a secretary

♦ *conj* **1** (*ainsi que*) as; **elle écrit comme elle parle** she writes as she talks; **comme si** as if

**2** (*au moment où, alors que*) as; **il est parti comme j'arrivais** he left as I arrived

**3** (*parce que, puisque*) as; **comme il était en retard, il ...** as he was late he ...

♦ *adv*: **comme il est fort/c'est bon!** he's so strong/it's so good!

**commémorer** [kɔmemɔre] *vt* to commemorate

**commencement** [kɔmɑ̃smɑ̃] *nm* beginning, start

**commencer** [kɔmɑ̃se] *vt, vi* to begin, start; ~ **à** *ou* **de faire** to begin *ou* start doing

**comment** [kɔmɑ̃] *adv* how; **~?** (*que dites-vous*) pardon?

**commentaire** [kɔmɑ̃tɛʀ] *nm* (*remarque*) comment, remark; (*exposé*) commentary

**commenter** [kɔmɑ̃te] *vt* (*jugement, événement*) to comment (up)on; (RADIO, TV: *match, manifestation*) to cover

**commérages** [kɔmeʀaʒ] *nmpl* gossip *sg*

**commerçant, e** [kɔmɛʀsɑ̃, ɑ̃t] *nm/f* shopkeeper, trader

**commerce** [kɔmɛʀs] *nm* (*activité*) trade, commerce; (*boutique*) business; **~ électronique** e-commerce; **commercial, e, -aux** *adj* commercial, trading; (*péj*) commercial; **les commerciaux** the sales people; **commercialiser** *vt* to market

**commère** [kɔmɛʀ] *nf* gossip

**commettre** [kɔmɛtʀ] *vt* to commit

**commis** [kɔmi] *nm* (*de magasin*) (shop) assistant; (*de banque*) clerk

**commissaire** [kɔmisɛʀ] *nm* (*de police*) ≃ (police) superintendent; **commissaire-priseur** *nm* auctioneer; **commissariat** *nm* police station

**commission** [kɔmisjɔ̃] *nf* (*comité, pourcentage*) commission; (*message*) message; (*course*) errand; **~s** *nfpl* (*achats*) shopping *sg*

**commode** [kɔmɔd] *adj* (*pratique*) convenient, handy; (*facile*) easy; (*personne*): **pas ~** awkward (to deal with) ♦ *nf* chest of drawers; **commodité** *nf* convenience

**commotion** [kɔmosjɔ̃] *nf:* **~ (cérébrale)** concussion; **commotionné, e** *adj* shocked, shaken

**commun, e** [kɔmœ̃, yn] *adj* common; (*pièce*) communal, shared; (*effort*) joint; **ça sort du ~** it's out of the ordinary; **le ~ des mortels** the common run of people; **en ~** (*faire*) jointly; **mettre en ~** to pool, share; *voir aussi* **communs**

**communauté** [kɔmynote] *nf* community

**commune** [kɔmyn] *nf* (*ADMIN*) commune, ≃ district; (: *urbaine*) ≃ borough

**communicatif, -ive** [kɔmynikatif, iv] *adj* (*rire*) infectious; (*personne*) communicative

**communication** [kɔmynikasjɔ̃] *nf* communication; **~ (téléphonique)** (telephone) call

**communier** [kɔmynje] *vi* (*REL*) to receive communion

**communion** [kɔmynjɔ̃] *nf* communion

**communiquer** [kɔmynike] *vt* (*nouvelle, dossier*) to pass on, convey; (*peur etc*) to communicate ♦ *vi* to communicate; **se ~ à** (*se propager*) to spread to

**communisme** [kɔmynism] *nm* communism; **communiste** *adj, nm/f* communist

**communs** [kɔmœ̃] *nmpl* (*bâtiments*) outbuildings

**commutateur** [kɔmytatœʀ] *nm* (*ÉLEC*) (change-over) switch, commutator

**compact, e** [kɔ̃pakt] *adj* (*dense*) dense; (*appareil*) compact

**compagne** [kɔ̃paɲ] *nf* companion

**compagnie** [kɔ̃paɲi] *nf* (*firme, MIL*) company; **tenir ~ à qn** to keep sb company; **fausser ~ à qn** to give sb the slip, slip *ou* sneak away from sb; **~ aérienne** airline (company)

**compagnon** [kɔ̃paɲɔ̃] *nm* companion

**comparable** [kɔ̃paʀabl] *adj:* **~ (à)** comparable (to)

**comparaison** [kɔ̃paʀɛzɔ̃] *nf* comparison

**comparaître** [kɔ̃paʀɛtʀ] *vi:* **~ (devant)** to appear (before)

**comparer** [kɔ̃paʀe] *vt* to compare; **~ qch/qn à** *ou* **et** (*pour choisir*) to compare sth/sb with *ou* and; (*pour établir une similitude*) to compare sth/sb to

**compartiment** [kɔ̃paʀtimɑ̃] *nm* compartment

**comparution** [kɔ̃paʀysjɔ̃] *nf* (*JUR*) appearance

**compas** [kɔ̃pa] *nm* (*GÉOM*) (pair of) compasses *pl*; (*NAVIG*) compass

**compatible** [kɔ̃patibl] *adj* compatible

**compatir** [kɔ̃patiʀ] *vi* to sympathize

**compatriote** [kɔ̃patʀijɔt] *nm/f* compatriot

**compensation** [kɔ̃pɑ̃sasjɔ̃] *nf* compensation

**compenser** [kɔ̃pɑ̃se] *vt* to compensate for, make up for

**compère** [kɔ̃pɛʀ] *nm* accomplice

**compétence** [kɔ̃petɑ̃s] *nf* competence

**compétent, e** [kɔ̃petɑ̃, ɑ̃t] *adj* (*apte*) competent, capable

**compétition** [kɔ̃petisjɔ̃] *nf* (*gén*) competition; (*SPORT*): *épreuve*) event; **la ~ automobile** motor racing

**complainte** [kɔ̃plɛ̃t] *nf* lament

**complaire** [kɔ̃plɛʀ]: **se ~** *vi*: **se ~ dans** to take pleasure in

**complaisance** [kɔ̃plɛzɑ̃s] *nf* kindness; **pavillon de ~** flag of convenience

**complaisant, e** [kɔ̃plɛzɑ̃, ɑ̃t] *adj* (*aimable*) kind, obliging

**complément** [kɔ̃plemɑ̃] *nm* complement; (*reste*) remainder; **~ d'information** (*ADMIN*) supplementary *ou* further information; **complémentaire** *adj* complementary; (*additionnel*) supplementary

**complet, -ète** [kɔ̃plɛ, ɛt] *adj* complete; (*plein*: *hôtel etc*) full ♦ *nm* (*aussi*: **~ veston**) suit; **pain ~** wholemeal bread; **complètement** *adv* completely; **compléter** *vt* (*porter à la quantité voulue*) to complete; (*augmenter*: *connaissances, études*) to complement, supplement; (*: garde-robe*) to add to; **se compléter** (*caractères*) to complement one another

**complexe** [kɔ̃plɛks] *adj*, *nm* complex; **complexé, e** *adj* mixed-up, hung-up

**complication** [kɔ̃plikasjɔ̃] *nf* complexity, intricacy; (*difficulté, ennui*) complication

**complice** [kɔ̃plis] *nm* accomplice; **complicité** *nf* complicity

**compliment** [kɔ̃plimɑ̃] *nm* (*louange*) compliment; **~s** *nmpl* (*félicitations*) congratulations

**compliqué, e** [kɔ̃plike] *adj* complicated, complex; (*personne*) complicated; **compliquer** [kɔ̃plike] *vt* to complicate; **se ~** to become complicated

**complot** [kɔ̃plo] *nm* plot

**comportement** [kɔ̃pɔʀtəmɑ̃] *nm* behaviour

**comporter** [kɔ̃pɔʀte] *vt* (*consister en*) to consist of, comprise; (*inclure*) to

have; **se ~** *vi* to behave

**composant** [kɔ̃pozɑ̃] *nm*, **composante** [kɔ̃pozɑ̃t] *nf* component

**composé** [kɔ̃poze] *nm* compound

**composer** [kɔ̃poze] *vt* (*musique, texte*) to compose; (*mélange, équipe*) to make up; (*numéro*) to dial; (*constituer*) to make up, form ♦ *vi* (*transiger*) to come to terms; **se ~ de** to be composed of, be made up of; **compositeur, -trice** *nm/f* (*MUS*) composer; **composition** *nf* composition; (*SCOL*) test

**composter** [kɔ̃pɔste] *vt* (*billet*) to punch

**compote** [kɔ̃pɔt] *nf* stewed fruit *no pl*; **~ de pommes** stewed apples

**compréhensible** [kɔ̃pʀeɑ̃sibl] *adj* comprehensible; (*attitude*) understandable

**compréhensif, -ive** [kɔ̃pʀeɑ̃sif, iv] *adj* understanding

**comprendre** [kɔ̃pʀɑ̃dʀ] *vt* to understand; (*se composer de*) to comprise, consist of

**compresse** [kɔ̃pʀɛs] *nf* compress

**compression** [kɔ̃pʀesjɔ̃] *nf* compression; (*de personnes*) reduction

**comprimé** [kɔ̃pʀime] *nm* tablet

**comprimer** [kɔ̃pʀime] *vt* to compress; (*fig*: *crédit etc*) to reduce, cut down

**compris, e** [kɔ̃pʀi, iz] *pp de* **comprendre** ♦ *adj* (*inclus*) included; **~ entre** (*situé*) contained between; **l'électricité ~e/non ~e, y/non ~ l'électricité** including/excluding electricity; **100 F tout ~** 100 F all inclusive *ou* all-in

**compromettre** [kɔ̃pʀɔmɛtʀ] *vt* to compromise; **compromis** *nm* compromise

**comptabilité** [kɔ̃tabilite] *nf* (*activité*) accounting, accountancy; (*comptes*) accounts *pl*, books *pl*; (*service*) accounts office

**comptable** [kɔ̃tabl] *nm/f* accountant

**comptant** [kɔ̃tɑ̃] *adv*: **payer ~** to pay cash; **acheter ~** to buy for cash

**compte** [kɔ̃t] *nm* count; (*total, mon-*

*tant)* count, (right) number; *(bancaire, facture)* account; **~s** *nmpl (FINANCE)* accounts, books; *(fig)* explanation *sg*; **en fin de ~** all things considered; **s'en tirer à bon ~** to get off lightly; **pour le ~ de** on behalf of; **pour son propre ~** for one's own benefit; **tenir ~ de** to take account of; **travailler à son ~** to work for oneself; **rendre ~ (à qn) de qch** to give (sb) an account of sth; *voir aussi* **rendre ~ à rebours** countdown; **~ chèques postaux** Post Office account; **~ courant** current account; **~ rendu** account, report; *(de film, livre)* review; **compte-gouttes** *nm inv* dropper

**compter** [kɔ̃te] *vt* to count; *(facturer)* to charge for; *(avoir à son actif, comporter)* to have; *(prévoir)* to allow, reckon; *(penser, espérer)*: **~ réussir** to expect to succeed ♦ *vi* to count; *(être économe)* to economize; *(figurer)*: **~ parmi** to be *ou* rank among; **~ sur** to count (up)on; **~ avec qch/qn** to reckon with *ou* take account of sth/sb; **sans ~ que** besides which

**compteur** [kɔ̃tœʀ] *nm* meter; **~ de vitesse** speedometer

**comptine** [kɔ̃tin] *nf* nursery rhyme

**comptoir** [kɔ̃twaʀ] *nm (de magasin)* counter; *(bar)* bar

**compulser** [kɔ̃pylse] *vt* to consult

**comte** [kɔ̃t] *nm* count; **comtesse** *nf* countess

**con, ne** [kɔ̃, kɔn] *(fam!) adj* damned *ou* bloody *(BRIT)* stupid *(!)*

**concéder** [kɔ̃sede] *vt* to grant; *(défaite, point)* to concede

**concentré, e** [kɔ̃sɑ̃tʀe] *adj (lait)* condensed ♦ *nm*: **~ de tomates** tomato purée

**concentrer** [kɔ̃sɑ̃tʀe] *vt* to concentrate; **se ~** *vi* to concentrate

**concept** [kɔ̃sɛpt] *nm* concept

**conception** [kɔ̃sɛpsjɔ̃] *nf* conception, *(d'une machine etc)* design; *(d'un problème, de la vie)* approach

**concerner** [kɔ̃sɛʀne] *vt* to concern; **en ce qui me concerne** as far as I am concerned

**concert** [kɔ̃sɛʀ] *nm* concert; **de ~** *(décider)* unanimously; **concerter: se concerter** *vi* to put their *etc* heads together

**concession** [kɔ̃sesjɔ̃] *nf* concession; **concessionnaire** *nm/f* agent, dealer

**concevoir** [kɔ̃s(ə)vwaʀ] *vt (idée, projet)* to conceive (of); *(comprendre)* to understand; *(enfant)* to conceive; **bien/mal conçu** well-/badly-designed

**concierge** [kɔ̃sjɛʀʒ] *nm/f* caretaker

**conciliabules** [kɔ̃siljabyl] *nmpl* (private) discussions, confabulations

**concilier** [kɔ̃silje] *vt* to reconcile; **se ~** *vt* to win over

**concis, e** [kɔ̃si, iz] *adj* concise

**concitoyen, ne** [kɔ̃sitwajɛ̃, jɛn] *nm/f* fellow citizen

**concluant, e** [kɔ̃klyɑ̃, ɑ̃t] *adj* conclusive

**conclure** [kɔ̃klyʀ] *vt* to conclude; **conclusion** *nf* conclusion

**conçois** *etc* [kɔ̃swa] *vb voir* **concevoir**

**concombre** [kɔ̃kɔ̃bʀ] *nm* cucumber

**concorder** [kɔ̃kɔʀde] *vi* to tally, agree

**concourir** [kɔ̃kuʀiʀ] *vi (SPORT)* to compete; **~ à** *(effet etc)* to work towards

**concours** [kɔ̃kuʀ] *nm* competition; *(SCOL)* competitive examination; *(assistance)* aid, help; **~ de circonstances** combination of circumstances; **~ hippique** horse show

**concret, -ète** [kɔ̃kʀɛ, ɛt] *adj* concrete; **concrétiser: se ~** *vi* to materialize

**conçu, e** [kɔ̃sy] *pp de* **concevoir**

**concubinage** [kɔ̃kybinaʒ] *nm (JUR)* cohabitation

**concurrence** [kɔ̃kyʀɑ̃s] *nf* competition; **faire ~ à** to be in competition with; **jusqu'à ~ de** up to

**concurrent, e** [kɔ̃kyʀɑ̃, ɑ̃t] *nm/f (SPORT, ÉCON etc)* competitor; *(SCOL)* candidate

**condamner** [kɔ̃dane] *vt (blâmer)* to

**condemn**; (JUR) to sentence; (porte, ouverture) to fill in, block up; **~ qn à 2 ans de prison** to sentence sb to 2 years' imprisonment

**condensation** [kɔ̃dɑ̃sasjɔ̃] nf condensation

**condenser** [kɔ̃dɑ̃se] vt to condense; **se ~ vi** to condense

**condisciple** [kɔ̃disipl] nm/f fellow student

**condition** [kɔ̃disjɔ̃] nf condition; **~s** nfpl (tarif, prix) terms; (circonstances) conditions; **à ~ de ou que** provided that; **conditionnel, le** nm conditional (tense)

**conditionnement** [kɔ̃disjɔnmã] nm (emballage) packaging

**conditionner** [kɔ̃disjɔne] vt (déterminer) to determine; (COMM: produit) to package; **air conditionné** air conditioning

**condoléances** [kɔ̃dɔleɑ̃s] nfpl condolences

**conducteur, -trice** [kɔ̃dyktœR, tRis] nm/f driver ♦ nm (ÉLEC etc) conductor

**conduire** [kɔ̃dɥiR] vt to drive; (délégation, troupeau) to lead; **se ~ vi** to behave; **~ à** to lead to; **~ qn quelque part** to take sb somewhere, to drive sb somewhere

**conduite** [kɔ̃dɥit] nf (comportement) behaviour; (d'eau, de gaz) pipe; **sous la ~ de** led by; **~ à gauche** left-hand drive

**cône** [kon] nm cone

**confection** [kɔ̃feksjɔ̃] nf (fabrication) making; (COUTURE): **la ~** the clothing industry

**confectionner** [kɔ̃feksjɔne] vt to make

**conférence** [kɔ̃feRɑ̃s] nf conference; (exposé) lecture; **~ de presse** press conference; **conférencier, -ière** nm/f speaker, lecturer

**confesser** [kɔ̃fese] vt to confess; **se ~ vi** (REL) to go to confession; **confession** nf confession; (culte: catholique etc) denomination

**confiance** [kɔ̃fjɑ̃s] nf (en l'honnêteté de qn) confidence, trust; (en la valeur de qch) confidence ou faith; **avoir ~ en** to have confidence ou faith in, to trust; **faire ~ à qn** to trust sb; **mettre qn en ~** to win sb's trust; **~ en soi** self-confidence

**confiant, e** [kɔ̃fjɑ̃, jɑ̃t] adj confident; trusting

**confidence** [kɔ̃fidɑ̃s] nf confidence; **confidentiel, le** adj confidential

**confier** [kɔ̃fje] vt: **~ à qn** (objet, travail) to entrust to sb; (secret, pensée) to confide to sb; **se ~ à qn** to confide in sb

**confins** [kɔ̃fɛ̃] nmpl: **aux ~ de** on the borders of

**confirmation** [kɔ̃fiRmasjɔ̃] nf confirmation

**confirmer** [kɔ̃fiRme] vt to confirm

**confiserie** [kɔ̃fizRi] nf (magasin) confectioner's ou sweet shop; **~s** nfpl (bonbons) confectionery sg

**confisquer** [kɔ̃fiske] vt to confiscate

**confit, e** [kɔ̃fi, it] adj: **fruits ~s** crystallized fruits ♦ nm: **~ d'oie** conserve of goose

**confiture** [kɔ̃fityR] nf jam; **~ d'oranges** (orange) marmalade

**conflit** [kɔ̃fli] nm conflict

**confondre** [kɔ̃fɔ̃dR] vt (jumeaux, faits) to confuse, mix up; (témoin, menteur) to confound; **se ~ vi** to merge; **se ~ en excuses** to apologize profusely; **confondu, e** adj (stupéfait) speechless, overcome

**conforme** [kɔ̃fɔRm] adj: **~ à** (loi, règle) in accordance with; **conformément** adv: **conformément à** in accordance with; **conformer** vt: **se conformer à** to conform to

**confort** [kɔ̃fɔR] nm comfort; **tout ~** (COMM) with all modern conveniences; **confortable** adj comfortable

**confrère** [kɔ̃fRɛR] nm colleague

**confronter** [kɔ̃fRɔ̃te] vt to confront

**confus, e** [kɔ̃fy, yz] adj (vague) confused; (embarrassé) embarrassed; **confusion** nf (voir confus) confusion;

embarrassment; (*voir* confondre) confusion, mixing up

**congé** [kɔ̃ʒe] *nm* (*vacances*) holiday; **en ~** on holiday; **semaine de ~** week off; **prendre ~ de qn** to take one's leave of sb; **donner son ~ à** to give in one's notice to; **~ de maladie** sick leave; **~ de maternité** maternity leave; **~s payés** paid holiday

**congédier** [kɔ̃ʒedje] *vt* to dismiss

**congélateur** [kɔ̃ʒelatœr] *nm* freezer

**congeler** [kɔ̃ʒ(ə)le] *vt* to freeze; **les produits congelés** frozen foods

**congestion** [kɔ̃ʒɛstjɔ̃] *nf* congestion; **~ cérébrale** stroke; **congestionner** *vt* (*rue*) to congest; (*visage*) to flush

**congrès** [kɔ̃grɛ] *nm* congress

**conifère** [kɔnifɛr] *nm* conifer

**conjecture** [kɔ̃ʒɛktyr] *nf* conjecture

**conjoint, e** [kɔ̃ʒwɛ̃, wɛ̃t] *adj* joint ♦ *nm/f* spouse

**conjonction** [kɔ̃ʒɔ̃ksjɔ̃] *nf* (LING) conjunction

**conjonctivite** [kɔ̃ʒɔ̃ktivit] *nf* conjunctivitis

**conjoncture** [kɔ̃ʒɔ̃ktyr] *nf* circumstances *pl*; **la ~ actuelle** the present (economic) situation

**conjugaison** [kɔ̃ʒygɛzɔ̃] *nf* (LING) conjugation

**conjuguer** [kɔ̃ʒyge] *vt* (LING) to conjugate; (*efforts etc*) to combine

**conjuration** [kɔ̃ʒyrasjɔ̃] *nf* conspiracy

**conjurer** [kɔ̃ʒyre] *vt* (*sort, maladie*) to avert; (*implorer*) to beseech, entreat

**connaissance** [kɔnɛsɑ̃s] *nf* (*savoir*) knowledge *no pl*; (*personne connue*) acquaintance; **être sans ~** to be unconscious; **perdre/reprendre ~** to lose/regain consciousness; **à ma/sa ~** to (the best of) my/his knowledge; **faire la ~ de qn** to meet sb

**connaisseur** [kɔnɛsœr, øz] *nm* connoisseur

**connaître** [kɔnɛtr] *vt* to know; (*éprouver*) to experience; (*avoir: succès*) to have, enjoy; **~ de nom/vue** to know

by name/sight; **ils se sont connus à Genève** they (first) met in Geneva; **s'y ~ en qch** to know a lot about sth

**connecter** [kɔnɛkte] *vt* to connect

**connerie** [kɔnri] (*fam!*) *nf* stupid thing (to do/say)

**connu, e** [kɔny] *adj* (*célèbre*) well-known

**conquérir** [kɔ̃kerir] *vt* to conquer; **conquête** *nf* conquest

**consacrer** [kɔ̃sakre] *vt* (*employer*) to devote, dedicate; (REL) to consecrate

**conscience** [kɔ̃sjɑ̃s] *nf* conscience; **avoir/prendre ~ de** to be/become aware of; **perdre ~** to lose consciousness; **avoir bonne/mauvaise ~** to have a clear/guilty conscience; **consciencieux, -euse** *adj* conscientious; **conscient, e** *adj* conscious

**conscrit** [kɔ̃skri] *nm* conscript

**consécutif, -ive** [kɔ̃sekytif, iv] *adj* consecutive; **~ à** following upon

**conseil** [kɔ̃sɛj] *nm* (*avis*) piece of advice; (*assemblée*) council; **des ~s** advice; **prendre ~ (auprès de qn)** to take advice (from sb); **~ d'administration** board (of directors); **le ~ des ministres** ≈ the Cabinet; **~ municipal** town council

**conseiller, -ère** [kɔ̃seje, ɛr] *nm/f* adviser ♦ *vt* (*personne*) to advise; (*méthode, action*) to recommend, advise; **~ à qn de** to advise sb to; **~ municipal** town councillor

**consentement** [kɔ̃sɑ̃tmɑ̃] *nm* consent

**consentir** [kɔ̃sɑ̃tir] *vt* to agree, consent

**conséquence** [kɔ̃sekɑ̃s] *nf* consequence; **en ~** (*donc*) consequently; (*de façon appropriée*) accordingly; **conséquent, e** *adj* logical, rational; (*fam: important*) substantial; **par conséquent** consequently

**conservateur, -trice** [kɔ̃sɛrvatœr, tris] *nm/f* (POL) conservative; (*de musée*) curator ♦ *nm* (*pour aliments*) preservative

**conservatoire** [kɔ̃sɛrvatwar] *nm* academy

**conserve** [kɔ̃sɛrv] *nf (gén pl)* canned *ou* tinned (BRIT) food; **en ~**, canned, tinned (BRIT)

**conserver** [kɔ̃sɛrve] *vt (faculté)* to retain, keep; *(amis, livres)* to keep; *(préserver, aussi* CULIN*)* to preserve

**considérable** [kɔ̃siderabl] *adj* considerable, significant, extensive

**considération** [kɔ̃siderasjɔ̃] *nf* consideration; *(estime)* esteem

**considérer** [kɔ̃sidere] *vt* to consider; **~ qch comme** to regard sth as

**consigne** [kɔ̃siɲ] *nf (de gare)* left luggage (office) (BRIT), checkroom (US); *(ordre, instruction)* instructions *pl*; **~ (automatique)** left-luggage locker;

**consigner** [kɔ̃siɲe] *vt (note, pensée)* to record; *(punir: élève)* to put in detention; (COMM) to put a deposit on

**consistant, e** [kɔ̃sistɑ̃, ɑ̃t] *adj (mélange)* thick; *(repas)* solid

**consister** [kɔ̃siste] *vi:* **~ en/à faire** to consist of/in doing

**consœur** [kɔ̃sœr] *nf (lady)* colleague

**console** [kɔ̃sɔl] *nf:* **~ de jeux** games console

**consoler** [kɔ̃sɔle] *vt* to console

**consolider** [kɔ̃sɔlide] *vt* to strengthen; *(fig)* to consolidate

**consommateur, -trice** [kɔ̃sɔmatœr, tris] *nm/f* (ÉCON) consumer; *(dans un café)* customer

**consommation** [kɔ̃sɔmasjɔ̃] *nf (boisson)* drink; (ÉCON) consumption

**consommer** [kɔ̃sɔme] *vt (suj: personne)* to eat ou drink, consume; (: *voiture, machine)* to use, consume; *(mariage)* to consummate ♦ *vi (dans un café)* to (have a) drink

**consonne** [kɔ̃sɔn] *nf* consonant

**conspirer** [kɔ̃spire] *vi* to conspire

**constamment** [kɔ̃stamɑ̃] *adv* constantly

**constant, e** [kɔ̃stɑ̃, ɑ̃t] *adj* constant; *(personne)* steadfast

**constat** [kɔ̃sta] *nm (de police, d'accident)* report; **~ (à l')amiable** jointly-agreed statement for insurance purposes; **~ d'échec** acknowledgement of failure

**constatation** [kɔ̃statasjɔ̃] *nf (observation)* (observed) fact, observation

**constater** [kɔ̃state] *vt (remarquer)* to note; (ADMIN, JUR: *attester)* to certify

**consterner** [kɔ̃stɛrne] *vt* to dismay

**constipé, e** [kɔ̃stipe] *adj* constipated

**constitué, e** [kɔ̃stitɥe] *adj:* **~ de** made up ou composed of

**constituer** [kɔ̃stitɥe] *vt (équipe)* to set up; *(dossier, collection)* to put together; *(suj: éléments: composer)* to make up, constitute; *(représenter, être)* to constitute; **se ~ prisonnier** to give o.s. up;

**constitution** [kɔ̃stitysjɔ̃] *nf (composition)* composition; *(santé,* POL*)* constitution

**constructeur** [kɔ̃stryktœr] *nm* manufacturer, builder

**constructif, -ive** [kɔ̃stryktif, iv] *adj* constructive

**construction** [kɔ̃stryksjɔ̃] *nf* construction, building

**construire** [kɔ̃strɥir] *vt* to build, construct

**consul** [kɔ̃syl] *nm* consul; **consulat** *nm* consulate

**consultant, e** [kɔ̃syltɑ̃, ɑ̃t] *adj, nm* consultant

**consultation** [kɔ̃syltasjɔ̃] *nf* consultation; **~s** *nfpl* (POL) talks; **heures de ~** (MÉD) surgery (BRIT) ou office (US) hours

**consulter** [kɔ̃sylte] *vt* to consult ♦ *vi (médecin)* to hold surgery (BRIT), be in (the office) (US); **se ~** to confer

**consumer** [kɔ̃syme] *vt* to consume; **se ~** vi to burn

**contact** [kɔ̃takt] *nm* contact; **au ~ de** *(air, peau)* on contact with; *(gens)* through contact with; **mettre/couper le ~** (AUTO) to switch on/off the ignition; **entrer en** ou **prendre ~ avec** to get in touch ou contact with; **contacter** *vt* to contact, get in touch with

**contagieux, -euse** [kɔ̃taʒjø, jøz] *adj* infectious; (*par le contact*) contagious

**contaminer** [kɔ̃tamine] *vt* to contaminate

**conte** [kɔ̃t] *nm* tale; ~ **de fées** fairy tale

**contempler** [kɔ̃tɑ̃ple] *vt* to contemplate, gaze at

**contemporain, e** [kɔ̃tɑ̃pɔʀɛ̃, ɛn] *adj, nm/f* contemporary

**contenance** [kɔ̃t(ə)nɑ̃s] *nf* (*d'un récipient*) capacity; (*attitude*) bearing, attitude; **perdre ~** to lose one's composure

**conteneur** [kɔ̃t(ə)nœʀ] *nm* container

**contenir** [kɔ̃t(ə)niʀ] *vt* to contain; (*avoir une capacité de*) to hold; **se ~** *vi* to contain o.s.

**content, e** [kɔ̃tɑ̃, ɑ̃t] *adj* pleased, glad; **~ de** pleased with; **contenter** *vt* to satisfy, please; **se contenter de** to content o.s. with

**contentieux** [kɔ̃tɑ̃sjø] *nm* (COMM) litigation; (*service*) litigation department

**contenu** [kɔ̃t(ə)ny] *nm* (*d'un récipient*) contents *pl*; (*d'un texte*) content

**conter** [kɔ̃te] *vt* to recount, relate

**contestable** [kɔ̃testabl] *adj* questionable

**contestation** [kɔ̃testasjɔ̃] *nf* (POL) protest

**conteste** [kɔ̃test]: **sans ~** *adv* unquestionably, indisputably; **contester** *vt* to question ♦ *vi* (POL, *gén*) to rebel (against established authority)

**contexte** [kɔ̃tekst] *nm* context

**contigu, ë** [kɔ̃tigy] *adj:* ~ **(à)** adjacent (to)

**continent** [kɔ̃tinɑ̃] *nm* continent

**continu, e** [kɔ̃tiny] *adj* continuous; **faire la journée ~e** to work without taking a full lunch break; **(courant) ~** direct current, DC

**continuel, le** [kɔ̃tinɥɛl] *adj* (*qui se répète*) constant, continual; (*continu*) continuous

**continuer** [kɔ̃tinɥe] *vt* (*travail, voyage etc*) to continue (with), carry on (with),

go on (with); (*prolonger: alignement, rue*) to continue ♦ *vi* (*vie, bruit*) to continue, go on; **~ à** ou **de faire** to go on ou continue doing

**contorsionner** [kɔ̃tɔʀsjɔne]: **se ~** *vi* to contort o.s., writhe about

**contour** [kɔ̃tuʀ] *nm* outline, contour; **contourner** *vt* to go round; (*difficulté*) to get round

**contraceptif, -ive** [kɔ̃tʀaseptif, iv] *adj, nm* contraceptive; **contraception** *nf* contraception

**contracté, e** [kɔ̃tʀakte] *adj* tense

**contracter** [kɔ̃tʀakte] *vt* (*muscle etc*) to tense, contract; (*maladie, dette*) to contract; (*assurance*) to take out; **se ~** *vi* (*muscles*) to contract

**contractuel, le** [kɔ̃tʀaktɥɛl] *nm/f* (*agent*) traffic warden

**contradiction** [kɔ̃tʀadiksjɔ̃] *nf* contradiction; **contradictoire** *adj* contradictory, conflicting

**contraignant, e** [kɔ̃tʀɛɲɑ̃, ɑ̃t] *adj* restricting

**contraindre** [kɔ̃tʀɛ̃dʀ] *vt:* ~ **qn à faire** to compel sb to do; **contrainte** *nf* constraint

**contraire** [kɔ̃tʀɛʀ] *adj, nm* opposite; **~ à** contrary to; **au ~** on the contrary

**contrarier** [kɔ̃tʀaʀje] *vt* (*personne: irriter*) to annoy; (*fig: projets*) to thwart, frustrate; **contrariété** *nf* annoyance

**contraste** [kɔ̃tʀast] *nm* contrast

**contrat** [kɔ̃tʀa] *nm* contract; **~ de travail** employment contract

**contravention** [kɔ̃tʀavɑ̃sjɔ̃] *nf* parking ticket

**contre** [kɔ̃tʀ] *prép* against; (*en échange*) (in exchange) for; **par ~** on the other hand

**contrebande** [kɔ̃tʀəbɑ̃d] *nf* (*trafic*) contraband, smuggling; (*marchandise*) contraband, smuggled goods *pl*; **faire la ~ de** to smuggle; **contrebandier, -ière** *nm/f* smuggler

**contrebas** [kɔ̃tʀəba]: **en ~** *adv* (down) below

**contrebasse** [kɔ̃tʀəbas] *nf* (double) bass

**contre...: contrecarrer** *vt* to thwart; **contrecœur: à contrecœur** *adv* (be)grudgingly, reluctantly; **contrecoup** *nm* repercussions *pl*; **contredire** *vt* (*personne*) to contradict; (*faits*) to refute

**contrée** [kɔ̃tʀe] *nf* (*région*) region; (*pays*) land

**contrefaçon** [kɔ̃tʀəfasɔ̃] *nf* forgery

**contrefaire** [kɔ̃tʀəfɛʀ] *vt* (*document, signature*) to forge, counterfeit

**contre...: contre-indication** (*pl* **contre-indications**) *nf* (MÉD) contra-indication; "**contre-indication en cas d'eczéma**" "should not be used by people with eczema"; **contreindiqué, e** *adj* (MÉD) contraindicated; (*déconseillé*) unadvisable, ill-advised; **contre-jour: à contre-jour** *adv* against the sunlight

**contremaître** [kɔ̃tʀəmɛtʀ] *nm* foreman

**contrepartie** [kɔ̃tʀəpaʀti] *nf*: **en ~** in return

**contre-pied** [kɔ̃tʀəpje] *nm*: **prendre le ~~ de** (*opinion*) to take the opposing view of; (*action*) to take the opposite course to

**contre-plaqué** [kɔ̃tʀəplake] *nm* plywood

**contrepoids** [kɔ̃tʀəpwa] *nm* counterweight, counterbalance

**contrepoison** [kɔ̃tʀəpwazɔ̃] *nm* antidote

**contrer** [kɔ̃tʀe] *vt* to counter

**contresens** [kɔ̃tʀəsɑ̃s] *nm* (*erreur*) misinterpretation; (*de traduction*) mistranslation; **à ~** the wrong way

**contretemps** [kɔ̃tʀətɑ̃] *nm* hitch; **à ~** (*fig*) at an inopportune moment

**contrevenir** [kɔ̃tʀəv(ə)niʀ]: **~ à** *vt* to contravene

**contribuable** [kɔ̃tʀibɥabl] *nm/f* taxpayer

**contribuer** [kɔ̃tʀibɥe]: **~ à** *vt* to contribute towards; **contribution** *nf* contribution; **contributions directes** direct/indirect taxation *sg*; **mettre à contribution** to call upon

**contrôle** [kɔ̃tʀol] *nm* checking *no pl*, check; (*des prix*) monitoring, control; (*test*) test, examination; **perdre le ~ de** (*véhicule*) to lose control of; **~ continu** (SCOL) continuous assessment; **~ d'identité** identity check

**contrôler** [kɔ̃tʀole] *vt* (*vérifier*) to check; (*surveiller: opérations*) to supervise; (: *prix*) to monitor, control; (*maîtriser , COMM: firme*) to control; **se ~** *vi* to control o.s.; **contrôleur, -euse** *nm/f* (*de train*) (ticket) inspector; (*de bus*) (bus) conductor(-tress)

**contrordre** [kɔ̃tʀɔʀdʀ] *nm*: **sauf ~** unless otherwise directed

**controversé, e** [kɔ̃tʀɔvɛʀse] *adj* (*personnage, question*) controversial

**contusion** [kɔ̃tyzjɔ̃] *nf* bruise, contusion

**convaincre** [kɔ̃vɛ̃kʀ] *vt*: **~ qn (de qch)** to convince sb (of sth); **~ qn (de faire)** to persuade sb (to do)

**convalescence** [kɔ̃valesɑ̃s] *nf* convalescence

**convenable** [kɔ̃vnabl] *adj* suitable; (*assez bon, respectable*) decent

**convenance** [kɔ̃vnɑ̃s] *nf*: **à ma/votre ~** to my/your liking; **~s** *nfpl* (*normes sociales*) proprieties

**convenir** [kɔ̃vniʀ] *vi* to be suitable; **~ à** to suit; **~ de** (*bien-fondé de qch*) to admit (to), acknowledge; (*date, somme etc*) to agree upon; **~ que** (*admettre*) to admit that; **~ de faire** to agree to do

**convention** [kɔ̃vɑ̃sjɔ̃] *nf* convention; **~s** *nfpl* (*convenances*) convention *sg*; **collective** (ÉCON) collective agreement; **conventionnel, e** *adj* (ADMIN) applying charges laid down by the state

**convenu, e** [kɔ̃vny] *pp de* **convenir** *adj* agreed

**conversation** [kɔ̃vɛʀsasjɔ̃] *nf* conversation

**convertir** [kɔ̃vɛʀtiʀ] vt: ~ qn (à) to convert sb (to); **se ~ (à)** to be converted (to); ~ **qch en** to convert sth into

**conviction** [kɔ̃viksjɔ̃] nf conviction

**convienne** etc [kɔ̃vjɛn] vb voir **convenir**

**convier** [kɔ̃vje] vt: ~ qn à (dîner etc) to (cordially) invite sb to

**convive** [kɔ̃viv] nm/f guest (at table)

**convivial, e, -aux** [kɔ̃vivjal, jo] adj (INFORM) user-friendly

**convocation** [kɔ̃vɔkasjɔ̃] nf (document) notification to attend; (: JUR) summons sg

**convoi** [kɔ̃vwa] nm convoy; (train) train

**convoiter** [kɔ̃vwate] vt to covet

**convoquer** [kɔ̃vɔke] vt (assemblée) to convene; (subordonné) to summon; (candidat) to ask to attend

**convoyeur** [kɔ̃vwajœʀ] nm: ~ de fonds security guard

**coopération** [kɔɔpeʀasjɔ̃] nf cooperation; (ADMIN): **la C~** ≈ Voluntary Service Overseas (BRIT), ≈ Peace Corps (US)

**coopérer** [kɔɔpeʀe] vi: ~ (à) to cooperate (in)

**coordonnées** [kɔɔʀdɔne] nfpl: **donnez-moi vos ~** (fam) can I have your details please?

**coordonner** [kɔɔʀdɔne] vt to coordinate

**copain** [kɔpɛ̃] (fam) nm mate, pal; (petit ami) boyfriend

**copeau, x** [kɔpo] nm shaving

**copie** [kɔpi] nf copy; (SCOL) script, paper; **copier** vt, vi to copy; **copier sur** to copy from; **copieur** nm (photo)copier

**copieux, -euse** [kɔpjø, jøz] adj copious

**copine** [kɔpin] (fam) nf mate, pal; (petite amie) girlfriend

**copropriété** [kɔpʀɔpʀijete] nf coownership, joint ownership

**coq** [kɔk] nm cock, rooster; **coq-à-**

**l'âne** inv abrupt change of subject

**coque** [kɔk] nf (de noix, mollusque) shell; (de bateau) hull; **à la ~** (CULIN) (soft-)boiled

**coquelicot** [kɔkliko] nm poppy

**coqueluche** [kɔklyʃ] nf whooping-cough

**coquet, te** [kɔke, ɛt] adj appearance-conscious; (logement) smart, charming

**coquetier** [kɔk(ə)tje] nm egg-cup

**coquillage** [kɔkijaʒ] nm (mollusque) shellfish inv; (coquille) shell

**coquille** [kɔkij] nf shell; (TYPO) misprint; ~ **St Jacques** scallop

**coquin, e** [kɔkɛ̃, in] adj mischievous, roguish; (polisson) naughty

**cor** [kɔʀ] nm (MUS) horn; (MÉD): ~ (au pied) corn

**corail, -aux** [kɔʀaj, o] nm coral no pl

**Coran** [kɔʀɑ̃] nm: **le ~** the Koran

**corbeau, x** [kɔʀbo] nm crow

**corbeille** [kɔʀbɛj] nf basket; ~ **à papier** waste paper basket ou bin

**corbillard** [kɔʀbijaʀ] nm hearse

**corde** [kɔʀd] nf rope; (de violon, raquette) string; **usé jusqu'à la ~** threadbare; ~ **à linge** washing ou clothes line; ~ **à sauter** skipping rope; **~s vocales** vocal cords

**cordée** [kɔʀde] nf (d'alpinistes) rope, roped party

**cordialement** [kɔʀdjalmɑ̃] adv (formule épistolaire) (kind) regards

**cordon** [kɔʀdɔ̃] nm cord, string; ~ **ombilical** umbilical cord; ~ **sanitaire/de police** sanitary/police cordon

**cordonnerie** [kɔʀdɔnʀi] nf shoe repairer's (shop); **cordonnier** nm shoe repairer

**Corée** [kɔʀe] nf: **la ~ du Sud/du Nord** South/North Korea

**coriace** [kɔʀjas] adj tough

**corne** [kɔʀn] nf horn; (de cerf) antler

**cornée** [kɔʀne] nf cornea

**corneille** [kɔʀnɛj] nf crow

**cornemuse** [kɔʀnəmyz] nf bagpipes pl

**cornet** [kɔʀne] nm (paper) cone; (de

*glace*) cornet, cone
**corniche** [kɔrniʃ] *nf* (*route*) coast road
**cornichon** [kɔrniʃɔ̃] *nm* gherkin
**Cornouailles** [kɔrnwaj] *nf* Cornwall
**corporation** [kɔrpɔrasjɔ̃] *nf* corporate body
**corporel, le** [kɔrpɔrɛl] *adj* bodily; (*punition*) corporal
**corps** [kɔr] *nm* body; **à ~ perdu** headlong; **prendre ~** to take shape; **~ à ~**
♦ *adv* hand-to-hand ♦ *nm* clinch; **le ~ électoral** the electorate; **le ~ enseignant** the teaching profession
**corpulent, e** [kɔrpylɑ̃, ɑ̃t] *adj* stout
**correct, e** [kɔrɛkt] *adj* correct; (*fam:
acceptable: salaire, hôtel*) reasonable, decent; **correcteur, -trice** *nm/f* (SCOL) examiner; **correction** *nf* (*voir corriger*) correction; (*voir correct*) correctness; (*coups*) thrashing; **correctionnel, le** *adj* (JUR): **tribunal correctionnel** ≈ criminal court
**correspondance** [kɔrɛspɔ̃dɑ̃s] *nf* correspondence; (*de train, d'avion*) connection; **cours par ~** correspondence course; **vente par ~** mail-order business
**correspondant, e** [kɔrɛspɔ̃dɑ̃, ɑ̃t] *nm/f* correspondent; (TÉL) person phoning (*ou* being phoned)
**correspondre** [kɔrɛspɔ̃dr] *vi* to correspond, tally; **~ à** to correspond to; **~ avec qn** to correspond with sb
**corrida** [kɔrida] *nf* bullfight
**corridor** [kɔridɔr] *nm* corridor
**corrigé** [kɔriʒe] *nm* (SCOL: *d'exercice*) correct version
**corriger** [kɔriʒe] *vt* (*devoir*) to correct; (*punir*) to thrash; **~ qn de** (*défaut*) to cure sb of
**corroborer** [kɔrɔbɔre] *vt* to corroborate
**corrompre** [kɔrɔ̃pr] *vt* to corrupt; (*acheter: témoin etc*) to bribe
**corruption** [kɔrypsjɔ̃] *nf* corruption; (*de témoins*) bribery
**corsage** [kɔrsaʒ] *nm* bodice; (*chemisier*) blouse

**corsaire** [kɔrsɛr] *nm* pirate
**corse** [kɔrs] *adj, nm/f* Corsican ♦ *nf*: **la C~** Corsica
**corsé, e** [kɔrse] *adj* (*café*) full-flavoured; (*sauce*) spicy; (*problème*) tough
**corset** [kɔrsɛ] *nm* corset
**cortège** [kɔrtɛʒ] *nm* procession
**cortisone** [kɔrtizɔn] *nf* cortisone
**corvée** [kɔrve] *nf* chore, drudgery *no pl*
**cosmétique** [kɔsmetik] *nm* beauty care product
**cosmopolite** [kɔsmɔpɔlit] *adj* cosmopolitan
**cossu, e** [kɔsy] *adj* (*maison*) opulent(-looking)
**costaud, e** [kɔsto, od] (*fam*) *adj* strong, sturdy
**costume** [kɔstym] *nm* (*d'homme*) suit; (*de théâtre*) costume; **costumé, e** *adj* dressed up; **bal costumé** fancy dress ball
**cote** [kɔt] *nf* (*en Bourse*) quotation; **~ d'alerte** danger *ou* flood level
**côte** [kot] *nf* (*rivage*) coast(line); (*pente*) hill; (ANAT) rib; (*d'un tricot, tissu*) rib, ribbing *no pl*; **~ à ~** side by side; **la C~ (d'Azur)** the (French) Riviera
**coté, e** [kɔte] *adj*: **être bien ~** to be highly rated
**côté** [kote] *nm* (*gén*) side; (*direction*) way, direction; **de chaque ~ (de)** on each side (of); **de tous les ~s** from all directions; **de quel ~ est-il parti?** which way did he go?; **de ce~/de l'autre ~** this/the other way; **du ~ de** (*provenance*) from; (*direction*) towards; (*proximité*) near; **de ~** (*regarder*) sideways; (*mettre*) aside; **mettre de l'argent de ~** to save some money; **à ~** (right) nearby; (*voisins*) next door; **à ~ de** beside, next to; (*en comparaison*) compared to; **être aux ~s de** to be by the side of
**coteau, x** [kɔto] *nm* hill
**côtelette** [kotlɛt] *nf* chop
**côtier, -ière** [kotje, jɛr] *adj* coastal

**cotisation** [kɔtizasjɔ̃] *nf* subscription, dues *pl*; (*pour une pension*) contributions *pl*

**cotiser** [kɔtize] *vi*: ~ (à) to pay contributions (to); **se** ~ *vi* to club together

**coton** [kɔtɔ̃] *nm* cotton; ~ **hydrophile** cotton wool (BRIT), absorbent cotton (US); **Coton-Tige** ® *nm* cotton bud

**côtoyer** [kotwaje] *vt* (*fréquenter*) to rub shoulders with

**cou** [ku] *nm* neck

**couchant** [kuʃɑ̃] *adj*: **soleil** ~ setting sun

**couche** [kuʃ] *nf* layer; (*de peinture, vernis*) coat; (*de bébé*) nappy (BRIT), diaper (US); ~ **d'ozone** ozone layer; ~**s sociales** social levels *ou* strata

**couché, e** [kuʃe] *adj* lying down; (*au lit*) in bed

**coucher** [kuʃe] *nm* (*du soleil*) setting ♦ *vt* (*personne*) to put to bed; (*objet*) to put up; (*objet*) to lay on its side ♦ *vi* to sleep; **se** ~ *vi* (*pour dormir*) to go to bed; (*pour se reposer*) to lie down; (*soleil*) to set; ~ **de soleil** sunset

**couchette** [kuʃɛt] *nf* couchette; (*pour voyageur, sur bateau*) berth

**coucou** [kuku] *nm* cuckoo

**coude** [kud] *nm* (ANAT) elbow; (*de tuyau, de la route*) bend; ~ **à** ~ shoulder to shoulder, side by side

**coudre** [kudʀ] *vt* (*bouton*) to sew on ♦ *vi* to sew

**couenne** [kwan] *nf* (*de lard*) rind

**couette** [kwɛt] *nf* duvet, quilt; ~**s** *nfpl* (*cheveux*) bunches

**couffin** [kufɛ̃] *nm* Moses basket

**couler** [kule] *vi* to flow, run; (*fuir: stylo, récipient*) to leak; (*nez*) to run; (*sombrer: bateau*) to sink ♦ *vt* (*cloche, sculpture*) to cast; (*bateau*) to sink; (*faire échouer: personne*) to bring down

**couleur** [kulœʀ] *nf* colour (BRIT), color (US); (CARTES) suit; **film/télévision en** ~**s** colo(u)r film/television

**couleuvre** [kulœvʀ] *nf* grass snake

**coulisse** [kulis] *nf*: ~ ♦ *nfpl* (THÉÂTRE)

wings; (*fig*): **dans les** ~**s** behind the scenes; **coulisser** *vi* to slide, run

**couloir** [kulwaʀ] *nm* corridor, passage; (*d'avion*) aisle; (*de bus*) gangway; ~ **aérien/de navigation** air/shipping lane

**coup** [ku] *nm* (*heurt, choc*) knock; (*affectif*) blow, shock; (*agressif*) blow; (*avec arme à feu*) shot; (*de l'horloge*) stroke; (*tennis, golf*) stroke; (*boxe*) blow; (*fam: fois*) time; ~ **de coude** nudge (with the elbow); ~ **de tonnerre** clap of thunder; ~ **de sonnette** ring of the bell; **donner un** ~ **de balai** to give the floor a sweep; **boire un** ~ (*fam*) to have a drink; **être dans le** ~ to be in on it; **du** ~ ... as a result; **d'un seul** ~ (*subitement*) suddenly; (*à la fois*) at one go; **du premier** ~ first time; **du même** ~ at the same time; **à tous les** ~**s** (*fam*) every time; **tenir le** ~ to hold out; **après** ~ afterwards; **à** ~ **sûr** definitely, without fail; **sur le** ~ in quick succession; **sur le** ~ outright; **sous le** ~ **de** (*surprise etc*) under the influence of; **en** ~ **de vent** in a tearing hurry; **de chance** stroke of luck; ~ **de couteau** stab (of a knife); ~ **d'État** coup; ~ **de feu** shot; ~ **de fil** (*fam*) phone call; ~ **de frein** (sharp) braking *no pl*; ~ **de main**: **donner un** ~ **de main à qn** to give sb a (helping) hand; ~ **d'œil** glance; ~ **de pied** kick; ~ **de poing** punch; ~ **de soleil** sunburn *no pl*; ~ **de téléphone** phone call; ~ **de tête** (*fig*) (sudden) impulse

**coupable** [kupabl] *adj* guilty ♦ *nm/f* (*gén*) culprit; (JUR) guilty party

**coupe** [kup] *nf* (*verre*) goblet; (*à fruits*) dish; (SPORT) cup; (*de cheveux, de vêtement*) cut; (*graphique, plan*) (cross) section

**coupe-papier** [kuppapje] *nm inv* paper knife

**couper** [kupe] *vt* to cut; (*retrancher*) to cut (out); (*route, courant*) to cut off; (*appétit*) to take away; (*vin à table*) to dilute ♦ vi to cut; (prendre un raccourci) to take a short-cut; se ~ vi (se blesser) to cut o.s.; ~ la parole à qn to cut sb short

**couple** [kupl] nm couple

**couplet** [kuplɛ] nm verse

**coupole** [kupɔl] nf dome

**coupon** [kupɔ̃] nm (ticket) coupon; (reste de tissu) remnant; **coupon-réponse** nm reply coupon

**coupure** [kupyr] nf cut; (billet de banque) note; (de journal) cutting; ~ de courant power cut

**cour** [kur] nf (de ferme, jardin) (court)yard; (d'immeuble) back yard; (JUR, royale) court; **faire la ~ à qn** to court sb; ~ **d'assises** court of assizes; ~ **de récréation** playground; ~ **martiale** court-martial

**courage** [kuraʒ] nm courage, bravery; **courageux, -euse** adj brave, courageous

**couramment** [kuramɑ̃] adv commonly; (parler) fluently

**courant, e** [kurɑ̃, ɑ̃t] adj (fréquent) common; (COMM, gén: normal) standard; (en cours) current ♦ nm current; (fig) movement; (: d'opinion) trend; **être au ~ (de)** (fait, nouvelle) to know (about); **mettre qn au ~ (de)** (fait) to tell sb (about); (nouveau travail etc) to teach sb the basics (of); **se tenir au ~ (de)** (techniques etc) to keep o.s. up-to-date (on); **dans le ~ (de)** (pendant) in the course of; **le 10 ~** (COMM) the 10th inst.; ~ **d'air** draught; ~ **électrique** (electric) current, power

**courbature** [kurbatyr] nf ache

**courbe** [kurb] adj curved ♦ nf curve; **courber** vt to bend; **se courber** vi (personne) to bend (down), stoop

**coureur, -euse** [kurœr, øz] nm/f (SPORT) runner (ou driver); (péj) womanizer; manhunter; ~ **automobile** racing driver

**courge** [kurʒ] nf (CULIN) marrow; **courgette** nf courgette (BRIT), zucchini (US)

**courir** [kurir] vi to run ♦ vt (SPORT: épreuve) to compete in; (risque) to run; (danger) to face; ~ **les magasins** to go round the shops; **le bruit court que** the rumour is going round that

**couronne** [kurɔn] nf crown; (de fleurs) wreath, crown

**courons** etc [kurɔ̃] vb voir **courir**

**courrier** [kurje] nm mail, post; (lettres à écrire) letters pl; ~ **électronique** E-mail

**courroie** [kurwa] nf strap; (TECH) belt

**courrons** etc [kurɔ̃] vb voir **courir**

**cours** [kur] nm (leçon) class; (: particulier) lesson; (série de leçons, cheminement) course; (écoulement) flow; (COMM: de devises) rate; (: de denrées) price; **donner libre ~ à** to give free expression to; **avoir ~** (SCOL) to have a class ou lecture; **en ~** (année) current; (travaux) in progress; **en ~ de route** on the way; **au ~ de** in the course of, during; ~ **d'eau** waterway; ~ **du soir** night school; ~ **intensif** crash course

**course** [kurs] nf running; (SPORT: épreuve) race; (d'un taxi) journey, trip; (commission) errand; ~**s** nfpl (achats) shopping sg; **faire des ~s** to do some shopping

**court, e** [kur, kurt(ə)] adj short ♦ adv short ♦ nm: ~ **(de tennis)** (tennis) court; **à ~ de** short of; **prendre qn de ~** to catch sb unawares; **court-circuit** nm short-circuit

**courtier, -ère** [kurtje, jɛr] nm/f broker

**courtiser** [kurtize] vt to court, woo

**courtois, e** [kurtwa, waz] adj courteous; **courtoisie** nf courtesy

**couru, e** [kury] pp de **courir**

**cousais** etc [kuze] vb voir **coudre**

**couscous** [kuskus] nm couscous

**cousin, e** [kuzɛ̃, in] nm/f cousin

**coussin** [kusɛ̃] nm cushion

**cousu, e** [kuzy] pp de **coudre**

**coût** [ku] nm cost; **le ~ de la vie** the cost of living; **coûtant** adj m: **au prix coûtant** at cost price

**couteau, x** [kuto] nm knife

**coûter** [kute] vt, vi to cost; **combien ça coûte?** how much is it?, what does it cost?; **coûte que coûte** at all costs; **coûteux, -euse** adj costly, expensive

**coutume** [kutym] nf custom

**couture** [kutyʀ] nf sewing; (profession) dressmaking; (points) seam; **couturier** nm fashion designer; **couturière** nf dressmaker

**couvée** [kuve] nf brood, clutch

**couvent** [kuvɑ̃] nm (de sœurs) convent; (de frères) monastery

**couver** [kuve] vt to hatch; (maladie) to be coming down with ♦ vi (feu) to smoulder; (révolte) to be brewing

**couvercle** [kuvɛʀkl] nm lid; (de bombe aérosol etc, qui se visse) cap, top

**couvert, e** [kuvɛʀ, ɛʀt] pp de **couvrir** ♦ adj (ciel) overcast ♦ nm place setting; (place à table) place; **~s** nmpl (ustensiles) cutlery sg; **~ de** covered with ou in; **mettre le ~** to lay the table

**couverture** [kuvɛʀtyʀ] nf blanket; (de livre, assurance, fig) cover; (presse) coverage; **~ chauffante** electric blanket

**couveuse** [kuvøz] nf (de maternité) incubator

**couvre-feu** [kuvʀəfø] nm curfew

**couvre-lit** [kuvʀəli] nm bedspread

**couvreur** [kuvʀœʀ] nm roofer

**couvrir** [kuvʀiʀ] vt to cover; **se ~** vi (s'habiller) to cover up; (se coiffer) to put on one's hat; (ciel) to cloud over

**cow-boy** [kɔbɔj] nm cowboy

**crabe** [kʀab] nm crab

**cracher** [kʀaʃe] vi, vt to spit

**crachin** [kʀaʃɛ̃] nm drizzle

**crack** [kʀak] nm (fam: as) ace

**craie** [kʀɛ] nf chalk

**craindre** [kʀɛ̃dʀ] vt to fear, be afraid of; (être sensible à: chaleur, froid) to be easily damaged by

**crainte** [kʀɛ̃t] nf fear; **de ~ de/que** for fear of/that; **craintif, -ive** adj timid

**cramoisi, e** [kʀamwazi] adj crimson

**crampe** [kʀɑ̃p] nf cramp

**crampon** [kʀɑ̃pɔ̃] nm (de chaussure de football) stud; (de chaussure de course) spike; (d'alpinisme) crampon; **cramponner** vb: **se cramponner (à)** to hang ou cling on (to)

**cran** [kʀɑ̃] nm (entaille) notch; (de courroie) hole; (fam: courage) guts pl; **~ d'arrêt** safety catch

**crâne** [kʀɑn] nm skull

**crâner** [kʀɑne] (fam) vi to show off

**crapaud** [kʀapo] nm toad

**crapule** [kʀapyl] nf villain

**craquement** [kʀakmɑ̃] nm crack, snap; (du plancher) creak, creaking noise

**craquer** [kʀake] vi (bois, plancher) to creak; (fil, branche) to snap; (couture) to come apart; (fig: accusé) to break down; (: fam) to crack up ♦ vt (allumette) to strike; **j'ai craqué** (fam) I couldn't resist it

**crasse** [kʀas] nf grime, filth; **crasseux, -euse** adj grimy, filthy

**cravache** [kʀavaʃ] nf (riding) crop

**cravate** [kʀavat] nf tie

**crawl** [kʀol] nm crawl; **dos ~é** backstroke

**crayon** [kʀɛjɔ̃] nm pencil; **~ à bille** ball-point pen; **~ de couleur** crayon, colouring pencil; **crayon-feutre** (pl **crayons-feutres**) nm felt(-tip) pen

**créancier, -ière** [kʀeɑ̃sje, jɛʀ] nm/f creditor

**création** [kʀeɑsjɔ̃] nf creation

**créature** [kʀeatyʀ] nf creature

**crèche** [kʀɛʃ] nf (de Noël) crib; (garderie) crèche, day nursery

**crédit** [kʀedi] nm (gén) credit; **~s** nmpl (fonds) funds; **payer/acheter à ~** to pay/buy on credit ou on easy terms; **faire ~ à qn** to give sb credit; **créditer** vt: **créditer un compte (de)** to credit an account (with)

**crédule** [kʀedyl] adj credulous, gullible

**créer** [kʀee] vt to create

**crémaillère** [kʀemajɛʀ] nf: **pendre la ~** to have a house-warming party

**crématoire** [kʀematwaʀ] adj: **four ~**

crematorium

**crème** [kʀɛm] nf cream; (entremets) cream dessert ♦ adj inv cream(-coloured); **un (café) ~** ≃ a white coffee; **~ anglaise** (egg) custard; **~ chantilly** whipped cream; **~ fouettée = crème chantilly; crémerie** nf dairy; **crémeux, -euse** adj creamy

**créneau, x** [kʀeno] nm (de fortification) crenel(le); (dans marché) gap, niche; (AUTO): **faire un ~** to reverse into a parking space (between two cars alongside the kerb)

**crêpe** [kʀɛp] nf (galette) pancake ♦ nm (tissu) crêpe; **crêpé, e** adj (cheveux) backcombed; **crêperie** nf pancake shop ou restaurant

**crépiter** [kʀepite] vi (friture) to sputter, splutter; (fire) to crackle

**crépu, e** [kʀepy] adj frizzy, fuzzy

**crépuscule** [kʀepyskyl] nm twilight, dusk

**cresson** [kʀesɔ̃] nm watercress

**crête** [kʀɛt] nf (de coq) comb; (de vague, montagne) crest

**creuser** [kʀøze] vt (trou, tunnel) to dig; (sol) to dig a hole in; (fig) to go (deeply) into; **ça creuse** that gives you a real appetite; **se ~ la cervelle** (fam) to rack one's brains

**creux, -euse** [kʀø, kʀøz] adj hollow ♦ nm hollow; **heures creuses** slack periods; (électricité, téléphone) off-peak periods; **avoir un ~** (fam) to be hungry

**crevaison** [kʀavɛzɔ̃] nf puncture

**crevasse** [kʀavas] nf (dans le sol, la peau) crack; (de glacier) crevasse

**crevé, e** [kʀave] (fam) adj (fatigué) all in, exhausted

**crever** [kʀave] vt (ballon) to burst ♦ vi (pneu) to burst; (automobiliste) to have a puncture (BRIT) ou a flat (tire) (US); (fam) to die

**crevette** [kʀavɛt] nf: **~ (rose)** prawn; **~ grise** shrimp

**cri** [kʀi] nm cry, shout; (d'animal: spécifique) cry, call; **c'est le dernier ~** (fig)

it's the latest fashion

**criant, e** [kʀijɑ̃, kʀijɑ̃t] adj (injustice) glaring

**criard, e** [kʀijaʀ, kʀijaʀd] adj (couleur) garish, loud; (voix) yelling

**crible** [kʀibl] nm riddle; **passer qch au ~** (fig) to go over sth with a fine-tooth comb; **criblé, e** adj: **criblé de** riddled with; (de dettes) crippled with

**cric** [kʀik] nm (AUTO) jack

**crier** [kʀije] vi (pour appeler) to shout, cry (out); (de douleur etc) to scream, yell ♦ vt (injure) to shout (out), yell (out)

**crime** [kʀim] nm crime; (meurtre) murder; **criminel, le** nm/f criminal; (assassin) murderer

**crin** [kʀɛ̃] nm (de cheval) hair no pl

**crinière** [kʀinjɛʀ] nf mane

**crique** [kʀik] nf creek, inlet

**criquet** [kʀikɛ] nm grasshopper

**crise** [kʀiz] nf crisis; (MÉD) attack; (: d'épilepsie) fit; **piquer une ~ de nerfs** to go hysterical; **~ cardiaque** heart attack; **~ de foie** bilious attack

**crisper** [kʀispe] vt (poings) to clench; **se ~** vi (visage) to tense; (personne) to get tense

**crisser** [kʀise] vi (neige) to crunch; (pneu) to screech

**cristal, -aux** [kʀistal, o] nm crystal; **cristallin, e** adj crystal-clear

**critère** [kʀitɛʀ] nm criterion

**critiquable** [kʀitikabl] adj open to criticism

**critique** [kʀitik] adj critical ♦ nm/f (de théâtre, musique) critic ♦ nf criticism; (THÉÂTRE etc: article) review

**critiquer** [kʀitike] vt (dénigrer) to criticize; (évaluer) to assess, examine (critically)

**croasser** [kʀɔase] vi to caw

**Croatie** [kʀɔasi] nf Croatia

**croc** [kʀo] nm (dent) fang; (de boucher) hook; **croc-en-jambe** nm: **faire un croc-en-jambe à qn** to trip sb up

**croche** [kʀɔʃ] nf (MUS) quaver (BRIT),

eighth note (US); **croche-pied** nm = **croc-en-jambe**

**crochet** [kʀɔʃɛ] nm hook; (détour) detour; (TRICOT: aiguille) crochet hook; (: technique) crochet; **vivre aux ~s de qn** to live ou sponge off sb

**crochu, e** [kʀɔʃy] adj (nez) hooked; (doigts) claw-like

**crocodile** [kʀɔkɔdil] nm crocodile

**croire** [kʀwaʀ] vt to believe; **se ~ fort** to think one is strong; **~ que** to believe ou think that; **~ à, ~ en** to believe in

**crois** [kʀwa] vb voir **croire**

**croisade** [kʀwazad] nf crusade

**croisé, e** [kʀwaze] adj (veste) double-breasted

**croisement** [kʀwazmɑ̃] nm (carrefour) crossroads sg; (BIO) crossing; (: résultat) crossbreed

**croiser** [kʀwaze] vt (personne, voiture) to pass; (route) to cross, cut across; (BIO) to cross; **se ~** vi (personnes, véhicules) to pass each other; (routes, lettres) to cross; (regards) to meet; **~ les jambes/bras** to cross one's legs/fold one's arms

**croisière** [kʀwazjɛʀ] nf cruise

**croissance** [kʀwasɑ̃s] nf growth

**croissant** [kʀwasɑ̃] nm (à manger) croissant; (motif) crescent

**croître** [kʀwatʀ] vi to grow

**croix** [kʀwa] nf cross; **~ gammée** swastika; **la C~ Rouge** the Red Cross

**croque-monsieur** [kʀɔkmɔsjø] nm inv toasted ham and cheese sandwich

**croquer** [kʀɔke] vt (manger) to crunch; (: fruit) to munch; (dessiner) to sketch; **chocolat à ~** plain dessert chocolate

**croquis** [kʀɔki] nm sketch

**cross** [kʀɔs] nm: **faire du ~ (à pied)** to do cross-country running

**crosse** [kʀɔs] nf (de fusil) butt; (de revolver) grip

**crotte** [kʀɔt] nf droppings pl; **crotté, e** adj muddy, mucky; **crottin** nm dung, manure; (fromage) (small round) cheese (made of goat's milk)

**crouler** [kʀule] vi (s'effondrer) to collapse; (être délabré) to be crumbling

**croupe** [kʀup] nf rump; **en ~** pillion

**croupir** [kʀupiʀ] vi to stagnate

**croustillant, e** [kʀustijɑ̃, ɑ̃t] adj crisp

**croûte** [kʀut] nf crust; (du fromage) rind; (MÉD) scab; **en ~** (CULIN) in pastry

**croûton** [kʀutɔ̃] nm (CULIN) crouton; (bout du pain) crust, heel

**croyable** [kʀwajabl] adj credible

**croyant, e** [kʀwajɑ̃, ɑ̃t] nm/f believer

**CRS** sigle fpl (= Compagnies républicaines de sécurité) state security police force ♦ sigle m member of the CRS

**cru, e** [kʀy] pp de **croire** ♦ adj (non cuit) raw; (lumière, couleur) harsh; (paroles) crude ♦ nm (vignoble) vineyard; (vin) wine; **un grand ~** a great vintage; **jambon ~** Parma ham

**crû** [kʀy] pp de **croître**

**cruauté** [kʀyote] nf cruelty

**cruche** [kʀyʃ] nf pitcher, jug

**crucifix** [kʀysifi] nm crucifix; **crucifixion** nf crucifixion

**crudités** [kʀydite] nfpl (CULIN) salads

**crue** [kʀy] nf (inondation) flood

**cruel, le** [kʀyɛl] adj cruel

**crus** etc [kʀy] vb voir **croire**; **croître**

**crûs** etc [kʀy] vb voir **croître**

**crustacés** [kʀystase] nmpl shellfish

**Cuba** [kyba] nf Cuba; **cubain, e** adj Cuban ♦ nm/f: **Cubain, e** Cuban

**cube** [kyb] nm cube; (jouet) brick; **mètre ~** cubic metre; **2 au ~** 2 cubed

**cueillette** [kœjɛt] nf picking; (quantité) crop, harvest

**cueillir** [kœjiʀ] vt (fruits, fleurs) to pick, gather; (fig) to catch

**cuiller** [kɥijɛʀ], **cuillère** [kɥijɛʀ] nf spoon; **~ à café** coffee spoon; (CULIN) teaspoonful; **~ à soupe** soup spoon; (CULIN) tablespoonful; **cuillerée** nf spoonful

**cuir** [kɥiʀ] nm leather; **~ chevelu** scalp

**cuire** [kɥiʀ] vt (aliments) to cook; (au four) to bake ♦ vi to cook; **bien cuit** (viande) well done; **trop cuit** overdone

**cuisant, e** [kɥizɑ̃, ɑ̃t] adj (douleur) stinging; (fig: souvenir, échec) bitter

**cuisine** [kɥizin] nf (pièce) kitchen; (art culinaire) cookery, cooking; (nourriture) cooking, food; **faire la ~** to cook; (fam) to grill ♦ vi to cook; **cuisinier, -ière** nm/f cook; **cuisinière** nf (poêle) cooker

**cuisse** [kɥis] nf thigh; (CULIN) leg

**cuisson** [kɥisɔ̃] nf cooking

**cuit, e** [kɥi, kɥit] pp de **cuire**

**cuivre** [kɥivʀ] nm copper; **les ~s** (MUS) the brass

**cul** [ky] (fam!) nm arse (!)

**culbute** [kylbyt] nf somersault; (accidentelle) tumble, fall

**culminant, e** [kylminɑ̃, ɑ̃t] adj: **point ~** highest point

**culminer** [kylmine] vi to reach its highest point

**culot** [kylo] (fam) nm (effronterie) cheek

**culotte** [kylɔt] nf (de femme) knickers pl (BRIT), panties pl

**culpabilité** [kylpabilite] nf guilt

**culte** [kylt] nm (religion) religion; (hommage, vénération) worship; (protestant) service

**cultivateur, -trice** [kyltivatœʀ, tʀis] nm/f farmer

**cultivé, e** [kyltive] adj (personne) cultured, cultivated

**cultiver** [kyltive] vt to cultivate; (légumes) to grow, cultivate

**culture** [kyltyʀ] nf cultivation; (connaissances etc) culture; **les ~s intensives** intensive farming; **~ physique** physical training; **culturel, le** adj cultural; **culturisme** nm body-building

**cumin** [kymɛ̃] nm cumin

**cumuler** [kymyle] vt (emplois) to hold concurrently; (salaires) to draw concurrently

**cupide** [kypid] adj greedy, grasping

**cure** [kyʀ] nf (MÉD) course of treatment

**curé** [kyʀe] nm parish priest

**cure-dent** [kyʀdɑ̃] nm toothpick

**cure-pipe** [kyʀpip] nm pipe cleaner

**curer** [kyʀe] vt to clean out

**curieusement** [kyʀjøzmɑ̃] adv curiously

**curieux, -euse** [kyʀjø, jøz] adj (indiscret) curious, inquisitive; (étrange) strange, curious ♦ nmpl (badauds) onlookers; **curiosité** nf curiosity; (site, spectacle) unusual feature

**curriculum vitae** [kyʀikylɔmvite] nm inv curriculum vitae

**curseur** [kyʀsœʀ] nm (INFORM) cursor

**cutané, e** [kytane] adj skin

**cuti-réaction** [kytiʀeaksjɔ̃] nf (MÉD) skin-test

**cuve** [kyv] nf vat; (à mazout etc) tank

**cuvée** [kyve] nf vintage

**cuvette** [kyvɛt] nf (récipient) bowl, basin; (GÉO) basin

**CV** sigle m (AUTO) = **cheval vapeur**; (COMM) = **curriculum vitae**

**cyanure** [sjanyʀ] nm cyanide

**cybercafé** [sibɛʀkafe] nm cybercafé

**cyclable** [siklabl] adj: **piste ~** cycle track

**cycle** [sikl] nm cycle; **cyclisme** nm cycling; **cycliste** nm/f cyclist ♦ adj cycle cpd; **coureur cycliste** racing cyclist

**cyclomoteur** [siklomotœʀ] nm moped

**cyclone** [siklon] nm hurricane

**cygne** [siɲ] nm swan

**cylindre** [silɛ̃dʀ] nm cylinder; **cylindrée** nf (AUTO) (cubic) capacity

**cymbale** [sɛ̃bal] nf cymbal

**cynique** [sinik] adj cynical

**cystite** [sistit] nf cystitis

# D, d

**d'** [d] prép voir **de**

**dactylo** [daktilo] nf (aussi: **~graphe**) typist; (aussi: **~graphie**) typing; **dactylographier** vt to type (out)

**dada** [dada] nm hobby-horse

**daigner** [deɲe] vt to deign

# daim

# débandade

**daim** [dɛ̃] *nm* (fallow) deer *inv*; (*cuir suédé*) suede

**dalle** [dal] *nf* paving stone, slab

**daltonien, ne** [daltɔnjɛ̃, jɛn] *adj* colour-blind

**dam** [dã] *nm*: **au grand ~ de** much to the detriment (*ou* annoyance) of

**dame** [dam] *nf* lady; (*CARTES, ÉCHECS*) queen; **~s** *nfpl* (*jeu*) draughts *sg* (*BRIT*), checkers *sg* (*US*)

**damner** [dane] *vt* to damn

**dancing** [dãsiŋ] *nm* dance hall

**Danemark** [danmark] *nm* Denmark

**danger** [dãʒe] *nm* danger; **dangereux, -euse** *adj* dangerous

**danois, e** [danwa, waz] *adj* Danish ♦ *nm*/f: **D~, e** Dane ♦ *nm* (*LING*) Danish

**dans** [dã] *prép* **1** (*position*) in; (*à l'intérieur de*) inside; **c'est dans le tiroir/le salon** it's in the drawer/ lounge; **dans la boîte** in *ou* inside the box; **marcher dans la ville** to walk about the town

**2** (*direction*) into; **elle a couru dans le salon** she ran into the lounge

**3** (*provenance*) out of, from; **je l'ai pris dans le tiroir/salon** I took it out of *ou* from the drawer/lounge; **boire dans un verre** to drink out of *ou* from a glass

**4** (*temps*) in; **dans 2 mois** in 2 months, in 2 months' time

**5** (*approximation*) about; **dans les 20 F** about 20F

**danse** [dãs] *nf*: **la ~ classique** dancing; **une ~** a dance; **la ~ classique** ballet; **danser** *vi, vt* to dance; **danseur, -euse** *nm/f* ballet dancer; (*au bal etc*) dancer; (: *cavalier*) partner

**dard** [dar] *nm* (*d'animal*) sting

**date** [dat] *nf* date; **de longue ~** long-standing; **~ de naissance** date of birth; **~ de péremption** expiry date; **~ limite** deadline; **dater** *vt, vi* to date;

**dater de** to date from; **à dater de** (as) from

**datte** [dat] *nf* date

**dauphin** [dofɛ̃] *nm* (*ZOOL*) dolphin

**davantage** [davãtaʒ] *adv* more; (*plus longtemps*) longer; **~ de** more

**de, d'** [də] (*de + le = du*, *de + les = des*) *prép* **1** (*appartenance*) of; **le toit de la maison** the roof of the house; **la voiture d'Ann/de mes parents** Ann's/my parents' car

**2** (*provenance*) from; **il vient de Londres** he comes from London; **elle est sortie du cinéma** she came out of the cinema

**3** (*caractérisation, mesure*): **un mur de brique/bureau d'acajou** a brick wall/ mahogany desk; **un billet de 50 F** a 50F note; **une pièce de 2 m de large** *ou* **large de 2 m** a room 2m wide, a 2m-wide room; **un bébé de 10 mois** a 10-month-old baby; **12 mois de crédit/travail** 12 months' credit/work; **de 14 à 18** from 14 to 18; **augmenter de 10 F** to increase by 10 F; **de 14 à 18** from 14 to 18

♦ *dét* **1** (*phrases affirmatives*) some (*souvent omis*); **du vin, de l'eau, des pommes** (some) wine, (some) water, (some) apples; **des enfants sont venus** some children came; **pendant des mois** for months

**2** (*phrases interrogatives et négatives*) any; **a-t-il du vin?** has he got any wine?; **il n'a pas de pommes/ d'enfants** he hasn't (got) any apples/ children, he has no apples/children

**dé** [de] *nm* (*à jouer*) die *ou* dice; (*aussi*: **~ à coudre**) thimble

**dealer** [dilœr] (*fam*) *nm* (drug) pusher

**déambuler** [deãbyle] *vi* to stroll about

**débâcle** [debakl] *nf* rout

**déballer** [debale] *vt* to unpack

**débandade** [debãdad] *nf* (*dispersion*) scattering

**débarbouiller** [debaʀbuje] vt to wash; **se ~** vi to wash (one's face)

**débarcadère** [debaʀkadɛʀ] nm wharf

**débardeur** [debaʀdœʀ] nm (maillot) tank top

**débarquer** [debaʀke] vt to unload, land ♦ vi to disembark; (fig: fam) to turn up

**débarras** [debaʀa] nm (pièce) lumber room; (placard) junk cupboard; **bon ~!** good riddance!; **débarrasser** vt to clear; **se débarrasser de** vt to get rid of; **débarrasser qn de** (vêtements, paquets) to relieve sb of

**débat** [deba] nm discussion, debate; **débattre** vt to discuss, debate; **se débattre** vi to struggle

**débaucher** [deboʃe] vt (licencier) to lay off, dismiss; (entraîner) to lead astray, debauch

**débile** [debil] (fam) adj (idiot) dim-witted

**débit** [debi] nm (d'un liquide, fleuve) flow; (d'un magasin) turnover (of goods); (élocution) delivery; (bancaire) debit; **~ de boissons** drinking establishment; **~ de tabac** tobacconist's; **débiter** vt (compte) to debit; (couper: bois, viande) to cut up; (péj: dire) to debt-or ♦ adj in debit; (compte) debit cpd

**déblayer** [debleje] vt to clear

**débloquer** [debloke] vt (prix, crédits) to free

**déboires** [debwaʀ] nmpl setbacks

**déboiser** [debwaze] vt to deforest

**déboîter** [debwate] vt (AUTO) to pull out; **se ~ le genou** etc to dislocate one's knee etc

**débonnaire** [debonɛʀ] adj easy-going, good-natured

**débordé, e** [debɔʀde] adj: **être ~ (de)** (travail, demandes) to be snowed under (with)

**déborder** [debɔʀde] vi to overflow; (lait etc) to boil over; **~ (de) qch** (dépasser) to extend beyond sth

**débouché** [debuʃe] nm (pour vendre) outlet; (perspective d'emploi) opening

**déboucher** [debuʃe] vt (évier, tuyau etc) to unblock; (bouteille) to uncork ♦ vi: **~ de** to emerge from; **~ sur** (études) to lead on to

**débourser** [debuʀse] vt to pay out

**déboussolé, e** [debusɔle] (fam) adj disorientated

**debout** [d(ə)bu] adv: **être ~** (personne) to be standing, stand; (: levé, éveillé) to be up; **se mettre ~** to stand up; **se tenir ~** to stand; **~!** stand up!; (du lit) get up!; **cette histoire ne tient pas ~** this story doesn't hold water

**déboutonner** [debutɔne] vt to undo, unbutton

**débraillé, e** [debʀaje] adj slovenly, untidy

**débrancher** [debʀɑ̃ʃe] vt to disconnect; (appareil électrique) to unplug

**débrayage** [debʀejaʒ] nm (AUTO) clutch; **débrayer** vi (AUTO) to declutch; (cesser le travail) to stop work

**débris** [debʀi] nmpl fragments; **des ~ de verre** bits of glass

**débrouillard, e** [debʀujaʀ, aʀd] (fam) adj smart, resourceful

**débrouiller** [debʀuje] vt to disentangle, untangle; **se ~** vi to manage; **débrouillez-vous** you'll have to sort things out yourself

**début** [deby] nm beginning, start; **~s** nmpl (de carrière) début sg; **~ juin** in early June; **débutant, e** nm/f beginner, novice; **débuter** vi to begin, start; (faire ses débuts) to start out

**deçà** [dəsa]: **en ~ de** prép this side of

**décadence** [dekadɑ̃s] nf decline

**décaféiné, e** [dekafeine] adj decaffeinated

**décalage** [dekalaʒ] nm gap; **~ horaire** time difference

**décaler** [dekale] vt to shift

**décalquer** [dekalke] vt to trace

**décamper** [dekɑ̃pe] (fam) vi to clear out ou off

**décaper** [dekape] vt (surface peinte) to strip

**décapiter** [dekapite] vt to behead; (par accident) to decapitate

**décapotable** [dekapɔtabl] adj convertible

**décapsuleur** [dekapsylœʀ] nm bottle-opener

**décarcasser** [dekaʀkase]: **se ~** (fam) vi to flog o.s. to death

**décédé, e** [desede] adj deceased

**décéder** [desede] vi to die

**déceler** [des(ə)le] vt (trouver) to discover, detect

**décembre** [desãbʀ] nm December

**décemment** [desamã] adv decently

**décennie** [deseni] nf decade

**décent, e** [desã, ãt] adj decent

**déception** [desɛpsjɔ̃] nf disappointment

**décerner** [deseʀne] vt to award

**décès** [desɛ] nm death

**décevant, e** [des(ə)vã, ãt] adj disappointing

**décevoir** [des(ə)vwaʀ] vt to disappoint

**déchaîner** [defene] vt (violence) to unleash; (enthousiasme) to arouse; **se ~** (tempête) to rage; (personne) to fly into a rage

**déchanter** [defãte] vi to become disillusioned

**décharge** [defaʀʒ] nf (dépôt d'ordures) rubbish tip ou dump; (électrique) electrical discharge; **décharger** vt (marchandise, véhicule) to unload; (tirer) to discharge; **se décharger** vi (batterie) to go flat; **décharger qn de** (responsabilité) to release sb from

**décharné, e** [defaʀne] adj emaciated

**déchausser** [defose] vt (skis) to take off; **se ~** vi to take off one's shoes; (dent) to come ou work loose

**déchéance** [defeãs] nf (physique) degeneration; (morale) decay

**déchet** [defɛ] nm (reste) scrap; **~s** nmpl (ordures) refuse sg, rubbish sg; **~s nucléaires** nuclear waste

**déchiffrer** [defifʀe] vt to decipher

**déchiqueter** [defik(ə)te] vt to tear ou pull to pieces

**déchirant, e** [defiʀã, ãt] adj heart-rending

**déchirement** [defiʀmã] nm (chagrin) wrench, heartbreak; (gén pl: conflit) rift, split

**déchirer** [defiʀe] vt to tear; (en morceaux) to tear up; (arracher) to tear out; (fig: conflit) to tear (apart); **se ~** vi to tear, rip; **se ~ un muscle** to tear a muscle

**déchirure** [defiʀyʀ] nf (accroc) tear, rip; **~ musculaire** torn muscle

**déchoir** [defwaʀ] vi (personne) to lower o.s., demean o.s.

**déchu, e** [defy] adj (roi) deposed

**décidé, e** [deside] adj (personne, air) determined; **c'est ~** it's decided; **décidément** adv really

**décider** [deside] vt: **~ qch** to decide on sth; **~ de faire** to decide (to do), make up one's mind (to do); **se ~ pour** to decide on ou in favour of; **~ de faire/que** to decide to do/that; **~ qn (à faire qch)** to persuade sb (to do sth)

**décimal, e, -aux** [desimal, o] adj decimal; **décimale** nf decimal

**décimètre** [desimɛtʀ] nm decimetre

**décisif, -ive** [desizif, iv] adj decisive

**décision** [desizjɔ̃] nf decision

**déclaration** [deklaʀasjɔ̃] nf declaration; (discours: POL etc) statement; **~ (d'impôts)** = tax return

**déclarer** [deklaʀe] vt to declare; (décès, naissance) to register; **se ~** vi (feu) to break out

**déclencher** [deklãʃe] vt (mécanisme etc) to release; (sonnerie) to set off; (attaque, grève) to launch; (provoquer) to trigger off; **se ~** vi (mécanisme etc) to go off

**déclic** [deklik] nm (bruit) click

**décliner** [dekline] vi to decline ♦ vt (invitation) to decline; (nom, adresse) to state

**décocher** [dekɔʃe] vt (coup de poing) to throw; (flèche, regard) to shoot

**décoiffer** [dekwafe] vt: ~ **qn** to mess up sb's hair; **je suis toute décoiffée** my hair is in a real mess

**déçois** etc [deswa] vb voir **décevoir**

**décollage** [dekɔlaʒ] nm (AVIAT) takeoff

**décoller** [dekɔle] vt to unstick ♦ vi (avion) to take off; **se ~** vi to come unstuck

**décolleté, e** [dekɔlte] adj low-cut ♦ nm low neck(line); (plongeant) cleavage

**décolorer** [dekɔlɔʀe]: **se ~** vi to fade; **se faire ~ les cheveux** to have one's hair bleached

**décombres** [dekɔ̃bʀ] nmpl rubble sg, debris sg

**décommander** [dekɔmɑ̃de] vt to cancel; **se ~** vi to cry off

**décomposé, e** [dekɔ̃poze] adj (pourri) decomposed; (visage) haggard, distorted

**décompte** [dekɔ̃t] nm deduction; (facture) detailed account

**déconcerter** [dekɔ̃sɛʀte] vt to disconcert, confound

**déconfit, e** [dekɔ̃fi, it] adj crestfallen

**décongeler** [dekɔ̃ʒ(ə)le] vt to thaw

**déconner** [dekɔne] (fam) vi to talk rubbish

**déconseiller** [dekɔ̃seje] vt: ~ **qch** (à **qn**) to advise (sb) against sth; **c'est déconseillé** it's not recommended

**décontracté, e** [dekɔ̃tʀakte] adj relaxed, laid-back (fam)

**décontracter** [dekɔ̃tʀakte]: **se ~** vi to relax

**déconvenue** [dekɔ̃v(ə)ny] nf disappointment

**décor** [dekɔʀ] nm décor; (paysage) scenery; **~s** nmpl (THÉÂTRE) scenery sg, décor sg; (CINÉMA) set sg; **décorateur** nm (interior) decorator; **décoration** nf decoration; **décorer** vt to decorate

**décortiquer** [dekɔʀtike] vt to shell; (fig: texte) to dissect

**découcher** [dekuʃe] vi to spend the

night away from home

**découdre** [dekudʀ]: **se ~** vi to come unstitched

**découler** [dekule] vi: ~ **de** to ensue ou follow from

**découper** [dekupe] vt (papier, tissu etc) to cut up; (viande) to carve; (article) to cut out; **se ~ sur** to stand out against

**décourager** [dekuʀaʒe] vt to discourage; **se ~** vi to lose heart, become discouraged

**décousu, e** [dekuzy] adj unstitched; (fig) disjointed, disconnected

**découvert, e** [dekuvɛʀ, ɛʀt] adj (tête) bare, uncovered; (lieu) open, exposed ♦ nm (bancaire) overdraft; **découverte** nf discovery; **faire la découverte de** to discover

**découvrir** [dekuvʀiʀ] vt to discover; (enlever ce qui couvre) to uncover; (dévoiler) to reveal; **se ~** vi (chapeau) to take off one's hat; (vêtement) to take something off; (ciel) to clear

**décret** [dekʀɛ] nm decree; **décréter** vt to decree

**décrié, e** [dekʀije] adj disparaged

**décrire** [dekʀiʀ] vt to describe

**décrocher** [dekʀɔʃe] vt (détacher) to take down; (téléphone) to take off the hook; (: pour répondre) to lift the receiver; (fam: contrat etc) to get, land ♦ vi (fam: abandonner) to drop out; (: cesser d'écouter) to switch off

**décroître** [dekʀwatʀ] vi to decrease, decline

**décrypter** [dekʀipte] vt to decipher

**déçu, e** [desy] pp de **décevoir**

**décupler** [dekyple] vt, vi to increase tenfold

**dédaigner** [dedeɲe] vt to despise, scorn; (négliger) to disregard, spurn; **dédaigneux, -euse** adj scornful, disdainful; **dédain** nm scorn, disdain

**dédale** [dedal] nm maze

**dedans** [dədɑ̃] adv inside; (pas en plein air) indoors, inside ♦ nm inside; **au ~** inside

**dédicacer** [dedikase] vt: ~ **(à qn)** to sign (for sb), autograph (for sb)

**dédier** [dedje] vt to dedicate

**dédire** [dediʀ]: **se ~** vi to go back on one's word, retract

**dédommagement** [dedɔmaʒmɑ̃] nm compensation

**dédommager** [dedɔmaʒe] vt: ~ **qn (de)** to compensate sb (for)

**dédouaner** [dedwane] vt to clear through customs

**dédoubler** [deduble] vt (classe, effectifs) to split (into two)

**déduire** [deduiʀ] vt: ~ **qch (de)** (ôter) to deduct sth (from); (conclure) to deduce ou infer sth (from)

**déesse** [dees] nf goddess

**défaillance** [defajɑ̃s] nf (syncope) blackout; (fatigue) (sudden) weakness no pl; (technique) fault, failure; ~ **cardiaque** heart failure

**défaillir** [defajiʀ] vi to feel faint; (mémoire etc) to fail

**défaire** [defɛʀ] vt to undo; (installation) to take down, dismantle; **se ~** vi to come undone; **se ~ de** to get rid of

**défait, e** [defɛ, ɛt] adj (visage) haggard, ravaged; **défaite** nf defeat

**défalquer** [defalke] vt to deduct

**défaut** [defo] nm (moral) fault, failing, defect; (tissus) fault, flaw; (manque, carence): ~ **de** shortage of; **prendre qn en ~** to catch sb out; **faire ~** (manquer) to be lacking; **à ~ de** for lack ou want of

**défavorable** [defavɔʀabl] adj unfavourable (BRIT), unfavorable (US)

**défavoriser** [defavɔʀize] vt to put at a disadvantage

**défection** [defɛksjɔ̃] nf defection, failure to give support

**défectueux, -euse** [defɛktɥø, øz] adj faulty, defective

**défendre** [defɑ̃dʀ] vt to defend; (interdire) to forbid; **se ~** vi to defend o.s.; ~ **à qn qch/de faire** to forbid sb sth/to do; **il se défend** (fam) he's doing ou se débrouille) he

can hold his own; **se ~ de/contre** (se protéger) to protect o.s. from/against; **se ~ de** (se garder de) to refrain from

**défense** [defɑ̃s] nf defence; (d'éléphant etc) tusk; "~ **de fumer**" "no smoking"

**déférer** [defeʀe] vt (JUR) to refer; ~ **à** (requête, décision) to defer to

**déferler** [defɛʀle] vi (vagues) to break; (fig: foule) to surge

**défi** [defi] nm challenge; **lancer un ~ à qn** to challenge sb; **sur un ton de ~** defiantly

**déficit** [defisit] nm (COMM) deficit; **déficitaire** adj in deficit

**défier** [defje] vt (provoquer) to challenge; (mort, autorité) to defy

**défigurer** [defigyʀe] vt to disfigure

**défilé** [defile] nm (GÉO) (narrow) gorge ou pass; (soldats) parade; (manifestants) procession, march; ~ **de mode** fashion parade

**défiler** [defile] vi (troupes) to march past; (sportifs) to parade; (manifestants) to march; (visiteurs) to pour, stream; **se ~** vi: **il s'est défilé** (fam) he wriggled out of it

**définir** [definiʀ] vt to define

**définitif, -ive** [definitif, iv] adj (final) final, definitive; (pour longtemps) permanent, definitive; (refus) definite; **définitive** nf: **en définitive** eventually; (somme toute) in fact; **définitivement** adv (partir, s'installer) for good

**déformer** [defɔʀse] vt (porte) to smash in ou down; **se ~** (fam) vi (travailler) to work like a dog; (drogué) to get high

**déformer** [defɔʀme] vt to put out of shape; (pensée, fait) to distort; **se ~** vi to lose its shape

**défouler** [defule]: **se ~** vi to unwind, let off steam

**défraîchir** [defʀeʃiʀ]: **se ~** vi to fade

**défricher** [defʀiʃe] vt to clear (for cultivation)

**défunt, e** [defœ̃, œ̃t] nm/f deceased

**dégagé, e** [degaʒe] adj (route, ciel) clear; **sur un ton ~**

**dégagement** [degaʒmã] nm: **voie de ~** slip road

**dégager** [degaʒe] vt (exhaler) to give off; (délivrer) to free, extricate; (désencombrer) to clear; (isoler: idée, aspect) to bring out; **se ~** (passage, ciel) to clear

**dégarnir** [degarnir] vt (vider) to empty, clear; **se ~** vi (tempes, crâne) to go bald

**dégâts** [dega] nmpl damage sg

**dégel** [deʒel] nm thaw; **dégeler** vt to thaw (out)

**dégénérer** [deʒenere] vi to degenerate

**dégingandé, e** [deʒɛ̃gɑ̃de] adj gangling

**dégivrer** [deʒivre] vt (frigo) to defrost; (vitres) to de-ice

**dégonflé, e** [degɔ̃fle] adj (pneu) flat

**dégonfler** [degɔ̃fle] vt (pneu, ballon) to let down, deflate; **se ~** vi (fam) to chicken out

**dégouliner** [deguline] vi to trickle, drip

**dégourdi, e** [degurdi] adj smart, resourceful

**dégourdir** [degurdir] vt: **se ~ les jambes** to stretch one's legs (fig)

**dégoût** [degu] nm disgust, distaste; **dégoûtant, e** adj disgusting; **dégoûté, e** adj disgusted; **dégoûté de** sick of; **dégoûter** vt to disgust; **dégoûter qn de qch** to put sb off sth

**dégrader** [degrade] vt (MIL: officier) to degrade; (abîmer) to damage, deface; **se ~** vi (relations, situation) to deteriorate

**dégrafer** [degrafe] vt to unclip, unhook

**degré** [dəgre] nm degree

**dégressif, -ive** [degresif, iv] adj on a decreasing scale

**dégringoler** [degrɛ̃gɔle] vi to tumble (down)

**dégrossir** [degrosir] vt (fig: projet) to work out roughly

**déguenillé, e** [deg(ə)nije] adj ragged, tattered

**déguerpir** [degerpir] vi to clear off

**dégueulasse** [degœlas] (fam) adj disgusting

**dégueuler** [degœle] (fam) vi to throw up

**déguisement** [degizmã] nm (pour s'amuser) fancy dress

**déguiser** [degize] vt: **se ~** (se costumer) to dress up; (pour tromper) to disguise o.s.

**dégustation** [degystasjɔ̃] nf (de fromages etc) sampling; **~ de vins** wine-tasting session

**déguster** [degyste] vt (vins) to taste; (fromages etc) to sample; (savourer) to enjoy, savour

**dehors** [dəɔr] adv outside; (en plein air) outdoors ♦ nm outside ♦ nmpl (apparences) appearances; **mettre** ou **jeter ~** (expulser) to throw out; **au ~** outside; **au ~ de** outside; **en ~ de** (hormis) apart from

**déjà** [deʒa] adv already; (auparavant) before, already

**déjeuner** [deʒœne] vi to (have) lunch; (le matin) to have breakfast ♦ nm lunch

**déjouer** [deʒwe] vt (complot) to foil

**delà** [dəla] adv: **en ~ (de)**, **au ~ (de)** beyond

**délabrer** [delabre] se ~ vi to fall into decay, become dilapidated

**délacer** [delase] vt (chaussures) to undo

**délai** [dele] nm (attente) waiting period; (sursis) extension of time; (temps accordé) time limit; **sans ~** without delay; **dans les ~s** within the time limit

**délaisser** [delese] vt to abandon, desert

**délasser** [delase] vt to relax; **se ~** vi to relax

**délavé, e** [delave] adj faded

**délayer** [deleje] vt (CULIN) to mix (with water etc); (peinture) to thin down

**delco** [dɛlko] nm (AUTO) distributor

**délecter** [delekte]: **se ~** vi to revel ou delight in

**délégué, e** [delege] *nm/f* representative

**déléguer** [delege] *vt* to delegate

**délibéré, e** [delibere] *adj* (*conscient*) deliberate

**délibérer** [delibere] *vi* to deliberate

**délicat, e** [delika, at] *adj* delicate; (*plein de tact*) tactful; (*attention*) thoughtful; **délicatement** *adv* delicately; (*avec douceur*) gently

**délice** [delis] *nm* delight

**délicieux, -euse** [delisjø, jøz] *adj* (*au goût*) delicious; (*sensation*) delightful

**délimiter** [delimite] *vt* (*terrain*) to delimit, demarcate

**délinquance** [delɛ̃kɑ̃s] *nf* criminality; **délinquant, e** *adj, nm/f* delinquent

**délirant, e** [delirɑ̃, ɑ̃t] *(fam) adj* wild

**délirer** [delire] *vi* to be delirious; **tu délires!** *(fam)* you're crazy!

**délit** [deli] *nm* (criminal) offence

**délivrer** [delivre] *vt* (*prisonnier*) to (set) free, release; (*passeport*) to issue

**déloger** [delɔʒe] *vt* (*objet coincé*) to dislodge

**déloyal, e, -aux** [delwajal, o] *adj* (*ami*) disloyal; (*procédé*) unfair

**deltaplane** [dɛltaplan] *nm* hang-glider

**déluge** [delyʒ] *nm* (*pluie*) downpour; (*biblique*) Flood

**déluré, e** [delyre] *(péj) adj* forward, pert

**demain** [d(ə)mɛ̃] *adv* tomorrow

**demande** [d(ə)mɑ̃d] *nf* (*requête*) request; (*revendication*) demand; (*d'emploi*) application; (ÉCON) **la ~** demand; **"~s d'emploi"** (*annonces*) "situations wanted"; **~ en mariage** proposal (of marriage)

**demandé, e** [d(ə)mɑ̃de] *adj* (*article etc*): **très ~** (*very*) much in demand

**demander** [d(ə)mɑ̃de] *vt* to ask for; (*chemin, heure etc*) to ask; (*nécessiter*) to require, demand; **se ~ si/pourquoi** *etc* to wonder whether/why *etc*; **~ qch à qn** to ask sb for sth; **~ un service à qn** to ask sb a favour; **~ à qn de faire qch** to ask sb to do; **demandeur, -euse**

*nm/f*: **demandeur d'emploi** job-seeker

**démangeaison** [demɑ̃ʒɛzɔ̃] *nf* itching; **avoir des ~s** to be itching

**démanger** [demɑ̃ʒe] *vi* to itch

**démanteler** [demɑ̃t(ə)le] *vt* to break up

**démaquillant** [demakijɑ̃] *nm* make-up remover

**démaquiller** [demakije] *vt*: **se ~** to remove one's make-up

**démarche** [demarʃ] *nf* (*allure*) gait, walk; (*intervention*) step; (*fig*: *intellectuelle*) thought processes *pl*; **faire les ~s nécessaires (pour obtenir qch)** to take the necessary steps (to obtain sth)

**démarcheur, -euse** [demarʃœr, øz] *nm/f* (COMM) door-to-door salesman/woman

**démarque** [demark] *nf* (*article*) markdown

**démarrage** [demaraʒ] *nm* start

**démarrer** [demare] *vi* (*conducteur*) to start (up); (*véhicule*) to move off; (*travaux*) to get moving; **démarreur** *nm* (AUTO) starter

**démêlant** [demelɑ̃] *nm* conditioner

**démêler** [demele] *vt* to untangle; **démêlés** *nmpl* problems

**déménagement** [demenaʒmɑ̃] *nm* move; **camion de ~** removal van

**déménager** [demenaʒe] *vt* (*meubles*) to (re)move ♦ *vi* to move (house); **déménageur** *nm* removal man

**démener** [dem(ə)ne]: **se ~** *vi* (*se dépenser*) to exert o.s.; (*pour obtenir qch*) to go to great lengths

**dément, e** [demɑ̃, ɑ̃t] *adj* (*fou*) mad, crazy; (*fam*) brilliant, fantastic

**démentiel, le** [demɑ̃sjɛl] *adj* insane

**démentir** [demɑ̃tir] *vt* to refute; **~ que** to deny that

**démerder** [demɛrde] *(fam)*: **se ~** *vi* to sort things out for o.s.

**démesuré, e** [dem(ə)zyre] *adj* immoderate

**démettre** [demɛtr] *vt*: **~ qn de** (*fonction, poste*) to dismiss sb from; **se ~**

l'épaule *etc* to dislocate one's shoulder *etc*

**demeurant** [d(ə)mœʀɑ̃]: **au ~** *adv* for all that

**demeure** [d(ə)mœʀ] *nf* residence; **demeurer** *vi* (*habiter*) to live; (*rester*) to remain

**demi, e** [dəmi] *adj* half ♦ *nm* (*bière*) ≈ half-pint (0,25 litres) ♦ *préfixe*: **~...** half-, semi-..., demi-; **trois heures/bouteilles et ~es** three and a half hours/bottles, three hours/bottles and a half; **il est 2 heures et ~e/midi et ~** it's half past 2/half past 12; **à ~** half-; **à la ~e** (*heure*) on the half-hour; **demi-cercle** *nm* semicircle; **en demi-cercle** ♦ *adj* semicircular ♦ *adv* in a half circle; **demi-douzaine** *nf* half-dozen, half a dozen; **demi-finale** *nf* semifinal; **demi-frère** *nm* half-brother; **demi-heure** *nf* half-hour, half an hour; **demi-journée** *nf* half-day, half a day; **demi-litre** *nm* half-litre, half a litre; **demi-livre** *nf* half-pound, half a pound; **demi-mot** *adv*: **à demi-mot** without having to spell things out; **demi-pension** *nf* (*à l'hôtel*) half-board; **demi-pensionnaire** *nm/f*: **être demi-pensionnaire** to take school lunches; **demi-place** *nf* half-fare

**démis, e** [demi, iz] *adj* (*épaule etc*) dislocated

**demi-sel** [dəmisɛl] *adj inv* (*beurre, fromage*) slightly salted

**demi-sœur** [dəmisœʀ] *nf* half-sister

**démission** [demisjɔ̃] *nf* resignation; **donner sa ~** to give *ou* hand in one's notice; **démissionner** *vi* to resign

**demi-tarif** [dəmitaʀif] *nm* half-price; **voyager à ~~** to travel half-fare

**demi-tour** [dəmituʀ] *nm* about-turn; **faire ~~** to turn (and go) back

**démocratie** [demɔkʀasi] *nf* democracy; **démocratique** *adj* democratic

**démodé, e** [demɔde] *adj* old-fashioned

**demoiselle** [d(ə)mwazɛl] *nf* (*jeune fille*) young lady; (*célibataire*) single lady,

maiden lady; **~ d'honneur** bridesmaid

**démolir** [demɔliʀ] *vt* to demolish

**démon** [demɔ̃] *nm* (*enfant turbulent*) devil, demon; **le D~** the Devil

**démonstration** [demɔ̃stʀasjɔ̃] *nf* demonstration

**démonté, e** [demɔ̃te] *adj* (*mer*) raging, wild

**démonter** [demɔ̃te] *vt* (*machine etc*) to take down, dismantle

**démontrer** [demɔ̃tʀe] *vt* to demonstrate

**démordre** [demɔʀdʀ] *vi*: **ne pas ~ de** to refuse to give up, stick to

**démouler** [demule] *vt* to turn out

**démuni, e** [demyni] *adj* (*sans argent*) impoverished; **~ de** without

**démunir** [demyniʀ] *vt*: **~ qn de** to deprive sb of; **se ~ de** to part with, give up

**dénaturer** [denatyʀe] *vt* (*goût*) to alter; (*pensée, fait*) to distort

**dénicher** [deniʃe] (*fam*) *vt* (*objet*) to unearth; (*restaurant etc*) to discover

**dénier** [denje] *vt* to deny

**dénigrer** [denigʀe] *vt* to denigrate, run down

**dénivellation** [denivelasjɔ̃] *nf* (*pente*) slope

**dénombrer** [denɔ̃bʀe] *vt* to count

**dénomination** [denɔminasjɔ̃] *nf* designation, appellation

**dénommé, e** [denɔme] *adj*: **un ~ Dupont** a certain Mr Dupont

**dénoncer** [denɔ̃se] *vt* to denounce

**dénouement** [denumɑ̃] *nm* outcome

**dénouer** [denwe] *vt* to unknot, undo; **se ~** *vi* (*nœud*) to come undone

**dénoyauter** [denwajote] *vt* to stone

**denrée** [dɑ̃ʀe] *nf*: **~s (alimentaires)** foodstuffs

**dense** [dɑ̃s] *adj* dense; **densité** *nf* density

**dent** [dɑ̃] *nf* tooth; **~ de lait/sagesse** milk/wisdom tooth; **dentaire** *adj* dental

**dentelé, e** [dɑ̃t(ə)le] *adj* jagged, indented

**dentelle** [dɑ̃tɛl] nf lace no pl

**dentier** [dɑ̃tje] nm denture

**dentifrice** [dɑ̃tifʀis] nm toothpaste

**dentiste** [dɑ̃tist] nm/f dentist

**dentition** [dɑ̃tisjɔ̃] nf teeth

**dénuder** [denyde] vt to bare

**dénué, e** [denye] adj: ~ **de** devoid of;

**dénuement** nm destitution

**déodorant** [deɔdɔʀɑ̃] nm deodorant

**déontologie** [deɔ̃tɔlɔʒi] nf code of practice

**dépannage** [depanaʒ] nm: **service de** ~ (AUTO) breakdown service

**dépanner** [depane] vt (voiture, télévision) to fix, repair; (fig) to bail out, help out; **dépanneuse** nf breakdown lorry (BRIT), tow truck (US)

**dépareillé, e** [depaʀeje] adj (collection, service) incomplete; (objet) odd

**départ** [depaʀ] nm departure; (SPORT) start; **au** ~ at the start; **la veille du son** ~ the day before he leaves/left

**départager** [depaʀtaʒe] vt to decide between

**département** [depaʀtəmɑ̃] nm department

---

**département**

France is divided into 96 administrative units called **départements**. These local government divisions are headed by a state-appointed **préfet**, and administered by an elected Conseil général. **Départements** are usually named after prominent geographical features such as rivers or mountain ranges; see also DOM-TOM.

---

**dépassé, e** [depase] adj superseded, outmoded; **il est complètement** ~ he's completely out of his depth, he can't cope

**dépasser** [depase] vt (véhicule, concurrent) to overtake; (endroit) to pass, go past; (somme, limite) to exceed; (fig: en beauté etc) to surpass, outshine ♦ vi (ju-

pon etc) to show

**dépaysé, e** [depeize] adj disoriented

**dépaysement** [depeizmɑ̃] nm (changement) change of scenery

**dépecer** [depəse] vt to joint, cut up

**dépêche** [depɛʃ] nf dispatch

**dépêcher** [depeʃe]: **se** ~ vi to hurry

**dépeindre** [depɛ̃dʀ] vt to depict

**dépendance** [depɑ̃dɑ̃s] nf dependence; (bâtiment) outbuilding

**dépendre** [depɑ̃dʀ]: ~ **de** vt to depend on; (financièrement etc) to be dependent on

**dépens** [depɑ̃] nmpl: **aux** ~ **de** at the expense of

**dépense** [depɑ̃s] nf spending no pl, expense, expenditure no pl; **dépenser** vt to spend; (énergie) to expend, use up; **se dépenser** vi to exert o.s.; **dépensier, -ière** adj: **il est dépensier** he's a spendthrift

**dépérir** [depeʀiʀ] vi (personne) to waste away; (plante) to wither

**dépêtrer** [depetʀe] vt: **se** ~ **de** to extricate o.s. from

**dépeupler** [depœple]: **se** ~ vi to become depopulated

**dépilatoire** [depilatwaʀ] adj depilatory, hair-removing

**dépister** [depiste] vt to detect; (voleur) to track down

**dépit** [depi] nm vexation, frustration; **en** ~ **de** in spite of; **en** ~ **du bon sens** contrary to all good sense; **dépité, e** adj vexed, frustrated

**déplacé, e** [deplase] adj (propos) out of place, uncalled-for

**déplacement** [deplasmɑ̃] nm (voyage) trip, travelling no pl

**déplacer** [deplase] vt (table, voiture) to move, shift; **se** ~ vi to move; (voyager) to travel; **se** ~ **une vertèbre** to slip a disc

**déplaire** [deplɛʀ] vt: **ça me déplaît** I don't like this, I dislike this; **se** ~ vi to be unhappy; **déplaisant, e** adj disagreeable

**dépliant** [deplijɑ̃] nm leaflet

**déplier** [deplije] vt to unfold

**déplorer** [deplɔʀe] vt to deplore

**déployer** [deplwaje] vt (carte) to open out; (ailes) to spread; (troupes) to deploy

**déporter** [depɔʀte] vt (exiler) to deport; (dévier) to carry off course

**déposer** [depoze] vt (gén: mettre, poser) to lay ou put down; (à la banque, à la consigne) to deposit; (passager) to drop (off), set down; (roi) to depose; (plainte) to lodge; (marque) to register; **se ~** vi to settle; **dépositaire** nm/f (COMM) agent; **déposition** nf statement

**dépôt** [depo] nm (à la banque, sédiment) deposit; (entrepôt) warehouse, store

**dépotoir** [depotwaʀ] nm dumping ground, rubbish dump

**dépouiller** [depuje] vt (documents) to go through, peruse; **~ qn/qch de** to strip sb/sth of; **~ le scrutin** to count the votes

**dépourvu, e** [depuʀvy] adj: **~ de** lacking in, without; **prendre qn au ~** to catch sb unprepared

**déprécier** [depʀesje]: **se ~** vi to depreciate

**dépression** [depʀesjɔ̃] nf depression; **(nerveuse)** (nervous) breakdown

**déprimant, e** [depʀimɑ̃, ɑ̃t] adj depressing

**déprimer** [depʀime] vi to be/get depressed

---

## MOT-CLÉ

**depuis** [dəpɥi] prép 1 (point de départ dans le temps) since; **il habite Paris depuis 1983/l'an dernier** he has been living in Paris since 1983/last year; **depuis quand le connaissez-vous?** how long have you known him?

2 (temps écoulé) for; **il habite Paris depuis 5 ans** he has been living in Paris for 5 years; **je le connais depuis**

**3 ans** I've known him for 3 years

3 (lieu): **il a plu depuis Metz** it's been raining since Metz; **elle a téléphoné depuis Valence** she rang from Valence

4 (quantité, rang) from; **depuis les plus petits jusqu'aux plus grands** from the youngest to the oldest

♦ adv (temps) since (then); **je ne lui ai pas parlé depuis** I haven't spoken to him since (then)

**depuis que** conj since; **depuis qu'il m'a dit ça** (ever) since he said that to me

---

**député, e** [depyte] nm/f (POL) ≈ Member of Parliament (BRIT), ≈ Member of Congress (US)

**députer** [depyte] vt to delegate

**déraciner** [deʀasine] vt to uproot

**dérailler** [deʀaje] vi (train) to be derailed; **faire ~** to derail

**déraisonner** [deʀezɔne] vi to talk nonsense, rave

**dérangement** [deʀɑ̃ʒmɑ̃] nm (gêne) trouble; (gastrique etc) disorder; **en ~** (téléphone, machine) out of order

**déranger** [deʀɑ̃ʒe] vt (personne) to trouble, bother; (projets) to disrupt, upset; (objets, vêtements) to disarrange; **se ~** vi: **surtout ne vous dérangez pas pour moi** please don't put yourself out on my account; **est-ce que cela vous dérange si ...?** do you mind if ...?

**déraper** [deʀape] vi (voiture) to skid; (personne, semelles) to slip

**dérégler** [deʀegle] vt (mécanisme) to put out of order; (estomac) to upset

**dérider** [deʀide]: **se ~** vi to brighten up

**dérision** [deʀizjɔ̃] nf: **tourner en ~** to deride; **dérisoire** adj derisory

**dérive** [deʀiv] nf: **aller à la ~** (NAVIG, fig) to drift

**dérivé, e** [deʀive] nm (TECH) by-product

**dériver** [deʀive] vt (MATH) to derive

(cours d'eau etc) to divert ♦ vi (bateau) to drift; ~ **de** to derive from

**dermatologue** [dɛʀmatɔlɔg] nm/f dermatologist

**dernier, -ière** [dɛʀnje, jɛʀ] adj last; (le plus récent) latest, last; **lundi/le mois ~** last Monday/month; **le ~ cri** it's the very latest thing; **en ~** last; **ce ~** the latter; **dernièrement** adv recently

**dérobé, e** [deʀɔbe] adj: **à la ~e** surreptitiously

**dérober** [deʀɔbe] vt to steal; **se ~** vi (s'esquiver) to slip away; **se ~ à** (justice, regards) to hide from; (obligation) to shirk

**dérogation** [deʀɔgasjɔ̃] nf (special) dispensation

**déroger** [deʀɔʒe]: ~ **à** vt to go against, depart from

**dérouiller** [deʀuje] vt: **se ~ les jambes** to stretch one's legs (fig)

**déroulement** [deʀulmɑ̃] nm (d'une opération etc) progress

**dérouler** [deʀule] vt (ficelle) to unwind; **se ~** vi (avoir lieu) to take place; (se passer) to go (off); **tout s'est déroulé comme prévu** everything went as planned

**dérouter** [deʀute] vt (avion, train) to reroute, divert; (étonner) to disconcert, throw (out)

**derrière** [dɛʀjɛʀ] adv, prép behind ♦ nm (d'une maison) back; (postérieur) behind, bottom; **les pattes de ~** the back ou hind legs; **par ~** from behind; (fig) behind one's back

**des** [de] dét voir **de** ♦ prép +dét = **de** +**les**

**dès** [dɛ] prép from; ~ **que** as soon as; ~ **son retour** as soon as he was (ou is) back

**désabusé, e** [dezabyze] adj disillusioned

**désaccord** [dezakɔʀ] nm disagreement; **désaccordé, e** adj (MUS) out of tune

**désaffecté, e** [dezafɛkte] adj disused

**désagréable** [dezagʀeabl] adj unpleas-

ant

**désagréger** [dezagʀeʒe]: **se ~** vi to disintegrate, break up

**désagrément** [dezagʀemɑ̃] nm annoyance, trouble no pl

**désaltérer** [dezaltere] vt: **se ~** to quench one's thirst

**désapprobateur, -trice** [dezapʀɔbatœʀ, tʀis] adj disapproving

**désapprouver** [dezapʀuve] vt to disapprove of

**désarmant, e** [dezaʀmɑ̃, ɑ̃t] adj disarming

**désarroi** [dezaʀwa] nm disarray

**désastre** [dezastʀ] nm disaster; **désastreux, -euse** adj disastrous

**désavantage** [dezavɑ̃taʒ] nm disadvantage; **désavantager** vt to put at a disadvantage

**descendre** [desɑ̃dʀ] vt (escalier, montagne) to go (ou come) down; (valise, paquet) to take ou get down; (étagère etc) to lower; (fam: abattre) to shoot down ♦ vi to go (ou come) down; (passager: s'arrêter) to get out, alight; ~ **à pied/en voiture** to walk/drive down; ~ **du train** to get out of ou get off the train; ~ **de cheval** to dismount; ~ **à l'hôtel** to stay at a hotel

**descente** [desɑ̃t] nf descent, going down; (chemin) way down; (ski) downhill (race); ~ **de lit** bedside rug; ~ **(de police)** (police) raid

**description** [dɛskʀipsjɔ̃] nf description

**désemparé, e** [dezɑ̃paʀe] adj bewildered, distraught

**désemplir** [dezɑ̃pliʀ] vi: **ne pas ~** to be always full

**déséquilibre** [dezekilibʀ] nm (position): **en ~** unsteady; (fig: des forces, du budget) imbalance; **déséquilibré, e** nm/f (PSYCH) unbalanced person; **déséquilibrer** vt to throw off balance

**désert, e** [dezɛʀ, ɛʀt] adj deserted ♦ nm desert; **déserter** vi, vt to desert; **désertique** adj desert cpd

**désespéré, e** [dezɛspeʀe] adj desperate

**désespérer** [dezespeʀe] vi: ~ **(de)** to despair (of); **désespoir** [dezespwaʀ] nm despair; **en désespoir de cause** in desperation

**déshabiller** [dezabije] vt to undress; **se ~** vi to undress (o.s.)

**déshériter** [dezeʀite] vt to disinherit; **déshérités** nmpl: **les déshérités** the underprivileged

**déshonneur** [dezɔnœʀ] nm dishonour

**déshydraté, e** [dezidʀate] adj dehydrated

**desiderata** [deziderata] nmpl requirements

**désigner** [deziɲe] vt (montrer) to point out, indicate; (dénommer) to denote; (candidat etc) to name

**désinfectant, e** [dezɛ̃fɛktɑ̃, ɑ̃t] adj, nm disinfectant

**désinfecter** [dezɛ̃fɛkte] vt to disinfect

**désintégrer** [dezɛ̃tegʀe]: **se ~** vi to disintegrate

**désintéressé, e** [dezɛ̃teʀese] adj disinterested, unselfish

**désintéresser** [dezɛ̃teʀese] vt: **se ~ (de)** to lose interest (in)

**désintoxication** [dezɛ̃tɔksikasjɔ̃] nf: **faire une cure de ~** to undergo treatment for alcoholism (ou drug addiction)

**désinvolte** [dezɛ̃vɔlt] adj casual, off-hand; **désinvolture** nf casualness

**désir** [deziʀ] nm wish; (sensuel) desire; **désirer** vt to want, wish for; (sexuellement) to desire; **je désire ...** (formule de politesse) I would like ...

**désister** [deziste]: **se ~** vi to stand down, withdraw

**désobéir** [dezɔbeiʀ] vi: **~ (à qn/qch)** to disobey (sb/sth); **désobéissant, e** adj disobedient

**désobligeant, e** [dezɔbliʒɑ̃, ɑ̃t] adj disagreeable

**désodorisant** [dezɔdɔʀizɑ̃] nm air freshener, deodorizer

**désœuvré, e** [dezœvʀe] adj idle

**désolé, e** [dezɔle] adj (paysage) desolate; **je suis ~** I'm sorry

**désoler** [dezɔle] vt to distress, grieve

**désopilant, e** [dezɔpilɑ̃, ɑ̃t] adj hilarious

**désordonné, e** [dezɔʀdɔne] adj untidy

**désordre** [dezɔʀdʀ] nm disorder(liness), untidiness; (anarchie) disorder; **en ~** in a mess, untidy

**désorienté, e** [dezɔʀjɑ̃te] adj disorientated

**désormais** [dezɔʀmɛ] adv from now on

**désossé, e** [dezɔse] adj (viande) boned

**desquelles** [dekɛl] prép +pron = **de +lesquelles**

**desquels** [dekɛl] prép +pron = **de +lesquels**

**desséché, e** [deseʃe] adj dried up

**dessécher** [deseʃe]: **se ~** vi to dry out

**dessein** [desɛ̃] nm: **à ~** intentionally, deliberately

**desserrer** [deseʀe] vt to loosen; (frein) to release

**dessert** [desɛʀ] nm dessert, pudding

**desserte** [desɛʀt] nf (table) side table; (transport): **la ~ du village est assurée par autocar** there is a coach service to the village

**desservir** [desɛʀviʀ] vt (ville, quartier) to serve; (débarrasser): **~ (la table)** to clear the table

**dessin** [desɛ̃] nm (œuvre, art) drawing; (motif) pattern, design; **~ animé** cartoon (film); **~ humoristique** cartoon; **dessinateur, -trice** nm/f drawer; (de bandes dessinées) cartoonist; (industriel) draughtsman(-woman) (BRIT), draftsman(-woman) (US); **dessiner** vt to draw; (concevoir) to design

**dessous** [d(ə)su] adv underneath, beneath ♦ nm underside ♦ nmpl (sous-vêtements) underwear sg; **en ~, par ~** underneath; **au-~ (de)** below; (péj: digne de) beneath; **avoir le ~** to get the worst of it; **les voisins du ~** the downstairs neighbours; **dessous-de-plat** nm inv tablemat

**dessus** [d(ə)sy] adv on top; (collé, écrit

on it ♦ *nm* top; **en ~** above; **par ~** ♦ *adv* over it ♦ *prép* over; **au-~ (de)** above; **avoir le ~** to get the upper hand; **dessus-de-lit** *nm inv* bedspread

**destin** [dɛstɛ̃] *nm* fate; (*avenir*) destiny

**destinataire** [dɛstinatɛʀ] *nm/f* (POSTES) addressee; (*d'un colis*) consignee

**destination** [dɛstinasjɔ̃] *nf* (*lieu*) destination; (*usage*) purpose; **à ~ de** bound for, travelling to

**destinée** [dɛstine] *nf* (*existence, avenir*) destiny

**destiner** [dɛstine] *vt*: **~ qch à qn** (*envisager de donner*) to intend sb to have sth; (*adresser*) to intend sth for sb; **être destiné à** (*usage*) to be meant for

**désuet, -ète** [dezɥɛ, ɛt] *adj* outdated, outmoded

**détachant** [detaʃɑ̃] *nm* stain remover

**détachement** [detaʃmɑ̃] *nm* detachment

**détacher** [detaʃe] *vt* (*enlever*) to detach, remove; (*délier*) to untie; (ADMIN): **~ qn (auprès de** *ou* **à)** to post sb (to); **se ~** *vi* (*se séparer*) to come off; (: *page*) to come out; (*se défaire*) to come undone; **se ~ sur** to stand out against; **se ~ de** (*se désintéresser*) to grow away from

**détail** [detaj] *nm* detail; (COMM): **le ~** retail; **en ~** in detail; **au ~** (COMM) retail

**détaillant** [detajɑ̃] *nm* retailer; **détaillé, e** [detaje] *adj* (*plan, explications*) detailed; (*facture*) itemized; **détailler** [detaje] *vt* (*expliquer*) to explain in detail

**détaler** [detale] *vi* (*fam*) (*personne*) to take off

**détartrant** [detartrɑ̃] *nm* scale remover

**détaxé, e** [detakse] *adj*: **produits ~s** tax-free goods

**détecter** [detɛkte] *vt* to detect

**détective** [detɛktiv] *nm*: **~ (privé)** private detective

**déteindre** [detɛ̃dʀ] *vi* (*au lavage*) to run, lose its colour

**détendre** [detɑ̃dʀ] *vt* (*corps, esprit*) to

relax; **se ~** *vi* (*ressort*) to lose its tension; (*personne*) to relax

**détenir** [det(ə)niʀ] *vt* (*record, pouvoir, secret*) to hold; (*prisonnier*) to detain, hold

**détente** [detɑ̃t] *nf* relaxation

**détention** [detɑ̃sjɔ̃] *nf* (*d'armes*) possession; (*captivité*) detention; **~ préventive** custody

**détenu, e** [det(ə)ny] *nm/f* prisoner

**détergent** [detɛʀʒɑ̃] *nm* detergent

**détériorer** [deteʀjɔʀe] *vt* to damage; **se ~** *vi* to deteriorate

**déterminé, e** [detɛʀmine] *adj* (*résolu*) determined; (*précis*) specific, definite

**déterminer** [detɛʀmine] *vt* (*fixer*) to determine; **se ~ à faire qch** to make up one's mind to do sth

**déterrer** [detɛʀe] *vt* to dig up

**détestable** [detɛstabl] *adj* foul, detestable

**détester** [detɛste] *vt* to hate, detest

**détonner** [detɔne] *vi* (*fig*) to clash

**détour** [detuʀ] *nm* detour; (*tournant*) bend, curve; **ça vaut le ~** it's worth the trip; **sans ~** (*fig*) plainly

**détourné, e** [deturne] *adj* (*moyen*) roundabout

**détournement** [deturnəmɑ̃] *nm*: **~ d'avion** hijacking

**détourner** [deturne] *vt* to divert; (*par la force*) to hijack; (*yeux, tête*) to turn away; (*de l'argent*) to embezzle; **se ~** *vi* to turn away

**détracteur, -trice** [detʀaktœʀ, tʀis] *nm/f* disparager, critic

**détraquer** [detʀake] *vt* to put out of order; (*estomac*) to upset; **se ~** *vi* (*machine*) to go wrong

**détrempé, e** [detʀɑ̃pe] *adj* (*sol*) sodden, waterlogged

**détresse** [detʀɛs] *nf* distress

**détriment** [detʀimɑ̃] *nm*: **au ~ de** to the detriment of

**détritus** [detʀity(s)] *nmpl* rubbish *sg*, refuse *sg*

**détroit** [detʀwa] *nm* strait

**détromper** [detʀɔpe] vt to disabuse

**détruire** [detʀɥiʀ] vt to destroy

**dette** [dɛt] nf debt

**DEUG** sigle m (= diplôme d'études universitaires générales) diploma taken after 2 years at university

**deuil** [dœj] nm (perte) bereavement; (période) mourning; **être en ~** to be in mourning

**deux** [dø] num two; **tous les ~** both; **ses ~ mains** both his hands, his two hands; **~ fois** twice; **deuxième** num second; **deuxièmement** adv secondly; **deux-pièces** nm inv (tailleur) two-piece suit; (de bain) two-piece (swimsuit); (appartement) two-roomed flat (BRIT) ou apartment (US); **deux-points** nm inv colon sg; **deux-roues** nm inv two-wheeled vehicle

**devais** etc [dəvɛ] vb voir **devoir**

**dévaler** [devale] vt to hurtle down

**dévaliser** [devalize] vt to rob, burgle

**dévaloriser** [devalɔʀize] vt to depreciate; **se ~** vi to depreciate

**dévaluation** [devalɥasjɔ̃] nf devaluation

**devancer** [d(ə)vɑ̃se] vt (coureur, rival) to get ahead of; (arriver) to arrive before; (prévenir: questions, désirs) to anticipate

**devant** [d(ə)vɑ̃] adv in front; (à distance: en avant) ahead ♦ prép in front of; (en avant) ahead of; (avec mouvement: passer) past; (en présence de) before, in front of; (étant donné) in view of ♦ nm front; **prendre les ~s** to make the first move; **les pattes de ~** the front legs, the forelegs; **par ~** (boutonner) at the front; (entrer) the front way; **aller au-~ de qn** to go out to meet sb; **aller au-~ de** (désirs de qn) to anticipate

**devanture** [d(ə)vɑ̃tyʀ] nf (étalage) display; (vitrine) (shop) window

**déveine** [devɛn] (fam) nf rotten luck no pl

**développement** [dev(ə)lɔpmɑ̃] nm development; **pays en voie de ~** developing countries

**développer** [dev(ə)lɔpe] vt to develop; **se ~** vi to develop

**devenir** [dəv(ə)niʀ] vb +attrib to become; **que sont-ils devenus?** what has become of them?

**dévergondé, e** [devɛʀɡɔ̃de] adj wild, shameless

**déverser** [devɛʀse] vt (liquide) to pour (out); (ordures) to tip (out); **se ~ dans** (fleuve) to flow into

**dévêtir** [devetiʀ] vt to undress

**devez** etc [dəve] vb voir **devoir**

**déviation** [devjasjɔ̃] nf (AUTO) diversion (BRIT), detour (US)

**devienne** etc [dəvjɛn] vb voir **devenir**

**dévier** [devje] vt (fleuve, circulation) to divert; (coup) to deflect ♦ vi to veer (off course)

**devin** [dəvɛ̃] nm soothsayer, seer

**deviner** [d(ə)vine] vt to guess; (apercevoir) to distinguish; **devinette** nf riddle

**devins** etc [dəvɛ̃] vb voir **devenir**

**devis** [d(ə)vi] nm estimate, quotation

**dévisager** [devizaʒe] vt to stare at

**devise** [dəviz] nf (formule) motto, watchword; **~s** nfpl (argent) currency sg

**deviser** [dəvize] vi to converse

**dévisser** [devise] vt to unscrew, undo

**dévoiler** [devwale] vt to unveil

**devoir** [dəvwaʀ] nm duty; (SCOL) homework no pl; (: en classe) exercise ♦ vt (argent, respect): **~ qch (à qn)** to owe (sb) sth; (+infin: obligation): **il doit le faire** he has to do it, he must do it (: intention): **le nouveau centre commercial doit ouvrir en mai** the new shopping centre is due to open in May; (: probabilité): **il doit être tard** it must be late

**dévolu, e** [devɔly] nm: **jeter son ~ sur** to fix one's choice on

**dévorer** [devɔʀe] vt to devour

**dévot, e** [devo, ɔt] adj devout, pious

**dévotion** nf devoutness

**dévoué, e** [devwe] *adj* devoted

**dévouement** [devumã] *nm* devotion

**dévouer** [devwe]: **se ~** *vi* (*se sacrifier*): **se ~ (pour)** to sacrifice o.s. (for); (*se consacrer*): **se ~ à** to devote ou dedicate o.s. to

**dévoyé, e** [devwaje] *adj* delinquent

**devrai** *etc* [dəvre] *vb voir* **devoir**

**diabète** [djabɛt] *nm* diabetes *sg*; **diabétique** *nm/f* diabetic

**diable** [djabl] *nm* devil

**diabolo** [djablo] *nm* (*boisson*) lemonade with fruit cordial

**diagnostic** [djagnɔstik] *nm* diagnosis *sg*; **diagnostiquer** *vt* to diagnose

**diagonal, e, -aux** [djagɔnal, o] *adj* diagonal; **diagonale** *nf* diagonal; **en diagonale** diagonally

**diagramme** [djagram] *nm* chart, graph

**dialecte** [djalɛkt] *nm* dialect

**dialogue** [djalɔg] *nm* dialogue

**diamant** [djamã] *nm* diamond

**diamètre** [djamɛtr] *nm* diameter

**diapason** [djapazɔ̃] *nm* tuning fork

**diaphragme** [djafragm] *nm* diaphragm

**diapo** [djapo] (*fam*) *nf* slide

**diapositive** [djapozitiv] *nf* transparency, slide

**diarrhée** [djare] *nf* diarrhoea

**dictateur** [diktatœr] *nm* dictator; **dictature** *nf* dictatorship

**dictée** [dikte] *nf* dictation

**dicter** [dikte] *vt* to dictate

**dictionnaire** [diksjɔnɛr] *nm* dictionary

**dicton** [diktɔ̃] *nm* saying, dictum

**dièse** [djɛz] *nm* sharp

**diesel** [djezɛl] *nm* diesel ♦ *adj inv* diesel

**diète** [djɛt] *nf* (*jeûne*) starvation diet; (*régime*) diet; **diététique** *adj*: **magasin diététique** health food shop

**dieu, x** [djø] *nm* god; **D~** God; **mon D~!** good heavens!

**diffamation** [difamasjɔ̃] *nf* slander; (*écrite*) libel

**différé** [difere] *nm* (*TV*): **en ~** (pre-)

recorded

**différemment** [diferamã] *adv* differently

**différence** [diferãs] *nf* difference; **à la ~ de** unlike; **différencier** *vt* to differentiate; **différend** *nm* difference (of opinion), disagreement

**différent, e** [diferã, ãt] *adj* (*dissemblable*) different; **~ de** different from; (*divers*) different, various

**différer** [difere] *vt* to postpone, put off ♦ *vi*: **~ (de)** to differ (from)

**difficile** [difisil] *adj* difficult; (*exigeant*) hard to please; **difficilement** *adv* with difficulty

**difficulté** [difikylte] *nf* difficulty; **en ~** (*bateau, alpiniste*) in difficulties

**difforme** [difɔrm] *adj* deformed, misshapen

**diffuser** [difyze] *vt* (*chaleur*) to diffuse; (*émission, musique*) to broadcast; (*nouvelle*) to circulate; (*COMM*) to distribute

**digérer** [diʒere] *vt* to digest; (*fam: accepter*) to stomach, put up with; **digestif** *nm* (after-dinner) liqueur; **digestion** *nf* digestion

**digne** [diɲ] *adj* dignified; **~ de** worthy of; **~ de foi** trustworthy; **dignité** *nf* dignity

**digue** [dig] *nf* dike, dyke

**dilapider** [dilapide] *vt* to squander

**dilemme** [dilɛm] *nm* dilemma

**dilettante** [diletɑ̃t] *nm/f*: **faire qch en ~** to dabble in sth

**diligence** [diliʒɑ̃s] *nf* stagecoach

**diluer** [dilɥe] *vt* to dilute

**diluvien, ne** [dilyvjɛ̃, jɛn] *adj*: **pluie ~ne** torrential rain

**dimanche** [dimɑ̃ʃ] *nm* Sunday

**dimension** [dimɑ̃sjɔ̃] *nf* (*grandeur*) size; (~**s**) dimensions

**diminué, e** [diminɥe] *adj*: **il est très ~ depuis son accident** he's not at all the man he was since his accident

**diminuer** [diminɥe] *vt* to reduce, decrease; (*ardeur etc*) to lessen; (*dénigrer*) to belittle ♦ *vi* to decrease, diminish;

**diminutif** nm (surnom) pet name; **diminution** nf decreasing, diminishing

**dinde** [dɛ̃d] nf turkey

**dindon** [dɛ̃dɔ̃] nm turkey

**dîner** [dine] nm dinner ♦ vi to have dinner

**dingue** [dɛ̃g] (fam) adj crazy

**dinosaure** [dinɔzɔʀ] nm dinosaur

**diplomate** [diplɔmat] adj diplomatic ♦ nm diplomat; (fig) diplomatist; **diplomatie** nf diplomacy

**diplôme** [diplom] nm diploma; **avoir des ~s** to have qualifications; **diplômé, e** adj qualified

**dire** [diʀ] nm: **au ~ de** according to ♦ vt to say; (secret, mensonge, heure) to tell; **~ qch à qn** to tell sb sth; **~ à qn qu'il fasse** ou **de faire** to tell sb to do; **on dit que** they say that; **ceci dit** that being said; **si cela lui dit** (plaire) if he fancies it; **que dites-vous de** (penser) what do you think of; **on dirait que** it looks (ou sounds etc) as if; **dis/dites (donc)!** I say!

**direct, e** [diʀɛkt] adj direct ♦ nm (TV): **en ~** live; **directement** adv directly

**directeur, -trice** [diʀɛktœʀ, tʀis] nm/f (d'entreprise) director; (de service) manager(-eress); (d'école) head(teacher) (BRIT), principal (US)

**direction** [diʀɛksjɔ̃] nf (sens) direction; (d'entreprise) management; (AUTO) steering; **"toutes ~s"** "all routes"

**dirent** [diʀ] vb voir **dire**

**dirigeant, e** [diʀiʒɑ̃, ɑ̃t] adj (classe) ruling ♦ nm/f (d'un parti etc) leader

**diriger** [diʀiʒe] vt (entreprise) to manage, run; (véhicule) to steer; (orchestre) to conduct; (recherches, travaux) to supervise; **se ~** vi (s'orienter) to find one's way; **se ~ vers** ou **sur** to make ou head for

**dis** etc [di] vb voir **dire**

**discernement** [disɛʀnəmɑ̃] nm (bon sens) discernment, judgement

**discerner** [disɛʀne] vt to discern, make out

**discipline** [disiplin] nf discipline; **discipliner** vt to discipline

**discontinu, e** [diskɔ̃tiny] adj intermittent

**discontinuer** [diskɔ̃tinɥe] vi: **sans ~** without stopping, without a break

**discordant, e** [diskɔʀdɑ̃, ɑ̃t] adj discordant

**discothèque** [diskɔtek] nf (boîte de nuit) disco(thèque)

**discours** [diskuʀ] nm speech

**discret, -ète** [diskʀɛ, ɛt] adj discreet; (parfum, maquillage) unobtrusive; **discrétion** nf discretion; **à discrétion** as much as one wants

**discrimination** [diskʀiminasjɔ̃] nf discrimination; **sans ~** indiscriminately

**disculper** [diskylpe] vt to exonerate

**discussion** [diskysjɔ̃] nf discussion

**discutable** [diskytabl] adj debatable

**discuté, e** [diskyte] adj controversial

**discuter** [diskyte] vt (débattre) to discuss; (contester) to question, dispute ♦ vi to talk; (protester) to argue; **~ de** to discuss

**dise** etc [diz] vb voir **dire**

**diseuse** [dizøz] nf: **~ de bonne aventure** fortuneteller

**disgracieux, -euse** [disgʀasjø, jøz] adj ungainly, awkward

**disjoindre** [disʒwɛ̃dʀ] vt to take apart; **se ~** to come apart

**disjoncteur** [disʒɔ̃ktœʀ] nm (ÉLEC) circuit breaker

**disloquer** [dislɔke]: **se ~** vi (parti, empire) to break up

**disons** [dizɔ̃] vb voir **dire**

**disparaître** [dispaʀɛtʀ] vi to disappear; (se perdre: traditions etc) to die out; **faire ~** (tache) to remove; (douleur) to get rid of

**disparition** [dispaʀisjɔ̃] nf disappearance; **espèce en voie de ~** endangered species

**disparu, e** [dispaʀy] nm/f missing person ♦ adj: **être porté ~** to be reported missing

**dispensaire** [dispɑ̃sɛʀ] nm community clinic

**dispenser** [dispɑ̃se] vt: ~ qn de to exempt sb from; **se ~ de** vt (corvée) to get out of

**disperser** [dispɛʀse] vt to scatter; **se ~** vi to break up

**disponibilité** [disponibilite] nf availability; **disponible** adj available

**dispos** [dispo] adj m: (**frais**) ~ fresh (as a daisy)

**disposé, e** [dispoze] adj: **bien/mal ~** (humeur) in a good/bad mood; ~ **à** (prêt à) willing ou prepared to

**disposer** [dispoze] vt to arrange ♦ vi: **vous pouvez ~** you may leave; ~ **de** to have (at one's disposal); **se ~ à faire** to prepare to do, be about to do

**dispositif** [dispozitif] nm device; (fig) system, plan of action

**disposition** [dispozisjɔ̃] nf (arrangement) arrangement, layout; (humeur) mood; **dispositions** nfpl to make arrangements; **avoir des ~s pour la musique** etc to have a special aptitude for music etc; **à la ~ de qn** at sb's disposal; **je suis à votre ~** I am at your service

**disproportionné, e** [dispʀɔpɔʀsjɔne] adj disproportionate, out of all proportion

**dispute** [dispyt] nf quarrel, argument; **disputer** vt (match) to play; (combat) to fight; **se disputer** vi to quarrel

**disquaire** [diskɛʀ] nm/f record dealer

**disqualifier** [diskalifje] vt to disqualify

**disque** [disk] nm (MUS) record; (forme, pièce) disc; (SPORT) discus; ~ **compact** compact disc; ~ **dur** hard disk; **disquette** nf floppy disk, diskette

**disséminer** [disemine] vt to scatter

**disséquer** [diseke] vt to dissect

**dissertation** [disɛʀtasjɔ̃] nf (SCOL) essay

**dissimuler** [disimyle] vt to conceal

**dissipé, e** [disipe] adj (élève) undisciplined, unruly

**dissiper** [disipe] vt to dissipate; (for-

tune) to squander; **se ~** vi (brouillard) to clear, disperse

**dissolvant** [disɔlvɑ̃] nm nail polish remover

**dissonant, e** [disɔnɑ̃, ɑ̃t] adj discordant

**dissoudre** [disudʀ] vt to dissolve; **se ~** vi to dissolve

**dissuader** [disɥade] vt: ~ **qn de faire** to dissuade sb from doing; **dissuasion** nf: **force de dissuasion** deterrent power

**distance** [distɑ̃s] nf distance; (fig: écart) gap; **à ~** at ou from a distance; **distancer** vt to outdistance

**distant, e** [distɑ̃, ɑ̃t] adj (réservé) distant; ~ **de** (lieu) far away from

**distendre** [distɑ̃dʀ]: **se ~** vi to distend

**distillerie** [distilʀi] nf distillery

**distinct, e** [distɛ̃(kt), ɛ̃kt] adj distinct; **distinctement** adv distinctly, clearly; **distinctif, -ive** adj distinctive

**distingué, e** [distɛ̃ge] adj distinguished

**distinguer** [distɛ̃ge] vt to distinguish

**distraction** [distʀaksjɔ̃] nf (inattention) absent-mindedness; (passe-temps) distraction, entertainment

**distraire** [distʀɛʀ] vt (divertir) to entertain, divert; (déranger) to distract; **se ~** vi to amuse ou enjoy o.s.; **distrait, e** adj absent-minded

**distrayant, e** [distʀɛjɑ̃, ɑ̃t] adj entertaining

**distribuer** [distʀibɥe] vt to distribute, hand out; (CARTES) to deal (out); (courrier) to deliver; **distributeur** (COMM) distributor; (automatique) (vending) machine; (: de billets) (cash) dispenser; **distribution** nf distribution; (postale) delivery; (choix d'acteurs) casting, cast

**dit, e** [di, dit] pp de **dire** ♦ adj (fixé): **le jour ~** the arranged day; (surnommé): **X, ~ Pierrot** X, known as Pierrot

**dites** [dit] vb voir **dire**

**divaguer** [divage] vi to ramble; (fam) to rave

**divan** [divɑ̃] nm divan

**diverger** [divɛʀʒe] vi to diverge

**divers, e** [divɛʀ, ɛʀs] adj (varié) diverse, varied; (différent) different, various; **~es personnes** various ou several people

**diversifier** [divɛʀsifje] vt to vary

**diversité** [divɛʀsite] nf (variété) diversity

**divertir** [divɛʀtiʀ]: **se ~** vi to amuse ou enjoy o.s.; **divertissement** nm distraction, entertainment

**divin, e** [divɛ̃, in] adj divine

**diviser** [divize] vt to divide; **division** nf division

**divorce** [divɔʀs] nm divorce; **divorcé, e** nm/f divorcee; **divorcer** vi to get a divorce, get divorced

**divulguer** [divylge] vt to disclose

**dix** [dis] num ten; **dixième** num tenth

**dizaine** [dizɛn] nf: **une ~ (de)** about ten, ten or so

**do** [do] nm (note) C; (en chantant la gamme) do(h)

**docile** [dɔsil] adj docile

**dock** [dɔk] nm dock; **docker** nm docker

**docteur** [dɔktœʀ] nm doctor; **doctorat** nm doctorate; **doctoresse** nf lady doctor

**doctrine** [dɔktʀin] nf doctrine

**document** [dɔkymɑ̃] nm document; **documentaire** adj, nm documentary; **documentaliste** nm/f (SCOL) librarian; **documentation** nf documentation, literature; **documenter** vt: **se documenter (sur)** to gather information (on)

**dodo** [dodo] nm (langage enfantin): **aller faire ~** to go to beddy-byes

**dodu, e** [dɔdy] adj plump

**dogue** [dɔg] nm mastiff

**doigt** [dwa] nm finger; **à deux ~s de** within an inch of; **~ de pied** toe; **doigté** nm (MUS) fingering; (fig: habileté) diplomacy, tact

**doit** etc [dwa] vb voir **devoir**

**doléances** [dɔleɑ̃s] nfpl grievances

**dollar** [dɔlaʀ] nm dollar

**domaine** [dɔmɛn] nm estate, property; (fig) domain, field

**domestique** [dɔmɛstik] adj domestic; nm/f servant, domestic; **domestiquer** vt to domesticate

**domicile** [dɔmisil] nm home, place of residence; **à ~** at home; **livrer à ~** to deliver; **domicilié, e** adj: **"domicilié à ..." "address ..."**

**dominant, e** [dɔminɑ̃, ɑ̃t] adj (opinion) predominant

**dominer** [dɔmine] vt to dominate; (su: sujet) to master; (surpasser) to outclass, surpass; (surplomber) to tower above, dominate ♦ vi to be in the dominant position; **se ~** vi to control o.s.

**domino** [dɔmino] nm domino

**dommage** [dɔmaʒ] nm: **~s** (dégâts) damage no pl; **c'est ~!** what a shame; **c'est ~ que** it's a shame ou pity that; **dommages-intérêts** nmpl damages

**dompter** [dɔ̃(p)te] vt to tame; **dompteur, -euse** nm/f trainer

**DOM-TOM** [dɔmtɔm] sigle m (= départements et territoires d'outre-mer) French overseas departments and territories

**don** [dɔ̃] nm gift; (charité) donation; **avoir des ~s pour** to have a gift ou talent for; **elle a le ~ de m'énerver** she's got a knack of getting on my nerves

**donc** [dɔ̃k] conj therefore, so; (après une digression) so, then

**donjon** [dɔ̃ʒɔ̃] nm keep

**donné, e** [dɔne] adj (convenu: lieu, heure) given; (pas cher: bien): **c'est ~** it's a gift; **étant ~ ...** given ...; **données** nfpl data

**donner** [dɔne] vt to give; (vieux habits etc) to give away; (spectacle) to put on; **~ qch à qn** to give sb sth, give sth to sb; **~ sur** (suj: fenêtre, chambre) to look (out) onto; **ça donne soif/faim** it makes you (feel) thirsty/hungry; **se ~** à fond to give one's all; **se donner du mal** to take (great) trouble; **s'en ~ à cœur**

joie (fam) to have a great time

**MOT-CLÉ**

**dont** [dɔ̃] pron relatif 1 (appartenance: objets) whose, of which; (appartenance: êtres animés) whose; **la maison dont le toit est rouge** the house the roof of which is red, the house whose roof is red; **l'homme dont je connais la sœur** the man whose sister I know

2 (parmi lesquel(le)s): **2 livres, dont l'un est ...** 2 books, one of which is ...; **il y avait plusieurs personnes, dont Gabrielle** there were several people, among them Gabrielle; **10 blessés, dont 2 grièvement** 10 injured, 2 of them seriously

3 (complément d'adjectif, de verbe): **le fils dont il est si fier** the son he's so proud of; **ce dont je parle** what I'm talking about

**doré, e** [dɔʀe] adj golden; (avec dorure) gilt, gilded

**dorénavant** [dɔʀenavɑ̃] adv henceforth

**dorer** [dɔʀe] vt to gild; (faire) ~ (CULIN) to brown

**dorloter** [dɔʀlɔte] vt to pamper

**dormir** [dɔʀmiʀ] vi to sleep; (être endormi) to be asleep

**dortoir** [dɔʀtwaʀ] nm dormitory

**dorure** [dɔʀyʀ] nf gilding

**dos** [do] nm back; (de livre) spine; **"voir au ~"** "see over"; **de ~** from the back

**dosage** [dozaʒ] nm mixture

**dose** [doz] nf dose; **doser** vt to measure out; **il faut savoir doser ses efforts** you have to be able to pace yourself

**dossard** [dosaʀ] nm number (worn by competitor)

**dossier** [dosje] nm (documents) file; (de chaise) back; (PRESSE) feature; **un ~ scolaire** a school report

**dot** [dɔt] nf dowry

**doter** [dɔte] vt: ~ **de** to equip with

**douane** [dwan] nf customs pl; **douanier, -ière** adj customs cpd ♦ nm customs officer

**double** [dubl] adj, adv double ♦ nm (2 fois plus): **le** ~ **(de)** twice as much (ou many) (as); (autre exemplaire) duplicate, copy; (sosie) double; (TENNIS) doubles sg; **en** ~ **(exemplaire)** in duplicate; **faire** ~ **emploi** to be redundant

**double-cliquer** [dublklike] vi (INFORM) to double-click

**doubler** [duble] vt (multiplier par 2) to double; (vêtement) to line; (dépasser) to overtake, pass; (film) to dub; (acteur) to stand in for ♦ vi to double

**doublure** [dublyʀ] nf lining; (CINÉMA) stand-in

**douce** [dus] adj voir **doux**; **douceâtre** adj sickly sweet; **doucement** adv gently; (lentement) slowly; **doucereux, -euse** (péj) adj sugary; **douceur** nf softness; (de quelqu'un) gentleness; (de climat) mildness

**douche** [duʃ] nf shower; **doucher: se doucher** vi to have ou take a shower

**doudoune** [dudun] nf padded jacket

**doué, e** [dwe] adj gifted, talented; **être** ~ **pour** to have a gift for

**douille** [duj] nf (ÉLEC) socket

**douillet, te** [duje, et] adj cosy; (péj: à la douleur) soft

**douleur** [dulœʀ] nf pain; (chagrin) grief, distress; **douloureux, -euse** adj painful

**doute** [dut] nm doubt; **sans** ~ no doubt; (probablement) probably; **sans aucun** ~ without a doubt; **douter** vt to doubt; **douter de** (sincérité de qn) to have (one's) doubts about; (réussite) to be doubtful of; **se douter de qch/que** to suspect sth/that; **je m'en doutais** I suspected as much; **douteux, -euse** adj (incertain) doubtful; (péj) dubious-looking

**Douvres** [duvʀ] n Dover

**doux, douce** [du, dus] adj soft; (sucré) sweet; (peu fort: moutarde, clément: cli-

mat) mild; (pas brusque) gentle
**douzaine** [duzɛn] nf (12) dozen; (environ 12): **une ~ (de)** a dozen or so
**douze** [duz] num twelve; **douzième** num twelfth
**doyen, ne** [dwajɛ̃, jɛn] nm/f (en âge) most senior member; (de faculté) dean
**dragée** [draʒe] nf sugared almond
**dragon** [dragɔ̃] nm dragon
**draguer** [drage] vt (rivière) to dredge; (fam) to try to pick up
**dramatique** [dramatik] adj dramatic; (tragique) tragic ♦ nf (TV) (television) drama
**dramaturge** [dramatyrʒ] nm dramatist, playwright
**drame** [dram] nm drama
**drap** [dra] nm (de lit) sheet; (tissu) woollen fabric
**drapeau, x** [drapo] nm flag
**drap-housse** [draus] nm fitted sheet
**dresser** [drese] vt (mettre vertical, monter) to put up, erect; (liste) to draw up; (animal) to train; **se ~** vi (obstacle) to stand; (personne) to draw s. o. up; **~ qn contre qn** to set sb against sb; **~ l'oreille** to prick up one's ears
**drogue** [drɔg] nf drug; **la ~** drugs pl; **drogué, e** nm/f drug addict; **droguer** vt (victime) to drug; **se droguer** vi (aux stupéfiants) to take drugs; (péj: de médicaments) to dose o. s. up; **droguerie** nf hardware shop; **droguiste** nm keeper/ owner of a hardware shop
**droit, e** [drwa, drwat] adj (non courbe) straight; (vertical) upright, straight; (fig: loyal) upright, straight(forward); (opposé à gauche) right, right-hand ♦ adv straight ♦ nm (prérogative) right; (taxe) duty, tax; (: d'inscription) fee; (JUR): **le ~** law; (taxe) **le ~ de** to be allowed to; **avoir ~ à** to be entitled to; **être dans son ~** to be within one's rights; **à ~e** on the right; (direction) to the right; **~s d'auteur** royalties; **~s de l'homme** human rights; **~s d'inscription** enrolment fee; **droite** (nf POL): **la droite** the

right (wing); **droitier, -ière** nm right-handed person; **droiture** nf uprightness, straightness
**drôle** [drol] adj funny; **une ~ d'idée** funny idea; **drôlement** (fam) adv (très) terribly, awfully
**dromadaire** [drɔmadɛr] nm dromedary
**dru, e** [dry] adj (cheveux) thick, bushy; (pluie) heavy
**du** [dy] dét voir **de** ♦ prép +dét = **de + le**
**dû, due** [dy] vb voir **devoir** ♦ adj (somme) owing, owed; (causé par): **~ due to** ♦ nm due
**duc** [dyk] nm duke; **duchesse** nf duchess
**dûment** [dymã] adv duly
**dune** [dyn] nf dune
**Dunkerque** [dœ̃kɛrk] n Dunkirk
**duo** [dyo] nm (MUS) duet
**dupe** [dyp] nf dupe ♦ adj: **(ne pas) être ~ de** (not) to be taken in by
**duplex** [dyplɛks] nm (appartement) split-level apartment, duplex
**duplicata** [dyplikata] nm duplicate
**duquel** [dykɛl] prép +pron = **de +lequel**
**dur, e** [dyr] adj (pierre, siège, travail, problème) hard; (viande, climat) harsh; (sévère) hard, harsh; (cruel) hard-hearted); (porte, col) stiff; (viande) tough ♦ adv hard ♦ nm (fam: meneur) tough nut; **~ d'oreille** hard of hearing
**durant** [dyrã] prép (au cours de) during; (pendant) for; **des mois ~** for months
**durcir** [dyrsir] vt, vi to harden; **se ~** to harden
**durée** [dyre] nf length; (d'une pile etc) life; **de courte ~** (séjour) short
**durement** [dyrmã] adv harshly
**durer** [dyre] vi to last
**dureté** [dyrte] nf hardness; harshness, stiffness; toughness
**durit** ® [dyrit] nf (car radiator) hose
**dus** etc [dy] vb voir **devoir**
**duvet** [dyvɛ] nm down; (sac de couchage) down-filled sleeping bag

DVD *sigle m* (= digital versatile disc) DVD

**dynamique** [dinamik] *adj* dynamic; **dynamisme** *nm* dynamism

**dynamite** [dinamit] *nf* dynamite

**dynamo** [dinamo] *nf* dynamo

**dyslexie** [disleksi] *nf* dyslexia, word-blindness

# E, e

**eau, x** [o] *nf/pl* water; ~**x** *nfpl* (MÉD) waters; **prendre l'~** to leak, let in water; **tomber à l'~** (*fig*) to fall through; ~ **courante** running water; ~ **de Javel** bleach; ~ **de toilette** toilet water; ~ **douce** fresh water; ~ **gazeuse** sparkling (mineral) water; ~ **minérale** mineral water; ~ **plate** still water; ~ **potable** drinking water; **eau-de-vie** *nf* brandy; **eau-forte** *nf* etching

**ébahi, e** [ebai] *adj* dumbfounded

**ébattre** [ebatʀ]: **s'~** *vi* to frolic

**ébaucher** [eboʃe] *vt* to sketch out, outline; **s'~** *vi* to take shape

**ébène** [eben] *nf* ebony; **ébéniste** *nm* cabinetmaker

**éberlué, e** [ebɛʀlye] *adj* astounded

**éblouir** [ebluiʀ] *vt* to dazzle

**éborgner** [ebɔʀɲe] *vt* to blind in one eye

**éboueur** [ebwœʀ] *nm* dustman (BRIT), garbageman (US)

**ébouillanter** [ebujɑ̃te] *vt* to scald; (CULIN) to blanch

**éboulement** [ebulmɑ̃] *nm* rock fall

**ébouler** [ebule]: **s'~** *vi* to crumble, collapse; **éboulis** *nmpl* fallen rocks

**ébouriffé, e** [eburife] *adj* tousled

**ébranler** [ebʀɑ̃le] *vt* to shake; (*affaiblir*) to weaken; **s'~** *vi* (*partir*) to move off

**ébrécher** [ebʀeʃe] *vt* to chip

**ébriété** [ebʀijete] *nf*: **en état d'~** in a state of intoxication

**ébrouer** [ebʀue]: **s'~** *vi* to shake o.s.

**ébruiter** [ebʀuite] *vt* to spread, disclose

**ébullition** [ebylisjɔ̃] *nf* boiling point

**écaille** [ekɑj] *nf* (*de poisson*) scale; (*matière*) tortoiseshell; **écailler** *vt* (*poisson*) to scale; **s'écailler** *vi* to flake *ou* peel (off)

**écarlate** [ekaʀlat] *adj* scarlet

**écarquiller** [ekaʀkije] *vt*: ~ **les yeux** to stare wide-eyed

**écart** [ekaʀ] *nm* gap; **à l'~** out of the way; **à l'~ de** away from; **faire un ~** (*voiture*) to swerve; ~ **de conduite** misdemeanour

**écarté, e** [ekaʀte] *adj* (*lieu*) out-of-the-way, remote; (*ouvert*): **les jambes ~es** legs apart; **les bras ~s** arms outstretched

**écarter** [ekaʀte] *vt* (*séparer*) to move apart, separate; (*éloigner*) to push back, move away; (*ouvrir: bras, jambes*) to spread, open; (: *rideau*) to draw (back); (*éliminer: candidat, possibilité*) to dismiss; **s'~** *vi* to part; (*s'éloigner*) to move away; **s'~ de** to wander from

**écervelé, e** [esɛʀvəle] *adj* scatterbrained, featherbrained

**échafaud** [eʃafo] *nm* scaffold

**échafaudage** [eʃafodaʒ] *nm* scaffolding

**échafauder** [eʃafode] *vt* (*plan*) to construct

**échalote** [eʃalɔt] *nf* shallot

**échancrure** [eʃɑ̃kʀyʀ] *nf* (*de robe*) scoop neckline

**échange** [eʃɑ̃ʒ] *nm* exchange; **en ~ de** in exchange *ou* return for; **échanger** *vt*: **échanger qch (contre)** to exchange sth (for); **échangeur** *nm* (AUTO) interchange

**échantillon** [eʃɑ̃tijɔ̃] *nm* sample

**échappement** [eʃapmɑ̃] *nm* (AUTO) exhaust

**échapper** [eʃape]: ~ **à** *vt* (*gardien*) to escape (from); (*punition, péril*) to escape; **s'~** *vi* to escape; ~ **à qn** (*détail, sens*) to escape sb; (*objet qu'on tient*) to slip out of sb's hands; **laisser** ~ (*cri etc*) to let out; **l'~ belle** to have a narrow escape

**écharde** [eʃaʀd] *nf* splinter (of wood)

**écharpe** [eʃaʀp] *nf* scarf; **avoir le bras en ~** to have one's arm in a sling

**échasse** [eʃas] *nf* stilt

**échassier** [eʃasje] *nm* wader

**échauffer** [eʃofe] *vt* (*moteur*) to overheat; **s'~** *vi* (SPORT) to warm up; (*dans la discussion*) to become heated

**échéance** [eʃeɑ̃s] *nf* (*d'un paiement*: *date*) settlement date; (*fig*) deadline; **à brève ~** in the short term; **à longue ~** in the long run

**échéant** [eʃeɑ̃]: **le cas ~** *adv* if the case arises

**échec** [eʃɛk] *nm* failure; (ÉCHECS): **~ et mat/au roi** checkmate/check; **~s** *nmpl* (*jeu*) chess *sg*; **tenir en ~** to hold in check

**échelle** [eʃɛl] *nf* ladder; (*fig*, *d'une carte*) scale

**échelon** [eʃ(ə)lɔ̃] *nm* (*d'échelle*) rung; (ADMIN) grade; **échelonner** *vt* to space out

**échevelé, e** [eʃəv(ə)le] *adj* tousled, dishevelled

**échine** [eʃin] *nf* backbone, spine

**échiquier** [eʃikje] *nm* chessboard

**écho** [eko] *nm* echo; **échographie** *nf*: **passer une échographie** to have a scan

**échoir** [eʃwaʀ] *vi* (*dette*) to fall due; (*délais*) to expire; **~ à** to fall to

**échouer** [eʃwe] *vi* to fail; **s'~** *vi* to run aground

**échu, e** [eʃy] *pp de* **échoir**

**éclabousser** [eklabuse] *vt* to splash

**éclair** [eklɛʀ] *nm* (*d'orage*) flash of lightning, lightning *no pl*; (*gâteau*) éclair

**éclairage** [eklɛʀaʒ] *nm* lighting

**éclaircie** [eklɛʀsi] *nf* bright interval

**éclaircir** [eklɛʀsiʀ] *vt* to lighten; (*fig*: *mystère*) to clear up; (: *point*) to clarify; **s'~** *vi* (*ciel*) to clear; **s'~ la voix** to clear one's throat; **éclaircissement** *nm* (*sur un point*) clarification

**éclairer** [eklɛʀe] *vt* (*lieu*) to light (up);

(*personne*: *avec une lampe etc*) to light the way for; (*fig*: *problème*) to shed light on ♦ *vi*: **~: mal/bien** to give poor/good light; **s'~ à la bougie** to use candlelight

**éclaireur, -euse** [eklɛʀœʀ, øz] *nm* (*scout*) (boy) scout/(girl) guide ♦ *nm* (MIL) scout

**éclat** [ekla] *nm* (*de bombe, de verre*) fragment; (*du soleil, d'une couleur etc*) brightness, brilliance; (*d'une cérémonie*) splendour; (*scandale*): **faire un ~** t cause a commotion; **~s de voi** shouts; **~ de rire** roar of laughter

**éclatant, e** [eklatɑ̃, ɑ̃t] *adj* brilliant

**éclater** [eklate] *vi* (*pneu*) to burst (*bombe*) to explode; (*guerre*) to brea "out; (*groupe, parti*) to break up; **~ e sanglots/de rire** to burst ou sobbing/laughing

**éclipser** [eklipse]: **s'~** *vi* to slip away

**éclore** [eklɔʀ] *vi* (*œuf*) to hatch; (*fleu* to open (out)

**écluse** [eklyz] *nf* lock

**écœurant, e** [ekœʀɑ̃, ɑ̃t] *adj* (*gâtea etc*) sickly; (*fig*) sickening

**écœurer** [ekœʀe] *vt*: **~ qn** (*nourritur* to make sb feel sick; (*conduite, pe sonne*) to disgust sb

**école** [ekɔl] *nf* school; **aller à l'~** to g to school; **~ maternelle/primair** nursery/primary school; **~ publiqu** state school; **écolier, -ière** *nm* schoolboy(-girl)

---

**école maternelle**

*Nursery school (l'école maternelle) is publicly funded in France and, though not compulsory, is attended b most children between the ages of tw and six. Statutory education begins with primary school (l'école primaire) from the age of six to ten or eleven.*

---

**écologie** [ekɔlɔʒi] *nf* ecology; **écolog que** *adj* environment-friendly; **écolc**

**giste** nm/f ecologist

**éconduire** [ekɔ̃dɥiʀ] vt to dismiss

**économe** [ekɔnɔm] adj thrifty ♦ nm/f (de lycée etc) bursar (BRIT), treasurer (US)

**économie** [ekɔnɔmi] nf economy; (gain: d'argent, de temps etc) saving; (science) economics sg; **~s** nfpl (pécule) savings; **économique** adj (avantageux) economical; (ÉCON) economic; **économiser** vt, vi to save; **économiseur** nm: **économiseur d'écran** screen saver

**écoper** [ekɔpe] vi to bale out; **~ de 3 ans de prison** (fig: fam) to get sentenced to 3 years

**écorce** [ekɔʀs] nf bark; (de fruit) peel

**écorcher** [ekɔʀʃe] vt: **s'~ le genou/la main** to graze one's knee/one's hand; **écorchure** nf graze

**écossais, e** [ekɔsɛ, ɛz] adj Scottish ♦ nm/f: **É~, e** Scot

**Écosse** [ekɔs] nf: **l'~** Scotland

**écosser** [ekɔse] vt to shell

**écoulement** [ekulmɑ̃] nm (d'eau) flow

**écouler** [ekule] vt (marchandise) to sell; **s'~** vi (eau) to flow (out); (jours, temps) to pass (by)

**écourter** [ekuʀte] vt to curtail, cut short

**écoute** [ekut] nf (RADIO, TV): **temps/heure d'~** listening (ou viewing) time/hour; **rester à l'~ (de)** to stay tuned in (to); **~s téléphoniques** phone tapping sg

**écouter** [ekute] vt to listen to; **écouteur** nm (TÉL) receiver; (RADIO) headphones pl, headset

**écoutille** [ekutij] nf hatch

**écran** [ekʀɑ̃] nm screen; **petit ~** television; **~ total** sunblock

**écrasant, e** [ekʀazɑ̃, ɑ̃t] adj overwhelming

**écraser** [ekʀaze] vt to crush; (piéton) to run over; **s'~** vi to crash; **s'~ contre** to crash into

**écrémé, e** [ekʀeme] adj (lait) skimmed

**écrevisse** [ekʀəvis] nf crayfish inv

**écrier** [ekʀije]: **s'~** vi to exclaim

**écrin** [ekʀɛ̃] nm case, box

**écrire** [ekʀiʀ] vt to write; **s'~** to write to each other; **ça s'écrit comment?** how is it spelt? **écrit** nm (examen) written paper; **par écrit** in writing

**écriteau, x** [ekʀito] nm notice, sign

**écriture** [ekʀityʀ] nf writing; **l'É~, les É~s** the Scriptures

**écrivain** [ekʀivɛ̃] nm writer

**écrou** [ekʀu] nm nut

**écrouer** [ekʀue] vt to imprison

**écrouler** [ekʀule]: **s'~** vi to collapse

**écru, e** [ekʀy] adj off-white, écru

**ECU** [eky] sigle m ECU

**écueil** [ekœj] nm reef; (fig) pitfall

**éculé, e** [ekyle] adj (chaussure) down-at-heel; (fig: péj) hackneyed

**écume** [ekym] nf foam; **écumer** (CULIN) to skim; **écumoire** nf skimmer

**écureuil** [ekyʀœj] nm squirrel

**écurie** [ekyʀi] nf stable

**écusson** [ekysɔ̃] nm badge

**écuyer, -ère** [ekɥije, jɛʀ] nm/f rider

**eczéma** [ɛgzema] nm eczema

**édenté, e** [edɑ̃te] adj toothless

**EDF** sigle f (= Électricité de France) national electricity company

**édifice** [edifis] nm edifice, building

**édifier** [edifje] vt to build, erect; (fig) to edify

**Édimbourg** [edɛ̃buʀ] n Edinburgh

**éditer** [edite] vt (publier) to publish; (annoter) to edit; **éditeur, -trice** nm/f publisher; **édition** nf edition; (industrie du livre) publishing

**édredon** [edʀadɔ̃] nm eiderdown

**éducateur, -trice** [edykatœʀ, tʀis] nm/f teacher; (in special school) instructor

**éducatif, -ive** [edykatif, iv] adj educational

**éducation** [edykasjɔ̃] nf education; (familiale) upbringing; (manières) (good) manners pl; **~ physique** physical education

**édulcorant** [edylkɔʀɑ̃] nm sweetener

**éduquer** [edyke] vt to educate; (élever)

to bring up

**effacé, e** [efase] adj unassuming

**effacer** [efase] vt to erase, rub out; **s'~** vi (inscription etc) to wear off; (pour laisser passer) to step aside

**effarant, e** [efarɑ̃, ɑ̃t] adj alarming

**effarer** [efare] vt to alarm

**effaroucher** [efaruʃe] vt to frighten ou scare away

**effectif, -ive** [efɛktif, iv] adj real ♦ nm (SCOL) (pupil) numbers pl; (entreprise) staff, workforce; **effectivement** adv (réellement) actually, really; (en effet) indeed

**effectuer** [efɛktɥe] vt (opération) to carry out; (trajet) to make

**efféminé, e** [efemine] adj effeminate

**effervescent, e** [efɛrvesɑ̃, ɑ̃t] adj effervescent

**effet** [efɛ] nm effect; (impression) impression; **~s** nmpl (vêtements etc) things; **faire ~** (médicament) to take effect; **faire bon/mauvais ~ sur qn** to make a good/bad impression on sb; **en ~** indeed; **~ de serre** greenhouse effect

**efficace** [efikas] adj (personne) efficient; (action, médicament) effective; **efficacité** nf efficiency; effectiveness

**effilocher** [efilɔʃe]: **s'~** vi to fray

**efflanqué, e** [eflɑ̃ke] adj emaciated

**effleurer** [eflœre] vt to brush (against); (sujet) to touch upon; (suj: idée, pensée): **ça ne m'a pas effleuré** it didn't cross my mind

**effluves** [eflyv] nmpl exhalation(s)

**effondrer** [efɔ̃dre]: **s'~** vi to collapse

**efforcer** [efɔrse]: **s'~ de** vt: **s'~ de faire** to try hard to do

**effort** [efɔr] nm effort

**effraction** [efraksjɔ̃] nf: **s'introduire par ~ dans** to break into

**effrayant, e** [efrɛjɑ̃, ɑ̃t] adj frightening

**effrayer** [efrɛje] vt to frighten, scare

**effréné, e** [efrene] adj wild

**effriter** [efrite]: **s'~** vi to crumble

**effroi** [efrwa] nm terror, dread no pl

**effronté, e** [efrɔ̃te] adj cheeky

**effroyable** [efrwajabl] adj horrifying, appalling

**effusion** [efyzjɔ̃] nf effusion; **sans ~ de sang** without bloodshed

**égal, e, -aux** [egal, o] adj equal; (constant: vitesse) steady ♦ nm/f equal; **être ~ à** (prix, nombre) to be equal to; **ça lui est ~** it's all the same to him, he doesn't mind; **sans ~** matchless, unequalled; **d'~ à ~** as equals; **également** adv equally; (aussi) too, as well

**égaler** vt to equal; **égaliser** vt (sol, salaires) to level (out); (chances) to equalize ♦ vi (SPORT) to equalize; **égalité** nf equality; **être à égalité** to be level

**égard** [egar] nm: **~s** consideration sg; **cet ~** in this respect; **par ~ pour** out of consideration for; **à l'~ de** towards

**égarement** [egarmɑ̃] nm distraction

**égarer** [egare] vt to mislay; **s'~** vi to get lost, lose one's way; (objet) to go astray

**égayer** [egeje] vt to cheer up; (pièce) to brighten up

**églantine** [eglɑ̃tin] nf wild ou dog rose

**églefin** [egləfɛ̃] nm haddock

**église** [egliz] nf church; **aller à l'~** to go to church

**égoïsme** [egɔism] nm selfishness

**égoïste** [egɔist] adj selfish

**égorger** [egɔrʒe] vt to cut the throat of

**égosiller** [egozije]: **s'~** vi to shout o.s. hoarse

**égout** [egu] nm sewer

**égoutter** [egute] vt to drip; **s'~** vi to drip; **égouttoir** nm draining board; (mobile) draining rack

**égratigner** [egratine] vt to scratch; **égratignure** nf scratch

**Égypte** [eʒipt] nf: **l'~** Egypt; **égyptien, ne** adj Egyptian ♦ nm/f: **Égyptien, ne** Egyptian

**eh** [e] excl hey!; **~ bien** well

**éhonté, e** [eɔ̃te] adj shameless, brazen

**jecter** [ʒɛkte] vt (TECH) to eject; (fam) to kick ou chuck out

**laborer** [elabɔʀe] vt to elaborate; (projet, stratégie) to work out; (rapport) to draft

**lan** [elɑ̃] nm (ZOOL) elk, moose; (SPORT) run up; (fig: de tendresse etc) surge; **prendre de l'~** to gather speed

**lancé, e** [elɑ̃se] adj slender

**lancement** [elɑ̃smɑ̃] nm shooting pain

**lancer** [elɑ̃se]: **s'~** vi to dash, rush o.s.

**largir** [elaʀʒiʀ] vt to widen; **s'~** vi to widen; (vêtement) to stretch

**lastique** [elastik] adj elastic ♦ nm (de bureau) rubber band; (pour la couture) elastic no pl

**lecteur, -trice** [elɛktœʀ, tʀis] nm/f elector, voter

**lection** [elɛksjɔ̃] nf election

**lectorat** [elɛktɔʀa] nm electorate

**lectricien, ne** [elɛktʀisjɛ̃, jɛn] nm/f electrician

**lectricité** [elɛktʀisite] nf electricity; **allumer/éteindre l'~** to put on/off the light

**lectrique** [elɛktʀik] adj electric(al)

**lectrocuter** [elɛktʀɔkyte] vt to electrocute

**lectroménager** [elɛktʀomenaʒe] adj, nm: **appareils ~s, l'~** domestic (electrical) appliances

**lectronique** [elɛktʀɔnik] adj electronic ♦ nf electronics sg

**lectrophone** [elɛktʀɔfɔn] nm record player

**légance** [elegɑ̃s] nf elegance

**légant, e** [elegɑ̃, ɑ̃t] adj elegant

**lément** [elemɑ̃] nm element; (pièce) component, part; **~s de cuisine** kitchen units; **élémentaire** adj elementary

**léphant** [elefɑ̃] nm elephant

**levage** [el(ə)vaʒ] nm breeding; (de bovins) cattle rearing; **truite d'~** farmed trout

**élévation** [elevasjɔ̃] nf (hausse) rise

**élevé, e** [el(ə)ve] adj high; **bien/mal ~** well-/ill-mannered

**élève** [elɛv] nm/f pupil

**élever** [el(ə)ve] vt (enfant) to bring up, raise; (animaux) to breed; (hausser: taux, niveau) to raise; (édifier: monument) to put up, erect; **s'~** vi (avion) to go up; (niveau, température) to rise; **s'~ à** (suj: frais, dégâts) to amount to, add up to; **s'~ contre qch** to rise up against sth; **~ la voix** to raise one's voice; **éleveur, -euse** nm/f breeder

**élimé, e** [elime] adj threadbare

**éliminatoire** [eliminatwaʀ] nf (SPORT) heat

**éliminer** [elimine] vt to eliminate

**élire** [eliʀ] vt to elect

**elle** [ɛl] pron (sujet) she; (: chose) it; (complément) her; it; **~s** (sujet) they; (complément) them; **~-même** herself; itself; **~s-mêmes** themselves; voir aussi **il**

**élocution** [elɔkysjɔ̃] nf delivery; **défaut d'~** speech impediment

**éloge** [elɔʒ] nm (gén no pl) praise; **faire l'~ de** to praise; **élogieux, -euse** adj laudatory, full of praise

**éloigné, e** [elwaɲe] adj distant, far-off; (parent) distant; **éloignement** nm (distance, aussi fig) distance

**éloigner** [elwaɲe] vt (échéance) to put off, postpone; (soupçons, danger) to ward off; (objet): **~ qch (de)** to move ou take sth away (from); (personne): **~ qn (de)** to take sb away ou remove sb (from); **s'~ (de)** (personne) to go away (from); (véhicule) to move away (from); (affectivement) to become estranged (from); **ne vous éloignez pas!** don't go far away!

**élu, e** [ely] pp de **élire** ♦ nm/f (POL) elected representative

**éluder** [elyde] vt to evade

**Élysée** [elize] nm: **(le palais de) l'~** the Élysée Palace (the French president's residence)

**émacié, e** [emasje] adj emaciated

**émail, -aux** [emaj, o] nm enamel

**e-mail** [imel] nm e-mail; **envoyer qch par ~** to e-mail sth

**émaillé, e** [emaje] adj (fig): **~ de** dotted with

**émanciper** [emɑ̃sipe] vt (fig) to become emancipated ou liberated

**émaner** [emane]: **~ de** vt to come from

**emballage** [ɑ̃balaʒ] nm (papier) wrapping; (boîte) packaging

**emballer** [ɑ̃bale] vt to wrap (up); (dans un carton) to pack (up); (fig: fam) to thrill to bits; **s'~** vi (moteur) to race; (cheval) to bolt; (fig: personne) to get carried away

**embarcadère** [ɑ̃baʀkadɛʀ] nm wharf, pier

**embarcation** [ɑ̃baʀkasjɔ̃] nf (small) boat, (small) craft inv

**embardée** [ɑ̃baʀde] nf: **faire une ~** to swerve

**embarquement** [ɑ̃baʀkəmɑ̃] nm (de passagers) boarding; (de marchandises) loading

**embarquer** [ɑ̃baʀke] vt (personne) to embark; (marchandise) to load; (fam) to cart off ♦ vi (passager) to board; **s'~** vi to board; **s'~ dans** (affaire, aventure) to embark upon

**embarras** [ɑ̃baʀa] nm (gêne) embarrassment; **mettre qn dans l'~** to put sb in an awkward position; **vous n'avez que l'~ du choix** the only problem is choosing

**embarrassant, e** [ɑ̃baʀasɑ̃, ɑ̃t] adj embarrassing

**embarrasser** [ɑ̃baʀase] vt (encombrer) to clutter (up); (gêner) to hinder, hamper; **~ qn** to put sb in an awkward position; **s'~ de** to burden o.s. with

**embauche** [ɑ̃boʃ] nf hiring; **embaucher** vt to take on, hire

**embaumer** [ɑ̃bome] vt: **~ la lavande** etc to be fragrant with lavender etc

**embellie** [ɑ̃beli] nf brighter period

**embellir** [ɑ̃beliʀ] vt to make more attractive; (une histoire) to embellish ♦ vi to grow lovelier ou more attractive

**embêtements** [ɑ̃betmɑ̃] nmpl trouble sg

**embêter** [ɑ̃bete] vt to bother; **s'~** (s'ennuyer) to be bored

**emblée** [ɑ̃ble]: **d'~** adv straightaway

**embobiner** [ɑ̃bɔbine] vt (fam) to get round

**emboîter** [ɑ̃bwate] vt to fit together; **s'~ (dans)** to fit (into); **~ le pas à qn** to follow in sb's footsteps

**embonpoint** [ɑ̃bɔ̃pwɛ̃] nm stoutness

**embouchure** [ɑ̃buʃyʀ] nf (Géo) mouth

**embourber** [ɑ̃buʀbe]: **s'~** vi to get stuck in the mud

**embourgeoiser** [ɑ̃buʀʒwaze]: **s'~** to become middle-class

**embouteillage** [ɑ̃butejaʒ] nm traffic jam

**emboutir** [ɑ̃butiʀ] vt (heurter) to crash into, ram

**embranchement** [ɑ̃bʀɑ̃ʃmɑ̃] nm (routier) junction

**embraser** [ɑ̃bʀaze]: **s'~** vi to flare up

**embrassades** [ɑ̃bʀasad] nfpl hugging and kissing

**embrasser** [ɑ̃bʀase] vt to kiss; (sujet, période) to embrace, encompass; **s'~** to kiss (each other)

**embrasure** [ɑ̃bʀazyʀ] nf: **dans l'~ de la porte** in the door(way)

**embrayage** [ɑ̃bʀejaʒ] nm clutch

**embrayer** [ɑ̃bʀeje] vi (Auto) to let in the clutch

**embrocher** [ɑ̃bʀɔʃe] vt to put on a spit

**embrouiller** [ɑ̃bʀuje] vt to muddle up; (fils) to tangle (up); **s'~** vi (personne) to get into a muddle

**embruns** [ɑ̃bʀɛ̃] nmpl sea spray sg

**embûches** [ɑ̃byʃ] nfpl pitfalls, traps

**embué, e** [ɑ̃bɥe] adj misted up

**embuscade** [ɑ̃byskad] nf ambush

**éméché, e** [emeʃe] adj tipsy, merry

**émeraude** [em(ə)ʀod] nf emerald

**émerger** [emɛʀʒe] vt to emerge; (fair

*saillie, aussi fig*) to stand out

**méri** [em(ə)ʀi] nm: **toile** *ou* **papier ~** emery paper

**merveillement** [emɛʀvɛjmɑ̃] nm wonder

**merveiller** [emɛʀveje] vt to fill with wonder; **s'~ de** to marvel at

**mettre** [emetʀ] vt (*son, lumière*) to give out, emit; (*message etc*: RADIO) to transmit; (*billet, timbre, emprunt*) to issue; (*hypothèse, avis*) to voice, put forward ♦ vi to broadcast

**meus** *etc* [emø] vb voir **émouvoir**

**meute** [emøt] nf riot

**mietter** [emjete] vt to crumble

**migrer** [emigʀe] vi to emigrate

**mincer** [emɛ̃se] vt to cut into thin slices

**minent, e** [eminɑ̃, ɑ̃t] adj distinguished

**mission** [emisjɔ̃] nf (RADIO, TV) programme, broadcast; (*d'un message*) transmission; (*de timbre*) issue

**mmagasiner** [emagazine] vt (*amasser*) to store up

**mmanchure** [emɑ̃ʃyʀ] nf armhole

**mmêler** [emele] vt to tangle (up); (*fig*) to muddle up; **s'~** to get in a tangle

**mménager** [emenaʒe] vi to move in; **~ dans** to move into

**mmener** [em(ə)ne] vt to take (with one); (*comme otage, capture*) to take away; **~ qn au cinéma** to take sb to the cinema

**mmerder** [emɛʀde] (*fam!*) vt to bug, bother; **s'~** vi to be bored stiff

**mmitoufler** [emitufle]: **s'~** vi to wrap up (warmly)

**moi** [emwa] nm commotion

**motif, -ive** [emɔtif, -iv] adj emotional

**motion** [emɔsjɔ̃] nf emotion

**mousser** [emuse] vt to blunt; (*fig*) to dull

**mouvoir** [emuvwaʀ] vt to move; **s'~** vi to be moved; (*s'indigner*) to be roused

**empailler** [ɑ̃paje] vt to stuff

**empaqueter** [ɑ̃pakte] vt to parcel up

**emparer** [ɑ̃paʀe]: **s'~ de** vt (*objet*) to seize, grab; (*comme otage*, MIL) to seize; (*suj: peur etc*) to take hold of

**empâter** [ɑ̃pɑte]: **s'~** vi to thicken out

**empêchement** [ɑ̃pɛʃmɑ̃] nm (*unexpected*) obstacle, hitch

**empêcher** [ɑ̃peʃe] vt to prevent; **~ qn de faire** to prevent *ou* stop sb (from) doing; **il n'empêche que** nevertheless; **il n'a pas pu s'~ de rire** he couldn't help laughing

**empereur** [ɑ̃pʀœʀ] nm emperor

**empester** [ɑ̃pɛste] vi to stink, reek

**empêtrer** [ɑ̃petʀe] vt: **s'~ dans** (*fils etc*) to get tangled up in

**emphase** [ɑ̃faz] nf pomposity, bombast

**empiéter** [ɑ̃pjete] vi: **~ sur** to encroach upon

**empiffrer** [ɑ̃pifʀe]: **s'~** (*fam*) vi to stuff o.s.

**empiler** [ɑ̃pile] vt to pile (up)

**empire** [ɑ̃piʀ] nm empire; (*fig*) influence

**empirer** [ɑ̃piʀe] vi to worsen, deteriorate

**emplacement** [ɑ̃plasmɑ̃] nm site

**emplettes** [ɑ̃plɛt] nfpl shopping sg

**emplir** [ɑ̃pliʀ] vt to fill; **s'~ (de)** to fill (with)

**emploi** [ɑ̃plwa] nm use; (COMM, ÉCON) employment; (*poste*) job, situation; **mode d'~** directions for use; **~ du temps** timetable, schedule

**employé, e** [ɑ̃plwaje] nm/f employee; **~ de bureau** office employee *ou* clerk

**employer** [ɑ̃plwaje] vt to use; (*ouvrier, main-d'œuvre*) to employ; **s'~ à faire** to apply ou devote o.s. to doing; **employeur, -euse** nm/f employer

**empocher** [ɑ̃pɔʃe] vt to pocket

**empoigner** [ɑ̃pwaɲe] vt to grab

**empoisonner** [ɑ̃pwazɔne] vt to poison; (*empester: air, pièce*) to stink out; (*fam*): **~ qn** to drive sb mad

**emporté, e** [ɑ̃pɔʀte] *adj* quick-tempered

**emporter** [ɑ̃pɔʀte] *vt* to take (with one); (*en dérobant ou enlevant, emmener: blessés, voyageurs*) to take away; (*entraîner*) to carry away; **s'~** *vi* (*de colère*) to lose one's temper; **l'~ (sur)** to get the upper hand (of); **plats à ~** take-away meals

**empreint, e** [ɑ̃pʀɛ̃, ɛ̃t] *adj:* **~ de** (*regret, jalousie*) marked with; **empreinte** *nf:* **empreinte (de pas)** footprint; **empreinte (digitale)** fingerprint

**empressé, e** [ɑ̃pʀese] *adj* attentive

**empressement** [ɑ̃pʀesmɑ̃] *nm* (*hâte*) eagerness

**empresser** [ɑ̃pʀese]: **s'~** *vi:* **s'~ auprès de qn** to surround sb with attentions; **s'~ de faire** (*se hâter*) to hasten to do

**emprise** [ɑ̃pʀiz] *nf* hold, ascendancy

**emprisonnement** [ɑ̃pʀizɔnmɑ̃] *nm* imprisonment

**emprisonner** [ɑ̃pʀizɔne] *vt* to imprison

**emprunt** [ɑ̃pʀœ̃] *nm* loan

**emprunté, e** [ɑ̃pʀœ̃te] *adj* (*fig*) ill-at-ease, awkward

**emprunter** [ɑ̃pʀœ̃te] *vt* to borrow; (*itinéraire*) to take, follow

**ému, e** [emy] *pp* de **émouvoir** ♦ *adj* (*gratitude*) touched; (*compassion*) moved

---

*MOT-CLÉ*

**en** [ɑ̃] *prép* 1 (*endroit, pays*) in; (*direction*) to; **habiter en France/ville** to live in France/town; **aller en France/ville** to go to France/town

2 (*moment, temps*) in; **en été/juin** in summer/June

3 (*moyen*) by; **en avion/taxi** by plane/taxi

4 (*composition*) made of; **c'est en verre** it's (made of) glass; **un collier en argent** a silver necklace

5 (*description, état*): **une femme (ha-**

**billée) en rouge** a woman (dressed) red; **peindre qch en rouge** to paint sth red; **en T/étoile** T/star-shaped; **en chemise/chaussettes** in one's shir sleeves/socks; **en soldat** as a soldie **cassé en plusieurs morceaux** broke into several pieces; **en réparatio** being repaired, under repair; **en v** **cances** on holiday; **en deuil** in mourn ing; **le même en plus grand** the sam but ou only bigger

6 (*avec gérondif*) while, on, by; **en do mant** while sleeping, as one sleeps; **e** **sortant** on going out, as he *etc* wen out; **sortir en courant** to run out

♦ *pron* 1 (*indéfini*): **j'en ai/veux** I have want some; **en as-tu?** have you got any?; **je n'en veux pas** I don't wan any; **j'en ai 2** I've got 2; **combien en a-t-il?** how many (of them) a there?; **j'en ai assez** I've got enoug (of it *ou* them); (*j'en ai marre*) I've ha enough

2 (*provenance*) from there; **j'en vien** I've come from there

3 (*cause*): **il en est malade/perd l** **sommeil** he is ill/can't sleep becaus of it

4 (*complément de nom, d'adjectif, d* *verbe*): **j'en connais les dangers** know its *ou* the dangers; **j'en sui** **fier/ai besoin** I am proud of it/need i

---

**ENA** *sigle f* (= École Nationale d'Administration) *one of the Grandes École*

**encadrement** [ɑ̃kadʀamɑ̃] *nm* (*cadre* managerial staff

**encadrer** [ɑ̃kadʀe] *vt* (*tableau, imag* to frame; (*fig: entourer*) to surroun (*personnel, soldats etc*) to train

**encaissé, e** [ɑ̃kese] *adj* (*vallée*) steep sided; (*rivière*) with steep banks

**encaisser** [ɑ̃kese] *vt* (*chèque*) to cash (*argent*) to collect; (*fam: coup, défait* to take

**encart** [ɑ̃kaʀ] *nm* insert

**en-cas** [ɑ̃kɑ] *nm* snack

**encastré, e** [ãkastʀe] *adj*: **four ~** built-in oven

**enceinte** [ãsɛ̃t] *adj f*: **~ (de 6 mois)** (6 months) pregnant ♦ *nf (mur)* wall; *(espace)* enclosure; *(aussi: ~ acoustique)* (loud)speaker

**encens** [ãsã] *nm* incense

**encercler** [ãsɛʀkle] *vt* to surround

**enchaîner** [ãʃene] *vt* to chain up; *(mouvements, séquences)* to link *(together)* ♦ *vi* to carry on

**enchanté, e** [ãʃãte] *adj (ravi)* delighted; *(magique)* enchanted; **~ (de faire votre connaissance)** pleased to meet you

**enchantement** [ãʃãtmã] *nm* delight; *(magie)* enchantment

**enchère** [ãʃɛʀ] *nf* bid; **mettre/vendre aux ~s** to put up for (sale by)/sell by auction

**enchevêtrer** [ãʃ(ə)vetʀe]: **s'~** *vi* to get in a tangle

**enclencher** [ãklãʃe] *vt (mécanisme)* to engage; **s'~** *vi* to engage

**enclin, e** [ãklɛ̃, in] *adj*: **~ à** inclined ou prone to

**enclos** [ãklo] *nm* enclosure

**enclume** [ãklym] *nf* anvil

**encoche** [ãkɔʃ] *nf* notch

**encoignure** [ãkɔɲyʀ] *nf* corner

**encolure** [ãkɔlyʀ] *nf (cou)* neck

**encombrant, e** [ãkɔ̃bʀã, ãt] *adj* cumbersome, bulky

**encombre** [ãkɔ̃bʀ]: **sans ~** *adv* without mishap *ou* incident; **encombrement** *nm*: **être pris dans un encombrement** to be stuck in a traffic jam

**encombrer** [ãkɔ̃bʀe] *vt* to clutter (up); *(gêner)* to hamper; **s'~ de** *(bagages etc)* to load *ou* burden o.s. with

**encontre** [ãkɔ̃tʀ]: **à l'~ de** *prép* against, counter to

MOT-CLÉ

**encore** [ãkɔʀ] *adv* **1** *(continuation)* still; **il y travaille encore** he's still working on it; **pas encore** not yet

**2** *(de nouveau)* again; **j'irai encore demain** I'll go again tomorrow; **encore une fois** (once) again; **encore deux jours** two more days

**3** *(intensif)* even, still; **encore plus fort/mieux** even louder/better, louder/better still

**4** *(restriction)* even so *ou* then, only; **encore pourrais-je le faire si ...** even so, I might be able to do it if ...; **si encore** if only

**encore que** *conj* although

**encouragement** [ãkuʀaʒmã] *nm* encouragement

**encourager** [ãkuʀaʒe] *vt* to encourage

**encourir** [ãkuʀiʀ] *vt* to incur

**encrasser** [ãkʀase] *vt* to make filthy

**encre** [ãkʀ] *nf* ink; **encrier** *nm* inkwell

**encroûter** [ãkʀute]: **s'~** *(fam)* vi *(fig)* to get into a rut, get set in one's ways

**encyclopédie** [ãsiklɔpedi] *nf* encyclopaedia

**endetter** [ãdete]: **s'~** *vi* to get into debt

**endiablé, e** [ãdjable] *adj (danse)* furious

**endimanché, e** [ãdimãʃe] *adj* in one's Sunday best

**endive** [ãdiv] *nf* chicory *no pl*

**endoctriner** [ãdɔktʀine] *vt* to indoctrinate

**endommager** [ãdɔmaʒe] *vt* to damage

**endormi, e** [ãdɔʀmi] *adj* asleep

**endormir** [ãdɔʀmiʀ] *vt (pour faire* to put to sleep; *(suj: chaleur etc)* to send to sleep; *(MÉD: dent, nerf)* to anaesthetize; *(fig: soupçons)* to allay; **s'~** *vi* to fall asleep, go to sleep

**endosser** [ãdose] *vt (responsabilité)* to take, shoulder; *(chèque)* to endorse; *(uniforme, tenue)* to put on

**endroit** [ãdʀwa] *nm* place; *(opposé à l'envers)* right side; **à l'~** *(vêtement)* the right way out; *(objet posé)* the right way round

**enduire** [ɑ̃dɥiʀ] vt to coat
**enduit** [ɑ̃dɥi] nm coating
**endurance** [ɑ̃dyʀɑ̃s] nf endurance
**endurant, e** [ɑ̃dyʀɑ̃, ɑ̃t] adj tough, hardy
**endurcir** [ɑ̃dyʀsiʀ]: **s'~** vi (physiquement) to become tougher; (moralement) to become hardened
**endurer** [ɑ̃dyʀe] vt to endure, bear
**énergétique** [enɛʀʒetik] adj (aliment) energy-giving
**énergie** [enɛʀʒi] nf (PHYSIQUE) energy; (TECH) power; (morale) vigour, spirit; **énergique** adj energetic, vigorous; (mesures) drastic, stringent
**énervant, e** [enɛʀvɑ̃, ɑ̃t] adj irritating, annoying
**énerver** [enɛʀve] vt to irritate, annoy; **s'~** vi to get excited, get worked up
**enfance** [ɑ̃fɑ̃s] nf childhood
**enfant** [ɑ̃fɑ̃] nm/f child; **~ de chœur ♦** nm (REL) altar boy; **enfantillage** (péj) nm childish behaviour no pl; **enfantin, e** adj (puéril) childlike; (langage, jeu etc) children's cpd
**enfer** [ɑ̃fɛʀ] nm hell
**enfermer** [ɑ̃fɛʀme] vt to shut up; (à clef, interner) to lock up
**enfiévré, e** [ɑ̃fjevʀe] adj feverish
**enfiler** [ɑ̃file] vt (vêtement) to slip on, slip into; (perles) to string; (aiguille) to thread
**enfin** [ɑ̃fɛ̃] adv at last; (en énumérant) lastly; (toutefois) still; (pour conclure) in a word; (somme toute) after all
**enflammer** [ɑ̃flame]: **s'~** vi to catch fire; (MÉD) to become inflamed
**enflé, e** [ɑ̃fle] adj swollen
**enfler** [ɑ̃fle] vi to swell (up)
**enfoncer** [ɑ̃fɔ̃se] vt (clou) to drive in; (faire pénétrer): **~ qch dans** to push (ou drive) sth into; (forcer: porte) to break open; **s'~** vi to sink; **s'~ dans** to sink into; (forêt, ville) to disappear into
**enfouir** [ɑ̃fwiʀ] vt (dans le sol) to bury; (dans un tiroir etc) to tuck away
**enfourcher** [ɑ̃fuʀʃe] vt to mount

**enfreindre** [ɑ̃fʀɛ̃dʀ] vt to infringe, break
**enfuir** [ɑ̃fɥiʀ]: **s'~** vi to run away ou off
**enfumer** [ɑ̃fyme] vt (pièce) to fill with smoke
**engageant, e** [ɑ̃gaʒɑ̃, ɑ̃t] adj attractive, appealing
**engagement** [ɑ̃gaʒmɑ̃] nm commitment
**engager** [ɑ̃gaʒe] vt (embaucher) to take on; (: artiste) to engage; (commencer) to start; (lier) to bind, commit; (impliquer) to involve; (investir) to invest, lay out; (inciter) to urge; (introduire: clé) to insert; **s'~** vi (promettre) to commit o.s.; (MIL) to enlist; **s'~ à faire** to undertake to do; **s'~ dans** (rue, passage) to turn into; (fig: affaire, discussion) to enter into, embark on
**engelures** [ɑ̃ʒlyʀ] nfpl chilblains
**engendrer** [ɑ̃ʒɑ̃dʀe] vt to breed, create
**engin** [ɑ̃ʒɛ̃] nm machine; (outil) instrument; (AUT) vehicle; (AVIAT) aircraft inv
**englober** [ɑ̃glɔbe] vt to include
**engloutir** [ɑ̃glutiʀ] vt to swallow up
**engoncé, e** [ɑ̃gɔ̃se] adj: **~ dans** cramped in
**engorger** [ɑ̃gɔʀʒe] vt to obstruct, block
**engouement** [ɑ̃gumɑ̃] nm (sudden) passion
**engouffrer** [ɑ̃gufʀe] vt to swallow up, devour; **s'~ dans** to rush into
**engourdir** [ɑ̃guʀdiʀ] vt to numb; (fig) to dull, blunt; **s'~** vi to go numb
**engrais** [ɑ̃gʀɛ] nm manure; **~ (chimique)** (chemical) fertilizer
**engraisser** [ɑ̃gʀese] vt to fatten (up)
**engrenage** [ɑ̃gʀənaʒ] nm gears pl, gearing; (fig) chain
**engueuler** [ɑ̃gœle] (fam) vt to bawl at
**enhardir** [ɑ̃aʀdiʀ]: **s'~** vi to grow bolder
**énigme** [enigm] nf riddle
**enivrer** [ɑ̃nivʀe]: **s'~** vi to get drunk
**enjambée** [ɑ̃ʒɑ̃be] nf stride

**enjamber** [ɑ̃ʒɑ̃be] *vt* to stride over

**enjeu, x** [ɑ̃ʒø] *nm* stakes *pl*

**enjôler** [ɑ̃ʒole] *vt* to coax, wheedle

**enjoliver** [ɑ̃ʒɔlive] *vt* to embellish; **enjoliveur** *nm* (AUTO) hub cap

**enjoué, e** [ɑ̃ʒwe] *adj* playful

**enlacer** [ɑ̃lase] *vt* (étreindre) to embrace, hug

**enlaidir** [ɑ̃lediʀ] *vt* to make ugly ♦ *vi* to become ugly

**enlèvement** [ɑ̃lɛvmɑ̃] *nm* (rapt) abduction, kidnapping

**enlever** [ɑ̃l(ə)ve] *vt* (ôter: gén) to remove; (: vêtement, lunettes) to take off; (emporter: ordures etc) to take away; (kidnapper) to abduct, kidnap; (obtenir: prix, contrat) to win; (prendre): **~ qch à qn** to take sth (away) from sb

**enliser** [ɑ̃lize]: **s'~** *vi* to sink, get stuck

**enneigé, e** [ɑ̃neʒe] *adj* (route, maison) snowed-up; (paysage) snowy

**ennemi, e** [ɛnmi] *adj* hostile; (MIL) enemy *cpd* ♦ *nm/f* enemy

**ennui** [ɑ̃nɥi] *nm* (lassitude) boredom; (difficulté) trouble *no pl*; **avoir des ~s** to have problems; **ennuyer** *vt* to bother; (lasser) to bore; **s'ennuyer** to be bored; **ennuyeux, -euse** *adj* boring, tedious; (embêtant) annoying

**énoncé** [enɔ̃se] *nm* (de problème) terms *pl*

**énoncer** [enɔ̃se] *vt* (faits) to set out, state

**enorgueillir** [ɑ̃nɔʀgœjiʀ]: **s'~ de** *vt* to pride o.s. on

**énorme** [enɔʀm] *adj* enormous, huge; **énormément** *adv* enormously; **énormément de neige/gens** an enormous amount of snow/number of people; **énormité** *nf* (propos) outrageous remark

**enquérir** [ɑ̃keʀiʀ]: **s'~ de** *vt* to inquire about

**enquête** [ɑ̃kɛt] *nf* (de journaliste, de police) investigation; (judiciaire, administrative) inquiry; (sondage d'opinion) survey; **enquêter** *vi* to investigate

**enquiers** *etc* [ɑ̃kje] *vb voir* **enquérir**

**enquiquiner** [ɑ̃kikine] *(fam) vt* to annoy, irritate, bother

**enracine, e** [ɑ̃ʀasine] *adj* deep-rooted

**enragé, e** [ɑ̃ʀaʒe] *adj* (MÉD) rabid, with rabies; (fig) fanatical

**enrageant, e** [ɑ̃ʀaʒɑ̃, ɑ̃t] *adj* infuriating

**enrager** [ɑ̃ʀaʒe] *vi* to be in a rage

**enrayer** [ɑ̃ʀeje] *vt* to check, stop

**enregistrement** [ɑ̃ʀ(ə)ʒistʀəmɑ̃] *nm* recording; **~ des bagages** (à l'aéroport) baggage check-in

**enregistrer** [ɑ̃ʀ(ə)ʒistʀe] *vt* (MUS etc) to record; (fig: mémoriser) to make a mental note of; (bagages: à l'aéroport) to check in

**enrhumer** [ɑ̃ʀyme] *vt*: **s'~, être enrhumé** to catch a cold

**enrichir** [ɑ̃ʀiʃiʀ] *vt* to make rich(er); (fig) to enrich; **s'~** *vi* to get rich(er)

**enrober** [ɑ̃ʀɔbe] *vt*: **~ qch de** to coat sth with

**enrôler** [ɑ̃ʀole] *vt* to enlist; **s'~ (dans)** to enlist (in)

**enrouer** [ɑ̃ʀwe]: **s'~** *vi* to go hoarse

**enrouler** [ɑ̃ʀule] *vt* (fil, corde) to wind (up)

**ensanglanté, e** [ɑ̃sɑ̃glɑ̃te] *adj* covered with blood

**enseignant, e** [ɑ̃sɛɲɑ̃, ɑ̃t] *nm/f* teacher

**enseigne** [ɑ̃sɛɲ] *nf* sign; **~ lumineuse** neon sign

**enseignement** [ɑ̃sɛɲ(ə)mɑ̃] *nm* teaching; (ADMIN) education

**enseigner** [ɑ̃seɲe] *vt, vi* to teach; **~ qch à qn** to teach sb sth

**ensemble** [ɑ̃sɑ̃bl] *adv* together ♦ *nm* (groupement) set; (vêtements) outfit; (totalité): **l'~ du/de la** the whole *ou* entire; (unité, harmonie) unity; **impression/idée d'~** overall *ou* general impression/idea; **dans l'~** (en gros) on the whole

**ensemencer** [ɑ̃s(ə)mɑ̃se] *vt* to sow

**ensevelir** [ɑ̃səv(ə)liʀ] *vt* to bury

**ensoleillé, e** [ɑ̃sɔleje] *adj* sunny

**ensommeillé, e** [ɑ̃sɔmeje] *adj* drowsy

**ensorceler** [ɑ̃sɔrsəle] *vt* to enchant, bewitch

**ensuite** [ɑ̃sɥit] *adv* then, next; (*plus tard*) afterwards, later

**ensuivre** [ɑ̃sɥivr]: **s'~** *vi* to follow, ensue; **et tout ce qui s'ensuit** and all that goes with it

**entaille** [ɑ̃taj] *nf* cut; (*sur un objet*) notch

**entamer** [ɑ̃tame] *vt* (*pain, bouteille*) to start; (*hostilités, pourparlers*) to open

**entasser** [ɑ̃tase] *vt* (*empiler*) to pile up, heap up; **s'~** *vi* (*s'amonceler*) to pile up; **s'~ dans** (*personnes*) to cram into

**entendre** [ɑ̃tɑ̃dr] *vt* to hear; (*comprendre*) to understand; (*vouloir dire*) to mean; **s'~** *vi* (*sympathiser*) to get on; (*se mettre d'accord*) to agree; **j'ai entendu dire que** I've heard (it said) that

**entendu, e** [ɑ̃tɑ̃dy] *adj* (*réglé*) agreed; (*au courant: air*) knowing; (**c'est**) **~** all right, agreed; **bien ~** of course

**entente** [ɑ̃tɑ̃t] *nf* understanding; (*accord, traité*) agreement; **à double ~** (*sens*) with a double meaning

**entériner** [ɑ̃terine] *vt* to ratify, confirm

**enterrement** [ɑ̃tɛrmɑ̃] *nm* (*cérémonie*) funeral, burial

**enterrer** [ɑ̃tere] *vt* to bury

**entêtant, e** [ɑ̃tɛtɑ̃, ɑ̃t] *adj* heady

**en-tête** [ɑ̃tɛt] *nm* heading; **papier à ~** headed notepaper

**entêter** [ɑ̃tete]: **s'~** *vi*: **s'~ (à faire)** to persist (in doing)

**enthousiasme** [ɑ̃tuzjasm] *nm* enthusiasm; **enthousiasmer** *vt* to fill with enthusiasm; **s'enthousiasmer (pour qch)** to get enthusiastic (about sth); **enthousiaste** *adj* enthusiastic

**enticher** [ɑ̃tiʃe]: **s'~ de** *vt* to become infatuated with

**entier, -ère** [ɑ̃tje, jɛr] *adj* whole; (*total: satisfaction etc*) complete; (*fig: caractère*) unbending ♦ *nm* (*MATH*) whole; **en ~** totally; **lait ~** full-cream milk; **en-**

**tièrement** *adv* entirely, wholly

**entonner** [ɑ̃tɔne] *vt* (*chanson*) to strike

**entonnoir** [ɑ̃tɔnwar] *nm* funnel

**entorse** [ɑ̃tɔrs] *nf* (*MÉD*) sprain; (*fig*): **~ au règlement** infringement of the rule

**entortiller** [ɑ̃tɔrtije] *vt* (*enrouler*) to twist, wind; (*fam: cajoler*) to get round

**entourage** [ɑ̃turaʒ] *nm* circle; (*famille*) circle of family/friends; (*ce qui enclôt*) surround

**entourer** [ɑ̃ture] *vt* to surround; (*apporter son soutien à*) to rally round; **~ de** to surround with

**entracte** [ɑ̃trakt] *nm* interval

**entraide** [ɑ̃trɛd] *nf* mutual aid; **s'~r** *vi* to help each other

**entrain** [ɑ̃trɛ̃] *nm* spirit; **avec/sans ~** spiritedly/half-heartedly

**entraînement** [ɑ̃trɛnmɑ̃] *nm* training

**entraîner** [ɑ̃trɛne] *vt* (*charrier*) to carry ou drag along; (*TECH*) to drive; (*emmener: personne*) to take (off); (*influencer*) to lead; (*SPORT*) to train; (*impliquer*) to entail; **s'~** *vi* (*SPORT*) to train; **s'~ à qch/à faire** to train o.s. for sth/to do; **~ qn à faire** (*inciter*) to lead sb to do; **entraîneur, -euse** *nf* (*SPORT*) coach, trainer ♦ *nm* (*HIPPISME*) trainer

**entraver** [ɑ̃trave] *vt* (*action, progrès*) to hinder

**entre** [ɑ̃tr] *prép* between; (*parmi*) among(st); **l'un d'~ eux/nous** one of them/us; **~ eux** among(st) themselves; **entrebâillé, e** *adj* half-open, ajar; **entrechoquer: s'entrechoquer** *vi* to knock ou bang together; **entrecôte** *nf* entrecôte ou rib steak; **entrecouper**: **entrecouper qch de** to intersperse sth with; **entrecroiser: s'entrecroiser** to intertwine

**entrée** [ɑ̃tre] *nf* entrance; (*accès: au cinéma etc*) admission; (*billet*) (admission) ticket; (*CULIN*) first course

**entre...: entrefaites: sur ces entrefaites** *adv* at this juncture; **entrefilet** *nm* paragraph (*short article*); **entre-**

**bes** *nm* crotch; **entrelacer** *vt* to intertwine; **entremêler**: **s'entremêler** *vi* to become entangled; **entremets** *nm* (cream) dessert; **entremise** *nf* intervention; **par l'entremise de** through

**ntreposer** [ɑ̃trəpoze] *vt* to store, put into storage

**ntrepôt** [ɑ̃trəpo] *nm* warehouse

**ntreprenant, e** [ɑ̃trəprənɑ̃, ɑ̃t] *adj* (*actif*) enterprising; (*trop galant*) forward

**ntreprendre** [ɑ̃trəprɑ̃dr] *vt* (*se lancer dans*) to undertake; (*commencer*) to begin *ou* start (upon)

**ntrepreneur** [ɑ̃trəprənœr, øz] *nm*: **~ (en bâtiment)** (building) contractor

**ntreprise** [ɑ̃trəpriz] *nf* (*société*) firm, concern; (*action*) undertaking, venture

**ntrer** [ɑ̃tre] *vi* to go (*ou* come) in, enter ♦ *vt* (*INFORM*) to enter, input; (*faire*) **~ qch dans** to get sth into; **~ dans** (*gén*) to enter; (*pièce*) to go (*ou* come) into, enter; (*club*) to join; (*heurter*) to run into; **~ à l'hôpital** to go into hospital; **faire ~** (*visiteur*) to show in

**ntresol** [ɑ̃trəsɔl] *nm* mezzanine

**ntre-temps** [ɑ̃trətɑ̃] *adv* meanwhile

**ntretenir** [ɑ̃trət(ə)nir] *vt* to maintain; (*famille, maîtresse*) to support, keep; **~ qn (de)** to speak to sb (about)

**ntretien** [ɑ̃trətjɛ̃] *nm* maintenance; (*discussion*) discussion, talk; (*pour un emploi*) interview

**ntrevoir** [ɑ̃trəvwar] *vt* (*à peine*) to make out; (*brièvement*) to catch a glimpse of

**ntrevue** [ɑ̃trəvy] *nf* (*audience*) interview

**ntrouvert, e** [ɑ̃truver, ɛrt] *adj* half-open

**numérer** [enymere] *vt* to list

**nvahir** [ɑ̃vair] *vt* to invade; (*suj: inquiétude, peur*) to come over; **envahissant, e** (*péj*) *adj* (*personne*) intrusive

**nveloppe** [ɑ̃v(ə)lɔp] *nf* (*de lettre*) envelope; (*crédits*) budget; **envelopper** *vt* to wrap; (*fig*) to envelop, shroud

**envenimer** [ɑ̃v(ə)nime] *vt* to aggravate

**envergure** [ɑ̃vɛrgyr] *nf* (*fig*) scope; (*personne*) calibre

**enverrai** *etc* [ɑ̃vɛre] *vb voir* **envoyer**

**envers** [ɑ̃vɛr] *prép* towards, to ♦ *nm* other side; (*d'une étoffe*) wrong side; **à l'~** (*verticalement*) upside down; (*pull*) back to front; (*chaussettes*) inside out

**envie** [ɑ̃vi] *nf* (*sentiment*) envy; (*souhait*) desire, wish; **avoir ~ de** (*faire*) to feel like (doing); (*plus fort*) to want (to do); **avoir ~ que** to wish that; **cette glace me fait ~** I fancy some of that ice cream; **envier** *vt* to envy; **envieux, -euse** *adj* envious

**environ** [ɑ̃virɔ̃] *adv*: **~ 3 h/2 km** (around) about 3 o'clock/2 km; *voir aussi* **environs**

**environnant, e** [ɑ̃virɔnɑ̃, ɑ̃t] *adj* surrounding

**environnement** [ɑ̃virɔnmɑ̃] *nm* environment

**environs** [ɑ̃virɔ̃] *nmpl* surroundings; **aux ~ de** (round) about

**envisager** [ɑ̃vizaʒe] *vt* to contemplate, envisage; **~ de faire** to consider doing

**envoi** [ɑ̃vwa] *nm* (*paquet*) parcel, consignment; **coup d'~** (*SPORT*) kick-off

**envoler** [ɑ̃vɔle]: **s'~** *vi* (*oiseau*) to fly away *ou* off; (*avion*) to take off; (*papier, feuille*) to blow away; (*fig*) to vanish (into thin air)

**envoûter** [ɑ̃vute] *vt* to bewitch

**envoyé, e** [ɑ̃vwaje] *nm/f* (*POL*) envoy; (*PRESSE*) correspondent

**envoyer** [ɑ̃vwaje] *vt* to send; (*lancer*) to hurl, throw; **~ chercher** to send for; **~ promener qn** (*fam*) to send sb packing

**Éole** [eɔl] *sigle m* (= *est-ouest-liaison-express*) Paris high-speed, east-west subway service

**épagneul, e** [epaɲœl] *nm/f* spaniel

**épais, se** [epɛ, ɛs] *adj* thick; **épaisseur** *nf* thickness

**épancher** [epɑ̃ʃe]: **s'~** *vi* to open one's heart

**épanouir** [epanwir]: **s'~** *vi* (*fleur*) to

bloom, open out; (*visage*) to light up; (*personne*) to blossom

**épargne** [eparɲ] *nf* saving

**épargner** [eparɲe] *vt* to save; (*ne pas tuer ou endommager*) to spare ♦ *vi* to save; ~ **qch à qn** to spare sb sth

**éparpiller** [eparpije] *vt* to scatter; **s'~** *vi* to scatter; (*fig*) to dissipate one's efforts

**épars, e** [epar, ars] *adj* scattered

**épatant, e** [epatã, ãt] (*fam*) *adj* super

**épater** [epate] (*fam*) *vt* (*étonner*) to amaze; (*impressionner*) to impress

**épaule** [epol] *nf* shoulder

**épauler** [epole] *vt* (*aider*) to back up, support; (*arme*) to raise (to one's shoulder) ♦ *vi* to (take) aim

**épaulette** [epolɛt] *nf* (MIL) epaulette; (*rembourrage*) shoulder pad

**épave** [epav] *nf* wreck

**épée** [epe] *nf* sword

**épeler** [ep(ə)le] *vt* to spell

**éperdu, e** [eperdy] *adj* distraught, overcome; (*amour*) passionate

**éperon** [eprɔ̃] *nm* spur

**épervier** [epervje] *nm* sparrowhawk

**épi** [epi] *nm* (*de blé, d'orge*) ear; (*de maïs*) cob

**épice** [epis] *nf* spice

**épicé, e** [epise] *adj* spicy

**épicer** [epise] *vt* to spice

**épicerie** [episri] *nf* grocer's shop; (*denrées*) groceries *pl*; ~ **fine** delicatessen; **épicier, -ière** *nm/f* grocer

**épidémie** [epidemi] *nf* epidemic

**épiderme** [epidɛrm] *nm* skin

**épier** [epje] *vt* to spy on, watch closely

**épilepsie** [epilɛpsi] *nf* epilepsy

**épiler** [epile] *vt* (*jambes*) to remove the hair from; (*sourcils*) to pluck

**épilogue** [epilɔg] *nm* (*fig*) conclusion, dénouement; **épiloguer** *vi*: **épiloguer sur** to hold forth on

**épinards** [epinar] *nmpl* spinach *sg*

**épine** [epin] *nf* thorn, prickle; (*d'oursin etc*) spine; ~ **dorsale** backbone; **épineux, -euse** *adj* thorny

**épingle** [epɛ̃gl] *nf* pin; ~ **à cheveux** hairpin; ~ **de nourrice** *ou* **de sûreté** safety pin; **épingler** *vt* (*badge, décoration*): **épingler qch sur** to pin sth on(to); (*fam*) to catch, nick

**épisode** [epizɔd] *nm* episode; **film/roman à ~s** serial; **épisodique** *adj* occasional

**éploré, e** [eplɔre] *adj* tearful

**épluche-légumes** [eplyʃlegym] *nm inv* (potato) peeler

**éplucher** [eplyʃe] *vt* (*fruit, légumes*) to peel; (*fig*) to go over with a fine-tooth comb; **épluchures** *nfpl* peelings

**éponge** [epɔ̃ʒ] *nf* sponge; **éponger** (*liquide*) to mop up; (*surface*) to sponge; (*fig: déficit*) to soak up

**épopée** [epɔpe] *nf* epic

**époque** [epɔk] *nf* (*de l'histoire*) age, era; (*de l'année, la vie*) time; **d'~** (*meuble*) period *cpd*

**époumoner** [epumɔne]: **s'~** *vi* to shout o.s. hoarse

**épouse** [epuz] *nf* wife; **épouser** *vt* to marry

**épousseter** [epuste] *vt* to dust

**époustouflant, e** [epustuflã, ãt] (*fam*) *adj* staggering, mind-boggling

**épouvantable** [epuvãtabl] *adj* appalling, dreadful

**épouvantail** [epuvãtaj] *nm* scarecrow

**épouvante** [epuvãt] *nf* terror; **film d'~** horror film; **épouvanter** *vt* to terrify

**époux** [epu] *nm* husband ♦ *nmpl* (*married*) couple

**éprendre** [eprãdr]: **s'~ de** *vt* to fall in love with

**épreuve** [eprœv] *nf* (*d'examen*) test; (*malheur, difficulté*) trial, ordeal; (PHOTO) print; (TYPO) proof; (SPORT) event; **à toute ~** unfailing; **mettre à l'~** to put to the test

**épris, e** [epri, iz] *pp* de **éprendre**

**éprouvant, e** [epruvã, ãt] *adj* trying, testing

**éprouver** [epruve] *vt* (*tester*) to test;

_marquer, faire souffrir_) to afflict, distress; (_ressentir_) to experience

**prouvette** [epʀuvɛt] _nf_ test tube

**puisé, e** [epɥize] _adj_ exhausted; (_livre_) out of print; **épuisement** _nm_ exhaustion

**puiser** [epɥize] _vt_ (_fatiguer_) to exhaust, wear _ou_ tire out; (_stock, sujet_) to exhaust; **s'~** _vi_ to wear _ou_ tire o.s. out, exhaust o.s.

**puisette** [epɥizɛt] _nf_ shrimping net

**purer** [epyʀe] _vt_ (_liquide_) to purify; (_parti etc_) to purge

**quateur** [ekwatœʀ] _nm_ equator; (**la république de**) **l'É~** Ecuador

**quation** [ekwasjɔ̃] _nf_ equation

**querre** [ekɛʀ] _nf_ (_à dessin_) (set) square

**garder/perdre l'~** to keep/lose one's balance; **être en ~** to be balanced; **équilibré, e** _adj_ well-balanced; **équilibrer** _vt_ to balance; **s'équilibrer** _vi_ (_poids_) to balance; (_fig: défauts etc_) to balance each other out

**quipage** [ekipaʒ] _nm_ crew

**quipe** [ekip] _nf_ team

**quipé, e** [ekipe] _adj_: **bien/mal ~** well-poorly-equipped; **équipée** _nf_ escapade

**quipement** [ekipmɑ̃] _nm_ equipment; **~s** _nmpl_ (_installations_) amenities, facilities

**quiper** [ekipe] _vt_ to equip; **~ qn/qch de** to equip sb/sth with

**quipier, -ière** [ekipje, jɛʀ] _nm/f_ team member

**quitable** [ekitabl] _adj_ fair

**quitation** [ekitasjɔ̃] _nf_ (horse-)riding; **faire de l'~** to go riding

**quivalent, e** [ekivalɑ̃, ɑ̃t] _adj, nm_ equivalent

**quivaloir** [ekivalwaʀ]: **~ à** _vt_ to be equivalent to

**quivoque** [ekivɔk] _adj_ equivocal, ambiguous; (_louche_) dubious ♦ _nf_ (_incertitude_) doubt

**rable** [eʀabl] _nm_ maple

**érafler** [eʀafle] _vt_ to scratch; **éraflure** _nf_ scratch

**éraillé, e** [eʀaje] _adj_ (_voix_) rasping

**ère** [ɛʀ] _nf_ era; **en l'an 1050 de notre ~** in the year 1050 A.D.

**érection** [eʀɛksjɔ̃] _nf_ erection

**éreinter** [eʀɛ̃te] _vt_ to exhaust, wear out; (_critiquer_) to pull to pieces

**ériger** [eʀiʒe] _vt_ (_monument_) to erect

**ermite** [ɛʀmit] _nm_ hermit

**éroder** [eʀɔde] _vt_ to erode

**érotique** [eʀɔtik] _adj_ erotic

**errer** [eʀe] _vi_ to wander

**erreur** [eʀœʀ] _nf_ mistake, error; **faire ~** to be mistaken; **par ~** by mistake; **~ judiciaire** miscarriage of justice

**érudit, e** [eʀydi, it] _adj_ erudite, learned

**éruption** [eʀypsjɔ̃] _nf_ eruption; (_MÉD_) rash

**es** [ɛ] _vb voir_ **être**

**ès** [ɛs] _prép_: **licencié ~ lettres/sciences** ≃ Bachelor of Arts/Science

**escabeau, x** [ɛskabo] _nm_ (_tabouret_) stool; (_échelle_) stepladder

**escadron** [ɛskadʀɔ̃] _nm_ squadron

**escalade** [ɛskalad] _nf_ climbing _no pl_; (_POL etc_) escalation; **escalader** _vt_ to climb

**escale** [ɛskal] _nf_ (_NAVIG: durée_) call; (_endroit_) port of call; (_AVIAT_) stop(over); **faire ~ à** (_NAVIG_) to put in at; (_AVIAT_) to stop over at; **vol sans ~** nonstop flight

**escalier** [ɛskalje] _nm_ stairs _pl_; **dans l'~** on the stairs; **~ roulant** escalator

**escamoter** [ɛskamɔte] _vt_ (_esquiver_) to get round, evade; (_faire disparaître_) to conjure away

**escapade** [ɛskapad] _nf_: **faire une ~** to go on a jaunt; (_s'enfuir_) to run away _ou_ off

**escargot** [ɛskaʀgo] _nm_ snail

**escarpé, e** [ɛskaʀpe] _adj_ steep

**escarpin** [ɛskaʀpɛ̃] _nm_ low-fronted shoe, court shoe (_BRIT_)

**escient** [esjɑ̃] _nm_: **à bon ~** advisedly

**esclaffer** [ɛsklafe]: **s'~** _vi_ to guffaw

**esclandre** [esklɑ̃dʀ] nm scene, fracas

**esclavage** [esklavaʒ] nm slavery

**esclave** [esklav] nm/f slave

**escompte** [eskɔ̃t] nm discount; **escompter** vt (fig) to expect

**escorte** [eskɔʀt] nf escort; **escorter** vt to escort

**escrime** [eskʀim] nf fencing

**escrimer** [eskʀime]: **s'~** vi: **s'~ à faire** to wear o.s. out doing

**escroc** [eskʀo] nm swindler, conman;

**escroquer** [eskʀɔke] vt: **escroquer qch (à qn)** to swindle sth (out of sb); **escroquerie** nf swindle

**espace** [espas] nm space

**espacer** vt to space out; **s'~** vi (visites etc) to become less frequent

**espadon** [espadɔ̃] nm swordfish inv

**espadrille** [espadʀij] nf rope-soled sandal

**Espagne** [espaɲ] nf: **l'~** Spain; **espagnol, e** adj Spanish ♦ nm/f: **Espagnol, e** Spaniard ♦ nm (LING) Spanish

**escouade** [eskwad] nf squad

**espèce** [espɛs] nf (BIO, BOT, ZOOL) species inv; (gén: sorte) sort, kind, type; (péj): **~ de maladroit!** you clumsy oaf!; **~s** nfpl (COMM) cash sg; **en ~** in cash

**espérance** [espeʀɑ̃s] nf hope; **~ de vie** life expectancy

**espérer** [espeʀe] vt to hope for; **j'espère (bien)** I hope so; **~ que/faire** to hope that/to do

**espiègle** [espjɛgl] adj mischievous

**espion, ne** [espjɔ̃, jɔn] nm/f spy; **espionnage** nm espionage, spying; **espionner** vt to spy (up)on

**esplanade** [esplanad] nf esplanade

**espoir** [espwaʀ] nm hope

**esprit** [espʀi] nm (intellect) mind; (humour) wit; (mentalité, d'une loi etc, fantôme etc) spirit; **faire de l'~** to try to be witty; **reprendre ses ~s** to come to; **perdre l'~** to lose one's mind

**esquimau, de, x** [eskimo, od] adj Eskimo ♦ nm/f: **E~, de** Eskimo ♦ nm: **E~** ® ice lolly (BRIT), popsicle (US)

**esquinter** [eskɛ̃te] (fam) vt to mess up

**esquisse** [eskis] nf sketch; **esquisse** vt to sketch; **esquisser un sourire** give a vague smile

**esquiver** [eskive] vt to dodge; **s'~** to slip away

**essai** [ese] nm (tentative) attempt, try; (de produit) testing; (RUGBY) try; (LITTÉRATURE) essay; **~s** nmpl (AUTO) trials; **gratuit** (COMM) free trial; **à l'~** on trial basis

**essaim** [esɛ̃] nm swarm

**essayer** [eseje] vt to try; (vêtement, chaussures) to try (on); (méthode, voiture) to try (out) ♦ vi to try; **~ de faire** to try ou attempt to do

**essence** [esɑ̃s] nf (de voiture) petrol (BRIT), gas(oline) (US); (extrait de plante) essence; (espèce: d'arbre) species inv

**essentiel, le** [esɑ̃sjɛl] adj essentiel; **c'est l'~** (ce qui importe) that's the main thing; **l'~ de** the main part of

**essieu, x** [esjø] nm axle

**essor** [esɔʀ] nm (de l'économie etc) rapid expansion

**essorer** [esɔʀe] vt (en tordant) to wring (out); (par la force centrifuge) to spin dry; **essoreuse** nf spin-dryer

**essouffler** [esufle]: **s'~** to get out of breath

**essuie-glace** [esɥiglas] nm inv windscreen (BRIT) ou windshield (US) wiper

**essuyer** [esɥije] vt to wipe; (fig: échec) to suffer; **s'~** vi (après le bain) to dry o.s.; **~ la vaisselle** to dry up

**est¹** [ɛ] vb voir **être**

**est²** [ɛst] nm east ♦ adj inv east; (région) east(ern); **à l'~** in the east; (direction) to the east, east(wards); **à l'~ de** (to the) east of

**estampe** [estɑ̃p] nf print, engraving

**est-ce que** [ɛska] adv: **~ c'est cher/c'était bon?** is it expensive/was it good?; **quand est-ce qu'il part?** when does he leave?; **où est-ce qu'il part?,** when is he leaving voir aussi **que**

**esthéticienne** [estetisjɛn] nf beau

**cian**

**sthétique** [estetik] *adj* attractive

**stimation** [estimasjɔ̃] *nf* valuation; (*chiffre*) estimate

**stime** [estim] *nf* esteem, regard; **estimer** *vt* (*respecter*) to esteem; (*expertiser: bijou etc*) to value; (*évaluer: coût etc*) to assess, estimate; (*penser*): **estimer que/être** to consider that/o.s. to be

**stival, e, -aux** [estival, o] *adj* summer *cpd*

**stivant, e** [estivɑ̃, ɑ̃t] *nm/f* (summer) holiday-maker

**stomac** [estɔma] *nm* stomach

**stomaqué, e** [estɔmake] (*fam*) *adj* flabbergasted

**stomper** [estɔ̃pe]: **s'~** *vi* (*sentiments*) to soften; (*contour*) to become blurred

**strade** [estrad] *nf* platform, rostrum

**stragon** [estragɔ̃] *nm* tarragon

**stuaire** [estɥɛr] *nm* estuary

**et** [e] *conj* and; **~ lui?** what about him?; **~ alors!** so what!

**table** [etabl] *nf* cowshed

**tabli** [etabli] *nm* (work)bench

**tablir** [etablir] *vt* (*papiers d'identité, facture*) to make out; (*liste, programme*) to draw up; (*entreprise*) to set up; (*réputation, usage, fait, culpabilité*) to establish; **s'~** *vi* to be established; **s'~** (*à son compte*) to set up in business; **s'~ à/près de** to settle in/near

**tablissement** [etablismɑ̃] *nm* (*entreprise, institution*) establishment; **~ scolaire** school, educational establishment

**tage** [etaʒ] *nm* (*d'immeuble*) storey, floor; **à l'~** upstairs; **au 2ème ~** on the 2nd (*BRIT*) ou 3rd (*US*) floor

**tagère** [etaʒɛr] *nf* (*rayon*) shelf; (*meuble*) shelves *pl*

**tai** [etɛ] *nm* stay, prop

**tain** [etɛ̃] *nm* pewter *no pl*

**tais** *etc* [etɛ] *vb voir* **être**

**tal** [etal] *nm* stall

**talage** [etalaʒ] *nm* display; (*devanture*) display window; **faire ~ de** to show

off, parade

**étaler** [etale] *vt* (*carte, nappe*) to spread (out); (*peinture*) to spread; (*échelonner: paiements, vacances*) to spread, stagger; (*marchandises*) to display; (*connaissances*) to parade; **s'~** *vi* (*liquide*) to spread out; (*fam*) to fall flat on one's face; **s'~ sur** (*suj: paiements etc*) to be spread out over

**étalon** [etalɔ̃] *nm* (*cheval*) stallion

**étanche** [etɑ̃ʃ] *adj* (*récipient*) watertight; (*montre, vêtement*) waterproof; **étancher** *vt*: **étancher sa soif** to quench one's thirst

**étang** [etɑ̃] *nm* pond

**étant** [etɑ̃] *vb voir* **être; donné**

**étape** [etap] *nf* stage; (*lieu d'arrivée*) stopping place; (: *CYCLISME*) staging point

**état** [eta] *nm* (*POL, condition*) state; **en mauvais ~** in poor condition; **en ~ (de marche)** in (working) order; **remettre en ~** to repair; **hors d'~** out of order; **être en ~/hors d'~ de faire** to be in a/in no fit state to do; **être dans tous ses ~s** to be in a state; **faire ~ de** (*alléguer*) to put forward; **l'É~** the State; **~ civil** civil status; **~ des lieux** inventory of fixtures; **étatiser** *vt* to bring under state control; **état-major** (*MIL*) staff; **États-Unis** *nmpl*: **les États-Unis** the United States

**étau, x** [eto] *nm* vice (*BRIT*), vise (*US*)

**étayer** [eteje] *vt* to prop ou shore up

**etc.** [etsetera] *abr etc*

**et c(a)etera** [etsetera] *adv* et cetera, and so on

**été** [ete] *pp de* **être ♦** *nm* summer

**éteindre** [etɛ̃dr] *vt* (*lampe, lumière, radio*) to turn ou switch off; (*cigarette, feu*) to put out, extinguish; **s'~** *vi* (*feu, lumière*) to go out; (*mourir*) to pass away; **éteint, e** *adj* (*fig*) lacklustre, dull; (*volcan*) extinct

**étendard** [etɑ̃dar] *nm* standard

**étendre** [etɑ̃dr] *vt* (*pâte, liquide*) to spread; (*carte etc*) to spread out; (*linge*) to hang up; (*bras, jambes*) to stretch out; (*fig: agrandir*) to extend; **s'~** *vi* (*augmenter, se propager*) to spread; (*terrain, forêt etc*) to stretch; (*s'allonger*) to stretch out; (*se coucher*) to lie down; (*fig: expliquer*) to elaborate

**étendu, e** [etɑ̃dy] *adj* extensive; **étendue** *nf* (*d'eau, de sable*) stretch, expanse; (*importance*) extent

**éternel, le** [etɛʀnɛl] *adj* eternal

**éterniser** [etɛʀnize]: **s'~** *vi* to last for ages; (*visiteur*) to stay for ages

**éternité** [etɛʀnite] *nf* eternity; **ça a duré une ~** it lasted for ages

**éternuement** [etɛʀnymɑ̃] *nm* sneeze

**éternuer** [etɛʀnɥe] *vi* to sneeze

**êtes** [ɛt(z)] *vb voir* **être**

**éthique** [etik] *adj* ethical

**ethnie** [etni] *nf* ethnic group

**éthylisme** [etilism] *nm* alcoholism

**étiez** [etje] *vb voir* **être**

**étinceler** [etɛ̃s(ə)le] *vi* to sparkle

**étincelle** [etɛ̃sɛl] *nf* spark

**étiqueter** [etik(ə)te] *vt* to label

**étiquette** [etikɛt] *nf* label; (*protocole*): **l'~** etiquette

**étirer** [etiʀe]: **s'~** *vi* (*personne*) to stretch; (*convoi, route*): **s'~ sur** to stretch out over

**étoffe** [etɔf] *nf* material, fabric

**étoffer** [etɔfe] *vt* to fill out

**étoile** [etwal] *nf* star; **à la belle ~** in the open; **~ de mer** starfish; **~ filante** shooting star; **étoilé, e** *adj* starry

**étonnant, e** [etɔnɑ̃, ɑ̃t] *adj* amazing

**étonnement** [etɔnmɑ̃] *nm* surprise, amazement

**étonner** [etɔne] *vt* to surprise, amaze; **s'~ que/de** to be amazed that/at; **cela m'~ait (que)** (*j'en doute*) I'd be very surprised (if)

**étouffant, e** [etufɑ̃, ɑ̃t] *adj* stifling

**étouffée** [etufe]: **à l'~** *adv* (*CULIN: légumes*) steamed; (*: viande*) braised

**étouffer** [etufe] *vt* to suffocate; (*bruit*) to muffle; (*scandale*) to hush up ♦ *vi* to suffocate; **s'~** *vi* (*en mangeant etc*) to

choke; **on étouffe** it's stifling

**étourderie** [etuʀdəʀi] *nf* (*caractère*) absent-mindedness *no pl*; (*faute*) thoughtless blunder

**étourdi, e** [etuʀdi] *adj* (*distrait*) scatterbrained, heedless

**étourdir** [etuʀdiʀ] *vt* (*assommer*) to stun, daze; (*griser*) to make dizzy ♦; **étourdissement** *nm* dizzy spel

**étourneau, x** [etuʀno] *nm* starling

**étrange** [etʀɑ̃ʒ] *adj* strange

**étranger, ère** [etʀɑ̃ʒe, ɛʀ] *adj* foreign; (*pas de la famille, non familier*) strang ♦ *nm/f* foreigner; stranger ♦ *nm*: **à l'~** abroad

**étrangler** [etʀɑ̃gle] *vt* to strangle; **s'~** *vi* (*en mangeant etc*) to choke

<hr>

MOT-CLÉ

**être** [ɛtʀ] *nm* being; **être humain** human being

♦ *vb +attrib* **1** (*état, description*) to be; **est instituteur** he is *ou* he's a teacher; **vous êtes grand/intelligent/fatigué** you are *ou* you're tall/clever/tired

**2** (*+à: appartenir*) to be; **le livre est à Paul** the book is Paul's *ou* belongs to Paul; **c'est à moi/eux** it is *ou* it's mine/theirs

**3** (*+de: provenance*): **il est de Paris** he is from Paris; (*: appartenance*): **il est des nôtres** he is one of us

**4** (*date*): **nous sommes le 10 janvier** it's the 10th of January (today)

♦ *vi* to be; **je ne serai pas ici demain** I won't be here tomorrow

♦ *vb aux* **1** to have; to be; **être arrivé/allé** to have arrived/gone; **il est parti** he has left, he has gone

**2** (*forme passive*) to be; **être fait par** to be made by; **il a été promu** he has been promoted

**3** (*+à: obligation*): **c'est à réparer** it needs repairing; **c'est à essayer** it should be tried

♦ *vb impers* **1**: **il est** +*adjectif* it is +*adjective*; **il est impossible de le faire** it

impossible to do it
**2** (*heure, date*): **il est 10 heures, c'est
10 heures** it is *ou* it's 10 o'clock
**3** (*emphatique*): **c'est moi** it's me;
**c'est à lui de le faire** it's up to him to
do it

**étreindre** [etʀɛ̃dʀ] *vt* to clutch, grip;
(*amoureusement, amicalement*) to embrace; **s'~** *vi* to embrace
**étrenner** [etʀene] *vt* to use (*ou* wear)
for the first time; **étrennes** *nfpl* Christmas box *sg*
**étrier** [etʀije] *nm* stirrup
**étriqué, e** [etʀike] *adj* skimpy
**étroit, e** [etʀwa, wat] *adj* narrow;
(*vêtement*) tight; (*fig: liens, collaboration*) close; **à l'~** cramped; **~ d'esprit**
narrow-minded
**étude** [etyd] *nf* studying; (*ouvrage, rapport*) study; (*SCOL: salle de travail*) study
room; **~s** *nfpl* (*SCOL*) studies; **être à l'~**
(*projet etc*) to be under consideration;
**faire des ~s** (*de droit/médecine*) to
study (law/medicine)
**étudiant, e** [etydjã, jãt] *nm/f* student
**étudier** [etydje] *vt, vi* to study
**étui** [etɥi] *nm* case
**étuve** [etyv] *nf* steamroom
**étuvée** [etyve]: **à l'~** *adv* braised
**eu, eue** [y] *pp de* **avoir**
**euh** [ø] *excl* er
**euro** [øʀo] *nm* euro
**Euroland** [øʀolɑ̃d] *nm* Euroland
**Europe** [øʀɔp] *nf*: **l'~** Europe; **euro-
péen, ne** *adj* European ♦ *nm/f*: **Euro-
péen, ne** European
**eus** *etc* [y] *vb voir* **avoir**
**eux** [ø] *pron* (*sujet*) they; (*objet*) them
**évacuer** [evakɥe] *vt* to evacuate
**évader** [evade]: **s'~** *vi* to escape
**évaluer** [evalɥe] *vt* (*expertiser*) to ap-
praise, evaluate; (*juger approximativement*) to estimate
**évangile** [evãʒil] *nm* gospel
**évanouir** [evanwiʀ]: **s'~** *vi* to faint;
(*disparaître*) to vanish, disappear; **éva-**

**nouissement** *nm* (*syncope*) fainting fit
**évaporer** [evapɔʀe]: **s'~** *vi* to evaporate
**évasé, e** [evɑze] *adj* (*manches, jupe*)
flared
**évasif, -ive** [evazif, iv] *adj* evasive
**évasion** [evazjɔ̃] *nf* escape
**évêché** [eveʃe] *nm* bishop's palace
**éveil** [evɛj] *nm* awakening; **être en ~**
to be alert; **éveillé, e** *adj* awake; (*vif*)
alert, sharp; **éveiller** *vt* to (a)waken;
(*soupçons etc*) to arouse; **s'éveiller** *vi* to
(a)waken; (*fig*) to be aroused
**événement** [evɛnmã] *nm* event
**éventail** [evãtaj] *nm* fan; (*choix*) range
**éventaire** [evãtɛʀ] *nm* stall, stand
**éventer** [evãte] *vt* (*secret*) to uncover;
**s'~** *vi* (*parfum*) to go stale
**éventualité** [evãtɥalite] *nf* eventuality,
possibility; **dans l'~ de** in the event of
**éventuel, le** [evãtɥɛl] *adj* possible;
**éventuellement** *adv* possibly
**évêque** [evɛk] *nm* bishop
**évertuer** [evɛʀtɥe]: **s'~** *vi*: **s'~ à faire**
to try very hard to do
**éviction** [eviksjɔ̃] *nf* (*de locataire*) evic-
tion
**évidemment** [evidamã] *adv* (*bien sûr*)
of course; (*certainement*) obviously
**évidence** [evidãs] *nf* obviousness; (*fait*)
obvious fact; **de toute ~** quite obviously *ou* evidently; **être en ~** to be
clearly visible; **mettre en ~** (*fait*) to
highlight; **évident, e** *adj* obvious, evident; **ce n'est pas évident!** (*fam*) it's
not that easy!
**évider** [evide] *vt* to scoop out
**évier** [evje] *nm* (kitchen) sink
**évincer** [evɛ̃se] *vt* to oust
**éviter** [evite] *vt* to avoid; **~ de faire** to
avoid doing; **~ qch à qn** to spare sb
sth
**évolué, e** [evɔlɥe] *adj* advanced
**évoluer** [evɔlɥe] *vi* (*enfant, maladie*) to
develop; (*situation, moralement*) to
evolve, develop; (*aller et venir*) to move
about; **évolution** *nf* development,

evolution

**évoquer** [evɔke] vt to call to mind, evoke; (*mentionner*) to mention

**ex...** [eks] *préfixe* ex-

**exact, e** [egza(kt), egzakt] adj exact; (*correct*) correct; (*ponctuel*) punctual; **l'heure ~** the right *ou* exact time; **exactement** adv exactly

**ex aequo** [egzeko] adj equally placed; **arriver ~** to finish neck and neck

**exagéré, e** [egzaʒere] adj (*prix etc*) excessive

**exagérer** [egzaʒere] vt to exaggerate ♦ vi to exaggerate; (*abuser*) to go too far

**exalter** [egzalte] vt (*enthousiasmer*) to excite, elate

**examen** [egzamɛ̃] nm examination; (SCOL) exam, examination; **à l'~** under consideration

**examinateur, -trice** [egzaminatœr, tris] nm/f examiner

**examiner** [egzamine] vt to examine

**exaspérant, e** [egzaspera, ɑ̃t] adj exasperating

**exaspérer** [egzaspere] vt to exasperate

**exaucer** [egzose] vt (*vœu*) to grant

**excédent** [eksedɑ̃] nm surplus; **en ~** surplus; **~ de bagages** excess luggage

**excéder** [eksede] vt (*dépasser*) to exceed; (*agacer*) to exasperate

**excellent, e** [ekselɑ̃, ɑ̃t] adj excellent

**excentrique** [eksɑ̃trik] adj eccentric

**excepté, e** [eksepte] adj, prép: **les élèves ~s, ~ les élèves** except for the pupils

**exception** [eksɛpsjɔ̃] nf exception; **à l'~ de** except for, with the exception of; **d'~** (*mesure, loi*) special, exceptional; **exceptionnel, le** adj exceptional; **exceptionnellement** adv exceptionally

**excès** [eksɛ] nm surplus ♦ nmpl excesses; **faire des ~** to overindulge; **~ de vitesse** speeding no pl; **excessif, -ive** adj excessive

**excitant, e** [eksitɑ̃, ɑ̃t] adj exciting ♦ nm stimulant; **excitation** nf (*état*)

excitement

**exciter** [eksite] vt to excite; (*suj: café etc*) to stimulate; **s'~** vi to get excited

**exclamation** [eksklamasjɔ̃] nf exclamation

**exclamer** [eksklame]: **s'~** vi to exclaim

**exclure** [eksklyr] vt (*faire sortir*) to expel; (*ne pas compter*) to exclude, leave out; (*rendre impossible*) to exclude, rule out; **il est exclu que** it's out of the question that ...; **il n'est pas exclu que** ... it's not impossible that ...; **exclusif, -ive** adj exclusive; **exclusion** nf exclusion; **à l'exclusion de** with the exclusion *ou* exception of; **exclusivité** nf (COMM) exclusive rights pl; **film passant en exclusivité à** film showing only at

**excursion** [ekskyrsjɔ̃] nf (*en autocar*) excursion, trip; (*à pied*) walk, hike

**excuse** [ekskyz] nf excuse; **~s** nfpl (*regret*) apology sg, apologies; **excuser** vt to excuse; **s'excuser (de)** to apologize (for); **"excusez-moi"** "I'm sorry"; (*pour attirer l'attention*) "excuse me"

**exécrable** [egzekrabl] adj atrocious

**exécuter** [egzekyte] vt (*tuer*) to execute; (*tâche etc*) to execute, carry out; (MUS: *jouer*) to perform, execute; **s'~** vi to comply; **exécutif, -ive** adj, nm (POL) executive; **exécution** nf execution; **mettre à exécution** to carry out

**exemplaire** [egzɑ̃pler] nm copy

**exemple** [egzɑ̃pl] nm example; **par ~** for instance, for example; **donner l'~** to set an example

**exempt, e** [egzɑ̃, ɑ̃(p)t] adj: **~ de** (*dispensé de*) exempt from; (*sans*) free from

**exercer** [egzerse] vt (*pratiquer*) to exercise, practise; (*influence, contrôle*) to exert; (*former*) to exercise, train; **s'~** vi (*sportif, musicien*) to practise

**exercice** [egzersis] nm exercise

**exhaustif, -ive** [egzostif, iv] adj exhaustive

**exhiber** [ɛgzibe] vt (montrer: papiers, certificat) to present, produce; (péj) to display, flaunt; **s'~** vi to parade; (suj: exhibitionniste) to expose o.s.; **exhibitionniste** [ɛgzibisjɔnist] nm/f flasher

**exhorter** [ɛgzɔʀte] vt to urge

**exigeant, e** [ɛgziʒɑ̃, ɑ̃t] adj demanding; (péj) hard to please

**exigence** [ɛgziʒɑ̃s] nf demand, requirement

**exiger** [ɛgziʒe] vt to demand, require

**exigu, ë** [ɛgzigy] adj cramped, tiny

**exil** [ɛgzil] nm exile; **exiler** vt to exile; **s'exiler** vi to go into exile

**existence** [ɛgzistɑ̃s] nf existence

**exister** [ɛgziste] vi to exist; **il existe un/des** there is a/are some

**exonérer** [ɛgzɔnere] vt: **~ de** to exempt from

**exorbitant, e** [ɛgzɔʀbitɑ̃, ɑ̃t] adj exorbitant

**exorbité, e** [ɛgzɔʀbite] adj: **yeux ~s** bulging eyes

**exotique** [ɛgzɔtik] adj exotic; **yaourt aux fruits ~s** tropical fruit yoghurt

**expatrier** [ɛkspatʀije] vt: **s'~** to leave one's country

**expectative** [ɛkspɛktativ] nf: **être dans l'~** to be still waiting

**expédient** [ɛkspedjɑ̃, jɑ̃t] (péj) nm: **vivre d'~s** to live by one's wits

**expédier** [ɛkspedje] vt (lettre, paquet) to send; (troupes) to dispatch; (fam: travail etc) to dispose of, dispatch; **expéditeur, -trice** nm/f sender; **expédition** nf sending; (scientifique, sportive, MIL) expedition

**expérience** [ɛksperjɑ̃s] nf (de la vie) experience; (scientifique) experiment; **expérimenté, e** adj experienced

**expérimenter** [ɛksperimɑ̃te] vt to test out, experiment with

**expert, e** [ɛkspɛʀ, ɛʀt] adj, nm expert; **expert-comptable** nm ≈ chartered accountant (BRIT), ≈ certified public accountant (US)

**expertise** [ɛkspɛʀtiz] nf (évaluation) expert evaluation

**expertiser** [ɛkspɛʀtize] vt (objet de valeur) to value; (voiture accidentée etc) to assess damage to

**expier** [ɛkspje] vt to expiate, atone for

**expirer** [ɛkspiʀe] vi (prendre fin, mourir) to expire; (respirer) to breathe out

**explicatif, -ive** [ɛksplikatif, iv] adj explanatory

**explication** [ɛksplikasjɔ̃] nf explanation; (discussion) discussion; (dispute) argument; **~ de texte** (SCOL) critical analysis

**explicite** [ɛksplisit] adj explicit

**expliquer** [ɛksplike] vt to explain; **s'~** to explain (o.s.); **s'~ avec qn** (discuter) to explain o.s. to sb; **son erreur s'explique** one can understand his mistake

**exploit** [ɛksplwa] nm exploit, feat; **exploitant, e** nm/f: **exploitant (agricole)** farmer

**exploitation** nf exploitation; (d'une entreprise) running; **~ agricole** farming concern; **exploiter** vt (personne, don) to exploit; (entreprise, ferme) to run, operate; (mine) to exploit, work

**explorer** [ɛksplɔʀe] vt to explore

**exploser** [ɛksploze] vi to explode, blow up; (engin explosif) to go off; (personne: de colère) to flare up; **explosif, -ive** adj, nm explosive; **explosion** nf explosion

**exportateur, -trice** [ɛkspɔʀtatœʀ, tʀis] adj export cpd, exporting ♦ nm exporter

**exportation** [ɛkspɔʀtasjɔ̃] nf (action) exportation; (produit) export

**exporter** [ɛkspɔʀte] vt to export

**exposant** [ɛkspozɑ̃] nm exhibitor

**exposé, e** [ɛkspoze] nm talk ♦ adj: **~ au sud** facing south

**exposer** [ɛkspoze] vt (marchandise) to display; (peinture) to exhibit, show; (parler de) to explain, set out; (mettre en danger, orienter, PHOTO) to expose;

# exprès

**exposition** nf (manifestation) exhibition; (PHOTO) exposure

**exprès¹** [ɛkspʀɛ] adv (délibérément) on purpose; (spécialement) specially

**exprès², -esse** [ɛkspʀɛs] adj (ordre, défense) express ♦ adj inv (PTT) express ♦ adv express

**express** [ɛkspʀɛs] adj, nm: (café) ~ espresso (coffee); (train) ~ fast train

**expressément** [ɛkspʀesemã] adv (spécialement) specifically

**expressif, -ive** [ɛkspʀesif, iv] adj expressive

**expression** [ɛkspʀesjɔ̃] nf expression

**exprimer** [ɛkspʀime] vt (sentiment, idée) to express; (jus, liquide) to press out; s'~ vi (personne) to express o.s

**exproprier** [ɛkspʀɔpʀije] vt to buy up by compulsory purchase, expropriate

**expulser** [ɛkspylse] vt to expel; (locataire) to evict; (SPORT) to send off

**exquis, e** [ɛkski, iz] adj exquisite

**extase** [ɛkstaz] nf ecstasy; **extasier**: s'extasier sur vt to go into raptures over

**extension** [ɛkstãsjɔ̃] nf (fig) extension

**exténuer** [ɛkstenɥe] vt to exhaust

**extérieur, e** [ɛksteʀjœʀ] adj (porte, mur etc) outer, outside; (au dehors: escalier, w.-c.) outside; (commerce: foreign; (influences) external; (apparent: calme, gaieté etc) surface cpd ♦ nm (d'une maison, d'un récipient etc) outside, exterior; (apparence) exterior; à l'~ outside; (à l'étranger) abroad; **extérieurement** adv on the outside; (en apparence) on the surface

**exterminer** [ɛkstɛʀmine] vt to exterminate, wipe out

**externat** [ɛkstɛʀna] nm day school

**externe** [ɛkstɛʀn] adj external, outer ♦ nm/f (MÉD) non-resident medical student (BRIT), extern (US); (SCOL) day pupil

**extincteur** [ɛkstɛ̃ktœʀ] nm (fire) extinguisher

**extinction** [ɛkstɛ̃ksjɔ̃] nf: ~ de voix loss of voice

**extorquer** [ɛkstɔʀke] vt to extort

**extra** [ɛkstʀa] adj inv first-rate; (fam) fantastic ♦ nm inv extra help

**extracommunautaire** [ɛkstʀakɔmynotɛʀ] adj non-EU

**extrader** [ɛkstʀade] vt to extradite

**extraire** [ɛkstʀɛʀ] vt to extract; **extrait** nm extract

**extraordinaire** [ɛkstʀaɔʀdinɛʀ] adj extraordinary; (POL: mesures etc) special

**extravagant, e** [ɛkstʀavagã, ãt] adj extravagant

**extraverti, e** [ɛkstʀavɛʀti] adj extrovert

**extrême** [ɛkstʀɛm] adj, nm extreme; **extrêmement** adv extremely; **extrême-onction** nf last rites pl; **Extrême-Orient** nm Far East

**extrémité** [ɛkstʀemite] nf end; (situation) straits pl, plight; (geste désespéré) extreme action; ~s nfpl (pieds et mains) extremities

**exubérant, e** [ɛgzybeʀã, ãt] adj exuberant

**exutoire** [ɛgzytwaʀ] nm outlet, release

# F, f

**F** abr = **franc**

**fa** [fa] nm inv (MUS) F; (en chantant la gamme) fa

**fable** [fabl] nf fable

**fabricant** [fabʀikã, ãt] nm manufacturer

**fabrication** [fabʀikasjɔ̃] nf manufacture

**fabrique** [fabʀik] nf factory; **fabriquer** vt to make; (industriellement) to manufacture; (fig): **qu'est-ce qu'il fabrique?** (fam) what is he doing?

**fabulation** [fabylasjɔ̃] nf fantasizing

**fac** [fak] (fam) abr f (SCOL) = **faculté**

**façade** [fasad] nf front, façade

**face** [fas] nf face; (fig: aspect) side ♦ adj: **le côté** ~ heads; **en** ~ **de** opposite; (fig) in front of; **de** ~ (voir) face on; ~ **à** facing; (fig) faced with, in the face of; **faire** ~ **à** to face; ~ **à** ~ adv facing

**fâché, e** [faʃe] *adj* angry; (*désolé*) sorry

**fâcher** [faʃe] *vt* to anger; **se ~** *vi* to get angry; **se ~ avec** (*se brouiller*) to fall out with

**fâcheux, -euse** [faʃø, øz] *adj* unfortunate, regrettable

**facile** [fasil] *adj* easy; (*caractère*) easygoing; **facilement** *adv* easily

**facilité** *nf* easiness; (*disposition, don*) aptitude; **facilités de paiement** easy terms; **faciliter** *vt* to make easier

**façon** [fasɔ̃] *nf* (*manière*) way; (*d'une robe etc*) making-up, cut; **~s** *nfpl* (*péj*) fuss *sg*; **de ~ à/à ce que** so as to/that; **de toute ~** anyway, in any case; **façonner** [fasɔne] *vt* (*travailler: matière*) to shape, fashion

**facteur, -trice** [faktœʀ, tʀis] *nm/f* postman(-woman) (BRIT), mailman(-woman) (US) ♦ *nm* (MATH, *fig*: élément) factor

**factice** [faktis] *adj* artificial

**faction** [faksjɔ̃] *nf* faction; **être de ~** to be on guard (duty)

**facture** [faktyʀ] *nf* (*à payer: gén*) bill; invoice; **facturer** *vt* to invoice

**facultatif, -ive** [fakyltatif, iv] *adj* optional

**faculté** [fakylte] *nf* (*intellectuelle, d'université*) faculty; (*pouvoir, possibilité*) power

**fade** [fad] *adj* insipid

**fagot** [fago] *nm* bundle of sticks

**faible** [fɛbl] *adj* weak; (voix, lumière, vent) faint; (rendement, revenu) low ♦ *nm* (pour quelqu'un) weakness, soft spot; **faiblesse** *nf* weakness; **faiblir** *vi* to weaken; (lumière) to dim; (vent) to drop

**faïence** [fajɑ̃s] *nf* earthenware *no pl*

**faignant, e** [fɛɲɑ̃, ɑ̃t] *nm/f* = **fainéant, e**

**faille** [faj] *vb voir* **falloir** ♦ *nf* (GÉO) fault; (*fig*) flaw, weakness

**faillir** [fajiʀ] *vi*: **j'ai failli tomber** I almost ou very nearly fell

**faillite** [fajit] *nf* bankruptcy

**faim** [fɛ̃] *nf* hunger; **avoir ~** to be hungry; **rester sur sa ~** (*aussi fig*) to be left wanting more

**fainéant, e** [feneɑ̃, ɑ̃t] *nm/f* idler, loafer

**faire** [fɛʀ] *vt* 1 (*fabriquer, être l'auteur de*) to make; **faire du vin/une offre/un film** to make wine/an offer/a film; **faire du bruit** to make a noise

2 (*effectuer: travail, opération*) to do; **que faites-vous?** (*quel métier etc*) what do you do?; (*quelle activité: au moment de la question*) what are you doing?; **faire la lessive** to do the washing

3 (*études*) to do; (*sport, musique*) to play; **faire du droit/du français** to do law/French; **faire du rugby/piano** to play rugby/the piano

4 (*simuler*): **faire le malade/l'ignorant** to act the invalid/the fool

5 (*transformer, avoir un effet sur*): **faire de qn un frustré/avocat** to make sb frustrated/a lawyer; **ça ne me fait rien** (*m'est égal*) I don't care ou mind; (*me laisse froid*) it has no effect on me; **ça ne fait rien** it doesn't matter; **faire que** (*impliquer*) to mean that

6 (*calculs, prix, mesures*): **2 et 2 font 4** 2 and 2 are ou make 4; **ça fait 10 m/15 F** it's 10 m/15F; **je vous le fais 10 F** I'll let you have it for 10F

7: **qu'a-t-il fait de sa valise?** what has he done with his case?

8: **ne faire que**: **il ne fait que critiquer** (*sans cesse*) all he (ever) does is criticize; (*seulement*) he's only criticizing

9 (*dire*) to say; **"vraiment?" fit-il** "really?" he said

10 (*maladie*) to have; **faire du diabète** to have diabetes *sg*

♦ *vi* 1 (*agir, s'y prendre*) to act, do; **il faut faire vite** we (ou you etc) must act quickly; **comment a-t-il fait pour?** how did he manage to?; **faites** comme chez vous make yourself at home

2 (*paraître*) to look; **faire vieux/démodé** to look old/old-fashioned; **ça fait bien** it looks good

♦ *vb substitut* to do; **ne le casse pas comme je l'ai fait** don't break it as I did; **je peux le voir? - faites!** can I see it? - please do!

♦ *vb impers*: **1: il fait beau** *etc* the weather is fine *etc*; *voir aussi* **jour**; **froid** *etc*

2 (*temps écoulé, durée*): **ça fait 2 ans qu'il est parti** it's 2 years since he left; **ça fait 2 ans qu'il y est** he's been there for 2 years

♦ *vb semi-aux* **1: faire** +*infinitif* (*action directe*) to make; **faire tomber/bouger qch** to make sth fall/move; **faire démarrer un moteur/chauffer de l'eau** to start up an engine/heat some water; **cela fait dormir** it makes you sleep; **faire travailler les enfants** to make the children work *ou* get the children to work

2 (*indirectement, par un intermédiaire*): **faire réparer qch** to get *ou* have sth repaired; **faire punir les enfants** to have the children punished; **se faire** *vi*

**1** (*vin, fromage*) to mature

**2: cela se fait beaucoup/ne se fait pas** it's done a lot/not done

**3: se faire** +*nom ou pron*: **se faire une jupe** to make o.s. a skirt; **se faire des amis** to make friends; **se faire du souci** to worry; **il ne s'en fait pas** he doesn't worry

**4: se faire** +*adj* (*devenir*): **se faire vieux** to be getting old; (*délibérément*): **se faire beau** to do o.s. up

**5: se faire à** (*s'habituer*) to get used to; **je n'arrive pas à me faire à la nourriture ou climat** I can't get used to the food/climate

**6: se faire** +*infinitif*: **se faire examiner la vue/opérer** to have one's eyes tested/to have an operation; **se faire**

**couper les cheveux** to get one's hair cut; **il va se faire tuer/punir** he's going to get himself killed/get (himself) punished; **il s'est fait aider** he got somebody to help him; **il s'est fait aider par Simon** he got Simon to help him; **se faire faire un vêtement** to get a garment made for o.s.

**7** (*impersonnel*): **comment se fait-il/faisait-il que?** how is it/was it that?

**faire-part** [fɛʀpaʀ] *nm inv* announcement (*of birth, marriage etc*)

**faisable** [fəzabl] *adj* feasible

**faisan, e** [fəzã, an] *nm/f* pheasant; **faisandé, e** *adj* high (*bad*)

**faisceau, x** [fɛso] *nm* (*de lumière etc*) beam

**faisons** [fəzõ] *vb voir* **faire**

**fait, e** [fɛ, fɛt] *adj* (*mûr: fromage, melon*) ripe ♦ *nm* (*événement*) event, occurrence; (*réalité, donnée*) fact; **être au ~** (**de**) to be informed (of); **au ~** (*à propos*) by the way; **en venir au ~** to get to the point; **du ~ de ceci/qu'il a menti** on account of this/his having lied; **de ce ~** for this reason; **en ~** in fact; **prendre qn sur le ~** to catch sb in the act; **~ divers** news item

**faîte** [fɛt] *nm* top; (*fig*) pinnacle, height

**faites** [fɛt] *vb voir* **faire**

**faîtout** [fetu] *nm*, **fait-tout** [fetu] *nm inv* stewpot

**falaise** [falɛz] *nf* cliff

**falloir** [falwaʀ] *vb impers*: **il faut qu'il parte/a fallu qu'il parte** (*obligation*) he has to *ou* must leave/had to leave; **il a fallu le faire** it had to be done; **il faut faire attention** you have to be careful; **il me faudrait 100 F** I would need 100 F; **il vous faut tourner à gauche après l'église** you have to turn left past the church; **nous avons ce qu'il (nous) faut** we have what we need; **s'en ~**: **il s'en est fallu de 100 F/5 minutes** we/they *etc* were only

**falsifier** [falsifje] vt to falsify, doctor

**famé, e** [fame] adj: **mal ~** disreputable, of ill repute

**famélique** [famelik] adj half-starved

**fameux, -euse** [famø, øz] adj (illustre) famous; (bon: repas, plat etc) first-rate, first-class; (valeur intensive) real, downright

**familial, e, -aux** [familjal, jo] adj family cpd

**familiarité** [familjarite] nf familiarity; **~s** nfpl (privautés) familiarities

**familier, -ère** [familje, jɛʀ] adj (connu) familiar; (atmosphère) informal, friendly; (LING) informal, colloquial ♦ nm regular (visitor)

**famille** [famij] nf family; **il a de la ~ à Paris** he has relatives in Paris

**famine** [famin] nf famine

**fanatique** [fanatik] adj fanatical ♦ nm/f fanatic; **fanatisme** nm fanaticism

**faner** [fane]: **se ~** vi to fade

**fanfare** [fɑ̃faʀ] nf (orchestre) brass band; (musique) fanfare

**fanfaron, ne** [fɑ̃faʀɔ̃, ɔn] nm/f braggart

**fantaisie** [fɑ̃tezi] nf (spontanéité) fancy, imagination; (caprice) whim ♦ adj: **bijou ~** costume jewellery; **fantaisiste** (péj) adj unorthodox, eccentric

**fantasme** [fɑ̃tasm] nm fantasy

**fantasque** [fɑ̃task] adj whimsical, capricious

**fantastique** [fɑ̃tastik] adj fantastic

**fantôme** [fɑ̃tom] nm ghost, phantom

**faon** [fɑ̃] nm fawn

**farce** [faʀs] nf (viande) stuffing; (blague) (practical) joke; (THÉÂTRE) farce; **farcir** vt (viande) to stuff

**fardeau, x** [faʀdo] nm burden

**farder** [faʀde]: **se ~** vi to make (o.s.) up

**farfelu, e** [faʀfəly] adj hare-brained

**farine** [faʀin] nf flour; **farineux, -euse** adj (sauce, pomme) floury

**farouche** [faʀuʃ] adj (timide) shy, timid

**fart** [faʀt] nm (ski) wax

**fascicule** [fasikyl] nm volume

**fascination** [fasinasjɔ̃] nf fascination

**fasciner** [fasine] vt to fascinate

**fascisme** [faʃism] nm fascism

**fasse** etc [fas] vb voir **faire**

**faste** [fast] nm splendour

**fastidieux, -euse** [fastidjø, jøz] adj tedious, tiresome

**fastueux, -euse** [fastyø, øz] adj sumptuous, luxurious

**fatal, e** [fatal] adj fatal; (inévitable) inevitable; **fatalité** (of destin) fate; (coïncidence) fateful coincidence

**fatidique** [fatidik] adj fateful

**fatigant, e** [fatigɑ̃, ɑ̃t] adj tiring; (agaçant) tiresome

**fatigue** [fatig] nf tiredness, fatigue; **fatigué, e** [fatige] adj tired; **fatiguer** vt to tire, make tired; (fig: agacer) to annoy ♦ vi (moteur) to labour, strain; **se fatiguer** to get tired

**fatras** [fatʀa] nm jumble, hotchpotch

**faubourg** [fobuʀ] nm suburb

**fauché, e** [foʃe] (fam) adj broke

**faucher** [foʃe] vt (herbe) to cut; (champs, blés) to reap; (fig: véhicule) to mow down; (fam: voler) to pinch

**faucille** [fosij] nf sickle

**faucon** [fokɔ̃] nm falcon, hawk

**faudra** [fodʀa] vb voir **falloir**

**faufiler** [fofile]: **se ~** vi: **se ~ dans** to edge one's way into; **se ~ parmi/entre** to thread one's way among/between

**faune** [fon] nf (ZOOL) wildlife, fauna

**faussaire** [fosɛʀ] nm forger

**fausse** [fos] adj voir **faux**; **faussement** adv (accuser) wrongly, wrongfully; (croire) falsely

**fausser** [fose] vt (objet) to bend, buckle; (fig) to distort; **~ compagnie à qn** to give sb the slip

**faut** [fo] vb voir **falloir**

**faute** [fot] nf (erreur) mistake, error; (mauvaise action) misdemeanour; (FOOTBALL etc) offence; **c'est de sa/ma ~** it's his/my fault; **être en ~** to be in the wrong; **~ de** (temps, argent) for ou through lack of; **sans ~** without fail; **~ de frappe** typing error; **~ de goût** error of taste; **~ professionnelle** professional misconduct no pl

**fauteuil** [fotœj] nm: armchair; **~ roulant** wheelchair

**fauteur** [fotœʀ] nm: **~ de troubles** trouble-maker

**fautif, -ive** [fotif, iv] adj (responsable) at fault, in the wrong; (incorrect) incorrect, inaccurate; **il se sentait ~** he felt guilty

**fauve** [fov] nm wildcat ♦ adj (couleur) fawn

**faux¹** [fo] nf scythe

**faux², fausse** [fo, fos] adj (inexact) wrong; (voix) out of tune; (billet) fake, forged; (sournois, postiche) false, artificial; (MUS) out of tune ♦ nm (copie) fake, forgery; (opposé au vrai): **le ~** falsehood; **faire ~ bond à qn** to stand sb up; **fausse alerte** false alarm; **fausse couche** miscarriage; **~ frais** ♦ nmpl extras, incidental expenses; **~ pas** tripping no pl; (fig) faux pas; **~ témoignage** (délit) perjury; **faux-filet** nm sirloin; **faux-monnayeur** nm counterfeiter, forger

**faveur** [favœʀ] nf favour; **traitement de ~** preferential treatment; **en ~ de** in favour of

**favorable** [favɔʀabl] adj favourable

**favori, te** [favɔʀi, it] adj, nm/f favourite

**favoriser** [favɔʀize] vt to favour

**fax** [faks] nm fax; **faxer** vt to fax

**fébrile** [febʀil] adj feverish, febrile

**fécond, e** [fekɔ̃, ɔ̃d] adj fertile; **féconder** vt to fertilize; **fécondité** nf fertility

**fécule** [fekyl] nf potato flour; **féculent** nm starchy food

**fédéral, e, -aux** [federal, o] adj fed-

eral

**fédération** [federasjɔ̃] nf federation; **la F~ française de football** the French football association

**fée** [fe] nf fairy; **féerique** adj magical, fairytale cpd

**feignant, e** [fɛɲɑ̃, ɑ̃t] nm/f = **fainéant, e**

**feindre** [fɛdʀ] vt to feign; **~ de faire** to pretend to do

**feinte** [fɛt] nf (SPORT) dummy

**fêler** [fele] vt to crack

**félicitations** [felisitasjɔ̃] nfpl congratulations

**féliciter** [felisite] vt: **~ qn (de)** to congratulate sb (on)

**félin, e** [felɛ̃, in] nm (big) cat

**fêlure** [felyʀ] nf crack

**femelle** [fəmɛl] adj, nf female

**féminin, e** [feminɛ̃, in] adj feminine; (sexe) female; (équipe, vêtements etc) women's ♦ nm (LING) feminine; **féministe** [feminist] adj feminist

**femme** [fam] nf woman; (épouse) wife; **~ au foyer** housewife; **~ de chambre** chambermaid; **~ de ménage** cleaning lady

**fémur** [femyʀ] nm femur, thighbone

**fendre** [fɑ̃dʀ] vt (couper en deux) to split; (fissurer) to crack; (traverser: foule, air) to cleave through; **se ~** vi to crack

**fenêtre** [f(ə)nɛtʀ] nf window

**fenouil** [fənuj] nm fennel

**fente** [fɑ̃t] nf (fissure) crack; (de boîte à lettres etc) slit

**fer** [fɛʀ] nm iron; **~ à cheval** horseshoe; **~ (à repasser)** iron; **~ forgé** wrought iron

**ferai** etc [fəʀe] vb voir **faire**

**fer-blanc** [fɛʀblɑ̃] nm tin(plate)

**férié, e** [feʀje] adj: **jour ~** public holiday

**ferions** etc [fəʀjɔ̃] vb voir **faire**

**ferme** [fɛʀm] adj firm ♦ adv (travailler etc) hard ♦ nf (exploitation) farm; (maison) farmhouse

**fermé, e** [fɛʀme] adj closed, shut; (gaz, eau etc) off; (fig: milieu) exclusive

**fermenter** [fɛʀmɑ̃te] vi to ferment

**fermer** [fɛʀme] vt to close, shut; (cesser l'exploitation de) to close down, shut down; (eau, électricité, robinet) to put off, turn off; (aéroport, route) to close ♦ vi to close, shut; (magasin: définitivement) to close down, shut down; **se ~** vi to close, to shut

**fermeté** [fɛʀmate] nf firmness

**fermeture** [fɛʀmatyʀ] nf closing; (dispositif) catch; **heures de ~** closing times; **~ éclair** ® zip (fastener) (BRIT), zipper (US)

**fermier, ière** [fɛʀmje, jɛʀ] nm farmer; **fermière** nf woman farmer; (épouse) farmer's wife

**fermoir** [fɛʀmwaʀ] nm clasp

**féroce** [feʀɔs] adj ferocious, fierce

**ferons** [faʀɔ̃] vb voir **faire**

**ferraille** [feʀaj] nf scrap iron; **mettre à la ~** to scrap

**ferrer** [feʀe] vt (cheval) to shoe

**ferronnerie** [feʀɔnʀi] nf ironwork

**ferroviaire** [feʀɔvjɛʀ] adj rail(way) cpd (BRIT), rail(road) cpd (US)

**ferry(boat)** [feʀe(bot)] nm ferry

**fertile** [fɛʀtil] adj fertile; **~ en incidents** eventful, packed with incidents

**féru, e** [feʀy] adj: **~ de** with a keen interest in

**fesse** [fɛs] nf buttock; **fessée** nf spanking

**festin** [fɛstɛ̃] nm feast

**festival** [fɛstival] nm festival

**festivités** [fɛstivite] nfpl festivities

**festoyer** [fɛstwaje] vi to feast

**fêtard** [fɛtaʀ, aʀd] nm (fam) high liver, merry-maker

**fête** [fɛt] nf (religieuse) feast; (publique) holiday; (réception) party; (kermesse) fête, fair; (du nom) feast day, name day; **faire la ~** to live it up; **faire ~ à qn** to give sb a warm welcome; **les ~s (de fin d'année)** the festive season; **la salle des ~s** the village hall; **~ foraine** (fun) fair; **fêter** vt to celebrate; (personne) to have a celebration for

**feu, x** [fø] nm (gén) fire; (signal lumi-

neux) light; (de cuisinière) ring; **~x** nmpl (AUTO) (traffic) lights; **au ~!** (incendie) fire!; **à ~ doux/vif** over a slow/brisk heat; **à petit ~** (CULIN) over a gentle heat; (fig) slowly; **faire ~** to fire; **prendre ~** to catch fire; **mettre le ~ à** to set fire to; **faire du ~** to make a fire; **avez-vous du ~?** (pour cigarette) have you (got) a light?; **~ arrière** rear light; **~ d'artifice** (spectacle) fireworks pl; **~ de joie** bonfire; **~ rouge/vert/orange** red/green/amber (BRIT) ou yellow (US) light; **~x de brouillard** fog-lamps; **~x de croisement** dipped (BRIT) ou dimmed (US) headlights; **~x de position** sidelights; **~x de route** headlights

**feuillage** [fœjaʒ] nm foliage, leaves pl

**feuille** [fœj] nf (d'arbre) leaf; (de papier) sheet; **~ de maladie** medical expenses claim form; **~ de paie** pay slip

**feuillet** [fœjɛ] nm leaf

**feuilleté, e** [fœjte] adj: **pâte ~** flaky pastry

**feuilleter** [fœjte] vt (livre) to leaf through

**feuilleton** [fœjtɔ̃] nm serial

**feutre** [føtʀ] nm felt; (chapeau) felt hat; (aussi: **stylo-~**) felt-tip pen; **feutré, e** adj (atmosphère) muffled

**fève** [fɛv] nf broad bean

**février** [fevʀije] nm February

**FF** abr = **franc français** FF

**FFF** sigle f = **Fédération française de football**

**fiable** [fjabl] adj reliable

**fiançailles** [fjãsaj] nfpl engagement sg

**fiancé, e** [fjãse] nm/f fiancé(e) ♦ adj: **être ~ (à)** to be engaged (to)

**fiancer** [fjãse]: **se ~** vi to become engaged

**fibre** [fibʀ] nf fibre; **~ de verre** fibreglass, glass fibre

**ficeler** [fis(ə)le] vt to tie up

**ficelle** [fisɛl] nf string no pl; (morceau) piece ou length of string

**fiche** [fiʃ] nf (pour fichier) (index) card; (formulaire) form; (ÉLEC) plug

**ficher** [fiʃe] vt (dans un fichier) to file; (POLICE) to put on file; (fam: faire) to do; (: donner) to give; (: mettre) to stick ou shove; **se ~ de** (fam: se gausser) to make fun of; **fiche(-moi) le camp** (fam) clear off; **fiche-moi la paix** (fam) leave me alone; **je m'en fiche!** (fam) I don't care!

**fichier** [fiʃje] nm file

**fichu, e** [fiʃy] pp de **ficher** (fam) ♦ adj (fam: fini, inutilisable) bust, done for; (: intensif) wretched, darned ♦ nm (fou-lard) (head)scarf; **mal ~** (fam) feeling lousy

**fictif, -ive** [fiktif, iv] adj fictitious

**fiction** [fiksjɔ̃] nf fiction; (fait imaginé) invention

**fidèle** [fidɛl] adj faithful ♦ nm/f (REL): **les ~s** (à l'église) the congregation sg; **fidélité** nf fidelity

**fier[1]** [fje]: **se ~ à** vt to trust

**fier[2], fière** [fjɛʀ] adj proud; **fierté** nf pride

**fièvre** [fjɛvʀ] nf fever; **avoir de la ~/39 de ~** to have a temperature/temperature of 39°C; **fiévreux, -euse** adj feverish

**figé, e** [fiʒe] adj (manières) stiff; (société) rigid; (sourire) set

**figer** [fiʒe]: **se ~** vi (huile) to congeal; (personne) to freeze

**fignoler** [finɔle] (fam) vt to polish up

**figue** [fig] nf fig; **figuier** nm fig tree

**figurant, e** [figyʀɑ̃, ɑ̃t] nm/f (THÉÂTRE) walk-on; (CINÉMA) extra

**figure** [figyʀ] nf (visage) face; (forme, personnage) figure; (illustration) picture, diagram

**figuré, e** [figyʀe] adj (sens) figurative

**figurer** [figyʀe] vi to appear ♦ vt to represent; **se ~ que** to imagine that

**fil** [fil] nm (brin, fig: d'une histoire) thread; (électrique) wire; (d'un couteau) edge; **au ~ des années** with the pass-ing of the years; **au ~ de l'eau** with the stream ou current; **coup de ~** (fam) phone call; **~ à coudre** (sewing)

thread; **~ de fer** wire; **~ de fer barbelé** barbed wire

**filament** [filamɑ̃] nm (ÉLEC) filament

**filandreux, -euse** [filɑ̃dʀø, øz] adj stringy

**filature** [filatyʀ] nf (fabrique) mill; (po-licière) shadowing no pl, tailing no pl

**file** [fil] nf line; (AUTO) lane; **en ~ in-dienne** in single file; **à la ~** (d'affilée) in succession; **~ (d'attente)** queue (BRIT), line (US)

**filer** [file] vt (tissu, toile) to spin; (pren-dre en filature) to shadow, tail; (fam: donner): **~ qch à qn** to slip sb sth ♦ vi (bas) to run; (aller vite) to fly past; (fam: partir) to make ou be off; **~ doux** to toe the line

**filet** [filɛ] nm net; (CULIN) fillet; (d'eau, de sang) trickle; **~ (à provisions)** string bag

**filiale** [filjal] nf (COMM) subsidiary

**filière** [filjɛʀ] nf (carrière) path; **suivre la ~** (dans sa carrière) to work one's way up (through the hierarchy)

**filiforme** [filifɔʀm] adj spindly

**filigrane** [filigʀan] nm (d'un billet, timbre) watermark

**fille** [fij] nf girl; (opposé à fils) daughter; **vieille ~** old maid; **fillette** nf (little) girl

**filleul, e** [fijœl] nm/f godchild, godson/daughter

**film** [film] nm (pour photo) (roll of) film; (œuvre) film, picture, movie; **~ d'épou-vante** horror film; **~ policier** thriller

**filon** [filɔ̃] nm vein, lode; (fig) lucrative line, money spinner

**fils** [fis] nm son; **~ à papa** daddy's boy

**filtre** [filtʀ] nm filter; **filtrer** vt to filter; (fig: candidats, visiteurs) to screen

**fin[1]** [fɛ̃] nf end; **~s** nfpl (but) ends; **prendre ~** to come to an end; **mettre ~ à** to put an end to; **à la ~** in the end, eventually; **en ~ de compte** in the end; **sans ~** endless; **~ juin** at the end of June

**fin[2], e** [fɛ̃, fin] adj (papier, couche, fil

thin; (cheveux, visage) fine; (taille) neat, slim; (esprit, remarque) subtle ♦ adv (couper) finely; ~ **prêt** ready; **~es herbes** mixed herbs

**final, e** [final, o] adj final ♦ nm (MUS) finale; **finale** nf final; **quarts de finale** quarter finals; **finalement** adv finally, in the end; (après tout) after all

**finance** [finɑ̃s]: **~s** nfpl (situation) finances; (activités) finance sg; **moyennant ~** for a fee; **financer** vt to finance; **financier, -ière** adj financial

**finaud, e** [fino, od] adj wily

**finesse** [fines] nf thinness; (raffinement) fineness; (subtilité) subtlety

**fini, e** [fini] adj finished; (MATH) finite ♦ nm (d'un objet manufacturé) finish

**finir** [finiʀ] vt to finish ♦ vi to finish, end; **~ par faire** to end up ou finish up doing; **~ de faire** to finish doing; (cesser) to stop doing; **il finit par m'agacer** he's beginning to get on my nerves; **en ~ avec** to be ou have done with; **il va mal ~** he will come to a bad end

**finition** [finisjɔ̃] nf (résultat) finish

**finlandais, e** [fɛ̃lɑ̃dɛ, ɛz] adj Finnish ♦ nm/f: **F~, e** Finn

**Finlande** [fɛ̃lɑ̃d] nf: **la ~** Finland

**fiole** [fjɔl] nf phial

**fisc** [fisk] nm tax authorities pl; **fiscal, e, -aux** [fiskal] adj tax cpd, fiscal; **fiscalité** nf tax system

**fissure** [fisyʀ] nf crack; **fissurer** vt to crack; **se fissurer** vi to crack

**fiston** [fistɔ̃] (fam) nm son, lad

**fit** [fi] vb voir **faire**

**fixation** [fiksasjɔ̃] nf (attache) fastening; (PSYCH) fixation

**fixe** [fiks] adj (fixé); (emploi) steady, regular ♦ nm (salaire) basic salary; **à heure ~** at a set time; **menu à prix ~** set menu

**fixé, e** [fikse] adj: **être ~ (sur)** (savoir à quoi s'en tenir) to have made up one's mind (about)

**fixer** [fikse] vt (attacher): **~ qch (à/sur)** to fix ou fasten sth (to/onto); (déterminer) to fix, set; (regarder) to stare at; **se ~ vi** (s'établir) to settle down; **se ~ sur** (suj: attention) to focus on

**flacon** [flakɔ̃] nm bottle

**flageoler** [flaʒɔle] vi (jambes) to sag

**flageolet** [flaʒɔlɛ] nm (CULIN) dwarf kidney bean

**flagrant, e** [flagʀɑ̃, ɑ̃t] adj flagrant, blatant; **en ~ délit** in the act

**flair** [flɛʀ] nm sense of smell; (fig) intuition; **flairer** vt (humer) to sniff (at); (détecter) to scent

**flamand, e** [flamɑ̃, ɑ̃d] adj Flemish ♦ nm (LING) Flemish ♦ nm/f: **F~, e** Fleming; **les F~s** the Flemish

**flamant** [flamɑ̃] nm flamingo

**flambant, e** [flɑ̃bɑ̃, ɑ̃t] adv: **~ neuf** brand new

**flambé, e** [flɑ̃be] adj (CULIN) flambé

**flambeau, x** [flɑ̃bo] nm (flaming) torch

**flambée** [flɑ̃be] nf blaze; (fig: des prix) explosion

**flamber** [flɑ̃be] vi to blaze (up)

**flamboyer** [flɑ̃bwaje] vi to blaze (up)

**flamme** [flam] nf flame; (fig) fire, fervour; **en ~s** on fire, ablaze

**flan** [flɑ̃] nm (CULIN) custard tart ou pie

**flanc** [flɑ̃] nm side; (MIL) flank

**flancher** [flɑ̃ʃe] (fam) vi to fail, pack up

**flanelle** [flanɛl] nf flannel

**flâner** [flane] vi to stroll; **flânerie** nf stroll

**flanquer** [flɑ̃ke] vt to flank; (fam: mettre) to chuck, shove; (: jeter): **~ par terre/à la porte** to fling to the ground/chuck out

**flaque** [flak] nf (d'eau) puddle; (d'huile, de sang etc) pool

**flash** [flaʃ] (pl **~es**) nm (PHOTO) flash; **~ (d'information)** newsflash

**flasque** [flask] adj flabby

**flatter** [flate] vt to flatter; **se ~ de qch** to pride o.s. on sth; **flatterie** nf flattery no pl; **flatteur, -euse** adj flattering

**fléau, x** [fleo] *nm* scourge

**flèche** [flɛʃ] *nf* arrow; (*de clocher*) spire; **monter en ~** (*fig*) to soar, rocket; **partir en ~** to be off like a shot; **fléchette** *nf* dart

**fléchir** [fleʃiʀ] *vt* (*corps, genou*) to bend; (*fig*) to sway, weaken ♦ *vi* (*fig*) to weaken, flag

**flemmard, e** [flemaʀ, aʀd] (*fam*) *nm/f* lazybones *sg*, loafer

**flemme** [flem] *nf* (*fam*) laziness; **j'ai la ~ de le faire** I can't be bothered doing it

**flétrir** [fletʀiʀ]: **se ~** *vi* to wither

**fleur** [flœʀ] *nf* flower; (*d'un arbre*) blossom; **en ~** (*arbre*) in blossom; **à ~s** flowery

**fleuri, e** [flœʀi] *adj* (*jardin*) in flower or bloom; (*tissu, papier*) flowery

**fleurir** [flœʀiʀ] *vi* (*rose*) to flower; (*arbre*) to blossom; (*fig*) to flourish ♦ *vt* (*tombe*) to put flowers on; (*chambre*) to decorate with flowers

**fleuriste** [flœʀist] *nm/f* florist

**fleuve** [flœv] *nm* river

**flexible** [fleksibl] *adj* flexible

**flic** [flik] (*fam: péj*) *nm* cop

**flipper** [flipœʀ] *nm* pinball (machine)

**flirter** [flœʀte] *vi* to flirt

**flocon** [flɔkɔ̃] *nm* flake

**flopée** [flɔpe] (*fam*) *nf*: **une ~ de** loads of, masses of

**floraison** [flɔʀɛzɔ̃] *nf* flowering

**flore** [flɔʀ] *nf* flora

**florissant, e** [flɔʀisɑ̃, ɑ̃t] *adj* (*économie*) flourishing

**flot** [flo] *nm* flood, stream; **~s** *nmpl* (*de la mer*) waves; **être à ~** (*NAVIG*) to be afloat; **entrer à ~s** to stream ou pour in

**flottant, e** [flɔtɑ̃, ɑ̃t] *adj* (*vêtement*) loose

**flotte** [flɔt] *nf* (*NAVIG*) fleet; (*fam: eau*) water; (*: pluie*) rain

**flottement** [flɔtmɑ̃] *nm* (*fig*) wavering, hesitation

**flotter** [flɔte] *vi* to float; (*nuage, odeur*) to drift; (*drapeau*) to fly; (*vêtements*) to

hang loose; (*fam: pleuvoir*) to rain; **faire ~** to float; **flotteur** *nm* float

**flou, e** [flu] *adj* fuzzy, blurred; (*fig*) woolly, vague

**fluctuation** [flyktɥasjɔ̃] *nf* fluctuation

**fluet, te** [flɥɛ, ɛt] *adj* thin, slight

**fluide** [flɥid] *adj* fluid; (*circulation etc*) flowing freely ♦ *nm* fluid

**fluor** [flyɔʀ] *nm*: **dentifrice au ~** fluoride toothpaste

**fluorescent, e** [flyɔʀesɑ̃, ɑ̃t] *adj* fluorescent

**flûte** [flyt] *nf* flute; (*verre*) flute glass; (*pain*) long loaf; **~!** drat it!; **~ à bec** recorder

**flux** [fly] *nm* incoming tide; (*écoulement*) flow; **le ~ et le reflux** the ebb and flow

**FM** *sigle f* (= *fréquence modulée*) FM

**foc** [fɔk] *nm* jib

**foi** [fwa] *nf* faith; **digne de ~** reliable; **être de bonne/mauvaise ~** to be sincere/insincere; **ma ~ ...** well ...

**foie** [fwa] *nm* liver; **crise de ~** stomach upset

**foin** [fwɛ̃] *nm* hay; **faire du ~** (*fig: fam*) to kick up a row

**foire** [fwaʀ] *nf* fair; (*fête foraine*) (fun) fair; **faire la ~** (*fig: fam*) to whoop it up; **~** (*exposition*) trade fair

**fois** [fwa] *nf* time; **une/deux ~** once/ twice; **2 ~ 2** 2 times 2; **une ~** (*passé*) once; (*futur*) sometime; **une ~ pour toutes** once and for all; **une ~ que** once; **des ~** (*parfois*) sometimes; **à la ~** (*ensemble*) at once

**foison** [fwazɔ̃] *nf*: **à ~** in plenty; **foisonner** *vi* to abound

**fol** [fɔl] *adj voir* **fou**

**folie** [fɔli] *nf* (*d'une décision, d'un acte*) madness, folly; (*état*) madness, insanity; **la ~ des grandeurs** delusions of grandeur; **faire des ~s** (*en dépenses*) to be extravagant

**folklorique** [fɔlklɔʀik] *adj* folk *cpd*; (*fam*) weird

**folle** [fɔl] *adj, e voir* **fou; follement**

**adv** (très) madly, wildly

**foncé, e** [fɔse] adj dark

**foncer** [fɔse] vi to go darker; (fam: aller vite) to tear ou belt along; ~ **sur** to charge at

**foncier, -ère** [fɔsje, jɛʀ] adj (honnêteté etc) basic, fundamental; (COMM) real estate cpd

**fonction** [fɔksjɔ] nf function; (emploi, poste) post, position; ~**s** nfpl (professionnelles) duties; **voiture de ~** company car; **en ~ de** (par rapport à) according to; **faire ~ de** to serve as; **la ~ publique** the state ou civil (BRIT) service; **fonctionnaire** nm/f state employee, local authority employee; (dans l'administration) ≈ civil servant; **fonctionner** vi to work, function

**fond** [fɔ̃] nm (d'un récipient, trou) bottom; (d'une salle, scène) back; (d'un tableau, décor) background; (opposé à la forme) content; (SPORT): **le ~** long distance (running); **au ~ de** at the bottom of; at the back of; **à ~** (connaître, soutenir) thoroughly; (appuyer, visser) right down ou home; **à ~** (de train) (fam) full tilt; **dans le ~, au ~** (en somme) basically, really; **de ~ en comble** from top to bottom; voir aussi **fonds; ~ de teint** foundation (cream)

**fondamental, e, -aux** [fɔdamɑ̃tal, o] adj fundamental

**fondant, e** [fɔdɑ̃, ɑ̃t] adj (neige) melting; (poire) that melts in the mouth

**fondateur, -trice** [fɔdatœʀ, tʀis] nm/f founder

**fondation** [fɔdasjɔ] nf founding; (établissement) foundation; ~**s** nfpl (d'une maison) foundations

**fondé, e** [fɔde] adj (accusation etc) well-founded; **être ~ à** to have grounds for ou good reason to

**fondement** [fɔdmɑ̃] nm: **sans ~** (rumeur etc) groundless, unfounded

**fonder** [fɔde] vt to found; (fig) to base; **se ~ sur** (suj: personne) to base o.s. on

**fonderie** [fɔdʀi] nf smelting works sg

**fondre** [fɔdʀ] vt (aussi: **faire ~**) to melt; (dans l'eau) to dissolve; (fig: mélanger) to merge, blend ♦ vi (à la chaleur) to melt; (dans l'eau) to dissolve; (fig) to melt away; (se précipiter): ~ **sur** to swoop down on; ~ **en larmes** to burst into tears

**fonds** [fɔ̃] nm (COMM): ~ **(de commerce)** business ♦ nmpl (argent) funds

**fondu, e** [fɔdy] adj (beurre, neige) melted; (métal) molten; **fondue** nf (CULIN) fondue

**font** [fɔ̃] vb voir **faire**

**fontaine** [fɔtɛn] nf fountain; (source) spring

**fonte** [fɔt] nf melting; (métal) cast iron; **la ~ des neiges** (the spring) thaw

**foot** [fut] (fam) nm football

**football** [futbol] nm football, soccer; **footballeur** nm footballer

**footing** [futiŋ] nm jogging; **faire du ~** to go jogging

**for** [fɔʀ] nm: **dans son ~ intérieur** in one's heart of hearts

**forain, e** [fɔʀɛ, ɛn] adj fairground cpd ♦ nm (marchand) stallholder; (acteur) fairground entertainer

**forçat** [fɔʀsa] nm convict

**force** [fɔʀs] nf strength; (PHYSIQUE, MÉCANIQUE) force; ~**s** nfpl (physiques) strength sg; (MIL) forces; **à ~ d'insister** by dint of insisting; as he (ou I etc) kept on insisting; **de ~** forcibly, by force; **les ~s de l'ordre** the police

**forcé, e** [fɔʀse] adj forced; **c'est ~** (fam) it's inevitable; **forcément** adv inevitably; **pas forcément** not necessarily

**forcené, e** [fɔʀsəne] nm/f maniac

**forcer** [fɔʀse] vt to force; (voix) to strain ♦ vi (SPORT) to overtax o.s.; ~ **la dose** (fam) to overdo it; **se ~ (à faire)** to force o.s. (to do)

**forcir** [fɔʀsiʀ] vi (grossir) to broaden out

**forer** [fɔʀe] vt to drill, bore

**forestier, -ère** [fɔʀɛstje, jɛʀ] adj forest

cpd

**forêt** [fɔʀɛ] nf forest

**forfait** [fɔʀfɛ] nm (COMM) all-in deal ou price; **forfaitaire** adj inclusive

**forge** [fɔʀʒ] nf forge, smithy; **forger** vt to forge; (fig: prétexte) to contrive, make up; **forgeron** nm (black)smith

**formaliser** [fɔʀmalize]: se ~ vi: se ~ (de) to take offence (at)

**formalité** [fɔʀmalite] nf formality; **simple ~** mere formality

**format** [fɔʀma] nm size; **formater** vt (disque) to format

**formation** [fɔʀmasjɔ̃] nf (développement) forming; (apprentissage) training; ~ **permanente** continuing education; ~ **professionnelle** vocational training

**forme** [fɔʀm] nf (gén) form; (d'un objet) shape, form; ~**s** nfpl (bonnes manières) proprieties; (d'une femme) figure sg; **être en ~** (SPORT etc) to be on form; **en bonne et due ~** in due form

**formel, le** [fɔʀmɛl] adj (catégorique) definite, positive; **formellement** adv (absolument) positively; **formellement interdit** strictly forbidden

**former** [fɔʀme] vt to form; (éduquer) to train; se ~ vi to form

**formidable** [fɔʀmidabl] adj tremendous

**formulaire** [fɔʀmylɛʀ] nm form

**formule** [fɔʀmyl] nf (gén) formula; (expression) phrase; ~ **de politesse** polite phrase; (en fin de lettre) letter ending; **formuler** vt (émettre) to formulate

**fort, e** [fɔʀ, fɔʀt] adj strong; (intensité, rendement) high, great; (corpulent) stout; (doué) good, able ♦ adv (serrer, frapper) hard; (parler) loud(ly); (beaucoup) greatly, very much; (très) very ♦ nm (édifice) fort; (point ~) strong point, forte; ~**e tête** rebel; **forteresse** nf stronghold

**fortifiant** [fɔʀtifjã, jãt] nm tonic

**fortifier** [fɔʀtifje] vt to strengthen

**fortiori** [fɔʀsjɔʀi]: **à ~** adv all the more so

**fortuit, e** [fɔʀtɥi, it] adj fortuitous, chance cpd

**fortune** [fɔʀtyn] nf fortune; **faire ~** to make one's fortune; **de ~** makeshift; **fortuné, e** adj wealthy

**fosse** [fos] nf (grand trou) pit; (tombe) grave

**fossé** [fose] nm ditch; (fig) gulf, gap

**fossette** [fosɛt] nf dimple

**fossile** [fosil] nm fossil

**fossoyeur** [foswajœʀ] nm gravedigger

**fou (fol), folle** [fu, fɔl] adj mad; (déréglé etc) wild, erratic; (fam: extrême, très grand) terrific, tremendous ♦ nm/f madman(-woman) ♦ nm (du roi) jester; **être ~de** to be mad ou crazy about; **avoir le ~rire** to have the giggles

**foudre** [fudʀ] nf: **la ~** lightning

**foudroyant, e** [fudʀwajã, ãt] adj (progrès) lightning cpd; (succès) stunning; (maladie, poison) violent

**foudroyer** [fudʀwaje] vt to strike down; **être foudroyé** to be struck by lightning; ~ **qn du regard** to glare at sb

**fouet** [fwɛ] nm whip; (CULIN) whisk; **de plein ~** (se heurter) head on; **fouetter** vt to whip; (crème) to whisk

**fougère** [fuʒɛʀ] nf fern

**fougue** [fug] nf ardour, spirit; **fougueux, -euse** adj fiery

**fouille** [fuj] nf search; ~**s** nfpl (archéologiques) excavations; **fouiller** vt to search; (creuser) to dig ♦ vi to rummage; **fouillis** nm jumble, muddle

**fouiner** [fwine] (péj) vi: ~ **dans** to nose around ou about in

**foulard** [fulaʀ] nm scarf

**foule** [ful] nf crowd; **la ~** crowds pl; **une ~ de** masses of

**foulée** [fule] nf stride

**fouler** [fule] vt to press; (sol) to tread upon; se ~ **la cheville** to sprain one's ankle; **ne pas se ~** not to overexert o.s.; **il ne se foule pas** he doesn't put himself out; **foulure** nf sprain

**four** [fuʀ] nm oven; (de potier) kiln;

(THÉÂTRE: échec) flop

**fourbe** [fuʀb] adj deceitful

**fourbu, e** [fuʀby] adj exhausted

**fourche** [fuʀʃ] nf pitchfork

**fourchette** [fuʀʃɛt] nf fork; (STATISTIQUE) bracket, margin

**fourgon** [fuʀgɔ̃] nm van; (RAIL) wag(g)on; **fourgonnette** nf (small) van

**fourmi** [fuʀmi] nf ant; **~s** nfpl (fig) pins and needles; **fourmilière** nf (ant-hill); **fourmiller** vi to swarm

**fournaise** [fuʀnɛz] nf blaze; (fig) furnace, oven

**fourneau, x** [fuʀno] nm stove

**fournée** [fuʀne] nf batch

**fourni, e** [fuʀni] adj (barbe, cheveux) thick; (magasin): **bien ~ (en)** well stocked (with)

**fournir** [fuʀniʀ] vt to supply; (preuve, exemple) to provide, supply; (effort) to put in; **fournisseur, -euse** nm/f supplier; (INTERNET): **fournisseur d'accès à Internet** (Internet) service provider, ISP; **fourniture** nf supply(ing); **fournitures scolaires** school stationery

**fourrage** [fuʀaʒ] nm fodder

**fourré, e** [fuʀe] adj (bonbon etc) filled; (manteau etc) fur-lined ♦ nm thicket

**fourrer** [fuʀe] (fam) vt to stick, shove; **se ~ dans/sous** to get into/under; **fourre-tout** nm inv (sac) holdall; (fig) rag-bag

**fourrière** [fuʀjɛʀ] nf pound

**fourrure** [fuʀyʀ] nf fur; (sur l'animal) coat

**fourvoyer** [fuʀvwaje]: **se ~** vi to go astray, stray

**foutre** [futʀ] (fam!) vt = **ficher**; **foutu, e** (fam!) adj = **fichu, e**

**foyer** [fwaje] nm (maison) home; (famille) family; (de cheminée) hearth; (de jeunes etc) (social) club; (résidence) hostel; (salon) foyer; **lunettes à double ~** bi-focal glasses

**fracas** [fʀaka] nm (d'objet qui tombe) crash; **fracassant, e** adj (succès) thun-

dering; **fracasser** vt to smash

**fraction** [fʀaksjɔ̃] nf fraction; **fractionner** vt to divide (up), split (up)

**fracture** [fʀaktyʀ] nf fracture; **~ du crâne** fractured skull; **fracturer** vt (coffre, serrure) to break open; (os, membre) to fracture

**fragile** [fʀaʒil] adj fragile, delicate; (fig) frail; **fragilité** nf fragility

**fragment** [fʀagmɑ̃] nm (d'un objet) fragment, piece

**fraîche** [fʀɛʃ] adj voir **frais**; **fraîcheur** nf coolness; (d'un aliment) freshness; **fraîchir** vi to get cooler; (vent) to freshen

**frais, fraîche** [fʀɛ, fʀɛʃ] adj fresh; (froid) cool ♦ adv (récemment) newly, freshly; **il fait ~** it's cool; **servir ~** serve chilled; **prendre le ~** to take a breath of cool air; **faire des ~** to go to a lot of expense; **~ de scolarité** school fees (BRIT), tuition (US); **~ généraux** overheads

**fraise** [fʀɛz] nf strawberry; **~ des bois** wild strawberry

**framboise** [fʀɑ̃bwaz] nf raspberry

**franc, franche** [fʀɑ̃, fʀɑ̃ʃ] adj (personne) frank, straightforward; (visage) open; (net: refus) clear; (: coupure) clean; (intensif) downright ♦ nm franc

**français, e** [fʀɑ̃sɛ, ɛz] adj French ♦ nm/f: **F~,** e Frenchman(-woman) ♦ nm (LING) French; **les F~** the French

**France** [fʀɑ̃s] nf: **la ~** France

**franche** [fʀɑ̃ʃ] adj voir **franc**; **franchement** adv frankly; (nettement) definitely; (tout à fait: mauvais etc) down-right

**franchir** [fʀɑ̃ʃiʀ] vt (obstacle) to clear, get over; (seuil, ligne, rivière) to cross; (distance) to cover

**franchise** [fʀɑ̃ʃiz] nf frankness; (douanière) exemption; (ASSURANCES) excess

**franc-maçon** [fʀɑ̃masɔ̃] nm freemason

**franco** [fʀɑ̃ko] adv (COMM): **~ (de port)**

postage paid

**francophone** [frɑ̃kɔfɔn] *adj* French-speaking

**franc-parler** [frɑ̃parle] *nm inv* outspokenness; **avoir son ~-~** to speak one's mind

**frange** [frɑ̃ʒ] *nf* fringe

**frangipane** [frɑ̃ʒipan] *nf* almond paste

**franquette** [frɑ̃kɛt]: **à la bonne ~** *adv* without any fuss

**frappant, e** [frapɑ̃, ɑ̃t] *adj* striking

**frappé, e** [frape] *adj* iced

**frapper** [frape] *vt* to hit, strike; (*étonner*) to strike; **~ dans ses mains** to clap one's hands; **frappé de stupeur** dumbfounded

**frasques** [frask] *nfpl* escapades

**fraternel, le** [fratɛrnɛl] *adj* brotherly, fraternal; **fraternité** *nf* brotherhood

**fraude** [frod] *nf* fraud; (*SCOL*) cheating; **passer qch en ~** to smuggle sth in (*ou* out); **~ fiscale** tax evasion; **frauder** *vi, vt* to cheat; **frauduleux, -euse** *adj* fraudulent

**frayer** [freje] *vt* to open up, clear ♦ *vi* to spawn; **se ~ un chemin dans la foule** to force one's way through the crowd

**frayeur** [frejœr] *nf* fright

**fredonner** [frədɔne] *vt* to hum

**freezer** [frizœr] *nm* freezing compartment

**frein** [frɛ̃] *nm* brake; **mettre un ~ à** (*fig*) to curb, check; **~ à main** handbrake; **freiner** *vi* to brake ♦ *vt* (*progrès etc*) to check

**frêle** [frɛl] *adj* frail, fragile

**frelon** [frəlɔ̃] *nm* hornet

**frémir** [fremir] *vi* (*de peur, d'horreur*) to shudder; (*de colère*) to shake; (*feuillage*) to quiver

**frêne** [frɛn] *nm* ash

**frénétique** [frenetik] *adj* frenzied, frenetic

**fréquemment** [frekamɑ̃] *adv* frequently

**fréquent, e** [frekɑ̃, ɑ̃t] *adj* frequent

**fréquentation** [frekɑ̃tasjɔ̃] *nf* frequenting; **~s** *nfpl* (*relations*) company *sg*

**fréquenté, e** [frekɑ̃te] *adj*: **très ~** (very) busy; **mal ~** patronized by disreputable elements

**fréquenter** [frekɑ̃te] *vt* (*lieu*) to frequent; (*personne*) to see; **se ~** to see each other

**frère** [frɛr] *nm* brother

**fresque** [frɛsk] *nf* (*ART*) fresco

**fret** [frɛ(t)] *nm* freight

**frétiller** [fretije] *vi* (*poisson*) to wriggle

**fretin** [frətɛ̃] *nm*: **menu ~** small fry

**friable** [frijabl] *adj* crumbly

**friand, e** [frijɑ̃, frijɑ̃d] *adj*: **~ de** very fond of ♦ *nm*: **~ au fromage** cheese puff

**friandise** [frijɑ̃diz] *nf* sweet

**fric** [frik] (*fam*) *nm* cash, bread

**friche** [friʃ]: **en ~** *adj, adv* (lying) fallow

**friction** [friksjɔ̃] *nf* (*massage*) rub, rubdown; (*TECH, fig*) friction; **frictionner** *vt* to rub (down)

**frigidaire** ® [friʒidɛr] *nm* refrigerator

**frigide** [friʒid] *adj* frigid

**frigo** [frigo] (*fam*) *nm* fridge

**frigorifié, e** [frigɔrifje] (*fam*) *adj*: **être ~** to be frozen stiff

**frigorifique** [frigɔrifik] *adj* refrigerating

**frileux, -euse** [frilø, øz] *adj* sensitive to (the) cold

**frime** [frim] (*fam*) *nf*: **c'est de la ~** it's a lot of eyewash, it's all put on; **frimer** (*fam*) *vi* to show off

**frimousse** [frimus] *nf* (sweet) little face

**fringale** [frɛ̃gal] (*fam*) *nf*: **avoir la ~** to be ravenous

**fringant, e** [frɛ̃gɑ̃, ɑ̃t] *adj* dashing

**fringues** [frɛ̃g] (*fam*) *nfpl* clothes

**fripé, e** [fripe] *adj* crumpled

**fripon, ne** [fripɔ̃, ɔn] *adj* roguish, mischievous ♦ *nm/f* rascal, rogue

**fripouille** [fripuj] *nf* scoundrel

**frire** [frir] *vt, vi*: **faire ~** to fry

**frisé, e** [fʀize] *adj* (*cheveux*) curly; (*personne*) curly-haired

**frisson** [fʀisɔ̃] *nm* (*de froid*) shiver; (*de peur*) shudder; **frissonner** *vi* (*de fièvre, froid*) to shiver; (*d'horreur*) to shudder

**frit, e** [fʀi, fʀit] *pp de* **frire; frite** *nf:* (**pommes**) **frites** chips (*BRIT*), French fries; **friture** *nf* chip pan; *(huile)* (deep) fat; *(plat):* **friture (de poissons)** fried fish

**frivole** [fʀivɔl] *adj* frivolous

**froid, e** [fʀwa, fʀwad] *adj, nm* cold; **il fait** ~ it's cold; **avoir/prendre** ~ to be/catch cold; **être en** ~ **avec** to be on bad terms with; **froidement** *adv* (*accueillir*) coldly; (*décider*) coolly

**froideur** [fʀwadœʀ] *nf* coldness

**froisser** [fʀwase] *vt* to crumple, crease, (*fig*) to hurt, offend; **se** ~ *vi* to crumple, crease; (*personne*) to take offence; **se** ~ **un muscle** to strain a muscle

**frôler** [fʀole] *vt* to brush against; (*suj: projectile*) to skim past; (*fig*) to come very close to

**fromage** [fʀɔmaʒ] *nm* cheese; ~ **blanc** soft white cheese

**froment** [fʀɔmɑ̃] *nm* wheat

**froncer** [fʀɔ̃se] *vt* to gather; ~ **les sourcils** to frown

**frondaisons** [fʀɔ̃dɛzɔ̃] *nfpl* foliage *sg*

**front** [fʀɔ̃] *nm* forehead, brow; (*MIL*) front; **de** ~ (*se heurter*) head-on; (*simultanément*) at once; **faire** ~ **à** to face up to

**frontalier, -ère** [fʀɔ̃talje, jɛʀ] *adj* border *cpd*, frontier *cpd*

**frontière** [fʀɔ̃tjɛʀ] *nf* frontier, border

**frotter** [fʀɔte] *vi* to rub, scrape ♦ *vt* to rub; (*pommes de terre, plancher*) to scrub; ~ **une allumette** to strike a match

**fructifier** [fʀyktifje] *vi* to yield a profit

**fructueux, -euse** [fʀyktɥø, øz] *adj* fruitful

**frugal, e, -aux** [fʀygal, o] *adj* frugal

**fruit** [fʀɥi] *nm* fruit *gen no pl;* ~ **de la passion** passion fruit; ~**s de mer** seafood(s); ~**s secs** dried fruit *sg;* **fruité, e** *adj* fruity; **fruitier, -ère** *adj:* **arbre fruitier** fruit tree

**fruste** [fʀyst] *adj* unpolished, uncultivated

**frustrer** [fʀystʀe] *vt* to frustrate

**FS** *abr* (= *franc suisse*) SF

**fuel(-oil)** [fjul(ɔjl)] *nm* fuel oil; (*domestique*) heating oil

**fugace** [fygas] *adj* fleeting

**fugitif, -ive** [fyʒitif, iv] *adj* (*fugace*) fleeting ♦ *nm/f* fugitive

**fugue** [fyg] *nf:* **faire une** ~ to run away, abscond

**fuir** [fɥiʀ] *vt* to flee from; (*éviter*) to shun ♦ *vi* to run away; (*gaz, robinet*) to leak

**fuite** [fɥit] *nf* flight; (*écoulement, divulgation*) leak; **être en** ~ to be on the run; **mettre en** ~ to put to flight

**fulgurant, e** [fylgyʀɑ̃, ɑ̃t] *adj* lightning *cpd,* dazzling

**fulminer** [fylmine] *vi* to thunder forth

**fumé, e** [fyme] *adj* (*CULIN*) smoked; (*verre*) tinted; **fumée** *nf* smoke

**fumer** [fyme] *vi* to smoke; (*soupe*) to steam ♦ *vt* to smoke

**fumes** *etc* [fym] *vb voir* **être**

**fumet** [fyme] *nm* aroma

**fumeur, -euse** [fymœʀ, øz] *nm/f* smoker

**fumeux, -euse** [fymø, øz] (*péj*) *adj* woolly, hazy

**fumier** [fymje] *nm* manure

**fumiste** [fymist] *nm/f* (*péj: paresseux*) shirker

**funèbre** [fynɛbʀ] *adj* funeral *cpd*; (*fig: atmosphère*) gloomy

**funérailles** [fyneʀaj] *nfpl* funeral *sg*

**funeste** [fynɛst] *adj* (*erreur*) disastrous

**fur** [fyʀ]: **au** ~ **et à mesure** *adv* as one goes along; **au** ~ **et à mesure que** as

**furet** [fyʀɛ] *nm* ferret

**fureter** [fyʀ(ə)te] (*péj*) *vi* to nose about

**fureur** [fyʀœʀ] *nf* fury; **être en** ~ to

be infuriated; **faire ~** to be all the rage

**furibond, e** [fyribɔ̃, ɔ̃d] *adj* furious

**furie** [fyri] *nf* fury; *(femme)* shrew, vixen; **en ~** *(mer)* raging; **furieux, -euse** *adj* furious

**furoncle** [fyrɔ̃kl] *nm* boil

**furtif, -ive** [fyrtif, iv] *adj* furtive

**fus** [fy] *vb voir* **être**

**fusain** [fyzɛ̃] *nm (ART)* charcoal

**fuseau, x** [fyzo] *nm (pour filer)* spindle; *(pantalon)* (ski) pants; **~ horaire** time zone

**fusée** [fyze] *nf* rocket; **~ éclairante** flare

**fuser** [fyze] *vi (rires etc)* to burst forth

**fusible** [fyzibl] *nm (ÉLEC)* fuse wire; *(: fiche)* fuse

**fusil** [fyzi] *nm (de guerre, à canon rayé)* rifle, gun; *(de chasse, à canon lisse)* shotgun, gun; **fusillade** *nf* gunfire *no pl*, shooting *no pl*; **fusiller** *vt* to shoot; **fusil-mitrailleur** *nm* machine gun

**fusionner** [fyzjɔne] *vi* to merge

**fut** [fy] *vb voir* **être**

**fût** [fy] *vb voir* **être** ♦ *nm (tonneau)* barrel, cask

**futé, e** [fyte] *adj* crafty; **Bison ~** ® *TV and radio traffic monitoring service*

**futile** [fytil] *adj* futile; frivolous

**futur, e** [fytyr] *adj,* nm future

**fuyant, e** [fɥijɑ̃, ɑ̃t] *vb voir* **fuir** ♦ *adj (regard etc)* evasive; *(lignes etc)* receding

**fuyard, e** [fɥijar, ard] *nm/f* runaway

# G, g

**gâcher** [gaʃe] *vt (gâter)* to spoil; *(gaspiller)* to waste; **gâchis** *nm* waste *no pl*

**gadoue** [gadu] *nf* sludge

**gaffe** [gaf] *nf* blunder; **faire ~** *(fam)* to be careful

**gage** [gaʒ] *nm (dans un jeu)* forfeit; *(fig: de fidélité, d'amour)* token

**gageure** [gaʒyr] *nf:* **c'est une ~** it's attempting the impossible

**gagnant, e** [gaɲɑ̃, ɑ̃t] *nm/f* winner

**gagne-pain** [gaɲpɛ̃] *nm inv* job

**gagner** [gaɲe] *vt* to win; *(somme d'argent, revenu)* to earn; *(aller vers, atteindre)* to reach; *(envahir: sommeil, peur)* to overcome; *(: mal)* to spread to ♦ *vi* to win; *(fig)* to gain; **~ du temps/de la place** to gain time/save space; **~ sa vie** to earn one's living

**gai, e** [ge] *adj* cheerful; *(un peu ivre)* merry; **gaiement** *adv* cheerfully; **gaieté** *nf* cheerfulness; **de gaieté de cœur** with a light heart

**gaillard, e** [gajar, ard] *nm (strapping)* fellow

**gain** [gɛ̃] *nm (revenu)* earnings *pl*; *(bénéfice: gén pl)* profits *pl*

**gaine** [gen] *nf (corset)* girdle; *(fourreau)* sheath

**gala** [gala] *nm* official reception; **de ~** *(soirée etc)* gala

**galant, e** [galɑ̃, ɑ̃t] *adj (courtois)* courteous, gentlemanly; *(entreprenant)* flirtatious, gallant; *(scène, rendez-vous)* romantic

**galère** [galɛr] *nf* galley; **quelle ~!** *(fam)* it's a real grind!; **galérer** *(fam)* *vi* to slog away, work hard; *(rencontrer des difficultés)* to have a hassle

**galerie** [galri] *nf* gallery; *(THÉÂTRE)* circle; *(de voiture)* roof rack; *(fig: spectateurs)* audience; **~ de peinture** *(privée)* art gallery; **~ marchande** shopping arcade

**galet** [galɛ] *nm* pebble

**galette** [galɛt] *nf* flat cake; **~ des Rois** cake eaten on Twelfth Night

**galipette** [galipɛt] *nf* somersault

**Galles** [gal] *nfpl:* **le pays de ~** Wales; **gallois, e** *adj* Welsh ♦ *nm/f:* **Gallois, e** Welshman(-woman) ♦ *nm (LING)* Welsh

**galon** [galɔ̃] *nm (MIL)* stripe; *(décoratif)* piece of braid

**galop** [galo] *nm* gallop; **galoper** *vi* to gallop

**galopin** [galɔpɛ̃] *nm* urchin, ragamuffin

**gambader** [gɑ̃bade] *vi (animal, enfant)*

to leap about

**gambas** [gɑ̃bas] *nfpl* Mediterranean prawns

**gamin, e** [gamɛ̃, in] *nm/f* kid ♦ *adj* childish

**gamme** [gam] *nf* (MUS) scale; (*fig*) range

**gammé, e** [game] *adj*: **croix ~e** swastika

**gang** [gɑ̃g] *nm* (*de criminels*) gang

**gant** [gɑ̃] *nm* glove; **~ de toilette** face flannel (BRIT), face cloth

**garage** [gaʀaʒ] *nm* garage; **garagiste** *nm/f* garage owner; (*employé*) garage mechanic

**garantie** [gaʀɑ̃ti] *nf* guarantee; (**bon de**) **~** guarantee *ou* warranty slip

**garantir** [gaʀɑ̃tiʀ] *vt* to guarantee

**garce** [gaʀs] (*fam*) *nf* bitch

**garçon** [gaʀsɔ̃] *nm* boy; (*célibataire*): **vieux ~** bachelor; (*serveur*): **~ (de café)** waiter; **~ de courses** messenger; **~ d'honneur** best man; **garçonnière** *nf* bachelor flat

**garde** [gaʀd(ə)] *nm* (*de prisonnier*) guard; (*de domaine etc*) warden; (*soldat, sentinelle*) guardsman ♦ *nf* (*soldats*) guard; **de ~** on duty; **monter la ~** to stand guard; **mettre en ~** to warn; **prendre ~ (à)** to be careful (of); **~ champêtre** ♦ *nm* rural policeman; **~ du corps** ♦ *nm* bodyguard; **~ des enfants** ♦ *nf* (*après divorce*) custody of the children; **~ à vue** ♦ *nf* (JUR) ≈ police custody; **garde-à-vous** *nm*: **être/se mettre au garde-à-vous** to be at/ stand to attention; **garde-barrière** *nm/f* level-crossing keeper; **garde-boue** *nm inv* mudguard; **garde-chasse** *nm* gamekeeper; **garde-malade** *nf* home nurse; **garde-manger** *nm inv* (*armoire*) meat safe; (*pièce*) pantry, larder

**garder** [gaʀde] *vt* (*conserver*) to keep; (*surveiller: enfants*) to look after; (: *immeuble, lieu, prisonnier*) to guard; **se ~** *vi* (*aliment: se conserver*) to keep; **se ~**

**de faire** to be careful not to do; **~ le lit/la chambre** to stay in bed/indoors; **pêche/chasse gardée** private fishing/ hunting (ground)

**garderie** [gaʀdəʀi] *nf* day nursery, crèche

**gardien, ne** [gaʀdjɛ̃, jɛn] *nm/f* (*garde*) guard; (*de prison*) warder; (*de domaine, réserve*) warden; (*de musée etc*) attendant; (*de phare, cimetière*) keeper; (*d'immeuble*) caretaker; (*fig*) guardian; **~ de but** goalkeeper; **~ de la paix** policeman; **~ de nuit** night watchman

**gare** [gaʀ] *nf* station; **~ routière** bus station

**garer** [gaʀe] *vt* to park; **se ~** *vi* to park

**gargariser** [gaʀgaʀize]: **se ~** *vi* to gargle

**gargote** [gaʀgɔt] *nf* cheap restaurant

**gargouille** [gaʀguj] *nf* gargoyle

**gargouiller** [gaʀguje] *vi* to gurgle

**garnement** [gaʀnəmɑ̃] *nm* rascal, scallywag

**garni, e** [gaʀni] *adj* (*plat*) served with vegetables (*and chips or rice etc*)

**garnison** [gaʀnizɔ̃] *nf* garrison

**garniture** [gaʀnityʀ] *nf* (CULIN) vegetables *pl*; **~ de frein** brake lining

**gars** [gɑ] (*fam*) *nm* guy

**Gascogne** [gaskɔɲ] *nf* Gascony; **le golfe de ~** the Bay of Biscay

**gas-oil** [gazɔjl] *nm* diesel (oil)

**gaspiller** [gaspije] *vt* to waste

**gastronome** [gastʀɔnɔm] *nm/f* gourmet; **gastronomie** *nf* gastronomy; **gastronomique** *adj* gastronomic

**gâteau, x** [gɑto] *nm* cake; **~ sec** biscuit

**gâter** [gɑte] *vt* to spoil; **se ~** *vi* (*dent, fruit*) to go bad; (*temps, situation*) to change for the worse

**gâterie** [gɑtʀi] *nf* little treat

**gâteux, -euse** [gɑtø, øz] *adj* senile

**gauche** [goʃ] *adj* left, left-hand; (*maladroit*) awkward, clumsy ♦ *nf* (POL) left (wing); **le bras ~** the left arm; **le côté ~** the left-hand side; **à ~** on the left;

(direction) (to the) left; **gaucher, -ère** adj left-handed; **gauchiste** nm/f leftist

**gaufre** [gofʀ] nf waffle

**gaufrette** [gofʀɛt] nf wafer

**gaulois, e** [golwa, waz] adj Gallic ♦ nm/f: **G~, e** Gaul

**gaver** [gave] vt to force-feed; **se ~ de** to stuff o.s. with

**gaz** [gɑz] nm inv gas

**gaze** [gɑz] nf gauze

**gazer** [gɑze] (fam) vi: **ça gaze?** how's things?

**gazette** [gɑzɛt] nf news sheet

**gazeux, -euse** [gɑzø, øz] adj (boisson) fizzy; (eau) sparkling

**gazoduc** [gɑzɔdyk] nm gas pipeline

**gazon** [gɑzɔ̃] nm (herbe) grass; (pelouse) lawn

**gazouiller** [gɑzuje] vi to chirp; (enfant) to babble

**geai** [ʒɛ] nm jay

**géant, e** [ʒeɑ̃, ɑ̃t] adj gigantic; (COMM) giant-size ♦ nm/f giant

**geindre** [ʒɛ̃dʀ] vi to groan, moan

**gel** [ʒɛl] nm frost; **~ douche** shower gel

**gélatine** [ʒelatin] nf gelatine

**gelée** [ʒ(ə)le] nf jelly; (gel) frost

**geler** [ʒ(ə)le] vt, vi to freeze; **il gèle** it's freezing

**gélule** [ʒelyl] nf (MÉD) capsule

**gelures** [ʒǎlyʀ] nfpl frostbite sg

**Gémeaux** [ʒemo] nmpl: **les ~** Gemini

**gémir** [ʒemiʀ] vi to groan, moan

**gênant, e** [ʒɛnɑ̃, ɑ̃t] adj (irritant) annoying; (embarrassant) embarrassing

**gencive** [ʒɑ̃siv] nf gum

**gendarme** [ʒɑ̃daʀm] nm gendarme; **gendarmerie** nf military police force in countryside and small towns; their police station or barracks

**gendre** [ʒɑ̃dʀ] nm son-in-law

**gêné, e** [ʒene] adj embarrassed

**gêner** [ʒene] vt (incommoder) to bother; (encombrer) to be in the way; (embarrasser): **~ qn** to make sb feel ill-at-ease

**général, e, -aux** [ʒeneʀal, o] adj, nm general; **en ~** usually, in general; **gé-**

**nérale** nf: (répétition) générale final dress rehearsal; **généralement** adv generally; **généraliser** vt, vi to generalize; **se généraliser** vi to become widespread; **généraliste** nm/f general practitioner; G.P.

**génération** [ʒeneʀasjɔ̃] nf generation

**généreux, -euse** [ʒeneʀø, øz] adj generous

**générique** [ʒeneʀik] nm (CINÉMA) credits pl

**générosité** [ʒeneʀozite] nf generosity

**genêt** [ʒ(ə)nɛ] nm broom no pl (shrub)

**génétique** [ʒenetik] adj genetic; **génétiquement** adv: **~ment modifié** genetically modified, GM

**Genève** [ʒ(ə)nɛv] n Geneva

**génial, e, -aux** [ʒenjal, jo] adj of genius; (fam: formidable) fantastic, brilliant

**génie** [ʒeni] nm genius; (MIL): **le ~** the Engineers pl; **~ civil** civil engineering

**genièvre** [ʒənjɛvʀ] nm juniper

**génisse** [ʒenis] nf heifer

**génital, e, -aux** [ʒenital, o] adj genital; **les parties ~es** the genitals

**génoise** [ʒenwaz] nf sponge cake

**genou, x** [ʒ(ə)nu] nm knee; **à ~x** on one's knees; **se mettre à ~x** to kneel down

**genre** [ʒɑ̃ʀ] nm kind, type, sort; (LING) gender; **avoir bon ~** to look a nice sort; **avoir mauvais ~** to be coarse-looking; **ce n'est pas son ~** it's not like him

**gens** [ʒɑ̃] nmpl (f in some phrases) people pl

**gentil, le** [ʒɑ̃ti, ij] adj kind; (enfant: sage) good; (endroit etc) nice; **gentillesse** nf kindness; **gentiment** adv kindly

**géographie** [ʒeɔgʀafi] nf geography

**geôlier** [ʒolje, jeʀ] nm jailer

**géologie** [ʒeɔlɔʒi] nf geology

**géomètre** [ʒeɔmɛtʀ] nm/f (arpenteur) (land) surveyor

**géométrie** [ʒeɔmetʀi] nf geometry; **géométrique** adj geometric

**gérant, e** [ʒeʀɑ̃, ɑ̃t] nm/f manager(-

eress)

**gerbe** [ʒɛʀb] *nf (de fleurs)* spray; *(de blé)* sheaf

**gercé, e** [ʒɛʀse] *adj* chapped

**gerçure** [ʒɛʀsyʀ] *nf* crack

**gérer** [ʒeʀe] *vt* to manage

**germain, e** [ʒɛʀmɛ̃, ɛn] *adj*: **cousin ~** first cousin

**germe** [ʒɛʀm] *nm* germ; **germer** *vi* to sprout; *(semence)* to germinate

**geste** [ʒɛst] *nm* gesture

**gestion** [ʒɛstjɔ̃] *nf* management

**ghetto** [geto] *nm* ghetto

**gibet** [ʒibɛ] *nm* gallows *pl*

**gibier** [ʒibje] *nm (animaux)* game

**giboulée** [ʒibule] *nf* sudden shower

**gicler** [ʒikle] *vi* to spurt, squirt

**gifle** [ʒifl] *nf* slap (in the face); **gifler** *vt* to slap (in the face)

**gigantesque** [ʒiɡɑ̃tɛsk] *adj* gigantic

**gigogne** [ʒiɡɔɲ] *adj*: **lits ~s** truckle *(BRIT)* ou trundle beds

**gigot** [ʒiɡo] *nm* leg (of mutton ou lamb)

**gigoter** [ʒiɡɔte] *vi* to wriggle (about)

**gilet** [ʒilɛ] *nm* waistcoat; *(pull)* cardigan; **~ de sauvetage** life jacket

**gin** [dʒin] *nm* gin; **~-tonic** gin and tonic

**gingembre** [ʒɛ̃ʒɑ̃bʀ] *nm* ginger

**girafe** [ʒiʀaf] *nf* giraffe

**giratoire** [ʒiʀatwaʀ] *adj*: **sens ~** roundabout

**girofle** [ʒiʀɔfl] *nf*: **clou de ~** clove

**girouette** [ʒiʀwɛt] *nf* weather vane ou cock

**gitan, e** [ʒitɑ̃, an] *nm/f* gipsy

**gîte** [ʒit] *nm (maison)* home; *(abri)* shelter; **~ (rural)** holiday cottage ou apartment

**givre** [ʒivʀ] *nm* (hoar) frost; **givré, e** *adj* covered in frost; *(fam: fou)* nuts; **orange givrée** orange sorbet *(served in peel)*

**glace** [ɡlas] *nf* ice; *(crème glacée)* ice cream; *(miroir)* mirror; *(de voiture)* window

**glacé, e** [ɡlase] *adj (mains, vent, pluie)* freezing; *(lac)* frozen; *(boisson)* iced

**glacer** [ɡlase] *vt* to freeze; *(gâteau)* to ice; *(fig)*: **~ qn** *(intimider)* to chill sb; *(paralyser)* to make sb's blood run cold

**glacial, e** [ɡlasjal, jo] *adj* icy

**glacier** [ɡlasje] *nm (GÉO)* glacier; *(marchand)* ice-cream maker

**glacière** [ɡlasjɛʀ] *nf* icebox

**glaçon** [ɡlasɔ̃] *nm* icicle; *(pour boisson)* ice cube

**glaïeul** [ɡlajœl] *nm* gladiolus

**glaise** [ɡlɛz] *nf* clay

**gland** [ɡlɑ̃] *nm* acorn; *(décoration)* tassel

**glande** [ɡlɑ̃d] *nf* gland

**glander** [ɡlɑ̃de] *(fam)* *vi* to fart around (!)

**glauque** [ɡlok] *adj* dull blue-green

**glissade** [ɡlisad] *nf (par jeu)* slide; *(chute)* slip; **faire des ~s sur la glace** to slide on the ice

**glissant, e** [ɡlisɑ̃, ɑ̃t] *adj* slippery

**glissement** [ɡlismɑ̃] *nm*: **~ de terrain** landslide

**glisser** [ɡlise] *vi (avancer)* to glide ou slide along; *(coulisser, tomber)* to slide; *(déraper)* to slip; *(être glissant)* to be slippery ♦ *vt* to slip; **se ~ dans** to slip into

**global, e, -aux** [ɡlɔbal, o] *adj* overall

**globe** [ɡlɔb] *nm* globe

**globule** [ɡlɔbyl] *nm (du sang)* corpuscle

**globuleux, -euse** [ɡlɔbylø, øz] *adj*: **yeux ~** protruding eyes

**gloire** [ɡlwaʀ] *nf* glory; **glorieux, -euse** *adj* glorious

**glousser** [ɡluse] *vi* to cluck; *(rire)* to chuckle; **gloussement** *nm* cluck; chuckle

**glouton, ne** [ɡlutɔ̃, ɔn] *adj* gluttonous

**gluant, e** [ɡlyɑ̃, ɑ̃t] *adj* sticky, gummy

**glucose** [ɡlykoz] *nm* glucose

**glycine** [ɡlisin] *nf* wisteria

**goal** [ɡol] *nm* goalkeeper

**GO** *sigle* (= **grandes ondes**) LW

**gobelet** [ɡɔblɛ] *nm (en étain, verre, ar-

**gent**) tumbler; (*d'enfant, de pique-nique*) beaker; (*à dés*) cup

**gober** [gɔbe] *vt* to swallow (whole)

**godasse** [gɔdas] (*fam*) *nf* shoe

**godet** [gɔdɛ] *nm* pot

**goéland** [gɔelɑ̃] *nm* (sea)gull

**goélette** [gɔelɛt] *nf* schooner

**gogo** [gɔgo]: **à ~** *adv* galore

**goguenard, e** [gɔg(ə)naʀ, aʀd] *adj* mocking

**goinfre** [gwɛ̃fʀ] *nm* glutton

**golf** [gɔlf] *nm* golf; (*terrain*) golf course

**golfe** [gɔlf] *nm* gulf; (*petit*) bay

**gomme** [gɔm] *nf* (*à effacer*) rubber (*BRIT*), eraser; **gommer** *vt* to rub out (*BRIT*), erase

**gond** [gɔ̃] *nm* hinge; **sortir de ses ~s** (*fig*) to fly off the handle

**gondoler** [gɔ̃dɔle]: **se ~** *vi* (*planche*) to warp; (*métal*) to buckle

**gonflé, e** [gɔ̃fle] *adj* swollen; **il est ~** (*fam: courageux*) he's got some nerve; (*impertinent*) he's got a nerve

**gonfler** [gɔ̃fle] *vt* (*pneu, ballon: en soufflant*) to blow up; (: *avec une pompe*) to pump up; (*nombre, importance*) to inflate ♦ *vi* to swell (up); (*CULIN: pâte*) to rise; **gonfleur** *nm* pump

**gonzesse** [gɔ̃zɛs] (*fam*) *nf* chick, bird (*BRIT*)

**goret** [gɔʀɛ] *nm* piglet

**gorge** [gɔʀʒ] *nf* (*ANAT*) throat; (*vallée*) gorge

**gorgé, e** [gɔʀʒe] *adj*: **~ de** filled with; (*eau*) saturated with; **gorgée** *nf* (*petite*) sip; (*grande*) gulp

**gorille** [gɔʀij] *nm* gorilla; (*fam*) bodyguard

**gosier** [gozje] *nm* throat

**gosse** [gɔs] (*fam*) *nm/f* kid

**goudron** [gudʀɔ̃] *nm* tar; **goudronner** *vt* to tar(mac) (*BRIT*), asphalt (*US*)

**gouffre** [gufʀ] *nm* abyss, gulf

**goujat** [guʒa] *nm* boor

**goulot** [gulo] *nm* neck; **boire au ~** to drink from the bottle

**goulu, e** [guly] *adj* greedy

**gourd, e** [guʀ, guʀd] *adj* numb (with cold)

**gourde** [guʀd] *nf* (*récipient*) flask; (*fam*) (*clumsy*) clot *ou* oaf ♦ *adj* oafish

**gourdin** [guʀdɛ̃] *nm* club, bludgeon

**gourer** [guʀe]: (*fam*): **se ~** *vi* to boob

**gourmand, e** [guʀmɑ̃, ɑ̃d] *adj* greedy; **gourmandise** [guʀmɑ̃diz] *nf* greed; (*bonbon*) sweet

**gourmet** [guʀmɛ] *nm* gourmet

**gourmette** [guʀmɛt] *nf* chain bracelet

**gousse** [gus] *nf*: **~ d'ail** clove of garlic

**goût** [gu] *nm* taste; **avoir bon ~** to taste good; **de bon ~** tasteful; **de mauvais ~** tasteless; **prendre ~ à** to develop a taste *ou* a liking for

**goûter** [gute] *vt* (*essayer*) to taste; (*apprécier*) to enjoy ♦ *vi* to have (afternoon) tea ♦ *nm* (afternoon) tea

**goutte** [gut] *nf* drop; (*MÉD*) gout; (*alcool*) brandy; **tomber ~ à ~** to drip; **goutte-à-goutte** *nm* (*MÉD*) drip

**gouttelette** [gut(ə)lɛt] *nf* droplet

**gouttière** [gutjɛʀ] *nf* gutter

**gouvernail** [guvɛʀnaj] *nm* rudder; (*barre*) helm, tiller

**gouvernante** [guvɛʀnɑ̃t] *nf* governess

**gouvernement** [guvɛʀnəmɑ̃] *nm* government

**gouverner** [guvɛʀne] *vt* to govern

**grabuge** [gʀabyʒ] (*fam*) *nm* mayhem

**grâce** [gʀɑs] *nf* (*charme*) grace; (*faveur*) favour; (*JUR*) pardon; **~s** *nfpl* (*REL*) grace *sg*; **faire ~ à qn de qch** to spare sb sth; **rendre ~(s) à** to give thanks to; **demander ~** to beg for mercy; **~ à** thanks to; **gracier** *vt* to pardon; **gracieux, -euse** *adj* graceful

**grade** [gʀad] *nm* rank; **monter en ~** to be promoted

**gradin** [gʀadɛ̃] *nm* tier; step; **~s** *nmpl* (*de stade*) terracing *sg*

**gradué, e** [gʀadɥe] *adj*: **verre ~** measuring jug

**graduel, le** [gʀadɥɛl] *adj* gradual

**graduer** [gʀadɥe] *vt* (*effort etc*) to increase gradually; (*règle, verre*) to graduate

**graffiti** [grafiti] nmpl graffiti

**grain** [grɛ̃] nm (gén) grain; (NAVIG) squall; ~ **de beauté** beauty spot; ~ **de café** coffee bean; ~ **de poivre** peppercorn; ~ **de poussière** speck of dust; ~ **de raisin** grape

**graine** [grɛn] nf seed

**graissage** [grɛsaʒ] nm lubrication, greasing

**graisse** [grɛs] nf fat; (lubrifiant) grease; **graisser** vt to lubricate, grease; (tacher) to make greasy; **graisseux, -euse** adj greasy

**grammaire** [gra(m)mɛr] nf grammar; **grammatical, e, -aux** adj grammatical

**gramme** [gram] nm gramme

**grand, e** [grɑ̃, grɑ̃d] adj (haut) tall; (gros, vaste, large) big, large; (long) long; (plus âgé) big; (adulte) grown-up; (sens abstraits) great ♦ adv: ~ **ouvert** wide open; **au** ~ **air** in the open (air); **les** ~s **blessés** the severely injured; ~ **ensemble** housing scheme; ~ **magasin** department store; ~ **personne** grown-up; ~ **surface** hypermarket; ~es **écoles** prestige schools of university level; ~es **lignes** (RAIL) main lines; ~es **vacances** summer holidays; **grand-chose** nm/f inv: **pas grand-chose** not much; **Grande-Bretagne** nf (Great) Britain; **grandeur** nf (dimension) size; **grandeur nature** life-size; **grandiose** adj imposing; **grandir** vi to grow ♦ vt: **grandir qn** (suj: vêtement, chaussure) to make sb look taller; **grand-mère** nf grandmother; **grand-messe** nf high mass; **grand-peine**: **à grand-peine** adv with difficulty; **grand-père** nm grandfather; **grand-route** nf main road; **grands-parents** nmpl grandparents

**grange** [grɑ̃ʒ] nf barn

**granit(e)** [granit] nm granite

**graphique** [grafik] adj graphic ♦ nm graph

**grappe** [grap] nf cluster; ~ **de raisin** bunch of grapes

**gras, se** [grɑ, grɑs] adj (viande, soupe) fatty; (personne) fat; (surface, main) greasy; (plaisanterie) coarse; (TYPO) bold ♦ nm (CULIN) fat; **faire la ~se matinée** to have a lie-in (BRIT), sleep late (US); **grassement** adv: **grassement payé** handsomely paid; **grassouillet, te** adj podgy, plump

**gratifiant, e** [gratifjɑ̃, jɑ̃t] adj gratifying, rewarding

**gratin** [gratɛ̃] nm (plat) cheese-topped dish; (croûte) cheese topping; **gratiné, e** adj (CULIN) au gratin

**gratis** [gratis] adv free

**gratitude** [gratityd] nf gratitude

**gratte-ciel** [gratsjɛl] nm inv skyscraper

**gratte-papier** [gratpapje] (péj) nm inv penpusher

**gratter** [grate] vt (avec un outil) to scrape; (enlever: avec un outil) to scrape off; (: avec un ongle) to scratch; (enlever avec un ongle) to scratch off ♦ vi (irriter) to be scratchy; (démanger) to itch; **se** ~ to scratch (o.s.)

**gratuit, e** [gratɥi, ɥit] adj (entrée, billet) free; (fig) gratuitous

**gravats** [grava] nmpl rubble sg

**grave** [grav] adj (maladie, accident) serious, bad; (sujet, problème) serious, grave; (air) grave, solemn; (voix, son) deep, low-pitched; **gravement** adv seriously; (parler, regarder) gravely

**graver** [grave] vt to engrave

**gravier** [gravje] nm gravel no pl; **gravillons** nmpl loose chippings ou gravel sg

**gravir** [gravir] vt to climb (up)

**gravité** [gravite] nf (de maladie, d'accident) seriousness; (de sujet, problème) gravity

**graviter** [gravite] vi to revolve

**gravure** [gravyr] nf engraving; (reproduction) print

**gré** [gre] nm: **de bon** ~ willingly; **contre le** ~ **de qn** against sb's will; **de**

**son (plein)** ~ of one's own free will; **bon** ~ **mal** ~ like it or not; **de** ~ **ou de force** whether one likes it or not; **savoir** ~ **à qn de qch** to be grateful to sb for sth

**grec, grecque** [gʀɛk] *adj* Greek; *(classique: vase etc)* Grecian ♦ *nm/f*: **G~, Grecque** Greek ♦ *nm* (LING) Greek

**Grèce** [gʀɛs] *nf*: **la** ~ Greece

**greffe** [gʀɛf] *nf* (BOT, MÉD: de tissu) graft; (MÉD: d'organe) transplant; **greffer** *vt* (BOT, MÉD: tissu) to graft; (MÉD: organe) to transplant

**greffier** [gʀefje, jɛʀ] *nm* clerk of the court

**grêle** [gʀɛl] *adj* (very) thin ♦ *nf* hail; **grêler** *vb impers*: **il grêle** it's hailing; **grêlon** [gʀɛlɔ̃] *nm* hailstone

**grelot** [gʀəlo] *nm* little bell

**grelotter** [gʀələte] *vi* to shiver

**grenade** [gʀənad] *nf* (explosive) grenade; (BOT) pomegranate; **grenadine** *nf* grenadine

**grenat** [gʀəna] *adj inv* dark red

**grenier** [gʀənje] *nm* attic; (de ferme) loft

**grenouille** [gʀənuj] *nf* frog

**grès** [gʀɛ] *nm* sandstone; (poterie) stoneware

**grésiller** [gʀezije] *vi* to sizzle; (RADIO) to crackle

**grève** [gʀɛv] *nf* (d'ouvriers) strike; (plage) shore; **se mettre en/faire** ~ to go on/be on strike; ~ **de la faim** hunger strike; ~ **du zèle** work-to-rule (BRIT); slowdown (US); ~ **sauvage** wildcat strike

**gréviste** [gʀevist] *nm/f* striker

**gribouiller** [gʀibuje] *vt* to scribble, scrawl

**grièvement** [gʀijɛvmɑ̃] *adv* seriously

**griffe** [gʀif] *nf* claw; (de couturier) label; **griffer** *vt* to scratch

**griffonner** [gʀifɔne] *vt* to scribble

**grignoter** [gʀiɲɔte] *vt* (personne) to nibble at; (souris) to gnaw at ♦ *vi* to nibble

**gril** [gʀil] *nm* steak *ou* grill pan; **faire cuire au** ~ to grill; **grillade** *nf* (viande etc) grill

**grillage** [gʀijaʒ] *nm* (treillis) wire netting; (clôture) wire fencing

**grille** [gʀij] *nf* (clôture) wire fence; (portail) (metal) gate; (d'égout) (metal) grate; (fig) grid

**grille-pain** [gʀijpɛ̃] *nm inv* toaster

**griller** [gʀije] *vt* (pain) to toast; (viande) to grill; (fig: ampoule etc) to blow; **faire** ~ to toast; to grill; (châtaignes) to roast; ~ **un feu rouge** to jump the lights

**grillon** [gʀijɔ̃] *nm* cricket

**grimace** [gʀimas] *nf* grimace; (pour faire rire): **faire des ~s** to pull *ou* make faces

**grimper** [gʀɛ̃pe] *vi*, *vt* to climb

**grincer** [gʀɛ̃se] *vi* (objet métallique) to grate; (plancher, porte) to creak; ~ **des dents** to grind one's teeth

**grincheux, -euse** [gʀɛ̃ʃø, øz] *adj* grumpy

**grippe** [gʀip] *nf* flu, influenza; **grippé, e** *adj*: **être grippé** to have flu

**gris, e** [gʀi, gʀiz] *adj* grey; (ivre) tipsy

**grisaille** [gʀizaj] *nf* greyness, dullness

**griser** [gʀize] *vt* to intoxicate

**grisonner** [gʀizɔne] *vi* to be going grey

**grisou** [gʀizu] *nm* firedamp

**grive** [gʀiv] *nf* thrush

**grivois, e** [gʀivwa, waz] *adj* saucy

**Groenland** [gʀɔɛnlɑ̃d] *nm* Greenland

**grogner** [gʀɔɲe] *vi* to growl; (fig) to grumble; **grognon, ne** *adj* grumpy

**groin** [gʀwɛ̃] *nm* snout

**grommeler** [gʀɔm(ə)le] *vi* to mutter to o.s.

**gronder** [gʀɔ̃de] *vi* to rumble; (fig: révolte) to be brewing ♦ *vt* to scold; **se faire** ~ to get a telling-off

**groom** [gʀum] *nm* bellboy

**gros, se** [gʀo, gʀos] *adj* big, large; (obèse) fat; (travaux, dégâts) extensive; (épais) thick; (rhume, averse) heavy

♦ *adv*: **risquer/gagner ~** to risk/win a lot ♦ *nm/f* fat man/woman ♦ *nm* (*COMM*): **le ~** the wholesale business; **prix de ~** wholesale price; **par ~ temps/grosse mer** in rough weather/heavy seas; **en ~** roughly; (*COMM*) wholesale; **~ lot** jackpot; **~ mot** coarse word; **~ plan** (*PHOTO*) close-up; **~ sel** cooking salt; **~ titre** headline; **~se caisse** big drum

**groseille** [gʀozɛj] *nf*: **~ (rouge/blanche)** red/white currant; **~ à maquereau** gooseberry

**grosse** [gʀos] *adj voir* **gros**; **grossesse** *nf* pregnancy; **grosseur** *nf* size; (*tumeur*) lump

**grossier, -ière** [gʀosje, jɛʀ] *adj* coarse; (*insolent*) rude; (*dessin*) rough; (*travail*) roughly done; (*imitation, instrument*) crude; (*évident: erreur*) gross; **grossièrement** *adv* (*sommairement*) roughly; (*vulgairement*) coarsely; **grossièretés** *nfpl*: **dire des grossièretés** to use coarse language

**grossir** [gʀosiʀ] *vi* (*personne*) to put on weight ♦ *vt* (*exagérer*) to exaggerate; (*au microscope*) to magnify; (*suj: vêtement*), to make sb look fatter **grossiste** [gʀosist] *nm/f* wholesaler **grosso modo** [gʀosomɔdo] *adv* roughly

**grotesque** [gʀɔtɛsk] *adj* (*extravagant*) grotesque; (*ridicule*) ludicrous **grotte** [gʀɔt] *nf* cave **grouiller** [gʀuje] *vi*: **~ de** to be swarming with; **se ~** (*fam*) ♦ *vi* to get a move on; **grouillant, e** *adj* swarming **groupe** [gʀup] *nm* group; **le ~ des 8** Group of 8; **~ de parole** support group; **~ sanguin** blood group; **groupement** *nm* (*action*) grouping; (*groupe*) grouping; **grouper** *vt* to group; **se grouper** *vi* to gather **grue** [gʀy] *nf* crane **grumeaux** [gʀymo] *nmpl* lumps **guenilles** [gənij] *nfpl* rags **guenon** [gənɔ̃] *nf* female monkey

**guépard** [gepaʀ] *nm* cheetah **guêpe** [gɛp] *nf* wasp **guêpier** [gepje] *nm* (*fig*) trap **guère** [gɛʀ] *adv* (*avec adjectif, adverbe*): **ne ... ~** hardly; (*avec verbe*): **ne ... ~** (*pas beaucoup*) *tournure négative +much*; (*pas souvent*) hardly ever; (*pas longtemps*) *tournure négative +(very) long*; **il n'y a ~ que/de** there's hardly anybody (*ou* anything) but/hardly any; **ce n'est ~ difficile** it's hardly difficult; **nous n'avons ~ de temps** we have hardly any time **guéridon** [geʀidɔ̃] *nm* pedestal table **guérilla** [geʀija] *nf* guerrilla warfare **guérillero** [geʀijeʀo] *nm* guerrilla **guérir** [geʀiʀ] *vt* (*personne, maladie*) to cure; (*membre, plaie*) to heal ♦ *vi* (*malade, maladie*) to be cured; (*blessure*) to heal; **guérison** *nf* (*de maladie*) curing; (*de membre, plaie*) healing; (*de malade*) recovery; **guérisseur, -euse** *nm/f* healer

**guerre** [gɛʀ] *nf* war; **~ civile** civil war; **en ~** at war; **faire la ~ à** to wage war against; **guerrier, -ière** *adj* warlike ♦ *nm/f* warrior **guet** [gɛ] *nm*: **faire le ~** to be on the look-out; **guet-apens** [gɛtapɑ̃] *nm* ambush; **guetter** *vt* (*épier*) to watch (intently); (*attendre*) to watch (out) for; (*hostilement*) to be lying in wait for **gueule** [gœl] *nf* (*d'animal*) mouth; (*fam: figure*) face; (: *bouche*) mouth; **ta ~!** (*fam*) shut up!; **~ de bois** (*fam*) hangover; **gueuler** (*fam*) *vi* to bawl; **gueuleton** (*fam*) *nm* blow-out **gui** [gi] *nm* mistletoe **guichet** [giʃɛ] *nm* (*de bureau, banque*) counter; **les ~s** (*à la gare, au théâtre*) the ticket office *sg*; **~ automatique** cash dispenser (*BRIT*), automatic telling machine (*US*) **guide** [gid] *nm* guide ♦ *nf* (*éclaireuse*) girl guide; **guider** *vt* to guide **guidon** [gidɔ̃] *nm* handlebars *pl* **guignol** [giɲɔl] *nm* ≈ Punch and Judy

show; (fig) clown
**guillemets** [gijmɛ] *nmpl:* **entre ~** in inverted commas
**guillotiner** [gijɔtine] *vt* to guillotine
**guindé, e** [gɛ̃de] *adj (personne, air)* stiff, starchy; *(style)* stilted
**guirlande** [gɪʀlɑ̃d] *nf (fleurs)* garland; **~ de Noël** tinsel garland; **~ lumineuse** string of fairy lights; **~ de papier** paper chain
**guise** [giz] *nf:* **à votre ~** as you wish *ou* please; **en ~ de** by way of
**guitare** [gitaʀ] *nf* guitar
**gym** [ʒim] *nf (exercices)* gym; **gymnase** [ʒimnɑz] *nm* gym(nasium); **gymnaste** *nm/f* gymnast; **gymnastique** *nf* gymnastics *sg;* (au réveil etc) keep-fit exercises *pl*
**gynécologie** [ʒinekɔlɔʒi] *nf* gynaecology; **gynécologique** *adj* gynaecological; **gynécologue** *nm/f* gynaecologist

# H, h

**habile** [abil] *adj* skilful; *(malin)* clever; **habileté** [abilte] *nf* skill, skilfulness; cleverness
**habillé, e** [abije] *adj* dressed; *(chic)* dressy
**habillement** [abijmɑ̃] *nm* clothes *pl*
**habiller** [abije] *vt* to dress; *(fournir en vêtements)* to clothe; **s'~** *vi* to dress (o.s.); *(se déguiser, mettre des vêtements chic)* to dress up
**habit** [abi] *nm* outfit; **~s** *nmpl (vêtements)* clothes *pl;* **~ (de soirée)** evening dress; *(pour homme)* tails *pl*
**habitant, e** [abitɑ̃, ɑ̃t] *nm/f* inhabitant; *(d'une maison)* occupant; **loger chez l'~** to stay with the locals
**habitation** [abitasjɔ̃] *nf* house; **~s à loyer modéré** (block of) council flats
**habiter** [abite] *vt* to live in ♦ *vi:* **~ à/ dans** to live in
**habitude** [abityd] *nf* habit; **avoir l'~ de faire** to be in the habit of doing; *(expérience)* to be used to doing; **d'~**

usually; **comme d'~** as usual
**habitué, e** [abitɥe] *nm/f (de maison)* regular visitor; *(de café)* regular (customer)
**habituel, le** [abitɥɛl] *adj* usual
**habituer** [abitɥe] *vt:* **~ qn à** to get sb used to; **s'~ à** to get used to
**'hache** [ʼaʃ] *nf* axe
**'hacher** [ʼaʃe] *vt (viande)* to mince; *(persil)* to chop; **'hachis** *nm* mince *no pl;* **hachis Parmentier** ≈ shepherd's pie
**'hachisch** [ʼaʃiʃ] *nm* hashish
**'hachoir** [ʼaʃwaʀ] *nm (couteau)* chopper; *(appareil)* (meat) mincer; *(planche)* chopping board
**'hagard, e** [ʼagaʀ, aʀd] *adj* wild, distraught
**'haie** [ʼɛ] *nf* hedge; *(SPORT)* hurdle
**'haillons** [ʼajɔ̃] *nmpl* rags
**'haine** [ʼɛn] *nf* hatred
**'haïr** [ʼaiʀ] *vt* to detest, hate
**'hâlé, e** [ʼɑle] *adj* (sun)tanned, sunburnt
**haleine** [alɛn] *nf* breath; **hors d'~** out of breath; **tenir en ~** *(attention)* to hold spellbound; *(incertitude)* to keep in suspense; **de longue ~** long-term
**'haleter** [ʼalte] *vi* to pant
**'hall** [ʼol] *nm* hall
**'halle** [ʼal] *nf* (covered) market; **~s** *nfpl (d'une grande ville)* central food market *sg*
**hallucinant, e** [alysinɑ̃, ɑ̃t] *adj* staggering
**hallucination** [alysinasjɔ̃] *nf* hallucination
**'halte** [ʼalt] *nf* stop, break; *(endroit)* stopping place ♦ *excl* stop!; **faire ~** to stop
**haltère** [altɛʀ] *nm* dumbbell, barbell; **~s** *nmpl:* **(poids et) ~s** *(activité)* weightlifting *sg;* **haltérophilie** *nf* weightlifting
**'hamac** [ʼamak] *nm* hammock
**'hamburger** [ʼɑ̃buʀɡœʀ] *nm* hamburger
**'hameau, x** [ʼamo] *nm* hamlet
**hameçon** [amsɔ̃] *nm* (fish) hook
**'hanche** [ʼɑ̃ʃ] *nf* hip

'**hand-ball** ['dbal] *nm* handball

'**handicapé, e** ['ɑ̃dikape] *nm/f* physically (*ou* mentally) handicapped person; **~ moteur** spastic

'**hangar** ['ɑ̃gaʀ] *nm* shed; (AVIAT) hangar

'**hanneton** ['antɔ̃] *nm* cockchafer

'**hanter** ['ɑ̃te] *vt* to haunt

'**hantise** ['ɑ̃tiz] *nf* obsessive fear

'**happer** ['ape] *vt* to snatch; (*suj: train etc*) to hit

'**haras** ['aʀɑ] *nm* stud farm

'**harassant, e** ['aʀasɑ̃, ɑ̃t] *adj* exhausting

'**harcèlement** ['aʀsɛlmɑ̃] *nm* harassment; **~ sexuel** sexual harassment

'**harceler** ['aʀsəle] *vt* to harass; **~ qn de questions** to plague sb with questions

'**hardi, e** ['aʀdi] *adj* bold, daring

'**hareng** ['aʀɑ̃] *nm* herring

'**hargne** ['aʀɲ] *nf* aggressiveness; '**hargneux, -euse** *adj* aggressive

'**haricot** ['aʀiko] *nm* bean; **~ blanc** haricot bean; **~ vert** green bean; **~ rouge** kidney bean

**harmonica** [aʀmɔnika] *nm* mouth organ

**harmonie** [aʀmɔni] *nf* harmony; **harmonieux, -euse** *adj* harmonious; (*couleurs, couple*) well-matched

'**harnacher** ['aʀnaʃe] *vt* to harness

'**harnais** ['aʀnɛ] *nm* harness

'**harpe** ['aʀp] *nf* harp

'**harponner** ['aʀpɔne] *vt* to harpoon; (*fam*) to collar

'**hasard** ['azaʀ] *nm*: **le ~** chance, fate; **un ~** a coincidence; **au ~** (*aller*) aimlessly; (*choisir*) at random; **par ~** by chance; **à tout ~** (*en cas de besoin*) just in case; (*en espérant trouver ce qu'on cherche*) on the off chance (BRIT); '**hasarder** *vt* (*mot*) to venture; **se hasarder à faire** to risk doing

'**hâte** ['ɑt] *nf* haste; **à la ~** hurriedly, hastily; **en ~** posthaste, with all possible speed; **avoir ~ de** to be eager *ou* anxious to; '**hâter** *vt* to hasten; **se hâter** *vi* to hurry; '**hâtif, -ive** *adj* (*tra-*

*vail*) hurried; (*décision, jugement*) hasty

'**hausse** ['os] *nf* rise, increase; **être en ~** to be going up; '**hausser** *vt* to raise; **hausser les épaules** to shrug (one's shoulders)

'**haut, e** ['o, 'ot] *adj* high; (*grand*) tall ♦ *adv* high ♦ *nm* top (part); **de 3 m de ~**, 3 m high, 3 m in height; **des ~s et des bas** ups and downs; **en ~ lieu** in high places; **à ~e voix, (tout) ~** aloud, out loud; **du ~ de** from the top of; **de ~ en bas** from top to bottom; **plus ~** higher up, further up; (*dans un texte*) above; (*parler*) louder; **en ~** (*être/aller*) at/to the top; (*dans une maison*) upstairs; **en ~ de** at the top of

'**hautain, e** ['otɛ̃, ɛn] *adj* haughty

'**hautbois** ['obwa] *nm* oboe

'**haut-de-forme** ['odfɔʀm] *nm* top hat

'**hauteur** ['otœʀ] *nf* height; **à la ~ de** (*accident*) near; (*fig: tâche, situation*) equal to; **à la ~** (*fig*) up to it

'**haut...**: '**haut-fourneau** *nm* blast *ou* smelting furnace; '**haut-le-cœur** *nm inv* retch, heave; '**haut-parleur** *nm* (loud)speaker

'**havre** ['avʀ] *nm* haven

'**Haye** ['ɛ] *n*: **la ~** the Hague

'**hayon** ['ɛjɔ̃] *nm* hatchback

**hebdo** [ɛbdo] (*fam*) *nm* weekly

**hebdomadaire** [ɛbdɔmadɛʀ] *adj, nm* weekly

**hébergement** [ebɛʀʒəmɑ̃] *nm* accommodation

**héberger** [ebɛʀʒe] *vt* (*touristes*) to accommodate, lodge; (*amis*) to put up; (*réfugiés*) to take in

**hébété, e** [ebete] *adj* dazed

**hébreu, x** [ebʀø] *adj m, nm* Hebrew

**hécatombe** [ekatɔ̃b] *nf* slaughter

**hectare** [ɛktaʀ] *nm* hectare

'**hein** ['ɛ̃] *excl* eh?

'**hélas** ['elas] *excl* alas! ♦ *adv* unfortunately

'**héler** [ele] *vt* to hail

**hélice** [elis] *nf* propeller

**hélicoptère** [elikɔptɛʀ] *nm* helicopter

**helvétique** [ɛlvetik] *adj* Swiss

**hématome** [ematom] *nm* nasty bruise

**hémicycle** [emisikl] *nm* (POL): **l'~** ≃ the benches of the Commons (BRIT), ≃ the floor of the House of Representatives (US)

**hémisphère** [emisfɛr] *nm*: **l'~ nord/ sud** the northern/southern hemisphere

**hémorragie** [emɔraʒi] *nf* bleeding no pl, haemorrhage

**hémorroïdes** [emɔrɔid] *nfpl* piles, haemorrhoids

**'hennir** ['enir] *vi* to neigh, whinny; **'hennissement** *nm* neigh, whinny

**hépatite** [epatit] *nf* hepatitis

**herbe** [ɛrb] *nf* grass; (CULIN, MÉD) herb; **~s de Provence** mixed herbs; **en ~** unripe; (fig) budding; **herbicide** *nm* weed-killer; **herboriste** *nm/f* herbalist

**'hère** ['ɛr] *nm*: **pauvre ~** poor wretch

**héréditaire** [erediter] *adj* hereditary

**'hérisser** ['erise] *vt*: **~ qn** (fig) to ruffle sb; **se ~** *vi* to bristle, bristle up;. **'hérisson** *nm* hedgehog

**héritage** [eritaʒ] *nm* inheritance; (coutumes, système) heritage, legacy

**hériter** [erite] *vi*: **~ de qch (de qn)** to inherit sth (from sb); **héritier, -ière** [eritje, jɛr] *nm/f* heir(-ess)

**hermétique** [ermetik] *adj* airtight; (fig: obscur) abstruse; (: impénétrable) impenetrable

**hermine** [ermin] *nf* ermine

**'hernie** ['erni] *nf* hernia

**héroïne** [erɔin] *nf* heroine; (drogue) heroin

**héroïque** [erɔik] *adj* heroic

**'héron** ['erɔ̃] *nm* heron

**'héros** ['ero] *nm* hero

**hésitant, e** [ezitɑ̃, ɑ̃t] *adj* hesitant

**hésitation** [ezitasjɔ̃] *nf* hesitation

**hésiter** [ezite] *vi*: **~ (à faire)** to hesitate (to do)

**hétéroclite** [eteroklit] *adj* heterogeneous; (objets) sundry

**hétérogène** [eterɔʒɛn] *adj* heterogeneous

**hétérosexuel, le** [eterɔsɛksɥɛl] *adj* heterosexual

**'hêtre** ['ɛtr] *nm* beech

**heure** [œr] *nf* hour; (SCOL) period; (moment) time; **c'est l'~** it's time; **quelle ~ est-il?** what time is it?; **2 ~s (du matin)** 2 o'clock (in the morning); **être à l'~** to be on time; (montre) to be right; **mettre à l'~** to set right; **à une ~ avancée (de la nuit)** at a late hour of the night; **à toute ~** at any time; **24 ~s sur 24** round the clock, 24 hours a day; **à l'~ qu'il est** at this time (of day); by now; **sur l'~** at once; **~ de pointe** rush hour; (téléphone) peak period; **~ d'affluence** rush hour; **~s creuses** slack periods; (pour électricité, téléphone etc) off-peak periods; **~s supplémentaires** overtime *sg*

**heureusement** [œrøzmɑ̃] *adv* (par bonheur) fortunately, luckily

**heureux, -euse** [œrø, øz] *adj* happy; (chanceux) lucky, fortunate

**heurter** ['œrte] *vt* (mur) to strike, hit; (personne) to collide with; **se ~ à** *vt* (fig) to come up against

**'heurts** ['œr] *nmpl* (fig) clashes

**hexagone** [egzagɔn] *nm* hexagon; (la France) France (because of its shape)

**hiberner** [ibɛrne] *vi* to hibernate

**'hibou, x** ['ibu] *nm* owl

**hideux, -euse** ['idø, øz] *adj* hideous

**hier** [jɛr] *adv* yesterday; **~ soir** last night, yesterday evening; **toute la journée d'~** all day yesterday; **toute la matinée d'~** all yesterday morning

**hiérarchie** ['jerarʃi] *nf* hierarchy

**hi-fi** ['ifi] *adj inv* hi-fi ♦ *nf* hi-fi

**hilare** [ilar] *adj* mirthful

**hindou, e** [ɛ̃du] *adj* Hindu ♦ *nm/f*: **H~, e** Hindu

**hippique** [ipik] *adj* equestrian, horse *cpd*; **un club ~** a riding centre; **un concours ~** a horse show; **hippisme** *nm* (horse)riding

**hippodrome** [ipɔdrom] *nm* racecourse

**hippopotame** [ipɔpɔtam] *nm* hippopotamus

**hirondelle** [iR5dɛl] nf swallow

**hirsute** [iRsyt] adj (personne) shaggy-haired; (barbe) shaggy; (tête) tousled

**'hisser** ['ise] vt to hoist, haul up; **se ~** vi to heave o.s. up

**histoire** [istwaR] nf (science, événements) history; (anecdote, récit, mensonge) story; (affaire) business no pl; **~s** nfpl (chichis) fuss no pl; (ennuis) trouble sg; **historique** adj historical; (important) historic

**'hit-parade** ['itpaRad] nm: **le ~~** the charts

**hiver** [ivɛR] nm winter; **hivernal, e, -aux** adj winter cpd; (glacial) wintry; **hiverner** vi to winter

**HLM** nm ou f (= habitation à loyer modéré) council flat; **des HLM** council housing

**'hobby** ['ɔbi] nm hobby

**hocher** ['ɔʃe] vt: **~ la tête** to nod; (signe négatif ou dubitatif) to shake one's head

**'hochet** ['ɔʃɛ] nm rattle

**'hockey** ['ɔkɛ] nm: **~ (sur glace/gazon)** (ice/field) hockey

**'hold-up** ['ɔldœp] nm inv hold-up

**'hollandais, e** ['ɔlɑ̃dɛ, ɛz] adj Dutch ♦ nm (LING) Dutch ♦ nm/f: **H~, e** Dutchman(-woman); **les H~** the Dutch

**'Hollande** ['ɔlɑ̃d] nf: **la ~** Holland

**'homard** ['ɔmaR] nm lobster

**homéopathique** [ɔmeɔpatik] adj homoeopathic

**homicide** [ɔmisid] nm murder; **~ involontaire** manslaughter

**hommage** [ɔmaʒ] nm tribute; **~s** nmpl: **présenter ses ~s** to pay one's respects; **rendre ~ à** to pay tribute ou homage to

**homme** [ɔm] nm man; **~ d'affaires** businessman; **~ d'État** statesman; **~ de main** hired man; **~ de paille** stooge; **~ politique** politician; **homme-grenouille** nm frogman

**homo...: homogène** adj homogeneous; **homologue** nm/f counterpart; **homologué, e** adj (SPORT) ratified; (tarif) authorized; **homonyme** nm (LING) homonym; (d'une personne) namesake; **homosexuel, le** adj homosexual

**'Hongrie** ['ɔ̃gri] nf: **la ~** Hungary; **'hongrois, e** adj Hungarian ♦ nm/f: **Hongrois, e** nm (LING) Hungarian ♦ nm (LING) Hungarian

**honnête** [ɔnɛt] adj (intègre) honest; (juste, satisfaisant) fair; **honnêtement** adv honestly; **honnêteté** nf honesty

**honneur** [ɔnœR] nm honour; (mérite) credit; **en l'~ de** in honour of; (événement) on the occasion of; **faire ~ à** (engagements) to honour; (famille) to be a credit to; (fig: repas etc) to do justice to

**honorable** [ɔnɔRabl] adj worthy, honourable; (suffisant) decent

**honoraire** [ɔnɔRɛR] adj honorary; **professeur ~** professor emeritus; **honoraires** nmpl fees pl

**honorer** [ɔnɔRe] vt to honour; (estimer) to hold in high regard; (faire honneur à) to do credit to; **honorifique** [ɔnɔRifik] adj honorary

**'honte** ['ɔ̃t] nf shame; **avoir ~ de** to be ashamed of; **faire ~ à qn** to make sb (feel) ashamed; **'honteux, -euse** adj ashamed; (conduite, acte) shameful, disgraceful

**hôpital, -aux** [ɔpital, o] nm hospital

**'hoquet** ['ɔkɛ] nm: **avoir le ~** to have (the) hiccoughs; **'hoqueter** vi to hiccough

**horaire** [ɔRɛR] adj hourly ♦ nm timetable, schedule; **~s** nmpl (d'employé) hours; **~ souple** flexitime

**horizon** [ɔRizɔ̃] nm horizon

**horizontal, e, -aux** [ɔRizɔ̃tal, o] adj horizontal

**horloge** [ɔRlɔʒ] nf clock; **l'~ parlante** the speaking clock; **horloger, -ère**

*nm/f* watchmaker; clockmaker

**'hormis** [ˈɔʀmi] *prép* save

**horoscope** [ɔʀɔskɔp] *nm* horoscope

**horreur** [ɔʀœʀ] *nf* horror; **quelle ~!** how awful!; **avoir ~ de** to loathe ou detest; **horrible** *adj* horrible; **horrifier** *vt* to horrify

**horripiler** [ɔʀipile] *vt* to exasperate

**hors** [ˈɔʀ] *prép*: **~ de** out of; **~ pair** outstanding; **~ de propos** inopportune; **être ~ de soi** to be beside o.s.; **~ d'usage** out of service; **'hors-bord** *nm inv* speedboat (*with outboard motor*); **'hors-d'œuvre** *nm inv* hors d'œuvre; **'hors-jeu** *nm inv* offside; **'hors-la-loi** *nm inv* outlaw; **'hors-taxe** *adj* (*boutique, articles*) duty-free

**hortensia** [ɔʀtɑ̃sja] *nm* hydrangea

**hospice** [ɔspis] *nm* (*de vieillards*) home

**hospitalier, -ière** [ɔspitalje, jɛʀ] *adj* (*accueillant*) hospitable; (*MÉD: service, centre*) hospital *cpd*

**hospitaliser** [ɔspitalize] *vt* to take/ send to hospital, hospitalize

**hospitalité** [ɔspitalite] *nf* hospitality

**hostie** [ɔsti] *nf* host (REL)

**hostile** [ɔstil] *adj* hostile; **hostilité** *nf* hostility

**hosto** [ɔsto] (*fam*) *nm* hospital

**hôte** [ot] *nm* (*maître de maison*) host ♦ (*invité*) guest

**hôtel** [otel] *nm* hotel; **aller à l'~** to stay in a hotel; **~ de ville** town hall; **~ (particulier)** (*private*) mansion; **hôtelier, -ière** *adj* hotel *cpd* ♦ *nm/f* hotelier; **hôtellerie** *nf* hotel business

**hôtesse** [otes] *nf* hostess; **~ de l'air** air stewardess; **~ (d'accueil)** receptionist

**'hotte** [ˈɔt] *nf* (*panier*) basket (*carried on the back*); **~ aspirante** cooker hood

**houblon** [ˈublɔ̃] *nm* (BOT) hop; (*pour la bière*) hops *pl*

**'houille** [ˈuj] *nf* coal; **~ blanche** hydro-electric power

**'houle** [ˈul] *nf* swell; **'houleux, -euse** *adj* stormy

**'houligan** [ˈuligɑ̃] *nm* hooligan

**'hourra** [ˈuʀa] *excl* hurrah!

**'houspiller** [ˈuspije] *vt* to scold

**'housse** [ˈus] *nf* cover

**'houx** [ˈu] *nm* holly

**hublot** [ˈyblo] *nm* porthole

**'huche** [ˈyʃ] *nf*: **~ à pain** bread bin

**'huer** [ˈɥe] *vt* to boo

**huile** [ɥil] *nf* oil; **~ solaire** suntan oil; **huiler** *vt* to oil; **huileux, -euse** *adj* oily

**huis** [ɥi] *nm*: **à ~ clos** in camera

**huissier** [ɥisje] *nm* usher; (JUR) ≃ bailiff

**'huit** [ˈɥi(t)] *num* eight; **samedi en ~** a week on Saturday; **dans ~ jours** in a week; **'huitaine** *nf*: **une huitaine (de jours)** a week or so; **'huitième** *num* eighth

**huître** [ɥitʀ] *nf* oyster

**humain, e** [ymɛ̃, ɛn] *adj* human; (*compatissant*) humane ♦ *nm* human (*being*); **humanitaire** *adj* humanitarian; **humanité** *nf* humanity

**humble** [œbl] *adj* humble

**humecter** [ymɛkte] *vt* to dampen

**'humer** [ˈyme] *vt* (*plat*) to smell; (*parfum*) to inhale

**humeur** [ymœʀ] *nf* mood; **de bonne/ mauvaise ~** in a good/bad mood

**humide** [ymid] *adj* damp; (*main, yeux*) moist; (*climat, chaleur*) humid; (*saison, route*) wet

**humilier** [ymilje] *vt* to humiliate

**humilité** [ymilite] *nf* humility, humbleness

**humoristique** [ymɔʀistik] *adj* humorous

**humour** [ymuʀ] *nm* humour; **avoir de l'~** to have a sense of humour; **~ noir** black humour

**'huppé, e** [ˈype] (*fam*) *adj* posh

**'hurlement** [ˈyʀləmɑ̃] *nm* howling *no pl*, howl, yelling *no pl*, yell

**'hurler** [ˈyʀle] *vi* to howl, yell

**hurluberlu** [yʀlybɛʀly] (*péj*) *nm* crank

**'hutte** [ˈyt] *nf* hut

**hybride** [ibʀid] *adj, nm* hybrid

**hydratant, e** [idʀatɑ̃, ɑ̃t] adj (crème) moisturizing

**hydraulique** [idʀolik] adj hydraulic

**hydravion** [idʀavjɔ̃] nm seaplane

**hydrogène** [idʀɔʒɛn] nm hydrogen

**hydroglisseur** [idʀɔɡlisœʀ] nm hydroplane

**hyène** [jɛn] nf hyena

**hygiénique** [iʒenik] adj hygienic

**hymne** [imn] nm hymn; **~ national** national anthem

**hypermarché** [ipɛʀmaʀʃe] nm hypermarket

**hypermétrope** [ipɛʀmetʀɔp] adj long-sighted

**hypertension** [ipɛʀtɑ̃sjɔ̃] nf high blood pressure

**hypertexte** [ipɛʀtɛkst] nm (INFORM) hypertext

**hypnose** [ipnoz] nf hypnosis; **hypnotiser** vt to hypnotize; **hypnotiseur** nm hypnotist

**hypocrisie** [ipɔkʀizi] nf hypocrisy; **hypocrite** adj hypocritical

**hypothèque** [ipɔtɛk] nf mortgage

**hypothèse** [ipɔtɛz] nf hypothesis

**hystérique** [isteʀik] adj hysterical

## I, i

**iceberg** [ajsbɛʀɡ] nm iceberg

**ici** [isi] adv here; **jusqu'~** (espace) as far as this; (temps) so far; **d'~ demain** by tomorrow; **d'~ là** by then, in the meantime; **d'~ peu** before long

**icône** [ikon] nf icon

**idéal, e, -aux** [ideal, o] adj ideal ♦ nm ideal; **idéaliste** adj idealistic ♦ nm/f idealist

**idée** [ide] nf idea; **avoir dans l'~ que** to have an idea that; **~ fixe** obsession; **~ reçue** generally accepted idea

**identifier** [idɑ̃tifje] vt to identify; **s'~ à** (héros etc) to identify with

**identique** [idɑ̃tik] adj: **~ (à)** identical (to)

**identité** [idɑ̃tite] nf identity

**idiot, e** [idjo, idjɔt] adj idiotic ♦ nm/f idiot; **idiotie** nf idiotic thing

**idole** [idɔl] nf idol

**if** [if] nm yew

**igloo** [iglu] nm igloo

**ignare** [iɲaʀ] adj ignorant

**ignifugé, e** [iɲifyʒe] adj fireproof

**ignoble** [iɲɔbl] adj vile

**ignorant, e** [iɲɔʀɑ̃, ɑ̃t] adj ignorant

**ignorer** [iɲɔʀe] vt not to know; (personne) to ignore

**il** [il] pron he; (animal, chose, en tournure impersonnelle) it; **~s** they; voir **avoir**

**île** [il] nf island; **l'~ Maurice** Mauritius; **les ~s anglo-normandes** the Channel Islands; **les ~s Britanniques** the British Isles

**illégal, e, -aux** [i(l)legal, o] adj illegal

**illégitime** [i(l)leʒitim] adj illegitimate

**illettré, e** [i(l)letʀe] adj, nm/f illiterate

**illimité, e** [i(l)limite] adj unlimited

**illisible** [i(l)lizibl] adj illegible; (roman) unreadable

**illogique** [i(l)lɔʒik] adj illogical

**illumination** [i(l)lyminasjɔ̃] nf illumination; (idée) flash of inspiration

**illuminer** [i(l)lymine] vt to light up; (monument, rue: pour une fête) to illuminate; (: au moyen de projecteurs) to floodlight

**illusion** [i(l)lyzjɔ̃] nf illusion; **se faire des ~s** to delude o.s.; **faire ~** to delude ou fool people; **illusionniste** nm/f conjuror

**illustration** [i(l)lystʀasjɔ̃] nf illustration

**illustre** [i(l)lystʀ] adj illustrious

**illustré, e** [i(l)lystʀe] adj illustrated ♦ nm comic

**illustrer** [i(l)lystʀe] vt to illustrate; **s'~** to become famous, win fame

**îlot** [ilo] nm small island, islet

**ils** [il] pron voir **il**

**image** [imaʒ] nf (gén) picture; (métaphore) image; **~ de marque** brand image; (fig) public image; **imagé, e** adj (texte) full of imagery; (langage) colourful

**imaginaire** [imaʒinɛʀ] *adj* imaginary

**imagination** [imaʒinɑsjɔ̃] *nf* imagination; **avoir de l'~** to be imaginative

**imaginer** [imaʒine] *vt* to imagine; (*inventer: expédient*) to devise, think up; **s'~** *vt* (*se figurer: scène etc*) to imagine, picture; **s'~ que** to imagine that

**imbattable** [ɛ̃batabl] *adj* unbeatable

**imbécile** [ɛ̃besil] *adj* idiotic ♦ *nm/f* idiot;

**imbécillité** *nf* idiocy; (*action*) idiotic thing; (*film, livre, propos*) rubbish

**imbiber** [ɛ̃bibe] *vt* to soak; **s'~ de** to become saturated with

**imbu, e** [ɛ̃by] *adj*: **~ de** full of

**imbuvable** [ɛ̃byvabl] *adj* undrinkable; (*personne, fam*) unbearable

**imitateur, -trice** [imitatœʀ, tʀis] *nm/f* (*gén*) imitator; (*MUSIC-HALL*) impersonator

**imitation** [imitasjɔ̃] *nf* imitation; (*de personnalité*) impersonation

**imiter** [imite] *vt* to imitate; (*contrefaire*) to forge; (*ressembler à*) to look like

**immaculé, e** [imakyle] *adj* (*linge, surface, réputation*) spotless; (*blancheur*) immaculate

**immangeable** [ɛ̃mɑ̃ʒabl] *adj* inedible

**immatriculation** [imatʀikylasjɔ̃] *nf* registration

**immatriculer** [imatʀikyle] *vt* to register; **faire/se faire ~** to register

**immédiat, e** [imedja, jat] *adj* immediate ♦ *nm*: **dans l'~** for the time being; **immédiatement** *adv* immediately

**immense** [i(m)mɑ̃s] *adj* immense

**immerger** [imɛʀʒe] *vt* to immerse, submerge

**immeuble** [imœbl] *nm* building; (*à usage d'habitation*) block of flats

**immigration** [imigʀasjɔ̃] *nf* immigration

**immigré, e** [imigʀe] *nm/f* immigrant

**imminent, e** [iminɑ̃, ɑ̃t] *adj* imminent

**immiscer** [imise]: **s'~** *vi*: **s'~ dans** to interfere in *ou* with

**immobile** [i(m)mɔbil] *adj* still, motionless

**immobilier, -ière** [imɔbilje, jɛʀ] *adj* property *cpd* ♦ *nm*: **l'~** the property business

**immobiliser** [imɔbilize] *vt* (*gén*) to immobilize; (*circulation, véhicule, affaires*) to bring to a standstill; **s'~** (*personne*) to stand still; (*machine, véhicule*) to come to a halt

**immonde** [imɔ̃d] *adj* foul

**immoral, e, -aux** [i(m)mɔʀal, o] *adj* immoral

**immortel, le** [imɔʀtɛl] *adj* immortal

**immuable** [imɥabl] *adj* unchanging

**immunisé, e** [im(m)ynize] *adj*: **~ contre** immune to

**immunité** [imynite] *nf* immunity

**impact** [ɛ̃pakt] *nm* impact

**impair, e** [ɛ̃pɛʀ] *adj* odd ♦ *nm* faux pas, blunder

**impardonnable** [ɛ̃paʀdɔnabl] *adj* unpardonable, unforgiving

**imparfait, e** [ɛ̃paʀfɛ, ɛt] *adj* imperfect

**impartial, e, -aux** [ɛ̃paʀsjal, jo] *adj* impartial, unbiased

**impasse** [ɛ̃pɑs] *nf* dead end, cul-de-sac; (*fig*) deadlock

**impassible** [ɛ̃pasibl] *adj* impassive

**impatience** [ɛ̃pasjɑ̃s] *nf* impatience

**impatient, e** [ɛ̃pasjɑ̃, jɑ̃t] *adj* impatient; **impatienter: s'impatienter** *vi* to get impatient

**impeccable** [ɛ̃pekabl] *adj* (*parfait*) perfect; (*propre*) impeccable; (*fam*) smashing

**impensable** [ɛ̃pɑ̃sabl] *adj* (*événement hypothétique*) unthinkable; (*événement qui a eu lieu*) unbelievable

**imper** [ɛ̃pɛʀ] (*fam*) *nm* raincoat

**impératif, -ive** [ɛ̃peʀatif, iv] *adj* imperative ♦ *nm* (*LING*) imperative; **~s** *nmpl* (*exigences: d'une fonction, d'une charge*) requirements; (: *de la mode*) demands

**impératrice** [ɛ̃peʀatʀis] *nf* empress

**imperceptible** [ɛ̃pɛʀseptibl] *adj* imperceptible

**impérial, e, -aux** [ɛ̃perjal, jo] adj imperial; **impériale** nf top deck

**impérieux, -euse** [ɛ̃perjø, jøz] adj (caractère, ton) imperious; (obligation, besoin) pressing, urgent

**impérissable** [ɛ̃perisabl] adj undying

**imperméable** [ɛ̃pɛrmeabl] adj waterproof; (fig): ~ à impervious to ♦ nm raincoat

**impertinent, e** [ɛ̃pɛrtinɑ̃, ɑ̃t] adj impertinent

**imperturbable** [ɛ̃pɛrtyrbabl] adj (personne, caractère) unperturbable; (sang-froid, gaieté, sérieux) unshakeable

**impétueux, -euse** [ɛ̃petɥø, øz] adj impetuous

**impitoyable** [ɛ̃pitwajabl] adj pitiless, merciless

**implanter** [ɛ̃plɑ̃te] vi to be set up

**impliquer** [ɛ̃plike] vt to imply; ~ qn (dans) to implicate sb (in)

**impoli, e** [ɛ̃poli] adj impolite, rude

**impopulaire** [ɛ̃popylɛr] adj unpopular

**importance** [ɛ̃portɑ̃s] nf importance; **sans ~** unimportant

**important, e** [ɛ̃portɑ̃, ɑ̃t] adj important; (en quantité: somme, retard) considerable, sizeable; (: dégâts) extensive; (péj: airs, ton) self-important ♦ nm: **l'~** the important thing

**importateur, -trice** [ɛ̃portatœr, tris] nm/f importer

**importation** [ɛ̃portasjɔ̃] nf importation; (produit) import

**importer** [ɛ̃porte] vt (COMM) to import; (maladies, plantes) to introduce ♦ vi (être important) to matter; **il importe qu'il fasse** it is important that he should do; **peu m'importe** (je n'ai pas de préférence) I don't mind; (je m'en moque) I don't care; **peu importe (que)** it doesn't matter (if); voir aussi **n'importe**

**importun, e** [ɛ̃portœ̃, yn] adj irksome, importunate; (arrivée, visite) inopportune, ill-timed ♦ nm intruder; **importuner** vt to bother

**imposable** [ɛ̃pozabl] adj taxable

**imposant, e** [ɛ̃pozɑ̃, ɑ̃t] adj imposing

**imposer** [ɛ̃poze] vt (taxer) to tax; **s'~** (être nécessaire) to be imperative; ~ **qch à qn** to impose sth on sb; **en ~ à** to impress; **s'~ comme** to emerge as; **s'~ par** to win recognition through

**impossibilité** [ɛ̃posibilite] nf impossibility; **être dans l'~ de faire qch** to be unable to do sth

**impossible** [ɛ̃posibl] adj impossible; **il m'est ~ de le faire** it is impossible for me to do it, I can't possibly do it; **faire l'~** to do one's utmost

**imposteur** [ɛ̃postœr] nm impostor

**impôt** [ɛ̃po] nm tax; **~s** nmpl (contributions) (income) tax sg; **payer 1000 F d'~s** to pay 1,000F in tax; ~ **foncier** land tax; ~ **sur le chiffre d'affaires** corporation (BRIT) ou corporate (US) tax; ~ **sur le revenu** income tax

**impotent, e** [ɛ̃potɑ̃, ɑ̃t] adj disabled

**impraticable** [ɛ̃pratikabl] adj (projet) impracticable, unworkable; (piste) impassable

**imprécis, e** [ɛ̃presi, iz] adj imprecise

**imprégner** [ɛ̃preɲe] vt (tissu) to impregnate; (lieu, air) to fill; **s'~ de** (fig) to absorb

**imprenable** [ɛ̃prənabl] adj (forteresse) impregnable; **vue ~** unimpeded outlook

**imprésario** [ɛ̃presarjo] nm manager

**impression** [ɛ̃presjɔ̃] nf impression; (d'un ouvrage, tissu) printing; **faire bonne ~** to make a good impression; **impressionnant, e** adj (imposant) impressive; (bouleversant) upsetting; **impressionner** vt (frapper) to impress; (bouleverser) to upset

**imprévisible** [ɛ̃previzibl] adj unforeseeable

**imprévoyant, e** [ɛ̃prevwajɑ̃, ɑ̃t] adj lacking in foresight; (en matière d'argent) improvident

**imprévu, e** [ɛ̃prevy] adj unforeseen, unexpected ♦ nm (incident) unexpected incident; **des vacances pleines d'~** holidays full of surprises; **en cas d'~** if anything unexpected happens; **sauf ~** unless anything unexpected crops up

**imprimante** [ɛ̃pʀimɑ̃t] nf printer

**imprimé** [ɛ̃pʀime] nm (formulaire) printed form; (POSTES) printed matter no pl; (tissu) printed fabric; **~ à fleur** floral print

**imprimer** [ɛ̃pʀime] vt to print; (publier) to publish; **imprimerie** nf printing; (établissement) printing works sg; **imprimeur** nm printer

**impromptu, e** [ɛ̃pʀɔ̃pty] adj (repas, discours) impromptu; (départ) sudden; (visite) surprise

**impropre** [ɛ̃pʀɔpʀ] adj inappropriate; **~ à** unfit for

**improviser** [ɛ̃pʀɔvize] vt, vi to improvise

**improviste** [ɛ̃pʀɔvist]: **à l'~** adv unexpectedly, without warning

**imprudence** [ɛ̃pʀydɑ̃s] nf (d'une personne, d'une action) carelessness no pl; (d'une remarque) imprudence no pl; **commettre une ~** to do something foolish

**imprudent, e** [ɛ̃pʀydɑ̃, ɑ̃t] adj (conducteur, geste, action) careless; (remarque) unwise, imprudent; (projet) foolhardy

**impudent, e** [ɛ̃pydɑ̃, ɑ̃t] adj impudent

**impudique** [ɛ̃pydik] adj shameless

**impuissant, e** [ɛ̃pɥisɑ̃, ɑ̃t] adj helpless; (sans effet) ineffectual; (sexuellement) impotent

**impulsif, -ive** [ɛ̃pylsif, iv] adj impulsive

**impulsion** [ɛ̃pylsjɔ̃] nf (ÉLEC, instinct) impulse; (élan, influence) impetus

**impunément** [ɛ̃pynemɑ̃] adv with impunity

**inabordable** [inabɔʀdabl] adj (cher) prohibitive

**inacceptable** [inaksɛptabl] adj unacceptable

**inaccessible** [inaksesibl] adj inaccessible

**inachevé, e** [inaʃ(ə)ve] adj unfinished

**inactif, -ive** [inaktif, iv] adj inactive; (remède) ineffective; (BOURSE): **marché** slack ♦ nm: **les ~s** the non-working population

**inadapté, e** [inadapte] adj (gén): **~ à** not adapted to, unsuited to; (PSYCH) maladjusted

**inadéquat, e** [inadekwa(t), kwat] adj inadequate

**inadmissible** [inadmisibl] adj inadmissible

**inadvertance** [inadvɛʀtɑ̃s]: **par ~** adv inadvertently

**inaltérable** [inalteʀabl] adj (matière) stable; (fig) unfailing; **~ à** unaffected by

**inanimé, e** [inanime] adj (matière) inanimate; (évanoui) unconscious; (sans vie) lifeless

**inanition** [inanisjɔ̃] nf: **tomber d'~** to faint with hunger (and exhaustion)

**inaperçu, e** [inapɛʀsy] adj: **passer ~** to go unnoticed

**inapte** [inapt] adj: **~ à** incapable of; (MIL) unfit for

**inattaquable** [inatakabl] adj (texte, preuve) irrefutable

**inattendu, e** [inatɑ̃dy] adj unexpected

**inattentif, -ive** [inatɑ̃tif, iv] adj inattentive; **~ à** (dangers, détails) heedless of; **inattention** nf: **faute d'inattention** careless mistake

**inauguration** [inogyʀasjɔ̃] nf inauguration

**inaugurer** [inogyʀe] vt (monument) to unveil; (exposition, usine) to open; (fig) to inaugurate

**inavouable** [inavwabl] adj shameful; (bénéfices) undisclosable

**incalculable** [ɛ̃kalkylabl] adj incalculable

**incandescence** [ɛ̃kɑ̃desɑ̃s] nf: **porter à ~** to heat white-hot

**incapable** [ɛ̃kapabl] adj incapable; **~ de faire** incapable of doing; (empêché) unable to do

**incapacité** [ɛ̃kapasite] *nf* (*incompétence*) incapability; (*impossibilité*) incapacity; **dans l'~ de faire** unable to do

**incarcérer** [ɛ̃karsere] *vt* to incarcerate, imprison

**incarné, e** [ɛ̃karne] *adj* (*ongle*) ingrown

**incarner** [ɛ̃karne] *vt* to embody, personify; (THÉÂTRE) to play

**incassable** [ɛ̃kasabl] *adj* unbreakable

**incendiaire** [ɛ̃sɑ̃djɛr] *adj* incendiary; (*fig: discours*) inflammatory

**incendie** [ɛ̃sɑ̃di] *nm* fire; **~ criminel** arson *no pl*; **~ de forêt** forest fire; **incendier** *vt* (*mettre le feu à*) to set fire to, set alight; (*brûler complètement*) to burn down; **se faire incendier** (*fam*) to get a rocket

**incertain, e** [ɛ̃sɛrtɛ̃, ɛn] *adj* uncertain; (*temps*) unsettled; (*imprécis: contours*) indistinct, blurred; **incertitude** *nf* uncertainty

**incessamment** [ɛ̃sesamɑ̃] *adv* very shortly

**incident** [ɛ̃sidɑ̃, ɑ̃t] *nm* incident; **~ de parcours** minor hitch *ou* setback; **~ technique** technical difficulties *pl*

**incinérer** [ɛ̃sinere] *vt* (*ordures*) to incinerate; (*mort*) to cremate

**incisive** [ɛ̃siziv] *nf* incisor

**inciter** [ɛ̃site] *vt*: **~ qn à (faire) qch** to encourage sb to do sth; (*à la révolte etc*) to incite sb to do sth

**inclinable** [ɛ̃klinabl] *adj*: **siège à dossier ~** reclining seat

**inclinaison** [ɛ̃klinɛzɔ̃] *nf* (*déclivité: d'une route etc*) incline; (: *d'un toit*) slope; (*état penché*) tilt

**inclination** [ɛ̃klinasjɔ̃] *nf* (*penchant*) inclination; **~ de la tête** nod (of the head); **~ (de buste)** bow

**incliner** [ɛ̃kline] *vt* (*pencher*) to tilt ♦ *vi*: **~ à qch/à faire** to incline towards sth/doing; **s'~ (devant)** to bow (before); (*céder*) to give in *ou* yield (to); **~ la tête** to give a slight bow

**inclure** [ɛ̃klyr] *vt* to include; (*joindre à un envoi*) to enclose; **jusqu'au 10 mars inclus** until 10th March inclusive

**incognito** [ɛ̃kɔɲito] *adv* incognito ♦ *nm*: **garder l'~** to remain incognito

**incohérent, e** [ɛ̃kɔerɑ̃, ɑ̃t] *adj* (*comportement*) inconsistent; (*geste, langage, texte*) incoherent

**incollable** [ɛ̃kɔlabl] *adj* (*riz*) non-stick; **il est ~** (*fam*) he's got all the answers

**incolore** [ɛ̃kɔlɔr] *adj* colourless

**incommoder** [ɛ̃kɔmɔde] *vt* (*chaleur, odeur*): **~ qn** to bother sb

**incomparable** [ɛ̃kɔ̃parabl] *adj* incomparable

**incompatible** [ɛ̃kɔ̃patibl] *adj* incompatible

**incompétent, e** [ɛ̃kɔ̃petɑ̃, ɑ̃t] *adj* incompetent

**incomplet, -ète** [ɛ̃kɔ̃plɛ, ɛt] *adj* incomplete

**incompréhensible** [ɛ̃kɔ̃preɑ̃sibl] *adj* incomprehensible

**incompris, e** [ɛ̃kɔ̃pri, iz] *adj* misunderstood

**inconcevable** [ɛ̃kɔ̃s(ə)vabl] *adj* inconceivable

**inconciliable** [ɛ̃kɔ̃siljabl] *adj* irreconcilable

**inconditionnel, le** [ɛ̃kɔ̃disjɔnɛl] *adj* unconditional; (*partisan*) unquestioning ♦ *nm/f* (*d'un homme politique*) ardent supporter; (*d'un écrivain, d'un chanteur*) ardent admirer; (*d'une activité*) fanatic

**inconfort** [ɛ̃kɔ̃fɔr] *nm* discomfort; **inconfortable** *adj* uncomfortable

**incongru, e** [ɛ̃kɔ̃gry] *adj* unseemly

**inconnu, e** [ɛ̃kɔny] *adj* unknown ♦ *nm/f* stranger ♦ *nm*: **l'~** the unknown; **inconnue** *nf* unknown factor

**inconsciemment** [ɛ̃kɔ̃sjamɑ̃] *adv* unconsciously

**inconscient, e** [ɛ̃kɔ̃sjɑ̃, ɑ̃t] *adj* unconscious; (*irréfléchi*) thoughtless, reckless; (*sentiment*) subconscious ♦ *nm* (PSYCH): **l'~** the unconscious; **~ de** unaware of

**inconsidéré, e** [ɛ̃kɔ̃sidere] *adj* ill-

considered
**inconsistant, e** [ɛ̃kɔ̃sistɑ̃, ɑ̃t] adj (fig)
flimsy, weak
**inconsolable** [ɛ̃kɔ̃sɔlabl] adj inconsolable
**incontestable** [ɛ̃kɔ̃tɛstabl] adj indisputable
**incontinent, e** [ɛ̃kɔ̃tinɑ̃, ɑ̃t] adj incontinent
**incontournable** [ɛ̃kɔ̃turnabl] adj unavoidable
**incontrôlable** [ɛ̃kɔ̃trolabl] adj unverifiable; (irrépressible) uncontrollable
**inconvenant, e** [ɛ̃kɔ̃v(ə)nɑ̃, ɑ̃t] adj unseemly, improper
**inconvénient** [ɛ̃kɔ̃venjɑ̃] nm disadvantage, drawback; **si vous n'y voyez pas d'~** if you have no objections
**incorporer** [ɛ̃kɔrpɔre] vt: ~ (à) to mix in (with); ~ (dans) (paragraphe etc) to incorporate (in); (MIL: appeler) to recruit (into); **il a très bien su s'~ à notre groupe** he was very easily incorporated into our group
**incorrect, e** [ɛ̃kɔrɛkt] adj (impropre, inconvenant) improper; (défectueux) faulty; (inexact) incorrect; (impoli) impolite; (déloyal) underhand
**incorrigible** [ɛ̃kɔriʒibl] adj incorrigible
**incrédule** [ɛ̃kredyl] adj incredulous; (REL) unbelieving
**increvable** [ɛ̃krəvabl] adj (fam) tireless
**incriminer** [ɛ̃krimine] vt (personne) to incriminate; (action, conduite) to bring under attack; (bonne foi, honnêteté) to call into question
**incroyable** [ɛ̃krwajabl] adj incredible
**incruster** [ɛ̃kryste] vt (ART) to inlay; **s'~ vi** (invité) to take root
**inculpé, e** [ɛ̃kylpe] nm/f accused
**inculper** [ɛ̃kylpe] vt: ~ **(de)** to charge (with)
**inculquer** [ɛ̃kylke] vt: ~ **qch à** to inculcate sth in ou instil sth into
**inculte** [ɛ̃kylt] adj uncultivated; (esprit, peuple) uncultured
**Inde** [ɛ̃d] nf: **l'~** India

**indécent, e** [ɛ̃desɑ̃, ɑ̃t] adj indecent
**indéchiffrable** [ɛ̃deʃifrabl] adj indecipherable
**indécis, e** [ɛ̃desi, iz] adj (par nature) indecisive; (temporairement) undecided
**indéfendable** [ɛ̃defɑ̃dabl] adj indefensible
**indéfini, e** [ɛ̃defini] adj (imprécis, incertain) undefined; (illimité, LING) indefinite; **indéfiniment** adv indefinitely; **indéfinissable** adj indefinable
**indélébile** [ɛ̃delebil] adj indelible
**indélicat, e** [ɛ̃delika, at] adj tactless
**indemne** [ɛ̃dɛmn] adj unharmed; **indemniser** vt: **indemniser qn (de)** to compensate sb (for)
**indemnité** [ɛ̃dɛmnite] nf (dédommagement) compensation no pl; (allocation) allowance; **indemnité de licenciement** redundancy payment
**indépendamment** [ɛ̃depɑ̃damɑ̃] adv independently; ~ **de** (abstraction faite de) irrespective of; (en plus de) over and above
**indépendance** [ɛ̃depɑ̃dɑ̃s] nf independence
**indépendant, e** [ɛ̃depɑ̃dɑ̃, ɑ̃t] adj independent; ~ **de** independent of
**indescriptible** [ɛ̃dɛskriptibl] adj indescribable
**indésirable** [ɛ̃dezirabl] adj undesirable
**indestructible** [ɛ̃dɛstryktibl] adj indestructible
**indétermination** [ɛ̃determinasjɔ̃] nf (irrésolution: chronique) indecision; (: temporaire) indecisiveness
**indéterminé, e** [ɛ̃determine] adj (date, cause, nature) unspecified; (forme, longueur, quantité) indeterminate
**index** [ɛ̃dɛks] nm (doigt) index finger; (d'un livre etc) index; **mettre à l'~** to blacklist; **indexé, e** adj (ÉCON): **indexé (sur)** index-linked (to)
**indic** [ɛ̃dik] nm (fam) (POLICE) grass
**indicateur** [ɛ̃dikatœr] nm (POLICE) informer; (TECH) gauge, indicator
**indicatif, -ive** [ɛ̃dikatif, iv] adj: **à titre**

~ for (your) information ♦ nm (LING) indicative; (RADIO) theme ou signature tune; (TÉL) dialling code

**indication** [ɛ̃dikasjɔ̃] nf indication; (renseignement) information no pl; **~s** nfpl (directives) instructions

**indice** [ɛ̃dis] nm (marque, signe) indication, sign; (POLICE: lors d'une enquête) clue; (JUR: présomption) piece of evidence; (SCIENCE, ÉCON, TECH) index

**indicible** [ɛ̃disibl] adj inexpressible

**indien, ne** [ɛ̃djɛ̃, jɛn] adj Indian ♦ nm/f: **I~, ne** Indian

**indifféremment** [ɛ̃diferamɑ̃] adv (sans distinction) equally (well)

**indifférence** [ɛ̃diferɑ̃s] nf indifference

**indifférent, e** [ɛ̃diferɑ̃, ɑ̃t] adj (peu intéressé) indifferent; **ça m'est** it doesn't matter to me; **elle m'est ~e** I am indifferent to her

**indigence** [ɛ̃diʒɑ̃s] nf poverty

**indigène** [ɛ̃diʒɛn] adj native, indigenous; (des gens du pays) local ♦ nm/f native

**indigeste** [ɛ̃diʒɛst] adj indigestible

**indigestion** [ɛ̃diʒɛstjɔ̃] nf indigestion no pl

**indigne** [ɛ̃diɲ] adj unworthy

**indigner** [ɛ̃diɲe] vt: **s'~ (de ou contre)** to get indignant (at)

**indiqué, e** [ɛ̃dike] adj (date, lieu) agreed; (traitement) appropriate; (conseillé) advisable

**indiquer** [ɛ̃dike] vt (suj: pendule, aiguille) to show; (: étiquette, panneau) to show, indicate; (renseigner sur) to point out, tell; (déterminer: date, lieu) to give, state; (signaler, dénoter) to indicate, point to; **~ qch/qn à qn** (montrer du doigt) to point sth/sb out to sb; (faire connaître: médecin, restaurant) to tell sb of sth/sb

**indirect, e** [ɛ̃dirɛkt] adj indirect

**indiscipliné, e** [ɛ̃disipline] adj undisciplined

**indiscret, -ète** [ɛ̃diskrɛ, ɛt] adj indiscreet

**indiscutable** [ɛ̃diskytabl] adj indisputable

**indispensable** [ɛ̃dispɑ̃sabl] adj indispensable, essential

**indisposé, e** [ɛ̃dispoze] adj indisposed

**indisposer** [ɛ̃dispoze] vt (incommoder) to upset; (déplaire à) to antagonize; (énerver) to irritate

**indistinct, e** [ɛ̃distɛ̃(kt), ɛkt] adj indistinct; **indistinctement** adv (voir, prononcer) indistinctly; (sans distinction) indiscriminately

**individu** [ɛ̃dividy] nm individual; **individuel, le** adj (gén) individual; (responsabilité, propriété, liberté) personal; **chambre individuelle** single room; **maison individuelle** detached house

**indolore** [ɛ̃dɔlɔr] adj painless

**indomptable** [ɛ̃dɔ̃(p)tabl] adj untameable; (fig) invincible

**Indonésie** [ɛ̃dɔnezi] nf Indonesia

**indu, e** [ɛ̃dy] adj: **à une heure ~e** at some ungodly hour

**induire** [ɛ̃dɥir] vt: **~ qn en erreur** to lead sb astray, mislead sb

**indulgent, e** [ɛ̃dylʒɑ̃, ɑ̃t] adj (parent, regard) indulgent; (juge, examinateur) lenient

**industrialisé, e** [ɛ̃dystrijalize] adj industrialized

**industrie** [ɛ̃dystri] nf industry; **industriel, le** adj industrial ♦ nm industrialist

**inébranlable** [inebrɑ̃labl] adj (masse, colonne) solid; (personne, certitude, foi) unshakeable

**inédit, e** [inedi, it] adj (correspondance, livre) hitherto unpublished; (spectacle, moyen) novel, original; (film) unreleased

**ineffaçable** [inefasabl] adj indelible

**inefficace** [inefikas] adj (remède, moyen) ineffective; (machine, employé) inefficient

**inégal, e, -aux** [inegal, o] adj unequal; (irrégulier) uneven; **inégalable** adj matchless; **inégalé, e** adj (record) unequalled; (beauté) unrivalled; **inégalité** nf inequality

**inépuisable** [inepɥizabl] adj inexhaustible

**inerte** [inɛʀt] adj (immobile) lifeless; (sans réaction) passive

**inespéré, e** [inespeʀe] adj unexpected, unhoped-for

**inestimable** [inɛstimabl] adj priceless; (fig: bienfait) invaluable

**inévitable** [inevitabl] adj unavoidable; (fatal, habituel) inevitable

**inexact, e** [inɛgza(kt), akt] adj inaccurate

**inexcusable** [inɛkskyzabl] adj unforgivable

**inexplicable** [inɛksplikabl] adj inexplicable

**in extremis** [inɛkstʀemis] adv at the last minute ♦ adj last-minute

**infaillible** [ɛ̃fajibl] adj infallible

**infâme** [ɛ̃fam] adj vile

**infarctus** [ɛ̃faʀktys] nm: ~ (du myocarde) coronary (thrombosis)

**infatigable** [ɛ̃fatigabl] adj tireless

**infect, e** [ɛ̃fɛkt] adj revolting; (personne) obnoxious; (temps) foul

**infecter** [ɛ̃fɛkte] vt (atmosphère, eau) to contaminate; (MÉD) to infect; **s'~** to become infected ou septic; **infection** nf infection; (puanteur) stench

**inférieur, e** [ɛ̃feʀjœʀ] adj lower; (en qualité, intelligence) inferior; **~ à** (somme, quantité) less ou smaller than; (moins bon que) inferior to

**infernal, e, -aux** [ɛ̃fɛʀnal, o] adj (insupportable: chaleur, rythme) infernal; (: enfant) horrid; (satanique, effrayant) diabolical

**infidèle** [ɛ̃fidɛl] adj unfaithful

**infiltrer** [ɛ̃filtʀe] vb: **s'~ dans** to get into; (liquide) to seep through; (fig: groupe, ennemi) to infiltrate

**infime** [ɛ̃fim] adj minute, tiny

**infini, e** [ɛ̃fini] adj infinite ♦ nm infinity; **à l'~** infinitely; **infiniment** adv infinitely; **infinité** nf: **une infinité de** an infinite number of

**infinitif** [ɛ̃finitif, iv] nm infinitive

**infirme** [ɛ̃fiʀm] adj disabled ♦ nm/f disabled person

**infirmerie** [ɛ̃fiʀməʀi] nf medical room

**infirmier, -ière** [ɛ̃fiʀmje] nm/f nurse; **infirmière chef** sister

**infirmité** [ɛ̃fiʀmite] nf disability

**inflammable** [ɛ̃flamabl] adj (in)flammable

**inflation** [ɛ̃flasjɔ̃] nf inflation

**infliger** [ɛ̃fliʒe] vt: **~ qch (à qn)** to inflict sth (on sb); (amende, sanction) to impose sth (on sb)

**influençable** [ɛ̃flyɑ̃sabl] adj easily influenced

**influence** [ɛ̃flyɑ̃s] nf influence; **influencer** vt to influence; **influent, e** adj influential

**informateur, -trice** [ɛ̃fɔʀmatœʀ, tʀis] nm/f (POLICE) informer

**informaticien, ne** [ɛ̃fɔʀmatisjɛ̃, jɛn] nm/f computer scientist

**information** [ɛ̃fɔʀmasjɔ̃] nf (renseignement) piece of information; (PRESSE, TV: nouvelle) item of news; (diffusion de renseignements, INFORM) information; (JUR) inquiry, investigation; **~s** nfpl (TV) news sg

**informatique** [ɛ̃fɔʀmatik] nf (technique) data processing; (science) computer science ♦ adj computer cpd; **informatiser** vt to computerize

**informe** [ɛ̃fɔʀm] adj shapeless

**informer** [ɛ̃fɔʀme] vt: **~ qn (de)** to inform sb (of); **s'~ (de/si)** to inquire ou find out (about/whether ou if)

**infos** [ɛ̃fo] nfpl: **les ~** the news sg

**infraction** [ɛ̃fʀaksjɔ̃] nf offence; **~ à** violation ou breach of; **être en ~** to be in breach of the law

**infranchissable** [ɛ̃fʀɑ̃ʃisabl] adj impassable; (fig) insuperable

**infrarouge** [ɛ̃fʀaʀuʒ] adj infrared

**infrastructure** [ɛ̃fʀastʀyktyʀ] nf (AVIAT, MIL) ground installations pl; (ÉCON: touristique etc) infrastructure

**infuser** [ɛ̃fyze] vt, vi (thé) to brew; (tisane) to infuse; **infusion** nf (tisane) herb tea

**ingénier** [ɛ̃ʒenje]: **s'~** vi: **s'~ à faire** to strive to do

**ingénierie** [ɛ̃ʒeniʀi] nf engineering; **~ génétique** genetic engineering

**ingénieur** [ɛ̃ʒenjœʀ] nm engineer; **in-génieur du son** sound engineer

**ingénieux, -euse** [ɛ̃ʒenjø, jøz] adj ingenious, clever

**ingénu, e** [ɛ̃ʒeny] adj ingenuous, artless

**ingérer** [ɛ̃ʒeʀe] vb: **s'~ dans** to interfere in

**ingrat, e** [ɛ̃gʀa, at] adj (personne) ungrateful; (travail, sujet) thankless; (visage) unprepossessing

**ingrédient** [ɛ̃gʀedjɑ̃] nm ingredient

**ingurgiter** [ɛ̃gyʀʒite] vt to swallow

**inhabitable** [inabitabl] adj uninhabitable

**inhabité, e** [inabite] adj uninhabited

**inhabituel, le** [inabituel] adj unusual

**inhibition** [inibisjɔ̃] nf inhibition

**inhumain, e** [inymɛ̃, ɛn] adj inhuman

**inhumation** [inymasjɔ̃] nf burial

**inhumer** [inyme] vt to inter, bury

**inimaginable** [inimaʒinabl] adj unimaginable

**ininterrompu, e** [inɛ̃teʀɔ̃py] adj (file, série) unbroken; (flot, vacarme) uninterrupted, non-stop; (effort) unremitting, continuous; (suite, ligne) unbroken

**initial, e, -aux** [inisjal, jo] adj initial; **initiale** nf initial; **initialiser** vt to initialize

**initiation** [inisjasjɔ̃] nf: **~ à** introduction to

**initiative** [inisjativ] nf initiative

**initier** [inisje] vt: **~ qn à** to initiate sb into; (faire découvrir: art, jeu) to introduce sb to

**injecté, e** [ɛ̃ʒekte] adj: **yeux ~s de sang** bloodshot eyes

**injecter** [ɛ̃ʒekte] vt to inject; **injection** nf injection; **à injection** (AUTO) fuel injection cpd

**injure** [ɛ̃ʒyʀ] nf insult, abuse no pl; **inju-**

rier vt to insult, abuse; **injurieux, -euse** adj abusive, insulting

**injuste** [ɛ̃ʒyst] adj unjust, unfair; **injus-tice** nf injustice

**inlassable** [ɛ̃lasabl] adj tireless

**inné, e** [i(n)ne] adj innate, inborn

**innocent, e** [inɔsɑ̃, ɑ̃t] adj innocent; **innocenter** vt to clear, prove innocent

**innombrable** [i(n)nɔ̃bʀabl] adj innumerable

**innommable** [i(n)nɔmabl] adj unspeakable

**innover** [inɔve] vi to break new ground

**inoccupé, e** [inɔkype] adj unoccupied

**inodore** [inɔdɔʀ] adj (gaz) odourless; (fleur) scentless

**inoffensif, -ive** [inɔfɑ̃sif, iv] adj harmless, innocuous

**inondation** [inɔ̃dasjɔ̃] nf flood

**inonder** [inɔ̃de] vt to flood; **~ de** to flood with

**inopiné, e** [inɔpine] adj unexpected; (mort) sudden

**inopportun, e** [inɔpɔʀtœ̃, yn] adj ill-timed, untimely

**inoubliable** [inublijabl] adj unforgettable

**inouï, e** [inwi] adj unheard-of, extraordinary

**inox** [inɔks] nm stainless steel

**inqualifiable** [ɛ̃kalifjabl] adj unspeakable

**inquiet, -ète** [ɛ̃kjɛ, ɛkjɛt] adj anxious; **inquiétant, e** adj worrying, disturbing; **inquiéter** vt to worry; **s'inquiéter** to worry; **s'inquiéter de** to worry about; (s'enquérir de) to inquire about; **inquiétude** nf anxiety

**insaisissable** [ɛ̃sezisabl] adj (fugitif, ennemi) elusive; (différence, nuance) imperceptible

**insalubre** [ɛ̃salybʀ] adj insalubrious

**insatisfaisant, e** [ɛ̃satisfazɑ̃, ɑ̃t] adj unsatisfactory

**insatisfait, e** [ɛ̃satisfɛ, ɛt] adj (non comblé) unsatisfied; (mécontent) dissatisfied

**inscription** [ɛ̃skʀipsjɔ̃] nf inscription; (immatriculation) enrolment

**inscrire** [ɛ̃skʀiʀ] vt (marquer: sur son calepin etc) to note ou write down; (: sur un mur, une affiche etc) to write; (: dans la pierre, le métal) to inscribe; (mettre: sur une liste, un budget etc) to put down; **s'~** (pour une excursion etc) to put one's name down; **s'~ (à)** (club, parti) to join; (université) to register ou enrol (at); (examen, concours) to register (for); **~ qn à** (club, parti) to enrol sb at

**insecte** [ɛ̃sɛkt] nm insect; **insecticide** nm insecticide

**insensé, e** [ɛ̃sɑ̃se] adj mad

**insensibiliser** [ɛ̃sɑ̃sibilize] vt to anaesthetize

**insensible** [ɛ̃sɑ̃sibl] adj (nerf, membre) numb; (dur, indifférent) insensitive

**inséparable** [ɛ̃sepaʀabl] adj inseparable ♦ nm: **~s** (oiseaux) lovebirds

**insigne** [ɛ̃siɲ] nm (d'un parti, club) badge; (d'une fonction) insignia ♦ adj distinguished

**insignifiant, e** [ɛ̃siɲifjɑ̃, jɑ̃t] adj insignificant; trivial

**insinuer** [ɛ̃sinɥe] vt to insinuate; **s'~ dans** (fig) to worm one's way into

**insipide** [ɛ̃sipid] adj insipid

**insister** [ɛ̃siste] vi to insist; (continuer à sonner) to keep on trying; **~ sur** (détail, sujet) to lay stress on

**insolation** [ɛ̃sɔlasjɔ̃] nf (MÉD) sunstroke no pl

**insolent, e** [ɛ̃sɔlɑ̃, ɑ̃t] adj insolent

**insolite** [ɛ̃sɔlit] adj strange, unusual

**insomnie** [ɛ̃sɔmni] nf insomnia no pl

**insonoriser** [ɛ̃sɔnɔʀize] vt to soundproof

**insouciant, e** [ɛ̃susjɑ̃, ɑ̃t] adj carefree; **~ du danger** heedless of (the) danger

**insoumis, e** [ɛ̃sumi, iz] adj (caractère, enfant) rebellious, refractory; (contrée, tribu) unsubdued

**insoupçonnable** [ɛ̃supsɔnabl] adj un-

suspected; (personne) above suspicion

**insoupçonné, e** [ɛ̃supsɔne] adj unsuspected

**insoutenable** [ɛ̃sut(ə)nabl] adj (argument) untenable; (chaleur) unbearable

**inspecter** [ɛ̃spɛkte] vt to inspect; **inspecteur, -trice** nm/f inspector; **inspecteur d'Académie** (regional) director of education; **inspecteur des finances** ≈ tax inspector (BRIT), ≈ Internal Revenue Service agent (US); **inspection** nf inspection

**inspirer** [ɛ̃spiʀe] vt (gén) to inspire ♦ vi (aspirer) to breathe in; **s'~ de** (suj: artiste) to draw one's inspiration from

**instable** [ɛ̃stabl] adj unstable; (meuble, équilibre) unsteady; (temps) unsettled

**installation** [ɛ̃stalasjɔ̃] nf installation; **~s** nfpl facilities

**installer** [ɛ̃stale] vt (loger, placer) to put; (meuble, gaz, électricité) to put in; (rideau, étagère, tente) to put up; (appartement) to fit out; **s'~** (s'établir: artisan, dentiste etc) to set o.s. up; (se loger) to settle; (emménager) to settle in; (sur un siège, à un emplacement) to settle (down); (fig: maladie, grève) to take a firm hold

**instance** [ɛ̃stɑ̃s] nf (ADMIN: autorité) authority; **affaire en ~** matter pending; **être en ~ de divorce** to be awaiting a divorce

**instant** [ɛ̃stɑ̃] nm moment, instant; **dans un ~** in a moment; **à l'~** this instant; **pour l'~** for the moment, for the time being

**instantané, e** [ɛ̃stɑ̃tane] adj (lait, café) instant; (explosion, mort) instantaneous ♦ nm snapshot

**instar** [ɛ̃staʀ]: **à l'~ de** prép following the example of, like

**instaurer** [ɛ̃stɔʀe] vt to institute; (couvre-feu) to impose

**instinct** [ɛ̃stɛ̃] nm instinct; **instinctivement** adv instinctively

**instit** [ɛ̃stit] (fam) nm/f (primary school) teacher

**nstituer** [ɛ̃stitɥe] vt to establish

**nstitut** [ɛ̃stity] nm institute; **~ de beauté** beauty salon; **Institut universitaire de technologie** ≈ polytechnic

**nstituteur, -trice** [ɛ̃stitytœʀ, tʀis] nm/f (primary school) teacher

**nstitution** [ɛ̃stitysjɔ̃] nf institution; (collège) private school

**nstructif, -ive** [ɛ̃stʀyktif, iv] adj instructive

**nstruction** [ɛ̃stʀyksjɔ̃] nf (enseignement, savoir) education; (JUR) (preliminary) investigation and hearing; **~s** nfpl (ordres, mode d'emploi) instructions; **~ civique** civics sg

**nstruire** [ɛ̃stʀɥiʀ] vt (élèves) to teach; (recrues) to train; (JUR: affaire) to conduct the investigation for; **s'~** to educate o.s.; **instruit, e** adj educated

**nstrument** [ɛ̃stʀymɑ̃] nm instrument; **~ à cordes/vent** stringed/wind instrument; **~ de mesure** measuring instrument; **~ de musique** musical instrument; **~ de travail** (working) tool

**nsu** [ɛ̃sy] nm: **à l'~ de qn** without sb knowing (it)

**nsubmersible** [ɛ̃sybmɛʀsibl] adj unsinkable

**nsuffisant, e** [ɛ̃syfizɑ̃, ɑ̃t] adj (en quantité) insufficient; (en qualité) inadequate; (sur une copie) poor

**nsulaire** [ɛ̃sylɛʀ] adj island cpd; (attitude) insular

**nsuline** [ɛ̃sylin] nf insulin

**nsulte** [ɛ̃sylt] nf insult; **insulter** vt to insult

**nsupportable** [ɛ̃sypɔʀtabl] adj unbearable

**nsurger** [ɛ̃syʀʒe] vb: **s'~ (contre)** to rise up ou rebel (against)

**nsurmontable** [ɛ̃syʀmɔ̃tabl] adj (difficulté) insuperable; (aversion) unconquerable

**nsurrection** [ɛ̃syʀɛksjɔ̃] nf insurrection

**ntact, e** [ɛ̃takt] adj intact

**ntangible** [ɛ̃tɑ̃ʒibl] adj intangible; (principe) inviolable

**intarissable** [ɛ̃taʀisabl] adj inexhaustible

**intégral, e, -aux** [ɛ̃tegʀal, o] adj complete; **texte ~** unabridged version; **bronzage ~** all-over suntan; **intégralement** adv in full; **intégralité** nf whole; **dans son intégralité** in full; **intégrant, e** adj: **faire partie intégrante de** to be an integral part of

**intègre** [ɛ̃tɛgʀ] adj upright

**intégrer** [ɛ̃tegʀe] vt: **bien s'~** to integrate well

**intégrisme** [ɛ̃tegʀism] nm fundamentalism

**intellectuel, le** [ɛ̃telektɥɛl] adj intellectual ♦ nm/f intellectual; (péj) highbrow

**intelligence** [ɛ̃teliʒɑ̃s] nf intelligence; (compréhension): **l'~ de** the understanding of; (complicité): **regard d'~** glance of complicity; (accord): **vivre en bonne ~ avec qn** to be on good terms with sb

**intelligent, e** [ɛ̃teliʒɑ̃, ɑ̃t] adj intelligent

**intelligible** [ɛ̃teliʒibl] adj intelligible

**intempéries** [ɛ̃tɑ̃peʀi] nfpl bad weather sg

**intempestif, -ive** [ɛ̃tɑ̃pɛstif, iv] adj untimely

**intenable** [ɛ̃t(ə)nabl] adj (chaleur) unbearable

**intendant, e** [ɛ̃tɑ̃dɑ̃] nm/f (MIL) quartermaster; (SCOL) bursar

**intense** [ɛ̃tɑ̃s] adj intense; **intensif, -ive** adj intensive; **un cours intensif** a crash course

**intenter** [ɛ̃tɑ̃te] vt: **~ un procès contre** ou **à** to start proceedings against

**intention** [ɛ̃tɑ̃sjɔ̃] nf intention; (JUR) intent; **avoir l'~ de faire** to intend to do; **à l'~ de** for; (renseignement) for the benefit of; (film, ouvrage) aimed at; **à cette ~** with this aim in view; **intentionné, e** adj: **bien intentionné** well-meaning ou -intentioned; **mal inten-**

**tionné** ill-intentioned

**interactif, -ive** [ɛteʀaktif, iv] adj (COMPUT) interactive

**intercalaire** [ɛteʀkaleʀ] nm divider

**intercaler** [ɛteʀkale] vt to insert

**intercepter** [ɛteʀsepte] vt to intercept; (lumière, chaleur) to cut off

**interchangeable** [ɛteʀʃɑ̃ʒabl] adj interchangeable

**interclasse** [ɛteʀklas] nm (SCOL) break (between classes)

**interdiction** [ɛteʀdiksjɔ̃] nf ban; **~ de stationner** no parking; **~ de fumer** no smoking

**interdire** [ɛteʀdiʀ] vt to forbid; (ADMIN) to ban, prohibit; (: journal, livre) to ban; **~ à qn de faire** to forbid sb to do; (suj: empêchement) to prevent sb from doing

**interdit, e** [ɛteʀdi, it] adj (stupéfait) taken aback

**intéressant, e** [ɛteʀesɑ̃, ɑ̃t] adj interesting; (avantageux) attractive

**intéressé, e** [ɛteʀese] adj (parties) involved, concerned; (amitié, motifs) self-interested

**intéresser** [ɛteʀese] vt (captiver) to interest; (toucher) to be of interest to; (ADMIN: concerner) to affect, concern; **s'~ à** to be interested in

**intérêt** [ɛteʀe] nm interest; (égoïsme) self-interest; **tu as ~ à accepter** it's in your interest to accept; **tu as ~ à te dépêcher** you'd better hurry

**intérieur, e** [ɛteʀjœʀ] adj (mur, escalier, poche) inside; (commerce, politique) domestic; (cour, calme, vie) inner; (navigation) inland ♦ nm (d'une maison, d'un récipient etc) inside; (d'un pays, aussi décor, mobilier) interior; **à l'~ (de)** inside; **intérieurement** adv inwardly

**intérim** [ɛteʀim] nm interim period; **faire de l'~** to temp; **assurer l'~ (de)** to deputize (for); **par ~** interim

**intérimaire** [ɛteʀimeʀ] adj (directeur, ministre) acting; (secrétaire, personnel) temporary ♦ nm/f (secrétaire) temporary

secretary, temp (BRIT)

**interlocuteur, -trice** [ɛteʀlɔkytœʀ, tʀis] nm/f speaker; **son ~** the person he was speaking to

**interloquer** [ɛteʀlɔke] vt to take aback

**intermède** [ɛteʀmɛd] nm interlude

**intermédiaire** [ɛteʀmedjeʀ] adj intermediate; (solution) temporary ♦ nm/f intermediary; (COMM) middleman; **sans ~** directly; **par l'~ de** through

**interminable** [ɛteʀminabl] adj endless

**intermittence** [ɛteʀmitɑ̃s] nf: **par ~** sporadically, intermittently

**internat** [ɛteʀna] nm boarding school

**international, e, -aux** [ɛteʀnasjɔnal, o] adj, nm/f international

**interne** [ɛteʀn] adj internal ♦ nm/f (SCOL) boarder; (MÉD) houseman

**interner** [ɛteʀne] vt (POL) to intern; (MÉD) to confine to a mental institution

**Internet** [ɛteʀnɛt] nm: **l'~** the Internet

**interpeller** [ɛteʀpəle] vt (appeler) to call out to; (apostropher) to shout at; (POLICE, POL) to question; (concerner) to concern

**interphone** [ɛteʀfɔn] nm intercom; (d'immeuble) entry phone

**interposer** [ɛteʀpoze] vt: **s'~** to intervene; **par personnes interposées** through a third party

**interprétation** [ɛteʀpʀetasjɔ̃] nf interpretation

**interprète** [ɛteʀpʀɛt] nm/f interpreter; (porte-parole) spokesperson

**interpréter** [ɛteʀpʀete] vt to interpret; (jouer) to play; (chanter) to sing

**interrogateur, -trice** [ɛteʀɔgatœʀ, tʀis] adj questioning, inquiring

**interrogatif, -ive** [ɛteʀɔgatif, iv] adj (LING) interrogative

**interrogation** [ɛteʀɔgasjɔ̃] nf question; (action) questioning; (SCOL) (written or oral) test

**interrogatoire** [ɛteʀɔgatwaʀ] nm (POLICE) questioning no pl; (JUR, aussi fig) cross-examination

**interroger** [ɛteʀɔʒe] vt to question; (IN-

_FORM_) to consult; (_SCOL_) to test

**interrompre** [ɛterɔ̃pr] _vt_ (_gén_) to interrupt; (_négociations_) to break off; (_match_) to stop; **s'~** to break off; **interrupteur** _nm_ switch; **interruption** _nf_ interruption; (_pause_) break; **sans interruption** without stopping

**intersection** [ɛterseksjɔ̃] _nf_ intersection

**interstice** [ɛterstis] _nm_ crack; (_de volet_) slit

**interurbain, e** [ɛteryrbɛ̃, ɛn] _adj_ (_TÉL_) long-distance

**intervalle** [ɛterval] _nm_ (_espace_) space; (_de temps_) interval; **à deux jours d'~** two days apart

**intervenir** [ɛtervənir] _vi_ (_gén_) to intervene; **~ auprès de qn** to intervene with sb

**intervention** [ɛtervɑ̃sjɔ̃] _nf_ intervention; (_discours_) speech; **intervention chirurgicale** (surgical) operation

**intervertir** [ɛtervertir] _vt_ to invert (the order of), reverse

**interview** [ɛtervju] _nf_ interview

**intestin** [ɛtestɛ̃, in] _nm_ intestine

**intime** [ɛtim] _adj_ intimate; (_vie_) private; (_conviction_) inmost; (_dîner, cérémonie_) quiet ♦ _nm/f_ close friend; **un journal ~** a diary

**intimider** [ɛtimide] _vt_ to intimidate

**intimité** [ɛtimite] _nf_: **dans l'~** in private; (_sans formalités_) with only a few friends, quietly

**intitulé, e** [ɛtityle] _adj_ entitled

**intolérable** [ɛtɔlerabl] _adj_ intolerable

**intox** [ɛtɔks] (_fam_) _nf_ brainwashing

**intoxication** [ɛtɔksikasjɔ̃] _nf_: **~ alimentaire** food poisoning

**intoxiquer** [ɛtɔksike] _vt_ to poison; (_fig_) to brainwash

**intraduisible** [ɛtradɥizibl] _adj_ untranslatable; (_fig_) inexpressible

**intraitable** [ɛtretabl] _adj_ inflexible, uncompromising

**intranet** [ɛtranɛt] _nm_ intranet

**intransigeant, e** [ɛtrɑ̃ziʒɑ̃, ɑ̃t] _adj_ intransigent

**intransitif, -ive** [ɛtrɑ̃zitif, iv] _adj_ (_LING_) intransitive

**intrépide** [ɛtrepid] _adj_ dauntless

**intrigue** [ɛtrig] _nf_ (_scénario_) plot; **intriguer** _vt_ to puzzle, intrigue

**intrinsèque** [ɛtrɛ̃sɛk] _adj_ intrinsic

**introduction** [ɛtrɔdyksjɔ̃] _nf_ introduction

**introduire** [ɛtrɔdɥir] _vt_ to introduce; (_visiteur_) to show in; (_aiguille, clef_): **~ qch dans** to insert ou introduce sth into; **s'~ (dans)** to get in(to); (_dans un groupe_) to get o.s. accepted (into)

**introuvable** [ɛtruvabl] _adj_ which cannot be found; (_COMM_) unobtainable

**introverti, e** [ɛtrɔverti] _nm/f_ introvert

**intrus, e** [ɛtry, yz] _nm/f_ intruder

**intrusion** [ɛtryzjɔ̃] _nf_ intrusion

**intuition** [ɛtɥisjɔ̃] _nf_ intuition

**inusable** [inyzabl] _adj_ hard-wearing

**inusité, e** [inyzite] _adj_ rarely used

**inutile** [inytil] _adj_ useless; (_superflu_) unnecessary; **inutilement** _adv_ unnecessarily; **inutilisable** _adj_ unusable

**invalide** [ɛ̃valid] _adj_ disabled ♦ _nm_: **~ de guerre** disabled ex-serviceman

**invariable** [ɛ̃varjabl] _adj_ invariable

**invasion** [ɛ̃vazjɔ̃] _nf_ invasion

**invectiver** [ɛ̃vɛktive] _vt_ to hurl abuse at

**invendable** [ɛ̃vɑ̃dabl] _adj_ unsaleable; (_COMM_) unmarketable; **invendus** _nmpl_ unsold goods

**inventaire** [ɛ̃vɑ̃ter] _nm_ inventory; (_COMM_: _liste_) stocklist; (: _opération_) stocktaking _no pl_

**inventer** [ɛ̃vɑ̃te] _vt_ to invent; (_subterfuge_) to devise, invent; (_histoire, excuse_) to make up, invent; **inventeur** _nm_ inventor; **inventif, -ive** _adj_ inventive; **invention** _nf_ invention

**inverse** [ɛ̃vɛrs] _adj_ opposite ♦ _nm_ opposite; **dans l'ordre ~** in the reverse order; **en sens ~** in the (_ou_ from) the opposite direction; **dans le sens ~ des aiguilles d'une montre** anticlockwise;

tu t'es trompé, c'est l'~ you've got it wrong, it's the other way round; **inversement** adv conversely; **inverser** vt to invert, reverse; (ÉLEC) to reverse

**investigation** [ɛ̃vɛstigasjɔ̃] nf investigation

**investir** [ɛ̃vɛstiʀ] vt to invest; **investissement** nm investment; **investiture** nf nomination

**invétéré, e** [ɛ̃vetere] adj inveterate

**invisible** [ɛ̃vizibl] adj invisible

**invitation** [ɛ̃vitasjɔ̃] nf invitation

**invité, e** [ɛ̃vite] nm/f guest

**inviter** [ɛ̃vite] vt to invite

**invivable** [ɛ̃vivabl] adj unbearable

**involontaire** [ɛ̃vɔlɔ̃tɛʀ] adj (mouvement) involuntary; (insulte) unintentional; (complice) unwitting

**invoquer** [ɛ̃vɔke] vt (Dieu, muse) to call upon, invoke; (prétexte) to put forward (as an excuse); (loi, texte) to refer to

**invraisemblable** [ɛ̃vʀɛsɑ̃blabl] adj (fait, nouvelle) unlikely, improbable; (insolence, habit) incredible

**iode** [jɔd] nm iodine

**irai** etc [iʀe] vb voir **aller**

**Irak** [iʀak] nm Iraq; **irakien, ne** adj Iraqi ♦ nm/f: **Irakien, ne** Iraqi

**Iran** [iʀɑ̃] nm Iran; **iranien, ne** adj Iranian ♦ nm/f: **Iranien, ne** Iranian

**irascible** [iʀasibl] adj short-tempered

**irions** etc [iʀjɔ̃] vb voir **aller**

**iris** [iʀis] nm iris

**irlandais, e** [iʀlɑ̃dɛ, ɛz] adj Irish ♦ nm/f: **Irlandais, e** Irishman(-woman); **les Irlandais** the Irish

**Irlande** [iʀlɑ̃d] nf Ireland; ~ **du Nord** Northern Ireland; **la République d'~** the Irish Republic

**ironie** [iʀɔni] nf irony; **ironique** adj ironical; **ironiser** vi to be ironical

**irons** etc [iʀɔ̃] vb voir **aller**

**irradier** [iʀadje] vt to irradiate

**irraisonné, e** [iʀezɔne] adj irrational

**irrationnel, le** [iʀasjɔnɛl] adj irrational

**irréalisable** [iʀealizabl] adj unrealizable; (projet) impracticable

**irrécupérable** [iʀekypeʀabl] adj beyond repair; (personne) beyond redemption

**irréductible** [iʀedyktibl] adj (volonté) indomitable; (ennemi) implacable

**irréel, le** [iʀeel] adj unreal

**irréfléchi, e** [iʀefleʃi] adj thoughtless

**irrégularité** [iʀegylaʀite] nf irregularity; (de travail, d'effort, de qualité) unevenness no pl

**irrégulier, -ière** [iʀegylje, jɛʀ] adj irregular; (travail, effort, qualité) uneven; (élève, athlète) erratic

**irrémédiable** [iʀemedjabl] adj irreparable

**irremplaçable** [iʀɑ̃plasabl] adj irreplaceable

**irréparable** [iʀepaʀabl] adj (objet) beyond repair; (dommage etc) irreparable

**irréprochable** [iʀepʀɔʃabl] adj irreproachable, beyond reproach; (tenue) impeccable

**irrésistible** [iʀezistibl] adj irresistible; (besoin, désir, preuve, logique) compelling; (amusant) hilarious

**irrésolu, e** [iʀezɔly] adj (personne) irresolute; (problème) unresolved

**irrespectueux, -euse** [iʀɛspɛktyø, øz] adj disrespectful

**irrespirable** [iʀespiʀabl] adj unbreathable; (fig) oppressive

**irresponsable** [iʀespɔ̃sabl] adj irresponsible

**irriguer** [iʀige] vt to irrigate

**irritable** [iʀitabl] adj irritable

**irriter** [iʀite] vt to irritate

**irruption** [iʀypsjɔ̃] nf: **faire ~ (chez qn)** to burst in (on sb)

**Islam** [islam] nm Islam; **islamique** adj Islamic; **islamiste** adj (militant) Islamic; (mouvement) Islamic fundamentalist ♦ nm/f Islamic fundamentalist

**Islande** [islɑ̃d] nf Iceland

**isolant, e** [izɔlɑ̃, ɑ̃t] adj insulating; (insonorisant) soundproofing

**isolation** [izɔlasjɔ̃] nf insulation

**isolé, e** [izole] adj isolated; (contre le

*froid)* insulated

**isoler** [izɔle] *vt* to isolate; *(prisonnier)* to put in solitary confinement; *(ville)* to cut off, isolate; *(contre le froid)* to insulate; **s'~** *vi* to isolate o.s.; **isoloir** [izɔlwaʀ] *nm* polling booth

**Israël** [israɛl] *nm* Israel; **israélien, ne** *adj* Israeli ♦ *nm/f:* **Israélien, ne** Israeli; **israélite** *adj* Jewish ♦ *nm/f:* **Israélite** Jew (Jewess)

**issu, e** [isy] *adj:* **~ de** *(né de)* descended from; *(résultant de)* stemming from; **issue** *nf (ouverture, sortie)* exit; *(solution)* way out, solution; *(dénouement)* outcome; **à l'issue de** at the conclusion *ou* close of; **voie sans issue** dead end; **issue de secours** emergency exit

**Italie** [itali] *nf* Italy; **italien, ne** *adj* Italian ♦ *nm/f:* **Italien, ne** Italian ♦ *nm (LING)* Italian

**italique** [italik] *nm:* **en ~** in italics

**itinéraire** [itineʀɛʀ] *nm* itinerary, route; **~ bis** diversion

**IUT** *sigle m* = **Institut universitaire de technologie**

**IVG** *sigle f (= interruption volontaire de grossesse)* abortion

**ivoire** [ivwaʀ] *nm* ivory

**ivre** [ivʀ] *adj* drunk; **~ de** *(colère, bonheur)* wild with; **ivresse** *nf* drunkenness; **ivrogne** *nm/f* drunkard

# J, j

**j'** [ʒ] *pron voir* **je**

**jacasser** [ʒakase] *vi* to chatter

**jacinthe** [ʒasɛ̃t] *nf* hyacinth

**jadis** [ʒadis] *adv* long ago

**jaillir** [ʒajiʀ] *vi (liquide)* to spurt out; *(cris, responses)* to burst forth

**jais** [ʒɛ] *nm* jet; **(d'un noir) de ~** jet-black

**jalousie** [ʒaluzi] *nf* jealousy; *(store)* slatted blind

**jaloux, -ouse** [ʒalu, uz] *adj* jealous

**jamais** [ʒamɛ] *adv* never; *(sans négation)* ever; **ne ... ~** never; **à ~** for ever

**jambe** [ʒɑ̃b] *nf* leg

**jambon** [ʒɑ̃bɔ̃] *nm* ham; **~ blanc** boiled *ou* cooked ham; **jambonneau, x** *nm* knuckle of ham

**jante** [ʒɑ̃t] *nf* (wheel) rim

**janvier** [ʒɑ̃vje] *nm* January

**Japon** [ʒapɔ̃] *nm* Japan; **japonais, e** *adj* Japanese ♦ *nm/f:* **Japonais, e** Japanese ♦ *nm (LING)* Japanese

**japper** [ʒape] *vi* to yap, yelp

**jaquette** [ʒakɛt] *nf (de cérémonie)* morning coat

**jardin** [ʒaʀdɛ̃] *nm* garden; **~ d'enfants** nursery school; **jardinage** *nm* gardening; **jardiner** *vi* to do some gardening; **jardinier, -ière** *nm/f* gardener; **jardinière** *nf* planter; *(de fenêtre)* window box; **jardinière de légumes** mixed vegetables

**jargon** [ʒaʀgɔ̃] *nm (baragouin)* gibberish; *(langue professionnelle)* jargon

**jarret** [ʒaʀɛ] *nm* back of knee; *(CULIN)* knuckle, shin

**jarretelle** [ʒaʀtɛl] *nf* suspender *(BRIT)*, garter *(US)*

**jarretière** [ʒaʀtjɛʀ] *nf* garter

**jaser** [ʒaze] *vi (médire)* to gossip

**jatte** [ʒat] *nf* basin, bowl

**jauge** [ʒoʒ] *nf (instrument)* gauge; **~ d'essence** petrol gauge; **~ d'huile** (oil) dipstick

**jaune** [ʒon] *adj, nm* yellow ♦ *adv (fam):* **rire ~** to laugh on the other side of one's face; **~ d'œuf** (egg) yolk; **jaunir** *vi, vt* to turn yellow; **jaunisse** *nf* jaundice

**Javel** [ʒavɛl] *nf voir* **eau**

**javelot** [ʒavlo] *nm* javelin

**J.-C.** *abr* = **Jésus-Christ**

**je, j'** [ʒ] *pron* I

**jean** [dʒin] *nm* jeans *pl*

**Jésus-Christ** [ʒezykʀi(st)] *n* Jesus Christ; **600 avant/après ~-~** *ou* **J.-C.** 600 B.C./A.D.

**jet¹** [ʒɛ] *nm (lancer: action)* throwing *no*

**jet** pl; (: résultat) throw; (jaillissement: d'eaux) jet; (: de sang) spurt; ~ **d'eau** spray

**jet²** [dʒɛt] nm (avion) jet

**jetable** [ʒ(ə)tabl] adj disposable

**jetée** [ʒəte] nf jetty; (grande) pier

**jeter** [ʒ(ə)te] vt (gén) to throw; (se défaire de) to throw away ou out; se ~ **dans** to flow into; ~ **qch à qn** to throw sth to sb; (de façon agressive) to throw sth at sb; ~ **un coup d'œil (à)** to take a look (at); ~ **un sort à qn** to cast a spell on sb; **se ~ sur qn** to rush at sb

**jeton** [ʒ(ə)tɔ̃] nm (au jeu) counter

**jette** etc [ʒɛt] vb voir jeter

**jeu, x** [ʒø] nm (divertissement, TECH: d'une pièce) play; (TENNIS: partie, FOOTBALL etc: façon de jouer) game; (THÉÂTRE etc) acting; (série d'objets, jouet) set; (CARTES) hand; (au casino): **le ~** gambling; **être en ~** to be at stake; **entrer/mettre en ~** to come/bring into play; ~ **de cartes** pack of cards; ~ **d'échecs** chess set; ~ **de hasard** game of chance; ~ **de mots** pun; ~ **de société** parlour game; ~ **télévisé** television quiz; ~ **vidéo** video game

**jeudi** [ʒødi] nm Thursday

**jeun** [ʒœ̃]: à ~ adv on an empty stomach; **être à** ~ to have eaten nothing; **rester à** ~ not to eat anything

**jeune** [ʒœn] adj young; **les ~s** young people; ~ **fille** girl; ~ **homme** young man; **~s mariés** newly-weds

**jeûne** [ʒøn] nm fast

**jeunesse** [ʒœnɛs] nf youth; (aspect) youthfulness

**joaillerie** [ʒɔajri] nf jewellery (magasin) jeweller's; **joaillier, -ière** nm/f jeweller

**jogging** [dʒɔgiŋ] nm jogging; (survêtement) tracksuit; **faire du** ~ to go jogging

**joie** [ʒwa] nf joy

**joindre** [ʒwɛ̃dʀ] vt to join; (à une lettre): ~ **qch à** to enclose sth with;

(contacter) to contact, get in touch with; **se ~ à** to join; ~ **les mains** to put one's hands together

**joint, e** [ʒwɛ̃, ɛt] adj: **pièce ~e** enclosure ♦ nm joint; (ligne) join; ~ **de culasse** cylinder head gasket; ~ **de robinet** washer

**joker** [ʒɔkɛʀ] nm (INFORM): (caractère m) ~ wildcard

**joli, e** [ʒɔli] adj pretty, attractive; **c'est du** ~! (ironique) that's very nice!; **c'est bien** ~, **mais ...** that's all very well but ...

**jonc** [ʒɔ̃] nm (bul)rush

**jonction** [ʒɔ̃ksjɔ̃] nf junction

**jongleur, -euse** [ʒɔ̃glœʀ, øz] nm/f juggler

**jonquille** [ʒɔ̃kij] nf daffodil

**Jordanie** [ʒɔʀdani] nf: **la** ~ Jordan

**joue** [ʒu] nf cheek

**jouer** [ʒwe] vt to play; (somme d'argent, réputation) to stake, wager; (simuler: sentiment) to affect, feign ♦ vi to play; (THÉÂTRE, CINÉMA) to act; (au casino) to gamble; (bois, porte: se voiler) to warp; (clef, pièce: avoir du jeu) to be loose; ~ **sur** (miser) to gamble on; ~ **de** (MUS) to play; ~ **à** (jeu, sport, roulette) to play; ~ **un tour à qn** to play a trick on sb; ~ **serré** to play a close game; ~ **la comédie** to put on an act; **bien joué!** well done!; **on joue Hamlet au théâtre X** Hamlet is on at the X theatre

**jouet** [ʒwɛ] nm toy; **être le ~ de** (illusion etc) to be the victim of

**joueur, -euse** [ʒwœʀ, øz] nm/f player; **être beau** ~ to be a good loser

**joufflu, e** [ʒufly] adj chubby-cheeked

**joug** [ʒu] nm yoke

**jouir** [ʒwiʀ] vi (sexe: fam) to come ♦ vt: ~ **de** to enjoy; **jouissance** nf pleasure; (JUR) use

**joujou** [ʒuʒu] (fam) nm toy

**jour** [ʒuʀ] nm day; (opposé à la nuit) day, daytime; (clarté) daylight; (fig: aspect) light; (ouverture) gap; **au** ~ **le**

from day to day; **de nos ~s** these days; **du ~ au lendemain** overnight; **il fait ~** it's daylight; **au grand ~** in the open; **mettre au ~** to disclose; **mettre à ~** to update; **donner le ~ à** to give birth to; **voir le ~** to be born; **~ férié** public holiday; **~ de fête** holiday; **~ ouvrable** working day

**journal, -aux** [ʒuʀnal, o] *nm* (news)paper; (spécialisé) journal; (intime) diary; **~ de bord** log; **~ télévisé** television news *sg*

**journalier, -ière** [ʒuʀnalje, jɛʀ] *adj* daily; (banal) everyday

**journalisme** [ʒuʀnalism] *nm* journalism; **journaliste** *nm/f* journalist

**journée** [ʒuʀne] *nf* day; **faire la ~ continue** to work over lunch

**journellement** [ʒuʀnɛlmɑ̃] *adv* daily

**joyau, x** [ʒwajo] *nm* gem, jewel

**joyeux, -euse** [ʒwajø, øz] *adj* joyful, merry; **~ Noël!** merry Christmas!; **~ anniversaire!** happy birthday!

**jubiler** [ʒybile] *vi* to be jubilant, exult

**jucher** [ʒyʃe] *vt, vi* to perch

**judas** [ʒyda] *nm* (trou) spy-hole

**judiciaire** [ʒydisjɛʀ] *adj* judicial

**judicieux, -euse** [ʒydisjø, jøz] *adj* judicious

**judo** [ʒydo] *nm* judo

**juge** [ʒyʒ] *nm* judge; **~ d'instruction** examining (BRIT) ou committing (US) magistrate; **~ de paix** justice of the peace; **~ de touche** linesman

**jugé** [ʒyʒe]: **au ~** *adv* by guesswork

**jugement** [ʒyʒmɑ̃] *nm* judgment; (JUR: au pénal) sentence; (: au civil) decision

**jugeote** [ʒyʒɔt] (fam) *nf* commonsense

**juger** [ʒyʒe] *vt* to judge; (estimer) to consider; **~ qn/qch satisfaisant** to consider sb/sth (to be) satisfactory; **~ bon de faire** to see fit to do; **~ de** to appreciate

**juif, -ive** [ʒɥif, ʒɥiv] *adj* Jewish ♦ *nm/f*: **J~, ive** Jew (Jewess)

**juillet** [ʒɥijɛ] *nm* July

**juin** [ʒɥɛ̃] *nm* June

**jumeau, -elle, x** [ʒymo, ɛl] *adj, nm/f* twin

**jumeler** [ʒym(ə)le] *vt* to twin

**jumelle** [ʒymɛl] *adj, nf* voir **jumeau**; **~s** *nfpl* (appareil) binoculars

**jument** [ʒymɑ̃] *nf* mare

**jungle** [ʒœ̃gl] *nf* jungle

**jupe** [ʒyp] *nf* skirt

**jupon** [ʒypɔ̃] *nm* waist slip

**juré, e** [ʒyʀe] *nm/f* juror

**jurer** [ʒyʀe] *vt* (obéissance etc) to swear, vow ♦ *vi* (dire des jurons) to swear, curse; (dissoner): **~ (avec)** to clash (with); **~ de faire/que** to swear to do/ that; **~ de qch** (s'en porter garant) to swear to sth

**juridique** [ʒyʀidik] *adj* legal

**juron** [ʒyʀɔ̃] *nm* curse, swearword

**jury** [ʒyʀi] *nm* (JUR; ART, SPORT) panel of judges; (SCOL) board of examiners

**jus** [ʒy] *nm* juice; (de viande) gravy; (meat) juice; **~ de fruit** fruit juice

**jusque** [ʒysk]: **jusqu'à** *prép* (lieu) as far as, (up) to; (moment) until, till; (limite) up to; **~ sur/dans** up to; (y compris) even on/in; **jusqu'à ce que** until; **jusqu'à présent** so far; **jusqu'où?** how far?

**justaucorps** [ʒystokɔʀ] *nm* leotard

**juste** [ʒyst] *adj* (équitable) just, fair; (légitime) just; (exact) right; (pertinent) apt; (étroit) tight; (insuffisant) on the short side ♦ *adv* rightly, correctly; (chanter) in tune; (exactement, seulement) just; **~ assez/au-dessus** just enough/above; **au ~** exactly; **le ~ mi-lieu** the happy medium; **c'était ~** it was a close thing; (*précisément*) just, precisely; **justes-se** nf (*précision*) accuracy; (*d'une remarque*) aptness; (*d'une opinion*) soundness; **de justesse** only just

**justice** [ʒystis] nf (*équité*) fairness, justice; (ADMIN) justice; **rendre ~ à qn** to do sb justice; **justicier, -ière** nm/f righter of wrongs

**justificatif, -ive** [ʒystifikatif, iv] adj (*document*) supporting; **pièce justificative** written proof

**justifier** [ʒystifje] vt to justify; **~ de** to prove

**juteux, -euse** [ʒytø, øz] adj juicy

**juvénile** [ʒyvenil] adj youthful

# K, k

**K** [ka] nm (INFORM) K

**kaki** [kaki] adj inv khaki

**kangourou** [kɑ̃guru] nm kangaroo

**karaté** [karate] nm karate

**karting** [kartiŋ] nm go-carting, karting

**kascher** [kaʃɛr] adj kosher

**kayak** [kajak] nm canoe, kayak; **faire du ~** to go canoeing

**kermesse** [kɛrmɛs] nf fair; (*fête de charité*) bazaar, (charity) fête

**kidnapper** [kidnape] vt to kidnap

**kilo** [kilo] nm = **kilogramme**

**kilo...: kilobit** nm kilobit; **kilogramme** nm kilogramme; **kilométrage** nm number of kilometres travelled, ≈ mileage; **kilomètre** nm kilometre; **kilométrique** adj (*distance*) in kilometres

**kinésithérapeute** [kineziterapøt] nm/f physiotherapist

**kiosque** [kjɔsk] nm kiosk, stall; **~ à musique** bandstand

**kir** [kir] nm kir (*white wine with blackcurrant liqueur*)

**kit** [kit] nm: **en ~** in kit form

**klaxon** [klaksɔn] nm horn; **klaxonner** vi, vt to hoot (BRIT), honk (US)

**km** abr = **kilomètre**

**km/h** abr (= *kilomètres/heure*) ≈ mph

**K.-O.** (*fam*) adj inv shattered, knackered

**Kosovo** [kɔsovo] nm Kosovo

**k-way** ® [kawe] nm (*lightweight nylon*) cagoule

**kyste** [kist] nm cyst

# L, l

**l'** [l] art déf voir **le**

**la** [la] art déf voir **le ♦** nm (MUS) A; (*en chantant la gamme*) la

**là** [la] adv there; (*ici*) here; (*dans le temps*) then; **elle n'est pas ~** she isn't here; **c'est ~ que** this is where; (*où*) where; **de ~** (*fig*) hence; **par ~** (*fig*) by that; *voir aussi* **-ci; ce; celui; là-bas** adv there

**label** [label] nm stamp, seal

**labeur** [labœr] nm toil no pl, toiling n pl.

**labo** [labo] (*fam*) nm (= *laboratoire*) lab

**laboratoire** [labɔratwar] nm laboratory; **~ de langues** language laboratory

**laborieux, -euse** [labɔrjø, jøz] adj (*tâche*) laborious

**labour** [labur] nm ploughing no pl; ~s nmpl (*champs*) ploughed fields; **cheval de ~** plough- ou cart-horse; **labourer** vt to plough

**labyrinthe** [labirɛ̃t] nm labyrinth, maze

**lac** [lak] nm lake

**lacer** [lase] vt to lace ou do up

**lacérer** [lasere] vt to tear to shreds

**lacet** [lasɛ] nm (*de chaussure*) lace; (*de route*) sharp bend; (*piège*) snare

**lâche** [lɑʃ] adj (*poltron*) cowardly; (*desserré*) loose, slack ♦ nm/f coward

**lâcher** [lɑʃe] vt to let go of; (*ce qui tombe, abandonner*) to drop; (*oiseau, animal: libérer*) to release, set free; (*fig: mot, remarque*) to let slip, come out with ♦ vi (freins) to fail; **~ les amarres** (NAVIG) to cast off (the moorings); **~ prise** to let go

**lâcheté** [loʃte] nf cowardice

**lacrymogène** [lakrimɔʒɛn] adj: **gaz ~** teargas

**lacté, e** [lakte] adj (produit, régime) milk cpd

**lacune** [lakyn] nf gap

**là-dedans** [ladədã] adv inside (there), in it; (fig) in that

**là-dessous** [ladsu] adv underneath, under there; (fig) behind that

**là-dessus** [ladsy] adv on there; (fig: sur ces mots) at that point; (: à ce sujet) about that

**ladite** [ladit] dét voir **ledit**

**lagune** [lagyn] nf lagoon

**là-haut** [lao] adv up there

**laïc** [laik] adj, nm/f= **laïque**

**laid, e** [lɛ, lɛd] adj ugly; **laideur** nf ugliness no pl

**lainage** [lɛnaʒ] nm (vêtement) woollen garment; (étoffe) woollen material

**laine** [lɛn] nf wool

**laïque** [laik] adj lay, civil; (SCOL) state cpd ♦ nm/f layman(-woman)

**laisse** [lɛs] nf (de chien) lead, leash; **tenir en ~** to keep on a lead ou leash

**laisser** [lese] vt to leave ♦ vb aux: **~ qn faire** to let sb do; **se ~ aller** to let o.s. go; **laisse-toi faire** let me (ou him etc) do it; **laisser-aller** nm carelessness, slovenliness; **laissez-passer** nm inv pass

**lait** [lɛ] nm milk; **frère/sœur de ~** foster brother/sister; **~ condensé/concentré** evaporated/condensed milk; **~ démaquillant** cleansing milk; **laiterie** nf dairy product; **laiterie** nf dairy; **laitier, -ière** adj dairy cpd ♦ nm/f milkman (dairywoman)

**laiton** [lɛtɔ̃] nm brass

**laitue** [lety] nf lettuce

**laïus** [lajys] (péj) nm spiel

**lambeau, x** [lãbo] nm scrap; **en ~x** in tatters, tattered

**lambris** [lãbri] nm panelling no pl

**lame** [lam] nf blade; (vague) wave; (~lle) strip; **~ de fond** ground swell no pl; **~ de rasoir** razor blade; **lamelle** nf thin strip ou blade

**lamentable** [lamãtabl] adj appalling

**lamenter** [lamãte] vb: **se ~ (sur)** to moan (over)

**lampadaire** [lãpadɛr] nm (de salon) standard lamp; (dans la rue) street lamp

**lampe** [lãp] nf lamp; (TECH) valve; **~ à souder** blowlamp; **~ de chevet** bedside lamp; **~ de poche** torch (BRIT), flashlight (US)

**lampion** [lãpjɔ̃] nm Chinese lantern

**lance** [lãs] nf spear; **~ d'incendie** fire hose

**lancée** [lãse] nf: **être/continuer sur sa ~** to be under way/keep going

**lancement** [lãsmã] nm launching

**lance-pierres** [lãspjɛr] nm inv catapult

**lancer** [lãse] nm (SPORT) throwing no pl, throw ♦ vt to throw; (émettre, projeter) to throw out, send out; (produit, fusée, bateau, artiste) to launch; (injure) to hurl, fling; **~** vi (prendre de l'élan) to build up speed; (se précipiter): **se ~ sur** ou **contre** to rush at; **se ~ dans** (discussion) to launch into; (aventure) to embark on; **~ qch à qn** to throw sth to sb; (de façon agressive) to throw sth at sb; **se ~ du poids** putting the shot

**lancinant, e** [lãsinã, ãt] adj (douleur) shooting

**landau** [lãdo] nm pram (BRIT), baby carriage (US)

**lande** [lãd] nf moor

**langage** [lãgaʒ] nm language

**langouste** [lãgust] nf crayfish inv; **langoustine** nf Dublin Bay prawn

**langue** [lãg] nf (ANAT, CULIN) tongue; (LING) language; **tirer la ~ (à)** to stick out one's tongue (at); **de ~ française** French-speaking; **~ maternelle** native language, mother tongue; **~ vivante/étrangère** modern/foreign language

**langueur** [lɑ̃gœʀ] *nf* languidness

**languir** [lɑ̃giʀ] *vi* to languish; *(conversation)* to flag; **faire ~ qn** to keep sb waiting

**lanière** [lanjɛʀ] *nf (de fouet)* lash; *(de sac, bretelle)* strap

**lanterne** [lɑ̃tɛʀn] *nf (portable)* lantern; *(électrique)* light, lamp; *(de voiture)* (side)light

**laper** [lape] *vt* to lap up

**lapidaire** [lapidɛʀ] *adj (fig)* terse

**lapin** [lapɛ̃] *nm* rabbit; *(peau)* rabbitskin; *(fourrure)* cony; **poser un ~ à qn** *(fam)* to stand sb up

**Laponie** [laponi] *nf* Lapland

**laps** [laps] *nm*: **~ de temps** space of time, time *no pl*

**laque** [lak] *nf (vernis)* lacquer; *(pour cheveux)* hair spray

**laquelle** [lakɛl] *pron voir* lequel

**larcin** [laʀsɛ̃] *nm* theft

**lard** [laʀ] *nm (bacon)* (streaky) bacon; *(graisse)* fat

**lardon** [laʀdɔ̃] *nm*: **~s** chopped bacon

**large** [laʀʒ] *adj* wide, broad; *(fig)* generous ♦ *adv*: **calculer/voir ~** to allow extra/think big ♦ *nm (largeur)*: **5 m de ~** 5 m wide *ou* in width; *(mer)*: **le ~** the open sea; **au ~ de** off; **~ d'esprit** broad-minded; **largement** *adv* widely; *(de loin)* greatly; *(au moins)* easily; *(généreusement)* generously; **c'est largement suffisant** that's ample; **largesse** *nf* generosity; **largesses** *nfpl (dons)* liberalities; **largeur** *nf (qu'on mesure)* width; *(impression visuelle)* wideness, width; *(d'esprit)* broadness

**larguer** [laʀge] *vt* to drop; **~ les amarres** to cast off (the moorings)

**larme** [laʀm] *nf* tear; *(fam: goutte)* drop; **en ~s** in tears; **larmoyer** [laʀmwaje] *vi (yeux)* to water; *(se plaindre)* to whimper

**larvé, e** [laʀve] *adj (fig)* latent

**laryngite** [laʀɛ̃ʒit] *nf* laryngitis

**las, lasse** [lɑ, lɑs] *adj* weary

**laser** [lazɛʀ] *nm*: **(rayon) ~** laser

*(beam)*; **chaîne ~** compact disc (player); **disque ~** compact disc

**lasse** [lɑs] *adj voir* **las**

**lasser** [lɑse] *vt* to weary, tire; **se ~ de** *vt* to grow weary *ou* tired of

**latéral, e, -aux** [lateʀal, o] *adj* side *cpd*, lateral

**latin, e** [latɛ̃, in] *adj* Latin ♦ *nm/f*: **L~, e** Latin ♦ *nm* (LING) Latin

**latitude** [latityd] *nf* latitude

**latte** [lat] *nf* lath, slat; *(de plancher)* board

**lauréat, e** [lɔʀea, at] *nm/f* winner

**laurier** [lɔʀje] *nm (BOT)* laurel; *(CULIN)* bay leaves *pl*

**lavable** [lavabl] *adj* washable

**lavabo** [lavabo] *nm* washbasin; **~s** *nmpl (toilettes)* toilet *sg*

**lavage** [lavaʒ] *nm* washing *no pl*, wash; **~ de cerveau** brainwashing *no pl*

**lavande** [lavɑ̃d] *nf* lavender

**lave** [lav] *nf* lava *no pl*

**lave-linge** [lavlɛ̃ʒ] *nm inv* washing machine

**laver** [lave] *vt* to wash; *(tache)* to wash off; **se ~** *vi* to have a wash, wash; **se ~ les mains/dents** to wash one's hands/clean one's teeth; **~ qn de** *(accusation)* to clear sb of; **laverie** *nf*: **laverie (automatique)** launderette; **lavette** *nf* dish cloth; *(fam)* drip; **laveur, -euse** *nm/f* cleaner; **lave-vaisselle** *nm inv* dishwasher; **lavoir** *nm* wash house; *(évier)* sink

**laxatif, -ive** [laksatif, iv] *adj, nm* laxative

**layette** [lɛjɛt] *nf* baby clothes

---MOT-CLÉ---

**le, la, l'** *(pl* **les)** *art déf* **1** the; **le livre/la pomme/l'arbre** the book/the apple/the tree; **les étudiants** the students

**2** *(noms abstraits)*: **le courage/l'amour/la jeunesse** courage/love/youth

**3** *(indiquant la possession)*: **se casser la**

**jambe** *etc* to break one's leg *etc*; **levez la main** put your hand up; **avoir les yeux gris/le nez rouge** to have grey eyes/a red nose

**4** (*temps*): **le matin/soir** in the morning/evening; **mornings/evenings**; **le jeudi** *etc* (*d'habitude*) on Thursdays *etc*; (*ce jeudi-là etc*) on (the) Thursday

**5** (*distribution, évaluation*), a, an; **10 F le mètre/kilo** 10F a *ou* per metre/kilo; **le tiers/quart de** a third/quarter of

♦ *pron* **1** (*personne: mâle*) him; (*personne: femelle*) her; (: *pluriel*) them; **je le/la/les vois** I can see him/her/them

**2** (*animal, chose: singulier*) it; (: *pluriel*) them; **je le** (*ou* **la**) **vois** I can see it; **je les vois** I can see them

**3** (*remplaçant une phrase*): **je ne le savais pas** I didn't know (about it); **il était riche et ne l'est plus** he was once rich but no longer is

---

**lécher** [leʃe] *vt* to lick; (*laper: lait, eau*) to lick *ou* lap up; **lèche-vitrines**: **faire du lèche-vitrines** to go window-shopping

**leçon** [l(ə)sɔ̃] *nf* lesson; **faire la ~ à** (*fig*) to give a lecture to; **~s de conduite** driving lessons

**lecteur, -trice** [lɛktœʀ, tʀis] *nm/f* reader; (*d'université*) foreign language assistant ♦ *nm* (*TECH*): **~ de cassettes/CD** cassette/CD player; **~ de disquette** disk drive

**lecture** [lɛktyʀ] *nf* reading

**ledit** [lədi], **ladite** (*mpl* **lesdits**, *fpl* **lesdites**) *dét* the aforesaid

**légal, e, -aux** [legal, o] *adj* legal; **légaliser** *vt* to legalize; **légalité** *nf* law

**légendaire** [leʒɑ̃dɛʀ] *adj* legendary

**légende** [leʒɑ̃d] *nf* (*mythe*) legend; (*de carte, plan*) key; (*de dessin*) caption

**léger, -ère** [leʒe, ɛʀ] *adj* light; (*bruit, retard*) slight; (*personne: superficiel*) thoughtless; (: *volage*) free and easy; **à la légère** (*parler, agir*) rashly, thoughtlessly; **légèrement** *adv* (*s'habiller, bou-*

---

*ger*) lightly; (*un peu*) slightly; **manger légèrement** to eat a light meal; **légèreté** *nf* lightness; (*d'une remarque*) flippancy

---

**Légion d'honneur**

*Created by Napoleon in 1802 to reward service to the state, the* **Légion d'honneur** *is a prestigious French order headed by the President of the Republic, the Grand Maître. Members receive an annual tax-free payment.*

---

**législatif, -ive** [leʒislatif, iv] *adj* legislative; **législatives** *nfpl* general election *sg*

**légitime** [leʒitim] *adj* (*JUR*) lawful, legitimate; (*fig*) rightful, legitimate; **en état de ~ défense** in self-defence

**legs** [leg] *nm* legacy

**léguer** [lege] *vt*: **~ qch à qn** (*JUR*) to bequeath sth to sb

**légume** [legym] *nm* vegetable

**lendemain** [lɑ̃dmɛ̃] *nm*: **le ~** the next *ou* following day; **le ~ matin/soir** the next *ou* following morning/evening; **le ~ de** the day after

**lent, e** [lɑ̃, lɑ̃t] *adj* slow; **lentement** *adv* slowly; **lenteur** *nf* slowness *no pl*

**lentille** [lɑ̃tij] *nf* (*OPTIQUE*) lens *sg*; (*CULIN*) lentil

**léopard** [leɔpaʀ] *nm* leopard

**lèpre** [lɛpʀ] *nf* leprosy

---

**MOT-CLÉ**

**lequel, laquelle** [ləkɛl, lakɛl] (*mpl* **lesquels**, *fpl* **lesquelles**) (*à + lequel* = **auquel**, *de + lequel* = **duquel** *etc*) *pron* **1** (*interrogatif*) which, which one

**2** (*relatif: personne: sujet*) who; (: *objet, après préposition*) whom; (: *chose*) which

♦ *adj*: **auquel cas** in which case

---

**les** [le] *dét voir* **le**

**lesbienne** [lɛsbjɛn] *nf* lesbian

**lesdites** [ledit], **lesdits** [ledi] *dét voir* **le**

*voir* **ledit**

**léser** [leze] *vt* to wrong

**lésiner** [lezine] *vi*: **ne pas ~ sur les moyens** (*pour mariage etc*) to push the boat out

**lésion** [lezjɔ̃] *nf* lesion, damage *no pl*

**lesquelles, lesquels** [lekɛl] *pron pl voir* **lequel**

**lessive** [lesiv] *nf* (*poudre*) washing powder; (*linge*) washing *no pl*, wash; **lessiver** *vt* to wash; (*fam: fatiguer*) to tire out, exhaust

**lest** [lɛst] *nm* ballast

**leste** [lɛst] *adj* sprightly, nimble

**lettre** [lɛtr] *nf* letter; **~s** *nfpl* (*littérature*) literature *sg*; (*SCOL*) arts (subjects); **à la ~** literally; **en toutes ~s** in full

**leucémie** [løsemi] *nf* leukaemia

---
MOT-CLÉ
---

**leur** [lœr] *adj possessif* their; **leur maison** their house; **leurs amis** their friends

♦ *pron* **1** (*objet indirect*) (to) them; **je leur ai dit la vérité** I told them the truth; **je le leur ai donné** I gave it to them, I gave them it

**2** (*possessif*): **le(la) leur, les leurs** theirs

---

**leurre** [lœr] *nm* (*fig: illusion*) delusion; (*: duperie*) deception; **leurrer** *vt* to delude, deceive

**leurs** [lœr] *adj voir* **leur**

**levain** [ləvɛ̃] *nm* leaven

**levé, e** [ləve] *adj*: **être ~** to be up; **levée** *nf* (*POSTES*) collection

**lever** [l(ə)ve] *vt* (*vitre, bras etc*) to raise; (*soulever de terre, supprimer: interdiction, siège*) to lift; (*impôts, armée*) to levy ♦ *vi* to rise ♦ *nm*: **au ~** on getting up; **se ~** *vi* to get up; (*soleil*) to rise; (*jour*) to break; (*brouillard*) to lift; **~ de soleil** sunrise; **~ du jour** daybreak

**levier** [ləvje] *nm* lever

**lèvre** [lɛvr] *nf* lip

**lévrier** [levrije] *nm* greyhound

**levure** [l(ə)vyr] *nf* yeast; **~ chimique** baking powder

**lexique** [lɛksik] *nm* vocabulary; (*glossaire*) lexicon

**lézard** [lezar] *nm* lizard

**lézarde** [lezard] *nf* crack

**liaison** [ljezɔ̃] *nf* (*rapport*) connection; (*transport*) link; (*amoureuse*) affair; (*PHONÉTIQUE*) liaison; **entrer/être en ~ avec** to get/be in contact with

**liane** [ljan] *nf* creeper

**liant, e** [ljɑ̃, ljɑ̃t] *adj* sociable

**liasse** [ljas] *nf* wad, bundle

**Liban** [libɑ̃] *nm*: **le ~** (the) Lebanon; **libanais, e** *adj* Lebanese ♦ *nm/f*: **Libanais, e** Lebanese

**libeller** [libele] *vt* (*chèque, mandat*): **~ (au nom de)** to make out (to); (*lettre*) to word

**libellule** [libelyl] *nf* dragonfly

**libéral, e, -aux** [liberal, o] *adj*, *nm/f* liberal; **profession ~e** (liberal) profession

**libérer** [libere] *vt* (*délivrer*) to free, liberate; (*relâcher: prisonnier*) to discharge, release; (: *d'inhibitions*) to liberate; (*gaz*) to release; **se ~** *vi* (*de rendez-vous*) to get out of previous engagements

**liberté** [liberte] *nf* freedom; (*loisir*) free time; **~s** *nfpl* (*privautés*) liberties; **mettre/être en ~** to set/be free; **en ~ provisoire/surveillée/conditionnelle** on bail/probation/parole

**libraire** [librɛr] *nm/f* bookseller

**librairie** [libreri] *nf* bookshop

**libre** [libr] *adj* free; (*route, voie*) clear; (*place, salle*) free; (*ligne*) not engaged; (*SCOL*) non-state; **~ de qch/de faire** free from sth/to do; **~ arbitre** free will; **libre-échange** *nm* free trade; **libre-service** *nm* self-service store

**Libye** [libi] *nf*: **la ~** Libya

**licence** [lisɑ̃s] *nf* (*permis*) permit; (*diplôme*) degree; (*liberté*) liberty; **licencié, e** *nm/f* (*SCOL*): **licencié ès lettres/ en droit** = Bachelor of Arts/Law

**licenciement** [lisɑ̃simɑ̃] nm redundancy

**licencier** [lisɑ̃sje] vt (débaucher) to make redundant; (renvoyer) to dismiss

**licite** [lisit] adj lawful

**lie** [li] nf dregs pl, sediment

**lié, e** [lje] adj: **très ~ avec** very friendly with ou close to

**liège** [ljɛʒ] nm cork

**lien** [ljɛ̃] nm (corde, fig: affectif) bond; (rapport) link, connection; **~ de parenté** family tie

**lier** [lje] vt (attacher) to tie up; (joindre) to link up; (fig: unir, engager) to bind; **se ~ avec** to make friends with; **~ qch à** to tie ou link sth to; **~ conversation avec** to strike up a conversation with

**lierre** [ljɛʀ] nm ivy

**liesse** [ljɛs] nf: **être en ~** to be celebrating ou jubilant

**lieu, x** [ljø] nm place; **~x** nmpl (locaux) premises; (endroit: d'un accident etc) scene sg; **en ~ sûr** in a safe place; **(signe) en premier ~** in the first place; **en dernier ~** lastly; **avoir ~** to take place; **tenir ~ de** to serve as; **donner ~ à** to give rise to; **au ~ de** instead of; **lieu-dit** (pl lieux-dits) nm locality

**lieutenant** [ljøt(ə)nɑ̃] nm lieutenant

**lièvre** [ljɛvʀ] nm hare

**ligament** [ligamɑ̃] nm ligament

**ligne** [liɲ] nf (gén) line; (TRANSPORTS: liaison) service; (: trajet) route; (silhouette) figure; **entrer en ~ de compte** to come into it; **en ~** (INFORM) online; **~ fixe** (TEL) fixed line (phone)

**lignée** [liɲe] nf line, lineage

**ligoter** [ligɔte] vt to tie up

**ligue** [lig] nf league; **liguer: se liguer contre** (fig) to combine against

**lilas** [lila] nm lilac

**limace** [limas] nf slug

**limande** [limɑ̃d] nf dab

**lime** [lim] nf file; **~ à ongles** nail file; **limer** vt to file

**limier** [limje] nm bloodhound; (détec-

tive) sleuth

**limitation** [limitasjɔ̃] nf: **~ de vitesse** speed limit

**limite** [limit] nf (de terrain) boundary; (partie ou point extrême) limit; **vitesse/charge ~** maximum speed/load; **cas ~** borderline case; **date ~** deadline; **limiter** vt (restreindre) to limit, restrict; (délimiter) to border; **limitrophe** adj border cpd

**limoger** [limɔʒe] vt to dismiss

**limon** [limɔ̃] nm silt

**limonade** [limɔnad] nf lemonade

**lin** [lɛ̃] nm (tissu) linen

**linceul** [lɛ̃sœl] nm shroud

**linge** [lɛ̃ʒ] nm (serviettes etc) linen; (lessive) washing; (aussi: **~ de corps**) underwear; **lingerie** nf lingerie, underwear

**lingot** [lɛ̃go] nm ingot

**linguistique** [lɛ̃gɥistik] adj linguistic ♦ nf linguistics sg

**lion, ne** [ljɔ̃, ljɔn] nm/f lion (lioness); **le L~** Leo; **lionceau, x** nm lion cub

**liqueur** [likœʀ] nf liqueur

**liquidation** [likidasjɔ̃] nf (vente) sale

**liquide** [likid] adj liquid ♦ nm liquid; (COMM): **en ~** in ready money ou cash; **liquider** vt to liquidate; (COMM: articles) to clear, sell off; **liquidités** nfpl (COMM) liquid assets

**lire** [liʀ] nf (monnaie) lira ♦ vt, vi to read

**lis** [lis] nm = **lys**

**lisible** [lizibl] adj legible

**lisière** [lizjɛʀ] nf (de forêt) edge

**lisons** [lizɔ̃] vb voir **lire**

**lisse** [lis] adj smooth

**liste** [list] nf list; **faire la ~ de** to list; **~ électorale** electoral roll; **listing** (INFORM) nm printout

**lit** [li] nm bed; **petit ~, lit à une place** single bed; **grand ~, lit à deux places** double bed; **faire son ~** to make one's bed; **aller/se mettre au ~** to go to/get into bed; **~ de camp** campbed; **~ d'enfant** cot (BRIT), crib (US)

**literie** [litʀi] *nf* bedding, bedclothes *pl*

**litière** [litjɛʀ] *nf* litter

**litige** [litiʒ] *nm* dispute

**litre** [litʀ] *nm* litre

**littéraire** [liteʀɛʀ] *adj* literary ♦ *nm/f* arts student; **elle est très ~** (*she's very literary*)

**littéral, e, -aux** [liteʀal, o] *adj* literal

**littérature** [liteʀatyʀ] *nf* literature

**littoral, -aux** [litɔʀal, o] *nm* coast

**liturgie** [lityʀʒi] *nf* liturgy

**livide** [livid] *adj* livid, pallid

**livraison** [livʀɛzɔ̃] *nf* delivery

**livre** [livʀ] *nm* book ♦ *nf* (*poids, mon-naie*) pound; **~ de bord** logbook; **~ de poche** paperback

**livré, e** [livʀe] *adj*: **~ à soi-même** left to o.s. *ou* one's own devices; **livrée** *nf* livery

**livrer** [livʀe] *vt* (*COMM*) to deliver; (*otage, coupable*) to hand over; (*secret, information*) to give away; **se ~ à** (*se confier*) to confide in; (*se rendre, s'abandonner*) to give o.s. up to; (*faire: pratiques, actes*) to indulge in; (*enquête*) to carry out

**livret** [livʀɛ] *nm* booklet; (*d'opéra*) li-bretto; **~ de caisse d'épargne** (sav-ings) bank-book; **~ de famille** (official) family record book; **~ scolaire** (school) report book

**livreur, -euse** [livʀœʀ, øz] *nm/f* deliv-ery boy *ou* man/girl *ou* woman

**local, e, -aux** [lɔkal] *adj* local ♦ *nm* (*salle*) premises *pl*; *voir aussi* **locaux**; **lo-caliser** *vt* (*repérer*) to locate, place; (*li-miter*) to confine; **localité** *nf* locality

**locataire** [lɔkatɛʀ] *nm/f* tenant; (*de chambre*) lodger

**location** [lɔkasjɔ̃] *nf* (*par le locataire, le loueur*) renting; (*par le propriétaire*) renting out, letting; (*THÉÂTRE*) booking office; **"~ de voitures"** "car rental"; **habiter en ~** to live in rented accom-modation; **prendre une ~** (*pour les vacances*) to rent a house *etc* (for the holidays)

**locaux** [lɔko] *nmpl* premises

**locomotive** [lɔkɔmɔtiv] *nf* locomotive, engine

**locution** [lɔkysjɔ̃] *nf* phrase

**loge** [lɔʒ] *nf* (*THÉÂTRE: d'artiste*) dressing room; (: *de spectateurs*) box; (*de con-cierge, franc-maçon*) lodge

**logement** [lɔʒmɑ̃] *nm* accommodation *no pl* (*BRIT*), accommodations *pl* (*US*); (*appartement*) flat (*BRIT*), apartment (*US*); (*hébergement*) housing *no pl*

**loger** [lɔʒe] *vt* to accommodate ♦ *vi* to live; **se ~ dans** (*suj: balle, flèche*) to lodge itself in; **trouver à se ~** to find accommodation; **logeur, -euse** *nm/f* landlord(-lady)

**logiciel** [lɔʒisjɛl] *nm* software

**logique** [lɔʒik] *adj* logical ♦ *nf* logic

**logis** [lɔʒi] *nm* abode, dwelling

**logo** [lɔɡo] *nm* logo

**loi** [lwa] *nf* law; **faire la ~** to lay down the law

**loin** [lwɛ̃] *adv* far; (*dans le temps: futur*) a long way off; (: *passé*) a long time ago; **plus ~** further; **~ de** far from; **au ~** far off; **de ~** from a distance; (*fig*: *de beaucoup*) by far

**lointain, e** [lwɛ̃tɛ̃, ɛn] *adj* faraway, dis-tant; (*dans le futur, passé*) distant; (*cause, parent*) remote, distant ♦ *nm*: **dans le ~** in the distance

**loir** [lwaʀ] *nm* dormouse

**loisir** [lwaziʀ] *nm*: **heures de ~** spare time; **~s** *nmpl* (*temps libre*) leisure *sg*; (*activités*) leisure activities; **avoir le ~ de faire** to have the time *ou* opportu-nity to do; **à ~** at leisure

**londonien, ne** [lɔ̃dɔnjɛ̃, jɛn] *adj* Lon-don *cpd*, of London ♦ *nm/f*: **L~, ne** Lon-doner

**Londres** [lɔ̃dʀ] *n* London

**long, longue** [lɔ̃, lɔ̃ɡ] *adj* long ♦ *adv*: **en savoir ~** to know a great deal ♦ *nm*: **de 3 m de ~** 3 m long, 3 m in length; **ne pas faire ~ feu** not to last long; **(tout) le ~ de** (all) along; **tout au ~ de** (*année, vie*) throughout; **de**

**en large** (marcher) to and fro, up and down; voir aussi **longue**

**onger** [lɔ̃ʒe] vt to go (ou walk ou drive) along(side); (suj: mur, route) to border

**ongiligne** [lɔ̃ʒiliɲ] adj long-limbed

**ongitude** [lɔ̃ʒityd] nf longitude

**ongtemps** [lɔ̃tɑ̃] adv (for) a long time, (for) long; **avant ~** before long; **pour ou pendant ~** for a long time; **mettre ~ à faire** to take a long time to do

**ongue** [lɔ̃g] adj voir **long** ♦ nf: **à la ~** in the end; **longuement** adv (long-temps) for a long time; (en détail) at length

**ongueur** [lɔ̃gœʀ] nf length; **~s** nfpl (fig: d'un film etc) tedious parts; **en ~** lengthwise; **tirer en ~** to drag on; **à ~ de journée** all day long; **~ d'onde** wavelength

**ongue-vue** [lɔ̃gvy] nf telescope

**ook** [luk] (fam) nm look, image

**opin** [lɔpɛ̃] nm: **~ de terre** patch of land

**oque** [lɔk] nf (personne) wreck; **~s** nfpl (habits) rags

**oquet** [lɔkɛ] nm latch

**orgner** [lɔʀɲe] vt to eye; (fig) to have one's eye on

**ors** [lɔʀ]: **~ de** prép at the time of; during

**orsque** [lɔʀsk] conj when, as

**osange** [lɔzɑ̃ʒ] nm diamond

**ot** [lo] nm (part) share; (de ~erie) prize; (fig: destin) fate, lot; (COMM, INFORM) batch; **le gros ~** the jackpot

**oterie** [lɔtʀi] nf lottery

**oti, e** [lɔti] adj: **bien/mal ~** well-/badly off

**otion** [losjɔ̃] nf lotion

**otissement** [lɔtismɑ̃] nm housing development; (parcelle) plot, lot

**oto** [lɔto] nm lotto

Loto

Le Loto is a state-run national lottery with large cash prizes. Participants select 7 numbers out of 49. The more correct numbers, the greater the prize. The draw is televised twice weekly.

**lotte** [lɔt] nf monkfish

**louable** [lwabl] adj commendable

**louanges** [lwɑ̃ʒ] nfpl praise sg

**loubard** [lubaʀ] (fam) nm lout

**louche** [luʃ] adj shady, fishy, dubious ♦ nf ladle; **loucher** vi to squint

**louer** [lwe] vt (maison: suj: propriétaire) to let, rent (out); (: locataire) to rent; (voiture ou: entreprise) to hire out (BRIT), rent (out); (: locataire) to hire, rent; (réserver) to book; (faire l'éloge de) to praise; **"à ~"** "to let" (BRIT), "for rent" (US)

**loup** [lu] nm wolf

**loupe** [lup] nf magnifying glass

**louper** [lupe] (fam) vt (manquer) to miss; (examen) to flunk

**lourd, e** [luʀ, luʀd] adj, adv heavy; **~ de** (conséquences, menaces) charged with; **il fait ~** the weather is close, it's sultry; **lourdaud, e** (péj) adj clumsy; **lourdement** adv heavily; **lourdeur** nf weight; **lourdeurs d'estomac** indigestion

**loutre** [lutʀ] nf otter

**louveteau, x** [luv(ə)to] nm wolf-cub; (scout) cub (scout)

**louvoyer** [luvwaje] vi (fig) to hedge, evade the issue

**loyal, e, -aux** [lwajal, o] adj (fidèle) loyal, faithful; (fair-play) fair; **loyauté** nf loyalty, faithfulness; fairness

**loyer** [lwaje] nm rent

**lu, e** [ly] pp de **lire**

**lubie** [lybi] nf whim, craze

**lubrifiant** [lybʀifjɑ̃, jɑ̃t] nm lubricant

**lubrifier** [lybʀifje] vt to lubricate

**lubrique** [lybʀik] adj lecherous

**lucarne** [lykaʀn] nf skylight

**lucide** [lysid] adj lucid; (accidenté) conscious

**lucratif, -ive** [lykʀatif, iv] adj lucrative, profitable; **à but non ~** non profit-making

**lueur** [lɥœʀ] nf (pâle) (faint) light; (chatoyante) glimmer no pl; (fig) glimmer; gleam

**luge** [lyʒ] nf sledge (BRIT), sled (US)

**lugubre** [lygybʀ] adj gloomy, dismal

---
MOT-CLÉ
---

**lui** [lɥi] pron 1 (objet indirect: mâle) (to) him; (: femelle) (to) her; (: chose, animal) (to) it; **je lui ai parlé** I have spoken to him (ou to her); **il lui a offert un cadeau** he gave him (ou her) a present

2 (après préposition, comparatif: personne) him; (: chose, animal) it; **elle est contente de lui** she is pleased with him; **je la connais mieux que lui** I know her better than he does; I know her better than him

3 (sujet, forme emphatique) he; **lui, il est à Paris** HE is in Paris

4: **lui-même** himself; itself

---

**luire** [lɥiʀ] vi to shine; (en rougeoyant) to glow

**lumière** [lymjɛʀ] nf light; **mettre en ~** (fig) to highlight; **~ du jour** daylight

**luminaire** [lyminɛʀ] nm lamp, light

**lumineux, -euse** [lyminø, øz] adj luminous; (éclairé) illuminated; (ciel, couleur) bright; (rayon) of light, light cpd; (fig: regard) radiant

**lunatique** [lynatik] adj whimsical, temperamental

**lundi** [lœdi] nm Monday; **~ de Pâques** Easter Monday

**lune** [lyn] nf moon; **~ de miel** honeymoon

**lunette** [lynɛt] nf: **~s** ♦ nfpl glasses, spectacles, and; (: protectrices) goggles; **~ arrière** (AUTO) rear window; **~s de soleil** sunglasses

**lus** etc [ly] vb voir **lire**

**lustre** [lystʀ] nm (de plafond) chandelier; (fig: éclat) lustre; **lustrer** vt to shine

**lut** [ly] vb voir **lire**

**luth** [lyt] nm lute

**lutin** [lytɛ̃] nm imp, goblin

**lutte** [lyt] nf (conflit) struggle; (sport, wrestling; **lutter** vi to fight, struggle

**luxe** [lyks] nm luxury; **de ~** luxury cpd

**Luxembourg** [lyksɑ̃buʀ] nm: **le ~** Luxembourg

**luxer** [lykse] vt: **se ~ l'épaule** to dislo-cate one's shoulder

**luxueux, -euse** [lyksɥø, øz] adj luxu-rious

**luxure** [lyksyʀ] nf lust

**luxuriant, e** [lyksyʀjɑ̃, jɑ̃t] adj luxu-riant

**lycée** [lise] nm secondary school; **ly-céen, ne** nm/f secondary school pupil

**lyophilisé, e** [ljɔfilize] adj (café) freeze-dried

**lyrique** [liʀik] adj lyrical; (OPÉRA) lyric **artiste ~** opera singer

**lys** [lis] nm lily

# M, m

**M** abr = **Monsieur**

**m'** [m] pron voir **me**

**ma** [ma] adj voir **mon**

**macaron** [makaʀɔ̃] nm (gâteau) maca-roon; (insigne) (round) badge

**macaroni** [makaʀɔni] nmpl macaroni sg

**macédoine** [masedwan] nf: **~ de fruits** fruit salad; **~ de légumes** mixed vegetables

**macérer** [maseʀe] vi, vt to macerate (dans du vinaigre) to pickle

**mâcher** [mɑʃe] vt to chew; **ne pas ~ ses mots** not to mince one's words

**machin** [maʃɛ̃] nm (fam) thing(umajig)

**machinal, e, -aux** [maʃinal, o] adj mechanical, automatic; **machinale-ment** adv mechanically, automatically

**machination** [maʃinasjɔ̃] nf frame-up

**machine** [maʃin] nf machine; (locomo-tive) engine; **~ à écrire** typewriter **~ à laver/coudre** washing/sewing machine; **~ à sous** fruit machine

**macho** [matʃo] (fam) nm male chauvinist

**mâchoire** [maʃwaʀ] nf jaw

**mâchonner** [maʃɔne] vt to chew (at)

**maçon** [masɔ̃] nm builder; (poseur de briques) bricklayer; **maçonnerie** nf (murs) brickwork; (pierres) masonry, stonework

**maculer** [makyle] vt to stain

**Madame** [madam] (pl **Mesdames**) nf: **~ X** Mrs X; **occupez-vous de ~/ Monsieur/Mademoiselle** please serve this lady/gentleman/(young) lady; **bonjour ~/Monsieur/Mademoiselle** good morning; (ton déférent) good morning Madam/Sir/Madam; (le nom est connu) good morning Mrs/Mr/Miss X; **~/ Monsieur/Mademoiselle!** (pour appeler) Madam/Sir/Miss!; **~/Monsieur/ Mademoiselle** (sur lettre) Dear Madam/Sir/Miss; **chère ~/cher Monsieur/chère Mademoiselle** Dear Mrs/Mr/Miss X; **Mesdames** Ladies

**madeleine** [madlɛn] nf madeleine; small sponge cake

**Mademoiselle** [madmwazɛl] (pl **Mesdemoiselles**) nf Miss; voir aussi **Madame**

**madère** [madɛʀ] nm Madeira (wine)

**magasin** [magazɛ̃] nm (boutique) shop; (entrepôt) warehouse; **en ~** (COMM) in stock

**magazine** [magazin] nm magazine

**Maghreb** [magʀɛb] nm: **le ~** North Africa; **maghrébin, e** adj North African ♦ nm/f: **Maghrébin, e** North African

**magicien, ne** [maʒisjɛ̃, jɛn] nm/f magician

**magie** [maʒi] nf magic; **magique** adj magic; (enchanteur) magical

**magistral, e, -aux** [maʒistʀal, o] adj (œuvre, adresse) masterly; (ton) authoritative; **cours ~** lecture

**magistrat** [maʒistʀa] nm magistrate

**magnat** [magna] nm tycoon

**magnétique** [maɲetik] adj magnetic

**magnétiser** [maɲetize] vt to magnetize; (fig) to mesmerize, hypnotize

**magnétophone** [maɲetɔfɔn] nm tape recorder; **~ à cassettes** cassette recorder

**magnétoscope** [maɲetɔskɔp] nm video-tape recorder

**magnifique** [maɲifik] adj magnificent

**magot** [mago] (fam) nm (argent) pile (of money); (économies) nest egg

**magouille** [maguj] (fam) nf scheming; **magouiller** (fam) vi to scheme

**magret** [magʀɛ] nm: **~ de canard** duck steaklet

**mai** [mɛ] nm May

---

**mai**

Le premier mai is a public holiday in France marking union demonstrations in the United States in 1886 to secure the eight-hour working day. It is traditional to exchange and wear sprigs of lily of the valley. Le 8 mai is a public holiday in France commemorating the surrender of the German army to Eisenhower on May 7, 1945. There are parades of ex-servicemen in most towns. The social upheavals of May and June 1968, marked by student demonstrations, strikes and rioting, are generally referred to as "les événements de mai 68". De Gaulle's government survived, but reforms in education and a move towards decentralization ensued.

---

**maigre** [mɛgʀ] adj (very) thin, skinny; (viande) lean; (fromage) low-fat; (végétation) thin, sparse; (fig) poor, meagre, skimpy; **jours ~s** days of abstinence, fish days; **maigreur** nf thinness; **maigrir** vi to get thinner, lose weight; **maigrir de 2 kilos** to lose 2 kilos

**maille** [maj] nf stitch; **avoir ~ à partir avec qn** to have a brush with sb; **~ à l'endroit/à l'envers** plain/purl stitch

**maillet** [majɛ] *nm* mallet

**maillon** [majɔ̃] *nm* link

**maillot** [majo] *nm* (*aussi:* ~ **de corps**) vest; (*de sportif*) jersey; ~ **de bain** swimsuit; (*d'homme*) bathing trunks *pl*

**main** [mɛ̃] *nf* hand; **à la** ~ in one's hand; **se donner la** ~ to hold hands; **donner** *ou* **tendre la** ~ **à qn** to hold out one's hand to sb; **serrer la** ~ **à qn** to shake hands with sb; **sous la** ~ *ou* **sous la** *ou* **à remettre en ~s propres** to be delivered personally; **mettre la dernière** ~ **à** to put the finishing touches to; **se faire/perdre la** ~ to get one's hand in/lose one's touch; **avoir qch bien en** ~ to have (got) the hang of sth; **main-d'œuvre** *nf* manpower, labour; **main-forte** *nf:* **prêter main-forte à qn** to come to sb's assistance; **mainmise** *nf* (*fig*): **mainmise sur** complete hold on

**maint, e** [mɛ̃, mɛ̃t] *adj* many a; ~s many; **à ~es reprises** time and (time) again

**maintenant** [mɛ̃t(ə)nɑ̃] *adv* now; (*actuellement*) nowadays

**maintenir** [mɛ̃t(ə)niʀ] *vt* (*retenir, soutenir*) to support; (*contenir: foule etc*) to hold back; (*conserver, affirmer*) to maintain; **se** ~ *vi* (*prix*) to keep steady; (*amélioration*) to persist

**maintien** [mɛ̃tjɛ̃] *nm* (*sauvegarde*) maintenance; (*attitude*) bearing

**maire** [mɛʀ] *nm* mayor; **mairie** *nf* (*bâtiment*) town hall; (*administration*) town council

**mais** [mɛ] *conj* but; ~ **non!** of course not!; ~ **enfin** but after all; (*indignation*) look here!

**maïs** [mais] *nm* maize (BRIT), corn (US)

**maison** [mɛzɔ̃] *nf* house; (*chez-soi*) home; (COMM) firm ♦ *adj inv* (CULIN) home-made; (*fig*) in-house, own; **à la** ~ at home; (*direction*) home; ~ **close** *ou* **de passe** brothel; ~ **de repos** convalescent home; ~ **de retraite** old people's home; ~ **de santé** mental

home; ~ **des jeunes** ≈ youth club; ~ **mère** parent company; **maisonnée** *nf* household, family; **maisonnette** *nf,* cottage

---

**maisons des jeunes et de la culture**

Maisons des jeunes et de la culture *are centres for young people which organize a wide range of sporting and cultural activities, and are also engaged in welfare work. The centres are, in part, publicly financed.*

---

**maître, -esse** [mɛtʀ, mɛtʀɛs] *nm/f* master (mistress); (SCOL) teacher, schoolmaster(-mistress) ♦ *nm* (*peintre etc*) master; (*titre*): **M~** Maître, term *ou* address gen for a barrister ♦ *adj* (*principal, essentiel*) main; **être** ~ **de** (*soi, situation*) to be in control of; **une maîtresse femme** a managing woman; ~ **chanteur** blackmailer; ~ **d'école** schoolmaster; ~ **d'hôtel** (*domestique*) butler; (*d'hôtel*) head waiter; ~ **nageur** lifeguard; **maîtresse** *nf* (*amante*) mistress; **maîtresse (d'école)** teacher, (school)mistress; **maîtresse de maison** hostess; (*ménagère*) housewife

**maîtrise** [mɛtʀiz] *nf* (*aussi:* ~ **de soi**) self-control, self-possession; (*habileté*) skill, mastery; (*suprématie*) mastery, command; (*diplôme*) ≈ master's degree; **maîtriser** *vt* (*cheval, incendie*) to (bring under) control; (*sujet*) to master; (*émotion*) to control, master; **se maîtriser** to control o.s.

**maïzena** ® [maizena] *nf* cornflour

**majestueux, -euse** [maʒɛstɥø, øz] *adj* majestic

**majeur, e** [maʒœʀ] *adj* (*important*) major; (JUR) of age ♦ *nm* (*doigt*) middle finger; **en** ~ **e partie** for the most part, **la** ~ **e partie de** most of

**majoration** [maʒɔʀasjɔ̃] *nf* rise, increase

**majorer** [maʒɔʀe] *vt* to increase

**majoritaire** [maʒɔʀitɛʀ] *adj*

**majorité** [maʒɔʀite] *nf* (*gén*) majority; (*parti*) party in power; **en ~** mainly

**majuscule** [maʒyskyl] *adj, nf*: **(lettre) ~** capital (letter)

**mal** [mal, mo] (*pl* **maux**) *nm* (*opposé au bien*) evil; (*tort, dommage*) harm; (*douleur physique*) pain, ache; (*~odie*) illness, sickness *no pl* ♦ *adv* badly ♦ *adj* bad, wrong; **être ~ à l'aise** to be uncomfortable; **être ~ avec qn** to be on bad terms with sb; **il a ~ compris** he misunderstood; **dire/penser du ~ de** to speak/think ill of; **ne voir aucun ~ à** to see no harm in, see nothing wrong in; **faire ~ à qn** to hurt sb; **se faire ~** to hurt o.s.; **se donner du ~ pour faire qch** to go to a lot of trouble to do sth; **ça fait ~** it hurts; **j'ai ~ au dos** my back hurts; **avoir ~ à la tête/à la gorge/aux dents** to have a headache/a sore throat/toothache; **avoir le ~ du pays** to be homesick; *voir aussi* **cœur; maux; ~ de mer** seasickness; **~ en point** in a bad state

**malade** [malad] *adj* ill, sick; (*poitrine, jambe*) bad; (*plante*) diseased ♦ *nm/f* invalid, sick person; (*à l'hôpital etc*) patient; **tomber ~** to fall ill; **être ~ du cœur** to have heart trouble *ou* a bad heart; **~ mental** mentally sick *ou* ill person; **maladie** *nf* (*spécifique*) disease, illness; (*mauvaise santé*) illness, sickness; **maladif, -ive** *adj* sickly; (*curiosité, besoin*) pathological

**maladresse** [maladʀɛs] *nf* clumsiness *no pl*; (*gaffe*) blunder

**maladroit, e** [maladʀwa, wat] *adj* clumsy

**malaise** [malɛz] *nm* (MÉD) feeling of faintness; (*fig*) uneasiness, malaise; **avoir un ~** to feel faint

**malaisé, e** [maleze] *adj* difficult

**malaxer** [malakse] *vt* (*pétrir*) to knead; (*mélanger*) to mix

**malbouffe** [malbuf] (*fam*) *nf*: **la ~** junk food

**malchance** [malʃɑ̃s] *nf* misfortune, ill luck *no pl*; **par ~** unfortunately; **malchanceux, -euse** *adj* unlucky

**mâle** [mɑl] *adj* (*aussi* ÉLEC, TECH) male; (*viril: voix, traits*) manly ♦ *nm* male

**malédiction** [malediksjɔ̃] *nf* curse

**mal...: malencontreux, -euse** *adj* unfortunate, untoward; **mal-en-point** *adj inv* in a sorry state; **malentendant, e** *nm/f*: **les malentendants** the hard of hearing; **malentendu** *nm* misunderstanding; **malfaçon** *nf* fault; **malfaisant, e** *adj* evil, harmful; **malfaiteur** *nm* lawbreaker, criminal; (*voleur*) burglar, thief; **malfamé, e** *adj* disreputable

**malgache** [malgaʃ] *adj* Madagascan, Malagasy ♦ *nm/f*: **M~** Madagascan, Malagasy ♦ *nm* (LING) Malagasy

**malgré** [malgʀe] *prép* in spite of, despite; **~ tout** all the same

**malhabile** [malabil] *adj* clumsy, awkward

**malheur** [malœʀ] *nm* (*situation*) adversity, misfortune; (*événement*) misfortune; (*: très grave*) disaster, tragedy; **faire un ~** to be a smash hit; **malheureusement** *adv* unfortunately; **malheureux, -euse** *adj* (*triste*) unhappy, miserable; (*infortuné, regrettable*) unfortunate; (*malchanceux*) unlucky; (*insignifiant*) wretched ♦ *nm/f* poor soul; **les malheureux** the destitute

**malhonnête** [malɔnɛt] *adj* dishonest; **malhonnêteté** *nf* dishonesty

**malice** [malis] *nf* mischievousness; (*méchanceté*) malice; **par ~** out of malice *ou* spite; **sans ~** guileless; **malicieux, -euse** *adj* mischievous

**malin, -igne** [malɛ̃, malin] *adj* (*futé: f gén: ~e*) smart, shrewd; (MÉD) malignant

**malingre** [malɛ̃gʀ] *adj* puny

**malle** [mal] *nf* trunk; **mallette** *nf* (small) suitcase; (*porte-documents*) attaché case

**malmener** [malməne] *vt* to manhandle; (*fig*) to give a rough handling to

**malodorant, e** [malɔdɔʀɑ̃, ɑ̃t] *adj* foul- *ou* ill-smelling

**malotru** [malɔtʀy] *nm* lout, boor

**malpoli, e** [malpɔli] *adj* impolite

**malpropre** [malpʀɔpʀ] *adj* dirty

**malsain, e** [malsɛ̃, ɛn] *adj* unhealthy

**malt** [malt] *nm* malt

**Malte** [malt] *nf* Malta

**maltraiter** [maltʀete] *vt* to manhandle, ill-treat

**malveillance** [malvejɑ̃s] *nf* (*animosité*) ill will; (*intention de nuire*) malevolence

**malversation** [malvɛʀsasjɔ̃] *nf* embezzlement

**maman** [mamɑ̃] *nf* mum(my), mother

**mamelle** [mamɛl] *nf* teat

**mamelon** [mam(ə)lɔ̃] *nm* (*ANAT*) nipple

**mamie** [mami] *nf* (*fam*) granny

**mammifère** [mamifɛʀ] *nm* mammal

**mammouth** [mamut] *nm* mammoth

**manche** [mɑ̃ʃ] *nf* (*de vêtement*) sleeve; (*d'un jeu, tournoi*) round; (*GÉO*): **la M~** the Channel ♦ *nm* (*d'outil, casserole*) handle; (*de pelle, pioche etc*) shaft; **à ~s courtes/longues** short-/long-sleeved

**manchette** [mɑ̃ʃɛt] *nf* (*de chemise*) cuff; (*coup*) forearm blow; (*titre*) headline

**manchot** [mɑ̃ʃo, ɔt] *nm* one-armed man; armless man; (*ZOOL*) penguin

**mandarin** [mɑ̃daʀɛ̃] *nm* mandarin (orange), tangerine

**mandat** [mɑ̃da] *nm* (*postal*) postal *ou* money order; (*d'un député etc*) mandate; (*procuration*) power of attorney, proxy; (*POLICE*) warrant; **~ d'arrêt** warrant for arrest; **mandataire** *nm/f* (*représentant*) representative; (*JUR*) proxy

**manège** [manɛʒ] *nm* riding school; (*à la foire*) roundabout, merry-go-round; (*fig*) game, ploy

**manette** [manɛt] *nf* lever, tap; **~ de jeu** joystick

**mangeable** [mɑ̃ʒabl] *adj* edible, eatable

**mangeoire** [mɑ̃ʒwaʀ] *nf* trough, manger

**manger** [mɑ̃ʒe] *vt* to eat; (*ronger: suj: rouille etc*) to eat into *ou* away ♦ *vi* to eat; **donner à ~ à** (*enfant*) to feed; **mangeur, -euse** *nm/f* eater; **gros mangeur** big eater

**mangue** [mɑ̃g] *nf* mango

**maniable** [manjabl] *adj* (*outil*) handy; (*voiture, voilier*) easy to handle

**maniaque** [manjak] *adj* finicky, fussy ♦ *nm/f* (*méticuleux*) fusspot; (*fou*) maniac

**manie** [mani] *nf* (*tic*) odd habit; (*obsession*) mania; **avoir la ~ de** to be obsessive about

**manier** [manje] *vt* to handle

**manière** [manjɛʀ] *nf* (*façon*) way, manner; **~s** *nfpl* (*attitude*) manners; (*chichis*) fuss *sg*; **de ~ à** so as to; **de cette ~** in this way *ou* manner; **d'une certaine ~** in a way; **de toute ~** in any case

**maniéré, e** [manjeʀe] *adj* affected

**manif** [manif] (*fam*) *nf* demo

**manifestant, e** [manifɛstɑ̃, ɑ̃t] *nm/f* demonstrator

**manifestation** [manifɛstasjɔ̃] *nf* (*de joie, mécontentement*) expression, demonstration; (*symptôme*) outward sign; (*culturelle etc*) event; (*POL*) demonstration

**manifeste** [manifɛst] *adj* obvious, evident ♦ *nm* manifesto; **manifester** *vt* (*volonté, intentions*) to show, indicate; (*joie, peur*) to express, show ♦ *vi* to demonstrate; **se manifester** *vi* (*émotion*) to show *ou* express itself; (*difficultés*) to arise; (*symptômes*) to appear

**manigance** [manigɑ̃s] *nf* scheme; **manigancer** *vt* to plot

**manipulation** [manipylasjɔ̃] *nf* handling; (*POL, génétique*) manipulation

**manipuler** [manipyle] *vt* to handle; (*fig*) to manipulate

**manivelle** [manivɛl] *nf* crank

**mannequin** [mankɛ̃] *nm* (*COUTURE*) dummy; (*MODE*) model

**manœuvre** [manœvʀ] *nf* (*gén*) manœuvre (*BRIT*), maneuver (*US*) ♦ *nm* labourer; **manœuvrer** *vt* to manœuvre

(BRIT), maneuver (US); (levier, machine) to operate ♦ vi to manoeuvre

**nanoir** [manwar] nm manor ou country house

**nanque** [mãk] nm (insuffisance): ~ de lack of; (vide) emptiness, gap; (MÉD) withdrawal; être en état de ~ to suffer withdrawal symptoms

**nanqué, e** [mãke] adj failed; garçon ~ tomboy

**nanquer** [mãke] vi (faire défaut) to be lacking; (être absent) to be missing; (échouer) to fail ♦ vt to miss ♦ vb impers: il (nous) manque encore 100 F we are still 100 F short; il manque des pages (au livre) there are some pages missing (from the book); il me manque 1 miss him/this; ~ à (règles etc) to be in breach of, fail to observe; ~ de to lack; je ne ~ai pas de le lui dire I'll be sure to tell him; il a manqué (de) se tuer he very nearly got killed

**nansarde** [mãsard] nf attic; mansardé, e adj: chambre mansardée attic room

**nanteau, x** [mãto] nm coat

**nanucure** [manykyr] nf manicurist

**nanuel, le** [manɥɛl] adj manual ♦ nm (ouvrage) manual, handbook

**nanufacture** [manyfaktyr] nf factory; manufacturé, e adj manufactured

**nanuscrit, e** [manyskri, it] adj handwritten ♦ nm manuscript

**nanutention** [manytãsjɔ̃] nf (COMM) handling

**nappemonde** [mapmɔ̃d] nf (plane) map of the world; (sphère) globe

**naquereau, x** [makro] nm (ZOOL) mackerel inv; (fam) pimp

**naquette** [makɛt] nf (à échelle réduite) (scale) model; (d'une page illustrée) paste-up

**naquillage** [makijaʒ] nm making up; (crème etc) make-up

**naquiller** [makije] vt (personne, visage) to make up; (truquer: passeport, statisti-

que) to fake; (: voiture volée) to do over (respray etc); se ~ vi to make up (one's face)

**maquis** [maki] nm (GÉO) scrub; (MIL) maquis, underground fighting no pl

**maraîcher, -ère** [mareʃe, ɛr] adj: cultures maraîchères market gardening sg ♦ nm/f market gardener

**marais** [mare] nm marsh, swamp

**marasme** [marasm] nm stagnation, slump

**marathon** [maratɔ̃] nm marathon

**maraudeur, euse** [marodœr, øz] nm prowler

**marbre** [marbr] nm marble

**marc** [mar] nm (de raisin, pommes) marc; ~ de café coffee grounds pl ou dregs pl

**marchand, e** [marʃã, ãd] nm/f shopkeeper, tradesman(-woman); (au marché) stallholder; (de vins, charbon) merchant ♦ adj: prix/valeur ~e market price/value; ~(e) de fruits fruiterer (BRIT), fruit seller (US); ~(e) de journaux newsagent; ~(e) de légumes greengrocer (BRIT), produce dealer (US); ~(e) de poissons fishmonger; marchander vi to bargain, haggle; marchandise nf goods pl, merchandise no pl

**marche** [marʃ] nf (d'escalier) step; (activité) walking; (promenade, trajet, allure) walk; (démarche) walk, gait; (MIL etc) march; (fonctionnement) running; (des événements) course; dans le sens de la ~ (RAIL) facing the engine; en ~ (monter etc) while the vehicle is moving ou in motion; mettre en ~ to start; se mettre en ~ (personne) to get moving; (machine) to start; être en état de ~ to be in working order; ~ à suivre (correct) procedure; ~ arrière reverse (gear); faire ~ arrière to reverse; (fig) to backtrack, back-pedal

**marché** [marʃe] nm market; (transaction) bargain, deal; faire du ~ noir to buy and sell on the black market; ~ aux puces flea market; M~ commun

Common Market

**marchepied** [maʀʃəpje] nm (RAIL) step

**marcher** [maʀʃe] vi to walk; (MIL) to march; (aller: voiture, train, affaires) to go; (prospérer) to go well; (fonctionner) to work, run; (fam: consentir) to go along, agree; (: croire naïvement) to be taken in; **faire ~ qn** (taquiner) to pull sb's leg; (tromper) to lead sb up the garden path; **marcheur, -euse** nm/f walker

**mardi** [maʀdi] nm Tuesday; **M~ gras** Shrove Tuesday

**mare** [maʀ] nf pond; (flaque) pool

**marécage** [maʀekaʒ] nm marsh, swamp; **marécageux, -euse** adj marshy

**maréchal, -aux** [maʀeʃal, o] nm marshal; **maréchal-ferrant** [maʀeʃalferɑ̃, maʀeʃo-] (pl maréchaux-ferrants) nm blacksmith, farrier

**marée** [maʀe] nf tide; (poissons) fresh (sea) fish; **~ haute/basse** high/low tide; **~ montante/descendante** rising/ebb tide; **~ noire** oil slick

**marelle** [maʀɛl] nf hopscotch

**margarine** [maʀgaʀin] nf margarine

**marge** [maʀʒ] nf margin; **en ~ de** (fig) on the fringe of; **~ bénéficiaire** profit margin

**marginal, e, -aux** [maʀʒinal, o] nm/f (original) eccentric; (déshérité) dropout

**marguerite** [maʀgəʀit] nf marguerite, (oxeye) daisy; (d'imprimante) daisy-wheel

**mari** [maʀi] nm husband

**mariage** [maʀjaʒ] nm marriage; (noce) wedding; **~ civil/religieux** registry office (BRIT) ou civil/church wedding

**marié, e** [maʀje] adj married ♦ nm (bride)groom; **les ~s** the bride and groom; **les (jeunes) ~s** the newly-weds; **mariée** nf bride

**marier** [maʀje] vt to marry; (fig) to blend; **se ~** vr to get married; **se ~ (avec)** to marry

**marin, e** [maʀɛ̃, in] adj sea cpd, marine

♦ nm sailor

**marine** [maʀin] adj voir **marin** ♦ adj in navy (blue) ♦ nm (MIL) marine ♦ nf navy; **~ de guerre** navy; **~ marchande** merchant navy

**mariner** [maʀine] vt: **faire ~** to marinade

**marionnette** [maʀjɔnɛt] nf puppet

**maritalement** [maʀitalmɑ̃] adv: **vivre ~** to live as husband and wife

**maritime** [maʀitim] adj sea cpd, maritime

**mark** [maʀk] nm mark

**marmelade** [maʀməlad] nf stewed fruit, compote; **~ d'oranges** marmalade

**marmite** [maʀmit] nf (cooking-)pot

**marmonner** [maʀmɔne] vt, vi to mumble, mutter

**marmot** [maʀmo] (fam) nm kid

**marmotter** [maʀmɔte] vt to mumble

**Maroc** [maʀɔk] nm: **le ~** Morocco

**marocain, e** [maʀɔkɛ̃, ɛn] adj Moroccan ♦ nm/f: **Marocain, e** Moroccan

**maroquinerie** [maʀɔkinʀi] nf (articles) fine leather goods pl; (boutique) shop selling fine leather goods

**marquant, e** [maʀkɑ̃, ɑ̃t] adj outstanding

**marque** [maʀk] nf mark; (COMM: de nourriture) brand; (: de voiture, produits manufacturés) make; (de disques) label **de ~** (produits) high-class; (visiteur etc) distinguished, well-known; **une grande ~ de vin** a well-known brand of wine **~ de fabrique** trademark; **~ déposée** registered trademark

**marquer** [maʀke] vt to mark; (inscrire) to write down; (bétail) to brand; (SPORT: but etc) to score; (: joueur) to mark (accentuer: taille etc) to emphasize; (manifester: refus, intérêt) to show ♦ vi (événement) to stand out, be outstanding; (SPORT) to score

**marqueterie** [maʀkɛtʀi] nf inlaid work, marquetry

**marquis** [maʀki] nm marquis, mar

quess; **marquise** nf marchioness; (auvent) glass canopy ou awning

**narraine** [maren] nf godmother

**narrant, e** [marɑ̃, ɑ̃t] (fam) adj funny

**narre** [mar] (fam) adv: **en avoir ~ de** to be fed up with

**narrer** [mare]: **se ~** (fam) vi to have a (good) laugh

**narron** [marɔ̃] nm (fruit) chestnut ♦ adj inv brown; **~s glacés** candied chestnuts; **marronnier** nm chestnut (tree)

**nars** [mars] nm March

**Marseille** [marsɛj] n Marseilles

**narsouin** [marswɛ̃] nm porpoise

**narteau, x** [marto] nm hammer; **être ~** (fam) to be nuts; **marteau-piqueur** nm pneumatic drill

**narteler** [martəle] vt to hammer

**martien, ne** [marsjɛ̃, jɛn] adj Martian, of ou from Mars

**martyr, e** [martir] nm/f martyr; **martyre** nm martyrdom; (fig: sens affaibli) agony, torture; **martyriser** vt (REL) to martyr; (fig) to bully; (enfant) to batter, beat

**narxiste** [marksist] adj, nm/f Marxist

**mascara** [maskara] nm mascara

**masculin, e** [maskylɛ̃, in] adj masculine; (sexe, population) male; (équipe, vêtements) men's; (viril) manly ♦ nm masculine; **masculinité** nf masculinity

**masochiste** [mazɔʃist] adj masochistic

**nasque** [mask] nm mask; **masquer** vt

(cacher: paysage, porte) to hide, conceal; (dissimuler: vérité, projet) to mask, obscure

**massacre** [masakr] nm massacre, slaughter; **massacrer** vt to massacre, slaughter; (fam: texte etc) to murder

**massage** [masaʒ] nm massage

**masse** [mas] nf mass; (ÉLEC) earth; (maillet) sledgehammer; (péj): **la ~** the masses pl; **une ~ de** (fam) masses ou loads of; **en ~** ♦ adv (acheter) in bulk; (en foule) en masse ♦ adj (exécutions, production) mass cpd

**masser** [mase] vt (assembler: gens) to gather; (pétrir) to massage; **se ~** vi (foule) to gather; **masseur, -euse** nm/f masseur(-euse)

**massif, -ive** [masif, iv] adj (porte) solid, massive; (visage) heavy, large; (bois, or) solid; (dose) massive; (déportations etc) mass cpd ♦ nm (montagneux) massif; (de fleurs) clump, bank

**massue** [masy] nf club, bludgeon

**mastic** [mastik] nm (pour vitres) putty; (pour fentes) filler

**mastiquer** [mastike] vt (aliment) to chew, masticate

**mat, e** [mat] adj (couleur, métal) mat(t); (bruit, son) dull ♦ adj inv (ÉCHECS): **être ~** to be checkmate

**mât** [mɑ] nm (NAVIG) mast; (poteau) pole, post

**match** [matʃ] nm match; **faire ~ nul** to draw; **~ aller** first leg; **~ retour** second leg, return match

**matelas** [mat(ə)la] nm mattress; **~ pneumatique** air bed ou mattress; **matelassé, e** adj (vêtement) padded; (tissu) quilted

**matelot** [mat(ə)lo] nm sailor, seaman

**mater** [mate] vt (personne) to bring to heel, subdue; (révolte) to put down

**matérialiser** [materjalize]: **se ~** vi to materialize

**matérialiste** [materjalist] adj materialistic

**matériaux** [materjo] nmpl material(s)

**matériel, le** [materjɛl] *adj* material
♦ *nm* equipment *no pl*; *(de camping etc)*
gear *no pl*; *(INFORM)* hardware

**maternel, le** [matɛrnɛl] *adj (amour,*
*geste)* motherly, maternal; *(grand-père,*
*oncle)* maternal; **maternelle** *nf (aussi:*
**école maternelle)** (state) nursery
school

**maternité** [matɛrnite] *nf (établisse-*
*ment)* maternity hospital; *(état de mère)*
motherhood, maternity; *(grossesse)*
pregnancy; **congé de ~** maternity
leave

**mathématique** [matematik] *adj*
mathematical; **mathématiques** *nfpl*
*(science)* mathematics *sg*

**maths** [mat] *(fam) nfpl* maths

**matière** [matjɛr] *nf; (COMM,*
*TECH)* material, matter *no pl*; *(fig: d'un*
*livre etc)* subject matter, material; *(SCOL)*
subject; **en ~ de** as regards; **~s gras-**
**ses** fat content *sg*; **~s premières** raw
materials

---

hôtel Matignon

**L'hôtel Matignon** *is the Paris office*
*and residence of the French Prime*
*Minister. By extension, the term "Ma-*
*tignon" is often used to refer to the*
*Prime Minister or his staff.*

---

**matin** [matɛ̃] *nm, adv* morning; **du ~**
**au soir** from morning till night; **de**
**bon** *ou* **grand ~** early in the morning;
**matinal, e, -aux** *adj (toilette, gym-*
*nastique)* morning *cpd*; **être matinal**
*(personne)* to be up early; to be an early riser; **matinée** *nf* morning; *(specta-*
*cle)* matinée

**matou** [matu] *nm* tom(cat)

**matraque** [matrak] *nf (de policier)*
truncheon *(BRIT)*, billy *(US)*

**matricule** [matrikyl] *nm (MIL)* regi-
mental number; *(ADMIN)* reference
number

**matrimonial, e, -aux** [matrimɔnjal,
jo] *adj* marital, marriage *cpd*

**maudire** [modir] *vt* to curse; **maudit,**
**e** *(fam) adj (satané)* blasted, confounded

**maugréer** [mogree] *vi* to grumble

**maussade** [mosad] *adj* sullen; *(temps)*
gloomy

**mauvais, e** [mɔvɛ, ɛz] *adj* bad; *(faux)*:
**le ~ numéro/moment** the wrong
number/moment; *(méchant, malveil-*
*lant)* malicious; sharp; **il fait ~** the
weather is bad; **la mer est ~e** the sea
is rough; **~ plaisant** hoaxer; **~e herbe**
weed; **~e langue** gossip, scandal-
monger *(BRIT)*; **~e passe** bad patch

**mauve** [mov] *adj* mauve

**maux** [mo] *nmpl de* **mal**; **~ de ventre**
stomachache *sg*

**maximum** [maksimɔm] *adj, nm* maximum; **au ~** *(le plus possible)* as much
as one can; *(tout au plus)* at the (very)
most *ou* maximum; **faire le ~** to do
one's level best

**mayonnaise** [majɔnɛz] *nf* mayonnaise

**mazout** [mazut] *nm* (fuel) oil

**Me** *abr* = **Maître**

**me, m'** [m(ə)] *pron (direct: téléphoner,*
*attendre etc)* me; *(indirect: parler, don-*
*ner etc)* (to) me; *(réfléchi)* myself

**mec** [mɛk] *(fam) nm* bloke, guy

**mécanicien, ne** [mekanisjɛ̃, jɛn] *nm/f*
mechanic; *(RAIL)* (train ou engine) driver

**mécanique** [mekanik] *adj* mechanical
♦ *nf (science)* mechanics *sg*; *(méca-*
*nisme)* mechanism; **ennui ~** engine
trouble *no pl*

**mécanisme** [mekanism] *nm* mechanism

**méchamment** [meʃamɑ̃] *adv* nastily,
maliciously, spitefully

**méchanceté** [meʃɑ̃ste] *nf* nastiness,
maliciousness; **dire des ~s à qn** to say
spiteful things to sb

**méchant, e** [meʃɑ̃, ɑ̃t] *adj* nasty, malicious, spiteful; *(enfant: pas sage)*
naughty; *(animal)* vicious

**mèche** [mɛʃ] *nf (de cheveux)* lock; *(de*
*lampe, bougie)* wick; *(d'un explosif)* fuse;

**de ~ avec** in league with

**méchoui** [meʃwi] *nm* barbecue of a whole roast sheep

**méconnaissable** [mekɔnɛsabl] *adj* unrecognizable

**méconnaître** [mekɔnɛtr] *vt* (*ignorer*) to be unaware of; (*mésestimer*) to misjudge

**mécontent, e** [mekɔ̃tɑ̃, ɑ̃t] *adj*: **~ (de)** discontented *ou* dissatisfied *ou* displeased (with); (*contrarié*) annoyed (at); **mécontentement** *nm* dissatisfaction, discontent, displeasure; (*irritation*) annoyance

**médaille** [medaj] *nf* medal

**médaillon** [medajɔ̃] *nm* (*bijou*) locket

**médecin** [med(ə)sɛ̃] *nm* doctor; **~ légiste** forensic medicine

**médecine** [med(ə)sin] *nf* medicine

**média** [medja] *nmpl*: **les ~** the media; **médiatique** *adj* media *cpd*; **médiatisé, e** *adj* reported in the media; **ce procès a été très médiatisé** (*péj*) this trial was turned into a media event

**médical, e, -aux** [medikal, o] *adj* medical; **passer une visite ~e** to have a medical

**médicament** [medikamɑ̃] *nm* medicine, drug

**médiéval, e, -aux** [medjeval, o] *adj* medieval

**médiocre** [medjɔkr] *adj* mediocre, poor

**médire** [medir] *vi*: **~ de** to speak ill of; **médisance** *nf* scandalmongering (BRIT)

**méditer** [medite] *vt* to meditate on

**Méditerranée** [mediterane] *nf*: **la (mer) ~** the Mediterranean (Sea); **méditerranéen, ne** *adj* Mediterranean ♦ *nm/f*: **Méditerranéen, ne** native *ou* inhabitant of a Mediterranean country

**méduse** [medyz] *nf* jellyfish

**meeting** [mitiŋ] *nm* (POL, SPORT) rally

**méfait** [mefɛ] *nm* (*faute*) misdemeanour, wrongdoing; **~s** *nmpl* (*ravages*) ravages, damage *sg*

**méfiance** [mefjɑ̃s] *nf* mistrust, distrust

**méfiant, e** [mefjɑ̃, jɑ̃t] *adj* mistrustful, distrustful

**méfier** [mefje]: **se ~** *vi* to be wary; to be careful; **se ~ de** to mistrust, distrust, be wary of

**mégarde** [megard] *nf*: **par ~** (*accidentellement*) accidentally; (*par erreur*) by mistake

**mégère** [meʒɛr] *nf* shrew

**mégot** [mego] (*fam*) *nm* cigarette end

**meilleur, e** [mɛjœr] *adj, adv* better ♦ *nm*: **le ~** the best; **le ~ des deux** the better of the two; **~ marché** (*inv*) cheaper; **meilleure** *nf*: **la meilleure** the best (one)

**mélancolie** [melɑ̃kɔli] *nf* melancholy, gloom; **mélancolique** *adj* melancholic, melancholy

**mélange** [melɑ̃ʒ] *nm* mixture; **mélanger** *vt* to mix; (*vins, couleurs*) to blend; (*mettre en désordre*) to mix up, muddle (up)

**mélasse** [melas] *nf* treacle, molasses *sg*

**mêlée** [mele] *nf* mêlée, scramble; (RUGBY) scrum(mage)

**mêler** [mele] *vt* (*unir*) to mix; (*embrouiller*) to muddle (up), mix up; **se ~** *vi* to mix, mingle; **se ~ à** (*personne*) to join; (: *s'associer à*) to mix with; **se ~ de** (*suj*: *personne*) to meddle with, interfere in; **mêle-toi de ce qui te regarde!** mind your own business!

**mélodie** [melɔdi] *nf* melody; **mélodieux, -euse** *adj* melodious

**melon** [m(ə)lɔ̃] *nm* (BOT) (honeydew) melon; (*aussi*: **chapeau ~**) bowler (hat)

**membre** [mɑ̃br] *nm* (ANAT) limb; (*personne, pays, élément*) member ♦ *adj* member *cpd*

**mémé** [meme] (*fam*) *nf* granny

MOT-CLÉ

**même** [mɛm] *adj* 1 (*avant le nom*) same; **en même temps** at the same time

2 (*après le nom: renforcement*): **il est la loyauté même** he is loyalty itself; **ce**

sont ses paroles/celles-là mêmes they are his very words/the very ones ♦ pron: le(la) même the same one ♦ adv 1 (renforcement): il n'a même pas pleuré he didn't even cry; même lui l'a dit even HE said it; ici même at this very place 2: à même: à même la bouteille straight from the bottle; à même la peau next to the skin; être à même de faire to be in a position to do, be able to do 3: de même: faire de même to do likewise; lui de même so does (ou did ou) is he); de même que just as; il en va de même pour the same goes for

**mémo** [memo] (fam) nm memo
**mémoire** [memwar] nf memory ♦ nm (SCOL) dissertation, paper; ~s nmpl (souvenirs) memoirs; à la ~ de to the ou in memory of; de ~ from memory; ~ morte/vive (INFORM) ROM/RAM
**mémorable** [memɔrabl] adj memorable, unforgettable

**menace** [mǝnas] nf threat; **menacer** vt to threaten
**ménage** [menaʒ] nm (travail) housework; (couple) (married) couple; (famille, ADMIN) household; faire le ~ to do the housework; **ménager, -ère** adj household cpd, domestic ♦ vt (traiter: personne) to handle with tact; (utiliser) to use sparingly; (prendre soin de) to take (great) care of, look after; (organiser) to arrange; **ménager qch à qn** (réserver) to have sth in store for sb; **ménagère** nf housewife
**mendiant, e** [mɑ̃djɑ̃, jɑ̃t] nm/f beggar
**mendier** [mɑ̃dje] vi to beg ♦ vt to beg (for)
**mener** [m(ǝ)ne] vt to lead; (enquête) to conduct; (affaires) to manage ♦ vi: ~ à/dans (emmener) to take to/into; ~ qch à bien to see sth through (to a successful conclusion), complete sth

successfully
**meneur, -euse** [mǝnœr, øz] nm/f leader; (péj) agitator
**méningite** [menɛ̃ʒit] nf meningitis no pl
**ménopause** [menopoz] nf menopause
**menottes** [mǝnɔt] nfpl handcuffs

**mensonge** [mɑ̃sɔ̃ʒ] nm lie; (action) lying no pl; **mensonger, -ère** adj false
**mensualité** [mɑ̃sɥalite] nf (traite) monthly payment
**mensuel, le** [mɑ̃sɥɛl] adj monthly
**mensurations** [mɑ̃syrasjɔ̃] nfpl measurements
**mental, e, -aux** [mɑ̃tal, o] adj mental; **mentalité** nf mentality
**menteur, -euse** [mɑ̃tœr, øz] nm/f liar
**menthe** [mɑ̃t] nf mint
**mention** [mɑ̃sjɔ̃] nf (annotation) note, comment; (SCOL) grade; ~ bien etc ≃ grade B etc (ou upper 2nd class etc) pass (BRIT), ≃ pass with (high) honors (US); (ADMIN): "rayer les ~s inutiles" "delete as appropriate"; **mentionner** vt to mention
**mentir** [mɑ̃tir] vi to lie
**menton** [mɑ̃tɔ̃] nm chin
**menu, e** [mǝny] adj (personne) slim, slight; (frais, difficulté) minor ♦ adv (couper, hacher) very fine ♦ nm menu; ~ touristique/gastronomique economy/gourmet's menu
**menuiserie** [mǝnɥizri] nf (métier) joinery, carpentry; (passe-temps) woodwork; **menuisier** nm joiner, carpenter
**méprendre** [meprɑ̃dr]: se ~ vi: se ~ sur to be mistaken (about)
**mépris** [mepri] nm (dédain) contempt, scorn; au ~ de regardless of, in defiance of; **méprisable** adj contemptible, despicable; **méprisant, e** adj scornful; **méprise** nf mistake, error; **mépriser** vt to scorn, despise; (gloire, danger) to scorn, spurn
**mer** [mɛr] nf sea; (marée) tide; en ~ at sea, on the open sea; la ~ du Nord/Rouge

the North/Red Sea

**mercenaire** [mɛʀsənɛʀ] *nm* mercenary, hired soldier

**mercerie** [mɛʀsəʀi] *nf (boutique)* haberdasher's shop *(BRIT)*, notions store *(US)*

**merci** [mɛʀsi] *excl* thank you ♦ *nf*: **à la ~ de qn/qch** at sb's mercy/the mercy of sth; **~ beaucoup** thank you very much; **~ de** thank you for; **sans ~** merciless(ly)

**mercredi** [mɛʀkʀədi] *nm* Wednesday

**mercure** [mɛʀkyʀ] *nm* mercury

**merde** [mɛʀd] *(fam!) nf* shit *(!)* ♦ *excl* (bloody) hell *(!)*

**mère** [mɛʀ] *nf* mother; **~ célibataire** unmarried mother

**merguez** [mɛʀgɛz] *nf* merguez sausage *(type of spicy sausage from N Africa)*

**méridional, e, -aux** [meʀidjɔnal, o] *adj* southern ♦ *nm/f* Southerner

**meringue** [məʀɛ̃g] *nf* meringue

**mérite** [meʀit] *nm* merit; **avoir du ~ (à faire qch)** to deserve credit for (doing sth); **mériter** *vt* to deserve

**merlan** [mɛʀlɑ̃] *nm* whiting

**merle** [mɛʀl] *nm* blackbird

**merveille** [mɛʀvɛj] *nf* marvel, wonder; **faire ~** to work wonders; **à ~** perfectly, wonderfully; **merveilleux, -euse** *adj* marvellous, wonderful

**mes** [me] *adj voir* **mon**

**mésange** [mezɑ̃ʒ] *nf* tit(mouse)

**mésaventure** [mezavɑ̃tyʀ] *nf* misadventure, misfortune

**Mesdames** [medam] *nfpl de* **Madame**

**Mesdemoiselles** [medmwazɛl] *nfpl de* **Mademoiselle**

**mesquin, e** [mɛskɛ̃, in] *adj* mean, petty; **mesquinerie** *nf* meanness; *(procédé)* mean trick

**message** [mesaʒ] *nm* message; **messager, -ère** *nm/f* messenger; **messagerie** *nf (INTERNET)* **messagerie électronique** bulletin board

**messe** [mɛs] *nf* mass

**Messieurs** [mesjø] *nmpl de* **Monsieur**

**mesure** [m(ə)zyʀ] *nf (évaluation, dimension)* measurement; *(récipient)* measure; *(MUS: cadence)* time, tempo; *(: division)* bar; *(retenue)* moderation; *(disposition)* measure, step; **sur ~** *(costume)* made-to-measure; **dans la ~ où** insofar as, inasmuch as; **à ~ que** as; **être en ~ de** to be in a position to; **dans une certaine ~** to a certain extent

**mesurer** [məzyʀe] *vt* to measure; *(juger)* to weigh up, assess; *(modérer: ses paroles etc)* to moderate; **se ~ avec** to have a confrontation with; **il mesure 1 m 80** he's 1 m 80 tall

**met** [me] *vb voir* **mettre**

**métal, -aux** [metal, o] *nm* metal; **métallique** *adj* metallic

**météo** [meteo] *nf (bulletin)* weather report

**météorologie** [meteɔʀɔlɔʒi] *nf* meteorology

**méthode** [metɔd] *nf* method; *(livre, ouvrage)* manual, tutor

**méticuleux, -euse** [metikylø, øz] *adj* meticulous

**métier** [metje] *nm (profession: gén)* job; *(: manuel)* trade; *(artisanal)* craft; *(technique, expérience)* (acquired) skill ou technique; *(aussi: ~ à tisser)* (weaving) loom; **avoir du ~** to have practical experience

**métis, se** [metis] *adj, nm/f* half-caste, half-breed

**métrage** [metʀaʒ] *nm*: **long/moyen/court ~** full-length/medium-length/short film

**mètre** [mɛtʀ] *nm (unité)* metre; *(règle)* (metre) rule; *(ruban)* tape measure; **métrique** *adj* metric

**métro** [metʀo] *nm* underground *(BRIT)*, subway

**métropole** [metʀɔpɔl] *nf (capitale)* metropolis; *(pays)* home country

**mets** [me] *nm* dish

**metteur** [metœʀ] *nm*: **~ en scène** *(THÉÂTRE)* producer; *(CINÉMA)* director

MOT-CLÉ

**mettre** [mɛtʀ] vt 1 (placer) to put; **mettre en bouteille/en sac** to bottle/put in bags ou sacks; **mettre en charge (pour)** to charge (with), indict (for)

2 (vêtements: revêtir) to put on; (: porter) to wear; **mets ton gilet** put your cardigan on; **je ne mets plus mon manteau** I no longer wear my coat

3 (faire fonctionner: chauffage, électricité) to put on; (: reveil, minuteur) to set; (: installer: gaz, eau) to put in, lay on; **mettre en marche** to start up

4 (consacrer): **mettre du temps à faire qch** to take time to do sth ou over sth

5 (noter, écrire) to say, put (down); **qu'est-ce qu'il a mis sur la carte?** what did he say ou write on the card?; **mettez au pluriel** ... put ... into the plural

6 (supposer): **mettons que** ... let's suppose ou say that ...

7: **y mettre du sien** to pull one's weight

**se mettre** vi 1 (se placer): **vous pouvez vous mettre là** you can sit (ou stand) there; **où ça se met?** where does it go?; **se mettre au lit** to get into bed; **se mettre au piano** to sit down at the piano; **se mettre de l'encre sur les doigts** to get ink on one's fingers

2 (s'habiller): **se mettre en maillot de bain** to get into ou put on a swimsuit; **n'avoir rien à se mettre** to have nothing to wear

3: **se mettre à** to begin, start; **se mettre à faire** to begin ou start doing ou to do; **se mettre au piano** to start learning the piano; **se mettre au travail/à l'étude** to get down to work/one's studies

**meuble** [mœbl] nm piece of furniture; **des ~s** furniture; **meublé** nm furnished

flatlet (BRIT) ou room; **meubler** vt to furnish

**meugler** [møgle] vi to low, moo

**meule** [møl] nf (de foin, blé) stack; (de fromage) round; (à broyer) millstone

**meunier** [mønje, jɛʀ] nm miller; **meunière** nf miller's wife

**meure** etc [mœʀ] vb voir **mourir**

**meurtre** [mœʀtʀ] nm murder; **meurtrier, -ière** adj (arme etc) deadly; (fureur, instincts) murderous ♦ nm/f murderer(-eress)

**meurtrir** [mœʀtʀiʀ] vt to bruise; (fig) to wound; **meurtrissure** nf bruise

**meus** etc [mœ] vb voir **mouvoir**

**meute** [møt] nf pack

**mexicain, e** [mɛksikɛ̃, ɛn] adj Mexican ♦ nm/f: **M~, e** Mexican

**Mexico** [mɛksiko] n Mexico City

**Mexique** [mɛksik] nm: **le ~** Mexico

**Mgr** abr = **Monseigneur**

**mi** [mi] nm (MUS) E; (en chantant la gamme) mi ♦ préfixe: **~...** half(-); mid(-); **la ~-janvier** in mid-January; **à ~-hauteur** halfway up; **mi-bas** nm inv knee sock

**miauler** [mjole] vi to mew

**miche** [miʃ] nf round ou cob loaf

**mi-chemin** [miʃmɛ̃]: **à ~-~** adv halfway, midway

**mi-clos, e** [miklo, kloz] adj half-closed

**micro** [mikʀo] nm mike, microphone; (INFORM) micro

**microbe** [mikʀɔb] nm germ, microbe

**micro...**: **micro-onde** nf: **four à micro-ondes** microwave oven; **micro-ordinateur** nm microcomputer; **microscope** nm microscope; **microscopique** adj microscopic

**midi** [midi] nm midday, noon; (moment du déjeuner) lunchtime; (sud) south; **à ~** at 12 (o'clock) ou midday ou noon; **le M~** the South (of France), the Midi

**mie** [mi] nf crumb (of the loaf)

**miel** [mjɛl] nm honey; **mielleux, -euse** adj (personne) unctuous, syrupy

**mien, ne** [mjɛ̃, mjɛn] pron: **le(la)**

~(ne), les ~(ne)s mine; les ~s my family

**miette** [mjɛt] *nf (de pain, gâteau)* crumb; *(fig: de la conversation etc)* scrap; **en ~s** in pieces *ou* bits

---
MOT-CLÉ
---

**mieux** [mjø] *adv* **1** *(d'une meilleure façon)*: **mieux (que)** better (than); **elle travaille/mange mieux** she works/ eats better; **elle va mieux** she is better **2** *(de la meilleure façon)* best; **ce que je sais le mieux** what I know best; **les livres les mieux faits** the best made books
**3**: **de mieux en mieux** better and better

♦ *adj inv* **1** *(plus à l'aise, en meilleure forme)* better; **se sentir mieux** to feel better **2** *(plus satisfaisant)* better; **c'est mieux ainsi** it's better like this; **c'est le mieux des deux** it's the better of the two; **le/la) mieux, les mieux** the best; **demandez-lui, c'est le mieux** ask him, it's the best thing
**3** *(plus joli)* better-looking
**4**: **au mieux** at best; **au mieux avec** on the best of terms with; **pour le mieux** for the best

♦ *nm* **1** *(progrès)* improvement
**2**: **de mon/ton mieux** as best I/you can *(ou could)*; **faire de son mieux** to do one's best

**mièvre** [mjɛvʀ] *adj* mawkish *(BRIT)*, sickly sentimental
**mignon, ne** [miɲɔ̃, ɔn] *adj* sweet, cute
**migraine** [migʀɛn] *nf* headache; *(MÉD)* migraine
**mijoter** [miʒɔte] *vt* to simmer; *(préparer avec soin)* to cook lovingly; *(fam: tramer)* to plot, cook up ♦ *vi* to simmer
**mil** [mil] *num* = **mille**
**milieu, x** [miljø] *nm (centre)* middle; *(BIO, GÉO)* environment; *(entourage social)* milieu; *(provenance)* background; *(pègre)*: **le ~** the underworld; **au ~ de** in the middle of; **au beau** *ou* **en plein ~ (de)** right in the middle (of); **un juste ~** a happy medium
**militaire** [militɛʀ] *adj* military, army *cpd* ♦ *nm* serviceman
**militant, e** [militã, ãt] *adj, nm/f* militant
**militer** [milite] *vi* to be a militant
**mille** [mil] *num* a *ou* one thousand
♦ *nm (mesure)*: **~ (marin)** nautical mile; **mettre dans le ~** *(fig)* to be bang on target; **millefeuille** *nm* cream *ou* vanilla slice; **millénaire** *nm* millennium
♦ *adj* thousand-year-old; *(fig)* ancient; **mille-pattes** *nm inv* centipede
**millésimé, e** [milezime] *adj* vintage *cpd*
**millet** [mijɛ] *nm*
**milliard** [miljaʀ] *nm* milliard, thousand million *(BRIT)*, billion *(US)*; **milliardaire** *nm/f* multimillionaire *(BRIT)*, billionaire *(US)*
**millier** [milje] *nm* thousand; **un ~ (de)** a thousand or so, about a thousand; **par ~s** in (their) thousands, by the thousand
**milligramme** [miligʀam] *nm* milligramme
**millimètre** [milimɛtʀ] *nm* millimetre
**million** [miljɔ̃] *nm* million; **deux ~s de** two million; **millionnaire** *nm/f* millionaire
**mime** [mim] *nm/f (acteur)* mime(r)
♦ *nm (art)* mime, miming; **mimer** *vt* to mime; *(singer)* to mimic, take off
**mimique** [mimik] *nf (grimace)* funny face; *(signes)* gesticulations *pl*, sign language *no pl*
**minable** [minabl] *adj (décrépit)* shabby(-looking); *(médiocre)* pathetic
**mince** [mɛ̃s] *adj (fin)*: *(personne, taille)* slim, slender; *(fig: profit, connaissances)* slight, small, weak ♦ *excl*: **~ alors!** drat it!, darn it! *(US)*; **minceur** *nf* thinness; *(d'une personne)* slimness, slenderness; **mincir** *vi* to get slimmer
**mine** [min] *nf (physionomie)* expression,

look; (allure) exterior, appearance; (de crayon) lead; (gisement, explosif, fig: source) mine; **avoir bonne ~** (personne) to look well; (ironique) to look an utter idiot; **avoir mauvaise ~** to look unwell ou poorly; **faire ~ de faire** to make a pretence of doing; **~ de rien** although you wouldn't think so

**miner** [mine] vt (saper) to undermine, erode; (MIL) to mine

**minerai** [minʀɛ] nm ore

**minéral, e, -aux** [mineʀal, o] adj, nm mineral

**minéralogique** [mineʀalɔʒik] adj: **numéro ~** registration number

**minet, te** [minɛ, ɛt] nm/f (chat) pussycat; (péj) young trendy

**mineur, e** [minœʀ] adj minor ♦ nm (JUR) minor, person under age ♦ nm (travailleur) miner

**miniature** [minjatyʀ] adj, nf miniature

**minibus** [minibys] nm minibus

**mini-cassette** [minikasɛt] nf cassette (recorder)

**minier, -ière** [minje, jɛʀ] adj mining

**mini-jupe** [miniʒyp] nf mini-skirt

**minime** [minim] adj minor, minimal

**minimiser** [minimize] vt to minimize; (fig) to play down

**minimum** [minimɔm] adj, nm minimum; **au ~** (au moins) at the very least

**ministère** [ministɛʀ] nm (aussi REL) ministry; (cabinet) government

**ministre** [ministʀ] nm (aussi REL) minister

**Minitel** ® [minitɛl] nm videotext terminal and service

stock market and situations vacant. Services are accessed by phoning the relevant number and charged to the subscriber's phone bill.
└──────────────────────

**minoritaire** [minɔʀitɛʀ] adj minority

**minorité** [minɔʀite] nf minority; **être en ~** to be in the ou a minority

**minuit** [minɥi] nm midnight

**minuscule** [minyskyl] adj minute, tiny ♦ nf: (lettre) ~ small letter

**minute** [minyt] nf minute; **à la ~** (just) this instant; (faire) there and then; **minuter** vt to time; **minuterie** nf time switch

**minutieux, -euse** [minysjø, jøz] adj (personne) meticulous; (travail) minutely detailed

**mirabelle** [miʀabɛl] nf (cherry) plum

**miracle** [miʀakl] nm miracle

**mirage** [miʀaʒ] nm mirage

**mire** [miʀ] nf: **point de ~** (fig) focal point

**miroir** [miʀwaʀ] nm mirror

**miroiter** [miʀwate] vi to sparkle, shimmer; **faire ~ qch à qn** to paint sth in glowing colours for sb, dangle sth in front of sb's eyes

**mis, e** [mi, miz] pp de **mettre** ♦ adj: **bien ~** well-dressed

**mise** [miz] nf (argent: au jeu) stake; (tenue) clothing, attire; **être de ~** to be acceptable ou in season; **~ au point** (fig) clarification; **~ de fonds** capital outlay; **~ en examen** charging, indictment; **~ en plis** set; **~ en scène** production

**miser** [mize] vt (enjeu) to stake, bet; **~ sur** (cheval, numéro) to bet on; (fig) to bank ou count on

**misérable** [mizeʀabl] adj (lamentable, malheureux) pitiful, wretched; (pauvre) poverty-stricken; (insignifiant, mesquin) miserable ♦ nm/f wretch

**misère** [mizɛʀ] nf (extreme) poverty, destitution; **~s** nfpl (malheurs) woes, miseries; (ennuis) little troubles; **salaire**

de ~ starvation wage

**missile** [misil] *nm* missile

**mission** [misjɔ] *nf* mission; **partir en** ~ (ADMIN, POL) to go on an assignment; **missionnaire** *nm/f* missionary

**mit** [mi] *vb voir* **mettre**

**mité, e** [mite] *adj* moth-eaten

**mi-temps** [mitɑ̃] *nf inv* (SPORT: *période*) half; (: *pause*) half-time; **à ~~** part-time

**miteux, -euse** [mitø, øz] *adj* (*lieu*) seedy

**mitigé, e** [mitiʒe] *adj*: **sentiments ~s** mixed feelings

**mitonner** [mitɔne] *vt* to cook with loving care; (*fig*) to cook up quietly

**mitoyen, ne** [mitwajɛ̃, jɛn] *adj* (*mur*) common, party *cpd*

**mitrailler** [mitraje] *vt* to machine-gun; (*fig*) to pelt, bombard; (: *photographier*) to take shot after shot of; **mitraillette** *nf* submachine gun; **mitrailleuse** *nf* machine gun

**mi-voix** [mivwa]: **à ~~** *adv* in a low *ou* hushed voice

**mixage** [miksaʒ] *nm* (CINÉMA) (sound) mixing

**mixer** [miksœr] *nm* (food) mixer

**mixte** [mikst] *adj* (*gén*) mixed; (SCOL) mixed, coeducational

**mixture** [mikstyr] *nf* mixture; (*fig*) concoction

**Mlle** (*pl* **Mlles**) *abr* = **Mademoiselle**

**MM** *abr* = **Messieurs**

**Mme** (*pl* **Mmes**) *abr* = **Madame**

**mobile** [mɔbil] *adj* mobile; (*pièce de machine*) moving ♦ *nm* (*motif*) motive; (*œuvre d'art*) mobile

**mobilier, -ière** [mɔbilje, jɛr] *nm* furniture

**mobiliser** [mɔbilize] *vt* to mobilize

**mocassin** [mɔkasɛ̃] *nm* moccasin

**moche** [mɔʃ] (*fam*) *adj* (*laid*) ugly; (*mauvais*) rotten

**modalité** [mɔdalite] *nf* form, mode; **~s de paiement** methods of payment

**mode** [mɔd] *nf* fashion ♦ *nm* (*manière*)

form, mode; **à la** ~ fashionable, in fashion; **~ d'emploi** directions *pl* (for use)

**modèle** [mɔdɛl] *nm* model; (*qui pose: de peintre*) sitter; **~ déposé** registered design; **~ réduit** small-scale model; **modeler** *vt* to model

**modem** [mɔdɛm] *nm* modem

**modéré, e** [mɔdere] *adj, nm/f* moderate

**modérer** [mɔdere] *vt* to moderate; **se ~** *vi* to restrain o.s.

**moderne** [mɔdɛrn] *adj* modern ♦ *nm* (*style*) modern style; (*meubles*) modern furniture; **moderniser** *vt* to modernize

**modeste** [mɔdɛst] *adj* modest; **modestie** *nf* modesty

**modifier** [mɔdifje] *vt* to modify, alter; **se ~** *vi* to alter

**modique** [mɔdik] *adj* modest

**modiste** [mɔdist] *nf* milliner

**module** [mɔdyl] *nm* module

**moelle** [mwal] *nf* marrow; **~ épinière** spinal cord

**moelleux, -euse** [mwalø, øz] *adj* soft; (*gâteau*) light and moist

**mœurs** [mœr] *nfpl* (*conduite*) morals; (*manières*) manners; (*pratiques sociales, mode de vie*) habits

**mohair** [mɔɛr] *nm* mohair

**moi** [mwa] *pron* me; (*emphatique*): ~, **je** ... for my part, I ...; ~ **aussi** ...; **à** ~ mine; **moi-même** *pron* myself; (*emphatique*) I myself

**moindre** [mwɛ̃dr] *adj* lesser; lower; **le(la)** ~, **les** ~**s** the least, the slightest; **merci – c'est la** ~ **des choses!** thank you – it's a pleasure!

**moine** [mwan] *nm* monk, friar

**moineau, x** [mwano] *nm* sparrow

---

*MOT-CLÉ*

**moins** [mwɛ̃] *adv* **1** (*comparatif*): **moins (que)** less (than); **moins grand que** less tall than, not as tall as; **moins je travaille, mieux je me porte** the less I work, the better I feel

**2** (superlatif): **le moins** (the) least;
**c'est ce que j'aime le moins** it's what
I like (the) least; **le(la) moins doué(e)**
the least gifted; **au moins, du moins**
at least; **pour le moins** at the very
least

**3: moins de** (quantité) less (than);
(nombre) fewer (than); **moins de
sable/d'eau** less sand/water; **moins
de livres/gens** fewer books/people;
**moins de 2 ans** less than 2 years;
**moins de midi** not yet midday

**4: de moins, en moins:** 100 F/3
**jours de moins** 100F/3 days less; **3 livres en moins** 3 books fewer; **3 books
too few; de l'argent en moins** less
money; **le soleil en moins** but for the
sun, minus the sun; **de moins en
moins** less and less

**5: à moins de, à moins que** unless; **à
moins de faire** unless we do (ou he
does etc); **à moins que tu ne fasses**
unless you do; **à moins d'un accident**
barring any accident

♦ prép: **4 moins 2** 4 minus 2; **il est
moins 5** it's 5 to; **il fait moins 5** it's 5
(degrees) below (freezing), it's minus 5

**mois** [mwa] nm month

**moisi** [mwazi] nm mould, mildew;
**odeur de ~** musty smell; **moisir** vi to
go mouldy; **moisissure** nf mould no pl

**moisson** [mwasɔ̃] nf harvest; **moissonner** vt to harvest, reap; **moisson-
neuse** nf (machine) harvester

**moite** [mwat] adj sweaty, sticky

**moitié** [mwatje] nf half; **la ~ half; la
~ de** half (of); **la ~ du temps** half the
time; **la ~ de** halfway through; **à ~**
(avant le verbe) half; (avant l'adjectif)
half-; **à ~ prix** (at) half-price; **~ moitié**
half-and-half

**moka** [mɔka] nm coffee gateau

**mol** [mɔl] adj voir **mou**

**molaire** [mɔlɛr] nf molar

**molester** [mɔleste] vt to manhandle,
maul (about)

**molle** [mɔl] adj voir **mou; mollement**
adv (péj: travailler) sluggishly; (protester)
feebly

**mollet** [mɔlɛ] nm calf ♦ adj m: **œuf ~**
soft-boiled egg

**molletonné, e** [mɔltɔne] adj fleece-
lined

**mollir** [mɔlir] vi (fléchir) to relent; (substance) to go soft

**mollusque** [mɔlysk] nm mollusc

**môme** [mom] (fam) nm/f (enfant) brat

**moment** [mɔmɑ̃] nm moment; **ce
n'est pas le ~** this is not the (right)
time; **pour un bon ~** for a good
while; **pour le ~** for the moment, for
the time being; **au ~ de** at the time of;
**au ~ où** just as; **à tout ~** (peut arriver
etc) at any time ou moment; (constamment) constantly, continually; **en ce ~**
at the moment; at present; **sur le ~** at
the time; **par ~s** now and then, at
times; **du ~ où** ou **que** seeing that,
since; **momentané, e** adj temporary,
momentary; **momentanément** adv
(court instant) for a short while

**momie** [mɔmi] nf mummy

**mon, ma** [mɔ̃, ma] (pl **mes**) adj my

**Monaco** [mɔnako] nm Monaco

**monarchie** [mɔnarʃi] nf monarchy

**monastère** [mɔnaster] nm monastery

**monceau, x** [mɔ̃so] nm heap

**mondain, e** [mɔ̃dɛ̃, ɛn] adj (vie) society
cpd

**monde** [mɔ̃d] nm world; (haute société): **le ~** (high) society; **il y a du ~**
(beaucoup de gens) there are a lot of
people; (quelques personnes) there are
some people; **beaucoup/peu de ~**
many/few people; **mettre au ~** to
bring into the world; **pas le moins du
~** not in the least; **se faire un ~ de
qch** to make a great deal of fuss about
sth; **mondial, e, -aux** adj (population)
world cpd; (influence) world-wide;
**mondialement** adv throughout the
world

**monégasque** [mɔnegask] adj Monegasque, of *ou* from Monaco

**monétaire** [mɔnetɛʀ] *adj* monetary

**moniteur, -trice** [mɔnitœʀ, tʀis] *nm/f* (SPORT) instructor(-tress); (*de colonie de vacances*) supervisor ♦ *nm* (*écran*) monitor

**monnaie** [mɔnɛ] *nf* (ÉCON, *gén: moyen d'échange*) currency; (*petites pièces*): **avoir de la ~** to have (some) change; **une pièce de ~** a coin; **faire de la ~** to get (some) change; **avoir/faire la ~ de 20 F** to have change of/get change for 20 F; **rendre à qn la ~ (sur 20 F)** to give sb the change (out of *ou* from 20 F); **monnayer** *vt* to convert into cash; (*talent*) to capitalize on

**monologue** [mɔnɔlɔg] *nm* monologue, soliloquy; **monologuer** *vi* to soliloquize

**monopole** [mɔnɔpɔl] *nm* monopoly

**monotone** [mɔnɔtɔn] *adj* monotonous

**Monsieur** [məsjø] (*pl* **Messieurs**) *titre* Mr ♦ *nm* (*homme quelconque*): **un/le m~** a/the gentleman; **M~, ...** (*en tête de lettre*) Dear Sir, ...; *voir aussi* **Madame**

**monstre** [mɔstʀ] *nm* monster ♦ *adj* (*fam: colossal*) monstrous; **un travail ~** a fantastic amount of work; **monstrueux, -euse** *adj* monstrous

**mont** [mɔ] *nm*: **par ~s et par vaux** up hill and down dale; **le M~ Blanc** Mont Blanc

**montage** [mɔtaʒ] *nm* (*assemblage: d'appareil*) assembly; (PHOTO) photomontage; (CINÉMA) editing

**montagnard, e** [mɔtaɲaʀ, aʀd] *adj* mountain ♦ *nm/f* mountain-dweller

**montagne** [mɔtaɲ] *nf* (*cime*) mountain; (*région*): **la ~** the mountains *pl*; **~s russes** big dipper *sg*, switchback *sg*; **montagneux, -euse** *adj* mountainous; (*basse montagne*) hilly

**montant, e** [mɔtɑ, ɑt] *adj* rising; **pull à col ~** high-necked jumper ♦ *nm* (*somme, total*) (sum) total, (total) amount; (*de fenêtre*) upright; (*de lit*) post

**monte-charge** [mɔtʃaʀʒ] *nm inv* goods lift, hoist

**montée** [mɔte] *nf* (*des prix, hostilités*) rise; (*escalade*) climb; (*côte*) hill; **au milieu de la ~** halfway up

**monter** [mɔte] *vt* (*escalier, côte*) to go (*ou* come) up; (*valise, paquet*) to take (*ou* bring) up; (*étagère*) to raise; (*tente, échafaudage*) to put up; (*machine*) to assemble; (CINÉMA) to edit; (THÉÂTRE) to put on, stage; (*société etc*) to set up ♦ *vi* to go (*ou* come) up; (*prix, niveau, température*) to go up, rise; (*passager*) to get on; **se ~ à** (*frais etc*) to add up to, come to; **~ à pied** to walk up, go up on foot; **~ dans le train/l'avion** to get into the train/plane, board the train/plane; **~ sur** to climb up onto; **~ à cheval** (*faire du cheval*) to ride, go riding

**montre** [mɔtʀ] *nf* watch; **contre la ~** (SPORT) against the clock; **montre-bracelet** *nf* wristwatch

**montrer** [mɔtʀe] *vt* to show; **~ qch à qn** to show sb sth

**monture** [mɔtyʀ] *nf* (*cheval*) mount; (*de lunettes*) frame; (*d'une bague*) setting

**monument** [mɔnymɑ] *nm* monument; **~ aux morts** war memorial

**moquer** [mɔke]: **se ~ de** *vt* to make fun of, laugh at; (*fam: se désintéresser de*) not to care about; (*tromper*): **se ~ de qn** to take sb for a ride; **moquerie** *nf* mockery

**moquette** [mɔkɛt] *nf* fitted carpet

**moqueur, -euse** [mɔkœʀ, øz] *adj* mocking

**moral, e, -aux** [mɔʀal, o] *adj* moral ♦ *nm* morale; **avoir le ~** (*fam*) to be in good spirits; **avoir le ~ à zéro** (*fam*) to be really down; **morale** *nf* (*mœurs*) morals *pl*; (*valeurs*) moral standards *pl*, morality; (*d'une fable etc*) moral; **faire la morale à** to lecture, preach at; **moralité** *nf* morality; (*de fable*) moral

**morceau, x** [mɔʀso] *nm* piece, bit;

(*d'une œuvre*) passage, extract; (*MUS*) piece; (*CULIN: de viande*) cut; (*de sucre*) lump; **mettre en ~x** to pull to pieces *ou* bits; **manger un ~** to have a bite (to eat)

**morceler** [mɔʀsəle] *vt* to break up, divide up

**mordant, e** [mɔʀdɑ̃, ɑ̃t] *adj* (*ton, remarque*) scathing, cutting; (*ironie, froid*) biting ♦ *nm* (*style*) bite, punch

**mordiller** [mɔʀdije] *vt* to nibble at, chew at

**mordre** [mɔʀdʀ] *vt* to bite ♦ *vi* (*poisson*) to bite; **~ sur** (*fig*) to go over into, overlap into; **~ à l'hameçon** to bite, rise to the bait

**mordu, e** [mɔʀdy] (*fam*) *nm/f* enthusiast; **un ~ de jazz** a jazz fanatic

**morfondre**: **se ~** *vi* to mope

**morgue** [mɔʀg] *nf* (*arrogance*) haughtiness; (*lieu: de la police*) morgue; (: *à l'hôpital*) mortuary

**morne** [mɔʀn] *adj* dismal, dreary

**morose** [mɔʀoz] *adj* sullen, morose

**mors** [mɔʀ] *nm* bit

**morse** [mɔʀs] *nm* (*ZOOL*) walrus; (*TÉL*) Morse (code)

**morsure** [mɔʀsyʀ] *nf* bite

**mort**[1] [mɔʀ] *nf* death

**mort**[2], **e** [mɔʀ, mɔʀt] *pp de* **mourir** ♦ *adj* dead ♦ *nm/f* (*défunt*) dead man/woman; (*victime*): **il y a eu plusieurs ~s** several people were killed, there were several killed; **~ de peur/fatigue** frightened to death/dead tired

**mortalité** [mɔʀtalite] *nf* mortality, death rate

**mortel, le** [mɔʀtɛl] *adj* (*poison etc*) deadly, lethal; (*accident, blessure*) fatal; (*silence, ennemi*) deadly; (*péché*) mortal; (*fam: ennuyeux*) deadly boring

**mortier** [mɔʀtje] *nm* (*gén*) mortar

**mort-né, e** [mɔʀne] *adj* (*enfant*) stillborn

**mortuaire** [mɔʀtɥɛʀ] *adj*: **avis ~** death announcement

**morue** [mɔʀy] *nf* (*ZOOL*) cod *inv*

**mosaïque** [mozaik] *nf* mosaic

**Moscou** [mɔsku] Moscow

**mosquée** [mɔske] *nf* mosque

**mot** [mo] *nm* word; (*message*) line, note; **~ à ~** word for word; **~ d'ordre** watchword; **~ de passe** password; **~s croisés** crossword (puzzle) *sg*

**motard** [mɔtaʀ] *nm* biker; (*policier*) motorcycle cop

**motel** [mɔtɛl] *nm* motel

**moteur, -trice** [mɔtœʀ, tʀis] *adj* (*ANAT, PHYSIOL*) motor; (*TECH*) driving; (*AUTO*): **à 4 roues motrices** 4-wheel drive ♦ *nm* engine, motor; **à ~** power-driven, motor *cpd*

**motif** [mɔtif] *nm* (*cause*) motive; (*décoratif*) design, pattern, motif; **sans ~** groundless

**motivation** [mɔtivasjɔ̃] *nf* motivation

**motiver** [mɔtive] *vt* to motivate; (*justifier*) to justify, account for

**moto** [mɔto] *nf* (*motor*)bike; **motocycliste** *nm/f* motorcyclist

**motorisé, e** [mɔtɔʀize] *adj* (*personne*) having transport *ou* a car

**motrice** [mɔtʀis] *adj voir* **moteur**

**motte** [mɔt] *nf*: **~ de terre** lump of earth, clod (of earth); **~ de beurre** lump of butter

**mou (mol), molle** [mu, mɔl] *adj* soft; (*personne*) lethargic; (*protestations*) weak ♦ *nm*: **avoir du mou** to be slack

**moucharder** [muʃaʀde] (*fam*) *vt* (*SCOL*) to sneak on; (*POLICE*) to grass on

**mouche** [muʃ] *nf* fly

**moucher** [muʃe]: **se ~** *vi* to blow one's nose

**moucheron** [muʃʀɔ̃] *nm* midge

**mouchoir** [muʃwaʀ] *nm* handkerchief, hanky; **~ en papier** tissue, paper hanky

**moudre** [mudʀ] *vt* to grind

**moue** [mu] *nf* pout; **faire la ~** to pout; (*fig*) to pull a face

**mouette** [mwɛt] *nf* (sea)gull

**moufle** [mufl] *nf* (*gant*) mitt(en)

**mouillé, e** [muje] *adj* wet

**mouiller** [muje] vt (humecter) to wet, moisten; (tremper): ~ **qn/qch** to make sb/sth wet ♦ vi (NAVIG) to lie ou be at anchor; **se** ~ to get wet; (fam: prendre des risques) to commit o.s.

**moulant, e** [mulɑ̃, ɑ̃t] adj figure-hugging

**moule** [mul] nf mussel ♦ nm (CULIN) mould; ~ **à gâteaux** ♦ nm cake tin (BRIT) ou pan (US)

**moulent** [mul] voir **moudre**; **mouler**

**mouler** [mule] vt (suj: vêtement): to hug, fit closely round

**moulin** [mulɛ̃] nm mill; ~ **à café/à poivre** coffee/pepper mill; ~ **à légumes** (vegetable) shredder; ~ **à paroles** (fig) chatterbox; ~ **à vent** windmill

**moulinet** [mulinɛ] nm (de canne à pêche) reel; (mouvement): **faire des ~s avec qch** to whirl sth around

**moulinette** ® [mulinɛt] nf (vegetable) shredder

**moulu, e** [muly] pp de **moudre**

**mourant, e** [murɑ̃, ɑ̃t] adj dying

**mourir** [muRiR] vi (personne) to die; (civilisation) to die out; ~ **de froid/faim** to die of exposure/hunger; ~ **de faim/d'ennui** (fig) to be starving/be bored to death; ~ **d'envie de faire** to be dying to do

**mousse** [mus] nf (BOT) moss; (de savon) lather; (écume: sur eau, bière) froth, foam; (CULIN) mousse ♦ nm (NAVIG) ship's boy; ~ **à raser** shaving foam

**mousseline** [muslin] nf muslin; **pommes ~** mashed potatoes

**mousser** [muse] vi (bière, détergent) to foam; (savon) to lather; **mousseux, -euse** adj frothy ♦ nm: **(vin) mousseux** sparkling wine

**mousson** [musɔ̃] nf monsoon

**moustache** [mustaʃ] nf moustache; ~**s** nfpl (du chat) whiskers pl; **moustachu, e** adj with a moustache

**moustiquaire** [mustikɛR] nf mosquito net

**moustique** [mustik] nm mosquito

**moutarde** [mutaRd] nf mustard

**mouton** [mutɔ̃] nm sheep inv; (peau) sheepskin; (CULIN) mutton

**mouvement** [muvmɑ̃] nm movement; (fig: impulsion) impulse; **avoir un bon ~** to make a nice generous gesture; **en ~** in motion; on the move; **mouvementé, e** adj (vie, poursuite) eventful; (réunion) turbulent

**mouvoir** [muvwaR]: **se** ~ vi to move

**moyen, ne** [mwajɛ̃, jɛn] adj average; (tailles, prix) medium; (de grandeur moyenne) medium-sized ♦ nm (façon) means sg, way; ~**s** nmpl (capacités) means; **très** ~ (résultats) pretty poor; **je n'en ai pas les ~s** I can't afford it; **au ~ de** by means of; **par tous les ~s** by every possible means, every possible way; **par ses propres ~s** all by one-self; ~ **âge** Middle Ages; ~ **de transport** means of transport

**moyennant** [mwajɛnɑ̃] prép (somme) for; (service, conditions) in return for; (travail, effort) with

**moyenne** [mwajɛn] nf average; (MATH) mean; (SCOL) pass mark; **en** ~ on (an) average; ~ **d'âge** average age

**Moyen-Orient** [mwajɛ̃nɔRjɑ̃] nm: **le** ~~ the Middle East

**moyeu, x** [mwajø] nm hub

**MST** sigle f (= maladie sexuellement transmissible) STD

**MTC** sigle m (= mécanisme du taux de change) ERM

**mû, mue** [my] pp de **mouvoir**

**muer** [mɥe] vi (oiseau, mammifère) to moult; (serpent) to slough; (jeune garçon): **il mue** his voice is breaking; **se** ~ **en** to transform into

**muet, te** [mɥɛ, mɥɛt] adj dumb; (fig): ~ **d'admiration** etc speechless with admiration etc; (CINÉMA) silent ♦ nm/f mute

**mufle** [myfl] nm muzzle; (fam: goujat) boor

**mugir** [myʒiR] vi (taureau) to bellow; (vache) to low; (fig) to howl

**muguet** [mygɛ] nm lily of the valley

**mule** [myl] nf (ZOOL) (she-)mule

**mulet** [mylɛ] nm (ZOOL) (he-)mule

**multinationale** [myltinasjɔnal] nf multinational

**multiple** [myltipl] adj multiple, numerous; (varié) many, manifold; **multiplication** nf multiplication; **multiplier** vt to multiply; **se multiplier** vi to multiply

**municipal, e, -aux** [mynisipal, o] adj (élections, stade) municipal; (conseil) town cpd; **piscine/bibliothèque ~e** public swimming pool/library; **municipalité** nf (ville) municipality; (conseil) town council

**munir** [mynir] vt: **~ qch de** to equip sth with; **se ~ de** to arm o.s. with

**munitions** [mynisjɔ̃] nfpl ammunition sg

**mur** [myr] nm wall; **~ du son** sound barrier

**mûr, e** [myr] adj ripe; (personne) mature

**muraille** [myrɑj] nf (high) wall

**mural, e, -aux** [myral, o] adj wall cpd; (art) mural

**mûre** [myr] nf blackberry

**muret** [myrɛ] nm low wall

**mûrir** [myrir] vi (fruit, blé) to ripen; (abcès) to come to a head; (fig: idée, personne) to mature ♦ vt (projet) to nurture; (personne) to (make) mature

**murmure** [myrmyr] nm murmur; **murmurer** vi to murmur

**muscade** [myskad] nf (aussi: **noix de ~**) nutmeg

**muscat** [myska] nm (raisins) muscat grape; (vin) muscatel (wine)

**muscle** [myskl] nm muscle; **musclé, e** adj muscular; (fig) strong-arm

**museau, x** [myzo] nm muzzle; (CULIN) brawn

**musée** [myze] nm museum; (de peinture) art gallery

**museler** [myz(ə)le] vt to muzzle; **muselière** nf muzzle

**musette** [myzɛt] nf (sac) lunchbag

**musical, e, -aux** [myzikal, o] adj musical

**music-hall** [myzikol] nm (salle) variety theatre; (genre) variety

**musicien, ne** [myzisjɛ̃, jɛn] adj musical ♦ nm/f musician

**musique** [myzik] nf music; **~ d'ambiance** background music

**musulman, e** [myzylmɑ̃, an] adj, nm/f Moslem, Muslim

**mutation** [mytasjɔ̃] nf (ADMIN) transfer

**muter** [myte] vt to transfer, move

**mutilé, e** [mytile] nm/f disabled person (through loss of limbs)

**mutiler** [mytile] vt to mutilate, maim

**mutin, e** [mytɛ̃, in] adj (air, ton) mischievous, impish ♦ nm/f (MIL, NAVIG) mutineer; **mutinerie** nf mutiny

**mutisme** [mytism] nm silence

**mutuel, le** [mytɥɛl] adj mutual; **mutuelle** nf voluntary insurance premiums for back-up health cover

**myope** [mjɔp] adj short-sighted

**myosotis** [mjɔzɔtis] nm forget-me-not

**myrtille** [mirtij] nf bilberry

**mystère** [mistɛr] nm mystery; **mystérieux, -euse** adj mysterious

**mystifier** [mistifje] vt to fool

**mythe** [mit] nm myth

**mythologie** [mitɔlɔʒi] nf mythology

# N, n

**n'** [n] adv voir **ne**

**nacre** [nakr] nf mother of pearl

**nage** [naʒ] nf swimming; (manière) style of swimming, stroke; **traverser/s'éloigner à la ~** to swim across/away; **en ~** bathed in sweat; **nageoire** nf fin; **nager** vi to swim; **nageur, -euse** nm/f swimmer

**naguère** [nagɛr] adv formerly

**naïf, -ive** [naif, naiv] adj naïve

**nain, e** [nɛ̃, nɛn] nm/f dwarf

**naissance** [nesɑ̃s] nf birth; **donner ~ à** to give birth to; (fig) to give rise to

**naître** [nɛtr] vi to be born; (fig): **~ de** to arise from, be born out of; **il est né**

**en 1960** he was born in 1960; **faire ~** (fig) to give rise to, arouse

**naïve** [najv] adj voir **naïf**

**naïveté** [naivte] nf naïvety

**nana** [nana] (fam) nf (fille) chick, bird (BRIT)

**nantir** [nɑ̃tiʀ] vt: **~ qn de** to provide sb with; **les nantis** (péj) the well-to-do

**nappe** [nap] nf tablecloth; (de pétrole, gaz) layer; **~ phréatique** ground water; **napperon** nm table-mat

**naquit** etc [naki] vb voir **naître**

**narcodollars** [naʀkɔdɔlaʀ] nmpl drug money sg

**narguer** [naʀge] vt to taunt

**narine** [naʀin] nf nostril

**narquois, e** [naʀkwa, waz] adj mocking

**natal, e** [natal] adj native; **natalité** nf birth rate

**natation** [natasjɔ̃] nf swimming

**natif, -ive** [natif, iv] adj native

**nation** [nasjɔ̃] nf nation; **national, e, -aux** adj national; **nationale** nf: (route) **nationale** ≃ A road (BRIT), ≃ state highway (US); **nationaliser** vt to nationalize; **nationalisme** nm nationalism; **nationalité** nf nationality

**natte** [nat] nf (cheveux) plait; (tapis) mat

**naturaliser** [natyʀalize] vt to naturalize

**nature** [natyʀ] nf nature ♦ adj, adv (CU-LIN) plain, without seasoning or sweetening; (café, thé) black, without sugar; (yaourt) natural; **payer en ~** to pay in kind; **~ morte** still-life; **naturel, le** adj (gén, aussi enfant) natural ♦ nm (absence d'affectation) naturalness; (caractère) disposition, nature; **naturellement** adv naturally; (bien sûr) of course

**naufrage** [nofʀaʒ] nm (ship)wreck; **faire ~** to be shipwrecked

**nauséabond, e** [nozeabɔ̃, ɔ̃d] adj foul

**nausée** [noze] nf nausea

**nautique** [notik] adj nautical, water cpd; **sports ~s** water sports

**naval, e** [naval] adj naval; (industrie) shipbuilding

**navet** [navɛ] nm turnip; (péj: film) rubbishy film

**navette** [navɛt] nf shuttle; **faire la ~ (entre)** to go to and fro ou shuttle (between)

**navigateur** [navigatœʀ, tʀis] nm (NA-VIG) seafarer; (INFORM) browser

**navigation** [navigasjɔ̃] nf navigation, sailing

**naviguer** [navige] vi to navigate, sail; **~ sur Internet** to browse the Internet

**navire** [naviʀ] nm ship

**navrer** [navʀe] vt to upset, distress; **je suis navré** I'm so sorry

**ne, n'** [n(ə)] adv voir **pas**; **plus**; **jamais** etc; (sans valeur négative: non traduit): **c'est plus loin que je ~ le croyais** it's further than I thought

**né, e** [ne] pp (voir **naître**): **~ en 1960** born in 1960; **~e Scott** née Scott

**néanmoins** [neɑ̃mwɛ̃] adv nevertheless

**néant** [neɑ̃] nm nothingness; **réduire à ~** to bring to nought; (espoir) to dash

**nécessaire** [neseseʀ] adj necessary ♦ nm necessary; (sac) kit; **je vais faire le ~** I'll see to it; **~ de couture** sewing kit; **nécessité** nf necessity; **nécessiter** vt to require

**nécrologique** [nekʀɔlɔʒik] adj: **rubrique ~** obituary column

**néerlandais, e** [neeʀlɑ̃dɛ, ɛz] adj Dutch

**nef** [nɛf] nf (d'église) nave

**néfaste** [nefast] adj (nuisible) harmful; (funeste) ill-fated

**négatif, -ive** [negatif, iv] adj negative ♦ nm (PHOTO) negative

**négligé, e** [negliʒe] adj (en désordre) slovenly ♦ nm (tenue) negligee

**négligeable** [negliʒabl] adj negligible

**négligent, e** [negliʒɑ̃, ɑ̃t] adj careless, negligent

**négliger** [negliʒe] vt (tenue) to be careless about; (avis, précautions) to disregard; (épouse, jardin) to neglect; **~ de**

**faire** to fail to do, not bother to do

**négoce** [negɔs] nm trade

**négociant, e** [negɔsjɑ̃, jɑ̃t] nm merchant

**négociation** [negɔsjasjɔ̃] nf negotiation; **négocier** vi, vt to negotiate

**nègre** [nɛgʀ] (péj) nm (écrivain) ghost (writer)

**neige** [nɛʒ] nf snow; **neiger** vi to snow

**nénuphar** [nenyfaʀ] nm water-lily

**néon** [neɔ̃] nm neon

**néo-zélandais, e** [neozelɑ̃dɛ, ɛz] adj New Zealand cpd ♦ nm/f: **N~-Z~, e** New Zealander

**nerf** [nɛʀ] nm nerve; **être sur les ~s** to be all keyed up; **allons, du ~!** come on, buck up!; **nerveux, -euse** adj nervous; (irritable) touchy, nervy; (voiture) nippy, responsive; **nervosité** nf excitability, tenseness; (irritabilité passagère) irritability, nerviness

**nervure** [nɛʀvyʀ] nf vein

**n'est-ce pas** [nɛspɑ] adv isn't it?, won't you? etc, selon le verbe qui précède

**Net** [nɛt] nm (Internet): **le ~** the Net

**net, nette** [nɛt] adj (sans équivoque, distinct) clear; (évident: amélioration, différence) marked, distinct; (propre) neat, clean; (COMM: prix, salaire) net ♦ adv (refuser) flatly ♦ nm: **mettre au ~** to copy out; **s'arrêter ~** to stop dead; **nettement** adv clearly, distinctly; (incontestablement) decidedly, distinctly; **netteté** nf clearness

**nettoyage** [netwajaʒ] nm cleaning; **~ à sec** dry cleaning

**nettoyer** [netwaje] vt to clean

**neuf¹** [nœf] num nine

**neuf², neuve** [nœf, nœv] adj new ♦ nm: **remettre à ~** to do up (as good as new), refurbish; **quoi de ~?** what's new?

**neutre** [nøtʀ] adj neutral; (LING) neuter

**neuve** [nœv] adj voir **neuf²**

**neuvième** [nœvjɛm] num ninth

**neveu, x** [n(ə)vø] nm nephew

**névrosé, e** [nevʀoze] adj, nm/f neurotic

**nez** [ne] nm nose; **~ à ~ avec** face to face with; **avoir du ~** to have flair

**ni** [ni] conj: **~ ... ~** neither ... nor; **je n'aime ~ les lentilles ~ les épinards** I like neither lentils nor spinach; **il n'a dit ~ oui ~ non** he didn't say either yes or no; **elles ne sont venues ~ l'une ~ l'autre** neither of them came

**niais, e** [njɛ, njɛz] adj silly, thick

**niche** [niʃ] nf (du chien) kennel; (de mur) recess, niche; **nicher** vi to nest

**nid** [ni] nm nest; **~ de poule** pothole

**nièce** [njɛs] nf niece

**nier** [nje] vt to deny

**nigaud, e** [nigo, od] nm/f booby, fool

**Nil** [nil] nm: **le ~** the Nile

**n'importe** [nɛ̃pɔʀt] adv: **~ qui/quoi/où** anybody/anything/anywhere; **~ quand** any time; **~ quel/quelle** any; **~ lequel/laquelle** any (one); **~ comment** (sans soin) carelessly

**niveau, x** [nivo] nm level; (des élèves, études) standard; **~ de vie** standard of living

**niveler** [niv(ə)le] vt to level

**NN** abr (= nouvelle norme) revised standard of hotel classification

**noble** [nɔbl] adj noble; **noblesse** nf nobility; (d'une action etc) nobleness

**noce** [nɔs] nf wedding; (gens) wedding party (ou guests pl); **faire la ~** (fam) to go on a binge

**nocif, -ive** [nɔsif, iv] adj harmful

**nocturne** [nɔktyʀn] adj nocturnal ♦ nf late-night opening

**Noël** [nɔɛl] nm Christmas

**nœud** [nø] nm knot; (ruban) bow; **~ papillon** bow tie

**noir, e** [nwaʀ] adj black; (obscur, sombre) dark ♦ nm/f black man/woman ♦ nm: **dans le ~** in the dark; **travail au ~** moonlighting; **travailler au ~** to work on the side; **noircir** vt, vi to blacken; **noire** nf (MUS) crotchet (BRIT), quarter note (US)

**noisette** [nwazɛt] nf hazelnut

**noix** [nwa] nf walnut; (CULIN): **une ~ de**

**beurre** a knob of butter; **~ de cajou** cashew nut; **~ de coco** coconut; **à la ~** *(fam)* worthless

**nom** [nɔ̃] *nm* name; *(LING)* noun; **~ de famille** surname; **~ de jeune fille** maiden name; **~ déposé** trade name; **~ propre** proper noun

**nomade** [nɔmad] *nm/f* nomad

**nombre** [nɔ̃bʀ] *nm* number; **venir en ~** to come in large numbers; **depuis ~ d'années** for many years; **au ~ de mes amis** among my friends; **nombreux, -euse** *adj* many, numerous; *(avec nom sg: foule etc)* large; **peu nombreux** few

**nombril** [nɔ̃bʀi(l)] *nm* navel

**nommer** [nɔme] *vt* to name; *(élire)* to appoint, nominate; **se ~: il se nomme Pascal** his name's Pascal, he's called Pascal

**non** [nɔ̃] *adv (réponse)* no; *(avec loin, sans, seulement)* not; **~ (pas) que** not that; **moi ~ plus** neither do I, I don't either; **c'est bon ~?** *(exprimant le doute)* it's good, isn't it?

**non-alcoolisé, e** [nɔ̃alkɔlize] *adj* non-alcoholic

**nonante** [nɔnɑ̃t] *(BELGIQUE, SUISSE)* num ninety

**non-fumeur** [nɔ̃fymœʀ, øz] *nm* non-smoker

**non-sens** [nɔ̃sɑ̃s] *nm* absurdity

**nonchalant, e** [nɔ̃ʃalɑ̃, ɑ̃t] *adj* nonchalant

**nord** [nɔʀ] *nm* North ♦ *adj* northern; north; **au ~** *(situation)* in the north; *(direction)* to the north; **au ~ de** *(to the)* north of; **nord-est** *nm* North-East; **nord-ouest** *nm* North-West

**normal, e, -aux** [nɔʀmal, o] *adj* normal; **c'est tout à fait ~** it's perfectly natural; **vous trouvez ça ~?** does it seem right to you?; **normale** *nf:* **la normale** the norm, the average; **normalement** *adv (en général)* normally

**normand, e** [nɔʀmɑ̃, ɑ̃d] *adj* of Normandy

**Normandie** [nɔʀmɑ̃di] *nf* Normandy

**norme** [nɔʀm] *nf* norm; *(TECH)* standard

**Norvège** [nɔʀvɛʒ] *nf* Norway; **norvégien, ne** *adj* Norwegian ♦ *nm/f:* **Norvégien, ne** Norwegian ♦ *nm (LING)* Norwegian

**nos** [no] *adj voir* **notre**

**nostalgie** [nɔstalʒi] *nf* nostalgia; **nostalgique** *adj* nostalgic

**notable** [nɔtabl] *adj (fait)* notable, noteworthy; *(marqué)* noticeable, marked ♦ *nm* prominent citizen

**notaire** [nɔtɛʀ] *nm* solicitor

**notamment** [nɔtamɑ̃] *adv* in particular, among others

**note** [nɔt] *nf (écrite, MUS)* note; *(SCOL)* mark *(BRIT)*, grade; *(facture)* bill; **~ de service** memorandum

**noté, e** [nɔte] *adj:* **être bien/mal ~** *(employé etc)* to have a good/bad record

**noter** [nɔte] *vt (écrire)* to write down; *(remarquer)* to note, notice; *(devoir)* to mark, grade

**notice** [nɔtis] *nf* summary, short article; *(brochure)* leaflet, instruction book

**notifier** [nɔtifje] *vt:* **~ qch à qn** to notify sb of sth, notify sth to sb

**notion** [nɔsjɔ̃] *nf* notion, idea

**notoire** [nɔtwaʀ] *adj* widely known; *(en mal)* notorious

**notre** [nɔtʀ] *(pl nos) adj* our

**nôtre** [notʀ] *pron:* **le ~, la ~, les ~s** ours ♦ *adj* ours; **les ~s** our own people; **soyez des ~s** join us

**nouer** [nwe] *vt* to tie, knot; *(fig: alliance etc)* to strike up

**noueux, -euse** [nwø, øz] *adj* gnarled

**nouilles** [nuj] *nfpl* noodles

**nourrice** [nuʀis] *nf (gardienne)* childminder

**nourrir** [nuʀiʀ] *vt* to feed; *(fig: espoir)* to harbour, nurse; **se ~** to eat; **se ~ de** to feed (o.s.) on; **nourrissant, e** *adj* nourishing, nutritious; **nourrisson** *nm* (unweaned) infant; **nourriture** *nf* food

**nous** [nu] *pron* (*sujet*) we; (*objet*) us; **nous-mêmes** *pron* ourselves

**nouveau** (**nouvel**), **-elle, x** [nuvo, nuvɛl] *adj* new ♦ *nm*: **y a-t-il de ~?** is there anything new on this? ♦ *nm/f* new pupil (*ou* employee); **de ~,** again; **~ venu, nouvelle venue** newcomer; **~x mariés** newly-weds; **nouveau-né, e** *nm/f* newborn baby; **nouveauté** *nf* novelty; (*objet*) new thing *ou* article

**nouvel** [nuvɛl] *adj voir* **nouveau; N~ An** New Year

**nouvelle** [nuvɛl] *adj voir* **nouveau** ♦ *nf* (*piece of*) news *sg*; (*LITTÉRATURE*) short story; **les ~s** the news; **je suis sans ~s de lui** I haven't heard from him; **Nouvelle-Calédonie** *nf* New Caledonia; **nouvellement** *adv* recently, newly; **Nouvelle-Zélande** *nf* New Zealand

**novembre** [nɔvãbʀ] *nm* November

**novice** [nɔvis] *adj* inexperienced

**noyade** [nwajad] *nf* drowning *no pl*

**noyau, x** [nwajo] *nm* (*de fruit*) stone; (*BIO, PHYSIQUE*) nucleus; (*fig: centre*) core; **noyauter** *vt* (*POL*) to infiltrate

**noyer** [nwaje] *nm* walnut (tree); (*bois*) walnut ♦ *vt* to drown; (*moteur*) to flood; **se ~** *vi* to be drowned, drown; (*suicide*) to drown o.s.

**nu, e** [ny] *adj* naked; (*membres*) naked, bare; (*pieds, mains, chambre, fil électrique*) bare ♦ *nm* (*ART*) nude; **tout ~** stark naked; **se mettre ~** to strip; **mettre à ~** to bare

**nuage** [nɥaʒ] *nm* cloud; **nuageux, -euse** *adj* cloudy

**nuance** [nɥãs] *nf* (*de couleur, sens*) shade; **il y a une ~ (entre)** there's a slight difference (between); **nuancer** *vt* (*opinion*) to bring some reservations *ou* qualifications to

**nucléaire** [nykleɛʀ] *adj* nuclear ♦ *nm*: **le ~** nuclear energy

**nudiste** [nydist] *nm/f* nudist

**nuée** [nɥe] *nf*: **une ~ de** a cloud *ou* host *ou* swarm of

**nues** [ny] *nfpl*: **tomber des ~** to be taken aback; **porter qn aux ~** to praise sb to the skies

**nuire** [nɥiʀ] *vi* to be harmful; **~ à** to harm, do damage to; **nuisible** *adj* harmful; **animal nuisible** pest

**nuit** [nɥi] *nf* night; **il fait ~** it's dark; **cette ~** (*hier*) last night; (*aujourd'hui*) tonight; **~ blanche** sleepless night

**nul, nulle** [nyl] *adj* (*aucun*) no; (*minime*) nil, non-existent; (*non valable*) null; (*péj*) useless, hopeless ♦ *pron* none, no one; **match** *ou* **résultat ~** draw; **~le part** nowhere; **nullement** *adv* by no means; **nullité** *nf* (*personne*) nonentity

**numérique** [nymeʀik] *adj* numerical; (*affichage*) digital

**numéro** [nymeʀo] *nm* number; (*spectacle*) act, turn; (*PRESSE*) issue, number; **~ de téléphone** (tele)phone number; **~ vert** freefone ® number (*BRIT*), ≈ toll-free number (*US*); **numéroter** *vt* to number

**nu-pieds** [nypje] *adj inv, adv* barefoot

**nuque** [nyk] *nf* nape of the neck

**nu-tête** [nytɛt] *adj inv, adv* bareheaded

**nutritif, -ive** [nytʀitif, iv] *adj* (*besoins, valeur*) nutritional; (*nourrissant*) nutritious

**nylon** [nilɔ̃] *nm* nylon

# O, o

**oasis** [ɔazis] *nf* oasis

**obéir** [ɔbeiʀ] *vi* to obey; **~ à** to obey; **obéissance** *nf* obedience; **obéissant, e** *adj* obedient

**obèse** [ɔbɛz] *adj* obese; **obésité** *nf* obesity

**objecter** [ɔbʒɛkte] *vt* (*prétexter*) to plead, put forward as an excuse; **objec- teur** *nm*: **objecteur de conscience** conscientious objector

**objectif, -ive** [ɔbʒɛktif, iv] *adj* objective ♦ *nm* objective; (*PHOTO*) lens *sg*, objective; **objectivité** nf objectivity

**objection** [ɔbʒɛksjɔ̃] nf objection

**objet** [ɔbʒɛ] nm object; (d'une discussion, recherche) subject; **être le l'~ de** (discussion) to be the subject of; (soins) to be given ou shown; **sans ~** purposeless; groundless; **~ d'art** objet d'art; **~s trouvés** lost property sg (BRIT), lost-and-found sg (US); **~s de valeur** valuables

**obligation** [ɔbligasjɔ̃] nf obligation; (COMM) bond, debenture; **obligatoire** adj compulsory, obligatory; **obligatoirement** adv necessarily; (fam: sans aucun doute) inevitably

**obligé, e** [ɔbliʒe] adj (redevable): **être très ~ à qn** to be most obliged to sb

**obligeance** [ɔbliʒɑ̃s] nf: **avoir l'~ de ... to** be kind ou good enough to ...; **obligeant, e** adj (personne) obliging, kind

**obliger** [ɔbliʒe] vt (contraindre): **~ qn à faire** to force ou oblige sb to do; **je suis bien obligé** I have to

**oblique** [ɔblik] adj oblique; **en ~** diagonally; **obliquer** vi: **obliquer vers** to turn off towards

**oblitérer** [ɔblitere] vt (timbre-poste) to cancel

**obnubiler** [ɔbnybile] vt to obsess

**obscène** [ɔpsɛn] adj obscene

**obscur, e** [ɔpskyr] adj dark; (méconnu) obscure; **obscurcir** vt to darken; (fig) to obscure; **s'obscurcir** vi to grow dark; **obscurité** nf darkness; **dans l'obscurité** in the dark, in darkness

**obsédé, e** [ɔpsede] nm/f: **un ~** (sexuel) a sex maniac

**obséder** [ɔpsede] vt to obsess, haunt

**obsèques** [ɔpsɛk] nfpl funeral sg

**observateur, -trice** [ɔpsɛrvatœr, tris] adj observant, perceptive ♦ nm/f observer

**observation** [ɔpsɛrvasjɔ̃] nf observation; (d'un règlement etc) observance; (reproche) reproof; **être en ~** (MÉD) to be under observation

**observatoire** [ɔpsɛrvatwar] nm observatory

**observer** [ɔpsɛrve] vt (regarder) to observe, watch; (scientifiquement; aussi règlement etc) to observe; (surveiller) to watch; (remarquer) to observe, notice; **faire ~ qch à qn** (dire) to point out sth to sb

**obsession** [ɔpsesjɔ̃] nf obsession

**obstacle** [ɔpstakl] nm obstacle; (ÉQUITATION) jump, hurdle; **faire ~ à** (projet) to hinder, put obstacles in the path of

**obstiné, e** [ɔpstine] adj obstinate

**obstiner** [ɔpstine]: **s'~** vi to insist, dig one's heels in; **s'~ à faire** to persist (obstinately) in doing

**obstruer** [ɔpstrye] vt to block, obstruct

**obtenir** [ɔptanir] vt to obtain, get; (résultat) to achieve, obtain; **~ de pouvoir faire** to obtain permission to do

**obturateur** [ɔptyratœr, tris] nm (PHOTO) shutter

**obus** [ɔby] nm shell

**occasion** [ɔkazjɔ̃] nf (aubaine, possibilité) opportunity; (circonstance) occasion; (COMM: article non neuf) secondhand buy; (: acquisition avantageuse) bargain; **à plusieurs ~s** on several occasions; **à l'~** sometimes, on occasions; **d'~** secondhand; **occasionnel, le** adj (non régulier) occasional; **occasionnellement** adv occasionally, from time to time

**occasionner** [ɔkazjɔne] vt to cause

**occident** [ɔksidɑ̃] nm: **l'O~** the West; **occidental, e, -aux** adj western; (POL) Western ♦ nm/f Westerner

**occupation** [ɔkypasjɔ̃] nf occupation

**occupé, e** [ɔkype] adj (personne) busy; (place, sièges) taken; (toilettes) engaged; (ligne) engaged (BRIT), busy (US); (MIL, POL) occupied

**occuper** [ɔkype] vt to occupy; (poste) to hold; (être responsable de) to be in charge of; **s'~ de** (être responsable de: affaire) to take charge of; (se charger de: deal with; (: clients *etc*) to attend to; **s'~ (à qch)** to occupy o.s. *ou* keep o.s. busy (with sth)

**occurrence** [ɔkyʀɑ̃s] *nf*: **en l'~** in this case

**océan** [ɔseɑ̃] *nm* ocean

**octante** [ɔktɑ̃t] *adj* (*regional*) eighty

**octet** [ɔkte] *nm* byte

**octobre** [ɔktɔbʀ] *nm* October

**octroyer** [ɔktʀwaje]: **s'~** *vt* (*vacances etc*) to treat o.s.

**oculiste** [ɔkylist] *nm/f* eye specialist

**odeur** [ɔdœʀ] *nf* smell

**odieux, -euse** [ɔdjø, jøz] *adj* hateful

**odorant, e** [ɔdɔʀɑ̃, ɑ̃t] *adj* sweet-smelling, fragrant

**odorat** [ɔdɔʀa] *nm* (sense of) smell

**œil** [œj] (*pl* **yeux**) *nm* eye; **à l'œil** (*fam*) for free; **à l'œil nu** with the naked eye; **tenir qn à l'œil** to keep an eye *ou* a watch on sb; **avoir l'œil à** to keep an eye on; **fermer les yeux (sur)** (*fig*) to turn a blind eye (to); **voir qch d'un bon/mauvais œil** to look on sth favourably/unfavourably

**œillères** [œjɛʀ] *nfpl* blinkers (*BRIT*), blinders (*US*)

**œillet** [œje] *nm* (*BOT*) carnation

**œuf** [œf, *pl* ø] *nm* egg; **œuf à la coque/sur le plat/dur** boiled/fried/hard-boiled egg; **œuf de Pâques** Easter egg; **œufs brouillés** scrambled eggs

**œuvre** [œvʀ] *nf* (*tâche*) task, undertaking; (*livre, tableau etc*) work; (*ensemble de la production artistique*) works *pl* ♦ *nm* (*CONSTR*): **le gros œuvre** the shell; **œuvre (de bienfaisance)** charity; **mettre en œuvre** (*moyens*) to make use of; **œuvre d'art** work of art

**offense** [ɔfɑ̃s] *nf* insult; **offenser** *vt* to offend, hurt

**offert, e** [ɔfɛʀ, ɛʀt] *pp de* **offrir**

**office** [ɔfis] *nm* (*agence*) bureau, agency; (*REL*) service ♦ *nm ou nf* (*pièce*) pantry; **faire ~ de** to act as; **d'~** automatically; **~ du tourisme** tourist bureau

**officiel, le** [ɔfisjɛl] *adj/nm/f* official

**officier** [ɔfisje] *nm* officer

**officieux, -euse** [ɔfisjø, jøz] *adj* unofficial

**offrande** [ɔfʀɑ̃d] *nf* offering

**offre** [ɔfʀ] *nf* offer; (*aux enchères*) bid; (*ADMIN: soumission*) tender; (*ÉCON*): **l'~ et la demande** supply and demand; **"~s d'emploi"** "situations vacant"; **~ d'emploi** job advertised

**offrir** [ɔfʀiʀ] *vt*: **~ (à qn)** to offer (to sb); (*faire cadeau de*) to give (to sb) **s'~** *vt* (*vacances, voiture*) to treat o.s. to; **~ (à qn) de faire qch** to offer to do sth (for sb); **~ à boire à qn** (*chez soi*) to offer sb a drink

**offusquer** [ɔfyske] *vt* to offend

**OGM** *sigle m* (= *organisme génétiquement modifié*) GMO

**oie** [wa] *nf* (*ZOOL*) goose

**oignon** [ɔɲɔ̃] *nm* onion; (*de tulipe etc*) bulb

**oiseau, x** [wazo] *nm* bird; **~ de proie** bird of prey

**oisif, -ive** [wazif, iv] *adj* idle

**oléoduc** [ɔleɔdyk] *nm* (oil) pipeline

**olive** [ɔliv] *nf* (*BOT*) olive; **olivier** *nm* olive (tree)

**OLP** *sigle f* (= *Organisation de libération de la Palestine*) PLO

**olympique** [ɔlɛ̃pik] *adj* Olympic

**ombragé, e** [ɔ̃bʀaʒe] *adj* shaded, shady; **ombrageux, -euse** *adj* (*personne*) touchy, easily offended

**ombre** [ɔ̃bʀ] *nf* (*espace non ensoleillé*) shade; (*~ portée, tache*) shadow; **à l'~** in the shade; **dans l'~** (*fig*) in the dark; **~ à paupières** eyeshadow; **ombrelle** *nf* parasol, sunshade

**omelette** [ɔmlɛt] *nf* omelette; **~ norvégienne** baked Alaska

**omettre** [ɔmɛtʀ] *vt* to omit, leave out

**omnibus** [ɔmnibys] *nm* slow *ou* stopping train

**omoplate** [ɔmɔplat] *nf* shoulder blade

── **MOT-CLÉ** ──────

**on** [ɔ̃] *pron* **1** (*indéterminé*) you, one; **on peut le faire ainsi** you *ou* one can do

it like this, it can be done like this
**2** (quelqu'un): **on les a attaqués** they were attacked; **on vous demande au téléphone** there's a phone call for you, you're wanted on the phone
**3** (nous) we: **on va y aller demain** we're going tomorrow
**4** (les gens) they; **autrefois, on croyait ...** they used to believe ...
**5: on ne peut plus**
♦ adv: **on ne peut plus stupide** as stupid as can be

**oncle** [5kl] nm uncle

**onctueux, -euse** [5ktɥø, øz] adj creamy, smooth

**onde** [5d] nf wave; **sur les ~s** on the radio; **sur ~s courtes** on short wave sg; **moyennes/longues ~s** medium/long wave sg

**ondée** [5de] nf shower

**on-dit** [5di] nm inv rumour

**onduler** [5dyle] vi to undulate; (cheveux) to wave

**onéreux, -euse** [ɔnerø, øz] adj costly

**ongle** [5gl] nm nail

**ont** [5] vb voir **avoir**

**ONU** sigle f (= Organisation des Nations Unies) UN

**onze** ['5z] num eleven; **onzième** num eleventh

**OPA** sigle f = offre publique d'achat

**opaque** [ɔpak] adj opaque

**opéra** [ɔpera] nm opera; opera house

**opérateur, -trice** [ɔperatœr, tris] nm/f operator; **~ (de prise de vues)** cameraman

**opération** [ɔperasjɔ] nf operation; (COMM) dealing

**opératoire** [ɔperatwar] adj (choc etc) post-operative

**opérer** [ɔpere] vt (personne) to operate on; (faire, exécuter) to carry out, make ♦ vi (remède: faire effet) to act, work; (MÉD) to operate; s'~ vi (avoir lieu) to occur, take place; **se faire ~** to have

an operation

**opérette** [ɔperet] nf operetta, light opera

**ophtalmologiste** [ɔftalmɔlɔʒist] nm/f ophthalmologist, optician

**opiner** [ɔpine] vi: **~ de la tête** to nod assent

**opinion** [ɔpinjɔ] nf opinion; **l'~ (publique)** public opinion

**opportun, e** [ɔpɔrtɶ, yn] adj timely, opportune; **opportuniste** nm/f opportunist

**opposant, e** [ɔpozɑ, ɑt] nm/f opponent

**opposé, e** [ɔpoze] adj (direction) opposite; (faction) opposing; (opinions, intérêts) conflicting; (contre): **~ à** opposed to, against ♦ nm: **l'~** the other ou opposite side (ou direction); (contraire) the opposite; **à l'~** (fig) on the other hand; **à l'~ de** (fig) contrary to, unlike

**opposer** [ɔpoze] vt (personnes, équipes) to oppose; (couleurs) to contrast; **s'~** vi (équipes) to confront each other; (opinions) to conflict; (couleurs, styles) to contrast; **s'~ à** (interdire) to oppose; **qch à** (comme obstacle, défense) to put sth against; (comme objection) to put sth forward against

**opposition** [ɔpozisjɔ] nf opposition; **par ~ à** as opposed to, **entrer en ~ avec** to come into conflict with; **faire ~ à un chèque** to stop a cheque

**oppressant, e** [ɔpresɑ, ɑt] adj oppressive

**oppresser** [ɔprese] vt to oppress; **oppression** nf oppression

**opprimer** [ɔprime] vt to oppress

**opter** [ɔpte] vi: **~ pour** to opt for

**opticien, ne** [ɔptisjɛ, jɛn] nm/f optician

**optimisme** [ɔptimism] nm optimism; **optimiste** nm/f optimist ♦ adj optimistic

**option** [ɔpsjɔ] nf option; **matière à ~** (SCOL) optional subject

**optique** [ɔptik] adj (nerf) optic; (verres) optical ♦ nf (fig: manière de voir) perspective

**opulent, e** [ɔpylɑ̃, ɑ̃t] *adj* wealthy, opulent; (*formes, poitrine*) ample, generous

**or** [ɔʀ] *nm* gold ♦ *conj* now, but; **en ~** (*objet*) gold *cpd*; **une affaire en ~** a real bargain; **il croyait gagner ~ il a perdu** he was sure he would win and yet he lost

**orage** [ɔʀaʒ] *nm* (thunder)storm; **orageux, -euse** *adj* stormy

**oral, e, -aux** [ɔʀal, o] *adj, nm* oral; **par voie ~e** (*MÉD*) orally

**orange** [ɔʀɑ̃ʒ] *nf* orange ♦ *adj inv* orange; **orangeade** *nf* orangeade; **orangé, e** *adj* orangey, orange-coloured; **oranger** *nm* orange tree

**orateur** [ɔʀatœʀ, tʀis] *nm* speaker

**orbite** [ɔʀbit] *nf* (*ANAT*) (eye-)socket; (*PHYSIQUE*) orbit

**orchestre** [ɔʀkɛstʀ] *nm* orchestra; (*de jazz*) band; (*places*) stalls *pl* (*BRIT*), orchestra (*US*); **orchestrer** *vt* to orchestrate

**orchidée** [ɔʀkide] *nf* orchid

**ordinaire** [ɔʀdinɛʀ] *adj* ordinary; (*qualité*) standard; (*péj: commun*) common ♦ *nm* ordinary; (*menus*) everyday fare ♦ *nf* (*essence*) ≈ two-star (petrol) (*BRIT*), ≈ regular gas (*US*); **d'~** usually, normally; **comme à l'~** as usual

**ordinateur** [ɔʀdinatœʀ] *nm* computer

**ordonnance** [ɔʀdɔnɑ̃s] *nf* (*MÉD*) prescription; (*MIL*) orderly, batman (*BRIT*)

**ordonné, e** [ɔʀdɔne] *adj* tidy, orderly

**ordonner** [ɔʀdɔne] *vt* (*agencer*) to organize, arrange; (*donner un ordre*): **~ à qn de faire** to order sb to do; (*REL*) to ordain; (*MÉD*) to prescribe

**ordre** [ɔʀdʀ] *nm* order; (*propreté et soin*) orderliness, tidiness; (*nature*): **d'~ pratique** of a practical nature; **~s** *nmpl* (*REL*) holy orders; **mettre en ~** to tidy (up), put in order; **à l'~ de qn** payable to sb; **être aux ~s de qn/sous les ~s de qn** to be at sb's disposal/under sb's command; **jusqu'à nouvel ~** until

further notice; **de premier ~** first-rate; **~ du jour** (*d'une réunion*) agenda; **à l'~ du jour** (*fig*) topical

**ordure** [ɔʀdyʀ] *nf* filth no pl; **~s** *nfpl* (*balayures, déchets*) rubbish *sg*, refuse *sg*; **~s ménagères** household refuse

**oreille** [ɔʀɛj] *nf* ear; **avoir de l'~** to have a good ear (for music)

**oreiller** [ɔʀeje] *nm* pillow

**oreillons** [ɔʀɛjɔ̃] *nmpl* mumps *sg*

**ores** [ɔʀ]: **d'~ et déjà** *adv* already

**orfèvrerie** [ɔʀfɛvʀəʀi] *nf* goldsmith's (*ou* silversmith's) trade; (*ouvrage*) gold (*ou* silver) plate

**organe** [ɔʀgan] *nm* organ; (*porte-parole*) representative, mouthpiece

**organigramme** [ɔʀganigʀam] *nm* (*tableau hiérarchique*) organization chart; (*schéma*) flow chart

**organique** [ɔʀganik] *adj* organic

**organisateur, -trice** [ɔʀganizatœʀ, tʀis] *nm/f* organizer

**organisation** [ɔʀganizasjɔ̃] *nf* organization

**organiser** [ɔʀganize] *vt* to organize; (*mettre sur pied: service etc*) to set up; **s'~** to get organized

**organisme** [ɔʀganism] *nm* (*BIO*) organism; (*corps, ADMIN*) body

**organiste** [ɔʀganist] *nm/f* organist

**orgasme** [ɔʀgasm] *nm* orgasm, climax

**orge** [ɔʀʒ] *nf* barley

**orgue** [ɔʀg] *nm* organ; **~s** *nfpl* (*MUS*) organ *sg*

**orgueil** [ɔʀgœj] *nm* pride; **orgueilleux, -euse** *adj* proud

**Orient** [ɔʀjɑ̃] *nm*: **l'~** the East, the Orient; **oriental, e, -aux** *adj* (*langue, produit*) oriental; (*frontière*) eastern

**orientation** [ɔʀjɑ̃tasjɔ̃] *nf* (*de recherches*) orientation; (*d'une maison etc*) aspect; (*d'un journal*) leanings *pl*; **avoir le sens de l'~** to have a (good) sense of direction; **~ professionnelle** careers advisory service

**orienté, e** [ɔʀjɑ̃te] *adj* (*fig: article, journal*) slanted; **bien/mal ~** (*apparte-*

ment) well/badly positioned; **~ au sud** facing south, with a southern aspect

**orienter** [ɔrjɑ̃te] *vt* (*tourner: antenne*) to direct, turn; (*personne, recherches*) to direct; (*fig: élève*) to orientate; **s'~** (*se repérer*) to find one's bearings; **s'~ vers** (*fig*) to turn towards

**origan** [ɔrigɑ̃] *nm* oregano

**originaire** [ɔriʒinɛr] *adj*: **être ~ de** to be a native of

**original, e, -aux** [ɔriʒinal, o] *adj* original; (*bizarre*) eccentric ♦ *nm/f* eccentric ♦ *nm* (*document etc, ART*) original

**origine** [ɔriʒin] *nf* origin; **dès l'~** from the outset; **à l'~** originally; **originel, le** *adj* original

**orme** [ɔrm] *nm* elm

**ornement** [ɔrnəmɑ̃] *nm* ornament

**orner** [ɔrne] *vt* to decorate, adorn

**ornière** [ɔrnjɛr] *nf* rut

**orphelin, e** [ɔrfəlɛ̃, in] *adj* orphan(ed) ♦ *nm/f* orphan; **~ de père/mère** fatherless/motherless; **orphelinat** [ɔrfəlina] *nm* orphanage

**orteil** [ɔrtɛj] *nm* toe; **gros ~** big toe

**orthographe** [ɔrtɔgraf] *nf* spelling

**ortie** [ɔrti] *nf* (stinging) nettle

**os** [ɔs] *nm* bone; **tomber sur un ~** (*fam*) to hit a snag

**osciller** [ɔsile] *vi* (*au vent etc*) to rock; (*fig*): **~ entre** to waver *ou* fluctuate between

**osé, e** [oze] *adj* daring, bold

**oseille** [ozɛj] *nf* sorrel

**oser** [oze] *vi, vt* to dare; **~ faire** to dare (to) do

**osier** [ozje] *nm* willow; **d'~, en ~** wicker(work)

**ossature** [ɔsatyr] *nf* (*ANAT*) frame, skeletal structure; (*fig*) framework

**osseux, -euse** [ɔsø, øz] *adj* bony; (*tissu, maladie, greffe*) bone *cpd*

**ostensible** [ɔstɑ̃sibl] *adj* conspicuous

**otage** [ɔtaʒ] *nm* hostage; **prendre qn comme ~** to take sb hostage

**OTAN** *sigle f* (= *Organisation du traité de l'Atlantique Nord*) NATO

**otarie** [ɔtari] *nf* sea-lion

**ôter** [ote] *vt* to remove; (*soustraire*) to take away; **~ qch à qn** to take sth (away) from sb; **~ qch de** to remove sth from

**otite** [ɔtit] *nf* ear infection

**ou** [u] *conj* or; **~ ... ~** either ... or; **~ bien** or (else)

---

MOT-CLÉ

**où** [u] *pron relatif* **1** (*position, situation*) where, that (*souvent omis*); **la chambre où il était** the room (that) he was in, the room where he was; **la ville où je l'ai rencontré** the town where I met him; **la pièce d'où il est sorti** the room he came out of; **le village d'où je viens** the village I come from; **les villes par où il est passé** the towns he went through

**2** (*temps, état*) that (*souvent omis*); **le jour où il est parti** the day (that) he left; **au prix où c'est** at the price it is

♦ *adv* **1** (*interrogation*) where; **où est-il/va-t-il?** where is he/is he going?; **par où?** which way?; **d'où vient que ...?** how come ...?

**2** (*position*) where; **je sais où il est** I know where he is; **où que l'on aille** wherever you go

---

**ouate** ['wat] *nf* cotton wool (*BRIT*), cotton (*US*)

**oubli** [ubli] *nm* (*acte*): **l'~ de** forgetting; (*trou de mémoire*) lapse of memory; (*négligence*) omission, oversight; **tomber dans l'~** to sink into oblivion

**oublier** [ublije] *vt* to forget; (*laisser quelque part: chapeau etc*) to leave behind; (*ne pas voir: erreurs etc*) to miss

**oubliettes** [ublijɛt] *nfpl* dungeon *sg*

**ouest** [wɛst] *nm* west ♦ *adj inv* west; (*région*) western; **à l'~** in the west; (*direction*) (to the) west, westwards; **à l'~ de** (to the) west of

**ouf** ['uf] *excl* phew!

**oui** ['wi] *adv* yes

**ouï-dire** [widir]: par ~~ adv by hear-say

**ouïe** [wi] nf hearing; ~s nfpl (de poisson) gills

**ouille** ['uj] excl ouch!

**ouragan** [uʀagã] nm hurricane

**ourlet** [uʀlɛ] nm hem

**ours** [uʀs] nm bear; ~ **brun/blanc** brown/polar bear; ~ **(en peluche)** teddy (bear)

**oursin** [uʀsɛ̃] nm sea urchin

**ourson** [uʀsɔ̃] nm (bear-)cub

**ouste** [ust] excl hop it!

**outil** [uti] nm tool; **outiller** vt to equip

**outrage** [utʀaʒ] nm insult; ~ **à la pudeur** indecent conduct no pl; **outrager** vt to offend gravely

**outrance** [utʀãs]: **à** ~ adv excessively, to excess

**outre** [utʀ] prép besides ♦ adv: **passer** ~ **à** to disregard, take no notice of; **en** ~ besides, moreover; ~ **mesure** to excess; (manger, boire) immoderately; **outre-Atlantique** adv across the Atlantic; **outre-Manche** adv across the Channel; **outre-mer** adv overseas; **outrepasser** vt to go beyond, exceed

**ouvert, e** [uvɛʀ, ɛʀt] pp de **ouvrir** ♦ adj open; (robinet, gaz etc) on; **ouvertement** adv openly; **ouverture** nf opening; (MUS) overture; **ouverture d'esprit** open-mindedness

**ouvrable** [uvʀabl] adj: **jour** ~ working day, weekday

**ouvrage** [uvʀaʒ] nm (tâche, de tricot etc) work; (objet: COUTURE, ART) piece of work; (livre) work; **ouvragé, e** adj finely embroidered (ou worked ou carved)

**ouvre-boîte(s)** [uvʀəbwat] nm inv tin (BRIT) ou can opener

**ouvre-bouteille(s)** [uvʀəbutɛj] nm inv bottle-opener

**ouvreuse** [uvʀøz] nf usherette

**ouvrier, -ière** [uvʀije, ijɛʀ] nm/f worker ♦ adj working-class; (conflit) industrial; (mouvement) labour cpd; **classe ouvrière** working class

**ouvrir** [uvʀiʀ] vt (gén) to open; (brèche, passage, MÉD: abcès) to open; (commencer l'exploitation de, créer) to open (up); (eau, électricité, chauffage, robinet) to turn on ♦ vi to open; to open up; **s'~** vi to open; **s'~ à qn** to open one's heart to sb; ~ **l'appétit à qn** to whet sb's appetite

**ovaire** [ɔvɛʀ] nm ovary

**ovale** [ɔval] adj oval

**ovni** [ɔvni] sigle m (= objet volant non identifié) UFO

**oxyder** [ɔkside]: **s'~** vi to become oxidized

**oxygène** [ɔksiʒɛn] nm oxygen

**oxygéné, e** [ɔksiʒene] adj: **eau ~e** hydrogen peroxide

**oxygéner** [ɔksiʒene]: **s'~** (fam) vi to get some fresh air

**ozone** [ozon] nf ozone; **la couche d'~** the ozone layer

# P, p

**pacifique** [pasifik] adj peaceful ♦ nm: **le P~**, **l'océan P~** the Pacific (Ocean)

**pacotille** [pakɔtij] nf cheap junk

**pack** [pak] nm pack

**pacte** [pakt] nm pact, treaty

**pagaie** [pagɛ] nf paddle

**pagaille** [pagaj] nf mess, shambles sg

**pagayer** vi to paddle

**page** [paʒ] nf page ♦ nm page (boy); **à la** ~ (fig) up-to-date; ~ **d'accueil** (INFORM) home page

**paiement** [pemã] nm payment

**païen, ne** [pajɛ̃, pajɛn] adj, nm/f pagan, heathen

**paillasson** [pajasɔ̃] nm doormat

**paille** [paj] nf straw

**paillettes** [pajɛt] nfpl (décoratives) sequins, spangles

**pain** [pɛ̃] nm (substance) bread; (unité) loaf (of bread); (morceau): ~ de savon etc bar of soap; ~ **au chocolat** chocolate-filled pastry; ~ **aux raisins**

currant bun; **~ bis/complet** brown/
wholemeal (BRIT) ou wholewheat (US)
bread; **~ d'épice** gingerbread; **~ de
mie** sandwich loaf; **~ grillé** toast

**pair, e** [pɛʀ] adj (nombre) even ♦ nm
peer; **aller de ~** to go hand in hand
ou together; **jeune fille au ~** au pair;
**paire** nf pair

**paisible** [pezibl] adj peaceful, quiet

**paître** [pɛtʀ] vi to graze

**paix** [pɛ] nf peace; **faire/avoir la ~** to
make/have peace; **fiche-lui la ~!** (fam)
leave him alone!

**Pakistan** [pakistɑ̃] nm: **le ~** Pakistan

**palace** [palas] nm luxury hotel

**palais** [palɛ] nm palace; (ANAT) palate

**pâle** [pɑl] adj pale; **bleu ~** pale blue

**Palestine** [palɛstin] nf: **la ~** Palestine

**palet** [palɛ] nm disc; (HOCKEY) puck

**paletot** [palto] nm (thick) cardigan

**palette** [palɛt] nf (de peintre) palette;
(produits) range

**pâleur** [pɑlœʀ] nf paleness

**palier** [palje] nm (d'escalier) landing;
(fig) level, plateau; **par ~s** in stages

**pâlir** [palɪʀ] vi to turn ou go pale; (couleur) to fade

**palissade** [palisad] nf fence

**pallier** [palje]: **~ à** vt to offset, make
up for

**palmarès** [palmaʀɛs] nm record (of
achievements); (SPORT) list of winners

**palme** [palm] nf (de plongeur) flipper;
**palmé, e** adj (pattes) webbed

**palmier** [palmje] nm palm tree;
(gâteau) heart-shaped biscuit made of flaky
pastry

**pâlot, te** [palo, ɔt] adj pale, peaky

**palourde** [paluʀd] nf clam

**palper** [palpe] vt to feel, finger

**palpitant, e** [palpitɑ̃, ɑ̃t] adj thrilling

**palpiter** [palpite] vi (cœur, pouls) to
beat; (+ plus fort) to pound, throb

**paludisme** [palydism] nm malaria

**pamphlet** [pɑ̃flɛ] nm lampoon, satirical
tract

**pamplemousse** [pɑ̃pləmus] nm grape-

fruit

**pan** [pɑ̃] nm section, piece ♦ excl bang!

**panache** [panaʃ] nm plume; (fig) spirit,
panache

**panaché, e** [panaʃe] adj: **glace ~e**
mixed-flavour ice cream ♦ nm (bière)
shandy

**pancarte** [pɑ̃kaʀt] nf sign, notice

**pancréas** [pɑ̃kʀeas] nm pancreas

**pané, e** [pane] adj fried in breadcrumbs

**panier** [panje] nm basket; **mettre au ~**
to chuck away; **~ à provisions** shopping basket; **panier-repas** nm packed
lunch

**panique** [panik] nf, adj panic; **paniquer** vi to panic

**panne** [pan] nf breakdown; **être/
tomber en ~** to have broken down/
break down; **être en ~ d'essence** ou
**sèche** to have run out of petrol (BRIT)
ou gas (US); **~ d'électricité** ou **de courant** power ou electrical failure

**panneau, x** [pano] nm (écriteau) sign,
notice; **~ d'affichage** notice board; **~
de signalisation** roadsign

**panoplie** [panɔpli] nf (jouet) outfit;
(fig) array

**panorama** [panɔʀama] nm panorama

**panse** [pɑ̃s] nf paunch

**pansement** [pɑ̃smɑ̃] nm dressing,
bandage; **~ adhésif** sticking plaster

**panser** [pɑ̃se] vt (plaie) to dress, bandage; (bras) to put a dressing on, bandage; (cheval) to groom

**pantalon** [pɑ̃talɔ̃] nm trousers pl, pair
of trousers; **~ de ski** ski pants pl

**panthère** [pɑ̃tɛʀ] nf panther

**pantin** [pɑ̃tɛ̃] nm puppet

**pantois** [pɑ̃twa] adj m: **rester ~** to be
flabbergasted

**pantoufle** [pɑ̃tufl] nf slipper

**paon** [pɑ̃] nm peacock

**papa** [papa] nm dad(dy)

**pape** [pap] nm pope

**paperasse** [papʀas] (péj) nf bumf no pl,
papers pl; **paperasserie** (péj) nf paper-
work no pl; (tracasserie) red tape no pl

**papeterie** [papetʀi] nf (magasin) stationer's (shop)

**papi** nm (fam) granddad

**papier** [papje] nm paper; (article) article; **~s** nmpl (aussi: **~s d'identité**) (identity) papers; **~ à lettres** writing paper, notepaper; **~ carbone** carbon paper; **~ (d')aluminium** aluminium (BRIT) ou aluminum (US) foil, tinfoil; **~ de verre** sandpaper; **~ hygiénique** ou **de toilette** toilet paper; **~ journal** newspaper; **~ peint** wallpaper

**papillon** [papijɔ̃] nm butterfly; (fam: contravention) (parking) ticket; **~ de nuit** moth

**papillote** [papijɔt] nf: **en ~** cooked in tinfoil

**papoter** [papɔte] vi to chatter

**paquebot** [pak(ə)bo] nm liner

**pâquerette** [pakʀɛt] nf daisy

**Pâques** [pak] nm, nfpl Easter

**paquet** [pake] nm packet; (colis) parcel; (fig: tas): **~ de** pile ou heap of; **paquet-cadeau** nm: **faites-moi un paquet-cadeau** gift-wrap it for me

**par** [paʀ] prép by; **finir** etc **~ to end** etc with; **~ amour** out of love; **passer ~ Lyon/la côte** to go via ou through Lyons/along by the coast; **~ la fenêtre** (jeter, regarder) out of the window; **3 ~ jour/personne** 3 a ou per day/head; **2 ~ 2** in twos; **~ ici** this way; (dans le coin) round here; **~-ci, ~-là** here and there; **~ temps de pluie** in wet weather

**parabolique** [paʀabɔlik] adj: **antenne ~** parabolic ou dish aerial

**parachever** [paʀaʃ(ə)ve] vt to perfect

**parachute** [paʀaʃyt] nm parachute; **parachutiste** nm/f parachutist; (MIL) paratrooper

**parade** [paʀad] nf (spectacle, défilé) parade; (ESCRIME, BOXE) parry

**paradis** [paʀadi] nm heaven, paradise

**paradoxe** [paʀadɔks] nm paradox

**paraffine** [paʀafin] nf paraffin

**parages** [paʀaʒ] nmpl: **dans les ~ (de)** in the area ou vicinity (of)

**paragraphe** [paʀagʀaf] nm paragraph

**paraître** [paʀɛtʀ] vb +attrib to seem, look, appear ♦ vi to appear; (être visible) to show; (PRESSE, ÉDITION) to be published, come out, appear ♦ vb impers: **il paraît que** it seems ou appears that, they say that; **chercher à ~** to show off

**parallèle** [paʀalɛl] adj parallel; (non officiel) unofficial ♦ nm (comparaison): **faire un ~ entre** to draw a parallel between ♦ nf parallel (line)

**paralyser** [paʀalize] vt to paralyse

**paramédical, e, -aux** [paʀamedikal, o] adj: **personnel ~** paramedics pl, paramedical workers pl

**paraphrase** [paʀafʀaz] nf paraphrase

**parapluie** [paʀaplɥi] nm umbrella

**parasite** [paʀazit] nm parasite; **~s** nmpl (TÉL) interference sg

**parasol** [paʀasɔl] nm parasol, sunshade

**paratonnerre** [paʀatɔnɛʀ] nm lightning conductor

**paravent** [paʀavɑ̃] nm folding screen

**parc** [paʀk] nm (public) park, gardens pl; (de château etc) grounds pl; (d'enfant) playpen; (ensemble d'unités) stock; (de voitures etc) fleet; **~ d'attractions** theme park; **~ de stationnement** car park

**parcelle** [paʀsɛl] nf fragment, scrap; (de terrain) plot, parcel

**parce que** [paʀs(ə)] conj because

**parchemin** [paʀʃəmɛ̃] nm parchment

**parcmètre** [paʀkmɛtʀ] nm parking meter

**parcourir** [paʀkuʀiʀ] vt (trajet, distance) to cover; (article, livre) to skim ou glance through; (lieu) to go all over, travel up and down; (suj: frisson) to run through

**parcours** [paʀkuʀ] nm (trajet) journey; (itinéraire) route

**par-derrière** [paʀdɛʀjɛʀ] adv round the back; **dire du mal de qn ~~** to speak ill of sb behind his back

**par-dessous** [pard(ə)su] *prép, adv* under(neath)

**pardessus** [pardəsy] *nm* overcoat

**par-dessus** [pard(ə)sy] *prép* over (the top of) ♦ *adv* over (the top); **le ~ marché** over and above all that; ~ **tout** above all; **en avoir ~~ la tête** to have had enough

**par-devant** [pard(ə)vã] *adv* (*passer*) round the front

**pardon** [pardɔ̃] *nm* forgiveness *no pl* ♦ *excl* sorry!; (*pour interpeller etc*) excuse me!; **demander ~ à qn (de)** to apologize to sb (for); **je vous demande ~** I'm sorry; (*pour interpeller*) excuse me!

**pardonner** *vt* to forgive; **pardonner qch à qn** to forgive sb for sth

**pare...: pare-balles** *adj inv* bulletproof; **pare-brise** *nm inv* windscreen (BRIT), windshield (US); **pare-chocs** *nm inv* bumper

**paré, e** [pare] *adj* ready, all set

**pareil, le** [parej] *adj* (*identique*) the same, alike; (*similaire*) similar; (*tel*): **un courage/livre ~** such courage/a book, courage/a book like this; **de ~s livres** such books; **ne pas avoir son(sa) ~(le)** to be second to none; **à la même as**; (*similaire*) similar to; **sans ~** unparalleled, unequalled

**parent, e** [parã, ãt] *nm/f*: **un(e) ~(e)** a relative *ou* relation; **~s** *nmpl* (*père et mère*) parents; **parenté** *nf* (*lien*) relationship

**parenthèse** [parãtɛz] *nf* (*ponctuation*) bracket, parenthesis; (*digression*) parenthesis, digression; **entre ~s** in brackets; (*fig*) incidentally

**parer** [pare] *vt* to adorn; (*éviter*) to ward off; ~ **au plus pressé** to attend to the most urgent things first

**paresse** [parɛs] *nf* laziness; **paresseux, -euse** *adj* lazy

**parfaire** [parfɛr] *vt* to perfect

**parfait, e** [parfɛ, ɛt] *adj* perfect ♦ *nm* (LING) perfect (tense); **parfaitement** *adv* perfectly ♦ *excl* (most) certainly

**parfois** [parfwa] *adv* sometimes

**parfum** [parfɛ̃] *nm* (*produit*) perfume, scent; (*odeur: de fleur*) scent, fragrance; (*goût*) flavour; **parfumé, e** *adj* (*fleur, fruit*) fragrant; (*femme*) perfumed; **parfumé au café** coffee-flavoured; **parfumer** *vt* (*suj: odeur, bouquet*) to perfume; (*crème, gâteau*) to flavour; **parfumerie** *nf* (*produits*) perfumes *pl*; (*boutique*) perfume shop

**pari** [pari] *nm* bet; **parier** *vt* to bet

**Paris** [pari] *n* Paris; **parisien, ne** *adj* Parisian; (GÉO, ADMIN) Paris *cpd* ♦ *nm/f*: **Parisien, ne** Parisian

**parjure** [parʒyr] *nm* perjury

**parking** [parkiŋ] *nm* (*lieu*) car park

**parlant, e** [parlã, ãt] *adj* (*regard*) eloquent; (CINÉMA) talking; **les chiffres sont ~s** the figures speak for themselves

**parlement** [parləmã] *nm* parliament; **parlementaire** *adj* parliamentary ♦ *nm/f* member of parliament; **parlementer** *vi* to negotiate, parley

**parler** [parle] *vi* to speak, talk; (*avouer*) to talk; ~ **(à qn) de** to talk *ou* speak (to sb) about; ~ **le/en français** to speak French/in French; ~ **affaires** to talk business; **sans ~ de** (*fig*) not to mention, to say nothing of; **tu parles!** (*fam: bien sûr*) you bet!

**parloir** [parlwar] *nm* (*de prison, d'hôpital*) visiting room

**parmi** [parmi] *prép* among(st)

**paroi** [parwa] *nf* wall; (*cloison*) partition; ~ **rocheuse** rock face

**paroisse** [parwas] *nf* parish

**parole** [parɔl] *nf* (*faculté*): **la ~** speech; (*mot, promesse*) word; **~s** *nfpl* (MUS) words, lyrics; **tenir ~** to keep one's word; **prendre la ~** to speak; **demander la ~** to ask for permission to speak; **je te crois sur ~** I'll take your word for it

**parquer** [parke] *vt* (*voiture, matériel*) to park; (*bestiaux*) to pen (in *ou* up)

**parquet** [parke] *nm* (*parquet*) floor;

**parrain** *(JUR):* **le** ~ the Public Prosecutor's department

**parrain** [paʀɛ̃] *nm* godfather; **parrainer** *vt (suj: entreprise)* to sponsor

**pars** [paʀ] *vb voir* **partir**

**parsemer** [paʀsəme] *vt (suj: feuilles, papiers)* to be scattered over; ~ **qch de** to scatter sth with

**part** [paʀ] *nf (gén) part (course, réunion)* share; *(fraction, ~ie)* part; **prendre ~ à** *(débat etc)* to take part in; *(soucis, douleur de qn)* to share in; **faire ~ de qch à qn** to announce sth to sb, inform sb of sth; **pour ma ~** as for me, as far as I'm concerned; **à ~ entière** full; **de la ~ de** *(au nom de)* on behalf of; *(donné par)* from; **de toute(s) ~(s)** from all sides ou quarters; **de ~ et d'autre** on both sides, on either side; **d'une ~ ... d'autre ~** on the one hand ... on the other hand; **d'autre ~** *(de plus)* moreover; **à ~** ♦ *adv (séparément)* separately; *(de côté)* aside ♦ *prép* apart from, except for; **faire la ~ des choses** to make allowances

**partage** [paʀtaʒ] *nm (fractionnement)* dividing up; *(répartition)* sharing out *no pl,* share-out

**partager** [paʀtaʒe] *vt* to share; *(distribuer, répartir)* to share (out); *(morceler, diviser)* to divide (up); **se ~** *vt (héritage etc)* to share between themselves *(ou* ourselves*)*

**partance** [paʀtɑ̃s]: **en ~** *adv:* **en ~ pour** (bound) for

**partenaire** [paʀtɑneʀ] *nm/f* partner

**parterre** [paʀtɛʀ] *nm (de fleurs)* (flowered) bed; *(THÉÂTRE)* stalls *pl*

**parti** [paʀti] *nm (POL)* party; *(décision)* course of action; *(personne à marier)* match; **tirer ~ de** to take advantage of, turn to good account; **prendre ~ (pour/contre)** to take sides *ou* a stand (for/against); ~ **pris** bias

**partial, e, -aux** [paʀsjal, jo] *adj* biased, partial

**participant, e** [paʀtisipɑ̃, ɑ̃t] *nm/f* participant; *(à un concours)* entrant

**participation** [paʀtisipasjɔ̃] *nf* participation; *(financière)* contribution

**participer** [paʀtisipe]: ~ **à** *vt (course, réunion)* to take part in; *(frais etc)* to contribute to; *(chagrin, succès de qn)* to share (in)

**particularité** [paʀtikylaʀite] *nf* (distinctive) characteristic

**particulier, -ière** [paʀtikylje, jɛʀ] *adj (spécifique)* particular; *(spécial)* special, particular; *(personnel, privé)* private; *(étrange)* peculiar, odd ♦ *nm (individu: ADMIN)* private individual; ~ **à** peculiar to; **en** ~ *(surtout)* in particular, particularly; *(en privé)* in private; **particulièrement** *adv* particularly

**partie** [paʀti] *nf (gén)* part; *(JUR etc: protagonistes)* party; *(de cartes, tennis etc)* game; **une ~ de pêche** a fishing party *ou* trip; **en ~** partly, in part; **faire ~ de** *(suj: chose)* to be part of; **prendre qn à ~** to take sb to task; **en grande ~** largely, in the main; ~ **civile** *(JUR)* party claiming damages in a criminal case

**partiel, le** [paʀsjɛl] *adj* partial ♦ *nm (SCOL)* class exam

**partir** [paʀtiʀ] *vi (gén)* to go; *(quitter)* to go, leave; *(tache)* to go, come out; ~ **de** *(lieu: quitter)* to leave; *(: commencer à)* to start from; **à ~ de** from

**partisan, e** [paʀtizɑ̃, an] *nm/f* partisan ♦ *adj:* **être ~ de qch/de faire** to be in favour of sth/doing

**partition** [paʀtisjɔ̃] *nf (MUS)* score

**partout** [paʀtu] *adv* everywhere; ~ **où** **il allait** everywhere *ou* wherever he went

**paru** [paʀy] *pp de* **paraître**

**parure** [paʀyʀ] *nf (bijoux etc)* finery *no pl;* jewellery *no pl; (assortiment)* set

**parution** [paʀysjɔ̃] *nf* publication

**parvenir** [paʀvəniʀ]: ~ **à** *vt (atteindre)* to reach; *(réussir)* to succeed; ~ **à faire** to manage to do, succeed in doing; ~ **à ses fins** to achieve one's ends

**pas¹** [pa] *nm (enjambée, DANSE)* step;

(allure, mesure) pace; (bruit) (foot)step; (trace) footprint; **~ à ~** step by step; **au ~** at walking pace; **faire les cent ~** to pace up and down; **faire les premiers ~** to make the first move; **sur le ~ de la porte** on the doorstep

---
MOT-CLÉ
---

**pas²** [pɑ] adv 1 (en corrélation avec ne, non etc) not; **il ne pleure pas** he does not ou doesn't cry; he's not ou isn't crying; **il n'a pas pleuré/ne pleurera pas** he did not ou didn't/will not ou won't cry; **ils n'ont pas de voiture/ d'enfants** they haven't got a car/any children, they have no car/children; **il m'a dit de ne pas le faire** he told me not to do it; **non pas que ... not that ...**

2 (employé sans ne etc): **pas moi** not me; not I, I don't (ou can't etc); **une pomme pas mûre** an apple which isn't ripe; **pas plus tard qu'hier** only yesterday; **pas du tout** not at all 3: **pas mal** not bad; not badly; **pas mal de** quite a lot of

---

**passage** [pɑsaʒ] nm (fait de passer) voir passer; (lieu, prix de la traversée, extrait) passage; (chemin) way; **de ~** (touristes) passing through; **~ à niveau** level crossing; **~ clouté** pedestrian crossing; **"~ interdit"** "no entry"; **~ souterrain** subway (BRIT); **~ clandestin** stowaway

**passager, -ère** [pɑsaʒe, ɛʀ] adj passing ♦ nm/f passenger; **~ clandestin** stowaway

**passant, e** [pɑsɑ̃, ɑ̃t] adj (rue, endroit) busy ♦ nm/f passer-by; **en ~** in passing

**passe¹** [pɑs] nf (SPORT, NAVIG) pass; **être en ~ de faire** to be on the way to doing; **être dans une mauvaise ~** to be going through a rough patch

**passe²** [pɑs] nm (~-partout) master ou skeleton key

**passé, e** [pɑse] adj (révolu) past; (dernier: semaine etc) last; (couleur) faded ♦

prép after ♦ nm past; (LING) past (tense); **~ de mode** out of fashion; **~ composé** perfect (tense); **~ simple** past historic

**passe-partout** [pɑspaʀtu] nm inv master ou skeleton key ♦ adj inv all-purpose

**passeport** [pɑspɔʀ] nm passport

**passer** [pɑse] vi (aller) to go; (voiture, piétons: défiler) to pass (by), go by; (facteur, laitier etc) to come, call; (pour rendre visite) to call ou drop in; (film, émission) to be on; (temps, jours) to pass, go by; (couleur) to fade; (mode) to die out; (douleur) to pass, go away; (SCOL) to go up (to the next class) ♦ vt (frontière, rivière etc) to cross; (douane) to go through; (examen) to sit, take; (visite médicale etc) to have; (journée, temps) to spend; (enfiler: vêtement) to slip on; (film, pièce) to show, put on; (disque) to play, put on; (marché, accord) to agree on; **se ~** vi (avoir lieu: scène, action) to take place; (se dérouler: entretien etc) to go; (s'écouler: semaine etc) to pass, go by; (arriver): **que s'est-il passé?** what happened?; **~ qch à qn** (sel etc) to pass sth to sb; (prêter) to lend sth to sb; (lettre, message) to pass sth on to sb; (tolérer) to let sb get away with sth; **~ par** to go through; **~ avant qch/qn** (fig) to come before sth/sb; **~ un coup de fil à qn** (fam) to give sb a ring; **laisser ~** (air, lumière, personne) to let through; (occasion) to let slip, miss; (erreur) to overlook; **~ la seconde** (AUTO) to change into second; **~ le balai/l'aspirateur** to sweep up/hoover; **je vous passe M. X** (je vous mets en communication avec M. X) I'm putting you through to Mr X; (je lui passe l'appareil) here is Mr X, I'll hand you over to Mr X; **se ~ de** to go ou do without

**passerelle** [pɑsʀɛl] nf footbridge; (de navire, avion) gangway

**passe-temps** [pɑstɑ̃] nm inv pastime

**passible** [pɑsibl] adj: **~ de** liable to

**passif, -ive** [pɑsif, iv] adj passive

**passion** [pasjɔ̃] *nf* passion; **passionnant, e** *adj* fascinating; **passionné, e** *adj* (*personne*) passionate; (*récit*) impassioned; **être passionné de** to have a passion for; **passionner** *vt* (*personne*) to fascinate, grip; **se passionner pour** (*sport*) to have a passion for

**passoire** [paswaʀ] *nf* sieve; (*à légumes*) colander; (*à thé*) strainer

**pastèque** [pastɛk] *nf* watermelon

**pasteur** [pastœʀ] *nm* (*protestant*) minister, pastor

**pasteurisé, e** [pastœrize] *adj* pasteurized

**pastille** [pastij] *nf* (*à sucer*) lozenge, pastille

**patate** [patat] *nf* (*fam*: *pomme de terre*) spud; **~ douce** sweet potato

**patauger** [patoʒe] *vi* to splash about

**pâte** [pat] *nf* (*à tarte*) pastry; (*à pain*) dough; (*à frire*) batter; **~s** *nfpl* (*macaroni etc*) pasta *sg*; **~ à modeler** modelling clay, Plasticine ® (*BRIT*); **~ brisée** shortcrust pastry; **~ d'amandes** almond paste; **~ de fruits** crystallized fruit *no pl*; **~ feuilletée** puff ou flaky pastry

**pâté** [pate] *nm* (*charcuterie*) pâté; (*tache*) ink blot; (*de sable*) sandpie; **~ de maisons** block (of houses); **~ en croûte** ≈ pork pie

**pâtée** [pate] *nf* mash, feed

**patente** [patɑ̃t] *nf* (*COMM*) trading licence

**paternel, le** [patɛʀnɛl] *adj* (*amour, soins*) fatherly; (*ligne, autorité*) paternal

**pâteux, -euse** [patø, øz] *adj* pasty; (*langue*) coated

**pathétique** [patetik] *adj* moving

**patience** [pasjɑ̃s] *nf* patience

**patient, e** [pasjɑ̃, jɑ̃t] *adj, nm/f* patient; **patienter** *vi* to wait

**patin** [patɛ̃] *nm* skate; (*sport*) skating; **~s (à glace)** (ice) skates; **~s à roulettes** roller skates

**patinage** [patinaʒ] *nm* skating

**patiner** [patine] *vi* to skate; (*roue, voiture*) to spin; **se ~** *vi* (*meuble, cuir*) to acquire a sheen; **patineur, -euse** *nm/f* skater; **patinoire** *nf* skating rink, (ice) rink

**pâtir** [patiʀ]: **~ de** *vt* to suffer because of

**pâtisserie** [patisʀi] *nf* (*boutique*) cake shop; (*gâteau*) cake, pastry; (*à la maison*) pastry- ou cake-making, baking; **pâtissier, -ière** *nm/f* pastrycook

**patois** [patwa, waz] *nm* dialect, patois

**patraque** [patʀak] (*fam*) *adj* peaky, off-colour

**patrie** [patʀi] *nf* homeland

**patrimoine** [patʀimwan] *nm* (*culture*) heritage

**patriotique** [patʀijɔtik] *adj* patriotic

**patron, ne** [patʀɔ̃, ɔn] *nm/f* boss; (*REL*) patron saint; (*COUTURE*) pattern; **patronat** *nm* employers *pl*; **patronner** *vt* to sponsor, support

**patrouille** [patʀuj] *nf* patrol

**patte** [pat] *nf* (*jambe*) leg; (*pied*: *de chien, chat*) paw; (: *d'oiseau*) foot

**pâturage** [patyʀaʒ] *nm* pasture

**paume** [pom] *nf* palm

**paumé, e** [pome] (*fam*) *nm/f* drop-out

**paumer** [pome] (*fam*) *vt* to lose

**paupière** [popjɛʀ] *nf* eyelid

**pause** [poz] *nf* (*arrêt*) break; (*en parlant, MUS*) pause

**pauvre** [povʀ] *adj* poor; **pauvreté** *nf* (*état*) poverty

**pavaner** [pavane]: **se ~** *vi* to strut about

**pavé, e** [pave] *adj* (*cour*) paved; (*chaussée*) cobbled ♦ *nm* (*bloc*) paving stone; cobblestone

**pavillon** [pavijɔ̃] *nm* (*de banlieue*) small (detached) house; pavilion; (*drapeau*) flag

**pavoiser** [pavwaze] *vi* (*fig*) to rejoice, exult

**pavot** [pavo] *nm* poppy

**payant, e** [pejɑ̃, ɑ̃t] *adj* (*spectateurs etc*) paying; (*fig*: *entreprise*) profitable; (*effort*) which pays off; **c'est ~** you have

**paye** [pɛj] *nf* pay, wages *pl*

**payer** [peje] *vt* (*créancier, employé, loyer*) to pay; (*achat, réparations, fig: faute*) to pay for ♦ *vi* to pay; (*métier*) to be well-paid; (*tactique etc*) to pay off; **il me l'a fait ~ 10 F** he charged me 10 F for it; **~ qch à qn** to buy sth for sb, buy sb sth; **se ~ la tête de qn** (*fam*) to take the mickey out of sb

**pays** [pei] *nm* country; (*région*) region; **du ~** local

**paysage** [peizaʒ] *nm* landscape

**paysan, ne** [peizɑ̃, an] *nm/f* farmer; (*péj*) peasant ♦ *adj* (*agricole*) farming; (*rural*) country

**Pays-Bas** [peiba] *nmpl*: **les ~~** the Netherlands

**PC** *nm* (*INFORM*) PC ♦ *sigle m* = **parti communiste**

**P.D.G.** *sigle m* = **président directeur général**

**péage** [peaʒ] *nm* toll; (*endroit*) tollgate

**peau, x** [po] *nf* skin; **gants de ~** fine leather gloves; **être bien/mal dans sa ~** to be quite at ease/ill-at-ease; **~ de chamois** (*chiffon*) chamois leather, shammy; **Peau-Rouge** *nm/f* Red Indian, redskin

**pêche** [pɛʃ] *nf* (*sport, activité*) fishing; (*poissons pêchés*) catch; (*fruit*) peach; **~ à la ligne** (*en rivière*) angling

**péché** [peʃe] *nm* sin

**pécher** [peʃe] *vi* (*REL*) to sin

**pêcher** [peʃe] *nm* peach tree ♦ *vi* to go fishing ♦ *vt* (*attraper*) to catch; (*être pêcheur de*) to fish for

**pêcheur, -eresse** [peʃœr, peʃrɛs] *nm/f* sinner

**pêcheur** [peʃœr] *nm* fisherman; (*à la ligne*) angler

**pécule** [pekyl] *nm* savings *pl*, nest egg

**pédagogie** [pedagoʒi] *nf* educational methods *pl*, pedagogy; **pédagogique** *adj* educational

**pédale** [pedal] *nf* pedal

**pédalo** [pedalo] *nm* pedal-boat

**pédant, e** [pedɑ̃, ɑ̃t] (*péj*) *adj* pedantic

**pédestre** [pedɛstʀ] *adj*: **randonnée ~** ramble; **sentier ~** pedestrian footpath

**pédiatre** [pedjatʀ] *nm/f* paediatrician, child specialist

**pédicure** [pedikyʀ] *nm/f* chiropodist

**pègre** [pɛgʀ] *nf* underworld

**peignais** *etc* [peɲɛ] *vb voir* **peindre**; **peigner**

**peigne** [peɲ] *nm* comb; **peigner** *vt* to comb (the hair of); **se peigner** *vi* to comb one's hair

**peignoir** [peɲwaʀ] *nm* dressing gown; **peignoir de bain** bathrobe

**peindre** [pɛ̃dʀ] *vt* to paint; (*fig*) to portray, depict

**peine** [pɛn] *nf* (*affliction*) sorrow, sadness *no pl*; (*mal, effort*) trouble *no pl*, effort; (*difficulté*) difficulty; (*JUR*) sentence; **avoir de la ~** to be sad; **faire de la ~ à qn** to distress *ou* upset sb; **prendre la ~ de faire** to go to the trouble of doing; **se donner de la ~** to make an effort; **ce n'est pas la ~ de faire** there's no point in doing, it's not worth doing; **à ~** scarcely, hardly, barely; **à ~ ... que** hardly ... than; **~ capitale** *ou* **de mort** capital punishment, death sentence; **peiner** *vi* (*personne*) to work hard; (*moteur, voiture*) to labour ♦ *vt* to grieve, sadden

**peintre** [pɛ̃tʀ] *nm* painter; **~ en bâtiment** house painter

**peinture** [pɛ̃tyʀ] *nf* painting; (*matière*) paint; (*surfaces peintes: aussi:* **~s**) paintwork; **"~ fraîche"** "wet paint"

**péjoratif, -ive** [peʒɔʀatif, iv] *adj* pejorative, derogatory

**pelage** [pəlaʒ] *nm* coat, fur

**pêle-mêle** [pɛlmɛl] *adv* higgledy-piggledy

**peler** [pəle] *vt, vi* to peel

**pèlerin** [pɛlʀɛ̃] *nm* pilgrim

**pèlerinage** [pɛlʀinaʒ] *nm* pilgrimage

**pelle** [pɛl] *nf* shovel; (*d'enfant, de terrassier*) spade

**pellicule** [pelikyl] *nf* film; **~s** *nfpl* (*MÉD*)

dandruff sg

**pelote** [p(ə)lɔt] nf (de fil, laine) ball

**peloton** [p(ə)lɔtɔ̃] nm group, squad; (CYCLISME) pack; ~ **d'exécution** firing squad

**pelotonner** [p(ə)lɔtɔne]: **se** ~ vi to curl (o.s.) up

**pelouse** [p(ə)luz] nf lawn

**peluche** [p(ə)lyʃ] nf: **(animal en)** ~ fluffy animal, soft toy; **chien/lapin en** ~ fluffy dog/rabbit

**pelure** [p(ə)lyr] nf peeling, peel no pl

**pénal, e, -aux** [penal, o] adj penal; **pénalité** nf penalty

**penaud, e** [pəno, od] adj sheepish, contrite

**penchant** [pɑ̃ʃɑ̃] nm (tendance) tendency, propensity; (faible) liking, fondness

**pencher** [pɑ̃ʃe] vi to tilt, lean over ♦ vt to tilt; **se** ~ vi to lean over; (se baisser) to bend down; **se** ~ **sur** (fig: problème) to look into; ~ **pour** to be inclined to favour

**pendaison** [pɑ̃dɛzɔ̃] nf hanging

**pendant** [pɑ̃dɑ̃] prép (au cours de) during; (indique la durée) for; ~ **que** while

**pendentif** [pɑ̃dɑ̃tif] nm pendant

**penderie** [pɑ̃dʀi] nf wardrobe

**pendre** [pɑ̃dʀ] vt, vi to hang; **se** ~ (se suicider) to hang o.s.; ~ **la crémaillère** to have a house-warming party

**pendule** [pɑ̃dyl] nf clock ♦ nm pendulum

**pénétrer** [penetre] vi, vt to penetrate; ~ **dans** to enter

**pénible** [penibl] adj (travail) hard; (sujet) painful; (personne) tiresome; **péniblement** adv with difficulty

**péniche** [peniʃ] nf barge

**pénicilline** [penisilin] nf penicillin

**péninsule** [penɛ̃syl] nf peninsula

**pénis** [penis] nm penis

**pénitence** [penitɑ̃s] nf (peine) penance; (repentir) penitence; **pénitencier** nm penitentiary

**pénombre** [penɔ̃bʀ] nf (faible clarté)

half-light; (obscurité) darkness

**pensée** [pɑ̃se] nf thought; (démarche, doctrine) thinking no pl; (fleur) pansy; **en** ~ in one's mind

**penser** [pɑ̃se] vi, vt to think; ~ **à** (ami, vacances) to think of ou about; (réfléchir à: problème, offre) to think about ou over; (prévoir) to think of; **faire** ~ **à** to remind one of; ~ **faire qch** to be thinking of doing sth, intend to do sth; **pensif, -ive** adj pensive, thoughtful

**pension** [pɑ̃sjɔ̃] nf (allocation) pension; (prix du logement) board and lodgings, bed and board; (école) boarding school; ~ **alimentaire** (de divorcée) maintenance allowance, alimony; ~ **complète** full board; ~ **(de famille)** boarding house, guesthouse; **pensionnaire** nm/f (SCOL) boarder; **pensionnat** nm boarding school

**pente** [pɑ̃t] nf slope; **en** ~ sloping

**Pentecôte** [pɑ̃tkot] nf: **la** ~ Whitsun (BRIT), Pentecost

**pénurie** [penyri] nf shortage

**pépé** [pepe] (fam) nm grandad

**pépin** [pepɛ̃] nm (BOT: graine) pip; (ennui) snag, hitch

**pépinière** [pepinjɛʀ] nf nursery

**perçant, e** [pɛʀsɑ̃, ɑ̃t] adj (cri) piercing, shrill; (regard) piercing

**percée** [pɛʀse] nf (trouée) opening; (MIL, technologique) breakthrough

**perce-neige** [pɛʀsənɛʒ] nf inv snowdrop

**percepteur** [pɛʀsɛptœʀ, tʀis] nm tax collector

**perception** [pɛʀsɛpsjɔ̃] nf perception; (bureau) tax office

**percer** [pɛʀse] vt to pierce; (ouverture etc) to make; (mystère, énigme) to penetrate ♦ vi to break through; **perceuse** nf drill

**percevoir** [pɛʀsəvwaʀ] vt (distinguer) to perceive, detect; (taxe, impôt) to collect; (revenu, indemnité) to receive

**perche** [pɛʀʃ] nf (bâton) pole

**percher** [pɛʀʃe] vt, vi to perch; **se** ~ vi

to perch; **perchoir** nm perch

**perçois** etc [pɛʀswa] vb voir **percevoir**

**percolateur** [pɛʀkɔlatœʀ] nm percolator

**perçu, e** [pɛʀsy] pp de **percevoir**

**percussion** [pɛʀkysjɔ̃] nf percussion

**percuter** [pɛʀkyte] vt to strike; (suj: véhicule) to crash into

**perdant, e** [pɛʀdɑ̃, ɑ̃t] nm/f loser

**perdre** [pɛʀdʀ] vt to lose; (gaspiller: temps, argent) to waste; (personne: moralement etc) to ruin ♦ vi to lose; (sur une vente etc) to lose out; **se ~** vi (s'égarer) to get lost, lose one's way; (denrées) to go to waste

**perdrix** [pɛʀdʀi] nf partridge

**perdu, e** [pɛʀdy] pp de **perdre** ♦ adj (isolé) out-of-the-way; (COMM: emballage) non-returnable; (malade): **il est ~** there's no hope left for him; **à vos moments ~s** in your spare time

**père** [pɛʀ] nm father; **~ de famille** father; **le ~ Noël** Father Christmas

**perfection** [pɛʀfɛksjɔ̃] nf perfection; **à la ~** to perfection; **perfectionné, e** adj sophisticated; **perfectionner** vt to improve, perfect

**perforatrice** [pɛʀfɔʀatʀis] nf (de bureau) punch

**perforer** [pɛʀfɔʀe] vt (poinçonner) to punch

**performant, e** [pɛʀfɔʀmɑ̃, ɑ̃t] adj: **très ~** high-performance cpd

**perfusion** [pɛʀfyzjɔ̃] nf: **faire une ~ à qn** to put sb on a drip

**péricliter** [pɛʀiklite] vi to collapse

**péril** [peʀil] nm peril

**périmé, e** [peʀime] adj (ADMIN) out-of-date, expired

**périmètre** [peʀimɛtʀ] nm perimeter

**période** [peʀjɔd] nf period; **périodique** adj periodic ♦ nm periodical

**péripéties** [peʀipesi] nfpl events, episodes

**périphérique** [peʀifeʀik] adj (quartiers) outlying ♦ nm (AUTO) ring road

**périple** [peʀipl] nm journey

**périr** [peʀiʀ] vi to die, perish

**périssable** [peʀisabl] adj perishable

**perle** [pɛʀl] nf pearl; (de plastique, métal, sueur) bead

**permanence** [pɛʀmanɑ̃s] nf permanence; (local) (duty) office; **assurer une ~** (service public, bureaux) to operate ou maintain a basic service; **être de ~** to be on call ou duty; **en ~** continuously

**permanent, e** [pɛʀmanɑ̃, ɑ̃t] adj permanent; (spectacle) continuous; **permanente** nf perm

**perméable** [pɛʀmeabl] adj (terrain) permeable; **~ à** (fig) receptive ou open to

**permettre** [pɛʀmɛtʀ] vt to allow, permit; **~ à qn de faire/qch** to allow sb to do/sth; **se ~ de faire** to take the liberty of doing

**permis** [pɛʀmi, iz] nm permit, licence; **~ de chasse** hunting permit; **~ (de conduire)** (driving) licence (BRIT), (driver's) license (US); **~ de construire** planning permission (BRIT), building permit (US); **~ de séjour** residence permit; **~ de travail** work permit

**permission** [pɛʀmisjɔ̃] nf permission; (MIL) leave; **avoir la ~ de faire** to have permission to do; **en ~** on leave

**permuter** [pɛʀmyte] vt to change around, permutate ♦ vi to change, swap

**Pérou** [peʀu] nm Peru

**perpétuel, le** [pɛʀpetɥɛl] adj perpetual; **perpétuité** nf: **à perpétuité** for life; **être condamné à perpétuité** to receive a life sentence

**perplexe** [pɛʀplɛks] adj perplexed, puzzled

**perquisitionner** [pɛʀkizisjɔne] vi to carry out a search

**perron** [peʀɔ̃] nm steps pl (leading to entrance)

**perroquet** [peʀɔkɛ] nm parrot

**perruche** [peʀyʃ] nf budgerigar (BRIT), budgie (BRIT), parakeet (US)

**perruque** [peʀyk] nf wig

**persan, e** [pεʀsɑ̃, an] adj Persian

**persécuter** [pεʀsekyte] vt to persecute

**persévérer** [pεʀsevεʀe] vi to persevere

**persiennes** [pεʀsjεn] nfpl shutters

**persil** [pεʀsi] nm parsley

**Persique** [pεʀsik] adj: **le golfe ~** the (Persian) Gulf

**persistant, e** [pεʀsistɑ̃, ɑ̃t] adj persistent

**persister** [pεʀsiste] vi to persist; **~ à faire qch** to persist in doing sth

**personnage** [pεʀsɔnaʒ] nm (individu) character, individual; (célébrité) important person; (de roman, film) character; (PEINTURE) figure

**personnalité** [pεʀsɔnalite] nf personality; (personnage) prominent figure

**personne** [pεʀsɔn] nf person ♦ pron nobody, no one; (avec négation en anglais) anybody, anyone; **~s** nfpl (gens) people pl; **il n'y a ~** there's nobody there, there isn't anybody there; **~ âgée** elderly person; **personnel, le** adj personal; (égoïste) selfish ♦ nm staff, personnel; **personnellement** adv personally

**perspective** [pεʀspεktiv] nf (ART) perspective; (vue) view; (point de vue) viewpoint, angle; (chose envisagée) prospect; **en ~** in prospect

**perspicace** [pεʀspikas] adj clearsighted, gifted with (ou showing) insight; **perspicacité** nf clearsightedness

**persuader** [pεʀsɥade] vt: **~ qn (de faire)** to persuade sb (to do); **persuasif, -ive** adj persuasive

**perte** [pεʀt] nf loss; (de temps) waste; (fig: morale) ruin; **à ~ de vue** as far as the eye can (ou could) see; **~s blanches** (vaginal) discharge sg

**pertinemment** [pεʀtinamɑ̃] adv (savoir) full well

**pertinent, e** [pεʀtinɑ̃, ɑ̃t] adj apt, relevant

**perturbation** [pεʀtyʀbasjɔ̃] nf: **~ (at-mosphérique)** atmospheric disturbance

**perturber** [pεʀtyʀbe] vt to disrupt; (PSYCH) to perturb, disturb

**pervers, e** [pεʀvεʀ, εʀs] adj perverted

**pervertir** [pεʀvεʀtiʀ] vt to pervert

**pesant, e** [pəzɑ̃, ɑ̃t] adj heavy; (fig: présence) burdensome

**pèse-personne** [pεzpεʀsɔn] nm (bathroom) scales pl

**peser** [pəze] vt to weigh ♦ vi to weigh; (fig: avoir de l'importance) to carry weight; **~ lourd** to be heavy

**pessimisme** [pesimism] nm pessimism

**pessimiste** [pesimist] adj pessimistic ♦ nm/f pessimist

**peste** [pεst] nf plague

**pester** [pεste] vi: **~ contre** to curse

**pétale** [petal] nm petal

**pétanque** [petɑ̃k] nf type of bowls

---

**pétanque**

Pétanque, which originated in the south of France, is a version of the game of boules played on a variety of hard surfaces. Standing with their feet together, players throw steel bowls towards a wooden jack.

---

**pétarader** [petaʀade] vi to backfire

**pétard** [petaʀ] nm banger (BRIT), firecracker

**péter** [pete] vi (fam: casser) to bust; (fam!) to fart (!)

**pétillant, e** [petijɑ̃, ɑ̃t] adj (eau etc) sparkling

**pétiller** [petije] vi (feu) to crackle; (champagne) to bubble; (yeux) to sparkle

**petit, e** [p(ə)ti, it] adj small; (avec nuance affective) little; (voyage) short, little; (bruit etc) faint, slight; **~s** nmpl (d'un animal) young pl; **les tout-~s** the little ones, the tiny tots; **~ à ~** bit by bit, gradually; **~(e) ami(e)** boyfriend/ girlfriend; **~ déjeuner** breakfast; **~ pain** (bread) roll; **les ~es annonces** the

small ads; **~s pois** garden peas;
**petite-fille** nf granddaughter; **petit-fils** nm grandson
**pétition** [petisjɔ̃] nf petition
**petits-enfants** [patizɑ̃fɑ̃] nmpl grandchildren
**petit-suisse** [pətisɥis] (pl **~s-~s**) nm small individual pot of cream cheese
**pétrin** [petʀɛ̃] nm (fig): **dans le ~** (fam) in a jam ou fix
**pétrir** [petʀiʀ] vt to knead
**pétrole** [petʀɔl] nm oil; (pour lampe, réchaud etc) paraffin (oil); **pétrolier, -ière** nm oil tanker

---

MOT-CLÉ

---

**peu** [pø] adv **1** (modifiant verbe, adjectif, adverbe): **il boit peu** he doesn't drink (very) much; **il est peu bavard** he's not very talkative; **peu avant/après** shortly before/afterwards

**2** (modifiant nom): **peu de**: **peu de gens/d'arbres** few ou not (very) many people/trees; **il a peu d'espoir** he hasn't (got) much hope, he has little hope; **pour peu de temps** for (only) a short while

**3**: **peu à peu** little by little; **à peu près** just about; more or less; **à peu près 10 kg/10 F** approximately 10 kg/10F
♦ nm **1**: **le peu de gens qui** the few people who; **le peu de sable qui** what little sand, the little sand which
**2**: **un peu** a little; **un petit peu** a little bit; **un peu d'espoir** a little hope
♦ pron: **peu le savent** few know (it); **avant** ou **sous peu** shortly, before long; **de peu** (only) just

---

**peuple** [pœpl] nm people; **peupler** vt (pays, région) to populate; (étang) to stock; (suj: hommes, poissons) to inhabit
**peuplier** [pœplije] nm poplar (tree)
**peur** [pœʀ] nf fear; **avoir ~** (de/de faire/que) to be frightened ou afraid (of/of doing/that); **faire ~ à** to frighten; **de ~ de/que** for fear of/that; **peu-**

**reux, -euse** adj fearful, timorous
**peut** [pø] vb voir **pouvoir**
**peut-être** [pøtɛtʀ] adv perhaps; maybe; **~~ que** perhaps, maybe; **~~ bien qu'il fera/est** he may well do/be
**peux** etc [pø] vb voir **pouvoir**
**phare** [faʀ] nm (en mer) lighthouse; (de véhicule) headlight; **~s de recul** reversing lights
**pharmacie** [faʀmasi] nf (magasin) chemist's (BRIT), pharmacy; (de salle de bain) medicine cabinet; **pharmacien, ne** nm pharmacist, chemist (BRIT)
**phénomène** [fenɔmɛn] nm phenomenon
**philatélie** [filateli] nf philately, stamp collecting
**philosophe** [filɔzɔf] nm/f philosopher
♦ adj philosophical
**philosophie** [filɔzɔfi] nf philosophy
**phobie** [fɔbi] nf phobia
**phonétique** [fɔnetik] nf phonetics sg
**phoque** [fɔk] nm seal
**phosphorescent, e** [fɔsfɔʀesɑ̃, ɑ̃t] adj luminous
**photo** [fɔto] nf photo(graph); **prendre en ~** to take a photo(graph); **faire de la ~** to take photos; **~ d'identité** passport photograph; **photocopie** nf photocopy; **photocopier** vt to photocopy; **photocopieuse** nf photocopier; **photographe** nm/f photographer; **photographie** nf (technique) photography; (cliché) photograph; **photographier** vt to photograph
**phrase** [fʀɑz] nf sentence
**physicien, ne** [fizisjɛ̃, jɛn] nm/f physicist
**physionomie** [fizjɔnɔmi] nf face
**physique** [fizik] adj physical ♦ nm physique ♦ nf physics sg; **au ~** physically; **physiquement** adv physically;
**piailler** [pjaje] vi to squawk
**pianiste** [pjanist] nm/f pianist
**piano** [pjano] nm piano; **pianoter** vi to tinkle away (at the piano)
**pic** [pik] nm (instrument) pick(axe);

(montagne) peak; (ZOOL) woodpecker; **à ~** vertically; (fig: tomber, arriver) just at the right time

**pichet** [piʃɛ] nm jug

**picorer** [pikɔʀe] vt to peck

**picoter** [pikɔte] vt (suj: oiseau) to peck ♦ vi (irriter) to smart, prickle

**pie** [pi] nf magpie

**pièce** [pjɛs] nf (d'un logement) room; (THÉÂTRE) play; (de machine) part; (de monnaie) coin; (document) document; (fragment, de collection) piece; **dix francs ~** ten francs each; **vendre à la ~** to sell separately; **travailler à la ~** to do piecework; **un maillot une ~** one-piece swimsuit; **un deux-~s cuisine** a two-room(ed) flat (BRIT) ou apartment (US) with kitchen; **un deux-~s** exhibit; **~ d'identité: avez-vous une ~ d'identité?** have you got any (means of) identification?; **~ montée** tiered cake; **~s détachées** spares, (spare) parts; **~s justificatives** supporting documents

**pied** [pje] nm foot; (de table) leg; (de lampe) base; **à ~** on foot; **au ~ de la lettre** literally; **avoir ~** to be able to touch the bottom, not to be out of one's depth; **avoir le ~ marin** to be a good sailor; **sur ~** (debout, rétabli) up and about; **mettre sur ~** (entreprise) to set up; **c'est le ~** (fam) it's brilliant; **mettre les ~s dans le plat** (fam) to put one's foot in it; **il se débrouille comme un ~** (fam) he's completely useless; **pied-noir** nm Algerian-born Frenchman

**piège** [pjɛʒ] nm trap; **prendre au ~** to trap; **piéger** vt (avec une bombe) to booby-trap; **lettre/voiture piégée** letter/car-bomb

**pierre** [pjɛʀ] nf stone; **~ précieuse** precious stone, gem; **~ tombale** tombstone; **pierreries** nfpl gems, precious stones

**piétiner** [pjetine] vi (trépigner) to stamp (one's foot); (fig) to be at a

standstill ♦ vt to trample on

**piéton, ne** [pjetɔ̃, ɔn] nm/f pedestrian; **piétonnier, -ière** adj: **rue** ou **zone piétonnière** pedestrian precinct

**pieu, x** [pjø] nm post; (pointu) stake

**pieuvre** [pjœvʀ] nf octopus

**pieux, -euse** [pjø, pjøz] adj pious

**piffer** [pife] (fam) vt: **je ne peux pas le ~** I can't stand him

**pigeon** [piʒɔ̃] nm pigeon

**piger** [piʒe] (fam) vi, vt to understand

**pigiste** [piʒist] nm/f freelance(r)

**pignon** [piɲɔ̃] nm (de mur) gable

**pile** [pil] nf (tas) pile; (ÉLEC) battery ♦ adv (fam: s'arrêter etc) dead; **à deux heures ~** at two on the dot; **jouer à ~ ou face** to toss up (for it); **~ ou face?** heads or tails?

**piler** [pile] vt to crush, pound

**pilier** [pilje] nm pillar

**piller** [pije] vt to pillage, plunder, loot

**pilote** [pilɔt] nm pilot; (de voiture) driver ♦ adj pilot cpd; **~ de course** racing driver; **~ de ligne/d'essai/de chasse** airline/test/fighter pilot; **piloter** vt (avion) to pilot, fly; (voiture) to drive

**pilule** [pilyl] nf pill; **prendre la ~** to be on the pill

**piment** [pimɑ̃] nm (aussi: **~ rouge**) chilli; (fig) spice, piquancy; **~ doux** pepper, capsicum; **pimenté, e** adj (plat) hot, spicy

**pimpant, e** [pɛ̃pɑ̃, ɑ̃t] adj spruce

**pin** [pɛ̃] nm pine

**pinard** [pinaʀ] (fam) nm (cheap) wine, plonk (BRIT)

**pince** [pɛ̃s] nf (outil) pliers pl; (de homard, crabe) pincer, claw; (COUTURE: pli) dart; **~ à épiler** tweezers pl; **~ à linge** clothes peg (BRIT) ou pin (US)

**pincé, e** [pɛ̃se] adj (air) stiff

**pinceau, x** [pɛ̃so] nm (paint)brush

**pincée** [pɛ̃se] nf: **une ~ de** a pinch of

**pincer** [pɛ̃se] vt to pinch; (fam) to nab

**pinède** [pinɛd] nf pinewood, pine forest

**pingouin** [pɛ̃gwɛ̃] nm penguin

**ping-pong** ® [piŋpɔ̃g] nm table tennis

**pingre** [pɛ̃gʀ] adj niggardly

**pinson** [pɛ̃sɔ̃] nm chaffinch

**pintade** [pɛ̃tad] nf guinea-fowl

**pioche** [pjɔʃ] nf pickaxe; **piocher** vt to dig up (with a pickaxe); **piocher dans** (le tas, ses économies) to dig into

**pion** [pjɔ̃] nm (ÉCHECS) pawn; (DAMES) piece; (SCOL) supervisor

**pionnier** [pjɔnje] nm pioneer

**pipe** [pip] nf pipe; **fumer la ~** to smoke a pipe

**pipeau, x** [pipo] nm (reed-)pipe

**piquant, e** [pikɑ̃, ɑ̃t] adj (barbe, rosier etc) prickly; (saveur, sauce) hot, pungent; (détail) titillating; (froid) biting ♦ nm (épine) thorn, prickle; (fig) spiciness, spice

**pique** [pik] nf (arme) pike; (fig) cutting remark ♦ nm (CARTES) spades pl

**pique-nique** [piknik] nm picnic; **pique-niquer** vi to have a picnic

**piquer** [pike] vt (suj: guêpe, fumée, orties) to sting; (: moustique) to bite; (: barbe) to prick; (: froid) to bite; (MÉD) to give a jab to; (: chien, chat) to put to sleep; (intérêt) to arouse; (fam: voler) to pinch ♦ vi (avion) to go into a dive; se ~ (avec une aiguille) to prick o.s.; (dans les orties) to get stung; (suj: toxicomane) to shoot up; **une colère** to fly into a rage

**piquet** [pikɛ] nm (pieu) post, stake; (de tente) peg; **~ de grève** (strike-)picket

**piqûre** [pikyʀ] nf (d'épingle) prick; (d'ortie) sting; (de moustique) bite; (MÉD) injection, shot (US); **faire une ~ à qn** to give sb an injection

**pirate** [piʀat] nm, adj pirate; **~ de l'air** hijacker

**pire** [piʀ] adj worse; (superlatif): **le(la) ~ ... the worst ...** ♦ nm: **le ~ (de)** the worst (of); **au ~** at the (very) worst

**pis** [pi] nm (de vache) udder; (pire): **le ~** the worst ♦ adj, adv worse; **de mal en ~** from bad to worse

**piscine** [pisin] nf (swimming) pool; **~ couverte** indoor (swimming) pool

**pissenlit** [pisɑ̃li] nm dandelion

**pistache** [pistaʃ] nf pistachio (nut)

**piste** [pist] nf (d'un animal, sentier) track, trail; (indice) lead; (de stade) track; (de cirque) ring; (de danse) floor; (de patinage) rink; (de ski) run; (AVIAT) runway; **~ cyclable** cycle track

**pistolet** [pistɔlɛ] nm (arme) pistol, gun; (à peinture) spray gun; **pistolet-mitrailleur** nm submachine gun

**piston** [pistɔ̃] nm (TECH) piston; **avoir du ~** (fam) to have friends in the right places; **pistonner** vt (candidat) to pull strings for

**piteux, -euse** [pitø, øz] adj pitiful, sorry (avant le nom)

**pitié** [pitje] nf pity; **il me fait ~** I feel sorry for him; **avoir ~ de** (compassion) to pity, feel sorry for; (merci) to have pity ou mercy on

**pitoyable** [pitwajabl] adj pitiful

**pitre** [pitʀ] nm clown; **pitrerie** nf tomfoolery no pl

**pittoresque** [pitɔʀɛsk] adj picturesque

**pivot** [pivo] nm pivot; **pivoter** vi to revolve; (fauteuil) to swivel

**P.J.** sigle f (= police judiciaire) ≈ CID (BRIT), ≈ FBI (US)

**placard** [plakaʀ] nm (armoire) cupboard; (affiche) poster, notice

**place** [plas] nf (emplacement, classement) place; (de ville, village) square; (espace libre) room, space; (de parking) space; (siège: de train, cinéma, voiture) seat; (emploi) job; **en ~** (mettre) in its place; **sur ~** on the spot; **faire ~ à** to give way to; **ça prend de la ~** it takes up a lot of room ou space; **à la ~ de** in place of, instead of; **à ta ~ ...** if I were you ...; **se mettre à la ~ de qn** to put o.s. in sb's place ou shoes

**placé, e** [plase] adj: **être bien/mal ~** (spectateur) to have a good/a poor seat; (concurrent) to be in a good/bad position; **il est bien ~ pour le savoir**

he is in a position to know

**placement** [plasmã] *nm* (*FINANCE*) investment; **bureau de ~** employment agency

**placer** [plase] *vt* to place; (*convive, spectateur*) to seat; (*argent*) to place, invest; **il n'a pas pu ~ un mot** he couldn't get a word in; **se ~ au premier rang** to go and stand (*ou* sit) in the first row

**plafond** [plafɔ̃] *nm* ceiling

**plage** [plaʒ] *nf* beach

**plagiat** [plaʒja] *nm* plagiarism

**plaid** [plɛd] *nm* (*tartan*) car rug

**plaider** [plede] *vi* (*avocat*) to plead ♦ *vt* to plead; **~ pour** (*fig*) to speak for; **plaidoyer** [pledwaje] *nm* (*JUR*) speech for the defence; (*fig*) plea

**plaie** [plɛ] *nf* wound

**plaignant, e** [plɛɲɑ̃, ɑ̃t] *nm/f* plaintiff

**plaindre** [plɛ̃dʀ] *vt* to pity, feel sorry for; **se ~** *vi* (*gémir*) to moan; (*protester*): **se ~ (à qn) (de)** to complain (to sb) (about); (*souffrir*): **se ~ de** to complain of

**plaine** [plɛn] *nf* plain

**plain-pied** [plɛ̃pje] *adv*: **de ~~ (avec)** on the same level (as)

**plainte** [plɛ̃t] *nf* (*gémissement*) moan, groan; (*doléance*) complaint; **porter ~** to lodge a complaint

**plaire** [plɛʀ] *vi* to be a success, be successful; **ça plaît beaucoup aux jeunes** it's very popular with young people; **~ à: cela me plaît** I like it; **se ~ quelque part** to like being somewhere *ou* like it somewhere; **j'irai si ça me plaît** I'll go if I feel like it; **s'il vous plaît** please

**plaisance** [plɛzɑ̃s] *nf* (*aussi*: **navigation de ~**) (pleasure) sailing, yachting

**plaisant, e** [plɛzɑ̃, ɑ̃t] *adj* pleasant; (*histoire, anecdote*) amusing

**plaisanter** [plɛzɑ̃te] *vi* to joke; **plaisanterie** *nf* joke

**plaise** *etc* [plɛz] *vb voir* **plaire**

**plaisir** [plɛziʀ] *nm* pleasure; **faire ~ à qn** (*délibérément*) to be nice to sb, please sb; **ça me fait ~** I like (doing)

it; **j'espère que ça te fera ~** I hope you'll like it; **pour le ~** for pleasure

**plaît** [plɛ] *vb voir* **plaire**

**plan, e** [plɑ̃, an] *adj* flat ♦ *nm* plan; (*fig*) level, plane; (*CINÉMA*) shot; **au premier/second ~** in the foreground/middle distance; **à l'arrière ~** in the background; **rester en ~** (*fam*) to be left stranded; **laisser en ~** (*fam: travail*) to drop, abandon; **d'eau** lake

**planche** [plɑ̃ʃ] *nf* (*pièce de bois*) plank, (wooden) board; (*illustration*) plate; **~ à repasser** ironing board; **~ à roulettes** skateboard; **~ à voile** (*sport*) windsurfing

**plancher** [plɑ̃ʃe] *nm* floor; floorboards *pl* ♦ *vi* (*fam*) to work hard

**planer** [plane] *vi* to glide; (*fam: rêveur*) to have one's head in the clouds; **~ sur** (*fig: danger*) to hang over

**planète** [planɛt] *nf* planet

**planeur** [planœʀ] *nm* glider

**planification** [planifikasjɔ̃] *nf* (economic) planning

**planifier** [planifje] *vt* to plan

**planning** [planiŋ] *nm* programme, schedule

**planque** [plɑ̃k] (*fam*) *nf* (*emploi peu fatigant*) cushy (*BRIT*) *ou* easy number; (*cachette*) hiding place

**plant** [plɑ̃] *nm* seedling, young plant

**plante** [plɑ̃t] *nf* plant; **~ d'appartement** house *ou* pot plant; **~ des pieds** sole of the foot

**planter** [plɑ̃te] *vt* (*plante*) to plant; (*enfoncer*) to hammer *ou* drive in; (*tente*) to put up, pitch; (*fam: personne*) to dump; **se ~** (*fam: se tromper*) to get it wrong

**plantureux, -euse** [plɑ̃tyʀø, øz] *adj* copious, lavish; (*femme*) buxom

**plaque** [plak] *nf* plate; (*de verglas, d'eczéma*) patch; (*avec inscription*) plaque; **~ chauffante** hotplate; **~ de chocolat** bar of chocolate; **~ (minéralogique *ou* d'immatriculation)** number

*(BRIT)* ou **license** *(US)* plate; ~ **tournante** *(fig)* centre

**plaqué, e** [plake] adj: ~ **or/argent** gold-/silver-plated

**plaquer** [plake] vt *(aplatir)*: ~ **qch sur** ou **contre** to make sth stick ou cling to; *(RUGBY)* to bring down; *(fam: laisser tomber)* to drop

**plaquette** [plaket] nf *(de chocolat)* bar; *(beurre)* pack(et); ~ **de frein** brake pad

**plastique** [plastik] adj, nm plastic; **plastiquer** vt to blow up *(with a plastic bomb)*

**plat, e** [pla, -at] adj flat; *(cheveux)* straight; *(style)* flat, dull ♦ nm *(récipient, CULIN)* dish; *(d'un repas)* course; **à ~ ventre** face down; **à ~** *(pneu, batterie)* flat; *(fam: personne)* dead beat; ~ **cuisiné** pre-cooked meal; ~ **de résistance** main course; ~ **du jour** dish of the day

**platane** [platan] nm plane tree

**plateau, x** [plato] nm *(support)* tray; *(GÉO)* plateau; *(CINÉMA)* set; ~ **de fromages** cheeseboard

**plate-bande** [platbɑ̃d] nf flower bed

**plate-forme** [platfɔrm] nf platform; ~~ **de forage/pétrolière** drilling/oil rig

**platine** [platin] nm platinum ♦ nf *(d'un tourne-disque)* turntable

**plâtre** [platʀ] nm *(matériau)* plaster; *(statue)* plaster statue; *(MÉD)* *(plaster)* cast; **avoir un bras dans le ~** to have an arm in plaster

**plein, e** [plɛ̃, plɛn] adj full ♦ nm: **faire le ~** *(d'essence)* to fill up *(with petrol)*; **à ~es mains** *(ramasser)* in handfuls; **à ~ temps** full-time; **en ~ air** in the open air; **en ~ soleil** in direct sunlight; **en ~ nuit/rue** in the middle of the night/street; **en ~ jour** in broad daylight

**pleurer** [plœre] vi to cry; *(yeux)* to water ♦ vt to mourn (for); ~ **sur** to lament (over), to bemoan

**pleurnicher** [plœrniʃe] vi to snivel, whine

**pleurs** [plœr] nmpl: **en ~** in tears

**pleut** [plø] vb voir **pleuvoir**

**pleuvoir** [pløvwar] vb impers to rain ♦ vi *(coups)* to rain down; *(critiques, invitations)* to shower down; **il pleut** it's raining

**pli** [pli] nm fold; *(de jupe)* pleat; *(de pantalon)* crease; **prendre le ~ de faire** to get into the habit of doing; **un mauvais ~** a bad habit

**pliant, e** [plijɑ̃, plijɑ̃t] adj folding

**plier** [plije] vt to fold; *(pour ranger)* to fold up; *(genou, bras)* to bend ♦ vi to bend; *(fig)* to yield; **se ~** vi to fold; **se ~ à** to submit to

**plinthe** [plɛ̃t] nf skirting board

**plisser** [plise] vt *(jupe)* to put pleats in; *(yeux)* to screw up; *(front)* to crease

**plomb** [plɔ̃] nm *(métal)* lead; *(d'une cartouche)* lead shot; *(PÊCHE)* sinker; *(ÉLEC)* fuse; **sans ~** *(essence etc)* unleaded

**plombage** [plɔ̃baʒ] nm *(de dent)* filling

**plomberie** [plɔ̃bʀi] nf plumbing

**plombier** [plɔ̃bje] nm plumber

**plonge** [plɔ̃ʒ] nf washing-up

**plongeant, e** [plɔ̃ʒɑ̃, ɑ̃t] adj *(vue)* from above; *(décolleté)* plunging

**plongée** [plɔ̃ʒe] nf *(SPORT)* diving no pl; *(sans scaphandre)* skin diving; ~ **sous-marine** diving

**plongeoir** [plɔ̃ʒwar] nm diving board

**plongeon** [plɔ̃ʒɔ̃] nm dive

**plonger** [plɔ̃ʒe] vi to dive ♦ vt: ~ **qch dans** to plunge sth into; **se ~ dans** *(études, lecture)* to bury o.s. in; **plongeur** nm diver

**ployer** [plwaje] vt, vi to bend

**plu** [ply] pp de **plaire**; **pleuvoir**

**pluie** [plɥi] nf rain

**plume** [plym] nf feather; *(pour écrire)* (pen) nib; *(fig)* pen

**plupart** [plypar]: **la ~** pron the majority, most (of them); **la ~ des**, most, the majority of; **la ~ du temps/d'entre nous** most of the time/of us; **pour la ~** for the most part, mostly

**pluriel** [plyrjel] nm plural

**plus¹** [ply] *vb voir* **plaire**

MOT-CLÉ

**plus²** [ply] *adv* **1** (*forme négative*): **ne ... plus** no more, no longer; **je n'ai plus d'argent** I've got no more money *ou* no money left; **il ne travaille plus** he's no longer working, he doesn't work any more **2** (*comparatif*) more, ...+er; (*superlatif*): **le plus** the most, the ...+est; **plus grand/intelligent (que)** bigger/more intelligent (than); **le plus grand/intelligent** the biggest/most intelligent; **tout au plus** at the very most **3** (*davantage*) more; **il travaille plus (que)** he works more (than); **plus il travaille, plus il est heureux** the more he works, the happier he is; **plus de pain** more bread; **plus de 10 personnes** more than 10 people, over 10 people; **3 heures de plus que** 3 hours more than; **de plus** what's more, moreover; **3 kilos en plus** 3 kilos more; **en plus de** in addition to; **de plus en plus** more and more; **plus ou moins** more or less; **ni plus ni moins** no more, no less

♦ *prép*: **4 plus 2** 4 plus 2

**plusieurs** [plyzjœʀ] *dét, pron* several; **ils sont** ~ there are several of them

**plus-value** [plyvaly] *nf* (*bénéfice*) surplus

**plut** [ply] *vb voir* **plaire**

**plutôt** [plyto] *adv* rather; **je préfère** ~ **celui-ci** I'd rather have this one; ~ **que (de) faire** rather than *ou* instead of doing

**pluvieux, -euse** [plyvjø, jøz] *adj* rainy, wet

**PME** *sigle f* (= **petite(s) et moyenne(s) entreprise(s)**) small business(es)

**PMU** *sigle m* (= **Pari mutuel urbain**) system of betting on horses; (*café*) betting agency

**PNB** *sigle m* (= **produit national brut**) GNP

**pneu** [pnø] *nm* tyre (*BRIT*), tire (*US*)

**pneumonie** [pnømɔni] *nf* pneumonia

**poche** [pɔʃ] *nf* pocket; (*sous les yeux*) bag, pouch; **argent de** ~ pocket money

**pocher** [pɔʃe] *vt* (*CULIN*) to poach

**pochette** [pɔʃɛt] *nf* (*d'aiguilles etc*) case; (*mouchoir*) breast pocket handkerchief; (*sac à main*) clutch bag; ~ **de disque** record sleeve

**poêle** [pwal] *nm* stove ♦ *nf*: ~ (**à frire**) frying pan

**poème** [pɔɛm] *nm* poem

**poésie** [pɔezi] *nf* (*poème*) poem; (*art*): **la** ~ poetry

**poète** [pɔɛt] *nm* poet

**poids** [pwa] *nm* weight; (*SPORT*) shot; **vendre au** ~ to sell by weight; **prendre du** ~ to put on weight; ~ **lourd** (*camion*) lorry (*BRIT*), truck (*US*)

**poignant, e** [pwaɲɑ̃, ɑ̃t] *adj* poignant

**poignard** [pwaɲaʀ] *nm* dagger; **poignarder** *vt* to stab, knife

**poigne** [pwaɲ] *nf* grip; **avoir de la** ~ (*fig*) to rule with a firm hand

**poignée** [pwaɲe] *nf* (*de sel etc, fig*) handful; (*de couvercle, porte*) handle; ~ **de main** handshake

**poignet** [pwaɲɛ] *nm* (*ANAT*) wrist; (*de chemise*) cuff

**poil** [pwal] *nm* (*ANAT*) hair; (*de pinceau, brosse*) bristle; (*de tapis*) strand; (*pelage*) coat; **à** ~ (*fam*) starkers; **au** ~ (*fam*) hunky-dory; **poilu, e** *adj* hairy

**poinçon** [pwɛ̃sɔ̃] *nm* (*marque*) hallmark; **poinçonner** [pwɛ̃sɔne] *vt* (*bijou*) to hallmark; (*billet*) to punch

**poing** [pwɛ̃] *nm* fist; **coup de** ~ punch

**point** [pwɛ̃] *nm* point; (*endroit*) spot; (*marque, signe*) dot; (: *de ponctuation*) full stop, period (*US*); (*COUTURE, TRICOT*) stitch ♦ *adv* = **pas²**; **faire le** ~ (*fig*) to take stock (of the situation); **sur le** ~ **de faire** (just) about to do; **à** ~ (*que* so much so that; **mettre au** ~ (*procédé*) to develop; (*affaire*) to settle; **à** ~

(CULIN: viande) medium; **à ~ (nommé)**
just at the right time; **deux ~s** colon;
**(de côté)** stitch (pain); **~ d'exclamation/d'interrogation** exclamation/
question mark; **~ de repère** landmark;
(dans le temps) point of reference; **~ de
suture** (MÉD) stitch; **~ de vente** retail
outlet; **~ de vue** viewpoint; (fig: opinion) point of view; **~ d'honneur:
mettre un ~ d'honneur à faire qch**
to make it a point of honour to do sth; **~
faible/fort** weak/strong point; **~ noir**
blackhead; **~s de suspension** suspension points

**pointe** [pwɛt] nf point; (clou) tack; (fig):
**une ~ de** a hint of; **être à la ~ de** (fig)
to be in the forefront of; **sur la ~ des
pieds** on tiptoe; **en ~** pointed, tapered; **de ~** (technique etc) leading;
**heures de ~** peak hours

**pointer** [pwɛte] vt (diriger: canon,
doigt): **~ sur** qch to point at sth ♦ vi
(employé) to clock in

**pointillé** [pwɛtije] nm (trait) dotted
line

**pointilleux, -euse** [pwɛtijø, øz] adj
particular, pernickety

**pointu, e** [pwɛty] adj pointed; (voix)
shrill; (analyse) precise

**pointure** [pwɛtyr] nf size

**point-virgule** [pwɛvirgyl] nm semi-colon

**poire** [pwar] nf pear; (fam: péj) mug

**poireau, x** [pwaro] nm leek

**poireauter** [pwarote] vi (fam) to be
left kicking one's heels

**poirier** [pwarje] nm pear tree

**pois** [pwa] nm (BOT) pea; (sur une
étoffe) dot, spot; **~ chiche** chickpea; **à
~** (cravate etc) spotted, polka-dot cpd

**poison** [pwazɔ̃] nm poison

**poisse** [pwas] (fam) nf rotten luck

**poisseux, -euse** [pwasø, øz] adj sticky

**poisson** [pwasɔ̃] nm fish gén inv; **les
P~s** (signe) Pisces; **~ d'avril!** April fool!;
**~ rouge** goldfish; **poissonnerie** nf
fish-shop; **poissonnier, -ière** nm/f

fishmonger (BRIT), fish merchant (US)

**poitrine** [pwatrin] nf chest; (seins)
bust, bosom; (CULIN) breast

**poivre** [pwavr] nm pepper

**poivron** [pwavrɔ̃] nm pepper, capsicum

**polaire** [pɔlɛr] adj polar

**polar** [pɔlar] (fam) nm detective novel

**pôle** [pol] nm (GÉO, ÉLEC) pole

**poli, e** [pɔli] adj polite; (lisse) smooth

**police** [pɔlis] nf police; **~ d'assurance**
insurance policy; **~ judiciaire** ≃ Criminal Investigation Department (BRIT), ≃
Federal Bureau of Investigation (US); **~
secours** ≃ emergency services pl (BRIT),
≃ paramedics pl (US); **policier, -ière**
adj police cpd ♦ nm policeman; (aussi:
**roman policier**) detective novel

**polir** [pɔlir] vt to polish

**polisson, e** [pɔlisɔ̃, ɔn] nm/f (enfant)
(little) rascal

**politesse** [pɔlites] nf politeness

**politicien, ne** [pɔlitisjɛ̃, jɛn] (péj) nm/f
politician

**politique** [pɔlitik] adj political ♦ nf politics sg; (mesures, méthode) policies pl

**pollen** [pɔlɛn] nm pollen

**polluant, e** [pɔlɥɑ̃, ɑ̃t] adj polluting ♦
nm: (produit) **~** pollutant; **non ~**
non-polluting

**polluer** [pɔlɥe] vt to pollute; **pollution**
nf pollution

**polo** [pɔlo] nm (chemise) polo shirt

**Pologne** [pɔlɔɲ] nf: **la ~** Poland; **polonais, e** adj Polish ♦ nm/f: **Polonais,
e**, Pole ♦ nm (LING) Polish

**poltron, ne** [pɔltrɔ̃, ɔn] adj cowardly

**polycopier** [pɔlikɔpje] vt to duplicate

**Polynésie** [pɔlinezi] nf: **la ~** Polynesia

**polyvalent, e** [pɔlivalɑ̃, ɑ̃t] adj (rôle)
varied; (salle) multi-purpose

**pommade** [pɔmad] nf ointment,
cream

**pomme** [pɔm] nf apple; **tomber dans
les ~s** (fam) to pass out; **~ d'Adam**
Adam's apple; **~ de pin** pine ou fir
cone; **~ de terre** potato

**pommeau, x** [pɔmo] nm (boule) knob; (de selle) pommel

**pommette** [pɔmɛt] nf cheekbone

**pommier** [pɔmje] nm apple tree

**pompe** [pɔ̃p] nf pump; (faste) pomp (and ceremony); ~ **à essence** petrol pump; ~**s funèbres** funeral parlour sg, undertaker's sg; **pomper** vt to pump; (aspirer) to pump up; (absorber) to soak up

**pompeux, -euse** [pɔ̃pø, øz] adj pompous

**pompier** [pɔ̃pje] nm fireman

**pompiste** [pɔ̃pist] nm/f petrol (BRIT) ou gas (US) pump attendant

**poncer** [pɔ̃se] vt to sand (down)

**ponctuation** [pɔ̃ktɥasjɔ̃] nf punctuation

**ponctuel, le** [pɔ̃ktɥɛl] adj punctual

**pondéré, e** [pɔ̃dere] adj level-headed, composed

**pondre** [pɔ̃dʀ] vt to lay

**poney** [pɔnɛ] nm pony

**pont** [pɔ̃] nm bridge; (NAVIG) deck; **faire le** ~ to take the extra day off; ~ **suspendu** suspension bridge; **pont-levis** nm drawbridge

---

**faire le pont**

The expression "faire le pont" refers to the practice of taking a Monday or Friday off to make a long weekend if a public holiday falls on a Tuesday or Thursday. The French often do this at l'Ascension, l'Assomption and le 14 juillet.

---

**pop** [pɔp] adj inv pop

**populace** [pɔpylas] (péj) nf rabble

**populaire** [pɔpylɛʀ] adj popular; (manifestation) mass cpd; (milieux, quartier) working-class; (expression) vernacular

**popularité** [pɔpylaʀite] nf popularity

**population** [pɔpylasjɔ̃] nf population; ~ **active** working population

**populeux, -euse** [pɔpylø, øz] adj densely populated

**porc** [pɔʀ] nm pig; (CULIN) pork

**porcelaine** [pɔʀsəlɛn] nf porcelain, china; piece of china(ware)

**porc-épic** [pɔʀkepik] nm porcupine

**porche** [pɔʀʃ] nm porch

**porcherie** [pɔʀʃəʀi] nf pigsty

**pore** [pɔʀ] nm pore

**porno** [pɔʀno] adj porno ♦ nm porn

**port** [pɔʀ] nm harbour, port; (ville) port; (de l'uniforme etc) wearing; (pour lettre) postage; (pour colis, aussi: posture) carriage; ~ **de pêche/de plaisance** fishing/sailing harbour

**portable** [pɔʀtabl] nm (COMPUT) laptop (computer)

**portail** [pɔʀtaj] nm gate

**portant, e** [pɔʀtɑ̃, ɑ̃t] adj: **bien/mal** ~ in good/poor health

**portatif, -ive** [pɔʀtatif, iv] adj portable

**porte** [pɔʀt] nf door; (de ville, jardin) gate; **mettre à la** ~ to throw out; ~ **à** ~ ♦ nm door-to-door selling; ~ **d'entrée** front door; **porte-avions** nm inv aircraft carrier; **porte-bagages** nm inv luggage rack; **porte-bonheur** nm inv lucky charm; **porte-clefs** nm inv key ring; **porte-documents** nm inv attaché ou document case

**porté, e** [pɔʀte] adj: **être ~ à faire** to be inclined to do; **être ~ sur qch** to be keen on sth; **portée** nf (d'une arme) range; (fig: effet) impact, import; (: capacité) scope, capability; (de chatte etc) litter; (MUS) stave, staff; **à/hors de portée (de)** within/out of reach (of); **à portée de (la) main** within (arm's) reach; **à la portée de qn** (fig) at sb's level, within sb's capabilities

**porte...: porte-fenêtre** nf French window; **portefeuille** nm wallet; **portemanteau, x** nm (cintre) coat hanger; (au mur) coat rack; **porte-monnaie** nm inv purse; **porte-parole** nm inv spokesman

**porter** [pɔʀte] vt to carry; (sur soi: vêtement, barbe, bague) to wear; (fig: responsabilité etc) to bear, carry; (inscription, nom, fruits) to bear; (coup) to deal; (attention) to turn; (argument) to put forward; **~ qch à qn** to take sth to sb ♦ vi (voix) to carry; (coup, argument) to hit home; **se ~** vi (se sentir): **se ~ bien/mal** to be well/unwell; **~ sur** (recherches) to be concerned with; **se faire ~ malade** to report sick

**porteur, euse** [pɔʀtœʀ, øz] nm (de bagages) porter; (de chèque) bearer

**porte-voix** [pɔʀtəvwa] nm inv megaphone

**portier** [pɔʀtje] nm doorman

**portière** [pɔʀtjɛʀ] nf door

**portillon** [pɔʀtijɔ̃] nm gate

**portion** [pɔʀsjɔ̃] nf (part) portion, share; (partie) portion, section

**porto** [pɔʀto] nm port (wine)

**portrait** [pɔʀtʀɛ] nm (peinture) portrait; (photo) photograph; **portrait-robot** nm Identikit ® ou photo-fit ® picture

**portuaire** [pɔʀtɥɛʀ] adj port cpd, harbour cpd

**portugais, e** [pɔʀtyɡɛ, ɛz] adj Portuguese ♦ nm/f: **P~, e** Portuguese ♦ nm (LING) Portuguese

**Portugal** [pɔʀtyɡal] nm: **le ~** Portugal

**pose** [poz] nf (de moquette) laying; (attitude, d'un modèle) pose; (PHOTO) exposure

**posé, e** [poze] adj serious

**poser** [poze] vt to put; (installer: moquette, carrelage) to lay; (rideaux, papier peint) to hang; (question) to ask; (principe, conditions) to lay ou set down; (problème) to formulate; (difficulté) to pose ♦ vi (modèle) to pose; **se ~** vi (oiseau, avion) to land; (question) to arise; **~ qch (sur)** (déposer) to put sth down (on); **~ qch sur/quelque part** (placer) to put sth on/somewhere; **sa candidature à un poste** to apply for a post

**positif, -ive** [pozitif, iv] adj positive

**position** [pozisjɔ̃] nf position; **prendre ~** (fig) to take a stand

**posologie** [pozɔlɔʒi] nf dosage

**posséder** [pɔsede] vt to own, possess; (qualité, talent) to have, possess; (sexuellement) to possess; **possession** nf ownership no pl, possession

**possibilité** [pɔsibilite] nf possibility; **~s** nfpl (potentiel) potential sg

**possible** [pɔsibl] adj possible; (projet, entreprise) feasible ♦ nm: **faire son ~** to do all one can, do one's utmost; **le plus/moins de livres ~** as many/few books as possible; **le plus vite ~** as quickly as possible; **dès que ~** as soon as possible

**postal, e, -aux** [pɔstal, o] adj postal

**poste** [pɔst] nf (service) post, postal service; (administration, bureau) post office ♦ nm (fonction, MIL) post; (TÉL) extension; (de radio etc) set; **mettre à la ~** to post; **~ (de police)** police station; **~ de secours** first-aid post; **~ restante** poste restante (BRIT), general delivery (US)

**poster¹** [pɔste] vt to post

**poster²** [pɔstɛʀ] nm poster

**postérieur, e** [pɔsteʀjœʀ] adj (date) later; (partie) back ♦ nm (fam) behind

**posthume** [pɔstym] adj posthumous

**postulant, e** [pɔstylɑ̃, ɑ̃t] nm/f applicant

**postuler** [pɔstyle] vi: **~ à** ou **pour un emploi** to apply for a job

**posture** [pɔstyʀ] nf position

**pot** [po] nm (en verre) jar; (en terre) pot; (en plastique, carton) carton; (en métal) tin; (fam: chance) luck; **avoir du ~** (fam) to be lucky; **boire** ou **prendre un ~** (fam) to have a drink; **petit ~** (pour bébé) (jar of) baby food; **~ catalytique** catalytic converter; **~ d'échappement** exhaust pipe; **~ de fleurs** plant pot, flowerpot; (plante) pot plant

**potable** [pɔtabl] adj: **eau (non) ~** (non-)drinking water

**potage** [pɔtaʒ] nm soup; **potager, -ère** adj: (jardin) **potager** kitchen ou vegetable garden

**pot-au-feu** [pɔtofø] nm inv (beef) stew

**pot-de-vin** [potdəvɛ̃] nm bribe

**pote** [pot] (fam) nm pal

**poteau, x** [poto] nm post; ~ **indicateur** signpost

**potelé, e** [pot(ə)le] adj plump, chubby

**potence** [potɑ̃s] nf gallows sg

**potentiel, le** [potɑ̃sjɛl] adj, nm potentiel

**poterie** [potʀi] nf pottery; (objet) piece of pottery

**potier** [potje] nm potter

**potins** [potɛ̃] (fam) nmpl gossip sg

**potiron** [potiʀɔ̃] nm pumpkin

**pou, x** [pu] nm louse

**poubelle** [pubɛl] nf (dust)bin

**pouce** [pus] nm thumb

**poudre** [pudʀ] nf powder; (fard) (face) powder; (explosif) gunpowder; **café en ~:** instant coffee; **lait en ~** dried ou powdered milk; **poudreuse** nf powder snow; **poudrier** (powder) compact

**pouffer** [pufe] vi: ~ **(de rire)** to burst out laughing

**poulailler** [pulaje] nm henhouse

**poulain** [pulɛ̃] nm foal; (fig) protégé

**poule** [pul] nf hen; (CULIN) (boiling) fowl

**poulet** [pulɛ] nm chicken; (fam) cop

**poulie** [puli] nf pulley

**pouls** [pu] nm pulse; **prendre le ~ de qn** to feel sb's pulse

**poumon** [pumɔ̃] nm lung

**poupe** [pup] nf stern; **en ~** astern

**poupée** [pupe] nf doll

**pouponnière** [pupɔnjɛʀ] nf crèche, day nursery

**pour** [puʀ] prép for ♦ nm: **le ~ et le contre** the pros and cons; ~ **faire** (so as) to do, in order to do; ~ **avoir fait** for having done; ~ **que** so that, in order that; ~ **100 francs d'essence** 100 francs' worth of petrol; ~ **cent** per cent; ~ **ce qui est de** as for

**pourboire** [puʀbwaʀ] nm tip

**pourcentage** [puʀsɑ̃taʒ] nm percentage

**pourchasser** [puʀʃase] vt to pursue

**pourparlers** [puʀpaʀle] nmpl talks, negotiations

**pourpre** [puʀpʀ] adj crimson

**pourquoi** [puʀkwa] adv, conj why ♦ nm inv: **le ~ (de)** the reason (for)

**pourrai** etc [puʀe] vb voir **pouvoir**

**pourri, e** [puʀi] adj rotten

**pourrir** [puʀiʀ] vi to rot; (fruit) to go rotten ou bad ♦ vt to rot; (fig) to spoil thoroughly; **pourriture** nf rot

**pourrons** etc [puʀɔ̃] vb voir **pouvoir**

**poursuite** [puʀsɥit] nf pursuit, chase; ~**s** nfpl (JUR) legal proceedings

**poursuivre** [puʀsɥivʀ] vt to pursue, chase (after); (obséder) to haunt; (JUR) to bring proceedings against, prosecute; (: au civil) to sue; (but) to strive towards; (continuer: études etc) to carry on with, continue; **se ~** vi to go on, continue

**pourtant** [puʀtɑ̃] adv yet; **c'est ~ facile** (and) yet it's easy

**pourtour** [puʀtuʀ] nm perimeter

**pourvoir** [puʀvwaʀ] vt: ~ **qch/qn de** to equip sth/sb with ♦ vi: ~ **à** to provide for; **pourvoyeur** nm supplier; **pourvu, e** adj: **pourvu de** equipped with; **pourvu que** (si) provided that, so long as; (espérons que) let's hope (that)

**pousse** [pus] nf growth; (bourgeon) shoot

**poussé, e** [puse] adj (enquête) exhaustive; (études) advanced; **poussée** nf thrust; (d'acné) eruption; (fig: prix) upsurge

**pousser** [puse] vt to push; (émettre: cri, soupir) to give; (stimuler: élève) to urge on; (poursuivre: études, discussion) to carry on (further); (croître) to grow; **se ~** vi to move over; ~ **qn à** (inciter) to urge ou press sb to; (acculer) to drive sb to; **faire ~** (plante) to grow

**poussette** [pusɛt] nf push chair (BRIT), stroller (US)

**poussière** [pusjɛʀ] nf dust; **poussié-**

**reux, -euse** adj dusty

**poussin** [pusɛ̃] nm chick

**poutre** [putʀ] nf beam

---
MOT-CLÉ
---

**pouvoir** [puvwaʀ] nm power; (POL: dirigeants): **le pouvoir** those in power; **les pouvoirs publics** the authorities; **pouvoir d'achat** purchasing power

♦ vb semi-aux **1** (être en état de) can, be able to; **je ne peux pas le réparer** I can't ou I am not able to repair it; **déçu de ne pas pouvoir le faire** disappointed not to be able to do it

**2** (avoir la permission) can, may, be allowed to; **vous pouvez aller au cinéma** you can ou may go to the pictures

**3** (probabilité, hypothèse) may, might, could; **il a pu avoir un accident** he may ou might ou could have had an accident; **il aurait pu le dire!** he might ou could have said (so)!

♦ vb impers may, might, could; **il peut arriver que** it may ou might ou could happen that

♦ vt can, be able to; **j'ai fait tout ce que j'ai pu** I did all I could; **je n'en peux plus** (épuisé) I'm exhausted; (à bout) I can't take any more; **se pouvoir** vi: **il se peut que** it may ou might be that; **cela se pourrait** that's quite possible

---

**prairie** [pʀeʀi] nf meadow

**praline** [pʀalin] nf sugared almond

**praticable** [pʀatikabl] adj passable, practicable

**pratiquant, e** [pʀatikɑ̃, ɑ̃t] nm/f (regular) churchgoer

**pratique** [pʀatik] nf practice ♦ adj practical; **pratiquement** adv (pour ainsi dire) practically, virtually; **pratiquer** vt to practise; (l'équitation, la pêche) to go in for; (le golf, football) to play; (intervention, opération) to carry out

**pré** [pʀe] nm meadow

**préados** [pʀeado] nmpl preteens

**préalable** [pʀealabl] adj preliminary; **au ~** beforehand

**préambule** [pʀeɑ̃byl] nm preamble; (fig) prelude; **sans ~** straight away

**préau** [pʀeo] nm (SCOL) covered playground

**préavis** [pʀeavi] nm notice

**précaution** [pʀekosjɔ̃] nf precaution; **avec ~** cautiously; **par ~** as a precaution

**précédemment** [pʀesedamɑ̃] adv before, previously

**précédent, e** [pʀesedɑ̃, ɑ̃t] adj previous ♦ nm precedent

**précéder** [pʀesede] vt to precede

**précepteur, -trice** [pʀesɛptœʀ, tʀis] nm/f (private) tutor

**prêcher** [pʀeʃe] vt to preach

**précieux, -euse** [pʀesjø, jøz] adj precious; (aide, conseil) invaluable

**précipice** [pʀesipis] nm drop, chasm

**précipitamment** [pʀesipitamɑ̃] adv hurriedly, hastily

**précipitation** [pʀesipitasjɔ̃] nf (hâte) haste; **~s** nfpl (pluie) rain sg

**précipité, e** [pʀesipite] adj hasty

**précipiter** [pʀesipite] vt (hâter: départ) to hasten; (faire tomber): **~ qn/qch du haut de** to throw ou hurl sb/sth off ou from; **se ~** vi to speed up; **se ~ sur/vers** to rush at/towards

**précis, e** [pʀesi, iz] adj precise; (mesures) accurate, precise; **à 4 heures ~es** at 4 o'clock sharp; **précisément** adv precisely; **préciser** vt (expliquer) to be more specific about, clarify; (spécifier) to state, specify; **se préciser** vi to become clear(er); **précision** nf precision; (détail) point ou detail; **demander des précisions** to ask for further explanation

**précoce** [pʀekɔs] adj early; (enfant) precocious

**préconçu, e** [pʀekɔ̃sy] adj preconceived

**préconiser** [pʀekɔnize] vt to advocate

**prédécesseur** [pʀedesesœʀ] nm predecessor

**prédilection** [predilɛksjɔ̃] nf: avoir une ~ pour to be partial to

**prédire** [predir] vt to predict

**prédominer** [predomine] vi to predominate

**préface** [prefas] nf preface

**préfecture** [prefɛktyr] nf prefecture; ~ de police police headquarters pl

**préférable** [preferabl] adj preferable

**préféré, e** [prefere] adj, nm/f favourite

**préférence** [preferɑ̃s] nf preference; de ~ preferably

**préférer** [prefere] vt: ~ qn/qch (à) to prefer sb/sth (to), like sb/sth better (than); ~ faire to prefer to do; je ~ais du thé I would rather have tea, I'd prefer tea

**préfet** [prefe] nm prefect

**préhistorique** [preistorik] adj prehistoric

**préjudice** [preʒydis] nm (matériel) loss; (moral) harm no pl; porter ~ à to harm, be detrimental to; au ~ de at the expense of

**préjugé** [preʒyʒe] nm prejudice; avoir un ~ contre to be prejudiced ou biased against

**préjuger** [preʒyʒe]: ~ de vt to prejudge

**prélasser** [prelase]: se ~ vi to lounge

**prélèvement** [prelɛvmɑ̃] nm (montant) deduction; faire un ~ de sang to take a blood sample

**prélever** [prel(ə)ve] vt (échantillon) to take; ~ (sur) (montant) to deduct (from); (argent: sur son compte) to withdraw (from)

**prématuré, e** [prematyre] adj premature ♦ nm premature baby

**premier, -ière** [prəmje, jɛr] adj first; (rang) front; (fig: objectif) basic; le ~ venu the first person to come along; de ~ ordre first-rate; P~ Ministre Prime Minister; **première** nf (SCOL) lower sixth form; (THÉÂTRE) first night; (AUTO) first (gear); (AVIAT, RAIL etc) first

class; (CINÉMA) première; (exploit) first; **premièrement** adv firstly

**prémonition** [premɔnisjɔ̃] nf premonition

**prémunir** [premynir]: se ~ vi: se ~ contre to guard against

**prenant, e** [prənɑ̃, ɑ̃t] adj absorbing, engrossing

**prénatal, e** [prenatal] adj (MÉD) antenatal

**prendre** [prɑ̃dr] vt to take; (repas) to have; (se procurer) to get; (malfaiteur, poisson) to catch; (passager) to pick up; (personnel) to take on; (traiter: personne) to handle; (voix, ton) to put on; (ôter): ~ qch à to take sth from; (coincer): se ~ les doigts dans to get one's fingers caught in ♦ vi (liquide, ciment) to set; (greffe, vaccin) to take; (feu: foyer) to go; (se diriger): ~ à gauche to turn (to the) left; ~ froid to catch cold; se ~ pour to think one is; s'en ~ à to attack; se ~ d'amitié pour to befriend; s'y ~ (procéder) to set about it

**preneur** [prənœr, øz] nm: être/trouver ~ to be willing to buy/find a buyer

**preniez** [prənje] vb voir **prendre**

**prenne** etc [prɛn] vb voir **prendre**

**prénom** [prenɔ̃] nm first ou Christian name

**préoccupation** [preɔkypasjɔ̃] nf (souci) concern; (idée fixe) preoccupation

**préoccuper** [preɔkype] vt (inquiéter) to worry; (absorber) to preoccupy; se ~ de to be concerned with

**préparatifs** [preparatif] nmpl preparations

**préparation** [preparasjɔ̃] nf preparation

**préparer** [prepare] vt to prepare; (café, thé) to make; (examen) to prepare for; (voyage, entreprise) to plan; se ~ vi (orage, tragédie) to brew, be in the air; ~ qch à qn (surprise etc) to have sth in store for sb; se ~ (à qch/ faire) to prepare (o.s.) ou get ready (for sth/to do)

**prépondérant, e** [prepɔ̃derɑ̃, ɑ̃t] adj major, dominating

**préposé, e** [prepoze] nm/f employee; (facteur) postman

**préposition** [prepozisjɔ̃] nf preposition

**près** [prɛ] adv near, close; **~ de** near (to), close to; (environ) nearly, almost; **de ~** closely; **à 5 kg ~** to within about 5 kg; **à cela ~ que** apart from the fact that; **il n'est pas à 10 minutes ~** he can spare 10 minutes

**présage** [prezaʒ] nm omen; **présager** vt to foresee

**presbyte** [prɛsbit] adj long-sighted

**presbytère** [prɛsbiter] nm presbytery

**prescription** [prɛskripsjɔ̃] nf prescription

**prescrire** [prɛskrir] vt to prescribe

**présence** [prezɑ̃s] nf presence; (au bureau, à l'école) attendance

**présent, e** [prezɑ̃, ɑ̃t] adj, nm present; **à ~ (que)** now (that)

**présentation** [prezɑ̃tasjɔ̃] nf presentation; (de nouveau venu) introduction; (allure) appearance; **faire les ~s** to do the introductions

**présenter** [prezɑ̃te] vt to present; (excuses, condoléances) to offer; (invité, conférencier): **~ qn (à)** to introduce sb (to) ♦ vi: **~ bien** to have a pleasing appearance; **se ~** vi (occasion) to arise; **se ~ à** (examen) to sit; (élection) to stand at, run for

**préservatif** [prezɛrvatif, iv] nm sheath, condom

**préserver** [prezɛrve] vt: **~ de** (protéger) to protect from

**président** [prezidɑ̃] nm (POL) president; (d'une assemblée, COMM) chairman; **~ directeur général** chairman and managing director; **présidentielles** nfpl presidential elections

**présider** [prezide] vt to preside over; (dîner) to be the guest of honour at

**présomptueux, -euse** [prezɔ̃ptuø,

øz] adj presumptuous

**presque** [prɛsk] adv almost, nearly; **~ personne** hardly anyone; **~ rien** hardly anything; **~ pas** hardly (at all); **~ pas (de)** hardly any

**presqu'île** [prɛskil] nf peninsula

**pressant, e** [presɑ̃, ɑ̃t] adj urgent

**presse** [prɛs] nf press; (affluence): **heures de ~** busy times

**pressé, e** [prese] adj in a hurry; (travail) urgent; **orange ~e** freshly-squeezed orange juice

**pressentiment** [presɑ̃timɑ̃] nm foreboding, premonition

**pressentir** [presɑ̃tir] vt to sense

**presse-papiers** [prɛspapje] nm inv paperweight

**presser** [prese] vt (fruit, éponge) to squeeze; (bouton) to press; (allure) to speed up; (inciter): **~ qn de faire** to urge ou press sb to do ♦ vi to be urgent; **se ~** vi (se hâter) to hurry (up); **se ~ contre qn** to squeeze up against sb; **rien ne presse** there's no hurry

**pressing** [presiŋ] nm (magasin) dry-cleaner's

**pression** [presjɔ̃] nf pressure; (bouton) press stud; (fam: bière) draught beer; **faire ~ sur** to put pressure on; **~ artérielle** blood pressure

**prestance** [prestɑ̃s] nf presence, imposing bearing

**prestataire** [prestater] nm/f supplier

**prestation** [prestasjɔ̃] nf (allocation) benefit; (d'une entreprise) service provided; (d'un artiste) performance

**prestidigitateur, -trice** [prestidiʒitatœr, tris] nm/f conjurer

**prestige** [prestiʒ] nm prestige; **prestigieux, -euse** adj prestigious

**présumer** [prezyme] vt: **~ que** to presume ou assume that

**prêt, e** [prɛ, prɛt] adj ready ♦ nm (somme) loan; **prêt-à-porter** nm ready-to-wear ou off-the-peg (BRIT) clothes pl

**prétendre** [pretɑ̃dr] vt (affirmer): **~**

que to claim that; (avoir l'intention de):
~ faire qch to mean ou intend to do
sth; **prétendu, e** adj (supposé) so-
called

**prétentieux, -euse** [pretɑ̃sjø, jøz] adj
pretentious

**prétention** [pretɑ̃sjɔ̃] nf claim; (vanité)
pretentiousness; ~s nfpl (salaire) expected salary

**prêter** [prete] vt (livres, argent): ~ qch
(à) to lend sth (to); (supposer): ~ à qn
(caractère, propos) to attribute to sb; se
~ à to lend o.s. (to); (se) itself) to; (pré-
gances etc) to go along with; ~ à (critique, commentaires etc) to be open to,
give rise to; ~ attention à to pay attention to; ~ serment to take the oath

**prétexte** [pretekst] nm pretext, excuse;
**sous aucun** ~ on no account; **prétexter** vt to give as a pretext ou an excuse

**prêtre** [prɛtr] nm priest

**preuve** [prœv] nf proof; (indice) proof,
evidence no pl; faire ~ de to show; faire ses ~s to prove o.s. (ou itself)

**prévaloir** [prevalwar] vi to prevail

**prévenant, e** [prev(ə)nɑ̃, ɑ̃t] adj
thoughtful, kind

**prévenir** [prev(ə)nir] vt (éviter: catastrophe etc) to avoid, prevent; (anticiper:
désirs, besoins) to anticipate; ~ qn (de)
(avertir) to warn sb (about); (informer)
to tell ou inform sb (about)

**préventif, -ive** [prevɑ̃tif, iv] adj pre-
ventive

**prévention** [prevɑ̃sjɔ̃] nf prevention; ~
**routière** road safety

**prévenu, e** [prev(ə)ny] nm/f (JUR) defendant, accused

**prévision** [previzjɔ̃] nf: ~s predictions;
(ÉCON) forecast sg; en ~ de in anticipation of; ~s météorologiques weather
forecast sg

**prévoir** [prevwar] vt (anticiper) to foresee; (s'attendre à) to expect, reckon on;
(organiser: voyage etc) to plan; (envisager) to allow; **comme prévu** as

planned; **prévoyant, e** adj gifted with
(rien showing) foresight; **prévu, e** pp de
**prévoir**

**prier** [prije] vi to pray (Dieu) to
pray to; (implorer) to beg; (demander):
~ qn de faire to ask sb to do; se faire
~ to need coaxing ou persuading; je
vous en prie (allez-y) please do; (de
rien) don't mention it; **prière** nf prayer;
**"prière de ..."** "please ..."

**primaire** [primɛr] adj primary ♦ nm
(SCOL) primary education

**prime** [prim] nf (bonus) bonus; (subvention) premium; (COMM: cadeau) free
gift; (ASSURANCES, BOURSE) premium ♦ adj:
de ~ abord at first glance; **primer** vt
(récompenser) to award a prize to ♦ vi
to dominate; to be most important

**primeurs** [primœr] nfpl early fruits
and vegetables

**primevère** [primvɛr] nf primrose

**primitif, -ive** [primitif, iv] adj primitive; (originel) original

**primordial, e, -iaux** [primɔrdjal, jo]
adj essential

**prince** [prɛ̃s] nm prince; **princesse** nf
princess

**principal, e, -aux** [prɛ̃sipal, o] adj
principal, main ♦ nm (SCOL) principal,
head(master); (essentiel) main thing

**principe** [prɛ̃sip] nm principle; **par** ~
on principle; **en** ~ (habituellement) as a
rule; (théoriquement) in principle

**printemps** [prɛ̃tɑ̃] nm spring

**priorité** [prijɔrite] nf priority; (AUTO)
right of way; ~ **à droite** right of way to
vehicles coming from the right

**pris, e** [pri, priz] pp de **prendre** ♦ adj
(place) taken; (mains) full; (personne)
busy; avoir le nez/la gorge ~(e) to
have a stuffy nose/a hoarse throat; **être**
~ **de panique** to be panic-stricken

**prise** [priz] nf (d'une ville) capture;
(PÊCHE, CHASSE) catch; (point d'appui ou
pour empoigner) hold; (ÉLEC: fiche) plug;
(: femelle) socket; être aux ~s avec to
be grappling with; ~ **de conscience**

awareness,' realization; ~ **de contact** (*rencontre*) initial meeting, first contact; ~ **de courant** power point; ~ **de sang** blood test; ~ **de vue** (*photo*) shot; ~ **multiple** adaptor

**priser** [prize] *vt* (*estimer*) to prize, value

**prison** [prizɔ̃] *nf* prison; **aller/être en** ~ to go to/be in prison *ou* jail; **prisonnier, -ière** *nm/f* prisoner ♦ *adj* captive

**prit** [pri] *vb voir* **prendre**

**privé, e** [prive] *adj* private ♦ *nm* (*COMM*) private sector; **en** ~ in private

**priver** [prive] *vt*: ~ **qn de** to deprive sb of; **se** ~ to go *ou* do without

**privilège** [privilɛʒ] *nm* privilege

**prix** [pri] *nm* price; (*récompense, SCOL*) prize; **hors de** ~ exorbitantly priced; **à aucun** ~ not at any price; **à tout** ~ at all costs; ~ **d'achat/de vente/de revient** purchasing/selling/cost price

**probable** [prɔbabl] *adj* likely, probable; **probablement** *adv* probably

**probant, e** [prɔbɑ̃, ɑ̃t] *adj* convincing

**problème** [prɔblɛm] *nm* problem

**procédé** [prɔsede] *nm* (*méthode*) process; (*comportement*) behaviour *no pl*

**procéder** [prɔsede] *vi* to proceed; (*moralement*) to behave; ~ **à** to carry out

**procès** [prɔsɛ] *nm* trial; (*poursuites*) proceedings *pl*; **être en** ~ **avec** to be involved in a lawsuit with

**processus** [prɔsesys] *nm* process

**procès-verbal, -aux** [prɔsɛvɛrbal, o] *nm* (*de réunion*) minutes *pl*; (*aussi*: P.V.) parking ticket

**prochain, e** [prɔʃɛ̃, ɛn] *adj* next; (*proche: départ, arrivée*) impending ♦ *nm* fellow man; **la ~e fois/semaine** ~**e** next time/week; **prochainement** *adv* soon, shortly

**proche** [prɔʃ] *adj* nearby; (*dans le temps*) imminent; (*parent, ami*) close; ~**s** *nmpl* (*parents*) close relatives; **être** ~ (**de**) to be near, be close (to); **le P~-Orient** the Middle East

**proclamer** [prɔklame] *vt* to proclaim

**procuration** [prɔkyrasjɔ̃] *nf* proxy

**procurer** [prɔkyre] *vt*: ~ **qch à qn** (*fournir*) to obtain sth for sb; (*causer: plaisir etc*) to bring sb sth; **se** ~ *vt* to get; **procureur** *nm* public prosecutor

**prodige** [prɔdiʒ] *nm* marvel, wonder; (*personne*) prodigy; **prodiguer** *vt* (*soins, attentions*): **prodiguer qch à qn** to give sb sth

**producteur, -trice** [prɔdyktœr, tris] *nm/f* producer

**productif, -ive** [prɔdyktif, iv] *adj* productive

**production** [prɔdyksjɔ̃] *nf* production; (*rendement*) output

**productivité** [prɔdyktivite] *nf* productivity

**produire** [prɔdɥir] *vt* to produce; **se** ~ *vi* (*événement*) to happen, occur; (*acteur*) to perform, appear

**produit** [prɔdɥi] *nm* product; ~ **chimique** chemical; ~ **d'entretien** cleaning product; ~ **national brut** gross national product; ~**s alimentaires** foodstuffs

**prof** [prɔf] (*fam*) *nm* teacher

**profane** [prɔfan] *adj* (*REL*) secular ♦ *nm/f* layman(-woman)

**proférer** [prɔfere] *vt* to utter

**professeur, e** [prɔfesœr] *nm/f* teacher; (*de faculté*) (university) lecturer; (: *titulaire d'une chaire*) professor

**profession** [prɔfesjɔ̃] *nf* occupation; ~ **libérale** (liberal) profession; **sans** ~ unemployed; **professionnel, le** *adj*, *nm/f* professional

**profil** [prɔfil] *nm* profile; **de** ~ in profile

**profit** [prɔfi] *nm* (*avantage*) benefit, advantage; (*COMM, FINANCE*) profit; **au** ~ **de** in aid of; **tirer** ~ **de** to profit from; **profitable** *adj* (*utile*) beneficial; (*lucratif*) profitable; **profiter**: **profiter de** (*situation, occasion*) to take advantage of; (*vacances, jeunesse etc*) to make the most of

**profond, e** [prɔfɔ̃, ɔ̃d] *adj* deep; (*senti-*

*ment, intérêt*) profound; **profondément** *adv* deeply; **il dort profondément** he is sound asleep; **profondeur** *nf* depth

**progéniture** [prɔʒenityr] *nf* offspring *inv*

**programme** [prɔgram] *nm* programme; (SCOL) syllabus, curriculum; (INFORM) program; **programmer** *vt* (*émission*) to schedule; (INFORM) to program; **programmeur, -euse** *nm/f* programmer

**progrès** [prɔgrɛ] *nm* progress *no pl*; **faire des ~** to make progress; **progresser** *vi* to progress; **progressif, -ive** *adj* progressive

**prohiber** [prɔibe] *vt* to prohibit, ban

**proie** [prwa] *nf* prey *no pl*

**projecteur** [prɔʒɛktœr] *nm* (*pour films*) projector; (*de théâtre, cirque*) spotlight

**projectile** [prɔʒɛktil] *nm* missile

**projection** [prɔʒɛksjɔ̃] *nf* projection; (*séance*) showing

**projet** [prɔʒɛ] *nm* plan; (*ébauche*) draft; **~ de loi** bill; **projeter** *vt* (*envisager*) to plan; (*film, photos*) to project; (*ombre, lueur*) to throw, cast; (*jeter*) to throw up (*ou* off *ou* out)

**prolétaire** [prɔleter] *adj, nmf* proletarian

**prolongement** [prɔlɔ̃ʒmɑ̃] *nm* extension; **dans le ~ de** running on from

**prolonger** [prɔlɔ̃ʒe] *vt* (*débat, séjour*) to prolong; (*délai, billet, rue*) to extend; **se ~** *vi* to go on

**promenade** [prɔm(ə)nad] *nf* walk (*ou* drive *ou* ride); **faire une ~** to go for a walk; **une ~ en voiture/à vélo** a drive/(bicycle) ride

**promener** [prɔm(ə)ne] *vt* (*chien*) to take out for a walk; (*doigts, regard*): **~ qch sur** to run sth over; **se ~** *vi* to go for (*ou* be out for) a walk

**promesse** [prɔmɛs] *nf* promise

**promettre** [prɔmɛtr] *vt* to promise ♦ *vi* to be *ou* look promising; **~ à qn de faire** to promise sb that one will do

**promiscuité** [prɔmiskɥite] *nf* (*chambre*) lack of privacy

**promontoire** [prɔmɔ̃twar] *nm* headland

**promoteur, -trice** [prɔmɔtœr, tris] *nm/f*: **~ (immobilier)** property developer (BRIT), real estate promoter (US)

**promotion** [prɔmosjɔ̃] *nf* promotion; **en ~** on special offer

**promouvoir** [prɔmuvwar] *vt* to promote

**prompt, e** [prɔ̃(pt), prɔ̃(p)t] *adj* swift, rapid

**prôner** [prone] *vt* (*préconiser*) to advocate

**pronom** [prɔnɔ̃] *nm* pronoun

**prononcer** [prɔnɔ̃se] *vt* to pronounce; (*dire*) to utter; (*discours*) to deliver; **se ~** *vi* to be pronounced; **se ~ (sur)** (*se décider*) to reach a decision (on *ou* about), give a verdict (on); **prononciation** *nf* pronunciation

**pronostic** [prɔnɔstik] *nm* (MÉD) prognosis; (*fig: aussi:* **~s**) forecast

**propagande** [prɔpagɑ̃d] *nf* propaganda

**propager** [prɔpaʒe] *vt* to spread; **se ~** *vi* to spread

**prophète** [prɔfɛt] *nm* prophet

**prophétie** [prɔfesi] *nf* prophecy

**propice** [prɔpis] *adj* favourable

**proportion** [prɔpɔrsjɔ̃] *nf* proportion; **toute(s) ~(s) gardée(s)** making due allowance(s)

**propos** [prɔpo] *nm* (*intention*) intention, aim; (*sujet*): **à quel ~?** what about? ♦ *nmpl* (*paroles*) talk *no pl*, remarks; **à ~ de** about, regarding; **à tout ~** for the slightest thing *ou* reason; **à ~** by the way; (*opportunément*) at the right moment

**proposer** [prɔpoze] *vt* to propose; **~ qch (à qn)** (*suggérer*) to suggest sth (to sb), propose sth (to sb); (*offrir*) to offer (sb) sth; **se ~** to offer one's services; **se ~ de faire** to intend *ou* propose to do; **proposition** (*suggestion*) *nf* proposal, suggestion; (LING) clause

**propre** [prɔpr] *adj* clean; (*net*) neat, tidy; (*possessif*) own; (*sens*) literal; (*particulier*): ~ à peculiar to; (*approprié*): ~ à suitable for ♦ *nm*: recopier au ~ to make a fair copy of; **proprement** *adv* (*avec propreté*) cleanly; **le village proprement dit** the village itself; à **proprement parler** strictly speaking; **propreté** *nf* cleanliness

**propriétaire** [prɔprijetɛr] *nm/f* owner; (*pour le locataire*) landlord(-lady)

**propriété** [prɔprijete] *nf* property; (*droit*) ownership

**propulser** [prɔpylse] *vt* to propel

**proroger** [prɔrɔʒe] *vt* (*prolonger*) to extend

**proscrire** [prɔskrir] *vt* (*interdire*) to ban, prohibit

**prose** [proz] *nf* (*style*) prose

**prospecter** [prɔspɛkte] *vt* to prospect; (*COMM*) to canvass

**prospectus** [prɔspɛktys] *nm* leaflet

**prospère** [prɔspɛr] *adj* prosperous; **prospérer** *vi* to prosper

**prosterner** [prɔstɛrne]: **se ~** *vi* to bow low, prostrate o.s.

**prostituée** [prɔstitɥe] *nf* prostitute

**prostitution** [prɔstitysjɔ̃] *nf* prostitution

**protecteur, -trice** [prɔtɛktœr, tris] *adj* protective; (*air, ton: péj*) patronizing ♦ *nm/f* protector

**protection** [prɔtɛksjɔ̃] *nf* protection; (*d'un personnage influent: aide*) patronage

**protéger** [prɔteʒe] *vt* to protect; **se ~ de ou contre** to protect o.s. from

**protéine** [prɔtein] *nf* protein

**protestant, e** [prɔtɛstɑ̃, ɑ̃t] *adj, nm/f* Protestant

**protestation** [prɔtɛstasjɔ̃] *nf* (*plainte*) protest

**protester** [prɔtɛste] *vi*: ~ (**contre**) to protest (against *ou* about); ~ **de** (*son innocence*) to protest

**prothèse** [prɔtɛz] *nf*: ~ **dentaire** den-

ture

**protocole** [prɔtɔkɔl] *nm* (*fig*) etiquette

**proue** [pru] *nf* bow(s *pl*), prow

**prouesse** [prues] *nf* feat

**prouver** [pruve] *vt* to prove

**provenance** [prɔv(ə)nɑ̃s] *nf* origin; **avion en ~ de** plane (arriving) from

**provenir** [prɔv(ə)nir]: ~ **de** *vt* to come from

**proverbe** [prɔvɛrb] *nm* proverb

**province** [prɔvɛ̃s] *nf* province

**proviseur** [prɔvizœr] *nm* ≈ head(teacher) (*BRIT*), ≈ principal (*US*)

**provision** [prɔvizjɔ̃] *nf* (*réserve*) stock, supply; ~**s** *nfpl* (*vivres*) provisions, food *no pl*

**provisoire** [prɔvizwar] *adj* temporary; **provisoirement** *adv* temporarily

**provocant, e** [prɔvɔkɑ̃, ɑ̃t] *adj* provocative

**provoquer** [prɔvɔke] *vt* (*défier*) to provoke; (*causer*) to cause, bring about; (*inciter*): ~ **qn à** to incite sb to

**proxénète** [prɔksenet] *nm* procurer

**proximité** [prɔksimite] *nf* nearness, closeness; (*dans le temps*) imminence, closeness; à ~ near *ou* close by; à ~ **de** near (to), close to

**prudemment** [prydamɑ̃] *adv* carefully; wisely, sensibly

**prudence** [prydɑ̃s] *nf* carefulness; **avec ~** carefully; **par ~** as a precaution

**prudent, e** [prydɑ̃, ɑ̃t] *adj* (*pas téméraire*) careful; (: *en général*) safetyconscious; (*sage, conseillé*) wise, sensible; **c'est plus ~** it's wiser

**prune** [pryn] *nf* plum

**pruneau, x** [pryno] *nm* prune

**prunelle** [prynɛl] *nf* (*BOT*) sloe; **il y tient comme à la ~ de ses yeux** he treasures *ou* cherishes it

**prunier** [prynje] *nm* plum tree

**PS** *sigle m* = **parti socialiste**

**psaume** [psom] *nm* psalm

**pseudonyme** [psødɔnim] *nm* (*gén*) fictitious name; (*d'écrivain*) pseudonym, pen name

**psychanalyse** [psikanaliz] *nf* psycho-analysis

**psychiatre** [psikjatʀ] *nm/f* psychiatrist; **psychiatrique** *adj* psychiatric

**psychique** [psiʃik] *adj* psychological

**psychologie** [psikɔlɔʒi] *nf* psychology; **psychologique** *adj* psychological; **psychologue** *nm/f* psychologist

**P.T.T.** *sigle fpl* = **Postes, Télécommunications et Télédiffusion**

**pu** [py] *pp de* **pouvoir**

**puanteur** [pɥɑ̃tœʀ] *nf* stink, stench

**pub** [pyb] *nf (fam: annonce)* ad, advert; *(pratique)* advertising

**public, -ique** [pyblik] *adj* public; *(école, instruction)* state *cpd ♦ nm* public; *(assistance)* audience; **en ~** in public

**publicitaire** [pyblisitɛʀ] *adj* advertising *cpd*; *(film)* publicity *cpd*

**publicité** [pyblisite] *nf (méthode, profession)* advertising; *(annonce)* advertisement; *(révélations)* publicity

**publier** [pyblije] *vt* to publish

**publique** [pyblik] *adj voir* **public**

**puce** [pys] *nf* flea; *(INFORM)* chip; **carte à ~** smart card; **~s** *nfpl (marché)* flea market *sg*

**pudeur** [pydœʀ] *nf* modesty; **pudique** *adj (chaste)* modest; *(discret)* discreet

**puer** [pɥe] *(péj) vi* to stink

**puériculture** [pɥeʀikyltʀis] *nf* p(a)ediatric nurse

**puéril, e** [pɥeʀil] *adj* childish

**puis** [pɥi] *vb voir* **pouvoir ♦** *adv* then

**puiser** [pɥize] *vt:* **~ (dans)** to draw (from)

**puisque** [pɥisk] *conj* since

**puissance** [pɥisɑ̃s] *nf* power; **en ~ ♦** *adj* potential

**puissant, e** [pɥisɑ̃, ɑ̃t] *adj* powerful

**puisse** *etc* [pɥis] *vb voir* **pouvoir**

**puits** [pɥi] *nm* well

**pull-(over)** [pyl(ɔvɛʀ)] *nm* sweater

**pulluler** [pylyle] *vi* to swarm

**pulvérisateur** [pylveʀizatœʀ] *nm* spray

**pulvériser** [pylveʀize] *vt* to pulverize; *(liquide)* to spray

**punaise** [pynɛz] *nf (ZOOL)* bug; *(clou)* drawing pin *(BRIT)*, thumbtack *(US)*

**punch¹** [pɔ̃ʃ] *nm (boisson)* punch

**punch²** [pœnʃ] *nm (BOXE, fig)* punch

**punir** [pyniʀ] *vt* to punish; **punition** *nf* punishment

**pupille** [pypij] *nf (ANAT)* pupil ♦ *nm/f (enfant)* ward

**pupitre** [pypitʀ] *nm (SCOL)* desk

**pur, e** [pyʀ] *adj* pure; *(vin)* undiluted; *(whisky)* neat; **en ~e perte** to no avail; **c'est de la folie ~e** it's sheer madness; **purement** *adv* purely

**purée** [pyʀe] *nf:* **~ (de pommes de terre)** mashed potatoes *pl*; **~ de marrons** chestnut purée

**purgatoire** [pyʀgatwaʀ] *nm* purgatory

**purger** [pyʀʒe] *vt (MÉD, POL)* to purge; *(JUR: peine)* to serve

**purin** [pyʀɛ̃] *nm* liquid manure

**pur-sang** [pyʀsɑ̃] *nm inv* thoroughbred

**putain** [pytɛ̃] *(fam!) nf* whore *(!)*

**puzzle** [pœzl] *nm* jigsaw (puzzle)

**P.-V.** *sigle m* = **procès-verbal**

**pyjama** [piʒama] *nm* pyjamas *pl (BRIT)*, pajamas *pl (US)*

**Pyrénées** [piʀene] *nfpl:* **les ~** the Pyrenees

## Q, q

**QI** *sigle m* (= quotient intellectuel) IQ

**quadra** [k(w)adʀa] *nm/f* man/woman in his/her forties; **les ~s** forty somethings *(fam)*

**quadragénaire** [k(w)adʀaʒenɛʀ] *nm/f* man/woman in his/her forties

**quadriller** [kadʀije] *vt (POLICE)* to keep under tight control

**quadruple** [k(w)adʀypl] *nm:* **le ~ de** four times as much as; **quadruplés, -ées** *nm/fpl* quadruplets, quads

**quai** [ke] *nm (de port)* quay; *(de gare)* platform; **être à ~** *(navire)* to be alongside

**qualification** [kalifikasjɔ̃] nf (aptitude) qualification

**qualifié, e** [kalifje] adj qualified; (main d'œuvre) skilled

**qualifier** [kalifje] vt to qualify; **se ~** vi to qualify; **~ qch/qn de** to describe sth/sb as

**qualité** [kalite] nf quality

**quand** [kɑ̃] conj, adv when; **~ je serai riche** when I'm rich; **~ même** all the same; **~ même, il exagère!** really, he overdoes it!; **~ bien même** even though

**quant** [kɑ̃]: **~ à** prép (pour ce qui est de) as for, as to; (au sujet de) regarding; **quant-à-soi** nm: **rester sur son quant-à-soi** to remain aloof

**quantité** [kɑ̃tite] nf quantity, amount; (grand nombre): **une** ou **des ~(s) de** a great deal of

**quarantaine** [karɑ̃tɛn] nf (MÉD) quarantine; **avoir la ~** (âge) to be around forty; **une ~ (de)** forty or so, about forty

**quarante** [karɑ̃t] num forty

**quart** [kaʀ] num (fraction) quarter; (surveillance) watch; **un ~ de vin** a quarter litre of wine; **le ~ de** a quarter of; **~ d'heure** quarter of an hour; **~s de finale** quarter finals

**quartier** [kaʀtje] nm (de ville) district, area; (de bœuf) quarter; (de fruit) piece; **cinéma de ~** local cinema; **avoir ~ libre** (fig) to be free; **~ général** headquarters pl

**quartz** [kwaʀts] nm quartz

**quasi** [kazi] adv almost, nearly; **quasiment** adv almost, nearly; **quasiment jamais** hardly ever

**quatorze** [katɔʀz] num fourteen

**quatre** [katʀ] num four; **à ~ pattes** on all fours; **se mettre en ~ pour** qn to go out of one's way for sb; **~ à ~** (monter, descendre) four at a time; **quatre-quarts** nm inv pound cake; **quatre-vingt-dix** num ninety;

**quatre-vingts** num eighty; **quatre-vingt-un** num eighty-one; **quatrième** num fourth ♦ nf (SCOL) third form ou year

**quatuor** [kwatɥɔʀ] nm quartet(te)

MOT-CLÉ

**que** [kə] conj 1 (introductive complétive) that; **il sait que tu es là** he knows (that) you're here; **je veux que tu acceptes** I want you to accept; **il a dit que oui** he said he would (ou it was) etc

2 (reprise d'autres conjonctions): **quand il rentrera et qu'il aura mangé** when he gets back and (when) he has eaten; **si vous y allez ou que vous ...** if you go there or if you ...

3 (en tête de phrase: hypothèse, souhait etc): **qu'il le veuille ou non** whether he likes it or not; **qu'il fasse ce qu'il voudra!** let him do as he pleases!

4 (après comparatif) than; ou: voir aussi **plus**; **aussi**; **autant** etc

5 (seulement): **ne ... que** only; **il ne boit que de l'eau** he only drinks water

♦ adv (exclamation): **qu'il** ou **qu'est-ce qu'il est bête/court vite!** he's so silly!/he runs so fast!; **que de livres!** what a lot of books!

♦ pron 1 (relatif: personne) whom; (: chose) that, which; **l'homme que je vois** the man (whom) I see; **le livre que tu vois** the book (that ou which) you see; **un jour que j'étais ...** a day when I was ...

2 (interrogatif) what; **que fais-tu?** what are you doing?; **qu'est-ce que tu fais?** what are you doing?; **qu'est-ce que c'est?** what is it?, what's that?; **que faire?** what can one do?

**Québec** [kebɛk] n: **le ~** Quebec; **québecois, e** adj Quebec ♦ nm/f: **Québecois, e** Quebecker ♦ nm (LING) Quebec French

MOT-CLÉ

**quel, quelle** [kɛl] *adj* 1 (*interrogatif:
personne*) who; (: *chose*) what; which;
**quel est cet homme?** who is this
man?; **quel est ce livre?** what is this
book?; **quel livre/homme?** what
book/man?; (*parmi un certain choix*)
which book/man?; **quels acteurs
préférez-vous?** which actors do you
prefer?; **dans quels pays êtes-vous
allé?** which *ou* what countries did you
go to?

2 (*exclamatif*): **quelle surprise!** what a
surprise!

3: **quel que soit le coupable** whoever
is guilty; **quel que soit votre avis**
whatever your opinion

**quelconque** [kɛlkɔ̃k] *adj* (*indéfini*): **un
ami/prétexte ~** some friend/pretext
or other; (*médiocre: repas*) indifferent,
poor; (*laid: personne*) plain-looking

MOT-CLÉ

**quelque** [kɛlk] *adj* 1 some; a few;
(*tournure interrogative*) any; **quelque
espoir** some hope; **il a quelques amis**
he has a few *ou* some friends; **a-t-il
quelques amis?** has he any friends?;
**les quelques livres qui** the few books
which; **20 kg et quelque(s)** a bit over
20 kg

2: **quelque ... que:** **quelque livre
qu'il choisisse** whatever (*ou* which-
ever) book he chooses

3: **quelque chose** something, (*tournure interrogative*) anything; **quelque
chose d'autre** something else; anything else; **quelque part** somewhere;
anywhere; **en quelque sorte** as it were
♦ *adv* 1 (*environ*): **quelque 100 mètres**
some 100 metres

2: **quelque peu** rather, somewhat

**quelquefois** [kɛlkəfwa] *adv* sometimes
**quelques-uns, -unes** [kɛlkəzœ̃, yn]

*pron* a few, some

**quelqu'un** [kɛlkœ̃] *pron* someone,
somebody; (*+tournure interrogative*)
anyone, anybody; **~ d'autre** someone
*ou* somebody else; (*+ tournure interrogative*) anybody else

**quémander** [kemɑ̃de] *vt* to beg for
**qu'en dira-t-on** [kɑ̃diraɑ̃tɔ̃] *nm inv*: **le
~ ~-~-~** gossip, what people say
**querelle** [kərɛl] *nf* quarrel; **quereller:
se quereller** *vi* to quarrel
**qu'est-ce que** [kɛskə] *voir* **que**
**qu'est-ce qui** [kɛski] *voir* **qui**
**question** [kɛstjɔ̃] *nf* question; (*fig*) matter, issue; **il a été ~ de** we (*ou* they)
spoke about; **de quoi est-il ~?** what is
it about?; **il n'en est pas ~** there's no
question of it; **hors de ~** out of the
question; **remettre en ~** to question;
**questionnaire** *nm* questionnaire;
**questionner** *vt* to question
**quête** [kɛt] *nf* collection; (*recherche*)
quest, search; **faire la ~** (*à l'église*) to
take the collection; (*artiste*) to pass the
hat round
**quetsche** [kwɛtʃ] *nf* kind of dark-red
plum
**queue** [kø] *nf* tail; (*fig: du classement*)
bottom; (: *de poêle*) handle; (: *de fruit,
feuille*) stalk; (: *de train, colonne, file*)
rear; **faire la ~** to queue (up) (*BRIT*),
line up (*US*); **~ de cheval** ponytail; **~
de poisson** (*AUT*): **faire une ~ de
poisson à qn** to cut in front of sb
**qui** [ki] *pron* (*personne*) who; (*+prép*)
whom; (*chose, animal*) which, that;
**qu'est-ce ~ est sur la table?** what is
on the table?; **~ est-ce ~?** who?; **~
est-ce que?** who?; **à ~ est ce sac?**
whose bag is this?; **à ~ parlais-tu?**
who were you talking to?, to whom
were you talking?; **amenez ~ vous
voulez** bring who you like; **~ que ce
soit** whoever it may be
**quiconque** [kikɔ̃k] *pron* (*celui qui*) whoever, anyone who; (*n'importe qui*) anyone, anybody

**quiétude** [kjetyd] *nf*: **en toute ~ in complete peace**

**quille** [kij] *nf*: **(jeu de) ~s** skittles (*BRIT*), bowling (*US*)

**quincaillerie** [kɛ̃kajʀi] *nf* (*ustensiles*) hardware; (*magasin*) hardware shop; **quincaillier, -ière** *nm/f* hardware dealer

**quinquagénaire** [kɛ̃kaʒenɛʀ] *nm/f* man/woman in his/her fifties

**quintal, -aux** [kɛ̃tal, o] *nm* quintal (*100 kg*)

**quinte** [kɛ̃t] *nf*: **~ (de toux)** coughing fit

**quintuple** [kɛ̃typl] *rfm*: **le ~ de** five times as much as; **quintuplés, -ées** *nm/fpl* quintuplets, quins

**quinzaine** [kɛ̃zɛn] *nf*: **une ~ (de)** about fifteen, fifteen or so; **une ~ (de jours)** a fortnight (*BRIT*), two weeks

**quinze** [kɛ̃z] *num* fifteen; **dans ~ jours** in a fortnight('s time), in two weeks(' time)

**quiproquo** [kipʀɔko] *nm* misunderstanding

**quittance** [kitɑ̃s] *nf* (*reçu*) receipt

**quitte** [kit] *adj*: **être ~ envers qn** to be no longer in sb's debt; (*fig*) to be quits with sb; **~ à faire** even if it means doing

**quitter** [kite] *vt* to leave; (*vêtement*) to take off; **se ~** *vi* (*couples, interlocuteurs*) to part; **ne quittez pas** (*au téléphone*) hold the line

**qui-vive** [kiviv] *nm*: **être sur le ~~** to be on the alert

**quoi** [kwa] *pron* (*interrogatif*) what; **~ de neuf?** what's the news?; **as-tu de ~ écrire?** have you anything to write with?; **~ qu'il arrive** whatever happens; **~ qu'il en soit** be that as it may; **~ que ce soit** anything at all; **"il n'y a pas de ~"** "(please) don't mention it"; **il n'y a pas de ~ rire** there's nothing to laugh about; **à ~ bon?** what's the use?; **en ~ puis-je vous aider?** how can I help you?

**quoique** [kwak] *conj* (al)though

**quote-part** [kɔtpaʀ] *nf* share

**quotidien, ne** [kɔtidjɛ̃, jɛn] *adj* daily; (*banal*) everyday ♦ *nm* (*journal*) daily (paper); **quotidiennement** *adv* daily

# R, r

**r.** *abr* = **route**; **rue**

**rab** [ʀab] (*fam*) *nm* (*nourriture*) extra; **est-ce qu'il y a du ~?** is there any extra (left)?

**rabâcher** [ʀabɑʃe] *vt* to keep on repeating

**rabais** [ʀabɛ] *nm* reduction, discount; **rabaisser** *vt* (*dénigrer*) to belittle; (*rabattre: prix*) to reduce

**rabat-joie** [ʀabaʒwa] *nm inv* killjoy

**rabattre** [ʀabatʀ] *vt* (*couvercle, siège*) to pull down; (*déduire*) to reduce; **se ~** *vi* (*se refermer: couvercle*) to fall shut; (*véhicule, coureur*) to cut in; **se ~ sur** to fall back on

**rabbin** [ʀabɛ̃] *nm* rabbi

**râblé, e** [ʀɑble] *adj* stocky

**rabot** [ʀabo] *nm* plane

**rabougri, e** [ʀabugʀi] *adj* stunted

**rabrouer** [ʀabʀue] *vt* to snub

**racaille** [ʀakaj] (*péj*) *nf* rabble, riffraff

**raccommoder** [ʀakɔmɔde] *vt* to mend, repair; **se ~** *vi* (*fam*) to make it up

**raccompagner** [ʀakɔ̃paɲe] *vt* to take ou see back

**raccord** [ʀakɔʀ] *nm* link; (*retouche*) touch up; **raccorder** *vt* to join (up), link up; (*suj: pont etc*) to connect, link

**raccourci** [ʀakuʀsi] *nm* short cut

**raccourcir** [ʀakuʀsiʀ] *vt* to shorten ♦ *vi* (*jours*) to grow shorter, draw in

**raccrocher** [ʀakʀɔʃe] *vt* (*tableau*) to hang back up; (*récepteur*) to put down ♦ *vi* (*TÉL*) to hang up, ring off; **se ~ à** vt to cling to, hang on to

**race** [ʀas] *nf* race; (*d'animaux, fig*) breed; **de ~** purebred, pedigree

**rachat** [ʀaʃa] nm buying; (du même objet) buying back

**racheter** [ʀaʃ(ə)te] vt (article perdu) to buy another; (après avoir vendu) to buy back; (d'occasion) to buy; (COMM: part, firme) to buy up; (davantage): ~ **du lait/3 œufs** to buy more milk/another 3 eggs ou 3 more eggs; **se** ~ vi (fig) to make amends

**racial, e, -aux** [ʀasjal, jo] adj racial

**racine** [ʀasin] nf root; ~ **carrée/cubique** square/cube root

**raciste** [ʀasist] adj, nm/f raci(al)ist

**racket** [ʀaket] nm racketeering no pl

**raclée** [ʀɑkle] nf (fam) hiding, thrashing

**racler** [ʀɑkle] vt (surface) to scrape; **se** ~ **la gorge** to clear one's throat

**racoler** [ʀɑkɔle] vt (suj: prostituée) to solicit; (: parti, marchand) to tout for

**racontars** [ʀɑkɔ̃taʀ] nmpl story, lie

**raconter** [ʀɑkɔ̃te] vt: ~ (**à qn**) (décrire) to relate (to sb), tell (sb) about; (dire de mauvaise foi) to tell (sb); ~ **une histoire** to tell a story

**racorni, e** [ʀakɔʀni] adj hard(ened)

**radar** [ʀadaʀ] nm radar

**rade** [ʀad] nf (natural) harbour; **rester en** ~ (fig) to be left stranded

**radeau, x** [ʀado] nm raft

**radiateur** [ʀadjatœʀ] nm radiator, heater; (AUTO) radiator; ~ **électrique/à gaz** electric/gas heater ou fire

**radiation** [ʀadjasjɔ̃] nf (PHYSIQUE) radiation

**radical, e, -aux** [ʀadikal, o] adj radical

**radier** [ʀadje] vt to strike off

**radieux, -euse** [ʀadjø, jøz] adj radiant

**radin, e** [ʀadɛ̃, in] (fam) adj stingy

**radio** [ʀadjo] nf radio; (MÉD) X-ray ♦ nm radio operator; **à la** ~ on the radio; **radioactif, -ive** adj radioactive; **radio-cassette** nm cassette radio, radio-cassette player; **radiodiffuser** vt to broadcast; **radiographie** nf radiography; (photo) X-ray photograph; **radiophonique** adj radio cpd; **radio-réveil** (pl

**radios-réveils**) nm radio alarm clock

**radis** [ʀadi] nm radish

**radoter** [ʀadɔte] vi to ramble on

**radoucir** [ʀadusiʀ]: **se** ~ vi (temps) to become milder; (se calmer) to calm down

**rafale** [ʀafal] nf (vent) gust of wind; (tir) burst of gunfire

**raffermir** [ʀafɛʀmiʀ] vt to firm up; **se** ~ vi (fig: autorité, prix) to strengthen

**raffiner** [ʀafine] vt to refine; **raffinerie** nf refinery

**raffoler** [ʀafɔle]: ~ **de** vt to be very keen on

**rafistoler** [ʀafistɔle] (fam) vt to patch up

**rafle** [ʀɑfl] nf (de police) raid; **rafler** (fam) vt to swipe, nick

**rafraîchir** [ʀafʀeʃiʀ] vt (atmosphère, température) to cool (down); (aussi: **mettre à** ~) to chill; (fig: rénover) to brighten up; **se** ~ vi (temps) to grow cooler; (en se lavant) to freshen up; (en buvant) to refresh o.s.; **rafraîchissant, e** adj refreshing; **rafraîchissement** nm (boisson) cool drink; **rafraîchissements** nmpl (boissons, fruits etc) refreshments

**rage** [ʀaʒ] nf (MÉD): **la** ~ rabies; (fureur) rage, fury; **faire** ~ to rage; ~ **de dents** (raging) toothache

**ragot** [ʀago] (fam) nm malicious gossip no pl

**ragoût** [ʀagu] nm stew

**raide** [ʀed] adj stiff; (câble) taut, tight; (escarpé) steep; (droit: cheveux) straight; (fam: sans argent) flat broke; (osé) daring, bold ♦ adv (en pente) steeply; ~ **mort** stone dead; **raidir** vt (muscles) to stiffen; **se raidir** vi (tissu) to stiffen; (personne) to tense up; (: se préparer moralement) to brace o.s.; (fig: position) to harden; **raideur** nf (rigidité) stiffness; **avec raideur** (répondre) stiffly, abruptly

**raie** [ʀe] nf (ZOOL) skate, ray; (rayure) stripe; (des cheveux) parting

**raifort** [ʀefɔʀ] nm horseradish

**rail** [ʀɑj] nm rail; (chemins de fer) railways pl; **par ~** by rail

**railler** [ʀɑje] vt to scoff at, jeer at

**rainure** [ʀenyʀ] nf groove

**raisin** [ʀezɛ̃] nm (aussi: **~s**) grapes pl; **~s secs** raisins

**raison** [ʀezɔ̃] nf reason; **avoir ~** to be right; **donner ~ à qn** to agree with sb; (événement) to prove sb right; **perdre la ~** to become insane; **~ de plus** all the more reason; **à plus forte ~** all the more so; **en ~ de** because of; **à ~ de** at the rate of; **sans ~** for no reason; **raisonnable** adj reasonable, sensible

**raisonnement** [ʀezɔnmɑ̃] nm (façon de réfléchir) reasoning; (argumentation) argument

**raisonner** [ʀezɔne] vi (penser) to reason; (argumenter, discuter) to argue ♦ vt (personne) to reason with

**rajeunir** [ʀaʒœniʀ] vt (suj: coiffure, robe): **~ qn** to make sb look younger; (fig: personnel) to inject new blood into ♦ vi to become (ou look) younger

**rajouter** [ʀaʒute] vt to add

**rajuster** [ʀaʒyste] vt (vêtement) to straighten, tidy; (salaires) to adjust

**ralenti** [ʀalɑ̃ti] nm: **au ~** (fig) at a slower pace; **tourner au ~** (AUTO) to tick over, idle

**ralentir** [ʀalɑ̃tiʀ] vt to slow down

**râler** [ʀɑle] vi to groan; (fam) to grouse, moan (and groan)

**rallier** [ʀalje] vt (rejoindre) to rejoin; (gagner à sa cause) to win over; **se ~ à** (avis) to come over ou round to

**rallonge** [ʀalɔ̃ʒ] nf (de table) (extra) leaf

**rallonger** [ʀalɔ̃ʒe] vt to lengthen

**rallye** [ʀali] nm rally; (POL) march

**ramassage** [ʀamasaʒ] nm: **~ scolaire** school bus service

**ramassé, e** [ʀamase] adj (trapu) squat

**ramasser** [ʀamase] vt (objet tombé ou par terre, fam) to pick up; (recueillir: copies, ordures) to collect; (récolter) to gather; **se ~** vi (sur soi-même) to huddle up; **ramassis** (péj) nm (de voyous) bunch; (d'objets) jumble

**rambarde** [ʀɑ̃baʀd] nf guardrail

**rame** [ʀam] nf (aviron) oar; (de métro) train; (de papier) ream

**rameau, x** [ʀamo] nm (small) branch; **les R~x** (REL) Palm Sunday sg

**ramener** [ʀam(ə)ne] vt to bring back; (reconduire) to take back; **~ qch à** (réduire à) to reduce sth to

**ramer** [ʀame] vi to row

**ramollir** [ʀamɔliʀ] vt to soften; **se ~** vi to go soft

**ramoner** [ʀamone] vt to sweep

**rampe** [ʀɑ̃p] nf (d'escalier) banister(s pl); (dans un garage) ramp; (THÉÂTRE): **la ~** the footlights pl; **~ de lancement** launching pad

**ramper** [ʀɑ̃pe] vi to crawl

**rancard** [ʀɑ̃kaʀ] nm (fam) rendez-vous) date

**rancart** [ʀɑ̃kaʀ] nm: **mettre au ~** (fam) to scrap

**rance** [ʀɑ̃s] adj rancid

**rancœur** [ʀɑ̃kœʀ] nf rancour

**rançon** [ʀɑ̃sɔ̃] nf ransom

**rancune** [ʀɑ̃kyn] nf grudge, rancour; **garder ~ à qn (de qch)** to bear sb a grudge (for sth); **sans ~!** no hard feelings!; **rancunier, -ière** adj vindictive, spiteful

**randonnée** [ʀɑ̃dɔne] nf ride; (pédestre) walk, ramble; (: en montagne) hike, hiking no pl

**rang** [ʀɑ̃] nm (rangée) row; (grade, classement) rank; **~s** nmpl (MIL) ranks; **se mettre en ~s** to get into ou form rows; **au premier ~** in the first row; (fig) ranking first

**rangé, e** [ʀɑ̃ʒe] adj (vie) well-ordered; (personne) steady

**rangée** [ʀɑ̃ʒe] nf row

**ranger** [ʀɑ̃ʒe] vt (mettre de l'ordre dans) to tidy up; (classer, grouper) to order, arrange; (mettre à sa place) to put away; (fig: classer): **~ qn/qch parmi** to rank sb/sth among; **se ~** vi (véhicule, conducteur) to pull over ou in; (piéton) to step aside; (s'asseoir) to settle down; **se ~ à** (avis) to come round to

**ranimer** [Ranime] vt (personne) to bring round; (douleur, souvenir) to revive; (feu) to rekindle

**rap** [Rap] nm rap (music)

**rapace** [Rapas] nm bird of prey

**râpe** [Rɑp] nf (CULIN) grater; **râper** (CULIN) to grate

**rapetisser** [Rap(ə)tise] vt to shorten

**rapide** [Rapid] adj fast; (prompt: coup d'œil, mouvement) quick ♦ nm express (train); (de cours d'eau) rapid; **rapidement** adv fast; quickly

**rapiécer** [Rapjese] vt to patch

**rappel** [Rapɛl] nm (THÉÂTRE) curtain call; (MÉD: vaccination) booster; (deuxième avis) reminder; **rappeler** vt to call back; (ambassadeur, MIL) to recall; (faire se souvenir): **rappeler qch à qn** to remind sb of sth; **se rappeler** vt (se souvenir de) to remember, recall

**rapport** [RapɔR] nm (lien, analogie) connection; (compte rendu) report; (profit) yield, return; **~s** nmpl (entre personnes, pays) relations; **avoir ~ à** to have something to do with; **être/se mettre en ~ avec qn** to be/get in touch with sb; **par ~ à** in relation to; **~s (sexuels)** (sexual) intercourse sg

**rapporter** [RapɔRte] vt (rendre, ramener) to bring back; (bénéfice) to yield, bring in; (mentionner, répéter) to report ♦ vi (investissement) to give a good return ou yield; (: activité) to be very profitable; **se ~ à** vt (correspondre à) to relate to; **rapporteur, -euse** nm/f (péj) telltale ♦ nm (GÉOM) protractor

**rapprochement** [RapRɔʃmɑ̃] nm (de nations) reconciliation; (rapport) parallel

**rapprocher** [RapRɔʃe] vt (deux objets) to bring closer together; (fig: ennemis, partis etc) to bring together; (comparer) to establish a parallel between; (chaise d'une table): **~ qch (de)** to bring sth

closer (to); **se ~** vi to draw closer ou nearer; **se ~ de** to come closer to; (présenter une analogie avec) to be close to

**rapt** [Rapt] nm abduction

**raquette** [Rakɛt] nf (de tennis) racket; (de ping-pong) bat

**rare** [RɑR] adj rare; **se faire ~** to become scarce; **rarement** adv rarely, seldom

**ras, e** [Rɑ, Rɑz] adj (poil, herbe) short; (tête) close-cropped ♦ adv short; **en ~e campagne** in open country; **à ~ bords** to the brim; **en avoir ~ le bol** (fam) to be fed up; **~ du cou** ♦ adj (pull, robe) crew-neck

**rasade** [Razad] nf glassful

**raser** [Raze] vt (barbe, cheveux) to shave off; (menton, personne) to shave; (fam: ennuyer) to bore; (démolir) to raze (to the ground); (frôler) to graze, skim; **se ~** vt to shave; (fam) to be bored (to tears); **rasoir** nm razor

**rassasier** [Rasazje] vt: **être rassasié** to have eaten one's fill

**rassemblement** [Rasɑ̃bləmɑ̃] nm (groupe) gathering; (POL) union

**rassembler** [Rasɑ̃ble] vt (réunir) to assemble, gather; (documents, notes) to gather together, collect; **se ~** vi to gather

**rassis, e** [Rasi, iz] adj (pain) stale

**rassurer** [RasyRe] vt to reassure; **se ~** vi to reassure o.s.; **rassure-toi** don't worry

**rat** [Ra] nm rat

**rate** [Rat] nf spleen

**raté, e** [Rate] adj (tentative) unsuccessful, failed ♦ nm/f (fam: personne) failure

**râteau, x** [Rato] nm rake

**rater** [Rate] vi (affaire, projet etc) to go wrong, fail ♦ vt (cible, train, occasion) to miss; (plat) to spoil; (examen) to fail

**ration** [Rasjɔ̃] nf ration

**ratisser** [Ratise] vt (allée) to rake; (feuilles) to rake up; (suj: armée, police) to comb

**RATP** sigle f (= Régie autonome des transports parisiens) Paris transport authority

**rattacher** [Rataʃe] vt (animal, cheveux) to tie up again; (fig: relier): ~ qch à to link with with

**rattrapage** [RatRapaʒ] nm: **cours de ~** remedial class

**rattraper** [RatRape] vt (fugitif) to recapture; (empêcher de tomber) to catch (hold of); (atteindre, rejoindre) to catch up with; (réparer: erreur) to make up for; **se ~** vi to make up for it; **se ~ (à)** (se raccrocher) to stop o.s. falling (by catching hold of)

**rature** [RatyR] nf deletion, erasure

**rauque** [Rok] adj (voix) hoarse

**ravages** [Ravaʒ] nmpl: **faire des ~** to wreak havoc

**ravaler** [Ravale] vt (mur, façade) to restore; (déprécier) to lower

**ravi, e** [Ravi] adj: **être ~ de/que** to be delighted with/that

**ravigoter** [Ravigɔte] (fam) vt to buck up

**ravin** [Ravɛ̃] nm gully, ravine

**ravir** [RaviR] vt (enchanter) to delight; **à ~** adv beautifully

**raviser** [Ravize]: **se ~** vi to change one's mind

**ravissant, e** [Ravisɑ̃, ɑ̃t] adj delightful

**ravisseur, -euse** [RavisœR, øz] nm/f abductor, kidnapper

**ravitaillement** [RavitajmÃ] nm (réserves) supplies pl

**ravitailler** [Ravitaje] vt (en vivres, munitions) to provide with fresh supplies; (avion) to refuel; **se ~** vi to get fresh supplies; (avion) to refuel

**raviver** [Ravive] vt (feu, douleur) to revive; (couleurs) to brighten up

**rayé, e** [Reje] adj (à rayures) striped

**rayer** [Reje] vt (érafler) to scratch; (barrer) to cross out; (d'une liste) to cross off

**rayon** [Rejɔ̃] nm (de soleil etc) ray; (GÉOM) radius; (de roue) spoke; (étagère)

shelf; (de grand magasin) department; **dans un ~ de** within a radius of; **~ de soleil** sunbeam; **~s X** X-rays

**rayonnement** [Rejɔnmã] nm (fig: d'une culture) influence

**rayonner** [Rejɔne] vi (fig) to shine forth; (personne: de joie, de beauté) to be radiant; (touriste) to go touring (from one base)

**rayure** [RejyR] nf (motif) stripe; (éraflure) scratch; **à ~s** striped

**raz-de-marée** [Rɑdmare] nm inv tidal wave

**ré** [Re] nm (MUS) D; (en chantant la gamme) re

**réacteur** [ReaktœR] nm (d'avion) jet engine; (nucléaire) reactor

**réaction** [Reaksjɔ̃] nf reaction

**réadapter** [Readapte]: **se ~ (à)** vi to readjust (to)

**réagir** [ReaʒiR] vi to react

**réalisateur, -trice** [RealizatœR, tRis] nm/f (TV, CINÉMA) director

**réalisation** [Realizasjɔ̃] nf realization; (cinéma) production; **en cours de ~** under way

**réaliser** [Realize] vt (projet, opération) to carry out, realize; (rêve, souhait) to realize, fulfil; (exploit) to achieve; (film) to produce; (se rendre compte de) to realize; **se ~** vi to be realized

**réaliste** [Realist] adj realistic

**réalité** [Realite] nf reality; **en ~** in (actual) fact; **dans la ~** in reality

**réanimation** [Reanimasjɔ̃] nf resuscitation; **service de ~** intensive care unit

**rébarbatif, -ive** [Rebarbatif, iv] adj forbidding

**rebattu, e** [R(ə)baty] adj hackneyed

**rebelle** [Rəbɛl] nm/f rebel ♦ adj (troupes) rebel; (enfant) rebellious; (mèche etc) unruly

**rebeller** [R(ə)bele]: **se ~** vi to rebel

**rebondi, e** [R(ə)bɔ̃di] adj (joues) chubby

**rebondir** [R(ə)bɔ̃diR] vi (ballon: au sol) to bounce; (: contre un mur) to rebound; (fig) to get moving again; **rebondissement** nm new development

**rebord** [R(ə)bɔR] nm edge; **le ~ de la fenêtre** the windowsill

**rebours** [R(ə)buR]: **à ~** adv the wrong way

**rebrousser** [R(ə)bRuse] vt: **~ chemin** to turn back

**rebut** [Raby] nm: **mettre au ~** to scrap; **rebutant, e** adj off-putting; **rebuter** vt to put off

**récalcitrant, e** [RekalsitRɑ̃, ɑ̃t] adj refractory

**recaler** [R(ə)kale] vt (SCOL) to fail; **se faire ~** to fail

**récapituler** [Rekapityle] vt to recapitulate, sum up

**receler** [R(ə)səle] vt (produit d'un vol) to receive; (fig) to conceal; **receleur, -euse** nm/f receiver

**récemment** [Resamɑ̃] adv recently

**recensement** [R(ə)sɑ̃smɑ̃] nm (population) census

**recenser** [R(ə)sɑ̃se] vt (population) to take a census of; (inventorier) to list

**récent, e** [Resɑ̃, ɑ̃t] adj recent

**récépissé** [Resepise] nm receipt

**récepteur** [ReseptœR, tRis] nm receiver

**réception** [Resepsjɔ̃] nf receiving no pl; (accueil, welcome; (bureau) reception desk; (réunion mondaine) reception, party; **réceptionniste** nm/f receptionist

**recette** [R(ə)sɛt] nf recipe; (COMM) takings pl; **~s** nfpl (COMM: rentrées) receipts

**receveur, -euse** [R(ə)səvœR, øz] nm/f (des contributions) tax collector; (des postes) postmaster(-mistress)

**recevoir** [R(ə)səvwaR] vt to receive; (client, patient) to see; **être reçu (à un examen)** to pass

**rechange** [R(ə)fɑ̃ʒ]: **de ~** adj (pièces) spare; (fig: solution) alternative; **des vêtements de ~** a change of clothes

**réchapper** [Refape]: **~ de** ou **à** vt (accident, maladie) to come through

**recharge** [R(ə)faRʒ] nf refill; **rechar-**

**geable** adj (stylo etc) refillable; **recharger** vt (stylo) to refill; (batterie) to recharge

**réchaud** [Refo] nm (portable) stove

**réchauffement** [Refofmɑ̃] nm: **le ~ climatique** global warming

**réchauffer** [Refofe] vt (plat) to reheat; (mains, personne) to warm; **se ~** vi (température) to get warmer; (personne) to warm o.s. (up)

**rêche** [Rɛʃ] adj rough

**recherche** [R(ə)fɛRʃ] nf (action) search; (raffinement) studied elegance; (scientifique etc): **la ~** research; **~s** nfpl (de la police) investigations; (scientifiques) research sg; **la ~ de** the search for; **être à la ~ de qch** to be looking for sth

**recherché, e** [R(ə)fɛRʃe] adj (rare, demandé) much sought-after; (raffiné: style) mannered; (: tenue) elegant

**rechercher** [R(ə)fɛRʃe] vt (objet égaré, personne) to look for; (causes, nouveau procédé) to try to find; (bonheur, compliments) to seek

**rechigner** [R(ə)fiɲe] vi: **~ à faire qch** to balk ou jib at doing sth

**rechute** [R(ə)fyt] nf (MÉD) relapse

**récidiver** [Residive] vi to commit a subsequent offence; (fig) to do it again

**récif** [Resif] nm reef

**récipient** [Resipjɑ̃] nm container

**récit** [Resi] nm story; **récital** nm recital; **réciter** vt to recite

**réclamation** [Reklamasjɔ̃] nf complaint; **~s** nfpl (bureau) complaints department sg

**réclame** [Reklam] nf ad, advert(isement); **en ~** on special offer; **réclamer** vt to ask for; (revendiquer) to claim, demand ♦ vi to complain

**réclusion** [Reklyzjɔ̃] nf imprisonment

**recoin** [Rəkwɛ̃] nm nook, corner

**reçois** etc [Rəswa] vb voir **recevoir**

**récolte** [Rekɔlt] nf harvesting, gathering; (produits) harvest, crop; **récolter** vt to harvest, gather (in); (fig) to collect

**recommandé** [R(ə)kɔmɑ̃de] nm

(POSTES): **en ~** by registered mail

**recommander** [R(ə)kɔmɑ̃de] vt to recommend; (POSTES) to register

**recommencer** [R(ə)kɔmɑ̃se] vt (reprendre: lutte, séance) to resume, start again; (refaire: travail, explications) to start afresh, start (over) again ♦ vi to start again; (récidiver) to do it again

**récompense** [Rekɔ̃pɑ̃s] nf reward; (prix) award; **récompenser** vt: récompenser qn (de ou pour) to reward sb (for)

**réconcilier** [Rekɔ̃silje] vt to reconcile; **se ~ (avec)** to be reconciled (with)

**reconduire** [R(ə)kɔ̃dɥiR] vt (raccompagner) to take ou see back; (renouveler) to renew

**réconfort** [Rekɔ̃fɔR] nm comfort; **réconforter** vt (consoler) to comfort

**reconnaissance** [R(ə)kɔnesɑ̃s] nf (gratitude) gratitude, gratefulness; (action de reconnaître) recognition; (MIL) reconnaissance, recce; **reconnaissant, e** adj grateful

**reconnaître** [R(ə)kɔnɛtR] vt to recognize; (MIL: lieu) to reconnoitre; (JUR: enfant, torts) to acknowledge; **~ que** to admit ou acknowledge that; **reconnu, e** adj (indiscuté, connu) recognized

**reconstituant, e** [R(ə)kɔ̃stituɑ̃, ɑ̃t] adj (aliment, régime) strength-building

**reconstituer** [R(ə)kɔ̃stitɥe] vt (événement, accident) to reconstruct; (fresque, vase brisé) to piece together, reconstitute

**reconstruction** [R(ə)kɔ̃stRyksjɔ̃] nf rebuilding

**reconstruire** [R(ə)kɔ̃stRɥiR] vt to rebuild

**reconvertir** [R(ə)kɔ̃vɛRtiR]: **se ~ dans** vt (un métier, une branche) to go into

**record** [R(ə)kɔR] nm, adj record

**recoupement** [R(ə)kupmɑ̃] nm: **par ~** by cross-checking

**recouper** [R(ə)kupe]: **se ~** vi (témoignages) to tie ou match up

**recourber** [R(ə)kuRbe]: **se ~** vi to

curve (up), bend (up)

**recourir** [R(ə)kuRiR]: **~ à** vt (ami, agence) to turn ou appeal to; (force, ruse, emprunt) to resort to

**recours** [R(ə)kuR] nm: **avoir ~ à = recourir à; en dernier ~** as a last resort

**recouvrer** [R(ə)kuvRe] vt (vue, santé etc) to recover, regain

**recouvrir** [R(ə)kuvRiR] vt (couvrir à nouveau) to re-cover; (couvrir entièrement, aussi fig) to cover

**récréation** [RekReasjɔ̃] nf (SCOL) break

**récrier** [RekRije]: **se ~** vi to exclaim

**récriminations** [RekRiminasjɔ̃] nfpl remonstrations, complaints

**recroqueviller** [R(ə)kRɔk(ə)vije]: **se ~** vi (personne) to huddle up

**recrudescence** [R(ə)kRydesɑ̃s] nf fresh outbreak

**recrue** [RəkRy] nf recruit

**recruter** [R(ə)kRyte] vt to recruit

**rectangle** [Rɛktɑ̃gl] nm rectangle; **rectangulaire** adj rectangular

**rectificatif, ive** [Rɛktifikatif, iv] nm correction

**rectifier** [Rɛktifje] vt (calcul, adresse, paroles) to correct; (erreur) to rectify

**rectiligne** [Rɛktilin] adj straight

**recto** [Rɛkto] nm front (of a page); **~ verso** on both sides (of the page)

**reçu, e** [R(ə)sy] pp de **recevoir** ♦ adj (candidat) successful; (admis, consacré) accepted ♦ nm (COMM) receipt

**recueil** [Rəkœj] nm collection; **recueillir** vt to collect; (voix, suffrages) to win; (accueillir: réfugiés, chat) to take in; **se recueillir** vi to gather one's thoughts, meditate

**recul** [R(ə)kyl] nm (éloignement) distance; (déclin) decline; **être en ~** to be on the decline; **avec du ~** with hindsight; **avoir un mouvement de ~** to recoil; **prendre du ~** to stand back; **reculé, e** adj remote; **reculer** vi to move back, back away; (AUTO) to reverse, back (up); (fig) to (be on the) decline ♦ vt to move back; (véhicule) to reverse, back (up); (*date, décision*) to postpone; **reculons: à reculons** *adv* backwards

**récupérer** [Rekypere] *vt* to recover, get back; (*heures de travail*) to make up; (*déchets*) to salvage ♦ *vi* to recover

**récurer** [Rekyre] *vt* to scour

**récuser** [Rekyze] *vt* to challenge; **se ~** *vi* to decline to give an opinion

**reçut** [Rəsy] *vb voir* recevoir

**recycler** [R(ə)sikle] *vt* (TECH) to recycle; **se ~** *vi* to retrain

**rédacteur, -trice** [Redaktœr, tris] *nm/f* (*journaliste*) writer; subeditor; (*d'ouvrage de référence*) editor, compiler; **~ en chef** chief editor

**rédaction** [Redaksjɔ̃] *nf* writing; (*rédacteurs*) editorial staff; (SCOL: *devoir*) essay, composition

**redemander** [Rədmɑ̃de] *vt* (*une nouvelle fois*) to ask again for; (*davantage*) to ask for more of

**redescendre** [R(ə)desɑ̃dR] *vi* to go back down ♦ *vt* (*pente etc*) to go down

**redevance** [R(ə)dəvɑ̃s] *nf* (TÉL) rental charge; (TV) licence fee

**rédiger** [Redize] *vt* to write; (*contrat*) to draw up

**redire** [R(ə)diR] *vt* to repeat; **trouver à ~ à** to find fault with

**redonner** [R(ə)dɔne] *vt* (*rendre*) to give back; (*resservir: nourriture*) to give more

**redoubler** [R(ə)duble] *vi* (*tempête, violence*) to intensify; (SCOL) to repeat a year; **~ de patience/prudence** to be doubly patient/careful

**redoutable** [R(ə)dutabl] *adj* formidable, fearsome

**redouter** [R(ə)dute] *vt* to dread

**redressement** [R(ə)dRɛsmɑ̃] *nm* (*économique*) recovery

**redresser** [R(ə)dRese] *vt* (*relever*) to set upright; (*pièce tordue*) to straighten out; (*situation, économie*) to put right; **se ~** *vi* (*personne*) to sit (*ou* stand) up (straight); (*économie*) to recover

**réduction** [Redyksjɔ̃] *nf* reduction

**réduire** [RedyiR] *vt* to reduce; (*prix, dépenses*) to cut, reduce; **se ~ à** (*revenir à*) to boil down to; **réduit** *nm* (*pièce*) tiny room

**rééducation** [Reedykasjɔ̃] *nf* (*d'un membre*) re-education; (*de délinquants, d'un blessé*) rehabilitation

**réel, le** [Reɛl] *adj* real; **réellement** *adv* really

**réexpédier** [Reɛkspedje] *vt* (*à l'envoyeur*) to return, send back; (*au destinataire*) to send on, forward

**refaire** [R(ə)fɛR] *vt* to do again; (*faire de nouveau: sport*) to take up again; (*réparer, restaurer*) to do up

**réfection** [Refɛksjɔ̃] *nf* repair

**réfectoire** [RefɛktwaR] *nm* refectory

**référence** [Referɑ̃s] *nf* reference; **~s** *nfpl* (*recommandations*) reference *sg*

**référer** [Refere]: **se ~ à** *vt* to refer to

**refermer** [R(ə)fɛRme] *vt* to close *ou* shut again; **se ~** *vi* (*porte*) to close *ou* shut (again)

**refiler** [R(ə)file] *vt* (*fam*) to palm off

**réfléchi, e** [Refleʃi] *adj* (*caractère*) thoughtful; (*action*) well-thought-out; (LING) reflexive; **c'est tout ~** my mind's made up

**réfléchir** [RefleʃiR] *vt* to reflect ♦ *vi* to think; **~ à** to think about

**reflet** [R(ə)flɛ] *nm* reflection; (*sur l'eau etc*) sheen *no pl*, glint; **refléter** *vt* to reflect; **se refléter** *vi* to be reflected

**réflexe** [Reflɛks] *nm, adj* reflex

**réflexion** [Reflɛksjɔ̃] *nf* (*de la lumière etc*) reflection; (*fait de penser*) thought; (*remarque*) remark; **~ faite, à la ~** on reflection

**refluer** [R(ə)flye] *vi* to flow back; (*foule*) to surge back

**reflux** [Rəfly] *nm* (*de la mer*) ebb

**réforme** [RefɔRm] *nf* reform; (REL): **la R~** the Reformation; **réformer** *vt* to reform; (MIL) to declare unfit for service

**refouler** [R(ə)fule] *vt* (*envahisseurs*) to drive back; (*larmes*) to force back; (*désir, colère*) to repress

**refrain** [ʀ(ə)fʀɛ̃] nm refrain, chorus

**refréner** [ʀəfʀene] vt, **réfréner** [ʀefʀene] vt to curb, check

**réfrigérateur** [ʀefʀiʒeʀatœʀ] nm refrigerator, fridge

**refroidir** [ʀ(ə)fʀwadiʀ] vt to cool; (fig: personne) to put off ♦ vi to cool (down); **se ~** vi (temps) to get cooler ou colder; (fig: ardeur) to cool (off); **refroidissement** nm (grippe etc) chill

**refuge** [ʀ(ə)fyʒ] nm refuge; **réfugié, e** adj, nm/f refugee; **réfugier: se réfugier** vi to take refuge

**refus** [ʀ(ə)fy] nm refusal; **ce n'est pas de ~** I won't say no, it's welcome; **refuser** vt to refuse; (SCOL: candidat) to fail; **refuser qch à qn** to refuse sb sth; **se refuser à faire** to refuse to do

**réfuter** [ʀefyte] vt to refute

**regagner** [ʀ(ə)gaɲe] vt (faveur) to win back; (lieu) to get back to

**regain** [ʀəgɛ̃] nm (renouveau): **un ~ de** renewed +nom

**régal** [ʀegal] nm treat; **régaler: se régaler** vi to have a delicious meal; (fig) to enjoy o.s.

**regard** [ʀ(ə)gaʀ] nm (coup d'œil), glance; (expression) look (in one's eye); **au ~ de** (loi, morale) from the point of view of; **en ~ de** in comparison with

**regardant, e** [ʀ(ə)gaʀdã, ãt] adj (économe) tight-fisted; **peu ~ (sur)** very free (about)

**regarder** [ʀ(ə)gaʀde] vt to look at; (film, télévision, match) to watch; (concerner) to concern ♦ vi to look; **ne pas ~ à la dépense** to spare no expense; **~ qn/qch comme** to regard sb/sth as

**régie** [ʀeʒi] nf (COMM, INDUSTRIE) state-owned company; (THÉÂTRE, CINÉMA) production; (RADIO, TV) control room

**regimber** [ʀ(ə)ʒɛ̃be] vi to balk, jib

**régime** [ʀeʒim] nm (POL) régime; (MÉD) diet; (ADMIN: carcéral, fiscal etc) system; (de bananes, dattes) bunch; **se mettre au/suivre un ~** to go on/be on a diet

**régiment** [ʀeʒimã] nm regiment

**région** [ʀeʒjɔ̃] nf region; **régional, e, -aux** adj regional

**régir** [ʀeʒiʀ] vt to govern

**régisseur** [ʀeʒisœʀ] nm (d'un domaine) steward; (CINÉMA, TV) assistant director; (THÉÂTRE) stage manager

**registre** [ʀəʒistʀ] nm register

**réglage** [ʀeglaʒ] nm adjustment

**règle** [ʀɛgl] nf (instrument) ruler; (loi) rule; **~s** nfpl (menstruation) period sg; **en ~** (papiers d'identité) in order; **en ~ générale** as a (general) rule

**réglé, e** [ʀegle] adj (vie) well-ordered; (arrangé) settled

**règlement** [ʀɛgləmã] nm (paiement) settlement; (arrêté) regulation; (règles, statuts) regulations pl, rules pl; **~ de compte(s)** settling of old scores; **réglementaire** adj conforming to the regulations; (tenue) regulation cpd; **réglementation** nf (règles, règlement) regulations; **réglementer** vt to regulate

**régler** [ʀegle] vt (conflit, facture) to settle; (personne) to settle up with; (mécanisme, machine) to regulate, adjust; (thermostat etc) to set, adjust

**réglisse** [ʀeglis] nf liquorice

**règne** [ʀɛɲ] nm (d'un roi etc, fig) reign; **régner** vi (roi) to rule, reign; (fig) to reign

**regorger** [ʀ(ə)gɔʀʒe] vi: **~ de** to overflow with, be bursting with

**regret** [ʀ(ə)gʀɛ] nm regret; **à ~** with regret; **sans ~** with no regrets; **regrettable** adj regrettable; **regretter** vt to regret; (personne) to miss; **je regrette mais ...** I'm sorry but ...

**regrouper** [ʀ(ə)gʀupe] vt (grouper) to group together; (contenir) to include, comprise; **se ~** vi to gather (together)

**régulier, -ière** [ʀegylje, jɛʀ] adj (gén) regular; (vitesse, qualité) steady; (égal: couche, ligne) even; (TRANSPORTS: ligne, service), scheduled, regular; (légal) lawful, in order; (honnête) straight, on the level; **régulièrement** adv regularly; (uniformément) evenly

**rehausser** [ʀəose] vt (relever) to heighten, raise; (fig: souligner) to set off, enhance

**rein** [ʀɛ̃] nm kidney; **~s** nmpl (dos) back sg

**reine** [ʀɛn] nf queen

**reine-claude** [ʀɛnklod] nf greengage

**réinsertion** [ʀeɛ̃sɛʀsjɔ̃] nf (de délinquant) reintegration, rehabilitation

**réintégrer** [ʀeɛ̃tegʀe] vt (lieu) to return to; (fonctionnaire) to reinstate

**rejaillir** [ʀ(ə)ʒajiʀ] vi to splash up; **~ sur** (fig: scandale) to rebound on; (: gloire) to be reflected on

**rejet** [ʀəʒɛ] nm rejection; **rejeter** vt (relancer) to throw back; (écarter) to reject; (déverser) to throw out, discharge; (vomir) to bring ou throw up; **rejeter la responsabilité de qch sur qn** to lay the responsibility for sth at sb's door

**rejoindre** [ʀ(ə)ʒwɛ̃dʀ] vt (famille, régiment) to rejoin, return to; (lieu) to get (back) to; (suj: route etc) to meet, join; (rattraper) to catch up (with); **se ~** vi to meet; **je te rejoins à la gare** I'll see ou meet you at the station

**réjouir** [ʀeʒwiʀ] vt to delight; **se ~** (de) vi to be delighted (about); **réjouissances** nfpl (fête) festivities

**relâche** [ʀəlɑʃ] nm ou nf: **sans ~** without respite ou a break; **relâché, e** adj loose, lax; **relâcher** vt (libérer) to release; (desserrer) to loosen; **se relâcher** vi (discipline) to become slack ou lax; (élève etc) to slacken off

**relais** [ʀ(ə)lɛ] nm (SPORT): **(course de) ~** relay (race); **prendre le ~ (de)** to take over (from); **~ routier** ≈ transport café (BRIT), ≈ truck stop (US)

**relancer** [ʀ(ə)lɑ̃se] vt (balle) to throw back; (moteur) to restart; (fig) to boost, revive; (harceler): **~ qn** to pester sb

**relatif, -ive** [ʀ(ə)latif, iv] adj relative

**relation** [ʀ(ə)lasjɔ̃] nf (rapport) relation(ship); (connaissance) acquaintance; **~s** nfpl (rapports) relations; (connaissances) connections; **être/entrer en**

**~(s) avec** to be/get in contact with

**relaxe** [ʀəlaks] (fam) adj (tenue) informal; (personne) relaxed; **relaxer: se relaxer** vi to relax

**relayer** [ʀ(ə)leje] vt (collaborateur, coureur etc) to relieve; **se ~** vi (dans une activité) to take it in turns

**reléguer** [ʀ(ə)lege] vt to relegate

**relent(s)** [ʀəlɑ̃] nm(pl) (foul) smell

**relevé, e** [ʀəl(ə)ve] adj (manches) rolled-up; (sauce) highly-seasoned ♦ nm (de compteur) reading; (bancaire) statement

**relève** [ʀəlɛv] nf (personne) relief; **prendre la ~** to take over

**relever** [ʀəl(ə)ve] vt (meuble) to stand up again; (personne tombée) to help up; (vitre, niveau de vie) to raise; (col) to turn up; (style) to elevate; (plat, sauce) to season; (sentinelle, équipe) to relieve, (fautes) to find out; (défi) to accept, take up; (noter: adresse etc) to take down, note; (: plan) to sketch; (compteur) to read; (ramasser: cahiers) to collect, take in; **se ~** vi (se remettre debout) to get up; **~ de** (maladie) to be recovering from; (être du ressort de) to be a matter for; (fig) to pertain to; **~ qn de** (fonctions) to relieve sb of

**relief** [ʀəljɛf] nm relief; **mettre en ~** (fig) to bring out, highlight

**relier** [ʀəlje] vt to link up; (livre) to bind; **~ qch à** to link sth to

**religieuse** [ʀ(ə)liʒjøz] nf nun; (gâteau) cream bun

**religieux, -euse** [ʀ(ə)liʒjø, jøz] adj religious ♦ nm monk

**religion** [ʀ(ə)liʒjɔ̃] nf religion

**relire** [ʀ(ə)liʀ] vt (à nouveau) to reread; (vérifier) to read over

**reliure** [ʀəljyʀ] nf binding

**reluire** [ʀ(ə)lɥiʀ] vi to gleam

**remanier** [ʀ(ə)manje] vt to reshape, recast; (POL) to reshuffle

**remarquable** [ʀ(ə)maʀkabl] adj remarkable

**remarque** [ʀ(ə)maʀk] nf remark

(*écrite*) note

**remarquer** [R(ə)maRke] *vt* (*voir*) to notice; **se ~** *vi* to be noticeable; **faire ~** (**à qn**) **que** to point out (to sb) that; **faire ~ qch** (**à qn**) to point sth out (to sb); **remarquez, ...** mind you ...; **se faire ~** to draw attention to o.s.

**rembourrer** [Rɑ̃buʀe] *vt* to stuff

**remboursement** [Rɑ̃buʀsəmɑ̃] *nm* (*de dette, d'emprunt*) repayment; (*de frais*) refund; **rembourser** *vt* to pay back, repay; (*frais, billet etc*) to refund; **se faire rembourser** to get a refund

**remède** [R(ə)mɛd] *nm* (*médicament*) medicine; (*traitement, fig*) remedy, cure

**remémorer** [R(ə)memɔʀe]: **se ~** *vt* to recall, recollect

**remerciements** [Rəmɛʀsimɑ̃] *nmpl* thanks

**remercier** [R(ə)mɛʀsje] *vt* to thank; (*congédier*) to dismiss; **~ qn de/d'avoir fait** to thank sb for/for having done

**remettre** [R(ə)mɛtʀ] *vt* (*replacer*) to put back; (*vêtement*) to put back on; (*ajouter*) to add; (*ajourner*) to postpone (until); **se ~** *vi*: **se ~** (**de**) to recover (from); **~ qch à qn** (*donner: lettre, clé etc*) to hand over sth to sb; (*: prix, décoration*) to present sb with sth; **se ~ à faire qch** to start doing sth again

**remise** [R(ə)miz] *nf* (*rabais*) discount; (*local*) shed; **~ de peine** reduction of sentence; **~ en jeu** (*FOOTBALL*) throw-in

**remontant** [R(ə)mɔ̃tɑ̃, ɑ̃t] *nm* tonic, pick-me-up

**remonte-pente** [R(ə)mɔ̃tpɑ̃t] *nm* ski-lift

**remonter** [R(ə)mɔ̃te] *vi* to go back up; (*prix, température*) to go up again ♦ *vt* (*pente*) to go up again; (*fleuve*) to sail (*ou* swim *etc*) up; (*manches, pantalon*) to roll up; (*col*) to turn up; (*niveau, limite*) to raise; (*fig: personne*) to buck up; (*qch de démonté*) to put back together, reassemble; (*montre*) to wind up; **~ le moral à qn** to raise sb's spirits; **~ à** (*dater*

*de*) to date *ou* go back to

**remontrance** [R(ə)mɔ̃tʀɑ̃s] *nf* reproof, reprimand

**remontrer** [R(ə)mɔ̃tʀe] *vt* (*fig*): **en ~ à** to prove one's superiority over

**remords** [R(ə)mɔʀ] *nm* remorse *no pl*; **avoir ~** to feel remorse

**remorque** [R(ə)mɔʀk] *nf* trailer; **remorquer** *vt* to tow; **remorqueur** *nm* tug(boat)

**remous** [Rəmu] *nm* (*d'un navire*) (back)wash *no pl*; (*de rivière*) swirl, eddy ♦ *nmpl* (*fig*) stir *sg*

**remparts** [Rɑ̃paʀ] *nmpl* walls, ramparts

**remplaçant, e** [Rɑ̃plasɑ̃, ɑ̃t] *nm/f* replacement, stand-in; (*SCOL*) supply teacher

**remplacement** [Rɑ̃plasmɑ̃] *nm* replacement; **faire des ~s** (*professeur*) to do supply teaching; (*secrétaire*) to temp

**remplacer** [Rɑ̃plase] *vt* to replace; **~ qch/qn par** to replace sth/sb with

**rempli, e** [Rɑ̃pli] *adj* (*emploi du temps*) full, busy; **~ de** full of, filled with

**remplir** [Rɑ̃pliʀ] *vt* to fill (up); (*questionnaire*) to fill out *ou* up; (*obligations, fonction, condition*) to fulfil; **se ~** *vi* to fill up

**remporter** [Rɑ̃pɔʀte] *vt* (*marchandise*) to take away; (*fig*) to win, achieve

**remuant, e** [Rəmɥɑ̃, ɑ̃t] *adj* restless

**remue-ménage** [R(ə)mymenaʒ] *nm inv* commotion

**remuer** [Rəmɥe] *vt* to move; (*café, sauce*) to stir ♦ *vi* to move; (*fam: s'activer*) to get a move on

**rémunérer** [Remyneʀe] *vt* to remunerate

**renard** [R(ə)naʀ] *nm* fox

**renchérir** [Rɑ̃feʀiʀ] *vi* (*fig*): **~** (**sur**) (*en paroles*) to add something (to)

**rencontre** [Rɑ̃kɔ̃tʀ] *nf* meeting; (*imprévue*) encounter; **aller à la ~ de qn** to go and meet sb; **rencontrer** *vt* to meet; (*mot, expression*) to come across; (*difficultés*) to meet with; **se rencontrer** *vi* to meet

**rendement** [Rɑ̃dmɑ̃] *nm* (*d'un travailleur, d'une machine*) output; (*d'un champ*) yield

**rendez-vous** [Rɑ̃devu] *nm* appointment; (*d'amoureux*) date; (*lieu*) meeting place; **donner ~ ~ à qn** to arrange to meet sb; **avoir/prendre ~ ~ (avec)** to have/make an appointment (with)

**rendre** [Rɑ̃dR] *vt* (*restituer*) to give back, return; (*invitation*) to return, repay; (*vomir*) to bring up; (*exprimer, traduire*) to render; (*faire devenir*): **~ qn célèbre/qch possible** to make sb famous/sth possible; **se ~ vi** (*capituler*) to surrender, give o.s. up; (*aller*): **se ~ quelque part** to go somewhere; **~ la monnaie à qn** to give sb his change; **se ~ compte de qch** to realize sth

**rênes** [Rɛn] *nfpl* reins

**renfermé, e** [Rɑ̃fɛRme] *adj* (*fig*) withdrawn ♦ *nm*: **sentir le ~** to smell stuffy

**renfermer** [Rɑ̃fɛRme] *vt* to contain

**renflouer** [Rɑ̃flue] *vt* to refloat; (*fig*) to set back on its (*ou* his/her *etc*) feet

**renfoncement** [Rɑ̃fɔ̃smɑ̃] *nm* recess

**renforcer** [Rɑ̃fɔRse] *vt* to reinforce; **renfort: renforts** *nmpl* reinforcements; **à grand renfort de** with a great deal of

**renfrogné, e** [Rɑ̃fRɔɲe] *adj* sullen

**rengaine** [Rɑ̃gɛn] (*péj*) *nf* old tune

**renier** [Rənje] *vt* (*personne*) to disown, repudiate; (*foi*) to renounce

**renifler** [R(ə)nifle] *vi, vt* to sniff

**renne** [Rɛn] *nm* reindeer *inv*

**renom** [Rənɔ̃] *nm* reputation; (*célébrité*) renown; **renommé, e** *adj* celebrated, renowned; **renommée** *nf* fame

**renoncer** [R(ə)nɔ̃se]: **~ à** *vt* to give up; **~ à faire** to give up the idea of doing

**renouer** [Rənwe] *vt*: **~ avec** (*habitude*) to take up again

**renouvelable** [R(ə)nuv(ə)labl] *adj* (*énergie etc*) renewable

**renouveler** [R(ə)nuv(ə)le] *vt* to renew; (*exploit, méfait*) to repeat; **se ~ vi** (*incident*) to recur, happen again; **renouvellement** *nm* (*remplacement*) renewal

**rénover** [Renɔve] *vt* (*immeuble*) to renovate, do up; (*quartier*) to redevelop

**renseignement** [Rɑ̃sɛɲmɑ̃] *nm* information *no pl*, piece of information; (**bureau des**) **~s** information office

**renseigner** [Rɑ̃seɲe] *vt*: **~ qn (sur)** to give information to sb (about); **se ~** to ask for information, make inquiries

**rentabilité** [Rɑ̃tabilite] *nf* profitability

**rentable** [Rɑ̃tabl] *adj* profitable

**rente** [Rɑ̃t] *nf* private income; (*pension*) pension

**rentrée** [Rɑ̃tRe] *nf*: **~ (d'argent)** cash *no pl* coming in; **la ~ (des classes)** the start of the new school year

┌─────────────────────────────┐
│ rentrée (des classes)        │
└─────────────────────────────┘

La **rentrée (des classes)** in September marks an important point in the French year. Children and teachers return to school, and political and social life begin again after the long summer break.

**rentrer** [Rɑ̃tRe] *vi* (*revenir chez soi*) to go (*ou* come) (back) home; (*entrer de nouveau*) to go (*ou* come) back in; (*entrer*) to go (*ou* come) in; (*air, clou: pénétrer*) to go in; (*revenu*) to come in ♦ *vt* to bring in; (: *véhicule*) to put away; (*chemise dans pantalon etc*) to tuck in; (*griffes*) to draw in; **~ le ventre** to pull in one's stomach; **~ dans** (*heurter*) to crash into; **~ dans l'ordre** to be back to normal; **~ dans ses frais** to recover one's expenses

**renverse** [Rɑ̃vɛRs]: **à la ~** *adv* backwards

**renverser** [Rɑ̃vɛRse] *vt* (*faire tomber*) *chaise, verre*) to knock over, overturn; (*liquide, contenu*) to spill, upset; (*piéton*) to knock down; (*retourner*) to turn upside down; (: *ordre des mots etc*) to reverse; (*fig: gouvernement etc*) to overthrow; (*fam: stupéfier*) to bowl over; **se ~ vi** (*verre, vase*) to fall over; (*contenu*) to spill

**envoi** [ɑ̃vwa] *nm* (d'employé) dismissal; (d'élève) expulsion; (référence) cross-reference; (éructation) belch; **envoyer** *vt* to send back; (congédier) to dismiss; (élève: définitivement) to expel; (lumière) to reflect; (ajourner): **renvoyer qch (à)** to put sth off *ou* postpone sth (until)

**epaire** [R(ə)pɛR] *nm* den

**épandre** [epɑ̃dR] *vt* (renverser) to spill; (étaler, diffuser) to spread; (odeur) to give off; **se ~** *vi* to spill; (se propager) to spread; **répandu, e** *adj* (opinion, usage) widespread

**éparation** [Repaʀasjɔ̃] *nf* repair

**éparer** [Repaʀe] *vt* to repair; (fig: offense) to make up for, atone for; (: oubli, erreur) to put right

**epartie** [Repaʀti] *nf* retort; **avoir de la ~** to be quick at repartee

**epartir** [R(ə)paʀtiʀ] *vi* to leave again; (voyageur) to set off again; (fig) to get going again; **~ à zéro** to start from scratch (again)

**épartir** [Repaʀtiʀ] *vt* (pour attribuer) to share out; (pour disperser, disposer) to divide up; (poids) to distribute; **se ~** *vt* (travail, rôles) to share out between themselves; **répartition** *nf* (des richesses etc) distribution

**epas** [R(ə)pɑ] *nm* meal

**epassage** [R(ə)pasaʒ] *nm* ironing

**epasser** [R(ə)pase] *vi* to come (ou go) back ♦ *vt* (vêtement, tissu) to iron; (examen) to retake, resit; (film) to show again; (leçon: revoir) to go over (again)

**epêcher** [R(ə)peʃe] *vt* to fish out; (candidat) to pass (by inflating marks)

**epentir** [Rapɑ̃tiʀ] *nm* repentance; **se ~** *vi* to repent; **se ~ d'avoir fait qch** (regretter) to regret having done sth

**répercussions** [Repɛʀkysjɔ̃] *nfpl* (fig) repercussions

**répercuter** [Repɛʀkyte] *vt* (son): **se ~** *vi* (bruit) to reverberate; (fig): **se ~ sur** to have repercussions on

**repère** [R(ə)pɛR] *nm* mark; (monument,

*événement)* landmark

**repérer** [R(ə)peʀe] *vt* (fam: erreur, personne) to spot; (: endroit) to locate; **se ~** *vi* to find one's way about

**répertoire** [RepɛʀtwaR] *nm* (liste) (alphabetical) list; (carnet) index notebook; (INFORM) folder, directory; (d'un artiste) repertoire

**répéter** [Repete] *vt* to repeat; (préparer: leçon) to learn, go over; (THÉÂTRE) to rehearse; **se ~** *vi* (redire) to repeat o.s.; (se reproduire) to be repeated, recur

**répétition** [Repetisjɔ̃] *nf* repetition; (THÉÂTRE) rehearsal

**répit** [Repi] *nm* respite

**replier** [R(ə)plije] *vt* (rabattre) to fold down *ou* over; **se ~** *vi* (troupes, armée) to withdraw, fall back; (sur soi-même) to withdraw into o.s.

**réplique** [Replik] *nf* (repartie, fig) reply; (THÉÂTRE) line; (copie) replica; **répliquer** *vi* to reply; (riposter) to retaliate

**répondeur** [RepɔdœR, øz] *nm*: **~ automatique** (TÉL) answering machine

**répondre** [RepɔdR] *vi* to answer, reply; (freins) to respond; **~ à** to reply to, answer; (affection, salut) to return; (provocation) to respond to; (correspondre à: besoin) to answer; (: conditions) to meet; (: description) to match; (avec impertinence): **~ à qn** to answer sb back; **~ de** to answer for

**réponse** [Repɔs] *nf* answer, reply; **en ~ à** in reply to

**reportage** [R(ə)pɔʀtaʒ] *nm* report; **~ en direct** (live) commentary

**reporter¹** [RapɔʀteR] *nm* reporter

**reporter²** [Rapɔʀte] *vt* (ajourner): **~ qch (à)** to postpone sth (until); (transférer): **~ qch sur** to transfer sth to; **se ~ à** (époque) to think back to; (document) to refer to

**repos** [R(ə)po] *nm* rest; (tranquillité) peace and quiet; (MIL): **~!** stand at ease!; **ce n'est pas de tout ~!** it's no picnic!

**reposant, e** [R(ə)pozɑ̃, ɑ̃t] *adj* restful

**reposer** [R(ə)poze] vt (verre, livre) to put down; (délasser) to rest ♦ vi: **laisser ~** (pâte) to leave to stand; **se ~** to rest; **se ~ sur qn** to rely on sb; **~ sur** (fig) to rest on

**repoussant, e** [R(ə)pusɑ̃, ɑ̃t] adj repulsive

**repousser** [R(ə)puse] vi to grow again ♦ vt to repel, repulse; (offre) to turn down, reject; (personne) to push back; (différer) to put back

**reprendre** [R(ə)pRɑ̃dR] vt (objet prêté, donné) to take back; (prisonnier, ville) to recapture; (firme, entreprise) to take over; (le travail) to resume; (emprunter: argument, idée) to take up, use; (refaire: article etc) to go over again; (vêtement) to alter; (réprimander) to tell off; (corriger) to correct; (chercher): **je viendrai te ~ à 4 h** I'll come and fetch you at 4; (se resservir de): **~ du pain/un œuf** to take (ou eat) more bread/another egg ♦ vi (classes, pluie) to start (up) again; (activités, travaux, combats) to resume, start (up) again; (affaires) to pick up; (dire): **reprit-il** he went on; **se ~** vi (se ressaisir) to recover; **~ des forces** to recover one's strength; **~ courage** to take new heart; **~ la route** to set off again; **~ haleine** ou **son souffle** to get one's breath back

**représailles** [R(ə)pRezaj] nfpl reprisals

**représentant, e** [R(ə)pRezɑ̃tɑ̃, ɑ̃t] nm/f representative

**représentation** [R(ə)pRezɑ̃tasjɔ̃] nf (symbole, image) representation; (spectacle) performance

**représenter** [R(ə)pRezɑ̃te] vt to represent; (donner: pièce, opéra) to perform; **se ~** vt (se figurer) to imagine

**répression** [RepResjɔ̃] nf repression

**réprimer** [RepRime] vt (émotions) to suppress; (peuple etc) to repress

**repris** [R(ə)pRi, iz] nm: **~ de justice** ex-prisoner, ex-convict

**reprise** [R(ə)pRiz] nf (recommencement) resumption; (économique) recovery; (TV)

repeat; (COMM) trade-in, part exchange; (raccommodage) mend; **à plusieurs ~** on several occasions

**repriser** [R(ə)pRize] vt (chaussette, lo nage) to darn; (tissu) to mend

**reproche** [R(ə)pRɔʃ] nm (remontrance reproach; **faire des ~s à qn** to re proach sb; **sans ~(s)** beyond reproach

**reprocher** vt: **reprocher qch à qn** reproach ou blame sb for sth; **repr cher qch à** (critiquer) to have s against

**reproduction** [R(ə)pRɔdyksjɔ̃] nf r production

**reproduire** [R(ə)pRɔdɥiR] vt to repro duce; **se ~** vi (BIO) to reproduce; (r commencer) to recur, re-occur

**réprouver** [RepRuve] vt to reprove

**reptile** [Reptil] nm reptile

**repu, e** [Rəpy] adj satisfied, sated

**république** [Repyblik] nf republic

**répugnant, e** [Repyñɑ̃, ɑ̃t] adj disgust ing

**répugner** [Repyñe]: **~ à** vt: **~ à qn** repel ou disgust sb; **~ à faire** to b loath ou reluctant to do

**réputation** [Repytasjɔ̃] nf reputatio

**réputé, e** adj renowned

**requérir** [RakeRiR] vt (nécessiter) to re quire, call for

**requête** [Raket] nf request

**requin** [Rakɛ̃] nm shark

**requis, e** [Raki, iz] adj required

**RER** sigle m (= réseau express régiona Greater Paris high-speed train service

**rescapé, e** [Reskape] nm/f survivor

**rescousse** [Reskus] nf: **aller à la ~ d qn** to go to sb's aid ou rescue

**réseau, x** [Rezo] nm network

**réservation** [RezeRvasjɔ̃] nf bookin reservation

**réserve** [RezeRv] nf (retenue) reserv (entrepôt) storeroom; (restrictio d'Indiens) reservation; (de pêche, chass preserve; **de ~** (provisions etc) in re serve

**réservé, e** [RezeRve] adj reserve

chasse/pêche ~e private hunting/ fishing

**réserver** [REZERVE] vt to reserve; (chambre, billet etc) to book, reserve; (fig: destiner) to have in store; (garder): ~ qch pour/à to keep ou save sth for

**réservoir** [REZERVWAR] nm tank

**résidence** [Rezidɑ̃s] nf residence; ~ secondaire second home; **résidentiel, le** adj residential; **résider** vi: **résider à/dans/en** to reside in; **résider dans** (fig) to lie in

**résidu** [Rezidy] nm residue no pl

**résigner** [Rezine]: **se** ~ vi: **se** ~ (à qch/à faire) to resign o.s. (to sth/to doing)

**résilier** [Rezilje] vt to terminate

**résistance** [Rezistɑ̃s] nf resistance; (de réchaud, bouilloire: fil) element

**résistant, e** [Rezistɑ̃, ɑ̃t] adj (personne) robust, tough; (matériau) strong, hard-wearing

**résister** [Reziste] vi to resist; ~ à (assaut, tentation) to resist; (supporter: gel etc) to withstand; (désobéir à) to stand up to, oppose

**résolu, e** [Rezɔly] pp de **résoudre**
♦ adj: **être** ~ **à qch/faire** to be set upon sth/doing

**résolution** [Rezɔlysjɔ̃] nf (fermeté, décision) resolution; (d'un problème) solution

**résolve** etc [Rezɔlv] vb voir **résoudre**

**résonner** [Rezɔne] vi (cloche, pas) to reverberate, resound; (salle) to be resonant

**résorber** [Rezɔrbe]: **se** ~ vi (fig: chômage) to be reduced; (: déficit) to be absorbed

**résoudre** [Rezudr] vt to solve; **se** ~ **à faire** to bring o.s. to do

**respect** [Respe] nm respect; **tenir en** ~ to keep at bay; **respecter** vt to respect; **respectueux, -euse** adj respectful

**respiration** [Respirasjɔ̃] nf breathing no pl

**respirer** [Respire] vi to breathe; (fig: se détendre) to get one's breath; (: se rassurer) to breathe again ♦ vt to breathe (in), inhale; (manifester: santé, calme etc) to exude

**resplendir** [Resplɑ̃dir] vi to shine; (fig): ~ (de) to be radiant (with)

**responsabilité** [Respɔ̃sabilite] nf responsibility; (légale) liability

**responsable** [Respɔ̃sabl] adj responsible ♦ nm/f (coupable) person responsible; (personne compétente) person in charge; (de parti, syndicat) official; ~ **de** responsible for

**resquiller** [REskije] (fam) vi to get in without paying; (ne pas faire la queue) to jump the queue

**ressaisir** [R(ə)sezir]: **se** ~ vi to regain one's self-control

**ressasser** [R(ə)sase] vt to keep going over

**ressemblance** [R(ə)sɑ̃blɑ̃s] nf resemblance, similarity, likeness

**ressemblant, e** [R(ə)sɑ̃blɑ̃, ɑ̃t] adj (portrait) lifelike, true to life

**ressembler** [R(ə)sɑ̃ble]: ~ **à** vt to be like, resemble; (visuellement) to look like; **se** ~ vi to be (ou look) alike

**ressemeler** [R(ə)sam(ə)le] vt to (re)sole

**ressentiment** [R(ə)sɑ̃timɑ̃] nm resentment

**ressentir** [R(ə)sɑ̃tir] vt to feel

**resserrer** [R(ə)sere] vt (nœud, boulon) to tighten (up); (fig: liens) to strengthen

**resservir** [R(ə)servir] vi to do ou serve again; **se** ~ vi to help o.s. again

**ressort** [R(ə)sɔr] nm (pièce) spring; (énergie) spirit; (recours): **en dernier** ~ as a last resort; (compétence): **être du** ~ **de** to fall within the competence of

**ressortir** [R(ə)sɔrtir] vi to go ou come out (again); (contraster) to stand out; ~ **de** to emerge from; **faire** ~ (fig: souligner) to bring out

**ressortissant, e** [R(ə)sɔrtisɑ̃, ɑ̃t] nm/f

national

**ressources** [R(ə)suRs] *nfpl* (*moyens*) resources

**ressusciter** [Resysite] *vt* (*fig*) to revive, bring back ♦ *vi* to rise (from the dead)

**restant, e** [Restã, ãt] *adj* remaining ♦ *nm*: **le ~ (de)** the remainder (of); **un ~ de** (*de trop*) some left-over

**restaurant** [RestɔRã] *nm* restaurant

**restauration** [RestɔRasjɔ̃] *nf* restoration; (*hôtellerie*) catering; **~ rapide** fast food

**restaurer** [RestɔRe] *vt* to restore; **se ~** *vi* to have something to eat

**reste** [Rest] *nm* (*restant*): **le ~ (de)** the rest (of); (*de trop*): **un ~ (de)** some left-over; **~s** *nmpl* (*nourriture*) left-overs; (*d'une cité etc, dépouille mortelle*) remains; **du ~, au ~** besides, moreover

**rester** [Reste] *vi* to stay, remain; (*subsister*) to remain, be left; (*durer*) to last, live on ♦ *vb impers*: **il reste du pain/2 œufs** there's some bread/2 eggs left (over); **restons-en là** let's leave it at that; **il me reste assez de temps** I have enough time left; **il ne me reste plus qu'à ...** I've just got to ...

**restituer** [Restitɥe] *vt* (*objet, somme*): **~ qch (à qn)** to return sth (to sb)

**restreindre** [RestRɛ̃dR] *vt* to restrict, limit

**restriction** [RestRiksjɔ̃] *nf* restriction

**résultat** [Rezylta] *nm* result; (*d'examen, d'élection*) results *pl*

**résulter** [Rezylte]: **~ de** *vt* to result from, be the result of

**résumé** [Rezyme] *nm* summary, résumé

**résumer** [Rezyme] *vt* (*texte*) to summarize; (*récapituler*) to sum up

**résurrection** [RezyRɛksjɔ̃] *nf* resurrection

**rétablir** [RetabliR] *vt* to restore, re-establish; **se ~** *vi* (*guérir*) to recover; (*silence, calme*) to return, be restored; **rétablissement** *nm* restoring; (*guéri-*

*son*) recovery

**retaper** [R(ə)tape] *vt* (*fam*) (*maison, voiture etc*) to do up; (*revigorer*) to buck up

**retard** [R(ə)taR] *nm* (*d'une personne attendue*) lateness *no pl*; (*sur l'horaire, un programme*) delay; (*fig: scolaire, mental etc*) backwardness; **en ~ (de 2 heures)** (2 hours) late; **avoir du ~** to be late; (*sur un programme*) to be behind (schedule); **prendre du ~** (*train, avion*) to be delayed; **sans ~** without delay

**retardataire** [R(ə)taRdatɛR] *nmf* latecomer

**retardement** [R(ə)taRdəmã]: **à ~** delayed action *cpd*; **bombe à ~** time bomb

**retarder** [R(ə)taRde] *vt* to delay; (*montre*) to put back ♦ *vi* (*montre*) to be slow; **~ qn (d'une heure)** (*sur un horaire*) to delay sb (an hour); **~ qch (de 2 jours)** (*départ, date*) to put sth back (2 days)

**retenir** [Rət(ə)niR] *vt* (*garder, retarder*) to keep, detain; (*maintenir: objet qui glisse, fig: colère, larmes*) to hold back; (*se rappeler*) to retain; (*réserver*) to reserve; (*accepter: proposition etc*) to accept; (*fig: empêcher d'agir*): **~ qn (de faire)** to hold sb back (from doing); (*prélever*): **~ qch (sur)** to deduct sth (from); **se ~** (*euphémisme*) to hold onto; (*se contenir*): **se ~ de faire** to restrain o.s. from doing; **~ son souffle** to hold one's breath

**retentir** [R(ə)tãtiR] *vi* to ring out; (*salle*): **~ de** to ring *ou* resound with; **retentissant, e** *adj* resounding; **retentissement** *nm* repercussion

**retenu, e** [Rət(ə)ny] *adj* (*place*) reserved; (*personne: empêché*) held up; **retenue** *nf* (*prélèvement*) deduction; (*SCOL*) detention; (*modération*) (self-)restraint

**réticence** [Retisãs] *nf* hesitation, reluctance *no pl*; **réticent, e** *adj* hesitant, reluctant

**rétine** [retin] *nf* retina

**retiré, e** [R(ə)tiRe] *adj* (*vie*) secluded; (*lieu*) remote

**retirer** [R(ə)tiRe] *vt* (*vêtement, lunettes*) to take off, remove; (*argent, plainte*) to withdraw; (*reprendre: bagages, billets*) to collect, pick up; (*extraire*): **~ qch de** to take sth out of, remove sth from

**retombées** [Rət5be] *nfpl* (*radioactives*) fallout *sg*; (*fig: répercussions*) effects

**retomber** [R(ə)t5be] *vi* (*à nouveau*) to fall again; (*atterrir: après un saut etc*) to land; (*échoir*): **~ sur qn** to fall on sb

**rétorquer** [RetɔRke] *vt*: **~ (à qn) que** to retort (to sb) that

**retouche** [R(ə)tuʃ] *nf* (*sur vêtement*) alteration; **retoucher** *vt* (*photographie*) to touch up; (*texte, vêtement*) to alter

**retour** [R(ə)tuR] *nm* return; **au ~** (*en route*) on the way back; **à mon ~** when I get/got back; **être de ~ (de)** to be back (from); **par ~ du courrier** by return of post

**retourner** [R(ə)tuRne] *vt* (*dans l'autre sens: matelas, crêpe etc*) to turn (over); (*: sac, vêtement*) to turn inside out; (*fam: bouleverser*) to shake; (*renvoyer, restituer*): **~ qch à qn** to return sth to sb ♦ *vi* (*aller, revenir*): **~ quelque part/ à** to go back *ou* return somewhere/to; **se ~** *vi* (*tourner la tête*) to turn round; **~ à** (*état, activité*) to return to, go back to; **se ~ contre** (*fig*) to turn against

**retrait** [R(ə)tRɛ] *nm* (*d'argent*) withdrawal; **en ~** set back; **~ du permis (de conduire)** (*BRIT*) disqualification from driving (*BRIT*), revocation of driver's license (*US*)

**retraite** [R(ə)tRɛt] *nf* (*d'un employé*) retirement; (*revenu*) pension; (*d'une armée, REL*) retreat; **prendre sa ~** to retire; **~ anticipée** early retirement; **retraité, e** *adj* retired ♦ *nm/f* pensioner

**retrancher** [R(ə)tRɑ̃ʃe] *vt* (*nombre, somme*): **~ qch de** to take *ou* deduct sth from; **se ~ derrière/dans** to take refuge behind/in

**retransmettre** [R(ə)tRɑ̃smɛtR] *vt* (*RADIO*) to broadcast; (*TV*) to show

**rétrécir** [RetResiR] *vt* to take in ♦ *vi* to shrink

**rétribution** [RetRibysjɔ̃] *nf* payment

**rétro** [RetRO] *adj inv*: **la mode ~** the nostalgia vogue

**rétrograde** [RetRɔgRad] *adj* reactionary, backward-looking

**rétroprojecteur** [RetRopRɔʒɛktœR] *nm* overhead projector

**rétrospective** [RetRɔspɛktiv] *nf* retrospective exhibition/season; **rétrospectivement** *adv* in retrospect

**retrousser** [R(ə)tRuse] *vt* to roll up

**retrouvailles** [R(ə)tRuvaj] *nfpl* reunion *sg*

**retrouver** [R(ə)tRuve] *vt* (*fugitif, objet perdu*) to find; (*calme, santé*) to regain; (*revoir*) to see again; (*rejoindre*) to meet (again), join; **se ~** *vi* to meet; (*s'orienter*) to find one's way; **se ~ quelque part** to find o.s. somewhere; **s'y ~** (*y voir clair*) to make sense of it; (*rentrer dans ses frais*) to break even

**rétroviseur** [RetRɔvizœR] *nm* (rear-view) mirror

**réunion** [Reynjɔ̃] *nf* (*séance*) meeting

**réunir** [ReyniR] *vt* (*rassembler*) to gather together; (*inviter: amis, famille*) to have round, have in; (*cumuler: qualités etc*) to combine; (*rapprocher: ennemis*) to bring together (again), reunite; (*rattacher: parties*) to join (together); **se ~** *vi* (*se rencontrer*) to meet

**réussi, e** [Reysi] *adj* successful

**réussir** [ReysiR] *vi* to succeed, be successful; (*à un examen*) to pass ♦ *vt* to make a success of; **~ à faire** to succeed in doing; **~ à qn** (*être bénéfique à*) to agree with sb; **réussite** *nf* success; (*CARTES*) patience

**revaloir** [R(ə)valwaR] *vt*: **je vous revaudrai cela** I'll repay you some day; (*en mal*) I'll pay you back for this

**revanche** [R(ə)vɑ̃ʃ] *nf* revenge; (*sport*) revenge match; **en ~** on the other hand

**rêve** [REV] nm dream; **de ~** dream cpd; **faire un ~** to have a dream

**revêche** [Rəvɛʃ] adj surly, sour-tempered

**réveil** [Revɛj] nm waking up no pl; (fig) awakening; (pendule) alarm (clock); **au ~** on waking (up); **réveille-matin** nm inv alarm clock; **réveiller** vt (personne) to wake up; (fig) to awaken, revive; **se réveiller** vi to wake up

**réveillon** [Revɛjɔ̃] nm Christmas Eve; (de la Saint-Sylvestre) New Year's Eve; **réveillonner** vi to celebrate Christmas Eve (ou New Year's Eve)

**révélateur, -trice** [Revelatœr, tris] adj: **~ (de qch)** revealing (sth)

**révéler** [Revele] vt to reveal; **se ~** vi to be revealed, reveal itself ♦ vb +attrib: **se ~ difficile/aisé** to prove difficult/easy

**revenant, e** [R(ə)vənɑ̃, ɑ̃t] nm/f ghost

**revendeur, -euse** [R(ə)vɑ̃dœr, øz] nm/f (détaillant) retailer; (de drogue) (drug-)dealer

**revendication** [R(ə)vɑ̃dikasjɔ̃] nf claim, demand

**revendiquer** [R(ə)vɑ̃dike] vt to claim, demand; (responsabilité) to claim

**revendre** [R(ə)vɑ̃dr] vt (d'occasion) to resell; (détailler) to sell; **à ~** (en abondance) to spare

**revenir** [Rəv(ə)nir] vi to come back; (coûter): **~ cher/à 100 F (à qn)** to cost (sb) a lot/100 F; **~ à** (reprendre: études, projet) to return to, go back to; (équivaloir à) to amount to; **~ à qn** (part, honneur) to go to sb, be sb's; (souvenir, nom) to come back to sb; **~ sur** (question, sujet) to go back over; (engagement) to go back on; **~ à soi** to come round; **n'en pas ~: je n'en reviens pas** I can't get over it; **~ sur ses pas** to retrace one's steps; **cela revient à dire que/au même** it amounts to say-ing that/the same thing; **faire ~** (CULIN) to brown

**revenu, e** [Rəv(ə)ny] nm income; **~s** nmpl

income sg

**rêver** [Reve] vi, vt to dream; **~ de/à** to dream of

**réverbère** [Reverbɛr] nm street lamp ou light; **réverbérer** vt to reflect

**révérence** [Reverɑ̃s] nf (salut) bow; (: de femme) curtsey

**rêverie** [Revri] nf daydreaming no pl, daydream

**revers** [R(ə)vɛr] nm (de feuille, main) back; (d'étoffe) wrong side; (de pièce, médaille) back, reverse; (TENNIS, PING-PONG) backhand; (de veste) lapel; (fig: échec) setback

**revêtement** [R(ə)vɛtmɑ̃] nm (des sols) flooring; (de chaussée) surface

**revêtir** [R(ə)vɛtir] vt (habit) to don, put on; (prendre: importance, apparence) to take on; **~ qch de** to cover sth with

**rêveur, -euse** [Revœr, øz] adj dreamy ♦ nm/f dreamer

**revient** [Rəvjɛ] vb voir **revenir**

**revigorer** [R(ə)vigɔre] vt (air frais) to invigorate, brace up; (repas, boisson) to revive, buck up

**revirement** [R(ə)virmɑ̃] nm change of mind; (d'une situation) reversal

**réviser** [Revize] vt to revise; (machine) to overhaul, service

**révision** [Revizjɔ̃] nf revision; (de voiture) servicing no pl

**revivre** [R(ə)vivr] vi (reprendre des forces) to come alive again ♦ vt (épreuve, moment) to relive

**revoir** [Rəvwar] vt to see again; (réviser) to revise ♦ nm: **au ~** goodbye

**révoltant, e** [Revɔltɑ̃, ɑ̃t] adj revolting, appalling

**révolte** [Revɔlt] nf rebellion, revolt

**révolter** [Revɔlte] vt to revolt; **se ~ (contre)** to rebel (against); **ça me révolte (de voir que ...)** I'm revolted ou appalled (to see that ...)

**révolu, e** [Revɔly] adj past; (ADMIN): **âgé de 18 ans ~s** over 18 years of age

**révolution** [Revɔlysjɔ̃] nf revolution; **révolutionnaire** [Revɔlysjɔnɛr] adj, nm/f revolutionary

**revolver** [ʀəvɔlveʀ] *nm* gun; *(à barillet)* revolver

**révoquer** [ʀevɔke] *vt (fonctionnaire)* to dismiss; *(arrêt, contrat)* to revoke

**revue** [ʀ(ə)vy] *nf* review; *(périodique)* review, magazine; *(de music-hall)* variety show; **passer en ~** *(mentalement)* to go through

**rez-de-chaussée** [ʀed(ə)ʃose] *nm inv* ground floor

**RF** *sigle f* = **République française**

**Rhin** [ʀɛ̃] *nm* Rhine

**rhinocéros** [ʀinɔseʀɔs] *nm* rhinoceros

**Rhône** [ʀon] *nm* Rhone

**rhubarbe** [ʀybaʀb] *nf* rhubarb

**rhum** [ʀɔm] *nm* rum

**rhumatisme** [ʀymatism] *nm* rheumatism *no pl*

**rhume** [ʀym] *nm* cold; **~ de cerveau** head cold; **le ~ des foins** hay fever

**ri** [ʀi] *pp de* **rire**

**riant, e** [ʀ(i)jɑ̃, ʀ(i)jɑ̃t] *adj* smiling, cheerful

**ricaner** [ʀikane] *vi (avec méchanceté)* to snigger; *(bêtement)* to giggle

**riche** [ʀiʃ] *adj (personne, pays)* rich, wealthy; **~ en** rich in; **richesse** *nf* wealth; *(fig: de sol, musée etc)* richness; **richesses** *nfpl (ressources, argent)* wealth *sg*; *(fig: trésors)* treasures

**ricochet** [ʀikɔʃɛ] *nm*: **faire des ~s** to skip stones; **par ~** *(fig)* as an indirect result

**rictus** [ʀiktys] *nm* grin

**ride** [ʀid] *nf* wrinkle

**rideau, x** [ʀido] *nm* curtain; **~ de fer** *(boutique)* metal shutter(s)

**rider** [ʀide] *vt* to wrinkle; **se ~** *vi* to become wrinkled

**ridicule** [ʀidikyl] *adj* ridiculous ♦ *nm*: **le ~** ridicule; **ridiculiser**: **se ridiculiser** *vi* to make a fool of o.s.

**MOT-CLÉ**

**rien** [ʀjɛ̃] *pron* **1**: *(ne)* **... rien** nothing; *tournure negative + anything;* **qu'est-ce que vous avez? – rien** what have you got? – nothing; **il n'a rien dit/fait** he said/did nothing; he hasn't said/done anything; **il n'a rien** *(n'est pas blessé)* he's all right; **de rien!** not at all!

**2** *(quelque chose):* **a-t-il jamais rien fait pour nous?** has he ever done anything for us?

**3**: **rien de**: **rien d'intéressant** nothing interesting; **rien d'autre** nothing else; **rien du tout** nothing at all

**4**: **rien que**: just, only; nothing but; **rien que pour lui faire plaisir** only *ou* just to please him; **rien que la vérité** nothing but the truth; **rien que cela** that alone

♦ *nm*: **un petit rien** *(cadeau)* a little something; **des riens** trivia *pl*; **un rien de** a hint of; **en un rien de temps** in no time at all

**rieur, -euse** [ʀ(i)jœʀ, ʀ(i)jøz] *adj* cheerful

**rigide** [ʀiʒid] *adj* stiff; *(fig)* rigid; strict

**rigole** [ʀigɔl] *nf (conduit)* channel

**rigoler** [ʀigɔle] *vi (fam: rire)* to laugh; *(s'amuser)* to have (some) fun; *(plaisanter)* to be joking *ou* kidding; **rigolo, -ote** *(fam) adj* funny ♦ *nm/f* comic; *(péj)* fraud, phoney

**rigoureusement** [ʀiguʀøzmɑ̃] *adv (vrai)* absolutely; *(interdit)* strictly

**rigoureux, -euse** [ʀiguʀø, øz] *adj* rigorous; *(hiver)* hard, harsh

**rigueur** [ʀigœʀ] *nf* rigour; **être de ~** to be the rule; **à la ~** at a pinch; **tenir ~ à qn de qch** to hold sth against sb

**rillettes** [ʀijɛt] *nfpl* potted meat *(made from pork or goose)*

**rime** [ʀim] *nf* rhyme

**rinçage** [ʀɛ̃saʒ] *nm* rinsing (out); *(opération)* rinse

**rincer** [ʀɛ̃se] *vt* to rinse; *(récipient)* to rinse out

**ring** [ʀiŋ] *nm* (boxing) ring

**ringard, e** [ʀɛ̃gaʀ, aʀd] *(fam) adj* old-fashioned

**rions** [ʀjɔ̃] vb voir **rire**

**rire** [ʀiʀ] vi to laugh; (se divertir) to have fun ♦ nm laugh; **le ~** laughter; **~ de** to laugh at; **pour ~** (pas sérieusement) for a joke ou a laugh

**risée** [ʀize] nf: **être la ~ de** to be the laughing stock of

**risible** [ʀizibl] adj laughable

**risque** [ʀisk] nm risk; **le ~** danger; **à ses ~s et périls** at his own risk; **risqué, e** adj risky; (plaisanterie) risqué, daring; **risquer** vt to risk; (allusion, question) to venture, hazard; **ça ne risque rien** it's quite safe; **risquer de**: **il risque de se tuer** he could get himself killed; **ce qui risque de se produire** what might ou could well happen; **il ne risque pas de recommencer** there's no chance of him doing that again; **se risquer à faire** (tenter) to venture ou dare to do

**rissoler** [ʀisɔle] vi, vt: **(faire) ~** to brown

**ristourne** [ʀistuʀn] nf discount

**rite** [ʀit] nm rite; (fig) ritual

**rivage** [ʀivaʒ] nm shore

**rival, e, -aux** [ʀival, o] adj, nm/f rival; **rivaliser**: **rivaliser avec** (personne) to rival, vie with; **rivalité** nf rivalry

**rive** [ʀiv] nf shore; (de fleuve) bank; **riverain, e** nm/f riverside (ou lakeside) resident; (d'une route) local resident

**rivet** [ʀivɛ] nm rivet

**rivière** [ʀivjɛʀ] nf river

**rixe** [ʀiks] nf brawl, scuffle

**riz** [ʀi] nm rice; **rizière** nf paddy-field, ricefield

**RMI** sigle m (= revenu minimum d'insertion) ≈ income support (BRIT), welfare (US)

**RN** sigle f = **route nationale**

**robe** [ʀɔb] nf dress; (de juge) robe; (pelage) coat; **~ de chambre** dressing gown; **~ de soirée/de mariée** evening/wedding dress

**robinet** [ʀɔbinɛ] nm tap

**robot** [ʀɔbo] nm robot

**robuste** [ʀɔbyst] adj robust, sturdy; **robustesse** nf robustness, sturdiness

**roc** [ʀɔk] nm rock

**rocade** [ʀɔkad] nf bypass

**rocaille** [ʀɔkaj] nf loose stones pl; (jardin) rockery, rock garden

**roche** [ʀɔʃ] nf rock

**rocher** [ʀɔʃe] nm rock

**rocheux, -euse** [ʀɔʃø, øz] adj rocky

**rodage** [ʀɔdaʒ] nm: **en ~** running in

**roder** [ʀɔde] vt (AUTO) to run in

**rôder** [ʀode] vi to roam about; (de façon suspecte) to lurk (about ou around); **rôdeur, -euse** nm/f prowler

**rogne** [ʀɔɲ] (fam) nf: **être en ~** to be in a temper

**rogner** [ʀɔɲe] vt to clip; **~ sur** (fig) to cut down ou back on

**rognons** [ʀɔɲɔ̃] nmpl (CULIN) kidneys

**roi** [ʀwa] nm king; **la fête des R~s, les R~s** Twelfth Night

La fête des Rois is celebrated on January 6. Figurines representing the magi are traditionally added to the Christmas crib and people eat la galette des Rois, a plain, flat cake in which a porcelain charm (la fève) is hidden. Whoever finds the charm is king or queen for the day and chooses a partner.

**rôle** [ʀol] nm role, part

**romain, e** [ʀɔmɛ̃, ɛn] adj Roman ♦ nm/f: **R~, e** Roman

**roman, e** [ʀɔmɑ̃, an] adj (ARCHIT) Romanesque ♦ nm novel; **~ d'espionnage** spy novel ou story; **~ policier** detective story

**romance** [ʀɔmɑ̃s] nf ballad

**romancer** [ʀɔmɑ̃se] vt (agrémenter) to romanticize; **romancier, -ière** nm/f novelist; **romanesque** adj (amours, aventures) storybook cpd; (sentimental *personne)* romantic

**roman-feuilleton** [ʀɔmɑ̃fœjtɔ̃] nm serialized novel

**romanichel, le** [ʀɔmaniʃɛl] *(péj)* nm/f gipsy

**romantique** [ʀɔmɑ̃tik] adj romantic

**romarin** [ʀɔmaʀɛ̃] nm rosemary

**rompre** [ʀɔ̃pʀ] vt to break; *(entretien, fiançailles)* to break off ♦ vi *(fiancés)* to break it off; **se ~** vi to break; **rompu, e** adj *(fourbu)* exhausted

**ronces** [ʀɔ̃s] nfpl brambles

**ronchonner** [ʀɔ̃ʃɔne] *(fam)* vi to grouse, grouch

**rond, e** [ʀɔ̃, ʀɔ̃d] adj round; *(joues, mollets)* well-rounded; *(fam: ivre)* tight ♦ nm *(cercle)* ring; *(fam: sou)*: **je n'ai plus un ~** I haven't a penny left; **en ~** *(s'asseoir, danser)* in a ring; **ronde** nf *(gén: de surveillance)* rounds pl, patrol; *(danse)* round dance; *(MUS)* semibreve *(BRIT)*, whole note *(US)*; **à la ronde** *(alentour)*: **à 10 km à la ronde** for 10 km round; **rondelet, te** adj plump

**rondelle** [ʀɔ̃dɛl] nf *(tranche)* slice, round; *(TECH)* washer

**rondement** [ʀɔ̃dmɑ̃] adv *(efficacement)* briskly

**rondin** [ʀɔ̃dɛ̃] nm log

**rond-point** [ʀɔ̃pwɛ̃] nm roundabout

**ronflant, e** [ʀɔ̃flɑ̃, ɑ̃t] *(péj)* adj high-flown, grand

**ronflement** [ʀɔ̃flɑmɑ̃] nm snore, snoring

**ronfler** [ʀɔ̃fle] vi to snore; *(moteur, poêle)* to hum

**ronger** [ʀɔ̃ʒe] vt to gnaw (at); *(suj: vers, rouille)* to eat into; **se ~ les ongles** to bite one's nails; **se ~ les sangs** to worry o.s. sick; **rongeur** nm rodent

**ronronner** [ʀɔ̃ʀɔne] vi to purr

**rosace** [ʀozas] nf *(vitrail)* rose window

**rosbif** [ʀɔsbif] nm: **du ~** roasting meat; *(cuit)* roast beef

**rose** [ʀoz] nf rose ♦ adj pink

**rosé, e** [ʀoze] adj pinkish; *(vin)* ~ rosé

**roseau, x** [ʀozo] nm reed

**rosée** [ʀoze] nf dew

**rosette** [ʀozɛt] nf *(nœud)* bow

**rosier** [ʀozje] nm rosebush, rose tree

**rosse** [ʀɔs] *(fam)* adj nasty, vicious

**rossignol** [ʀɔsiɲɔl] nm *(zool)* nightingale

**rotatif, -ive** [ʀɔtatif, iv] adj rotary

**rotation** [ʀɔtasjɔ̃] nf rotation

**roter** [ʀɔte] *(fam)* vi to burp, belch

**rôti** [ʀoti] nm: **du ~** roasting meat; *(cuit)* roast meat; **~ de bœuf/porc** joint of beef/pork

**rotin** [ʀɔtɛ̃] nm rattan (cane); **fauteuil en ~** cane (arm)chair

**rôtir** [ʀotiʀ] vt *(aussi:* **faire ~**) to roast; **rôtisserie** nf *(restaurant)* steakhouse; *(traiteur)* roast meat shop; **rôtissoire** nf *(roasting)* spit

**rotule** [ʀɔtyl] nf kneecap

**roturier, -ière** [ʀɔtyʀje, jɛʀ] nm/f commoner

**rouage** [ʀwaʒ] nm cog(wheel), gearwheel; **les ~s de l'État** the wheels of State

**roucouler** [ʀukule] vi to coo

**roue** [ʀu] nf wheel; **~ de secours** spare wheel

**roué, e** [ʀwe] adj wily

**rouer** [ʀwe] vt: **~ qn de coups** to give sb a thrashing

**rouge** [ʀuʒ] adj, nm/f red ♦ nm red; *(vin)* ~ red wine; **sur la liste ~** *(BRIT)*, unlisted *(US)*; **passer au ~** *(signal)* to go red; *(automobiliste)* to go through a red light; **~ (à lèvres)** lipstick; **rouge-gorge** nm robin (redbreast)

**rougeole** [ʀuʒɔl] nf measles sg

**rougeoyer** [ʀuʒwaje] vi to glow red

**rouget** [ʀuʒɛ] nm mullet

**rougeur** [ʀuʒœʀ] nf redness; *(MÉD: tache)* red blotch

**rougir** [ʀuʒiʀ] vi to turn red; *(de honte, timidité)* to blush, flush; *(de plaisir, colère)* to flush

**rouille** [ʀuj] nf rust; **rouillé, e** adj

**rusty; rouiller** vt to rust ♦ vi to rust, go rusty; **se rouiller** vi to rust

**roulant, e** [ʀulɑ̃, ɑ̃t] adj (meuble) on wheels; (tapis etc) moving; **escalier ~** escalator

**rouleau, x** [ʀulo] nm roll; (à mise en plis, à peinture, vague) roller; **~ à pâtisserie** rolling pin

**roulement** [ʀulmɑ̃] nm (rotation) rotation; (bruit) rumbling no pl, rumble; **travailler par ~** to work on a rota (BRIT) ou rotation (US) basis; **~ (à billes)** ball bearings pl; **~ de tambour** drum roll

**rouler** [ʀule] vt to roll; (papier, tapis) to roll up; (CULIN: pâte) to roll out; (fam: duper) to do, con ♦ vi (bille, boule) to roll; (voiture, train) to go, run; (automobiliste) to drive; (bateau) to roll; **se ~ dans** (boue) to roll in; (couverture) to roll o.s. (up) in

**roulette** [ʀulɛt] nf (de table, fauteuil) castor; (de dentiste) drill; (jeu) roulette; **à ~s** on castors; **ça a marché comme sur des ~s** (fam) it went off very smoothly

**roulis** [ʀuli] nm roll(ing)

**roulotte** [ʀulɔt] nf caravan

**roumain, e** [ʀumɛ̃, ɛn] adj Rumanian ♦ nm/f: **R~, e** Rumanian

**Roumanie** [ʀumani] nf Rumania

**rouquin, e** [ʀukɛ̃, in] (péj) nm/f redhead

**rouspéter** [ʀuspete] (fam) vi to moan

**rousse** [ʀus] adj voir **roux**

**roussir** [ʀusir] vt to scorch ♦ vi (CULIN): **faire ~** to brown

**route** [ʀut] nf road; (fig: chemin) way; (itinéraire, parcours) route; (fig: voie) road, path; **il y a 3h de ~** it's a 3-hour ride ou journey; **en ~** on the way; **mettre en ~** to start up; **se mettre en ~** to set off; **~ nationale** ≈ A road (BRIT), ≈ state highway (US); **routier, -ière** adj road cpd ♦ nm (camionneur) (long-distance) lorry (BRIT) ou truck (US) driver; (restaurant) ≈ transport café

(BRIT), ≈ truck stop (US)

**routine** [ʀutin] nf routine; **routinier, -ière** (péj) adj (activité) humdrum; (personne) addicted to routine

**rouvrir** [ʀuvʀiʀ] vt, vi to reopen, open again; **se ~** vi to reopen, open again

**roux, rousse** [ʀu, ʀus] adj red; (cheveux) red-haired ♦ nm/f redhead

**royal, e, -aux** [ʀwajal, o] adj royal; (cadeau etc) fit for a king

**royaume** [ʀwajom] nm kingdom; (fig) realm; **le R~-Uni** the United Kingdom

**royauté** [ʀwajote] nf (régime) monarchy

**RPR** sigle m: **Rassemblement pour la République** French right-wing political party

**ruban** [ʀybɑ̃] nm ribbon; **~ adhésif** adhesive tape

**rubéole** [ʀybeɔl] nf German measles sg, rubella

**rubis** [ʀybi] nm ruby

**rubrique** [ʀybʀik] nf (titre, catégorie) heading; (PRESSE: article) column

**ruche** [ʀyʃ] nf hive

**rude** [ʀyd] adj (au toucher) rough; (métier, tâche) hard, tough; (climat) severe, harsh; (bourru) harsh; (fruste: manières) rugged, tough; (fam: fameux) jolly good; **rudement** (fam) adv (très) terribly

**rudimentaire** [ʀydimɑ̃tɛʀ] adj rudimentary, basic

**rudiments** [ʀydimɑ̃] nmpl: **avoir des ~ d'anglais** to have a smattering of English

**rudoyer** [ʀydwaje] vt to treat harshly

**rue** [ʀy] nf street

**ruée** [ʀɥe] nf rush

**ruelle** [ʀɥɛl] nf alley(-way)

**ruer** [ʀɥe] vi (cheval) to kick out; **se ~** vi: **se ~ sur** to pounce on; **se ~ vers/dans/hors de** to rush ou dash towards/into/out of

**rugby** [ʀygbi] nm rugby (football)

**rugir** [ʀyʒiʀ] vi to roar

**rugueux, -euse** [ʀygø, øz] adj rough

**ruine** [ʀɥin] *nf* ruin; **ruiner** *vt* to ruin; **ruineux, -euse** *adj* ruinous

**ruisseau, x** [ʀɥiso] *nm* stream, brook

**ruisseler** [ʀɥis(ə)le] *vi* to stream

**rumeur** [ʀymœʀ] *nf* (*nouvelle*) rumour; (*bruit confus*) rumbling

**ruminer** [ʀymine] *vt* (*herbe*) to ruminate; (*fig*) to ruminate on *ou* over, chew over

**rupture** [ʀyptyʀ] *nf* (*séparation, désunion*) break-up, split; (*de négociations etc*) breakdown; (*de contrat*) breach; (*dans continuité*) break

**rural, e, -aux** [ʀyʀal, o] *adj* rural, country *cpd*

**ruse** [ʀyz] *nf*: **la ~** cunning, craftiness; (*pour tromper*) trickery; **une ~** a trick, a ruse; **rusé, e** *adj* cunning, crafty

**russe** [ʀys] *adj* Russian ♦ *nm/f*: **R~** Russian ♦ *nm* (*LING*) Russian

**Russie** [ʀysi] *nf*: **la ~** Russia

**rustine** ® [ʀystin] *nf* rubber repair patch (*for bicycle tyre*)

**rustique** [ʀystik] *adj* rustic

**rustre** [ʀystʀ] *nm* boor

**rutilant, e** [ʀytilɑ̃, ɑ̃t] *adj* gleaming

**rythme** [ʀitm] *nm* rhythm; (*vitesse*) rate; (: *de la vie*) pace, tempo; **rythmé, e** *adj* rhythmic(al)

## S, s

**s'** [s] *pron voir* **se**

**sa** [sa] *adj voir* **son**[1]

**SA** *sigle* (= *société anonyme*) ≃ Ltd (*BRIT*), ≃ Inc. (*US*)

**sable** [sabl] *nm* sand; **~s mouvants** quicksand(s)

**sablé** [sable] *nm* shortbread biscuit

**sabler** [sable] *vt* (*contre le verglas*) to grit; **~ le champagne** to drink champagne

**sablier** [sablije] *nm* hourglass; (*de cuisine*) egg timer

**sablonneux, -euse** [sablɔnø, øz] *adj* sandy

**saborder** [sabɔʀde] *vt* (*navire*) to scuttle; (*fig: projet*) to put paid to, scupper

**sabot** [sabo] *nm* clog; (*de cheval*) hoof; **~ de frein** brake shoe

**saboter** [sabɔte] *vt* to sabotage; (*bâcler*) to make a mess of, botch

**sac** [sak] *nm* bag; (*à charbon etc*) sack; **~ à dos** rucksack; **~ à main** handbag; **~ de couchage** sleeping bag; **~ de voyage** travelling bag; **~ poubelle** bin liner

**saccadé, e** [sakade] *adj* jerky; (*respiration*) spasmodic

**saccager** [sakaʒe] *vt* (*piller*) to sack; (*dévaster*) to create havoc in

**saccharine** [sakaʀin] *nf* saccharin

**sacerdoce** [sasɛʀdɔs] *nm* priesthood; (*fig*) calling, vocation

**sache** *etc* [saʃ] *vb voir* **savoir**

**sachet** [saʃɛ] *nm* (*small*) bag; (*de sucre, café*) sachet; **du potage en ~** packet soup; **~ de thé** tea bag

**sacoche** [sakɔʃ] *nf* (*gén*) bag; (*de bicyclette*) saddlebag

**sacquer** [sake] *vt* (*fam: employé*) to fire; (*détester*): **je ne peux pas le ~** I can't stand him

**sacre** [sakʀ] *nm* (*roi*) coronation

**sacré, e** [sakʀe] *adj* sacred; (*fam: satané*) blasted; (*fam: fameux*): **un ~ toupé** a heck of a cheek

**sacrement** [sakʀəmɑ̃] *nm* sacrament

**sacrifice** [sakʀifis] *nm* sacrifice; **sacrifier** *vt* to sacrifice

**sacristie** [sakʀisti] *nf* (*catholique*) sacristy; (*protestante*) vestry

**sadique** [sadik] *adj* sadistic

**safran** [safʀɑ̃] *nm* saffron

**sage** [saʒ] *adj* wise; (*enfant*) good

**sage-femme** [saʒfam] *nf* midwife

**sagesse** [saʒɛs] *nf* wisdom

**Sagittaire** [saʒitɛʀ] *nm*: **le ~** Sagittarius

**Sahara** [saaʀa] *nm*: **le ~** the Sahara (desert)

**saignant, e** [sɛɲɑ̃, ɑ̃t] *adj* (*viande*) rare

**saignée** [seɲe] *nf* (*fig*) heavy losses *pl*

**saigner** [sɛɲe] *vi* to bleed ♦ *vt* to bleed; (*animal*) to kill (by bleeding); ~ **du nez** to have a nosebleed

**saillie** [saji] *nf* (*sur un mur etc*) projection

**saillir** [sajiʀ] *vi* to project, stick out; (*veine, muscle*) to bulge

**sain, e** [sɛ̃, sɛn] *adj* healthy; ~ **d'esprit** sound in mind, sane; ~ **et sauf** safe and sound, unharmed

**saindoux** [sɛ̃du] *nm* lard

**saint, e** [sɛ̃, sɛ̃t] *adj* holy ♦ *nm/f* saint; **le S~ Esprit** the Holy Spirit *ou* Ghost; **la S~e Vierge** the Blessed Virgin; **la S~-Sylvestre** New Year's Eve; **sainteté** *nf* holiness

**sais** *etc* [sɛ] *vb voir* **savoir**

**saisi, e** [sezi] *adj*: ~ **de panique** panic-stricken; **être** ~ **(par le froid)** to be struck by the sudden cold; **saisie** *nf* seizure; ~**e (de données)** (data) capture

**saisir** [seziʀ] *vt* to take hold of, grab; (*fig: occasion*) to seize; (*comprendre*) to grasp; (*entendre*) to get, catch; (*données*) to capture; (*CULIN*) to fry quickly; (*JUR: biens, publication*) to seize; **se** ~ **de** *vt* to seize; **saisissant, e** *adj* startling, striking

**saison** [sezɔ̃] *nf* season; **morte** ~ slack season; **saisonnier, -ière** *adj* seasonal

**sait** [sɛ] *vb voir* **savoir**

**salade** [salad] *nf* (*BOT*) lettuce *etc*; (*CULIN*) (green) salad; (*fam: confusion*) tangle, muddle; ~ **composée** mixed salad; ~ **de fruits** fruit salad; **saladier** *nm* (salad) bowl

**salaire** [salɛʀ] *nm* (*annuel, mensuel*) salary; (*hebdomadaire, journalier*) pay, wages *pl*; ~ **minimum interprofessionnel de croissance** index-linked *guaranteed minimum wage*

**salarié, e** [salaʀje] *nm/f* salaried employee; wage-earner

**salaud** [salo] (*fam!*) *nm* sod (*!*), bastard (*!*)

**sale** [sal] *adj* dirty, filthy; (*fam: mauvais*) nasty

**salé, e** [sale] *adj* (*mer, goût*) salty; (*CULIN: amandes, beurre etc*) salted; (: *gâteaux*) savoury; (*fam: grivois*) spicy; (: *facture*) steep

**saler** [sale] *vt* to salt

**saleté** [salte] *nf* (*saleté*) dirtiness; (*crasse*) dirt, filth; (*tache etc*) dirt *no pl*; (*fam: méchanceté*) dirty trick; (: *camelote*) rubbish *no pl*; (: *obscénité*) filthy thing (to say)

**salière** [saljɛʀ] *nf* saltcellar

**salir** [saliʀ] *vt* to (make) dirty; (*fig: quelqu'un*) to soil the reputation of; **se** ~ *vi* to get dirty; **salissant, e** *adj* (*tissu*) which shows the dirt; (*travail*) messy

**salle** [sal] *nf* room; (*d'hôpital*) ward; (*de restaurant*) dining room; (*d'un cinéma*) auditorium; (: *public*) audience; ~ **à manger** dining room; ~ **d'attente** waiting room; ~ **de bain(s)** bathroom; ~ **de classe** classroom; ~ **de concert** concert hall; ~ **d'eau** shower-room; ~ **d'embarquement** (*à l'aéroport*) departure lounge; ~ **de jeux** (*pour enfants*) playroom; ~ **d'opération** (*d'hôpital*) operating theatre; ~ **de séjour** living room; ~ **des ventes** saleroom

**salon** [salɔ̃] *nm* lounge, sitting room; (*mobilier*) lounge suite; (*exposition*) exhibition, show; ~ **de beauté** beauty salon; ~ **de coiffure** hairdressing salon; ~ **de thé** tearoom

**salope** [salɔp] (*fam!*) *nf* bitch (*!*); **saloperie** (*fam!*) *nf* (*action*) dirty trick; (*chose sans valeur*) rubbish *no pl*

**salopette** [salɔpɛt] *nf* dungarees *pl*; (*d'ouvrier*) overall(s)

**salsifis** [salsifi] *nm* salsify

**salubre** [salybʀ] *adj* healthy, salubrious

**saluer** [salɥe] *vt* (*pour dire bonjour, fig*) to greet; (*pour dire au revoir*) to take one's leave; (*MIL*) to salute

**salut** [saly] *nm* (*geste*) wave; (*parole*) greeting; (*MIL*) salute; (*sauvegarde*) safety; (*REL*) salvation ♦ *excl* (*fam: bonjour*) hi (there); (: *au revoir*) see you, bye

**salutations** [salytasjɔ̃] *nfpl* greetings; **Veuillez agréer, Monsieur, mes ~ distinguées** yours faithfully

**samedi** [samdi] *nm* Saturday

**SAMU** [samy] *sigle m* (= *service d'assistance médicale d'urgence*) ≃ ambulance (service) (*BRIT*), ≃ paramedics *pl* (*US*)

**sanction** [sɑ̃ksjɔ̃] *nf* sanction; **sanctionner** *vt* (*loi, usage*) to sanction; (*punir*) to punish

**sandale** [sɑ̃dal] *nf* sandal; **~s à lanières** strappy sandals

**sandwich** [sɑ̃dwi(t)ʃ] *nm* sandwich

**sang** [sɑ̃] *nm* blood; **en ~** covered in blood; **se faire du mauvais ~** to fret, get in a state; **sang-froid** *nm* calm, sangfroid; **de sang-froid** in cold blood; **sanglant, e** *adj* bloody

**sangle** [sɑ̃gl] *nf* strap

**sanglier** [sɑ̃glije] *nm* (wild) boar

**sanglot** [sɑ̃glo] *nm* sob; **sangloter** *vi* to sob

**sangsue** [sɑ̃sy] *nf* leech

**sanguin, e** [sɑ̃gɛ̃, in] *adj* blood *cpd*; **sanguinaire** *adj* bloodthirsty

**sanitaire** [sanitɛʀ] *adj* health *cpd*; **~s** *nmpl* (*lieu*) bathroom *sg*

**sans** [sɑ̃] *prép* without; **un pull ~ manches** a sleeveless jumper; **~ faute** without fail; **~ arrêt** without a pause; **~ ça** (*fam*) otherwise; **~ qu'il s'en aperçoive** without him ou his noticing; **sans-abri** *nmpl* homeless; **sans-emploi** *nm/f inv* unemployed person; **les sans-emploi** the unemployed; **sans-gêne** *adj inv* inconsiderate

**santé** [sɑ̃te] *nf* health; **en bonne ~** in good health; **boire à la ~ de qn** to drink (to) sb's health; **à la/votre ~!** cheers!

**saoudien, ne** [saudjɛ̃, jɛn] *adj* Saudi Arabian ♦ *nm/f:* **S~, ne** Saudi Arabian

**saoul, e** [su, sul] *adj* = **soûl**

**sape** [sap] *vt* to undermine, sap

**sapeur-pompier** [sapœʀpɔ̃pje] *nm*

fireman

**saphir** [safiʀ] *nm* sapphire

**sapin** [sapɛ̃] *nm* fir (tree); (*bois*) fir; **~ de Noël** Christmas tree

**sarcastique** [saʀkastik] *adj* sarcastic

**sarcler** [saʀkle] *vt* to weed

**Sardaigne** [saʀdɛɲ] *nf*: **la ~** Sardinia

**sarrasin** [saʀazɛ̃] *nm* buckwheat

**SARL** *sigle f* (= *société à responsabilité limitée*) ≃ plc (*BRIT*), ≃ Inc. (*US*)

**sas** [sɑs] *nm* (*de sous-marin, d'engin spatial*) airlock; (*d'écluse*) lock

**satané, e** [satane] (*fam*) *adj* confounded

**satellite** [satelit] *nm* satellite

**satin** [satɛ̃] *nm* satin

**satire** [satiʀ] *nf* satire; **satirique** *adj* satirical

**satisfaction** [satisfaksjɔ̃] *nf* satisfaction

**satisfaire** [satisfɛʀ] *vt* to satisfy; **~ à** (*conditions*) to meet; **satisfaisant, e** *adj* (*acceptable*) satisfactory; **satisfait, e** *adj* satisfied; **satisfait de** happy ou satisfied with

**saturer** [satyʀe] *vt* to saturate

**sauce** [sos] *nf* sauce; (*avec un rôti*) gravy; **saucière** *nf* sauceboat

**saucisse** [sosis] *nf* sausage

**saucisson** [sosisɔ̃] *nm* (slicing) sausage

**sauf, sauve** [sof, sov] *adj* unharmed, unhurt; (*fig: honneur*) intact, saved ♦ *prép* except; **laisser la vie sauve à qn** to spare sb's life; **~ si** (*à moins que*) unless; **~ erreur** if I'm not mistaken; **~ avis contraire** unless you hear to the contrary

**sauge** [soʒ] *nf* sage

**saugrenu, e** [sogʀany] *adj* preposterous

**saule** [sol] *nm* willow (tree)

**saumon** [somɔ̃] *nm* salmon *inv*

**saumure** [somyʀ] *nf* brine

**saupoudrer** [sopudʀe] *vt*: **~ qch de** to sprinkle sth with

**saur** [sɔʀ] *adj m*: **hareng ~** smoked ou red herring, kipper

**saurai** *etc* [sɔʀe] *vb voir* **savoir**

**saut** [so] nm jump; (discipline sportive) jumping; **faire un ~ chez qn** to pop over to sb's (place); **~ à l'élastique** bungee jumping; **~ à la perche** pole vaulting; **~ en hauteur/longueur** high/long jump; **~ périlleux** somersault

**saute** [sot] nf: **~ d'humeur** sudden change of mood

**sauter** [sote] vi to jump, leap; (exploser) to blow up, explode; (: fusibles) to blow; (se détacher) to pop out (ou off) ♦ vt to jump (over), leap (over); (fig: omettre) to skip, miss (out); **faire ~** to blow up; (CULIN) to sauté; **~ au cou de qn** to fly into sb's arms; **~ sur une occasion** to jump at an opportunity; **~ aux yeux** to be (quite) obvious

**sauterelle** [sotRɛl] nf grasshopper

**sautiller** [sotije] vi (oiseau) to hop; (enfant) to skip

**sauvage** [sovaʒ] adj (gén) wild; (peuplade) savage; (farouche: personne) unsociable; (barbare) wild, savage; (non officiel) unauthorized, unofficial; **faire du camping ~** to camp in the wild ♦ nm/f savage; (timide) unsociable type

**sauve** [sov] adj f voir **sauf**

**sauvegarde** [sovgard] nf safeguard; (INFORM) backup; **sauvegarder** vt to safeguard; (INFORM: enregistrer) to save; (: copier) to back up

**sauve-qui-peut** [sovkipø] excl run for your life!

**sauver** [sove] vt to save; (porter secours à) to rescue; (récupérer) to salvage, rescue; **se ~** vi (s'enfuir) to run away; (fam: partir) to be off; **sauvetage** nm rescue; **sauveteur** nm rescuer; **sauvette: à la sauvette** adv (se marier etc) hastily, hurriedly; **sauveur** nm saviour

**savais** etc [save] vb voir **savoir**

**savamment** [savamɑ̃] adv (avec érudition) learnedly; (habilement) skilfully, cleverly

**savant, e** [savɑ̃, ɑ̃t] adj scholarly, learned ♦ nm scientist

**saveur** [savœr] nf flavour; (fig) savour

**savoir** [savwar] vt to know; (être capable de): **il sait nager** he can swim ♦ nm knowledge; **se ~** vi (être connu) to be known; **à ~** that is, namely; **faire ~ qch à qn** to let sb know sth; **pas que je sache** not as far as I know

**savon** [savɔ̃] nm (produit) soap; (morceau) bar of soap; (fam): **passer un ~ à qn** to give sb a good dressing-down; **savonner** vt to soap; **savonnette** nf bar of soap

**savons** [savɔ̃] vb voir **savoir**

**savourer** [savure] vt to savour; **savoureux, -euse** adj tasty; (fig: anecdote) spicy, juicy

**saxo(phone)** [saksɔ(fɔn)] nm sax(ophone)

**scabreux, -euse** [skabrø, øz] adj risky; (indécent) improper, shocking

**scandale** [skɑ̃dal] nm scandal; (tapage) **faire un ~** to make a scene, create a disturbance; **faire ~** to scandalize people; **scandaleux, -euse** adj scandalous, outrageous

**scandinave** [skɑ̃dinav] adj Scandinavian ♦ nm/f: **S~** Scandinavian

**Scandinavie** [skɑ̃dinavi] nf Scandinavia

**scaphandre** [skafɑ̃dr] nm (de plongeur) diving suit

**scarabée** [skarabe] nm beetle

**scarlatine** [skarlatin] nf scarlet fever

**scarole** [skarɔl] nf endive

**sceau, x** [so] nm seal

**scélérat, e** [selera, at] nm/f villain

**sceller** [sele] vt to seal

**scénario** [senarjo] nm scenario

**scène** [sɛn] nf (gén) scene; (estrade, fig: théâtre) stage; **entrer en ~** to come on stage; **mettre en ~** (THÉÂTRE) to stage; (CINÉMA) to direct; **~ de ménage** domestic scene

**sceptique** [sɛptik] adj sceptical

**schéma** [ʃema] nm (diagramme) diagram, sketch; **schématique** adj diagrammatic(al), schematic; (*fig*) oversimplified

**sciatique** [sjatik] *nf* sciatica

**scie** [si] *nf* saw; **~ à métaux** hacksaw

**sciemment** [sjamã] *adv* knowingly

**science** [sjãs] *nf* science; (*savoir*) knowledge; **~s naturelles** (SCOL) natural science *sg*, biology *sg*; **~s po** political science *ou* studies *pl*; **science-fiction** *nf* science fiction; **scientifique** *adj* scientific ♦ *nm/f* scientist; (*étudiant*) science student

**scier** [sje] *vt* to saw; (*retrancher*) to saw off; **scierie** *nf* sawmill

**scinder** [sɛ̃de] *vt* to split up; **se ~** *vi* to split up

**scintiller** [sɛ̃tije] *vi* to sparkle; (*étoile*) to twinkle

**scission** [sisjɔ̃] *nf* split

**sciure** [sjyʀ] *nf*: **~ (de bois)** sawdust

**sclérose** [skleʀoz] *nf*: **~ en plaques** multiple sclerosis

**scolaire** [skɔlɛʀ] *adj* school *cpd*; **scolariser** *vt* to provide with schooling/schools; **scolarité** *nf* schooling

**scooter** [skutœʀ] *nm* (motor) scooter

**score** [skɔʀ] *nm* score

**scorpion** [skɔʀpjɔ̃] *nm* (*signe*): **le S~** Scorpio

**Scotch** ® [skɔtʃ] *nm* adhesive tape

**scout, e** [skut] *adj, nm* scout

**script** [skʀipt] *nm* (*écriture*) printing; (*CINÉMA*) (shooting) script

**scrupule** [skʀypyl] *nm* scruple

**scruter** [skʀyte] *vt* to scrutinize; (*l'obscurité*) to peer into

**scrutin** [skʀytɛ̃] *nm* (*vote*) ballot; (*ensemble des opérations*) poll

**sculpter** [skylte] *vt* to sculpt; (*bois*) to carve; **sculpteur** *nm* sculptor; **sculpture** *nf* sculpture; **sculpture sur bois** wood carving

**SDF** *sigle m* (= *sans domicile fixe*) homeless person; **les SDF** the homeless

---MOT-CLÉ---

**se** [sə], **s'** *pron* **1** (*emploi réfléchi*) oneself;

(*: masc*) himself; (*: fém*) herself; (*: sujet non humain*) itself; (*: pl*) themselves; **se voir comme l'on est** to see o.s. as one is

**2** (*réciproque*) one another, each other; **ils s'aiment** they love one another *ou* each other

**3** (*passif*): **cela se répare facilement** it is easily repaired

**4** (*possessif*): **se casser la jambe/laver les mains** to break one's leg/wash one's hands

**séance** [seãs] *nf* (*d'assemblée*) meeting, session; (*de tribunal*) sitting, session; (*musicale, CINÉMA, THÉÂTRE*) performance; **~ tenante** forthwith

**seau, x** [so] *nm* bucket, pail

**sec, sèche** [sɛk, sɛʃ] *adj* dry; (*raisins, figues*) dried; (*cœur: insensible*) hard, cold ♦ *nm*: **tenir au ~** to keep in a dry place ♦ *adv* hard; **je le bois ~** I drink it straight *ou* neat; **à ~** (*puits*) dried up

**sécateur** [sekatœʀ] *nm* secateurs *pl* (BRIT), shears *pl*

**sèche** [sɛʃ] *adj f voir* **sec**; **sèche-cheveux** *nm inv* hair-drier; **sèche-linge** *nm inv* tumble dryer; **sèchement** *adv* (*répondre*) drily

**sécher** [seʃe] *vt* to dry; (*dessécher: peau, blé*) to dry (out); (*: étang*) to dry up; (*fam: cours*) to skip ♦ *vi* to dry; to dry out; to dry up; (*fam: candidat*) to be stumped; **se ~** (*après le bain*) to dry o.s.; **sécheresse** *nf* dryness; (*absence de pluie*) drought; **séchoir** *nm* drier

**second, e** [s(ə)gɔ̃, 5d] *adj* second ♦ *nm* (*assistant*) second in command; (*NAVIG*) first mate; **voyager en ~e** to travel second-class; **secondaire** *adj* secondary; **seconde** *nf* second; **seconder** *vt* to assist

**secouer** [s(ə)kwe] *vt* to shake; (*passagers*) to rock; (*traumatiser*) to shake (up); **se ~** *vi* (*fam: faire un effort*) to shake o.s. up; (*: se dépêcher*) to get a move on

**secourir** [s(ə)kuʀiʀ] vt (venir en aide à) to assist, aid; **secourisme** nm first aid; **secouriste** nm/f first-aid worker

**secours** [s(ə)kuʀ] nm help, aid, assistance ♦ nmpl aid sg; **au ~!** help!; **appeler au ~** to shout ou call for help; **porter ~ à qn** to give sb assistance, help sb; **les premiers ~** first aid sg

**secousse** [s(ə)kus] nf jolt, bump; (électrique) shock; (fig: psychologique) jolt, shock; **~ sismique** earth tremor

**secret, -ète** [sakʀɛ, ɛt] adj secret; (fig: renfermé) reticent, reserved ♦ nm secret; (discrétion absolue): **le ~** secrecy

**secrétaire** [s(ə)kʀetɛʀ] nm/f secretary ♦ nm (meuble) writing desk; **~ de direction** private ou personal secretary; **~ d'État** junior minister; **~ général** (COMM) company secretary; **secrétariat** nm (profession) secretarial work; (bureau) office; (: d'organisation internationale) secretariat

**secteur** [sɛktœʀ] nm sector; (zone) area; (ÉLEC): **branché sur ~** plugged into the mains (supply)

**section** [sɛksjɔ̃] nf section; (de parcours d'autobus) fare stage; (MIL: unité) platoon; **sectionner** vt to sever

**Sécu** [seky] abr f = **sécurité sociale**

**séculaire** [sekylɛʀ] adj (très vieux) age-old

**sécuriser** [sekyʀize] vt to give a (feeling of) security to

**sécurité** [sekyʀite] nf (absence de danger) safety; (absence de troubles) security; **système de ~** security system; **être en ~** to be safe; **la ~ routière** road safety; **la ~ sociale** ≈ (the) Social Security (BRIT), ≈ Welfare (US)

**sédentaire** [sedɑ̃tɛʀ] adj sedentary

**séduction** [sedyksjɔ̃] nf seduction; (charme, attrait) appeal, charm

**séduire** [seduiʀ] vt to charm; (femme: abuser de) to seduce; **séduisant, e** (femme) seductive; (homme, offre) very attractive

**ségrégation** [segʀegasjɔ̃] nf segrega-tion

**seigle** [sɛgl] nm rye

**seigneur** [sɛɲœʀ] nm lord

**sein** [sɛ̃] nm breast; (entrailles) womb; **au ~ de** (équipe, institution) within

**séisme** [seism] nm earthquake

**seize** [sɛz] num sixteen; **seizième** num sixteenth

**séjour** [seʒuʀ] nm stay; (pièce) living room; **séjourner** vi to stay

**sel** [sɛl] nm salt; (fig: piquant) spice

**sélection** [seleksjɔ̃] nf selection; **sélectionner** vt to select

**self-service** [sɛlfsɛʀvis] adj, nm self-service

**selle** [sɛl] nf saddle; **~s** nfpl (MÉD) stools; **seller** vt to saddle

**sellette** [sɛlɛt] nf: **être sur la ~** to be in the hot seat

**selon** [s(ə)lɔ̃] prép according to; (en se conformant à) in accordance with; **~ que** according to whether; **~ moi** as I see it

**semaine** [s(ə)mɛn] nf week; **en ~** during the week, on weekdays

**semblable** [sɑ̃blabl] adj similar; (de ce genre): **de ~s mésaventures** such mishaps ♦ nm fellow creature ou man; **~ à** similar to, like

**semblant** [sɑ̃blɑ̃] nm: **un ~ de ...** a semblance of ...; **faire ~ (de faire)** to pretend (to do)

**sembler** [sɑ̃ble] vb +attrib to seem ♦ vb impers: **il semble (bien) que/inutile de** it (really) seems ou appears that/ useless to; **il me semble que** it seems to me that; **comme bon lui semble** as he sees fit

**semelle** [s(ə)mɛl] nf sole; (intérieure) insole, inner sole

**semence** [s(ə)mɑ̃s] nf (graine) seed

**semer** [s(ə)me] vt to sow; (fig: éparpiller) to scatter; (: confusion) to spread; (fam: poursuivants) to lose, shake off; **semé de** (difficultés) riddled with

**semestre** [s(ə)mɛstʀ] nm half-year; (SCOL) semester

**séminaire** [seminɛʀ] nm seminar

**semi-remorque** [səmiʀəmɔʀk] nm articulated lorry (BRIT), semi(trailer) (US)

**semoule** [s(ə)mul] nf semolina

**sempiternel, le** [sɑ̃pitɛʀnɛl] adj eternal, never-ending

**sénat** [sena] nm senate; **sénateur** [senatœʀ] nm senator

**sens** [sɑ̃s] nm (PHYSIOL, instinct) sense; (signification) meaning, sense; (direction) direction; **à mon ~** to my mind; **dans le ~ des aiguilles d'une montre** clockwise; **~ dessus dessous** upside down; **~ interdit** one-way street; **~ unique** one-way street

**sensation** [sɑ̃sasjɔ̃] nf sensation; **à ~** (péj) sensational; **faire ~** to cause ou create a sensation; **sensationnel, le** adj (fam) fantastic, terrific

**sensé, e** [sɑ̃se] adj sensible

**sensibiliser** [sɑ̃sibilize] vt: **~ qn à** to make sb sensitive to

**sensibilité** [sɑ̃sibilite] nf sensitivity

**sensible** [sɑ̃sibl] adj sensitive; (aux sens) perceptible; (appréciable: différence, progrès) appreciable, noticeable; **sensiblement** adv (à peu près): **ils sont sensiblement du même âge** they are approximately the same age; **sensiblerie** nf sentimentality

**sensuel, le** [sɑ̃sɥɛl] adj (personne) sensual; (musique) sensuous

**sentence** [sɑ̃tɑ̃s] nf (jugement) sentence

**sentier** [sɑ̃tje] nm path

**sentiment** [sɑ̃timɑ̃] nm feeling; **sentimental, e, -aux** adj sentimental; (vie, aventure) love cpd

**sentinelle** [sɑ̃tinɛl] nf sentry

**sentir** [sɑ̃tiʀ] vt (par l'odorat) to smell; (par le goût) to taste; (au toucher, fig) to feel; (répandre une odeur de) to smell of; (: ressemblance) to smell like ♦ vi to smell; **~ mauvais** to smell bad; **se ~ bien** to feel good; **se ~ mal** (être indisposé) to feel unwell ou ill; **se ~ le courage/la force de faire** to feel

brave/strong enough to do; **il ne peut pas le ~** (fam) he can't stand him

**séparation** [separasjɔ̃] nf separation; (cloison) division, partition

**séparé, e** [separe] adj (distinct) separate; (époux) separated; **séparément** adv separately

**séparer** [separe] vt to separate; (désunir) to drive apart; (détacher): **~ qch de** to pull sth (off) from; **se ~** vi (époux, amis) to separate, part; (se diviser: route etc) to divide; **se ~ de** (époux) to separate ou part from; (employé, objet personnel) to part with

**sept** [sɛt] num seven; **septante** (BELGIQUE, SUISSE) adj num seventy

**septembre** [sɛptɑ̃bʀ] nm September

**septennat** [septena] nm seven year term of office (of French President)

**septentrional, e, -aux** [sɛptɑ̃tʀijɔnal, o] adj northern

**septicémie** [sɛptisemi] nf blood poisoning, septicaemia

**septième** [sɛtjɛm] num seventh

**septique** [sɛptik] adj: **fosse ~** septic tank

**sépulture** [sepyltyʀ] nf (tombeau) burial place, grave

**séquelles** [sekɛl] nfpl after-effects; (fig) aftermath sg

**séquestrer** [sekɛstʀe] vt (personne) to confine illegally; (biens) to impound

**serai** etc [səʀe] vb voir **être**

**serein, e** [səʀɛ̃, ɛn] adj serene

**serez** [səʀe] vb voir **être**

**sergent** [sɛʀʒɑ̃] nm sergeant

**série** [seʀi] nf series inv; (de clés, casseroles, outils) set; (catégorie: SPORT) rank; **en ~** in quick succession; (COMM) mass cpd; **hors ~** (COMM) custom-built

**sérieusement** [seʀjøzmɑ̃] adv seriously

**sérieux, -euse** [seʀjø, jøz] adj serious; (élève, employé) reliable, responsible; (client, maison) reliable; dependable ♦ nm seriousness; (d'une entreprise etc) reliability; **garder son ~** to keep a straight face; **prendre qch/qn au ~** to take sth/sb seriously

**serin** [s(ə)Rɛ̃] nm canary

**seringue** [s(ə)Rɛ̃g] nf syringe

**serions** [səRjɔ̃] vb voir **être**

**serment** [sɛRmɑ̃] nm (juré) oath; (promesse) pledge, vow

**séronégatif, -ive** [seRonegatif, iv] adj (MÉD) HIV negative

**séropositif, -ive** [seRopozitif, iv] adj (MÉD) HIV positive

**serpent** [sɛRpɑ̃] nm snake; **serpenter** vi to wind

**serpillière** [sɛRpijɛR] nf floorcloth

**serre** [sɛR] nf (AGR) greenhouse; **~s** nfpl (griffes) claws, talons

**serré, e** [seRe] adj (habits) tight; (fig: lutte, match) tight, close-fought; (passagers etc) (tightly) packed; (réseau) dense; **avoir le cœur ~** to have a heavy heart

**serrer** [seRe] vt (tenir) to grip ou hold tight; (comprimer, coincer) to squeeze; (poings, mâchoires) to clench; (suj: vêtement) to be too tight for; (ceinture, nœud, vis) to tighten ♦ vi: **~ à droite** to keep ou get over to the right; **se ~** vi (se rapprocher) to squeeze up; **se ~ contre qn** to huddle up to sb; **~ la main à qn** to shake sb's hand; **~ qn dans ses bras** to hug sb, clasp sb in one's arms

**serrure** [seRyR] nf lock; **serrurier** nm locksmith

**sert** etc [sɛR] vb voir **servir**

**servante** [sɛRvɑ̃t] nf (maid)servant

**serveur, -euse** [sɛRvœR, øz] nm/f waiter (waitress)

**serviable** [sɛRvjabl] adj obliging, willing to help

**service** [sɛRvis] nm service; (assortiment de vaisselle) set, service; (bureau: de la vente etc) department, section; (travail) duty; **premier ~** (série de repas) first sitting; **être de ~** to be on duty; **faire le ~** to serve; **rendre un ~ à qn** to do sb a favour; (objet: s'avérer utile) to

come in useful ou handy for sb; **mettre en ~** to put into service ou operation; **~ compris/non compris** service included/not included; **hors ~** out of order; **~ après-vente** after-sales service; **~ d'ordre** police (ou stewards) in charge of maintaining order; **~ militai-re** military service; **~s secrets** secret service sg

service militaire

*French men over eighteen are required to do ten months' service militaire if pronounced fit. The call-up can be delayed if the conscript is in full-time higher education. Conscientious objectors are required to do two years' public service. Since 1970, women have been able to do military service, though few do.*

**serviette** [sɛRvjɛt] nf (de table) (table) napkin, serviette; (de toilette) towel; (porte-documents) briefcase; **~ de plage** beach towel; **~ hygiénique** sanitary towel

**servir** [sɛRviR] vt to serve; (au restaurant) to wait on; (au magasin) to serve, attend to ♦ vi (TENNIS) to serve; (CARTES) to deal; **~** (prendre d'un plat) to help o.s.; **vous êtes servi?** are you being served?; **~ à qn** (diplôme, livre) to be of use to sb; **~ à qch/faire** (outil etc) to be used for sth/doing; **ça ne sert à rien** it's no use; **~ (à qn) de** to serve as (for sb); **se ~ de** (plat) to help o.s. to; (voiture, outil, relations) to use

**serviteur** [sɛRvitœR] nm servant

**ses** [se] adj voir **son[1]**

**set** [sɛt] nm: **~ (de table)** tablemat, place mat

**seuil** [sœj] nm doorstep; (fig) threshold

**seul, e** [sœl] adj (sans compagnie) alone; (unique): **un ~ livre** only one book, a single book ♦ adv (vivre) alone, on one's own ♦ nm, nf: **il en reste un(e) ~(e)** there's only one left; **le ~ li-**

vre the only book; **parler tout** ~ to talk to oneself; **faire qch (tout)** ~ to do sth (all) on one's own *ou* (all) by oneself; **à lui (tout)** ~ single-handed, on his own; **se sentir** ~ to feel lonely; **seulement** *adv* only; **non seulement ... mais aussi** *ou* **encore** not only ... but also

**sève** [sεv] *nf* sap

**sévère** [sevεʀ] *adj* severe

**sévices** [sevis] *nmpl* (*punir*) cruelty *sg*, ill treatment *sg*

**sévir** [seviʀ] *vi* (*suj: fléau*) to rage, be rampant

**sevrer** [səvʀe] *vt* (*enfant etc*) to wean

**sexe** [sεks] *nm* sex; (*organes génitaux*) genitals, sex organs; **sexuel, le** *adj* sexual

**seyant, e** [sεjɑ̃, ɑ̃t] *adj* becoming

**shampooing** [ʃɑ̃pwε̃] *nm* shampoo

**short** [ʃɔʀt] *nm* (pair of) shorts *pl*

---

MOT-CLÉ

**si** [si] *nm* (MUS) B; (*en chantant la gamme*) ti

♦ **adv 1** (*oui*) yes

**2** (*tellement*) so; **si gentil/rapidement** so kind/fast; (**tant et**) **si bien que** so much so that; **si rapide qu'il soit** however fast he may be

♦ *conj* if; **si tu veux** if you want; **je me demande si** I wonder if *ou* whether; **si seulement** if only

---

**Sicile** [sisil] *nf*: **la** ~ Sicily

**SIDA** [sida] *sigle m* (= *syndrome immuno-déficitaire acquis*) AIDS *sg*

**sidéré, e** [sideʀe] *adj* staggered

**sidérurgie** [sideʀyʀʒi] *nf* steel industry

**siècle** [sjεkl] *nm* century

**siège** [sjεʒ] *nm* seat; (*d'entreprise*) head office; (*d'organisation*) headquarters *pl*, (MIL) siege; ~ **social** registered office; **siéger** *vi* to sit

**sien, ne** [sjε̃, sjεn] *pron*: **le(la)** ~**(ne)**, **les** ~**(ne)s** (*homme*) his; (*femme*) hers;

(*chose, animal*) its; **les** ~**s** (*sa famille*) one's family; **faire des** ~**nes** (*fam*) to be up to one's (usual) tricks

**sieste** [sjεst] *nf* (afternoon) nap *ou* nap; **faire la** ~ to have a snooze *ou* nap

**sifflement** [sifləmɑ̃] *nm*: **un** ~ a whistle

**siffler** [sifle] *vi* (*gén*) to whistle; (*en respirant*) to wheeze; (*serpent, vapeur*) to hiss ♦ *vt* (*chanson*) to whistle; (*chien etc*) to whistle for; (*fille*) to whistle at; (*pièce, orateur*) to hiss, boo; (*fin du match, départ*) to blow one's whistle for; (*fam: verre*) to guzzle

**sifflet** [sifle] *nm* whistle; **coup de** ~ whistle

**siffloter** [siflɔte] *vi*, *vt* to whistle

**sigle** [sigl] *nm* acronym

**signal, -aux** [siɲal, o] *nm* signal; (*indice, écriteau*) sign; **donner le** ~ **de** to give the signal for; ~ **d'alarme** alarm signal; **signaux (lumineux)** (AUTO) traffic signals; **signalement** *nm* description, particulars *pl*

**signaler** [siɲale] *vt* to indicate; (*personne: faire un signe*) to signal; (*vol, perte*) to report; (*faire remarquer*): ~ **qch à qn/à qn que** to point out sth to sb/(to sb) that; **se** ~ **(par)** to distinguish o.s. (by)

**signature** [siɲatyʀ] *nf* signature; (*action*) signing

**signe** [siɲ] *nm* sign; (TYPO) mark; **faire un** ~ **de la main** to give a sign with one's hand; **faire** ~ **à qn** (*fig: contacter*) to get in touch with sb; **faire** ~ **à qn d'entrer** to motion (to) sb to come in; **signer** *vt* to sign; **se signer** *vi* to cross o.s.

**significatif, -ive** [siɲifikatif, iv] *adj* significant

**signification** [siɲifikasjɔ̃] *nf* meaning

**signifier** [siɲifje] *vt* (*vouloir dire*) to mean; (*faire connaître*): ~ **qch (à qn)** to make sth known (to sb)

**silence** [silɑ̃s] *nm* silence; (MUS) rest;

garder le ~ to keep silent, say nothing; **silencieux, -euse** adj quiet, silent ♦ nm silencer

**silex** [silɛks] nm flint

**silhouette** [silwɛt] nf outline, silhouette; (allure) figure

**silicium** [silisjɔm] nm silicon

**sillage** [sijaʒ] nm wake

**sillon** [sijɔ̃] nm furrow; (de disque) groove; **sillonner** vt to criss-cross

**simagrées** [simagʀe] nfpl fuss sg

**similaire** [similɛʀ] adj similar; **similicuir** nm imitation leather; **similitude** nf similarity

**simple** [sɛ̃pl] adj simple; (non multiple) single; ~ **messieurs** nm (TENNIS) men's singles sg; ~ **soldat** private

**simplicité** [sɛ̃plisite] nf simplicity

**simplifier** [sɛ̃plifje] vt to simplify

**simulacre** [simylakʀ] nm (péj): un ~ **de** a pretence of

**simuler** [simyle] vt to sham, simulate

**simultané, e** [simyltane] adj simultaneous

**sincère** [sɛ̃sɛʀ] adj sincere; **sincèrement** adv sincerely; (pour parler franchement) honestly, really; **sincérité** nf sincerity

**sine qua non** [sinekwanɔn] adj: **condition** ~ indispensable condition

**singe** [sɛ̃ʒ] nm monkey; (de grande taille) ape; **singer** vt to ape, mimic; **singeries** nfpl antics

**singulariser** [sɛ̃gylaʀize]: **se** ~ vi to call attention to o.s.

**singularité** [sɛ̃gylaʀite] nf peculiarity

**singulier, -ière** [sɛ̃gylje, jɛʀ] adj remarkable, singular ♦ nm singular

**sinistre** [sinistʀ] adj sinister ♦ nm (incendie) blaze; (catastrophe) disaster; (ASSURANCES) damage (giving rise to a claim); **sinistré, e** adj disaster-stricken ♦ nm/f disaster victim

**sinon** [sinɔ̃] conj (autrement, sans quoi) otherwise, or else; (sauf) except, other than; (si ce n'est) if not

**sinueux, -euse** [sinɥø, øz] adj winding

**sinus** [sinys] nm (ANAT) sinus; (GÉOM) sine; **sinusite** nf sinusitis

**siphon** [sifɔ̃] nm (tube, d'eau gazeuse) siphon; (d'évier etc) U-bend

**sirène** [siʀɛn] nf siren; ~ **d'alarme** fire alarm; (en temps de guerre) air-raid siren

**sirop** [siʀo] nm (à diluer: de fruit etc) syrup; (pharmaceutique) syrup, mixture; ~ **pour la toux** cough mixture

**siroter** [siʀɔte] vt to sip

**sismique** [sismik] adj seismic

**site** [sit] nm (paysage, environnement) setting; (d'une ville etc: emplacement) site; (pittoresque) beauty spot; ~s **touristiques** places of interest; ~ **Web** (INFORM) website

**sitôt** [sito] adv: ~ **parti** as soon as he etc had left; ~ **que** as soon as; **pas de** ~ not for a long time

**situation** [sitɥasjɔ̃] nf situation; (d'un édifice, d'une ville) position, location; ~ **de famille** marital status

**situé, e** [sitɥe] adj situated

**situer** [sitɥe] vt to site, situate; (en pensée) to set, place; **se** ~ vi to be situated

**six** [sis] num six; **sixième** num sixth ♦ nf (SCOL) first form

**Skaï** ® [skaj] nm Leatherette ®

**ski** [ski] nm (objet) ski; (sport) skiing; **faire du** ~ to ski; ~ **de fond** cross-country skiing; ~ **nautique** water-skiing; ~ **de piste** downhill skiing; ~ **de randonnée** cross-country skiing; **skier** vi to ski; **skieur, -euse** nm/f skier

**slip** [slip] nm (sous-vêtement) pants pl, briefs pl; (de bain: d'homme) trunks pl; (: du bikini) (bikini) briefs pl

**slogan** [slɔgɑ̃] nm slogan

**SMIC** [smik] sigle m = **salaire minimum interprofessionnel de croissance**

> SMIC

*In France, the SMIC is the minimum*

*legal hourly rate for workers over eighteen. It is index-linked and is raised each time the cost of living rises by 2%.*

**smicard, e** [smikar, aRd] (*fam*) *nm/f* minimum wage earner

**smoking** [smɔkiŋ] *nm* dinner *ou* evening suit

**SNCF** *sigle f* (= *Société nationale des chemins de fer français*) French railways

**snob** [snɔb] *adj* snobbish ♦ *nm/f* snob; **snobisme** *nm* snobbery, snobbishness

**sobre** [sɔbR] *adj* (*personne*) temperate, abstemious; (*élégance, style*) sober

**sobriquet** [sɔbRikɛ] *nm* nickname

**social, e, -aux** [sɔsjal, o] *adj* social

**socialisme** [sɔsjalism] *nm* socialism; **socialiste** *nm/f* socialist

**société** [sɔsjete] *nf* society; (*sportive*) club; (COMM) company; **la ~ de consommation** the consumer society; **~ anonyme** ≈ limited (BRIT) *ou* incorporated (US) company

**sociologie** [sɔsjɔlɔʒi] *nf* sociology

**socle** [sɔkl] *nm* (*de colonne, statue*) plinth, pedestal; (*de lampe*) base

**socquette** [sɔkɛt] *nf* ankle sock

**sœur** [sœR] *nf* sister; (*religieuse*) nun, sister

**soi** [swa] *pron* oneself; **en ~** (*intrinsèquement*) in itself; **cela va de ~** that *ou* it goes without saying; **soi-disant** *adj inv* so-called ♦ *adv* supposedly

**soie** [swa] *nf* silk; **soierie** *nf* (*tissu*) silk

**soif** [swaf] *nf* thirst; **avoir ~** to be thirsty; **donner ~ à qn** to make sb thirsty

**soigné, e** [swaɲe] *adj* (*tenue*) well-groomed, neat; (*travail*) careful, meticulous

**soigner** [swaɲe] *vt* (*malade, maladie: suj: docteur*) to treat; (*suj: infirmière, mère*) to nurse, look after; (*travail, détails*) to take care over; (*jardin, invités*) to look after; **soigneux, -euse** *adj* (*propre*) tidy, neat; (*appliqué*) painstaking, careful

**soi-même** [swamɛm] *pron* oneself

**soin** [swɛ̃] *nm* (*application*) care; (*propreté, ordre*) tidiness, neatness; **~s** *nmpl* (*à un malade, blessé*) treatment *sg*, medical attention *sg*; (*hygiène*) care *sg*; **prendre ~ de** to take care of, look after; **prendre ~ de faire** to take care to do; **les premiers ~s** first aid *sg*

**soir** [swaR] *nm* evening; **ce ~** this evening, tonight; **demain ~** tomorrow evening, tomorrow night; **soirée** *nf* evening; (*réception*) party

**soit** [swa] *vb voir* **être** ♦ *conj* (*à savoir*) namely; (*ou*): **~ ... ~** either ... *ou* ♦ *adv* so be it, very well; **~ que ... ~ que** *ou* **ou que** whether ... *ou* whether

**soixantaine** [swasɑ̃tɛn] *nf*: **une ~ (de)** sixty *ou* so, about sixty; **avoir la ~** (*âge*) to be around sixty

**soixante** [swasɑ̃t] *num* sixty; **soixante-dix** *num* seventy

**soja** [sɔʒa] *nm* soya; (*graines*) soya beans *pl*; **germes de ~** beansprouts

**sol** [sɔl] *nm* ground; (*de logement*) floor; (AGR) soil; (MUS) G; (: *en chantant la gamme*) so(h)

**solaire** [sɔlɛR] *adj* (*énergie etc*) solar; (*crème etc*) sun *cpd*

**soldat** [sɔlda] *nm* soldier

**solde** [sɔld] *nf* pay ♦ *nm* (COMM) balance; **~s** *nm ou f pl* (*articles*) sale goods; (*vente*) sales; **en ~** at sale price; **solder** *vt* (*marchandise*) to sell at sale price, sell off; **se solder par** (*fig*) to end in; **article soldé (à) 10 F** item reduced to 10 F

**sole** [sɔl] *nf* sole *inv* (*fish*)

**soleil** [sɔlɛj] *nm* sun; (*lumière*) sunshine; (*temps ensoleillé*) sun(shine); **il fait du ~** it's sunny; **au ~** in the sun

**solennel, le** [sɔlanɛl] *adj* solemn

**solfège** [sɔlfɛʒ] *nm* musical theory

**solidaire** [sɔlidɛR] *adj*: **être ~s** to show solidarity, stand *ou* stick together; **être ~ de** (*collègues*) to stand by; **solidarité** *nf* solidarity; **par solidarité (avec)** in sympathy with

**solide** [sɔlid] *adj* solid; (*mur, maison, meuble*) solid, sturdy; (*connaissances, argument*) sound; (*personne, estomac*) robust, sturdy ♦ *nm* solid

**soliste** [sɔlist] *nm/f* soloist

**solitaire** [sɔlitɛʀ] *adj* (*sans compagnie*) solitary, lonely; (*lieu*) lonely ♦ *nm/f* (*ermite*) recluse; (*fig: ours*) loner

**solitude** [sɔlityd] *nf* loneliness; (*tranquillité*) solitude

**solive** [sɔliv] *nf* joist

**solliciter** [sɔlisite] *vt* (*personne*) to appeal to; (*emploi, faveur*) to seek

**sollicitude** [sɔlisityd] *nf* concern

**soluble** [sɔlybl] *adj* soluble

**solution** [sɔlysjɔ̃] *nf* solution; ~ **de facilité** easy way out

**solvable** [sɔlvabl] *adj* solvent

**sombre** [sɔ̃bʀ] *adj* dark; (*fig*) gloomy; **sombrer** *vi* (*bateau*) to sink; **sombrer dans** (*misère, désespoir*) to sink into

**sommaire** [sɔmɛʀ] *adj* (*simple*) basic; (*expéditif*) summary ♦ *nm* summary

**sommation** [sɔmasjɔ̃] *nf* (*JUR*) summons *sg*; (*avant de faire feu*) warning

**somme** [sɔm] *nf* (*MATH*) sum; (*quantité*) amount; (*argent*) sum, amount ♦ *nm*: **faire un** ~ to have a (short) nap; **en** ~ all in all; ~ **toute** all in all

**sommeil** [sɔmɛj] *nm* sleep; **avoir** ~ to be sleepy; **sommeiller** *vi* to doze

**sommer** [sɔme] *vt*: ~ **qn de faire** to command *ou* order sb to do

**sommes** [sɔm] *vb voir* **être**

**sommet** [sɔmɛ] *nm* top; (*d'une montagne*) summit, top; (*fig: de la perfection, gloire*) height

**sommier** [sɔmje] *nm* (bed) base

**somnambule** [sɔmnɑ̃byl] *nm/f* sleepwalker

**somnifère** [sɔmnifɛʀ] *nm* sleeping drug *no pl* (*ou* pill)

**somnoler** [sɔmnɔle] *vi* to doze

**somptueux, -euse** [sɔ̃ptɥø, øz] *adj* sumptuous

**son¹, sa** [sɔ̃, sa] (*pl* **ses**) *adj* (*antécédent humain: mâle*) his; (: *femelle*) her; (: *va-*

*leur indéfinie*) one's, his/her; (*antécédent non humain*) its

**son²** [sɔ̃] *nm* sound; (*de blé*) bran

**sondage** [sɔ̃daʒ] *nm*: ~ **(d'opinion)** (opinion) poll

**sonde** [sɔ̃d] *nf* (*NAVIG*) lead *ou* sounding line; (*MÉD*) probe; (*TECH: de forage*) borer, driller

**sonder** [sɔ̃de] *vt* (*NAVIG*) to sound; (*TECH*) to bore, drill; (*fig: personne*) to sound out; ~ **le terrain** (*fig*) to test the ground

**songe** [sɔ̃ʒ] *nm* dream; **songer** *vi*: **songer à** (*penser à*) to think over; (*envisager*) to consider, think of; **songer que** to think that; **songeur, -euse** *adj* pensive

**sonnant, e** [sɔnɑ̃, ɑ̃t] *adj*: **à 8 heures** ~**es** on the stroke of 8

**sonné, e** [sɔne] *adj* (*fam*) cracked; **il est midi** ~ it's gone twelve

**sonner** [sɔne] *vi* to ring ♦ *vt* (*cloche*) to ring; (*glas, tocsin*) to sound; (*portier, infirmière*) to ring for; ~ **faux** (*instrument*) to sound out of tune; (*rire*) to ring false

**sonnerie** [sɔnʀi] *nf* (*son*) ringing; (*sonnette*) bell; ~ **d'alarme** alarm bell

**sonnette** [sɔnɛt] *nf* bell; ~ **d'alarme** alarm bell

**sono** [sɔno] *abr f* = **sonorisation**

**sonore** [sɔnɔʀ] *adj* (*voix*) sonorous, ringing; (*salle*) resonant; (*film, signal*) sound *cpd*; **sonorisation** *nf* (*équipement: de salle de conférences*) public address system, P.A. system; (: *de discothèque*) sound system; **sonorité** *nf* (*de piano, violon*) tone; (*d'une salle*) acoustics *pl*

**sont** [sɔ̃] *vb voir* **être**

**sophistiqué, e** [sɔfistike] *adj* sophisticated

**sorbet** [sɔʀbɛ] *nm* water ice, sorbet

**sorcellerie** [sɔʀsɛlʀi] *nf* witchcraft *no pl*

**sorcier** [sɔʀsje] *nm* sorcerer; **sorcière** *nf* witch *ou* sorceress

**sordide** [sɔʀdid] *adj* (*lieu*) squalid; (*action*) sordid

**sornettes** [sɔʀnɛt] *nfpl* twaddle *sg*

**sort** [sɔʀ] *nm* (*destinée*) fate; (*condition*) lot; (*magique*) curse, spell; **tirer au ~** to draw lots

**sorte** [sɔʀt] *nf* sort, kind; **de la ~** in that way; **de (telle) ~ que** so that; **en quelque ~** in a way; **faire en ~ que** to see to it that

**sortie** [sɔʀti] *nf* (*issue*) way out, exit; (*remarque drôle*) sally; (*promenade*) outing; (*le soir: au restaurant etc*) night out; (COMM: *d'un disque*) release; (: *d'un livre*) publication; (: *d'un modèle*) launching; **~s** *nfpl* (COMM: *somme*) items of expenditure, outgoings; **~ de bain** (*vêtement*) bathrobe; **~ de secours** emergency exit

**sortilège** [sɔʀtilɛʒ] *nm* (magic) spell

**sortir** [sɔʀtiʀ] *vi* (*gén*) to come out; (*partir, se promener, aller au spectacle*) to go out; (*numéro gagnant*) to come up ♦ *vt* (*gén*) to take out; (*produit, modèle*) to bring out; (*fam: dire*) to come out with; **~ avec qn** to be going out with sb; **s'en ~** (*malade*) to pull through; (*d'une difficulté etc*) to get through; **~ de** (*endroit*) to go ou come) out of, leave; (*provenir de*) to come from; (*compétence*) to be outside

**sosie** [sɔzi] *nm* double

**sot, sotte** [so, sɔt] *adj* silly, foolish ♦ *nm/f* fool; **sottise** *nf* (*caractère*) silliness, foolishness; (*action*) silly *ou* foolish thing

**sou** [su] *nm*: **près de ses ~s** tight-fisted; **sans le ~** penniless

**soubresaut** [subʀəso] *nm* start; (*cahot*) jolt

**souche** [suʃ] *nf* (*d'arbre*) stump; (*de carnet*) counterfoil (BRIT), stub

**souci** [susi] *nm* (*inquiétude*) worry; (*préoccupation*) concern; (BOT) marigold; **se faire du ~** to worry; **soucier**: **se soucier de** *vt* to care about; **soucieux, -euse** *adj* concerned, worried

**soucoupe** [sukup] *nf* saucer; **~ volante** flying saucer

**soudain, e** [sudɛ̃, ɛn] *adj* (*douleur,*

*mort*) sudden ♦ *adv* suddenly, all of a sudden

**soude** [sud] *nf* soda

**souder** [sude] *vt* (*avec fil à ~*) to solder; (*par soudure autogène*) to weld; (*fig*) to bind together

**soudoyer** [sudwaje] (*péj*) *vt* to bribe

**soudure** [sudyʀ] *nf* soldering; welding; (*joint*) soldered joint; weld

**souffle** [sufl] *nm* (*en expirant*) breath; (*en soufflant*) puff, blow; (*respiration*) breathing; (*d'explosion, de ventilateur*) blast; (*du vent*) blowing; **être à bout de ~** to be out of breath; **un ~ d'air** a breath of air

**soufflé, e** [sufle] *adj* (*fam: stupéfié*) staggered ♦ *nm* (CULIN) soufflé

**souffler** [sufle] *vi* (*gén*) to blow; (*haleter*) to puff (and blow) ♦ *vt* (*feu, bougie*) to blow out; (*chasser: poussière etc*) to blow away; (TECH: *verre*) to blow; (*dire*): **~ qch à qn** to whisper sth to sb; **soufflet** *nm* (*instrument*) bellows *pl*; (*gifle*) slap (in the face); **souffleur** *nm* (THÉÂTRE) prompter

**souffrance** [sufʀɑ̃s] *nf* suffering; **en ~** (*affaire*) pending

**souffrant, e** [sufʀɑ̃, ɑ̃t] *adj* unwell

**souffre-douleur** [sufʀədulœʀ] *nm inv* butt, underdog

**souffrir** [sufʀiʀ] *vi* to suffer, be in pain ♦ *vt* to suffer, endure; (*supporter*) to bear, stand; **~ de** (*maladie, froid*) to suffer from; **elle ne peut pas le ~** she can't stand ou bear him

**soufre** [sufʀ] *nm* sulphur

**souhait** [swɛ] *nm* wish; **tous nos ~ de** good wishes *ou* our best wishes for; **à vos ~s!** bless you!; **souhaitable** *adj* desirable

**souhaiter** [swete] *vt* to wish for; **~ la bonne année à qn** to wish sb a happy New Year; **~ que** to hope that

**souiller** [suje] *vt* to dirty, soil; (*fig: réputation etc*) to sully, tarnish

**soûl, e** [su, sul] *adj* drunk ♦ *nm*: **tout**

**son ~** to one's heart's content

**soulagement** [sulaʒmɑ̃] *nm* relief

**soulager** [sulaʒe] *vt* to relieve

**soûler** [sule] *vt*: **~ qn** to get sb drunk; (*suj: boisson*) to make sb drunk; (*fig*) to make sb's head spin *ou* reel; **se ~** *vi* to get drunk

**soulever** [sul(ə)ve] *vt* to lift; (*poussière*) to send up; (*enthousiasme*) to arouse; (*question, débat*) to raise; **se ~** *vi* (*peuple*) to rise up; (*personne couchée*) to lift o.s. up

**soulier** [sulje] *nm* shoe

**souligner** [suliɲe] *vt* to underline; (*fig*) to emphasize, stress

**soumettre** [sumɛtr] *vt* (*pays*) to subject, subjugate; (*rebelle*) to put down, subdue; **se ~ (à)** to submit (to); **~ qch à qn** (*projet etc*) to submit sth to sb

**soumis, e** [sumi, iz] *adj* submissive; **soumission** *nf* submission

**soupape** [supap] *nf* valve

**soupçon** [supsɔ̃] *nm* suspicion; (*petite quantité*): **un ~ de** a hint *ou* touch of; **soupçonner** *vt* to suspect; **soupçonneux, -euse** *adj* suspicious

**soupe** [sup] *nf* soup

**souper** [supe] *vi* to have supper ♦ *nm* supper

**soupeser** [supaze] *vt* to weigh in one's hand(s); (*fig*) to weigh up

**soupière** [supjɛr] *nf* (soup) tureen

**soupir** [supir] *nm* sigh; **pousser un ~ de soulagement** to heave a sigh of relief

**soupirail, -aux** [supiraj, o] *nm* (small) basement window

**soupirer** [supire] *vi* to sigh

**souple** [supl] *adj* supple; (*fig: règlement, caractère*) flexible; (: *démarche, taille*) lithe, supple; **souplesse** *nf* suppleness; (*de caractère*) flexibility

**source** [surs] *nf* (*point d'eau*) spring; (*d'un cours d'eau*) source; **de bonne ~** on good authority

**sourcil** [sursi] *nm* (eye)brow; **sourciller** *vi*: **sans sourciller** without turning

a hair *ou* batting an eyelid

**sourd, e** [sur, surd] *adj* deaf; (*bruit*) muffled; (*douleur*) dull ♦ *nm/f* deaf person; **faire la ~e oreille** to turn a deaf ear; **sourdine** *nf* (MUS) mute; **en sourdine** softly, quietly; **sourd-muet, sourde-muette** *adj* deaf-and-dumb ♦ *nm/f* deaf-mute

**souriant, e** [surjɑ̃, ɑ̃t] *adj* cheerful

**souricière** [surisjɛr] *nf* mousetrap; (*fig*) trap

**sourire** [surir] *nm* smile ♦ *vi* to smile; **~ à qn** to smile at sb; (*fig: plaire à*) to appeal to sb; (*suj: chance*) to smile on sb; **garder le ~** to keep smiling

**souris** [suri] *nf* mouse

**sournois, e** [surnwa, waz] *adj* deceitful, underhand

**sous** [su] *prép* under; **~ la pluie** in the rain; **~ terre** underground; **~ peu** shortly, before long; **sous-bois** *nm inv* undergrowth

**souscrire** [suskrir]: **~ à** *vt* to subscribe to

**sous...**: **sous-directeur, -trice** *nm/f* assistant manager(-manageress); **sous-entendre** *vt* to imply, infer; **sous-entendu, e** *adj* implied ♦ *nm* innuendo, insinuation; **sous-estimer** *vt* to underestimate; **sous-jacent, e** *adj* underlying; **sous-louer** *vt* to sublet; **sous-marin, e** *adj* (*flore, faune*) submarine; (*pêche*) underwater ♦ *nm* submarine; **sous-officier** *nm* ≃ non-commissioned officer (N.C.O.); **sous-produit** *nm* by-product; **sous-pull** *nm* thin poloneck jersey; **soussigné, e** *adj*: **je soussigné** I the undersigned; **sous-sol** *nm* basement; **sous-titre** *nm* subtitle

**soustraction** [sustraksjɔ̃] *nf* subtraction

**soustraire** [sustrɛr] *vt* to subtract, take away; (*dérober*): **~ qch à qn** to remove sth from sb; **se ~ à** (*autorité etc*) to elude, escape from

**sous...**: **sous-traitant** *nm* subcontractor; **sous-traiter** vt to sub-contract; **sous-vêtements** nmpl underwear sg

**soutane** [sutan] nf cassock, soutane

**soute** [sut] nf hold

**soutenir** [sut(ə)niR] vt to support; (assaut, choc) to stand up to, withstand; (intérêt, effort) to keep up; (assurer): ~ **que** to maintain that; **soutenu, e** (efforts) sustained, unflagging; (style) elevated

**souterrain, e** [suteRɛ̃, ɛn] adj underground ♦ nm underground passage

**soutien** [sutjɛ̃] nm support; **soutien-gorge** nm bra

**soutirer** [sutiʀe] vt: ~ **qch à qn** to squeeze ou get sth out of sb

**souvenir** [suv(ə)niR] nm memory; (objet) souvenir ♦ vb: **se ~ de** to remember; **se ~ que** to remember that; **en ~ de** in memory ou remembrance of

**souvent** [suvã] adv often; **peu ~** seldom, infrequently

**souverain, e** [suv(ə)Rɛ̃, ɛn] nm/f sovereign, monarch

**soyeux, -euse** [swajø, øz] adj silky

**soyons** etc [swajɔ̃] vb voir **être**

**spacieux, -euse** [spasjø, jøz] adj spacious, roomy

**spaghettis** [spageti] nmpl spaghetti sg

**sparadrap** [spaRadRa] nm sticking plaster (BRIT), Bandaid ® (US)

**spatial, e, -aux** [spasjal, jo] adj (AVIAT) space cpd

**speaker, ine** [spikœʀ, kRin] nm/f announcer

**spécial, e, -aux** [spesjal, jo] adj special; (bizarre) peculiar; **spécialement** adv especially, particularly; (tout exprès) specially; **spécialiser: se spécialiser** vi to specialize; **spécialiste** nm/f specialist; **spécialité** nf speciality; (branche) special field

**spécifier** [spesifje] vt to specify, state

**spécimen** [spesimɛn] nm specimen

**spectacle** [spɛktakl] nm (scène) sight; (représentation) show; (industrie) show business; **spectaculaire** adj spectacular

**spectateur, -trice** [spɛktatœR, tRis] nm/f (CINÉMA etc) member of the audience; (SPORT) spectator; (d'un événement) onlooker, witness

**spéculer** [spekyle] vi to speculate

**spéléologie** [speleɔlɔʒi] nf potholing

**sperme** [spɛRm] nm semen, sperm

**sphère** [sfɛR] nf sphere

**spirale** [spiʀal] nf spiral

**spirituel, le** [spiʀitɥɛl] adj spiritual; (fin, piquant) witty

**splendide** [splãdid] adj splendid

**sponsoring** [spɔ̃sɔRiŋ] nm sponsorship

**sponsoriser** [spɔ̃sɔRize] vt to sponsor

**spontané, e** [spɔ̃tane] adj spontaneous; **spontanéité** nf spontaneity

**sport** [spɔR] nm sport ♦ adj inv (vêtement) casual; **faire du ~** to do sport; **~s d'hiver** winter sports; **sportif, -ive** adj (journal, association, épreuve) sports cpd; (allure, démarche) athletic; (attitude, esprit) sporting

**spot** [spɔt] nm (lampe) spot(light); ~ (publicitaire) commercial (break)

**square** [skwaR] nm public garden(s)

**squelette** [skəlɛt] nm skeleton; **squelettique** adj scrawny

**stabiliser** [stabilize] vt to stabilize

**stable** [stabl] adj stable, steady

**stade** [stad] nm (SPORT) stadium; (phase, niveau) stage; **stadier** nm steward (working in a stadium)

**stage** [staʒ] nm (cours) training course; ~ **de formation (professionnelle)** vocational (training) course; ~ **de perfectionnement** advanced training course; **stagiaire** nm/f, adj trainee

**stagner** [stagne] vi to stagnate

**stalle** [stal] nf stall, box

**stand** [stãd] nm (d'exposition) stand; (de foire) stall; ~ **de tir** (à la foire, SPORT) shooting range

**standard** [stãdaR] adj inv standard ♦ nm switchboard; **standardiste** nm/f switchboard operator

**standing** [stãdiŋ] nm standing; **de grand ~** luxury

**starter** [stαʀtɛʀ] nm (AUTO) choke

**station** [stasjɔ̃] nf station; (de bus) stop; (de villégiature) resort; **~ balnéaire** seaside resort; **~ de ski** ski resort; **~ de taxis** taxi rank (BRIT) ou stand (US); **stationnement** nm parking; **stationner** vi to park; **station-service** nf service station

**statistique** [statistik] nf (science) statistics sg; (rapport, étude) statistic ♦ adj statistical

**statue** [staty] nf statue

**statu quo** [statykwo] nm status quo

**statut** [staty] nm status; **~s** nmpl (JUR, ADMIN) statutes; **statutaire** adj statutory

**Sté** abr = **société**

**steak** [stɛk] nm steak; **~ haché** hamburger

**sténo(dactylo)** [steno(daktilo)] nf shorthand typist (BRIT), stenographer (US)

**sténo(graphie)** [steno(gʀafi)] nf shorthand

**stéréo** [steʀeo] adj stereo

**stérile** [steʀil] adj sterile

**stérilet** [steʀilɛ] nm coil, loop

**stériliser** [steʀilize] vt to sterilize

**stigmates** [stigmat] nmpl scars, marks

**stimulant** [stimylã] nm (fig) stimulus, incentive; (physique) stimulant

**stimuler** [stimyle] vt to stimulate

**stipuler** [stipyle] vt to stipulate

**stock** [stɔk] nm stock; **stocker** vt to stock

**stop** [stɔp] nm (AUTO: écriteau) stop sign; (: feu arrière) brake-light; **faire du ~** (fam) to hitch(hike); **stopper** vt, vi to stop, halt

**store** [stɔʀ] nm blind; (de magasin) shade, awning

**strabisme** [stʀabism] nm squinting

**strapontin** [stʀapɔ̃tɛ̃] nm jump ou foldaway seat

**stratégie** [stʀateʒi] nf strategy; **straté-**

**gique** adj strategic

**stress** [stʀɛs] nm stress; **stressant, e** adj stressful; **stresser** vt: **stresser qn** to make sb (feel) tense

**strict, e** [stʀikt] adj strict; (tenue, décor) severe, plain; **le ~ nécessaire/minimum** the bare essentials/minimum

**strident, e** [stʀidã, ãt] adj shrill, strident

**strophe** [stʀɔf] nf verse, stanza

**structure** [stʀyktyʀ] nf structure

**studieux, -euse** [stydjø, jøz] adj studious

**studio** [stydjo] nm (logement) (one-roomed) flatlet (BRIT) ou apartment (US); (d'artiste, TV etc) studio

**stupéfait, e** [stypefɛ, ɛt] adj astonished

**stupéfiant, e** [stypefjã, jãt] adj (étonnant) stunning, astounding ♦ nm (MÉD) drug, narcotic

**stupéfier** [stypefje] vt (étonner) to stun, astonish

**stupeur** [stypœʀ] nf astonishment

**stupide** [stypid] adj stupid; **stupidité** nf stupidity; (parole, acte) stupid thing (to do ou say)

**style** [stil] nm style

**stylé, e** [stile] adj well-trained

**styliste** [stilist] nm/f designer

**stylo** [stilo] nm: **~ (à encre)** (fountain) pen; **~ (à) bille** ball-point pen; **~-feutre** felt-tip pen

**su, e** [sy] pp de **savoir** ♦ nm: **au ~ de** with the knowledge of

**suave** [sɥav] adj sweet

**subalterne** [sybaltɛʀn] adj (employé, officier) junior; (rôle) subordinate, subsidiary ♦ nm/f subordinate

**subconscient** [sypkɔ̃sjã] nm subconscious

**subconscient** [sypkɔ̃sjã] nm subconscious

**subir** [sybiʀ] vt (affront, dégâts) to suffer; (opération, châtiment) to undergo

**subit, e** [sybi, it] adj sudden; **subitement** adv suddenly, all of a sudden

**subjectif, -ive** [sybʒɛktif, iv] adj subjective

**subjonctif** [sybʒɔ̃ktif] *nm* subjunctive

**subjuguer** [sybʒyge] *vt* to captivate

**submerger** [sybmɛʀʒe] *vt* to submerge; *(fig)* to overwhelm

**subordonné, e** [sybɔʀdɔne] *adj, nm/f* subordinate

**subrepticement** [sybʀɛptismɑ̃] *adv* surreptitiously

**subside** [sybzid] *nm* grant

**subsidiaire** [sybzidjɛʀ] *adj*: **question ~** deciding question

**subsister** [sybziste] *vi (rester)* to remain, subsist; *(survivre)* to live on

**substance** [sypstɑ̃s] *nf* substance

**substituer** [sypstitɥe] *vt*: **~ qn/qch à** to substitute sb/sth for; **se ~ à qn** *(évincer)* to substitute o.s. for sb

**substitut** [sypstity] *nm (succédané)* substitute

**subterfuge** [sypteʀfyʒ] *nm* subterfuge

**subtil, e** [syptil] *adj* subtle

**subtiliser** [syptilize] *vt*: **~ qch (à qn)** to spirit sth away (from sb)

**subvenir** [sybvəniʀ]: **~ à** *vt* to meet

**subvention** [sybvɑ̃sjɔ̃] *nf* subsidy, grant; **subventionner** *vt* to subsidize

**suc** [syk] *nm (BOT)* sap; *(de viande, fruit)* juice

**succédané** [syksedane] *nm* substitute

**succéder** [syksede]: **~ à** *vt* to succeed; **se ~ à** *vi (accidents, années)* to follow one another

**succès** [syksɛ] *nm* success; **avoir du ~** to be a success, be successful; **à ~** *adj* successful; **~ de librairie** bestseller; **~ (féminins)** conquests

**successif, -ive** [syksesif, iv] *adj* successive

**successeur** [syksesœʀ] *nm* successor

**succession** [syksesjɔ̃] *nf (série, POL)* succession; *(JUR: patrimoine)* estate, inheritance

**succomber** [sykɔ̃be] *vi* to die, succumb; *(fig)*: **~ à** to succumb to

**succulent, e** [sykylɑ̃, ɑ̃t] *adj (repas, mets)* delicious

**succursale** [sykyʀsal] *nf* branch

**sucer** [syse] *vt* to suck; **sucette** *nf (bonbon)* lollipop; *(de bébé)* dummy *(BRIT)*, pacifier *(US)*

**sucre** [sykʀ] *nm (substance)* sugar; *(morceau)* lump of sugar, sugar lump *ou* cube; **~ d'orge** barley sugar; **~ en morceaux/en poudre** lump/caster sugar; **~ glace/roux** icing/brown sugar; **sucré, e** *adj (produit alimentaire)* sweetened; *(au goût)* sweet; **sucrer** *vt (thé, café)* to sweeten, put sugar in; **sucreries** *nfpl (bonbons)* sweets, sweet things; **sucrier** *nm (récipient)* sugar bowl

**sud** [syd] *nm*: **le ~** the south ♦ *adj inv* south; *(côte)* south, southern; **au ~** *(situation)* in the south; *(direction)* to the south; **au ~ de** *(to the)* south of; **sud-africain, e** *adj* South African ♦ *nm/f*: **Sud-Africain, e** South African; **sud-américain, e** *adj* South American ♦ *nm/f*: **Sud-Américain, e** South American; **sud-est** *nm inv* south-east; **sud-ouest** *nm, adj inv* south-west

**Suède** [sɥɛd] *nf*: **la ~** Sweden; **suédois, e** *adj* Swedish ♦ *nm/f*: **Suédois, e** Swede ♦ *nm (LING)* Swedish

**suer** [sɥe] *vi* to sweat; *(suinter)* to ooze; **sueur** *nf* sweat; **en sueur** sweating, in a sweat; **donner des sueurs froids à qn** to put sb in(to) a cold sweat

**suffire** [syfiʀ] *vi (être assez)*: **~ (à qn/ pour qch/pour faire)** to be enough *ou* sufficient (for sb/for sth/to do); **il suffit d'une négligence ...** it only takes one act of carelessness ...; **il suffit qu'on oublie pour que ...** one only needs to forget for ...; **ça suffit!** that's enough!

**suffisamment** [syfizamɑ̃] *adv* sufficiently, enough; **~ de** sufficient, enough

**suffisant, e** [syfizɑ̃, ɑ̃t] *adj* sufficient; *(résultats)* satisfactory; *(vaniteux)* self-important, bumptious

**suffixe** [syfiks] *nm* suffix

**suffoquer** [syfɔke] *vt* to choke, suffocate; *(stupéfier)* to stagger, astound ♦ *vi* to choke, suffocate

**suffrage** [syfʀaʒ] *nm* (POL: *voix*) vote

**suggérer** [sygʒeʀe] *vt* to suggest; **suggestion** *nf* suggestion

**suicide** [sɥisid] *nm* suicide; **suicider: se suicider** *vi* to commit suicide

**suie** [sɥi] *nf* soot

**suinter** [sɥɛ̃te] *vi* to ooze

**suis** [sɥi] *vb voir* être; suivre

**suisse** [sɥis] *adj* Swiss ♦ *nm:* **S~** Swiss *pl inv* ♦ *nf:* **la** S~ Switzerland; **la** S~ **romande/allemande** French-speaking/German-speaking Switzerland; **Suissesse** *nf* Swiss (woman *ou* girl)

**suite** [sɥit] *nf* (*continuation:* d'énumération etc) rest, remainder; (: de feuilleton) continuation; (: film etc sur le même thème) sequel; (série) series, succession; (conséquence) result; (ordre, liaison logique) coherence; (appartement , MUS) suite; (escorte) retinue, suite; *nfpl* (d'une maladie etc) effects; **prendre la ~ de** (directeur etc) to succeed, take over from; **donner ~ à** (requête, projet) to follow up; **faire ~ à** to follow; **(faisant) ~ à votre lettre du ...** further to your letter of the ...; **de ~** (d'affilée) in succession; (immédiatement) at once; **par la ~** afterwards, subsequently; **à la ~** one after the other; **à la ~ de** (derrière) behind; (en conséquence de) following

**suivant, e** [sɥivɑ̃, ɑ̃t] *adj* next, following ♦ *prép* (selon) according to; **au ~!** next!

**suivi, e** [sɥivi] *adj* (effort, qualité) consistent; (cohérent) coherent; **très/peu ~** (cours) well-/poorly-attended

**suivre** [sɥivʀ] *vt* (gén) to follow; (SCOL: cours) to attend; (comprendre) to keep up with; (COMM: article) to continue to stock ♦ *vi* to follow; (élève: assimiler) to keep up; **se ~** *vi* (accidents etc) to follow one after the other; **faire ~** (lettre) to forward; **"à ~"** "to be continued"

**sujet, te** [syʒɛ, ɛt] *adj:* **être ~ à** (vertige etc) to be liable *ou* subject to ♦

*nm/f* (d'un souverain) subject ♦ *nm* subject; **au ~ de** about; **~ de conversation** topic *ou* subject of conversation; **~ d'examen** (SCOL) examination question

**summum** [sɔ(m)mɔm] *nm:* **le ~ de** the height of

**super** [sypɛʀ] (fam) *adj inv* terrific, great, fantastic, super

**superbe** [sypɛʀb] *adj* magnificent, superb

**super(carburant)** [sypɛʀ(kaʀbyʀɑ̃)] *nm* ≈ 4-star petrol (BRIT), ≈ high-octane gasoline (US)

**supercherie** [sypɛʀʃəʀi] *nf* trick

**supérette** [sypeʀɛt] *nf* (COMM) minimarket, superette (US)

**superficie** [sypɛʀfisi] *nf* (surface) area

**superficiel, le** [sypɛʀfisjɛl] *adj* superficial

**superflu, e** [sypɛʀfly] *adj* superfluous

**supérieur, e** [sypeʀjœʀ] *adj* (lèvre, étages, classes) upper; (plus élevé: température, niveau, enseignement): **~ (à)** higher (than); (meilleur: qualité, produit): **~ (à)** superior (to); (excellent, hautain) superior ♦ *nm, nf* superior; **supériorité** *nf* superiority

**superlatif** [sypɛʀlatif] *nm* superlative

**supermarché** [sypɛʀmaʀʃe] *nm* supermarket

**superposer** [sypɛʀpoze] *vt* (faire chevaucher) to superimpose; **lits superposés** bunk beds

**superproduction** [sypɛʀpʀɔdyksjɔ̃] *nf* (film) spectacular

**superpuissance** [sypɛʀpɥisɑ̃s] *nf* super-power

**superstitieux, -euse** [sypɛʀstisjø, jøz] *adj* superstitious

**superviser** [sypɛʀvize] *vt* to supervise

**supplanter** [syplɑ̃te] *vt* to supplant

**suppléance** [sypleɑ̃s] *nf:* **faire des ~s** (professeur) to do supply teaching; **suppléant, e** *adj* (professeur) supply *cpd*; (juge, fonctionnaire) deputy *cpd* ♦ *nm/f* (professeur) supply teacher

**suppléer** [syplee] vt (ajouter: mot manquant etc) to supply, provide; (compenser: lacune) to fill in; ~ **à** to make up for

**supplément** [syplemɑ̃] nm supplement; (de frites etc) extra portion; **un ~ de travail** extra ou additional work; **payer un ~** to pay an additional charge; **le vin est en ~** wine is extra; **supplémentaire** adj additional, further; (train, bus) relief cpd, extra

**supplications** [syplikasjɔ̃] nfpl pleas, entreaties

**supplice** [syplis] nm torture no pl

**supplier** [syplije] vt to implore, beseech

**support** [sypɔr] nm support; (publicitaire) medium; (audio-visuel) aid

**supportable** [sypɔrtabl] adj (douleur) bearable

**supporter**[1] [sypɔrtɛr] nm supporter, fan

**supporter**[2] [sypɔrte] vt (conséquences, épreuve) to bear, endure; (défauts, personne) to put up with; (suj: chose: chaleur etc) to withstand; (: personne: chaleur, vin) to be able to take

**supposer** [sypoze] vt to suppose; (impliquer) to presuppose; **à ~ que** supposing (that)

**suppositoire** [sypozitwar] nm suppository

**suppression** [sypresjɔ̃] nf (voir supprimer) cancellation; removal; deletion

**supprimer** [syprime] vt (congés, service d'autobus etc) to cancel; (emplois, privilèges, témoin gênant) to do away with; (cloison, cause, anxiété) to remove; (clause, mot) to delete

**suprême** [syprɛm] adj supreme

_MOT-CLÉ_

**sur** [syr] prép **1** (position) on; (par-dessus) over; (au-dessus) above; **pose-le sur la table** put it on the table; **je n'ai pas d'argent sur moi** I haven't any money on me

**2** (direction) towards; **en allant sur Paris** going towards Paris; **sur votre droite** to ou towards your right

**3** (à propos de) on, about; **un livre/une conférence sur Balzac** a book/lecture on ou about Balzac

**4** (proportion, mesures) out of, by; **un sur 10** one in 10; (SCOL) one out of 10; **4 m sur 2** 4 m by 2

**sur ce** adv hereupon

**sûr, e** [syr] adj sure, certain; (digne de confiance) reliable; (sans danger) safe; (diagnostic, goût) reliable; **le plus ~ est de** the safest thing is to; ~ **de soi** self-confident; ~ **et certain** absolutely certain

**surcharge** [syrʃarʒ] nf (de passagers, marchandises) excess load; **surcharger** vt to overload

**surchoix** [syrʃwa] adj inv top-quality

**surclasser** [syrklase] vt to outclass

**surcroît** [syrkrwa] nm: **un ~ de** additional +nom; **par ou de ~** moreover; **en ~** in addition

**surdité** [syrdite] nf deafness

**surélever** [syrel(ə)ve] vt to raise, heighten

**sûrement** [syrmɑ̃] adv (certainement) certainly; (sans risques) safely

**surenchère** [syrɑ̃ʃɛr] nf (aux enchères) higher bid; **surenchérir** vi to bid higher; (fig) to try and outbid each other

**surent** [syr] vb voir **savoir**

**surestimer** [syrɛstime] vt to overestimate

**sûreté** [syrte] nf (sécurité) safety; (exactitude: de renseignements etc) reliability; (d'un geste) steadiness; **mettre en ~** to put in a safe place; **pour plus de ~** as an extra precaution, to be on the safe side

**surf** [sœrf] nm surfing

**surface** [syrfas] nf surface; (superficie) surface area; **une grande ~** supermarket; **faire ~** to surface; **en ~** near the surface; (fig) superficially

**surfait, e** [syrfɛ, ɛt] *adj* overrated

**surfer** [syrfe] *vi*: **~ sur Internet** to surf *ou* browse the Internet

**surgelé, e** [syrʒəle] *adj* (deep-)frozen ♦ *nm*: **les ~s** (deep-)frozen food

**surgir** [syrʒir] *vi* to appear suddenly; *(fig: problème, conflit)* to arise

**sur...: surhumain, e** *adj* superhuman; **sur-le-champ** *adv* immediately; **surlendemain** *nm*: **le surlendemain (soir)** two days later (in the evening); **le surlendemain de** two days after; **surmenage** *nm* overwork(ing); **surmener: se surmener** *vi* to overwork

**surmonter** [syrmɔ̃te] *vt (vaincre)* to overcome; *(être au-dessus de)* to top

**surnaturel, le** [syrnatyrɛl] *adj, nm* supernatural

**surnom** [syrnɔ̃] *nm* nickname

**surnombre** [syrnɔ̃br] *nm*: **être en ~** to be too many *(ou* one too many)

**surpeuplé, e** [syrpœple] *adj* overpopulated

**sur-place** [syrplas] *nm*: **faire du ~~** to mark time

**surplomber** [syrplɔ̃be] *vt, vi* to overhang

**surplus** [syrply] *nm (COMM)* surplus; *(reste)*: **~ de bois** wood left over

**surprenant, e** [syrprənɑ̃, ɑ̃t] *adj* amazing

**surprendre** [syrprɑ̃dr] *vt (étonner)* to surprise; *(tomber sur: intrus etc)* to catch; *(entendre)* to overhear

**surpris, e** [syrpri, iz] *adj*: **~ (de/que)** surprised (at/that); **surprise** *nf* surprise; **faire une surprise à qn** to give sb a surprise; **surprise-partie** *nf* party

**surréservation** [syrrezervasjɔ̃] *nf* double booking, overbooking

**sursaut** [syrso] *nm* start, jump; **~ de** *(énergie, indignation)* sudden fit *ou* burst of; **en ~** with a start; **sursauter** *vi* to (give a) start, jump

**sursis** [syrsi] *nm (JUR: gén)* suspended sentence; *(fig)* reprieve

**surtaxe** [syrtaks] *nf* surcharge

**surtout** [syrtu] *adv (avant tout, d'abord)* above all; *(spécialement, particulièrement)* especially; **~, ne dites rien!** whatever you do don't say anything!; **~ pas!** certainly *ou* definitely not!; **~ que** ... especially as ...

**surveillance** [syrvɛjɑ̃s] *nf* watch; *(POLICE, MIL)* surveillance; **sous ~ médicale** under medical supervision

**surveillant, e** [syrvɛjɑ̃, ɑ̃t] *nm/f (de prison)* warder; *(SCOL)* monitor

**surveiller** [syrveje] *vt (enfant, bagages)* to watch, keep an eye on; *(prisonnier, suspect)* to keep a watch on; *(territoire, bâtiment)* to keep watch over; *(travaux)* to supervise; *(SCOL: examen)* to invigilate; **~ son langage/sa ligne** to watch one's language/figure

**survenir** [syrvənir] *vi (incident, retards)* to occur, arise; *(événement)* to take place

**survêt(ement)** [syrvɛt(mɑ̃)] *nm* tracksuit

**survie** [syrvi] *nf* survival; **survivant, e** *nm/f* survivor; **survivre** *vi* to survive; **survivre à** *(accident etc)* to survive

**survoler** [syrvɔle] *vt* to fly over; *(fig: livre)* to skim through

**survolté, e** [syrvɔlte] *adj (fig)* worked up

**sus** [sy(s)]: **en ~ de** *prép* in addition to, over and above; **en ~** in addition

**susceptible** [sysɛptibl] *adj* touchy, sensitive; **~ de faire** liable to do

**susciter** [sysite] *vt (admiration)* to arouse; *(ennuis)*: **~ (à qn)** to create (for sb)

**suspect, e** [syspɛ, ɛkt] *adj* suspicious; *(témoignage, opinions)* suspect ♦ *nm/f* suspect; **suspecter** *vt* to suspect; *(honnêteté de qn)* to question, have one's suspicions about

**suspendre** [syspɑ̃dr] *vt (accrocher: vêtement)*: **~ qch (à)** to hang sth up (on); *(interrompre, démettre)* to suspend; **se ~ à** to hang from

**suspendu, e** [syspɑ̃dy] *adj (accroché:*

~ **à** hanging on (ou from); (perché) ~ **au-dessus de** suspended over

**suspens** [syspɑ̃]: **en** ~ adv (affaire) in abeyance; **tenir en** ~ to keep in suspense

**suspense** [syspɛns, syspãs] nm suspense

**suspension** [syspɑ̃sjɔ̃] nf suspension; (lustre) light fitting ou fitment

**sut** [sy] vb voir **savoir**

**suture** [sytyʀ] nf (MÉD): **point de** ~ stitch

**svelte** [svɛlt] adj slender, svelte

**SVP** abr (= s'il vous plaît) please

**sweat-shirt** [switʃœʀt] (pl ~-~s) nm sweatshirt

**syllabe** [si(l)lab] nf syllable

**symbole** [sɛ̃bɔl] nm symbol; **symbolique** adj symbolic(al); (geste, offrande) token cpd; **symboliser** vt to symbolize

**symétrique** [simetʀik] adj symmetrical

**sympa** [sɛ̃pa] (fam) adj inv nice; **sois ~, prête-le moi** be a pal and lend it to me

**sympathie** [sɛ̃pati] nf (inclination) liking; (affinité) friendship; (condoléances) sympathy; **j'ai beaucoup de ~ pour lui** I like him a lot; **sympathique** adj nice, friendly

**sympathisant, e** [sɛ̃patizɑ̃, ɑ̃t] nm/f sympathizer

**sympathiser** [sɛ̃patize] vi (voisins etc: s'entendre) to get on (BRIT) ou along (US) (well)

**symphonie** [sɛ̃fɔni] nf symphony

**symptôme** [sɛ̃ptom] nm symptom

**synagogue** [sinagɔg] nf synagogue

**syncope** [sɛ̃kɔp] nf (MÉD) blackout; **tomber en ~** to faint, pass out

**syndic** [sɛ̃dik] nm (d'immeuble) managing agent

**syndical, e, -aux** [sɛ̃dikal, o] adj (trade) union cpd; **syndicaliste** nm/f trade unionist

**syndicat** [sɛ̃dika] nm (d'ouvriers, employés) (trade) union; ~ **d'initiative** tourist office; **syndiqué, e** adj belong-

ing to a (trade) union; **syndiquer: se syndiquer** vi to form a trade union; (adhérer) to join a trade union

**synonyme** [sinɔnim] adj synonymous ♦ nm synonym; ~ **de** synonymous with

**syntaxe** [sɛ̃taks] nf syntax

**synthèse** [sɛ̃tɛz] nf synthesis

**synthétique** [sɛ̃tetik] adj synthetic

**Syrie** [siʀi] nf: **la ~** Syria

**systématique** [sistematik] adj systematic

**système** [sistɛm] nm system; ~ **D** (fam) resourcefulness

# T, t

**t'** [t] pron voir **te**

**ta** [ta] adj voir **ton**[1]

**tabac** [taba] nm (magasin) tobacconist's (shop); ~ **blond/brun** light/dark tobacco

**tabagisme** [tabaʒism] nm: ~ **passif** passive smoking

**tabasser** [tabase] (fam) vt to beat up

**table** [tabl] nf table; **à ~!** dinner etc is ready!; **se mettre à ~** to sit down to eat; **mettre la ~** to lay the table; **faire ~ rase de** to make a clean sweep of; ~ **à repasser** ironing board; ~ **de cuisson** (à l'électricité) hotplate; (au gaz) gas ring; ~ **de nuit** ou **de chevet** bedside table; ~ **des matières** (table of) contents pl; ~ **d'orientation** viewpoint indicator; ~ **roulante** trolley

**tableau, x** [tablo] nm (peinture) painting; (reproduction, fig) picture; (panneau) board; (schéma) table, chart; ~ **d'affichage** notice board; ~ **de bord** dashboard; (AVIAT) instrument panel; ~ **noir** blackboard

**tabler** [table] vi: ~ **sur** to bank on

**tablette** [tablɛt] nf (planche) shelf; ~ **de chocolat** bar of chocolate

**tableur** [tablœʀ] nm spreadsheet

**tablier** [tablije] nm apron

**tabou** [tabu] nm taboo

**tabouret** [tabuʀɛ] *nm* stool

**tac** [tak] *nm*: **il a répondu du ~ au ~** he answered me right back

**tache** [taʃ] *nf* (saleté) stain, mark; (ART, de couleur, lumière) spot; **~ de rousseur** freckle

**tâche** [tɑʃ] *nf* task

**tacher** [taʃe] *vt* to stain, mark

**tâcher** [tɑʃe] *vi*: **~ de faire** to try ou endeavour to do

**tacheté, e** [taʃte] *adj* spotted

**tacot** [tako] (péj) *nm* banger (BRIT), (old) heap

**tact** [takt] *nm* tact; **avoir du ~** to be tactful

**tactique** [taktik] *adj* tactical ♦ *nf* (technique) tactics *sg*; (plan) tactic

**taie** [tɛ] *nf*: **~ (d'oreiller)** pillowslip, pillowcase

**taille** [tɑj] *nf* cutting; (d'arbre etc) pruning; (milieu du corps) waist; (hauteur) height; (grandeur) size; **de ~ à faire** capable of doing; **de ~** sizeable; **taille-crayon(s)** *nm* pencil sharpener

**tailler** [tɑje] *vt* (pierre, diamant) to cut; (arbre, plante) to prune; (vêtement) to cut out; (crayon) to sharpen

**tailleur** [tɑjœʀ] *nm* (couturier) tailor; (vêtement) suit; **en ~** (assis) crosslegged

**taillis** [tɑji] *nm* copse

**taire** [tɛʀ] *vi*: **faire ~ qn** to make sb be quiet; **se ~** *vi* to be silent ou quiet

**talc** [talk] *nm* talc, talcum powder

**talent** [talɑ̃] *nm* talent

**talkie-walkie** [tokiwoki] *nm* walkietalkie

**taloche** [taloʃ] *nf* (fam) clout, cuff

**talon** [talɔ̃] *nm* heel; (de chèque, billet) stub, counterfoil (BRIT); **~s plats/aiguilles** flat/stiletto heels

**talonner** [talɔne] *vt* (suivre) to follow hot on the heels of; (harceler) to hound

**talus** [taly] *nm* embankment

**tambour** [tɑ̃buʀ] *nm* (MUS, aussi) drum; (musicien) drummer; (porte) revolving door(s pl); **tambourin** *nm* tambourine;

**tambouriner** *vi* to drum; **tambouriner à/sur** to drum on

**tamis** [tami] *nm* sieve

**Tamise** [tamiz] *nf*: **la ~** the Thames

**tamisé, e** [tamize] *adj* (fig) subdued, soft

**tampon** [tɑ̃pɔ̃] *nm* (de coton, d'ouate) wad, pad; (amortisseur) buffer; (bouchon) plug, stopper; (cachet, timbre) stamp; (mémoire) ~ (INFORM) buffer; **~ (hygiénique)** tampon; **tamponner** *vt* (timbres) to stamp; (heurter) to crash ou ram into; **tamponneuse** *adj f*: **autos tamponneuses** dodgems

**tandem** [tɑ̃dɛm] *nm* tandem

**tandis** [tɑ̃di]: **~ que** *conj* while

**tanguer** [tɑ̃ge] *vi* to pitch (and toss)

**tanière** [tanjɛʀ] *nf* lair, den

**tanné, e** [tane] *adj* weather-beaten

**tanner** [tane] *vt* to tan; (fam: harceler) to badger

**tant** [tɑ̃] *adv* so much; **~ de** (sable, eau) so much; (gens, livres) so many; **~ que** as long as; (autant que) as much as; **~ mieux** that's great; (avec une certaine réserve) so much the better; **~ pis** too bad; (conciliant) never mind

**tante** [tɑ̃t] *nf* aunt

**tantôt** [tɑ̃to] *adv* (parfois): **~ ... ~** now ... now; (cet après-midi) this afternoon

**taon** [tɑ̃] *nm* horsefly

**tapage** [tapaʒ] *nm* uproar, din

**tapageur, -euse** [tapaʒœʀ, øz] *adj* noisy; (voyant) loud, flashy

**tape** [tap] *nf* slap

**tape-à-l'œil** [tapalœj] *adj inv* flashy, showy

**taper** [tape] *vt* (porte) to bang, slam; (enfant) to slap; (dactylographier) to type (out); (fam: emprunter): **~ qn de 10 F** to touch sb for 10 F ♦ *vi* (soleil) to beat down; **se ~** *vt* (repas) to put away; (fam: corvée) to get landed with; **~ sur qn** to thump sb; (fig) to run sb down; **~ sur un clou** to hit a nail; **~ sur la table** to bang on the table; **~ à** (porte etc) to knock on; **~ dans** (se ser-

*vir*) to dig into; **~ des mains/pieds** to clap one's hands/stamp one's feet; (**à la machine**) to type; **se ~ un travail** (*fam*) to land o.s. a job

**tapi, e** [tapi] *adj* (*blotti*) crouching; (*caché*) hidden away

**tapis** [tapi] *nm* carpet; (*petit*) rug; **mettre sur le ~** (*fig*) to bring up for discussion; **~ de bain** bath mat; **~ de sol** (*de tente*) groundsheet; **~ de souris** (*INFORM*) mouse mat; **~ roulant** (*pour piétons*) moving walkway; (*pour bagages*) carousel

**tapisser** [tapise] *vt* (*avec du papier peint*) to paper; (*recouvrir*): **~ qch (de)** to cover sth (with); **tapisserie** *nf* (*tenture, broderie*) tapestry; (*papier peint*) wallpaper; **tapissier-décorateur** *nm* interior decorator

**tapoter** [tapɔte] *vt* (*joue, main*) to pat; (*objet*) to tap

**taquin, e** [takɛ̃, in] *adj* teasing; **taquiner** *vt* to tease

**tarabiscoté, e** [tarabiskɔte] *adj* overornate, fussy

**tard** [tar] *adv* late; **plus ~** later (on); **au plus ~** at the latest; **sur le ~** late in life

**tarder** [tarde] *vi* (*chose*) to be a long time coming; (*personne*): **~ à faire** to delay doing; **il me tarde d'être** I am longing to be; **sans (plus) ~** without (further) delay

**tardif, -ive** [tardif, iv] *adj* late

**taré, e** [tare] *nm/f* cretin

**tarif** [tarif] *nm*: **~ des consommations** price list; **~s postaux/douaniers** postal/customs rates; **~ des taxis** taxi fares; **~ plein/réduit** (*train*) full/reduced fare; (*téléphone*) peak/off-peak rate

**tarir** [tarir] *vi* to dry up, run dry

**tarte** [tart] *nf* tart; **~ aux fraises** strawberry tart; **~ Tatin** ≈ apple upside-down tart

**tartine** [tartin] *nf* slice of bread; **~ de miel** slice of bread and honey; **tarti-**

**ner** *vt* to spread; **fromage à tartiner** cheese spread

**tartre** [tartr] *nm* (*des dents*) tartar; (*de bouilloire*) fur, scale

**tas** [ta] *nm* heap, pile; (*fig*): **un ~ de** heaps of, lots of; **en ~** in a heap *ou* pile; **formé sur le ~** trained on the job

**tasse** [tas] *nf* cup; **~ à café** coffee cup

**tassé, e** [tase] *adj*: **bien ~** (*café etc*) strong

**tasser** [tase] *vt* (*terre, neige*) to pack down; (*entasser*): **~ qch dans** to cram sth into; **~ vi** (*se serrer*) to squeeze up; (*s'affaisser*) to settle; (*fig*) to settle down

**tata** [tata] *nf* auntie

**tâter** [tate] *vt* to feel; (*fig*) to try out; **se ~** (*hésiter*) to be in two minds; **~ de** (*prison etc*) to have a taste of

**tatillon, ne** [tatijɔ̃, ɔn] *adj* pernickety

**tâtonnement** [tatɔnmɑ̃] *nm*: **par ~s** (*fig*) by trial and error

**tâtonner** [tatɔne] *vi* to grope one's way along

**tâtons** [tatɔ̃]: **à ~** *adv*: **chercher/avancer à ~** to grope around for/grope one's way forward

**tatouage** [tatwaʒ] *nm* tattoo

**tatouer** [tatwe] *vt* to tattoo

**taudis** [todi] *nm* hovel, slum

**taule** [tol] *nf* nick (*fam*), prison

**taupe** [top] *nf* mole

**taureau, x** [tɔro] *nm* bull; (*signe*): **le T~** Taurus

**tauromachie** [tɔromaʃi] *nf* bullfighting

**taux** [to] *nm* rate; (*d'alcool*) level; **~ de change** exchange rate; **~ d'intérêt** interest rate

**taxe** [taks] *nf* tax; (*douanière*) duty; **toutes ~s comprises** inclusive of tax; **la boutique hors ~** the duty free shop; **~ à la valeur ajoutée** value added tax

**taxer** [takse] *vt* (*personne*) to tax; (*produit*) to put a tax on, tax

**taxi** [taksi] *nm* taxi; (*chauffeur: fam*) taxi

driver

**Tchécoslovaquie** [tʃekɔslɔvaki] nf Czechoslovakia; **tchèque** adj Czech ♦ nm/f: **Tchèque** Czech ♦ nm (LING) Czech; **la République tchèque** the Czech Republic

**te, t'** [tə] pron you; (réfléchi) yourself

**technicien, ne** [tɛknisjɛ̃, jɛn] nm/f technician

**technico-commercial, e, -aux** [tɛknikokɔmɛrsjal, jo] adj: **agent ~-~** sales technician

**technique** [tɛknik] adj technical ♦ nf technique; **techniquement** adv technically

**technologie** [tɛknɔlɔʒi] nf technology; **technologique** adj technological

**teck** [tɛk] nm teak

**tee-shirt** [tiʃœrt] nm T-shirt, tee-shirt

**teignais** etc [tɛɲɛ] vb voir **teindre**

**teindre** [tɛdr] vt to dye; **se ~ les cheveux** to dye one's hair; **teint, e** adj dyed ♦ nm (du visage) complexion; (momentané) colour ♦ nf shade; **grand teint** colourfast

**teinté, e** [tɛ̃te] adj: **~ de** (fig) tinged with

**teinter** [tɛ̃te] vt (verre, papier) to tint; (bois) to stain

**teinture** [tɛ̃tyr] nf dye; **~ d'iode** tincture of iodine; **teinturerie** nf dry cleaner's; **teinturier** nm dry cleaner

**tel, telle** [tɛl] adj (pareil) such; (comme): **~ un/des** ... like a/like ...; (indéfini) such-and-such a; (intensif): **un ~/de tels** ... such (a)/such ...; **rien de ~** nothing like it; **~ que** like, such as; **~ quel** as it is ou stands (ou was etc); **venez ~ jour** come on such-and-such a day

**télé** [tele] (fam) nf TV

**télé...: télécabine** nf (benne) cable car; **télécarte** nf phonecard; **télécommande** nf remote control; **télécopie** nf fax; **envoyer qch par télécopie** to fax sth; **télécopieur** nm fax machine; **télédistribution** nf cable TV; **téléférique** nm = **téléphérique**;

**télégramme** nm telegram; **télégraphier** vt to telegraph, cable; **téléguider** vt to radio-control; **télématique** nf telematics sg; **téléobjectif** nm telephoto lens sg; **télépathie** nf telepathy; **téléphérique** nm cable car

**téléphone** [telefɔn] nm telephone; **avoir le ~** to be on the (tele)phone; **au ~** on the phone; **~ mobile** mobile phone; **~ rouge** hot line; **~ sans fil** cordless (tele)phone; **~ de voiture** car phone; **téléphoner** vi to make a phone call; **téléphoner à** to phone, call up; **téléphonique** adj (tele)phone cpd

**télescope** [telɛskɔp] nm telescope

**télescoper** [telɛskɔpe] vt to smash up; **se ~** (véhicules) to concertina

**télé...: téléscripteur** nm teleprinter; **télésiège** nm chairlift; **téléski** nm ski-tow; **téléspectateur, -trice** nm/f (television) viewer; **télévente** nf telesales; **téléviseur** nm television set; **télévision** nf television; **à la télévision** on television; **télévision numérique** digital TV

**télex** [telɛks] nm telex

**telle** [tɛl] adj voir **tel**; **tellement** adv (tant) so much; (si) so; **tellement de** (sable, eau) so much; (gens, livres) so many; **il s'est endormi tellement il était fatigué** he was so tired (that) he fell asleep; **pas tellement** not (all) that much; not (all) that +adjectif

**téméraire** [temerɛr] adj reckless, rash; **témérité** nf recklessness, rashness

**témoignage** [temwaɲaʒ] nm (JUR: déclaration) testimony no pl, evidence no pl; (rapport, récit) account; (fig: d'affection etc: cadeau) token, mark; (: geste) expression

**témoigner** [temwaɲe] vt (intérêt, gratitude) to show ♦ vi (JUR) to testify, give evidence; **~ de** to bear witness to, testify to

**témoin** [temwɛ̃] nm witness ♦ adj: **appartement ~** show flat (BRIT); **être ~**

**de** to witness; **~ oculaire** eyewitness strap

**tempe** [tɑ̃p] *nf* temple

**tempérament** [tɑ̃peʀamɑ̃] *nm* temperament, disposition; **à ~** (*vente*) on deferred (payment) terms; (*achat*) by instalments, hire purchase *cpd*

**température** [tɑ̃peʀatyʀ] *nf* temperature; **avoir** *ou* **faire de la ~** to be running *ou* have a temperature

**tempéré, e** [tɑ̃peʀe] *adj* temperate

**tempête** [tɑ̃pɛt] *nf* storm; **~ de sable/neige** sand/snowstorm

**temple** [tɑ̃pl] *nm* temple; (*protestant*) church

**temporaire** [tɑ̃pɔʀɛʀ] *adj* temporary

**temps** [tɑ̃] *nm* (*atmosphérique*) weather; (*durée*) time; (*époque*) time, times *pl*; (*LING*) tense; (*MUS*) beat; (*TECH*) stroke; **un ~ de chien** (*fam*) rotten weather; **quel ~ fait-il?** what's the weather like?; **il fait beau/mauvais ~** the weather is fine/bad; **avoir le ~/tout son ~** to have time/plenty of time; **en ~ de paix/guerre** in peacetime/wartime; **en ~ utile** *ou* **voulu** in due time *ou* course; **ces derniers ~** lately; **dans quelque ~** in a (little) while; **de ~ en ~, de ~ à autre** from time to time; **à ~** (*partir, arriver*) in time; **à ~ complet, à plein ~** fulltime; **à ~ partiel** part-time; **à ~** at one time; **~ d'arrêt** pause, halt; **~ mort** (*COMM*) slack period

**tenable** [t(ə)nabl] *adj* bearable

**tenace** [tənas] *adj* persistent

**tenailler** [tənaje] *vt* (*fig*) to torment

**tenailles** [tənaj] *nfpl* pincers

**tenais** *etc* [t(ə)nɛ] *vb voir* **tenir**

**tenancier, -ière** [tənɑ̃sje] *nm/f* manager/manageress

**tenant, e** [tənɑ̃, ɑ̃t] *nm/f* (*SPORT*): **~ du titre** title-holder

**tendance** [tɑ̃dɑ̃s] *nf* tendency; (*opinions*) leanings *pl*, sympathies *pl*; (*évolution*) trend; **avoir ~ à** to have a tendency to, tend to

**tendeur** [tɑ̃dœʀ] *nm* (*attache*) elastic

**tendre** [tɑ̃dʀ] *adj* tender; (*bois, roche, couleur*) soft ♦ *vt* (*élastique, peau*) to stretch; (*corde*) to tighten; (*muscle*) to tense; (*fig: piège*) to set, lay; (*donner*): **~ qch à qn** to hold sth out to sb; (*offrir*) to offer sb sth; **se ~** *vi* (*corde*) to tighten; (*relations*) to become strained; **~ à qch/à faire** to tend towards sth/to do; **~ l'oreille** to prick up one's ears; **~ la main/le bras** to hold out one's hand/stretch out one's arm; **tendrement** *adv* tenderly; **tendresse** *nf* tenderness

**tendu, e** [tɑ̃dy] *pp de* **tendre** ♦ *adj* (*corde*) tight; (*muscles*) tensed; (*relations*) strained

**ténèbres** [tenɛbʀ] *nfpl* darkness *sg*

**teneur** [tənœʀ] *nf* content; (*d'une lettre*) terms *pl*, content

**tenir** [t(ə)niʀ] *vt* to hold; (*magasin, hôtel*) to run; (*promesse*) to keep ♦ *vi* to hold; (*neige, gel*) to hold; **se ~** *vi* (*avoir lieu*) to be held, take place; (*être: personne*) to stand; **~ à** (*personne, objet*) to be attached to; (*réputation*) to care about; **~ à faire** to be determined to do; **~ de** (*ressembler à*) to take after; **ça ne tient qu'à lui** it is entirely up to him; **~ qn pour** to regard sb as; **~ qch de qn** (*histoire*) to have heard *ou* learnt sth from sb; (*qualité, défaut*) to have inherited *ou* got sth from sb; **~ dans** to fit into; **~ compte de qch** to take sth into account; **~ les comptes** to keep the books; **~ bon** to stand fast; **~ le coup** to hold out; **~ au chaud** to keep hot; **tiens/tenez, voilà le stylo** there's the pen!; **tiens, voilà Alain!** look, here's Alain!; **tiens?** (*surprise*) really?; **se ~ droit** to stand (*ou* sit) up straight; **bien se ~** to behave well; **se ~ à qch** to hold on to sth; **s'en ~ à qch** to confine o.s. to sth

**tennis** [tenis] *nm* tennis; (*court*) tennis court ♦ *nm ou pl* (*aussi*: **chaussures de ~**) tennis *ou* gym shoes; **~ de table** table tennis; **tennisman** *nm* tennis player

**tension** [tɑ̃sjɔ̃] nf tension; (MÉD) blood pressure; **avoir de la ~** to have high blood pressure

**tentation** [tɑ̃tasjɔ̃] nf temptation

**tentative** [tɑ̃tativ] nf attempt

**tente** [tɑ̃t] nf tent

**tenter** [tɑ̃te] vt (éprouver, attirer) to tempt; (essayer): to attempt ou to do; **~ sa chance** to try one's luck

**tenture** [tɑ̃tyr] nf hanging

**tenu, e** [t(ə)ny] pp de **tenir ♦** adj (maison, comptes): **bien ~** well-kept; (obligé): **~ de faire** obliged to do **♦** nf (vêtements) clothes pl; (comportement) (good) manners pl, good behaviour; (d'une maison) upkeep; **en petite ~** scantily dressed ou clad; **~e de route** (AUTO) road-holding; **~e de soirée** evening dress

**ter** [tɛr] adj: **16 ~ 16b** ou B

**térébenthine** [terebɑ̃tin] nf: **(essence de) ~** (oil of) turpentine

**Tergal** ® [tɛrgal] nm Terylene ®

**terme** [tɛrm] nm term; (fin) end; **à court/long ~ ♦** adj short-/long-term **♦** adv in the short/long term; **avant ~** (MÉD) prematurely; **mettre un ~ à** to put an end ou a stop to; **en bons ~s** on good terms

**terminaison** [tɛrminɛzɔ̃] nf (LING) ending

**terminal** [tɛrminal, o] nm terminal; **terminale** nf (SCOL) ≈ sixth form ou year (BRIT), ≈ twelfth grade (US)

**terminer** [tɛrmine] vt to finish; **se ~** vi to end

**terne** [tɛrn] adj dull

**ternir** [tɛrnir] vt to dull; (fig) to sully, tarnish; **se ~** vi to become dull

**terrain** [tɛrɛ̃] nm (sol, fig) ground; (COMM: étendue de terre) land no pl; (parcelle) plot (of land); (à bâtir) site; **sur le ~** (fig) on the field; **~ d'aviation** airfield; **~ de camping** campsite; **~ de football/rugby** football/rugby

pitch (BRIT) ou field (US); **~ de golf** golf course; **~ de jeu** games field; (pour les petits) playground; **~ de sport** sports ground; **~ vague** waste ground no pl

**terrasse** [tɛras] nf terrace; **à la ~** (café) outside; **terrasser** vt (adversaire) to floor; (suj: maladie etc) to strike down

**terre** [tɛr] nf (gén, aussi ÉLEC) earth; (substance) soil, earth; (opposé à mer) land no pl; (contrée) land; **~s** nfpl (terrains) lands, land sg; **en ~** (pipe, poterie) clay cpd; **à ~** ou **par ~** (mettre, être, s'asseoir) on the ground (ou floor); (jeter, tomber) to the ground, down; **~ à ~** adj inv down-to-earth; **~ cuite** terracotta; **la ~ ferme** dry land; **~ glaise** clay

**terreau** [tɛro] nm compost

**terre-plein** [tɛrplɛ̃] nm platform; (sur chaussée) central reservation

**terrer** [tɛre]: **se ~** vi to hide away

**terrestre** [tɛrɛstr] adj (surface) earth's, of the earth; (BOT, ZOOL, MIL) land cpd; (REL) earthly

**terreur** [tɛrœr] nf terror no pl

**terrible** [tɛribl] adj terrible, dreadful; (fam) terrific; **pas ~** nothing special

**terrien, ne** [tɛrjɛ̃, jɛn] adj: **propriétaire ~** landowner **♦** nm/f (non martien etc) earthling

**terrier** [tɛrje] nm burrow, hole; (chien) terrier

**terrifier** [tɛrifje] vt to terrify

**terrine** [tɛrin] nf (récipient) terrine; (CULIN) pâté

**territoire** [tɛritwar] nm territory

**terroir** [tɛrwar] nm: **accent du ~** country accent

**terroriser** [tɛrɔrize] vt to terrorize

**terrorisme** [tɛrɔrism] nm terrorism; **terroriste** nm/f terrorist

**tertiaire** [tɛrsjɛr] adj tertiary **♦** nm (ÉCON) service industries pl

**tertre** [tɛrtr] nm hillock, mound

**tes** [te] adj voir **ton**[^1]

**tesson** [tesɔ̃] nm: **~ de bouteille** piece

of broken bottle

**test** [tɛst] *nm* test

**testament** [tɛstamɑ̃] *nm* (*JUR*) will; (*REL*) Testament; (*fig*) legacy

**tester** [tɛste] *vt* to test

**testicule** [tɛstikyl] *nm* testicle

**têtard** [tɛtaʀ] *nm* tadpole

**tête** [tɛt] *nf* head; (*cheveux*) hair *no pl*; (*visage*) face; **de ~** *adj* (*wagon etc*) front *cpd* ♦ *adv* (*calculer*) in one's head, mentally; **tenir ~ à qn** to stand up to sb; **la ~ en bas** with one's head down; **la ~ la première** (*tomber*) headfirst; **faire une ~** (*FOOTBALL*) to head the ball; **faire la ~** (*fig*) to sulk; **en ~** (*SPORT*) in the lead; **à la ~ de** at the head of; (*SPORT*) in the lead; **à la ~ de** at the head of; **à ~ reposée** in a more leisurely moment; **n'en faire qu'à sa ~** to do as one pleases; **en avoir par-dessus la ~** to be fed up; **en ~ à ~** in private, alone together; **de la ~ aux pieds** from head to toe; **~ de lecture** (playback) head; **~ de liste** (*POL*) chief candidate; **~ de série** (*TENNIS*) seeded player, seed; **tête-à-queue** *nm inv:* **faire un tête-à-queue** to spin round

**téter** [tete] *vt:* **~ (sa mère)** to suck at one's mother's breast, feed

**tétine** [tetin] *nf* teat; (*sucette*) dummy (*BRIT*), pacifier (*US*)

**têtu, e** [tety] *adj* stubborn, pigheaded

**texte** [tɛkst] *nm* text; (*morceau choisi*) passage

**textile** [tɛkstil] *adj* textile *cpd* ♦ *nm* textile; **le ~** the textile industry

**Texto** ® [tɛksto] *nm* text message

**texto** [tɛksto] (*fam*) *nm* word for word ♦ *nm* text message

**texture** [tɛkstyʀ] *nf* texture

**thaïlandais, e** [tajlɑ̃dɛ, ɛz] *adj* Thai ♦ *nm/f:* **T~, e** Thai

**Thaïlande** [tajlɑ̃d] *nf* Thailand

**TGV** *sigle m* (= *train à grande vitesse*) high-speed train

**thé** [te] *nm* tea; **au citron** lemon tea; **~ au lait** tea with milk; **prendre le ~** to have tea; **faire le ~** to make the tea

**théâtral, e, -aux** [teatʀal, o] *adj* theatrical

**théâtre** [teatʀ] *nm* theatre; (*péj:* simulation) playacting; (*fig: lieu*) scene of the action; **faire du ~** to act

**théière** [tejɛʀ] *nf* teapot

**thème** [tɛm] *nm* theme; (*SCOL:* traduction) prose (composition)

**théologie** [teɔlɔʒi] *nf* theology

**théorie** [teɔʀi] *nf* theory; **théorique** *adj* theoretical

**thérapie** [teʀapi] *nf* therapy

**thermal, e, -aux** [tɛʀmal, o] *adj:* **station ~e** spa; **cure ~e** water cure

**thermes** [tɛʀm] *nmpl* thermal baths

**thermomètre** [tɛʀmɔmɛtʀ] *nm* thermometer

**thermos** ® [tɛʀmos] *nm ou nf:* (**bouteille**) **~** vacuum *ou* Thermos ® flask

**thèse** [tɛz] *nf* thesis

**thon** [tɔ̃] *nm* tuna (fish)

**thym** [tɛ̃] *nm* thyme

**tibia** [tibja] *nm* shinbone, tibia; (*partie antérieure de la jambe*) shin

**TIC** [teise] *sigle f* (= technologies de l'information et de la communication) ICT

**tic** [tik] *nm* tic, (nervous) twitch; (*de langage etc*) mannerism

**ticket** [tikɛ] *nm* ticket; **~ de caisse** receipt; **~ de quai** platform ticket

**tic-tac** [tiktak] *nm inv* ticking; **faire ~~** to tick

**tiède** [tjɛd] *adj* lukewarm; (*vent, air*) mild, warm; **tiédir** *vi* to cool; (*se réchauffer*) to grow warmer

**tien, ne** [tjɛ̃, tjɛn] *pron:* **le(la) ~(ne), les ~(ne)s** yours; **à la ~ne!** cheers!

**tiens** [tjɛ̃] *vb, excl voir* **tenir**

**tierce** [tjɛʀs] *adj voir* **tiers**

**tiercé** [tjɛʀse] *nm* system of forecast betting giving first 3 horses

**tiers, tierce** [tjɛʀ, tjɛʀs] *adj* third ♦ *nm* (*JUR*) third party; (*fraction*) third; **le ~ monde** the Third World

**tifs** [tif] (*fam*) *nmpl* hair

**tige** [tiʒ] *nf* stem; (*baguette*) rod

**tignasse** [tiɲas] (*péj*) *nf* mop of hair

**tigre** [tigʀ] *nm* tiger; **tigresse** *nf* tigress; **tigré, e** adj (rayé) striped; (tacheté) spotted; (chat) tabby

**tilleul** [tijœl] nm lime (tree), linden (tree); (boisson) lime-blossom) tea

**timbale** [tɛ̃bal] nf (metal) tumbler; ~s nfpl (MUS) timpani, kettledrums

**timbre** [tɛ̃bR] nm (tampon) stamp; (aussi: ~-poste) (postage) stamp; (MUS: de voix, instrument) timbre, tone

**timbré, e** [tɛ̃bRe] (fam) adj cracked

**timide** [timid] adj shy; (timoré) timid; **timidement** adv shyly; timidly; **timidité** nf shyness; timidity

**tins** etc [tɛ̃] vb voir **tenir**

**tintamarre** [tɛ̃tamaR] nm din, uproar

**tinter** [tɛ̃te] vi to ring, chime; (argent, clefs) to jingle

**tique** [tik] nf (parasite) tick

**tir** [tiR] nm (sport) shooting; (fait ou manière de ~) firing no pl; (rafale) fire; (stand) shooting gallery; ~ **à l'arc** archery; ~ **au pigeon** clay pigeon shooting

**tirage** [tiRaʒ] nm (action) printing; (PHOTO) print; (de journal) circulation; (de livre: nombre d'exemplaires) (print) run; (: édition) edition; (de loterie) draw; **par ~ au sort** by drawing lots

**tirailler** [tiRaje] vt: **être tiraillé entre** to be torn between

**tire** [tiR] nf: **vol à la ~** pickpocketing

**tiré, e** [tiRe] adj (traits) drawn; ~ **par les cheveux** far-fetched

**tire-au-flanc** [tiRoflɑ̃] (péj) nm inv skiver

**tire-bouchon** [tiRbuʃɔ̃] nm corkscrew

**tirelire** [tiRliR] nf moneybox

**tirer** [tiRe] vt (gén) to pull; (extraire): ~ **qch de** to take ou pull sth out of; (trait, rideau, carte, conclusion, chèque) to draw; (langue) to stick out; (en faisant feu: balle, coup) to fire; (: animal) to shoot; (journal, livre, photo) to print; (FOOTBALL: corner etc) to take ♦ vi (faire feu) to fire; (faire du tir , FOOTBALL) to shoot; **se ~** vi (fam) to push off; **s'en ~** (éviter le pire) to get off; (survivre) to

pull through; (se débrouiller) to manage; ~ **sur** (corde) to pull on ou at; (faire feu sur) to shoot ou fire at; (pipe) to draw on; (approcher de: couleur) to verge ou border on; ~ **qn de** (embarras etc) to help ou get sb out of; ~ **à l'arc/ la carabine** to shoot with a bow and arrow/with a rifle; ~ **à sa fin** to be drawing to a close; ~ **qch au clair** to clear sth up; ~ **au sort** to draw lots; ~ **parti de** to take advantage of; ~ **profit de** to profit from

**tiret** [tiRɛ] nm dash

**tireur** [tiRœR] nm gunman; ~ **d'élite** marksman

**tiroir** [tiRwaR] nm drawer; **tiroir-caisse** nm till

**tisane** [tizan] nf herb tea

**tisonnier** [tizɔnje] nm poker

**tisser** [tise] vt to weave; **tisserand** nm weaver

**tissu** [tisy] nm fabric, material, cloth no pl; (ANAT, BIO) tissue; **tissu-éponge** nm (terry) towelling no pl

**titre** [titR] nm (gén) title; (de journal) headline; (diplôme) qualification; (COMM) security; **en ~** (champion) official; **à juste ~** rightly; **à quel ~?** on what grounds?; **à aucun ~** on no account; **au même ~ (que)** in the same way (as); **à ~ d'information** for (your) information; **à ~ gracieux** free of charge; **à ~ d'essai** on a trial basis; **à ~ privé** in a private capacity; ~ **de propriété** title deed; ~ **de transport** ticket

**tituber** [titybe] vi to stagger (along)

**titulaire** [titylɛR] adj (ADMIN) with tenure ♦ nm/f (de permis) holder

**toast** [tost] nm slice ou piece of toast; (de bienvenue) (welcoming) toast; **porter un ~ à qn** to propose ou drink a toast to sb

**toboggan** [tɔbɔgã] nm slide; (AUTO) flyover

**toc** [tɔk] excl: ~, **toc** knock knock ♦ nm: **en ~** fake

**tocsin** [tɔksɛ̃] nm alarm (bell)

**toge** [tɔʒ] nf toga; (de juge) gown

**tohu-bohu** [tɔybɔy] nm hubbub

**toi** [twa] pron you

**toile** [twal] nf (tableau) canvas; **de** ou **en ~** (pantalon) cotton; (sac) canvas; **~ cirée** oilcloth; **~ d'araignée** cobweb; **~ de fond** (fig) backdrop

**toilette** [twalɛt] nf (habits) outfit; **~s** nfpl (w.-c.) toilet sg; **faire sa ~** to have a wash, get washed; **articles de ~** toiletries

**toi-même** [twamɛm] pron yourself

**toiser** [twaze] vt to eye up and down

**toison** [twazɔ̃] nf (de mouton) fleece

**toit** [twa] nm roof; **~ ouvrant** sunroof

**toiture** [twatyr] nf roof

**tôle** [tol] nf (plaque) steel ou iron sheet; **~ ondulée** corrugated iron

**tolérable** [tɔlerabl] adj tolerable

**tolérant, e** [tɔlerɑ̃, ɑ̃t] adj tolerant

**tolérer** [tɔlere] vt to tolerate; (ADMIN: hors taxe etc) to allow

**tollé** [tɔ(l)le] nm outcry

**tomate** [tɔmat] nf tomato; **~s farcies** stuffed tomatoes

**tombe** [tɔ̃b] nf (sépulture) grave; (avec monument) tomb

**tombeau, x** [tɔ̃bo] nm tomb

**tombée** [tɔ̃be] nf: **à la ~ de la nuit** at nightfall

**tomber** [tɔ̃be] vi to fall; (fièvre, vent) to drop; **laisser ~** (objet) to drop; (personne) to let down; (activité) to give up; **laisse ~!** forget it!; **faire ~** to knock over; **~ sur** (rencontrer) to bump into; **~ de fatigue/sommeil** to drop from exhaustion/be falling asleep on one's feet; **ça tombe bien** that's come at the right time; **il est bien tombé** he's been lucky; **~ à l'eau** (projet) to fall through; **~ en panne** to break down

**tombola** [tɔ̃bɔla] nf raffle

**tome** [tɔm] nm volume

**ton¹, ta** [tɔ̃, ta] (pl **tes**) adj your

**ton²** [tɔ̃] nm (gén) tone; (couleur) shade, tone; **de bon ~** in good taste

**tonalité** [tɔnalite] nf (au téléphone) dialling tone

**tondeuse** [tɔ̃døz] nf (à gazon) (lawn)mower; (du coiffeur) clippers pl; (pour les moutons) shears pl

**tondre** [tɔ̃dr] vt (pelouse, herbe) to mow; (haie) to cut, clip; (mouton, toison) to shear; (cheveux) to crop

**tongs** [tɔ̃g] nfpl flip-flops

**tonifier** [tɔnifje] vt (peau, organisme) to tone up

**tonique** [tɔnik] adj fortifying ♦ nm tonic

**tonne** [tɔn] nf metric ton, tonne

**tonneau, x** [tɔno] nm (à vin, cidre) barrel; **faire des ~x** (voiture, avion) to roll over

**tonnelle** [tɔnɛl] nf bower, arbour

**tonner** [tɔne] vi to thunder; **il tonne** it is thundering, there's some thunder

**tonnerre** [tɔnɛʀ] nm thunder

**tonton** [tɔ̃tɔ̃] nm uncle

**tonus** [tɔnys] nm energy

**top** [tɔp] nm: **au 3ème ~** at the 3rd stroke

**topinambour** [tɔpinɑ̃buʀ] nm Jerusalem artichoke

**topo** [tɔpo] (fam) nm rundown; **c'est le même ~** it's the same old story

**toque** [tɔk] nf (de fourrure) fur hat; **~ de cuisinier** chef's hat; **~ de jockey/juge** jockey's/judge's cap

**toqué, e** [tɔke] (fam) adj cracked

**torche** [tɔʀʃ] nf torch

**torchon** [tɔʀʃɔ̃] nm cloth; (à vaisselle) tea towel ou cloth

**tordre** [tɔʀdʀ] vt (chiffon) to wring; (barre, fig: visage) to twist; **se ~: se ~ le poignet/la cheville** to twist one's wrist/ankle; **se ~ de douleur/rire** to be doubled up with pain/laughter; **tordu, e** adj bent; (fig) crazy

**tornade** [tɔʀnad] nf tornado

**torpille** [tɔʀpij] nf torpedo

**torréfier** [tɔʀefje] vt to roast

**torrent** [tɔʀɑ̃] nm mountain stream

**torsade** [tɔʀsad] nf: **un pull à ~s** a

cable sweater

**torse** [tɔʀs] *nm* chest; (ANAT, SCULPTURE) torso; ~ **stripped to the waist**

**tort** [tɔʀ] *nm* (défaut) fault; ~s *nmpl* (JUR) fault *sg*; **avoir** ~ to be wrong; **être dans son** ~ to be in the wrong; **donner** ~ **à qn** to lay the blame on sb; **causer du** ~ **à** to harm; **à** ~ wrongly; **à** ~ **et à travers** wildly

**torticolis** [tɔʀtikɔli] *nm* stiff neck

**tortiller** [tɔʀtije] *vt* to twist; (moustache) to twirl; **se** ~ *vi* to wriggle; (en dansant) to wiggle

**tortionnaire** [tɔʀsjɔnɛʀ] *nm* torturer

**tortue** [tɔʀty] *nf* tortoise; (d'eau douce) terrapin; (d'eau de mer) turtle

**tortueux, -euse** [tɔʀtɥø, øz] *adj* (rue) twisting; (fig) tortuous

**torture** [tɔʀtyʀ] *nf* torture; **torturer** *vt* to torture; (fig) to torment

**tôt** [to] *adv* early; ~ **ou tard** sooner or later; **si** ~ so early; (déjà) so soon; **plus** ~ earlier; **au plus** ~ at the earliest; **il eut** ~ **fait de faire** he soon did

**total, e, -aux** [tɔtal, o] *adj, nm* total; **au** ~ in total; (fig) on the whole; **faire le** ~ to work out the total; **totalement** *adv* totally; **totaliser** *vt* to total; **totalitaire** *adj* totalitarian; **totalité** *nf*: **la totalité de** all (of); the whole +*sg*; **en totalité** entirely

**toubib** [tubib] (fam) *nm* doctor

**touchant, e** [tuʃɑ̃, ɑ̃t] *adj* touching

**touche** [tuʃ] *nf* (de piano, de machine à écrire) key; (de téléphone) button; (PEIN-TURE etc) stroke, touch; (fig: de nostalgie) touch; (FOOTBALL: aussi: **remise en** ~) throw-in; (aussi: **ligne de** ~) touch-line

**toucher** [tuʃe] *nm* touch ♦ *vt* to touch; (palper) to feel; (atteindre: d'un coup de feu etc) to hit; (concerner) to concern, affect; (contacter) to reach, contact; (recevoir: récompense) to receive, get; (: salaire) to draw, get; (: chèque) to cash; **se** ~ (être en contact) to touch; **au** ~

to the touch; ~ **à** to touch; (concerner) to have to do with, concern; **je vais lui en** ~ **un mot** I'll have a word with him about it; ~ **à sa fin** to be drawing to a close

**touffe** [tuf] *nf* tuft

**touffu, e** [tufy] *adj* thick, dense

**toujours** [tuʒuʀ] *adv* always; (encore) still; (constamment) forever; ~ **plus** more and more; **pour** ~ forever; ~ **est-il que** the fact remains that; **essaie** ~ (you can) try anyway

**toupet** [tupɛ] (fam) *nm* cheek

**toupie** [tupi] *nf* (spinning) top

**tour** [tuʀ] *nf* tower; (immeuble) high-rise block (BRIT) ou building (US); (ÉCHECS) castle, rook ♦ *nm* (excursion) trip; (à pied) stroll, walk; (en voiture) run, ride; (SPORT: aussi: ~ **de piste**) lap; (d'être servi ou de jouer etc) turn; (de roue etc) revolution; (POL: aussi: ~ **de scrutin**) ballot; (ruse, de prestidigitation) trick; (de potier) wheel; (à bois, métaux) lathe; (circonférence): **de 3 m de** ~ 3 m round, with a circumference ou girth of 3 m; **faire le** ~ **de** to go round; (à pied) to walk round; **c'est au** ~ **de Renée** it's Renée's turn; **à** ~ **de rôle**, ~ **à** ~ in turn; ~ **de chant** *nm* song recital; ~ **de contrôle** *nm* control tower; ~ **de garde** *nm* spell of duty; ~ **d'horizon** *nm* (fig) general survey; ~ **de taille/tête** *nm* waist/head measurement; **un 33** ~**s un LP; un 45** ~**s a single**

**tourbe** [tuʀb] *nf* peat

**tourbillon** [tuʀbijɔ̃] *nm* whirlwind; (d'eau) whirlpool; (fig) whirl, swirl; **tourbillonner** *vi* to whirl (round)

**tourelle** [tuʀɛl] *nf* turret

**tourisme** [tuʀism] *nm* tourism; **agence de** ~ tourist agency; **faire du** ~ to go touring; (en ville) to go sightseeing; **touriste** *nm/f* tourist; **touristique** *adj* tourist *cpd*; (région) touristic

**tourment** [tuʀmɑ̃] *nm* torment; **tourmenter** *vt* to torment; **se tourmenter** *vi* to fret, worry o.s.

**tournage** [turnaʒ] nm (CINÉMA) shooting

**tournant** [turnɑ̃] nm (de route) bend; (fig) turning point

**tournebroche** [turnəbrɔʃ] nm roasting spit

**tourne-disque** [turnədisk] nm record player

**tournée** [turne] nf (du facteur etc) round; (d'artiste, politicien) tour; (au café) round of drinks

**tournemain** [turnəmɛ̃]: **en un ~** adv (as) quick as a flash

**tourner** [turne] vt to turn; (sauce, mélange) to stir; (CINÉMA: faire les prises de vues) to shoot; (: produire) to make ♦ vi to turn; (moteur) to run; (taximètre) to tick away; (lait etc) to turn (sour); **se ~** vi to turn round; **mal ~** to go wrong; **~ autour de** to go round; **~ à/en** to turn into; **~ à gauche/droite** to turn left/right; **~ le dos à** to turn one's back on; to have one's back to; **~ de l'œil** to pass out; **se ~ vers** to turn towards; (fig) to turn to

**tournesol** [turnəsɔl] nm sunflower

**tournevis** [turnəvis] nm screwdriver

**tourniquet** [turnikɛ] nm (pour arroser) sprinkler; (portillon) turnstile; (présentoir) revolving stand

**tournoi** [turnwa] nm tournament

**tournoyer** [turnwaje] vi to swirl (round)

**tournure** [turnyr] nf (LING) turn of phrase; (évolution): **la ~ de qch** the way sth is developing; **~ d'esprit** turn ou cast of mind; **la ~ des événements** the turn of events

**tourte** [turt] nf pie

**tourterelle** [turtərɛl] nf turtledove

**tous** [tu] adj, pron voir **tout**

**Toussaint** [tusɛ̃] nf: **la ~** All Saints' Day

La Toussaint, November 1, is a pub-

lic holiday in France. People traditionally visit the graves of friends and relatives to lay wreaths of heather and chrysanthemums.

**tousser** [tuse] vi to cough

**tout, e** [tu, tut] (mpl **tous**, fpl **toutes**) adj 1 (avec article singulier) all; **tout le lait** all the milk; **toute la nuit** all night, the whole night; **tout le livre** the whole book; **tout un pain** a whole loaf; **tout le temps** all the time; the whole time; **c'est tout le contraire** it's quite the opposite

2 (avec article pluriel) every, all; **tous les livres** all the books; **toutes les nuits** every night; **toutes les fois** every time; **toutes les trois/deux semaines** every third/other ou second week, every three/two weeks; **tous les deux** both ou each of us (ou them ou you); **toutes les trois** all three of us (ou them ou you)

3 (sans article): **à tout âge** at any age; **pour toute nourriture, il avait ...** his only food was ...

♦ pron everything, all; **il a tout fait** he's done everything; **je les vois tous** I can see them all ou all of them; **nous y sommes tous allés** all of us went, we all went; **en tout** in all; **tout ce qu'il sait** all he knows

♦ nm whole; **le tout** all of it (ou them); **le tout est de ...** the main thing is to ...; **pas du tout** not at all

♦ adv 1 (très, complètement) very; **tout près** very near; **le tout premier** the very first; **tout seul** all alone; **le livre tout entier** the whole book; **tout en haut** right at the top; **tout droit** straight ahead

2: **tout en** while; **tout en travaillant** while working, as he etc works

3: **tout d'abord** first of all; **tout à coup** suddenly; **tout à fait** absolutely;

**tout à l'heure** a short while ago; *(futur)* in a short while, shortly; **à tout à l'heure!** see you later!; **tout de même** all the same; **tout le monde** everybody; **tout de suite** immediately, straight away; **tout terrain** *ou* **tous terrains** all-terrain

**toutefois** [tutfwa] *adv* however

**toutes** [tut] *adj, pron voir* **tout**

**toux** [tu] *nf* cough

**toxicomane** [tɔksikɔman] *nm/f* drug addict

**toxique** [tɔksik] *adj* toxic

**trac** [trak] *nm (au théâtre, en public)* stage fright; *(aux examens)* nerves *pl*; **avoir le ~** *(au théâtre, en public)* to have stage fright; *(aux examens)* to be feeling nervous

**tracasser** [trakase] *vt* to worry, bother; **se ~** to worry

**trace** [tras] *nf (empreintes)* tracks *pl*; *(marques, aussi fig)* mark; *(quantité infime, indice, vestige)* trace; **~s de pas** footprints

**tracé** [trase] *nm (parcours)* line; *(plan)* layout

**tracer** [trase] *vt* to draw; *(piste)* to open up

**tract** [trakt] *nm* tract, pamphlet

**tractations** [traktasjɔ̃] *nfpl* dealings, bargaining *sg*

**tracteur** [traktœr] *nm* tractor

**traction** [traksjɔ̃] *nf*: **~ avant/arrière** front-wheel/rear-wheel drive

**tradition** [tradisjɔ̃] *nf* tradition; **traditionnel, le** *adj* traditional

**traducteur, -trice** [tradyktœr, tris] *nm/f* translator

**traduction** [tradyksjɔ̃] *nf* translation

**traduire** [traduir] *vt* to translate; *(exprimer)* to convey; **~ qn en justice** to bring sb before the courts

**trafic** [trafik] *nm* traffic; **~ d'armes** arms dealing; **trafiquant, e** *nm/f* trafficker; *(d'armes)* dealer; **trafiquer** *(péj)* *vt (vin)* to doctor; *(moteur, docu-*

*ment)* to tamper with

**tragédie** [traʒedi] *nf* tragedy; **tragique** *adj* tragic

**trahir** [trair] *vt* to betray; **trahison** *nf* betrayal; *(jur)* treason

**train** [trɛ̃] *nm (rail)* train; *(allure)* pace; **être en ~ de faire qch** to be doing sth; **mettre qn en ~** to put sb in good spirits; **se sentir en ~** to feel in good form; **~ d'atterrissage** undercarriage; **~ de vie** style of living; **~ électrique** *(jouet)* (electric) train set; **~ autos-couchettes** car-sleeper train

**traîne** [trɛn] *nf (de robe)* train; **être à la ~** to lag behind

**traîneau, x** [trɛno] *nm* sleigh, sledge

**traînée** [trɛne] *nf* trail; *(sur un mur, dans le ciel)* streak; *(péj)* slut

**traîner** [trɛne] *vt (remorque)* to pull; *(enfant, chien)* to drag *ou* trail along ♦ *vi (robe, manteau)* to trail; *(être en désordre)* to lie around; *(aller lentement)* to dawdle (along); *(vagabonder, agir lentement)* to hang about; *(durer)* to drag on; **se ~** *vi* to drag o.s. along; **~ les pieds** to drag one's feet

**train-train** [trɛ̃trɛ̃] *nm* humdrum routine

**traire** [trɛr] *vt* to milk

**trait** [trɛ] *nm (ligne)* line; *(de dessin)* stroke; *(caractéristique)* feature, trait; **~s** *nmpl (du visage)* features; **d'un ~** *(boire)* in one gulp; **de ~** *(animal)* draught; **avoir ~ à** to concern; **~ d'union** hyphen

**traitant, e** [trɛtɑ̃, ɑ̃t] *adj (shampooing)* medicated; **votre médecin ~** your usual *ou* family doctor

**traite** [trɛt] *nf (comm)* draft; *(agr)* milking; **d'une ~** without stopping; **la ~ des noirs** the slave trade

**traité** [trɛte] *nm* treaty

**traitement** [trɛtmɑ̃] *nm* treatment; *(salaire)* salary; **~ de données** data processing; **~ de texte** word processing; *(logiciel)* word processing package

**traiter** [trete] *vt* to treat; *(qualifier)*: **~**

**qn d'idiot** to call sb a fool ♦ vi to deal; **~ de** to deal with

**traiteur** [tʀɛtœʀ] nm caterer

**traître, -esse** [tʀɛtʀ, tʀɛtʀɛs] adj (dangereux) treacherous ♦ nm traitor

**trajectoire** [tʀaʒɛktwaʀ] nf path

**trajet** [tʀaʒɛ] nm (parcours, voyage) journey; (itinéraire) route; (distance à parcourir) distance

**trame** [tʀam] nf (de tissu) weft; (fig) framework; **usé jusqu'à la ~** threadbare

**tramer** [tʀame] vt: **il se trame quelque chose** there's something brewing

**trampoline** [tʀɑ̃pɔlin] nm trampoline

**tramway** [tʀamwɛ] nm tram(way); (voiture) tram(car) (BRIT), streetcar (US)

**tranchant, e** [tʀɑ̃ʃɑ̃, ɑ̃t] adj sharp; (fig) peremptory ♦ nm (d'un couteau) cutting edge; (de la main) edge; **à double ~** double-edged

**tranche** [tʀɑ̃ʃ] nf (morceau) slice; (arête) edge; **~ d'âge/de salaires** age/wage bracket

**tranché, e** [tʀɑ̃ʃe] adj (couleurs) distinct; (opinions) clear-cut; **tranchée** nf trench

**trancher** [tʀɑ̃ʃe] vt to cut, sever ♦ vi to take a decision; **~ avec** to contrast sharply with

**tranquille** [tʀɑ̃kil] adj quiet; (rassuré) easy in one's mind, with one's mind at rest; **se tenir ~** (enfant) to be quiet; **laisse-moi/laisse-ça ~** leave me/it alone; **avoir la conscience ~** to have a clear conscience; **tranquillisant** nm tranquillizer; **tranquillité** nf peace (and quiet); (d'esprit) peace of mind

**transat** [tʀɑ̃zat] nm deckchair

**transborder** [tʀɑ̃sbɔʀde] vt to tran(s)ship

**transcription** [tʀɑ̃skʀipsjɔ̃] nf transcription; (copie) transcript

**transférer** [tʀɑ̃sfeʀe] vt to transfer; **transfert** nm transfer

**transformation** [tʀɑ̃sfɔʀmasjɔ̃] nf change; transformation; alteration;

(RUGBY) conversion

**transformer** [tʀɑ̃sfɔʀme] vt to change; (radicalement) to transform; (vêtement) to alter; (matière première, appartement, RUGBY) to convert; (se) **~ en** to turn into

**transfusion** [tʀɑ̃sfyzjɔ̃] nf: **~ sanguine** blood transfusion

**transgresser** [tʀɑ̃sɡʀese] vt to contravene

**transi, e** [tʀɑ̃zi] adj numb (with cold), chilled to the bone

**transiger** [tʀɑ̃ziʒe] vi to compromise

**transit** [tʀɑ̃zit] nm transit; **transiter** vi to pass in transit

**transitif, -ive** [tʀɑ̃zitif, iv] adj transitive

**transition** [tʀɑ̃zisjɔ̃] nf transition; **transitoire** adj transitional

**translucide** [tʀɑ̃slysid] adj translucent

**transmettre** [tʀɑ̃smɛtʀ] vt (passer): **~ qch à qn** to pass sth on to sb; (TECH, TÉL, MÉD) to transmit; (TV, RADIO: retransmettre) to broadcast; **transmission** nf transmission

**transparent, e** [tʀɑ̃spaʀɑ̃, ɑ̃t] adj transparent

**transpercer** [tʀɑ̃spɛʀse] vt (froid, pluie) to go through, pierce; (balle) to go through

**transpiration** [tʀɑ̃spiʀasjɔ̃] nf perspiration

**transpirer** [tʀɑ̃spiʀe] vi to perspire

**transplanter** [tʀɑ̃splɑ̃te] vt (MÉD, BOT) to transplant; **transplantation** nf (MÉD) transplant

**transport** [tʀɑ̃spɔʀ] nm transport; **~s en commun** public transport sg; **transporter** vt to carry, move; (COMM) to transport, convey; **transporteur** nm haulage contractor (BRIT), trucker (US)

**transvaser** [tʀɑ̃svaze] vt to decant

**transversal, e, -aux** [tʀɑ̃svɛʀsal, o] adj (rue) which runs across; **coupe ~e** cross section

**trapèze** [tʀapɛz] nm (au cirque) trapeze

**trappe** [tʀap] nf trap door

**trapu, e** [trapy] adj squat, stocky

**traquenard** [traknar] nm trap

**traquer** [trake] vt to track down; (harceler) to hound

**traumatiser** [tromatize] vt to traumatize

**travail, -aux** [travaj] nm (gén) work; (tâche, métier) work no pl, job; (ÉCON, MÉD) labour; **être sans ~** (employé) to be unemployed; voir aussi **travaux; ~ (au) noir** moonlighting

**travailler** [travaje] vi to work; (bois) to warp ♦ vt (bois, métal) to work; (objet d'art, discipline) to work on; **cela le travaille** it is on his mind; **travailleur, -euse** adj hard-working ♦ nm/f worker; **travailliste** adj ≈ Labour cpd

**travaux** [travo] nmpl (de réparation, agricoles etc) work sg; (sur route) roadworks pl; (de construction) building (work); **travaux des champs** farmwork sg; **travaux dirigés** (SCOL) tutorial; **travaux forcés** hard labour sg; **travaux manuels** (SCOL) handicrafts; **travaux ménagers** housework sg; **travaux pratiques** (SCOL) practical work; (en laboratoire) lab work

**travers** [traver] nm fault, failing; **en ~ (de)** across; **au ~ (de)/à ~** through; **de ~** (nez, bouche) crooked; (chapeau) askew; **comprendre de ~** to misunderstand; **regarder de ~** (fig) to look askance at

**traverse** [travers] nf (de voie ferrée) sleeper; **chemin de ~** shortcut

**traversée** [traverse] nf crossing

**traverser** [traverse] vt (gén) to cross; (ville, tunnel, aussi: percer, fig) to go through; (suj: ligne, trait) to run across

**traversin** [travers] nm bolster

**travesti** [travesti] nm transvestite

**trébucher** [trebyfe] vi: **~ (sur)** to stumble (over), trip (against)

**trèfle** [trefl] nm (BOT) clover; (CARTES: couleur) clubs pl; (: carte) club

**treille** [trej] nf vine arbour

**treillis** [treji] nm (métallique) wire-

mesh; (MIL: tenue) combat uniform; (pantalon) combat trousers pl

**treize** [trez] num thirteen; **treizième** num thirteenth

---

**treizième mois**

Le **treizième mois** is an end-of-year bonus roughly equal to one month's salary. For many employees it is a standard part of their salary package.

---

**tréma** [trema] nm diaeresis

**tremblement** [trãblǝmã] nm: **~ de terre** earthquake

**trembler** [trãble] vi to tremble, shake; **~ de** (froid, fièvre) to shiver ou tremble with; (peur) to shake ou tremble with; **~ pour qn** to fear for sb

**trémousser** [tremuse]: **se ~** vi to jig about, wriggle about

**trempe** [trãp] nf (fig): **de cette/sa ~** of this/his calibre

**trempé, e** [trãpe] adj soaking (wet), drenched; (TECH) tempered

**tremper** [trãpe] vt to soak, drench; (aussi: **faire ~, mettre à ~**) to soak; (plonger): **~ qch dans** to dip sth in(to) ♦ vi to soak; (fig): **~ dans** to be involved ou have a hand in; **se ~** vi to have a quick dip; **trempette** nf: **faire ~** to go paddling

**tremplin** [trãplɛ̃] nm springboard; (SKI) ski-jump

**trentaine** [trãten] nf: **une ~ (de)** thirty or so, about thirty; **avoir la ~** (âge) to be around thirty

**trente** [trãt] num thirty; **être sur son ~ et un** to be wearing one's Sunday best; **trentième** num thirtieth

**trépidant, e** [trepidã, ãt] adj (fig: rythme) pulsating; (: vie) hectic

**trépied** [trepje] nm tripod

**trépigner** [trepiɲe] vi to stamp (one's feet)

**très** [tre] adv very; much +pp, highly +pp

**trésor** [trezɔr] nm treasure; **T~** (public) public revenue; **trésorerie** nf (gestion) accounts pl; (bureaux) accounts department; **difficultés de trésorerie** cash problems, shortage of cash ou funds; **trésorier, -ière** nm/f treasurer

**tressaillir** [tʀesajiʀ] vi to shiver, shudder

**tressauter** [tʀesote] vi to start, jump

**tresse** [tʀɛs] nf braid, plait; **tresser** vt (cheveux) to braid, plait; (fil, jonc) to plait; (corbeille) to weave; (corde) to twist

**tréteau, x** [tʀeto] nm trestle

**treuil** [tʀœj] nm winch

**trêve** [tʀɛv] nf (MIL, POL) truce; (fig) respite; ~ **de ...** enough of this ...

**tri** [tʀi] nm: **faire le ~** (de) to sort out; **le (bureau de) ~** (POSTES) the sorting office

**triangle** [tʀijɑ̃gl] nm triangle; **triangulaire** adj triangular

**tribord** [tʀibɔʀ] nm: **à ~** to starboard, on the starboard side

**tribu** [tʀiby] nf tribe

**tribunal, -aux** [tʀibynal, o] nm (JUR) court; (MIL) tribunal

**tribune** [tʀibyn] nf (estrade) platform, rostrum; (débat) forum; (d'église, de tribunal) gallery; (de stade) stand

**tribut** [tʀiby] nm tribute

**tributaire** [tʀibytɛʀ] adj: **être ~ de** to be dependent on

**tricher** [tʀiʃe] vi to cheat; **tricheur, -euse** nm/f cheat(er)

**tricolore** [tʀikɔlɔʀ] adj three-coloured; (français) red, white and blue

**tricot** [tʀiko] nm (technique, ouvrage) knitting no pl; (vêtement) jersey, sweater; ~ **de peau** vest; **tricoter** vt to knit

**trictrac** [tʀiktʀak] nm backgammon

**tricycle** [tʀisikl] nm tricycle

**triennal, e, -aux** [tʀijenal, o] adj three-year

**trier** [tʀije] vt to sort out; (POSTES, fruits) to sort

**trimestre** [tʀimɛstʀ] nm (SCOL) term;

(COMM) quarter; **trimestriel, le** adj quarterly; (SCOL) end-of-term

**tringle** [tʀɛ̃gl] nf rod

**trinquer** [tʀɛ̃ke] vi to clink glasses

**triomphe** [tʀijɔ̃f] nm triumph; **triompher** vi to triumph, win; **triompher de** to triumph over, overcome

**tripes** [tʀip] nfpl (CULIN) tripe sg

**triple** [tʀipl] adj triple ♦ nm: **le ~ (de)** (comparaison) three times as much (as); **en ~ exemplaire** in triplicate; **tripler** vi, vt to triple, treble

**triplés, -ées** [tʀiple] nm/fpl triplets

**tripoter** [tʀipɔte] vt to fiddle with

**triste** [tʀist] adj sad; (couleur, temps, journée) dreary; (péj): ~ **personnage/affaire** sorry individual/affair; **tristesse** nf sadness

**trivial, e, -aux** [tʀivjal, jo] adj coarse, crude; (commun) mundane

**troc** [tʀɔk] nm barter

**troène** [tʀɔɛn] nm privet

**trognon** [tʀɔɲɔ̃] nm (de fruit) core; (de légume) stalk

**trois** [tʀwa] num three; **troisième** num third; **trois quarts** nmpl: **les trois quarts de** three-quarters of

**trombe** [tʀɔ̃b] nf: **des ~s d'eau** a downpour; **en ~** like a whirlwind

**trombone** [tʀɔ̃bɔn] nm (MUS) trombone; (de bureau) paper clip

**trompe** [tʀɔ̃p] nf (d'éléphant) trunk; (MUS) trumpet, horn

**tromper** [tʀɔ̃pe] vt to deceive; (vigilance, poursuivants) to elude; **se ~** vi to make a mistake, be mistaken; **se ~ de voiture/jour** to take the wrong car/the day wrong; **se ~ de 3 cm/20 F** to be out by 3 cm/20 F; **tromperie** nf deception, trickery no pl

**trompette** [tʀɔ̃pɛt] nf trumpet; **en ~** (nez) turned-up

**trompeur, -euse** [tʀɔ̃pœʀ, øz] adj deceptive

**tronc** [tʀɔ̃] nm (BOT, ANAT) trunk; (d'église) collection box

**tronçon** [tʀɔ̃sɔ̃] nm section; **tron-**

**çonner** vt to saw up

**trône** [tʀon] nm throne

**trop** [tʀo] adv (+vb) too much; (+adjectif, adverbe) too; ~ **(nombreux)** too many; ~ **peu (nombreux)** too few; ~ **(souvent)** too often; ~ **(longtemps)** (for) too long; ~ **de** (nombre) too many; (quantité) too much; **de** ~, **en** ~: **des livres en** ~ a few books too many; **du lait en** ~ too much milk; **3 livres/3 F de** ~ 3 books too many/3 F too much

**tropical, e, -aux** [tʀɔpikal, o] adj tropical

**tropique** [tʀɔpik] nm tropic

**trop-plein** [tʀoplɛ̃] nm (tuyau) overflow ou outlet (pipe); (liquide) overflow

**troquer** [tʀɔke] vt: ~ **qch contre** to barter ou trade sth for; (fig) to swap sth for

**trot** [tʀo] nm trot; **trotter** vi to trot

**trotteuse** [tʀɔtøz] nf (sweep) second hand

**trottinette** [tʀɔtinɛt] nf (child's) scooter

**trottoir** [tʀɔtwaʀ] nm pavement; **faire le** ~ (péj) to walk the streets; ~ **roulant** moving walkway, travellator

**trou** [tʀu] nm hole; (fig) gap; (COMM) deficit; ~ **d'air** air pocket; ~ **d'ozone** ozone hole; **le** ~ **de la serrure** the keyhole; ~ **de mémoire** blank, lapse of memory

**troublant, e** [tʀublɑ̃, ɑ̃t] adj disturbing

**trouble** [tʀubl] adj (liquide) cloudy; (image, photo) blurred; (affaire) shady, murky ♦ nm agitation; ~**s** nmpl (POL) disturbances, troubles, unrest sg; (MÉD) trouble sg, disorders; **trouble-fête** nm spoilsport

**troubler** [tʀuble] vt to disturb; (liquide) to make cloudy; (intriguer) to bother; **se** ~ vi (personne) to become flustered ou confused

**trouer** [tʀue] vt to make a hole (ou holes) in

**trouille** [tʀuj] (fam) nf: **avoir la** ~ to

be scared to death

**troupe** [tʀup] nf troop; ~ **(de théâtre)** (theatrical) company

**troupeau, x** [tʀupo] nm (de moutons) flock; (de vaches) herd

**trousse** [tʀus] nf case, kit; (d'écolier) pencil case; **aux** ~**s de** (fig) on the heels ou tail of; ~ **à outils** toolkit; ~ **de toilette** toilet bag

**trousseau, x** [tʀuso] nm (de mariée) trousseau; ~ **de clefs** bunch of keys

**trouvaille** [tʀuvaj] nf find

**trouver** [tʀuve] vt to find; (rendre visite): **aller/venir** ~ **qn** to go/come and see sb; **se** ~ vi (être) to be; **je trouve que** I find ou think that; ~ **à boire/critiquer** to find something to drink/criticize; **se** ~ **bien** to feel well; **se** ~ **mal** to pass out

**truand** [tʀyɑ̃] nm gangster; **truander** vt: **se faire truander** to be swindled

**truc** [tʀyk] nm (astuce) way, trick; (de cinéma, prestidigitateur) trick, effect; (chose) thing, thingumajig; **avoir le** ~ to have the knack

**truelle** [tʀyɛl] nf trowel

**truffe** [tʀyf] nf truffle; (nez) nose

**truffé, e** [tʀyfe] adj: ~ **de** (fig) peppered with; (fautes) riddled with; (pièges) bristling with

**truie** [tʀɥi] nf sow

**truite** [tʀɥit] nf trout inv

**truquage** [tʀykaʒ] nm special effects

**truquer** [tʀyke] vt (élections, serrure, dés) to fix

**TSVP** sigle (= tournez svp) PTO

**TTC** sigle (= toutes taxes comprises) inclusive of tax

**tu¹** [ty] pron you

**tu², e** [ty] pp de **taire**

**tuba** [tyba] nm (MUS) tuba; (SPORT) snorkel

**tube** [tyb] nm tube; (chanson) hit

**tuberculose** [tybɛʀkyloz] nf tuberculosis

**tuer** [tɥe] vt to kill; **se** ~ vi to be killed;

(suicide) to kill o.s.; **tuerie** nf slaughter no pl

**tue-tête** [tytɛt]: **à ~~** adv at the top of one's voice

**tueur** [tɥœʀ] nm killer; **~ à gages** hired killer

**tuile** [tɥil] nf tile; (fam) spot of bad luck, blow

**tulipe** [tylip] nf tulip

**tuméfié, e** [tymefje] adj puffed-up, swollen

**tumeur** [tymœʀ] nf growth, tumour

**tumulte** [tymylt] nm commotion; **tumultueux, -euse** [tymyltɥø, øz] adj stormy, turbulent

**tunique** [tynik] nf tunic

**Tunisie** [tynizi] nf: **la ~** Tunisia; **tunisien, ne** adj Tunisian ♦ nm/f: **Tunisien, ne** Tunisian

**tunnel** [tynɛl] nm tunnel; **le ~ sous la Manche** the Channel Tunnel

**turbulences** [tyʀbylɑ̃s] nfpl (AVIAT) turbulence sg

**turbulent, e** [tyʀbylɑ̃, ɑ̃t] adj boisterous, unruly

**turc, turque** [tyʀk] adj Turkish ♦ nm/f: **T~, -que** Turk/Turkish woman ♦ nm (LING) Turkish

**turf** [tyʀf] nm racing; **turfiste** nm/f racegoer

**Turquie** [tyʀki] nf: **la ~** Turkey

**turquoise** [tyʀkwaz] nf turquoise ♦ adj inv turquoise

**tus** etc [ty] vb voir **taire**

**tutelle** [tytɛl] nf (JUR) guardianship; (POL) trusteeship; **sous la ~ de** (fig) under the supervision of

**tuteur** [tytœʀ] nm (JUR) guardian; (de plante) stake, support

**tutoyer** [tytwaje] vt: **~ qn** to address sb as "tu"

**tuyau, x** [tɥijo] nm pipe; (flexible) tube; (fam) tip; **~ d'arrosage** hosepipe; **~ d'échappement** exhaust pipe; **tuyauterie** nf piping no pl

**TVA** sigle f (= taxe à la valeur ajoutée) VAT

**tympan** [tɛ̃pɑ̃] nm (ANAT) eardrum

**type** [tip] nm type; (fam) chap, guy ♦ adj typical, classic

**typé, e** [tipe] adj ethnic

**typique** [tipik] adj typical

**tyran** [tirɑ̃] nm tyrant; **tyrannique** adj tyrannical

**tzigane** [dzigan] adj gipsy, tzigane

# U, u

**UEM** sigle f (= union économique et monétaire) EMU

**ulcère** [ylsɛʀ] nm ulcer; **ulcérer** vt (fig) to sicken, appal

**ultérieur, e** [ylteʀjœʀ] adj later, subsequent; **remis à une date ~e** postponed to a later date; **ultérieurement** adv later, subsequently

**ultime** [yltim] adj final

**ultra...** [yltʀa] préfixe: **~moderne/ ~rapide** ultra-modern/-fast

MOT-CLÉ

**un, une** [œ̃, yn] art indéf a; (devant voyelle) an; **un garçon/vieillard** a boy/an old man; **une fille** a girl
♦ pron one; **l'un des meilleurs** one of the best; **l'un ..., l'autre** (the) one ..., the other; **les uns ..., les autres** some ..., others; **l'un et l'autre** both (of them); **l'un ou l'autre** either (of them); **l'un l'autre, les uns les autres** each other, one another; **pas un seul** not a single one; **un par un** one by one
♦ num one; **une pomme seulement** one apple only

**unanime** [ynanim] adj unanimous; **unanimité** nf: **à l'unanimité** unanimously

**uni, e** [yni] adj (ton, tissu) plain; (surface) smooth, even; (famille) close (-knit); (pays) united

**unifier** [ynifje] vt to unite, unify

**uniforme** [ynifɔʀm] *adj* uniform; (*surface, ton*) even ♦ *nm* uniform; **uniformiser** *vt* (*systèmes*) to standardize

**union** [ynjɔ̃] *nf* union; **~ de consommateurs** consumers' association; **~ européenne** European Union; **U~ soviétique** Soviet Union

**unique** [ynik] *adj* (*seul*) only; (*exceptionnel*) unique; (*le même*): **un prix/système ~** a single price/system; **fils/fille ~** only son/daughter, only child; **sens ~** one-way street; **uniquement** *adv* only, solely; (*juste*) only, merely

**unir** [yniʀ] *vt* (*nations*) to unite; (*en mariage*) to unite, join together; **s'~** *vi* to unite; (*en mariage*) to be joined together

**unitaire** [yniteʀ] *adj*: **prix ~** unit price

**unité** [ynite] *nf* unit; (*harmonie, cohésion*) unity

**univers** [yniveʀ] *nm* universe; **universel, le** *adj* universal

**universitaire** [yniveʀsiteʀ] *adj* university *cpd*; (*diplôme, études*) academic, university *cpd* ♦ *nm/f* academic

**université** [yniveʀsite] *nf* university

**urbain, e** [yʀbɛ̃, ɛn] *adj* urban, city *cpd*, town *cpd*; **urbanisme** *nm* town planning

**urgence** [yʀʒɑ̃s] *nf* urgency; (*MÉD etc*) emergency; **d'~** *adj* emergency *cpd* ♦ *adv* as a matter of urgency; (*service des*) **~s** casualty

**urgent, e** [yʀʒɑ̃, ɑ̃t] *adj* urgent

**urine** [yʀin] *nf* urine; **urinoir** *nm* (public) urinal

**urne** [yʀn] *nf* (*électorale*) ballot box; (*vase*) urn

**urticaire** [yʀtikɛʀ] *nf* nettle rash

**us** [ys] *nmpl*: **~ et coutumes** (habits and) customs

**USA** *sigle mpl*: **les USA** the USA

**usage** [yzaʒ] *nm* (*emploi, utilisation*) use; (*coutume*) custom; **à l'~** with use; **à l'~ de** (*pour*) for (use of); **hors d'~** out of service; **à ~ interne** (*MÉD*) to be taken; **à ~ externe** (*MÉD*) for external

use only; **usagé, e** *adj* (*usé*) worn; **usager, -ère** *nm/f* user

**usé, e** [yze] *adj* worn; (*banal: argument etc*) hackneyed

**user** [yze] *vt* (*outil*) to wear down; (*vêtement*) to wear out; (*matière*) to wear away; (*consommer: charbon etc*) to use; **s'~** *vi* (*tissu, vêtement*) to wear out; **~ de** (*moyen, procédé*) to use, employ; (*droit*) to exercise

**usine** [yzin] *nf* factory

**usité, e** [yzite] *adj* common

**ustensile** [ystɑ̃sil] *nm* implement; **~ de cuisine** kitchen utensil

**usuel, le** [yzɥɛl] *adj* everyday, common

**usure** [yzyʀ] *nf* wear

**utérus** [yteʀys] *nm* uterus, womb

**utile** [ytil] *adj* useful

**utilisation** [ytilizasjɔ̃] *nf* use

**utiliser** [ytilize] *vt* to use

**utilitaire** [ytilitɛʀ] *adj* utilitarian

**utilité** [ytilite] *nf* usefulness *no pl*; **de peu d'~** of little use *ou* help

**utopie** [ytɔpi] *nf* utopia

---

## V, v

**va** [va] *vb voir* **aller**

**vacance** [vakɑ̃s] *nf* (*ADMIN*) vacancy; **~s** *nfpl* holiday(s *pl*), vacation *sg*; **les grandes ~s** the summer holidays; **prendre des/ses ~s** to take a holiday/one's holiday(s); **aller en ~s** to go on holiday; **vacancier, -ière** *nm/f* holiday-maker

**vacant, e** [vakɑ̃, ɑ̃t] *adj* vacant

**vacarme** [vakaʀm] *nm* (*bruit*) racket

**vaccin** [vaksɛ̃] *nm* vaccine; (*opération*) vaccination; **vaccination** *nf* vaccination; **vacciner** *vt* to vaccinate; **être vacciné contre qch** (*fam*) to be cured of sth

**vache** [vaʃ] *nf* (*ZOOL*) cow; (*cuir*) cowhide ♦ *adj* (*fam*) rotten, mean; **vachement** (*fam*) *adv* (*très*) really; (*pleuvoir, travailler*) a hell of a lot, a lot; **vacherie** *nf* (*action*) dirty trick; (*remarque*) nasty remark

**vaciller** [vasije] vi to sway, wobble; (bougie, lumière) to flicker; (fig) to be failing, falter

**va-et-vient** [vaevjɛ̃] nm inv (de personnes, véhicules) comings and goings pl, to-ings and fro-ings pl

**vagabond** [vagabɔ̃] nm (rôdeur) tramp, vagrant; (voyageur) wanderer; **vagabonder** vi to roam, wander

**vagin** [vaʒɛ̃] nm vagina

**vague** [vag] nf wave ♦ adj vague; (regard) faraway; (manteau, robe) loose (-fitting); (quelconque): **un ~ bureau/cousin** some office/cousin or other; **~ de fond** ground swell; **~ de froid** cold spell

**vaillant, e** [vajɑ̃, ɑ̃t] adj (courageux) gallant; (robuste) hale and hearty

**vaille** [vaj] vb voir **valoir**

**vain, e** [vɛ̃, vɛn] adj vain; **en ~** in vain

**vaincre** [vɛ̃kʀ] vt to defeat; (fig) to conquer, overcome; **vaincu, e** nm/f defeated party; **vainqueur** nm victor; (SPORT) winner

**vais** [vɛ] vb voir **aller**

**vaisseau, x** [vɛso] nm (ANAT) vessel; (NAVIG) ship, vessel; **~ spatial** spaceship

**vaisselier** [vɛsəlje] nm dresser

**vaisselle** [vɛsɛl] nf (service) crockery; (plats etc à laver) (dirty) dishes pl; **faire la ~** to do the washing-up (BRIT) or the dishes

**val** [val, vo] (pl **vaux** ou **~s**) nm valley

**valable** [valabl] adj valid; (acceptable) decent, worthwhile

**valent** etc [val] vb voir **valoir**

**valet** [valɛ] nm manservant; (CARTES) jack

**valeur** [valœʀ] nf (gén) value; (mérite) worth, merit; (COMM: titre) security; **mettre en ~** (détail) to highlight; (objet décoratif) to show off to advantage; **avoir de la ~** to be valuable; **sans ~** worthless; **prendre de la ~** to go up ou gain in value

**valide** [valid] adj (en bonne santé) fit;

(valable) valid; **valider** vt to validate

**valions** [valjɔ̃] vb voir **valoir**

**valise** [valiz] nf (suit)case; **faire ses ~s** to pack one's bags

**vallée** [vale] nf valley

**vallon** [valɔ̃] nm small valley; **vallonné, e** adj hilly

**valoir** [valwaʀ] vi (être valable) to hold, apply ♦ vt (prix, valeur, effort) to be worth; (causer): **~ qch à qn** to earn sb sth; **♦ ~** vi to be of equal merit; (pé) to be two of a kind; **faire ~** (droits, prérogatives) to assert; **faire ~ que** to point out that; **à ~ sur** to be deducted from; **vaille que vaille** somehow or other; **cela ne me dit rien qui vaille** I don't like the look of it at all; **ce climat ne me vaut rien** this climate doesn't suit me; **~ le coup** ou **la peine** to be worth the trouble ou worth it; **~ mieux: il vaut mieux se taire** it's better to say nothing; **ça ne vaut rien** it's worthless; **que vaut ce candidat?** how good is this applicant?

**valse** [vals] nf waltz

**valu, e** [valy] pp de **valoir**

**vandalisme** [vɑ̃dalism] nm vandalism

**vanille** [vanij] nf vanilla

**vanité** [vanite] nf vanity; **vaniteux, -euse** adj vain, conceited

**vanne** [van] nf gate; (fig) joke

**vannerie** [vanʀi] nf basketwork

**vantard, e** [vɑ̃taʀ, aʀd] adj boastful

**vanter** [vɑ̃te] vt to speak highly of, praise; **se ~** vi to boast, brag; **se ~ de** to pride o.s. on; (pé) to boast of

**vapeur** [vapœʀ] nf steam; (émanation) vapour, fumes pl; **~s** nfpl (bouffées) vapours; **à ~** steam-powered, steam cpd; **cuit à la ~** steamed; **vaporeux, -euse** adj (flou) hazy, misty; (léger) filmy; **vaporisateur** nm spray; **vaporiser** vt (parfum etc) to spray

**varappe** [vaʀap] nf rock climbing

**vareuse** [vaʀøz] nf (blouson) pea jacket; (d'uniforme) tunic

**variable** [vaʀjabl] adj variable; (temps,

*humeur*) changeable; (*divers: résultats*) varied, various

**varice** [vaʀis] *nf* varicose vein

**varicelle** [vaʀisɛl] *nf* chickenpox

**varié, e** [vaʀje] *adj* varied; (*divers*) various

**varier** [vaʀje] *vi* to vary; (*temps, humeur*) to change ♦ *vt* to vary; **variété** *nf* variety; **variétés** *nfpl*: **spectacle/émission de variétés** variety show

**variole** [vaʀjɔl] *nf* smallpox

**vas** [va] *vb voir* **aller**

**vase** [vaz] *nm* vase ♦ *nf* silt, mud; **vaseux, -euse** *adj* silty, muddy; (*fig: confus*) woolly, hazy; (: *fatigué*) woozy

**vasistas** [vazistas] *nm* fanlight

**vaste** [vast] *adj* vast, immense

**vaudrai** *etc* [vodʀe] *vb voir* **valoir**

**vaurien, ne** [voʀjɛ̃, jɛn] *nm/f* good-for-nothing

**vaut** [vo] *vb voir* **valoir**

**vautour** [votuʀ] *nm* vulture

**vautrer** [votʀe] *vb*: **se ~ dans/sur** to wallow in/sprawl on

**vaux** [vo] *nmpl de* **val** ♦ *vb voir* **valoir**

**va-vite** [vavit]: **à la ~~** *adv* in a rush ou hurry

**veau, x** [vo] *nm* (*ZOOL*) calf; (*CULIN*) veal; (*peau*) calfskin

**vécu, e** [veky] *pp de* **vivre**

**vedette** [vədɛt] *nf* (*artiste etc*) star; (*canot*) motor boat; (*police*) launch

**végétal, e, -aux** [veʒetal, o] *adj* vegetable ♦ *nm* vegetable, plant; **végétalien, ne** *adj, nm/f* vegan

**végétarien, ne** [veʒetaʀjɛ̃, jɛn] *adj, nm/f* vegetarian

**végétation** [veʒetasjɔ̃] *nf* vegetation; **~s** *nfpl* (*MÉD*) adenoids

**véhicule** [veikyl] *nm* vehicle; **~ utilitaire** commercial vehicle

**veille** [vɛj] *nf* (*état*) wakefulness; (*jour*): **la ~ (de)** the day before; **la ~ au soir** the previous evening; **à la ~ de** on the eve of; **la ~ de Noël** Christmas Eve; **la ~ du jour de l'An** New Year's Eve

**veillée** [veje] *nf* (*soirée*) evening; (*réunion*) evening gathering; **~ (funèbre)** wake

**veiller** [veje] *vi* to stay up ♦ *vt* (*malade, mort*) to watch over, sit up with; **~ à** to attend to, see to; **~ à ce que** to make sure that; **~ sur** to watch over; **veilleur** *nm*: **veilleur de nuit** night watchman; **veilleuse** *nf* (*lampe*) night light; (*AUTO*) sidelight; (*flamme*) pilot light

**veinard, e** [vɛnaʀ, aʀd] *nm/f* lucky devil

**veine** [vɛn] *nf* (*ANAT, du bois etc*) vein; (*filon*) vein, seam; (*fam: chance*): **avoir de la ~** to be lucky

**véliplanchiste** [veliplɑ̃ʃist] *nm/f* windsurfer

**vélo** [velo] *nm* bike, cycle; **faire du ~** to go cycling; **~ tout-terrain** mountain bike; **vélomoteur** *nm* moped

**velours** [v(ə)luʀ] *nm* velvet; **~ côtelé** corduroy; **velouté, e** *adj* velvety ♦ *nm*: **velouté de tomates** cream of tomato soup

**velu, e** [vəly] *adj* hairy

**venais** *etc* [vənɛ] *vb voir* **venir**

**venaison** [vənɛzɔ̃] *nf* venison

**vendange** [vɑ̃dɑ̃ʒ] *nf* (*aussi: ~s*) grape harvest; **vendanger** *vi* to harvest the grapes

**vendeur, -euse** [vɑ̃dœʀ, øz] *nm/f* shop assistant ♦ *nm* (*JUR*) vendor, seller; **~ de journaux** newspaper seller

**vendre** [vɑ̃dʀ] *vt* to sell; **~ qch à qn** to sell sb sth; **"à ~"** "for sale"

**vendredi** [vɑ̃dʀədi] *nm* Friday; **V~ saint** Good Friday

**vénéneux, -euse** [venenø, øz] adj poisonous

**vénérien, ne** [venerjɛ̃, jɛn] adj venereal

**vengeance** [vɑ̃ʒɑ̃s] nf vengeance no pl, revenge no pl

**venger** [vɑ̃ʒe] vt to avenge; **se ~** vi to avenge o.s.; **se ~ de qch** to avenge o.s. for sth, take one's revenge for sth; **se ~ de qn** to take revenge on sb; **se ~ sur** to take revenge on

**venimeux, -euse** [vanimø, øz] adj poisonous, venomous; (fig: haineux) venomous, vicious

**venin** [vanɛ̃] nm venom, poison

**venir** [v(ə)niʀ] vi to come; **~ de** to come from; **~ de faire: je viens d'y aller/de le voir** I've just been there/seen him; **s'il vient à pleuvoir** if it should rain; **j'en viens à croire que** I have come to believe that; **faire ~** (docteur, plombier) to call (out)

**vent** [vɑ̃] nm wind; **il y a du ~** it's windy; **c'est du ~** it's all hot air; **au ~** to windward; **sous le ~** to leeward; **avoir le ~ debout/arrière** to head into the wind/have the wind astern; **dans le ~** (fam) trendy

**vente** [vɑ̃t] nf sale; **la ~** (activité) selling; (secteur) sales pl; **mettre en ~** (produit) to put on sale; (maison, objet personnel) to put up for sale; **~ aux enchères** auction sale; **~ de charité** jumble sale

**venteux, -euse** [vɑ̃tø, øz] adj windy

**ventilateur** [vɑ̃tilatœʀ] nm fan

**ventiler** [vɑ̃tile] vt to ventilate

**ventouse** [vɑ̃tuz] nf (de caoutchouc) suction pad

**ventre** [vɑ̃tʀ] nm (ANAT) stomach; (légèrement péj) belly; (utérus) womb; **avoir mal au ~** to have stomach ache (BRIT) ou a stomach ache (US)

**ventriloque** [vɑ̃tʀilɔk] nm/f ventriloquist

**venu, e** [v(ə)ny] pp de **venir** ♦ adj: **bien ~** timely; **mal ~** out of place;

**être mal ~ à ou de faire** to have no grounds for doing, be in no position to do

**ver** [vɛʀ] nm worm; (des fruits etc) maggot; (du bois) woodworm no pl; voir aussi **vers**; **~ à soie** silkworm; **~ de terre** earthworm; **~ luisant** glowworm; **~ solitaire** tapeworm

**verbaliser** [vɛʀbalize] vi (POLICE) to book ou report an offender

**verbe** [vɛʀb] nm verb

**verdâtre** [vɛʀdɑtʀ] adj greenish

**verdict** [vɛʀdik(t)] nm verdict

**verdir** [vɛʀdiʀ] vi, vt to turn green;

**verdure** [vɛʀdyʀ] nf greenery

**véreux, -euse** [veʀø, øz] adj wormeaten; (malhonnête) shady, corrupt

**verge** [vɛʀʒ] nf (ANAT) penis

**verger** [vɛʀʒe] nm orchard

**verglacé, e** [vɛʀglase] adj icy, icedover

**verglas** [vɛʀgla] nm (black) ice

**vergogne** [vɛʀgɔɲ]: **sans ~** adv shamelessly

**véridique** [veʀidik] adj truthful

**vérification** [veʀifikasjɔ̃] nf (action) checking no pl; (contrôle) check

**vérifier** [veʀifje] vt to check; (corroborer) to confirm, bear out

**véritable** [veʀitabl] adj real; (ami, amour) true

**vérité** [veʀite] nf truth; **en ~** really, actually

**vermeil, le** [vɛʀmɛj] adj ruby red

**vermine** [vɛʀmin] nf vermin pl

**vermoulu, e** [vɛʀmuly] adj wormeaten

**verni, e** [vɛʀni] adj (fam) lucky; **cuir ~** patent leather

**vernir** [vɛʀniʀ] vt (bois, tableau, ongles) to varnish; (poterie) to glaze

**vernis** [vɛʀni] nm (enduit) varnish; glaze; (fig) veneer; **~ à ongles** nail polish ou varnish; **vernissage** nm (d'une exposition) preview

**vérole** [veʀɔl] nf (variole) smallpox

**verrai** etc [veʀe] vb voir **voir**

**verre** [vɛʀ] nm glass; (de lunettes) lens sg; **boire** ou **prendre un ~** to have a drink; **~ dépoli** frosted glass; **~s de contact** contact lenses; **verrerie** nf (fabrique) glassworks sg; (activité) glassmaking; (objets) glassware; **verrière** nf (paroi vitrée) glass wall; (toit vitré) glass roof

**verrons** etc vb voir **voir**

**verrou** [vɛʀu] nm (targette) bolt; **mettre qn sous les ~s** to put sb behind bars; **verrouillage** nm locking; **verrouillage centralisé** central locking; **verrouiller** vt (porte) to bolt; (ordinateur) to lock

**verrue** [vɛʀy] nf wart

**vers** [vɛʀ] nm line ♦ nmpl (poésie) verse sg ♦ prép (en direction de) toward(s); (près de) around (about); (temporel) about, around

**versant** [vɛʀsɑ̃] nm slopes pl, side

**versatile** [vɛʀsatil] adj fickle, changeable

**verse** [vɛʀs]: **à ~** adv: **il pleut à ~** it's pouring (with rain)

**Verseau** [vɛʀso] nm: **le ~** Aquarius

**versement** [vɛʀsəmɑ̃] nm payment; **en 3 ~s** in 3 instalments

**verser** [vɛʀse] vt (liquide, grains) to pour; (larmes, sang) to shed; (argent) to pay ♦ vi (véhicule) to overturn; (fig): **~ dans** to lapse into

**verset** [vɛʀsɛ] nm verse

**version** [vɛʀsjɔ̃] nf version; (SCOL) translation (into the mother tongue); **film en ~ originale** film in the original language

**verso** [vɛʀso] nm back; **voir au ~** see over(leaf)

**vert, e** [vɛʀ, vɛʀt] adj green; (vin) young; (vigoureux) sprightly ♦ nm green

**vertèbre** [vɛʀtɛbʀ] nf vertebra

**vertement** [vɛʀtəmɑ̃] adv (réprimander) sharply

**vertical, e, -aux** [vɛʀtikal, o] adj vertical; **verticale** nf vertical; **à la verticale** vertically; **verticalement** adv vertically

**vertige** [vɛʀtiʒ] nm (peur du vide) vertigo; (étourdissement) dizzy spell; (fig) fever; **vertigineux, -euse** adj breathtaking

**vertu** [vɛʀty] nf virtue; **en ~ de** in accordance with; **vertueux, -euse** adj virtuous

**verve** [vɛʀv] nf witty eloquence; **être en ~** to be in brilliant form

**verveine** [vɛʀvɛn] nf (BOT) verbena, vervain; (infusion) verbena tea

**vésicule** [vezikyl] nf vesicle; **~ biliaire** gall-bladder

**vessie** [vesi] nf bladder

**veste** [vɛst] nf jacket; **~ droite/croisée** single-/double-breasted jacket

**vestiaire** [vɛstjɛʀ] nm (au théâtre etc) cloakroom; (de stade etc) changing-room (BRIT), locker-room (US)

**vestibule** [vɛstibyl] nm hall

**vestige** [vɛstiʒ] nm relic; (fig) vestige; **~s** nmpl (de ville) remains

**vestimentaire** [vɛstimɑ̃tɛʀ] adj (détail) of dress; (élégance) sartorial; **dépenses ~s** clothing expenditure

**veston** [vɛstɔ̃] nm jacket

**vêtement** [vɛtmɑ̃] nm garment, item of clothing; **~s** nmpl clothes

**vétérinaire** [veteʀinɛʀ] nm/f vet, veterinary surgeon

**vêtir** [vetiʀ] vt to clothe, dress

**veto** [veto] nm veto; **opposer un ~ à** to veto

**vêtu, e** [vety] pp de **vêtir**

**vétuste** [vetyst] adj ancient, timeworn

**veuf, veuve** [vœf, vœv] adj widowed ♦ nm widower

**veuille** [vœj] vb voir **vouloir**

**veuillez** [vœje] vb voir **vouloir**

**veule** [vøl] adj spineless

**veuve** [vœv] nf widow

**veux** [vø] vb voir **vouloir**

**vexant, e** [vɛksɑ̃, ɑ̃t] adj (contrariant) annoying; (blessant) hurtful

**vexation** [vɛksasjɔ̃] nf humiliation

**vexer** [vɛkse] vt: **~ qn** to hurt sb's feelings; **se ~** vi to be offended

**viable** [vjabl] *adj* viable; *(économie, industrie etc)* sustainable

**viaduc** [vjadyk] *nm* viaduct

**viager, -ère** [vjaʒe, ɛʁ] *adj*: **rente viagère** life annuity

**viande** [vjɑ̃d] *nf* meat

**vibrer** [vibʁe] *vi* to vibrate; *(son, voix)* to be vibrant; *(fig)* to be stirred; **faire ~** (*to cause to*) vibrate; *(fig)* to stir, thrill

**vice** [vis] *nm* vice; *(défaut)* fault ♦ *préfixe*: **~... vice-**; **~ de forme** legal flaw *ou* irregularity

**vichy** [viʃi] *nm (toile)* gingham

**vicié, e** [visje] *adj (air)* polluted, tainted; *(JUR)* invalidated

**vicieux, -euse** [visjø, øz] *adj (pervers)* lecherous; *(rétif)* unruly ♦ *nm/f* lecher

**vicinal, e, -aux** [visinal, o] *adj*: **chemin ~** by-road, byway

**victime** [viktim] *nf* victim; *(d'accident)* casualty

**victoire** [viktwaʁ] *nf* victory

**victuailles** [viktɥaj] *nfpl* provisions

**vidange** [vidɑ̃ʒ] *nf (d'un fossé, réservoir)* emptying; *(AUTO)* oil change; *(de la cuba: bonde)* waste outlet; **~s** *nfpl (matières)* sewage *sg*; **vidanger** *vt* to empty

**vide** [vid] *adj* empty ♦ *nm (PHYSIQUE)* vacuum; *(espace)* (empty) space, gap; *(futilité, néant)* void; **avoir peur du ~** to be afraid of heights; **emballé sous ~** vacuum packed; **à ~** *(sans occupants)* empty; *(sans charge)* unladen

**vidéo** [video] *nf* video ♦ *adj*: **cassette ~** video cassette; **jeu ~** video game; **vidéoclip** *nm* music video; **vidéoclub** *nm* video shop

**vide-ordures** [vidɔʁdyʁ] *nm inv* (rubbish) chute

**vidéothèque** [videotɛk] *nf* video library

**vide-poches** [vidpɔʃ] *nm inv* tidy; *(AUTO)* glove compartment

**vider** [vide] *vt* to empty; *(CULIN: volaille, poisson)* to gut, clean out; **se ~** *vi* to empty; **~ les lieux** to quit *ou* vacate the premises; **videur** *nm (de boîte de* nuit) bouncer, doorman

**vie** [vi] *nf* life; **être en ~** to be alive; **sans ~** lifeless; **à ~** for life

**vieil** [vjɛj] *adj m voir* **vieux**; **vieillard** *nm* old man; **les vieillards** old people, the elderly; **vieille** *adj, nf voir* **vieux**; **vieilleries** *nfpl* old things; **vieillesse** *nf* old age; **vieillir** *vi (prendre de l'âge)* to grow old; *(population, vin)* to age; *(doctrine, auteur)* to become dated ♦ *vt* to age; **vieillissement** *nm* growing old; ageing

**Vienne** [vjɛn] *nf* Vienna

**viens** [vjɛ̃] *vb voir* **venir**

**vierge** [vjɛʁʒ] *adj* virgin; *(page)* clean, blank ♦ *nf* virgin; *(signe)*: **la V~** Virgo

**Vietnam, Viet-Nam** [vjetnam] *nm* Vietnam; **vietnamien, ne** *adj* Vietnamese ♦ *nm/f*: **Vietnamien, ne** Vietnamese

**vieux (vieil), vieille** [vjø, vjɛj] *adj* old ♦ *nm/f* old man (woman) ♦ *nmpl* old people; **mon ~/ma vieille** *(fam)* old man/girl; **prendre un coup de ~** to put years on; **vieille fille** spinster; **~ garçon** bachelor; **~ jeu** *adj inv* old-fashioned

**vif, vive** [vif, viv] *adj (animé)* lively; *(alerte, brusque, aigu)* sharp; *(lumière, couleur)* bright; *(air)* crisp; *(vent, émotion)* keen; *(fort: regret, déception)* great, deep; *(vivant)*: **brûlé ~** burnt alive; **de vive voix** personally; **avoir l'esprit ~** to be quick-witted; **piquer qn au ~** to cut sb to the quick; **à ~** *(plaie)* open; **avoir les nerfs à ~** to be on edge

**vigne** [viɲ] *nf (plante)* vine; *(plantation)* vineyard; **vigneron** *nm* wine grower

**vignette** [viɲet] *nf (ADMIN)* ≈ (road) tax disc (*BRIT*), ≈ license plate sticker (*US*); *(de médicament)* price label (*used for reimbursement*)

**vignoble** [viɲɔbl] *nm (plantation)* vineyard; *(vignes d'une région)* vineyards *pl*

**vigoureux, -euse** [viguʁø, øz] *adj* vigorous, robust

**vigueur** [vigœr] nf vigour; **entrer en ~** to come into force; **en ~** current

**vil, e** [vil] adj vile, base

**vilain, e** [vilɛ̃, ɛn] adj (laid) ugly; (affaire, blessure) nasty; (pas sage: enfant) naughty

**villa** [villa] nf (detached) house; **~ en multipropriété** time-share villa

**village** [vilaʒ] nm village; **villageois, e** adj village cpd ♦ nm/f villager

**ville** [vil] nf town; (importante) city; (administration): **la ~** ≈ the Corporation; ≈ the (town) council; **~ d'eaux** spa

**villégiature** [vi(l)leʒjatyʀ] nf holiday; **(lieu de) ~** (holiday) resort

**vin** [vɛ̃] nm wine; **avoir le ~ gai** to get happy after a few drinks; **~ d'honneur** reception (with wine and snacks); **~ de pays** local wine; **~ ordinaire** table wine

**vinaigre** [vinɛgʀ] nm vinegar; **vinaigrette** nf vinaigrette, French dressing

**vindicatif, -ive** [vɛ̃dikatif, iv] adj vindictive

**vineux, -euse** [vinø, øz] adj wine(e)y

**vingt** [vɛ̃] num twenty; **vingtaine** nf: **une vingtaine (de)** about twenty, twenty or so; **vingtième** num twentieth

**vinicole** [vinikɔl] adj wine cpd, wine-growing

**vins** etc [vɛ̃] vb voir **venir**

**vinyle** [vinil] nm vinyl

**viol** [vjɔl] nm (d'une femme) rape; (d'un lieu sacré) violation

**violacé, e** [vjɔlase] adj purplish, mauvish

**violemment** [vjɔlamɑ̃] adv violently

**violence** [vjɔlɑ̃s] nf violence

**violent, e** [vjɔlɑ̃, ɑ̃t] adj violent; (remède) drastic

**violer** [vjɔle] vt (femme) to rape; (sépulture, loi, traité) to violate

**violet, te** [vjɔlɛ, ɛt] adj, nm purple, mauve; **violette** nf (fleur) violet

**violon** [vjɔlɔ̃] nm violin; (fam: prison) lock-up; **~ d'Ingres** hobby; **violoncel-**

**le** [vjɔlɔ̃sɛl] nm cello; **violoniste** nm/f violinist

**vipère** [vipɛʀ] nf viper, adder

**virage** [viʀaʒ] nm (d'un véhicule) turn; (d'une route, piste) bend

**virée** [viʀe] nf trip; (à pied) walk; (longue) walking tour; (dans les cafés) tour

**virement** [viʀmɑ̃] nm (COMM) transfer

**virent** [viʀ] vb voir **voir**

**virer** [viʀe] vt (COMM): **~ qch (sur)** to transfer sth (into); (fam: expulser): **~ qn** to kick sb out ♦ vi to turn; (CHIMIE) to change colour; **~ de bord** to tack

**virevolter** [viʀvɔlte] vi to twirl around

**virgule** [viʀgyl] nf comma; (MATH) point

**viril, e** [viʀil] adj (propre à l'homme) masculine; (énergique, courageux) manly, virile

**virtuel, le** [viʀtɥɛl] adj potential; (théorique) virtual

**virtuose** [viʀtɥoz] nm/f (MUS) virtuoso; (gén) master

**virus** [viʀys] nm virus

**vis¹** [vi] vb voir **voir**; **vivre**

**vis²** [vis] nf screw

**visa** [viza] nm (sceau) stamp; (validation de passeport) visa

**visage** [vizaʒ] nm face

**vis-à-vis** [vizavi] prép: **~-~-~ de qn** to(wards) sb; **en ~-~-~** facing each other

**viscéral, e, -aux** [viseʀal, o] adj (fig) deep-seated, deep-rooted

**visées** [vize] nfpl (intentions) designs

**viser** [vize] vi to aim ♦ vt to aim at; (concerner) to be aimed ou directed at; (apposer un visa sur) to stamp, visa; **~ à qch/faire** to aim at sth/at doing ou to do; **viseur** nm (d'arme) sights pl; (PHOTO) viewfinder

**visibilité** [vizibilite] nf visibility

**visible** [vizibl] adj visible; (disponible): **est-il ~?** can he see me?, will he see visitors?

**visière** [vizjɛʀ] nf (de casquette) peak; (qui s'attache) eyeshade

**vision** [vizjɔ̃] nf vision; (sens) (eye)sight,

**vision**; (*fait de voir*): **la ~ de** the sight of; **visionneuse** *nf* viewer

**visite** [vizit] *nf* visit; **~ médicale** medical examination; **~ accompagnée** *ou* **guidée** guided tour; **faire une ~ à qn** to call on sb, pay sb a visit; **rendre ~ à qn** to visit sb, pay sb a visit; **être en ~ (chez qn)** to be visiting (sb); **avoir de la ~** to have visitors; **heures de ~** (*hôpital, prison*) visiting hours

**visiter** [vizite] *vt* to visit; **visiteur, -euse** *nm/f* visitor

**vison** [vizɔ̃] *nm* mink

**visser** [vise] *vt*: **~ qch** (*fixer, serrer*) to screw sth on

**visuel, le** [vizɥɛl] *adj* visual

**vit** [vi] *vb voir* **voir; vivre**

**vital, e, -aux** [vital, o] *adj* vital

**vitamine** [vitamin] *nf* vitamin

**vite** [vit] *adv* (*rapidement*) quickly, fast; (*sans délai*) quickly; (*sous peu*) soon; **~!** quick!; **faire ~** to be quick; **le temps passe ~** time flies

**vitesse** [vites] *nf* speed; (*AUTO: dispositif*) gear; **prendre de la ~** to pick up *ou* gather speed; **à toute ~** at full *ou* top speed; **en ~** (*rapidement*) quickly; (*en hâte*) in a hurry

**viticole** [vitikɔl] *adj* wine *cpd*, wine-growing; **viticulteur** *nm* wine grower

**vitrage** [vitʀaʒ] *nm*: **double ~** double glazing

**vitrail, -aux** [vitʀaj, o] *nm* stained-glass window

**vitre** [vitʀ] *nf* (*window*) pane; (*de portière, voiture*) window; **vitré, e** *adj* glass *cpd*; **vitrer** *vt* to glaze; **vitreux, -euse** *adj* (*terne*) glassy

**vitrine** [vitʀin] *nf* (*shop*) window; (*petite armoire*) display cabinet; **en ~** in the window; **~ publicitaire** display case, showcase

**vivable** [vivabl] *adj* (*personne*) livable-with; (*maison*) fit to live in

**vivace** [vivas] *adj* (*arbre, plante*) hardy, perennial; (*fig*) indestructible, inveterate

**vivacité** [vivasite] *nf* liveliness, vivacity

**vivant, e** [vivɑ̃, ɑ̃t] *adj* (*qui vit*) living, alive; (*animé*) lively; (*preuve, exemple*) living ♦ *nm*: **du ~ de qn** in sb's lifetime; **les ~s** the living

**vive** [viv] *adj voir* **vif** ♦ *vb voir* **vivre** ♦ *excl*: **~ le roi!** long live the king!; **vivement** *adv* deeply ♦ *excl*: **vivement les vacances!** roll on the holidays!

**vivier** [vivje] *nm* (*étang*) fish tank; (*réservoir*) fishpond

**vivifiant, e** [vivifjɑ̃, jɑ̃t] *adj* invigorating

**vivions** [vivjɔ̃] *vb voir* **vivre**

**vivoter** [vivɔte] *vi* (*personne*) to scrape a living, get by; (*fig: affaire etc*) to struggle along

**vivre** [vivʀ] *vi, vt* to live; (*période*) to live through; **~ de** to live on; **il vit encore** he is still alive; **se laisser ~** to take life as it comes; **ne plus ~** (*être anxieux*) to live on one's nerves; **il a vécu** (*eu une vie aventureuse*) he has seen life; **être facile à ~** to be easy to get on with; **faire ~ qn** (*pourvoir à sa subsistance*) to provide (a living) for sb; **vivres** *nmpl* provisions, food supplies

**vlan** [vlɑ̃] *excl* wham!, bang!

**VO** [veo] *nf*: **film en ~** film in the original version; **en ~ sous-titrée** in the original version with subtitles

**vocable** [vɔkabl] *nm* term

**vocabulaire** [vɔkabylɛʀ] *nm* vocabulary

**vocation** [vɔkasjɔ̃] *nf* vocation, calling

**vociférer** [vɔsifeʀe] *vi, vt* to scream

**vœu, x** [vø] *nm* wish; (*promesse*) vow; **faire ~ de** to take a vow of; **tous nos ~x de bonne année, meilleurs ~x** best wishes for the New Year

**vogue** [vɔg] *nf* fashion, vogue

**voguer** [vɔge] *vi* to sail

**voici** [vwasi] *prép* (*pour introduire, désigner*) here is *+sg*, here are *+pl*; **et ~ que ...** and now it (*ou* he) ...; *voir aussi* **voilà**

**voie** [vwa] *nf* way; (*RAIL*) track, line; (*AUTO*) lane; **être en bonne ~** to be going well; **mettre qn sur la ~** to put sb on the right track; **pays en ~ de développement** developing country; **être en ~ d'achèvement/de rénovation** to be nearing completion/in the process of renovation; **par ~ buccale** *ou* **orale** orally; **à ~ étroite** narrow-gauge; **~ d'eau** (NAVIG) leak; **~ de garage** (RAIL) siding; **~ ferrée** track; railway line; **la ~ publique** the public highway

**voilà** [vwala] *prép* (*en désignant*) there is +*sg*, there are +*pl*; **les ~** *ou* **voici** here *ou* there they are; **en ~ un** here's one, there's one; **voici mon frère et ~ ma sœur** this is my brother and that's my sister; **~** *ou* **voici deux ans** two years ago; **~** *ou* **voici deux ans que** it's two years since; **et ~!** there we are!; **tout** that's all; **~** *ou* **voici** (*en offrant etc*) there *ou* here you are; **tiens! ~ Paul** look! there's Paul

**voile** [vwal] *nm* veil; (*tissu léger*) net ♦ *nf* sail; (*sport*) sailing; **voiler** *vt* to veil; (*fausser: roue*) to buckle; (*: bois*) to warp; **se voiler** *vi* (*lune, regard*) to mist over; (*voix*) to become husky; (*roue, disque*) to buckle; (*planche*) to warp; **voilier** *nm* sailing ship; (*de plaisance*) sailing boat; **voilure** *nf* (*de voilier*) sails *pl*

**voir** [vwar] *vi, vt* to see; **se ~** *vt* (*être visible*) to show; (*se fréquenter*) to see each other; (*se produire*) to happen; **se ~ critiquer/transformer** to be criticized/transformed; **cela se voit** (*c'est visible*) that's obvious, it shows; **faire ~ qch à qn** to show sb sth; **en faire ~ à qn** (*fig*) to give sb a hard time; **ne pas pouvoir ~ qn** not to be able to stand sb; **voyons!** let's see now; (*indignation etc*) come on!; **avoir quelque chose à ~ avec** to have something to do with

**voire** [vwar] *adv* even

**voisin, e** [vwazɛ̃, in] *adj* (*proche*) neighbouring; (*contigu*) next; (*ressemblant*) connected ♦ *nm/f* neighbour;

**voisinage** *nm* (*proximité*) proximity; (*environs*) vicinity; (*quartier, voisins*) neighbourhood

**voiture** [vwatyr] *nf* car; (*wagon*) coach, carriage; **~ de course** racing car; **~ de sport** sports car

**voix** [vwa] *nf* voice; (POL) vote; **à haute ~** aloud; **à ~ basse** in a low voice; **à 2/4 ~** (MUS) in 2/4 parts; **avoir ~ au chapitre** to have a say in the matter

**vol** [vɔl] *nm* (*d'oiseau, d'avion*) flight; (*larcin*) theft; **~ régulier** scheduled flight; **à ~ d'oiseau** as the crow flies; **au ~: attraper qch au ~** to catch sth as it flies past; **en ~** in flight; **~ à main armée** armed robbery; **~ à voile** gliding; **~ libre** hang-gliding

**volage** [vɔlaʒ] *adj* fickle

**volaille** [vɔlaj] *nf* (*oiseaux*) poultry *pl*; (*viande*) poultry *no pl*; (*oiseau*) fowl

**volant, e** [vɔlɑ̃, ɑ̃t] *adj voir* **feuille** *etc* ♦ *nm* (*d'automobile*) (steering) wheel; (*de commande*) wheel; (*objet lancé*) shuttlecock; (*bande de tissu*) flounce

**volcan** [vɔlkɑ̃] *nm* volcano

**volée** [vɔle] *nf* (TENNIS) volley; **à la ~: rattraper à la ~** to catch in mid-air; **à toute ~** (*sonner les cloches*) vigorously; (*lancer un projectile*) with full force; **~ de coups/de flèches** volley of blows/arrows

**voler** [vɔle] *vi* (*avion, oiseau, fig*) to fly; (*voleur*) to steal ♦ *vt* (*objet*) to steal; (*personne*) to rob; **~ qch à qn** to steal sth from sb; **il ne l'a pas volé!** he asked for it!

**volet** [vɔlɛ] *nm* (*de fenêtre*) shutter; (*de feuillet, document*) section

**voleur, -euse** [vɔlœr, øz] *nm/f* thief ♦ *adj* thieving; **"au ~!"** "stop thief!"

**volière** [vɔljɛr] *nf* aviary

**volley** [vɔlɛ] *nm* volleyball

**volontaire** [vɔlɔ̃tɛr] *adj* (*acte, enrôlement, prisonnier*) voluntary; (*oubli*) intentional; (*caractère, personne: décidé*) self-willed ♦ *nm/f* volunteer

**volonté** [vɔlɔ̃te] *nf* (*faculté de vouloir*)

will; (*énergie, fermeté*) will(power); (*souhait, désir*) wish; **à ~** as much as one likes; **bonne ~** goodwill, willingness; **mauvaise ~** lack of goodwill, unwillingness

**volontiers** [vɔlɔ̃tje] *adv* (*avec plaisir*) willingly, gladly; (*habituellement, souvent*) readily, willingly; **voulez-vous boire quelque chose?** - ~! would you like something to drink? - yes, please!

**volt** [vɔlt] *nm* volt

**volte-face** [vɔltəfas] *nf inv*: **faire ~~** to turn round

**voltige** [vɔltiʒ] *nf* (*ÉQUITATION*) trick riding; (*au cirque*) acrobatics *sg*; **voltiger** *vi* to flutter (about)

**volubile** [vɔlybil] *adj* voluble

**volume** [vɔlym] *nm* volume; (*GÉOM: solide*) solid; **volumineux, -euse** *adj* voluminous, bulky

**volupté** [vɔlypte] *nf* sensual delight *ou* pleasure

**vomi** [vɔmi] *nm* vomit; **vomir** *vi* to vomit, be sick ♦ *vt* to vomit, bring up; (*fig*) to belch out, spew out; (*exécrer*) to loathe, abhor; **vomissements** *nmpl*: **être pris de vomissements** to (suddenly) start vomiting

**vont** [vɔ̃] *vb voir* **aller**

**vorace** [vɔras] *adj* voracious

**vos** [vo] *adj voir* **votre**

**vote** [vɔt] *nm* vote; **~ par correspondance/procuration** postal/proxy vote; **voter** *vi* to vote ♦ *vt* (*projet de loi*) to vote for; (*loi, réforme*) to pass

**votre** [vɔtʀ] (*pl* **vos**) *adj* your

**vôtre** [votʀ] *pron*: **le ~, la ~, les ~s** yours; **les ~s** (*fig*) your family *ou* folks; **à la ~** (*toast*) your (good) health!

**voudrai** *etc* [vudʀe] *vb voir* **vouloir**

**voué, e** [vwe] *adj*: **~ à** doomed to

**vouer** [vwe] *vt*: **~ qch à** (*Dieu, un saint*) to dedicate sth to; **~ sa vie à** (*étude, cause etc*) to devote one's life to; **~ une amitié éternelle à qn** to vow undying friendship to sb

---

| MOT-CLÉ |
| --- |

**vouloir** [vulwaʀ] *nm*: **le bon vouloir de qn** sb's goodwill; sb's pleasure
♦ *vt* **1** (*exiger, désirer*) to want; **vouloir faire/que qn fasse** to want to do/sb to do; **voulez-vous du thé?** would you like ou do you want some tea?; **que me veut-il?** what does he want with me?; **sans le vouloir** (*involontairement*) without meaning to, unintentionally; **je voudrais ceci/faire** I would ou I'd like this/to do

**2** (*consentir*): **je veux bien** (*bonne volonté*) I'll be happy to; (*concession*) fair enough, that's fine; **oui, si on veut** (*en quelque sorte*) yes, if you like; **veuillez attendre** please wait; **veuillez agréer ...** (*formule épistolaire*) yours faithfully

**3**: **en vouloir à qn** to bear sb a grudge; **s'en vouloir (de)** to be annoyed with o.s. (for); **il en veut à mon argent** he's after my money

**4**: **vouloir de**: **l'entreprise ne veut plus de lui** the firm doesn't want him any more; **elle ne veut pas de son aide** she doesn't want his help

**5**: **vouloir dire** to mean

---

**voulu, e** [vuly] *adj* (*requis*) required, requisite; (*délibéré*) deliberate, intentional; *voir aussi* **vouloir**

**vous** [vu] *pron* you; (*objet indirect*) (to) you; (*réfléchi*) yourself; (: *pl*) yourselves; (*réciproque*) each other; **~-même** yourself; **~-mêmes** yourselves

**voûte** [vut] *nf* vault; **voûter**: **se voûter** *vi* (*dos, personne*) to become stooped

**vouvoyer** [vuvwaje] *vt*: **~ qn** to address sb as "vous"

**voyage** [vwajaʒ] *nm* journey, trip; (*fait de ~r*): **le ~** travel(ling); **partir/être en ~** to go off/be away on a journey *ou* trip; **faire bon ~** to have a good journey; **~ d'agrément/d'affaires** pleasure/business trip; **~ de noces** honeymoon; **~ organisé** package tour

**voyager** [vwajaʒe] *vi* to travel; **voyageur, -euse** *nm/f* traveller; *(passager)* passenger

**voyant, e** [vwajɑ̃, ɑ̃t] *adj (couleur)* loud, gaudy ♦ *nm (signal)* (warning) light; **voyante** *nf* clairvoyant

**voyelle** [vwajɛl] *nf* vowel

**voyons** *etc* [vwajɔ̃] *vb voir* **voir**

**voyou** [vwaju] *nm* hooligan

**vrac** [vʀak]: **en ~** *adv (au détail)* loose; *(en gros)* in bulk; *(en désordre)* in a jumble

**vrai, e** [vʀe] *adj (véridique: récit, faits)* true; *(non factice, authentique)* real; **à ~ dire** to tell the truth; **vraiment** *adv* really; **vraisemblable** *adj* likely; *(excuse)* convincing; **vraisemblablement** *adj* probably; **vraisemblance** *nf* likelihood; *(romanesque)* verisimilitude

**vrille** [vʀij] *nf (de plante)* tendril; *(outil)* gimlet; *(spirale)* spiral; *(AVIAT)* spin

**vrombir** [vʀɔ̃biʀ] *vi* to hum

**VRP** *sigle m* (= *voyageur, représentant, placier*) sales rep *(fam)*

**VTT** *sigle m* (= *vélo tout-terrain*) mountain bike

**vu, e** [vy] *pp de voir* ♦ *adj*: **bien/mal ~** *(fig: personne)* popular/unpopular; *(: chose)* approved/disapproved of ♦ *prép (en raison de)* in view of; **~ que** in view of the fact that

**vue** [vy] *nf (fait de voir)*: **la ~ de** the sight of; *(sens, faculté)* (eye)sight; *(panorama, image, photo)* view; **~s** *nfpl (idées)* views; *(dessein)* designs; **hors de ~** out of sight; **avoir en ~** to have in mind; **tirer à ~** to shoot on sight; **à ~ d'œil** visibly; **de ~** by sight; **perdre de ~** to lose sight of; **en ~** *(visible)* in sight; *(célèbre)* in the public eye; **en ~ de faire** with a view to doing

**vulgaire** [vylgɛʀ] *adj (grossier)* vulgar, coarse; *(ordinaire)* commonplace; *(péj: quelconque)*: **de ~s touristes** common tourists; *(BOT, ZOOL: non latin)* common; **vulgariser** *vt* to popularize

**vulnérable** [vylneʀabl] *adj* vulnerable

# W, w

**wagon** [vagɔ̃] *nm (de voyageurs)* carriage; *(de marchandises)* truck, wagon; **wagon-lit** *nm* sleeper, sleeping car; **wagon-restaurant** *nm* restaurant *ou* dining car

**wallon, ne** [walɔ̃, ɔn] *adj* Walloon

**waters** [watɛʀ] *nmpl* toilet *sg*

**watt** [wat] *nm* watt

**WC** *sigle mpl* (= *water-closet(s)*) toilet

**Web** [wɛb] *nm inv*: **le ~** (the World Wide) Web

**week-end** [wikɛnd] *nm* weekend

**western** [wɛstɛʀn] *nm* western

**whisky** [wiski] *(pl* **whiskies)** *nm* whisky

# X, x

**xénophobe** [gzenɔfɔb] *adj* xenophobic ♦ *nm/f* xenophobe

**xérès** [gzeʀɛs] *nm* sherry

**xylophone** [gzilɔfɔn] *nm* xylophone

# Y, y

**y** [i] *adv (à cet endroit)* there; *(dessus)* on it *(ou* them); *(dedans)* in it *(ou* them) ♦ *pron (about ou on ou of)* it *(d'après le verbe employé)*; **j'~ pense** I'm thinking about it; **ça ~ est!** that's it!; *voir aussi* **aller; avoir**

**yacht** [jɔt] *nm* yacht

**yaourt** [jauʀt] *nm* yoghourt; **~ nature/aux fruits** plain/fruit yogurt

**yeux** [jø] *nmpl de* **œil**

**yoga** [jɔga] *nm* yoga

**yoghourt** [jɔguʀt] *nm* = **yaourt**

**yougoslave** [jugɔslav] *(HISTOIRE)* *adj* Yugoslav(ian) ♦ *nm/f*: **Y~** Yugoslav

**Yougoslavie** [jugɔslavi] *(HISTOIRE)* *nf* Yugoslavia

# Z, z

**zapper** [zape] vi to zap

**zapping** [zapiŋ] nm: **faire du ~** to flick through the channels

**zèbre** [zɛbʀ(ə)] nm (ZOOL) zebra; **zébré, e** adj striped, streaked

**zèle** [zɛl] nm zeal; **faire du ~** (péj) to be over-zealous; **zélé, e** adj zealous

**zéro** [zeʀo] nm zero, nought (BRIT); **au-dessous de ~** below zero (Centigrade) ou freezing; **partir de ~** to start from scratch; **trois (buts) à ~** 3 (goals to) nil

**zeste** [zɛst] nm peel, zest

**zézayer** [zezeje] vi to have a lisp

**zigzag** [zigzag] nm zigzag; **zigzaguer** vi to zigzag

**zinc** [zɛ̃g] nm (CHIMIE) zinc

**zizanie** [zizani] nf: **semer la ~** to stir up ill-feeling

**zizi** [zizi] nm (langage enfantin) willy

**zodiaque** [zɔdjak] nm zodiac

**zona** [zona] nm shingles sg

**zone** [zon] nf zone, area; **~ bleue** ≈ restricted parking area; **~ industrielle** industrial estate

**zoo** [zo(o)] nm zoo

**zoologie** [zɔɔlɔʒi] nf zoology; **zoologique** adj zoological

**zut** [zyt] excl dash (it)! (BRIT), nuts! (US)

# ENGLISH – FRENCH
# ANGLAIS – FRANÇAIS

## A, a

**A** [eɪ] n (MUS) la m

**KEYWORD**

**a** [eɪ, ə] (before vowel or silent h: an) indef art **1** (un(e): **a book** un livre; **an apple** une pomme; **she's a doctor** elle est médecin
**2** (instead of the number "one") un(e);
**a year ago** il y a un an; **a hundred/ thousand** etc **pounds** cent/mille etc livres
**3** (in expressing ratios, prices etc): **3 a day/week** 3 par jour/semaine; **10 km an hour** 10 km à l'heure; **30p a kilo** 30p le kilo

**A.A.** n abbr = **Alcoholics Anonymous**;
(BRIT: Automobile Association) ≃ TCF m
**A.A.A.** (US) n abbr (= American Automobile Association) ≃ TCF m
**aback** [əˈbæk] adv: **to be taken ~** être stupéfait(e), être déconcerté(e)
**abandon** [əˈbændən] vt abandonner
**abate** [əˈbeɪt] vi s'apaiser, se calmer
**abbey** [ˈæbɪ] n abbaye f
**abbot** [ˈæbət] n père supérieur
**abbreviation** [əbriːvɪˈeɪʃən] n abréviation f
**abdicate** [ˈæbdɪkeɪt] vt, vi abdiquer
**abdomen** [ˈæbdəmɛn] n abdomen m
**abduct** [æbˈdʌkt] vt enlever
**aberration** [æbəˈreɪʃən] n anomalie f
**abide** [əˈbaɪd] vt: **I can't ~ it/him** je ne peux pas le souffrir or supporter; **~ by** vt fus observer, respecter
**ability** [əˈbɪlɪtɪ] n compétence f; capacité f; (skill) talent m
**abject** [ˈæbdʒɛkt] adj (poverty) sordide;
(apology) plat(e)
**ablaze** [əˈbleɪz] adj en feu, en flammes

**able** [ˈeɪbl] adj capable, compétent(e);
**to be ~ to do sth** être capable de faire qch, pouvoir faire qch; **~-bodied** adj robuste; **ably** adv avec compétence or talent, habilement
**abnormal** [æbˈnɔːməl] adj anormal(e)
**aboard** [əˈbɔːd] adv à bord ♦ prep à bord de
**abode** [əˈbəud] n (LAW): **of no fixed ~** sans domicile fixe
**abolish** [əˈbɒlɪʃ] vt abolir
**aborigine** [æbəˈrɪdʒɪnɪ] n aborigène m/f
**abort** [əˈbɔːt] vt faire avorter; **~ion** n avortement m; **to have an ~ion** se faire avorter; **~ive** [əˈbɔːtɪv] adj manqué(e)

**KEYWORD**

**about** [əˈbaut] adv **1** (approximately) environ, à peu près; **about a hundred/thousand** etc environ cent/ mille etc, une centaine/un millier etc; **it takes about 10 hours** ça prend environ or à peu près 10 heures; **at about 2 o'clock** vers 2 heures; **I've just about finished** j'ai presque fini
**2** (referring to place) çà et là, de côté et d'autre; **to run about** courir çà et là; **to walk about** se promener, aller et venir
**3: to be about to do sth** être sur le point de faire qch
♦ prep **1** (relating to) au sujet de, à propos de; **a book about London** un livre sur Londres; **what is it about?** de quoi s'agit-il? **we talked about it** nous en avons parlé; **what** or **how about doing this?** et si nous faisions ceci?
**2** (referring to place) dans; **to walk**

**about the town** se promener dans la ville

**about-face** [ə'baut'feɪs] n demi-tour m
**about-turn** [ə'baut'tɜ:n] n (MIL) demi-tour m; (fig) volte-face f

**above** [ə'bʌv] adv au-dessus ♦ prep au-dessus de; (more) plus de; **mentioned** ~ mentionné ci-dessus; ~ **all** par-dessus tout, surtout; **~board** adj franc (franche); honnête

**abrasive** [ə'breɪzɪv] adj abrasif(-ive); (fig) caustique, agressif(-ive)

**abreast** [ə'brest] adv de front; **to keep ~ of** se tenir au courant de

**abroad** [ə'brɔ:d] adv à l'étranger

**abrupt** [ə'brʌpt] adj (steep, blunt) abrupt(e); (sudden, gruff) brusque; **~ly** adv (speak, end) brusquement

**abscess** ['æbsɪs] n abcès m

**absence** ['æbsəns] n absence f

**absent** ['æbsənt] adj absent(e); **~ee** [æbsən'ti:] n absent(e); (habitual absentéiste m/f; **~-minded** adj distrait(e)

**absolute** ['æbsəlu:t] adj absolu(e); **~ly** [æbsə'lu:tlɪ] adv absolument

**absolve** [əb'zɔlv] vt: **to ~ sb (from)** (blame, responsibility, sin) absoudre qn (de)

**absorb** [əb'zɔ:b] vt absorber; **to be ~ed in a book** être plongé(e) dans un livre; **~ent cotton** (US) n coton m hydrophile

**abstain** [əb'steɪn] vi: **to ~ (from)** s'abstenir (de)

**abstract** ['æbstrækt] adj abstrait(e)

**absurd** [əb'sɜ:d] adj absurde

**abundant** [ə'bʌndənt] adj abondant(e)

**abuse** [n ə'bju:s, vb ə'bju:z] n abus m; (insults) insultes fpl ♦ vt abuser de; (insult) insulter; **abusive** [ə'bju:sɪv] adj grossier(-ère), injurieux(-euse)

**abysmal** [ə'bɪzməl] adj exécrable; (ignorance etc) sans bornes

**abyss** [ə'bɪs] n abîme m, gouffre m

**AC** abbr (= alternating current) courant

alternatif

**academic** [ækə'demɪk] adj universitaire; (person: scholarly) intellectuel(le); (pej: issue) oiseux(-euse), purement théorique ♦ n universitaire m/f; **~ year** n année f universitaire

**academy** [ə'kædəmɪ] n (learned body) académie f; (school) collège m; **~ of music** conservatoire m

**accelerate** [æk'seləreɪt] vt, vi accélérer; **accelerator** n accélérateur m

**accent** ['æksent] n accent m

**accept** [ək'sept] vt accepter; **~able** adj acceptable; **~ance** n acceptation f

**access** ['ækses] n accès m; (LAW: in divorce) droit m de visite; **~ible** [æk'sesəbl] adj accessible

**accessory** [æk'sesərɪ] n accessoire m

**accident** ['æksɪdənt] n accident m; (chance) hasard m; **by ~** accidentellement; par hasard; **~al** [æksɪ'dentl] adj accidentel(le); **~ally** [æksɪ'dentəlɪ] adv accidentellement; **~ insurance** n assurance f accident; **~-prone** adj sujet(te) aux accidents

**acclaim** [ə'kleɪm] n acclamations fpl ♦ vt acclamer

**accommodate** [ə'kɔmədeɪt] vt loger, recevoir; (oblige, help) obliger; (car etc) contenir; **accommodating** adj obligeant(e), arrangeant(e); **accommodation** [əkɔmə'deɪʃən] (US **accommodations**) n logement m

**accompany** [ə'kʌmpənɪ] vt accompagner

**accomplice** [ə'kʌmplɪs] n complice m/f

**accomplish** [ə'kʌmplɪʃ] vt accomplir; **~ment** n accomplissement m; réussite f; (skill: gen pl) talent m

**accord** [ə'kɔ:d] n accord m ♦ vt accorder; **of his own ~** de son plein gré; **~ance** n: **in ~ance with** conformément à; **~ing: ~ing to** prep selon; **~ingly** adv en conséquence

**accordion** [ə'kɔ:dɪən] n accordéon m

**account** [ə'kaunt] n (COMM) compte m; (report) compte rendu; récit m; **~s npl** (COMM)

**accrued interest** [ə'kru:d-] *n* intérêt *m* cumulé

**accumulate** [ə'kju:mjuleɪt] *vt* accumuler, amasser ♦ *vi* s'accumuler, s'amasser

**accuracy** ['ækjurəsɪ] *n* exactitude *f*, précision *f*

**accurate** ['ækjurɪt] *adj* exact(e), précis(e); **~ly** *adv* avec précision

**accusation** [ækju'zeɪʃən] *n* accusation *f*

**accuse** [ə'kju:z] *vt*: **to ~ sb (of sth)** accuser qn (de qch); **the ~d** l'accusé(e)

**accustom** [ə'kʌstəm] *vt* accoutumer, habituer; **~ed** *adj* (*usual*) habituel(le); (*in the habit*): **~ed to** habitué(e) or accoutumé(e) à

**ace** [eɪs] *n* as *m*

**ache** [eɪk] *n* mal *m*, douleur *f* ♦ *vi* (*yearn*): **to ~ to do sth** mourir d'envie de faire qch; **my head ~s** j'ai mal à la tête

**achieve** [ə'tʃi:v] *vt* (*aim*) atteindre; (*victory*, *success*) remporter, obtenir; **~ment** *n* exploit *m*, réussite *f*

**acid** ['æsɪd] *adj* acide ♦ *n* acide *m*; **~ rain** *n* pluies *fpl* acides

**acknowledge** [ək'nɔlɪdʒ] *vt* (*letter*: *also*: **~ receipt of**) accuser réception de; (*fact*) reconnaître; **~ment** *n* (*of letter*) accusé *m* de réception

**acne** ['æknɪ] *n* acné *m*

**acorn** ['eɪkɔ:n] *n* gland *m*

**acoustic** [ə'ku:stɪk] *adj* acoustique; **~s** *n*, *npl* acoustique *f*

**acquaint** [ə'kweɪnt] *vt*: **to ~ sb with sth** mettre qn au courant de qch; **to be ~ed with** connaître; **~ance** *n* connaissance *f*

**acquire** [ə'kwaɪə*r*] *vt* acquérir

**acquit** [ə'kwɪt] *vt* acquitter; **to ~ o.s. well** bien se comporter, s'en tirer très honorablement

**acre** ['eɪkə*r*] *n* acre *f* (= 4047 m²)

**acrid** ['ækrɪd] *adj* âcre

**acrobat** ['ækrəbæt] *n* acrobate *m/f*

**across** [ə'krɔs] *prep* (*on the other side*) de l'autre côté de; (*crosswise*) en travers de ♦ *adv* de l'autre côté; en travers; **to run/swim ~** traverser en courant/à la nage; **~ from** en face de

**acrylic** [ə'krɪlɪk] *adj* acrylique

**act** [ækt] *n* acte *m*, action *f*; (*of play*) acte; (*in music-hall etc*) numéro *m*; (*LAW*) loi *f* ♦ *vi* agir; (*THEATRE*) jouer; (*pretend*) jouer la comédie ♦ *vt* (*part*) jouer, tenir; **in the ~ of** en train de; **to ~** servir de; **~ing** *adj* suppléant(e), par intérim ♦ *n* (*activity*): **to do some ~ing** faire du théâtre (*or* du cinéma)

**action** ['ækʃən] *n* action *f*; (*MIL*) combat(s) *m(pl)*; **out of ~** hors de combat; (*machine*) hors d'usage; **to take ~** agir, prendre des mesures; **~ replay** *n* (*TV*) ralenti *m*

**activate** ['æktɪveɪt] *vt* (*mechanism*) actionner, faire fonctionner

**active** ['æktɪv] *adj* actif(-ive); (*volcano*) en activité; **~ly** *adv* activement; **activity** [æk'tɪvɪtɪ] *n* activité *f*; **activity holiday** *n* vacances actives

**actor** ['æktə*r*] *n* acteur *m*

**actress** ['æktrɪs] *n* actrice *f*

**actual** ['æktjuəl] *adj* réel(le), véritable; **~ly** *adv* (*really*) réellement, véritablement; (*in fact*) en fait

**acute** [ə'kju:t] *adj* aigu(ë); (*mind*, *observer*) pénétrant(e), perspicace

**ad** [æd] *n abbr* = **advertisement**

**A.D.** *adv abbr* (= *anno Domini*) ap. J.-C.

**adamant** ['ædəmənt] *adj* inflexible

**adapt** [ə'dæpt] *vt* adapter ♦ *vi*: **to ~ (to)** s'adapter (à); **~able** *adj* (*device*) adaptable; (*person*) qui s'adapte facile-

---

(*COMM*) comptabilité *f*, comptes; **of no ~** sans importance; **on ~** en acompte; **on no ~** en aucun cas; **on ~ of** à cause de; **to take into ~, take ~ of** tenir compte de; **~ for** *vt fus* expliquer, rendre compte de; **~able** *adj*: **~able (to)** responsable (devant); **~ancy** *n* comptabilité *f*; **~ant** *n* comptable *m/f*; **~ number** *n* (*at bank etc*) numéro *m* de compte

ment; **~er, ~or** n (ELEC) adaptateur m

**add** [æd] vt (figures: also: **~ up**) additionner ♦ vi: **to ~** (to) (increase) ajouter à, accroître

**adder** ['ædə'] n vipère f

**addict** ['ædɪkt] n intoxiqué(e); (fig) fanatique m/f; **~ed** [ə'dɪktɪd] adj: **to be ~ed to** (drugs, drink etc) être adonné(e) à; (fig: football etc) être un(e) fanatique de; **~ion** n (MED) dépendance f; **~ive** adj qui crée une dépendance

**addition** [ə'dɪʃən] n addition f; (thing added) ajout m; **in ~** de plus; de surcroît; **in ~ to** en plus de; **~al** adj supplémentaire

**additive** ['ædɪtɪv] n additif m

**address** [ə'dres] n adresse f; (talk) discours m, allocution f ♦ vt adresser; (speak to) s'adresser à; **to ~ (o.s. to) a problem** s'attaquer à un problème

**adept** ['ædept] adj: **~ at** expert(e) à or en

**adequate** ['ædɪkwɪt] adj adéquat(e); suffisant(e)

**adhere** [əd'hɪə'] vi: **to ~ to** adhérer à; (fig: rule, decision) se tenir à

**adhesive** [əd'hi:zɪv] n adhésif m; **~ tape** n (BRIT) ruban adhésif m; (US: MED) sparadrap m

**ad hoc** [æd'hɔk] adj improvisé(e), ad hoc

**adjacent** [ə'dʒeɪsənt] adj: **~** (to) adjacent(e) (à)

**adjective** ['ædʒektɪv] n adjectif m

**adjoining** [ə'dʒɔɪnɪŋ] adj voisin(e), adjacent(e), attenant(e)

**adjourn** [ə'dʒə:n] vt ajourner ♦ vi suspendre la séance; clore la session

**adjust** [ə'dʒʌst] vt (machine) ajuster, régler; (prices, wages) rajuster ♦ vi: **to ~ (to)** s'adapter (à); **~able** adj réglable; **~ment** n (PSYCH) adaptation f; (to machine) ajustage m, réglage m; (of prices, wages) rajustement m

**ad-lib** [æd'lɪb] vt, vi improviser; **ad lib** adv à volonté, à loisir

**administer** [əd'mɪnɪstə'] vt adminis-

trer; (justice) rendre; **administration** [ədmɪnɪs'treɪʃən] n administration f; **administrative** [əd'mɪnɪstrətɪv] adj administratif(-ive)

**admiral** ['ædmərəl] n amiral m; **A~ty** ['ædmərəltɪ] (BRIT) n: **the A~ty** ministère m de la Marine

**admire** [əd'maɪə'] vt admirer

**admission** [əd'mɪʃən] n admission f; (to exhibition, night club etc) entrée f; (confession) aveu m; **~ charge** n droits mpl d'admission

**admit** [əd'mɪt] vt laisser entrer; admettre; (agree) reconnaître, admettre; **~ to** vt fus reconnaître, avouer; **~tance** n admission f, (droit m d')entrée f; **~tedly** adv il faut en convenir

**ado** [ə'du:] n: **without (any) more ~** sans plus de cérémonies

**adolescence** [ædəu'lesns] n adolescence f; **adolescent** adj, n adolescent(e)

**adopt** [ə'dɔpt] vt adopter; **~ed** adj adoptif(-ive), adopté(e); **~ion** n adoption f

**adore** [ə'dɔ:'] vt adorer

**adorn** [ə'dɔ:n] vt orner

**Adriatic (Sea)** [eɪdrɪ'ætɪk-] n Adriatique f

**adrift** [ə'drɪft] adv à la dérive

**adult** ['ædʌlt] n adulte m/f ♦ adj adulte; (literature, education) pour adultes

**adultery** [ə'dʌltərɪ] n adultère m

**advance** [əd'vɑ:ns] n avance f ♦ adj: **~ booking** réservation f ♦ vt avancer ♦ vi avancer; s'avancer; **~ notice** avertissement m; **to make ~s (to sb)** faire des propositions (à qn); (amorously) faire des avances (à qn); **in ~** à l'avance, d'avance; **~d** adj avancé(e); (SCOL: studies) supérieur(e)

**advantage** [əd'vɑ:ntɪdʒ] n (also TENNIS) avantage m; **to take ~ of** (person) exploiter

**advent** ['ædvənt] n avènement m, venue f; **A~** Avent m

**adventure** [əd'ventʃə'] n aventure f

**adverb** ['ædvə:b] n adverbe m

**adverse** ['ædvɜːs] *adj* défavorable, contraire

**advert** ['ædvɜːt] (BRIT) *n abbr* = **advertisement**

**advertise** ['ædvətaɪz] *vi, vt* faire de la publicité (pour); (*in classified ads etc*) mettre une annonce (pour vendre); **to ~ for** (*staff, accommodation*) faire paraître une annonce pour trouver; **~ment** [əd'vɜːtɪsmənt] (n COMM) réclame *f*, publicité *f*; (*in classified ads*) annonce *f*; **advertising** *n* publicité *f*

**advice** [əd'vaɪs] *n* conseils *mpl*; (*notification*) avis *m*; **piece of ~** conseil; **to take legal ~** consulter un avocat

**advisable** [əd'vaɪzəbl] *adj* conseillé(e), indiqué(e)

**advise** [əd'vaɪz] *vt* conseiller; **to ~ sb of sth** aviser or informer qn de qch; **to ~ against sth/doing sth** déconseiller qch/conseiller à ne pas faire qch; **~r, advisor** *n* conseiller(-ère); **advisory** *adj* consultatif(-ive)

**advocate** [*n* 'ædvəkɪt, *vb* 'ædvəkeɪt] *n* (*upholder*) défenseur *m*, avocat(e); (LAW) avocat(e) ♦ *vt* recommander, prôner

**Aegean (Sea)** [iː'dʒiːən-] *n* (mer *f*) Égée *f*

**aerial** ['ɛərɪəl] *n* antenne *f* ♦ *adj* aérien(ne)

**aerobics** [ɛə'rəʊbɪks] *n* aérobic *f*

**aeroplane** ['ɛərəpleɪn] (BRIT) *n* avion *m*

**aerosol** ['ɛərəsɔl] *n* aérosol *m*

**aesthetic** [iːs'θetɪk] *adj* esthétique

**afar** [ə'fɑː<sup>r</sup>] *adv*: **from ~** de loin

**affair** [ə'fɛə<sup>r</sup>] *n* affaire *f*; (*also*: **love ~**) liaison *f*; aventure *f*

**affect** [ə'fekt] *vt* affecter; (*disease*) atteindre; **~ed** *adj* affecté(e); **~ion** *n* affection *f*; **~ionate** *adj* affectueux(-euse)

**affinity** [ə'fɪnɪtɪ] *n* (*bond, rapport*): **to have an ~ with/for** avoir une affinité avec/pour

**afflict** [ə'flɪkt] *vt* affliger

**affluence** ['æfluəns] *n* abondance *f*, opulence *f*

**affluent** ['æfluənt] *adj* (*person, family,*

surroundings*) aisé(e), riche; **the ~ society** la société d'abondance

**afford** [ə'fɔːd] *vt* se permettre; (*provide*) fournir, procurer

**afloat** [ə'fləut] *adj, adv* à flot; **to stay ~** surnager

**afoot** [ə'fut] *adv*: **there is something ~** il se prépare quelque chose

**afraid** [ə'freɪd] *adj* effrayé(e); **to be ~ of** or **to** avoir peur de; **I am ~ that ...** je suis désolé(e) mais ...; **I am ~ so/ not** hélas oui/non

**Africa** ['æfrɪkə] *n* Afrique *f*; **~n** *adj* africain(e) ♦ *n* Africain(e)

**after** ['ɑːftə<sup>r</sup>] *prep, adv* après ♦ *conj* après que, après avoir or être *+pp*; **what/who are you ~?** que/qui cherchez-vous?; **he left/having done** après qu'il fut parti/après avoir fait; **ask ~ him** demandez de ses nouvelles; **to name sb ~ sb** donner à qn le nom de qn; **twenty ~ eight** (US) huit heures vingt; **~ all** après tout; **~ you!** après vous, Monsieur (or Madame *etc*); **~effects** *npl* (*of disaster, radiation, drink etc*) répercussions *fpl*; (*of illness*) séquelles *fpl*, suites *fpl*; **~math** *n* conséquences *fpl*, suites *fpl*; **~noon** *n* après-midi *m* or *f*; **~s** (*inf*) *n* (*dessert*) dessert *m*; **~-sales service** (BRIT) *n* (*for car, washing machine etc*) service *m* après-vente; **~-shave (lotion)** *n* after-shave *m*; **~sun** *n* après-soleil *m inv*; **~thought** *n*: **I had an ~thought** il m'est venu une idée après coup; **~wards** (US **afterward**) *adv* après

**again** [ə'gen] *adv* de nouveau; encore (une fois); **to do sth ~** refaire qch; **not ... ~** ne ... plus; **~ and ~** à plusieurs reprises

**against** [ə'genst] *prep* contre; (*compared to*) par rapport à

**age** [eɪdʒ] *n* âge *m* ♦ *vt, vi* vieillir; **it's been ~s since** ça fait une éternité que ... ne; **he is 20 years of ~** il a 20 ans; **to come of ~** atteindre sa majorité; **~d** [*adj* eɪdʒd, *npl* 'eɪdʒɪd] *adj*: **~d 10**

**âgé(e)** de 10 ans ♦ npl: **the ~d** les personnes âgées; **~ group** n tranche f d'âge; **~ limit** n limite f d'âge

**agency** ['eɪdʒənsɪ] n agence f; (government body) organisme m, office m

**agenda** [ə'dʒɛndə] n ordre m du jour

**agent** ['eɪdʒənt] n agent m, représentant m; (firm) concessionnaire m

**aggravate** ['ægrəveɪt] vt aggraver; (annoy) exaspérer

**aggressive** [ə'grɛsɪv] adj agressif(-ive)

**agitate** ['ædʒɪteɪt] vt (person) agiter, émouvoir, troubler ♦ vi: **to ~ for/ against** faire campagne pour/contre

**AGM** n abbr (= annual general meeting) AG f

**ago** [ə'gəu] adv: **2 days ~** il y a deux jours; **not long ~** il n'y a pas longtemps; **how long ~?** il y a combien de temps (de cela)?

**agony** ['ægənɪ] n (pain) douleur f atroce; **to be in ~** souffrir le martyre

**agree** [ə'griː] vi (price) convenir de ♦ vi: **to ~ with** (person) être d'accord avec; (statements etc) concorder avec; (LING) s'accorder avec; **to ~ to sth** accepter de or consentir à faire; **to ~ to sth** consentir à qch; **to ~ that** (admit) convenir or reconnaître que; **garlic doesn't ~ with me** je ne supporte pas l'ail; **~able** adj agréable; (willing) consentant(e), d'accord; **~d** adj (time, place) convenu(e); **~ment** n accord m; **in ~ment** d'accord

**agricultural** [ægrɪˈkʌltʃərəl] adj agricole

**agriculture** ['ægrɪkʌltʃər] n agriculture f

**aground** [ə'graund] adv: **to run ~** échouer, s'échouer

**ahead** [ə'hɛd] adv (in front: of position, place) devant; (: at the head) en avant; (look, plan, think) en avant; **~ of** devant; (fig: schedule etc) en avance sur; **~ of time** en avance; **go right or straight ~** allez tout droit; **go ~!** (fig: permission) allez-y!

**aid** [eɪd] n aide f; (device) appareil m ♦ vt aider; **in ~ of** en faveur de; see also **hearing**

**aide** [eɪd] n (person) aide mf, assistant(e)

**AIDS** [eɪdz] n abbr (= acquired immune deficiency syndrome) SIDA m; **AIDS-related** adj associé(e) au sida

**aim** [eɪm] vt: **to ~ sth (at)** (gun, camera) braquer or pointer qch (sur); (missile) lancer qch (à or contre or en direction de); (blow) allonger qch (à); (remark) destiner or adresser qch (à) ♦ vi (also: **to take ~**) viser ♦ n but m; (skill): **his ~ is bad** il vise mal; **to ~ at** viser; (fig) viser (à); **to ~ to do** avoir l'intention de faire; **~less** adj sans but

**ain't** [eɪnt] (inf) = **am not**; **aren't**; **isn't**

**air** [eər] n air m ♦ vt (room, bed, clothes) aérer; (grievances, views, ideas) exposer, faire connaître ♦ cpd (currents, attack etc) aérien(ne); **to throw sth into the ~** jeter qch en l'air; **by ~** (travel) par avion; **to be on the ~** (RADIO, TV: programme) être diffusé; (: station) diffuser; **~bed** n matelas m pneumatique; **~-conditioned** adj climatisé(e); **~ conditioning** n climatisation f; **~craft** n inv avion m; **~craft carrier** n porteavions m inv; **~field** n terrain m d'aviation; **A~ Force** n armée f de l'air; **~ freshener** n désodorisant m; **~gun** n fusil m à air comprimé; **~ hostess** (BRIT) n hôtesse f de l'air; **~ letter** (BRIT) n aérogramme m; **~lift** n pont aérien; **~line** n ligne aérienne, compagnie f d'aviation; **~liner** n avion m de ligne; **~mail** n: **by ~mail** par avion; **~ mile** n air mile m; **~plane** n (US) avion m; **~port** n aéroport m; **~ raid** n attaque or raid aérien(ne); **~sick** adj: **to be ~sick** avoir le mal de l'air; **~tight** adj hermétique; **~-traffic controller** n aiguilleur m du ciel; **~y** adj bien aéré(e); (manners) dégagé(e)

**aisle** [aɪl] n (of church) allée centrale, nef latérale; (of theatre etc) couloir m, passage *m*, allée; **~ seat** *n* place *f* côté couloir

**ajar** [əˈdʒɑːʳ] *adj* entrouvert(e)

**akin** [əˈkɪn] *adj*: **~ to** (*similar*) qui tient de *or* ressemble à

**alarm** [əˈlɑːm] *n* alarme *f* ♦ *vt* alarmer; **~ call** *n* coup de fil *m* pour réveiller; **~ clock** *n* réveille-matin *m inv*, réveil *m*

**alas** [əˈlæs] *excl* hélas!

**album** [ˈælbəm] *n* album *m*

**alcohol** [ˈælkəhɔl] *n* alcool *m*; **~-free** *adj* sans alcool; **~ic** [ælkəˈhɔlɪk] *adj* alcoolique ♦ *n* alcoolique *m/f*; **A~ics Anonymous** Alcooliques anonymes

**ale** [eɪl] *n* bière *f*

**alert** [əˈlɜːt] *adj* alerte, vif (vive); vigilant(e) ♦ *n* alerte *f* ♦ *vt* alerter; **on the ~** sur le qui-vive; (*MIL*) en état d'alerte

**algebra** [ˈældʒɪbrə] *n* algèbre *m*

**Algeria** [ælˈdʒɪərɪə] *n* Algérie *f*

**alias** [ˈeɪlɪəs] *adv* alias ♦ *n* faux nom, nom d'emprunt; (*writer*) pseudonyme *m*

**alibi** [ˈælɪbaɪ] *n* alibi *m*

**alien** [ˈeɪlɪən] *n* étranger(-ère); (*from outer space*) extraterrestre *mf* ♦ *adj*: **~ (to)** étranger(-ère) (à)

**alight** [əˈlaɪt] *adj*, *adv* en feu ♦ *vi* mettre pied à terre; (*passenger*) descendre

**alike** [əˈlaɪk] *adj* semblable, pareil(le) ♦ *adv* de même; **to look ~** se ressembler

**alimony** [ˈælɪmənɪ] *n* (*payment*) pension *f* alimentaire

**alive** [əˈlaɪv] *adj* vivant(e); (*lively*) plein(e) de vie

---

**KEYWORD**

**all** [ɔːl] *adj* (*singular*) tout(e); (*plural*) tous (toutes); **all day** toute la journée; **all night** toute la nuit; **all men** tous les hommes; **all five** tous les cinq; **all the food** toute la nourriture; **all the books** tous les livres; **all the time** tout le temps; **all his life** toute sa vie

♦ *pron* **1** tout; **I ate it all**, **I ate all of it** j'ai tout mangé; **all of us went** nous y sommes tous allés; **all of the boys**

went tous les garçons y sont allés

**2** (*in phrases*): **above all** surtout, pardessus tout; **after all** après tout; **not at all** (*in answer to question*) pas du tout; (*in answer to thanks*) je vous en prie!; **I'm not at all tired** je ne suis pas du tout fatigué(e); **anything at all will do** n'importe quoi fera l'affaire; **all in all** bien considéré, en fin de compte

♦ *adv*: **all alone** tout(e) seul(e); **it's not as hard as all that** ce n'est pas si difficile que ça; **all the more/better** d'autant plus/mieux; **all but** presque, pratiquement; **the score is 2 all** le score est de 2 partout

**allege** [əˈledʒ] *vt* alléguer, prétendre; **~dly** [əˈledʒɪdlɪ] *adv* à ce que l'on prétend, paraît-il

**allegiance** [əˈliːdʒəns] *n* allégeance *f*, fidélité *f*, obéissance *f*

**allergic** [əˈlɜːdʒɪk] *adj*: **~ to** allergique à

**allergy** [ˈælədʒɪ] *n* allergie *f*

**alleviate** [əˈliːvɪeɪt] *vt* soulager, adoucir

**alley** [ˈælɪ] *n* ruelle *f*

**alliance** [əˈlaɪəns] *n* alliance *f*

**allied** [ˈælaɪd] *adj* allié(e)

**all-in** [ˈɔːlɪn] (*BRIT*) *adj* (*also adv*: *charge*) tout compris

**all-night** [ˈɔːlˈnaɪt] *adj* ouvert(e) *or* qui dure toute la nuit

**allocate** [ˈæləkeɪt] *vt* (*share out*) répartir, distribuer; **to ~ sth to** (*duties*) assigner *or* attribuer qch à; (*sum*, *time*) allouer qch à

**allot** [əˈlɔt] *vt*: **to ~ (to)** (*money*) répartir (entre), distribuer (à); (*time*) allouer (à); **~ment** *n* (*share*) part *f*; (*garden*) lopin *m* de terre (loué à la municipalité)

**all-out** [ˈɔːlaʊt] *adj* (*effort etc*) total(e) ♦ *adv*: **all out** à fond

**allow** [əˈlaʊ] *vt* (*practice*, *behaviour*) permettre, autoriser; (*sum to spend etc*) accorder; allouer; (*sum*, *time estimated*) compter, prévoir; (*claim*, *goal*) admettre; (*concede*): **to ~ that** convenir que; **to ~ sb to do** permettre à qn de faire, autoriser qn à faire; **he is ~ed to ...** on lui permet de ...; ~ **for** vt fus tenir compte de; **~ance** [ə'lauəns] n (money received) allocation f; subside m; indemnité f; (TAX) somme f déductible du revenu imposable, abattement m; **to make ~ances for** tenir compte de

**alloy** ['ælɔɪ] n alliage m

**all:** ~ **right** adv (feel, work) bien; (as answer) d'accord; **~-rounder** n: **to be a good ~-rounder** être doué(e) en tout; **~-time** adj (record) sans précédent, absolu(e)

**ally** [n 'ælaɪ, vb ə'laɪ] n allié m ♦ vt: **to ~ o.s. with** s'allier avec

**almighty** [ɔːl'maɪtɪ] adj tout-puissant; (tremendous) énorme

**almond** ['ɑːmənd] n amande f

**almost** ['ɔːlməust] adv presque

**alone** [ə'ləun] adj, adv seul(e); **to leave sb ~** laisser qn tranquille; **to leave sth ~** ne pas toucher à qch; **let ~ ...** sans parler de ...; encore moins ...

**along** [ə'lɔŋ] prep le long de ♦ adv: **is he coming ~ with us?** vient-il avec nous?; **he was hopping/limping ~** il avançait en sautillant/boitant; ~ **with** (together with: person) en compagnie de; (: thing) avec, en plus de; **all ~** (all the time) depuis le début; **~side** prep le long de, à côté de ♦ adv bord à bord

**aloof** [ə'luːf] adj distant(e) ♦ adv: **to stand ~** se tenir à distance or à l'écart

**aloud** [ə'laud] adv à haute voix

**alphabet** ['ælfəbet] n alphabet m; **~ical** [ælfə'betɪkl] adj alphabétique

**alpine** ['ælpaɪn] adj alpin(e), alpestre

**Alps** [ælps] npl: **the ~** les Alpes fpl

**already** [ɔːl'redɪ] adv déjà

**alright** ['ɔːl'raɪt] (BRIT) adv = **all right**

**Alsatian** [æl'seɪʃən] (BRIT) n (dog) berger allemand

**also** ['ɔːlsəu] adv aussi

**altar** ['ɔːltər] n autel m

**alter** ['ɔːltər] vt, vi changer

**alternate** [adj ɔl'təːnɪt, vb 'ɔːltəːneɪt] adj alterné(e), alternant(e), alternatif(-ive) ♦

vi alterner; **on ~ days** un jour sur deux, tous les deux jours; **alternating current** n courant alternatif

**alternative** [ɔl'təːnətɪv] adj (solutions) possible, au choix; (plan) autre, de rechange; (lifestyle etc) parallèle ♦ n (choice) alternative f; (other possibility) solution f de remplacement or de rechange, autre possibilité f; ~ **medicine** médecines fpl parallèles or douces; **~ly** adv: **~ly one could** une autre or l'autre solution serait de, on pourrait aussi

**alternator** ['ɔːltəːneɪtər] n (AUT) alternateur m

**although** [ɔːl'ðəu] conj bien que +sub

**altitude** ['æltɪtjuːd] n altitude f

**alto** ['æltəu] n (female) contralto m; (male) haute-contre f

**altogether** [ɔːltə'geðər] adv entièrement, tout à fait; (on the whole) tout compte fait; (in all) en tout

**aluminium** [ælju'mɪnɪəm] (BRIT), **aluminum** [ə'luːmɪnəm] (US) n aluminium m

**always** ['ɔːlweɪz] adv toujours

**Alzheimer's (disease)** ['æltshaɪməz-] n maladie f d'Alzheimer

**AM** n abbr (= Assembly Member) député m au Parlement gallois

**am** [æm] vb see **be**

**a.m.** adv abbr (= ante meridiem) du matin

**amalgamate** [ə'mælgəmeɪt] vt, vi fusionner

**amateur** ['æmətər] n amateur m; **~ish** (pej) adj d'amateur

**amaze** [ə'meɪz] vt stupéfier; **to be ~d (at)** être stupéfait(e) (de); **~ment** n stupéfaction f, stupeur f; **amazing** adj étonnant(e); exceptionnel(le)

**ambassador** [æm'bæsədər] n ambassadeur m

**amber** ['æmbər] n ambre m; **at ~** (BRIT: AUT) à l'orange

**ambiguous** [æm'bɪgjuəs] adj ambigu(ë)

**ambition** [æm'bɪʃən] n ambition f;

**ambitious** adj ambitieux(-euse)

**ambulance** ['æmbjʊləns] n ambulance f

**ambush** ['æmbʊʃ] n embuscade f ♦ vt tendre une embuscade à

**amenable** [ə'miːnəbl] adj: ~ to (advice etc) disposé(e) à écouter

**amend** [ə'mɛnd] vt (law) amender; (text) corriger; to make ~s réparer ses torts, faire amende honorable

**amenities** [ə'miːnɪtɪz] npl aménagements mpl, équipements mpl

**America** [ə'mɛrɪkə] n Amérique f; ~n adj américain(e) ♦ n Américain(e)

**amiable** ['eɪmɪəbl] adj aimable, affable

**amicable** ['æmɪkəbl] adj amical(e); (LAW) à l'amiable

**amid(st)** [ə'mɪd(st)] prep parmi, au milieu de

**amiss** [ə'mɪs] adj, adv: there's something ~ il y a quelque chose qui ne va pas or qui cloche; to take sth ~ prendre qch mal or de travers

**ammonia** [ə'məʊnɪə] n (gas) ammoniac m; (liquid) ammoniaque f

**ammunition** [æmjʊ'nɪʃən] n munitions fpl

**amok** [ə'mɔk] adv: to run ~ être pris(e) d'un accès de folie furieuse

**among(st)** [ə'mʌŋ(st)] prep parmi, entre

**amorous** ['æmərəs] adj amoureux(-euse)

**amount** [ə'maʊnt] n (sum) somme f, montant m; (quantity) quantité f, nombre m ♦ vi: to ~ to (total) s'élever à; (be same as) équivaloir à, revenir à

**amp(ere)** ['æmp(ɛər)] n ampère m

**ample** ['æmpl] adj ample; spacieux(-euse); (enough): this is ~ c'est largement suffisant; to have ~ time/room avoir bien assez de temps/place

**amplifier** ['æmplɪfaɪər] n amplificateur m

**amuse** [ə'mjuːz] vt amuser, divertir; ~ment n amusement m; ~ment arcade n salle f de jeu; ~ment park n

parc m d'attractions

**an** [æn, ən] indef art see a

**anaemic** [ə'niːmɪk] (US **anemic**) adj anémique

**anaesthetic** [ænɪs'θɛtɪk] (US **anesthetic**) n anesthésique m

**analog(ue)** ['ænəlɔg] adj (watch, computer) analogique

**analyse** ['ænəlaɪz] (US **analyze**) vt analyser; **analysis** [ə'næləsɪs] (pl **analyses**) n analyse f; **analyst** ['ænəlɪst] n (POL etc) spécialiste m/f; (US) psychanalyste m/f

**analyze** ['ænəlaɪz] (US) vt = **analyse**

**anarchist** ['ænəkɪst] n anarchiste m/f

**anarchy** ['ænəkɪ] n anarchie f

**anatomy** [ə'nætəmɪ] n anatomie f

**ancestor** ['ænsɪstər] n ancêtre m

**anchor** ['æŋkər] n ancre f ♦ vi (also: to drop ~) jeter l'ancre, mouiller ♦ vt mettre à l'ancre; (fig): to ~ sth to fixer qch à

**anchovy** ['æntʃəvɪ] n anchois m

**ancient** ['eɪnʃənt] adj ancien(ne), antique; (person) d'un âge vénérable; (car) antédiluvien(ne)

**ancillary** [æn'sɪlərɪ] adj auxiliaire

**and** [ænd] conj et; ~ so on et ainsi de suite; try ~ come tâchez de venir; he talked ~ talked il n'a pas arrêté de parler; better ~ better de mieux en mieux

**anew** [ə'njuː] adv à nouveau

**angel** ['eɪndʒəl] n ange m

**anger** ['æŋgər] n colère f

**angina** [æn'dʒaɪnə] n angine f de poitrine

**angle** ['æŋgl] n angle m; from their ~ de leur point de vue

**angler** ['æŋglər] n pêcheur(-euse) à la ligne

**Anglican** ['æŋglɪkən] adj, n anglican(e)

**angling** ['æŋglɪŋ] n pêche f à la ligne

**Anglo-** ['æŋgləʊ] prefix anglo(-)

**angrily** ['æŋgrɪlɪ] adv avec colère

**angry** ['æŋgrɪ] adj en colère, furieux(-euse); (wound) enflammé(e); to be ~

with sb/at sth être furieux contre qn/ de qch; **to get ~** se fâcher, se mettre en colère

**anguish** ['æŋgwɪʃ] n (mental) angoisse f

**animal** ['ænɪməl] n animal m ♦ adj animal(e)

**animate** [vb 'ænɪmeɪt, adj 'ænɪmɪt] vt animer ♦ adj animé(e), vivant(e); **~d** adj animé(e)

**aniseed** ['ænɪsiːd] n anis m

**ankle** ['æŋkl] n cheville f; **~ sock** n socquette f

**annex** ['æneks] n (BRIT: ~e) annexe f

**anniversary** [ænɪ'vəːsərɪ] n anniversaire m

**announce** [ə'naʊns] vt annoncer; (birth, death) faire part de; **~ment** n annonce f; (for births etc: in newspaper) avis m de faire-part; (: letter, card) faire-part m; **~r** n (RADIO, TV: between programmes) speaker(ine)

**annoy** [ə'nɔɪ] vt agacer, ennuyer, contrarier; **don't get ~ed!** ne vous fâchez pas!; **~ance** n mécontentement m, contrariété f; **~ing** adj agaçant(e), contrariant(e)

**annual** ['ænjuəl] adj annuel(le) ♦ n (BOT) plante annuelle; (children's book) album m

**annul** [ə'nʌl] vt annuler

**annum** ['ænəm] n see per

**anonymous** [ə'nɒnɪməs] adj anonyme

**anorak** ['ænəræk] n anorak m

**anorexia** [ænə'reksɪə] n anorexie f

**another** [ə'nʌðə*] adj: **~ book** (one more) un autre livre, encore un livre, un livre de plus; (a different one) un autre livre ♦ pron un(e) autre, encore un(e), un(e) de plus; see also **one**

**answer** ['ɑːnsə*] n réponse f; (to problem) solution f ♦ vi répondre ♦ vt (reply to) répondre à; (problem) résoudre; (prayer) exaucer; **in ~ to your letter** en réponse à votre lettre; **to ~ the phone** répondre (au téléphone); **to ~ the bell** or **the door** aller or venir

ouvrir (la porte); **~ back** vi répondre, répliquer; **~ for** vt fus (person) répondre de, se porter garant de; (crime, one's actions) être responsable de; **~ to** vt fus (description) répondre or correspondre à; **~able** adj: **~able (to sb/for sth)** responsable (devant qn/de qch); **~ing machine** n répondeur m automatique

**ant** [ænt] n fourmi f

**antagonism** [æn'tægənɪzm] n antagonisme m

**antagonize** [æn'tægənaɪz] vt éveiller l'hostilité de, contrarier

**Antarctic** [ænt'ɑːktɪk] n: **the ~** l'Antarctique m

**antenatal** ['æntɪ'neɪtl] adj prénatal(e); **~ clinic** n service m de consultation prénatale

**anthem** ['ænθəm] n: **national ~** hymne national

**anti...** [ænti] prefix: **~-aircraft** adj (missile) antiaérien(ne); **~biotic** ['æntɪbaɪ'ɔtɪk] n antibiotique m; **~body** n anticorps m

**anticipate** [æn'tɪsɪpeɪt] vt s'attendre à; prévoir; (wishes, request) aller au devant de, devancer

**anticipation** [æntɪsɪ'peɪʃən] n attente f; **in ~** par anticipation, à l'avance

**anticlimax** ['æntɪ'klaɪmæks] n déception f, douche froide (fam)

**anticlockwise** ['æntɪ'klɒkwaɪz] adj, adv dans le sens inverse des aiguilles d'une montre

**antics** ['æntɪks] npl singeries fpl

**antidepressant** ['æntɪdɪ'presnt] n antidépresseur m

**antifreeze** ['æntɪfriːz] n antigel m

**antihistamine** ['æntɪ'hɪstəmɪn] n antihistaminique m

**antiquated** ['æntɪkweɪtɪd] adj vieilli(e), suranné(e), vétuste f

**antique** [æn'tiːk] n objet m d'art ancien, meuble ancien or d'époque, antiquité f ♦ adj ancien(ne); **~ dealer** n antiquaire m; **~ shop** n magasin m d'antiquités

**anti...: ~-Semitism** ['æntɪ'semɪtɪzəm] n

antisémitisme m; **~septic** [ˈæntɪˈsɛptɪk] n antiseptique m; **~social** [ˈæntɪˈsəʊʃəl] adj peu liant(e), sauvage, insociable; (against society) antisocial(e)

**antlers** [ˈæntləz] npl bois mpl, ramure f

**anvil** [ˈænvɪl] n enclume f

**anxiety** [æŋˈzaɪətɪ] n anxiété f; (keenness): **~ to do** grand désir or impatience f de faire

**anxious** [ˈæŋkʃəs] adj anxieux(-euse), angoissé(e); (worrying: time, situation) inquiétant(e); (keen): **~ to do/that** qui tient beaucoup à faire/à ce que; impatient(e) de faire/que

---

KEYWORD

**any** [ˈɛnɪ] adj 1 (in questions etc: singular) du, de l', de la, (: plural) des; **have you any butter/children/ink?** avez-vous du beurre/des enfants/de l'encre?

2 (with negative: du, de l'): **I haven't any money/books** je n'ai pas d'argent/de livres

3 (no matter which) n'importe quel(le); **choose any book you like** vous pouvez choisir n'importe quel livre

4 (in phrases): **in any case** de toute façon; **any day now** d'un jour à l'autre; **at any moment** à tout moment, d'un instant à l'autre; **at any rate** en tout cas

♦ pron 1 (in questions etc) en; **have you got any?** est-ce que vous en avez?; **can any of you sing?** est-ce que parmi vous il y en a qui savent chanter?

2 (with negative) en; **I haven't any (of them)** je n'en ai pas, je n'en ai aucun

3 (no matter which one(s)) n'importe lequel (or laquelle); **take any of these books (you like)** vous pouvez prendre n'importe lequel de ces livres

♦ adv 1 (in questions etc): **do you want any more soup/sandwiches?** voulez-vous encore de la soupe/des sandwichs?; **are you feeling any better?** est-ce que vous vous sentez mieux?

2 (with negative): **I can't hear him any more** je ne l'entends plus; **don't wait any longer** n'attendez pas plus longtemps

**any: ~body** pron n'importe qui; (in interrogative sentences) quelqu'un; (in negative sentences): **I don't see ~body** je ne vois personne; **~how** adv (at any rate) de toute façon, quand même; (haphazard) n'importe comment; **~one** pron = **anybody**; **~thing** pron n'importe quoi, quelque chose, ne ... rien; **~way** adv de toute façon; **~where** adv n'importe où, quelque part; **I don't see him ~where** je ne le vois nulle part

**apart** [əˈpɑːt] adv (to one side) à part; de côté; à l'écart; (separately) séparément; **10 miles ~** à 10 miles l'un de l'autre; **to take ~** démonter; **~ from** à part, excepté

**apartheid** [əˈpɑːteɪt] n apartheid m

**apartment** [əˈpɑːtmənt] n (US) appartement m, logement m; (room) chambre f; **~ building** (US) n immeuble m; (divided house) maison divisée en appartements

**ape** [eɪp] n (grand) singe ♦ vt singer

**apéritif** [əˈperitif] n apéritif m

**aperture** [ˈæpətʃʊəf] n orifice m, ouverture f; (PHOT) ouverture f (du diaphragme)

**APEX** [ˈeɪpɛks] n abbr (AVIAT) (= advance purchase excursion) APEX m

**apologetic** [əpɔləˈdʒɛtɪk] adj (tone, letter) d'excuse; (person): **to be ~** s'excuser

**apologize** [əˈpɒlədʒaɪz] vi: **to ~ (for sth to sb)** s'excuser (de qch auprès de qn), présenter les excuses (à qn pour qch)

**apology** [əˈpɒlədʒɪ] n excuses fpl

**apostle** [əˈpɒsl] n apôtre m

**apostrophe** [əˈpɒstrəfɪ] n apostrophe f

**appalling** [əˈpɔːlɪŋ] adj épouvantable; (stupidity) consternant(e)

**apparatus** [æpəˈreɪtəs] n appareil m, dispositif m; (in gymnasium) agrès mpl; (of government) dispositif m

**apparel** [əˈpærəl] (US) n habillement m

**apparent** [əˈpærənt] adj apparent(e); **~ly** adv apparemment

**appeal** [əˈpiːl] vi (LAW) faire or interjeter appel ♦ n appel m; (request) prière f; appel m; (charm) attrait m, charme m; **to ~ for** lancer un appel pour; **to ~ to** (beg) supplier; (be attractive) plaire à; **it doesn't ~ to me** cela ne m'attire pas; **~ing** adj (attractive) attrayant(e)

**appear** [əˈpɪəʳ] vi apparaître, se montrer; (LAW) comparaître; (publication) paraître, sortir, être publié(e); (seem) paraître, sembler; **it would ~ that** il semble que; **to ~ in Hamlet** jouer dans Hamlet; **to ~ on TV** passer à la télé; **~ance** n apparition f; parution f; (look, aspect) apparence f, aspect m

**appease** [əˈpiːz] vt apaiser, calmer

**appendicitis** [əpendɪˈsaɪtɪs] n appendicite f

**appendix** [əˈpendɪks] (pl **appendices**) n appendice m

**appetite** [ˈæpɪtaɪt] n appétit m; **appetizer** n amuse-gueule m; (drink) apéritif m

**applaud** [əˈplɔːd] vt, vi applaudir

**applause** [əˈplɔːz] n applaudissements mpl

**apple** [ˈæpl] n pomme f; **~ tree** n pommier m

**appliance** [əˈplaɪəns] n appareil m

**applicable** [əˈplɪkəbl] adj (relevant): **to be ~ to** valoir pour

**applicant** [ˈæplɪkənt] n: **~ (for)** candidat(e) (à)

**application** [æplɪˈkeɪʃən] n application f; (for a job, a grant etc) demande f; candidature f; **~ form** n formulaire m de demande

**applied** [əˈplaɪd] adj appliqué(e)

**apply** [əˈplaɪ] vt: **to ~ (to)** (paint, ointment) appliquer (sur); (law etc) appli-

quer (à) ♦ vi: **to ~ to** (be suitable for, relevant to) s'appliquer à; (ask) s'adresser à; **to ~ (for)** (permit, grant) faire une demande en vue d'obtenir; (job) poser sa candidature (pour), faire une demande d'emploi (concernant); **to ~ o.s. to** s'appliquer à

**appoint** [əˈpɔɪnt] vt nommer, engager; **~ed** adj: **at the ~ed time** à l'heure dite; **~ment** n nomination f; (meeting) rendez-vous m; **to make an ~ment (with)** prendre rendez-vous (avec)

**appraisal** [əˈpreɪzl] n évaluation f

**appreciate** [əˈpriːʃɪeɪt] vt (like) apprécier; (be grateful for) être reconnaissant(e) de; (understand) comprendre; se rendre compte de ♦ vi (FINANCE) prendre de la valeur

**appreciation** [əpriːʃɪˈeɪʃən] n appréciation f; (gratitude) reconnaissance f; (COMM) hausse f, valorisation f

**appreciative** [əˈpriːʃɪətɪv] adj (person) sensible; (comment) élogieux(-euse)

**apprehensive** [æprɪˈhensɪv] adj inquiet(-ète), appréhensif(-ive)

**apprentice** [əˈprentɪs] n apprenti m; **~ship** n apprentissage m

**approach** [əˈprəʊtʃ] vi approcher ♦ vt (come near) approcher de; (ask, apply to) s'adresser à; (situation, problem) aborder ♦ n approche f; (access) accès m; **~able** adj accessible

**appropriate** [adj əˈprəʊprɪɪt, vb əˈprəʊprɪeɪt] adj (moment, remark) opportun(e); (tool etc) approprié(e) ♦ vt (take) s'approprier

**approval** [əˈpruːvəl] n approbation f; **on ~** (COMM) à l'examen

**approve** [əˈpruːv] vt approuver; **~ of** vt fus approuver

**approximate** [adj əˈprɒksɪmɪt, vb əˈprɒksɪmeɪt] adj approximatif(-ive) ♦ vt se rapprocher de, être proche de; **~ly** adv approximativement

**apricot** [ˈeɪprɪkɒt] n abricot m

**April** [ˈeɪprəl] n avril m; **~ Fool's Day** n le premier avril

---
**April Fool's Day**

April Fool's Day est le 1er avril, à l'occasion duquel on fait des farces de toutes sortes. Les victimes de ces farces sont les "April fools". Les médias britanniques se prennent aussi au jeu, diffusant de fausses nouvelles, comme la découverte d'îles de la taille de l'Irlande, ou faisant des reportages bidon, montrant par exemple la culture d'arbres à spaghettis en Italie.

---

**apron** ['eɪprən] n tablier m

**apt** [æpt] adj (suitable) approprié(e); (likely): ~ **to do** susceptible de faire; qui a tendance à faire

**Aquarius** [ə'kwɛərɪəs] n le Verseau

**Arab** ['ærəb] adj arabe ♦ n Arabe m/f; **~ian** [ə'reɪbɪən] adj arabe; **~ic** adj arabe ♦ n arabe m

**arbitrary** ['ɑːbɪtrərɪ] adj arbitraire

**arbitration** [ɑːbɪ'treɪʃən] n arbitrage m

**arcade** [ɑː'keɪd] n arcade f; (passage with shops) passage m, galerie marchande; (with video games) salle f de jeu

**arch** [ɑːtʃ] n arc m, (of foot) cambrure f, voûte f plantaire ♦ vt arquer, cambrer

**archaeologist** [ɑːkɪ'ɔlədʒɪst] n archéologue m/f

**archaeology** [ɑːkɪ'ɔlədʒɪ] n archéologie f

**archbishop** [ɑːtʃ'bɪʃəp] n archevêque m

**archeology** etc (US) [ɑːkɪ'ɔlədʒɪ] = **archaeology** etc

**archery** ['ɑːtʃərɪ] n tir m à l'arc

**architect** ['ɑːkɪtekt] n architecte m; **~ure** n architecture f

**archives** ['ɑːkaɪvz] npl archives fpl

**Arctic** ['ɑːktɪk] adj arctique ♦ n Arctique m

**ardent** ['ɑːdənt] adj fervent(e)

**are** [ɑː] vb see **be**

**area** ['ɛərɪə] n (GEOM) superficie f; (zone) région f; (: smaller) secteur m, partie f

(in room) coin m; (knowledge, research) domaine m; ~ **code** (US) n (TEL) indicatif m téléphonique

**aren't** [ɑːnt] = **are not**

**Argentina** [ɑːdʒən'tiːnə] n Argentine f; **Argentinian** [ɑːdʒən'tɪnɪən] adj argentin(e) ♦ n Argentin(e)

**arguably** ['ɑːgjuəblɪ] adv: **it is ~** ... on peut soutenir que c'est ...

**argue** [ɑːgjuː] vi (quarrel) se disputer; (reason) argumenter; **to ~ that** objecter or alléguer que

**argument** ['ɑːgjumənt] n (reasons) argument m; (quarrel) dispute f; **~ative** [ɑːgju'mentətɪv] adj ergoteur(-euse), raisonneur(-euse)

**Aries** ['ɛərɪz] n le Bélier

**arise** [ə'raɪz] (pt arose, pp arisen) vi survenir, se présenter

**aristocrat** ['ærɪstəkræt] n aristocrate m/f

**arithmetic** [ə'rɪθmətɪk] n arithmétique f

**ark** [ɑːk] n: **Noah's A~** l'Arche f de Noé

**arm** [ɑːm] n bras m ♦ vt armer; **~s** npl (weapons, HERALDRY) armes fpl; **~ in ~** bras dessus bras dessous

**armaments** ['ɑːməmənts] npl armement m

**armchair** [ɑːm'tʃeər] n fauteuil m

**armed** [ɑːmd] adj armé(e); **~ robbery** n vol m à main armée

**armour** ['ɑːmər] (US **armor**) n armure f; (MIL: tanks) blindés mpl; **~ed car** n véhicule blindé

**armpit** ['ɑːmpɪt] n aisselle f

**armrest** ['ɑːmrɛst] n accoudoir m

**army** ['ɑːmɪ] n armée f

**A road** (BRIT) n (AUT) route nationale

**aroma** [ə'rəumə] n arôme m; **~therapy** n aromathérapie f

**arose** [ə'rəuz] pt of **arise**

**around** [ə'raund] adv autour; (nearby) dans les parages ♦ prep autour de; (near) près de; (fig: about) environ; (date, time) vers

**arouse** [əˈrauz] vt (sleeper) éveiller; (curiosity, passions) éveiller, susciter; (anger) exciter

**arrange** [əˈreɪndʒ] vt arranger; **to ~ to do sth** prévoir de faire qch; **~ment** n arrangement m; **~ments** npl (plans etc) arrangements mpl, dispositions fpl

**array** [əˈreɪ] n: **~ of** déploiement m or étalage m de

**arrears** [əˈrɪəz] npl arriéré m; **to be in ~ with one's rent** devoir un arriéré de loyer

**arrest** [əˈrɛst] vt arrêter; (sb's attention) retenir, attirer ♦ n arrestation f; **under ~** en état d'arrestation

**arrival** [əˈraɪvl] n arrivée f; **new ~** nouveau venu, nouvelle venue; (baby) nouveau-né(e)

**arrive** [əˈraɪv] vi arriver

**arrogant** [ˈærəgənt] adj arrogant(e)

**arrow** [ˈærəu] n flèche f

**arse** [ɑːs] (BRIT: infl) n cul m (!)

**arson** [ˈɑːsn] n incendie criminel

**art** [ɑːt] n art m; **A~s** (SCOL) les lettres fpl

**artery** [ˈɑːtərɪ] n artère f

**art gallery** n musée m d'art; (small and private) galerie f de peinture

**arthritis** [ɑːˈθraɪtɪs] n arthrite f

**artichoke** [ˈɑːtɪtʃəuk] n (also: **globe ~**) artichaut m; (also: **Jerusalem ~**) topinambour m

**article** [ˈɑːtɪkl] n article m; **~s** npl (BRIT: LAW: training) ≃ stage m; **~ of clothing** vêtement m

**articulate** [adj ɑːˈtɪkjulɪt, vb ɑːˈtɪkjuleɪt] adj (person) qui s'exprime bien; (speech) bien articulé(e), prononcé(e) clairement ♦ vt exprimer; **~d lorry** (BRIT) n (camion m) semi-remorque m

**artificial** [ɑːtɪˈfɪʃəl] adj artificiel(le); **~ respiration** n respiration artificielle

**artist** [ˈɑːtɪst] n artiste m/f; **~ic** [ɑːˈtɪstɪk] adj artistique; **~ry** n art m, talent m

**art school** n ≃ école f des beaux-arts

**as** [æz, əz] conj **1** (referring to time) comme, alors que; à mesure que; **he came in as I was leaving** il est arrivé comme je partais; **as the years went by** à mesure que les années passaient; **as from tomorrow** à partir de demain

**2** (in comparisons): **as big as** aussi grand que; **twice as big as** deux fois plus grand que; **as much** or **many as** autant que; **as much money/many books** autant d'argent/de livres que; **as soon as** dès que

**3** (since, because) comme, puisque; **as he had to be home by 10 ...** comme il or puisqu'il devait être de retour avant 10 h ...

**4** (referring to manner, way) comme; **do as you wish** faites comme vous voudrez

**5** (concerning): **as for** or **to that** quant à cela, pour ce qui est de cela

**6: as if** or **though** comme si; **he looked as if he was ill** il avait l'air d'être malade; see also **long; such; well**

♦ prep: **he works as a driver** il travaille comme chauffeur; **as chairman of the company, he ...** en tant que président de la société, il ...; **dressed up as a cowboy** déguisé en cowboy; **he gave me it as a present** il me l'a offert, il m'en a fait cadeau

**a.s.a.p.** abbr (= as soon as possible) dès que possible

**asbestos** [æzˈbɛstəs] n amiante f

**ascend** [əˈsɛnd] vt gravir; (throne) monter sur

**ascertain** [æsəˈteɪn] vt vérifier

**ash** [æʃ] n (dust) cendre f; (also: **~ tree**) frêne m

**ashamed** [əˈʃeɪmd] adj honteux(-euse), confus(e); **to be ~ of** avoir honte de

**ashore** [əˈʃɔː] adv à terre

**ashtray** [ˈæʃtreɪ] n cendrier m

**Ash Wednesday** n mercredi m des cendres

**Asia** ['eɪʃə] n Asie f; **~n** n Asiatique m/f ♦ adj asiatique

**aside** [ə'saɪd] adv de côté; à l'écart ♦ n aparté m

**ask** [ɑːsk] vt demander; (invite) inviter; **to ~ sb sth/to do sth** demander qch à qn/à qn de faire qch; **to ~ sb about sth** questionner qn sur qch; **to ~** se renseigner auprès de qn sur qch; **to ~ (sb) a question** poser une question (à qn); **to ~ sb out to dinner** inviter qn au restaurant; **~ after** vt fus demander des nouvelles de; **~ for** vt fus demander; (trouble) chercher

**asking price** ['ɑːskɪŋ-] n: **the ~** le prix de départ

**asleep** [ə'sliːp] adj endormi(e); **to fall ~** s'endormir

**asparagus** [əs'pærəgəs] n asperges fpl

**aspect** ['æspekt] n aspect m; (direction in which a building etc faces) orientation f, exposition f

**aspire** [əs'paɪə] vi: **to ~** aspirer à

**aspirin** ['æsprɪn] n aspirine f

**ass** [æs] n âne m; (inf) imbécile m/f; (US: inf!) cul m (!)

**assailant** [ə'seɪlənt] n agresseur m; assaillant m

**assassinate** [ə'sæsɪneɪt] vt assassiner; **assassination** [əsæsɪ'neɪʃən] n assassinat m

**assault** [ə'sɔːlt] n (MIL) assaut m; (gen: attack) agression f ♦ vt attaquer; (sexually) violenter

**assemble** [ə'sembl] vt assembler ♦ vi s'assembler, se rassembler; **assembly** n assemblée f, réunion f; (institution) assemblée; (construction) assemblage m; **assembly line** n chaîne f de montage

**assent** [ə'sent] n assentiment m, consentement m

**assert** [ə'sɜːt] vt affirmer, déclarer; (one's authority) faire valoir; (one's innocence) protester de

**assess** [ə'ses] vt évaluer; (tax, payment)

établir or fixer le montant de; (property etc: for tax) calculer la valeur imposable de; (person) juger la valeur de; **~ment** n évaluation f, fixation f, calcul m de la valeur imposable de, jugement m; **~or** n expert m (impôt and assurance)

**asset** ['æset] n avantage m, atout m; **~s** npl (FINANCE) capital m; avoir(s) m(pl); actif m

**assign** [ə'saɪn] vt (date) fixer; (task) assigner à; (resources) affecter à; **~ment** n tâche f, mission f

**assist** [ə'sɪst] vt aider, assister; **~ance** n aide f, assistance f; **~ant** n assistant(e), adjoint(e); (BRIT: also: **shop ~ant**) vendeur(-euse)

**associate** [n, adj ə'səʊʃɪɪt, vb ə'səʊʃɪeɪt] adj, n associé(e) ♦ vt associer ♦ vi: **to ~ with sb** fréquenter qn; **association** [əsəʊsɪ'eɪʃən] n association f

**assorted** [ə'sɔːtɪd] adj assorti(e)

**assortment** [ə'sɔːtmənt] n assortiment m

**assume** [ə'sjuːm] vt supposer; (responsibilities etc) assumer; (attitude, name) prendre, adopter; **assumption** [ə'sʌmpʃən] n supposition f, hypothèse f; (of power) assomption f, prise f

**assurance** [ə'ʃʊərəns] n assurance f

**assure** [ə'ʃʊə] vt assurer

**asthma** ['æsmə] n asthme m

**astonish** [ə'stɒnɪʃ] vt étonner, stupéfier; **~ment** n étonnement m

**astound** [ə'staʊnd] vt stupéfier, sidérer

**astray** [ə'streɪ] adv: **to go ~** s'égarer; (fig) quitter le droit chemin; **to lead ~** détourner du droit chemin

**astride** [ə'straɪd] prep à cheval sur

**astrology** [əs'trɒlədʒɪ] n astrologie f

**astronaut** ['æstrənɔːt] n astronaute m/f

**astronomy** [əs'trɒnəmɪ] n astronomie f

**asylum** [ə'saɪləm] n asile m

```
KEYWORD
```

**at** [æt] prep **1** (referring to position, direction) à; **at the top** au sommet; **at home/school** à la maison or chez soi/à

l'école; **at the baker's** à la boulangerie, chez le boulanger; **to look at sth** regarder qch
**2** (referring to time): **at 4 o'clock** à 4 heures; **at Christmas** à Noël; **at night** la nuit; **at times** par moments, parfois
**3** (referring to rates, speed etc) à; **at £1 a kilo** une livre le kilo; **two at a time** deux à la fois; **at 50 km/h** à 50 km/h
**4** (referring to manner): **at a stroke** d'un seul coup; **at peace** en paix
**5** (referring to activity): **to be at work** être au travail, travailler; **to play at cowboys** jouer aux cowboys; **to be good at sth** être bon en qch
**6** (referring to cause): **shocked/surprised/annoyed at sth** choqué par/étonné de/agacé par qch; **I went at his suggestion** j'y suis allé sur son conseil

**ate** [eɪt] pt of **eat**
**atheist** ['eɪθɪɪst] n athée m/f
**Athens** ['æθɪnz] n Athènes
**athlete** ['æθliːt] n athlète m/f; **athletic** [æθ'letɪk] adj athlétique ♦ n: **athletics** [æθ'letɪks] n athlétisme m
**Atlantic** [ət'læntɪk] adj atlantique ♦ n: **the ~ (Ocean)** l'(océan m) Atlantique m
**atlas** ['ætləs] n atlas m
**ATM** n abbr (= automated telling machine) guichet m automatique
**atmosphere** ['ætməsfɪə'] n atmosphère f
**atom** ['ætəm] n atome m; **~ic** [ə'tɒmɪk] adj atomique; **~(ic) bomb** n bombe f atomique; **~izer** n atomiseur m
**atone** [ə'təʊn] vi: **to ~ for** expier, racheter
**atrocious** [ə'trəʊʃəs] adj (very bad) atroce, exécrable
**attach** [ə'tætʃ] vt attacher; (document, letter) joindre; **to be ~ed to sb/sth** être attaché à qn/qch
**attaché case** [ə'tæʃeɪ] n mallette f, attaché-case m

**attachment** [ə'tætʃmənt] n (tool) accessoire m; (love): **~ (to)** affection f (pour), attachement m (à)
**attack** [ə'tæk] vt attaquer; (task etc) s'attaquer à ♦ n attaque f; (also: **heart ~**) crise f cardiaque
**attain** [ə'teɪn] vt (also: **to ~ to**) parvenir à, atteindre; (: knowledge) acquérir
**attempt** [ə'tempt] n tentative f, essai m ♦ vt essayer, tenter; **to make an ~ on sb's life** attenter à la vie de qn; **~ed** adj: **~ed murder/suicide** tentative f de meurtre/suicide
**attend** [ə'tend] vt (course) suivre; (meeting, talk) assister à; (school, church) aller à, fréquenter; (patient) soigner, s'occuper de; **~ to** vt fus (needs, affairs etc) s'occuper de; (customer, patient) s'occuper de; **~ance** n (being present) présence f; (people present) assistance f; **~ant** n employé(e) ♦ adj (dangers) inhérent(e), concomitant(e)
**attention** [ə'tenʃən] n attention f; **~!** (MIL) garde-à-vous!; **for the ~ of** (ADMIN) à l'attention de
**attentive** [ə'tentɪv] adj attentif(-ive); (kind) prévenant(e)
**attest** [ə'test] vi: **to ~ to** (demonstrate) démontrer; (confirm) témoigner
**attic** ['ætɪk] n grenier m
**attitude** ['ætɪtjuːd] n attitude f; pose f, maintien m
**attorney** [ə'tɜːnɪ] n (US: lawyer) avoué m; **A~ General** (BRIT) ≈ procureur général; (US) ≈ garde m des Sceaux, ministre m de la Justice
**attract** [ə'trækt] vt attirer; **~ion** (gen pl: pleasant things) attraction f, attrait m; (PHYSICS) attraction f; (fig: towards sb or sth) attirance f; **~ive** adj attrayant(e); (person) séduisant(e)
**attribute** [n 'ætrɪbjuːt, vb ə'trɪbjuːt] n attribut m ♦ vt: **to ~ sth to** attribuer qch à
**attrition** [ə'trɪʃən] n: **war of ~** guerre f d'usure
**aubergine** ['əʊbəʒiːn] n aubergine f

**auction** ['ɔːkʃən] n (also: **sale by ~**) vente f aux enchères ♦ vt (also: **sell by ~**) vendre aux enchères; (also: **put up for ~**) mettre aux enchères; **~eer** [ɔːkʃə'nɪə*] n commissaire-priseur m

**audience** ['ɔːdɪəns] n (people) assistance f; public m; spectateurs mpl; (interview) audience f

**audiovisual** ['ɔːdɪəu'vɪzjuəl] adj audiovisuel(le); **~ aids** npl supports ou moyens audiovisuels

**audit** ['ɔːdɪt] vt vérifier

**audition** [ɔː'dɪʃən] n audition f

**auditor** ['ɔːdɪtə*] n vérificateur m des comptes

**augur** ['ɔːgə*] vi: **it ~s well** c'est bon signe ou de bon augure

**August** ['ɔːgəst] n août m

**aunt** [ɑːnt] n tante f; **~ie**, **~y** ['ɑːntɪ] n dimin of **aunt**

**au pair** ['əu'peə*] n (also: **~ girl**) jeune fille f au pair

**auspicious** [ɔːs'pɪʃəs] adj de bon augure, propice

**Australia** [ɔs'treɪlɪə] n Australie f; **~n** adj australien(ne) ♦ n Australien(ne)

**Austria** ['ɔstrɪə] n Autriche f; **~n** adj autrichien(ne) ♦ n Autrichien(ne)

**authentic** [ɔː'θentɪk] adj authentique

**author** ['ɔːθə*] n auteur m

**authoritarian** [ɔːθɔrɪ'teərɪən] adj autoritaire

**authoritative** [ɔː'θɔrɪtətɪv] adj (account) digne de foi; (study, treatise) qui fait autorité; (person, manner) autoritaire

**authority** [ɔː'θɔrɪtɪ] n autorité f; (permission) autorisation (formelle); **the authorities** npl (ruling body) les autorités fpl, l'administration f

**authorize** ['ɔːθəraɪz] vt autoriser

**auto** ['ɔːtəu] (US) n auto f, voiture f

**auto-**: **~biography** [ɔːtəbaɪ'ɔgrəfɪ] n autobiographie f; **~graph** ['ɔːtəgrɑːf] n autographe m ♦ vt signer, dédicacer; **~mated** ['ɔːtəmeɪtɪd] adj automatisé(e), automatique; **~matic** [ɔːtə'mæt-

ɪk] adj automatique ♦ n (gun) automatique m; (washing machine) machine f à laver automatique; (BRIT: AUT) voiture f à transmission automatique; **~matically** adv automatiquement; **~mation** [ɔːtə'meɪʃən] n automatisation f (électronique); **~mobile** [ɔːtəmə'biːl] (US) n automobile f; **~nomy** [ɔː'tɔnəmɪ] n autonomie f

**autumn** ['ɔːtəm] n automne m; **in ~** en automne

**auxiliary** [ɔːg'zɪlɪərɪ] adj auxiliaire ♦ n auxiliaire m/f

**avail** [ə'veɪl] vt: **to ~ o.s. of** profiter de ♦ n: **to no ~** sans résultat, en vain, en pure perte

**availability** [əveɪlə'bɪlɪtɪ] n disponibilité f

**available** [ə'veɪləbl] adj disponible

**avalanche** ['ævəlɑːnʃ] n avalanche f

**Ave** abbr = **avenue**

**avenge** [ə'vendʒ] vt venger

**avenue** ['ævənjuː] n avenue f; (fig) moyen m

**average** ['ævərɪdʒ] n moyenne f; (fig) moyen ♦ adj moyen(ne) ♦ vt (a certain figure) atteindre ou faire etc en moyenne; **on ~** en moyenne; **~ out** vi: **to ~ out at** représenter en moyenne, donner une moyenne de

**averse** [ə'vɜːs] adj: **to be ~ to sth/ doing** sth éprouver une forte répugnance envers qch/à faire qch

**avert** [ə'vɜːt] vt (danger) prévenir, écarter; (one's eyes) détourner

**aviary** ['eɪvɪərɪ] n volière f

**avocado** [ævə'kɑːdəu] n (BRIT: ~ pear) avocat m

**avoid** [ə'vɔɪd] vt éviter

**await** [ə'weɪt] vt attendre

**awake** [ə'weɪk] (pt **awoke**, pp **awoken**) adj éveillé(e) ♦ vt éveiller ♦ vi s'éveiller; **~ to** (dangers, possibilities) conscient(e) de; **to be ~** être réveillé(e); **he was still ~** il ne dormait pas encore; **~ning** n réveil m

**award** [ə'wɔːd] n récompense f, prix m;

(LAW: *damages*) dommages-intérêts *mpl*
♦ *vt* (*prize*) décerner; (LAW: *damages*)
accorder

**aware** [əˈwɛəʳ] *adj*: ~ **(of)** (*conscious*)
conscient(e) (de); (*informed*) au courant
(de); **to become ~ of/that** prendre
conscience de/que; **to realize** se
rendre compte de/que; **~ness** *n* conscience *f*, connaissance *f*

**away** [əˈweɪ] *adj, adv* (au) loin; absent(e); **two kilometres ~** à (une distance de) deux kilomètres, à deux kilomètres de distance; **two hours ~ by
car** à deux heures de voiture or de route; **the holiday was two weeks ~** il
restait deux semaines jusqu'aux vacances; **~ from** loin de; **he's ~ for a week**
il est parti (pour) une semaine; **to
pedal/work/laugh ~** être en train de
pédaler/travailler/rire; **to fade ~**
(*sound*) s'affaiblir; (*colour*) s'estomper;
**to wither ~** (*plant*) se dessécher;
**to take ~** emporter; (*subtract*) enlever; **~
game** *n* (SPORT) match *m* à l'extérieur

**awe** [ɔː] *n* respect mêlé de crainte; **~-
inspiring** [ˈɔːɪnspaɪərɪŋ] *adj* impressionnant(e)

**awful** [ˈɔːfəl] *adj* affreux(-euse); **an ~
lot (of)** un nombre incroyable (de); **~ly**
*adv* (*very*) terriblement, vraiment

**awkward** [ˈɔːkwəd] *adj* (*clumsy*) gauche, maladroit(e); (*inconvenient*) peu
pratique; (*embarrassing*) gênant(e), délicat(e)

**awning** [ˈɔːnɪŋ] *n* (*of tent*) auvent *m*;
(*of shop*) store *m*; (*of hotel etc*) marquise *f*

**awoke** [əˈwəuk] *pt of* **awake**; **~n**
[əˈwəukən] *pp of* **awake**

**axe** [æks] (*US* **ax**) *n* hache *f* ♦ *vt* (*project
etc*) abandonner; (*jobs*) supprimer

**axes¹** [ˈæksɪz] *npl of* **axe**

**axes²** [ˈæksiːz] *npl of* **axis**

**axis** [ˈæksɪs] (*pl* **axes**) *n* axe *m*

**axle** [ˈæksl] *n* (*also*: **~-tree** AUT) essieu *m*

**ay(e)** [aɪ] *excl* (*yes*) oui

## B, b

**B** [biː] *n* (MUS) si *m*; **~ road** (BRIT) route
départementale

**B.A.** *abbr* = **Bachelor of Arts**

**babble** [ˈbæbl] *vi* bredouiller; (*baby,
stream*) gazouiller

**baby** [ˈbeɪbɪ] *n* bébé *m*; (*US: inf: darling*): **come on, ~!** viens ma belle/mon
gars!; **~ carriage** (US) *n* voiture *f* d'enfant; **~ food** *n* aliments *mpl* pour bébé(s); **~-sit** *vi* garder les enfants; **~-
sitter** *n* baby-sitter *m/f*; **~ wipe** *n* lingette *f* (*pour bébé*)

**bachelor** [ˈbætʃələʳ] *n* célibataire *m*; **B~
of Arts/Science** ≃ licencié(e) ès or en
lettres/sciences

**back** [bæk] *n* (*of person, horse, book*)
dos *m*; (*of hand*) dos, revers *m*; (*of
house*) derrière *m*; (*of car, train*) arrière
*m*; (*of chair*) dossier *m*; (*of page*) verso
*m*; (*of room, audience*) fond *m*; (SPORT)
arrière *m* ♦ *vt* (*candidate: also*: **~ up**)
soutenir, appuyer; (*horse: at races*) parier or miser sur; (*car*) (faire) reculer ♦ *vi*
(*also*: **~ up**) reculer; (*also*: **~ up**: *car etc*)
faire marche arrière ♦ *adj* (*in compounds*)
de derrière, à l'arrière ♦ *adv* (*not forward*) en arrière; (*returned*): **he's ~** il
est rentré, il est de retour; (*restitution*):
**throw the ball ~** renvoie la balle;
(*again*): **he called ~** il a rappelé;
**~ seat/wheel** (AUT) siège *m*/roue *f* arrière
*inv*; **~ payments/rent** arriéré *m* de
paiements/loyer; **he ran ~** il est revenu en courant; **~ down** *vi* rabattre de
ses prétentions; **~ out** *vi* (*of promise*) se
dédire; **~ up** *vi* (*candidate etc*) soutenir,
appuyer; (COMPUT) sauvegarder; **~ache**
*n* mal *m* de dos; **~bencher** (BRIT) *n*
membre du parlement sans portefeuille;
**~bone** *n* colonne vertébrale, épine
dorsale; **~date** *vt* (*letter*) antidater;
**~dated pay rise** augmentation *f* avec
effet rétroactif; **~fire** *vi* (AUT) pétarader;

(*plans*) mal tourner; **~ground** *n* arrière-plan *m*; (*of events*) situation *f*, conjecture *f*; (*basic knowledge*) éléments *mpl* de base; (*experience*) formation *f*; **family ~ground** milieu familial; **~hand** *t* (TENNIS: *also*: **~hand stroke**) revers *m*; **~hander** (BRIT) *n* (*bribe*) pot-de-vin *m*; **~ing** *n* (*fig*) soutien *m*, appui *m*; **~lash** *n* contre-coup *m*, répercussion *f*; **~log** *n*: **~log of work** travail *m* en retard; **~ number** *n* (*of magazine etc*) vieux numéro; **~pack** *n* sac *m* à dos; **~packer** randonneur(-euse); **~ pain** *n* mal *m* de dos; **~ pay** *n* rappel *m* de salaire; **~side** (*inf*) *n* derrière *m*, postérieur(-euse); **~stage** *adv* ♦ *n* derrière la scène, dans la coulisse; **~stroke** *n* dos crawlé; **~up** *adj* (*train, plane*) supplémentaire, de réserve; (COMPUT) de sauvegarde ♦ *n* (*support*) appui *m*, soutien *m*; (*also*: **~up disk/file**) sauvegarde *f*; **~ward** *adj* (*movement*) en arrière; (*person, country*) arriéré(e); attardé(e); **~wards** *adv* (*move, go*) en arrière; (*read a list*) à l'envers, à rebours; (*fall*) à la renverse; (*walk*) à reculons; **~water** *n* (*fig*) coin reculé, bled perdu (*péj*); **~yard** *n* arrière-cour *f*

**bacon** ['beɪkən] *n* bacon *m*, lard *m*

**bacteria** [bæk'tɪərɪə] *npl* bactéries *fpl*

**bad** [bæd] *adj* mauvais(e); (*child*) vilain(e); (*mistake, accident etc*) grave; (*meat, food*) gâté(e), avarié(e); **his ~ leg** sa jambe malade; **to go ~** (*meat, food*) se gâter

**badge** [bædʒ] *n* insigne *m*; (*of policeman*) plaque *f*

**badger** ['bædʒə*r*] *n* blaireau *m*

**badly** ['bædlɪ] *adv* (*work, dress etc*) mal; **~ wounded** grièvement blessé; **he needs it ~** il en a absolument besoin; **~ off** *adj, adv* dans la gêne

**badminton** ['bædmɪntən] *n* badminton *m*

**bad-tempered** ['bæd'tempəd] *adj* (*person: by nature*) ayant mauvais caractère; (: *on one occasion*) de mauvaise

**baffle** ['bæfl] *vt* (*puzzle*) déconcerter

**bag** [bæg] *n* sac *m* ♦ *vt* (*inf: take*) empocher; s'approprier; **~s of** (*inf: lots of*) des masses de; **~gage** *n* bagages *mpl*; **~gage allowance** *n* franchise *f* de bagages; **~gage reclaim** *n* livraison *f* de bagages; **~gy** *adj* avachi(e), qui fait des poches; **~pipes** *npl* cornemuse *f*

**bail** [beɪl] *n* (*payment*) caution *f*; (*release*) mise *f* en liberté sous caution ♦ *vt* (*prisoner: also*: **grant ~ to**) mettre en liberté sous caution; (*boat: also*: **~ out**) écoper; **on ~** (*prisoner*) sous caution; *see also* **bale**; **~ out** *vt* (*prisoner*) payer la caution de

**bailiff** ['beɪlɪf] *n* (BRIT) ≃ huissier *m*; (US) ≃ huissier-audiencier *m*

**bait** [beɪt] *n* appât *m* ♦ *vt* appâter; (*fig: tease*) tourmenter

**bake** [beɪk] *vt* (*faire*) cuire au four ♦ *vi* (*bread etc*) cuire (au four); (*make cakes etc*) faire de la pâtisserie; **~d beans** *npl* haricots blancs à la sauce tomate; **~d potato** *n* pomme *f* de terre en robe des champs; **~r** *n* boulanger *m*; **~ry** *n* boulangerie *f*; boulangerie industrielle; **baking** *n* cuisson *f*; **baking powder** *n* levure *f* (chimique)

**balance** ['bæləns] *n* équilibre *m*; (COMM: *sum*) solde *m*; (*remainder*) reste *m*; (*scales*) balance *f* ♦ *vt* mettre ou faire tenir en équilibre; (*pros and cons*) peser; (*budget*) équilibrer; (*account*) balancer; **~ of trade/payments** balance commerciale/des comptes *ou* paiements; **~d** *adj* (*personality, diet*) équilibré(e); (*report*) objectif(-ive); **~ sheet** *n* bilan *m*

**balcony** ['bælkənɪ] *n* balcon *m*; (*in theatre*) deuxième balcon

**bald** [bɔ:ld] *adj* chauve; (*tyre*) lisse

**bale** [beɪl] *n* balle *f*, ballot *m*; **~ out** *vi* (*of a plane*) sauter en parachute

**ball** [bɔ:l] *n* boule *f*; (*football*) ballon *m*; (*for tennis, golf*) balle *f*; (*of wool*) pelote *f*; (*of string*) bobine *f*; (*dance*) bal *m*; **to**

play ~ (with sb) (fig) coopérer (avec qn)

**ballast** ['bæləst] n lest m

**ball bearings** npl roulement m à billes

**ballerina** [bælə'ri:nə] n ballerine f

**ballet** ['bæleɪ] n ballet m; (art) danse f (classique); ~ **dancer** n danceur(-euse) m/f de ballet; ~ **shoe** n chausson m de danse

**balloon** [bə'lu:n] n ballon m; (in comic strip) bulle f

**ballot** ['bælət] n scrutin m; ~ **paper** n bulletin m de vote

**ballpoint (pen)** ['bɔ:lpɔɪnt(-)] n stylo m à bille

**ballroom** ['bɔ:lrum] n salle f de bal

**ban** [bæn] n interdiction f ♦ vt interdire

**banana** [bə'nɑ:nə] n banane f

**band** [bænd] n bande f; (at a dance) orchestre m; (MIL) musique f, fanfare f; ~ **together** vi se liguer

**bandage** ['bændɪdʒ] n bandage m, pansement m ♦ vt bander

**Bandaid** ® ['bændeɪd] (US) n pansement adhésif

**bandit** n bandit m

**bandy-legged** ['bændɪ'legɪd] adj aux jambes arquées

**bang** [bæŋ] n détonation f; (of door) claquement m; (blow) coup (violent) m ♦ vt frapper (violemment); (door) claquer ♦ vi détoner; claquer ♦ excl pan!; ~s (US) npl (fringe) frange f

**banish** ['bænɪʃ] vt bannir

**banister(s)** ['bænɪstə(z)] n(pl) rampe f (d'escalier)

**bank** [bæŋk] n banque f; (of river, lake) bord m, rive f; (of earth) talus m, remblai m ♦ vi (AVIAT) virer sur l'aile; ~ **on** vt fus miser or tabler sur; ~ **account** n compte m en banque; ~ **card** n carte d'identité bancaire; ~**er** n banquier m; ~**er's card** (BRIT) n = bank card; ~ **holiday** (BRIT) n jour férié (les banques sont fermées); ~**ing** n opérations fpl bancaires; profession f de banquier; ~**note** n billet m de banque; ~ **rate** n

taux m de l'escompte

---
**bank holiday**
---

Un bank holiday en Grande-Bretagne est un lundi férié et donc l'occasion d'un week-end prolongé. La circulation sur les routes et le trafic dans les gares et les aéroports augmentent considérablement à ces périodes. Les principaux bank holidays, à part Pâques et Noël, ont lieu au mois de mai et fin août.

---

**bankrupt** ['bæŋkrʌpt] adj en faillite; **to go ~** faire faillite; ~**cy** n faillite f

**bank statement** n relevé m de compte

**banner** ['bænə'] n bannière f

**bannister(s)** ['bænɪstə(z)] n(pl) = **banister(s)**

**baptism** ['bæptɪzəm] n baptême m

**bar** [bɑ:'] n (pub) bar m; (counter: in pub) comptoir m, bar m; (rod: of metal etc) barre f; (on window etc) barreau m; (of chocolate) tablette f, plaque f; (fig) obstacle m; (prohibition) mesure f d'exclusion; (MUS) mesure f ♦ vt (road) barrer; (window) munir de barreaux; (person) exclure; (activity) interdire; ~ **of soap** savonnette f; **the B~** (LAW) le barreau; **behind ~s** (prisoner) sous les verrous; ~ **none** sans exception

**barbaric** [bɑ:'bærɪk] adj barbare

**barbecue** ['bɑ:bɪkju:] n barbecue m

**barbed wire** ['bɑ:bd-] n fil m de fer barbelé

**barber** ['bɑ:bə'] n coiffeur m (pour hommes)

**bar code** n (on goods) code m à barres

**bare** [bɛə'] adj nu(e) ♦ vt mettre à nu, dénuder; (teeth) montrer; **the ~ necessities** le strict nécessaire; ~**back** adv à cru, sans selle; ~**faced** adj impudent(e), effronté(e); ~**foot** adj, adv nu-pieds, (les) pieds nus; ~**ly** adv à peine

**bargain** ['bɑ:gɪn] n (transaction) marché m; (good buy) affaire f, occasion f ♦

*vi* (*haggle*) marchander; (*negotiate*): to ~ (with sb) négocier (avec qn), traiter (avec qn); **into the ~** par-dessus le marché; ~ **for** *vt fus*: **he got more than he ~ed for** il ne s'attendait pas à un coup pareil

**barge** [bɑːdʒ] *n* péniche *f*; ~ **in** *vi* (*walk in*) faire irruption; (*interrupt talk*) intervenir mal à propos

**bark** [bɑːk] *n* (*of tree*) écorce *f*; (*of dog*) aboiement *m* ♦ *vi* aboyer

**barley** [ˈbɑːlɪ] *n* orge *f*; ~ **sugar** *n* sucre *m* d'orge

**bar:** ~**maid** *n* serveuse *f* de bar, barmaid *f*; ~**man** (*irreg*) *n* barman *m*; ~ **meal** *n* repas *m* de bistrot; **to go for a ~ meal** aller manger au bistrot

**barn** [bɑːn] *n* grange *f*

**barometer** [bəˈrɔmɪtəʳ] *n* baromètre *m*

**baron** [ˈbærən] *n* baron *m*; ~**ess** [ˈbærənɪs] *n* baronne *f*

**barracks** [ˈbærəks] *npl* caserne *f*

**barrage** [ˈbærɑːʒ] *n* (*MIL*) tir *m* de barrage; (*dam*) barrage *m*; (*fig*) pluie *f*

**barrel** [ˈbærəl] *n* tonneau *m*; (*of oil*) baril *m*; (*of gun*) canon *m*

**barren** [ˈbærən] *adj* stérile

**barricade** [bærɪˈkeɪd] *n* barricade *f*

**barrier** [ˈbærɪəʳ] *n* barrière *f*; (*fig*: *to progress etc*) obstacle *m*

**barring** [ˈbɑːrɪŋ] *prep* sauf

**barrister** [ˈbærɪstəʳ] (*BRIT*) *n* avocat (plaidant)

**barrow** [ˈbærəu] *n* (*wheelbarrow*) charrette *f* à bras

**bartender** [ˈbɑːtendəʳ] (*US*) *n* barman *m*

**barter** [ˈbɑːtəʳ] *vt*: **to ~ sth for** échanger qch contre

**base** [beɪs] *n* base *f*; (*of tree, post*) pied *m* ♦ *vt*: **to ~ sth on** baser *or* fonder qch sur ♦ *adj* vil(e), bas(se)

**baseball** [ˈbeɪsbɔːl] *n* base-ball *m*

**basement** [ˈbeɪsmənt] *n* sous-sol *m*

**bases¹** [ˈbeɪsɪz] *npl of* **base**

**bases²** [ˈbeɪsiːz] *npl of* **basis**

**bash** [bæʃ] (*inf*) *vt* frapper, cogner

**bashful** [ˈbæʃful] *adj* timide; modeste

**basic** [ˈbeɪsɪk] *adj* fondamental(e), de base; (*minimal*) rudimentaire; ~**ally** *adv* fondamentalement, à la base; (*in fact*) en fait, au fond; ~**s** *npl*: **the ~s** l'essentiel *m*

**basil** [ˈbæzl] *n* basilic *m*

**basin** [ˈbeɪsn] *n* (*vessel, also* GEO) cuvette *f*, bassin *m*; (*also*: **washbasin**) lavabo *m*

**basis** [ˈbeɪsɪs] (*pl* **bases**) *n* base *f*; **on a trial ~** à titre d'essai; **on a part-time ~** à temps partiel

**bask** [bɑːsk] *vi*: **to ~ in the sun** se chauffer au soleil

**basket** [ˈbɑːskɪt] *n* corbeille *f*; (*with handle*) panier *m*; ~**ball** *n* basket-ball *m*

**bass** [beɪs] *n* (*MUS*) basse *f*; ~ **drum** *n* grosse caisse *f*

**bassoon** [bəˈsuːn] *n* (*MUS*) basson *m*

**bastard** [ˈbɑːstəd] *n* enfant naturel(le), bâtard(e); (*inf!*) salaud *m* (!)

**bat** [bæt] *n* chauve-souris *f*; (*for baseball etc*) batte *f*; (*BRIT*: *for table tennis*) raquette *f* ♦ *vt*: **he didn't ~ an eyelid** il n'a pas sourcillé *or* bronché

**batch** [bætʃ] *n* (*of bread*) fournée *f*; (*of papers*) liasse *f*

**bated** [ˈbeɪtɪd] *adj*: **with ~ breath** en retenant son souffle

**bath** [bɑːθ] *n* bain *m*; (~*tub*) baignoire *f* ♦ *vt* baigner, donner un bain à; **to have a ~** prendre un bain; *see also* **baths**

**bathe** [beɪð] *vi* se baigner ♦ *vt* (*wound*) laver; **bathing** *n* baignade *f*; **bathing costume, bathing suit** (*US*) *n* maillot *m* (de bain)

**bath:** ~**robe** *n* peignoir *m* de bain; ~**room** *n* salle *f* de bains; ~**s** *npl* (*also*: **swimming ~s**) piscine *f*; ~ **towel** *n* serviette *f* de bain

**baton** [ˈbætən] *n* bâton *m*; (*MUS*) baguette *f*; (*club*) matraque *f*

**batter** [ˈbætəʳ] *vt* battre ♦ *n* pâte *f* à frire; ~**ed** [ˈbætəd] *adj* (*hat, pan*) cabossé(e)

**battery** ['bætərɪ] n batterie f; (of torch) pile f; ~ **farming** n élevage en batterie

**battle** ['bætl] n bataille f, combat m ♦ vi se battre, lutter; ~**field** n champ m de bataille; ~**ship** n cuirassé m

**Bavaria** [bə'vɛərɪə] n Bavière f

**bawl** [bɔːl] vi hurler; (child) brailler

**bay** [beɪ] n (of sea) baie f; **to hold sb at** ~ tenir qn à distance or en échec; ~ **leaf** n laurier m; ~ **window** n baie vitrée

**bazaar** [bə'zɑːʳ] n bazar m; vente f de charité

**B & B** n abbr = **bed and breakfast**

**BBC** n abbr (= British Broadcasting Corporation) la BBC

**B.C.** adv abbr (= before Christ) av. J.-C.

**be** [biː] (pt **was, were,** pp **been**) aux vb
**1** (with present participle: forming continuous tenses): **what are you doing?** que faites-vous?; **they're coming tomorrow** ils viennent demain; **I've been waiting for you for 2 hours** je t'attends depuis 2 heures
**2** (with pp: forming passives) être; **to be killed** être tué(e); **he was nowhere to be seen** on ne le voyait nulle part
**3** (in tag questions): **it was fun, wasn't it?** c'était drôle, n'est-ce pas?; **she's back, is she?** elle est rentrée, n'est-ce pas or alors?
**4** (+to + infinitive): **the house is to be sold** la maison doit être vendue; **he's not to open it** il ne doit pas l'ouvrir

♦ vb + complement **1** (gen) être; **I'm English** je suis anglais(e); **I'm tired** je suis fatigué(e); **I'm hot/cold** j'ai chaud/froid; **he's a doctor** il est médecin; **2 and 2 are 4** 2 et 2 font 4
**2** (of health) aller; **how are you?** comment allez-vous?; **he's fine now** il va bien maintenant; **he's very ill** il est très malade

**3** (of age) avoir; **how old are you?** quel âge avez-vous?; **I'm sixteen (years old)** j'ai seize ans
**4** (cost) coûter; **how much was the meal?** combien a coûté le repas?; **that'll be £5, please** ça fera 5 livres, s'il vous plaît

♦ vi **1** (exist, occur etc) être, exister; **the prettiest girl that ever was** la fille la plus jolie qui ait jamais existé; **be that as it may** quoi qu'il en soit; **so be it** soit
**2** (referring to place) être, se trouver; **I won't be here tomorrow** je ne serai pas ici demain; **Edinburgh is in Scotland** Édimbourg est or se trouve en Écosse
**3** (referring to movement) aller; **where have you been?** où êtes-vous allé(s)?

♦ impers vb **1** (referring to time, distance) être; **it's 5 o'clock** il est 5 heures; **it's the 28th of April** c'est le 28 avril; **it's 10 km to the village** le village est à 10 km
**2** (referring to the weather) faire; **it's too hot/cold** il fait trop chaud/froid; **it's windy** il y a du vent
**3** (emphatic): **it's me/the postman** c'est moi/le facteur

**beach** [biːtʃ] n plage f ♦ vt échouer; ~ **towel** n serviette f de plage

**beacon** ['biːkən] n (lighthouse) fanal m; (marker) balise f

**bead** [biːd] n perle f

**beak** [biːk] n bec m

**beaker** ['biːkəʳ] n gobelet m

**beam** [biːm] n poutre f; (of light) rayon m ♦ vi rayonner

**bean** [biːn] n haricot m; (of coffee) grain m; **runner** ~ haricot m (à rames); **broad** ~ fève f; ~**sprouts** npl germes mpl de soja

**bear** [bɛəʳ] (pt **bore,** pp **borne**) n ours m ♦ vt porter; (endure) supporter ♦ vi: **to** ~ **right/left** obliquer à droite/gauche, se diriger vers la droite/gauche; **~ out** vt corroborer, confirmer; **~ up** vi (person) tenir le coup

**beard** [bɪəd] n barbe f; **~ed** adj barbu(e)

**bearer** ['bɛərə*] n porteur m; (of passport) titulaire m/f

**bearing** ['bɛərɪŋ] n maintien m, allure f; (connection) rapport m; **~s** npl (also: **ball ~s**) roulement m (à billes); **to take a ~** faire le point

**beast** [biːst] n bête f; (inf: person) brute f; **~ly** adj infect(e)

**beat** [biːt] (pt **beat**, pp **beaten**) n battement m; (MUS) temps m, mesure f; (of policeman) ronde f ♦ vt, vi battre; **off the ~en track** hors des chemins or sentiers battus; **~ it!** (inf) fiche(-moi) le camp!; **~ off** vt repousser; **~ up** vt (inf: person) tabasser; (eggs) battre; **~ing** n raclée f

**beautiful** ['bjuːtɪful] adj beau (belle); **~ly** adv admirablement

**beauty** ['bjuːtɪ] n beauté f; **~ parlour** n institut m de beauté; **~ salon** n, **~ shop** n = **~ parlour**; **~ spot** (BRIT) n (TOURISM) site naturel (d'une grande beauté)

**beaver** ['biːvə*] n castor m

**because** [bɪ'kɔz] conj parce que; **~ of** prep à cause de

**beck** [bɛk] n: **to be at sb's ~ and call** être à l'entière disposition de qn

**beckon** ['bɛkən] vt (also: **~ to**) faire signe (de venir) à

**become** [bɪ'kʌm] (irreg: like **come**) vi devenir; **to ~ fat/thin** grossir/maigrir; **becoming** adj (behaviour) convenable, bienséant(e); (clothes) seyant(e)

**bed** [bɛd] n lit m; (of flowers) parterre m; (of coal, clay) couche f; (of sea) fond m; **to go to ~** aller se coucher; **~ and breakfast** n (terms) chambre et petit déjeuner; (place) voir encadré; **~clothes** npl couvertures fpl et draps mpl; **~ding** n literie f; **~ linen** n draps mpl de lit (et taies fpl d'oreillers), literie f

---

**bed and breakfast**

*Un* **bed and breakfast** *est une petite pension dans une maison particulière ou une ferme où l'on peut louer une chambre avec petit déjeuner compris pour un prix modique par rapport à ce que l'on paierait dans un hôtel. Ces établissements sont communément appelés B & B, et sont signalés par une pancarte dans le jardin ou au-dessus de la porte.*

---

**bedraggled** [bɪ'dræɡld] adj (person, clothes) débraillé(e); (hair: wet) trempé(e)

**bed:** **~ridden** adj cloué(e) au lit; **~room** n chambre f (à coucher); **~side** n: **at sb's ~side** au chevet de qn; **~sit(ter)** n (BRIT) chambre meublée, studio m; **~spread** n couvre-lit m, dessus-de-lit m inv; **~time** n heure f du coucher

**bee** [biː] n abeille f

**beech** [biːtʃ] n hêtre m

**beef** [biːf] n bœuf m; **roast ~** rosbif m; **~burger** n hamburger m; **~eater** n hallebardier de la Tour de Londres

**bee:** **~hive** n ruche f; **~line** n: **to make a ~line for** se diriger tout droit vers

**been** [biːn] pp of **be**

**beer** [bɪə*] n bière f

**beet** [biːt] n (vegetable) betterave f; (US: also: **red ~**) betterave (potagère)

**beetle** ['biːtl] n scarabée m

**beetroot** ['biːtruːt] n (BRIT) betterave f

**before** [bɪ'fɔː*] prep (in time) avant; (in space) devant ♦ conj avant que +sub; avant de ♦ adv avant; devant; **~ going** avant de partir; **~ she goes** avant qu'elle ne parte; **the week ~** la semaine précédente or d'avant; **I've seen it ~** je l'ai déjà vu; **~hand** adv au préalable, à l'avance

**beg** [bɛɡ] vi mendier ♦ vt mendier; (forgiveness, mercy etc) demander; (entreat) supplier; see also **pardon**

**began** [bɪ'gæn] *pt of* begin

**beggar** ['begə'] *n* mendiant(e)

**begin** [bɪ'gɪn] (*pt* began, *pp* begun) *vt, vi* commencer; **to ~ doing** or **to do sth** commencer à or de faire qch; **~ner** *n* débutant(e); **~ning** *n* commencement *m*, début *m*

**behalf** [bɪ'hɑ:f] *n*: **on ~ of**, (US) **in ~ of** (*representing*) de la part de; (*for benefit of*) pour le compte de; **on my/his ~** pour moi/lui

**behave** [bɪ'heɪv] *vi* se conduire, se comporter; (*well: also*: **~ o.s.**) se conduire bien or comme il faut; **behaviour** (US **behavior**) [bɪ'heɪvjə'] *n* comportement *m*, conduite *f*

**behead** [bɪ'hed] *vt* décapiter

**behind** [bɪ'haɪnd] *prep* derrière; (*time, progress*) en retard sur; (*work, studies*) en retard dans ♦ *adv* derrière ♦ *n* derrière *m*; **to be ~** (**schedule**) avoir du retard; **~ the scenes** dans les coulisses

**behold** [bɪ'həuld] (*irreg: like* hold) *vt* apercevoir, voir

**beige** [beɪʒ] *adj* beige

**Beijing** ['beɪ'dʒɪŋ] *n* Bei-jing, Pékin

**being** ['biːɪŋ] *n* être *m*

**Beirut** [beɪ'ruːt] *n* Beyrouth

**Belarus** [belə'rus] *n* Bélarus *m*

**belated** [bɪ'leɪtɪd] *adj* tardif(-ive)

**belch** [beltʃ] *vi* avoir un renvoi, roter ♦ *vt* (*also*: **~ out**: *smoke etc*) vomir, cracher

**Belgian** ['beldʒən] *adj* belge, de Belgique ♦ *n* Belge *m/f*

**Belgium** ['beldʒəm] *n* Belgique *f*

**belie** [bɪ'laɪ] *vt* démentir

**belief** [bɪ'liːf] *n* (*opinion*) conviction *f*; (*trust, faith*) foi *f*

**believe** [bɪ'liːv] *vt, vi* croire; **to ~ in** (*God*) croire en; (*method, ghosts*) croire à; **~r** *n* (*in idea, activity*) **~r in** partisan(e) de; (*REL*) croyant(e)

**belittle** [bɪ'lɪtl] *vt* déprécier, rabaisser

**bell** [bel] *n* cloche *f*; (*small*) clochette *f*, grelot *m*; (*on door*) sonnette *f*; (*electric*) sonnerie *f*

**belligerent** [bɪ'lɪdʒərənt] *adj* (*person, attitude*) agressif(-ive)

**bellow** ['beləu] *vi* (*bull*) meugler; (*person*) brailler

**belly** ['belɪ] *n* ventre *m*

**belong** [bɪ'lɒŋ] *vi*: **to ~ to** appartenir à; (*club etc*) faire partie de; **this book ~s here** ce livre va ici; **~ings** *npl* affaires *fpl*, possessions *fpl*

**beloved** [bɪ'lʌvɪd] *adj* (bien-)aimé(e)

**below** [bɪ'ləu] *prep* sous, au-dessous de ♦ *adv* en dessous; **see** ~ voir plus bas or plus loin or ci-dessous

**belt** [belt] *n* ceinture *f*; (*of land*) région *f*; (*TECH*) courroie *f* ♦ *vt* (*thrash*) donner une raclée à; **~way** (US) *n* (AUT) route *f* de ceinture; (: *motorway*) périphérique *m*

**bemused** [bɪ'mjuːzd] *adj* stupéfié(e)

**bench** [bentʃ] *n* (*gen, also* BRIT: *seat*) banc *m*; (*in workshop*) établi *m*; **the B~** (LAW: *judge*) le juge; (: *judges collectively*) la magistrature, la Cour

**bend** [bend] (*pt, pp* bent) *vt* courber; (*leg, arm*) plier ♦ *vi* se courber ♦ *n* (BRIT: *in road*) virage *m*, tournant *m*; (*in pipe, river*) coude *m*; **~ down** *vi* se baisser; **~ over** *vi* se pencher

**beneath** [bɪ'niːθ] *prep* sous, au-dessous de; (*unworthy of*) indigne de ♦ *adv* dessous, au-dessous, en bas

**benefactor** ['benɪfæktə'] *n* bienfaiteur *m*

**beneficial** [benɪ'fɪʃəl] *adj* salutaire; avantageux(-euse); **~ to the health** bon(ne) pour la santé

**benefit** ['benɪfɪt] *n* avantage *m*, profit *m*; (*allowance of money*) allocation *f* ♦ *vt* faire du bien à, profiter à ♦ *vi*: **he'll ~ from it** cela lui fera du bien, il y gagnera or s'en trouvera bien

**Benelux** ['benɪlʌks] *n* Bénélux *m*

**benevolent** [bɪ'nevələnt] *adj* bienveillant(e); (*organization*) bénévole

**benign** [bɪ'naɪn] *adj* (*person, smile*) bienveillant(e), affable; (MED) bénin(-igne)

**bent** [bɛnt] pt, pp of **bend** ♦ n inclination f, penchant m; **to be ~ on** être résolu(e) à

**bequest** [bɪ'kwɛst] n legs m

**bereaved** [bɪ'riːvd] n: **the ~** la famille du disparu

**beret** ['bɛreɪ] n béret m

**Berlin** [bəː'lɪn] n Berlin

**berm** [bəːm] (US) n (AUT) accotement m

**Bermuda** [bəː'mjuːdə] n Bermudes fpl

**berry** ['bɛrɪ] n baie f

**berserk** [bə'səːk] adj: **to go ~** (madman, crowd) se déchaîner

**berth** [bəːθ] n (bed) couchette f; (for ship) poste m d'amarrage, mouillage m ♦ vi (in harbour) venir à quai; (at anchor) mouiller

**beseech** [bɪ'siːtʃ] (pt, pp **besought**) vt implorer, supplier

**beset** [bɪ'sɛt] (pt, pp **beset**) vt assaillir

**beside** [bɪ'saɪd] prep à côté de; **to be ~ o.s. (with anger)** être hors de soi; **that's ~ the point** cela n'a rien à voir; **~s** adv en outre, de plus; (in any case) d'ailleurs ♦ prep (as well as) en plus de

**besiege** [bɪ'siːdʒ] vt (town) assiéger; (fig) assaillir

**best** [bɛst] adj meilleur(e) ♦ adv le mieux; **the ~ part of** (quantity) la plus clair de, la plus grande partie de; **at ~** au mieux; **to make the ~ of sth** s'accommoder de qch (du mieux que l'on peut); **to do one's ~** faire de son mieux; **to the ~ of my knowledge** pour autant que je sache; **to the ~ of my ability** du mieux que je pourrai; **~ before date** n date f de limite d'utilisation or de consommation; **~ man** n garçon m d'honneur

**bestow** [bɪ'stəu] vt: **to ~ sth on sb** accorder qch à qn; (title) conférer qch à qn

**bet** [bɛt] (pt, pp **bet** or **betted**) n pari m ♦ vt, vi parier

**betray** [bɪ'treɪ] vt trahir

**better** ['bɛtə*] adj meilleur(e) ♦ adv mieux ♦ vt améliorer ♦ n: **to get the ~**

**of** triompher de, l'emporter sur; **you had ~ do it** vous feriez mieux de le faire; **he thought ~ of it** il s'est ravisé; **to get ~** aller mieux; s'améliorer; **~ off** adj plus à l'aise financièrement; (fig): **you'd be ~ off this way** vous vous en trouveriez mieux ainsi

**betting** ['bɛtɪŋ] n paris mpl; **~ shop** (BRIT) n bureau m de paris

**between** [bɪ'twiːn] prep entre ♦ adv: **(in) ~** au milieu; dans l'intervalle; (in time) dans l'intervalle

**beverage** ['bɛvərɪdʒ] n boisson f (gén sans alcool)

**beware** [bɪ'wɛə*] vi: **to ~** prendre garde (à); **"~ of the dog"** "(attention) chien méchant"

**bewildered** [bɪ'wɪldəd] adj dérouté(e), ahuri(e)

**beyond** [bɪ'jɔnd] prep (in space, time) au-delà de; (exceeding) au-dessus de ♦ adv au-delà; **~ doubt** hors de doute; **~ repair** irréparable

**bias** ['baɪəs] n (prejudice) préjugé m, parti pris; (~(s)ed adj partial(e), montrant un parti pris

**bib** [bɪb] n bavoir m, bavette f

**Bible** ['baɪbl] n Bible f

**bicarbonate of soda** [baɪ'kɑːbənɪt-] n bicarbonate m de soude

**bicker** ['bɪkə*] vi se chamailler

**bicycle** ['baɪsɪkl] n bicyclette f

**bid** [bɪd] (pt **bid** or **bade**, pp **bid(den)**) n offre f; (at auction) enchère f; (attempt) tentative f ♦ vi faire une enchère or offre ♦ vt faire une enchère or offre de; **to ~ sb good day** souhaiter le bonjour à qn; **~der** n: **the highest ~der** le plus offrant; **~ding** n enchères fpl

**bide** [baɪd] vt: **to ~ one's time** attendre son heure

**bifocals** [baɪ'fəuklz] npl verres mpl à double foyer, lunettes bifocales

**big** [bɪg] adj grand(e); gros(se); **~-headed** adj prétentieux(-euse)

**bigot** ['bɪgət] n fanatique m/f, sectaire m/f; **~ed** adj fanatique, sectaire; **~ry** n fanatisme *m*, sectarisme *m*

**big top** *n* grand chapiteau

**bike** [baɪk] *n* vélo *m*, bécane *f*

**bikini** [bɪˈkiːnɪ] *n* bikini *m*

**bilingual** [baɪˈlɪŋgwəl] *adj* bilingue

**bill** [bɪl] *n* note *f*, facture *f*; (POL) projet *m* de loi; **"post no ~s"** "défense d'afficher"; **to fit** *or* **fill the ~** (fig) faire l'affaire; **~board** *n* panneau *m* d'affichage

**billet** [ˈbɪlɪt] *n* cantonnement *m* (chez l'habitant)

**billfold** [ˈbɪlfəuld] (US) *n* portefeuille *m*

**billiards** [ˈbɪljədz] *n* (jeu *m* de) billard *m*

**billion** [ˈbɪljən] *n* (BRIT) billion *m* (million de millions); (US) milliard *m*

**bimbo** [ˈbɪmbəu] (inf) *n* ravissante idiote *f*, potiche *f*

**bin** [bɪn] *n* boîte *f*; (also: **dustbin**) poubelle *f*; (for coal) coffre *m*

**bind** [baɪnd] (pt, pp **bound**) *vt* attacher; (book) relier; (oblige) obliger, contraindre ♦ *n* (inf: nuisance) scie *f*; **~ing** (contract) constituant une obligation

**binge** [bɪndʒ] (inf) *n*: **to go on a/the ~** aller faire la bringue

**bingo** [ˈbɪŋgəu] *n* jeu de loto pratiqué dans les établissements publics

**binoculars** [bɪˈnɔkjuləz] *npl* jumelles *fpl*

**bio** *prefix*: **~chemistry** *n* biochimie *f*; **~degradable** *adj* biodégradable; **~graphy** *n* biographie *f*; **~logical** *adj* biologique; **~logy** *n* biologie *f*

**birch** [bəːtʃ] *n* bouleau *m*

**bird** [bəːd] *n* oiseau *m*; (BRIT: inf: girl) nana *f*; **~'s-eye view** *n* vue *f* à vol d'oiseau; (fig) vue d'ensemble *or* générale; **~watcher** *n* ornithologue *m/f* amateur

**Biro** [ˈbaɪərəu] ® *n* stylo *m* à bille

**birth** [bəːθ] *n* naissance *f*; **to give ~ to** (subj: woman) donner naissance à; (: animal) mettre bas; **~ certificate** *n*

acte *m* de naissance; **~ control** *n* (policy) limitation *f* des naissances; (method) méthode(s) *f* contraceptive(s); **~day** *n* anniversaire *m* ♦ *cpd* d'anniversaire; **~place** *n* lieu *m* de naissance; (fig) berceau *m*; **~ rate** *n* (taux *m* de) natalité *f*

**biscuit** [ˈbɪskɪt] *n* (BRIT) biscuit *m*; (US) petit pain au lait

**bisect** [baɪˈsɛkt] *vt* couper *or* diviser en deux

**bishop** [ˈbɪʃəp] *n* évêque *m*; (CHESS) fou *m*

**bit** [bɪt] *pt of* **bite** *n* morceau *m*; (of tool) mèche *f*; (of horse) mors *m*; (COMPUT) élément *m* binaire; **a ~ of** un peu de; **a ~ mad** un peu fou; **~ by ~** petit à petit

**bitch** [bɪtʃ] *n* (dog) chienne *f*; (inf!) salope *f* (!), garce *f*

**bite** [baɪt] (pt **bit**, pp **bitten**) *vt, vi* mordre; (insect) piquer ♦ *n* (insect ~) piqûre *f*; (mouthful) bouchée *f*; **let's have a ~ (to eat)** (inf) mangeons un morceau; **to ~ one's nails** se ronger les ongles

**bitter** [ˈbɪtə] *adj* amer(-ère); (weather, wind) glacial(e); (criticism) cinglant(e); (struggle) acharné(e) ♦ *n* (BRIT: beer) bière *f* (forte); **~ness** *n* amertume *f*; (taste) goût amer

**black** [blæk] *adj* noir(e) ♦ *n* (colour) noir *m*; (person): **B~** noir(e) ♦ *vt* (BRIT: INDUSTRY) boycotter; **to give sb a ~ eye** pocher l'œil à qn, faire un œil au beurre noir à qn; **~ and blue** couvert(e) de bleus; **to be in the ~** (in credit) être créditeur(-trice); **~berry** *n* mûre *f*; **~bird** *n* merle *m*; **~board** *n* tableau noir; **~ coffee** *n* café noir; **~currant** *n* cassis *m*; **~en** *vt* noircir; **~ ice** *n* verglas *m*; **~leg** (BRIT) *n* briseur *m* de grève, jaune *m*; **~list** *n* liste noire; **~mail** *n* chantage *m* ♦ *vt* faire chanter, soumettre au chantage; **~ market** *n* marché noir; **~out** *n* panne *f* d'électricité; (TV etc) interruption *f* d'émission; (fainting) syncope *f*; **~ pudding** *n* boudin (noir); **B~ Sea** *n*: **the B~ Sea** la mer Noire; **~**

**sheep** n brebis galeuse; **~smith** n forgeron m; **~ spot** (AUT) point noir

**bladder** ['blædə*r*] n vessie f

**blade** [bleɪd] n lame f; (of propeller) pale f; **~ of grass** brin m d'herbe

**blame** [bleɪm] n faute f, blâme m ♦ vt: **to ~ sb/sth for sth** attribuer à qn/qch la responsabilité de qch; reprocher qch à qn/qch; **who's to ~?** qui est le fautif or coupable or responsable?

**bland** [blænd] adj (taste, food) doux (douce), fade

**blank** [blæŋk] adj blanc (blanche); (look) sans expression, dénué(e) d'expression ♦ n espace m vide, blanc m; (cartridge) cartouche f à blanc; **his mind was a ~** il avait la tête vide; **~ cheque** chèque m en blanc

**blanket** ['blæŋkɪt] n couverture f; (of snow, cloud) couche f

**blare** [blɛə*r*] vi beugler

**blast** [blɑːst] n souffle m; (of explosive) explosion f ♦ vt faire sauter or exploser; **~-off** n (SPACE) lancement m

**blatant** ['bleɪtənt] adj flagrant(e), criant(e)

**blaze** [bleɪz] n (fire) incendie m, (fig) flamboiement m ♦ vi (fire) flamber; (fig: eyes) flamboyer; (: guns) crépiter ♦ vt: **to ~ a trail** (fig) montrer la voie

**blazer** ['bleɪzə*r*] n blazer m

**bleach** [bliːtʃ] n (also: household ~) eau f de Javel ♦ vt (linen etc) blanchir; **~ed** adj (hair) oxygéné(e), décoloré(e)

**bleak** [bliːk] adj morne, triste; (countryside) désolé(e)

**bleat** [bliːt] vi bêler

**bleed** [bliːd] (pt, pp **bled**) vt, vi saigner; **my nose is ~ing** je saigne du nez

**bleeper** ['bliːpə*r*] n (device) bip m

**blemish** ['blemɪʃ] n défaut m; (on fruit, reputation) tache f

**blend** [blend] n mélange m ♦ vt mélanger ♦ vi (colours etc: also: **~ in**) se mélanger, se fondre; **~er** n mixeur m

**bless** [bles] (pt, pp **blessed** or **blest**) vt bénir; **~ you!** (after sneeze) à vos sou-

haits!; **~ing** n bénédiction f; (godsend) bienfait m

**blew** [bluː] pt of **blow**

**blight** [blaɪt] vt (hopes etc) anéantir; (life) briser

**blimey** ['blaɪmɪ] (BRIT: inf) excl mince alors!

**blind** [blaɪnd] adj aveugle ♦ n (for window) store m ♦ vt aveugler; **~ alley** n impasse f; **~ corner** (BRIT) n virage m sans visibilité; **~fold** n bandeau m ♦ adj, adv les yeux bandés ♦ vt bander les yeux à; **~ly** adv aveuglément; **~ness** n cécité f; **~ spot** n (AUT etc) angle mort; **that is her ~ spot** (fig) elle refuse d'y voir clair sur ce point

**blink** [blɪŋk] vi cligner des yeux; (light) clignoter; **~ers** npl œillères fpl

**bliss** [blɪs] n félicité f, bonheur m sans mélange

**blister** ['blɪstə*r*] n (on skin) ampoule f, cloque f; (on paintwork, rubber) boursouflure f ♦ vi (paint) se boursoufler, se cloquer

**blizzard** ['blɪzəd] n blizzard m, tempête f de neige

**bloated** ['bləʊtɪd] adj (face) bouffi(e); (stomach, person) gonflé(e)

**blob** [blɔb] n (drop) goutte f; (stain, spot) tache f

**block** [blɔk] n bloc m; (in pipes) obstruction f; (toy) cube m; (of buildings) pâté m (de maisons) ♦ vt bloquer; (fig) faire obstacle à; **~ of flats** (BRIT) immeuble (locatif); **~age** n obstruction f; **~buster** n (film, book) grand succès; **~ letters** npl majuscules fpl

**bloke** [bləʊk] (BRIT: inf) n type m

**blond(e)** [blɔnd] adj, n blond(e)

**blood** [blʌd] n sang m; **~ donor** n donneur(-euse) de sang; **~ group** n groupe sanguin; **~hound** n limier m; **~ poisoning** n empoisonnement m du sang; **~ pressure** n tension f (artérielle); **~shed** n effusion f de sang, carnage m; ~ **sports** npl sports mpl sanguinaires; ~**shot** adj: ~**shot eyes** yeux injectés de sang; ~**stream** n sang m, système sanguin; ~ **test** n prise f de sang; ~**thirsty** adj sanguinaire; ~ **vessel** n vaisseau sanguin; ~**y** adj sanglant(e); (nose) ensanglanté(e); **this** ~y ... ce foutu ... (!), ce putain de ... (!); ~**y strong/good** sacrément fort/bon; ~**y-minded** (BRIT: inf) adj contrariant(e), obstiné(e)

**bloom** [bluːm] n fleur f ♦ vi être en fleur

**blossom** ['blɒsəm] n fleur(s) f(pl) ♦ vi être en fleurs; (fig) s'épanouir; **to ~ into** devenir

**blot** [blɒt] n tache f ♦ vt tacher; ~ **out** vt (memories) effacer; (view) cacher, masquer

**blotchy** ['blɒtʃɪ] adj (complexion) couvert(e) de marbrures

**blotting paper** ['blɒtɪŋ-] n buvard m

**blouse** [blauz] n chemisier m, corsage m

**blow** [blau] (pt blew, pp blown) n coup m ♦ vi souffler ♦ vt souffler; (fuse) faire sauter; (instrument) jouer de; **to ~ one's nose** se moucher; **to ~ a whistle** siffler; ~ **away** vt chasser, faire s'envoler; ~ **down** vt faire tomber, renverser; ~ **off** vt emporter; ~ **out** vi (fire, flame) s'éteindre; ~ **over** vi s'apaiser; ~ **up** vi faire sauter (tyre) gonfler; (PHOT) agrandir ♦ vi exploser, sauter; ~**dry** n brushing m; ~**lamp** n (BRIT) chalumeau m; ~**out** n (of tyre) éclatement m; ~**torch** n = blowlamp

**blue** [bluː] adj bleu(e); (fig) triste; ~**s** n (MUS) the ~**s** le blues; ~ **film/joke** n film m/histoire f pornographique; **to come out of the ~** (fig) être complètement inattendu; ~**bell** n jacinthe f des bois; ~**bottle** n mouche f à viande; ~**print** n (fig) projet m, plan directeur

**bluff** [blʌf] vi bluffer ♦ n bluff m; **to call sb's ~** mettre qn au défi d'exécuter ses menaces

**blunder** ['blʌndəʳ] n gaffe f, bévue f ♦ vi faire une gaffe or une bévue

**blunt** [blʌnt] adj (person) brusque, ne mâchant pas ses mots; (knife) émoussé(e), peu tranchant(e); (pencil) mal taillé

**blur** [bləːʳ] n tache or masse floue or confuse ♦ vt brouiller

**blush** [blʌʃ] vi rougir ♦ n rougeur f

**blustery** ['blʌstərɪ] adj (weather) à bourrasques

**boar** [bɔːʳ] n sanglier m

**board** [bɔːd] n planche f, panneau m; (for chess) échiquier m; (cardboard) carton m; (committee) conseil m, comité m; (in firm) conseil d'administration; (NAUT, AVIAT): **on** ~ à bord de; (ship) monter à bord de; (train) monter dans; **full** ~ (BRIT) pension complète; **half** ~ demi-pension f; ~ **and lodging** chambre f avec pension; **which goes by the** ~ (fig) qu'on laisse tomber, qu'on abandonne; **to** ~ **up** vt (door, window) boucher; ~**er** n (SCOL) interne m/f, pensionnaire; ~ **game** n jeu m de société; ~**ing card** n = boarding pass; ~**ing house** n pension f; ~**ing pass** n (AVIAT, NAUT) carte f d'embarquement; ~**ing school** n internat m, pensionnat m; ~ **room** n salle f du conseil d'administration

**boast** [bəust] vi: **to** ~ (**about** or **of**) se vanter (de)

**boat** [bəut] n bateau m; (small) canot m; barque f; ~ **train** n train m (qui assure correspondance avec le ferry)

**bob** [bɒb] vi (boat, cork on water. also: ~ **up and down**) danser, se balancer

**bobby** ['bɒbɪ] n (BRIT: inf) = agent m (de police)

**bobsleigh** ['bɒbsleɪ] n bob m

**bode** [bəud] vi: **to** ~ **well/ill (for)** être de bon/mauvais augure (pour)

**bodily** ['bɒdɪlɪ] adj corporel(le) ♦ adv dans ses bras

**body** ['bɒdɪ] n corps m; (of car) carrosserie f; (of plane) fuselage m; (fig: society) organe *m*, organisme *m*; (: *quanti-ty*) ensemble *m*, masse *f*; (: *of wine*) corps; **~-building** *n* culturisme *m*; **~guard** *n* garde *m* du corps; **~work** *n* carrosserie *f*

**bog** [bɔg] *n* tourbière *f* ♦ *vt*: **to get ~ged down** (*fig*) s'enliser

**bog-standard** (*inf*) *adj* tout à fait ordinaire

**bogus** ['bəʊgəs] *adj* bidon *inv*; fantôme

**boil** [bɔɪl] *vt* (faire) bouillir ♦ *vi* bouillir ♦ *n* (*MED*) furoncle *m*; **to come to the** (*BRIT*) **~ or a** (*US*) **~** bouillir; **~ down to** *vt fus* (*fig*) se réduire or ramener à; **~ over** *vi* déborder; **~ed egg** *n* œuf *m* à la coque; **~ed potatoes** *npl* pommes *fpl* à l'anglaise or à l'eau; **~er** *n* chaudière *f*; **~ing point** *n* point *m* d'ébullition

**boisterous** ['bɔɪstərəs] *adj* bruyant(e), tapageur(-euse)

**bold** [bəʊld] *adj* hardi(e), audacieux(-euse); (*pej*) effronté(e); (*outline, colour*) franc (franche), tranché(e), marqué(e); (*pattern*) grand(e)

**bollard** ['bɔləd] (*BRIT*) *n* (*AUT*) borne lumineuse *or* de signalisation

**bolt** [bəʊlt] *n* (*lock*) verrou *m*; (*with nut*) boulon *m* ♦ *adv*: **~ upright** droit(e) comme un piquet ♦ *vt* verrouiller; (*TECH: also: ~ on, ~ together*) boulonner; (*food*) engloutir ♦ *vi* (*horse*) s'emballer

**bomb** [bɔm] *n* bombe *f* ♦ *vt* bombarder; **~ing** *n* (*by terrorist*) attentat *m* à la bombe; **~ disposal unit** *n* section *f* de déminage; **~er** *n* (*AVIAT*) bombardier *m*; **~shell** *n* (*fig*) bombe *f*

**bond** [bɔnd] *n* lien *m*; (*binding promise*) engagement *m*, obligation *f*; (*COMM*) obligation *f*; **in ~** (*of goods*) en douane

**bondage** ['bɔndɪdʒ] *n* esclavage *m*

**bone** [bəʊn] *n* os *m*; (*of fish*) arête *f* ♦ *vt* désosser; ôter les arêtes de; **~ dry** *adj* complètement sec (sèche); **~ idle** *adj* fainéant(e); **~ marrow** *n* moelle *f* osseuse

**bonfire** ['bɔnfaɪə'] *n* feu *m* (de joie);

(*for rubbish*) feu

**bonnet** ['bɔnɪt] *n* bonnet *m*; (*BRIT: of car*) capot *m*

**bonus** ['bəʊnəs] *n* prime *f*, gratification *f*

**bony** ['bəʊnɪ] *adj* (*arm, face, MED: tissue*) osseux(-euse); (*meat*) plein(e) d'os; (*fish*) plein d'arêtes

**boo** [bu:] *excl* hou!, peuh! ♦ *vt* huer

**booby trap** ['bu:bɪ-] *n* engin piégé

**book** [buk] *n* livre *m*; (*of stamps, tickets*) carnet *m* ♦ *vt* (*ticket*) prendre; (*seat, room*) réserver; (*driver*) dresser un procès-verbal à; (*football player*) prendre le nom de; **~s** *npl* (*accounts*) comptes *mpl*, comptabilité *f*; **~case** *n* bibliothèque *f* (*meuble*); **~ing office** (*BRIT*) *n* bureau *m* de location; **~keeping** *n* comptabilité *f*; **~let** *n* brochure *f*; **~maker** *n* bookmaker *m*; **~seller** *n* libraire *m/f*; **~shelf** *n* (*single*) étagère *f* (à livres); **~shop** *n* librairie *f*; **~store** *n* librairie *f*

**boom** [bu:m] *n* (*noise*) grondement *m*; (*busy period*) vague *f or* poussée *f* (*montante*); (*in prices, population*) forte augmentation *f* ♦ *vi* gronder; prospérer

**boon** [bu:n] *n* bénédiction *f*, grand avantage

**boost** [bu:st] *n* stimulant *m*, remontant *m* ♦ *vt* stimuler; **~er** *n* (*MED*) rappel *m*

**boot** [bu:t] *n* botte *f*; (*for hiking*) chaussure *f* (de marche); (*for football etc*) soulier *m*; (*BRIT: of car*) coffre *m* ♦ *vt* (*COMPUT*) amorcer, initialiser; **to ~** (*in addition*) par-dessus le marché

**booth** [bu:ð] *n* (*at fair*) baraque (foraine); (*telephone etc*) cabine *f*; (*also: voting ~*) isoloir *m*

**booze** [bu:z] (*inf*) *n* boissons *fpl* alcooliques, alcool *m*

**border** ['bɔːdə'] *n* bordure *f*; bord *m*; (*of a country*) frontière *f* ♦ *vt* border; (*also: ~ on*) être limitrophe de; **B~s** *n* (*GEO*): **the B~s** la région frontière entre l'Écosse et l'Angleterre; **~ on** *vt fus* être voisin(e) de, toucher à; **~line** *n* (*fig*) ligne *f* de démarcation; **~line case**

cas *m* limite
**bore** [bɔːr] *pt of* **bear** ♦ *vt* (*hole*) percer; (*oil well, tunnel*) creuser; (*person*) ennuyer, raser ♦ *n* raseur(-euse); (*of gun*) calibre *m*; **to be ~d** s'ennuyer; **~dom** *n* ennui *m*; **boring** *adj* ennuyeux(-euse)

**born** [bɔːn] *adj*: **to be ~** naître; **I was ~ in 1960** je suis né en 1960

**borne** [bɔːn] *pp of* **bear**

**borough** ['bʌrə] *n* municipalité *f*

**borrow** ['bɔrəu] *vt*: **to ~ sth (from sb)** emprunter qch (à qn)

**Bosnia (and) Herzegovina** ['bɔznɪə(ənd)hɜːtsəgəu'viːnə] *n* Bosnie-Herzégovine *f*; **Bosnian** *adj* bosniaque, bosnien(ne) ♦ *n* Bosniaque *m/f*

**bosom** ['buzəm] *n* poitrine *f*, (*fig*) sein *m*

**boss** [bɔs] *n* patron(ne) ♦ *vt* (*also: ~ around/about*) mener à la baguette; **~y** *adj* autoritaire

**bosun** ['bəusn] *n* maître *m* d'équipage

**botany** ['bɔtənɪ] *n* botanique *f*

**botch** [bɔtʃ] *vt* (*also: ~ up*) saboter, bâcler

**both** [bəuθ] *adj* les deux, l'un(e) et l'autre ♦ *pron*: **~ (of them)** les deux, tous (toutes) (les) deux, l'un(e) et l'autre; **they sell ~ the fabric and the finished curtains** ils vendent (et) le tissu et les rideaux (finis), ils vendent à la fois le tissu et les rideaux (finis); **~ of us went, we ~ went** nous y sommes allés (tous les deux)

**bother** ['bɔðər] *vt* (*worry*) tracasser; (*disturb*) déranger ♦ *vi* (*also: ~ o.s.*) se tracasser, se faire du souci ♦ *n*: **it is a ~ to have to do** c'est vraiment ennuyeux d'avoir à faire; **it's no ~** aucun problème; **to ~ doing** prendre la peine de faire

**bottle** ['bɔtl] *n* bouteille *f*; (*baby's*) biberon *m* ♦ *vt* mettre en bouteille(s); **~d beer** bière *f* en canette; **~d water** eau minérale; **~ up** *vt* refouler, contenir; **~ bank** *n* conteneur à verre; **~neck** *n* étranglement *m*; **~-opener** *n* ouvre-

bouteille *m*

**bottom** ['bɔtəm] *n* (*of container, sea etc*) fond *m*; (*buttocks*) derrière *m*; (*of page, list*) bas *m* ♦ *adj* du fond; du bas; **the ~ of the class** le dernier de la classe

**bough** [bau] *n* branche *f*, rameau *m*

**bought** [bɔːt] *pt, pp of* **buy**

**boulder** ['bəuldər] *n* gros rocher

**bounce** [bauns] *vi* (*ball*) rebondir; (*cheque*) être refusé(e) (*étant sans provision*) ♦ *vt* faire rebondir ♦ *n* (*rebound*) rebond *m*; **~r** (*inf*) *n* (*at dance, club*) videur *m*

**bound** [baund] *pt, pp of* **bind** ♦ *n* (*gen pl*) limite *f*; (*leap*) bond *m* ♦ *vi* (*leap*) bondir ♦ *vt* (*limit*) borner ♦ *adj*: **to be ~ to do sth** (*obliged*) être obligé(e) or avoir obligation de faire qch; **he's ~ to fail** (*likely*) il est sûr d'échouer, son échec est inévitable or assuré; **~ by** (*law, regulation*) engagé(e) par; **~ for** à destination de; **out of ~s** dont l'accès est interdit

**boundary** ['baundrɪ] *n* frontière *f*

**bout** [baut] *n* période *f*; (*of malaria etc*) accès *m*, crise *f*, attaque *f*; (*BOXING etc*) combat *m*, match *m*

**bow**[1] [bəu] *n* nœud *m*; (*weapon*) arc *m*; (*MUS*) archet *m*

**bow**[2] [bau] *n* (*with body*) révérence *f*, inclination *f* (du buste or corps); (*NAUT: also: ~s*) proue *f* ♦ *vi* faire une révérence, s'incliner; (*yield*): **to ~ to** or **before** s'incliner devant, se soumettre à

**bowels** [bauəlz] *npl* intestins *mpl*; (*fig*) entrailles *fpl*

**bowl** [bəul] *n* (*for eating*) bol *m*; (*ball*) boule *f* ♦ *vt* (*CRICKET*) lancer (la balle)

**bow-legged** ['bəu'legɪd] *adj* aux jambes arquées

**bowler** ['bəulər] *n* (*CRICKET, BASEBALL*) lanceur *m* (de la balle); (*BRIT: also: ~ hat*) (chapeau *m*) melon *m*

**bowling** ['bəulɪŋ] *n* (*game*) jeu *m* de boules; jeu *m* de quilles; **~ alley** *n* bowling m; ~ green n terrain m de boules (gazonné et carré)

bowls [bəʊlz] n (game) (jeu m de) boules fpl

bow tie [bəʊ-] n nœud m papillon

box [bɒks] n boîte f; (also: cardboard ~) carton m; (THEATRE) loge f ♦ vt mettre en boîte; (SPORT) boxer avec ♦ vi boxer, faire de la boxe; ~er n (person) boxeur m; ~er shorts npl caleçon msg; ~ing n (SPORT) boxe f; B~ing Day (BRIT) n le lendemain de Noël; ~ing gloves npl gants mpl de boxe; ~ing ring n ring m; ~ office n bureau m de location; ~room n débarras m; chambrette f

Boxing Day

Boxing Day est le lendemain de Noël, férié en Grande-Bretagne. Si Noël tombe un samedi, un jour férié est reculé jusqu'au lundi suivant. Ce nom vient d'une coutume du XIXe siècle qui consistait à donner des cadeaux de Noël (dans des boîtes) à ses employés etc le 26 décembre.

boy [bɔɪ] n garçon m

boycott ['bɔɪkɒt] n boycottage m ♦ vt boycotter

boyfriend ['bɔɪfrɛnd] n (petit) ami

boyish ['bɔɪɪʃ] adj (behaviour) de garçon; (girl) garçonnier(-ière)

BR n abbr = British Rail

bra [brɑ:] n soutien-gorge m

brace [breɪs] n (on teeth) appareil m (dentaire); (tool) vilbrequin m ♦ vt (knees, shoulders) appuyer; ~s npl (BRIT: for trousers) bretelles fpl; to ~ o.s. (lit) s'arc-bouter; (fig) se préparer mentalement

bracelet ['breɪslɪt] n bracelet m

bracing ['breɪsɪŋ] adj tonifiant(e), tonique

bracket ['brækɪt] n (TECH) tasseau m, support m; (group) classe f, tranche f; (also: brace ~) accolade f; (also: round ~) parenthèse f; (also: square ~) cro-

chet m ♦ vt mettre entre parenthèse(s); (fig: also: ~ together) regrouper

brag [bræg] vi se vanter

braid [breɪd] n (trimming) galon m; (of hair) tresse f

brain [breɪn] n cerveau m; ~s npl (intellect, CULIN) cervelle f; he's got ~s il est intelligent; ~wash vt faire subir un lavage de cerveau à; ~wave n idée géniale; ~y adj intelligent(e), doué(e)

braise [breɪz] vt braiser

brake [breɪk] n (on vehicle, also fig) frein m ♦ vi freiner; ~ light n feu m de stop

bran [bræn] n son m

branch [brɑ:ntʃ] n branche f; (COMM) succursale f ♦ vi bifurquer; ~ out vi (fig): to ~ out into étendre ses activités à

brand [brænd] n marque (commerciale) ♦ vt (cattle) marquer (au fer rouge); ~new adj tout(e) neuf (neuve), flambant neuf (neuve)

brandy ['brændɪ] n cognac m, fine f

brash [bræʃ] adj effronté(e)

brass [brɑ:s] n cuivre m (jaune), laiton m; the ~ (MUS) les cuivres; ~ band n fanfare f

brat [bræt] (pej) n mioche m/f, môme m/f

brave [breɪv] adj courageux(-euse), brave ♦ n guerrier m indien ♦ vt braver, affronter; ~ry n bravoure f, courage m

brawl [brɔ:l] n rixe f, bagarre f

brazen ['breɪzn] adj impudent(e), effronté(e) ♦ vt: to ~ it out payer d'effronterie, crâner

brazier ['breɪzɪə] n brasero m

Brazil [brə'zɪl] n Brésil m

breach [bri:tʃ] vt ouvrir une brèche dans ♦ n (gap) brèche f; (breaking): ~ of contract rupture f de contrat; ~ of the peace attentat m à l'ordre public

bread [brɛd] n pain m; ~ and butter n tartines (beurrées) fpl; (fig) subsistance f; ~bin (BRIT) n boîte f à pain; (bigger) huche f à pain; ~crumbs npl miettes fpl

de pain; (CULIN) chapelure f, panure f;
**~line n: to be on the ~line** être sans
le sou or dans l'indigence

**breadth** [bretθ] n largeur f; (fig) ampleur f

**breadwinner** ['brɛdwɪnəʳ] n soutien m
de famille

**break** [breɪk] (pt **broke**, pp **broken**) vt
casser, briser; (promise) rompre; (law)
violer ♦ vi (se) casser, se briser; (weather) tourner; (story, news) se répandre;
(day) se lever ♦ n (gap) brèche f (fracture) cassure f; (pause, interval) interruption f, arrêt m; (: short) pause f; (: at
school) récréation f; (chance) chance f,
occasion f favorable; **to ~ one's leg** etc
se casser la jambe etc; **to ~ a record**
battre un record; **to ~ the news to sb**
annoncer la nouvelle à qn; **even
return dans ses frais; ~ free** or **loose** se
dégager, s'échapper; **~ open** (door etc)
forcer, fracturer; **~ down** vt (figures,
data) décomposer, analyser ♦ vi s'effondrer; (MED) faire une dépression (nerveuse); (AUT) tomber en panne; **~ in** vt
(horse etc) dresser ♦ vi (burglar) entrer
par effraction; (interrupt) interrompre; **~
into** vt fus (house) s'introduire ou pénétrer par effraction dans; **~ off** vi (speaker) s'interrompre; (branch) se rompre; **~
out** vi éclater, se déclarer; (prisoner)
s'évader; **to ~ out in spots** or **a rash**
avoir une éruption de boutons; **~ up** vi
(ship) se disloquer; (crowd, meeting) se
disperser, se séparer; (marriage) se briser; (SCOL) entrer en vacances ♦ vt casser; (fight etc) interrompre, faire cesser;
**~age** n casse f; **~down** n (AUT) panne
f; (in communications, marriage) rupture
f; (MED: also: **nervous ~down**) dépression (nerveuse); (of statistics) ventilation
f; **~down van** (BRIT) n dépanneuse f;
**~er** n brisant m

**breakfast** ['brɛkfəst] n petit déjeuner

**break: ~-in** n cambriolage m; **~ing
and entering** n (LAW) effraction f;
**~through** n percée f; **~water** n brise-

lames m inv, digue f

**breast** [brɛst] n (of woman) sein m;
(chest, of meat) poitrine f; **~-feed** (irreg:
like **feed**) vt, vi allaiter; **~stroke** n brasse f

**breath** [brɛθ] n haleine f; **out of ~** à
bout de souffle, essoufflé(e); **B~alyser**
® ['brɛθəlaɪzəʳ] n Alcootest ® m

**breathe** [briːð] vt, vi respirer; **~ in** vt, vi
aspirer, inspirer; **~ out** vt, vi expirer; **~r**
n moment de repos or de répit;
**breathing** n respiration f

**breathless** ['brɛθlɪs] adj essoufflé(e),
haletant(e)

**breathtaking** ['brɛθteɪkɪŋ] adj stupéfiant(e)

**breed** [briːd] (pt, pp **bred**) vt élever, faire
l'élevage de ♦ vi se reproduire ♦ n race
f, variété f; **~ing** n (upbringing) éducation f

**breeze** [briːz] n brise f; **breezy** adj frais
(fraîche); aéré(e); (manner etc) désinvolte, jovial(e)

**brevity** ['brɛvɪtɪ] n brièveté f

**brew** [bruː] vt (tea) faire infuser; (beer)
brasser ♦ vi (fig) se préparer, couver;
**~ery** n brasserie f (fabrique)

**bribe** [braɪb] n pot-de-vin m ♦ vt acheter; soudoyer; **~ry** n corruption f

**brick** [brɪk] n brique f; **~layer** n maçon
m

**bridal** ['braɪdl] adj nuptial(e)

**bride** [braɪd] n mariée f, épouse f;
**~groom** n marié m, époux m; **~smaid**
n demoiselle f d'honneur

**bridge** [brɪdʒ] n pont m; (NAUT) passerelle f (de commandement); (of nose)
arête f; (CARDS, DENTISTRY) bridge m ♦ vt
(fig: gap, gulf) combler

**bridle** ['braɪdl] n bride f; **~ path** n piste
or allée cavalière

**brief** [briːf] adj bref (brève) ♦ n (LAW)
dossier m, cause f; (gen) tâche f ♦ vt
mettre au courant; **~s** npl (undergarment) slip m; **~case** n serviette f,
porte-documents m inv; **~ly** adv
brièvement

**bright** [braɪt] adj brillant(e); (room, weather) clair(e); (clever: person, idea) intelligent(e); (cheerful: colour, person) vif (vive)

**brighten** ['braɪtn] (also: ~ up) vt (room) éclaircir, égayer; (event) égayer ♦ vi s'éclaircir; (person) retrouver un peu de sa gaieté; (face) s'éclairer; (prospects) s'améliorer

**brilliance** ['brɪljəns] n éclat m

**brilliant** ['brɪljənt] adj brillant(e); (sunshine, light) éclatant(e); (inf: holiday etc) super

**brim** [brɪm] n bord m

**brine** [braɪn] n (CULIN) saumure f

**bring** [brɪŋ] (pt, pp **brought**) vt apporter; (person) amener; ~ **about** vt provoquer, entraîner; ~ **back** vt rapporter; ramener; (restore: hanging) réinstaurer; ~ **down** vt (price) faire baisser; (enemy plane) descendre; (government) faire tomber; ~ **forward** vt avancer; ~ **off** vt (task, plan) réussir, mener à bien; ~ **out** vt (meaning) faire ressortir; (new book) publier; (object) sortir; ~ **round** vt (unconscious person) ranimer; ~ **up** vt (child) élever; (carry up) monter; (question) soulever; (food: vomit) vomir, rendre

**brink** [brɪŋk] n bord m

**brisk** [brɪsk] adj vif (vive)

**bristle** ['brɪsl] n poil m ♦ vi se hérisser

**Britain** ['brɪtən] n (also: **Great ~**) Grande-Bretagne f

**British** ['brɪtɪʃ] adj britannique ♦ npl: **the ~** les Britanniques mpl; **~ Isles** npl: **the ~ Isles** les Iles fpl Britanniques; **~ Rail** n compagnie ferroviaire britannique

**Briton** ['brɪtən] n Britannique m/f

**Brittany** ['brɪtənɪ] n Bretagne f

**brittle** ['brɪtl] adj cassant(e), fragile

**broach** [brəutʃ] vt (subject) aborder

**broad** [brɔːd] adj large; (general: outlines) grand(e); (: distinction) général(e); (accent) prononcé(e); **in ~ daylight** en plein jour; **~cast** (pt, pp **broadcast**) n émission f ♦ vt radiodiffuser; téléviser ♦

vi émettre; **~en** vt élargir ♦ vi s'élargir; **to ~en one's mind** élargir ses horizons; **~ly** adv en gros, généralement; **~-minded** adj large d'esprit

**broccoli** ['brɒkəlɪ] n brocoli m

**brochure** ['brəuʃjuər] n prospectus m, dépliant m

**broil** [brɔɪl] vt griller

**broke** [brəuk] pt of **break** ♦ adj (inf) fauché(e)

**broken** ['brəukn] pp of **break** ♦ adj cassé(e); (machine: also: ~ **down**) fichu(e); **in ~ English/French** dans un anglais/français approximatif or hésitant; **~ leg** etc jambe etc cassée; **~-hearted** adj (ayant) le cœur brisé

**broker** ['brəukər] n courtier m

**brolly** ['brɒlɪ] (BRIT: inf) n pépin m, parapluie m

**bronchitis** [brɒŋ'kaɪtɪs] n bronchite f

**bronze** [brɒnz] n bronze m

**brooch** [brəutʃ] n broche f

**brood** [bruːd] n couvée f ♦ vi (person) méditer (sombrement), ruminer

**broom** [brum] n balai m; (BOT) genêt m; **~stick** n manche m à balai

**Bros.** abbr = **Brothers**

**broth** [brɔθ] n bouillon m de viande et de légumes

**brothel** ['brɔθl] n maison close f

**brother** ['brʌðər] n frère m; **~-in-law** n beau-frère m

**brought** [brɔːt] pt, pp of **bring**

**brow** [brau] n front m; (eyebrow) sourcil m; (of hill) sommet m

**brown** [braun] adj brun(e), marron inv; (hair) châtain inv, brun; (eyes) marron inv; (tanned) bronzé(e) ♦ n (colour) brun m ♦ vt (CULIN) faire dorer; **~ bread** n pain m bis; **B~ie** n (also: **B~ie Guide**) jeannette f, éclaireuse (cadette); **~ie** n (US) (cake) gâteau m au chocolat et aux noix; **~ paper** n papier m d'emballage; **~ sugar** n cassonade f

**browse** [brauz] vi (among books) bouquiner, feuilleter les livres; (COMPUT) surfer ou naviguer sur le Net; **to ~**

**through a book** feuilleter un livre

**browser** ['brauzə<sup>r</sup>] *n* (COMPUT) navigateur *m*

**bruise** [bruːz] *n* bleu *m*, contusion *f* ♦ *vt* contusionner, meurtrir

**brunette** [bruːˈnet] *n* (femme) brune

**brunt** [brʌnt] *n*: **the ~ of** (attack, criticism etc) le plus gros de

**brush** [brʌʃ] *n* brosse *f*; (painting) pinceau *m*; (shaving) blaireau *m*; (quarrel) accrochage *m*, prise *f* de bec ♦ *vt* brosser; (also: ~ **against**) effleurer, frôler; **~ aside** *vt* écarter, balayer; **~ up** *vt* (knowledge) rafraîchir, réviser; **~wood** *n* broussailles *fpl*, taillis *m*

**Brussels** ['brʌslz] *n* Bruxelles; **~ sprout** *n* chou *m* de Bruxelles

**brutal** ['bruːtl] *adj* brutal(e)

**brute** [bruːt] *n* brute *f* ♦ *adj*: **by ~ force** par la force

**BSc** *abbr* = **Bachelor of Science**

**BSE** *n abbr* (= bovine spongiform encephalopathy) ESB *f*, BSE *f*

**bubble** ['bʌbl] *n* bulle *f* ♦ *vi* bouillonner, faire des bulles; (sparkle) pétiller; **~ bath** *n* bain moussant; **~ gum** *n* bubblegum *m*

**buck** [bʌk] *n* mâle *m* (d'un lapin, daim etc); (us: inf) dollar *m* ♦ *vi* ruer, lancer une ruade; **to pass the ~ (to sb)** se décharger de la responsabilité (sur qn); **~ up** *vi* (cheer up) reprendre du poil de la bête, se remonter

**bucket** ['bʌkɪt] *n* seau *m*

Buckingham Palace

Buckingham Palace *est la résidence officielle londonienne du souverain britannique depuis 1762. Construit en 1703, il fut à l'origine le palais du duc de Buckingham. Il a été partiellement reconstruit au début du siècle.*

**buckle** ['bʌkl] *n* boucle *f* ♦ *vt* (belt etc) boucler, attacher ♦ *vi* (warp) tordre, gauchir; (: wheel) se voiler, se déformer

**bud** [bʌd] *n* bourgeon *m*; (of flower)

bouton *m* ♦ *vi* bourgeonner; (flower) éclore

**Buddhism** ['budɪzəm] *n* bouddhisme *m*

**Buddhist** *adj* bouddhiste ♦ *n* Bouddhiste *m/f*

**budding** ['bʌdɪŋ] *adj* (poet etc) en herbe; (passion etc) naissant(e)

**buddy** ['bʌdɪ] *n* (us) copain *m*

**budge** [bʌdʒ] *vt* faire bouger; (fig: person) faire changer d'avis ♦ *vi* bouger; changer d'avis

**budgerigar** ['bʌdʒərɪgɑːʳ] (BRIT) *n* perruche *f*

**budget** ['bʌdʒɪt] *n* budget *m* ♦ *vi*: **to ~ for sth** inscrire qch au budget

**budgie** ['bʌdʒɪ] (BRIT) *n* = **budgerigar**

**buff** [bʌf] *adj* (colour *f*) chamois *m* ♦ *n* (inf: enthusiast) mordu(e); **he's a ... ~** c'est un mordu de ...

**buffalo** ['bʌfələu] (pl ~ or ~es) *n* buffle *m*; (us) bison *m*

**buffer** ['bʌfəʳ] *n* tampon *m*; (COMPUT) mémoire *f* tampon

**buffet**[1] ['bʌfɪt] *vt* secouer, ébranler

**buffet**[2] ['bufeɪ] *n* (food, BRIT: bar) buffet *m*; **~ car** (BRIT) *n* (RAIL) voiture-buffet *f*

**bug** [bʌg] *n* (insect) punaise *f*; (: gen) insecte *m*, bestiole *f*; (fig: germ) virus *m*, microbe *m*; (COMPUT) erreur *f*; (fig: spy device) dispositif *m* d'écoute (électronique) ♦ *vt* garnir de dispositifs d'écoute; (inf: annoy) embêter; **~ged** *adj* sur écoute

**bugle** ['bjuːgl] *n* clairon *m*

**build** [bɪld] (pt, pp **built**) *n* (of person) carrure *f*, charpente *f* ♦ *vt* construire, bâtir; **~ up** *vt* accumuler, amasser, accroître; **~er** *n* entrepreneur *m*; **~ing** *n* (trade) construction *f*; (house, structure) bâtiment *m*, construction *f*; (offices, flats) immeuble *m*; **~ing society** (BRIT) *n* société *f* de crédit immobilier

building society

*Une building society est une mutuelle dont les épargnants et emprunteurs sont les propriétaires. Ces mu-*

tuelles offrent deux services principaux: on peut y avoir un compte d'épargne duquel on peut retirer son argent sur demande ou moyennant un court préavis; et on peut également y faire des emprunts à long terme, par exemple pour acheter une maison.

**built** [bɪlt] pt, pp of **build**; **~-in** ['bɪlt'ɪn] adj (cupboard, oven) encastré(e); (device) incorporé(e); intégré(e); **~-up area** ['bɪltʌp-] n zone urbanisée

**bulb** [bʌlb] n (BOT) bulbe m, oignon m; (ELEC) ampoule f

**Bulgaria** [bʌl'geərɪə] n Bulgarie f

**bulge** [bʌldʒ] n renflement m, gonflement m ♦ vi (pocket, file etc) être plein(e) à craquer; (cheeks) être gonflé(e)

**bulk** [bʌlk] n masse f, volume m; (of person) corpulence f; **in ~** (COMM) en vrac; **the ~ of** la plus grande partie de; **~y** adj volumineux(-euse), encombrant(e)

**bull** [bul] n taureau m; (male elephant/whale) mâle m; **~dog** n bouledogue m

**bulldozer** ['buldəʊzə] n bulldozer m

**bullet** ['bulɪt] n balle f (de fusil etc)

**bulletin** ['bulɪtɪn] n bulletin m, communiqué m; (news ~) (bulletin d')informations fpl; **~ board** n (INTERNET) messagerie f électronique

**bulletproof** ['bulɪtpru:f] adj (car) blindé(e); (vest etc) pare-balles inv

**bullfight** ['bulfaɪt] n corrida f, course f de taureaux; **~er** n torero m; **~ing** n tauromachie f

**bullion** ['buljən] n or m or argent m en lingots

**bullock** ['bulək] n bœuf m

**bullring** ['bulrɪŋ] n arènes fpl

**bull's-eye** ['bulzaɪ] n centre m (de la cible)

**bully** ['bulɪ] n brute f, tyran m ♦ vt tyranniser, rudoyer

**bum** [bʌm] n (inf: backside) derrière m; (esp US: tramp) vagabond(e), traîne-savates m/f inv

**bumblebee** ['bʌmblbi:] n bourdon m

**bump** [bʌmp] n (in car: minor accident) accrochage m; (jolt) cahot m; (on road etc, on head) bosse f ♦ vt heurter, cogner; **~ into** vt fus rentrer dans, tamponner; (meet) tomber sur; **~er** n pare-chocs m inv ♦ adj: **~er crop/harvest** récolte/moisson exceptionnelle; **~er cars** (US) npl autos tamponneuses; **~y** adj cahoteux(-euse)

**bun** [bʌn] n petit pain au lait; (of hair) chignon m

**bunch** [bʌntʃ] n (of flowers) bouquet m; (of keys) trousseau m; (of bananas) régime m; (of people) groupe m; **~es** npl (in hair) couettes fpl; **~ of grapes** grappe f de raisin

**bundle** ['bʌndl] n paquet m ♦ vt (also: **~ up**) faire un paquet de; (put): **to ~ sth/sb into** fourrer ou enfourner qch/qn dans

**bungalow** ['bʌngələʊ] n bungalow m

**bungle** ['bʌngl] vt bâcler, gâcher

**bunion** ['bʌnjən] n oignon m (au pied)

**bunk** [bʌŋk] n couchette f; **~ beds** npl lits superposés

**bunker** ['bʌŋkə] n (coal store) soute f à charbon; (MIL, GOLF) bunker m

**bunting** ['bʌntɪŋ] n pavoisement m, drapeaux mpl

**buoy** [bɔɪ] n bouée f; **~ up** vt faire flotter; (fig) soutenir, épauler; **~ant** adj capable de flotter; (carefree) gai(e), plein(e) d'entrain; (economy) ferme, actif

**burden** ['bə:dn] n fardeau m ♦ vt (trouble) accabler, surcharger

**bureau** ['bjuərəu] n (pl **~x**) (BRIT: writing desk) bureau m, secrétaire m; (US: chest of drawers) commode f; (office) bureau, office m; **~cracy** [bjuə'rɔkrəsɪ] n bureaucratie f

**burglar** ['bə:glə] n cambrioleur m; **~ alarm** n sonnerie f d'alarme

**Burgundy** ['bə:gəndɪ] n Bourgogne f

**burial** ['berɪəl] n enterrement m

**burly** ['bɜ:lɪ] *adj* de forte carrure, costaud(e)

**Burma** ['bɜ:mə] *n* Birmanie *f*

**burn** [bɜ:n] (*pt,pp* **burned** *or* **burnt**) *vt, vi* brûler ♦ *n* brûlure *f*; **~ down** *vt* incendier, détruire par le feu; **~er** *n* brûleur *m*; **~ing** *adj* brûlant(e); (*house*) en flammes; (*ambition*) dévorant(e)

**burrow** ['bʌrəʊ] *n* terrier *m* ♦ *vt* creuser

**bursary** ['bɜ:sərɪ] (*BRIT*) *n* bourse *f* (d'études)

**burst** [bɜ:st] (*pt,pp* **burst**) *vt* crever; faire éclater; (*subj: river: banks etc*) rompre ♦ *vi* éclater; (*tyre*) crever ♦ *n* (*of gunfire*) rafale *f* (de tir); (*also:* **~ pipe**) rupture *f*; fuite *f*; **a ~ of enthusiasm/energy** un accès d'enthousiasme/d'énergie; **to ~ into flames** s'enflammer soudainement; **to ~ out laughing** éclater de rire; **to ~ into tears** fondre en larmes; **to be ~ing with** être plein (à craquer) de; (*fig*) être débordant(e) de; **~ into** *vt fus* (*room etc*) faire irruption dans

**bury** ['berɪ] *vt* enterrer

**bus** [bʌs] (*pl* **~es**) *n* autobus *m*

**bush** [bʊʃ] *n* buisson *m*; (*scrubland*) brousse *f*; **to beat about the ~** tourner autour du pot; **~y** *adj* broussailleux(-euse), touffu(e)

**busily** ['bɪzɪlɪ] *adv* activement

**business** ['bɪznɪs] *n* (*matter, firm*) affaire *f*; (*trading*) affaires *fpl*; (*job, duty*) travail *m*; **to be away on ~** être en déplacement d'affaires; **it's none of my ~** cela ne me regarde pas, ce ne sont pas mes affaires; **he means ~** il ne plaisante pas, il est sérieux; **~like** *adj* (*firm*) sérieux(-euse); (*method*) efficace; **~man** (*irreg*) *n* homme *m* d'affaires; **~ trip** *n* voyage *m* d'affaires; **~woman** (*irreg*) *n* femme *f* d'affaires

**busker** ['bʌskəʳ] (*BRIT*) *n* musicien *m* ambulant

**bus:** **~ shelter** *n* abribus *m*; **~ station** *n* gare routière; **~ stop** *n* arrêt *m* d'autobus

**bust** [bʌst] *n* buste *m*; (*measurement*)

tour *m* de poitrine ♦ *adj* (*inf: broken*) fichu(e), fini(e); **to go ~** faire faillite

**bustle** ['bʌsl] *n* remue-ménage *m*, affairement *m* ♦ *vi* s'affairer, se démener; **bustling** *adj* (*town*) bruyant(e), affairé(e)

**busy** ['bɪzɪ] *adj* occupé(e); (*shop, street*) très fréquenté(e) ♦ *vt:* **to ~ o.s.** s'occuper; **~body** *n* mouche *f* du coche, âme *f* charitable; **~ signal** (*US*) *n* (*TEL*) tonalité *f* occupé *inv*

**but** [bʌt] *conj* mais; **I'd love to come, but I'm busy** j'aimerais venir mais je suis occupé

♦ *prep* (*apart from, except*) sauf, excepté; **we've had nothing but trouble** nous n'avons eu que des ennuis; **no-one but him can do it** lui seul peut le faire; **but for you/your help** sans toi/ton aide; **anything but that** tout sauf or excepté ça, tout mais pas ça

♦ *adv* (*just, only*) ne ... que; **she's but a child** elle n'est qu'une enfant; **had I but known** si seulement j'avais su; **all but finished** pratiquement terminé

**butcher** ['bʊtʃəʳ] *n* boucher *m* ♦ *vt* massacrer; (*cattle etc for meat*) tuer; **~'s (shop)** *n* boucherie *f*

**butler** ['bʌtləʳ] *n* maître d'hôtel

**butt** [bʌt] *n* (*large barrel*) gros tonneau; (*of gun*) crosse *f*; (*of cigarette*) mégot *m*; (*BRIT: fig: target*) cible *f* ♦ *vt* donner un coup de tête à; **~ in** *vi* (*interrupt*) s'immiscer dans la conversation

**butter** ['bʌtəʳ] *n* beurre *m* ♦ *vt* beurrer; **~cup** *n* bouton *m* d'or

**butterfly** ['bʌtəflaɪ] *n* papillon *m*; (*SWIMMING: also:* **~ stroke**) brasse *f* papillon

**buttocks** ['bʌtəks] *npl* fesses *fpl*

**button** ['bʌtn] *n* bouton *m*; (*US: badge*) pin *m* ♦ *vt* (*also:* **~ up**) boutonner ♦ *vi* se boutonner

**buttress** ['bʌtrɪs] *n* contrefort *m*

**buy** [baɪ] (pt, pp **bought**) vt acheter ♦ n achat m; **to ~ sb sth/sth from sb** acheter qch à qn; **to ~ sb a drink** offrir un verre or à boire à qn; **~er** n acheteur(-euse)

**buzz** [bʌz] n bourdonnement m; (inf: phone call): **to give sb a ~** passer un coup m de fil à qn ♦ vi bourdonner; **~er** n timbre m électrique; **~ word** (inf) mot m à la mode

---
KEYWORD
---

**by** [baɪ] prep **1** (referring to cause, agent) par, de; **killed by lightning** tué par la foudre; **surrounded by a fence** entouré d'une barrière; **a painting by Picasso** un tableau de Picasso

**2** (referring to method, manner, means): **by bus/car** en autobus/voiture; **by train** par le or en train; **to pay by cheque** payer par chèque; **by saving hard, he ...** à force d'économiser, il ...

**3** (via, through) par; **we came by Dover** nous sommes venus par Douvres

**4** (close to, past) à côté de; **the house by the school** la maison à côté de l'école; **a holiday by the sea** des vacances au bord de la mer; **she sat by his bed** elle était assise à son chevet; **she went by me** elle est passée à côté de moi; **I go by the post office every day** je passe devant la poste tous les jours

**5** (with time: not later than) avant; (: during): **by daylight** à la lumière du jour; **by night** la nuit, de nuit; **by 4 o'clock** avant 4 heures; **by this time tomorrow** d'ici demain à la même heure; **by the time I got here it was too late** lorsque je suis arrivé il était déjà trop tard

**6** (amount) à; **by the kilo/metre** au kilo/au mètre; **paid by the hour** payé à l'heure

**7** (MATH, measure): **to divide/multiply by 3** diviser/multiplier par 3; **a room 3 metres by 4** une pièce de 3 mètres sur 4; **it's broader by a metre** c'est plus large d'un mètre; **one by one** un à un; **little by little** petit à petit, peu à peu

**8** (according to) d'après, selon; **it's 3 o'clock by my watch** il est 3 heures à ma montre; **it's all right by me** je n'ai rien contre

**9: (all) by oneself** etc tout(e) seul(e)

**10: by the way** au fait, à propos

♦ adv **1** see go; pass etc

**2: by and by** un peu plus tard, bientôt; **by and large** dans l'ensemble

**bye(-bye)** ['baɪ('baɪ)] excl au revoir!, salut!

**bye(e)-law** ['baɪlɔː] n arrêté municipal

**by:** **~-election** (BRIT) n élection (législative) partielle; **~gone** adj passé(e) ♦ n: **let ~gones be ~gones** passons l'éponge, oublions le passé; **~pass** n (route f de) contournement m; (MED) pontage m ♦ vt éviter; **~-product** n sous-produit m, dérivé m; (fig) conséquence f secondaire, retombée f; **~stander** n spectateur(-trice), badaud(e)

**byte** [baɪt] n (COMPUT) octet m

**byword** ['baɪwɜːd] n: **to be a ~ for** être synonyme de (fig)

# C, c

**C** [siː] n (MUS) do m

**CA** abbr = chartered accountant

**cab** [kæb] n taxi m; (of train, truck) cabine f

**cabaret** ['kæbəreɪ] n (show) spectacle m de cabaret

**cabbage** ['kæbɪdʒ] n chou m

**cabin** ['kæbɪn] n (house) cabane f, hutte f; (on ship) cabine f; (on plane) compartiment m; **~ crew** n (AVIAT) équipage m; **~ cruiser** n cruiser m

**cabinet** ['kæbɪnɪt] n (POL) cabinet m; (furniture) petit meuble à tiroirs et rayons; (also: **display ~**) vitrine f, petite armoire vitrée

**cable** ['keɪbl] n câble m ♦ vt câbler, télégraphier; **~-car** n téléphérique m; **~ television** n télévision f par câble

**cache** [kæʃ] n stock m

**cackle** ['kækl] vi caqueter

**cactus** ['kæktəs] (pl **cacti**) n cactus m

**cadet** [kə'dɛt] n (MIL) élève m officier

**cadge** [kædʒ] (inf) vt: **to ~ (from** or **off)** se faire donner

**Caesarian** [sɪ'zɛərɪən] n (also: **~ section**) césarienne f

**café** ['kæfeɪ] n ≈ café(-restaurant) m (sans alcool)

**cage** [keɪdʒ] n cage f

**cagey** ['keɪdʒɪ] (inf) adj réticent(e); méfiant(e)

**cagoule** [kə'gu:l] n K-way ® m

**Cairo** ['kaɪərəu] n le Caire

**cajole** [kə'dʒəul] vt couvrir de flatteries or de gentillesses

**cake** [keɪk] n gâteau m; **~d** adj: **~d with** raidi(e) par, couvert(e) d'une croûte de

**calculate** ['kælkjuleɪt] vt calculer; (estimate: chances, effect) évaluer; **calculation** n calcul m; **calculator** n machine f à calculer, calculatrice f; (pocket) calculette f

**calendar** ['kæləndər] n calendrier m; **~ year** n année civile

**calf** [kɑ:f] (pl **calves**) n (of cow) veau m; (of other animals) petit m; (also: **~skin**) veau m, vachette f; (ANAT) mollet m

**calibre** ['kælɪbər] (US **caliber**) n calibre m

**call** [kɔ:l] vt appeler; (meeting) convoquer ♦ vi appeler; (visit: also: **~ in, ~ round**) passer ♦ n (shout) appel m, cri m; (also: **telephone ~**) coup m de téléphone; (visit) visite f; **she's ~ed Suzanne** elle s'appelle Suzanne; **to be on ~** être de permanence; **~ back** vi (return) repasser; (TEL) rappeler; **~ for** vt fus (demand) demander; (fetch) passer prendre; **~ off** vt annuler; **~ on** vt fus (visit) rendre visite à, passer voir; (re-

quest): **to ~ on sb to do** inviter qn à faire; **~ out** vi pousser un cri or des cris; **~ up** vt (MIL) appeler, mobiliser; (TEL) appeler; **~box** n (BRIT) cabine f téléphonique; **~ centre** n centre m d'appels; **~er** n (TEL) personne f qui appelle; (visitor) visiteur m; **~ girl** n call-girl f; **~-in** (US) n (RADIO, TV: phone-in) programme m à ligne ouverte; **~ing** n vocation f; (trade, occupation) état m; **~ing card** (US) n carte f de visite

**callous** ['kæləs] adj dur(e), insensible

**calm** [kɑ:m] adj calme ♦ n calme m ♦ vt calmer, apaiser; **~ down** vi se calmer ♦ vt calmer, apaiser

**Calor gas** ® ['kælər-] n butane m, butagaz m ®

**calorie** ['kælərɪ] n calorie f

**calves** [kɑ:vz] npl of **calf**

**camber** ['kæmbər] n (of road) bombement m

**Cambodia** [kæm'bəudɪə] n Cambodge m

**camcorder** ['kæmkɔ:dər] n caméscope m

**came** [keɪm] pt of **come**

**camel** ['kæməl] n chameau m

**camera** ['kæmərə] n (PHOT) appareil-photo m; (also: **cine-~, movie ~**) caméra f; **in ~** à huis clos; **~man** (irreg) n caméraman m

**camouflage** ['kæməflɑ:ʒ] n camouflage m ♦ vt camoufler

**camp** [kæmp] n camp m ♦ vi camper ♦ adj (man) efféminé(e)

**campaign** [kæm'peɪn] n (MIL, POL etc) campagne f ♦ vi faire campagne

**camp: ~bed** (BRIT) n lit m de camp; **~er** n campeur(-euse); (vehicle) camping-car m; **~ing** n camping m; **to go ~ing** faire du camping; **~ing gas** ® n butane m; **~site** n campement m, (terrain m de) camping m

**campus** ['kæmpəs] n campus m

**can**[1] [kæn] n (of milk, oil, water) bidon m; (tin) boîte f de conserve ♦ vt mettre en conserve

---
KEYWORD
---

**can²** [kæn] *(negative* **cannot, can't,** *conditional and pt* **could)** *aux vb* **1** *(be able to)* pouvoir; **you can do it if you try** vous pouvez le faire si vous essayez; **I can't hear you** je ne t'entends pas
**2** *(know how to)* savoir; **I can swim/play tennis/drive** je sais nager/jouer au tennis/conduire; **can you speak French?** parlez-vous français?
**3** *(may)* pouvoir; **can I use your phone?** puis-je me servir de votre téléphone?
**4** *(expressing disbelief, puzzlement etc)*: **it can't be true!** ce n'est pas possible!; **what CAN he want?** qu'est-ce qu'il peut bien vouloir?
**5** *(expressing possibility, suggestion etc)*: **he could be in the library** il est peut-être dans la bibliothèque; **she could have been delayed** il se peut qu'elle ait été retardée

---

**Canada** ['kænədə] *n* Canada *m*; **Canadian** [kə'neɪdɪən] *adj* canadien(ne) ♦ *n* Canadien(ne)
**canal** [kə'næl] *n* canal *m*
**canapé** ['kænəpeɪ] *n* canapé *m*
**canary** [kə'nɛərɪ] *n* canari *m*, serin *m*
**cancel** ['kænsəl] *vt* annuler; *(train)* supprimer; *(party, appointment)* décommander; *(cross out)* barrer, rayer; **~lation** [-'leɪʃən] *n* annulation *f*, suppression *f*
**cancer** ['kænsə'] *n* *(MED)* cancer *m*; **C~** *(ASTROLOGY)* le Cancer
**candid** ['kændɪd] *adj* (très) franc (franche), sincère
**candidate** ['kændɪdeɪt] *n* candidat(e)
**candle** ['kændl] *n* bougie *f*; *(of tallow)* chandelle *f*; *(in church)* cierge *m*; **~light** *n*: **by ~light** à la lumière d'une bougie; *(dinner)* aux chandelles; **~stick** *n* *(also: ~ holder)* bougeoir *m*; *(bigger, ornate)* chandelier *m*
**candour** ['kændə'] *(US* **candor)** *n*

(grande) franchise *or* sincérité
**candy** ['kændɪ] *n* sucre candi; *(US)* bonbon *m*; **~-floss** *(BRIT)* *n* barbe *f* à papa
**cane** [keɪn] *n* canne *f*; *(for furniture, baskets etc)* rotin *m* ♦ *vt* *(BRIT: SCOL)* administrer des coups de bâton à
**canister** ['kænɪstə'] *n* boîte *f*; *(of gas, pressurized substance)* bombe *f*
**cannabis** ['kænəbɪs] *n* *(drug)* cannabis *m*
**canned** [kænd] *adj* *(food)* en boîte, en conserve
**cannon** ['kænən] *(pl ~ or ~s)* *n* *(gun)* canon *m*
**cannot** ['kænɔt] = **can not**
**canoe** [kə'nuː] *n* pirogue *f*; *(SPORT)* canoë *m*; **~ing** *n*: **to go ~ing** faire du canoë
**canon** ['kænən] *n* *(clergyman)* chanoine *m*; *(standard)* canon *m*
**can-opener** ['kænəʊpnə'] *n* ouvre-boîte *m*
**canopy** ['kænəpɪ] *n* baldaquin *m*; dais *m*
**can't** [kænt] = **cannot**
**canteen** [kæn'tiːn] *n* cantine *f*; *(BRIT: of cutlery)* ménagère *f*
**canter** ['kæntə'] *vi* *(horse)* aller au petit galop
**canvas** ['kænvəs] *n* toile *f*
**canvass** ['kænvəs] *vi* *(POL)*: **to ~ for** faire campagne pour ♦ *vt* *(investigate: opinions etc)* sonder
**canyon** ['kænjən] *n* cañon *m*, gorge *f* (profonde)
**cap** [kæp] *n* casquette *f*; *(of pen)* capuchon *m*; *(of bottle)* capsule *f*; *(contraceptive: also:* **Dutch ~)** diaphragme *m*; *(for toy gun)* amorce *f* ♦ *vt* *(outdo)* surpasser; *(put limit on)* plafonner
**capability** [keɪpə'bɪlɪtɪ] *n* aptitude *f*, capacité *f*
**capable** ['keɪpəbl] *adj* capable
**capacity** [kə'pæsɪtɪ] *n* capacité *f*; *(capability)* aptitude *f*; *(of factory)* rendement *m*
**cape** [keɪp] *n* *(garment)* cape *f*; *(GEO)*

cap *m*

**caper** ['keɪpə<sup>r</sup>] *n* (CULIN: gen pl) câpre *f*; (prank) farce *f*

**capital** ['kæpɪtl] *n* (also: ~ city) capitale *f*; (money) capital *m*; (also: ~ letter) majuscule *f*; ~ **gains tax** *n* (COMM) impôt *m* sur les plus-values; ~**ism** *n* capitalisme *m*; ~**ist** *adj* capitaliste ♦ *n* capitaliste *m/f*; ~**ize** ['kæpɪtəlaɪz] *vi*: to ~**ize on** tirer parti de; ~ **punishment** *n* peine capitale

**Capitol**

Le **Capitol** est le siège du **Congress**, à Washington. Il est situé sur Capitol Hill.

**Capricorn** ['kæprɪkɔ:n] *n* le Capricorne

**capsize** [kæp'saɪz] *vt* faire chavirer ♦ *vi* chavirer

**capsule** ['kæpsju:l] *n* capsule *f*

**captain** ['kæptɪn] *n* capitaine *m*

**caption** ['kæpʃən] *n* légende *f*

**captive** ['kæptɪv] *adj, n* captif(-ive)

**capture** ['kæptʃə<sup>r</sup>] *vt* capturer, prendre; (attention) capter; (COMPUT) saisir ♦ *n* capture *f*; (data ~) saisie *f* de données

**car** [kɑ:<sup>r</sup>] *n* voiture *f*, auto *f*; (RAIL) wagon *m*, voiture

**caramel** ['kærəməl] *n* caramel *m*

**caravan** ['kærəvæn] *n* caravane *f*; ~**ning** *n*: to go ~**ning** faire du caravaning; ~ **site** (BRIT) *n* camping *m* pour caravanes

**carbohydrate** [kɑ:bəu'haɪdreɪt] *n* hydrate *m* de carbone; (food) féculent *m*

**carbon** ['kɑ:bən] *n* carbone *m*; ~ **diox-ide** *n* gaz *m* carbonique; ~ **monoxide** *n* oxyde *m* de carbone; ~ **paper** *n* papier *m* carbone

**car boot sale** *n* marché aux puces où les particuliers vendent des objets entreposés dans le coffre de leur voiture

**carburettor** [kɑ:bju'retə<sup>r</sup>] (US **carburetor**) *n* carburateur *m*

**card** [kɑ:d] *n* carte *f*; (material) carton *m*; ~**board** *n* carton *m*; ~ **game** *n* jeu

*m* de cartes

**cardiac** ['kɑ:dɪæk] *adj* cardiaque

**cardigan** ['kɑ:dɪgən] *n* cardigan *m*

**cardinal** ['kɑ:dɪnl] *adj* cardinal(e) ♦ *n* cardinal *m*

**card index** *n* fichier *m*

**cardphone** *n* téléphone *m* à carte

**care** [keə<sup>r</sup>] *n* soin *m*, attention *f*; (worry) souci *m*; (charge) charge *f*, garde *f* ♦ *vi*: to ~ **about** se soucier de, s'intéresser à; (person) être attaché(e) à; ~ **of** chez, aux bons soins de; **in sb's** ~ à la garde de *qn*, confié(e) à *qn*; **to take** ~ (**to do**) faire attention (à faire); **to take** ~ **of** s'occuper de; **I don't** ~ ça m'est bien égal; **I couldn't** ~ **less** je m'en fiche complètement (inf); ~ **for** *vt fus* s'occuper de; (like) aimer

**career** [kə'rɪə<sup>r</sup>] *n* carrière *f* ♦ *vi* (also: ~ **along**) aller à toute allure; ~ **woman** (irreg) *n* femme ambitieuse

**care**: ~**free** *adj* sans souci, insouciant(e); ~**ful** *adj* (thorough) soigneux(-euse); (cautious) prudent(e); (**be**) ~**ful!** (fais) attention!; ~**fully** *adv* avec soin, soigneusement; prudemment; ~**less** *adj* négligent(e); (heedless) insouciant(e); ~**r** *n* (MED) aide *f*

**caress** [kə'res] *n* caresse *f* ♦ *vt* caresser

**caretaker** ['keəteɪkə<sup>r</sup>] *n* gardien(ne), concierge *m/f*

**car-ferry** [kɑ:feri] *n* (on sea) ferry(-boat) *m*

**cargo** ['kɑ:gəu] (*pl* ~**es**) *n* cargaison *f*, chargement *m*

**car hire** *n* location *f* de voitures

**Caribbean** [kærɪ'bi:ən] *adj*: **the** ~ (**Sea**) la mer des Antilles or Caraïbes

**caring** ['keərɪŋ] *adj* (person) bienveillant(e); (society, organization) humanitaire

**carnation** [kɑ:'neɪʃən] *n* œillet *m*

**carnival** ['kɑ:nɪvl] *n* (public celebration) carnaval *m*; (US: funfair) fête foraine

**carol** ['kærəl] *n*: **(Christmas)** ~ chant *m* de Noël

**carp** [kɑ:p] *n* (fish) carpe *f*

**car park** (BRIT) n parking m, parc m de stationnement

**carpenter** ['kɑ:pɪntə'] n charpentier m; **carpentry** n menuiserie f

**carpet** ['kɑ:pɪt] n tapis m ♦ vt recouvrir d'un tapis; ~ **sweeper** n balai m mécanique

**car phone** n (TEL) téléphone m de voiture

**car rental** n location f de voitures

**carriage** ['kærɪdʒ] n voiture f; (of goods) transport m; (: cost) port m; **~way** (BRIT) n (part of road) chaussée f

**carrier** ['kærɪə'] n transporteur m, camionneur m; (company) entreprise f de transport; (MED) porteur(-euse); **~ bag** (BRIT) n sac m (en papier ou en plastique)

**carrot** ['kærət] n carotte f

**carry** ['kærɪ] vt (subj: person) porter; (vehicle) transporter; (involve: responsibilities etc) comporter, impliquer ♦ vi (sound) porter; **to get carried away** (fig) s'emballer, s'enthousiasmer; **~ on** vi: **to ~ on with sth/doing** continuer qch/de faire ♦ vt poursuivre; **~ out** vt (orders) exécuter; (investigation) mener; **~cot** (BRIT) n porte-bébé m; **~-on** (inf) n (fuss) histoires fpl

**cart** [kɑ:t] n charrette f ♦ vt (inf) transporter, trimballer (inf)

**carton** ['kɑ:tən] n (box) carton m; (of yogurt) pot m; (of cigarettes) cartouche f

**cartoon** [kɑ:'tu:n] n (PRESS) dessin m (humoristique), caricature f; (BRIT: comic strip) bande dessinée; (CINEMA) dessin animé

**cartridge** ['kɑ:trɪdʒ] n cartouche f

**carve** [kɑ:v] vt (meat) découper; (wood, stone) tailler, sculpter; **~ up** vt découper; (fig: country) morceler; **carving** n sculpture f; **carving knife** n couteau m à découper

**car wash** n station f de lavage (de voitures)

**case** [keɪs] n cas m; (LAW) affaire f, pro-

cès m; (box) caisse f, boîte f, étui m; (BRIT: also: suitcase) valise f; **in ~ of** en cas de; **in ~ he** ... au cas où il ...; **just in ~** à tout hasard; **in any ~** en tout cas, de toute façon

**cash** [kæʃ] n argent m; (COMM) argent liquide, espèces fpl ♦ vt encaisser; **to pay (in) ~** payer comptant; **~ on delivery** payable ou paiement à la livraison; **~book** n livre m de caisse; **~ card** (BRIT) n carte f de retrait; **~ desk** (BRIT) n caisse f; **~ dispenser** (BRIT) n distributeur m automatique de billets, billeterie f

**cashew** [kæ'ʃu:] n (also: **~ nut**) noix f de cajou

**cashier** [kæ'ʃɪə'] n caissier(-ère)

**cashmere** ['kæʃmɪə'] n cachemire m

**cash register** n caisse (enregistreuse)

**casing** ['keɪsɪŋ] n revêtement (protecteur), enveloppe (protectrice)

**casino** [kə'si:nəu] n casino m

**casket** ['kɑ:skɪt] n coffret m; (US: coffin) cercueil m

**casserole** ['kæsərəul] n (container) cocotte f; (food) ragoût m (en cocotte)

**cassette** [kæ'set] n cassette f, musicassette f; **~ player** n lecteur m de cassettes; **~ recorder** n magnétophone m à cassettes

**cast** [kɑ:st] (pt, pp **cast**) vt (throw) jeter; (shed) perdre; se dépouiller de; (statue) mouler; (THEATRE): **to ~ sb as Hamlet** attribuer à qn le rôle de Hamlet ♦ n (THEATRE) distribution f; (also: **plaster ~**) plâtre m; **to ~ one's vote** voter; **~ off** vi (NAUT) larguer les amarres; (KNITTING) arrêter les mailles; **~ on** vi (KNITTING) monter les mailles

**castaway** ['kɑ:stəweɪ] n naufragé(e)

**caster sugar** ['kɑ:stə-] (BRIT) n sucre m semoule

**casting vote** (BRIT) n voix prépondérante (pour départager)

**cast iron** n fonte f

**castle** ['kɑ:sl] n château (fort); (CHESS) tour f

**castor** ['kɑ:stə'] n (wheel) roulette f; **~**

**oil** *n* huile *f* de ricin

**castrate** [kæs'treɪt] *vt* châtrer

**casual** ['kæʒjul] *adj* (*by chance*) de hasard, fait(e) au hasard, fortuit(e); (*irregular: work etc*) temporaire; (*unconcerned*) désinvolte; **~ly** *adv* avec désinvolture, négligemment; (*dress*) de façon décontractée

**casualty** ['kæʒjultɪ] *n* accidenté(e), blessé(e); (*dead*) victime *f*, mort(e); (*MED: department*) urgences *fpl*

**casual wear** *n* vêtements *mpl* décontractés

**cat** [kæt] *n* chat *m*

**catalogue** ['kætəlɒg] (*US* **catalog**) *n* catalogue *m* ♦ *vt* cataloguer

**catalyst** ['kætəlɪst] *n* catalyseur *m*

**catalytic converter** [kætə'lɪtɪk kən'vɜːtər] *n* pot *m* catalytique

**catapult** ['kætəpʌlt] (*BRIT*) *n* (*sling*) lance-pierres *m inv*, fronde *f*

**catarrh** [kə'tɑːr] *n* rhume *m* chronique, catarrhe *m*

**catastrophe** [kə'tæstrəfɪ] *n* catastrophe *f*

**catch** [kætʃ] (*pt, pp* **caught**) *vt* attraper; (*person: by surprise*) prendre, surprendre; (*understand, hear*) saisir ♦ *vi* (*fire*) prendre; (*become trapped*) se prendre, s'accrocher ♦ *n* prise *f*, (*trick*) attrape *f*; (*of lock*) loquet *m*; **to ~ sb's attention** *or* **eye** attirer l'attention de qn; **to ~ one's breath** retenir son souffle; **to ~ fire** prendre feu; **to ~ sight of** apercevoir; **~ on** *vi* saisir; (*grow popular*) prendre; **~ up** *vi* se rattraper, combler son retard ♦ *vt* (*also:* **~ up with**) rattraper; **~ing** *adj* (*MED*) contagieux(-euse); **~ment area** [kætʃmənt-] (*BRIT*) *n* (*SCOL*) secteur *m* de recrutement; **~ phrase** *n* slogan *m*; expression *f* (à la mode); **~y** *adj* (*tune*) facile à retenir

**category** ['kætɪgərɪ] *n* catégorie *f*

**cater** ['keɪtər] *vi* (*provide food*): **to ~ (for)** préparer des repas (pour), se charger de la restauration (pour); **~ for** (*BRIT*) *vt fus* (*needs*) satisfaire, pourvoir à;

(*readers, consumers*) s'adresser à, pourvoir aux besoins de; **~er** *n* traiteur *m*; fournisseur *m*; **~ing** *n* restauration *f*; approvisionnement *m*, ravitaillement *m*

**caterpillar** ['kætəpɪlər] *n* chenille *f*

**cathedral** [kə'θiːdrəl] *n* cathédrale *f*

**catholic** ['kæθəlɪk] *adj* (*tastes*) éclectique, varié(e); **C~** *adj* catholique ♦ *n* catholique *m/f*

**Catseye** ® ['kæts'aɪ] (*BRIT*) *n* (*AUT*) catadioptre *m*

**cattle** ['kætl] *npl* bétail *m*

**catty** ['kætɪ] *adj* méchant(e)

**caucus** ['kɔːkəs] *n* (*POL: group*) comité local d'un parti politique; (*US: POL*) comité électoral (pour désigner des candidats)

**caught** [kɔːt] *pt, pp* of **catch**

**cauliflower** ['kɒlɪflaʊər] *n* chou-fleur *m*

**cause** [kɔːz] *n* cause *f* ♦ *vt* causer

**caution** ['kɔːʃən] *n* prudence *f*; (*warning*) avertissement *m* ♦ *vt* avertir, donner un avertissement à; **cautious** *adj* prudent(e)

**cavalry** ['kævəlrɪ] *n* cavalerie *f*

**cave** [keɪv] *n* caverne *f*, grotte *f*; **~ in** *vi* (*roof etc*) s'effondrer; **~man** (*irreg*) *n* homme *m* des cavernes

**caviar(e)** ['kævɪɑːr] *n* caviar *m*

**CB** *n abbr* (= *Citizens' Band (Radio)*) CB *f*

**CBI** *n abbr* (= *Confederation of British Industries*) groupement du patronat

**cc** *abbr* = **carbon copy; cubic centimetres**

**CD** *n abbr* (= *compact disc (player)*) CD *m*; **CDI** *n abbr* (= *Compact Disk Interactive*) CD-I *m*; **CD player** *n* platine *f* laser; **CD-ROM** [siːdiː'rɒm] *n abbr* (= *compact disc read-only memory*) CD-Rom *m*

**CDT** *BRIT abbr SCOL* (= *Craft, Design and Technology*) EMT *f*

**cease** [siːs] *vt, vi* cesser; **~fire** *n* cessez-le-feu *m*; **~less** *adj* incessant(e), continuel(le)

**cedar** ['siːdər] *n* cèdre *m*

**ceiling** ['siːlɪŋ] *n* plafond *m*

**celebrate** ['sɛlɪbreɪt] vt, vi célébrer; **~d** adj célèbre; **celebration** [sɛlɪ'breɪʃən] n célébration f; **celebrity** [sɪ'lɛbrɪtɪ] n célébrité f

**celery** ['sɛlərɪ] n céleri m (à côtes)

**cell** [sɛl] n cellule f; (ELEC) élément m (de pile)

**cellar** ['sɛlə'] n cave f

**cello** ['tʃɛləʊ] n violoncelle m

**cellphone** ['sɛlfəʊn] n téléphone m cellulaire

**Celt** [kɛlt, sɛlt] n Celte m/f; **~ic** adj celte

**cement** [sə'mɛnt] n ciment m; **~ mixer** n bétonnière f

**cemetery** ['sɛmɪtrɪ] n cimetière m

**censor** ['sɛnsə'] n censeur m ♦ vt censurer; **~ship** n censure f

**censure** ['sɛnʃə'] vt blâmer, critiquer

**census** ['sɛnsəs] n recensement m

**cent** [sɛnt] n (US, euro etc: coin) cent m (= un centième du dollar, de l'euro etc); see also **per**

**centenary** [sɛn'ti:nərɪ] n centenaire m

**center** ['sɛntə'] n, vt (US) = **centre**

**centigrade** ['sɛntɪgreɪd] adj centigrade

**centimetre** ['sɛntɪmi:tə'] (US **centimeter**) n centimètre m

**centipede** ['sɛntɪpi:d] n mille-pattes m inv

**central** ['sɛntrəl] adj central(e); **C~ America** n Amérique centrale; **~ heating** n chauffage central; **~ reservation** (BRIT) n (AUT) terre-plein central

**centre** ['sɛntə'] (US **center**) n centre m ♦ vt centrer; **~forward** n (SPORT) avant-centre m; **~half** n (SPORT) demi-centre m

**century** ['sɛntjʊrɪ] n siècle m; **20th ~** XXe siècle

**ceramic** [sɪ'ræmɪk] adj céramique

**cereal** ['si:rɪəl] n céréale f

**ceremony** ['sɛrɪmənɪ] n cérémonie f; **to stand on ~** faire des façons

**certain** ['sɜ:tən] adj certain(e); **for ~** certainement, sûrement; **~ly** adv certainement; **~ty** n certitude f

**certificate** [sə'tɪfɪkɪt] n certificat m

**certified** ['sɜ:tɪfaɪd] adj: **by ~ mail** (US) en recommandé, avec avis de réception; **~ public accountant** (US) expert-comptable m

**certify** ['sɜ:tɪfaɪ] vt certifier; (award diploma) to) conférer un diplôme etc à; (declare insane) déclarer malade mental(e)

**cervical** ['sɜ:vɪkl] adj: **~ cancer** cancer m du col de l'utérus; **~ smear** frottis vaginal

**cervix** ['sɜ:vɪks] n col m de l'utérus

**cf.** abbr (= compare) cf., voir

**CFC** n abbr (= chlorofluorocarbon) CFC m (gen pl)

**ch.** abbr (= chapter) chap

**chafe** [tʃeɪf] vt irriter, frotter contre

**chain** [tʃeɪn] n chaîne f ♦ vt (also: **~ up**) enchaîner, attacher (avec une chaîne); **~ reaction** n réaction f en chaîne; **~smoke** vi fumer cigarette sur cigarette; **~ store** n magasin m à succursales multiples

**chair** [tʃɛə'] n chaise f; (armchair) fauteuil m; (of university) chaire f; (of meeting, committee) présidence f ♦ vt (meeting) présider; **~lift** n télésiège m; **~man** (irreg) n président m

**chalet** ['ʃæleɪ] n chalet m

**chalk** [tʃɔ:k] n craie f

**challenge** ['tʃælɪndʒ] n défi m ♦ vt défier; (statement, right) mettre en question, contester; **to ~ sb to do** mettre qn au défi de faire; **challenging** adj (tone, look) de défi, provocateur(-trice); (task, career) qui représente un défi or une gageure

**chamber** ['tʃeɪmbə'] n chambre f; **~ of commerce** chambre de commerce; **~maid** n femme f de chambre; **~ music** n musique f de chambre

**champagne** [ʃæm'peɪn] n champagne m

**champion** ['tʃæmpɪən] n champion(ne); **~ship** n championnat m

**chance** [tʃɑ:ns] n (opportunity) occasion f, possibilité f; (hope, likelihood) chance f; (risk) risque m ♦ vt: **to ~ it** risquer (le coup), essayer ♦ *adj* fortuit(e), de hasard; **to take a ~** prendre un risque; **by ~** par hasard

**chancellor** ['tʃɑːnsələ'] *n* chancelier *m*; **C~ of the Exchequer** (BRIT) chancelier *m* de l'Échiquier; ≃ ministre des Finances

**chandelier** [ʃændə'lɪə'] *n* lustre *m*

**change** [tʃeɪndʒ] *vt* (alter, replace, COMM: money) changer; (hands, trains, clothes, one's name) changer de; (transform): **to ~ sb into** changer or transformer qn en ♦ *vi* (gen) changer; (one's clothes) se changer; (be transformed): **to ~ into** se changer or transformer en ♦ *n* changement *m*; (money) monnaie *f*; **to ~ gear** (AUT) changer de vitesse; **to ~ one's mind** changer d'avis; **a ~ of clothes** des vêtements de rechange; **for a ~** pour changer; **~able** *adj* (weather) variable; **~ machine** *n* distributeur *m* de monnaie; **~over** *n* (to new system) changement *m*, passage *m*; **changing** *adj* changeant(e); **changing room** (BRIT) *n* (in shop) salon *m* d'essayage; (SPORT) vestiaire *m*

**channel** ['tʃænl] *n* (TV) chaîne *f*; (navigable passage) chenal *m*; (irrigation) canal *m* ♦ *vt* canaliser; **the (English) C~** la Manche; **the C~ Islands** les îles de la Manche, les îles Anglo-Normandes; **the C~ Tunnel** le tunnel sous la Manche; **~-hopping** *n* (TV) zapping *m*

**chant** [tʃɑːnt] *n* chant *m*; (REL) psalmodie *f* ♦ *vt* chanter, scander

**chaos** ['keɪɔs] *n* chaos *m*

**chap** [tʃæp] (BRIT: inf) *n* (man) type *m*

**chapel** ['tʃæpl] *n* chapelle *f*; (BRIT: nonconformist ~) église *f*

**chaplain** ['tʃæplɪn] *n* aumônier *m*

**chapped** [tʃæpt] *adj* (skin, lips) gercé(e)

**chapter** ['tʃæptə'] *n* chapitre *m*

**char** [tʃɑː'] *vt* (burn) carboniser

**character** ['kærɪktə'] *n* caractère *m*; (in novel, film) personnage *m*; (eccentric) numéro *m*, phénomène *m*; **~istic** [kærɪktə'rɪstɪk] *adj* caractéristique ♦ *n*

caractéristique *f*

**charcoal** ['tʃɑːkəul] *n* charbon *m* de bois; (for drawing) charbon *m*

**charge** [tʃɑːdʒ] *n* (cost) prix (demandé); (accusation) accusation *f*; (LAW) inculpation *f* ♦ *vt*: **to ~ sb (with)** inculper qn (de); (battery, enemy) charger; (customer, sum) faire payer ♦ *vi* foncer; **~s** *npl* (costs) frais *mpl*; **to reverse the ~s** (TEL) téléphoner en P.C.V.; **to take ~ of** se charger de; **to be in ~ of** être responsable de, s'occuper de; **how much do you ~?** combien prenezvous?; **to ~ an expense (up) to sb** mettre une dépense sur le compte de qn; **~ card** *n* carte *f* de client

**charity** ['tʃærɪtɪ] *n* charité *f*; (organization) institution *f* charitable or de bienfaisance, œuvre *f* (de charité)

**charm** [tʃɑːm] *n* charme *m*; (on bracelet) breloque *f* ♦ *vt* charmer, enchanter; **~ing** *adj* charmant(e)

**chart** [tʃɑːt] *n* tableau *m*, diagramme *m*; graphique *m*; (map) carte marine ♦ *vt* dresser or établir la carte de; **~s** *npl* (MUS) hit-parade *m*

**charter** ['tʃɑːtə'] *vt* (plane) affréter ♦ *n* (document) charte *f*; **~ed accountant** (BRIT) *n* expert-comptable *m*; **~ flight** *n* charter *m*

**chase** [tʃeɪs] *vt* poursuivre, pourchasser; (also: **~ away**) chasser ♦ *n* poursuite *f*, chasse *f*

**chasm** ['kæzəm] *n* gouffre *m*, abîme *m*

**chat** [tʃæt] *vi* (also: **have a ~**) bavarder, causer ♦ *n* conversation *f*; **~ show** (BRIT) *n* causerie télévisée

**chatter** ['tʃætə'] *vi* (person) bavarder; (animal) jacasser ♦ *n* bavardage *m*; jacassement *m*; **my teeth are ~ing** je claque des dents; **~box** (inf) *n* moulin *m* à paroles

**chatty** ['tʃætɪ] *adj* (style) familier(-ère); (person) bavard(e)

**chauffeur** ['ʃəufə'] *n* chauffeur *m* (de maître)

**chauvinist** ['ʃəuvɪnɪst] *n* (male ~) phallocrate m; (nationalist) chauvin(e)

**cheap** [tʃiːp] adj bon marché inv, pas cher (chère); (joke) facile, d'un goût douteux; (poor quality) à bon marché, de qualité médiocre ♦ adv à bon marché, pour pas cher; **~ day return** billet m d'aller et retour réduit (valable pour la journée); **~er** adj moins cher (chère); **~ly** adv à bon marché, à bon compte

**cheat** [tʃiːt] vi tricher ♦ vt tromper, duper; (rob): **to ~ sb out of sth** escroquer qch à qn ♦ n tricheur(-euse); escroc m

**check** [tʃɛk] vt vérifier; (passport, ticket) contrôler; (halt) arrêter; (restrain) maîtriser ♦ n vérification f; contrôle m; (curb) frein m; (us: bill) addition f; (pattern: gen pl) carreaux mpl; (US): = **cheque** ♦ adj (pattern, cloth) à carreaux; **~ in** vi (in hotel) remplir sa fiche (d'hôtel); (at airport) se présenter à l'enregistrement ♦ vt (luggage) (faire) enregistrer; **~ out** vi (in hotel) régler sa note; **~ up** vi: **to ~ up (on sth)** vérifier (qch); **to ~ up on sb** se renseigner sur le compte de qn; **~ered** (US) adj = **chequered**; **~ers** (US) npl jeu m de dames; **~-in (desk)** n enregistrement m; **~ing account** (US) n (current account) compte courant; **~mate** n échec et mat m; **~out** n (in shop) caisse f; **~point** n contrôle m; **~room** (US) n (left-luggage office) consigne f; **~up** n (MED) examen médical, check-up m

**cheek** [tʃiːk] n joue f; (impudence) toupet m, culot m; **~bone** n pommette f; **~y** adj effronté(e), culotté(e)

**cheep** [tʃiːp] vi piailler

**cheer** [tʃɪə*] vt acclamer, applaudir; (gladden) réjouir, réconforter ♦ vi applaudir ♦ n (gen pl) acclamations fpl, applaudissements mpl; bravos mpl, hourras mpl; **~s!** à la vôtre!; **~ up** vi se dérider, reprendre courage ♦ vt remonter le moral à or de, dérider; **~ful** adj gai(e), joyeux(-euse)

**cheerio** [tʃɪərɪˈəu] (BRIT) excl salut!, au revoir!

**cheese** [tʃiːz] n fromage m; **~board** n plateau m de fromages

**cheetah** [ˈtʃiːtə] n guépard m

**chef** [ʃɛf] n chef (cuisinier)

**chemical** [ˈkɛmɪkl] adj chimique ♦ n produit m chimique

**chemist** [ˈkɛmɪst] n (BRIT: pharmacist) pharmacien(ne); (scientist) chimiste m/f; **~ry** n chimie f; **~'s (shop)** (BRIT) n pharmacie f

**cheque** [tʃɛk] (BRIT) n chèque m; **~book** n chéquier m, carnet m de chèques; **~ card** n carte f (d'identité) bancaire

**chequered** [ˈtʃɛkəd] (US **checkered**) adj (fig) varié(e)

**cherish** [ˈtʃɛrɪʃ] vt chérir

**cherry** [ˈtʃɛrɪ] n cerise f; (also: ~ **tree**) cerisier m

**chess** [tʃɛs] n échecs mpl; **~board** n échiquier m

**chest** [tʃɛst] n poitrine f; (box) coffre m, caisse f; **~ of drawers** n commode f

**chestnut** [ˈtʃɛsnʌt] n châtaigne f; (also: ~ **tree**) châtaignier m

**chew** [tʃuː] vt mâcher; **~ing gum** n chewing-gum m

**chic** [ʃiːk] adj chic inv, élégant(e)

**chick** [tʃɪk] n poussin m; (inf) nana f

**chicken** [ˈtʃɪkɪn] n poulet m; (inf: coward) poule mouillée; **~ out** (inf) vi se dégonfler; **~pox** n varicelle f

**chicory** [ˈtʃɪkərɪ] n (for coffee) chicorée f; (salad) endive f

**chief** [tʃiːf] n chef ♦ adj principal(e); **~ executive** (US **chief executive officer**) n directeur(-trice) général(e); **~ly** adv principalement, surtout

**chiffon** [ˈʃɪfɔn] n mousseline f de soie

**chilblain** [ˈtʃɪlbleɪn] n engelure f

**child** [tʃaɪld] (pl **~ren**) n enfant m/f; **~birth** n accouchement m; **~hood** n enfance f; **~ish** adj puéril(e), enfantin(e); **~like** adj d'enfant, innocent(e); **~ minder** (BRIT) n garde f d'enfants; **~ren** [ˈtʃɪldrən] npl of **child**

**Chile** ['tʃɪlɪ] *n* Chili *m*

**chill** [tʃɪl] *n* (*of water*) froid *m*; (*of air*) fraîcheur *f*; (*MED*) refroidissement *m*, coup *m* de froid ♦ *vt* (*person*) faire frissonner; (*CULIN*) mettre au frais, rafraîchir

**chil(l)i** ['tʃɪlɪ] *n* piment *m* (rouge)

**chilly** ['tʃɪlɪ] *adj* froid(e), glacé(e); (*sensitive to cold*) frileux(-euse); **to feel ~** avoir froid

**chime** [tʃaɪm] *n* carillon *m* ♦ *vi* carillonner, sonner

**chimney** ['tʃɪmnɪ] *n* cheminée *f*; **~ sweep** *n* ramoneur *m*

**chimpanzee** [tʃɪmpæn'zi:] *n* chimpanzé *m*

**chin** [tʃɪn] *n* menton *m*

**China** ['tʃaɪnə] *n* Chine *f*

**china** ['tʃaɪnə] *n* porcelaine *f*; (*crockery*) (vaisselle *f* en) porcelaine

**Chinese** [tʃaɪ'ni:z] *adj* chinois(e) ♦ *n inv* (*person*) Chinois(e); (*LING*) chinois *m*

**chink** [tʃɪŋk] *n* (*opening*) fente *f*, fissure *f*; (*noise*) tintement *m*

**chip** [tʃɪp] *n* (*gen pl*: *CULIN*: *BRIT*) frite *f*; (: *US*: *potato*) ~) chip *m*; (*of wood*) copeau *m*; (*of glass, stone*) éclat *m*; (*also*: *microchip*) puce *f* ♦ *vt* (*cup, plate*) ébrécher

---

### chip shop

*Un chip shop, que l'on appelle également un "fish-and-chip shop", est un magasin où l'on vend des plats à emporter. Les chip shops sont d'ailleurs à l'origine des takeaways. On y achète en particulier du poisson frit et des frites, mais on y trouve également des plats traditionnels britanniques (steak pies, saucisses, etc). Tous les plats étaient à l'origine emballés dans du papier journal. Dans certains de ces magasins, on peut s'asseoir pour consommer sur place.*

---

**chiropodist** [kɪ'rɔpədɪst] (*BRIT*) *n* pédicure *m/f*

**chirp** [tʃə:p] *vi* pépier, gazouiller

**chisel** ['tʃɪzl] *n* ciseau *m*

**chit** [tʃɪt] *n* mot *m*, note *f*

**chitchat** ['tʃɪtʃæt] *n* bavardage *m*

**chivalry** ['ʃɪvəlrɪ] *n* esprit *m* chevaleresque, galanterie *f*

**chives** [tʃaɪvz] *npl* ciboulette *f*, civette *f*

**chock-a-block** ['tʃɔkə'blɔk], **chock-full** [tʃɔk'ful] *adj* plein(e) à craquer

**chocolate** ['tʃɔklɪt] *n* chocolat *m*

**choice** [tʃɔɪs] *n* choix *m* ♦ *adj* de choix

**choir** ['kwaɪə<sup>r</sup>] *n* chœur *m*, chorale *f*; **~boy** *n* jeune choriste *m*

**choke** [tʃəuk] *vi* étouffer ♦ *vt* étrangler; étouffer ♦ *n* (*AUT*) starter *m*; **street with traffic** rue engorgée *or* embouteillée

**cholesterol** [kə'lestərɔl] *n* cholestérol *m*

**choose** [tʃu:z] (*pt* **chose**, *pp* **chosen**) *vt* choisir; **to ~ to do** décider de faire, juger bon de faire; **choosy** *adj*: **(to be) choosy** (faire le/la) difficile

**chop** [tʃɔp] *vt* (*wood*) couper (à la hache); (*CULIN*: *also*: **~ up**) couper (fin), émincer, hacher (en morceaux) ♦ *n* (*CULIN*) côtelette *f*; **~s** *npl* (*jaws*) mâchoires *fpl*

**chopper** ['tʃɔpə<sup>r</sup>] *n* (*helicopter*) hélicoptère *m*, hélico *m*

**choppy** ['tʃɔpɪ] *adj* (*sea*) un peu agité(e)

**chopsticks** ['tʃɔpstɪks] *npl* baguettes *fpl*

**chord** [kɔ:d] *n* (*MUS*) accord *m*

**chore** [tʃɔ:<sup>r</sup>] *n* travail *m* de routine; **household ~s** travaux *mpl* du ménage

**chortle** ['tʃɔ:tl] *vi* glousser

**chorus** ['kɔ:rəs] *n* chœur *m*; (*repeated part of song*: *also fig*) refrain *m*

**chose** [tʃəuz] *pt of* **choose**; **~n** *pp of* **choose**

**chowder** ['tʃaudə<sup>r</sup>] *n* soupe *f* de poisson

**Christ** [kraɪst] *n* Christ *m*

**christen** ['krɪsn] *vt* baptiser

**christening** ['krɪsnɪŋ] *n* baptême *m*

**Christian** ['krɪstɪən] *adj*, *n* chrétien(ne); **~ity** [krɪstɪ'ænɪtɪ] *n* christianisme *m*; **~**

**name** n prénom m

**Christmas** ['krɪsməs] n Noël m or f; **Happy** or **Merry ~!** joyeux Noël!; **~ card** n carte f de Noël; **~ Day** n le jour de Noël; **~ Eve** n la veille de Noël; la nuit de Noël; **~ tree** n arbre m de Noël

**chrome** [krəʊm] n chrome m

**chromium** ['krəʊmɪəm] n chrome m

**chronic** ['krɒnɪk] adj chronique

**chronicle** ['krɒnɪkl] n chronique f

**chronological** [krɒnə'lɒdʒɪkl] adj chronologique

**chrysanthemum** [krɪ'sænθəməm] n chrysanthème m

**chubby** ['tʃʌbɪ] adj potelé(e), rondelet(te)

**chuck** [tʃʌk] (inf) vt (throw) lancer, jeter; (BRIT: person) plaquer; (: also: **~ up**: job) lâcher; **~ out** vt flanquer dehors or à la porte; (rubbish) jeter

**chuckle** ['tʃʌkl] vi glousser

**chug** [tʃʌg] vi faire teuf-teuf; (also: **~ along**) avancer en faisant teuf-teuf

**chum** [tʃʌm] n copain (copine)

**chunk** [tʃʌŋk] n gros morceau

**church** [tʃəːtʃ] n église f; **~yard** n cimetière m

**churn** [tʃəːn] n (for butter) baratte f; (also: **milk ~**) (grand) bidon à lait; **~ out** vt débiter

**chute** [ʃuːt] n glissoire f; (also: **rubbish ~**) vide-ordures m inv

**chutney** ['tʃʌtnɪ] n condiment m à base de fruits au vinaigre

**CIA** n abbr (= Central Intelligence Agency) CIA f

**CID** (BRIT) n abbr (= Criminal Investigation Department) P.J. f

**cider** ['saɪdə*] n cidre m

**cigar** [sɪ'gɑː*] n cigare m

**cigarette** [sɪgə'rɛt] n cigarette f; **~ case** n étui m à cigarettes; **~ end** n mégot m

**Cinderella** [sɪndə'rɛlə] n Cendrillon f

**cinders** ['sɪndəz] npl cendres fpl

**cine-camera** ['sɪnɪ'kæmərə] (BRIT) n caméra f

**cinema** ['sɪnəmə] n cinéma m

**cinnamon** ['sɪnəmən] n cannelle f

**circle** ['səːkl] n cercle m; (in cinema, theatre) balcon m ♦ vi faire or décrire des cercles ♦ vt (move round) faire le tour de, tourner autour de; (surround) entourer, encercler

**circuit** ['səːkɪt] n circuit m; **~ous** [səː'kjuːtəs] adj indirect(e), qui fait un détour

**circular** ['səːkjʊlə*] adj circulaire ♦ n circulaire f

**circulate** ['səːkjʊleɪt] vi circuler ♦ vt faire circuler; **circulation** [səːkjʊ'leɪʃən] n circulation f; (of newspaper) tirage m

**circumflex** ['səːkəmflɛks] n (also: **~ accent**) accent m circonflexe

**circumstances** ['səːkəmstənsɪz] npl circonstances fpl; (financial condition) moyens mpl, situation financière

**circus** ['səːkəs] n cirque m

**CIS** n abbr (= Commonwealth of Independent States) CEI f

**cistern** ['sɪstən] n réservoir m (d'eau); (in toilet) réservoir de la chasse d'eau

**citizen** ['sɪtɪzn] n citoyen(ne); (resident): **the ~s of this town** les habitants de cette ville; **~ship** n citoyenneté f

**citrus fruit** ['sɪtrəs-] n agrume m

**city** ['sɪtɪ] n ville f, cité f; **the C~** la Cité de Londres (centre des affaires); **~ technology college** n établissement m d'enseignement technologique

**civic** ['sɪvɪk] adj civique; (authorities) municipal(e); **~ centre** (BRIT) n centre administratif (municipal)

**civil** ['sɪvɪl] adj civil(e); (polite) poli(e), courtois(e); (disobedience, defence) passif(-ive); **~ engineer** n ingénieur m des travaux publics; **~ian** [sɪ'vɪlɪən] n civil(e)

**civilization** [sɪvɪlaɪ'zeɪʃən] n civilisation f

**civilized** ['sɪvɪlaɪzd] adj civilisé(e); (fig) où règnent les bonnes manières

**civil: ~ law** n code civil; (study) droit civil; **~ servant** n fonctionnaire m/f; **C~**

**Service** n fonction publique, administration f; ~ **war** n guerre civile

**clad** [klæd] adj: ~ **(in)** habillé(e) (de)

**claim** [kleɪm] vt revendiquer; (rights, inheritance) demander, prétendre à; (assert) déclarer, prétendre ♦ vi (for insurance) faire une déclaration de sinistre ♦ n revendication f; demande f; prétention f; déclaration f; (right) droit m, titre m; ~**ant** n (ADMIN, LAW) requérant(e)

**clairvoyant** [klɛəˈvɔɪənt] n voyant(e)

**clam** [klæm] n palourde f

**clamber** [ˈklæmbəʳ] vi grimper, se hisser

**clammy** [ˈklæmɪ] adj humide (et froid(e)), moite

**clamour** [ˈklæməʳ] (US **clamor**) vi: to ~ **for** réclamer à grands cris

**clamp** [klæmp] n agrafe f, crampon m ♦ vt serrer; (sth to sth) fixer; (wheel) mettre un sabot à; ~ **down on** vt fus sévir or prendre des mesures draconiennes contre

**clan** [klæn] n clan m

**clang** [klæŋ] vi émettre un bruit or fracas métallique

**clap** [klæp] vi applaudir; ~**ping** n applaudissements mpl

**claret** [ˈklærət] n (vin m de) bordeaux m (rouge)

**clarinet** [klærɪˈnet] n clarinette f

**clarity** [ˈklærɪtɪ] n clarté f

**clash** [klæʃ] n choc m; (fig) conflit m ♦ vi se heurter; être or entrer en conflit; (colours) jurer; (two events) tomber en même temps

**clasp** [klɑːsp] n (of necklace, bag) fermoir m; (hold, embrace) étreinte f ♦ vt serrer, étreindre

**class** [klɑːs] n classe f ♦ vt classer, classifier

**classic** [ˈklæsɪk] adj classique ♦ n (author, work) classique m; ~**al** adj classique

**classified** [ˈklæsɪfaɪd] adj (information) secret(-ète); ~ **advertisement** n petite annonce

**classmate** [ˈklɑːsmeɪt] n camarade m/f de classe

**classroom** [ˈklɑːsrʊm] n (salle f de) classe f; ~ **assistant** n aide-éducateur(-trice)

**clatter** [ˈklætəʳ] n cliquetis m ♦ vi cliqueter

**clause** [klɔːz] n clause f; (LING) proposition f

**claw** [klɔː] n griffe f; (of bird of prey) serre f; (of lobster) pince f

**clay** [kleɪ] n argile f

**clean** [kliːn] adj propre; (clear, smooth) net(te); (record, reputation) sans tache; (joke, story) correct(e) ♦ vt nettoyer; ~ **out** vt nettoyer (à fond); ~ **up** vt nettoyer; (fig) remettre de l'ordre dans; ~**cut** adj (person) net(te), soigné(e); ~**er** n (person) nettoyeur(-euse), femme f de ménage; (product) détachant m; ~**er's** n (also: **dry ~er's**) teinturier m; ~**ing** n nettoyage m; ~**liness** [ˈklɛnlɪnɪs] n propreté f

**cleanse** [klɛnz] vt nettoyer; (purify) purifier; ~**r** n (for face) démaquillant m

**clean-shaven** [ˈkliːnˈʃeɪvn] adj rasé(e) de près

**cleansing department** [ˈklɛnzɪŋ-] (BRIT) n service m de voirie

**clear** [klɪəʳ] adj clair(e); (glass, plastic) transparent(e); (road, way) libre, dégagé(e); (conscience) net(te) ♦ vt (room) débarrasser; (of people) faire évacuer; (cheque) compenser; (LAW: suspect) innocenter; (obstacle) franchir or sauter sans heurter ♦ vi (weather) s'éclaircir; (fog) se dissiper ♦ adv: ~ **of** à distance de, à l'écart de; to ~ **the table** débarrasser la table, desservir; ~ **up** vt ranger, mettre en ordre; (mystery) éclaircir, résoudre; ~**ance** n (removal) déblaiement m; (permission) autorisation f; ~**cut** adj clair(e), nettement défini(e); ~**ing** n (in forest) clairière f; ~**ing bank** (BRIT) n banque qui appartient à une chambre de compensation; ~**ly** adv clairement; (evidently) de toute évidence;

**~way** (*BRIT*) *n* route *f* à stationnement interdit
**clef** [klɛf] *n* (*MUS*) clé *f*
**cleft** [klɛft] *n* (*in rock*) crevasse *f*, fissure *f*
**clementine** ['klɛməntaɪn] *n* clémentine *f*
**clench** [klɛntʃ] *vt* serrer
**clergy** ['klə:dʒɪ] *n* clergé *m*; **~man** (*irreg*) *n* ecclésiastique *m*
**clerical** ['klɛrɪkl] *adj* de bureau, d'employé de bureau; (*REL*) clérical(e), du clergé
**clerk** [klɑ:k, (*US*) klə:rk] *n* employé(e) de bureau; (*US*: *salesperson*) vendeur (-euse)
**clever** ['klɛvə^r] *adj* (*mentally*) intelligent(e); (*deft, crafty*) habile, adroit(e); (*device, arrangement*) ingénieux(-euse), astucieux(-euse)
**click** [klɪk] *vi* faire un bruit sec *or* un déclic
**client** ['klaɪənt] *n* client(e)
**cliff** [klɪf] *n* falaise *f*
**climate** ['klaɪmɪt] *n* climat *m*
**climax** ['klaɪmæks] *n* apogée *m*, point culminant; (*sexual*) orgasme *m*
**climb** [klaɪm] *vi* grimper, monter ♦ *vt* gravir, escalader, monter sur ♦ *n* montée *f*, escalade *f*; **~-down** *n* reculade *f*, dérobade *f*; **~er** *n* (*mountaineer*) grimpeur(-euse), varappeur(-euse); (*plant*) plante grimpante; **~ing** *n* (*mountaineering*) escalade *f*, varappe *f*
**clinch** [klɪntʃ] *vt* (*deal*) conclure, sceller
**cling** [klɪŋ] (*pt, pp* **clung**) *vi*: **to ~ (to)** se cramponner (à), s'accrocher (à); (*of clothes*) coller (à)
**clinic** ['klɪnɪk] *n* centre médical; **~al** *adj* clinique; (*attitude*) froid(e), détaché(e)
**clink** [klɪŋk] *vi* tinter, cliqueter
**clip** [klɪp] *n* (*for hair*) barrette *f*; (*also*: **paper ~**) trombone *m* ♦ *vt* (*fasten*) attacher; (*hair, nails*) couper; (*hedge*) tailler; **~pers** *npl* (*for hedge*) sécateur *m*; (*also*: **nail ~pers**) coupe-ongles *m inv*; **~ping** *n* (*from newspaper*) coupure *f* de journal
**cloak** [kləuk] *n* grande cape ♦ *vt* (*fig*) masquer, cacher; **~room** *n* (*for coats etc*) vestiaire *m*; (*BRIT*: *WC*) toilettes *fpl*
**clock** [klɔk] *n* (*large*) horloge *f*; (*small*) pendule *f*; **~ in** (*BRIT*) *vi* pointer (en arrivant); **~ off** (*BRIT*) *vi* pointer (en partant); **~ on** (*BRIT*) *vi* = **clock in**; **~ out** (*BRIT*) *vi* = **clock off**; **~wise** *adv* dans le sens des aiguilles d'une montre; **~work** *n* rouages *mpl*, mécanisme *m*; (*of clock*) mouvement *m* (d'horlogerie) ♦ *adj* mécanique
**clog** [klɔg] *n* sabot *m* ♦ *vt* boucher ♦ *vi* (*also*: **~ up**) se boucher
**cloister** ['klɔɪstə^r] *n* cloître *m*
**close¹** [kləus] *adj* (*near*) près, proche; (*contact, link*) étroit(e); (*contest*) très serré(e); (*watch*) étroit(e), strict(e); (*examination*) attentif(-ive), minutieux (-euse); (*weather*) lourd(e), étouffant(e) ♦ *adv* près, à proximité; **~ to** près de, proche de; **~ by** *adj* proche ♦ *adv* tout(e) près; **~ at hand** = **close by**; **a ~ friend** un ami intime; **to have a ~ shave** (*fig*) l'échapper belle
**close²** [kləuz] *vt* fermer ♦ *vi* (*shop etc*) fermer; (*lid, door etc*) se fermer; (*end*) se terminer, se conclure ♦ *n* (*end*) conclusion *f*, fin *f*; **~ down** *vt, vi* fermer (*définitivement*); **~d** *adj* fermé(e); **~d shop** *n* organisation *f* qui n'admet que des travailleurs syndiqués
**close-knit** ['kləus'nɪt] *adj* (*family, community*) très uni(e)
**closely** ['kləuslɪ] *adv* (*examine, watch*) de près
**closet** ['klɔzɪt] *n* (*cupboard*) placard *m*, réduit *m*
**close-up** ['kləusʌp] *n* gros plan
**closure** ['kləuʒə^r] *n* fermeture *f*
**clot** [klɔt] *n* (*gen*: *blood ~*) caillot *m*; (*inf*: *person*) ballot *m* ♦ *vi* (*blood*) se coaguler; **~ted cream** *crème fraîche très épaisse*
**cloth** [klɔθ] *n* (*material*) tissu *m*, étoffe *f*; (*also*: **teacloth**) torchon *m*; lavette *f*
**clothe** [kləuð] *vt* habiller, vêtir; **~s** *npl*

vêtements *mpl*, habits *mpl*; **~s brush** *n*
brosse *f* à habits; **~s line** *n* corde *f* (à
linge); **~s peg** (US **clothes pin**) *n* pince
*f* à linge; **clothing** *n* = **clothes**

**cloud** [klaud] *n* nuage *m*; **~burst** *n*
grosse averse; **~y** *adj* nuageux(-euse),
couvert(e); (*liquid*) trouble

**clout** [klaut] *vt* flanquer une taloche à

**clove** [klauv] *n* (*CULIN: spice*) clou *m* de
girofle; **~ of garlic** gousse *f* d'ail

**clover** ['klauvə⁸] *n* trèfle *m*

**clown** [klaun] *n* clown *m* ♦ *vi* (*also:*
**~ about, ~ around**) faire le clown

**cloying** ['klɔɪɪŋ] *adj* (*taste, smell*) écœu-
rant(e)

**club** [klʌb] *n* (*society, place: also:* **golf ~**)
club *m*; (*weapon*) massue *f*, matraque *f*
♦ *vt* matraquer ♦ *vi*: **to ~ together**
s'associer; **~s** *npl* (*CARDS*) trèfle *m*; **~
class** *n* (*AVIAT*) classe *f* club; **~house** *n*
club *m*

**cluck** [klʌk] *vi* glousser

**clue** [kluː] *n* indice *m*; (*in crosswords*)
définition *f*; **I haven't a ~** je n'en ai
pas la moindre idée

**clump** [klʌmp] *n*: **~ of trees** bouquet
*m* d'arbres

**clumsy** ['klʌmzɪ] *adj* gauche, mala-
droit(e)

**clung** [klʌŋ] *pt, pp* of **cling**

**cluster** ['klʌstə⁸] *n* (*of people*) (petit)
groupe; (*of flowers*) grappe *f*; (*of stars*)
amas *m* ♦ *vi* se rassembler

**clutch** [klʌtʃ] *n* (*grip, grasp*) étreinte *f*,
prise *f*; (*AUT*) embrayage *m* ♦ *vt* (*grasp*)
agripper; (*hold tightly*) serrer fort; (*hold
on to*) se cramponner à

**clutter** ['klʌtə⁸] *vt* (*also:* **~ up**) encombrer

**CND** *n abbr* (= Campaign for Nuclear Disarmament) mouvement pour le désarmement nucléaire

**Co.** *abbr* = **county; company**

**c/o** *abbr* (= care of) aux bons soins de

**coach** [kəutʃ] *n* (*bus*) autocar *m*;
(*horse-drawn*) diligence *f*; (*of train*) voiture *f*, wagon *m*; (*SPORT: trainer*)

entraîneur(-euse); (*SCOL: tutor*) répéti-
teur(-trice) ♦ *vt* entraîner; (*student*)
faire travailler; **~ trip** *n* excursion *f* en
car

**coal** [kəul] *n* charbon *m*; **~ face** *n* front
*m* de taille; **~field** *n* bassin houiller

**coalition** [kəuə'lɪʃən] *n* coalition *f*

**coalman** (*irreg*) *n* charbonnier *m*, marchand *m* de charbon

**coalmine** *n* mine *f* de charbon

**coarse** [kɔːs] *adj* grossier(-ère), rude

**coast** [kəust] *n* côte *f* ♦ *vi* (*car, cycle
etc*) descendre en roue libre; **~al** *adj*
côtier(-ère); **~guard** *n* garde-côte *m*;
(*service*) gendarmerie *f* maritime; **~line**
*n* côte *f*, littoral *m*

**coat** [kəut] *n* manteau *m*; (*of animal*)
pelage *m*, poil *m*; (*of paint*) couche *f*
♦ *vt* couvrir; **~ hanger** *n* cintre *m*; **~ing**
*n* couche *f*, revêtement *m*; **~ of arms** *n*
blason *m*, armoiries *fpl*

**coax** [kəuks] *vt* persuader par des cajoleries

**cobbler** ['kɔblə⁸] *n* cordonnier *m*

**cobbles** ['kɔblz] *npl* (*also:* **~tones**) *npl* pa-
vés (ronds)

**cobweb** ['kɔbwɛb] *n* toile *f* d'araignée

**cocaine** [kə'keɪn] *n* cocaïne *f*

**cock** [kɔk] *n* (*rooster*) coq *m*; (*male bird*)
mâle *m* ♦ *vt* (*gun*) armer; **~erel** *n* jeune
coq *m*

**cockle** ['kɔkl] *n* coque *f*

**cockney** ['kɔknɪ] *n* cockney *m*, habitant
des quartiers populaires de l'East End de
Londres, ≈ faubourien(ne)

**cockpit** ['kɔkpɪt] *n* (*in aircraft*) poste *m*
de pilotage, cockpit *m*

**cockroach** ['kɔkrəutʃ] *n* cafard *m*

**cocktail** ['kɔkteɪl] *n* cocktail *m*; (*fruit ~
etc*) salade *f*; **~ cabinet** *n* (*meuble-)bar
*m*; **~ party** *n* cocktail *m*

**cocoa** ['kəukau] *n* cacao *m*

**coconut** ['kəukənʌt] *n* noix *f* de coco

**COD** *abbr* = **cash on delivery**

**cod** [kɔd] *n* morue fraîche, cabillaud *m*

**code** [kəud] *n* code *m*; (*TEL: area code*)
indicatif *m*

**cod-liver oil** n huile f de foie de morue
**coercion** [kəʊˈəːʃən] n contrainte f
**coffee** [ˈkɔfɪ] n café m; ~ **bar** (BRIT) n café m; ~ **bean** n grain m de café; ~ **break** n pause-café f; ~**pot** n cafetière f; ~ **table** n (petite) table basse
**coffin** [ˈkɔfɪn] n cercueil m
**cog** [kɔg] n dent f (d'engrenage); (wheel) roue dentée
**cogent** [ˈkəʊdʒənt] adj puissant(e), convaincant(e)
**coil** [kɔɪl] n rouleau m, bobine f; (contraceptive) stérilet m ♦ vt enrouler
**coin** [kɔɪn] n pièce f de monnaie ♦ vt (word) inventer; ~**age** n monnaie f, système m monétaire; ~ **box** (BRIT) n cabine f téléphonique
**coincide** [kəʊɪnˈsaɪd] vi coïncider; ~**nce** [kəʊˈɪnsɪdəns] n coïncidence f
**Coke** [kəʊk] ® n coca m
**coke** [kəʊk] n coke m
**colander** [ˈkɔləndəʳ] n passoire f
**cold** [kəʊld] adj froid(e) ♦ n froid m; (MED) rhume m; **it's** ~ il fait froid; **to be** or **feel** ~ (person) avoir froid; **to catch** ~ prendre or attraper froid; **to catch a** ~ attraper un rhume; **in** ~ **blood** de sang-froid; ~**-shoulder** vt se montrer froid(e) envers, snober; ~ **sore** n bouton m de fièvre
**coleslaw** [ˈkəʊlslɔː] n sorte de salade de chou cru
**colic** [ˈkɔlɪk] n colique(s) f(pl)
**collapse** [kəˈlæps] vi s'effondrer, s'écrouler ♦ n effondrement m, écroulement m; **collapsible** adj pliant(e); télescopique
**collar** [ˈkɔləʳ] n (of coat, shirt) col m; (for animal) collier m; ~**bone** n clavicule f
**collateral** [kəˈlætərl] n nantissement m
**colleague** [ˈkɔliːg] n collègue m/f
**collect** [kəˈlekt] vt rassembler; ramasser; (as a hobby) collectionner; (BRIT: call and pick up) (passer) prendre; (mail) faire la levée de, ramasser; (money owed) encaisser; (donations, subscriptions) re-

cueillir ♦ vi (people) se rassembler; (things) s'amasser; **to call** ~ (US: TEL) téléphoner en P.C.V.; ~**ion** n collection f; (of mail) levée f; (for money) collecte f, quête f; ~**or** n collectionneur m
**college** [ˈkɔlɪdʒ] n collège m
**collide** [kəˈlaɪd] vi entrer en collision
**colliery** [ˈkɔlɪərɪ] (BRIT) n mine f de charbon, houillère f
**collision** [kəˈlɪʒən] n collision f
**colloquial** [kəˈləʊkwɪəl] adj familier (-ère)
**colon** [ˈkəʊlən] n (sign) deux-points m inv; (MED) côlon m
**colonel** [ˈkəːnl] n colonel m
**colony** [ˈkɔlənɪ] n colonie f
**colour** [ˈkʌləʳ] (US **color**) n couleur f ♦ vt (paint) peindre; (dye) teindre; (news) fausser, exagérer ♦ vi (blush) rougir; ~**s** npl (of party, club) couleurs fpl; ~ **in** vt colorier; ~ **bar** n discrimination raciale (dans un établissement); ~**-blind** adj daltonien(ne); ~**ed** adj (person) de couleur; (illustration) en couleur; ~ **film** n (for camera) pellicule f (en) couleur; ~**ful** adj coloré(e), vif(-vive); (personality) pittoresque, haut(e) en couleurs; ~**ing** n colorant m; (complexion) teint m; ~ **scheme** n combinaison f de(s) couleurs; ~ **television** n télévision f (en) couleur
**colt** [kəʊlt] n poulain m
**column** [ˈkɔləm] n colonne f; ~**ist** [ˈkɔləmnɪst] n chroniqueur(-euse)
**coma** [ˈkəʊmə] n coma m
**comb** [kəʊm] n peigne m ♦ vt (hair) peigner; (area) ratisser, passer au peigne fin
**combat** [ˈkɔmbæt] n combat m ♦ vt combattre, lutter contre
**combination** [kɔmbɪˈneɪʃən] n combinaison f
**combine** [vb kəmˈbaɪn, n ˈkɔmbaɪn] vt: **to** ~ **sth with sth** combiner qch avec qch; (one quality with another) joindre or allier qch à qch ♦ vi s'associer; (CHEM) se combiner ♦ n (ECON) trust m; ~ (har-

vester) n moissonneuse-batteuse(-lieuse) f

**come** [kʌm] (pt **came**, pp **come**) vi venir, arriver; **to ~ to** (decision etc) parvenir or arriver à; **to ~ undone/loose** se défaire/desserrer; **~ about** vi se produire, arriver; **~ across** vi fus rencontrer par hasard, tomber sur; **~ along** vi = **come on**; **~ away** vi partir, s'en aller, se détacher; **~ back** vi revenir; **~ by** vt fus (acquire) obtenir, se procurer; **~ down** vi descendre; (prices) baisser; (buildings) s'écrouler, être démoli(e); **~ forward** vi s'avancer, se présenter, s'annoncer; **~ from** vt fus être originaire de, venir de; **~ in** vi entrer; **~ in for** vi (criticism etc) être l'objet de; **~ into** vt fus (money) hériter de; **~ off** vi (button) se détacher; (stain) s'enlever; (attempt) réussir; **~ on** vi (pupil, work, project) faire des progrès, s'avancer; (lights, electricity) s'allumer; (central heating) se mettre en marche; **~ on!** viens!, allons!, allez!; **~ out** vi sortir; (book) paraître; (strike) cesser le travail, se mettre en grève; **~ round** vi (after faint, operation) revenir à soi, reprendre connaissance; **~ to** vi revenir à soi; **~ up** vi monter; **~ up against** vt fus (resistance, difficulties) rencontrer; **~ up with** vt fus: he came up with an idea il a eu une idée, il a proposé quelque chose; **~ upon** vt fus tomber sur; **~back** n (THEATRE etc) rentrée f

**comedian** [kə'miːdɪən] n (in music hall etc) comique m; (THEATRE) comédien m

**comedy** ['kɒmɪdɪ] n comédie f

**comeuppance** [kʌm'ʌpəns] n: **to get one's ~** recevoir ce qu'on mérite

**comfort** ['kʌmfət] n confort m, bien-être m; (relief) soulagement m, réconfort m ♦ vt consoler, réconforter; **the ~s of home** les commodités fpl de la maison; **~able** adj confortable; (person) à l'aise; (patient) dont l'état est stationnaire; (walk etc) facile; **~ably** adv (sit) confortablement; (live) à l'aise;

**comic** ['kɒmɪk] adj (also: **~al**) comique ♦ n comique m; (BRIT: magazine) illustré m; **~ strip** n bande dessinée

**coming** ['kʌmɪŋ] n arrivée f ♦ adj prochain(e), à venir; **~(s) and going(s)** n(pl) va-et-vient m inv

**comma** ['kɒmə] n virgule f

**command** [kə'mɑːnd] n ordre m, commandement m; (MIL: authority) commandement; (mastery) maîtrise f ♦ vt (troops) commander; **to ~ sb to do** ordonner à qn de faire; **~eer** [kɒmən'dɪə*] vt réquisitionner; **~er** n (MIL) commandant m

**commando** [kə'mɑːndəʊ] n commando m; membre m d'un commando

**commemorate** [kə'meməreɪt] vt commémorer

**commence** [kə'mens] vt, vi commencer

**commend** [kə'mend] vt louer; (recommend) recommander

**commensurate** [kə'menʃərɪt] adj: **~ with** or **to** en proportion de, proportionné(e) à

**comment** ['kɒment] n commentaire m ♦ vi: **to ~ (on)** faire des remarques (sur); **"no ~"** "je n'ai rien à dire"; **~ary** ['kɒməntərɪ] n commentaire m; (SPORT) reportage m (en direct); **~ator** ['kɒmənteɪtə*] n commentateur m; reporter m

**commerce** ['kɒmɜːs] n commerce m

**commercial** [kə'mɜːʃəl] adj commercial(e) ♦ n (TV, RADIO) annonce f publicitaire, spot m (publicitaire)

**commiserate** [kə'mɪzəreɪt] vi: **to ~ with sb** témoigner de la sympathie pour qn

**commission** [kə'mɪʃən] n (order for work) commande f; (committee, fee) commission f ♦ vt (work of art) commander, charger un artiste de l'exécution de; **out of ~** (not working) hors service; **~aire** [kəmɪʃə'neə*] n (at shop, cinema etc) portier m (en uniforme); **~er** n (POLICE) préfet m (de police)

**commit** [kə'mɪt] vt (act) commettre; (resources) consacrer; (to sb's care) confier (à); **to ~ o.s. (to do)** s'engager (à faire); **to ~ suicide** se suicider; **~ment** n engagement m; (obligation) responsabilité(s) f(pl)

**committee** [kə'mɪtɪ] n comité m

**commodity** [kə'mɔdɪtɪ] n produit m, marchandise f, article m

**common** ['kɔmən] adj commun(e); (usual) courant(e) ♦ n terrain communal; **the C~s** (BRIT) npl la chambre des Communes; **in ~** en commun; **~er** n roturier(-ière); **~ law** n droit coutumier; **~ly** adv communément, généralement; couramment; **C~ Market** n Marché commun; **~place** adj banal(e), ordinaire; **~ room** n salle commune; **~ sense** n bon sens; **C~wealth** (BRIT) n Commonwealth m

**commotion** [kə'məuʃən] n désordre m, tumulte m

**communal** ['kɔmjuːnl] adj (life) communautaire; (for common use) commun(e)

**commune** [n 'kɔmjuːn, vb kə'mjuːn] n (group) communauté f ♦ vi: **to ~ with** communier avec

**communicate** [kə'mjuːnɪkeɪt] vt, vi communiquer; **communication** [kəmjuːnɪ'keɪʃən] n communication f; **communication cord** (BRIT) n sonnette f d'alarme

**communion** [kə'mjuːnɪən] n (also: **Holy C~**) communion f

**communism** ['kɔmjunɪzəm] n communisme m; **communist** adj communiste ♦ n communiste m/f

**community** [kə'mjuːnɪtɪ] n communauté f; **~ centre** n centre m de loisirs; **~ chest** (US) n fonds commun

**commutation ticket** [kɔmjuː'teɪʃən-] (US) n carte f d'abonnement

**commute** [kə'mjuːt] vi faire un trajet journalier pour se rendre à son travail ♦

vt (LAW) commuer; **~r** n banlieusard(e) (qui fait un trajet journalier pour se rendre à son travail)

**compact** [adj kəm'pækt, n 'kɔmpækt] adj compact(e) ♦ n (also: **powder ~**) poudrier m; **~ disc** n disque compact; **~ disc player** n lecteur m de disque compact

**companion** [kəm'pænjən] n compagnon (compagne); **~ship** n camaraderie f

**company** ['kʌmpənɪ] n compagnie f; **to keep sb ~** tenir compagnie à qn; **~ secretary** (BRIT) n (COMM) secrétaire général (d'une société)

**comparative** [kəm'pærətɪv] adj (study) comparatif(-ive); (relative) relatif(-ive); **~ly** adv (relatively) relativement

**compare** [kəm'pɛəʳ] vt: **to ~ sth/sb with/to** comparer qch/qn avec et/à ♦ vi: **to ~ (with)** se comparer (à); être comparable (à); **comparison** [kəm'pærɪsn] n comparaison f

**compartment** [kəm'pɑːtmənt] n compartiment m

**compass** ['kʌmpəs] n boussole f; **~es** npl (GEOM: also: **pair of ~es**) compas m

**compassion** [kəm'pæʃən] n compassion f; **~ate** adj compatissant(e)

**compatible** [kəm'pætɪbl] adj compatible

**compel** [kəm'pɛl] vt contraindre, obliger

**compensate** ['kɔmpənseɪt] vt compenser, dédommager ♦ vi: **to ~ for** compenser; **compensation** [kɔmpən'seɪʃən] n compensation f; (money) dédommagement m, indemnité f

**compère** ['kɔmpɛəʳ] n (TV) animateur(-trice)

**compete** [kəm'piːt] vi: **to ~ (with)** rivaliser (avec), faire concurrence (à)

**competent** ['kɔmpɪtənt] adj compétent(e), capable

**competition** [kɔmpɪ'tɪʃən] n (contest) compétition f, concours m; (ECON) concurrence f

**competitive** [kəmˈpetɪtɪv] adj (ECON) concurrentiel(le); (sport) de compétition; (person) qui a l'esprit de compétition; **competitor** n concurrent(e)

**complacency** [kəmˈpleɪsnsɪ] n suffisance f, vaine complaisance

**complain** [kəmˈpleɪn] vi: to ~ (about) se plaindre (de); (in shop etc) réclamer (au sujet de); to ~ of (pain) se plaindre de; **~t** n plainte f; réclamation f; (MED) affection f

**complement** [n ˈkɒmplɪmənt, vb ˈkɒmplɪment] n complément m; (especially of ship's crew etc) effectif complet ♦ vt (enhance) compléter; **~ary** [kɒmplɪˈmentərɪ] adj complémentaire

**complete** [kəmˈpliːt] adj complet(-ète) ♦ vt achever, parachever; (set, group) compléter; (a form) remplir; **~ly** adv complètement; **completion** n achèvement m; (of contract) exécution f

**complex** [ˈkɒmpleks] adj complexe ♦ n complexe m

**complexion** [kəmˈplekʃən] n (of face) teint m

**compliance** [kəmˈplaɪəns] n (submission) docilité f; (agreement): ~ with le fait de se conformer à; **in ~ with** en accord avec

**complicate** [ˈkɒmplɪkeɪt] vt compliquer; **~d** adj compliqué(e); **complication** [kɒmplɪˈkeɪʃən] n complication f

**compliment** [n ˈkɒmplɪmənt, vb ˈkɒmplɪment] n compliment m ♦ vt complimenter; **~s** npl (respects) compliments mpl, hommages mpl; **to pay sb a ~** faire or adresser un compliment à qn; **~ary** [kɒmplɪˈmentərɪ] adj flatteur(-euse); (free) (offert(e)) à titre gracieux; **~ary ticket** n billet m de faveur

**comply** [kəmˈplaɪ] vi: to ~ with se soumettre à, se conformer à

**component** [kəmˈpəʊnənt] n composant m, élément m

**compose** [kəmˈpəʊz] vt composer;

(form): **to be ~d of** se composer de; **to ~ o.s.** se calmer, se maîtriser; prendre une contenance; **~d** adj calme, posé(e); **~r** n (MUS) compositeur m; **composition** [kɒmpəˈzɪʃən] n composition f; **composure** [kəmˈpəʊʒəʳ] n calme m, maîtrise f de soi

**compound** [ˈkɒmpaʊnd] n composé m; (enclosure) enclos m, enceinte f; (LING) mot composé ♦ adj composé(e); **~ fracture** n fracture compliquée; **~ interest** n intérêt composé

**comprehend** [kɒmprɪˈhend] vt comprendre; **comprehension** n compréhension f

**comprehensive** [kɒmprɪˈhensɪv] adj (très) complet(-ète); **~ policy** n (INSURANCE) assurance f tous risques; **~ (school)** n (BRIT) n école secondaire polyvalente; ≈ C.E.S. m

**compress** [vb kəmˈpres, n ˈkɒmpres] vt comprimer; (text, information) condenser ♦ n (MED) compresse f

**comprise** [kəmˈpraɪz] vt (also: **be ~d of**) comprendre; (constitute) constituer, représenter

**compromise** [ˈkɒmprəmaɪz] n compromis m ♦ vt compromettre ♦ vi transiger, accepter un compromis

**compulsion** [kəmˈpʌlʃən] n contrainte f, force f

**compulsive** [kəmˈpʌlsɪv] adj (PSYCH) compulsif(-ive); (book, film etc) captivant(e)

**compulsory** [kəmˈpʌlsərɪ] adj obligatoire

**computer** [kəmˈpjuːtəʳ] n ordinateur m; **~ game** n jeu m vidéo; **~-generated** adj de synthèse; **~ize** vt informatiser; **~ programmer** n programmeur(-euse); **~ programming** n programmation f; **~ science** n informatique f; **computing** n = **computer science**

**comrade** [ˈkɒmrɪd] n camarade m/f

**con** [kɒn] vt duper; (cheat) escroquer ♦ n escroquerie f

**conceal** [kənˈsiːl] vt cacher, dissimuler

**conceit** [kən'si:t] n vanité f, suffisance f, prétention f; **~ed** adj vaniteux(-euse), suffisant(e)

**conceive** [kən'si:v] vt, vi concevoir

**concentrate** ['kɔnsəntreɪt] vi se concentrer ♦ vt concentrer; **concentration** n concentration f; **concentration camp** n camp m de concentration

**concept** ['kɔnsept] n concept m

**concern** [kən'sə:n] n affaire f; (COMM) entreprise f, firme f; (anxiety) inquiétude f, souci m ♦ vt concerner; **to be ~ed (about)** s'inquiéter (de), être inquiet (-ète) (au sujet de); **~ing** prep en ce qui concerne, à propos de

**concert** ['kɔnsət] n concert m; **~ed** [kən'sə:tɪd] adj concerté(e); **~ hall** n salle f de concert

**concerto** [kən'tʃə:təu] n concerto m

**concession** [kən'seʃən] n concession f; **tax ~** dégrèvement fiscal

**conclude** [kən'klu:d] vt conclure; **conclusion** [kən'klu:ʒən] n conclusion f; **conclusive** [kən'klu:sɪv] adj concluant(e), définitif(-ive)

**concoct** [kən'kɔkt] vt confectionner, composer; (fig) inventer; **~ion** n mélange m

**concourse** ['kɔŋkɔ:s] n (hall) hall m, salle f des pas perdus

**concrete** ['kɔŋkri:t] n béton m ♦ adj concret(-ète); (floor etc) en béton

**concur** [kən'kə:r] vi (agree) être d'accord

**concurrently** [kən'kʌrntlɪ] adv simultanément

**concussion** [kən'kʌʃən] n (MED) commotion f (cérébrale)

**condemn** [kən'dem] vt condamner

**condensation** [kɔndɛn'seɪʃən] n condensation f

**condense** [kən'dɛns] vi se condenser ♦ vt condenser; **~d milk** n lait concentré (sucré)

**condition** [kən'dɪʃən] n condition f; (MED) état m ♦ vt déterminer, condition-

ner; **on ~ that** à condition que +sub, à condition de; **~al** adj conditionnel(le); **~er** n (for hair) baume après-shampooing m; (for fabrics) assouplissant m

**condolences** [kən'dəulənsɪz] npl condoléances fpl

**condom** ['kɔndəm] n préservatif m

**condominium** [kɔndə'mɪnɪəm] n (US) (building) immeuble m (en copropriété)

**condone** [kən'dəun] vt fermer les yeux sur, approuver (tacitement)

**conducive** [kən'dju:sɪv] adj: **~ to** favorable à, qui contribue à

**conduct** [n 'kɔndʌkt, vb kən'dʌkt] n conduite f ♦ vt conduire; (MUS) diriger; **to ~ o.s.** se conduire, se comporter; **~ed tour** n voyage organisé; (of building) visite guidée; **~or** n (of orchestra) chef m d'orchestre; (on bus) receveur m; (US: on train) chef m de train; (ELEC) conducteur m; **~ress** n (on bus) receveuse f

**cone** [kəun] n cône m; (for ice-cream) cornet m; (BOT) pomme f de pin, cône

**confectioner** [kən'fekʃənər] n confiseur(-euse); **~'s (shop)** n confiserie f; **~y** n confiserie f

**confer** [kən'fə:r] vt: **to ~ sth on** conférer qch à ♦ vi conférer, s'entretenir

**conference** ['kɔnfərəns] n conférence f

**confess** [kən'fes] vt confesser, avouer ♦ vi se confesser; **~ion** n confession f

**confetti** [kən'fetɪ] n confettis mpl

**confide** [kən'faɪd] vi: **to ~ in** se confier à

**confidence** ['kɔnfɪdns] n confiance f; (also: **self-~**) assurance f, confiance en soi; (secret) confidence f; **in ~** (speak, write) en confidence, confidentiellement; **~ trick** n escroquerie f; **confident** adj sûr(e), assuré(e); **confidential** [kɔnfɪ'denʃəl] adj confidentiel(le)

**confine** [kən'faɪn] vt limiter, borner; (shut up) confiner, enfermer; **~d** adj (space) restreint(e), réduit(e); **~ment** n emprisonnement m, détention f; **~s**

['kɒnfaɪnz] npl confins mpl, bornes fpl

**confirm** [kən'fɜːm] vt confirmer; (appointment) ratifier; **~ation** [kɒnfə'meɪʃən] n confirmation f; **~ed** adj invétéré(e), incorrigible

**confiscate** ['kɒnfɪskeɪt] vt confisquer

**conflict** [n 'kɒnflɪkt, vb kən'flɪkt] n conflit m, lutte f ♦ vi être or entrer en conflit; (opinions) s'opposer, se heurter; **~ing** [kən'flɪktɪŋ] adj contradictoire

**conform** [kən'fɔːm] vi: to ~ (to) se conformer (à)

**confound** [kən'faʊnd] vt confondre

**confront** [kən'frʌnt] vt confronter, mettre en présence; (enemy, danger) affronter, faire face à; **~ation** [kɒnfrən'teɪʃən] n confrontation f

**confuse** [kən'fjuːz] vt (person) troubler; (situation) embrouiller; (one thing with another) confondre; **~d** adj (person) dérouté(e), désorienté(e); **confusing** adj peu clair(e), déroutant(e); **confusion** [kən'fjuːʒən] n confusion f

**congeal** [kən'dʒiːl] vi (blood) se coaguler; (oil etc) se figer

**congenial** [kən'dʒiːnɪəl] adj sympathique, agréable

**congested** [kən'dʒestɪd] adj (MED) congestionné(e); (area) surpeuplé(e); (road) bloqué(e); **congestion** n congestion f; (fig) encombrement m

**congratulate** [kən'grætjuleɪt] vt: to ~ sb (on) féliciter qn (de); **congratulations** [kəngrætju'leɪʃənz] npl félicitations fpl

**congregate** ['kɒngrɪgeɪt] vi se rassembler, se réunir; **congregation** [kɒngrɪ'geɪʃən] n assemblée f (des fidèles)

**congress** ['kɒngres] n congrès m; **~man** (irreg) (US) ♦ n membre m du Congrès

**conjunction** [kən'dʒʌŋkʃən] n (LING) conjonction f

**conjunctivitis** [kəndʒʌŋktɪ'vaɪtɪs] n conjonctivite f

**conjure** ['kʌndʒər] vi faire des tours de

passe-passe; **~ up** vt (ghost, spirit) faire apparaître; (memories) évoquer; **~r** n prestidigitateur m, illusionniste m/f

**con man** (irreg) n escroc m

**connect** [kə'nekt] vt joindre, relier; (ELEC) connecter; (TEL: caller) mettre en connection (with avec); (: new subscriber) brancher; (fig) établir un rapport entre, faire un rapprochement entre ♦ vi (train): to ~ with assurer la correspondance avec; to be ~ed with (fig) avoir un rapport avec, avoir des rapports avec, être en relation avec; **~ion** n relation f, lien m; (ELEC) connexion f; (train, plane etc) correspondance f; (TEL) branchement m, communication f

**connive** [kə'naɪv] vi: to ~ at se faire le complice de

**conquer** ['kɒŋkər] vt conquérir; (feelings) vaincre, surmonter; **conquest** ['kɒŋkwest] n conquête f

**cons** [kɒnz] npl see **convenience**; **pro**

**conscience** ['kɒnʃəns] n conscience f; **conscientious** [kɒnʃɪ'enʃəs] adj consciencieux(-euse)

**conscious** ['kɒnʃəs] adj conscient(e); **~ness** n conscience f; (MED) connaissance f

**conscript** ['kɒnskrɪpt] n conscrit m

**consent** [kən'sent] n consentement m ♦ vi: to ~ (to) consentir (à)

**consequence** ['kɒnsɪkwəns] n conséquence f, suites fpl; (significance) importance f; **consequently** adv par conséquent, donc

**conservation** [kɒnsə'veɪʃən] n préservation f, protection f

**conservative** [kən'sɜːvətɪv] adj conservateur(-trice); at a ~ estimate au bas mot; **C~** (BRIT) adj, n (POL) conservateur(-trice)

**conservatory** [kən'sɜːvətrɪ] n (greenhouse) serre f

**conserve** [kən'sɜːv] vt conserver, préserver; (supplies, energy) économiser ♦ n confiture f

**consider** [kən'sɪdər] vt (study) considérer, réfléchir à; (take into account) penser à, prendre en considération; (regard, judge) considérer, estimer; **to ~ doing sth** envisager de faire qch; **~able** adj considérable; **~ably** adv nettement; **~ate** adj prévenant(e), plein(e) d'égards; **~ation** [kənsidəˈreiʃən] n considération f; **~ing** prep étant donné

**consign** [kənˈsain] vt expédier; (to sb's care) confier; (fig) livrer; **~ment** n arrivage m, envoi m

**consist** [kənˈsist] vi: **to ~ of** consister en, se composer de

**consistency** [kənˈsistənsi] n consistance f; (fig) cohérence f

**consistent** [kənˈsistənt] adj logique, cohérent(e)

**consolation** [kɔnsəˈleiʃən] n consolation f

**console**[1] [kənˈsəul] vt consoler

**console**[2] [ˈkɔnsəul] (COMPUT) console f

**consonant** [ˈkɔnsənənt] n consonne f

**conspicuous** [kənˈspikjuəs] adj voyant(e), qui attire l'attention

**conspiracy** [kənˈspirəsi] n conspiration f, complot m

**constable** [ˈkʌnstəbl] (BRIT) n ≈ agent m de police, gendarme m; **chief ~** ≈ préfet m de police; **constabulary** [kənˈstæbjuləri] (BRIT) n ≈ police f, gendarmerie f

**constant** [ˈkɔnstənt] adj constant(e); incessant(e); **~ly** adv constamment, sans cesse

**constipated** [ˈkɔnstipeitid] adj constipé(e); **constipation** [kɔnstiˈpeiʃən] n constipation f

**constituency** [kənˈstitjuənsi] n circonscription électorale

**constituent** [kənˈstitjuənt] n (POL) électeur(-trice); (part) élément constitutif, composant m

**constitution** [kɔnstiˈtjuːʃən] n constitution f; **~al** adj constitutionnel(le)

**constraint** [kənˈstreint] n contrainte f

**construct** [kənˈstrʌkt] vt construire;

**~ion** n construction f; **~ive** adj constructif(-ive); **~ive dismissal** démission forcée

**consul** [ˈkɔnsl] n consul m; **~ate** [ˈkɔnsjulit] n consulat m

**consult** [kənˈsʌlt] vt consulter; **~ant** n (MED) médecin consultant; (other specialist) consultant m, (expert-)conseil m; **~ing room** (BRIT) n cabinet m de consultation

**consume** [kənˈsjuːm] vt consommer; **~r** n consommateur(-trice); **~r goods** npl biens mpl de consommation; **~r society** n société f de consommation

**consummate** [ˈkɔnsʌmeit] vt consommer

**consumption** [kənˈsʌmpʃən] n consommation f

**cont.** abbr (= continued) suite

**contact** [ˈkɔntækt] n contact m; (person) connaissance f, relation f ♦ vt contacter, se mettre en contact or en rapport avec; **~ lenses** npl verres mpl de contact, lentilles fpl

**contagious** [kənˈteidʒəs] adj contagieux(-euse)

**contain** [kənˈtein] vt contenir; **to ~ o.s.** se contenir, se maîtriser; **~er** n récipient m; (for shipping etc) container m

**contaminate** [kənˈtæmineit] vt contaminer

**cont'd** abbr (= continued) suite

**contemplate** [ˈkɔntəmpleit] vt contempler; (consider) envisager

**contemporary** [kənˈtempərəri] adj contemporain(e); (design, wallpaper) moderne ♦ n contemporain(e)

**contempt** [kənˈtempt] n mépris m, dédain m; **~ of court** (LAW) outrage m à l'autorité de la justice; **~uous** [kənˈtemptjuəs] adj dédaigneux(-euse), méprisant(e)

**contend** [kənˈtend] vt: **to ~ that** soutenir or prétendre que ♦ vi: **to ~ with** (compete) rivaliser avec; (struggle) lutter avec; **~er** n concurrent(e); (POL) candidat(e)

**content** [adj, vb kən'tent, n 'kɔntent] adj content(e), satisfait(e) ♦ vt contenter, satisfaire ♦ n contenu m; (of fat, moisture) teneur f; ~s npl (of container etc) contenu m; (table of) ~s table f des matières; ~ed adj content(e), satisfait(e)

**contention** [kən'tenʃən] n dispute f, contestation f; (argument) assertion f, affirmation f

**contest** [n 'kɔntest, vb kən'test] n combat m, lutte f; (competition) concours m ♦ vt (decision, statement) contester, discuter; (compete for) disputer; ~ant [kən'testənt] n concurrent(e); (in fight) adversaire m/f

**context** ['kɔntekst] n contexte m

**continent** ['kɔntɪnənt] n continent m; the C~ (BRIT) l'Europe continentale; ~al [kɔntɪ'nentl] adj continental(e); ~al breakfast n petit déjeuner m à la française; ~al quilt (BRIT) n couette f

**contingency** [kən'tɪndʒənsɪ] n éventualité f, événement imprévu

**continual** [kən'tɪnjuəl] adj continuel(le)

**continuation** [kəntɪnju'eɪʃən] n continuation f; (after interruption) reprise f; (of story) suite f

**continue** [kən'tɪnju:] vi, vt continuer; (after interruption) reprendre, poursuivre; **continuity** [kɔntɪ'njuːɪtɪ] n continuité f; (TV etc) enchaînement m; **continuous** [kən'tɪnjuəs] adj continu(e); (LING) progressif(-ive)

**contort** [kən'tɔːt] vt tordre, crisper

**contour** ['kɔntuə] n contour m, profil m; (on map: also: ~ line) courbe f de niveau

**contraband** ['kɔntrəbænd] n contrebande f

**contraceptive** [kɔntrə'septɪv] n contraceptif(-ive), anticonceptionnel(le) ♦ n contraceptif m

**contract** [n 'kɔntrækt, vb kən'trækt] n contrat m ♦ vi (become smaller) se contracter, se resserrer; (COMM): **to ~ to do sth** s'engager (par contrat) à faire qch; ~**ion** [kən'trækʃən] n contraction f; ~**or** [kən'træktə] n entrepreneur m

**contradict** [kɔntrə'dɪkt] vt contredire

**contraflow** ['kɔntrəflau] n (AUT): ~ **lane** voie f à contresens; **there's a ~ system in operation on ...** une voie a été mise en opération en sens inverse sur ...

**contraption** [kən'træpʃən] (pej) n machin m, truc m

**contrary**¹ ['kɔntrərɪ] adj contraire, opposé(e) ♦ n contraire m; **on the ~** au contraire; **unless you hear to the ~** sauf avis contraire

**contrary**² [kən'treərɪ] adj (perverse) contrariant(e), entêté(e)

**contrast** [n 'kɔntrɑːst, vb kən'trɑːst] n contraste m ♦ vt mettre en contraste, contraster; **in ~ to** or **with** contrairement à

**contravene** [kɔntrə'viːn] vt enfreindre, violer, contrevenir à

**contribute** [kən'trɪbjuːt] vi contribuer ♦ vt: **to ~ £10/an article to** donner 10 livres/un article à; **to ~ to** contribuer à; (newspaper) collaborer à; **contribution** [kɔntrɪ'bjuːʃən] n contribution f; **contributor** [kən'trɪbjutə] n (to newspaper) collaborateur(-trice)

**contrive** [kən'traɪv] vt: **to ~ to do** s'arranger pour faire, trouver le moyen de faire

**control** [kən'trəul] vt maîtriser, commander; (check) contrôler ♦ n contrôle m, autorité f; maîtrise f; ~**s** npl (of machine etc) commandes fpl; (on radio, TV etc) boutons mpl de réglage; ~**led substance** narcotique m; **everything is under ~** tout va bien, j'ai (or il a etc) la situation en main; **to be in ~ of** être maître de, maîtriser; **the car went out of ~** j'ai (or il a etc) perdu le contrôle du véhicule; ~ **panel** n tableau m de commandes; ~ **room** n salle f des commandes; ~ **tower** n (AVIAT) tour f de contrôle

**controversial** [kɔntrə'vɜːʃl] adj (topic)

discutable, controversé(e); (person) qui fait beaucoup parler de lui; **controversy** ['kɒntrəvɜːsɪ] n controverse f, polémique f

**convalesce** [kɒnvə'les] vi relever de maladie, se remettre (d'une maladie)

**convector** [kən'vektə*] n (heater) radiateur m (à convexion)

**convene** [kən'viːn] vt convoquer, assembler ♦ vi se réunir, s'assembler

**convenience** [kən'viːnɪəns] n commodité f; **at your ~** quand ou comme cela vous convient; **all modern ~s**, (BRIT) **all mod cons** avec tout le confort moderne, tout confort

**convenient** [kən'viːnɪənt] adj commode

**convent** ['kɒnvənt] n couvent m; **~ school** n couvent m

**convention** [kən'venʃən] n convention f; **~al** adj conventionnel(le)

**conversant** [kən'vɜːsnt] adj: **to be ~ with** s'y connaître en; être au courant de

**conversation** [kɒnvə'seɪʃən] n conversation f

**converse** [n 'kɒnvɜːs, vb kən'vɜːs] n contraire m, inverse m ♦ vi s'entretenir; **~ly** [kɒn'vɜːslɪ] adv inversement, réciproquement

**convert** [vb kən'vɜːt, n 'kɒnvɜːt] vt (REL, COMM) convertir; (alter) transformer; (house) aménager ♦ n converti(e); **~ible** [kən'vɜːtəbl] n (voiture f) décapotable f

**convey** [kən'veɪ] vt transporter; (thanks) transmettre; (idea) communiquer; **~or belt** n convoyeur m, tapis roulant

**convict** [vb kən'vɪkt, n 'kɒnvɪkt] vt déclarer (or reconnaître) coupable ♦ n forçat m, détenu m; **~ion** [-ʃən] n (LAW) condamnation f; (belief) conviction f

**convince** [kən'vɪns] vt convaincre, persuader; **convincing** adj persuasif(-ive), convaincant(e)

**convoluted** ['kɒnvəluːtɪd] adj (argu-

ment) compliqué(e)

**convulse** [kən'vʌls] vt: **to be ~d with laughter/pain** se tordre de rire/douleur

**cook** [kuk] vt (faire) cuire ♦ vi cuire; (person) faire la cuisine ♦ n cuisinier (-ière); **~book** n livre m de cuisine; **~er** n cuisinière f; **~ery** n cuisine f; **~ery book** (BRIT) n = **cookbook**; **~ie** (US) n biscuit m, petit gâteau (sec); **~ing** n cuisine f

**cool** [kuːl] adj frais (fraîche); (calm, unemotional) calme; (unfriendly) froid(e) ♦ vt, vi rafraîchir, refroidir

**coop** [kuːp] n poulailler m; (for rabbits) clapier m ♦ vt: **to ~ up** (fig) cloîtrer, enfermer

**cooperate** [kəu'ɔpəreɪt] vi coopérer, collaborer; **cooperation** [kəuɔpə'reɪʃən] n coopération f, collaboration f; **cooperative** [kəu'ɔprətɪv] adj coopératif(-ive) ♦ n coopérative f

**coordinate** [vb kəu'ɔːdɪneɪt, n kəu'ɔːdɪmət] vt coordonner ♦ n (MATH) coordonnée f; **~s** npl (clothes) ensemble m, coordonnés mpl

**co-ownership** [kəu'əunəʃɪp] n copropriété f

**cop** [kɒp] (inf) n flic m

**cope** [kəup] vi: **to ~ with** faire face à; (solve) venir à bout de

**copper** ['kɒpə*] n cuivre m; (BRIT: inf: policeman) flic m; **~s** npl (coins) petite monnaie

**copy** ['kɒpɪ] n copie f; (of book etc) exemplaire m ♦ vt copier; **~right** n droit m d'auteur, copyright m

**coral** ['kɒrəl] n corail m

**cord** [kɔːd] n corde f; (fabric) velours côtelé; (ELEC) cordon m, fil m

**cordial** ['kɔːdɪəl] adj cordial(e), chaleureux(-euse) ♦ n cordial m

**cordon** ['kɔːdn] n cordon m; **~ off** vt boucler (par cordon de police)

**corduroy** ['kɔːdərɔɪ] n velours côtelé

**core** [kɔː*] n noyau m; (of fruit) trognon m, cœur m; (of building, problem) cœur

♦ vt enlever le trognon or le cœur de

**cork** [kɔːk] n liège m; (of bottle) bouchon m; **~screw** n tire-bouchon m

**corn** [kɔːn] n (BRIT: wheat) blé m; (US: maize) maïs m; (on foot) cor m; **~ on the cob** (CULIN) épi m de maïs; **~ed beef** n corned-beef m

**corner** [ˈkɔːnəʳ] n coin m; (AUT) tournant m, virage m; (FOOTBALL: also: **~ kick**) corner m ♦ vt acculer, mettre au pied du mur; coincer; (COMM: market) accaparer ♦ vi prendre un virage; **~stone** n pierre f angulaire

**cornet** [ˈkɔːnɪt] n (MUS) cornet m à pistons; (BRIT: of ice-cream) cornet (de glace)

**cornflakes** [ˈkɔːnfleɪks] npl corn-flakes mpl

**cornflour** [ˈkɔːnflauəʳ] (BRIT), **cornstarch** [ˈkɔːnstɑːtʃ] (US) n farine f de maïs, maïzena f ®

**Cornwall** [ˈkɔːnwəl] n Cornouailles f

**corny** [ˈkɔːnɪ] (inf) adj rebattu(e)

**coronary** [ˈkɒrənərɪ] n (also: **~ thrombosis**) infarctus m (du myocarde), thrombose f coronarienne

**coronation** [kɒrəˈneɪʃən] n couronnement m

**coroner** [ˈkɒrənəʳ] n officier chargé de déterminer les causes d'un décès

**corporal** [ˈkɔːpərəl] n caporal m, brigadier m ♦ adj: **~ punishment** châtiment corporel

**corporate** [ˈkɔːpərɪt] adj en commun, collectif(-ive); (COMM) de l'entreprise

**corporation** [kɔːpəˈreɪʃən] n (of town) municipalité f, conseil municipal; (COMM) société f

**corps** [kɔːʳ] (pl **~**) n corps m

**corpse** [kɔːps] n cadavre m

**correct** [kəˈrekt] adj (accurate) correct(e), exact(e); (proper) correct, convenable ♦ vt corriger; **~ion** n correction f

**correspond** [kɒrɪsˈpɒnd] vi correspondre; **~ence** n correspondance f, **~ence course** n cours m par correspondance

**~ent** n correspondant(e)

**corridor** [ˈkɒrɪdɔːʳ] n couloir m, corridor m

**corrode** [kəˈraud] vt corroder, ronger ♦ vi se corroder

**corrugated** [ˈkɒrəgeɪtɪd] adj plissé(e); ondulé(e); **~ iron** n tôle ondulée

**corrupt** [kəˈrʌpt] adj corrompu(e) ♦ vt corrompre; **~ion** n corruption f

**Corsica** [ˈkɔːsɪkə] n Corse f

**cosmetic** [kɒzˈmetɪk] n produit de beauté, cosmétique m

**cost** [kɒst] n (pt, pp **cost**) n coût m ♦ vt coûter à or calculer le prix de revient; **~s** npl (COMM) frais mpl; (LAW) dépens mpl; **it ~s £5/too much** cela coûte cinq livres/c'est trop cher; **at all ~s** coûte que coûte, à tout prix

**co-star** [ˈkaustɑːʳ] n partenaire m/f

**cost: ~-effective** adj rentable; **~ly** adj coûteux(-euse); **~-of-living** adj: **~-of-living allowance** indemnité f de vie chère; **~-of-living index** index m du coût de la vie; **~ price** (BRIT) n prix coûtant or de revient

**costume** [ˈkɒstjuːm] n costume m; (lady's suit) tailleur m; (BRIT: also: **swimming ~**) maillot m (de bain); **~ jewellery** n bijoux mpl fantaisie

**cosy** [ˈkəuzɪ] (US **cozy**) adj douillet(te); (person) à l'aise, au chaud

**cot** [kɒt] n (BRIT: child's) lit m d'enfant, petit lit; (US: campbed) lit de camp

**cottage** [ˈkɒtɪdʒ] n petite maison (à la campagne), cottage m; **~ cheese** n fromage blanc (maigre)

**cotton** [ˈkɒtn] n coton m; **~ on** (inf) vi: **to ~ on to** piger; **~ candy** (US) n barbe f à papa; **~ wool** (BRIT) n ouate f, coton m hydrophile

**couch** [kautʃ] n canapé m; divan m

**couchette** [kuːˈʃet] n couchette f

**cough** [kɒf] vi tousser ♦ n toux f; **~ sweet** n pastille f pour or contre la toux

**could** [kud] pt of **can²**; **~n't** = **could not**

**council** ['kaunsl] n conseil m; **city** or **town** ~ conseil municipal; ~ **estate** (BRIT) n (zone f de) logements loués à/ par la municipalité; ~ **house** (BRIT) n maison f (à loyer modéré) louée par la municipalité; **~lor** n conseiller(-ère)

**counsel** ['kaunsl] n (lawyer) avocat(e); (advice) conseil m, consultation f; **~lor** n conseiller(-ère); (US: lawyer) avocat(e)

**count** [kaunt] vt, vi compter ♦ n compte m; (nobleman) comte m; **~ on** vt fus compter sur; **~down** n compte m à rebours

**countenance** ['kauntinəns] n expression f ♦ vt approuver

**counter** ['kauntər] n comptoir m; (in post office, bank) guichet m; (in game) jeton m ♦ vt aller à l'encontre de, opposer ♦ adv: **~ to** contrairement à; **~act** vt neutraliser, contrebalancer; **~feit** n faux m, contrefaçon f ♦ vt contrefaire ♦ adj faux (fausse); **~foil** n talon m, souche f; **~part** n (of person etc) homologue m/f

**countess** ['kauntis] n comtesse f

**countless** ['kauntlis] adj innombrable

**country** ['kʌntri] n pays m; (native land) patrie f; (as opposed to town) campagne f; (region) région f, pays; **~ dancing** (BRIT) n danse f folklorique; **~ house** n manoir m, (petit) château; **~man** (irreg) n (compatriot) compatriote m; (country dweller) habitant m de la campagne, campagnard m; **~side** n campagne f

**county** ['kaunti] n comté m

**coup** [ku:] (pl **~s**) n beau coup m; (also: ~ **d'état**) coup d'État

**couple** ['kʌpl] n couple m; **a ~ of** deux; (a few) quelques

**coupon** ['ku:pɔn] n coupon m, bon-prime m, bon-réclame m; (COMM) coupon

**courage** ['kʌridʒ] n courage m

**courier** ['kuriər] n messager m, courrier m; (for tourists) accompagnateur(-trice), guide m/f

**course** [kɔ:s] n cours m; (of ship) route

f; (for golf) terrain m; (part of meal) plat m; **first ~** entrée f; **of ~** bien sûr; **~ of action** parti m, ligne f de conduite; **of treatment** (MED) traitement m

**court** [kɔ:t] n cour f; (LAW) cour, tribunal m; (TENNIS) court m ♦ vt (woman) courtiser, faire la cour à; **to take to ~** actionner ou poursuivre en justice

**courteous** ['kɔ:tiəs] adj courtois(e), poli(e); **courtesy** ['kɔ:təsi] n courtoisie f, politesse f; **(by) courtesy of** avec l'aimable autorisation de; **courtesy bus** or **coach** n navette gratuite

**court:** **~-house** (US) n palais m de justice; **~ier** n courtisan m, dame f de la cour; **~ martial** (pl **courts martial**) n cour martiale, conseil m de guerre; **~room** n salle f de tribunal; **~yard** n cour f

**cousin** ['kʌzn] n cousin(e); **first ~** cousin(e) germain(e)

**cove** [kəuv] n petite baie, anse f

**covenant** ['kʌvənənt] n engagement m

**cover** ['kʌvər] vt couvrir ♦ n couverture f; (of pan) couvercle m; (over furniture) housse f; (shelter) abri m; **to take ~** se mettre à l'abri; **under ~** à l'abri; **under ~ of darkness** à la faveur de la nuit; **under separate ~** (COMM) sous pli séparé; **to ~ up for sb** couvrir qn; **~age** n (TV, PRESS) reportage m; **~ charge** n couvert m (supplément à payer); **~ing** n couche f; **~ing letter** (US **cover letter**) n lettre explicative; **~ note** n (INSURANCE) police f provisoire

**covert** ['kʌvət] adj (threat) voilé(e), caché(e); (glance) furtif(-ive)

**cover-up** ['kʌvərʌp] n tentative f pour étouffer une affaire

**covet** ['kʌvit] vt convoiter

**cow** [kau] n vache f ♦ vt effrayer, intimider

**coward** ['kauəd] n lâche m/f; **~ice** n lâcheté f; **~ly** adj lâche

**cowboy** ['kaubɔi] n cow-boy m

**cower** ['kauər] vi se recroqueviller

**coy** [kɔɪ] adj faussement effarouché(e) or timide

**cozy** ['kəʊzɪ] (US) adj = **cosy**

**CPA** (US) n abbr = **certified public accountant**

**crab** [kræb] n crabe m; **~ apple** n pomme f sauvage

**crack** [kræk] n (split) fente f, fissure f; (in cup, bone etc) fêlure f; (in wall) lézarde f; (noise) craquement m, coup (sec); (drug) crack m ♦ vt fendre, fissurer; fêler; lézarder; (whip) faire claquer; (nut) casser; (code) déchiffrer; (problem) résoudre ♦ adj (athlete) de première classe, d'élite; **~ down** on vt fus mettre un frein à; **~ up** vi être au bout du rouleau, s'effondrer; **~ed** adj (cup, bone) fêlé(es); (broken) cassé(e); (wall) lézardé(e); (surface) craquelé(e); (inf: mad) cinglé(e); **~er** n (Christmas cracker) pétard m; (biscuit) biscuit (salé)

**crackle** ['krækl] vi crépiter, grésiller

**cradle** ['kreɪdl] n berceau m

**craft** [krɑːft] n métier (artisanal); (pl inv: boat) embarcation f, barque f; (: plane) appareil m; **~sman** (irreg) n artisan m, ouvrier (qualifié); **~smanship** n travail m; **~y** adj rusé(e), malin(-igne)

**crag** [kræg] n rocher escarpé

**cram** [kræm] vt (fill): **to ~ sth with** bourrer qch de; (put): **to ~ sth into** fourrer qch dans ♦ vi (for exams) bachoter

**cramp** [kræmp] n crampe f ♦ vt gêner, entraver; **~ed** adj à l'étroit, très serré(e)

**cranberry** ['krænbərɪ] n canneberge f

**crane** [kreɪn] n grue f

**crank** [kræŋk] n manivelle f; (person) excentrique m/f

**cranny** ['krænɪ] n see **nook**

**crash** [kræʃ] n fracas m; (of car) collision f; (of plane) accident m ♦ vt avoir un accident avec ♦ vi (plane) s'écraser; (two cars) se percuter, s'emboutir; (COMM) s'effondrer; **to ~ into** se jeter or se fracasser contre; **~ course** n cours intensif; **~ helmet** n casque (protecteur); **~**

**landing** n atterrissage forcé or en catastrophe

**crate** [kreɪt] n cageot m; (for bottles) caisse f

**cravat(e)** [krə'væt] n foulard (noué autour du cou)

**crave** [kreɪv] vt, vi: **to ~ (for)** avoir une envie irrésistible de

**crawl** [krɔːl] vi ramper; (vehicle) avancer au pas ♦ n (SWIMMING) crawl m

**crayfish** ['kreɪfɪʃ] n inv (freshwater) écrevisse f; (saltwater) langoustine f

**crayon** ['kreɪən] n crayon m (de couleur)

**craze** [kreɪz] n engouement m

**crazy** ['kreɪzɪ] adj fou (folle)

**creak** [kriːk] vi grincer, craquer

**cream** [kriːm] n crème f ♦ adj (colour) crème inv; **~ cake** n (petit) gâteau m à la crème; **~ cheese** n fromage m à la crème, fromage blanc; **~y** adj crémeux(-euse)

**crease** [kriːs] n pli m ♦ vt froisser, chiffonner ♦ vi se froisser, se chiffonner

**create** [kriː'eɪt] vt créer; **creation** n création f; **creative** adj (artistic) créatif(-ive); (ingenious) ingénieux (-euse)

**creature** ['kriːtʃə] n créature f

**crèche** [kreʃ] n garderie f, crèche f

**credence** ['kriːdns] n: **to lend** or **give ~ to** ajouter foi à

**credentials** [krɪ'denʃlz] npl (references) références fpl; (papers of identity) pièce f d'identité

**credit** ['kredɪt] n crédit m; (recognition) honneur m ♦ vt (COMM) créditer; (believe: also: **give ~ to**) ajouter foi à, croire; **~s** npl (CINEMA, TV) générique m; **to be in ~** (person, bank account) être créditeur(-trice); **to ~ sb with** (fig) prêter or attribuer à qn; **~ card** n carte f de crédit; **~or** n créancier(-ière)

**creed** [kriːd] n croyance f; credo m

**creek** [kriːk] n crique f, anse f; (US: stream) ruisseau m, petit cours d'eau

**creep** [kriːp] (pt, pp **crept**) vi ramper;

**~er** n plante grimpante; **~y** adj (frightening) qui fait frissonner, qui donne la chair de poule

**cremate** [krɪ'meɪt] vt incinérer; **crematorium** [kremə'tɔːrɪəm] (pl **crematoria**) n four m crématoire

**crêpe** [kreɪp] n crêpe m; **~ bandage** (BRIT) n bande f Velpeau ®

**crept** [krept] pt, pp of **creep**

**crescent** ['kresnt] n croissant m; (street) rue f (en arc de cercle)

**cress** [kres] n cresson m

**crest** [krest] n crête f; **~fallen** adj déconfit(e), découragé(e)

**Crete** [kriːt] n Crète f

**crevice** ['krevɪs] n fissure f, lézarde f, fente f

**crew** [kruː] n équipage m; (CINEMA) équipe f; **~-cut** n: **to have a ~-cut** avoir les cheveux en brosse; **~-neck** n col ras du cou

**crib** [krɪb] n lit m d'enfant; (for baby) berceau m ♦ vt (inf) copier

**crick** [krɪk] n: **~ in the neck** torticolis m; **~ in the back** tour m de reins

**cricket** ['krɪkɪt] n (insect) grillon m, cri-cri m inv; (game) cricket m

**crime** [kraɪm] n crime m; **criminal** ['krɪmɪnl] adj, n criminel(le)

**crimson** ['krɪmzn] adj cramoisi(e)

**cringe** [krɪndʒ] vi avoir un mouvement de recul

**crinkle** ['krɪŋkl] vt froisser, chiffonner

**cripple** ['krɪpl] n boiteux(-euse), infirme m/f ♦ vt estropier

**crisis** ['kraɪsɪs] (pl **crises**) n crise f

**crisp** [krɪsp] adj croquant(e); (weather) vif (vive); (manner etc) brusque; **~s** (BRIT) npl (pommes) chips fpl

**crisscross** ['krɪskrɔs] adj entrecroisé(e)

**criterion** [kraɪ'tɪərɪən] (pl **criteria**) n critère m

**critic** ['krɪtɪk] n critique m; **~al** adj critique; **~ally** adv (examine) d'un œil critique; (speak etc) sévèrement; **~ally ill** gravement malade; **~ism** ['krɪtɪsɪzm] n critique f; **~ize** ['krɪtɪsaɪz] vt critiquer

**croak** [krəuk] vi (frog) coasser; (raven) croasser; (person) parler d'une voix rauque

**Croatia** [krəu'eɪʃə] n Croatie f

**crochet** ['krəuʃeɪ] n travail m au crochet

**crockery** ['krɔkərɪ] n vaisselle f

**crocodile** ['krɔkədaɪl] n crocodile m

**crocus** ['krəukəs] n crocus m

**croft** [krɔft] (BRIT) n petite ferme

**crony** ['krəunɪ] (inf: pej) n copain (copine)

**crook** [kruk] n escroc m; (of shepherd) houlette f; **~ed** ['krukɪd] adj courbé(e), tordu(e); (action) malhonnête

**crop** [krɔp] n (produce) culture f; (amount produced) récolte f; (riding ~) cravache f ♦ vt (hair) tondre; **~ up** vi surgir, se présenter, survenir

**cross** [krɔs] n croix f; (BIO etc) croisement m ♦ vt (street etc) traverser; (arms, legs, BIO) croiser; (cheque) barrer ♦ adj en colère, fâché(e); **~ out** vt barrer, biffer; **~ over** vi traverser; **~bar** n barre (transversale); **~-country (race)** n cross(-country); **~-examine** vt (LAW) faire subir un examen contradictoire à; **~-eyed** adj qui louche; **~fire** n feux croisés; **~ing** n (sea passage) traversée f; (also: **pedestrian ~ing**) passage clouté; **~ing guard** (US) n contractuel qui fait traverser la rue aux enfants; **~ purposes** npl: **to be at ~ purposes with sb** comprendre qn de travers; **~-reference** n renvoi m, référence f; **~roads** n carrefour m; **~ section** n (of object) coupe transversale; (in population) échantillon m; **~walk** (US) n passage clouté; **~wind** n vent m de travers; **~word** n mots mpl croisés

**crotch** [krɔtʃ] n (ANAT, of garment) entre-jambes m inv

**crouch** [krautʃ] vi s'accroupir; se tapir

**crow** [krəu] n (bird) corneille f; (of cock) chant m du coq, cocorico m ♦ vi (cock) chanter

**crowbar** ['krəubɑː] n levier m

**crowd** [kraud] *n* foule *f* ♦ *vt* remplir ♦ *vi* affluer, s'attrouper, s'entasser; **to ~ in** entrer en foule; **~ed** *adj* bondé(e), plein(e)

**crown** [kraun] *n* couronne *f*; (*of head*) sommet *m* de la tête; (*of hill*) sommet ♦ *vt* couronner; **~ jewels** *npl* joyaux *mpl* de la Couronne

**crow's-feet** ['krəuzfi:t] *npl* pattes *fpl* d'oie

**crucial** ['kru:ʃl] *adj* crucial(e), décisif (-ive)

**crucifix** ['kru:sɪfɪks] *n* (REL) crucifix *m*; **~ion** [kru:sɪ'fɪkʃən] *n* (REL) crucifixion *f*

**crude** [kru:d] *adj* (*materials*) brut(e); non raffiné(e); (*fig: basic*) rudimentaire, sommaire; (: *vulgar*) cru(e), grossier (-ère); **~ (oil)** *n* (pétrole) brut *m*

**cruel** ['kruəl] *adj* cruel(le); **~ty** *n* cruauté *f*

**cruise** [kru:z] *n* croisière ♦ *vi* (*ship*) croiser; (*car*) rouler; **~r** *n* croiseur *m*; (*motorboat*) yacht *m* de croisière

**crumb** [krʌm] *n* miette *f*

**crumble** ['krʌmbl] *vt* émietter ♦ *vi* (*plaster etc*) s'effriter; (*land, earth*) s'ébouler; (*building*) s'écrouler, crouler; (*fig*) s'effondrer; **crumbly** *adj* friable

**crumpet** ['krʌmpɪt] *n* petite crêpe (épaisse)

**crumple** ['krʌmpl] *vt* froisser, friper

**crunch** [krʌntʃ] *vt* croquer; (*underfoot*) faire craquer ou crisser, écraser ♦ *n* (*fig*) instant *m* ou moment *m* critique, moment *m* de vérité; **~y** *adj* croquant(e), croustillant(e)

**crusade** [kru:'seɪd] *n* croisade *f*

**crush** [krʌʃ] *n* foule *f*, cohue *f*; (*love*): **to have a ~ on sb** avoir le béguin pour qn (*inf*); (*drink*): **lemon ~** citron pressé ♦ *vt* écraser; (*crumple*) froisser; (*fig: hopes*) anéantir

**crust** [krʌst] *n* croûte *f*

**crutch** [krʌtʃ] *n* béquille *f*

**crux** [krʌks] *n* point crucial

**cry** [kraɪ] *vi* pleurer; (*shout: also: ~ out*) crier ♦ *n* cri *m*; **~ off** (*inf*) *vi* se dédire,

se décommander

**cryptic** ['krɪptɪk] *adj* énigmatique

**crystal** ['krɪstl] *n* cristal *m*; **~-clear** *adj* clair(e) comme de l'eau de roche

**CSA** *n abbr* (= *Child Support Agency*) *organisme pour la protection des enfants de parents séparés, qui contrôle le versement des pensions alimentaires*

**CTC** *n abbr* = **city technology college**

**cub** [kʌb] *n* petit *m* (*d'un animal*); (*also:* **C~ scout**) louveteau *m*

**Cuba** ['kju:bə] *n* Cuba *m*

**cube** [kju:b] *n* cube *m* ♦ *vt* (MATH) élever au cube; **cubic** *adj* cubique; **cubic metre** *etc* mètre *m etc* cube; **cubic capacity** *n* cylindrée *f*

**cubicle** ['kju:bɪkl] *n* (*in hospital*) box *m*; (*at pool*) cabine *f*

**cuckoo** ['kuku:] *n* coucou *m*; **~ clock** *n* (pendule *f* à) coucou *m*

**cucumber** ['kju:kʌmbər] *n* concombre *m*

**cuddle** ['kʌdl] *vt* câliner, caresser ♦ *vi* se blottir l'un contre l'autre

**cue** [kju:] *n* (*snooker ~*) queue *f* de billard; (THEATRE *etc*) signal *m*

**cuff** [kʌf] *n* (BRIT: *of shirt, coat etc*) poignet *m*, manchette *f*; (US: *of trousers*) revers *m*; (*blow*) tape *f*; **off the ~** à l'improviste; **~ links** *npl* boutons *mpl* de manchette

**cul-de-sac** ['kʌldəsæk] *n* cul-de-sac *m*, impasse *f*

**cull** [kʌl] *vt* sélectionner ♦ *n* (*of animals*) massacre *m*

**culminate** ['kʌlmɪneɪt] *vi*: **to ~ in** finir or se terminer par; (*end in*) mener à; **culmination** [kʌlmɪ'neɪʃən] *n* point culminant

**culottes** [kju:'lɔts] *npl* jupe-culotte *f*

**culprit** ['kʌlprɪt] *n* coupable *m/f*

**cult** [kʌlt] *n* culte *m*

**cultivate** ['kʌltɪveɪt] *vt* cultiver; **cultivation** [kʌltɪ'veɪʃən] *n* culture *f*

**cultural** ['kʌltʃərəl] *adj* culturel(le)

**culture** ['kʌltʃər] *n* culture *f*; **~d** *adj* (*person*) cultivé(e)

**cumbersome** ['kʌmbəsəm] adj encombrant(e), embarrassant(e)

**cunning** ['kʌnɪŋ] n ruse f, astuce f ♦ adj rusé(e), malin(-igne); (device, idea) astucieux(-euse)

**cup** [kʌp] n tasse f; (as prize) coupe f; (of bra) bonnet m

**cupboard** ['kʌbəd] n armoire f; (built-in) placard m

**cup tie** (BRIT) n match m de coupe

**curate** ['kjuərɪt] n vicaire m

**curator** [kjuə'reɪtər] n conservateur m (d'un musée etc)

**curb** [kə:b] vt refréner, mettre un frein à ♦ n (fig) frein m, restriction f; (US: kerb) bord m du trottoir

**curdle** ['kə:dl] vi se cailler

**cure** [kjuər] vt guérir; (CULIN: salt) saler; (: smoke) fumer; (: dry) sécher ♦ n remède m

**curfew** ['kə:fju:] n couvre-feu m

**curiosity** [kjuərɪ'ɒsɪtɪ] n curiosité f

**curious** ['kjuərɪəs] adj curieux(-euse)

**curl** [kə:l] n boucle f (de cheveux) ♦ vt, vi boucler; (tightly) friser; **~ up** vi s'enrouler; se pelotonner; **~er** n bigoudi m, rouleau m; **~y** adj bouclé(e); frisé(e)

**currant** ['kʌrnt] n (dried) raisin m de Corinthe, raisin sec; (bush) groseillier m; (fruit) groseille f

**currency** ['kʌrnsɪ] n monnaie f; **to gain ~** (fig) s'accréditer

**current** ['kʌrnt] n courant m ♦ adj courant(e); **~ account** n (BRIT) compte courant; **~ affairs** npl (questions fpl d'actualité f; **~ly** adv actuellement

**curriculum** [kə'rɪkjuləm] (pl **~s** or **curricula**) n programme m d'études; **~ vitae** n curriculum vitae m

**curry** ['kʌrɪ] n curry m ♦ vt: **to ~ favour with** chercher à s'attirer les bonnes grâces de

**curse** [kə:s] vi jurer, blasphémer ♦ vt maudire ♦ n (spell) malédiction f; (problem, scourge) fléau m; (swearword) juron m

**cursor** ['kə:sər] n (COMPUT) curseur m

**cursory** ['kə:sərɪ] adj superficiel(le), hâtif(-ive)

**curt** [kə:t] adj brusque, sec (sèche)

**curtail** [kə:'teɪl] vt (visit etc) écourter; (expenses, freedom etc) réduire

**curtain** ['kə:tn] n rideau m

**curts(e)y** ['kə:tsɪ] vi faire une révérence

**curve** [kə:v] n courbe f; (in the road) tournant m, virage m ♦ vi se courber; (road) faire une courbe

**cushion** ['kuʃən] n coussin m ♦ vt (fall, shock) amortir

**custard** ['kʌstəd] n (for pouring) crème anglaise

**custody** ['kʌstədɪ] n (of child) garde f; **to take sb into ~** (suspect) placer qn en détention préventive

**custom** ['kʌstəm] n coutume f, usage m; (COMM) clientèle f; **~ary** adj habituel(le)

**customer** ['kʌstəmər] n client(e)

**customized** ['kʌstəmaɪzd] adj (car etc) construit(e) sur commande

**custom-made** ['kʌstəm'meɪd] adj (clothes) fait(e) sur mesure; (other goods) hors série, fait(e) sur commande

**customs** ['kʌstəmz] npl douane f; **~ officer** n douanier(-ière)

**cut** [kʌt] (pt, pp **cut**) vt couper; (meat) découper; (reduce) réduire ♦ vi couper ♦ n coupure f; (of clothes) coupe f; (in salary etc) réduction f; (of meat) morceau m; **to ~ one's hand** se couper la main; **to ~ a tooth** percer une dent; **~ down** vt fus (tree etc) couper, abattre; (consumption) réduire; **~ off** vt couper; (fig) isoler; **~ out** vt découper; (stop) arrêter; (remove) ôter; **~ up** vt (paper, meat) découper; **~back** n réduction f

**cute** [kju:t] adj mignon(ne), adorable

**cutlery** ['kʌtlərɪ] n couverts mpl

**cutlet** ['kʌtlɪt] n côtelette f

**cut:** **~out** n (switch) coupe-circuit m inv; (cardboard cutout) découpage m; **~-price** (US **cut-rate**) adj au rabais, à prix réduit; **~throat** n assassin m ♦ adj acharné(e); **~ting** adj tranchant(e), coupant(e); (fig) cinglant(e), mordant(e) ♦ n (BRIT: from newspaper) coupure f (de journal); (from plant) bouture f

**CV** n abbr = **curriculum vitae**

**cwt** abbr = **hundredweight(s)**

**cyanide** ['saɪənaɪd] n cyanure m

**cybercafé** ['saɪbəkæfeɪ] n cybercafé m

**cyberspace** ['saɪbəspeɪs] n cyberspace m

**cycle** ['saɪkl] n cycle m; (bicycle) bicyclette f, vélo m ♦ vi faire de la bicyclette; ~ **hire** n location f de vélos; ~ **lane** or **path** n piste f cyclable; **cycling** n cyclisme m; **cyclist** ['saɪklɪst] n cycliste m/f

**cygnet** ['sɪgnɪt] n jeune cygne m

**cylinder** ['sɪlɪndə'] n cylindre m; ~**head gasket** n joint m de culasse

**cymbals** ['sɪmblz] npl cymbales fpl

**cynic** ['sɪnɪk] n cynique m/f; ~**al** adj cynique; ~**ism** ['sɪnɪsɪzəm] n cynisme m

**Cypriot** ['sɪprɪət] adj cypriote, chypriote ♦ n Cypriote m/f, Chypriote m/f

**Cyprus** ['saɪprəs] n Chypre f

**cyst** [sɪst] n kyste m

**cystitis** [sɪs'taɪtɪs] n cystite f

**czar** [zɑː'] n tsar m

**Czech** [tʃɛk] adj tchèque ♦ n Tchèque m/f; (LING) tchèque m

**Czechoslovak** [tʃɛkə'sləʊvæk] adj tchécoslovaque ♦ n Tchécoslovaque m/f

**Czechoslovakia** [tʃɛkəslə'vækɪə] n Tchécoslovaquie f

---

# D, d

**D** [diː] n (MUS) ré m

**dab** [dæb] vt (eyes, wound) tamponner; (paint, cream) appliquer (par petites touches or rapidement)

**dabble** ['dæbl] vi: **to ~ in** faire or se mêler or s'occuper un peu de

**dad** [dæd] n, **daddy** [dædɪ] n papa m

**daffodil** ['dæfədɪl] n jonquille f

**daft** [dɑːft] adj idiot(e), stupide

---

**dagger** ['dægə'] n poignard m

**daily** ['deɪlɪ] adj quotidien(ne), journalier(-ère) ♦ n quotidien m ♦ adv tous les jours

**dainty** ['deɪntɪ] adj délicat(e), mignon(ne)

**dairy** ['dɛərɪ] n (BRIT: shop) crémerie f, laiterie f; (on farm) laiterie; ~ **products** npl produits laitiers; ~ **store** (US) n crémerie f, laiterie f

**daisy** ['deɪzɪ] n pâquerette f

**dale** [deɪl] n vallon m

**dam** [dæm] n barrage m ♦ vt endiguer

**damage** ['dæmɪdʒ] n dégâts mpl, dommages mpl; (fig) tort m ♦ vt endommager, abîmer; (fig) faire du tort à; ~**s** npl (LAW) dommages-intérêts mpl

**damn** [dæm] vt condamner; (curse) maudire ♦ n (inf): **I don't give a ~** je m'en fous ♦ adj (inf: also: ~**ed**): **this ~** ... ce sacré or foutu ...; ~ **(it)!** zut!; ~**ing** adj accablant(e)

**damp** [dæmp] adj humide ♦ n humidité f ♦ vt (also: ~**en**: cloth, rag) humecter; (: enthusiasm) refroidir

**damson** ['dæmzən] n prune f de Damas

**dance** [dɑːns] n danse f; (social event) bal m ♦ vi danser; ~ **hall** n salle f de bal, dancing m; ~**r** n danseur(-euse)

**dancing** n danse f

**dandelion** ['dændɪlaɪən] n pissenlit m

**dandruff** ['dændrəf] n pellicules fpl

**Dane** [deɪn] n Danois(e)

**danger** ['deɪndʒə'] n danger m; **there is a ~ of fire** il y a (un) risque d'incendie; **in ~** en danger; **he was in ~ of falling** il risquait de tomber; ~**ous** adj dangereux(-euse)

**dangle** ['dæŋgl] vt balancer ♦ vi pendre

**Danish** ['deɪnɪʃ] adj danois(e) ♦ n (LING) danois m

**dare** [dɛə'] vt: **to ~ sb to do** défier qn de faire ♦ vi: **to ~ (to) do sth** oser faire qch; **I ~ say** (I suppose) il est probable (que); **daring** adj hardi(e), audacieux(-euse); (dress) osé(e) ♦ n audace f, hardiesse f

**dark** [dɑːk] *adj* (*night, room*) obscur(e), sombre; (*colour, complexion*) foncé(e), sombre ♦ *n*: **in the ~** dans le noir; **in the ~ about** (*fig*) ignorant tout de; **after ~** après la tombée de la nuit; **~en** *vt* obscurcir, assombrir ♦ *vi* s'obscurcir, s'assombrir; **~ glasses** *npl* lunettes noires; **~ness** *n* obscurité f; **~room** *n* chambre noire

**darling** [ˈdɑːlɪŋ] *adj* chéri(e) ♦ *n* chéri(e); (*favourite*): **to be the ~ of** être la coqueluche de

**darn** [dɑːn] *vt* repriser, raccommoder

**dart** [dɑːt] *n* fléchette f; (*sewing*) pince f ♦ *vi*: **to ~ towards** (*also*: **make a ~ towards**) se précipiter *or* s'élancer vers; **to ~ away/along** partir/passer comme une flèche; **~board** *n* cible f (de jeu de fléchettes); **~s** *n* (jeu m de) fléchettes *fpl*

**dash** [dæʃ] *n* (*sign*) tiret m; (*small quantity*) goutte f, larme f ♦ *vt* (*missile*) jeter *or* lancer violemment; (*hopes*) anéantir ♦ *vi*: **to ~ towards** (*also*: **make a ~ towards**) se précipiter *or* se ruer vers; **~ away** *vi* partir à toute allure, filer; **~ off** *vi* = dash away

**dashboard** [ˈdæʃbɔːd] *n* (*AUT*) tableau m de bord

**dashing** [ˈdæʃɪŋ] *adj* fringant(e)

**data** [ˈdeɪtə] *npl* données *fpl*; **~base** *n* (*COMPUT*) base f de données; **~ processing** *n* traitement m de données

**date** [deɪt] *n* date f; (*with sb*) rendez-vous m; (*fruit*) datte f ♦ *vt* dater; (*person*) sortir avec; **~ of birth** date de naissance; **to ~** (*until now*) à ce jour; **out of ~** (*passport*) périmé(e); (*theory etc*) dépassé(e); (*clothes etc*) démodé(e); **up to ~** moderne; (*news*) très récent; **~d** [ˈdeɪtɪd] *adj* démodé(e); **~ rape** *n* viol m (à l'issue d'un rendez-vous galant)

**daub** [dɔːb] *vt* barbouiller

**daughter** [ˈdɔːtər] *n* fille f; **~-in-law** *n* belle-fille f, bru f

**daunting** [ˈdɔːntɪŋ] *adj* décourageant(e)

**dawdle** [ˈdɔːdl] *vi* traîner, lambiner

**dawn** [dɔːn] *n* aube f, aurore f ♦ *vi* (*day*) se lever, poindre; (*fig*): **it ~ed on him that ...** il lui vint à l'esprit que ...

**day** [deɪ] *n* jour m; (*as duration*) journée f; (*period of time, age*) époque f, temps m; **the ~ before** la veille, le jour précédent; **the ~ after, the following ~** le lendemain, le jour suivant; **the ~ after tomorrow** après-demain; **the ~ before yesterday** avant-hier; **by ~** de jour; **~break** n point m du jour; **~dream** *vi* rêver (tout éveillé); **~light** n (lumière f du) jour m; **~ return** (BRIT) n billet m d'aller-retour (valable pour la journée); **~time** n jour m, journée f; **~-to-** *adj* quotidien(ne); (*event*) journalier(-ère)

**daze** [deɪz] *vt* (*stun*) étourdir ♦ *n*: **in a ~** étourdi(e), hébété(e)

**dazzle** [ˈdæzl] *vt* éblouir, aveugler

**DC** *abbr* (= *direct current*) courant continu

**D-day** [ˈdiːdeɪ] n le jour J

**dead** [ded] *adj* mort(e); (*numb*) engourdi(e), insensible; (*battery*) à plat; (*telephone*): **the line is ~** la ligne est coupée ♦ *adv* absolument, complètement ♦ *npl*: **the ~** les morts; **he was shot ~** il a été tué d'un coup de revolver; **~ on time** à l'heure pile; **~ tired** éreinté(e), complètement fourbu(e); **to stop ~** s'arrêter pile *or* net; **~en** *vt* (*blow, sound*) amortir; (*pain*) calmer; **~ end** n impasse f; **~ heat** n (*SPORT*): **to finish in a ~ heat** terminer ex-æquo; **~line** n date f *or* heure f limite; **~lock** (*fig*) n impasse f; **~ loss** n: **to be a ~ loss** (*inf: person*) n'être bon(ne) à rien; **~ly** *adj* mortel(le); (*weapon*) meurtrier(-ère); (*accuracy*) extrême; **~pan** *adj* impassible; **D~ Sea** n: **the D~ Sea** la mer Morte

**deaf** [def] *adj* sourd(e); **~en** *vt* rendre sourd; **~ening** *adj* assourdissant(e); **~-**

**mute** n sourd(e)-muet(te); **~ness** n surdité f

**deal** [di:l] (pt, pp dealt) n affaire f, marché m ♦ vt (blow) porter; (cards) donner, distribuer; **a great ~ (of)** beaucoup (de); **~ in** vt fus faire le commerce de; **~ with** vt fus (person, problem) s'occuper de, se charger de; (be about: book etc) traiter de; **~er** n marchand m; **~ings** npl (COMM) transactions fpl; (relations) relations fpl, rapports mpl

**dean** [di:n] n (REL, BRIT: SCOL) doyen m; (US: SCOL) conseiller(-ère) (principal(e)) d'éducation

**dear** [dɪəʳ] adj cher (chère); (expensive) cher, coûteux(-euse) ♦ n: **my ~** mon cher/ma chère; **~ me!** mon Dieu!; **D~ Sir/Madam** (in letter) Monsieur/ Madame; **D~ Mr/Mrs X** Cher Monsieur/Chère Madame; **~ly** adv (love) tendrement; (pay) cher

**death** [deθ] n mort f; (fatality) mort m; (ADMIN) décès m; **~ certificate** n acte m de décès; **~ly** adj de mort; **~ penalty** n peine f de mort; **~ rate** n (taux m de) mortalité f; **~ toll** n nombre m de morts

**debase** [dɪˈbeɪs] vt (value) déprécier, dévaloriser

**debatable** [dɪˈbeɪtəbl] adj discutable

**debate** [dɪˈbeɪt] n discussion f, débat m ♦ vt discuter, débattre

**debit** [ˈdebɪt] n débit m ♦ vt: **to ~ a sum to sb or to sb's account** porter une somme au débit de qn, débiter qn d'une somme; see also **direct**

**debt** [det] n dette f; **to be in ~** avoir des dettes, être endetté(e); **~or** n débiteur(-trice)

**decade** [ˈdekeɪd] n décennie f, décade f

**decadence** [ˈdekədəns] n décadence f

**decaff** [ˈdiːkæf] (inf) n déca m

**decaffeinated** [dɪˈkæfɪneɪtɪd] adj décaféiné(e)

**decanter** [dɪˈkæntəʳ] n carafe f

**decay** [dɪˈkeɪ] n (of building) délabrement m; (also: **tooth ~**) carie f (dentai-

re) ♦ vi (rot) se décomposer, pourrir; (: teeth) se carier

**deceased** [dɪˈsiːst] n défunt(e)

**deceit** [dɪˈsiːt] n tromperie f, supercherie f; **~ful** adj trompeur(-euse); **deceive** vt tromper

**December** [dɪˈsembəʳ] n décembre m

**decent** [ˈdiːsənt] adj décent(e), convenable

**deception** [dɪˈsepʃən] n tromperie f

**deceptive** [dɪˈseptɪv] adj trompeur (-euse)

**decide** [dɪˈsaɪd] vt (person) décider; (question, argument) trancher, régler ♦ vi se décider, décider; **to ~ to do/that** décider de faire/que; **to ~ on** décider, se décider pour; **~d** adj (resolute) résolu(e), décidé(e); (clear, definite) net(te), marqué(e); **~dly** adv résolument; (distinctly) incontestablement, nettement

**deciduous** [dɪˈsɪdjuəs] adj à feuilles caduques

**decimal** [ˈdesɪml] adj décimal(e) ♦ n décimale f; **~ point** n ≈ virgule f

**decipher** [dɪˈsaɪfəʳ] vt déchiffrer

**decision** [dɪˈsɪʒən] n décision f

**decisive** [dɪˈsaɪsɪv] adj décisif(-ive); (person) décidé(e)

**deck** [dek] n (NAUT) pont m; (verandah) véranda f; (of bus): **top ~** impériale f; (of cards) jeu m; (record) platine f; **~chair** n chaise longue

**declare** [dɪˈklɛəʳ] vt déclarer

**decline** [dɪˈklaɪn] n (decay) déclin m; (lessening) baisse f ♦ vt refuser, décliner ♦ vi décliner; (business) baisser

**decoder** [diːˈkəʊdəʳ] n (TV) décodeur m

**decorate** [ˈdekəreɪt] vt (adorn, give a medal to) décorer; (paint and paper) peindre et tapisser; **decoration** [dekəˈreɪʃən] n (medal etc, adornment) décoration f; **decorator** n peintre-décorateur m

**decoy** [ˈdiːkɔɪ] n piège m; (person) compère m

**decrease** [n ˈdiːkriːs, vb dɪˈkriːs] n: **~ (in)** diminution f (de) ♦ vt, vi diminuer

**decree** [dɪˈkriː] n (POL, REL) décret m; (LAW) arrêt m, jugement m; ~ **nisi** [-ˈnaɪsaɪ] n jugement m provisoire de divorce

**dedicate** [ˈdedɪkeɪt] vt consacrer; (book etc) dédier; ~**d** adj (person) dévoué(e); (COMPUT) spécialisé(e), dédié(e); **dedication** [dedɪˈkeɪʃən] n (devotion) dévouement m; (in book) dédicace f

**deduce** [dɪˈdjuːs] vt déduire, conclure

**deduct** [dɪˈdʌkt] vt: **to ~ sth (from)** déduire qch (de), retrancher qch (de); ~**ion** n (deducting, deducing) déduction f; (from wage etc) prélèvement m, retenue f

**deed** [diːd] n action f, acte m; (LAW) acte notarié, contrat m

**deep** [diːp] adj profond(e); (voice) grave ♦ adv: spectators stood 20 ~ il y avait 20 rangs de spectateurs; **4 metres** ~ de 4 mètres de profondeur; ~ **end** (of swimming pool) grand bain; ~**en** vt approfondir ♦ vi (fig) s'approfondir; ~**freeze** n congélateur m; ~**fry** vt faire frire (en friteuse); ~**ly** adv profondément; (interested) vivement; ~**sea diver** n sous-marin(e); ~**sea diving** n plongée sous-marine; ~**sea fishing** n grande pêche; ~**seated** adj profond(e), profondément enraciné(e)

**deer** [dɪəʳ] n inv: (**red**) ~ cerf m, biche f; (**fallow**) ~ daim m; (**roe**) ~ chevreuil m; ~**skin** n daim

**deface** [dɪˈfeɪs] vt dégrader; (notice, poster) barbouiller

**default** [dɪˈfɔːlt] n (COMPUT: also: ~ **value**) valeur f par défaut; **by ~** (LAW) par défaut, par contumace; (SPORT) par forfait

**defeat** [dɪˈfiːt] n défaite f ♦ vt (team, opponents) battre

**defect** [n ˈdiːfekt, vb dɪˈfekt] n défaut m ♦ vi: **to ~ to the enemy** passer à l'ennemi; ~**ive** [dɪˈfektɪv] adj défectueux(-euse)

**defence** [dɪˈfens] (US **defense**) n défense f; ~**less** adj sans défense

**defend** [dɪˈfend] vt défendre; ~**ant** n défendeur(-deresse); (in criminal case) accusé(e), prévenu(e); ~**er** n défenseur m

**defer** [dɪˈfəːʳ] vt (postpone) différer, ajourner

**defiance** [dɪˈfaɪəns] n défi m; **in ~ of** au mépris de; **defiant** adj provocant(e), de défi; (person) rebelle, intraitable

**deficiency** [dɪˈfɪʃənsɪ] n insuffisance f, déficience f; **deficient** adj (inadequate) insuffisant(e); **to be deficient in** manquer de

**deficit** [ˈdefɪsɪt] n déficit m

**define** [dɪˈfaɪn] vt définir

**definite** [ˈdefɪnɪt] adj (fixed) défini(e), (bien) déterminé(e); (clear, obvious) net(te), manifeste; (certain) sûr(e); **he was ~ about it** il a été catégorique; ~**ly** adv sans aucun doute

**definition** [defɪˈnɪʃən] n définition f; (clearness) netteté f

**deflate** [diːˈfleɪt] vt dégonfler

**deflect** [dɪˈflekt] vt détourner, faire dévier

**deformed** [dɪˈfɔːmd] adj difforme

**defraud** [dɪˈfrɔːd] vt frauder; **to ~ sb of sth** escroquer qch à qn

**defrost** [diːˈfrɒst] vt dégivrer; (food) décongeler; ~**er** (US) n (demister) dispositif m anti-buée inv

**deft** [deft] adj adroit(e), preste

**defunct** [dɪˈfʌŋkt] adj défunt(e)

**defuse** [diːˈfjuːz] vt désamorcer

**defy** [dɪˈfaɪ] vt défier; (efforts etc) résister à

**degenerate** [vb dɪˈdʒenəreɪt, adj dɪˈdʒenərɪt] vi dégénérer ♦ adj dégénéré(e)

**degree** [dɪˈgriː] n degré m; (SCOL) diplôme m (universitaire); **a (first) ~ in maths** une licence en maths; **by ~s** (gradually) par degrés; **to some ~, to a certain ~** jusqu'à un certain point, dans une certaine mesure

**dehydrated** [diːhaɪˈdreɪtɪd] adj déshydraté(e); *(milk, eggs)* en poudre

**de-ice** [diːˈaɪs] *vt (windscreen)* dégivrer

**deign** [deɪn] *vi:* to ~ to do daigner faire

**dejected** [dɪˈdʒektɪd] *adj* abattu(e), déprimé(e)

**delay** [dɪˈleɪ] *vt* retarder ♦ *vi* s'attarder ♦ *n* délai *m*, retard *m*; to be ~ed être en retard

**delectable** [dɪˈlektəbl] *adj* délicieux (-euse)

**delegate** [*n* ˈdelɪgɪt, *vb* ˈdelɪgeɪt] *n* délégué(e) ♦ *vt* déléguer

**delete** [dɪˈliːt] *vt* rayer, supprimer

**deliberate** [*adj* dɪˈlɪbərɪt, *vb* dɪˈlɪbəreɪt] *adj (intentional)* délibéré(e); *(slow)* mesuré(e) ♦ *vi* délibérer, réfléchir; **~ly** [dɪˈlɪbərɪtlɪ] *adv (on purpose)* exprès, délibérément

**delicacy** [ˈdelɪkəsɪ] *n* délicatesse *f*; *(food)* mets *m* fin ou délicat, friandise *f*

**delicate** [ˈdelɪkɪt] *adj* délicat(e)

**delicatessen** [delɪkəˈtesn] *n* épicerie fine

**delicious** [dɪˈlɪʃəs] *adj* délicieux(-euse)

**delight** [dɪˈlaɪt] *n* (grande) joie, grand plaisir *m* ♦ *vt* enchanter; **to take (a)** ~ **in** prendre grand plaisir à; **~ed** *adj:* **~ed (at** *ou* **with/to do)** ravi(e) (de/de faire); **~ful** *adj (person)* adorable; *(meal, evening)* merveilleux(-euse)

**delinquent** [dɪˈlɪŋkwənt] *adj, n* délinquant(e)

**delirious** [dɪˈlɪrɪəs] *adj:* **to be** ~ délirer

**deliver** [dɪˈlɪvəʳ] *vt (mail)* distribuer; *(goods)* livrer; *(message)* remettre; *(speech)* prononcer; *(MED: baby)* mettre au monde; **~y** *n* distribution *f*; livraison *f*; *(of speaker)* élocution *f*; *(MED)* accouchement *m*; **to take ~y of** prendre livraison de

**delude** [dɪˈluːd] *vt* tromper, leurrer; **delusion** *n* illusion *f*

**demand** [dɪˈmɑːnd] *vt* réclamer, exiger ♦ *n* exigence *f*; *(claim)* revendication *f*; *(ECON)* demande *f*; **in** ~ demandé(e), recherché(e); **on** ~ sur demande; **~ing**

*adj (person)* exigeant(e); *(work)* astreignant(e)

**demean** [dɪˈmiːn] *vt:* **to** ~ **o.s.** s'abaisser

**demeanour** [dɪˈmiːnəʳ] *(US* **demeanor)** *n* comportement *m*; maintien *m*

**demented** [dɪˈmentɪd] *adj* dément(e), fou (folle)

**demise** [dɪˈmaɪz] *n* mort *f*

**demister** [diːˈmɪstəʳ] *(BRIT) n (AUT)* dispositif *m* anti-buée *inv*

**demo** [ˈdeməu] *(inf) n abbr (=* demonstration) manif *f*

**democracy** [dɪˈmɔkrəsɪ] *n* démocratie *f*; **democrat** [ˈdeməkræt] *n* démocrate *m/f*; **democratic** [deməˈkrætɪk] *adj* démocratique

**demolish** [dɪˈmɔlɪʃ] *vt* démolir

**demonstrate** [ˈdemənstreɪt] *vt* démontrer, prouver; *(show)* faire une démonstration de ♦ *vi:* **to** ~ **(for/against)** manifester (en faveur de/contre); **demonstration** [demənˈstreɪʃən] *n* démonstration *f*, manifestation *f*; **demonstrator** *n (POL)* manifestant(e)

**demote** [dɪˈməut] *vt* rétrograder

**demure** [dɪˈmjuəʳ] *adj* sage, réservé(e)

**den** [den] *n* tanière *f*, antre *m*

**denial** [dɪˈnaɪəl] *n* démenti *m*; *(refusal)* dénégation *f*

**denim** [ˈdenɪm] *n* jean *m*; **~s** *npl (jeans)* (blue-)jean(s) *m(pl)*

**Denmark** [ˈdenmɑːk] *n* Danemark *m*

**denomination** [dɪnɔmɪˈneɪʃən] *n (of money)* valeur *f*; *(REL)* confession *f*

**denounce** [dɪˈnauns] *vt* dénoncer

**dense** [dens] *adj* dense; *(stupid)* obtus(e), bouché(e); **~ly** *adv:* **~ly populated** à forte densité de population; **density** [ˈdensɪtɪ] *n* densité *f*; **double/high-density diskette** disquette *f* double densité/haute densité

**dent** [dent] *n* bosse *f* ♦ *vt (also:* **make a** ~ **in)** cabosser

**dental** [ˈdentl] *adj* dentaire; ~ **surgeon** *n* (chirurgien(ne)) dentiste

**dentist** [ˈdentɪst] *n* dentiste *m/f*

**dentures** ['dɛntʃəz] *npl* dentier *m sg*

**deny** [dɪ'naɪ] *vt* nier; (*refuse*) refuser

**deodorant** [di:'əʊdərənt] *n* déodorant *m*, désodorisant *m*

**depart** [dɪ'pɑ:t] *vi* partir; **to ~ from** (*fig: differ from*) s'écarter de

**department** [dɪ'pɑ:tmənt] *n* (COMM) rayon *m*; (SCOL) section *f*; (POL) ministère *m*, département *m*; **~ store** *n* grand magasin

**departure** [dɪ'pɑ:tʃə] *n* départ *m*; **a new ~** une nouvelle voie; **~ lounge** *n* (*at airport*) salle *f* d'embarquement

**depend** [dɪ'pɛnd] *vi*: **to ~ on** dépendre de; (*rely on*) compter sur; **it ~s** cela dépend; **~ing on the result** selon le résultat; **~able** *adj* (*person*) sérieux (-euse), sûr(e); (*car, watch*) solide, fiable; **~ant** *n* personne *f* à charge; **~ent** *adj*: **to be ~ent (on)** dépendre (de) ♦ *n* = **dependant**

**depict** [dɪ'pɪkt] *vt* (CHEM, COMM, GEO) (*in picture*) représenter; (*in words*) (dé)peindre, décrire

**depleted** [dɪ'pli:tɪd] *adj* (*considerably*) réduit(e) or diminué(e)

**deport** [dɪ'pɔ:t] *vt* expulser

**deposit** [dɪ'pɒzɪt] *n* (CHEM, COMM, GEO) dépôt *m*; (*of ore, oil*) gisement *m*; (*part payment*) arrhes *fpl*, acompte *m*; (*on bottle etc*) consigne *f*; (*for hired goods etc*) cautionnement *m*, garantie *f* ♦ *vt* déposer; **~ account** *n* compte *m* sur livret

**depot** ['dɛpəʊ] *n* dépôt *m*; (US: RAIL) gare *f*

**depress** [dɪ'prɛs] *vt* déprimer; (*press down*) appuyer sur, abaisser; (*prices, wages*) faire baisser; **~ed** *adj* (*person*) déprimé(e); (*area*) en déclin, touché(e) par le sous-emploi; **~ing** *adj* déprimant(e); **~ion** *n* dépression *f*; (*hollow*) creux *m*

**deprivation** [dɛprɪ'veɪʃən] *n* privation *f*; (*loss*) perte *f*

**deprive** [dɪ'praɪv] *vt*: **to ~ sb of** priver qn de; **~d** *adj* déshérité(e)

**depth** [dɛpθ] *n* profondeur *f*; **in the ~s**

of despair au plus profond du désespoir; **to be out of one's ~** avoir perdu pied, nager

**deputize** ['dɛpjʊtaɪz] *vi*: **to ~ for** assurer l'intérim de

**deputy** ['dɛpjʊtɪ] *adj* adjoint(e) ♦ *n* (*second in command*) adjoint(e); (US: *also*: **~ sheriff**) shérif adjoint; **~ head** directeur adjoint, sous-directeur *m*

**derail** [dɪ'reɪl] *vt*: **to be ~ed** dérailler

**deranged** [dɪ'reɪndʒd] *adj*: **to be (mentally) ~** avoir le cerveau dérangé

**derby** ['dɑ:rbɪ] (US) *n* (*bowler hat*) (chapeau *m*) melon *m*

**derelict** ['dɛrɪlɪkt] *adj* abandonné(e), à l'abandon

**derisory** [dɪ'raɪsərɪ] *adj* (*sum*) dérisoire; (*smile, person*) moqueur(-euse)

**derive** [dɪ'raɪv] *vt*: **to ~ sth from** tirer qch de; trouver qch dans ♦ *vi*: **to ~ from** provenir de, dériver de

**derogatory** [dɪ'rɒgətərɪ] *adj* désobligeant(e); péjoratif(-ive)

**descend** [dɪ'sɛnd] *vt, vi* descendre; **to ~ from** descendre de, être issu(e) de; **to ~ to (doing) sth** s'abaisser à (faire) qch; **descent** *n* descente *f*; (*origin*) origine *f*

**describe** [dɪs'kraɪb] *vt* décrire; **description** [dɪs'krɪpʃən] *n* description *f*; (*sort*) sorte *f*, espèce *f*

**desecrate** ['dɛsɪkreɪt] *vt* profaner

**desert** [*n* 'dɛzət, *vb* dɪ'zɜ:t] *n* désert *m* ♦ *vt* déserter, abandonner ♦ *vi* (MIL) déserter; **~s** *npl*: **to get one's just ~s** n'avoir que ce qu'on mérite; **~er** [dɪ'zɜ:tə] *n* déserteur *m*; **~ion** [dɪ'zɜ:ʃən] *n* (MIL) désertion *f*; (LAW: *of spouse*) abandon *m* du domicile conjugal; **~ island** *n* île déserte

**deserve** [dɪ'zɜ:v] *vt* mériter; **deserving** *adj* (*person*) méritant(e); (*action, cause*) méritoire

**design** [dɪ'zaɪn] *n* (*sketch*) plan *m*, dessin *m*; (*layout, shape*) conception *f*, ligne *f*; (*pattern*) dessin *m*, motif(s) *m(pl)*; (COMM, art) design *m*, stylisme *m*; (*in-*

tention) dessein m ♦ vt dessiner; élaborer; **~er** n (TECH) concepteur-projeteur m; (ART) dessinateur(-trice), designer m; (fashion) styliste m/f

**desire** [dı'zaıə<sup>r</sup>] n désir m ♦ vt désirer

**desk** [desk] n (in office) bureau m; (for pupil) pupitre m; (BRIT: in shop, restaurant) caisse f; (in hotel, at airport) réception f; **~-top publishing** n publication assistée par ordinateur, PAO f

**desolate** ['desəlıt] adj désolé(e); (person) affligé(e)

**despair** [dıs'peə<sup>r</sup>] n désespoir m ♦ vi: to ~ of désespérer de

**despatch** [dıs'pætʃ] n, vt = **dispatch**

**desperate** ['despərıt] adj désespéré(e); (criminal) prêt(e) à tout; **to be ~ for sth/to do sth** avoir désespérément besoin de qch/de faire qch; **~ly** adv désespérément; (very) terriblement, extrêmement; **desperation** [despə'reıʃən] n désespoir m; **in (sheer) desperation** en désespoir de cause

**despicable** [dıs'pıkəbl] adj méprisable

**despise** [dıs'paız] vt mépriser

**despite** [dıs'paıt] prep malgré, en dépit de

**despondent** [dıs'pɔndənt] adj découragé(e), abattu(e)

**dessert** [dı'zə:t] n dessert m; **~spoon** n cuiller f à dessert

**destination** [destı'neıʃən] n destination f

**destined** ['destınd] adj: **to be ~ to do/for sth** être destiné(e) à faire/à qch

**destiny** ['destını] n destinée f, destin m

**destitute** ['destıtju:t] adj indigent(e)

**destroy** [dıs'trɔı] vt détruire; (injured horse) abattre; (dog) faire piquer; **~er** n (NAUT) contre-torpilleur m

**destruction** [dıs'trʌkʃən] n destruction f

**detach** [dı'tætʃ] vt détacher; **~ed** adj (attitude, person) détaché(e); **~ed house** n pavillon m, maison(nette) f (individuelle); **~ment** n (MIL) détachement m; (fig) détachement, indifférence

**detail** ['di:teıl] n détail m ♦ vt raconter en détail, énumérer; **in ~** en détail; **~ed** adj détaillé(e)

**detain** [dı'teın] vt retenir; (in captivity) détenir; (in hospital) hospitaliser

**detect** [dı'tɛkt] vt déceler, percevoir; (MED, POLICE) dépister; (MIL, RADAR, TECH) détecter; **~ion** n découverte f; **~ive** n agent m de la sûreté, policier m; **private ~ive** détective privé; **~ive story** n roman policier

**detention** [dı'tɛnʃən] n détention f; (SCOL) retenue f, consigne f

**deter** [dı'tə:<sup>r</sup>] vt dissuader

**detergent** [dı'tə:dʒənt] n détergent m, détersif m

**deteriorate** [dı'tıərıəreıt] vi se détériorer, se dégrader

**determine** [dı'tə:mın] vt déterminer; **to ~ to do** résoudre de faire, se déterminer à faire; **~d** adj (person) déterminé(e), décidé(e)

**deterrent** [dı'tɛrənt] n effet m de dissuasion; force f de dissuasion

**detest** [dı'tɛst] vt détester, avoir horreur de

**detonate** ['detəneıt] vt faire détoner or exploser

**detour** ['di:tuə<sup>r</sup>] n détour m; (US: AUT: diversion) déviation f

**detract** [dı'trækt] vt: **to ~ from** (quality, pleasure) diminuer; (reputation) porter atteinte à

**detriment** ['detrımənt] n: **to the ~ of** au détriment de, au préjudice de; **~al** [detrı'mɛntl] adj: **~al to** préjudiciable or nuisible à

**devaluation** [dıvælju'eıʃən] n dévaluation f

**devastate** ['devəsteıt] vt dévaster; **~d** adj (fig) anéanti(e); **devastating** adj dévastateur(-trice); (news) accablant(e)

**develop** [dı'vɛləp] vt (gen) développer; (disease) commencer à souffrir de; (resources) mettre en valeur, exploiter ♦ vi se développer; (situation, disease:

*evolve*) évoluer; (*facts, symptoms: appear*) se manifester; se produire; **~ing country** pays m en voie de développement; **the machine has ~ed a fault** un problème s'est manifesté dans cette machine; **~er** [dɪ'veləpər] n (*also:* **property ~er**) promoteur m; **~ment** [dɪ'veləpmənt] n développement m; (*of affair, case*) rebondissement m, fait(s) nouveau(x)

**device** [dɪ'vaɪs] n (*apparatus*) engin m, dispositif m

**devil** ['devl] n diable m; démon m

**devious** ['di:vɪəs] adj (*person*) sournois(e), dissimulé(e)

**devise** [dɪ'vaɪz] vt imaginer, concevoir

**devoid** [dɪ'vɔɪd] adj: **~ of** dépourvu(e) de, dénué(e) de

**devolution** [di:və'lu:ʃən] n (*POL*) décentralisation f

**devote** [dɪ'vəut] vt: **to ~ sth to** consacrer qch à; **~d** [dɪ'vəutɪd] adj dévoué(e); **to be ~d to** (*book etc*) être consacré(e) à; (*person*) être très attaché(e) à; **~e** [devəu'ti:] n (*REL*) adepte m/f; (*MUS, SPORT*) fervent(e) **devotion** n dévouement m, attachement m; (*REL*) dévotion f, piété f

**devour** [dɪ'vauər] vt dévorer

**devout** [dɪ'vaut] adj pieux(-euse), dévot(e)

**dew** [dju:] n rosée f

**diabetes** [daɪə'bi:ti:z] n diabète m; **diabetic** [daɪə'betɪk] adj diabétique ♦ n diabétique m/f

**diabolical** [daɪə'bɒlɪkl] (*inf*) adj (*weather*) atroce; (*behaviour*) infernal(e)

**diagnosis** [daɪəg'nəusɪs] (*pl* **diagnoses**) n diagnostic m

**diagonal** [daɪ'ægənl] adj diagonal(e) ♦ n diagonale f

**diagram** ['daɪəgræm] n diagramme m, schéma m

**dial** ['daɪəl] n cadran m ♦ vt (*number*) faire, composer

**dialect** ['daɪəlekt] n dialecte m

**dialling code** (*BRIT*) n indicatif m (téléphonique)

**dialling tone** (*BRIT*) n tonalité f

**dialogue** ['daɪəlɒg] n dialogue m

**dial tone** (*US*) n = **dialling tone**

**diameter** [daɪ'æmɪtər] n diamètre m

**diamond** ['daɪəmənd] n diamant m; (*shape*) losange m; **~s** npl (*CARDS*) carreau m

**diaper** ['daɪəpər] (*US*) n couche f

**diaphragm** ['daɪəfræm] n diaphragme m

**diarrhoea** [daɪə'ri:ə] (*US* **diarrhea**) n diarrhée f

**diary** ['daɪərɪ] n (*daily account*) journal m; (*book*) agenda m

**dice** [daɪs] n inv dé m ♦ vt (*CULIN*) couper en dés or en cubes

**dictate** [dɪk'teɪt] vt dicter; **dictation** n dictée f

**dictator** [dɪk'teɪtər] n dictateur m; **~ship** n dictature f

**dictionary** ['dɪkʃənrɪ] n dictionnaire m

**did** [dɪd] pt of **do**; **~n't** = **did not**

**die** [daɪ] vi mourir; **to be dying for sth** avoir une envie folle de qch; **to be dying to do sth** mourir d'envie de faire qch; **~ away** vi s'éteindre; **~ down** vi se calmer, s'apaiser; **~ out** vi disparaître

**diesel** ['di:zl] n (*vehicle*) diesel m; (*also:* **~ oil**) carburant m diesel, gas-oil m; **~ engine** n moteur m diesel

**diet** ['daɪət] n alimentation f; (*restricted food*) régime m ♦ vi (*also:* **be on a ~**) suivre un régime

**differ** ['dɪfər] vi (*be different*): **to ~ (from)** être différent(e); différer (de); (*disagree*): **to ~ (from sb over sth)** ne pas être d'accord (avec qn au sujet de qch); **~ence** n différence f; (*quarrel*) différend m, désaccord m; **~ent** adj différent(e); **~entiate** [dɪfə'renʃieɪt] vi: **to ~entiate (between)** faire une différence (entre)

**difficult** ['dɪfɪkəlt] adj difficile; **~y** n difficulté f

**diffident** ['dɪfɪdənt] adj qui manque de

confiance or d'assurance

**dig** [dɪg] (pt, pp **dug**) vt (hole) creuser; (garden) bêcher ♦ n (prod) coup m de coude; (fig) coup de griffe or de patte; (archeological) fouilles fpl; **~ in** vi (MIL: also: **~ o.s. in**) se retrancher; **~ into** vt fus (savings) puiser dans; **to ~ one's nails into sth** enfoncer ses ongles dans qch; **~ up** vt déterrer

**digest** [vb daɪˈdʒɛst, daˈdʒɛst] vt digérer ♦ n sommaire m, résumé m; **~ion** [dɪˈdʒɛstʃən] n digestion f

**digit** [ˈdɪdʒɪt] n (number) chiffre m; (finger) doigt m; **~al** adj digital(e), à affichage numérique or digital; **~al computer** calculateur m numérique; **~al TV** n télévision f numérique; **~al watch** montre f à affichage numérique

**dignified** [ˈdɪgnɪfaɪd] adj digne

**dignity** [ˈdɪgnɪtɪ] n dignité f

**digress** [daɪˈgrɛs] vi: **to ~ from** s'écarter de, s'éloigner de

**digs** [dɪgz] (BRIT: inf) npl piaule f, chambre meublée

**dilapidated** [dɪˈlæpɪdeɪtɪd] adj délabré(e)

**dilemma** [daɪˈlɛmə] n dilemme m

**diligent** [ˈdɪlɪdʒənt] adj appliqué(e), assidu(e)

**dilute** [daɪˈluːt] vt diluer

**dim** [dɪm] adj (light) faible; (memory, outline) vague, indécis(e); (figure) vague, indistinct(e); (room) sombre; (stupid) borné(e), obtus(e) ♦ vt (light) réduire, baisser; (US: AUT) mettre en code

**dime** [daɪm] (US) n = **10 cents**

**dimension** [daɪˈmɛnʃən] n dimension f

**diminish** [dɪˈmɪnɪʃ] vt, vi diminuer

**diminutive** [dɪˈmɪnjʊtɪv] adj minuscule, tout(e) petit(e)

**dimmers** [ˈdɪməz] (US) npl (AUT) phares mpl code inv; feux mpl de position

**dimple** [ˈdɪmpl] n fossette f

**din** [dɪn] n vacarme m

**dine** [daɪn] vi dîner; **~r** n (person) dîneur(-euse); (US: restaurant) petit restaurant

**dinghy** [ˈdɪŋgɪ] n youyou m; (also: **rubber ~**) canot m pneumatique; (also: **sailing ~**) voilier m, dériveur m

**dingy** [ˈdɪndʒɪ] adj miteux(-euse), minable

**dining car** (BRIT) n wagon-restaurant m

**dining room** n salle f à manger

**dinner** [ˈdɪnə*] n dîner m; (lunch) déjeuner m; (public) banquet m; **~ jacket** n smoking m; **~ party** n dîner m; **~ time** n heure f du dîner; (midday) heure f du déjeuner

**dinosaur** [ˈdaɪnəsɔː*] n dinosaure m

**dip** [dɪp] n déclivité f; (in sea) baignade f, bain m; (CULIN) ≈ sauce f ♦ vt tremper, plonger; (BRIT: AUT: lights) mettre en code, baisser ♦ vi plonger

**diploma** [dɪˈpləʊmə] n diplôme m

**diplomacy** [dɪˈpləʊməsɪ] n diplomatie f

**diplomat** [ˈdɪpləmæt] n diplomate m; **~ic** [dɪplə'mætɪk] adj diplomatique

**dipstick** [ˈdɪpstɪk] n (AUT) jauge f de niveau d'huile

**dipswitch** [ˈdɪpswɪtʃ] (BRIT) (AUT) interrupteur m de lumière réduite

**dire** [daɪə*] adj terrible, extrême, affreux(-euse)

**direct** [daɪˈrɛkt] adj direct(e) ♦ vt diriger, orienter; (letter, remark) adresser; (film, programme) réaliser; (play) mettre en scène; (order): **to ~ sb to do sth** ordonner à qn de faire qch ♦ adv directement; **can you ~ me to ...?** pouvez-vous m'indiquer le chemin de ...?; **~ debit** (BRIT) n prélèvement m automatique

**direction** [dɪˈrɛkʃən] n direction f; **~s** npl (advice) indications fpl; **sense of ~** sens m de l'orientation; **~s for use** mode m d'emploi

**directly** [dɪˈrɛktlɪ] adv (in a straight line) directement, tout droit; (at once) tout de suite, immédiatement

**director** [dɪˈrɛktə*] n directeur m; (THEATRE) metteur m en scène; (CINEMA, TV) réalisateur(-trice)

**directory** [dɪˈrɛktərɪ] *n* annuaire *m*; (COMPUT) répertoire *m*; ~ **enquiries** (US **directory assistance**) *n* renseignements *mpl*

**dirt** [dəːt] *n* saleté *f*; crasse *f*; (earth) terre *f*, boue *f*; **~-cheap** *adj* très bon marché *inv*; **~y** *adj* sale ♦ *vt* salir; **~y trick** coup tordu

**disability** [dɪsəˈbɪlɪtɪ] *n* invalidité *f*, infirmité *f*

**disabled** [dɪsˈeɪbld] *adj* infirme, invalide ♦ *npl*: **the ~** les handicapés

**disadvantage** [dɪsədˈvɑːntɪdʒ] *n* désavantage *m*, inconvénient *m*

**disagree** [dɪsəˈɡriː] *vi* (be different) ne pas concorder; (be against, think otherwise): **to ~ (with)** ne pas être d'accord (avec); **~able** *adj* désagréable; **~ment** *n* désaccord *m*, différend *m*

**disallow** [ˈdɪsəˈlaʊ] *vt* rejeter

**disappear** [dɪsəˈpɪəʳ] *vi* disparaître; **~ance** *n* disparition *f*

**disappoint** [dɪsəˈpɔɪnt] *vt* décevoir; **~ed** *adj* déçu(e); **~ing** *adj* décevant(e); **~ment** *n* déception *f*

**disapproval** [dɪsəˈpruːvəl] *n* désapprobation *f*

**disapprove** [dɪsəˈpruːv] *vi*: **to ~ (of)** désapprouver

**disarmament** [dɪsˈɑːməmənt] *n* désarmement *m*

**disarray** [dɪsəˈreɪ] *n*: **in ~** (army) en déroute; (organization) en désarroi; (hair, clothes) en désordre

**disaster** [dɪˈzɑːstəʳ] *n* catastrophe *f*, désastre *m*; **disastrous** *adj* désastreux(-euse)

**disband** [dɪsˈbænd] *vt* démobiliser; disperser ♦ *vi* se séparer; se disperser

**disbelief** [ˈdɪsbəˈliːf] *n* incrédulité *f*

**disc** [dɪsk] *n* disque *m*; (COMPUT) = **disk**

**discard** [dɪsˈkɑːd] *vt* (old things) se débarrasser de; (fig) écarter, renoncer à

**discern** [dɪˈsəːn] *vt* discerner, distinguer; **~ing** *adj* perspicace

**discharge** [vb dɪsˈtʃɑːdʒ, n ˈdɪstʃɑːdʒ] *vt* décharger; (duties) s'acquitter de;

(patient) renvoyer (chez lui); (employee) congédier, licencier; (soldier) rendre à la vie civile, réformer; (defendant) relaxer, élargir *n* décharge *f*; (dismissal) renvoi *m*; licenciement *m*; élargissement *m*; (MED) écoulement *m*

**discipline** [ˈdɪsɪplɪn] *n* discipline *f*

**disc jockey** *n* disc-jockey *m*

**disclaim** [dɪsˈkleɪm] *vt* nier

**disclose** [dɪsˈkləʊz] *vt* révéler, divulguer; **disclosure** *n* révélation *f*

**disco** [ˈdɪskəʊ] *n abbr* = **discotheque**

**discomfort** [dɪsˈkʌmfət] *n* malaise *m*, gêne *f*; (lack of comfort) manque *m* de confort

**disconcert** [dɪskənˈsəːt] *vt* déconcerter

**disconnect** [dɪskəˈnɛkt] *vt* (ELEC, RADIO, pipe) débrancher; (TEL, water) couper

**discontent** [dɪskənˈtɛnt] *n* mécontentement *m*; **~ed** *adj* mécontent(e)

**discontinue** [dɪskənˈtɪnjuː] *vt* cesser, interrompre; **"~d"** (COMM) "fin de série"

**discord** [ˈdɪskɔːd] *n* discorde *f*, dissension *f*; (MUS) dissonance *f*

**discotheque** [ˈdɪskəʊtɛk] *n* discothèque *f*

**discount** [*n* ˈdɪskaʊnt, *vb* dɪsˈkaʊnt] *n* remise *f*, rabais *m* ♦ *vt* (sum) faire une remise de; (fig) ne pas tenir compte de

**discourage** [dɪsˈkʌrɪdʒ] *vt* décourager

**discover** [dɪsˈkʌvəʳ] *vt* découvrir; **~y** *n* découverte *f*

**discredit** [dɪsˈkrɛdɪt] *vt* (idea) mettre en doute; (person) discréditer

**discreet** [dɪsˈkriːt] *adj* discret(-ète)

**discrepancy** [dɪsˈkrɛpənsɪ] *n* divergence *f*, contradiction *f*

**discretion** [dɪsˈkrɛʃən] *n* discrétion *f*; **use your own ~** à vous de juger

**discriminate** [dɪsˈkrɪmɪneɪt] *vi*: **to ~ between** établir une distinction entre, faire la différence entre; **to ~ against** pratiquer la discrimination contre; **discriminating** *adj* qui a du discernement; **discrimination** [dɪskrɪmɪˈneɪʃən] *n* discrimination *f*; (judgment) discernement *m*

**discuss** [dɪsˈkʌs] *vt* discuter de; (*debate*) discuter; **~ion** *n* discussion *f*

**disdain** [dɪsˈdeɪn] *n* dédain *m*

**disease** [dɪˈziːz] *n* maladie *f*

**disembark** [dɪsɪmˈbɑːk] *vi* débarquer

**disentangle** [dɪsɪnˈtæŋɡl] *vt* (*wool, wire*) démêler, débrouiller; (*from wreckage*) dégager

**disfigure** [dɪsˈfɪɡəʳ] *vt* défigurer

**disgrace** [dɪsˈɡreɪs] *n* honte *f*; (*disfavour*) disgrâce *f* ♦ *vt* déshonorer, couvrir de honte; **~ful** *adj* scandaleux(-euse), honteux(-euse)

**disgruntled** [dɪsˈɡrʌntld] *adj* mécontent(e)

**disguise** [dɪsˈɡaɪz] *n* déguisement *m* ♦ *vt* déguiser; **in ~** déguisé(e)

**disgust** [dɪsˈɡʌst] *n* dégoût *m*, aversion *f* ♦ *vt* dégoûter, écœurer; **~ing** *adj* dégoûtant(e); révoltant(e)

**dish** [dɪʃ] *n* plat *m*; **to do** *or* **wash the ~es** faire la vaisselle; **~ out** *vt* servir, distribuer; **~ up** *vt* servir; **~cloth** *n* (*for washing*) lavette *f*

**dishearten** [dɪsˈhɑːtn] *vt* décourager

**dishevelled** [dɪˈʃevəld] (*US* **disheveled**) *adj* ébouriffé(e); décoiffé(e); débraillé(e)

**dishonest** [dɪsˈɒnɪst] *adj* malhonnête

**dishonour** [dɪsˈɒnəʳ] (*US* **dishonor**) *n* déshonneur *m*; **~able** *adj* (*behaviour*) déshonorant(e); (*person*) peu honorable

**dishtowel** [ˈdɪʃtauəl] (*US*) *n* torchon *m*

**dishwasher** [ˈdɪʃwɒʃəʳ] *n* lave-vaisselle *m*

**disillusion** [dɪsɪˈluːʒən] *vt* désabuser, désillusionner

**disinfect** [dɪsɪnˈfekt] *vt* désinfecter; **~ant** *n* désinfectant *m*

**disintegrate** [dɪsˈɪntɪɡreɪt] *vi* se désintégrer

**disinterested** [dɪsˈɪntrəstɪd] *adj* désintéressé(e)

**disjointed** [dɪsˈdʒɔɪntɪd] *adj* décousu(e), incohérent(e)

**disk** [dɪsk] *n* (*COMPUT*) disque *m*; (: *flop-*

*py ~*) disquette *f*; **single-/double-sided ~** disquette simple/double face; **~ drive** *n* lecteur *m* de disquettes; **~ette** [dɪsˈket] *n* disquette *f*, disque *m* souple

**dislike** [dɪsˈlaɪk] *n* aversion *f*, antipathie *f* ♦ *vt* ne pas aimer

**dislocate** [ˈdɪsləkeɪt] *vt* disloquer; déboiter

**dislodge** [dɪsˈlɒdʒ] *vt* déplacer, faire bouger

**disloyal** [dɪsˈlɔɪəl] *adj* déloyal(e)

**dismal** [ˈdɪzml] *adj* lugubre, maussade

**dismantle** [dɪsˈmæntl] *vt* démonter

**dismay** [dɪsˈmeɪ] *n* consternation *f*

**dismiss** [dɪsˈmɪs] *vt* congédier, renvoyer; (*soldiers*) faire rompre les rangs à; (*idea*) écarter; (*LAW*): **to ~ a case** rendre une fin de non-recevoir; **~al** *n* renvoi *m*

**dismount** [dɪsˈmaunt] *vi* mettre pied à terre, descendre

**disobedient** [dɪsəˈbiːdɪənt] *adj* désobéissant(e)

**disobey** [dɪsəˈbeɪ] *vt* désobéir à

**disorder** [dɪsˈɔːdəʳ] *n* désordre *m*; (*rioting*) désordres *mpl*; (*MED*) troubles *mpl*; **~ly** *adj* en désordre; désordonné(e)

**disorientated** [dɪsˈɔːrɪenteɪtd] *adj* désorienté(e)

**disown** [dɪsˈəun] *vt* renier

**disparaging** [dɪsˈpærɪdʒɪŋ] *adj* désobligeant(e)

**dispassionate** [dɪsˈpæʃənət] *adj* calme, froid(e); impartial(e), objectif(-ive)

**dispatch** [dɪsˈpætʃ] *vt* expédier, envoyer ♦ *n* envoi *m*, expédition *f*; (*MIL, PRESS*) dépêche *f*

**dispel** [dɪsˈpel] *vt* dissiper, chasser

**dispense** [dɪsˈpens] *vt* distribuer, administrer; **~ with** *vt fus* se passer de; **~r** *n* (*machine*) distributeur *m*; **dispensing chemist** (*BRIT*) *n* pharmacie *f*

**disperse** [dɪsˈpɜːs] *vt* disperser ♦ *vi* se disperser

**dispirited** [dɪsˈpɪrɪtɪd] *adj* découragé(e), déprimé(e)

**displace** [dɪs'pleɪs] vt déplacer

**display** [dɪs'pleɪ] n étalage m; déploiement m; affichage m; (screen) écran m, visuel m; (of feeling) manifestation f ♦ vt montrer; (goods) mettre à l'étalage, exposer; (results, departure times) afficher; (pej) faire étalage de

**displease** [dɪs'pliːz] vt mécontenter, contrarier; **~d** adj: **~d with** mécontent(e) de; **displeasure** [dɪs'plɛʒəʳ] n mécontentement m

**disposable** [dɪs'pəuzəbl] adj (pack etc) jetable, à jeter; (income) disponible; **~ nappy** (BRIT) n couche f à jeter, couche-culotte f

**disposal** [dɪs'pəuzl] n (of goods for sale) vente f; (of property) disposition f, cession f; (of rubbish) enlèvement m, destruction f; **at one's ~** à sa disposition

**dispose** [dɪs'pəuz] vt disposer; **~ of** vt fus (unwanted goods etc) se débarrasser de, se défaire de; (problem) expédier; **~d** adj: **to be ~d to do sth** être disposé(e) à faire qch; **disposition** [dɪspə'zɪʃən] n disposition f; (temperament) naturel m

**disprove** [dɪs'pruːv] vt réfuter

**dispute** [dɪs'pjuːt] n discussion f; (also: **industrial ~**) conflit m ♦ vt contester; (matter) discuter; (victory) disputer

**disqualify** [dɪs'kwɔlɪfaɪ] vt (SPORT) disqualifier; **to ~ sb for sth/from doing** rendre qn inapte à qch/à faire

**disquiet** [dɪs'kwaɪət] n inquiétude f, trouble m

**disregard** [dɪsrɪ'gɑːd] vt ne pas tenir compte de

**disrepair** ['dɪsrɪ'pɛəʳ] n: **to fall into ~** (building) tomber en ruine

**disreputable** [dɪs'rɛpjutəbl] adj (person) de mauvaise réputation; (behaviour) déshonorant(e)

**disrespectful** [dɪsrɪ'spɛktful] adj irrespectueux(-euse)

**disrupt** [dɪs'rʌpt] vt (plans) déranger; (conversation) interrompre

**dissatisfied** [dɪs'sætɪsfaɪd] adj: **~ (with)** insatisfait(e) (de)

**dissect** [dɪ'sɛkt] vt disséquer

**dissent** [dɪ'sɛnt] n dissentiment m, différence f d'opinion

**dissertation** [dɪsə'teɪʃən] n mémoire m

**disservice** [dɪs'sɜːvɪs] n: **to do sb a ~** rendre un mauvais service à qn

**dissimilar** [dɪ'sɪmɪləʳ] adj: **~ (to)** dissemblable (à), différent(e) (de)

**dissipate** ['dɪsɪpeɪt] vt dissiper; (money, efforts) disperser

**dissolute** ['dɪsəluːt] adj débauché(e), dissolu(e)

**dissolve** [dɪ'zɔlv] vt dissoudre ♦ vi se dissoudre, fondre; **to ~ in(to) tears** fondre en larmes

**distance** ['dɪstns] n distance f; **in the ~** au loin

**distant** ['dɪstnt] adj lointain(e), éloigné(e); (manner) distant(e), froid(e)

**distaste** [dɪs'teɪst] n dégoût m; **~ful** adj déplaisant(e), désagréable

**distended** [dɪs'tɛndɪd] adj (stomach) dilaté(e)

**distil** [dɪs'tɪl] (US **distill**) vt distiller; **~lery** n distillerie f

**distinct** [dɪs'tɪŋkt] adj distinct(e); (clear) marqué(e); **as ~ from** par opposition à; **~ion** n distinction f; (in exam) mention f très bien; **~ive** adj distinctif(-ive)

**distinguish** [dɪs'tɪŋgwɪʃ] vt distinguer; **~ed** adj (eminent) distingué(e); **~ing** adj (feature) distinctif(-ive), caractéristique

**distort** [dɪs'tɔːt] vt déformer

**distract** [dɪs'trækt] vt distraire, déranger; **~ed** adj (anxious) éperdu(e), égaré(e); **~ion** n distraction f; égarement m

**distraught** [dɪs'trɔːt] adj éperdu(e)

**distress** [dɪs'trɛs] n détresse f ♦ vt affliger; **~ing** adj douloureux(-euse), pénible

**distribute** [dɪs'trɪbjuːt] vt distribuer; **distribution** [dɪstrɪ'bjuːʃən] n distribution f; **distributor** n distributeur m

**district** ['dɪstrɪkt] n (of country) région f; (of town) quartier m; (ADMIN) district m; ~ **attorney** (US) n ≃ procureur m de la République; ~ **nurse** (BRIT) n infirmière visiteuse

**distrust** [dɪs'trʌst] n méfiance f ♦ vt se méfier de

**disturb** [dɪs'tɜːb] vt troubler; (inconvenience) déranger; ~**ance** n dérangement m; (violent event, political etc) troubles mpl; ~**ed** adj (worried, upset) agité(e), troublé(e); **to be emotionally ~ed** avoir des problèmes affectifs; ~**ing** adj troublant(e), inquiétant(e)

**disuse** [dɪs'juːs] n: **to fall into ~**. tomber en désuétude; ~**d** [dɪs'juːzd] adj désaffecté(e)

**ditch** [dɪtʃ] n fossé m; (irrigation) rigole f ♦ vt (inf) abandonner; (person) plaquer

**dither** ['dɪðəʳ] vi hésiter

**ditto** ['dɪtəu] adv idem

**dive** [daɪv] n plongeon m; (of submarine) plongée f ♦ vi plonger; **to ~ into** (bag, drawer etc) plonger la main dans; (shop, car etc) se précipiter dans; ~**r** n plongeur m

**diversion** [daɪ'vɜːʃən] n (BRIT: AUT) déviation f; (distraction, MIL) diversion f

**divert** [daɪ'vɜːt] vt (funds, BRIT: traffic) dévier; (river, attention) détourner

**divide** [dɪ'vaɪd] vt diviser; (separate) séparer ♦ vi se diviser; ~**d highway** (US) n route f à quatre voies

**dividend** ['dɪvɪdend] n dividende m

**divine** [dɪ'vaɪn] adj divin(e)

**diving** ['daɪvɪŋ] n plongée (sousmarine); ~ **board** n plongeoir m

**divinity** [dɪ'vɪnɪtɪ] n divinité f; (SCOL) théologie f

**division** [dɪ'vɪʒən] n division f

**divorce** [dɪ'vɔːs] n divorce m ♦ vt divorcer d'avec; (dissociate) séparer; ~**d** adj divorcé(e); ~**e** n divorcé(e)

**D.I.Y.** (BRIT) n abbr = **do-it-yourself**

**dizzy** ['dɪzɪ] adj: **to make sb ~** donner le vertige à qn; **to feel ~** avoir la tête

qui tourne

**DJ** n abbr = **disc jockey**

**DNA fingerprinting** n technique f des empreintes génétiques

**do** [duː] (pt **did**, pp **done**) n (inf: party etc) soirée f, fête f

♦ vb 1 (in negative constructions) non traduit; **I don't understand** je ne comprends pas

2 (to form questions) non traduit; **didn't you know?** vous ne le saviez pas?; **why didn't you come?** pourquoi n'êtes-vous pas venu?

3 (for emphasis, in polite expressions): **she does seem rather late** je trouve qu'elle est bien en retard; **do sit down/help yourself** asseyez-vous/servez-vous je vous en prie

4 (used to avoid repeating vb): **she swims better than I do** elle nage mieux que moi; **do you agree? - yes, I do/no, I don't** vous êtes d'accord? - oui/non; **she lives in Glasgow - so do I** elle habite Glasgow - moi aussi; **who broke it? - I did** qui l'a cassé? - c'est moi

5 (in question tags): **he laughed, didn't he?** il a ri, n'est-ce pas?; **I don't know him, do I?** je ne crois pas le connaître

♦ vt (gen: carry out, perform etc) faire; **what are you doing tonight?** qu'estce que vous faites ce soir?; **to do the cooking/washing-up** faire la cuisine/la vaisselle; **to do one's teeth/hair/nails** se brosser les dents/se coiffer/se faire les ongles; **the car was doing 100** ≈ la voiture faisait du 160 (à l'heure)

♦ vi 1 (act, behave) faire; **do as I do** faites comme moi

2 (get on, fare) marcher; **the firm is doing well** l'entreprise marche bien; **how do you do?** comment allez-vous?; (on being introduced) enchanté(e)!

**3** (*suit*) aller; **will it do?** est-ce que ça ira?

**4** (*be sufficient*) suffire, aller; **will £10 do?** est-ce que 10 livres suffiront?; **that'll do** ça suffit, ça va; **that'll do!** (*in annoyance*) ça va ou suffit comme ça!; **to make do (with)** se contenter (de)

**do away with** *vt fus* supprimer

**do up** *vt* (*laces, dress*) attacher; (*buttons*) boutonner; (*zip*) fermer; (*renovate: room*) refaire; (*: house*) remettre à neuf

**do with** *vt fus* (*need*): **I could do with a drink/some help** quelque chose à boire/un peu d'aide ne serait pas de refus; (*be connected*): **that has nothing to do with you** cela ne vous concerne pas; **I won't have anything to do with it** je ne veux pas m'en mêler

**do without** *vi* s'en passer ♦ *vt fus* se passer de

---

**dock** [dɔk] *n* dock *m*; (*LAW*) banc *m* des accusés ♦ *vi* se mettre à quai; (*SPACE*) s'arrimer; **~er** *n* docker *m*; **~yard** *n* chantier *m* de construction navale

**doctor** ['dɔktər] *n* médecin *m*, docteur *m*; (*PhD etc*) docteur ♦ *vt* (*drink*) frelater; **D~ of Philosophy** (*degree*) doctorat *m*; (*person*) Docteur *m* en Droit ou Lettres *etc*, titulaire *m/f* d'un doctorat

**document** ['dɔkjumənt] *n* document *m*; **~ary** [dɔkju'mɛntəri] *adj* documentaire ♦ *n* documentaire *m*

**dodge** [dɔdʒ] *n* truc *m*; combine *f* ♦ *vt* esquiver, éviter

**dodgems** ['dɔdʒəmz] (*BRIT*) *npl* autos tamponneuses

**doe** [dəu] *n* (*deer*) biche *f*; (*rabbit*) lapine *f*

**does** [dʌz] *vb see* **do**; **~n't** = **does not**

**dog** [dɔg] *n* chien(ne) *m* ♦ *vt* suivre de près; poursuivre, harceler; **~ collar** *n* collier *m* de chien; (*fig*) faux-col *m* d'ecclésiastique; **~-eared** *adj* corné(e).

**~ged** ['dɔgid] *adj* obstiné(e), opiniâtre; **~sbody** *n* bonne *f* à tout faire, tâcheron *m*

**doings** ['duːŋz] *npl* activités *fpl*

**do-it-yourself** ['duːitjɔː'self] *n* bricolage *m*

**doldrums** ['dɔldrəmz] *npl*: **to be in the ~** avoir le cafard; (*business*) être dans le marasme

**dole** [dəul] *n* (*BRIT: payment*) allocation *f* de chômage; **on the ~** au chômage; **~ out** *vt* donner au compte-goutte

**doll** [dɔl] *n* poupée *f*

**dollar** ['dɔlər] *n* dollar *m*

**dolled up** (*inf*) *adj*: **(all) ~** sur son trente et un

**dolphin** ['dɔlfin] *n* dauphin *m*

**dome** [dəum] *n* dôme *m*

**domestic** [də'mɛstik] *adj* (*task, appliances*) ménager(-ère); (*of country: trade, situation etc*) intérieur(e); (*animal*) domestique; **~ated** *adj* (*animal*) domestiqué(e); (*husband*) pantouflard(e)

**dominate** ['dɔmineit] *vt* dominer

**domineering** [dɔmi'niəriŋ] *adj* dominateur(-trice), autoritaire

**dominion** [də'miniən] *n* (*territory*) territoire *m*; **to have ~ over** contrôler

**domino** ['dɔminəu] (*pl* **~es**) *n* domino *m*; **~es** *n* (*game*) dominos *mpl*

**don** [dɔn] (*BRIT*) *n* professeur *m* d'université

**donate** [də'neit] *vt* faire don de, donner

**done** [dʌn] *pp of* **do**

**donkey** ['dɔŋki] *n* âne *m*

**donor** ['dəunər] *n* (*of blood etc*) donneur(-euse); (*to charity*) donateur(-trice); **~ card** *n* carte *f* de don d'organes

**don't** [dəunt] *vb* = **do not**

**donut** ['dəunʌt] (*US*) *n* = **doughnut**

**doodle** ['duːdl] *vi* griffonner, gribouiller

**doom** [duːm] *n* destin *m* ♦ *vt*: **to be ~ed (to failure)** être voué(e) à l'échec

**door** [dɔːr] *n* porte *f*; (*RAIL, of car*) portière *f*; **~bell** *n* sonnette *f*; **~handle** *n* poignée f de la porte; (car) poignée de portière; **~man** (irreg) n (in hotel) portier m; (in nightclub etc) videur m; **~mat** n paillasson m; **~step** n pas m de (la) porte, seuil m; **~way** n (embrasure f de la) porte f

**dope** [dəup] n (inf: drug) drogue f; (: person) andouille f ♦ vt (horse etc) doper

**dormant** ['dɔːmənt] adj assoupi(e)

**dormitory** ['dɔːmɪtrɪ] n dortoir m; (US: building) résidence f universitaire

**dormouse** ['dɔːmaus] (pl **dormice**) n loir m

**DOS** [dɒs] n abbr (= disk operating system) DOS

**dose** [dəus] n dose f

**dosh** [dɒʃ] (inf) n fric m

**doss house** ['dɒs-] (BRIT) n asile m de nuit

**dot** [dɒt] n point m; (on material) pois m ♦ vt: **~ted with** parsemé(e) de; **on the ~** à l'heure tapante or pile; **~ted line** n pointillé(s) m(pl)

**double** ['dʌbl] adj double ♦ adv (twice): **to cost ~** (sth) coûter le double (de qch) or deux fois plus (que qch) ♦ n double m ♦ vt doubler; (fold) plier en deux ♦ vi doubler; **~s** n (TENNIS) double m; on or (BRIT) at the **~** au pas de course; **~ bass** (BRIT) n contrebasse f; **~ bed** n grand lit; **~ bend** (BRIT) n virage m en S; **~-breasted** adj croisé(e); **~ click** vi (COMPUT) double-cliquer; **~-cross** vt doubler, trahir; **~-decker** n autobus m à impériale; **~ glazing** (BRIT) n double vitrage m; **~ room** n chambre f pour deux personnes; **doubly** adv doublement, deux fois plus

**doubt** [daut] n doute m ♦ vt douter de; **to ~ that** douter que; **~ful** adj douteux(-euse); (person) incertain(e); **~less** adv sans doute, sûrement

**dough** [dəu] n pâte f; (US donut) **~nut** n beignet m

**dove** [dʌv] n colombe f

**Dover** ['dəuvər] n Douvres

**dovetail** ['dʌvteɪl] vi (fig) concorder

**dowdy** ['daudɪ] adj démodé(e); mal fagoté(e) (inf)

**down** [daun] n (soft feathers) duvet m ♦ adv en bas, vers le bas; (on the ground) par terre ♦ prep en bas de; (along) le long de ♦ vt (inf: drink, food) s'envoyer; **~ with X!** à bas X!; **~-and-out** n clochard(e); **~-at-heel** adj éculé(e); (fig) miteux(-euse); **~cast** adj démoralisé(e); **~fall** n chute f; ruine f; **~hearted** adj découragé(e); **~hill** adv: **to go ~hill** descendre; (fig) péricliter; **~ payment** n acompte m; **~pour** n pluie torrentielle, déluge m; **~right** adj (lie etc) effronté(e); (refusal) catégorique; **~size** vt (ECON) réduire ses effectifs

**Down's syndrome** [daunz-] n (MED) trisomie f

**down:** **~stairs** adv au rez-de-chaussée; à l'étage inférieur; **~stream** adv en aval; **~-to-earth** adj terre à terre inv; **~town** adv en ville; **~ under** adv (in Australie/Nouvelle-Zélande, adj) adj, adv vers le bas; **~ward** adj, adv vers le bas; **~wards** adv vers le bas

**dowry** ['dauri] n dot f

**doz.** abbr = dozen

**doze** [dəuz] vi sommeiller; **~ off** vi s'assoupir

**dozen** ['dʌzn] n douzaine f; **a ~ books** une douzaine de livres; **~s of** des centaines de

**Dr.** abbr = doctor; drive

**drab** [dræb] adj terne, morne

**draft** [drɑːft] n ébauche f; (of letter, essay etc) brouillon m; (COMM) traite f

(US: call-up) conscription f ♦ vt faire le brouillon or un projet de; (MIL: send) détacher; see also **draught**

**draftsman** ['drɑːftsmən] (irreg) (US) n = **draughtsman**

**drag** [dræg] vt traîner; (river) draguer ♦ vi traîner ♦ n (inf) casse-pieds m/f; (women's clothing): **in** ~ (en) travesti; ~ **on** vi s'éterniser

**dragon** ['drægn] n dragon m

**dragonfly** ['drægənflaɪ] n libellule f

**drain** [dreɪn] n égout m, canalisation f; (on resources) saignée f ♦ vt (land, marshes etc) drainer, assécher; (vegetables) égoutter; (glass) vider ♦ vi (water) s'écouler; ~**age** n drainage m; système m d'égouts or de canalisations; ~**ing board** (US **drain board**) n égouttoir m; ~**pipe** n tuyau m d'écoulement

**drama** ['drɑːmə] n (art) théâtre m, art m dramatique; (play) pièce f (de théâtre); (event) drame m; ~**tic** [drəˈmætɪk] adj dramatique; spectaculaire; ~**tist** ['dræmətɪst] n auteur m dramatique; ~**tize** ['dræmətaɪz] vt (events) dramatiser; (adapt: for TV/cinema) adapter pour la télévision/pour l'écran

**drank** [dræŋk] pt of **drink**

**drape** [dreɪp] vt draper; ~**s** (US) npl rideaux mpl

**drastic** ['dræstɪk] adj sévère; énergique; (change) radical(e)

**draught** [drɑːft] (US **draft**) n courant m d'air; (NAUT) tirant m d'eau; **on** ~ (beer) à la pression; ~**board** (BRIT) n damier m; ~**s** (BRIT) n (jeu m de) dames fpl

**draughtsman** ['drɑːftsmən] (irreg) n dessinateur(-trice) (industriel(le))

**draw** [drɔː] (pt **drew**, pp **drawn**) vt tirer; (tooth) arracher, extraire; (attract) attirer; (picture) dessiner; (line, circle) tracer; (money) retirer; (wages) toucher ♦ vi (SPORT) faire match nul ♦ n match nul; (lottery) tirage au sort; loterie f; **to** ~ **near** s'approcher; approcher; ~ **out** vi (lengthen) s'allonger ♦ vt (money) retirer; ~ **up** vi (stop) s'arrêter ♦ vt

(chair) approcher; (document) établir, dresser; ~**back** n inconvénient m, désavantage m; ~**bridge** n pont-levis m

**drawer** [drɔːr] n tiroir m

**drawing** ['drɔːɪŋ] n dessin m; ~ **board** n planche f à dessin; ~ **pin** (BRIT) n punaise f; ~ **room** n salon m

**drawl** [drɔːl] n accent traînant

**drawn** [drɔːn] pp of **draw**

**dread** [dred] n terreur f, effroi m ♦ vt redouter, appréhender; ~**ful** adj affreux (-euse)

**dream** [driːm] (pt, pp **dreamed** or **dreamt**) n rêve m ♦ vt, vi rêver; ~**y** adj rêveur(-euse); (music) langoureux (-euse)

**dreary** ['drɪərɪ] adj morne; monotone

**dredge** [dredʒ] vt draguer

**dregs** [dregz] npl lie f

**drench** [drentʃ] vt tremper

**dress** [dres] n robe f; (no pl: clothing) habillement m, tenue f ♦ vi s'habiller ♦ vt habiller; (wound) panser; **to get** ~**ed** s'habiller; ~ **up** vi s'habiller; (in fancy ~) se déguiser; ~ **circle** (BRIT) n (THEATRE) premier balcon; ~**er** n (furniture) vaisselier m; (: US) coiffeuse f, commode f; ~**ing** n (MED) pansement m; (CULIN) sauce f, assaisonnement m; ~**ing gown** (BRIT) n robe f de chambre; ~**ing room** n (THEATRE) loge f; (SPORT) vestiaire m; ~**ing table** n coiffeuse f; ~**maker** n couturière f; ~ **rehearsal** n (répétition) générale f

**drew** [druː] pt of **draw**

**dribble** ['drɪbl] vi (baby) baver ♦ vt (ball) dribbler

**dried** [draɪd] adj (fruit, beans) sec (sèche); (eggs, milk) en poudre

**drier** ['draɪər] n = **dryer**

**drift** [drɪft] n (of current etc) force f, direction f, mouvement m; (of snow) rafale f; (: on ground) congère f; (general meaning) sens (général) m ♦ vi (boat) aller à la dérive, dériver; (sand, snow) s'amonceler, s'entasser; ~**wood** n bois flotté

**drill** [drɪl] n perceuse f; (~ bit) foret m, mèche f; (of dentist) roulette f, fraise f; (MIL) exercice m ♦ vt percer; (troops) entraîner ♦ vi (for oil) faire un or des forage(s)

**drink** [drɪŋk] (pt **drank**, pp **drunk**) n boisson f; (alcoholic) verre m ♦ vt, vi boire; **to have a ~** boire quelque chose, boire un verre; prendre l'apéritif; **a ~ of water** un verre d'eau; **~er** n buveur(-euse); **~ing water** n eau f potable

**drip** [drɪp] n goutte f; (MED) goutte-à-goutte m inv, perfusion f ♦ vi tomber goutte à goutte; (tap) goutter; **~-dry** adj (shirt) sans repassage; **~ping** n graisse f (de rôti)

**drive** [draɪv] (pt **drove**, pp **driven**) n promenade f or trajet m en voiture; (also: **~way**) allée f; (energy) dynamisme m, énergie f; (push) effort (concerté), campagne f; (also: **disk ~**) lecteur m de disquettes ♦ vt conduire; (push) chasser, pousser; (TECH: motor, wheel) faire fonctionner; entraîner; (nail, stake etc): **to ~ sth into sth** enfoncer qch dans qch ♦ vi (AUT: at controls) conduire; (: travel) aller en voiture; **left-/right-hand ~** conduite f à gauche/droite; **to ~ sb mad** rendre qn fou (folle); **to ~ sb home/to the airport** reconduire qn chez lui/conduire qn à l'aéroport; **~-by shooting** n (tentative d')assassinat par coups de feu tirés d'un voiture

**drivel** ['drɪvl] (inf) n idioties fpl

**driver** ['draɪvə*] n conducteur(-trice); (of taxi, bus) chauffeur m; **~'s license** (US) n permis m de conduire

**driveway** ['draɪvweɪ] n allée f

**driving** ['draɪvɪŋ] n conduite f; **~ instructor** n moniteur m d'auto-école; **~ lesson** n leçon f de conduite; **~ licence** (BRIT) n permis m de conduire; **~ school** n auto-école f; **~ test** n examen m du permis de conduire

**drizzle** ['drɪzl] n bruine f, crachin m

**drool** [druːl] vi baver

**droop** [druːp] vi (shoulders) tomber; (head) pencher; (flower) pencher la tête

**drop** [drɔp] n goutte f; (fall) baisse f; (also: **parachute ~**) saut m ♦ vt laisser tomber; (voice, eyes, price) baisser; (set down from car) déposer ♦ vi tomber; **~s** npl (MED) gouttes; **~ off** vi (sleep) s'assoupir ♦ vt (passenger) déposer; **~ out** vi (withdraw) se retirer; (student etc) abandonner, décrocher; **~out** n marginal(e); **~per** n compte-gouttes m inv; **~pings** npl crottes fpl

**drought** [draut] n sécheresse f

**drove** [drəuv] pt of **drive**

**drown** [draun] vt noyer ♦ vi se noyer

**drowsy** ['drauzɪ] adj somnolent(e)

**drug** [drʌg] n médicament m; (narcotic) drogue f ♦ vt droguer; **to be on ~s** se droguer; **~ addict** n toxicomane m/f; **~gist** (US) n pharmacien(ne)-droguiste; **~store** (US) n pharmacie-droguerie f, drugstore m

**drum** [drʌm] n tambour m; (for oil, petrol) bidon m; **~s** npl (kit) batterie f; **~mer** n (joueur m de) tambour m

**drunk** [drʌŋk] pp of **drink** ♦ adj ivre, soûl(e) ♦ n (also: **~ard**) ivrogne m/f; **~en** adj (person) ivre, soûl(e); (rage, stupor) ivrogne, d'ivrogne

**dry** [draɪ] adj sec (sèche); (day) sans pluie; (humour) pince-sans-rire (inv); (lake, riverbed, well) à sec ♦ vt sécher; (clothes) faire sécher ♦ vi sécher; **~ up** vi tarir; **~-cleaner's** n teinturerie f; **~er** n séchoir m; (spin-dryer) essoreuse f; **~ness** n sécheresse f; **~ rot** n pourriture sèche (du bois)

**DSS** n abbr (= Department of Social Security) ≈ Sécurité sociale

**DTP** n abbr (= desk-top publishing) PAO f

**dual** ['djuəl] adj double; **~ carriageway** (BRIT) n route f à quatre voies or à chaussées séparées; **~-purpose** adj à double usage

**dubbed** [dʌbd] adj (CINEMA) doublé(e)

**dubious** ['djuːbɪəs] adj hésitant(e), incertain(e); *(reputation, company)* douteux(-euse)

**duchess** ['dʌtʃis] n duchesse f

**duck** [dʌk] n canard m ♦ vi se baisser vivement, baisser subitement la tête; **~ling** ['dʌklɪŋ] n caneton m

**duct** [dʌkt] n conduite f, canalisation f; *(ANAT)* conduit m

**dud** [dʌd] n *(object, tool)*: **it's a ~** c'est de la camelote, ça ne marche pas ♦ adj: **~ cheque** *(BRIT)* chèque sans provision

**due** [djuː] adj dû (due); *(expected)* attendu(e); *(fitting)* qui convient ♦ n: **to give sb his** *(or* **her) ~** être juste envers qn ♦ adv: **~ north** droit vers le nord; **~s** npl *(for club, union)* cotisation f; **in ~ course** en temps utile or voulu; finalement; **~ to** due (à); causé(e) par; **he's ~ to finish tomorrow** normalement il doit finir demain

**duet** [djuː'et] n duo m

**duffel bag** ['dʌfl-] n sac m marin

**duffel coat** n duffel-coat m

**dug** [dʌg] pt, pp of **dig**

**duke** [djuːk] n duc m

**dull** [dʌl] adj terne, morne; *(boring)* ennuyeux(-euse); *(sound, pain)* sourd(e); *(weather, day)* gris(e), maussade ♦ vt *(pain, grief)* atténuer; *(mind, senses)* engourdir

**duly** ['djuːlɪ] adv *(on time)* en temps voulu; *(as expected)* comme il se doit

**dumb** [dʌm] adj muet(te); *(stupid)* bête; **~founded** adj sidéré(e)

**dummy** ['dʌmɪ] n *(tailor's model)* mannequin m; *(mock-up)* factice m, maquette f; *(BRIT: for baby)* tétine f ♦ adj faux (fausse), factice

**dump** [dʌmp] n *(also:* **rubbish ~)** décharge (publique); *(pej)* trou m ♦ vt *(put down)* déposer; déverser; *(get rid of)* se débarrasser de; *(COMPUT: data)* vider, transférer

**dumpling** ['dʌmplɪŋ] n boulette f *(de pâte)*

**dumpy** ['dʌmpɪ] adj boulot(te)

**dunce** [dʌns] n âne m, cancre m

**dune** [djuːn] n dune f

**dung** [dʌŋ] n fumier m

**dungarees** [dʌŋgə'riːz] npl salopette f; bleu(s) m(pl)

**dungeon** ['dʌndʒən] n cachot m

**duplex** ['djuːpleks] *(US)* n maison jumelée; *(apartment)* duplex m

**duplicate** [n 'djuːplɪkət, vb 'djuːplɪkeɪt] n double m ♦ vt faire un double de; *(on machine)* polycopier; photocopier; **in ~** en deux exemplaires

**durable** ['djuərəbl] adj durable; *(clothes, metal)* résistant(e), solide

**duration** [djuə'reɪʃən] n durée f

**during** ['djuərɪŋ] prep pendant, au cours de

**dusk** [dʌsk] n crépuscule m

**dust** [dʌst] n poussière f ♦ vt *(furniture)* épousseter, essuyer; *(cake etc)*: **to ~ with** saupoudrer de; **~bin** *(BRIT)* n poubelle f; **~er** n chiffon m; **~man** *(BRIT)* *(irreg)* n boueux m, éboueur m; **~y** adj poussiéreux(-euse)

**Dutch** [dʌtʃ] adj hollandais(e), néerlandais(e) ♦ n *(LING)* hollandais m ♦ adv *(inf):* **to go ~** partager les frais; **the ~** npl *(people)* les Hollandais; **~man** *(irreg)* n Hollandais; **~woman** *(irreg)* n Hollandaise f

**duty** ['djuːtɪ] n devoir m; *(tax)* droit m, taxe f; **on ~** de service; *(at night etc)* de garde; **off ~** libre, pas de service or de garde; **~-free** adj exempté(e) de douane, hors taxe m

**duvet** ['duːveɪ] *(BRIT)* n couette f

**DVD** [diːviːdiː] n abbr (= digital versatile disc) DVD m

**dwarf** [dwɔːf] *(pl* **dwarves)** n nain(e) ♦ vt écraser

**dwell** [dwel] *(pt, pp* **dwelt)** vi demeurer; **~ on** vt fus s'appesantir sur

**dwindle** ['dwɪndl] vi diminuer

**dye** [daɪ] n teinture f ♦ vt teindre

**dying** ['daɪɪŋ] adj mourant(e), agonisant(e)

**dyke** [daɪk] *(BRIT)* n digue f

**dynamic** [daɪ'næmɪk] adj dynamique

**dynamite** ['daɪnəmaɪt] n dynamite f

**dynamo** ['daɪnəməʊ] n dynamo f

**dyslexia** [dɪs'leksɪə] n dyslexie f

# E, e

**E** [iː] n (MUS) mi m

**each** [iːtʃ] adj chaque ♦ pron chacun(e); ~ **other** l'un(e) l'autre; **they hate** ~ **other** ils se détestent (mutuellement); **you are jealous of** ~ **other** vous êtes jaloux l'un de l'autre; **they have 2 books** ~ ils ont 2 livres chacun

**eager** ['iːɡə'] adj (keen) avide; **to be** ~ **to do sth** avoir très envie de faire qch; **to be** ~ **for** désirer vivement, être avide de

**eagle** ['iːɡl] n aigle m

**ear** [ɪə'] n oreille f; (of corn) épi m; **~ache** n mal m aux oreilles; **~drum** n tympan m

**earl** [əːl] (BRIT) n' comte m

**earlier** ['əːlɪə'] adj (date etc) plus rapproché(e); (edition, fashion etc) plus ancien(ne), antérieur(e) ♦ adv plus tôt

**early** ['əːlɪ] adv tôt, de bonne heure; (ahead of time) en avance; (near the beginning) au début ♦ adj qui se manifeste (or se fait) tôt or de bonne heure; (work) de jeunesse; (settler, Christian) premier(-ère); (reply) rapide; (death, birth) prématuré(e); **to have an** ~ **night** se coucher tôt or de bonne heure; **in the** ~ **or** ~ **in the spring/19th century** au début du printemps/19ème siècle; ~ **retirement** n: **to take** ~ **retirement** prendre sa retraite anticipée

**earmark** ['ɪəmɑːk] vt: **to** ~ **sth for** réserver or destiner qch à

**earn** [əːn] vt gagner; (COMM: yield) rapporter

**earnest** ['əːnɪst] adj sérieux(-euse); **in** ~ ♦ adv sérieusement

**earnings** ['əːnɪŋz] npl salaire m; (of company) bénéfices mpl

**ear: ~phones** npl écouteurs mpl; **~ring** n

**n** boucle f d'oreille; **~shot** n: **within** **~shot** à portée de voix

**earth** [əːθ] n (gen, also BRIT: ELEC) terre f ♦ vt relier à la terre; **~enware** n poterie f; faïence f; **~quake** n tremblement m de terre, séisme m; **~y** adj (vulgar: humour) truculent(e)

**ease** [iːz] n facilité f, aisance f; (comfort) bien-être m ♦ vt (soothe) calmer; (loosen) relâcher, détendre; **to** ~ **sth in/out** faire pénétrer/sortir qch délicatement or avec douceur; faciliter la pénétration/la sortie de qch; **at** ~! (MIL) repos!; ~ **off** vi diminuer; (slow down) ralentir; ~ **up** vi = ease off

**easel** ['iːzl] n chevalet m

**easily** ['iːzɪlɪ] adv facilement

**east** [iːst] n est m ♦ adj (wind) d'est; (side) est inv ♦ adv à l'est, vers l'est; **the** **E~** l'Orient m; **les pays** mpl **de l'Est**

**Easter** ['iːstə'] n Pâques fpl; ~ **egg** n œuf m de Pâques

**east: ~erly** ['iːstəlɪ] adj (wind) d'est, (direction) est inv; (point) vers l'est; **~ern** ['iːstən] adj de l'est, oriental(e); **~ward(s)** ['iːstwəd(z)] adv vers l'est, à l'est

**easy** ['iːzɪ] adj facile; (manner) aisé(e) ♦ adv: **to take it** or **things** ~ ne pas se fatiguer; (not worry) ne pas (trop) s'en faire; ~ **chair** n fauteuil m; **~-going** adj accommodant(e), facile à vivre

**eat** [iːt] (pt ate, pp eaten) vt, vi manger; ~ **away** or, ~ **into** vt fus ronger, attaquer; (savings) entamer

**eaves** [iːvz] npl avant-toit m

**eavesdrop** ['iːvzdrɔp] vi: **to** ~ **(on a conversation)** écouter (une conversation) de façon indiscrète

**ebb** [ɛb] n reflux m ♦ vi refluer; (fig: also: ~ **away**) décliner

**ebony** ['ɛbənɪ] n ébène f

**EC** n abbr (= European Community) C.E. f

**ECB** n abbr (= European Central Bank) BCE f

**eccentric** [ɪk'sɛntrɪk] adj excentrique ♦ n excentrique m/f

**echo** ['ɛkəʊ] (pl ~es) n écho m ♦ vt ré-

**péter ♦** vi résonner, faire écho

**eclipse** [ɪ'klɪps] n éclipse f

**ecology** [ɪ'kɔlədʒɪ] n écologie f

**e-commerce** ['iːkɔmɜːs] n commerce m électronique

**economic** [iːkə'nɔmɪk] adj économique; (business etc) rentable; **~al** adj économique; (person) économe

**economics** [iːkə'nɔmɪks] n économie f politique ♦ npl (of project, situation) aspect m financier

**economize** [ɪ'kɔnəmaɪz] vi économiser, faire des économies

**economy** [ɪ'kɔnəmɪ] n économie f; **~ class** n classe f touriste; **~ size** n format m économique

**ecstasy** ['ekstəsɪ] n extase f (drogue aussi); **ecstatic** [eks'tætɪk] adj extatique

**ECU** ['eɪkjuː] n abbr (= European Currency Unit) ECU m

**eczema** ['eksɪmə] n eczéma m

**edge** [edʒ] n bord m; (of knife etc) tranchant m, fil m ♦ vt border; **on** ~ (fig) crispé(e), tendu(e); **to ~ away from** s'éloigner furtivement de; **~ways** adv: **he couldn't get a word in ~ways** il ne pouvait pas placer un mot

**edgy** ['edʒɪ] adj crispé(e), tendu(e)

**edible** ['edɪbl] adj comestible

**Edinburgh** ['edɪnbərə] n Édimbourg

**edit** ['edɪt] vt (text, book) éditer; (report) préparer; (film) monter; (broadcast) réaliser; **~ion** [ɪ'dɪʃən] n édition f; **~or** n (of column) rédacteur(-trice); (of newspaper) rédacteur(-trice) en chef; (of sb's work) éditeur(-trice); **~orial** [edɪ'tɔːrɪəl] adj de la rédaction, éditorial(e) ♦ n éditorial m

**educate** ['edjukeɪt] vt (teach) instruire; (instruct) éduquer; **~d** adj (person) cultivé(e); **education** [edju'keɪʃən] n éducation f; (studies) études fpl; (teaching) enseignement m, instruction f; **educational** adj (experience, toy) pédagogique; (institution) scolaire; (policy) d'éducation

**eel** [iːl] n anguille f

**eerie** ['ɪərɪ] adj inquiétant(e)

**effect** [ɪ'fekt] n effet m ♦ vt effectuer; **to take ~** (law) entrer en vigueur; (drug) agir, faire son effet; **in ~** en réalité; **~ive** [ɪ'fektɪv] adj efficace; (actual) véritable; **~ively** adv efficacement; (in reality) effectivement; **~iveness** n efficacité f

**effeminate** [ɪ'femɪnɪt] adj efféminé(e)

**effervescent** [efə'vesnt] adj (drink) gazeux(-euse)

**efficiency** [ɪ'fɪʃənsɪ] n efficacité f; (of machine) rendement m

**efficient** [ɪ'fɪʃənt] adj efficace; (machine) qui a un bon rendement

**effort** ['efət] n effort m; **~less** adj (style) aisé(e); (achievement) facile

**effusive** [ɪ'fjuːsɪv] adj chaleureux(-euse)

**e.g.** adv abbr (= exempli gratia) par exemple, p. ex.

**egg** [eg] n œuf m; **hard-boiled/soft-boiled ~** œuf dur/à la coque; **~ on** vt pousser; **~cup** n coquetier m; **~plant** n (esp US) aubergine f; **~shell** n coquille f d'œuf

**ego** ['iːgəu] n (self-esteem) amour-propre m

**egotism** ['egəutɪzəm] n égotisme m

**egotist** ['egəutɪst] n égocentrique m/f

**Egypt** ['iːdʒɪpt] n Égypte f; **~ian** [ɪ'dʒɪpʃən] adj égyptien(ne) ♦ n Égyptien(ne)

**eiderdown** ['aɪdədaun] n édredon m

**Eiffel Tower** ['aɪfəl-] n tour f Eiffel

**eight** [eɪt] num huit; **~een** [eɪ'tiːn] num dix-huit; **~h** [eɪtθ] num huitième; **~y** ['eɪtɪ] num quatre-vingt(s)

**Eire** ['eərə] n République f d'Irlande

**either** ['aɪðə] adj l'un ou l'autre; (both, each) chaque ♦ pron: **~ (of them)** l'un ou l'autre ♦ adv non plus ♦ conj: **~ good or bad** ou bon ou mauvais, soit bon soit mauvais; **on ~ side** de chaque côté; **I don't like ~** je n'aime ni l'un ni l'autre; **no, I don't ~** moi non plus

**eject** [ɪ'dʒekt] vt (tenant etc) expulser

(object) éjecter

**elaborate** [adj ɪˈlæbərɪt, vb ɪˈlæbəreɪt] adj compliqué(e), recherché(e) ♦ vt élaborer ♦ vi: **to ~ (on)** entrer dans les détails (de)

**elastic** [ɪˈlæstɪk] adj élastique ♦ n élastique m; **~ band** n élastique m

**elated** [ɪˈleɪtɪd] adj transporté(e) de joie

**elation** [ɪˈleɪʃən] n allégresse f

**elbow** [ˈelbəʊ] n coude m

**elder** [ˈeldər] adj aîné(e) ♦ n (tree) sureau m; **one's ~s** ses aînés; **~ly** adj âgé(e) ♦ npl: **the ~ly** les personnes âgées

**eldest** [ˈeldɪst] adj, n: **the ~ (child)** l'aîné(e) (de) (enfants)

**elect** [ɪˈlekt] vt élire ♦ adj: **the president ~** le président désigné; **to ~ to do** choisir de faire; **~ion** n élection f; **~ioneering** [ɪlekʃəˈnɪərɪŋ] n propagande électorale, manœuvres électorales; **~or** n électeur(-trice); **~orate** n électorat m

**electric** [ɪˈlektrɪk] adj électrique; **~al** adj électrique; **~ blanket** n couverture chauffante; **~ fire** (BRIT) n radiateur m électrique; **~ian** [ɪlekˈtrɪʃən] n électricien m; **~ity** [ɪlekˈtrɪsɪtɪ] n électricité f

**electrify** [ɪˈlektrɪfaɪ] vt (RAIL, fence) électrifier; (audience) électriser

**electronic** [ɪlekˈtrɔnɪk] adj électronique; **~ mail** n courrier m électronique; **~s** n électronique f

**elegant** [ˈelɪɡənt] adj élégant(e)

**element** [ˈelɪmənt] n (gen) élément m; (of heater, kettle etc) résistance f; **~ary** [elɪˈmentərɪ] adj élémentaire; (school, education) primaire

**elephant** [ˈelɪfənt] n éléphant m

**elevation** [elɪˈveɪʃən] n (raising, promotion) avancement m, promotion f; (height) hauteur f

**elevator** [ˈelɪveɪtər] n (in warehouse etc) élévateur m, monte-charge m inv; (US: lift) ascenseur m

**eleven** [ɪˈlevn] num onze; **~ses** [ɪˈlevnzɪz] npl ≃ pause-café f; **~th** num

onzième

**elicit** [ɪˈlɪsɪt] vt: **to ~ (from)** obtenir (de), arracher (à)

**eligible** [ˈelɪdʒəbl] adj: **to be ~ for** remplir les conditions requises pour; **an ~ young man/woman** un beau parti

**elm** [elm] n orme m

**elongated** [ˈiːlɔŋɡeɪtɪd] adj allongé(e)

**elope** [ɪˈləʊp] vi (lovers) s'enfuir (ensemble)

**eloquent** [ˈeləkwənt] adj éloquent(e)

**else** [els] adv d'autre; **something ~** quelque chose d'autre, autre chose; **somewhere ~** ailleurs, autre part; **everywhere ~** partout ailleurs; **nobody ~** personne d'autre; **where ~?** à quel autre endroit?; **little ~** pas grand-chose d'autre; **~where** adv ailleurs, autre part

**elude** [ɪˈluːd] vt échapper à

**elusive** [ɪˈluːsɪv] adj insaisissable

**emaciated** [ɪˈmeɪsɪeɪtɪd] adj émacié(e), décharné(e)

**e-mail** [ˈiːmeɪl] n courrier m électronique ♦ vt (person) envoyer un message électronique à

**emancipate** [ɪˈmænsɪpeɪt] vt émanciper

**embankment** [ɪmˈbæŋkmənt] n (of road, railway) remblai m, talus m; (of river) berge f, quai m

**embark** [ɪmˈbɑːk] vi embarquer; **to ~ on** (journey) entreprendre; (fig) se lancer or s'embarquer dans; **~ation** [embɑːˈkeɪʃən] n embarquement m

**embarrass** [ɪmˈbærəs] vt embarrasser, gêner; **~ed** adj gêné(e); **~ing** adj gênant(e), embarrassant(e); **~ment** n embarras m, gêne f

**embassy** [ˈembəsɪ] n ambassade f

**embedded** [ɪmˈbedɪd] adj enfoncé(e)

**embellish** [ɪmˈbelɪʃ] vt orner, décorer; (fig: account) enjoliver

**embers** [ˈembəz] npl braise f

**embezzle** [ɪmˈbezl] vt détourner; **~ment** n détournement m de fonds

**embitter** [ɪmˈbɪtər] vt (person) aigrir;

(relations) envenimer

**embody** [ɪm'bɒdɪ] vt (features) réunir, comprendre; (ideas) formuler, exprimer

**embossed** [ɪm'bɒst] adj (metal) estampé(e); (leather) frappé(e); ~ **wallpaper** papier gaufré

**embrace** [ɪm'breɪs] vt embrasser, étreindre; (include) embrasser ♦ vi s'étreindre, s'embrasser ♦ n étreinte f

**embroider** [ɪm'brɔɪdə'] vt broder; ~**y** n broderie f

**emerald** ['emərəld] n émeraude f

**emerge** [ɪ'mɜːdʒ] vi apparaître; (from room, car) surgir; (from sleep, imprisonment) sortir

**emergency** [ɪ'mɜːdʒənsɪ] n urgence f; **in an ~** en cas d'urgence; ~ **cord** n (US) sonnette f d'alarme; ~ **exit** n sortie f de secours; ~ **landing** n atterrissage forcé; ~ **services** npl: **the ~ services** (fire, police, ambulance) les services mpl d'urgence

**emery board** ['eməri-] n lime f à ongles (en carton émerisé)

**emigrate** ['emɪɡreɪt] vi émigrer

**eminent** ['emɪnənt] adj éminent(e)

**emissions** [ɪ'mɪʃənz] npl émissions fpl

**emit** [ɪ'mɪt] vt émettre

**emotion** [ɪ'məʊʃən] n émotion f; ~**al** adj (person) émotif(-ive), très sensible; (needs, exhaustion) affectif(-ive); (scene) émouvant(e); (tone, speech) qui fait appel aux sentiments; **emotive** adj chargé(e) d'émotion; (subject) sensible

**emperor** ['empərə'] n empereur m

**emphasis** ['emfəsɪs] n (pl **-ases**) (stress) accent m; (importance) insistance f

**emphasize** ['emfəsaɪz] vt (syllable, word, point) appuyer or insister sur; (feature) souligner, accentuer

**emphatic** [em'fætɪk] adj (strong) énergique, vigoureux(-euse); (unambiguous, clear) catégorique

**empire** ['empaɪə'] n empire m

**employ** [ɪm'plɔɪ] vt employer; ~**ee** n employé(e); ~**er** n employeur(-euse);

~**ment** n emploi m; ~**ment agency** n agence f or bureau m de placement

**empower** [ɪm'paʊə'] vt: **to ~ sb to do** autoriser or habiliter qn à faire

**empress** ['emprɪs] n impératrice f

**emptiness** ['emptɪnɪs] n (of area, region) aspect m désertique m; (of life) vide m, vacuité f

**empty** ['emptɪ] adj vide; (threat, promise) en l'air, vain(e) ♦ vt vider; ♦ vi se vider; (liquid) s'écouler; ~**-handed** adj les mains vides

**EMU** n abbr (= economic and monetary union) UME f

**emulate** ['emjʊleɪt] vt rivaliser avec, imiter

**emulsion** [ɪ'mʌlʃən] n émulsion f; (also: ~ **paint**) peinture mate

**enable** [ɪ'neɪbl] vt: **to ~ sb to do** permettre à qn de faire

**enamel** [ɪ'næməl] n émail m; (also: ~ **paint**) peinture laquée

**enchant** [ɪn'tʃɑːnt] vt enchanter; ~**ing** adj ravissant(e), enchanteur(-teresse)

**encl.** abbr = **enclosed**

**enclose** [ɪn'kləʊz] vt (land) clôturer; (space, object) entourer; (letter etc): **to ~ (with)** joindre (à); **please find ~d** veuillez trouver ci-joint; **enclosure** n enceinte f

**encompass** [ɪn'kʌmpəs] vt (include) contenir, inclure

**encore** [ɒŋ'kɔː'] excl bis ♦ n bis m

**encounter** [ɪn'kaʊntə'] n rencontre f ♦ vt rencontrer

**encourage** [ɪn'kʌrɪdʒ] vt encourager; ~**ment** n encouragement m

**encroach** [ɪn'krəʊtʃ] vi: **to ~ (up)on** empiéter sur

**encyclop(a)edia** [ensaɪklə'piːdɪə] n encyclopédie f

**end** [end] n (gen, also: aim) fin f; (of table, street, rope etc) bout m, extrémité f ♦ vt terminer; (also: **bring to an ~, put an ~ to**) mettre fin à ♦ vi se terminer, finir; **in the ~** finalement; **on ~** (object) debout, dressé(e); **to stand on ~**

(hair) se dresser sur la tête; **for hours on ~** pendant des heures et des heures; **~ up** vi: **to ~ up in** (condition) finir or se terminer par; (place) finir or aboutir à

**endanger** [ɪnˈdeɪndʒəʳ] vt mettre en danger; **an ~ed species** une espèce en voie de disparition

**endearing** [ɪnˈdɪərɪŋ] adj attachant(e)

**endeavour** [ɪnˈdevəʳ] (US **endeavor**) n tentative f, effort m ♦ vi: **to ~ to do** tenter or s'efforcer de faire

**ending** [ˈendɪŋ] n dénouement m, fin f; (LING) terminaison f

**endive** [ˈendaɪv] n chicorée f; (smooth) endive f

**endless** [ˈendlɪs] adj sans fin, interminable

**endorse** [ɪnˈdɔːs] vt (cheque) endosser; (approve) appuyer, approuver, sanctionner; **~ment** n (approval) appui m, aval m; (BRIT: on driving licence) contravention portée au permis de conduire

**endure** [ɪnˈdjuəʳ] vt supporter, endurer ♦ vi durer

**enemy** [ˈenəmɪ] adj, n ennemi(e)

**energetic** [enəˈdʒetɪk] adj énergique; (activity) qui fait se dépenser (physiquement)

**energy** [ˈenədʒɪ] n énergie f

**enforce** [ɪnˈfɔːs] vt (law) appliquer, faire respecter

**engage** [ɪnˈɡeɪdʒ] vt engager; (attention etc) retenir ♦ vi (TECH) s'enclencher, s'engrener; **to ~ in** se lancer dans; **~d** adj (BRIT: busy, in use) occupé(e); (betrothed) fiancé(e); **to get ~d** se fiancer; **~d tone** n (TEL) tonalité f occupé inv or pas libre; **~ment** n obligation f, engagement m; rendez-vous m inv; (to marry) fiançailles fpl; **~ment ring** n bague f de fiançailles; **engaging** adj engageant(e), attirant(e)

**engine** [ˈendʒɪn] n (AUT) moteur m; (RAIL) locomotive f; **~ driver** n mécanicien m

**engineer** [endʒɪˈnɪəʳ] n ingénieur m;

(BRIT: repairer) dépanneur m; (NAVY, US RAIL) mécanicien m; **~ing** n engineering m, ingénierie f; (of bridges, ships) génie m; (of machine) mécanique f

**England** [ˈɪŋɡlənd] n Angleterre f

**English** adj anglais(e) ♦ n (LING) anglais m; **the English** npl (people) les Anglais; **the English Channel** la Manche; **Englishman** (irreg) n Anglais m; **Englishwoman** (irreg) n Anglaise f

**engraving** [ɪnˈɡreɪvɪŋ] n gravure f

**engrossed** [ɪnˈɡrəust] adj: **~ in** absorbé(e) par, plongé(e) dans

**engulf** [ɪnˈɡʌlf] vt engloutir

**enhance** [ɪnˈhɑːns] vt rehausser, mettre en valeur

**enjoy** [ɪnˈdʒɔɪ] vt aimer, prendre plaisir à; (have, fortune) jouir de; (: success) connaître; **to ~ o.s.** s'amuser; **~able** adj agréable; **~ment** n plaisir m

**enlarge** [ɪnˈlɑːdʒ] vt accroître; (PHOT) agrandir ♦ vi: **to ~ on** (subject) s'étendre sur; **~ment** n (PHOT) agrandissement m

**enlighten** [ɪnˈlaɪtn] vt éclairer; **~ed** adj éclairé(e); **~ment** n: **the E~ment** (HISTORY) ≈ le Siècle des lumières

**enlist** [ɪnˈlɪst] vt recruter; (support) s'assurer ♦ vi s'engager

**enmity** [ˈenmɪtɪ] n inimitié f

**enormous** [ɪˈnɔːməs] adj énorme

**enough** [ɪˈnʌf] adj, pron: **~ time/books** assez or suffisamment de temps/livres ♦ adv: **big ~** assez or suffisamment grand; **have you got ~?** en avez-vous assez?; **he has not worked ~** il n'a pas assez or suffisamment travaillé; **~ to eat** assez à manger; **~! assez!, ça suffit!; that's ~, thanks** cela suffit or c'est assez, merci; **I've had ~ of him** j'en ai assez de lui; **... which, funnily** or **oddly ~** ... qui, chose curieuse

**enquire** [ɪnˈkwaɪəʳ] vt, vi = **inquire**

**enrage** [ɪnˈreɪdʒ] vt mettre en fureur or en rage, rendre furieux(-euse)

**enrol** [ɪnˈrəul] (US **enroll**) vt inscrire ♦ vi s'inscrire; **~ment** n (US **enrollment**) n inscription f

**en suite** ['ɒnswi:t] *adj*: **with ~ bathroom** avec salle de bains en attenante

**ensure** [ɪn'ʃuə] *vt* assurer; garantir; **to ~ that** s'assurer que

**entail** [ɪn'teɪl] *vt* entraîner, occasionner

**entangled** [ɪn'tæŋɡld] *adj*: **to become ~ (in)** s'empêtrer (dans)

**enter** ['entə] *vt* (room) entrer dans, pénétrer dans; (club, army) entrer à; (competition) s'inscrire à or pour; (sb for a competition) (faire) inscrire; (write down) inscrire, noter; (COMPUT) entrer, introduire ♦ *vi* entrer; **~ for** *vt fus* s'inscrire à, se présenter pour or à; **~ into** *vt fus* (explanation) se lancer dans; (discussion, negotiations) entamer; (agreement) conclure

**enterprise** ['entəpraɪz] *n* entreprise f; (initiative) (esprit m d')initiative f; **free ~** libre entreprise; **private ~** entreprise privée; **enterprising** *adj* entreprenant(e), dynamique; (scheme) audacieux(-euse)

**entertain** [entə'teɪn] *vt* amuser, distraire; (invite) recevoir (à dîner); (idea, plan) envisager; **~er** *n* artiste m/f de variétés; **~ing** *adj* amusant(e), distrayant(e); **~ment** *n* (amusement) divertissement m, amusement m; (show) spectacle m

**enthralled** [ɪn'θrɔ:ld] *adj* captivé(e)

**enthusiasm** [ɪn'θu:zɪæzəm] *n* enthousiasme m

**enthusiast** [ɪn'θu:zɪæst] *n* enthousiaste m/f; **~ic** [ɪnθu:zɪ'æstɪk] *adj* enthousiaste; **to be ~ic about** être enthousiasmé(e) par

**entire** [ɪn'taɪə] *adj* (tout) entier(-ère); **~ly** *adv* entièrement, complètement; **~ty** [ɪn'taɪərətɪ] *n*: **in its ~ty** dans sa totalité

**entitle** [ɪn'taɪtl] *vt*: **to ~ sb to sth** donner droit à qch à qn; **~d** [ɪn'taɪtld] *adj* (book) intitulé(e); **to be ~d to do** avoir le droit de or être habilité à faire

**entrance** [*n* 'entrns, *vb* ɪn'trɑ:ns] *n* en-

trée f ♦ *vt* enchanter, ravir; **to gain ~ to** (university etc) être admis à; **~ examination** *n* examen d'entrée; **~ fee** *n* (to museum etc) prix m d'entrée; (to join club etc) droit m d'inscription; **~ ramp** (US) *n* (AUT) bretelle f d'accès; **entrant** *n* participant(e); concurrent(e); (BRIT: in exam) candidat(e)

**entrenched** [en'trentʃt] *adj* retranché(e); (ideas) arrêté(e)

**entrepreneur** ['ɒntrəprə'nə:] *n* entrepreneur m

**entrust** [ɪn'trʌst] *vt*: **to ~ sth to** confier qch à

**entry** ['entrɪ] *n* entrée f; (in register) inscription f; **no ~** défense d'entrer, entrée interdite; (AUT) sens interdit; **~ form** (BRIT) *n* feuille f d'inscription; **~ phone** (BRIT) *n* interphone m

**envelop** [ɪn'veləp] *vt* envelopper

**envelope** ['envələup] *n* enveloppe f

**envious** ['envɪəs] *adj* envieux(-euse)

**environment** [ɪn'vaɪərnmənt] *n* environnement m; (social, moral) milieu m; **~al** [ɪnvaɪərn'mentl] *adj* écologique; du milieu; **~-friendly** *adj* écologique

**envisage** [ɪn'vɪzɪdʒ] *vt* (foresee) prévoir

**envoy** ['envɔɪ] *n* (diplomat) ministre m plénipotentiaire

**envy** ['envɪ] *n* envie f ♦ *vt* envier; **to ~ sb sth** envier qch à qn

**epic** ['epɪk] *n* épopée f ♦ *adj* épique

**epidemic** [epɪ'demɪk] *n* épidémie f

**epilepsy** ['epɪlepsɪ] *n* épilepsie f; **epileptic** [epɪ'leptɪk] *adj* épileptique m/f

**episode** ['epɪsəud] *n* épisode m

**epitome** [ɪ'pɪtəmɪ] *n* modèle m; **epitomize** [ɪ'pɪtəmaɪz] *vt* incarner

**equal** ['i:kwl] *adj* égal(e) ♦ *n* égal(e) ♦ *vt* égaler; **~ to** (task) à la hauteur de; **~ity** [i:'kwɒlɪtɪ] *n* égalité f; **~ize** *vi* (SPORT) égaliser; **~ly** *adv* également; (just as) tout aussi

**equanimity** [ekwə'nɪmɪtɪ] *n* égalité f d'humeur

**equate** [ɪ'kweɪt] *vt*: **to ~ sth with** comparer qch à; assimiler qch à; **equa-**

**tion** n (MATH) équation f

**equator** [ɪ'kweɪtə*] n équateur m

**equilibrium** [iːkwɪ'lɪbrɪəm] n équilibre m

**equip** [ɪ'kwɪp] vt: **to ~ (with)** équiper (de); **to be well ~ped** être bien équipé(e); **~ment** n équipement m; (electrical etc) appareillage m, installation f

**equities** ['ekwɪtɪz] (BRIT) npl (COMM) actions cotées en Bourse

**equivalent** [ɪ'kwɪvələnt] adj: **~ (to)** équivalent(e) (à) ♦ n équivalent m

**era** ['ɪərə] n ère f, époque f

**eradicate** [ɪ'rædɪkeɪt] vt éliminer

**erase** [ɪ'reɪz] vt effacer; **~r** n gomme f

**erect** [ɪ'rekt] adj droit(e) ♦ vt construire; (monument) ériger, élever; (tent etc) dresser; **~ion** n (PHYSIOL) érection f

**ERM** n abbr (= Exchange Rate Mechanism) MTC m

**erode** [ɪ'rəʊd] vt éroder; (metal) ronger

**erotic** [ɪ'rɒtɪk] adj érotique

**errand** ['erənd] n course f, commission f

**erratic** [ɪ'rætɪk] adj irrégulier(-ère); inconstant(e)

**error** ['erə*] n erreur f

**erupt** [ɪ'rʌpt] vi entrer en éruption; (fig) éclater; **~ion** n éruption f

**escalate** ['eskəleɪt] vi s'intensifier

**escalator** ['eskəleɪtə*] n escalier roulant

**escapade** [eskə'peɪd] n (misdeed) fredaine f; (adventure) équipée f

**escape** [ɪs'keɪp] n fuite f; (from prison) évasion f ♦ vi s'échapper, fuir; (from jail) s'évader; (fig) s'en tirer; (leak) s'échapper ♦ vt échapper à; **to ~ from** (person) échapper à; (place) s'échapper de; (fig) fuir; **escapism** n (fig) évasion f

**escort** [n 'eskɔːt, vb ɪs'kɔːt] n escorte f ♦ vt escorter

**Eskimo** ['eskɪməʊ] n Esquimau(de)

**especially** [ɪs'peʃlɪ] adv (particularly) particulièrement; (above all) surtout

**espionage** ['espɪənɑːʒ] n espionnage m

**Esquire** [ɪs'kwaɪə*] n: **J Brown, ~** Monsieur J. Brown

**essay** ['eseɪ] n (SCOL) dissertation f; (LITERATURE) essai m

**essence** ['esns] n essence f

**essential** [ɪ'senʃl] adj essentiel(le); (basic) fondamental(e) ♦ n: **~s** éléments essentiels; **~ly** adv essentiellement

**establish** [ɪs'tæblɪʃ] vt établir; (business) fonder, créer; (one's power etc) asseoir, affermir; **~ed** adj bien établi(e); **~ment** n établissement m; (founding) création f

**estate** [ɪs'teɪt] n (land) domaine m, propriété f; (LAW) biens mpl, succession f; (BRIT: also: **housing ~**) lotissement m, cité f; **~ agent** n agent immobilier; **~ car** (BRIT) n break m

**esteem** [ɪs'tiːm] n estime f

**esthetic** [ɪs'θetɪk] (US) adj = **aesthetic**

**estimate** [n 'estɪmət, vb 'estɪmeɪt] n estimation f; (COMM) devis m ♦ vt estimer; **estimation** [estɪ'meɪʃən] n opinion f; (calculation) estimation f

**estranged** [ɪs'treɪndʒd] adj séparé(e); dont on s'est séparé(e)

**etc.** abbr (= et cetera) etc

**eternal** [ɪ'tɜːnl] adj éternel(le)

**eternity** [ɪ'tɜːnɪtɪ] n éternité f

**ethical** ['eθɪkl] adj moral(e); **ethics** n éthique f ♦ npl moralité f

**Ethiopia** [iːθɪ'əʊpɪə] n Éthiopie f

**ethnic** ['eθnɪk] adj ethnique; (music etc) folklorique; **~ minority** minorité f ethnique

**ethos** ['iːθɒs] n génie m

**etiquette** ['etɪket] n convenances fpl, étiquette f

**EU** n abbr (= European Union) UE f

**euro** ['juərəʊ] n (currency) euro m

**Euroland** ['juərəʊlænd] n Euroland m

**Eurocheque** ['juərəʊtʃek] n eurochèque m

**Europe** ['juərəp] n Europe f; **~an** [juərə'piːən] adj européen(ne) ♦ n Européen(ne); **~an Community** Communauté européenne

**evacuate** [ɪ'vækjueɪt] vt évacuer

**evade** [ɪ'veɪd] vt échapper à; (question etc) éluder; (duties) se dérober à; **to ~ tax** frauder le fisc

**evaporate** [ɪ'væpəreɪt] vi s'évaporer; **~d milk** n lait condensé non sucré

**evasion** [ɪ'veɪʒən] n dérobade f; **tax ~** fraude fiscale

**eve** [iːv] n: **on the ~ of** à la veille de

**even** [ˈiːvn] adj (level, smooth) régulier(-ère); (equal) égal(e); (number) pair(e) ♦ adv même; **~ if** même si +indic; **~ though** alors même que +cond; **~ more** encore plus; **~ so** quand même; **not ~** pas même; **to get ~ with sb** prendre sa revanche sur qn

**evening** [ˈiːvnɪŋ] n soir m; (as duration, event) soirée f; **in the ~** le soir; **~ class** n cours m du soir; **~ dress** n tenue f de soirée

**event** [ɪ'vent] n événement m; (SPORT) épreuve f; **in the ~ of** en cas de; **~ful** adj mouvementé(e)

**eventual** [ɪ'ventʃuəl] adj final(e); **~ity** [ɪventʃu'ælɪtɪ] n possibilité f, éventualité f; **~ly** adv finalement

**ever** [ˈevəʳ] adv jamais; (at all times) toujours; **the best ~** le meilleur qu'on ait jamais vu; **have you ~ seen it?** l'as-tu déjà vu?, as-tu eu l'occasion or c'est-il arrivé de le voir?; **why ~ not?** mais enfin, pourquoi pas?; **~ since** adv depuis ♦ conj depuis que; **~green** n arbre m à feuilles persistantes; **~lasting** adj éternel(le)

**every** [ˈevrɪ] adj chaque; **~ day** tous les jours, chaque jour; **~ other/third day** tous les deux/trois jours; **~ other car** une voiture sur deux; **~ now and then** de temps en temps; **~body** pron tout le monde, tous pl; **~day** adj quotidien(ne), de tous les jours; **~one** pron = **everybody**; **~thing** pron tout; **~where** adv partout

**evict** [ɪ'vɪkt] vt expulser; **~ion** n expulsion f

**evidence** [ˈevɪdns] n (proof) preuve(s)

f(pl); (of witness) témoignage m; (sign): **to show ~ of** présenter des signes de; **to give ~** témoigner, déposer

**evident** [ˈevɪdnt] adj évident(e); **~ly** adv de toute évidence; (apparently) apparemment

**evil** [ˈiːvl] adj mauvais(e) ♦ n mal m

**evoke** [ɪ'vəuk] vt évoquer

**evolution** [iːvə'luːʃən] n évolution f

**evolve** [ɪ'vɔlv] vt élaborer ♦ vi évoluer

**ewe** [juː] n brebis f

**ex-** [eks] prefix ex-

**exact** [ɪg'zækt] adj exact(e) ♦ vt: **to ~ sth (from)** extorquer qch (à); exiger qch (de); **~ing** adj exigeant(e); (work) astreignant(e); **~ly** adv exactement

**exaggerate** [ɪg'zædʒəreɪt] vt, vi exagérer; **exaggeration** [ɪgzædʒə'reɪʃən] n exagération f

**exalted** [ɪg'zɔːltɪd] adj (prominent) élevé(e); (: person) haut placé(e)

**exam** [ɪg'zæm] n abbr (SCOL) = **examination**

**examination** [ɪgzæmɪ'neɪʃən] n (SCOL, MED) examen m

**examine** [ɪg'zæmɪn] vt (gen) examiner; (SCOL: person) interroger; **~r** n examinateur(-trice)

**example** [ɪg'zɑːmpl] n exemple m; **for ~** par exemple

**exasperate** [ɪg'zɑːspəreɪt] vt exaspérer; **exasperation** [ɪgzɑːspə'reɪʃən] n exaspération f, irritation f

**excavate** [ˈekskəveɪt] vt excaver; **excavation** [ekskə'veɪʃən] n fouilles fpl

**exceed** [ɪk'siːd] vt dépasser; (one's powers) outrepasser; **~ingly** adv extrêmement

**excellent** [ˈeksələnt] adj excellent(e)

**except** [ɪk'sept] prep (also: **~ for, ~ing**) sauf, excepté ♦ vt excepter; **~ if/when** sauf si/quand; **~ that** sauf que, si ce n'est que; **~ion** n exception f; **to take ~ion to** s'offusquer de; **~ional** adj exceptionnel(le)

**excerpt** [ˈeksəːpt] n extrait m

**excess** [ɪk'ses] n excès m; **~ baggage**

n excédent m de bagages; ~ **fare** (BRIT) n supplément m; **~ive** adj excessif(-ive)

**exchange** [ɪks'tʃeɪndʒ] n échange m; (also: **telephone ~**) central m ♦ vt: **to ~ (for)** échanger (contre); **~ rate** n taux m de change

**Exchequer** [ɪks'tʃekə*] (BRIT) n: **the ~** l'Échiquier m, ≈ le ministère des Finances

**excise** [n 'eksaɪz, vb ek'saɪz] n taxe f ♦ vt exciser

**excite** [ɪk'saɪt] vt exciter; **to get ~d** s'exciter; **~ment** n excitation f; **exciting** adj passionnant(e)

**exclaim** [ɪks'kleɪm] vi s'exclamer; **exclamation** [ekskləˈmeɪʃən] n exclamation f; **exclamation mark** n point m d'exclamation

**exclude** [ɪks'kluːd] vt exclure; **exclusion zone** n zone interdite; **exclusive** adj exclusif(-ive); (club, district) sélect(e); (item of news) en exclusivité; **exclusive of VAT** TVA non comprise; **mutually exclusive** qui s'excluent l'un(e) l'autre

**excruciating** [ɪks'kruːʃieɪtɪŋ] adj atroce

**excursion** [ɪks'kəːʃən] n excursion f

**excuse** [n ɪks'kjuːs, vb ɪks'kjuːz] n excuse f ♦ vt excuser; **to ~ sb from** (activity) dispenser qn de ♦ **~ me!** excusez-moi, pardon!; **now if you will ~ me, ...** maintenant, si vous (le) permettez ...

**ex-directory** ['eksdɪ'rektərɪ] (BRIT) adj sur la liste rouge

**execute** ['eksɪkjuːt] vt exécuter; **execution** n exécution f

**executive** [ɪg'zekjutɪv] n (COMM) cadre m; (of organization, political party) bureau m ♦ adj exécutif(-ive)

**exemplify** [ɪg'zemplɪfaɪ] vt illustrer; (typify) incarner

**exempt** [ɪg'zempt] adj: **~ from** exempté(e) or dispensé(e) de ♦ vt: **to ~ sb from** exempter or dispenser qn de

**exercise** ['eksəsaɪz] n exercice m ♦ vt exercer; (patience etc) faire preuve de; (dog) promener ♦ vi prendre de l'exercice; **~ book** n cahier m

**exert** [ɪg'zəːt] vt exercer, employer; **to ~ o.s.** se dépenser; **~ion** n effort m

**exhale** [eks'heɪl] vt exhaler ♦ vi expirer

**exhaust** [ɪg'zɔːst] n (also: **~ fumes**) gaz mpl d'échappement; (also: **~ pipe**) tuyau m d'échappement ♦ vt épuiser; **~ed** adj épuisé(e); **~ion** n épuisement m; **nervous ~ion** fatigue nerveuse; surmenage mental; **~ive** adj très complet(-ète)

**exhibit** [ɪg'zɪbɪt] n (ART) pièce exposée, objet exposé; (LAW) pièce à conviction ♦ vt exposer; (courage, skill) faire preuve de; **~ion** [eksɪ'bɪʃən] n exposition f; (of ill-temper, talent etc) démonstration f

**exhilarating** [ɪg'zɪləreɪtɪŋ] adj grisant(e); stimulant(e)

**ex-husband** n ex-mari m

**exile** ['eksaɪl] n exil m; (person) exilé(e) ♦ vt exiler

**exist** [ɪg'zɪst] vi exister; **~ence** n existence f; **~ing** adj actuel(le)

**exit** ['eksɪt] n sortie f ♦ vi (COMPUT, THEATRE) sortir; **~ poll** n sondage m (fait à la sortie de l'isoloir); **~ ramp** n (AUT) bretelle f d'accès

**exodus** ['eksədəs] n exode m

**exonerate** [ɪg'zɔnəreɪt] vt: **to ~ from** disculper de

**exotic** [ɪg'zɔtɪk] adj exotique

**expand** [ɪks'pænd] vt agrandir; accroître ♦ vi (trade etc) se développer, s'accroître; (gas, metal) se dilater

**expanse** [ɪks'pæns] n étendue f

**expansion** [ɪks'pænʃən] n développement m, accroissement m

**expect** [ɪks'pekt] vt (anticipate) s'attendre à, s'attendre à ce que +sub; (count on) compter sur, escompter; (require) demander, exiger; (suppose) supposer; (await, also baby) attendre ♦ vi: **to be ~ing** être enceinte; **~ancy** n (anticipation) attente f; **life ~ancy** espérance f de vie; **~ant mother** n future maman; **~ation** [ekspek'teɪʃən] n attente f; espérance(s) f(pl)

**expedient** [ɪks'piːdɪənt] adj indiqué(e),

opportun(e) ♦ *n* expédient *m*

**expedition** [ɛkspə'dɪʃən] *n* expédition *f*

**expel** [ɪks'pɛl] *vt* chasser, expulser; (SCOL) renvoyer

**expend** [ɪks'pɛnd] *vt* consacrer; (money) dépenser; **~iture** [ɪks'pɛndɪtʃər] *n* dépense *f*; dépenses *fpl*

**expense** [ɪks'pɛns] *n* dépense *f*, frais *mpl*; (high cost) coût *m*; **~s** *npl* (COMM) frais *mpl*; **at the ~ of** aux dépens de; **~ account** *n* (note *f* de) frais *mpl*; **expensive** *adj* cher (chère), coûteux (-euse); **to be expensive** coûter cher

**experience** [ɪks'pɪərɪəns] *n* expérience *f* ♦ *vt* connaître, faire l'expérience de; (feeling) éprouver; **~d** *adj* expérimenté(e)

**experiment** [ɪks'pɛrɪmənt] *n* expérience *f* ♦ *vi* faire une expérience; **to ~ with** expérimenter

**expert** ['ɛkspə:t] *adj* expert(e) ♦ *n* expert *m*; **~ise** [ɛkspə:'ti:z] *n* (grande) compétence

**expire** [ɪks'paɪər] *vi* expirer; **expiry** *n* expiration *f*

**explain** [ɪks'pleɪn] *vt* expliquer; **explanation** [ɛksplə'neɪʃən] *n* explication *f*; **explanatory** [ɪks'plænətrɪ] *adj* explicatif(-ive)

**explicit** [ɪks'plɪsɪt] *adj* explicite; (definite) formel(le)

**explode** [ɪks'pləud] *vi* exploser

**exploit** [*n* 'ɛksplɔɪt, *vb* ɪks'plɔɪt] *n* exploit *m* ♦ *vt* exploiter; **~ation** [ɛksplɔɪ'teɪʃən] *n* exploitation *f*

**exploratory** [ɪks'plɔrətrɪ] *adj* (expedition) d'exploration; (fig: talks) préliminaire

**explore** [ɪks'plɔ:r] *vt* explorer; (possibilities) étudier, examiner; **~r** *n* explorateur(-trice)

**explosion** [ɪks'pləuʒən] *n* explosion *f*; **explosive** *adj* explosif(-ive) ♦ *n* explosif *m*

**exponent** [ɪks'pəunənt] *n* (of school of thought etc) interprète *m*, représentant

**export** [*vb* ɛks'pɔ:t, *n* 'ɛkspɔ:t] *vt* exporter ♦ *n* exportation *f* ♦ *cpd* d'exportation; **~er** *n* exportateur *m*

**expose** [ɪks'pəuz] *vt* exposer; (unmask) démasquer, dévoiler; **~d** *adj* (position, house) exposé(e); **exposure** *n* exposition *f*; (PUBLICITY) couverture *f*; (PHOT) (temps *m* de) pose *f*; (: shot) pose; **to die from exposure** (MED) mourir de froid; **exposure meter** *n* posemètre *m*

**express** [ɪks'prɛs] *adj* (definite) formel(le), exprès(-esse); (BRIT: letter etc) exprès *inv* ♦ *n* (train) rapide *m*; (bus) car *m* ♦ *vt* exprimer; **~ion** *n* expression *f*; **~ly** *adv* expressément, formellement; **~way** (US) *n* (urban motorway) voie *f* express (à plusieurs files)

**exquisite** [ɛks'kwɪzɪt] *adj* exquis(e)

**extend** [ɪks'tɛnd] *vt* (visit, street) prolonger; (building) agrandir; (offer) présenter, offrir; (hand, arm) tendre ♦ *vi* s'étendre; **extension** *n* prolongation *f*; agrandissement *m*; (building) annexe *f*; (to wire, cable) rallonge *f*; (telephone: in offices) poste *m*; (: in private house) téléphone *m* supplémentaire; **extensive** *adj* étendu(e), vaste; (damage, alterations) considérable; (inquiries) approfondi(e); **extensively** *adv*: **he's travelled extensively** il a beaucoup voyagé

**extent** [ɪks'tɛnt] *n* étendue *f*; **to some ~** dans une certaine mesure; **to what ~?** dans quelle mesure?, jusqu'à quel point?; **to the ~ of ...** au point de ...; **to such an ~ that ...** à tel point que ...

**extenuating** [ɪks'tɛnjueɪtɪŋ] *adj*: **~ circumstances** circonstances atténuantes

**exterior** [ɛks'tɪərɪər] *adj* extérieur(e) ♦ *n* extérieur *m*; dehors *m*

**external** [ɛks'tə:nl] *adj* externe

**extinct** [ɪks'tɪŋkt] *adj* éteint(e)

**extinguish** [ɪks'tɪŋgwɪʃ] *vt* éteindre

**extort** [ɪks'tɔ:t] *vt*: **~ sth (from)** extorquer qch (à); **~ionate** *adj* exorbitant(e)

**extra** ['ɛkstrə] *adj* supplémentaire, de plus ♦ *adv* (in addition) en plus ♦ *n* sup-

plément m; (perk) à-côté m; (THEATRE)
figurant(e) ♦ prefix extra...
**extract** [vb iks'trækt, n 'ekstrækt] vt extraire; (tooth) arracher; (money, promise) soutirer ♦ n extrait m
**extracurricular** ['ekstrəkə'rıkjulə°] adj
parascolaire
**extradite** ['ekstrədait] vt extrader
**extra...**: **~marital** ['ekstrə'mærit]
adj extra-conjugal(e); **~mural** ['ekstrə-
'mjuərl] adj hors faculté inv; (lecture)
public(-que); **~ordinary** [iks'trɔ:dnrı]
adj extraordinaire
**extravagance** [iks'trævəgəns] n prodi-
galités fpl; (thing bought) folie f, dépense excessive; **extravagant** adj extrava-
gant(e); (in spending: person) prodigue,
dépensier(-ère); (: tastes) dispendieux
(-euse)
**extreme** [iks'tri:m] adj extrême ♦ n extrême m; **~ly** adv extrêmement; **ex-
tremist** n, adj extrémiste m/f
**extricate** ['ekstrikeit] vt: **to ~ sth
(from)** dégager qch de
**extrovert** ['ekstrəvə:t] n extraverti(e)
**ex-wife** n ex-femme f
**eye** [ai] n œil m (pl yeux); (of needle)
trou m, chas m ♦ vt examiner; **to keep
an ~ on** surveiller; **~brow** n sourcil m;
**~drops** n gouttes fpl pour les yeux;
**~lash** n cil m; **~lid** n paupière f; **~liner**
n eye-liner m; **~-opener** n révélation f;
**~shadow** n ombre f à paupières;
**~sight** n vue f; **~sore** n horreur f; **~
witness** n témoin m oculaire

# F, f

**F** [ef] n (MUS) fa m
**fable** ['feibl] n fable f
**fabric** ['fæbrik] n tissu m
**fabulous** ['fæbjuləs] adj fabuleux
(-euse); (inf: super) formidable
**face** [feis] n visage m, figure f; (expression) expression f; (of clock) cadran m;
(of cliff) paroi f; (of mountain) face f; (of

building) façade f ♦ vt faire face à; **~
down** (person) à plat ventre; (card)
face en dessous; **to lose/save ~**
perdre/sauver la face; **to make or pull
a ~** faire une grimace; **in the ~ of**
(difficulties etc) face à, devant; **on the ~
of it** à première vue; **~ to ~** face à
face; **~ up to** vt fus faire face à, affronter; **~ cloth** (BRIT) n gant m de toilette;
**~ cream** n crème f pour le visage; **~
lift** n lifting m; (of building etc) ravale-
ment m, retapage m; **~ powder** n
poudre f de riz; **~ value** n (of coin) valeur nominale; **to take sth at ~ value**
(fig) prendre qch pour argent comptant
**facilities** [fə'sılıtız] npl installations fpl,
équipement m; **credit ~** facilités fpl de
paiement
**facing** ['feisiŋ] prep face à, en face de
**facsimile** [fæk'sımılı] n (exact replica)
fac-similé m; (fax) télécopie f
**fact** [fækt] n fait m; **in ~** en fait
**factor** ['fæktə°] n facteur m
**factory** ['fæktərı] n usine f, fabrique f
**factual** ['fæktjuəl] adj basé(e) sur les
faits
**faculty** ['fækəltı] n faculté f; (US: teaching staff) corps enseignant
**fad** [fæd] n (craze) engouement m
**fade** [feid] vi se décolorer, passer; (light,
sound) s'affaiblir; (flower) se faner
**fag** [fæg] (BRIT: inf) n (cigarette) sèche f
**fail** [feil] vt (exam) échouer à; (candidate) recaler; (subj: courage, memory) faire
défaut à ♦ vi échouer; (brakes) lâcher;
(eyesight, health, light) baisser, s'affaiblir; **to ~ to do sth** (neglect) négliger
de faire qch; (be unable) ne pas arriver
or parvenir à faire qch; **without ~** à
coup sûr; sans faute; **~ing** n défaut m ♦
prep faute de; **~ure** n échec m; (person)
raté(e) f; (mechanical etc) défaillance f
**faint** [feint] adj faible; (recollection) vague; (mark) à peine visible ♦ n éva-
nouissement m ♦ vi s'évanouir; **to feel
~** défaillir

**fair** [feəʳ] *adj* équitable, juste, impartial(e); *(hair)* blond(e); *(skin, complexion)* pâle, blanc (blanche); *(weather)* beau (belle); *(good enough)* assez bon(ne); *(sizeable)* considérable ♦ *adv*: **to play** ~ jouer franc-jeu ♦ *n* ♦ *f*; *(BRIT: funfair)* fête (foraine); **~ly** *adv* équitablement; *(quite)* assez; **~ness** *n* justice *f*, équité *f*, impartialité *f*

**fairy** [feərɪ] *n* fée *f*; ~ **tale** *n* conte *m* de fées

**faith** [feɪθ] *n* foi *f*; *(trust)* confiance *f*; *(specific religion)* religion *f*; **~ful** *adj* fidèle; **~fully** *adv* see **yours**

**fake** [feɪk] *n* (painting etc) faux *m*; (person) imposteur *m* ♦ *adj* faux (fausse); (painting) faire un faux de

**falcon** [fɔːlkən] *n* faucon *m*

**fall** [fɔːl] (*pt* **fell**, *pp* **fallen**) *n* chute *f*; *(US: autumn)* automne *m* ♦ *vi* tomber; *(price, temperature, dollar)* baisser; ~**s** *npl* *(waterfall)* chute *f* d'eau, cascade *f*; **to ~ flat** (one's face) tomber de tout son long, s'étaler; (joke) tomber à plat; (plan) échouer; ~ **back** *vi* reculer, se retirer; ~ **back on** *vt fus* se rabattre sur; ~ **behind** *vi* prendre du retard; ~ **down** *vi* (person) tomber; (building) s'écrouler; ~ **for** *vt fus* (trick, story etc) se laisser prendre à; (person) tomber amoureux de; ~ **in** *vi* s'effondrer; (MIL) se mettre en rangs; ~ **off** *vi* tomber; (diminish) baisser, diminuer; ~ **out** *vi* (hair, teeth) tomber; (MIL) rompre les rangs; (friends etc) se brouiller; ~ **through** *vi* (plan, project) tomber à l'eau

**fallacy** [fæləsɪ] *n* erreur *f*, illusion *f*

**fallout** [fɔːlaʊt] *n* retombées (radioactives)

**fallow** [fæləʊ] *adj* en jachère; en friche

**false** [fɔːls] *adj* faux (fausse); ~ **alarm** *n* fausse alerte; ~ **pretences** *npl*: **under** ~ **pretences** sous un faux prétexte; ~ **teeth** (BRIT) *npl* fausses dents

**falter** [fɔːltəʳ] *vi* chanceler, vaciller

**fame** [feɪm] *n* renommée *f*, renom *m*

**familiar** [fəmɪlɪəʳ] *adj* familier(-ère); **to be ~ with** (subject) connaître

**family** [fæmɪlɪ] *n* famille *f* ♦ *cpd* (business, doctor etc) de famille; **has he any ~?** (children) a-t-il des enfants?

**famine** [fæmɪn] *n* famine *f*

**famished** [fæmɪʃt] (inf) *adj* affamé(e)

**famous** [feɪməs] *adj* célèbre; **~ly** *adv* (get on) fameusement, à merveille

**fan** [fæn] *n* (folding) éventail *m*; (ELEC) ventilateur *m*; (of person) fan *m*, admirateur(-trice); (of team, sport etc) supporter *m/f* ♦ *vt* éventer; (fire, quarrel) attiser

**fanatic** [fənætɪk] *n* fanatique *m/f*

**fan belt** *n* courroie *f* de ventilateur

**fancy** [fænsɪ] *n* fantaisie *f*, envie *f*; imagination *f* ♦ *adj* (de) fantaisie *inv* ♦ *vt* (feel like, want) avoir envie de; (imagine, think) imaginer; **to take a ~ to** se prendre d'affection pour; s'enticher de; **he fancies her** (inf) elle lui plaît; ~ **dress** *n* déguisement *m*, travesti *m*; ~ **dress ball** *n* bal masqué ou costumé

**fang** [fæŋ] *n* croc *m*; (of snake) crochet *m*

**fantastic** [fæntæstɪk] *adj* fantastique

**fantasy** [fæntəsɪ] *n* imagination *f*, fantaisie *f*; (dream) chimère *f*

**far** [fɑːʳ] *adj* lointain(e), éloigné(e) ♦ *adv* loin; ~ **away** ou **off** au loin, dans le lointain; **at the ~ side/end** à l'autre côté/bout; ~ **better** beaucoup mieux; ~ **from** loin de; **by** ~ de loin, beaucoup; **go as ~ as the ~m** allez jusqu'à la ferme; **as ~ as I know** pour autant que je sache; **how ~ is it to ...?** combien y a-t-il jusqu'à ...?; **how have you got?** où en êtes-vous?; **~away** [fɑːrəweɪ] *adj* lointain(e); (look) distrait(e)

**farce** [fɑːs] *n* farce *f*

**fare** [feəʳ] *n* (on trains, buses) prix *m* du billet; (in taxi) prix de la course; (food) table *f*, chère *f*; **half** ~ demi-tarif; **full** ~ plein tarif

**Far East** *n* Extrême-Orient *m*

**farewell** [feə'wel] *excl* adieu ♦ *n* adieu *m*

**farm** [faːm] *n* ferme *f* ♦ *vt* cultiver; **~er** *n* fermier(-ère); cultivateur(-trice); **~hand** *n* ouvrier(-ère) agricole; **~house** *n* (maison *f* de) ferme *f*; **~ing** *n* agriculture *f*; (*of animals*) élevage *m*; **~land** *n* terres cultivées; **~ worker** *n* = **farmhand**; **~yard** *n* cour *f* de ferme

**far-reaching** [faː'riːtʃɪŋ] *adj* d'une grande portée

**fart** [faːt] (*inf!*) *vi* péter

**farther** ['faːðə*] *adv* plus loin ♦ *adj* plus éloigné(e), plus lointain(e)

**farthest** ['faːðɪst] *superl* of **far**

**fascinate** ['fæsɪneɪt] *vt* fasciner; **fascinating** *adj* fascinant(e)

**fascism** ['fæʃɪzəm] *n* fascisme *m*

**fashion** ['fæʃən] *n* mode *f*; (*manner*) façon *f*, manière *f* ♦ *vt* façonner; **in ~** à la mode; **out of ~** démodé(e); **~able** *adj* à la mode; **~ show** *n* défilé *m* de mannequins *or* de mode

**fast** [faːst] *adj* rapide; (*clock*): **to be ~** avancer; (*dye, colour*) grand *or* bon teint *inv* ♦ *adv* vite, rapidement; (*stuck, held*) solidement ♦ *n* jeûne *m* ♦ *vi* jeûner; **~ asleep** profondément endormi

**fasten** ['faːsn] *vt* attacher, fixer; (*coat*) attacher, fermer ♦ *vi* se fermer, s'attacher; **~er**, **~ing** *n* attache *f*

**fast food** *n* fast food *m*, restauration *f* rapide

**fastidious** [fæs'tɪdɪəs] *adj* exigeant(e), difficile

**fat** [fæt] *adj* gros(se) ♦ *n* graisse *f*; (*on meat*) gras *m*; (*for cooking*) matière grasse

**fatal** ['feɪtl] *adj* (*injury etc*) mortel(le); (*mistake*) fatal(e); **~ity** [fə'tælɪtɪ] *n* (*road death etc*) victime *f*, décès *m*

**fate** [feɪt] *n* destin *m*; (*of person*) sort *m*; **~ful** *adj* fatidique

**father** ['faːðə*] *n* père *m*; **~-in-law** *n* beau-père *m*; **~ly** *adj* paternel(le)

**fathom** ['fæðəm] *n* brasse *f* (= 1828 mm) ♦ *vt* (*mystery*) sonder, pénétrer

**fatigue** [fə'tiːg] *n* fatigue *f*

**fatten** ['fætn] *vt*, *vi* engraisser

**fatty** ['fætɪ] *adj* (*food*) gras(se) ♦ *n* (*inf*) gros(se)

**fatuous** ['fætjuəs] *adj* stupide

**faucet** ['fɔːsɪt] (*US*) *n* robinet *m*

**fault** [fɔːlt] *n* faute *f*; (*defect*) défaut *m*; (*GEO*) faille *f* ♦ *vt* trouver des défauts à; **it's my ~** c'est de ma faute; **to find ~ with** trouver à redire *or* à critiquer à; **at ~** fautif(-ive), coupable; **~y** *adj* défectueux(-euse)

**fauna** ['fɔːnə] *n* faune *f*

**favour** ['feɪvə*] (*US* **favor**) *n* faveur *f*; (*help*) service *m* ♦ *vt* (*proposition*) être en faveur de; (*pupil etc*) favoriser; (*team, horse*) donner gagnant; **to do sb a ~** rendre un service à qn; **to find ~ with** trouver grâce aux yeux de; **in ~ of** en faveur de; **~able** *adj* favorable; **~ite** [feɪvrɪt] *adj*, *n* favori(te)

**fawn** [fɔːn] *n* faon *m* ♦ *adj* (*colour*) fauve ♦ *vi*: **to ~ (up)on** flatter servilement

**fax** [fæks] *n* (*document*) télécopie *f*; (*machine*) télécopieur *m* ♦ *vt* envoyer par télécopie

**FBI** *n abbr* (*US: Federal Bureau of Investigation*) F.B.I. *m*

**fear** [fɪə*] *n* crainte *f*, peur *f* ♦ *vt* craindre; **for ~ of** de peur que +*sub*, de peur de +*infin*; **~ful** *adj* craintif(-ive); (*sight, noise*) affreux(-euse), épouvantable; **~less** *adj* intrépide

**feasible** ['fiːzəbl] *adj* faisable, réalisable

**feast** [fiːst] *n* festin *m*, banquet *m*; (*REL: also*: **~ day**) fête *f* ♦ *vi* festoyer

**feat** [fiːt] *n* exploit *m*, prouesse *f*

**feather** ['feðə*] *n* plume *f*

**feature** ['fiːtʃə*] *n* caractéristique *f*; (*article*) chronique *f*, rubrique *f* ♦ *vt* (*subj: film*) avoir pour vedette(s) ♦ *vi*: **to ~ in** figurer (en bonne place) dans; (*in film*) jouer dans; **~s** *npl* (*of face*) traits *mpl*; **~ film** *n* long métrage *m*

**February** ['februərɪ] *n* février *m*

**fed** [fed] *pt*, *pp* of **feed**

**federal** ['fedərəl] *adj* fédéral(e); **~ holiday** (*US*) *n* jour *m* férié

**fed up** adj: **to be ~** en avoir marre, en avoir plein le dos

**fee** [fi:] n rémunération f; (of doctor, lawyer) honoraires mpl; (for examination) droits mpl; **school ~s** frais mpl de scolarité

**feeble** ['fi:bl] adj faible; (pathetic: attempt, excuse) pauvre; (: joke) piteux (-euse)

**feed** [fi:d] (pt, pp **fed**) n (of animal) fourrage m; pâture f; (of printer) mécanisme m d'alimentation ♦ vt (gen) nourrir; (BRIT: baby) allaiter; (: with bottle) donner le biberon à; (horse etc) donner à manger à; (machine) alimenter; (data, information): **to ~ sth into** fournir qch à; **~ on** vt fus se nourrir de; **~back** n feed-back m

**feel** [fi:l] (pt, pp **felt**) n sensation f; (impression) impression f ♦ vt toucher; (explore) tâter, palper; (cold, pain) sentir; (grief, anger) ressentir, éprouver; (think, believe) trouver; **to ~ hungry/better** avoir faim/froid; **to ~ lonely/better** se sentir seul/mieux; **I don't ~ well** je ne me sens pas bien; **it ~s soft** c'est doux (douce) au toucher; **to ~ like** (want) avoir envie de; **~ about** vi fouiller, tâtonner; **~ing** n (of insect) antenne f; **~ing** n (physical) sensation f; (emotional) sentiment m

**feet** [fi:t] npl of **foot**

**feign** [feɪn] vt feindre, simuler

**fell** [fel] pt of **fall** ♦ vt (tree, person) abattre

**fellow** ['feləʊ] n type m; (comrade) compagnon m; (of learned society) membre m ♦ cpd: **their ~ prisoners/students** leurs camarades prisonniers/d'étude; **~ citizen** n concitoyen/ne; **~ countryman** (irreg) n compatriote m; **~ men** npl semblables mpl; **~ship** n (society) association f; (comradeship) amitié f, camaraderie f; (grant) sorte de bourse universitaire

**felony** ['feləni] n crime m, forfait m

**felt** [felt] pt, pp of **feel** ♦ n feutre m; **~-**

**tip pen** n stylo-feutre m

**female** ['fi:meɪl] n (ZOOL) femelle f; (pej: woman) bonne femme ♦ adj (BIO) femelle; (sex, character) féminin(e); (vote etc) des femmes

**feminine** ['femɪnɪn] adj féminin(e)

**feminist** ['femɪnɪst] n féministe m/f

**fence** [fens] n barrière f ♦ vt (also: **~ in**) clôturer ♦ vi faire de l'escrime; **fencing** n escrime m

**fend** [fend] vi: **to ~ for o.s.** se débrouiller (tout seul); **~ off** vt (attack etc) parer

**fender** ['fendər] n garde-feu m inv; (on boat) défense f; (US: of car) aile f

**ferment** [vb fə'ment, n 'fə:ment] vi fermenter ♦ n agitation f, effervescence f

**fern** [fə:n] n fougère f

**ferocious** [fə'rəʊʃəs] adj féroce

**ferret** ['ferɪt] n furet m

**ferry** ['ferɪ] n (small) bac m; (large: also: **~boat**) ferry(-boat) m ♦ vt transporter

**fertile** ['fə:taɪl] adj fertile; (BIO) fécond(e); **fertilizer** ['fə:tɪlaɪzər] n engrais m

**fester** ['festər] vi suppurer

**festival** ['festɪvəl] n (REL) fête f; (ART, MUS) festival m

**festive** ['festɪv] adj de fête; **the ~ season** (BRIT: Christmas) la période des fêtes; **festivities** npl réjouissances fpl

**festoon** [fes'tu:n] vt: **~ with** orner de

**fetch** [fetʃ] vt aller chercher; (sell for) se vendre

**fête** [feɪt] n fête f, kermesse f

**feud** [fju:d] n dispute f, dissension f

**fever** ['fi:vər] n fièvre f; **~ish** adj fiévreux(-euse), fébrile

**few** [fju:] adj (not many) peu de; **a ~** adj quelques ♦ pron quelques-uns (-unes); **~er** ['fju:ər] adj moins de; moins (nombreux); **~est** ['fju:ɪst] adj le moins (de)

**fiancé** [fɪ'ɑ̃:nseɪ] n fiancé(e) m/f

**fib** [fɪb] n bobard m

**fibre** ['faɪbər] (US **fiber**) n fibre f; **~glass**

['faɪbɡlɑːs] (**Fiberglass** ® *US*) *n* fibre de verre

**fickle** ['fɪkl] *adj* inconstant(e), volage, capricieux(-euse)

**fiction** ['fɪkʃən] *n* romans *mpl*, littérature *f* romanesque; (*invention*) fiction *f*; **~al** *adj* fictif(-ive)

**fictitious** *adj* fictif(-ive), imaginaire

**fiddle** ['fɪdl] *n* (*MUS*) violon *m*; (*cheating*) combine *f*, escroquerie *f* ♦ *vt* (*BRIT: accounts*) falsifier, maquiller; **~ with** *vt fus* tripoter

**fidget** ['fɪdʒɪt] *vi* se trémousser, remuer

**field** [fiːld] *n* champ *m*; (*fig*) domaine *m*, champ; (*SPORT: ground*) terrain *m*; **~work** *n* travaux *mpl* pratiques (sur le terrain)

**fiend** [fiːnd] *n* démon *m*

**fierce** [fɪəs] *adj* (*look, animal*) féroce, sauvage; (*wind, attack, person*) (très) violent(e); (*fighting, enemy*) acharné(e)

**fiery** ['faɪərɪ] *adj* ardent(e), brûlant(e); (*temperament*) fougueux(-euse)

**fifteen** [fɪf'tiːn] *num* quinze

**fifth** [fɪfθ] *num* cinquième

**fifty** ['fɪftɪ] *num* cinquante; **~-fifty** *adj*: a **~-fifty chance** *etc* une chance *etc* sur deux ♦ *adv* moitié-moitié

**fig** [fɪɡ] *n* figue *f*

**fight** [faɪt] (*pt, pp* **fought**) *n* (*MIL*) combat *m*; (*between persons*) bagarre *f*; (*against cancer etc*) lutte *f* ♦ *vt* se battre contre; (*cancer, alcoholism, emotion*) combattre, lutter contre; (*election*) se présenter à ♦ *vi* se battre; **~er** *n* (*fig*) lutteur *m*; (*plane*) chasseur *m*; **~ing** *n* combats *mpl*; (*brawl*) bagarres *fpl*

**figment** ['fɪɡmənt] *n*: a **~ of the imagination** une invention

**figurative** ['fɪɡjʊrətɪv] *adj* figuré(e)

**figure** ['fɪɡə*] *n* figure *f*; (*number, cipher*) chiffre *m*; (*body, outline*) silhouette *f*; (*shape*) ligne *f*, formes *fpl* ♦ *vt* (*think: esp US*) supposer ♦ *vi* (*appear*) figurer; **~ out** *vt* (*work out*) calculer; **~head** *n* (*NAUT*) figure *f* de proue; prête-nom *m*; **~ of speech** *n* figure *f* de rhétorique

**file** [faɪl] *n* (*dossier*) dossier *m*; (*folder*) dossier, chemise *f*; (: *with hinges*) classeur *m*; (*COMPUT*) fichier *m*; (*row*) file *f*; (*tool*) lime *f* ♦ *vt* (*nails, wood*) limer; (*papers*) classer; (*LAW: claim*) faire enregistrer; déposer ♦ *vi*: **to ~ in/out** entrer/sortir l'un derrière l'autre; **to ~ for divorce** faire une demande en divorce; **filing cabinet** *n* classeur *m* (*meuble*)

**fill** [fɪl] *vt* remplir; (*need*) répondre à ♦ *n*: **to eat one's ~** manger à sa faim; **to ~ with** remplir de; **~ in** *vt* (*hole*) boucher; (*form*) remplir; **~ up** *vt* remplir; **~ it up, please** (*AUT*) le plein, s'il vous plaît

**fillet** [ˈfɪlɪt] *n* filet *m*; **~ steak** *n* filet de bœuf, tournedos *m*

**filling** ['fɪlɪŋ] *n* (*CULIN*) garniture *f*, farce *f*; (*for tooth*) plombage *m*; **~ station** *n* station-service *f*

**film** [fɪlm] *n* film *m*; (*PHOT*) pellicule *f*, film; (*of powder, liquid*) couche *f*, pellicule *f* ♦ *vt* (*scene*) filmer ♦ *vi* tourner; **~ star** *n* vedette *f* de cinéma

**filter** ['fɪltə*] *n* filtre *m* ♦ *vt* filtrer; **~ lane** *n* (*AUT*) voie *f* de sortie; **~-tipped** *adj* à bout filtre

**filth** [fɪlθ] *n* saleté *f*; **~y** *adj* sale, dégoûtant(e); (*language*) ordurier(-ère)

**fin** [fɪn] *n* (*of fish*) nageoire *f*

**final** ['faɪnl] *adj* final(e); (*definitive*) définitif(-ive) ♦ *n* (*SPORT*) finale *f*; **~s** *npl* (*SCOL*) examens *mpl* de dernière année; **~e** [fɪˈnɑːlɪ] *n* finale *m*; **~ist** *n* finaliste *m/f*; **~ize** *vt* mettre au point; **~ly** *adv* (*eventually*) enfin, finalement; (*lastly*) en dernier lieu

**finance** [faɪˈnæns] *n* finance *f* ♦ *vt* financer; **~s** *npl* (*financial position*) finances *fpl*; **financial** [faɪˈnænʃəl] *adj* financier(-ère)

**find** [faɪnd] (*pt, pp* **found**) *vt* trouver; (*lost object*) retrouver ♦ *n* trouvaille *f*, découverte *f*; **to ~ sb guilty** (*LAW*) déclarer qn coupable; **~ out** *vt* (*truth, se-*

cret) découvrir; (*person*) démasquer ♦
*vi*: **to ~ out about** (*make enquiries*) se
renseigner; (*by chance*) apprendre;
**~ings** *npl* (*LAW*) conclusions *fpl*, verdict
*m*; (*of report*) conclusions *fpl*

**fine** [faɪn] *adj* (*excellent*) excellent(e);
(*thin, not coarse, subtle*) fin(e); (*weather*) beau (belle) ♦ *adv* (*well*) très bien
♦ *n* (*LAW*) amende *f*; contravention *f*
♦ *vt* (*LAW*) condamner à une amende;
donner une contravention à; **to be ~**
(*person*) aller bien; (*weather*) être beau;
**~ arts** *npl* beaux-arts *mpl*; **~ry** *n* parure
*f*

**finger** ['fɪŋɡə'] *n* doigt *m* ♦ *vt* palper,
toucher; **little ~** auriculaire *m*, petit
doigt; **index ~** index *m*; **~nail** *n* ongle
*m* (de la main); **~print** *n* empreinte digitale; **~tip** *n* bout *m* du doigt

**finish** ['fɪnɪʃ] *n* fin *f*; (*SPORT*) arrivée *f*;
(*polish etc*) finition *f* ♦ *vt* finir, terminer
♦ *vi* finir, se terminer; **to ~ doing sth**
finir de faire qch; **to ~ third** arriver or
terminer troisième; **~ off** *vt* finir, terminer; (*kill*) achever; **~ up** *vi, vt* finir; **~ing
line** *n* ligne *f* d'arrivée

**finite** ['faɪnaɪt] *adj* fini(e); (*verb*) conjugué(e)

**Finland** ['fɪnlənd] *n* Finlande *f*; **Finn**
[fɪn] *n* Finlandais(e); **Finnish** *adj* finlandais(e) ♦ *n* (*LING*) finnois *m*

**fir** [fɜː'] *n* sapin *m*

**fire** ['faɪə'] *n* feu *m*; (*accidental*) incendie
*m*; (*heater*) radiateur *m* ♦ *vt* (*fig*) enflammer, animer; (*inf: dismiss*) mettre à
la porte, renvoyer; (*discharge*): **to ~ a
gun** tirer un coup de feu ♦ *vi* (*shoot*) tirer, faire feu; **on ~** en feu; **~ alarm** *n*
avertisseur *m* d'incendie; **~arm** *n* arme
*f* à feu; **~ brigade** *n* (sapeurs-)
pompiers *mpl*; **~ department** (*US*) *n* =
**fire brigade**; **~ engine** *n* (*vehicle*) voiture *f* des pompiers; **~ escape** *n* escalier *m* de secours; **~ extinguisher** *n*
extincteur *m*; **~man** *n* pompier *m*;
**~place** *n* cheminée *f*; **~side** *n* foyer *m*,
coin *m* du feu; **~ station** *n* caserne *f*

de pompiers; **~wood** *n* bois *m* de
chauffage; **~works** *npl* feux *mpl* d'artifice; (*display*) feu(x) d'artifice

**firing squad** ['faɪərɪŋ-] *n* peloton *m*
d'exécution

**firm** [fɜːm] *adj* ferme ♦ *n* compagnie *f*,
firme *f*

**first** [fɜːst] *adj* premier(-ère) ♦ *adv* (*before all others*) le premier, la première;
(*before all other things*) en premier,
d'abord; (*when listing reasons etc*) en
premier lieu, premièrement ♦ *n* (*person: in race*) premier(-ère); (*BRIT: SCOL*) mention *f* très bien; (*AUT*) première *f*; **at ~**
au commencement, au début; **~ of all**
tout d'abord, pour commencer; **~ aid**
*n* premiers secours or soins; **~-aid kit** *n*
trousse *f* à pharmacie; **~-class** *adj* de
première classe; (*excellent*) excellent(e),
exceptionnel(le); **~-hand** *adj* de première main; **~ lady** (*US*) *n* femme *f* du
président; **~ly** *adv* premièrement, en
premier lieu; **~ name** *n* prénom *m*; **~-rate** *adj* excellent(e)

**fish** [fɪʃ] *n inv* poisson *m* ♦ *vt, vi* pêcher;
**to go ~ing** aller à la pêche; **~erman** *n*
pêcheur *m*; **~ farm** *n* établissement *m*
piscicole; **~ fingers** (*BRIT*) *npl* bâtonnets
de poisson (congelés); **~ing boat** *n*
barque *f* or bateau *m* de pêche; **~ing
line** *n* ligne *f* (de pêche); **~ing rod** *n*
canne *f* à pêche; **~ing tackle** *n* attirail
*m* de pêche; **~monger's (shop)** *n*
poissonnerie *f*; **~ slice** *n* pelle *f* à poisson; **~ sticks** (*US*) *npl* = **fish fingers**;
**~y** (*inf*) *adj* suspect(e), louche

**fist** [fɪst] *n* poing *m*

**fit** [fɪt] *adj* (*healthy*) en (bonne) forme;
(*proper*) convenable; approprié(e) ♦ *vt*
(*subj: clothes*) aller à; (*put in, attach*)
installer, poser; adapter; (*equip*) équiper, garnir, munir; (*suit*) convenir à ♦
*vi* (*clothes*) aller; (*parts*) s'adapter; (*in
space, gap*) entrer, s'adapter ♦ *n* (*MED*)
accès *m*, crise *f*; (*of anger*) accès; (*of
hysterics, jealousy*) crise; **~** en état
de; **~ for** digne de; apte à; **~ of**

**coughing** quinte f de toux; **a ~ of giggles** le fou rire; **this dress is a good ~** cette robe (me) va très bien; **by ~s and starts** par à-coups; **~ in** vi s'accorder; s'adapter; **~ful** adj (sleep) agité(e); **~ment** n meuble encastré, élément m; **~ness** n (MED) forme f physique; **~ted carpet** n moquette f; **~ted kitchen** (BRIT) n cuisine équipée; **~ter** n monteur m; **~ting** adj approprié(e) ♦ n (of dress) essayage m, (of piece of equipment) pose f, installation f; **~tings** npl (in building) installations fpl; **~ting room** n cabine f d'essayage

**five** [faiv] num cinq; **~r** n (inf) (BRIT) billet m de cinq livres; (US) billet m de cinq dollars

**fix** [fiks] vt (date, amount etc) fixer; (organize) arranger; (mend) réparer; (meal, drink) préparer ♦ n: **to be in a ~** être dans le pétrin; **~ up** vt (meeting) arranger; **to ~ sb up with sth** faire avoir qch à qn; **~ation** [fik'seiʃən] n (PSYCH) fixation f; (fig) obsession f; **~ed** adj (prices etc) fixe; (smile) figé(e); **~ture** f installation f (fixe); (SPORT) rencontre f (au programme)

**fizzy** ['fizi] adj pétillant(e); gazeux(-euse)

**flabbergasted** ['flæbəga:stid] adj sidéré(e), ahuri(e)

**flabby** ['flæbi] adj mou (molle)

**flag** [flæg] n drapeau m; (also: **~stone**) dalle f ♦ vi faiblir; fléchir; **~ down** vt héler, faire signe de (s'arrêter) à; **~pole** n mât m; **~ship** n vaisseau m amiral; (fig) produit m vedette

**flair** [fleə] n flair m

**flak** [flæk] n (MIL) tir antiaérien; (inf: criticism) critiques fpl

**flake** [fleik] n (of rust, paint) écaille f (of snow, soap powder) flocon m ♦ vi (also: **~ off**) s'écailler

**flamboyant** [flæm'bɔiənt] adj flamboyant(e), éclatant(e); (person) haut(e) en couleur

**flame** [fleim] n flamme f

**flamingo** [flə'miŋgəu] n flamant m (rose)

**flammable** ['flæməbl] adj inflammable

**flan** [flæn] (BRIT) n tarte f

**flank** [flæŋk] n flanc m ♦ vt flanquer

**flannel** ['flænl] n (fabric) flanelle f; (BRIT: also: **face ~**) gant m de toilette

**flap** [flæp] n (of pocket, envelope) rabat m ♦ vt (wings) battre (de) ♦ vi (sail, flag) claquer; (inf: also: **be in a ~**) paniquer

**flare** [fleə] n (signal) signal lumineux; (in skirt etc) évasement m; **~ up** vi s'embraser; (fig: person) se mettre en colère, s'emporter; (: revolt etc) éclater

**flash** [flæʃ] n éclair m; (also: **news ~**) flash m (d'information); (PHOT) flash m ♦ vt (light) projeter; (send: message) câbler; (look) jeter; (smile) lancer ♦ vi (light) clignoter; **a ~ of lightning** un éclair; **in a ~** en un clin d'œil; **to ~ one's headlights** faire un appel de phares; **to ~ by** or **past** (person) passer (devant) comme un éclair; **~bulb** n ampoule f de flash; **~cube** n cube-flash m; **~light** n lampe f de poche, flash m; **~y** (pej) adj tape-à-l'œil inv, tapageur(-euse)

**flask** [fla:sk] n flacon m, bouteille f; (also: **vacuum ~**) thermos ® m or f

**flat** [flæt] adj plat(e); (tyre) dégonflé(e), à plat; (beer) éventé(e); (denial) catégorique; (MUS) bémol inv; (: voice) faux (fausse); (fee, rate) fixe ♦ n (BRIT: apartment) appartement m; (AUT) crevaison f; (MUS) bémol m; **to work ~ out** travailler d'arrache-pied; **~ly** adv catégoriquement; **~ten** vt (also: **~ten out**) aplatir; (crop) coucher; (building(s)) raser

**flatter** ['flætə] vt flatter; **~ing** adj flatteur(-euse); **~y** n flatterie f

**flaunt** [flɔ:nt] vt faire étalage de

**flavour** ['fleivə] (US **flavor**) n goût m, saveur f; (of ice cream etc) parfum m ♦ vt parfumer; **vanilla-~ed** à l'arôme de vanille, à la vanille; **~ing** n arôme m

**flaw** [flɔ:] n défaut m; **~less** adj sans défaut

**flax** [flæks] n lin m

**flea** [fliː] n puce f

**fleck** [flɛk] n tacheture f; moucheture f

**flee** [fliː] (pt, pp **fled**) vt fuir ♦ vi fuir, s'enfuir

**fleece** [fliːs] n toison f ♦ vt (inf) voler, filouter

**fleet** [fliːt] n flotte f; (of lorries etc) parc m, convoi m

**fleeting** ['fliːtɪŋ] adj fugace, fugitif (-ive); (visit) très bref (brève)

**Flemish** ['flɛmɪʃ] adj flamand(e)

**flesh** [flɛʃ] n chair f; ~ **wound** n blessure superficielle

**flew** [fluː] pt of **fly**

**flex** [flɛks] n fil m or câble m électrique ♦ vt (knee) fléchir; (muscles) tendre; ~**ible** adj flexible

**flick** [flɪk] n petite tape; chiquenaude f; (of duster) petit coup ♦ vt donner un petit coup à; (switch) appuyer sur; ~ **through** vt fus feuilleter

**flicker** ['flɪkər] vi (light) vaciller; **his eyelids ~ed** il a cillé

**flier** ['flaɪər] n aviateur m

**flight** [flaɪt] n vol m; (escape) fuite f; (also: ~ **of steps**) escalier m; ~ **attendant** (US) n steward m, hôtesse f de l'air; ~ **deck** n (AVIAT) poste m de pilotage; (NAUT) pont m d'envol

**flimsy** ['flɪmzɪ] adj peu solide; (clothes) trop léger(-ère); (excuse) pauvre, mince

**flinch** [flɪntʃ] vi tressaillir; **to ~ from** se dérober à, reculer devant

**fling** [flɪŋ] (pt, pp **flung**) vt jeter, lancer

**flint** [flɪnt] n silex m; (in lighter) pierre f (à briquet)

**flip** [flɪp] vt (throw) lancer (d'une chiquenaude); **to ~ sth over** retourner qch

**flippant** ['flɪpənt] adj désinvolte, irrévérencieux(-euse)

**flipper** ['flɪpər] n (of seal etc) nageoire f; (for swimming) palme f

**flirt** [fləːt] vi flirter ♦ n flirteur(-euse) m/f

**float** [fləʊt] n flotteur m; (in procession) char m; (money) réserve f ♦ vi flotter

**flock** [flɔk] n troupeau m; (of birds) vol

m; (REL) ouailles fpl ♦ vi: **to ~** se rendre en masse à

**flog** [flɔg] vt fouetter

**flood** [flʌd] n inondation f; (of letters, refugees etc) flot m ♦ vt inonder ♦ vi (people): **to ~ in** envahir; ~**ing** n inondation f; ~**light** n projecteur m

**floor** [flɔːr] n sol m; (storey) étage m; (of sea, valley) fond m ♦ vt (subj: question) déconcerter; (: blow) terrasser; **on the ~** par terre; (ground) rez-de-chaussée m inv; **first ~**, (US) **second ~** premier étage; ~**board** n planche f (du plancher); ~ **show** n spectacle m de variétés

**flop** [flɔp] n fiasco m ♦ vi être un fiasco; (fall: into chair) s'affaler, s'effondrer; ~**py** adj lâche, flottant(e) ♦ n (COMPUT: also: ~**py disk**) disquette f

**flora** ['flɔːrə] n flore f

**floral** ['flɔːrl] adj (dress) à fleurs

**florid** ['flɔrɪd] adj (complexion) coloré(e); (style) plein(e) de fioritures

**florist** ['flɔrɪst] n fleuriste m/f; ~**'s (shop)** n magasin m or boutique f de fleuriste

**flounder** ['flaʊndər] vi patauger ♦ n (ZOOL) flet m

**flour** ['flaʊər] n farine f

**flourish** ['flʌrɪʃ] vi prospérer ♦ n (gesture) moulinet m

**flout** [flaʊt] vt se moquer de, faire fi de

**flow** [fləʊ] n (ELEC, of river) courant m; (of blood in veins) circulation f; (of tide) flux m; (of orders, data) flot m ♦ vi couler; (traffic) s'écouler; (clothes, hair) flotter; **the ~ of traffic** l'écoulement de la circulation; ~ **chart** n organigramme m

**flower** ['flaʊər] n fleur f ♦ vi fleurir; ~ **bed** n plate-bande f; ~**pot** n pot m (de fleurs); ~**y** adj fleuri(e)

**flown** [fləʊn] pp of **fly**

**flu** [fluː] n grippe f

**fluctuate** ['flʌktjʊeɪt] vi varier, fluctuer

**fluent** ['fluːənt] adj (speech) coulant(e), aisé(e); **he speaks ~ French, he's ~ in**

French: il parle couramment le français

**fluff** [flʌf] n duvet m; (on jacket, carpet) peluche f; **~y** adj duveteux(-euse); (toy) en peluche

**fluid** ['fluːɪd] adj fluide ♦ n fluide m

**fluke** [fluːk] (inf) n (luck) coup m de veine

**flung** [flʌŋ] pt, pp of **fling**

**fluoride** ['fluəraɪd] n fluorure f; **~ toothpaste** dentifrice m au fluor

**flurry** ['flʌrɪ] n (of snow) rafale f, bourrasque f; **~ of activity/excitement** affairement m/excitation f soudain(e)

**flush** [flʌʃ] n (on face) rougeur f; (fig: of youth, beauty etc) éclat m ♦ vt nettoyer à grande eau ♦ vi rougir ♦ adj: **~ with** au ras de, de niveau avec; **to ~ the toilet** tirer la chasse (d'eau); **~ed** adj (tout(e)) rouge

**flustered** ['flʌstəd] adj énervé(e)

**flute** [fluːt] n flûte f

**flutter** ['flʌtər] n (of panic, excitement) agitation f; (of wings) battement m ♦ vi (bird) battre des ailes, voleter

**flux** [flʌks] n: **in a state of ~** fluctuant sans cesse

**fly** [flaɪ] (pt **flew**, pp **flown**) n (insect) mouche f; (on trousers: also: **flies**) braguette f ♦ vt piloter; (passengers, cargo) transporter (par avion); (distances) parcourir ♦ vi voler; (passengers) aller en avion; (escape) s'enfuir, fuir; (flag) se déployer; **~ away** vi (bird, insect) s'envoler; **~ off** vi = **fly away**; **~-drive** n formule f avion plus voiture; **~ing** n (activity) aviation f; (action) vol m ♦ adj: **a ~ing visit** une visite éclair; **with ~ing colours** haut la main; **~ing saucer** n soucoupe volante; **~ing start** n: **to get off to a ~ing start** prendre un excellent départ; **~over** (BRIT) n (bridge) saut-de-mouton m; **~sheet** n (for tent) double toit m

**foal** [fəul] n poulain m

**foam** [fəum] n écume f; (on beer) mousse f; (also: **~ rubber**) caoutchouc mousse m ♦ vi (liquid) écumer; (soapy water) mousser

**fob** [fɔb] vt: **to ~ sb off** se débarrasser de qn

**focal point** ['fəukl-] n (fig) point central

**focus** ['fəukəs] (pl **~es**) n foyer m; (of interest) centre m ♦ vt (field glasses etc) mettre au point ♦ vi: **to ~ (on)** (with camera) régler la mise au point (sur); (person) fixer son regard (sur); **out of/ in ~** (picture) flou(e)/net(te); (camera) pas au point/au point

**fodder** ['fɔdər] n fourrage m

**foe** [fəu] n ennemi m

**fog** [fɔg] n brouillard m; **~gy** adj: **it's ~gy** il y a du brouillard; **~ lamp** (US **~light**) n (AUT) phare m antibrouillard

**foil** [fɔɪl] vt déjouer, contrecarrer ♦ n feuille f de métal; (kitchen ~) papier m alu(minium); (complement) repoussoir m

**fold** [fəuld] n (bend, crease) pli m; (AGR) parc m à moutons; (fig) bercail m ♦ vt plier; (arms) croiser; **~ up** vi (map, table etc) se plier; (business) fermer boutique ♦ vt (map, clothes) plier; **~er** n (for papers) chemise f; (: with hinges) classeur m; (COMPUT) répertoire m; **~ing** adj (chair, bed) pliant(e)

**foliage** ['fəulɪɪdʒ] n feuillage m

**folk** [fəuk] npl gens mpl ♦ cpd folklorique; **~s** (inf) npl (parents) parents mpl; **~lore** ['fəuklɔːr] n folklore m; **~ song** n chanson f folklorique

**follow** ['fɔləu] vt suivre ♦ vi suivre; (result) s'ensuivre; **to ~ suit** (fig) faire de même; **~ up** vt (letter, offer) donner suite à; (case) suivre; **~er** n disciple m/f, partisan(e); **~ing** adj suivant(e) ♦ n partisans mpl, disciples mpl

**folly** ['fɔlɪ] n inconscience f, folie f

**fond** [fɔnd] adj (memory, look) tendre; (hopes, dreams) un peu fou (folle); **to be ~ of** aimer beaucoup

**fondle** ['fɔndl] vt caresser

**font** [fɔnt] n (in church: for baptism) fonts baptismaux; (TYP) fonte f

**food** [fuːd] n nourriture f; **~ mixer** n

mixer m; ~ **poisoning** n intoxication f alimentaire; ~ **processor** n robot m de cuisine; **~stuffs** npl denrées fpl alimentaires; ~ **technology** BRIT n (SCOL) technologie f des produits alimentaires

**fool** [fu:l] n idiot(e); (CULIN) mousse f de fruits ♦ vt berner, duper ♦ vi faire l'idiot or l'imbécile; **~hardy** adj téméraire, imprudent(e); **~ish** adj idiot(e), stupide; (rash) imprudent(e); insensé(e); **~proof** adj (plan etc) infaillible

**foot** [fut] (pl **feet**) n pied m; (of animal) patte f; (measure) pied m (= 30,48 cm, 12 inches) ♦ vt (bill) payer; **on** ~ à pied; **~age** n (CINEMA: length) ≈ métrage m; (: material) séquences fpl; **~ball** n ballon m (de football); (sport: BRIT) football m, foot m; (: US) football américain; **~ball player** (BRIT) n (also: **~baller**) joueur m de football; **~brake** n pédale f; **~hills** npl contreforts mpl; **~hold** n prise f (de pied); **~ing** n (fig) position f; **to lose one's ~ing** perdre pied; **~lights** npl rampe f; **~note** n note f (en bas de page); **~path** n sentier m; (in street) trottoir m; **~print** n trace f (de pas); **~step** n pas m; **~wear** n chaussure(s) f(pl)

---

**football pools**

*Les football pools - ou plus familièrement les "pools" - consistent à parier sur les résultats des matches de football qui se jouent tous les samedis. L'expression consacrée en anglais est "to do the pools". Les parieurs envoient à l'avance les fiches qu'ils ont complétées à l'organisme qui gère les paris et ils attendent 17 h le samedi que les résultats soient annoncés. Les sommes gagnées se comptent parfois en milliers (ou même en millions) de livres sterling.*

---

KEYWORD

**for** [fɔːʳ] prep **1** (indicating destination,

intention, purpose) pour; **the train for London** le train pour or (à destination) de Londres; **he went for the paper** il est allé chercher le journal; **it's time for lunch** c'est l'heure du déjeuner; **what's it for?** ça sert à quoi?; **what for?** (why) pourquoi?

**2** (on behalf of, representing) pour; **the MP for Hove** le député de Hove; **to work for sb/sth** travailler pour qn/qch; **G for George** G comme Georges

**3** (because of) pour; **for this reason** pour cette raison; **for fear of being criticized** de peur d'être critiqué

**4** (with regard to) pour; **it's cold for July** il fait froid pour juillet; **a gift for languages** un don pour les langues

**5** (in exchange for): **I sold it for £5** je l'ai vendu 5 livres; **to pay 50 pence for a ticket** payer un billet 50 pence

**6** (in favour of) pour; **are you for or against us?** êtes-vous pour ou contre nous?

**7** (referring to distance) pendant, sur; **there are roadworks for 5 km** il y a des travaux sur 5 km; **we walked for miles** nous avons marché pendant des kilomètres

**8** (referring to time) pendant; depuis; pour; **he was away for 2 years** il a été absent pendant 2 ans; **she will be away for a month** elle sera absente (pendant) un mois; **I have known her for years** je la connais depuis des années; **can you do it for tomorrow?** est-ce que tu peux le faire pour demain?

**9** (with infinitive clauses): **it is not for me to decide** ce n'est pas à moi de décider; **it would be best for you to leave** le mieux serait que vous partiez; **there is still time for you to do it** vous avez encore le temps de le faire; **for this to be possible** ... pour que cela soit possible ...

**10** (in spite of): **for all his work/**

efforts malgré tout son travail/tous ses efforts; **for all his complaints, he's very fond of her** il a beau se plaindre, il l'aime beaucoup
♦ conj (since, as: rather formal) car

**forage** ['fɒrɪdʒ] vi fourrager

**foray** ['fɒreɪ] n incursion f

**forbid** [fə'bɪd] (pt **forbad(e)**, pp **forbidden**) vt défendre, interdire; **to ~ sb to do** défendre or interdire à qn de faire; **~ding** adj sévère, sombre

**force** [fɔːs] n force f ♦ vt forcer; (push) pousser (de force); **the F~s** npl (MIL) l'armée f; **in ~** en vigueur; **~-feed** vt nourrir de force; **~ful** adj énergique, volontaire; **forcibly** adv par la force, de force; (express) énergiquement

**ford** [fɔːd] n gué m

**fore** [fɔːr] n: **to come to the ~** se faire remarquer; **~arm** n avant-bras m inv; **~boding** n pressentiment m (néfaste); **~cast** (irreg: like **cast**) n prévision f ♦ vt prévoir; **~court** n (of garage) devant m; **~finger** n index m; **~front** n: **in the ~front of** au premier rang or plan de

**foregone** ['fɔːgɒn] adj: **it's a ~ conclusion** c'est couru d'avance

**foreground** ['fɔːgraʊnd] n premier plan

**forehead** ['fɒrɪd] n front m

**foreign** ['fɒrɪn] adj étranger(-ère); (trade) extérieur(-e); **~er** n étranger(-ère); **~ exchange** n change m; **F~ Office** (BRIT) n ministère m des Affaires étrangères; **F~ Secretary** (BRIT) n ministre m des Affaires étrangères

**fore:** **~leg** n (of cat, dog) patte f de devant; (of horse) jambe f antérieure; **~man** (irreg) n (of factory, building site) contremaître m, chef m d'équipe; **~most** adj le (la) plus en vue; premier(-ère) ♦ adv: **first and ~most** avant tout, tout d'abord

**forensic** [fə'rensɪk] adj: **~ medicine** médecine légale; **~ scientist** médecin

m légiste

**fore:** **~runner** n précurseur m; **~see** (irreg: like **see**) vt prévoir; **~seeable** adj prévisible; **~shadow** vt présager, annoncer, laisser prévoir; **~sight** n prévoyance f

**forest** ['fɒrɪst] n forêt f; **~ry** n sylviculture f

**foretaste** ['fɔːteɪst] n avant-goût m

**foretell** [fɔː'tel] (irreg: like **tell**) vt prédire

**forever** [fə'revər] adv pour toujours; (fig) continuellement

**foreword** ['fɔːwəːd] n avant-propos m inv

**forfeit** ['fɔːfɪt] vt (lose) perdre

**forgave** [fə'geɪv] pt of **forgive**

**forge** [fɔːdʒ] n forge f ♦ vt (signature) contrefaire; (wrought iron) forger; **to ~ money** (BRIT) fabriquer de la fausse monnaie; **~ ahead** vi pousser de l'avant, prendre de l'avance; **~d** adj faux (fausse); **~r** n faussaire m; **~ry** n faux m, contrefaçon f

**forget** [fə'get] (pt **forgot**, pp **forgotten**) vt, vi oublier; **~ful** adj distrait(e), étourdi(e); **~-me-not** n myosotis m

**forgive** [fə'gɪv] (pt **forgave**, pp **forgiven**) vt pardonner; **to ~ sb for sth/for doing sth** pardonner qch à qn/à qn de faire qch; **~ness** n pardon m

**forgo** [fɔː'gəʊ] (pt **forwent**, pp **forgone**) vt renoncer à

**fork** [fɔːk] n (for eating) fourchette f; (for gardening) fourche f; (of roads) bifurcation f; (of railways) embranchement m ♦ vi (road) bifurquer; **~ out** (inf) vt allonger; **~-lift truck** n chariot élévateur

**forlorn** [fə'lɔːn] adj (deserted) abandonné(e); (attempt, hope) désespéré(e)

**form** [fɔːm] n forme f; (SCOL) classe f; (questionnaire) formulaire m ♦ vt former; (habit) contracter; **in top ~** en pleine forme

**formal** ['fɔːml] adj (offer, receipt) en bonne et due forme; (person)

**format** cérémonieux(-euse); (*dinner*) officiel(le); (*clothes*) de soirée; (*garden*) à la française; (*education*) à proprement parler; **~ly** *adv* officiellement; cérémonieusement

**format** ['fɔːmæt] *n* format *m* ♦ *vt* (COMPUT) formater

**formation** [fɔː'meɪʃən] *n* formation *f*

**formative** ['fɔːmətɪv] *adj*: **~ years** années *fpl* d'apprentissage *or* de formation

**former** ['fɔːmər] *adj* ancien(ne) (*before n*), précédent(e); **the ~ ... the latter** le premier ... le second, celui-là ... celui-ci; **~ly** *adv* autrefois

**formidable** ['fɔːmɪdəbl] *adj* redoutable

**formula** ['fɔːmjulə] (*pl* **~e**) *n* formule *f*

**forsake** [fə'seɪk] (*pt* **forsook**, *pp* **forsaken**) *vt* abandonner

**fort** [fɔːt] *n* fort *m*

**forte** ['fɔːtɪ] *n* (point) fort *m*

**forth** [fɔːθ] *adv* en avant; **to go back and ~** aller et venir; **and so ~** et ainsi de suite; **~coming** *adj* (*event*) qui va avoir lieu prochainement; (*character*) ouvert(e), communicatif(-ive); (*available*) disponible; **~right** *adj* franc (franche), direct(e); **~with** *adv* sur-le-champ

**fortify** ['fɔːtɪfaɪ] *vt* fortifier

**fortitude** ['fɔːtɪtjuːd] *n* courage *m*

**fortnight** ['fɔːtnaɪt] (BRIT) *n* quinzaine *f*, quinze jours *mpl*; **~ly** (BRIT) *adj* bimensuel(le) ♦ *adv* tous les quinze jours

**fortunate** ['fɔːtʃənɪt] *adj* heureux(-euse); (*person*) chanceux(-euse); **it is ~ that** c'est une chance que; **~ly** *adv* heureusement

**fortune** ['fɔːtʃən] *n* chance *f*; (*wealth*) fortune *f*; **~-teller** *n* diseuse *f* de bonne aventure

**forty** ['fɔːtɪ] *num* quarante

**forward** ['fɔːwəd] *adj* (*ahead of schedule*) en avance; (*movement, position*) en avant, vers l'avant; (*not shy*) direct(e); effronté(e) ♦ *n* (SPORT) avant *m* ♦ *vt* (*letter*) faire suivre; (*parcel, goods*) expédier; (*fig*) promouvoir, favoriser; **~(s)**

*adv* en avant; **to move ~** avancer

**fossil** ['fɔsl] *n* fossile *m*

**foster** ['fɔstər] *vt* encourager, favoriser; (*child*) élever (*sans obligation d'adopter*); **~ child** *n* enfant adoptif(-ive); **~ mother** *n* mère *f* nourricière *or* adoptive

**fought** [fɔːt] *pt, pp* of **fight**

**foul** [faul] *adj* (*weather, smell etc*) infect(e); (*language*) ordurier(-ère) ♦ *n* (SPORT) faute *f* ♦ *vt* (*dirty*) salir, encrasser; **he's got a ~ temper** il a un caractère de chien; **~ play** *n* (LAW) acte criminel

**found** [faund] *pt, pp* of **find** ♦ *vt* (*establish*) fonder; **~ation** [faun'deɪʃən] *n* (*act*) fondation *f*; (*base*) fondement *m*; (*also*: **~ation cream**) fond *m* de teint; **~ations** *npl* (*of building*) fondations *fpl*

**founder** ['faundər] *n* fondateur *m* ♦ *vi* couler, sombrer

**foundry** ['faundrɪ] *n* fonderie *f*

**fountain** ['fauntɪn] *n* fontaine *f*; **~ pen** *n* stylo *m* (à encre)

**four** [fɔːr] *num* quatre; **on all ~s** à quatre pattes; **~-poster** *n* (*also*: **~-poster bed**) lit *m* à baldaquin; **~teen** *num* quatorze; **~th** *num* quatrième

**fowl** [faul] *n* volaille *f*

**fox** [fɔks] *n* renard *m* ♦ *vt* mystifier

**foyer** ['fɔɪeɪ] *n* (*hotel*) hall *m*; (THEATRE) foyer *m*

**fraction** ['frækʃən] *n* fraction *f*

**fracture** ['fræktʃər] *n* fracture *f*

**fragile** ['frædʒaɪl] *adj* fragile

**fragment** ['frægmənt] *n* fragment *m*

**fragrant** ['freɪgrənt] *adj* parfumé(e), odorant(e)

**frail** [freɪl] *adj* fragile, délicat(e)

**frame** [freɪm] *n* charpente *f*; (*of picture, bicycle*) cadre *m*; (*of door, window*) encadrement *m*, chambranle *m*; (*of spectacles: also*: **~s**) monture *f* ♦ *vt* encadrer; **~ of mind** disposition *f* d'esprit; **~work** *n* structure *f*

**France** [frɑːns] *n* France *f*

**franchise** ['fræntʃaɪz] *n* (POL) droit *m* de vote; (COMM) franchise *f*

# frank

**frank** [fræŋk] adj franc (franche) ♦ vt (letter) affranchir; **~ly** adv franchement

**frantic** ['fræntɪk] adj (hectic) frénétique; (distraught) hors de soi

**fraternity** [frə'tɜːnɪtɪ] n (spirit) fraternité f; (club) communauté f, confrérie f

**fraud** [frɔːd] n supercherie f, fraude f, tromperie f; (person) imposteur m

**fraught** [frɔːt] adj: **~ with** chargé(e) de, plein(e) de

**fray** [freɪ] vi s'effilocher

**freak** [friːk] n (also cpd) phénomène m, créature ou événement exceptionnel par sa rareté

**freckle** ['frekl] n tache f de rousseur

**free** [friː] adj libre; (gratis) gratuit(e) ♦ vt (prisoner etc) libérer; (jammed object or person) dégager; (of charge), for **~** gratuitement; **~dom** n liberté f; **F~fone** ® n numéro vert; **~for-all** n mêlée générale; **~ gift** n prime f; **~hold** n propriété foncière libre; **~ kick** n coup franc; **~lance** adj indépendant(e); **~ly** adv librement, (liberally) libéralement; **F~mason** n franc-maçon m; **F~post** ® n port payé; **~range** adj (hen, eggs) de ferme; **~ trade** n libre-échange m; **~way** (US) n autoroute f; **~ will** n libre arbitre m; **of one's own ~ will** de son plein gré

**freeze** [friːz] (pt froze, pp frozen) vi geler ♦ vt (food) congeler; (prices, salaries) bloquer, geler ♦ n gel m; (fig) blocage m; **~-dried** adj lyophilisé(e); **~r** n congélateur m; **freezing** adj: **freezing (cold)** (weather, water) glacial(e) ♦ n: **3 degrees below freezing** 3 degrés au-dessous de zéro; **freezing point** n point m de congélation

**freight** [freɪt] n (goods) fret m, cargaison f; (money charged) fret, prix m du transport; **~ train** n train m de marchandises

**French** [frentʃ] adj français(e) ♦ n (LING) français m; **the ~** npl (people) les Français; **~ bean** n haricot vert; **~ fried (potatoes)** (US **~ fries**) npl (pommes

de terre fpl) frites fpl; **~ horn** n (MUS) cor m (d'harmonie); **~ kiss** n baiser profond; **~ loaf** n baguette f; **~man** (irreg) n Français m; **~ window** n porte-fenêtre f; **~woman** (irreg) n Française f

**frenzy** ['frenzɪ] n frénésie f

**frequency** ['friːkwənsɪ] n fréquence f

**frequent** [adj 'friːkwənt, vb frɪ'kwent] adj fréquent(e) ♦ vt fréquenter; **~ly** adv fréquemment

**fresh** [freʃ] adj frais (fraîche); (new) nouveau (nouvelle); (cheeky) familier(-ère), culotté(e); **~en** vi (wind, air) fraîchir; **~en up** vi faire un brin de toilette; **~er** n (BRIT: inf) n (SCOL) bizuth m, étudiant(e) de 1ère année; **~ly** adv nouvellement, récemment; **~man** (US) (irreg) n = fresher; **~ness** n fraîcheur f; **~water** adj (fish) d'eau douce

**fret** [fret] vi s'agiter, se tracasser

**friar** ['fraɪə*] n moine m, frère m

**friction** ['frɪkʃən] n friction f

**Friday** ['fraɪdɪ] n vendredi m

**fridge** [frɪdʒ] (BRIT) n frigo m, frigidaire ® m

**fried** [fraɪd] adj frit(e); **~ egg** œuf m sur le plat

**friend** [frend] n ami(e); **~ly** adj amical(e); gentil(le); (place) accueillant(e); **they were killed by ~ly fire** ils sont morts sous les tirs de leur propre camp; **~ship** n amitié f

**frieze** [friːz] n frise f

**fright** [fraɪt] n peur f, effroi m; **to take ~** prendre peur, s'effrayer; **~en** vt effrayer, faire peur à; **~ened** adj: **to be ~ened (of)** avoir peur (de); **~ening** adj effrayant(e); **~ful** adj affreux(-euse)

**frigid** ['frɪdʒɪd] adj frigide

**frill** [frɪl] n (on dress) volant m; (on shirt) jabot m

**fringe** [frɪndʒ] n (BRIT: of hair) frange f; (edge: of forest etc) bordure f; **~ benefits** npl avantages sociaux ou en nature

**Frisbee** ® ['frɪzbɪ] n Frisbee ® m

# frisk 409 full

**frisk** [frɪsk] vt fouiller

**fritter** ['frɪtər] n beignet m; ~ **away** vt gaspiller

**frivolous** ['frɪvələs] adj frivole

**frizzy** ['frɪzɪ] adj crépu(e)

**fro** [frəu] adv: **to go to and** ~ aller et venir

**frock** [frɔk] n robe f

**frog** [frɔg] n grenouille f; ~**man** n homme-grenouille m

**frolic** ['frɔlɪk] vi folâtrer, batifoler

KEYWORD

**from** [frɔm] prep 1 (indicating starting place, origin etc) de; **where do you come from?**, **where are you from?** d'où venez-vous?; **from London to Paris** de Londres à Paris; **a letter from my sister** une lettre de ma sœur; **to drink from the bottle** boire à (même) la bouteille

2 (indicating time) (à partir) de; **from one o'clock** to or until or till **two** d'une heure à deux heures; **from January (on)** à partir de janvier

3 (indicating distance) de; **the hotel is one kilometre from the beach** l'hôtel est à un kilomètre de la plage

4 (indicating price, number etc) de; **the interest rate was increased from 9% to 10%** le taux d'intérêt est passé de 9 à 10%

5 (indicating difference) de; **he can't tell red from green** il ne peut pas distinguer le rouge du vert

6 (because of, on the basis of): **from what he says** d'après ce qu'il dit; **weak from hunger** affaibli par la faim

**front** [frʌnt] n (of house, dress) devant m; (of coach, train) avant m; (promenade: also: **sea** ~) bord m de mer; (MIL, METEOROLOGY) front m; (fig: appearances) contenance f, façade f ♦ adj de devant; (seat) avant inv; **in** ~ (of) devant; ~ **age** n (of building) façade f; ~ **door** n porte f d'entrée; (of car) portière f avant; ~**ier**

**[frʌntɪər]** n frontière f; ~ **page** n première page; ~ **room** (BRIT) n pièce f de devant, salon m; ~-**wheel drive** n traction f avant

**frost** [frɔst] n gel m, gelée f; (also: **hoar-frost**) givre m; ~**bite** n gelures fpl; ~**ed** adj (glass) dépoli(e); ~**y** adj (weather, welcome) glacial(e)

**froth** [frɔθ] n mousse f, écume f

**frown** [fraun] vi froncer les sourcils

**froze** [frəuz] pt of **freeze**

**frozen** ['frəuzn] pp of **freeze**

**fruit** [fru:t] n inv fruit m; ~**erer** n fruitier m, marchand(e) de fruits; ~**ful** adj (fig) fructueux(-euse); ~**ion** [fru:'ɪʃən] n: **to come to** ~**ion** se réaliser; ~ **juice** n jus m de fruit; ~ **machine** (BRIT) n machine f à sous; ~ **salad** n salade f de fruits

**frustrate** [frʌs'treɪt] vt frustrer

**fry** [fraɪ] (pt, pp **fried**) vt (faire) frire; see also **small**; ~**ing pan** n poêle f (à frire)

**ft.** abbr = **foot**; **feet**

**fudge** [fʌdʒ] n (CULIN) caramel m

**fuel** ['fjuəl] n (for heating) combustible m; (for propelling) carburant m; ~ **oil** n mazout m; ~ **tank** n (in vehicle) réservoir m

**fugitive** ['fju:dʒɪtɪv] n fugitif(-ive)

**fulfil** [ful'fɪl] (US **fulfill**) vt (function, condition) remplir; (order) exécuter; (wish, desire) satisfaire, réaliser; ~**ment** (US **fulfillment**) n (of wishes etc) réalisation f; (feeling) contentement m

**full** [ful] adj plein(e); (details, information) complet(-ète); (skirt) ample, large ♦ adv: **to know** ~ **well that** savoir fort bien que; **I'm** ~ **(up)** j'ai bien mangé; **a** ~ **two hours** deux bonnes heures; **at** ~ **speed** à toute vitesse; **in** ~ (reproduce, quote) intégralement; (write) en toutes lettres; ~ **employment** plein emploi; **to pay in** ~ tout payer; ~-**length** adj (film) long métrage; (portrait, mirror) en pied; (coat) long(ue); ~ **moon** n pleine lune; ~-**scale** adj (attack, war) complet(-ète), total(e); (model) grandeur nature inv; ~ **stop** n point m; ~-

**time** adj, adv (work) à plein temps; **~y** adv entièrement, complètement; (at least) au moins; **~y licensed** (hotel, restaurant) autorisé(e) à vendre des boissons alcoolisées; **~y-fledged** adj (barrister etc) diplômé(e); (citizen, member) à part entière

**fumble** ['fʌmbl] vi: **~ with** tripoter

**fume** [fjuːm] vi rager; **~s** npl vapeurs fpl, émanations fpl, gaz mpl

**fun** [fʌn] n amusement m, divertissement m; **to have ~** s'amuser; **for ~** pour rire; **to make ~ of** se moquer de

**function** ['fʌŋkʃən] n fonction f; (social occasion) cérémonie f, soirée officielle f ♦ vi fonctionner; **~al** adj fonctionnel(le)

**fund** [fʌnd] n caisse f, fonds m; (source, store) source f, mine f; **~s** npl (money) fonds mpl

**fundamental** [fʌndə'mentl] adj fondamental(e)

**funeral** ['fjuːnərəl] n enterrement m, obsèques fpl; **~ parlour** n entreprise f de pompes funèbres; **~ service** n service m funèbre

**funfair** ['fʌnfɛəʳ] (BRIT) n fête (foraine)

**fungi** ['fʌŋgaɪ] npl of **fungus**

**fungus** ['fʌŋgəs] (pl fungi) n champignon m; (mould) moisissure f

**funnel** ['fʌnl] n entonnoir m; (of ship) cheminée f

**funny** ['fʌnɪ] adj amusant(e), drôle; (strange) curieux(-euse), bizarre

**fur** [fəːʳ] n fourrure f; (BRIT: in kettle etc) (dépôt m de) tartre m

**furious** ['fjuərɪəs] adj furieux(-euse); (effort) acharné(e)

**furlong** ['fəːlɔŋ] n = 201,17 m

**furnace** ['fəːnɪs] n fourneau m

**furnish** ['fəːnɪʃ] vt meubler; (supply): **to ~ sb with sth** fournir qch à qn; **~ings** npl mobilier m, ameublement m

**furniture** ['fəːnɪtʃəʳ] n meubles mpl, mobilier m; **piece of ~** meuble m

**furrow** ['fʌrəu] n sillon m

**furry** ['fəːrɪ] adj (animal) à fourrure; (toy) en peluche

**further** ['fəːðəʳ] adj (additional) supplémentaire, autre; nouveau (nouvelle) ♦ adv plus loin; (more) davantage; (moreover) de plus ♦ vt faire avancer ou progresser, promouvoir; **~ education** n enseignement m postscolaire; **~more** adv de plus, en outre

**furthest** ['fəːðɪst] superl of **far**

**fury** ['fjuərɪ] n fureur f

**fuse** [fjuːz] (US **fuze**) n fusible m; (for bomb etc) amorce f, détonateur m ♦ vt, vi (metal) fondre; **to ~ the lights** (BRIT) faire sauter les plombs; **~ box** n boîte f à fusibles

**fuss** [fʌs] n (excitement) agitation f; (complaining) histoire(s) f(pl); **to make a ~** faire des histoires; **to make a ~ of sb** être aux petits soins pour qn; **~y** adj (person) tatillon(ne), difficile; (dress, style) tarabiscoté(e)

**future** ['fjuːtʃəʳ] adj futur(e) ♦ n avenir m; (LING) futur m; **in ~** à l'avenir

**fuze** [fjuːz] (US) n, vi, vt =**fuse**

**fuzzy** ['fʌzɪ] adj (PHOT) flou(e); (hair) crépu(e)

# G, g

**G** [dʒiː] n (MUS) sol m

**G7** n abbr (= Group of 7) le groupe des 7

**gabble** ['gæbl] vi bredouiller

**gable** ['geɪbl] n pignon m

**gadget** ['gædʒɪt] n gadget m

**Gaelic** ['geɪlɪk] adj gaélique ♦ n (LING) gaélique m

**gag** [gæg] n (on mouth) bâillon m; (joke) gag m ♦ vt bâillonner

**gaiety** ['geɪətɪ] n gaieté f

**gain** [geɪn] n (improvement) gain m; (profit) gain, profit m; (increase): **~ (in)** augmentation f (de) ♦ vt gagner ♦ vi (watch) avancer; **to ~ 3 lbs (in weight)** prendre 3 livres; **to ~ on sb** (catch up) rattraper qn; **to ~ from/by** gagner de/à

**gal.** abbr = **gallon**

**gale** [geɪl] n coup m de vent

**gallant** ['gælənt] adj vaillant(e), brave; (towards ladies) galant

**gall bladder** ['gɔːl-] n vésicule f biliaire

**gallery** ['gælərɪ] n galerie f; (also: **art ~**) musée m; (: private) galerie

**gallon** ['gæln] n gallon m (BRIT = 4,5 l; US = 3,8 l)

**gallop** ['gæləp] n galop m ♦ vi galoper

**gallows** ['gæləuz] n potence f

**gallstone** ['gɔːlstəun] n calcul m biliaire

**galore** [gə'lɔːr] adv en abondance, à gogo

**Gambia** ['gæmbɪə] n: (**The**) ~ la Gambie

**gambit** ['gæmbɪt] n (fig): (**opening**) ~ manœuvre f stratégique

**gamble** ['gæmbl] n pari m, risque calculé ♦ vt, vi jouer; **to ~ on** (fig) miser sur; **~r** n joueur m; **gambling** n jeu m

**game** [geɪm] n jeu m; (match) match m; (strategy, scheme) plan m; projet m; (HUNTING) gibier m ♦ adj (willing): **to be ~ (for)** être prêt(e) (à or pour); **big ~** gros gibier; **~keeper** n garde-chasse m

**gammon** ['gæmən] n (bacon) quartier m de lard fumé; (ham) jambon fumé

**gamut** ['gæmət] n gamme f

**gang** [gæŋ] n bande f; (of workmen) équipe f; **~ up** vi: **to ~ up on sb** se liguer contre qn; **~ster** n gangster m; **~way** ['gæŋweɪ] n passerelle f; (BRIT: of bus, plane) couloir central; (: in cinema) allée centrale

**gaol** [dʒeɪl] (BRIT) n = **jail**

**gap** [gæp] n trou m; (in time) intervalle m; (difference): **~ between** écart m entre

**gape** [geɪp] vi (person) être or rester bouche bée; (hole, shirt) être ouvert(e); **gaping** adj (hole) béant(e)

**garage** ['gærɑːʒ] n garage m

**garbage** ['gɑːbɪdʒ] n (US: rubbish) ordures fpl, détritus mpl; (inf: nonsense) foutaises fpl; **~ can** (US) n poubelle f, boîte f à ordures

**garbled** ['gɑːbld] adj (account, message) embrouillé(e)

**garden** ['gɑːdn] n jardin m; **~s** npl jardin public; **~er** n jardinier m; **~ing** n jardinage m

**gargle** ['gɑːgl] vi se gargariser

**garish** ['gɛərɪʃ] adj criard(e), voyant(e); (light) cru(e)

**garland** ['gɑːlənd] n guirlande f; couronne f

**garlic** ['gɑːlɪk] n ail m

**garment** ['gɑːmənt] n vêtement m

**garrison** ['gærɪsn] n garnison f

**garter** ['gɑːtər] n jarretière f; (US) jarretelle f

**gas** [gæs] n gaz m; (US: gasoline) essence f ♦ vt asphyxier; **~ cooker** (BRIT) n cuisinière f à gaz; **~ cylinder** n bouteille f de gaz; **~ fire** (BRIT) n radiateur m à gaz

**gash** [gæʃ] n entaille f; (on face) balafre f

**gasket** ['gæskɪt] n (AUT) joint m de culasse

**gas mask** n masque m à gaz

**gas meter** n compteur m à gaz

**gasoline** [gæsə'liːn] (US) n essence f

**gasp** [gɑːsp] vi haleter

**gas: ~ ring** n brûleur m; **~ station** (US) n station-service f; **~ tap** n bouton m (de cuisinière à gaz); (on pipe) robinet m à gaz

**gastric** ['gæstrɪk] adj gastrique; **~ flu** n grippe f intestinale

**gate** [geɪt] n (of garden) portail m; (of field) barrière f; (of building, at airport) porte f

**gateau** ['gætəu] n (pl **~x**) (gros) gâteau m à la crème

**gatecrash** vt s'introduire sans invitation dans

**gateway** n porte f

**gather** ['gæðər] vt (flowers, fruit) cueillir; (pick up) ramasser; (assemble) rassembler, réunir; recueillir; (understand) comprendre; (SEWING) froncer ♦ vi (assemble) se rassembler; **to ~ speed** prendre de la vitesse; **~ing** n rassemblement m

**gaudy** ['gɔːdɪ] adj voyant(e)

**gauge** [geɪdʒ] n (instrument) jauge f ♦ vt jauger

**gaunt** [gɔːnt] adj (thin) décharné(e); (grim, desolate) désolé(e)

**gauntlet** ['gɔːntlɪt] n (glove) gant m

**gauze** [gɔːz] n gaze f

**gave** [geɪv] pt of **give**

**gay** [geɪ] adj (homosexual) homosexuel(le); (cheerful) gai(e), réjoui(e); (colour etc) gai, vif (vive)

**gaze** [geɪz] n regard m fixe ♦ vi: **to ~ at** fixer du regard

**gazump** [gə'zʌmp] (BRIT) vi revenir sur une promesse de vente (pour accepter une offre plus intéressante)

**GB** abbr = **Great Britain**

**GCE** n abbr (BRIT) = **General Certificate of Education**

**GCSE** n abbr (BRIT) = **General Certificate of Secondary Education**

**gear** [gɪə*] n matériel m, équipement m; attirail m; (TECH) engrenage m; (AUT) vitesse f ♦ vt (fig: adapt): **to ~ sth to** adapter qch à; **top** or (US) **high ~** quatrième (or cinquième) vitesse; **low ~** première vitesse; **in ~** en prise; **~ box** n boîte f de vitesses; **~ lever** (US **gear shift**) n levier m de vitesse

**geese** [giːs] npl of **goose**

**gel** [dʒel] n gel m

**gem** [dʒem] n pierre précieuse

**Gemini** ['dʒemɪnaɪ] n les Gémeaux mpl

**gender** ['dʒendə*] n genre m

**gene** [dʒiːn] n gène m

**general** ['dʒenərəl] n général m ♦ adj général(e); **in ~** en général; **~ delivery** n poste restante; **~ election** n élection(s) législative(s); **~ knowledge** n connaissances générales; **~ly** adv généralement; **~ practitioner** n généraliste m/f

**generate** ['dʒenəreɪt] vt engendrer; (electricity etc) produire; **generation** n génération f; (of electricity etc) production f; **generator** n générateur m

**generosity** [dʒenə'rɒsɪtɪ] n générosité f

**generous** ['dʒenərəs] adj généreux (-euse); (copious) copieux(-euse)

**genetic** [dʒɪ'netɪk] adj: **~ engineering** ingénierie f génétique; **~ fingerprinting** système m d'empreinte génétique

**genetically modified** (food etc) adj génétiquement modifié(e)

**genetics** [dʒɪ'netɪks] n génétique f

**Geneva** [dʒɪ'niːvə] n Genève

**genial** ['dʒiːnɪəl] adj cordial(e)

**genitals** ['dʒenɪtlz] npl organes génitaux

**genius** ['dʒiːnɪəs] n génie m

**genteel** [dʒen'tiːl] adj distingué(e)

**gentle** ['dʒentl] adj doux (douce)

**gentleman** ['dʒentlmən] n monsieur m; (well-bred man) gentleman m

**gently** ['dʒentlɪ] adv doucement

**gentry** ['dʒentrɪ] n inv: **the ~** la petite noblesse

**gents** [dʒents] n W.-C. mpl (pour hommes)

**genuine** ['dʒenjuɪn] adj véritable, authentique; (person) sincère

**geographical** [dʒɪə'græfɪkl] adj géographique

**geography** [dʒɪ'ɒɡrəfɪ] n géographie f

**geology** [dʒɪ'ɒlədʒɪ] n géologie f

**geometric(al)** [dʒɪə'metrɪk(l)] adj géométrique

**geometry** [dʒɪ'ɒmɪtrɪ] n géométrie f

**geranium** [dʒɪ'reɪnɪəm] n géranium m

**geriatric** [dʒerɪ'ætrɪk] adj gériatrique

**germ** [dʒəːm] n (MED) microbe m

**German** ['dʒəːmən] adj allemand(e) ♦ n Allemand(e); (LING) allemand m; **~ measles** (BRIT) n rubéole f

**Germany** ['dʒəːmənɪ] n Allemagne f

**gesture** ['dʒestʃə*] n geste m

KEYWORD

**get** [ɡet] (pt, pp **got**, pp **gotten** (US)) vi 1 (become, be) devenir; **to get old/tired** devenir vieux/fatigué, vieillir/se fatiguer; **to get drunk** s'enivrer; **to get killed** se faire tuer; **when do I get**

**paid?** quand est-ce que je serai payé?; **it's getting late** il se fait tard

**2** (go): **to get to/from** aller à/de; **to get home** rentrer chez soi; **how did you get here?** comment es-tu arrivé ici?

**3** (begin) commencer or se mettre à; **I'm getting to like him** je commence à l'apprécier; **let's get going or started** allons-y

♦ vt (modal aux vb): **you've got to do it** il faut que vous le fassiez; **I've got to tell the police** je dois le dire à la police

♦ vt **1: to get sth done** (do) faire qch; (have done) faire faire qch; **to get one's hair cut** se faire couper les cheveux; **to get sb to do sth** faire faire qch à qn; **to get sb drunk** enivrer qn

**2** (obtain: money, permission, results) obtenir, avoir; (find: job, flat) trouver; (fetch: person, doctor, object) aller chercher; **to get sth for sb** procurer qch à qn; **get me Mr Jones, please** (on phone) passez-moi Mr Jones, s'il vous plaît; **can I get you a drink?** est-ce que je peux vous servir à boire?

**3** (receive: present, letter) recevoir, avoir; (acquire: reputation) avoir; (: prize) obtenir; **what did you get for your birthday?** qu'est-ce que tu as eu pour ton anniversaire?

**4** (catch) saisir, attraper; (hit: target etc) atteindre; **to get sb by the arm/throat** prendre or saisir or attraper qn par le bras/à la gorge; **get him!** arrête-le!

**5** (take, move) faire parvenir; **do you think we'll get it through the door?** on arrivera à le faire passer par la porte?; **I'll get you there somehow** je me débrouillerai pour t'y emmener

**6** (catch, take: plane, bus etc) prendre

**7** (understand) comprendre, saisir; (hear) entendre; **I've got it!** j'ai compris!, je saisis!; **I didn't get your name** je n'ai pas entendu votre nom

**8** (have, possess): **to have got** avoir; **how many have you got?** vous en avez combien?

**get about** vi se déplacer; (news) se répandre

**get along** vi (agree) s'entendre; (depart) s'en aller; (manage) = **get by**

**get at** vt fus (attack) s'en prendre à; (reach) atteindre, parvenir à

**get away** vi partir, s'en aller; (escape) s'échapper

**get away with** vt fus en être quitte pour; se faire passer or pardonner

**get back** vi (return) rentrer ♦ vt récupérer, recouvrer

**get by** vi (pass) passer; (manage) se débrouiller

**get down** vi, vt fus descendre ♦ vt descendre; (depress) déprimer

**get down to** vt fus (work) se mettre à (faire)

**get in** vi rentrer; (train) arriver

**get into** vt fus entrer dans; (car, train etc) monter dans; (clothes) mettre, enfiler, endosser; **to get into bed/a rage** se mettre au lit/en colère

**get off** vi (from train etc) descendre; (depart: person, car) s'en aller; (escape) s'en tirer ♦ vt (remove: clothes, stain) enlever ♦ vt fus (train, bus) descendre de

**get on** vi (at exam etc) se débrouiller; (agree): **to get on (with)** s'entendre (avec) ♦ vt fus monter dans; (horse) monter sur

**get out** vi sortir; (of vehicle) descendre ♦ vt sortir

**get out of** vt fus sortir de; (duty etc) échapper à, se soustraire à

**get over** vt fus (illness) se remettre de

**get round** vt fus contourner; (fig: person) entortiller

**get through** vi (TEL) avoir la communication; **to get through to sb** atteindre qn

**get together** vi se réunir ♦ vt assembler

**get up** vi (rise) se lever ♦ vt fus monter

**get up to** vt fus (reach) arriver à; (prank etc) faire

**getaway** ['getəweɪ] n (escape) fuite f
**geyser** ['giːzə⁴] n (GEO) geyser m; (BRIT: water heater) chauffe-eau m inv
**Ghana** ['gɑːnə] n Ghana m
**ghastly** ['gɑːstlɪ] adj atroce, horrible; (pale) livide, blême
**gherkin** ['gəːkɪn] n cornichon m
**ghetto blaster** ['getəʊ'blɑːstə⁴] n stéréo f portable
**ghost** [gəʊst] n fantôme m, revenant m
**giant** ['dʒaɪənt] n géant(e) ♦ adj géant(e), énorme
**gibberish** ['dʒɪbərɪʃ] n charabia m
**giblets** ['dʒɪblɪts] npl abats mpl
**Gibraltar** [dʒɪ'brɔːltə⁴] n Gibraltar
**giddy** ['gɪdɪ] adj (dizzy): **to be** or **feel** ~ avoir le vertige
**gift** [gɪft] n cadeau m; (donation, ability) don m; ~**ed** adj doué(e); ~ **shop** n boutique f de cadeaux; ~ **token** n chèque-cadeau m
**gigantic** [dʒaɪ'gæntɪk] adj gigantesque
**giggle** ['gɪgl] vi pouffer (de rire), rire sottement
**gill** [dʒɪl] n (measure) = 0.25 pints (BRIT = 0.15 l, US = 0.12 l)
**gills** [gɪlz] npl (of fish) ouïes fpl, branchies fpl
**gilt** [gɪlt] adj doré(e) ♦ n dorure f; ~-**edged** adj (COMM) de premier ordre
**gimmick** ['gɪmɪk] n truc m
**gin** [dʒɪn] n (liquor) gin m
**ginger** ['dʒɪndʒə⁴] n gingembre m; ~ **ale, ~ beer** n boisson gazeuse au gingembre; ~**bread** n pain m d'épices
**gingerly** ['dʒɪndʒəlɪ] adv avec précaution
**gipsy** ['dʒɪpsɪ] n = **gypsy**
**giraffe** [dʒɪ'rɑːf] n girafe f
**girder** ['gəːdə⁴] n poutrelle f
**girl** [gəːl] n fille f, fillette f; (young un-

married woman) jeune fille; (daughter) fille; **an English** ~ une jeune Anglaise; ~**friend** n (of girl) amie f; (of boy) petite amie; ~**ish** adj de petite or de jeune fille; (for a boy) efféminé(e)
**giro** ['dʒaɪrəʊ] n (bank ~) virement m bancaire; (post office ~) mandat m; (BRIT: welfare cheque) mandat m d'allocation chômage
**gist** [dʒɪst] n essentiel m
**give** [gɪv] (pt **gave**, pp **given**) vt donner ♦ vi (break) céder; (stretch: fabric) se prêter; **to ~ sb sth**, ~ **sth to sb** donner qch à qn; **to ~ a cry/sigh** pousser un cri/un soupir; ~ **away** vt donner; (free) faire cadeau de; (betray) donner, trahir; (disclose) révéler; (bride) conduire à l'autel; ~ **back** vt rendre; ~ **in** vi céder ♦ vt donner; ~ **off** vt dégager; ~ **out** vt distribuer; annoncer; ~ **up** vi renoncer ♦ vt renoncer à; **to ~ up smoking** arrêter de fumer; **to o.s. up** se rendre; ~ **way** (BRIT) vi céder; (AUT) céder la priorité
**GLA** (BRIT) n abbr (= Greater London Authority) conseil municipal de Londres
**glacier** ['glæsɪə⁴] n glacier m
**glad** [glæd] adj content(e); ~**ly** adv volontiers
**glamorous** ['glæmərəs] adj (person) séduisant(e); (job) prestigieux(-euse)
**glamour** ['glæmə⁴] n éclat m, prestige m
**glance** [glɑːns] n coup m d'œil ♦ vi: **to** ~ **at** jeter un coup d'œil à; **glancing** adj (blow) oblique
**gland** [glænd] n glande f
**glare** [glεə⁴] n (of anger) regard furieux; (of light) lumière éblouissante; (of publicity) feux mpl ♦ vi briller d'un éclat aveuglant; **to ~ at** lancer un regard furieux à; **glaring** adj (mistake) criant(e), qui saute aux yeux
**glass** [glɑːs] n verre m; ~**es** npl (spectacles) lunettes fpl; ~**house** (BRIT) n (for plants) serre f; ~**ware** n verrerie f
**glaze** [gleɪz] vt (door, window) vitrer;

*(pottery)* vernir ♦ *n (on pottery)* vernis *m*; **~d** *adj (pottery)* verni(e); *(eyes)* vitreux(-euse)

**glazier** ['gleɪzɪəʳ] *n* vitrier *m*

**gleam** [gliːm] *vi* luire, briller

**glean** [gliːn] *vt (information)* glaner

**glee** [gliː] *n* joie *f*

**glib** [glɪb] *adj (person)* qui a du bagou; *(response)* désinvolte, facile

**glide** [glaɪd] *vi* glisser; *(AVIAT, birds)* planer; **~r** *n (AVIAT)* planeur *m*; **gliding** *n (SPORT)* vol *m* à voile

**glimmer** ['glɪməʳ] *n* lueur *f*

**glimpse** [glɪmps] *n* vision passagère, aperçu *m* ♦ *vt* entrevoir, apercevoir

**glint** [glɪnt] *vi* étinceler

**glisten** ['glɪsn] *vi* briller, luire

**glitter** ['glɪtəʳ] *vi* scintiller, briller

**gloat** [gləut] *vi*: **to ~ (over)** jubiler à propos de)

**global** ['gləubl] *adj* mondial(e); **~ warming** *n* réchauffement *m* de la planète

**globe** [gləub] *n* globe *m*

**gloom** [gluːm] *n* obscurité *f*; *(sadness)* tristesse *f*, mélancolie *f*; **~y** *adj* sombre, triste, lugubre

**glorious** ['glɔːrɪəs] *adj* glorieux(-euse); splendide

**glory** ['glɔːrɪ] *n* gloire *f*; splendeur *f*

**gloss** [glɔs] *n (shine)* brillant *m*, vernis *m*; **~ over** *vt fus* glisser sur

**glossary** ['glɔsərɪ] *n* glossaire *m*

**glossy** ['glɔsɪ] *adj* brillant(e); **~ maga-zine** magazine *m* de luxe

**glove** [glʌv] *n* gant *m*; **~ compart-ment** *n (AUT)* boîte *f* à gants, vide-poches *m inv*

**glow** [gləu] *vi* rougeoyer; *(face)* rayonner; *(eyes)* briller

**glower** ['glauəʳ] *vi*: **to ~ (at)** lancer des regards mauvais (à)

**glucose** ['gluːkəus] *n* glucose *m*

**glue** [gluː] *n* colle *f* ♦ *vt* coller

**glum** [glʌm] *adj* sombre, morne

**glut** [glʌt] *n* surabondance *f*

**glutton** ['glʌtn] *n* glouton(ne); **a ~ for**

**work** un bourreau de travail; **a ~ for punishment** un masochiste *(fig)*

**GM** *abbr* (= genetically modified) généti-quement modifié(e)

**gnat** [næt] *n* moucheron *m*

**gnaw** [nɔː] *vt* ronger

**go** [gəu] *(pt* **went**, *pp* **gone**, *pl* **~es**) *vi* aller; *(depart)* partir, s'en aller; *(work)* marcher; *(break etc)* céder; *(be sold)*: **to ~ for £10** se vendre 10 livres; *(fit, suit)*: **to ~ with** aller avec; *(become)*: **to ~ pale/mouldy** pâlir/moisir ♦ *n*: **to have a ~ (at)** essayer (de faire); **to be on the ~** être en mouvement; **whose ~ is it?** à qui est-ce de jouer?; **he's ~ing to do it** il va le faire, il est sur le point de faire; **to ~ for a walk** aller se promener; **to ~ dancing** aller danser; **how did it ~?** comment est-ce que ça s'est passé?; **to ~ round the back/by the shop** passer par derrière/devant le maga-sin; **~ about** *vi (rumour)* se répandre ♦ *vt fus*: **how do I ~ about this?** comment dois-je m'y prendre (pour fai-re ceci)?; **~ after** *vt fus (pursue)* pour-suivre, courir après; *(job, record etc)* es-sayer d'obtenir; **~ ahead** *vi (make pro-gress)* avancer; *(get going)* y aller; **~ along** *vi* aller, avancer ♦ *vt fus* longer, parcourir; **~ away** *vi* partir, s'en aller; **~ back** *vi* rentrer; revenir; *(~ again)* re-tourner; **~ back on** *vt fus (promise)* re-venir sur; **~ by** *vi (years, time)* passer, s'écouler ♦ *vt fus* se tenir à; en croire; **~ down** *vi* descendre; *(ship)* couler; *(sun)* se coucher ♦ *vt fus* descendre; **~ for** *vt fus (fetch)* aller chercher; *(like)* aimer; *(attack)* s'en prendre à, attaquer; **~ in** *vi* entrer; **~ in for** *vt fus (competi-tion)* se présenter à; *(like)* aimer; **~ into** *vt fus* entrer dans; *(investigate)* étudier, examiner; *(embark on)* se lan-cer dans; **~ off** *vi* partir, s'en aller; *(food)* se gâter; *(explode)* sauter; *(event)* se dérouler ♦ *vt fus* ne plus aimer; **the gun went off** le coup est parti; **~ on** *vi* continuer; *(happen)* se passer; **to ~**

**on doing** continuer à faire; **~ out** vi sortir; (fire, light) s'éteindre; **~ over** vi fus (check) revoir, vérifier; **~ past** vt fus: **to ~ past sth** passer devant qch; **~ round** vi (circulate: news, rumour) circuler; (revolve) tourner; (suffice) suffire (pour tout le monde); **to ~ round to sb's** (visit) passer chez qn; **to ~ round (by)** (make a detour) faire un détour (par); **~ through** vt fus (town etc) traverser; **~ up** vt fus gravir; (price) augmenter **♦** vt fus gravir; **~ with** vt fus aller avec; **~ without** vt fus se passer de

**goad** [gəud] vt aiguillonner

**go-ahead** adj dynamique, entreprenant(e) **♦** n feu vert

**goal** [gəul] n but m; **~keeper** n gardien m de but; **~post** n poteau m de but

**goat** [gəut] n chèvre f

**gobble** ['gɔbl] vt (also: **~ down**, **~ up**) engloutir

**go-between** ['gəubɪtwiːn] n intermédiaire m/f

**god** [gɔd] n dieu m; **G~** n Dieu m; **~child** n filleul(e); **~daughter** n filleule f; **~dess** n déesse f; **~father** n parrain m; **~forsaken** adj abandonné(e); **~mother** n marraine f; **~send** n aubaine f; **~son** n filleul m

**goggles** ['gɔglz] npl (for skiing etc) lunettes protectrices

**going** ['gəuɪŋ] n (conditions) état m du terrain **♦** adj: **the ~ rate** le tarif (en vigueur)

**gold** [gəuld] n or m **♦** adj en or; (reserves) d'or; **~en** adj (made of gold) en or; (gold in colour) doré(e); **~fish** n poisson m rouge; **~-plated** adj plaqué(e) or inv; **~smith** n orfèvre m

**golf** [gɔlf] n golf m; **~ ball** n balle f de golf; (on typewriter) boule m; **~ club** n club m de golf; (stick) club m, crosse f de golf; **~ course** n (terrain m de) golf m; **~er** n joueur(-euse) de golf

**gone** [gɔn] pp of **go**

**gong** [gɔŋ] n gong m

**good** [gud] adj bon(ne); (kind) gentil(le); (child) sage **♦** n bien m; **~s** npl (COMM) marchandises fpl, articles mpl; **~!** bon!, très bien!; **to be ~ at** être bon en; **to be ~ for** être bon pour; **would you be ~ enough to ...?** auriez-vous la bonté or l'amabilité de ...?; **a ~ deal (of)** beaucoup (de); **a ~ many** beaucoup (de); **to make ~** vi (succeed) faire son chemin, réussir **♦** vt (deficit) combler; (losses) compenser; **it's no ~ complaining** cela ne sert à rien de se plaindre; **for ~** pour de bon, une fois pour toutes; **~ morning/afternoon!** bonjour!; **~ evening!** bonsoir!; **~ night!** bonsoir!; (on going to bed) bonne nuit!; **~bye** excl au revoir!; **G~ Friday** n Vendredi saint; **~-looking** adj beau (belle), bien inv; **~-natured** adj (person) qui a un bon naturel; **~ness** n (of person) bonté f; **for ~ness sake!** je vous en prie!; **~ness gracious!** mon Dieu!; **~s train** (BRIT) n train m de marchandises; **~will** n bonne volonté

**goose** [guːs] (pl **geese**) n oie f

**gooseberry** ['guzbərɪ] n groseille f à maquereau; **to play ~** (BRIT) tenir la chandelle

**gooseflesh** ['guːsfleʃ] n, **goose pimples** npl chair f de poule

**gore** [gɔːr] vt encorner **♦** n sang m

**gorge** [gɔːdʒ] n gorge f **♦** vt: **to ~ o.s. (on)** se gorger (de)

**gorgeous** ['gɔːdʒəs] adj splendide, superbe

**gorilla** [gə'rɪlə] n gorille m

**gorse** [gɔːs] n ajoncs mpl

**gory** ['gɔːrɪ] adj sanglant(e); (details) horrible

**go-slow** ['gəu'sləu] (BRIT) n grève perlée

**gospel** ['gɔspl] n évangile m

**gossip** ['gɔsɪp] n (chat) bavardages mpl; commérage, cancans mpl; (person) commère f **♦** vi bavarder; (maliciously) cancaner, faire des commérages

**got** [gɔt] pt, pp of **get**; **~ten** (US) pp of

get

**gout** [gaut] n goutte f

**govern** ['gʌvən] vt gouverner; **~ess** n gouvernante f; **~ment** n gouvernement m; (BRIT: ministers) ministère m; **~or** n (of state, bank) gouverneur m; (of school, hospital) ≃ membre m/f du conseil d'établissement; (BRIT: of prison) directeur(-trice)

**gown** [gaun] n robe f; (of teacher, BRIT: of judge) toge f

**GP** n abbr = **general practitioner**

**grab** [græb] vt saisir, empoigner ♦ vi: **to ~** essayer de saisir

**grace** [greis] n grâce f ♦ vt honorer; (adorn) orner; **5 days' ~** cinq jours de répit; **~ful** adj gracieux(-euse), élégant(e); **gracious** ['greiʃəs] adj bienveillant(e)

**grade** [greid] n (COMM) qualité f; (in hierarchy) catégorie f, grade m, échelon m; (SCOL) note f; (US: school class) classe f ♦ vt classer; **~ crossing** (US) n passage m à niveau; **~ school** (US) n école f primaire

**gradient** ['greidiənt] n inclinaison f, pente f

**gradual** ['grædjuəl] adj graduel(le), progressif(-ive); **~ly** adv peu à peu, graduellement

**graduate** [n 'grædjuit, vb 'grædjueit] n diplômé(e), licencié(e); (US: of high school) bachelier(-ère) ♦ vi obtenir un diplôme; (US) obtenir son baccalauréat; **graduation** [grædju'eiʃən] n (cérémonie f de) remise f des diplômes

**graffiti** [grə'fi:ti] npl graffiti mpl

**graft** [grɑ:ft] n (AGR, MED) greffe f; (bribery) corruption f ♦ vt greffer; **hard ~** (BRIT: inf) boulot acharné

**grain** [grein] n grain m

**gram** [græm] n gramme m

**grammar** ['græmə[r]] n grammaire f; **~ school** (BRIT) n ≃ lycée m; **grammatical** [grə'mætikl] adj grammatical(e)

**gramme** [græm] n = **gram**

**grand** [grænd] adj magnifique, splendi-

de; (gesture etc) noble; **~children** npl petits-enfants mpl; **~dad** (inf) n grandpapa m; **~daughter** n petite-fille f; **~father** n grand-père m; **~ma** (inf) n grand-maman f; **~mother** n grandmère f; **~pa** (inf) n = **granddad**; **~parents** npl grands-parents mpl; **~ piano** n piano m à queue; **~son** n petit-fils m; **~stand** n (SPORT) tribune f

**granite** ['grænit] n granit m

**granny** ['græni] (inf) n grand-maman f

**grant** [grɑ:nt] vt accorder; (a request) accéder à; (admit) concéder ♦ n (SCOL) bourse f; (ADMIN) subside m, subvention f; **to take it for ~ed that** trouver tout naturel que +sub; **to take sb for ~ed** considérer qn comme faisant partie du décor

**granulated sugar** ['grænjuleitid-] n sucre m en poudre

**grape** [greip] n raisin m

**grapefruit** ['greipfru:t] n pamplemousse m

**graph** [grɑ:f] n graphique m; **~ic** ['græfik] adj graphique; (account, description) vivant(e); **~ics** n arts mpl graphiques; graphisme m ♦ npl représentations fpl graphiques

**grapple** ['græpl] vi: **to ~ with** être aux prises avec

**grasp** [grɑ:sp] vt saisir ♦ n (grip) prise f; (understanding) compréhension f, connaissance f; **~ing** adj cupide

**grass** [grɑ:s] n herbe f; (lawn) gazon m; **~hopper** n sauterelle f; **~-roots** adj de la base, du peuple

**grate** [greit] n grille f de cheminée ♦ vi grincer ♦ vt (CULIN) râper

**grateful** ['greitful] adj reconnaissant(e)

**grater** ['greitə[r]] n râpe f

**gratifying** ['grætifaiiŋ] adj agréable

**grating** ['greitiŋ] n (iron bars) grille f ♦ adj (noise) grinçant(e)

**gratitude** ['grætitju:d] n gratitude f

**gratuity** [grə'tju:iti] n pourboire m

**grave** [greiv] n tombe f ♦ adj grave, sérieux(-euse)

**gravel** ['grævl] n gravier m

**gravestone** ['greivstəun] n pierre tombale

**graveyard** ['greivjɑːd] n cimetière m

**gravity** ['græviti] n (PHYSICS) gravité f; pesanteur f; (seriousness) gravité

**gravy** ['greivi] n jus m (de viande); sauce f

**gray** [grei] (US) adj = **grey**

**graze** [greiz] vi paître, brouter ♦ vt (touch lightly) frôler, effleurer; (scrape) écorcher ♦ n écorchure f

**grease** [griːs] n (fat) graisse f; (lubricant) lubrifiant m ♦ vt graisser; lubrifier; **~proof paper** (BRIT) n papier sulfurisé; **greasy** adj gras(se), graisseux(-euse)

**great** [greit] adj grand(e); (inf) formidable; **G~ Britain** n Grande-Bretagne f; **~-grandfather** n arrière-grand-père m; **~-grandmother** n arrière-grand-mère f; **~ly** adv très, grandement; (with verbs) beaucoup; **~ness** n grandeur f

**Greece** [griːs] n Grèce f

**greed** [griːd] n (also: **~iness**) avidité f; (for food) gourmandise f, gloutonnerie f; **~y** adj avide; gourmand(e), glouton(ne)

**Greek** [griːk] adj grec (grecque) ♦ n Grec (Grecque); (LING) grec m

**green** [griːn] adj vert(e); (inexperienced) (bien) jeune, naïf (naïve); (POL) vert(e), écologiste; (ecological) écologique ♦ n vert m; (stretch of grass) pelouse f; **~s** npl (vegetables) légumes verts; (POL): **the G~s** les Verts mpl; **the G~ Party** (BRIT: POL) le parti écologiste; **~ belt** n (round town) ceinture verte; **~ card** n (AUT) carte verte; (US) permis m de travail; **~ery** n verdure f; **~grocer's** (BRIT) n marchand m de fruits et légumes; **~house** n serre f; **~house effect** n effet m de serre; **~house gas** n gas m à effet de serre; **~ish** adj verdâtre

**Greenland** ['griːnlənd] n Groenland m

**greet** [griːt] vt accueillir; **~ing** n salutation f; **~ing(s) card** n carte f de vœux

**gregarious** [grə'gɛəriəs] adj (person)

sociable

**grenade** [grə'neid] n grenade f

**grew** [gruː] pt of **grow**

**grey** [grei] (US **gray**) adj gris(e); (dismal) sombre; **~-haired** adj grisonnant(e); **~hound** n lévrier m

**grid** [grid] n grille f; (ELEC) réseau m; **~lock** n (traffic jam) embouteillage m; **~locked** adj: **to be ~locked** (roads) être bloqué par un embouteillage; (talks etc) être suspendu

**grief** [griːf] n chagrin m, douleur f

**grievance** ['griːvəns] n doléance f, grief m

**grieve** [griːv] vi avoir du chagrin; se désoler ♦ vt faire de la peine à, affliger; **to ~ for sb** (dead person) pleurer qn; ~s

**grievous** [griːvəs] adj (LAW): **grievous bodily harm** coups mpl et blessures fpl

**grill** [gril] n (on cooker) gril m; (food: also mixed ~) grillade(s f(pl) ♦ vt (BRIT) griller; (inf: question) cuisiner

**grille** [gril] n grille f, grillage m; (AUT) calandre f

**grim** [grim] adj sinistre, lugubre; (serious, stern) sévère

**grimace** [gri'meis] n grimace f ♦ vi grimacer, faire une grimace

**grime** [graim] n crasse f, saleté f

**grin** [grin] n large sourire m ♦ vi sourire

**grind** [graind] (pt, pp **ground**) vt écraser; (coffee, pepper etc) moudre; (US: meat) hacher; (make sharp) aiguiser ♦ n (work) corvée f

**grip** [grip] n (hold) prise f, étreinte f; (control) emprise f; (grasp) connaissance f; (handle) poignée f; (holdall) sac m de voyage ♦ vt saisir, empoigner; **to come to ~s with** en venir aux prises avec; **~ping** adj prenant(e), palpitant(e)

**grisly** ['grizli] adj sinistre, macabre

**gristle** ['grisl] n cartilage m

**grit** [grit] n gravillon m; (courage) cran m ♦ vt (road) sabler; **to ~ one's teeth** serrer les dents

**groan** [grəun] n (of pain) gémissement

m ♦ vi gémir

**grocer** ['grəusə<sup>r</sup>] n épicier m; **~ies** npl provisions fpl; **~'s (shop)** n épicerie f

**groin** [grɔɪn] n aine f

**groom** [gru:m] n palefrenier m; (also: **bridegroom**) marié m ♦ vt (horse) panser; (fig): **to ~ sb for** former qn pour; **well-~ed** très soigné(e)

**groove** [gru:v] n rainure f

**grope** [grəup] vi: **to ~ for** chercher à tâtons

**gross** [grəus] adj grossier(-ère); (COMM) brut(e); **~ly** adv (greatly) très, grandement

**grotto** ['grɔtəu] n grotte f

**grotty** ['grɔtɪ] (inf) adj minable, affreux(-euse)

**ground** [graund] pt, pp of **grind** ♦ n sol m, terre f; (land) terrain m, terres fpl; (SPORT) terrain; (US: also: **~ wire**) terre; (reason: gen pl) raison f ♦ vt (plane) empêcher de décoller, retenir au sol; (US: ELEC) équiper d'une prise de terre; **~s** npl (of coffee etc) marc m; (gardens etc) parc m, domaine m; **on the ~, to the ~** par terre; **to gain/lose ~** gagner/perdre du terrain; **~ cloth** (US) n = **~sheet**; **~ing** n (in education) connaissances fpl de base; **~less** adj sans fondement; **~sheet** (BRIT) n tapis m de sol; **~ staff** n personnel m au sol; **~work** n préparation f

**group** [gru:p] n groupe m ♦ vt (also: **~ together**) grouper ♦ vi se grouper

**grouse** [graus] n inv (bird) grouse f ♦ vi (complain) rouspéter, râler

**grove** [grəuv] n bosquet m

**grovel** ['grɔvl] vi (fig) ramper

**grow** [grəu] (pt grew, pp grown) vi pousser, croître; (person) grandir; (increase) augmenter, se développer; (become): **to ~ rich/weak** s'enrichir/s'affaiblir; (develop): **he's ~n out of his jacket** sa veste est (devenue) trop petite pour lui ♦ vt cultiver, faire pousser; (beard) laisser pousser; **he'll ~ out of it!** ça lui passera!; **~ up** vi grandir; **~er**

n producteur m; **~ing** adj (fear, amount) croissant(e), grandissant(e)

**growl** [graul] vi grogner

**grown** [grəun] pp of **grow**; **~-up** n adulte m/f; grande personne

**growth** [grəuθ] n croissance f, développement m; (what has grown) poussée f, poussée f; (MED) grosseur f, tumeur f

**grub** [grʌb] n larve f; (inf: food) bouffe f

**grubby** ['grʌbɪ] adj crasseux(-euse)

**grudge** [grʌdʒ] n rancune f ♦ vt: **to ~ sb sth** (in giving) donner qch à qn à contre-cœur; (resent) reprocher qch à qn; **to bear sb a ~ (for)** garder rancune or en vouloir à qn (de)

**gruelling** ['gruəlɪŋ] (US **grueling**) adj exténuant(e)

**gruesome** ['gru:səm] adj horrible

**gruff** [grʌf] adj bourru(e)

**grumble** ['grʌmbl] vi rouspéter, ronchonner

**grumpy** ['grʌmpɪ] adj grincheux(-euse)

**grunt** [grʌnt] vi grogner

**G-string** ['dʒi:strɪŋ] n (garment) cache-sexe m inv

**guarantee** [gærən'ti:] n garantie f ♦ vt garantir

**guard** [gɑ:d] n garde f; (one man) garde m; (BRIT: RAIL) chef m de train; (on machine) dispositif m de sûreté; (also: **fireguard**) garde-feu m ♦ vt garder, surveiller; (protect): **to ~ (against** or **from**) protéger (contre); **~ against** vt (prevent) empêcher, se protéger de; **~ed** adj (fig) prudent(e); **~ian** n gardien(ne); (of minor) tuteur(-trice); **~'s van** (BRIT) n (RAIL) fourgon m

**guerrilla** [gə'rɪlə] n guérillero m

**guess** [ges] vt (estimate) évaluer; (US) croire, penser ♦ vi deviner ♦ n supposition f, hypothèse f; **to take** or **have a ~** essayer de deviner; **~work** n hypothèse f

**guest** [gest] n invité(e); (in hotel) client(e); **~-house** n pension f; **~ room** n chambre f d'amis

**guffaw** [gʌ'fɔ:] vi pouffer de rire

**guidance** ['gaɪdəns] n conseils mpl

**guide** [gaɪd] n (person, book etc) guide m; (BRIT: also: **girl**) guide f ♦ vt guider; **~book** n guide m; **~ dog** n chien d'aveugle; **~lines** npl (fig) instructions (générales), conseils mpl

**guild** [gɪld] n corporation f; cercle m, association f

**guillotine** ['gɪlətiːn] n guillotine f

**guilt** [gɪlt] n culpabilité f; **~y** adj coupable

**guinea pig** ['gɪnɪ-] n cobaye m

**guise** [gaɪz] n aspect m, apparence f

**guitar** [gɪ'tɑː] n guitare f

**gulf** [gʌlf] n golfe m; (abyss) gouffre m

**gull** [gʌl] n mouette f; (larger) goéland m

**gullible** ['gʌlɪbl] adj crédule

**gully** ['gʌlɪ] n ravin m; ravine f; couloir m

**gulp** [gʌlp] vi avaler sa salive ♦ vt (also: **~ down**) avaler

**gum** [gʌm] n (ANAT) gencive f; (glue) colle f; (sweet: also **~drop**) boule f de gomme; (also: **chewing ~**) chewing-gum m ♦ vt coller; **~boots** (BRIT) npl bottes fpl en caoutchouc

**gun** [gʌn] n (small) revolver m, pistolet m; (rifle) fusil m, carabine f; (cannon) canon m; **~boat** n canonnière f; **~fire** n fusillade f; **~man** n bandit armé; **~point** n: **at ~point** sous la menace du pistolet (or fusil); **~powder** n poudre f à canon; **~shot** n coup m de feu

**gurgle** ['gəːgl] vi gargouiller; (baby) gazouiller

**gush** [gʌʃ] vi jaillir; (fig) se répandre en effusions

**gust** [gʌst] n (of wind) rafale f; (of smoke) bouffée f

**gusto** ['gʌstəu] n enthousiasme m

**gut** [gʌt] n intestin m, boyau m; **~s** npl (inf: courage) cran m

**gutter** ['gʌtə] n (in street) caniveau m; (of roof) gouttière f

**guy** [gaɪ] n (inf: man) type m; (also: **~rope**) corde f; (BRIT: figure) effigie de Guy Fawkes (brûlée en plein air le 5 novembre)

**guzzle** ['gʌzl] vt avaler gloutonnement

**gym** [dʒɪm] n (also: **~nasium**) gymnase m; (also: **~nastics**) gym f; **~nast** n gymnaste m/f; **~nastics** [dʒɪm'næstɪks] n, npl gymnastique f; **~ shoes** npl chaussures fpl de gym; **~slip** (BRIT) n tunique f (d'écolière)

**gynaecologist** [gaɪnɪ'kɔlədʒɪst] (US **gynecologist**) n gynécologue m/f

**gypsy** ['dʒɪpsɪ] n gitan(e), bohémien(ne)

# H, h

**haberdashery** [hæbə'dæʃərɪ] (BRIT) n mercerie f

**habit** ['hæbɪt] n habitude f; (REL: costume) habit m; **~ual** adj habituel(le); (drinker, liar) invétéré(e)

**hack** [hæk] vt hacher, tailler ♦ n (pej: writer) nègre m; **~er** n (COMPUT) pirate m (informatique); (: enthusiast) passionné(e) m/f des ordinateurs

**hackneyed** ['hæknɪd] adj usé(e), rebattu(e)

**had** [hæd] *pt, pp of* **have**

**haddock** ['hædək] (*pl* ~ *or* ~**s**) *n* églefin *m; smoked* ~ haddock *m*

**hadn't** ['hædnt] = **had not**

**haemorrhage** ['hɛmərɪdʒ] (*us* **hemorrhage**) *n* hémorragie *f*

**haemorrhoids** ['hɛmərɔɪdz] (*us* **hemorrhoids**) *npl* hémorroïdes *fpl*

**haggle** ['hægl] *vi* marchander

**Hague** [heɪg] *n:* **The ~** La Haye

**hail** [heɪl] *n* grêle *f ♦ vt* (*call*) héler; (*acclaim*) acclamer *♦ vi* grêler; ~**stone** *n* grêlon *m*

**hair** [hɛər] *n* cheveux *mpl;* (*of animal*) pelage *m;* (*single:* ~ *on head*) cheveu *m;* (: *on body; of animal*) poil *m;* **to do one's** ~ se coiffer; ~**brush** *n* brosse *f* à cheveux; ~**cut** *n* coupe *f* (de cheveux); ~**do** *n* coiffure *f;* ~**dresser** *n* coiffeur (-euse); ~**dresser's** *n* salon *m* de coiffure, coiffeur *m;* ~ **dryer** *n* sèche-cheveux *m;* ~ **gel** *n* gel *m* pour cheveux; ~**grip** *n* pince *f* à cheveux; ~**net** *n* filet *m* à cheveux; ~**piece** *n* perruque *f;* ~**pin** *n* épingle *f* à cheveux; ~**pin bend** (*us* **hairpin curve**) *n* virage *m* en épingle à cheveux; ~**-raising** *adj* à (vous) faire dresser les cheveux sur la tête; ~ **removing cream** *n* crème *f* dépilatoire; ~ **spray** *n* laque *f* (pour les cheveux); ~**style** *n* coiffure *f;* ~**y** *adj* poilu(e); (*inf: fig*) effrayant(e)

**hake** [heɪk] (*pl* ~ *or* ~**s**) *n* colin *m,* merlu *m*

**half** [hɑːf] (*pl* **halves**) *n* moitié *f;* (*of beer: also:* ~ **pint**) ≈ demi *m;* (*RAIL, bus: also:* ~ **fare**) demi-tarif *m ♦ adj* demi(e) *♦ adv* (à) moitié, à demi; ~ **a dozen** une demi-douzaine; ~ **a pound** une demi-livre, ≈ 250 g; **two and a** ~ deux et demi; **to cut sth in** ~ couper qch en deux; ~**-caste** ['hɑːfkɑːst] *n* métis(se); ~**-hearted** *adj* tiède, sans enthousiasme; ~**-hour** *n* demi-heure *f;* ~**-mast**: **at** ~**-mast** *adv* (*flag*) en berne; ~**-penny** (*BRIT*) *n* demi-penny *m;* ~-

**price** *adj, adv:* (**at**) ~**-price** à moitié prix; ~ **term** (*BRIT*) *n* (*SCOL*) congé *m* de demi-trimestre; ~**-time** *n* mi-temps *f;* ~**way** *adv* à mi-chemin

**hall** [hɔːl] *n* salle *f;* (*entrance way*) hall *m,* entrée *f;* (*us*) = **corridor**

**hallmark** ['hɔːlmɑːk] *n* poinçon *m;* (*fig*) marque *f*

**hallo** [hə'ləu] *excl* = **hello**

**hall of residence** (*BRIT*) (*pl* **halls of residence**) *n* résidence *f* universitaire

**Hallowe'en** ['hæləu'iːn] *n* veille *f* de la Toussaint

**hallucination** [həluːsɪ'neɪʃən] *n* hallucination *f*

**hallway** ['hɔːlweɪ] *n* vestibule *m*

**halo** ['heɪləu] *n* (*of saint etc*) auréole *f*

**halt** [hɔːlt] *n* halte *f,* arrêt *m ♦ vt* (*progress etc*) interrompre *♦ vi* faire halte, s'arrêter

**halve** [hɑːv] *vt* (*apple etc*) partager ou diviser en deux; (*expense*) réduire de moitié; ~**s** *npl of* **half**

**ham** [hæm] *n* jambon *m*

**hamburger** ['hæmbɜːgər] *n* hamburger *m*

**hamlet** ['hæmlɪt] *n* hameau *m*

**hammer** ['hæmər] *n* marteau *m ♦ vt* (*nail*) enfoncer; (*fig*) démolir *♦ vi* (*on door*) frapper à coups redoublés; **to ~ an idea into sb** faire entrer de force une idée dans la tête de qn

**hammock** ['hæmək] *n* hamac *m*

**hamper** ['hæmpər] *vt* gêner *♦ n* panier *m* (d'osier)

**hamster** ['hæmstər] *n* hamster *m*

**hand** [hænd] n main f; (of clock) aiguille f; (~writing) écriture f; (worker) ouvrier(-ère); (at cards) jeu m ♦ vt passer, donner; **to give** or **lend sb a ~** donner un coup de main à qn; **at ~** à portée de la main; **in ~** (time) à disposition; (job, situation) en main; **to be on ~** (person) être disponible; (emergency services) être prêt(e) à intervenir); **to ~** (information etc) sous la main, à portée de la main; **on the one ~ ..., on the other ~ ...** d'une part ..., d'autre part; **~ in** vt remettre; **~ out** vt distribuer; **~ over** vt transmettre; céder; **~bag** n sac m à main; **~book** n manuel m; **~brake** n frein m à main; **~cuffs** npl menottes fpl; **~ful** n poignée f

**handicap** ['hændɪkæp] n handicap m ♦ vt handicaper; **mentally/physically ~ped** handicapé(e) mentalement/physiquement

**handicraft** ['hændɪkrɑːft] n (travail m d')artisanat m, technique artisanale; (object) objet artisanal

**handiwork** ['hændɪwɜːk] n ouvrage m

**handkerchief** ['hæŋkətʃɪf] n mouchoir m

**handle** ['hændl] n (of door etc) poignée f; (of cup etc) anse f; (of knife etc) manche m; (of saucepan) queue f; (for winding) manivelle f ♦ vt toucher, manier; (deal with) s'occuper de; (treat: people) prendre; **"~ with care"** "fragile"; **to fly off the ~** s'énerver; **~bar(s)** n(pl) guidon m

**hand:** **~luggage** n bagages mpl à main; **~made** adj fait(e) à la main; **~out** n (from government, parents) aide f, don m; (leaflet) documentation f, prospectus m; (summary of lecture) polycopié m; **~rail** n rampe f, main courante; **~set** n (TEL) combiné m; **please replace the ~set** raccrochez s'il vous plaît; **~shake** n poignée f de main

**handsome** ['hænsəm] adj beau (belle); (profit, return) considérable

**handwriting** ['hændraɪtɪŋ] n écriture f

**handy** ['hændɪ] adj (person) adroit(e); (close at hand) sous la main; (convenient) pratique

**hang** [hæŋ] (pt, pp hung) vt accrocher; (criminal: pt, pp: ~ed) pendre ♦ vi pendre; (hair, drapery) tomber; **to get the ~ of (doing) sth** (inf) attraper le coup pour faire qch; **~ about** vi traîner; **~ around** vi = hang about; **~ on** vi (wait) attendre; **~ up** vi (TEL): **to ~ up (on sb)** raccrocher (au nez de qn) ♦ vt (coat, painting etc) accrocher, suspendre

**hangar** ['hæŋə'] n hangar m

**hanger** ['hæŋə'] n cintre m, portemanteau m; **~-on** n parasite m

**hang:** **~-gliding** n deltaplane m, vol m libre; **~over** n (after drinking) gueule f de bois; **~-up** n complexe m

**hanker** ['hæŋkə'] vi: **to ~ after** avoir envie de

**hankie, hanky** ['hæŋkɪ] n abbr = handkerchief

**haphazard** [hæp'hæzəd] adj fait(e) au hasard, fait(e) au petit bonheur

**happen** ['hæpən] vi arriver; se passer, se produire; **if so ~s that** il se trouve que; **as it ~s** justement; **~ing** n événement m

**happily** ['hæpɪlɪ] adv heureusement; (cheerfully) joyeusement

**happiness** ['hæpɪnɪs] n bonheur m

**happy** ['hæpɪ] adj heureux(-euse); **~ with** (arrangements etc) satisfait(e) de; **to be ~ to do** faire volontiers; **~ birthday!** bon anniversaire!; **~-go-lucky** adj insouciant(e); **~ hour** n heure pendant laquelle les consommations sont à prix réduit

**harass** ['hærəs] vt accabler, tourmenter; **~ment** n tracasseries fpl

**harbour** ['hɑːbə'] (US harbor) n port m ♦ vt héberger, abriter; (hope, fear etc) entretenir

**hard** [hɑːd] adj dur(e); (question, problem) difficile, dur(e); (facts, evidence) concret(-ète) ♦ adv (work) dur; (think, try) sérieusement; **to look ~** at regarder fixement; (thing) regarder de près; **no ~ feelings!** sans rancune!; **to be ~ of hearing** être dur(e) d'oreille; **to be ~ done by** être traité(e) injustement; **~back** n livre relié; **~ cash** n espèces fpl; **~ disk** n (COMPUT) disque dur; **~en** vt durcir; (fig) endurcir ♦ vi durcir; **~headed** adj réaliste; décidé(e); **~ labour** n travaux forcés

**hardly** ['hɑːdlɪ] adv (scarcely, no sooner) à peine; **~ anywhere/ever** presque nulle part/jamais

**hard**: **~ship** n épreuves fpl; **~ shoulder** (BRIT) n (AUT) accotement stabilisé; **~ up** (inf) adj fauché(e); **~ware** n quincaillerie f; (COMPUT, MIL) matériel m; **~ware shop** n quincaillerie f; **~wearing** adj solide; **~working** adj travailleur(-euse)

**hardy** ['hɑːdɪ] adj robuste; (plant) résistant(e) au gel

**hare** [heəʳ] n lièvre m; **~brained** adj farfelu(e)

**harm** [hɑːm] n mal m; (wrong) tort m ♦ vt (person) faire du mal or du tort à; (thing) endommager; **out of ~'s way** à l'abri du danger, en lieu sûr; **~ful** adj nuisible; **~less** adj inoffensif(-ive); sans méchanceté

**harmony** ['hɑːmənɪ] n harmonie f

**harness** ['hɑːnɪs] n harnais m; (safety ~) harnais de sécurité ♦ vt (horse) harnacher; (resources) exploiter

**harp** [hɑːp] n harpe f ♦ vi: **to ~ on about** rabâcher

**harrowing** ['hærəʊɪŋ] adj déchirant(e), très pénible

**harsh** [hɑːʃ] adj (hard) dur(e); (severe) sévère; (unpleasant: sound) discordant(e); (: light) cru(e)

**harvest** ['hɑːvɪst] n (of corn) moisson f; (of fruit) récolte f; (of grapes) vendange f ♦ vt moissonner; récolter; vendanger

**has** [hæz] vb see **have**

**hash** [hæʃ] n (CULIN) hachis m; (fig: mess) gâchis m

**hasn't** ['hæznt] = **has not**

**hassle** ['hæsl] (inf) n (fuss) histoires fpl, tracas mpl

**haste** [heɪst] n hâte f; précipitation f; **~n** ['heɪsn] vt hâter, accélérer ♦ vi se hâter, s'empresser; **hastily** adv à la hâte; précipitamment; **hasty** adj hâtif(-ive); précipité(e)

**hat** [hæt] n chapeau m

**hatch** [hætʃ] n (NAUT: also: **~way**) écoutille f; (also: **service ~**) passe-plats m inv ♦ vi éclore; **~back** n (AUT) modèle m avec hayon arrière

**hatchet** ['hætʃɪt] n hachette f

**hate** [heɪt] vt haïr, détester ♦ n haine f; **~ful** adj odieux(-euse), détestable; **hatred** ['heɪtrɪd] n haine f

**haughty** ['hɔːtɪ] adj hautain(e), arrogant(e)

**haul** [hɔːl] vt traîner, tirer ♦ n (of fish) prise f; (of stolen goods etc) butin mc; **~age** n transport routier; (costs) frais mpl de transport; **~ier** ['hɔːlɪəʳ] (US **hauler**) n (company) transporteur (routier); (driver) camionneur m

**haunch** [hɔːntʃ] n hanche f; (of meat) cuissot m

**haunt** [hɔːnt] vt (subj: ghost, fear) hanter; (: person) fréquenter ♦ n repaire m

KEYWORD

**have** [hæv] (pt, pp **had**) aux vb **1** (gen) avoir; être; **to have arrived/gone** être arrivé(e)/allé(e); **to have eaten/slept** avoir mangé/dormi; **he has been promoted** il a eu une promotion

**2** (in tag questions): **you've done it, haven't you?** vous l'avez fait, n'est-ce pas?

**3** (in short answers and questions): **no I haven't!/yes we have!** mais non!/mais si!; **so I have!** ah oui, oui c'est vrai!; **I've been there before, have you?** j'y suis déjà allé, et vous?

♦ modal aux vb (be obliged): **to have (got) to do sth** devoir faire qch; être obligé(e) de faire qch; **she has (got)**

**to do it** elle doit le faire, il faut qu'elle le fasse; **you haven't to tell her** vous ne devez pas le lui dire

♦ vt 1 (possess, obtain) avoir; **he has (got) blue eyes/dark hair** il a les yeux bleus/les cheveux bruns; **may I have your address?** puis-je avoir votre adresse?

2 (+noun: take, hold etc): **to have breakfast/a bath/a shower** prendre le petit déjeuner/un bain/une douche; **to have dinner/lunch** dîner/déjeuner; **to have a swim** nager; **to have a meeting** se réunir; **to have a party** organiser une fête

3: **to have sth done** faire faire qch; **to have one's hair cut** se faire couper les cheveux; **to have sb do sth** faire faire qch à qn

4 (experience, suffer) avoir; **to have a cold/flu** avoir un rhume/la grippe; **to have an operation** se faire opérer

5 (inf: dupe) avoir; **he's been had** il s'est fait avoir ou rouler

**have out** vt: **to have it out with sb** (settle a problem etc) s'expliquer (franchement) avec qn

**haven** ['heɪvn] n port m; (fig) havre m

**haven't** ['hævnt] = **have not**

**havoc** ['hævək] n ravages mpl

**hawk** [hɔːk] n faucon m

**hay** [heɪ] n foin m; ~ **fever** n rhume m des foins; **~stack** n meule f de foin

**haywire** (inf) adj: **to go** ~ (machine) se détraquer; (plans) mal tourner

**hazard** ['hæzəd] n (danger) danger m, risque m ♦ vt risquer, hasarder; ~ (warning) lights npl (AUT) feux mpl de détresse

**haze** [heɪz] n brume f

**hazelnut** ['heɪzlnʌt] n noisette f

**hazy** ['heɪzɪ] adj brumeux(-euse); (idea) vague

**he** [hiː] pron il; **it is** ~ **who** ... c'est lui qui ...

**head** [hɛd] n tête f; (leader) chef m; (of

school) directeur(-trice) ♦ vt (list) être en tête de; (group) être à la tête de; ~s (or tails) pile (ou face); ~ **first** la tête la première; ~ **over heels in love** follement or éperdument amoureux(-euse); **to ~ a ball** faire une tête; ~ **for** vt fus se diriger vers; ~**ache** n mal m de tête; ~**dress** (BRIT) n (of Red Indian etc) coiffure f; ~**ing** n titre m; ~**lamp** (BRIT) n = headlight; ~**land** n promontoire m, cap m; ~**light** n phare m; ~**line** n titre m; ~**long** adv (fall) la tête la première; (rush) tête baissée; ~**master** n directeur m; ~**mistress** n directrice f; ~ **office** n bureau central, siège m; ~**-on** adj (collision) de plein fouet; (confrontation) en face à face; ~**phones** npl casque m (à écouteurs); ~**quarters** npl bureau or siège central; (MIL) quartier général; ~**rest** n appui-tête m; ~**room** n (in car) hauteur f de plafond; (under bridge) hauteur limite; ~**scarf** n foulard m; ~**strong** adj têtu(e), entêté(e); ~ **teacher** n directeur(-trice); (of secondary school) proviseur m; ~ **waiter** n maître d'hôtel; ~**way** n: **to make** ~**way** avancer, faire des progrès; ~**wind** n vent m contraire; (NAUT) vent debout; ~**y** adj capiteux(-euse); enivrant(e); (experience) grisant(e)

**heal** [hiːl] vt, vi guérir

**health** [hɛlθ] n santé f; ~ **food** n aliment(s) naturel(s); ~ **food shop** n magasin m diététique; **H~ Service** (BRIT) n: **the H~ Service** ≈ la Sécurité sociale; ~**y** adj (person) en bonne santé; (climate, food, attitude etc) sain(e), bon(ne) pour la santé

**heap** [hiːp] n tas m ♦ vt: **to** ~ (**up**) entasser, amonceler; **she** ~**ed her plate with cakes** elle a chargé son assiette de gâteaux

**hear** [hɪə*] (pt, pp **heard**) vt entendre; (news) apprendre ♦ vi entendre; ~ **about** entendre parler de; avoir des nouvelles de; **to** ~ **from sb** recevoir or avoir des nouvelles de qn; ~**ing** n (*sense*) ouïe f; (*of witnesses*) audition f; (*of a case*) audience f; (*of appareil m acoustique*); **~say: by ~say** *adv* par ouï-dire m

**hearse** [hɑːs] *n* corbillard m

**heart** [hɑːt] *n* cœur m; **~s** *npl* (CARDS) cœur m; **to lose/take ~** perdre/prendre courage; **at ~** au fond; **by ~** (*learn, know*) par cœur; **~ attack** *n* crise f cardiaque; **~beat** *n* battement m du cœur; **~breaking** *adj* déchirant(e), qui fend le cœur; **~broken** *adj*: **to be ~broken** avoir beaucoup de chagrin ou le cœur brisé; **~burn** *n* brûlures f d'estomac; **~ failure** *n* arrêt m du cœur; **~felt** *adj* sincère

**hearth** [hɑːθ] *n* foyer m, cheminée f

**heartily** ['hɑːtɪlɪ] *adv* chaleureusement; (*laugh*) de bon cœur; (*eat*) de bon appétit; **to agree ~** être entièrement d'accord

**hearty** ['hɑːtɪ] *adj* chaleureux(-euse); (*appetite*) robuste; (*dislike*) cordial(e)

**heat** [hiːt] *n* chaleur f; (*fig*) feu m, agitation f; (SPORT: *also*: **qualifying ~**) éliminatoire f ♦ *vt* chauffer; **~ up** *vi* (*water*) chauffer; (*room*) se réchauffer ♦ *vt* réchauffer; **~ed** *adj* chauffé(e); (*fig*) passionné(e), échauffé(e); **~er** *n* appareil m de chauffage; radiateur m; (*in car*) chauffage m; (*water heater*) chauffe-eau m

**heath** [hiːθ] (BRIT) *n* lande f

**heather** ['heðəʳ] *n* bruyère f

**heating** ['hiːtɪŋ] *n* chauffage m

**heatstroke** ['hiːtstrəʊk] *n* (MED) coup m de chaleur

**heat wave** *n* vague f de chaleur

**heave** [hiːv] *vt* soulever (avec effort); (*drag*) traîner ♦ *vi* se soulever; (*retch*) avoir un haut-le-cœur; **to ~ a sigh** pousser un soupir

**heaven** ['hevn] *n* ciel m, paradis m; (*fig*) paradis; **~ly** *adj* céleste, divin(e)

**heavily** ['hevɪlɪ] *adv* lourdement; (*drink, smoke*) beaucoup; (*sleep, sigh*) profondément

**heavy** ['hevɪ] *adj* lourd(e); (*work, sea, rain, eater*) gros(se); (*snow*) beaucoup de; (*drinker, smoker*) grand(e); (*breathing*) bruyant(e); (*schedule, week*) chargé(e); **~ goods vehicle** *n* poids lourd; **~weight** *n* (SPORT) poids lourd

**Hebrew** ['hiːbruː] *adj* hébraïque ♦ *n* (LING) hébreu m

**Hebrides** ['hebrɪdiːz] *npl*: **the ~ les** Hébrides *fpl*

**heckle** ['hekl] *vt* interpeller (*un orateur*)

**hectic** ['hektɪk] *adj* agité(e), trépidant(e)

**he'd** [hiːd] = **he would**; **he had**

**hedge** [hedʒ] *n* haie f ♦ *vi* se dérober; **to ~ one's bets** (*fig*) se couvrir

**hedgehog** ['hedʒhɒg] *n* hérisson m

**heed** [hiːd] *vt* (*also*: **take ~ of**) tenir compte de; **~less** *adj* insouciant(e)

**heel** [hiːl] *n* talon m ♦ *vt* retalonner

**hefty** ['heftɪ] *adj* (*person*) costaud(e); (*parcel*) lourd(e); (*profit*) gros(se)

**heifer** ['hefəʳ] *n* génisse f

**height** [haɪt] *n* (*of person*) taille f, grandeur f; (*of object*) hauteur f; (*of plane, mountain*) altitude f; (*high ground*) hauteur, éminence f; (*fig: of glory*) sommet m; (: *of luxury, stupidity*) comble m; **~en** *vt* (*fig*) augmenter

**heir** [ɛəʳ] *n* héritier m; **~ess** *n* héritière f; **~loom** *n* héritage m, meuble m (or bijou m or tableau m) de famille

**held** [held] *pt, pp of* **hold**

**helicopter** ['helɪkɒptəʳ] *n* hélicoptère m

**hell** [hel] *n* enfer m; **~!** (*inf!*) merde!

**he'll** [hiːl] = **he will**; **he shall**

**hellish** ['helɪʃ] (*inf*) *adj* infernal(e)

**hello** [hə'ləʊ] *excl* bonjour!; (*to attract attention*) hé!; (*surprise*) tiens!

**helm** [helm] *n* (NAUT) barre f

**helmet** ['helmɪt] *n* casque m

**help** [help] *n* aide f; (*charwoman*) femme f de ménage ♦ *vt* aider; **~!** au secours!; **~ yourself** servez-vous!; **he can't ~ it** il ne peut pas s'en empêcher; **~er** *n* aide m/f, assistant(e); **~ful** *adj* serviable, obligeant(e); (*useful*) utile;

**~ing** n portion f; **~less** adj impuissant(e); (defenceless) faible

**hem** [hem] n ourlet m ♦ vt ourler; **~ in** vt cerner

**hemorrhage** ['hemərɪdʒ] (US) n = **haemorrhage**

**hemorrhoids** ['hemərɔɪdz] (US) npl = **haemorrhoids**

**hen** [hen] n poule f

**hence** [hens] adv (therefore) d'où, de là; **2 years ~** d'ici 2 ans, dans 2 ans; **~forth** adv dorénavant

**her** [hɑːr] pron (direct) la, l'; (stressed, after prep) elle ♦ adj son (sa), ses pl; see also **me; my**

**herald** ['herəld] n héraut m ♦ vt annoncer; **~ry** n (study) héraldique f; (coat of arms) blason m

**herb** [hɜːb] n herbe f

**herd** [hɜːd] n troupeau m

**here** [hɪər] adv ici; (time) alors ♦ excl tiens!, tenez!; **~I** présent!; **~ is, ~ are** voici; **~ he/she is** le/la voici!; **~after** adv après, plus tard; **~by** adv (formal: in letter) par la présente

**hereditary** [hɪˈredɪtrɪ] adj héréditaire

**heresy** ['herəsɪ] n hérésie f

**heritage** ['herɪtɪdʒ] n (of country) patrimoine m

**hermit** ['hɜːmɪt] n ermite m

**hernia** ['hɜːnɪə] n hernie f

**hero** ['hɪərəʊ] (pl **~es**) n héros m

**heroin** ['herəʊɪn] n héroïne f

**heroine** ['herəʊɪn] n héroïne f

**heron** ['herən] n héron m

**herring** ['herɪŋ] n hareng m

**hers** [hɜːz] pron la sien(ne), les siens (siennes); see also **mine**[1]

**herself** [hɜːˈself] pron (reflexive) se; (emphatic) elle-même; (after prep) elle; see also **oneself**

**he's** [hiːz] = **he is; he has**

**hesitant** ['hezɪtənt] adj hésitant(e), indécis(e)

**hesitate** ['hezɪteɪt] vi hésiter; **hesitation** [hezɪˈteɪʃən] n hésitation f

**heterosexual** ['hetərəʊˈseksjʊəl] adj, n

hétérosexuel(le)

**heyday** ['heɪdeɪ] n: **the ~ of** l'âge m d'or de, les beaux jours de

**HGV** n abbr = **heavy goods vehicle**

**hi** [haɪ] excl salut!; (to attract attention) hé!

**hiatus** [haɪˈeɪtəs] n (gap) lacune f; (interruption) pause f

**hibernate** ['haɪbəneɪt] vi hiberner

**hiccough, hiccup** ['hɪkʌp] vi hoqueter; **~s** npl hoquet m

**hide** [haɪd] (pt **hid**, pp **hidden**) n (skin) peau f ♦ vt cacher ♦ vi: **to ~ (from sb)** se cacher (de qn); **~-and-seek** n cache-cache m

**hideous** ['hɪdɪəs] adj hideux(-euse)

**hiding** ['haɪdɪŋ] n (beating) correction f, volée f de coups; **to be in ~** (concealed) se tenir caché(e)

**hierarchy** ['haɪərɑːkɪ] n hiérarchie f

**hi-fi** ['haɪfaɪ] n hi-fi f inv ♦ adj hi-fi inv

**high** [haɪ] adj haut(e); (speed, respect, number) grand(e); (price) élevé(e); (wind) fort(e), violent(e); (voice) aigu (aiguë) ♦ adv haut; **20 m ~** haut(e de 20 m; **~brow** adj n intellectuel(le); **~chair** n (child's) chaise haute; **~er education** n études supérieures; **~handed** adj très autoritaire; très cavalier(-ère); **~heeled** adj à hauts talons; **~ jump** n (SPORT) saut m en hauteur; **~lands** npl Highlands mpl; **~light** n (fig: of event) point culminant ♦ vt faire ressortir, souligner; **~lights** npl (in hair) reflets mpl; **~ly** adv très, fort, hautement; **to speak/think ~ly of sb** dire/penser beaucoup de bien de qn; **~ly paid** adj très bien payé(e); **~ly strung** adj nerveux(-euse), toujours tendu(e); **~ness** n: **Her** (or **His**) **H~ness** Son Altesse f; **~pitched** adj aigu (aiguë); **~rise** adj: **~rise block, ~rise flats** tour f (d'habitation); **~school** n lycée m; (US) établissement m d'enseignement supérieur; **~ season** (BRIT) n haute saison; **~ street** (BRIT) n grand-rue f; **~way** n route nationale;

**H~way Code** (BRIT) n code m de la route

**hijack** ['haɪdʒæk] vt (plane) détourner; **~er** n pirate m de l'air

**hike** [haɪk] vi aller ou faire des excursions à pied ♦ n excursion f à pied, randonnée f; **~r** n promeneur(-euse), excursionniste m/f; **hiking** n excursions fpl à pied

**hilarious** [hɪ'lɛərɪəs] adj (account, event) désopilant(e)

**hill** [hɪl] n colline f; (fairly high) montagne f; (on road) côte f; **~side** n (flanc m de) coteau m; **~walking** n randonnée f de basse montagne; **~y** adj vallonné(e); montagneux(-euse)

**hilt** [hɪlt] n (of sword) garde f; **to the ~** (fig: support) à fond

**him** [hɪm] pron (direct) le, l'; (stressed, indirect, after prep) lui; see also **me**; **~self** pron (reflexive) se; (emphatic) lui-même; (after prep) lui; see also **oneself**

**hinder** ['hɪndər] vt gêner; (delay) retarder; **hindrance** n gêne f, obstacle m

**hindsight** ['haɪndsaɪt] n: **with ~** avec du recul, rétrospectivement

**Hindu** ['hɪnduː] adj hindou(e)

**hinge** [hɪndʒ] n charnière f ♦ vi (fig): **to ~ on** dépendre de

**hint** [hɪnt] n allusion f; (advice) conseil m ♦ vt: **to ~ that** insinuer que ♦ vi: **to ~ at** faire une allusion à

**hip** [hɪp] n hanche f

**hippie** ['hɪpɪ] n hippie m/f

**hippo** ['hɪpəu] (pl **~s**), **hippopotamus** [hɪpə'pɔtəməs] (pl **~potamuses** ou **~potami**) n hippopotame m

**hire** ['haɪər] vt (BRIT: car, equipment) louer; (worker) embaucher, engager ♦ n location f; **for ~** à louer; (taxi) libre; **~(d) car** n voiture f de location; **~ purchase** (BRIT) n achat m (ou vente f) à tempérament ou crédit

**his** [hɪz] pron le (la) sien(ne), les siens (siennes) ♦ adj son (sa), ses pl; see also **my; mine¹**

**hiss** [hɪs] vi siffler

**historic** [hɪ'stɔrɪk] adj historique; **~al** adj historique

**history** ['hɪstərɪ] n histoire f

**hit** [hɪt] (pt, pp hit) vt frapper; (reach: target) atteindre, toucher; (collide with: car) entrer en collision avec, heurter; (fig: affect) toucher ♦ n coup m; (success) succès m; (: song) tube m; **to ~ it off with sb** bien s'entendre avec qn; **~-and-run driver** n chauffard m (coupable du délit de fuite)

**hitch** [hɪtʃ] vt (fasten) accrocher, attacher; (also: **~ up**) remonter d'une saccade ♦ n (difficulty) anicroche f, contretemps m; **to ~ a lift** faire du stop; **~hike** vi faire de l'auto-stop; **~hiker** n auto-stoppeur(-euse)

**hi-tech** ['haɪ'tek] adj de pointe

**hitherto** [hɪðə'tuː] adv jusqu'ici

**hit man** n tueur m à gages

**HIV** n: **~-negative/-positive** adj séronégatif(-ive)/-positif(-ive)

**hive** [haɪv] n ruche f

**HMS** abbr = Her/His Majesty's Ship

**hoard** [hɔːd] n (of food) provisions fpl, réserves fpl; (of money) trésor m ♦ vt amasser; **~ing** (BRIT) n (for posters) panneau m d'affichage ou publicitaire

**hoarse** [hɔːs] adj enroué(e)

**hoax** [həuks] n canular m

**hob** [hɔb] n plaque (chauffante)

**hobble** ['hɔbl] vi boitiller

**hobby** ['hɔbɪ] n passe-temps favori

**hobo** ['həubəu] (US) n vagabond m

**hockey** ['hɔkɪ] n hockey m

**hog** [hɔg] n porc (châtré) m ♦ vt (fig) accaparer; **to go the whole ~** aller jusqu'au bout

**hoist** [hɔɪst] n (apparatus) palan m ♦ vt hisser

**hold** [həuld] (pt, pp held) vt tenir; (contain) contenir; (believe) considérer; (possess) avoir; (detain) détenir ♦ vi (withstand pressure) tenir (bon); (be valid) valoir ♦ n prise f; (NAUT) cale f; **~ the line!** (TEL) ne quittez pas!; **to ~ one's own** (fig) (bien) se défendre; **to catch** or **get (a) ~ of** saisir; **to get ~ of** (*fig*) trouver; **~ back** vt tenir; (*secret*) taire; **~ down** vt (*person*) maintenir à terre; (*job*) occuper; **~ off** vt tenir à distance; **~ on** vi tenir bon; (*wait*) attendre; **~ on!** (*TEL*) ne quittez pas!; **~ on to** vt fus se cramponner à; (*keep*) conserver, garder; **~ out** vt offrir ♦ vi (*resist*) tenir bon; **~ up** vt (*raise*) lever; (*support*) soutenir; (*delay*) retarder; (*rob*) braquer; **~all** (*BRIT*) n fourre-tout m inv; **~er** n (*of ticket, record*) détenteur(-trice); (*of office, title etc*) titulaire m/f; (*container*) support m; **~ing** n (*share*) intérêts mpl; (*farm*) ferme f; **~-up** n (*robbery*) hold-up m; (*delay*) retard m; (*BRIT: in traffic*) bouchon m

**hole** [həul] n trou m; **~-in-the-wall** n (*cash dispenser*) distributeur m de billets

**holiday** ['hɔlɪdeɪ] n vacances fpl; (*day off*) jour de congé; (*public*) jour férié; **on ~** en congé; **~ camp** n (*also: ~ centre*) camp m de vacances; **~maker** (*BRIT*) n vacancier(-ère); **~ resort** n centre m de villégiature or de vacances

**Holland** ['hɔlənd] n Hollande f

**hollow** ['hɔləu] adj creux(-euse) ♦ n creux m ♦ vt: **to ~ out** creuser, évider

**holly** ['hɔlɪ] n houx m

**holocaust** ['hɔləkɔːst] n holocauste m

**holster** ['həulstəʳ] n étui m de revolver

**holy** ['həulɪ] adj saint(e); (*bread, water*) bénit(e); (*ground*) sacré(e); **H~ Ghost** n Saint-Esprit m

**homage** ['hɔmɪdʒ] n hommage m; **to pay ~** rendre hommage à

**home** [həum] n foyer m, maison f; (*country*) pays natal, patrie f; (*institution*) maison ♦ adj de famille; (*ECON, POL*) national(e), intérieur(e); (*SPORT: game*) sur leur or notre terrain; (*team*) qui reçoit ♦ adv chez soi, à la maison; au pays natal; (*right in: nail etc*) à fond; **at ~** chez soi, à la maison; **make yourself at ~** faites comme chez vous; **~ address** n domicile permanent;

**~land** n patrie f; **~less** adj sans foyer; sans abri; **~ly** adj (*plain*) simple, sans prétention; **~-made** adj fait(e) à la maison; **~ match** n match m à domicile; **H~ Office** n (*BRIT*) ministère m de l'Intérieur; **~ page** n (*COMPUT*) page f d'accueil; **~ rule** n autonomie f; **H~ Secretary** (*BRIT*) n ministre m de l'Intérieur; **~sick** adj: **to be ~sick** avoir le mal du pays; s'ennuyer de sa famille; **~ town** n ville natale; **~ward** adj (*journey*) du retour; **~work** n devoirs mpl

**homoeopathic** [həumɪəu'pæθɪk] (*US* **homeopathic**) adj (*medicine, methods*) homéopathique; (*doctor*) homéopathe

**homogeneous** [hɔmau'dʒiːnɪəs] adj homogène

**homosexual** [hɔmau'sɛksjuəl] adj, n homosexuel(le)

**honest** ['ɔnɪst] adj honnête; (*sincere*) franc (franche); **~ly** adv honnêtement; franchement; **~y** n honnêteté f

**honey** ['hʌnɪ] n miel m; **~comb** n rayon m de miel; **~moon** n lune f de miel, voyage m de noces; **~suckle** (*BOT*) n chèvrefeuille m

**honk** [hɔŋk] vi (*AUT*) klaxonner

**honorary** ['ɔnərərɪ] adj honoraire; (*duty, title*) honorifique

**honour** ['ɔnəʳ] (*US* **honor**) vt honorer ♦ n honneur m; **hono(u)rable** adj honorable; **hono(u)rs degree** n (*SCOL*) licence avec mention

**hood** [hud] n capuchon m; (*of cooker*) hotte f; (*AUT: BRIT*) capote f; (*: US*) capot m

**hoof** [huːf] (*pl* **hooves**) n sabot m

**hook** [huk] n crochet m; (*on dress*) agrafe f; (*for fishing*) hameçon m ♦ vt accrocher; (*fish*) prendre

**hooligan** ['huːlɪgən] n voyou m

**hoop** [huːp] n cerceau m

**hooray** [huː'reɪ] excl hourra

**hoot** [huːt] vi (*AUT*) klaxonner; (*siren*) mugir; (*owl*) hululer; **~er** n (*BRIT: AUT*) klaxon m; (*NAUT, factory*) sirène f

**Hoover** ® ['huːvəʳ] (*BRIT*) n aspirateur

*m* ♦ *vt*: **h~** passer l'aspirateur dans or sur

**hooves** [hu:vz] *npl* of **hoof**

**hop** [hɔp] *vi* (on one foot) sauter à cloche-pied; (bird) sautiller

**hope** [həup] *vt, vi* espérer ♦ *n* espoir *m*; **I ~ so** je l'espère; **I ~ not** j'espère que non; **~ful** *adj* (person) plein(e) d'espoir; (situation) prometteur(-euse), encourageant(e); **~fully** *adv* (expectantly) avec espoir, avec optimisme; (one hopes) avec un peu de chance; **~less** *adj* désespéré(e); (useless) nul(le)

**hops** [hɔps] *npl* houblon *m*

**horizon** [hə'raızn] *n* horizon *m*; **~tal** [hɔrı'zɔntl] *adj* horizontal(e)

**horn** [hɔ:n] *n* corne *f*; (MUS: also: French **~**) cor *m*; (AUT) klaxon *m*

**hornet** ['hɔ:nıt] *n* frelon *m*

**horoscope** ['hɔrəskəup] *n* horoscope *m*

**horrendous** [hə'rendəs] *adj* horrible, affreux(-euse)

**horrible** ['hɔrıbl] *adj* horrible, affreux(-euse)

**horrid** ['hɔrıd] *adj* épouvantable

**horrify** ['hɔrıfaı] *vt* horrifier

**horror** ['hɔrə*] *n* horreur *f*; **~ film** *n* film *m* d'épouvante

**hors d'oeuvre** [ɔ:'də:vrə] *n* (CULIN) hors-d'œuvre *m*

**horse** [hɔ:s] *n* cheval *m*; **~back** *n*: **on ~back** à cheval; **~chestnut** *n* marron *m* (d'Inde); **~man** (irreg) *n* cavalier *m*; **~power** *n* puissance *f* (en chevaux), **~-racing** *n* courses *fpl* de chevaux; **~radish** *n* raifort *m*; **~shoe** *n* fer *m* à cheval

**hose** [həuz] *n* (also: **~pipe**) tuyau *m*; (also: **garden ~**) tuyau d'arrosage

**hospitable** ['hɔspıtəbl] *adj* hospitalier(-ère)

**hospital** ['hɔspıtl] *n* hôpital *m*; **in ~** à l'hôpital

**hospitality** [hɔspı'tælıtı] *n* hospitalité *f*

**host** [həust] *n* hôte *m*; (TV, RADIO) animateur(-trice); (REL) hostie *f*; (large number): **a ~ of** une foule de ♦ *vt*

(conference, games etc) accueillir

**hostage** ['hɔstıdʒ] *n* otage *m*

**hostel** ['hɔstl] *n* foyer *m*; (also: **youth ~**) auberge *f* de jeunesse

**hostess** ['həustıs] *n* hôtesse *f*; (TV, RADIO) animatrice *f*

**hostile** ['hɔstaıl] *adj* hostile; **hostility** [hɔ'stılıtı] *n* hostilité *f*

**hot** [hɔt] *adj* chaud(e); (as opposed to only warm) très chaud; (spicy) fort(e); (contest etc) acharné(e); (temper) passionné(e); **to be ~** (person) avoir chaud; (object) être (très) chaud; **it is ~** (weather) il fait chaud; **~bed** *n* (fig) foyer *m*, pépinière *f*; **~ dog** *n* hot-dog *m*

**hotel** [həu'tel] *n* hôtel *m*

**hot: ~house** *n* serre (chaude); **~line** *n* (POL) téléphone *m* rouge, ligne directe; **~ly** *adv* passionnément, violemment; **~plate** *n* (on cooker) plaque chauffante; **~pot** (BRIT) *n* ragoût *m*; **~-water bottle** *n* bouillotte *f*

**hound** [haund] *vt* poursuivre avec acharnement ♦ *n* chien courant

**hour** ['auə*] *n* heure *f*; **~ly** *adj, adv* toutes les heures; (rate) horaire

**house** [*n* haus, *vb* hauz] *n* maison *f*; (POL) chambre *f*; (THEATRE) salle *f*, auditorium *m* ♦ *vt* (person) loger, héberger; (objects) abriter; **on the ~** (fig) aux frais de la maison; **~ arrest** *n* assignation *f* à résidence; **~boat** *n* bateau *m* (aménagé en habitation); **~bound** *adj* confiné(e) chez soi; **~breaking** *n* cambriolage *m* (avec effraction); **~hold** *n* (persons) famille *f*, maisonnée *f*; (ADMIN etc) ménage *m*; **~keeper** *n* gouvernante *f*; **~keeping** *n* (work) ménage *m*; **~keeping (money)** argent *m* du ménage; **~warming (party)** *n* pendaison *f* de crémaillère; **~wife** (irreg) *n* ménagère *f*; femme *f* au foyer; **~work** *n* (travaux *mpl* du) ménage *m*

**housing** ['hauzıŋ] *n* logement *m*; **~ development, ~ estate** *n* lotissement *m*

**hovel** ['hɔvl] n taudis m

**hover** ['hɔvə*] vi planer; **~craft** n aéroglisseur m

**how** [hau] adv comment; **~ are you?** comment allez-vous?; **~ do you do?** bonjour; enchanté(e); **~ far is it to?** combien y a-t-il jusqu'à ...?; **~ long have you been here?** depuis combien de temps êtes-vous là?; **~ lovely!** que or comme c'est joli!; **~ many/much?** combien?; **~ many people/much milk?** combien de gens/lait?; **~ old are you?** quel âge avez-vous?

**however** [hau'evə*] adv de quelque façon or manière que +subj; (+adj) quelque or si ... que +subj; (in questions) comment ♦ conj pourtant, cependant

**howl** [haul] vi hurler

**H.P.** abbr = hire purchase

**h.p.** abbr = horsepower

**HQ** abbr = headquarters

**hub** [hʌb] n (of wheel) moyeu m; (fig) centre m, foyer m; **~cap** n enjoliveur m

**huddle** ['hʌdl] vi: **to ~ together** se blottir les uns contre les autres

**hue** [hju:] n teinte f, nuance f

**huff** [hʌf] n: **in a ~** fâché(e)

**hug** [hʌg] vt serrer dans ses bras; (shore, kerb) serrer

**huge** [hju:dʒ] adj énorme, immense

**hulk** [hʌlk] n (ship) épave f; (car, building) carcasse f; (person) mastodonte m

**hull** [hʌl] n coque f

**hullo** ['hʌ'ləu] excl = hello

**hum** [hʌm] vt (tune) fredonner ♦ vi fredonner; (insect) bourdonner; (plane, tool) vrombir

**human** ['hju:mən] adj humain(e) ♦ n: **~ being** être humain; **~e** [hju:'meɪn] adj humain(e), humanitaire; **~itarian** [hju:mænɪ'teərɪən] adj humanitaire; **~ity** [hju:'mænɪtɪ] n humanité f

**humble** ['hʌmbl] adj humble, modeste ♦ vt humilier

**humdrum** ['hʌmdrʌm] adj monotone, banal(e)

**humid** ['hju:mɪd] adj humide

**humiliate** [hju:'mɪlɪeɪt] vt humilier; **humiliation** [hju:mɪlɪ'eɪʃən] n humiliation f

**humorous** ['hju:mərəs] adj humoristique; (person) plein(e) d'humour

**humour** ['hju:mə*] (US **humor**) n humour m; (mood) humeur f ♦ vt (person) faire plaisir à; se prêter aux caprices de

**hump** [hʌmp] n bosse f

**hunch** [hʌntʃ] n (premonition) intuition f; **~back** n bossu(e); **~ed** adj voûté(e)

**hundred** ['hʌndrəd] num cent; **~s of** des centaines de; **~weight** n (BRIT) 50.8 kg, 112 lb; (US) 45.3 kg, 100 lb

**hung** [hʌŋ] pt, pp of hang

**Hungary** ['hʌŋgərɪ] n Hongrie f

**hunger** ['hʌŋgə*] n faim f ♦ vi: **to ~ for** avoir faim de, désirer ardemment

**hungry** ['hʌŋgrɪ] adj affamé(e); (keen): **~ for** avide de; **to be ~** avoir faim

**hunk** [hʌŋk] n (of bread etc) gros morceau

**hunt** [hʌnt] vt chasser; (criminal) pourchasser ♦ vi chasser; (search): **to ~ for** chercher (partout) ♦ n chasse f; **~er** n chasseur m; **~ing** n chasse f

**hurdle** ['hɜ:dl] n (SPORT) haie f; (fig) obstacle m

**hurl** [hɜ:l] vt lancer (avec violence); (abuse, insults) lancer

**hurrah** [hu'rɑ:] excl = hooray

**hurray** [hu'reɪ] excl = hooray

**hurricane** ['hʌrɪkən] n ouragan m

**hurried** ['hʌrɪd] adj pressé(e), précipité(e); (work) fait(e) à la hâte; **~ly** adv précipitamment, à la hâte

**hurry** ['hʌrɪ] (vb: also: **~ up**) n hâte f, précipitation f ♦ vi se presser, se dépêcher ♦ vt (person) faire presser, faire se dépêcher; (work) presser; **to be in a ~** être pressé(e); **to do sth in a ~** faire qch en vitesse; **to ~ in/out** entrer/sortir précipitamment

**hurt** [hɜ:t] (pt, pp **hurt**) vt (cause pain to) faire mal à; (injure, fig) blesser ♦ vi faire mal ♦ adj blessé(e); **~ful** adj (remark) blessant(e)

**urtle** ['hɜːtl] *vi*: **to ~ past** passer en trombe; **to ~ down** dégringoler

**usband** ['hʌzbənd] *n* mari *m*

**ush** [hʌʃ] *n* calme *m*, silence *m* ♦ *vt* faire taire; **~!** chut!; **~ up** *vt* (*scandal*) étouffer

**usk** [hʌsk] *n* (*of wheat*) balle *f*; (*of rice, maize*) enveloppe *f*

**usky** ['hʌskɪ] *adj* rauque ♦ *n* chien *m* esquimau *or* de traîneau

**ustle** ['hʌsl] *vt* pousser, bousculer ♦ *n*: **~ and bustle** tourbillon *m* (d'activité)

**ut** [hʌt] *n* hutte *f*; (*shed*) cabane *f*

**utch** [hʌtʃ] *n* clapier *m*

**yacinth** ['haɪəsɪnθ] *n* jacinthe *f*

**ydrant** ['haɪdrənt] *n* (*also*: **fire ~**) bouche *f* d'incendie

**ydraulic** [haɪ'drɔːlɪk] *adj* hydraulique

**ydroelectric** ['haɪdrəʊ'lektrɪk] *adj* hydro-électrique

**ydrofoil** ['haɪdrəfɔɪl] *n* hydrofoil *m*

**ydrogen** ['haɪdrədʒən] *n* hydrogène *m*

**yena** [haɪ'iːnə] *n* hyène *f*

**ygiene** ['haɪdʒiːn] *n* hygiène *f*; **hygienic** *adj* hygiénique

**ymn** [hɪm] *n* hymne *m*; cantique *m*

**ype** [haɪp] (*inf*) *n* battage *m* publicitaire

**ypermarket** ['haɪpəmɑːkɪt] (*BRIT*) *n* hypermarché *m*

**ypertext** ['haɪpətekst] *n* (*COMPUT*) hypertexte *m*

**yphen** ['haɪfn] *n* trait *m* d'union

**ypnotize** ['hɪpnətaɪz] *vt* hypnotiser

**ypocrisy** [hɪ'pɒkrɪsɪ] *n* hypocrisie *f*; **hypocrite** ['hɪpəkrɪt] *n* hypocrite *m/f*; **hypocritical** *adj* hypocrite

**ypothesis** [haɪ'pɒθɪsɪs] *n* (*pl* hypotheses) *n* hypothèse *f*

**ysterical** [hɪ'sterɪkl] *adj* hystérique; (*funny*) hilarant(e); **~ laughter** fou rire *m*

**ysterics** [hɪ'sterɪks] *npl*: **to be in/ have ~** (*anger, panic*) avoir une crise de nerfs; (*laughter*) attraper un fou rire

# I, i

**I** [aɪ] *pron* je; (*before vowel*) j'; (*stressed*) moi

**ice** [aɪs] *n* glace *f*; (*on road*) verglas *m* ♦ *vt* (*cake*) glacer ♦ *vi* (*also*: **~ over**, **~ up**) geler; (*window*) se givrer; **~berg** *n* iceberg *m*; **~box** *n* (*US*) réfrigérateur *m*; (*BRIT*) compartiment *m* à glace; (*insulated box*) glacière *f*; **~ cream** *n* glace *f*; **~ cube** *n* glaçon *m*; **~d** *adj* glacé(e); **~ hockey** *n* hockey *m* sur glace; **Iceland** *n* Islande *f*; **~ lolly** *n* (*BRIT*) esquimau *m* (glace); **~ rink** *n* patinoire *f*; **~-skating** *n* patinage *m* (sur glace)

**icicle** ['aɪsɪkl] *n* glaçon *m* (*naturel*)

**icing** ['aɪsɪŋ] *n* (*CULIN*) glace *f*; **~ sugar** *n* (*BRIT*) *n* sucre *m* glace

**ICT** (*BRIT*) *abbr* (*SCOL* = *Information and Communications Technology*) TIC *f*

**icy** ['aɪsɪ] *adj* glacé(e); (*road*) verglacé(e); (*weather, temperature*) glacial(e)

**I'd** [aɪd] = **I would; I had**

**idea** [aɪ'dɪə] *n* idée *f*

**ideal** [aɪ'dɪəl] *n* idéal *m* ♦ *adj* idéal(e)

**identical** [aɪ'dentɪkl] *adj* identique

**identification** [aɪdentɪfɪ'keɪʃən] *n* identification *f*; **means of ~** pièce *f* d'identité

**identify** [aɪ'dentɪfaɪ] *vt* identifier

**Identikit picture** ® [aɪ'dentɪkɪt-] *n* portrait-robot *m*

**identity** [aɪ'dentɪtɪ] *n* identité *f*; **~ card** *n* carte *f* d'identité

**ideology** [aɪdɪ'ɒlədʒɪ] *n* idéologie *f*

**idiom** ['ɪdɪəm] *n* expression *f* idiomatique; (*style*) style *m*

**idiosyncrasy** [ɪdɪəʊ'sɪŋkrəsɪ] *n* (*of person*) particularité *f*, petite manie

**idiot** ['ɪdɪət] *n* idiot(e), imbécile *m/f*; **~ic** [ɪdɪ'ɒtɪk] *adj* idiot(e), bête, stupide

**idle** ['aɪdl] *adj* sans occupation, désœuvré(e); (*lazy*) oisif(-ive), paresseux(-euse); (*unemployed*) au chômage; (*question, pleasures*) vain(e), futile ♦ *vi* (*engine*) tourner au ralenti; **to lie ~** être arrêté(e), ne pas fonctionner

**idol** [ˈaɪdl] *n* idole *f*; **~ize** *vt* idolâtrer, adorer

**i.e.** *adv abbr* (= *id est*) c'est-à-dire

**if** [ɪf] *conj* si; **~ so** si c'est le cas; **~ not** sinon; **~ only** si seulement

**ignite** [ɪgˈnaɪt] *vt* mettre le feu à, enflammer ♦ *vi* s'enflammer; **ignition** *n* (AUT) allumage *m*; **to switch on/off the ignition** mettre/couper le contact; **ignition key** *n* clé *f* de contact

**ignorant** [ˈɪgnərənt] *adj* ignorant(e); **to be ~ of** (*subject*) ne rien connaître à; (*events*) ne pas être au courant de

**ignore** [ɪgˈnɔː] *vt* ne tenir aucun compte de; (*person*) faire semblant de ne pas reconnaître, ignorer; (*fact*) méconnaître

**ill** [ɪl] *adj* (*sick*) malade; (*bad*) mauvais(e) ♦ *n* mal *m* ♦ *adv*: **to speak/think ~ of** dire/penser du mal de; **~s** *npl* (*misfortunes*) maux *mpl*, malheurs *mpl*; **to be taken ~** tomber malade; **~-advised** *adj* (*decision*) peu judicieux(-euse); (*person*) malavisé(e); **~-at-ease** *adj* mal à l'aise

**I'll** [aɪl] = **I will**; **I shall**

**illegal** [ɪˈliːgl] *adj* illégal(e)

**illegible** [ɪˈledʒɪbl] *adj* illisible

**illegitimate** [ɪlɪˈdʒɪtɪmət] *adj* illégitime

**ill-fated** [ɪlˈfeɪtɪd] *adj* malheureux (-euse); (*day*) néfaste

**ill feeling** *n* ressentiment *m*, rancune *f*

**illiterate** [ɪˈlɪtərət] *adj* illettré(e)

**ill: ~-mannered** *adj* (*child*) mal élevé(e); **~ness** *n* maladie *f*; **~-treat** *vt* maltraiter

**illuminate** [ɪˈluːmɪneɪt] *vt* (*room, street*) éclairer; (*for special effect*) illuminer; **illumination** [ɪluːmɪˈneɪʃən] *n* éclairage *m*; illumination *f*

**illusion** [ɪˈluːʒən] *n* illusion *f*

**illustrate** [ˈɪləstreɪt] *vt* illustrer; **illustration** [ɪləˈstreɪʃən] *n* illustration *f*

**ill will** *n* malveillance *f*

**I'm** [aɪm] = **I am**

**image** [ˈɪmɪdʒ] *n* image *f*; (*public face*)

image de marque; **~ry** *n* images *fpl*

**imaginary** [ɪˈmædʒɪnərɪ] *adj* imaginaire

**imagination** [ɪmædʒɪˈneɪʃən] *n* imagination *f*

**imaginative** [ɪˈmædʒɪnətɪv] *adj* imaginatif(-ive); (*person*) plein(e) d'imagination

**imagine** [ɪˈmædʒɪn] *vt* imaginer, s'imaginer; (*suppose*) imaginer, supposer

**imbalance** [ɪmˈbæləns] *n* déséquilibre *m*

**imitate** [ˈɪmɪteɪt] *vt* imiter; **imitation** [ɪmɪˈteɪʃən] *n* imitation *f*

**immaculate** [ɪˈmækjulət] *adj* impeccable; (REL) immaculé(e)

**immaterial** [ɪməˈtɪərɪəl] *adj* sans importance, insignifiant(e)

**immature** [ɪməˈtjuə] *adj* (*fruit*) qui n'est pas mûr(e); (*person*) qui manque de maturité

**immediate** [ɪˈmiːdɪət] *adj* immédiat(e); **~ly** *adv* (*at once*) immédiatement; **~ next to** juste à côté de

**immense** [ɪˈmens] *adj* immense; énorme

**immerse** [ɪˈmɜːs] *vt* immerger, plonger; **immersion heater** (BRIT) *n* chauffe-eau *m* électrique

**immigrant** [ˈɪmɪgrənt] *n* immigrant(e); immigré(e); **immigration** [ɪmɪˈgreɪʃən] *n* immigration *f*

**imminent** [ˈɪmɪnənt] *adj* imminent(e)

**immoral** [ɪˈmɔrl] *adj* immoral(e)

**immortal** [ɪˈmɔːtl] *adj, n* immortel(le)

**immune** [ɪˈmjuːn] *adj*: **~ (to)** immunisé(e) (contre); (*fig*) à l'abri de; **immunity** *n* immunité *f*

**impact** [ˈɪmpækt] *n* choc *m*, impact *m*; (*fig*) impact

**impair** [ɪmˈpɛə] *vt* détériorer, diminuer

**impart** [ɪmˈpɑːt] *vt* communiquer, transmettre; (*flavour*) donner

**impartial** [ɪmˈpɑːʃl] *adj* impartial(e)

**impassable** [ɪmˈpɑːsəbl] *adj* infranchissable; (*road*) impraticable

**impassive** [ɪmˈpæsɪv] *adj* impassible

**impatience** [ɪmˈpeɪʃəns] *n* impatience

**impatient** [ɪmˈpeɪʃənt] *adj* impatient(e); **to get** *or* **grow ~** s'impatienter; **~ly** *adv* avec impatience

**impeccable** [ɪmˈpɛkəbl] *adj* impeccable, parfait(e)

**impede** [ɪmˈpiːd] *vt* gêner; **impediment** *n* obstacle *m*; *(also:* **speech impediment)** défaut *m* d'élocution

**impending** [ɪmˈpɛndɪŋ] *adj* imminent(e)

**imperative** [ɪmˈpɛrətɪv] *adj (need)* urgent(e), pressant(e); *(tone)* impérieux (-euse) ♦ *n* (LING) impératif *m*

**imperfect** [ɪmˈpəːfɪkt] *adj* imparfait(e); *(goods etc)* défectueux(-euse)

**imperial** [ɪmˈpɪərɪəl] *adj* impérial(e); *(BRIT: measure)* légal(e)

**impersonal** [ɪmˈpəːsənl] *adj* impersonnel(le)

**impersonate** [ɪmˈpəːsəneɪt] *vt* se faire passer pour; *(THEATRE)* imiter

**impertinent** [ɪmˈpəːtɪnənt] *adj* impertinent(e), insolent(e)

**impervious** [ɪmˈpəːvɪəs] *adj (fig):* **~ to** insensible à

**impetuous** [ɪmˈpɛtjuəs] *adj* impétueux(-euse), fougueux(-euse)

**impetus** [ˈɪmpətəs] *n* impulsion *f*; *(of runner)* élan *m*

**impinge** [ɪmˈpɪndʒ]: **to ~ on** *vt fus (person)* affecter, toucher; *(rights)* empiéter sur

**implement** [*n* ˈɪmplɪmənt, *vb* ˈɪmplɪment] *n* outil *m*, instrument *m*; *(for cooking)* ustensile *m* ♦ *vt* exécuter

**implicit** [ɪmˈplɪsɪt] *adj* implicite; *(complete)* absolu(e), sans réserve

**imply** [ɪmˈplaɪ] *vt* suggérer, laisser entendre; indiquer, supposer

**impolite** [ɪmpəˈlaɪt] *adj* impoli(e)

**import** [*vb* ɪmˈpɔːt, *n* ˈɪmpɔːt] *vt* importer ♦ *n* (COMM) importation *f*

**importance** [ɪmˈpɔːtns] *n* importance *f*

**important** [ɪmˈpɔːtənt] *adj* important(e)

**importer** [ɪmˈpɔːtəʳ] *n* importateur (-trice)

**impose** [ɪmˈpəuz] *vt* imposer ♦ *vi:* **to ~ on sb** abuser de la gentillesse de qn; **imposing** *adj* imposant(e), impressionnant(e); **imposition** [ɪmpəˈzɪʃən] *n (of tax etc)* imposition *f*; **to be an imposition on** *(person)* abuser de la gentillesse *or* la bonté de

**impossible** [ɪmˈpɔsɪbl] *adj* impossible

**impotent** [ˈɪmpətnt] *adj* impuissant(e)

**impound** [ɪmˈpaund] *vt* confisquer, saisir

**impoverished** [ɪmˈpɔvərɪʃt] *adj* appauvri(e), pauvre

**impractical** [ɪmˈpræktɪkl] *adj* pas pratique; *(person)* qui manque d'esprit pratique

**impregnable** [ɪmˈprɛgnəbl] *adj (fortress)* imprenable

**impress** [ɪmˈprɛs] *vt* impressionner, faire impression sur; *(mark)* imprimer, marquer; **to ~ sth on sb** faire bien comprendre qch à qn; **~ed** *adj* impressionné(e)

**impression** [ɪmˈprɛʃən] *n* impression *f*; *(of stamp, seal)* empreinte *f*; *(imitation)* imitation *f*; **to be under the ~ that** avoir l'impression que; **~ist** *n (ART)* impressionniste *m/f*; *(entertainer)* imitateur(-trice) *m/f*

**impressive** [ɪmˈprɛsɪv] *adj* impressionnant(e)

**imprint** [ˈɪmprɪnt] *n (outline)* marque *f*, empreinte *f*

**imprison** [ɪmˈprɪzn] *vt* emprisonner, mettre en prison

**improbable** [ɪmˈprɔbəbl] *adj* improbable; *(excuse)* peu plausible

**improper** [ɪmˈprɔpəʳ] *adj (unsuitable)* déplacé(e), de mauvais goût; indécent(e); *(dishonest)* malhonnête

**improve** [ɪmˈpruːv] *vt* améliorer ♦ *vi* s'améliorer; *(pupil etc)* faire des progrès; **~ment** *n* amélioration *f (in de)*; progrès *m*

**improvise** [ˈɪmprəvaɪz] *vt, vi* improviser

**impudent** [ˈɪmpjudnt] *adj* impudent(e)

**impulse** [ˈɪmpʌls] *n* impulsion *f*; **on ~**

impulsivement, sur un coup de tête; **impulsive** adj impulsif(-ive)

---
KEYWORD
---

**in** [ɪn] prep **1** (indicating place, position) dans; **in the house/the fridge** dans la maison/le frigo; **in the garden** dans le or au jardin; **in town** en ville; **in the country** à la campagne; **in school** à l'école; **in here/there** ici/là

**2** (with place names: of town, region, country): **in London** à Londres; **in England** en Angleterre; **in Japan** au Japon; **in the United States** aux États-Unis

**3** (indicating time: during): **in spring** au printemps; **in summer** en été; **in May/1992** en mai/1992; **in the afternoon** (dans) l'après-midi; **at 4 o'clock in the afternoon** à 4 heures de l'après-midi

**4** (indicating time: in the space of) 3 hours/days (future): **I did it in 3 hours/days** je l'ai fait en 3 heures/jours; **I'll see you in 2 weeks** or **in 2 weeks' time** je te verrai dans 2 semaines

**5** (indicating manner etc): **in a loud/soft voice** à voix haute/basse; **in pencil** au crayon; **in French** en français; **the boy in the blue shirt** le garçon à or avec la chemise bleue

**6** (indicating circumstances): **in the sun** au soleil; **in the shade** à l'ombre; **in the rain** sous la pluie

**7** (indicating mood, state): **in tears** en larmes; **in anger** sous le coup de la colère; **in despair** au désespoir; **in good condition** en bon état; **to live in luxury** vivre dans le luxe

**8** (with ratios, numbers): **1 in 10** (households), **1 (household) in 10** (ménage) sur 10; **20 pence in the pound** 20 pence par livre sterling; **they lined up in twos** ils se mirent en rangs (deux) par deux; **in hundreds** par centaines

**9** (referring to people, works) chez; **the disease is common in children** c'est

une maladie courante chez les enfants; **in (the works of) Dickens** chez Dickens, dans (l'œuvre de) Dickens

**10** (indicating profession etc) dans; **to be in teaching** être dans l'enseignement

**11** (after superlative) de; **the best pupil in the class** le meilleur élève de la classe

**12** (with present participle): **in saying this** en disant ceci

♦ adv: **to be in** (person: at home, work) être là; (train, ship, plane) être arrivé(e); (in fashion) être à la mode; **to ask sb in** inviter qn à entrer; **to run/limp etc in** entrer en courant/boitant etc

♦ n: **the ins and outs (of)** (of proposal, situation etc) les tenants et aboutissants (de)

---

**in.** abbr = **inch**

**inability** [ɪnəˈbɪlɪtɪ] n incapacité f

**inaccurate** [ɪnˈækjʊrət] adj inexact(e); (person) qui manque de précision

**inadequate** [ɪnˈædɪkwət] adj insuffisant(e), inadéquat(e)

**inadvertently** [ɪnədˈvəːtntlɪ] adv par mégarde

**inadvisable** [ɪnədˈvaɪzəbl] adj (action) à déconseiller

**inane** [ɪˈneɪn] adj inepte, stupide

**inanimate** [ɪnˈænɪmət] adj inanimé(e)

**inappropriate** [ɪnəˈprəʊprɪət] adj inopportun(e), mal à propos; (word, expression) impropre

**inarticulate** [ɪnɑːˈtɪkjʊlət] adj (person) qui s'exprime mal; (speech) indistinct(e)

**inasmuch as** [ɪnəzˈmʌtʃ-] adv (insofar as) dans la mesure où; (seeing that) attendu que

**inauguration** [ɪnɔːgjʊˈreɪʃən] n inauguration f; (of president) investiture f

**inborn** [ɪnˈbɔːn] adj (quality) inné(e)

**inbred** [ɪnˈbrɛd] adj inné(e), naturel(le); (family) consanguin(e)

**Inc.** abbr = **incorporated**

**incapable** [ɪnˈkeɪpəbl] adj incapable

**incapacitate** [ɪnkə'pæsɪteɪt] vt: **to ~ sb from doing** rendre qn incapable de faire

**incense** [n 'ɪnsɛns, vb ɪn'sɛns] n encens m ♦ vt (anger) mettre en colère

**incentive** [ɪn'sɛntɪv] n encouragement m, raison f de se donner de la peine

**incessant** [ɪn'sɛsnt] adj incessant(e); **~ly** adv sans cesse, constamment

**inch** [ɪntʃ] n pouce m (= 25 mm; 12 in a foot); **within an ~ of** à deux doigts de; **he didn't give an ~** (fig) il n'a pas voulu céder d'un pouce

**incident** ['ɪnsɪdnt] n incident m; **~al** [ɪnsɪ'dɛntl] adj (additional) accessoire; **~al to** qui accompagne; **~ally** adv (by the way) à propos

**inclination** [ɪnklɪ'neɪʃən] n (fig) inclination f

**incline** [n 'ɪnklaɪn, vb ɪn'klaɪn] n pente f ♦ vt incliner ♦ vi (surface) s'incliner; **to be ~d to do** avoir tendance à faire

**include** [ɪn'kluːd] vt inclure, comprendre; **including** prep y compris; **inclusive** adj inclus(e), compris(e); **inclusive of tax** etc taxes etc comprises

**income** ['ɪnkʌm] n revenu m; **~ tax** n impôt m sur le revenu

**incoming** ['ɪnkʌmɪŋ] adj qui arrive; (president) entrant(e); **~ mail** courrier m du jour; **~ tide** marée montante

**incompetent** [ɪn'kɔmpɪtnt] adj incompétent(e), incapable

**incomplete** [ɪnkəm'pliːt] adj incomplet(-ète)

**incongruous** [ɪn'kɔŋgruəs] adj incongru(e)

**inconsiderate** [ɪnkən'sɪdərət] adj (person) qui manque d'égards; (action) inconsidéré(e)

**inconsistency** [ɪnkən'sɪstənsɪ] n (of actions etc) inconséquence f; (of work) irrégularité f; (of statement etc) incohérence f

**inconsistent** [ɪnkən'sɪstnt] adj inconséquent(e); irrégulier(-ère); peu cohérent(e); **~ with** incompatible avec

**inconspicuous** [ɪnkən'spɪkjuəs] adj qui passe inaperçu(e); (colour, dress) discret(-ète)

**inconvenience** [ɪnkən'viːnjəns] n inconvénient m; (trouble) dérangement m ♦ vt déranger

**inconvenient** [ɪnkən'viːnjənt] adj (house) malcommode; (time, place) mal choisi(e), qui ne convient pas; (visitor) importun(e)

**incorporate** [ɪn'kɔːpəreɪt] vt incorporer; (contain) contenir; **~d company** (US) n ≈ société f anonyme

**incorrect** [ɪnkə'rɛkt] adj incorrect(e)

**increase** [n 'ɪnkriːs, vb ɪn'kriːs] n augmentation f ♦ vi, vt augmenter; **increasing** adj (number) croissant(e); **increasingly** adv de plus en plus

**incredible** [ɪn'krɛdɪbl] adj incroyable

**incubator** ['ɪnkjubeɪtə'] n (for babies) couveuse f

**incumbent** [ɪn'kʌmbənt] n (president) président m en exercice; (REL) titulaire m/f ♦ adj: **it is ~ on him to ...** il lui incombe or appartient de ...

**incur** [ɪn'kəː'] vt (expenses) encourir; (anger, risk) s'exposer à; (debt) contracter; (loss) subir

**indebted** [ɪn'dɛtɪd] adj: **to be ~ to sb (for)** être redevable à qn (de)

**indecent** [ɪn'diːsnt] adj indécent(e), inconvenant(e); **~ assault** (BRIT) n attentat m à la pudeur; **~ exposure** n outrage m (public) à la pudeur

**indecisive** [ɪndɪ'saɪsɪv] adj (person) indécis(e)

**indeed** [ɪn'diːd] adv vraiment; en effet; (furthermore) d'ailleurs; **yes ~!** certainement!

**indefinitely** [ɪn'dɛfɪnɪtlɪ] adv (wait) indéfiniment

**indemnity** [ɪn'dɛmnɪtɪ] n (safeguard) assurance f, garantie f; (compensation) indemnité f

**independence** [ɪndɪ'pɛndns] n indépendance f

---
**Independence Day**

L'**Independence Day** *est la fête nationale aux États-Unis, le 4 juillet. Il commémore l'adoption de la déclaration d'Indépendance, en 1776, écrite par Thomas Jefferson et proclamant la séparation des 13 colonies américaines de la Grande-Bretagne.*

---

**independent** [ɪndɪˈpɛndnt] *adj* indépendant(e); *(school)* privé(e); *(radio)* libre

**index** [ˈɪndeks] *n (pl: ~es: in book)* index *m*; (: *in library etc)* catalogue *m*; *(pl: indices: ratio, sign)* indice *m*; **~ card** *n* fiche *f*; **~ finger** *n* index *m*; **~-linked** *adj* indexé(e) *(sur le coût de la vie etc)*

**India** [ˈɪndɪə] *n* Inde *f*; **~n** ♦ *adj* Indien(ne); **(American)** **~n** Indien(ne) *(d'Amérique)*; **~n Ocean** *n* océan Indien

**indicate** [ˈɪndɪkeɪt] *vt* indiquer; **indication** [ɪndɪˈkeɪʃən] *n* indication *f*, signe *m*; **indicative** [ɪnˈdɪkətɪv] *adj*: **indicative of** symptomatique de ♦ *n (LING)* indicatif *m*; **indicator** *n (sign)* indicateur *m*; *(AUT)* clignotant *m*

**indices** [ˈɪndɪsiːz] *npl of* **index**

**indictment** [ɪnˈdaɪtmənt] *n* accusation *f*

**indifferent** [ɪnˈdɪfrənt] *adj* indifférent(e); *(poor)* médiocre, quelconque

**indigenous** [ɪnˈdɪdʒɪnəs] *adj* indigène

**indigestion** [ɪndɪˈdʒɛstʃən] *n* indigestion *f*, mauvaise digestion

**indignant** [ɪnˈdɪgnənt] *adj*: **~ (at sth/with sb)** indigné(e) *(de qch/contre qn)*

**indignity** [ɪnˈdɪgnɪtɪ] *n* indignité *f*, affront *m*

**indirect** [ɪndɪˈrɛkt] *adj* indirect(e)

**indiscreet** [ɪndɪsˈkriːt] *adj* indiscret (-ète); *(rash)* imprudent(e)

**indiscriminate** [ɪndɪsˈkrɪmɪnət] *adj (person)* qui manque de discernement; *(killings)* commis(e) au hasard

**indisputable** [ɪndɪsˈpjuːtəbl] *adj* in-

contestable, indiscutable

**individual** [ɪndɪˈvɪdjuəl] *n* individu *m* ♦ *adj* individuel(le); *(characteristic)* particulier(-ère), original(e)

**indoctrination** [ɪndɒktrɪˈneɪʃən] *n* endoctrinement *m*

**Indonesia** [ɪndəˈniːzɪə] *n* Indonésie *f*

**indoor** [ˈɪndɔːˀ] *adj (plant)* d'appartement; *(swimming pool)* couvert(e); *(sport, games)* pratiqué(e) en salle; **~s** *adv* à l'intérieur

**induce** [ɪnˈdjuːs] *vt (persuade)* persuader; *(bring about)* provoquer; **~ment** *n (incentive)* récompense *f*; *(pej: bribe)* pot-de-vin *m*

**indulge** [ɪnˈdʌldʒ] *vt (whim)* céder à, satisfaire; *(child)* gâter ♦ *vi*: **to ~ in sth** *(luxury)* se permettre qch; *(fantasies etc)* se livrer à qch; **~nce** *n* fantaisie *f (que l'on s'offre)*; *(leniency)* indulgence *f*; **~nt** *adj* indulgent(e)

**industrial** [ɪnˈdʌstrɪəl] *adj* industriel(le); *(injury)* du travail; **~ action** *n* action revendicative; **~ estate** *(BRIT) n* zone industrielle; **~ist** *n* industriel *m*; **~ park** *(US) n* = **industrial estate**

**industrious** [ɪnˈdʌstrɪəs] *adj* travailleur(-euse)

**industry** [ˈɪndəstrɪ] *n* industrie *f*; *(diligence)* zèle *m*, application *f*

**inebriated** [ɪˈniːbrɪeɪtɪd] *adj* ivre

**inedible** [ɪnˈɛdɪbl] *adj* immangeable; *(plant etc)* non comestible

**ineffective** [ɪnɪˈfɛktɪv], **ineffectual** [ɪnɪˈfɛktʃuəl] *adj* inefficace

**inefficient** [ɪnɪˈfɪʃənt] *adj* inefficace

**inequality** [ɪnɪˈkwɔlɪtɪ] *n* inégalité *f*

**inescapable** [ɪnɪsˈkeɪpəbl] *adj* inéluctable, inévitable

**inevitable** [ɪnˈɛvɪtəbl] *adj* inévitable; **inevitably** *adv* inévitablement

**inexpensive** [ɪnɪkˈspɛnsɪv] *adj* bon marché *inv*

**inexperienced** [ɪnɪkˈspɪərɪənst] *adj* inexpérimenté(e)

**infallible** [ɪnˈfælɪbl] *adj* infaillible

**infamous** [ˈɪnfəməs] *adj* infâme, abominable

**infancy** [ˈɪnfənsɪ] n petite enfance, bas âge

**infant** [ˈɪnfənt] n (baby) nourrisson m; (young child) petit(e) enfant; ~ **school** (BRIT) n classes fpl préparatoires (entre 5 et 7 ans)

**infatuated** [ɪnˈfætjuertɪd] adj: ~ **with** entiché(e) de; **infatuation** [ɪnfætju'eɪʃən] n engouement m

**infect** [ɪnˈfɛkt] vt infecter, contaminer; ~**ion** n infection f; (contagion) contagion f; ~**ious** adj infectieux(-euse); (also fig) contagieux(-euse)

**infer** [ɪnˈfəːʳ] vt conclure, déduire

**inferior** [ɪnˈfɪərɪəʳ] adj inférieur(e); (goods) de qualité inférieure ♦ n: inférieur(e); (in rank) subalterne m/f; ~**ity** [ɪnfɪərɪˈɔrɪtɪ] n infériorité f

**infertile** [ɪnˈfəːtaɪl] adj stérile

**infighting** [ˈɪnfaɪtɪŋ] n querelles fpl internes

**infinite** [ˈɪnfɪnɪt] adj infini(e)

**infinitive** [ɪnˈfɪnɪtɪv] n infinitif m

**infinity** [ɪnˈfɪnɪtɪ] n infinité f; (also MATH) infini m

**infirmary** [ɪnˈfəːmərɪ] n (hospital) hôpital m

**inflamed** [ɪnˈfleɪmd] adj enflammé(e)

**inflammable** [ɪnˈflæməbl] (BRIT) adj inflammable

**inflammation** [ɪnfləˈmeɪʃən] n inflammation f

**inflatable** [ɪnˈfleɪtəbl] adj gonflable

**inflate** [ɪnˈfleɪt] vt (tyre, balloon) gonfler; (price) faire monter; **inflation** [ɪnˈfleɪʃən] n (ECON) inflation f; **inflationary** adj inflationniste

**inflict** [ɪnˈflɪkt] vt: **to ~ on** infliger à

**influence** [ˈɪnfluəns] n influence f ♦ vt influencer; **under the ~ of alcohol** en état d'ébriété; **influential** [ɪnfluˈɛnʃl] adj influent(e)

**influenza** [ɪnfluˈɛnzə] n grippe f

**influx** [ˈɪnflʌks] n afflux m

**infomercial** [ˈɪnfəʊmɜːʃl] (US) n (for product) publi-information f; (POL) émis-

sion ou un candidat présente son programme électoral

**inform** [ɪnˈfɔːm] vt: **to ~ sb (of)** informer ou avertir qn (de) ♦ vi: **to ~ on sb** dénoncer qn

**informal** [ɪnˈfɔːml] adj (person, manner, party) simple; (visit, discussion) dénué(e) de formalités; (announcement, invitation) non officiel(le); (colloquial) familier(-ère); ~**ity** [ɪnfɔːˈmælɪtɪ] n simplicité f, absence f de cérémonie; caractère non officiel

**informant** [ɪnˈfɔːmənt] n informateur(-trice)

**information** [ɪnfəˈmeɪʃən] n information f; renseignements mpl; (knowledge) connaissances fpl; **a piece of ~** un renseignement; ~ **desk** n accueil m; ~ **office** n bureau m de renseignements

**informative** [ɪnˈfɔːmətɪv] adj instructif(-ive)

**informer** [ɪnˈfɔːməʳ] n (also: **police ~**) indicateur(-trice)

**infringe** [ɪnˈfrɪndʒ] vt enfreindre ♦ vi: **to ~ on** empiéter sur; ~**ment** n: ~**ment (of)** infraction f (à)

**infuriating** [ɪnˈfjuərɪeɪtɪŋ] adj exaspérant(e)

**ingenious** [ɪnˈdʒiːnjəs] adj ingénieux(-euse); **ingenuity** [ɪndʒɪˈnjuːɪtɪ] n ingéniosité f

**ingenuous** [ɪnˈdʒɛnjuəs] adj naïf (naïve), ingénu(e)

**ingot** [ˈɪŋgət] n lingot m

**ingrained** [ɪnˈgreɪnd] adj enraciné(e)

**ingratiate** [ɪnˈgreɪʃɪeɪt] vt: **to ~ o.s. with** s'insinuer dans les bonnes grâces de, se faire bien voir de

**ingredient** [ɪnˈgriːdɪənt] n ingrédient m; (fig) élément m

**inhabit** [ɪnˈhæbɪt] vt habiter; ~**ant** n habitant(e)

**inhale** [ɪnˈheɪl] vt respirer; (smoke) avaler ♦ vi aspirer; (in smoking) avaler la fumée

**inherent** [ɪnˈhɪərənt] adj: ~ **(in** ou **to)** inhérent(e) (à)

**inherit** [ɪn'hɛrɪt] vt hériter (de); **~ance** n héritage m

**inhibit** [ɪn'hɪbɪt] vt (PSYCH) inhiber; (growth) freiner; **~ion** [ɪnhɪ'bɪʃən] n inhibition f

**inhuman** [ɪn'hjuːmən] adj inhumain(e)

**initial** [ɪ'nɪʃl] adj initial(e) ♦ n initiale f ♦ vt parafer; **~s** npl (letters) initiales fpl; (as signature) parafe m; **~ly** adv initialement, au début

**initiate** [ɪ'nɪʃɪeɪt] vt (start) entreprendre, amorcer; (entreprise) lancer; (person) initier; **to ~ proceedings against sb** intenter une action à qn; **initiative** n initiative f

**inject** [ɪn'dʒɛkt] vt injecter; (person): **to ~ sb with sth** faire une piqûre de qch à qn; **~ion** n injection f, piqûre f

**injure** [ˈɪndʒər] vt blesser; (reputation etc) compromettre; **~d** adj blessé(e); **injury** n blessure f; **~ time** n (SPORT) arrêts mpl de jeu

**injustice** [ɪn'dʒʌstɪs] n injustice f

**ink** [ɪŋk] n encre f

**inkling** [ˈɪŋklɪŋ] n: **to have an/no ~ of** avoir une (vague) idée de/n'avoir aucune idée de

**inlaid** [ˈɪnleɪd] adj incrusté(e); (table etc) marqueté(e)

**inland** adj [ˈɪnlənd], adv ɪn'lænd] adj intérieur(e) ♦ adv à l'intérieur, dans les terres; **Inland Revenue** (BRIT) n fisc m

**in-laws** [ˈɪnlɔːz] npl beaux-parents mpl; belle famille

**inlet** [ˈɪnlɛt] n (GEO) crique f

**inmate** [ˈɪnmeɪt] n (in prison) détenu(e); (in asylum) interné(e)

**inn** [ɪn] n auberge f

**innate** [ɪ'neɪt] adj inné(e)

**inner** [ˈɪnər] adj intérieur(e); **~ city** n centre m de zone urbaine; **~ tube** n (of tyre) chambre f à air

**innings** [ˈɪnɪŋz] n (CRICKET) tour m de batte

**innocent** [ˈɪnəsnt] adj innocent(e)

**innocuous** [ɪ'nɔkjuəs] adj inoffensif(-ive)

**innuendo** [ɪnju'ɛndəu] (pl **~es**) n insinuation f, allusion (malveillante)

**innumerable** [ɪ'njuːmrəbl] adj innombrable

**inpatient** [ˈɪnpeɪʃənt] n malade hospitalisé(e)

**input** [ˈɪnput] n (resources) ressources fpl; (COMPUT) entrée f (de données); (: data) données fpl

**inquest** [ˈɪnkwɛst] n enquête f; (coroner's) ~ enquête judiciaire

**inquire** [ɪn'kwaɪər] vi demander ♦ vt demander; **to ~ about** se renseigner sur; **~ into** vt fus faire une enquête sur; **inquiry** n demande f de renseignements; (investigation) enquête f, investigation f; **inquiries** npl: **the inquiries** (RAIL etc) les renseignements; **inquiry** or **inquiries office** (BRIT) n bureau m des renseignements

**inquisitive** [ɪn'kwɪzɪtɪv] adj curieux(-euse)

**ins** abbr = **inches**

**insane** [ɪn'seɪn] adj fou (folle); (MED) aliéné(e); **insanity** [ɪn'sænɪtɪ] n folie f; (MED) aliénation (mentale)

**inscription** [ɪn'skrɪpʃən] n inscription f; (in book) dédicace f

**inscrutable** [ɪn'skruːtəbl] adj impénétrable; (comment) obscur(e)

**insect** [ˈɪnsɛkt] n insecte m; **~icide** [ɪn'sɛktɪsaɪd] n insecticide m; **~ repellent** n crème f anti-insecte

**insecure** [ɪnsɪ'kjuər] adj peu solide; peu sûr(e); (person) anxieux(-euse)

**insensitive** [ɪn'sɛnsɪtɪv] adj insensible

**insert** [ɪn'səːt] vt insérer; **~ion** n insertion f

**in-service** [ˈɪnˈsəːvɪs] adj (training) continu(e), en cours d'emploi; (course) de perfectionnement ou de recyclage

**inshore** [ˈɪnˈʃɔːr] adj côtier(-ère) ♦ adv près de la côte; (move) vers la côte

**inside** [ˈɪnˈsaɪd] n intérieur m ♦ adj intérieur(e) ♦ adv à l'intérieur, dedans ♦ prep à l'intérieur de; (of time): **~ 10 minutes** en moins de 10 minutes; **~**

npl (inf) intestins mpl; ~ **information** n renseignements obtenus à la source; ~ **lane** n (AUT: in Britain) voie f de gauche; (: in US, Europe etc) voie de droite; ~ **out** adv à l'envers; (know) à fond; ~ **dealing**, ~r **trading** n (St Ex) délit m d'initié

**insight** ['ɪnsaɪt] n perspicacité f; (glimpse, idea) aperçu m

**insignificant** [ɪnsɪg'nɪfɪknt] adj insignifiant(e)

**insincere** [ɪnsɪn'sɪə] adj hypocrite

**insinuate** [ɪn'sɪnjueɪt] vt insinuer

**insist** [ɪn'sɪst] vi insister; to ~ **on doing** insister pour faire; to ~ **on sth** exiger qch; to ~ **that** insister pour que; (claim) maintenir ou soutenir que; ~**ent** adj insistant(e), pressant(e); (noise, action) ininterrompu(e)

**insole** ['ɪnsəul] n (removable) semelle intérieure

**insolent** ['ɪnsələnt] adj insolent(e)

**insolvent** [ɪn'sɔlvənt] adj insolvable

**insomnia** [ɪn'sɔmnɪə] n insomnie f

**inspect** [ɪn'spekt] vt inspecter; (ticket) contrôler; ~**ion** n inspection f, contrôle m; ~**or** n inspecteur(-trice); (BRIT: on buses, trains) contrôleur(-euse)

**inspire** [ɪn'spaɪə] vt inspirer

**install** [ɪn'stɔːl] vt installer; ~**ation** [ɪnstə'leɪʃən] n installation f

**instalment** [ɪn'stɔːlmənt] (US **installment**) n acompte m, versement partiel; (of TV serial etc) épisode m; **in ~s** (pay) à tempérament; (receive) en plusieurs fois

**instance** ['ɪnstəns] n exemple m; **for ~** par exemple; **in the first ~** tout d'abord, en premier lieu

**instant** ['ɪnstənt] n instant m ♦ adj immédiat(e); (coffee, food) instantané(e), en poudre; ~**ly** adv immédiatement, tout de suite

**instead** [ɪn'sted] adv au lieu de cela; ~ **of** au lieu de; ~ **of sb** à la place de qn

**instep** ['ɪnstep] n cou-de-pied m; (of shoe) cambrure f

**instigate** ['ɪnstɪgeɪt] vt (rebellion) fo-

menter, provoquer; (talks etc) promouvoir

**instil** [ɪn'stɪl] vt: to ~ (**into**) inculquer (à); (courage) insuffler (à)

**instinct** ['ɪnstɪŋkt] n instinct m

**institute** ['ɪnstɪtjuːt] n institut m ♦ vt instituer, établir; (inquiry) ouvrir; (proceedings) entamer

**institution** [ɪnstɪ'tjuːʃən] n institution f; (educational) établissement m (scolaire); (mental home) établissement (psychiatrique)

**instruct** [ɪn'strʌkt] vt: to ~ **sb in sth** enseigner qch à qn; to ~ **sb to do** charger qn ou ordonner à qn de faire; ~**ion** n instruction f; ~**ions** npl (orders) directives fpl; ~**ions (for use)** mode m d'emploi; ~**or** n professeur m; (for skiing, driving) moniteur m

**instrument** ['ɪnstrumənt] n instrument m; ~**al** [ɪnstru'mentl] adj: **to be ~al in** contribuer à; ~ **panel** n tableau m de bord

**insufficient** [ɪnsə'fɪʃənt] adj insuffisant(e)

**insular** ['ɪnsjulə] adj (outlook) borné(e); (person) aux vues étroites

**insulate** ['ɪnsjuleɪt] vt isoler; (against sound) insonoriser; **insulation** [ɪnsju'leɪʃən] n isolation f; insonorisation f

**insulin** ['ɪnsjulɪn] n insuline f

**insult** [n 'ɪnsʌlt, vb ɪn'sʌlt] n insulte f, affront m ♦ vt insulter, faire affront à

**insurance** [ɪn'ʃuərəns] n assurance f; **fire/life ~** assurance-incendie-/vie; ~ **policy** n police f d'assurance

**insure** [ɪn'ʃuə] vt assurer; to ~ (**o.s.**) **against** (fig) parer à

**intact** [ɪn'tækt] adj intact(e)

**intake** ['ɪnteɪk] n (of food, oxygen) consommation f; (BRIT: SCOL): **an ~ of 200 a year** 200 admissions fpl par an

**integral** ['ɪntɪgrəl] adj (part) intégrant(e)

**integrate** ['ɪntɪgreɪt] vt intégrer ♦ vi s'intégrer

**intellect** ['ɪntəlekt] n intelligence f; **~ual** [ɪntə'lektjuəl] adj, n intellectuel(le)

**intelligence** [ɪn'telɪdʒəns] n intelligence f; (MIL etc) informations fpl, renseignements mpl; **~ service** n services secrets; **intelligent** adj intelligent(e)

**intend** [ɪn'tend] vt (gift etc): to **~ sth for** destiner qch à; **to ~ to do** avoir l'intention de faire

**intense** [ɪn'tens] adj intense; (person) véhément(e); **~ly** adv intensément; profondément

**intensive** [ɪn'tensɪv] adj intensif(-ive); **~ care unit** n service m de réanimation

**intent** [ɪn'tent] n intention f ♦ adj attentif(-ive); **to all ~s and purposes** en fait, pratiquement; **to be ~ on doing sth** être (bien) décidé à faire qch; **~ion** n intention f; **~ional** adj intentionnel(le), délibéré(e); **~ly** adv attentivement

**interact** [ɪntər'ækt] vi avoir une action réciproque; (people) communiquer; **~ive** adj (COMPUT) interactif(-ive)

**interchange** [n 'ɪntətfeɪndʒ, vb ɪntə'tfeɪndʒ] n (exchange) échange m; (on motorway) échangeur m; **~able** adj interchangeable

**intercom** ['ɪntəkɔm] n interphone m

**intercourse** ['ɪntəkɔːs] n (sexual) rapports mpl

**interest** ['ɪntrɪst] n intérêt m; (pastime): **my main ~** ce qui m'intéresse le plus; (COMM) intérêts mpl ♦ vt intéresser; **to be ~ed in** s'intéresser à qch; **I am ~ed in going** ça m'intéresse d'y aller; **~ing** adj intéressant(e); **~ rate** n taux m d'intérêt

**interface** ['ɪntəfeɪs] n (COMPUT) interface f

**interfere** [ɪntə'fɪər] vi: **to ~ in** (quarrel) s'immiscer dans; (other people's business) se mêler de; **to ~ with** (object) toucher à; (plans) contrecarrer; (duty) être en conflit avec; **~nce** n (in affairs)

ingérance f; (RADIO, TV) parasites mpl

**interim** ['ɪntərɪm] adj provisoire ♦ n: **in the ~** dans l'intérim, entre-temps

**interior** [ɪn'tɪərɪə] n intérieur m ♦ adj intérieur(e); (minister, department) de l'Intérieur; **~ designer** n styliste m/f, designer m/f

**interjection** [ɪntə'dʒekʃən] n (interruption) interruption f; (LING) interjection f

**interlock** [ɪntə'lɔk] vi s'enclencher

**interlude** ['ɪntəluːd] n intervalle m; (THEATRE) intermède m

**intermediate** [ɪntə'miːdɪət] adj intermédiaire; (SCOL) moyen(ne)

**intermission** [ɪntə'mɪʃən] n pause f; (THEATRE, CINEMA) entracte m

**intern** [vb ɪn'tɔːn, n 'ɪntɔːn] vt interner ♦ n (US) interne m/f

**internal** [ɪn'tɔːnl] adj interne; (politics) intérieur(e); **~ly** adv: **"not to be taken ~ly"** "pour usage externe"; **I~ Revenue Service** (US) n fisc m

**international** [ɪntə'næʃənl] adj international(e)

**Internet** ['ɪntənet] n Internet m; **~ café** n cybercafé m; **~ service provider** n fournisseur m d'accès à Internet

**interplay** ['ɪntəpleɪ] n effet m réciproque, interaction f

**interpret** [ɪn'tɔːprɪt] vt interpréter ♦ vi servir d'interprète; **~er** n interprète m/f

**interrelated** [ɪntərɪ'leɪtɪd] adj en corrélation, en rapport étroit

**interrogate** [ɪn'terəugeɪt] vt interroger; (suspect etc) soumettre à un interrogatoire; **interrogation** [ɪnterəu'geɪʃən] n interrogation f; interrogatoire m

**interrupt** [ɪntə'rʌpt] vt, vi interrompre; **~ion** n interruption f

**intersect** [ɪntə'sekt] vi (roads) se croiser, se couper; **~ion** n (of roads) croisement m

**intersperse** [ɪntə'spɔːs] vt: **to ~ with** parsemer de

**intertwine** [ɪntə'twaɪn] vi s'entrelacer

**interval** ['ɪntəvl] n intervalle m; (BRIT: THEATRE) entracte m; (: SPORT) mi-temps f; **at ~s** par intervalles

**intervene** [ɪntəˈviːn] vi (person) intervenir; (event) survenir; (time) s'écouler (entre-temps); **intervention** n intervention f

**interview** [ˈɪntəvjuː] n (RADIO, TV etc) interview f; (for job) entrevue f ♦ vt interviewer; avoir une entrevue avec; **~er** n (RADIO, TV) interviewer m

**intestine** [ɪnˈtɛstɪn] n intestin m

**intimacy** [ˈɪntɪməsɪ] n intimité f

**intimate** [adj ˈɪntɪmət, vb ˈɪntɪmeɪt] adj intime; (friendship) profond(e); (knowledge) approfondi(e) ♦ vt (hint) suggérer, laisser entendre

**into** [ˈɪntu] prep dans; **~ pieces/French** en morceaux/français

**intolerant** [ɪnˈtɔlərənt] adj: **~ (of)** intolérant(e) (de)

**intoxicated** [ɪnˈtɔksɪkeɪtɪd] adj (drunk) ivre

**intractable** [ɪnˈtræktəbl] adj (child) indocile, insoumis(e); (problem) insoluble

**intranet** [ˈɪntrənɛt] n intranet m

**intransitive** [ɪnˈtrænsɪtɪv] adj intransitif(-ive)

**intravenous** [ɪntrəˈviːnəs] adj intraveineux(-euse)

**in-tray** [ˈɪntreɪ] n courrier m "arrivée"

**intricate** [ˈɪntrɪkət] adj complexe, compliqué(e)

**intrigue** [ɪnˈtriːg] n intrigue f ♦ vt intriguer; **intriguing** adj fascinant(e)

**intrinsic** [ɪnˈtrɪnsɪk] adj intrinsèque

**introduce** [ɪntrəˈdjuːs] vt introduire; (TV show, people to each other) présenter; **to ~ sb to** (pastime, technique) initier qn à; **introduction** n introduction f; (of person) présentation f; (to new experience) initiation f; **introductory** adj préliminaire, d'introduction; **introductory offer** n (COMM) offre f de lancement

**intrude** [ɪnˈtruːd] vi (person) être importun(e); **to ~ on** (conversation etc) s'immiscer dans; **~r** n intrus(e)

**intuition** [ɪntjuːˈɪʃən] n intuition f

**inundate** [ˈɪnʌndeɪt] vt: **to ~ with**

inonder de

**invade** [ɪnˈveɪd] vt envahir

**invalid** [n ˈɪnvəlɪd, adj ɪnˈvælɪd] n malade m/f; (with disability) invalide m/f ♦ adj (not valid) non valide or valable

**invaluable** [ɪnˈvæljuəbl] adj inestimable, inappréciable

**invariably** [ɪnˈvɛərɪəbl] adv invariablement; toujours

**invent** [ɪnˈvɛnt] vt inventer; **~ion** n invention f; **~ive** adj inventif(-ive); **~or** n inventeur(-trice)

**inventory** [ˈɪnvəntrɪ] n inventaire m

**invert** [ɪnˈvəːt] vt intervertir; (cup, object) retourner; **~ed commas** (BRIT) npl guillemets mpl

**invest** [ɪnˈvɛst] vt investir ♦ vi: **to ~ in** sth placer son argent dans qch; (fig) s'offrir qch

**investigate** [ɪnˈvɛstɪgeɪt] vt (crime etc) faire une enquête sur; **investigation** [ɪnvɛstɪˈgeɪʃən] n (of crime) enquête f

**investment** [ɪnˈvɛstmənt] n investissement m, placement m

**investor** [ɪnˈvɛstər] n investisseur m; actionnaire m/f

**invigilator** [ɪnˈvɪdʒɪleɪtər] n surveillant(e)

**invigorating** [ɪnˈvɪgəreɪtɪŋ] adj vivifiant(e); (fig) stimulant(e)

**invisible** [ɪnˈvɪzɪbl] adj invisible

**invitation** [ɪnvɪˈteɪʃən] n invitation f

**invite** [ɪnˈvaɪt] vt inviter; (opinions etc) demander; **inviting** adj engageant(e), attrayant(e)

**invoice** [ˈɪnvɔɪs] n facture f

**involuntary** [ɪnˈvɔləntrɪ] adj involontaire

**involve** [ɪnˈvɔlv] vt (entail) entraîner, nécessiter; (concern) concerner; (associate): **to ~ sb (in)** impliquer qn (dans), mêler qn (à); faire participer qn (à); **~d** adj (complicated) complexe; **to be ~d in** participer à; **~ment** n: **~ment (in)** participation f (à); rôle m (dans); (enthusiasm) enthousiasme m (pour)

**inward** [ˈɪnwəd] adj (thought, feeling)

profond(e), intime; (*movement*) vers
l'intérieur; **~(s)** adv vers l'intérieur

**iodine** ['aɪəʊdiːn] n iode m

**iota** [aɪ'əʊtə] n (*fig*) brin m, grain m

**IOU** n abbr (= I owe you) reconnaissance
f de dette

**IQ** n abbr (= intelligence quotient) Q.I. m

**IRA** n abbr (= Irish Republican Army) IRA
f

**Iran** [ɪ'rɑːn] n Iran m

**Iraq** [ɪ'rɑːk] n Irak m

**irate** [aɪ'reɪt] adj courroucé(e)

**Ireland** ['aɪələnd] n Irlande f

**iris** ['aɪrɪs] (pl **~es**) n iris m

**Irish** ['aɪrɪʃ] adj irlandais(e) ♦ npl: **the ~**
les Irlandais; **~man** (irreg) n Irlandais m;
**~ Sea** n mer f d'Irlande; **~woman** (irreg) n Irlandaise f

**iron** ['aɪən] n fer m; (*for clothes*) fer m à
repasser ♦ cpd de or en fer; (*fig*) de fer ♦
vt (*clothes*) repasser; **~ out** vt (*fig*) aplanir; faire disparaître

**ironic(al)** [aɪ'rɒnɪk(l)] adj ironique

**ironing** ['aɪənɪŋ] n repassage m; **~**
**board** n planche f à repasser

**ironmonger's (shop)** ['aɪənmʌŋɡəz-]
n quincaillerie f

**irony** ['aɪrənɪ] n ironie f

**irrational** [ɪ'ræʃənl] adj irrationnel(le)

**irregular** [ɪ'reɡjʊlə*] adj irrégulier(-ère);
(*surface*) inégal(e)

**irrelevant** [ɪ'reləvnt] adj sans rapport,
hors de propos

**irresistible** [ɪrɪ'zɪstɪbl] adj irrésistible

**irrespective** [ɪrɪ'spektɪv]: **~ of** prep sans
tenir compte de

**irresponsible** [ɪrɪ'spɒnsɪbl] adj (*act*) ir-
réfléchi(e); (*person*) irresponsable

**irrigate** ['ɪrɪɡeɪt] vt irriguer; **irrigation**
[ɪrɪ'ɡeɪʃən] n irrigation f

**irritate** ['ɪrɪteɪt] vt irriter

**irritating** adj irritant(e); **irritation**
[ɪrɪ'teɪʃən] n irritation f

**IRS** n abbr = Internal Revenue Service

**is** [ɪz] vb see **be**

**Islam** ['ɪzlɑːm] n Islam m; **~ic** adj islamique; **~ic fundamentalists** intégris-

tes mpl musulmans

**island** ['aɪlənd] n île f; **~er** n habi-
tant(e) d'une île, insulaire m/f

**isle** [aɪl] n île f

**isn't** ['ɪznt] = is not

**isolate** ['aɪsəleɪt] vt isoler; **~d** adj iso-
lé(e); **isolation** n isolation f

**ISP** n abbr = Internet service provider

**Israel** ['ɪzreɪl] n Israël m; **~i** [ɪz'reɪlɪ] adj
israélien(ne) ♦ n Israélien(ne)

**issue** ['ɪʃuː] n question f, problème m;
(*of book*) publication f, parution f; (*of
banknotes etc*) émission f; (*of newspaper
etc*) numéro m ♦ vt (*rations, equipment*)
distribuer; (*statement*) publier; faire;
(*banknotes etc*) émettre, mettre en circulation; **at ~** en jeu, en cause; **to
take ~ with sb (over)** exprimer son
désaccord avec qn (sur); **to make an ~
of sth** faire une montagne de qch

_KEYWORD_

**it** [ɪt] pron **1** (*specific: subject*) il (elle); (:
*direct object*) le (la) (l'); (: *indirect object*) lui; **it's on the table** c'est or il (or
elle) est sur la table; **about/from/of it**
en; **I spoke to him about it** je lui en
ai parlé; **what did you learn from it?**
qu'est-ce que vous en avez retiré?; **I'm
proud of it** j'en suis fier; **in/to it** y;
**put the book in it** mettez-y le livre;
**he agreed to it** il y a consenti; **did
you go to it?** (*party, concert etc*) est-ce
que vous y êtes allé(s)?

**2** (*impersonal*) il; ce; **it's raining** il
pleut; **it's Friday tomorrow** demain
c'est vendredi or nous sommes vendredi; **it's 6 o'clock** il est 6 heures; **who
is it? - it's me** qui est-ce? - c'est moi

**Italian** [ɪ'tæljən] adj italien(ne) ♦ n Ita-
lien(ne); (*LING*) italien m

**italics** [ɪ'tælɪks] npl italiques fpl

**Italy** ['ɪtəlɪ] n Italie f

**itch** [ɪtʃ] n démangeaison f ♦ vi (*person*)
éprouver des démangeaisons; (*part of*

body) démanger; **I'm ~ing to do** l'envie me démange de faire; **~y** adj qui
démange; **to be ~y** avoir des démangeaisons

**it'd** ['ɪtd] = **it would**; **it had**

**item** ['aɪtəm] n article m; (on agenda)
question f, point m; (also: **news ~**)
nouvelle f; **~ize** vt détailler, faire une
liste de

**itinerary** [aɪ'tɪnərərɪ] n itinéraire m

**it'll** ['ɪtl] = **it will**; **it shall**

**its** [ɪts] adj son (sa), ses pl

**it's** [ɪts] = **it is**; **it has**

**itself** [ɪt'self] pron (reflexive) se; (emphatic) lui-même (elle-même)

**ITV** n abbr (BRIT: Independent Television)
chaîne privée

**IUD** n abbr (= intra-uterine device) DIU m,
stérilet m

**I've** [aɪv] = **I have**

**ivory** ['aɪvərɪ] n ivoire m

**ivy** ['aɪvɪ] n lierre m

## J, j

**jab** [dʒæb] vt: **to ~ sth into** enfoncer or
planter qch dans ♦ n (inf: injection) piqûre f

**jack** [dʒæk] n (AUT) cric m; (CARDS) valet
m; **~ up** vt soulever (au cric)

**jackal** ['dʒækl] n chacal m

**jacket** ['dʒækɪt] n veste f, veston m; (of
book) jaquette f, couverture f; **~ potato** n pomme f de terre en robe des
champs

**jack**: **~knife** vi: **the lorry ~knifed** la remorque (du camion) s'est mise en tra-
vers; **~ plug** n (ELEC) prise jack mâle f;
**~pot** n gros lot

**jaded** ['dʒeɪdɪd] adj éreinté(e), fati-
gué(e)

**jagged** ['dʒægɪd] adj dentelé(e)

**jail** [dʒeɪl] n prison f ♦ vt emprisonner,
mettre en prison

**jam** [dʒæm] n confiture f; (also: **traffic
~**) embouteillage m ♦ vt (passage etc)

encombrer, obstruer; (mechanism,
drawer etc) bloquer, coincer; (RADIO)
brouiller ♦ vi se coincer, se bloquer;
(gun) s'enrayer; **to be in a ~** (inf) être
dans le pétrin; **to ~ into** entasser
qch dans; enfoncer qch dans

**Jamaica** [dʒə'meɪkə] n Jamaïque f

**jam**: **~ jar** n pot m à confiture; **~med**
adj (window etc) coincé(e); **~-packed**
adj: **~-packed (with)** bourré(e) (de)

**jangle** ['dʒæŋgl] vi cliqueter

**janitor** ['dʒænɪtə*] n concierge m

**January** ['dʒænjuərɪ] n janvier m

**Japan** [dʒə'pæn] n Japon m; **~ese**
[dʒæpə'niːz] adj japonais(e) ♦ n inv Ja-
ponais(e); (LING) japonais m

**jar** [dʒɑː*] n (stone, earthenware) pot m;
(glass) bocal m ♦ vi (sound discordant)
produire un son grinçant or discordant;
(colours etc) jurer

**jargon** ['dʒɑːgən] n jargon m

**jaundice** ['dʒɔːndɪs] n jaunisse f

**javelin** ['dʒævlɪn] n javelot m

**jaw** [dʒɔː] n mâchoire f

**jay** [dʒeɪ] n geai m; **~walker** n piéton m
indiscipliné

**jazz** [dʒæz] n jazz m; **~ up** vt animer,
égayer

**jealous** ['dʒeləs] adj jaloux(-ouse); **~y** n
jalousie f

**jeans** [dʒiːnz] npl jean m

**jeer** [dʒɪə*] vi: **to ~ (at)** se moquer
cruellement (de), railler

**Jehovah's Witness** [dʒɪ'həuvəz-] n
témoin m de Jéhovah

**jelly** ['dʒelɪ] n gelée f; **~fish** ['dʒelɪfɪʃ] n
méduse f

**jeopardy** ['dʒepədɪ] n: **to be in ~** être
en danger or péril

**jerk** [dʒɜːk] n secousse f; saccade f; sursaut m, spasme m; (inf: idiot) pauvre
type m ♦ vt (pull) tirer brusquement ♦
vi (vehicles) cahoter

**jersey** ['dʒɜːzɪ] n (pullover) tricot m;
(fabric) jersey m

**Jesus** ['dʒiːzəs] n Jésus m

**jet** [dʒet] n (gas, liquid) jet m; (AVIAT)

avion m à réaction, jet m; **~-black** *adj* (d'un noir) de jais; **~ engine** n moteur m à réaction; **~ lag** n (fatigue due au) décalage m horaire

**jettison** ['dʒɛtɪsn] *vt* jeter par-dessus bord

**jetty** ['dʒɛtɪ] n jetée f, digue f

**Jew** [dʒuː] n juif m

**jewel** ['dʒuːəl] n bijou m, joyau m; (*in watch*) rubis m; **~ler** (US **jeweler**) n bijoutier(-ère), joaillier m; **~ler's (shop)** n bijouterie f, joaillerie f; **~lery** (US **jewelry**) n bijoux mpl

**Jewess** ['dʒuːɪs] n juive f

**Jewish** ['dʒuːɪʃ] *adj* juif (juive)

**jibe** [dʒaɪb] n sarcasme m

**jiffy** ['dʒɪfɪ] (*inf*) n: **in a ~** en un clin d'œil

**jigsaw** ['dʒɪgsɔː] n (*also*: **~ puzzle**) puzzle m

**jilt** [dʒɪlt] *vt* laisser tomber, plaquer

**jingle** ['dʒɪŋgl] n (*for advert*) couplet m publicitaire ♦ *vi* cliqueter, tinter

**jinx** [dʒɪŋks] (*inf*) n (mauvais) sort

**jitters** ['dʒɪtəz] (*inf*) npl: **to get the ~** (*inf*) avoir la trouille or la frousse

**job** [dʒɔb] n (*chore, task*) travail m, tâche f; (*employment*) emploi m, poste m, place f; **it's a good ~ that ...** c'est heureux or c'est une chance que ...; **just the ~!** (c'est) juste or exactement ce qu'il faut!; **~ centre** (*BRIT*) n agence f pour l'emploi; **~less** *adj* sans travail, au chômage

**jockey** ['dʒɔkɪ] n jockey m ♦ *vi*: **to ~ for position** manœuvrer pour être bien placé

**jog** [dʒɔg] *vt* secouer ♦ *vi* (*SPORT*) faire du jogging; **to ~ sb's memory** rafraîchir la mémoire de qn; **~ along** *vi* cheminer; trotter; **~ging** n jogging m

**join** [dʒɔɪn] *vt* (*put together*) unir, assembler; (*become member of*) s'inscrire à; (*meet*) rejoindre, retrouver; (*queue*) se joindre à ♦ *vi* (*roads, rivers*) se rejoindre, se rencontrer ♦ n raccord m; **~ in** *vi* se mettre de la partie, participer ♦

*vt fus* participer à, se mêler à; **~ up** *vi* (*meet*) se rejoindre; (*MIL*) s'engager

**joiner** ['dʒɔɪnəʳ] (*BRIT*) n menuisier m

**joint** [dʒɔɪnt] n (*TECH*) jointure f; joint m; (*ANAT*) articulation f, joint m; (*CULIN*) rôti m; (*inf: place*) boîte f; (*: of cannabis*) joint m ♦ *adj* commun(e); **~ account** n (*with bank etc*) compte joint

**joke** [dʒəuk] n plaisanterie f; (*also*: **practical ~**) farce f ♦ *vi* plaisanter; **to play a ~ on** jouer un tour à, faire une farce à; **~r** n (*CARDS*) joker m

**jolly** ['dʒɔlɪ] *adj* gai(e), enjoué(e); (*enjoyable*) amusant(e), plaisant(e) ♦ *adv* (*BRIT: inf*) rudement, drôlement

**jolt** [dʒəult] n cahot m, secousse f; (*shock*) choc m ♦ *vt* cahoter, secouer

**Jordan** ['dʒɔːdən] n (*country*) Jordanie f

**jostle** ['dʒɔsl] *vt* bousculer, pousser

**jot** [dʒɔt] n: **not one ~** pas un brin; **~ down** *vt* noter; **~ter** (*BRIT*) n cahier m (de brouillon); (*pad*) bloc-notes m

**journal** ['dʒəːnl] n journal m; **~ism** n journalisme m; **~ist** n journaliste m/f

**journey** ['dʒəːnɪ] n voyage m; (*distance covered*) trajet m

**joy** [dʒɔɪ] n joie f; **~ful** *adj* joyeux (-euse); **~rider** n personne qui fait une virée dans une voiture volée; **~stick** n (*AVIAT, COMPUT*) manche m à balai

**JP** n abbr = **Justice of the Peace**

**Jr** abbr = **junior**

**jubilant** ['dʒuːbɪlnt] *adj* triomphant(e); réjoui(e)

**judge** [dʒʌdʒ] n juge m ♦ *vt* juger; **judg(e)ment** n jugement m

**judicial** [dʒuːˈdɪʃl] *adj* judiciaire; **judiciary** n (*pouvoir m*) judiciaire m

**judo** ['dʒuːdəu] n judo m

**jug** [dʒʌg] n pot m, cruche f

**juggernaut** ['dʒʌgənɔːt] (*BRIT*) n (*huge truck*) énorme poids lourd

**juggle** ['dʒʌgl] *vi* jongler; **~r** n jongleur m

**juice** [dʒuːs] n jus m; **juicy** *adj* juteux (-euse)

**jukebox** ['dʒuːkbɒks] n juke-box m

**July** [dʒuː'laɪ] n juillet m

**jumble** ['dʒʌmbl] n fouillis m ♦ vt (also: ~ **up**) mélanger, brouiller; ~ **sale** (BRIT) n vente f de charité

___

jumble sale
___

Les **jumble sales** ont lieu dans les églises, salles de fêtes ou halls d'écoles, et l'on y vend des articles de toutes sortes, en général bon marché et surtout d'occasion, pour collecter des fonds pour une œuvre de charité, une école ou encore une église.

___

**jumbo (jet)** ['dʒʌmbəu-] n jumbo-jet m, gros porteur

**jump** [dʒʌmp] vi sauter, bondir; (start) sursauter; (increase) monter en flèche ♦ vt sauter, franchir ♦ n saut m, bond m; sursaut m; **to ~ the queue** (BRIT) passer avant son tour

**jumper** ['dʒʌmpər] n (BRIT: pullover) pull-over m; (US: dress) robe-chasuble f

**jumper cables** (US: BRIT **jump leads**) npl câbles mpl de démarrage

**jumpy** ['dʒʌmpɪ] adj nerveux(-euse), agité(e)

**Jun.** abbr = **junior**

**junction** ['dʒʌŋkʃən] n (BRIT: of roads) carrefour m; (of rails) embranchement m

**juncture** ['dʒʌŋktʃər] n: **at this ~** à ce moment-là, sur ces entrefaites

**June** [dʒuːn] n juin m

**jungle** ['dʒʌŋgl] n jungle f

**junior** ['dʒuːnɪər] adj, n: **he's ~ to me (by 2 years)** il est mon cadet (de 2 ans), il est plus jeune que moi (de 2 ans); **he's ~ to me** (seniority) il est en dessous de moi (dans la hiérarchie), j'ai plus d'ancienneté que lui; ~ **school** (BRIT) n ≃ école f primaire

**junk** [dʒʌŋk] n (rubbish) camelote f; (cheap goods) bric-à-brac m inv; ~ **food** n aliments mpl sans grande valeur nutri-

tive; ~ **mail** n prospectus mpl (non sollicités); ~ **shop** n (boutique f de) brocanteur m

**Junr** abbr = **junior**

**juror** ['dʒuərər] n juré m

**jury** ['dʒuərɪ] n jury m

**just** [dʒʌst] adj juste ♦ adv: **he's ~ done it/left** il vient de le faire/partir; ~ **right/two o'clock** exactement or juste ce qu'il faut/deux heures; **she's ~ as clever as you** elle est tout aussi intelligente que vous; **it's ~ as well (that)** ... heureusement que ...; ~ **as he was leaving** au moment or à l'instant précis où il partait; ~ **before/enough/here** juste avant/assez/ici; **it's ~ me/a mistake** ce n'est que moi/(rien) qu'une erreur; ~ **missed/caught** manqué/attrapé de justesse; ~ **listen to this!** écoutez un peu ça!

**justice** ['dʒʌstɪs] n justice f; (US: judge) juge m de la Cour suprême; **J~ of the Peace** n juge m de paix

**justify** ['dʒʌstɪfaɪ] vt justifier

**jut** [dʒʌt] vi (also: ~ **out**) dépasser, faire saillie

**juvenile** ['dʒuːvənaɪl] adj juvénile; (court, books) pour enfants ♦ n adolescent(e)

# K, k

**K** abbr (= one thousand) K; (= kilobyte) Ko

**kangaroo** [kæŋgə'ruː] n kangourou m

**karate** [kə'rɑːtɪ] n karaté m

**kebab** [kə'bæb] n kébab m

**keel** [kiːl] n quille f; **on an even ~** (fig) à flot

**keen** [kiːn] adj (eager) plein(e) d'enthousiasme; (interest, desire, competition) vif (vive); (eye, intelligence) pénétrant(e); (edge) effilé(e); **to be ~ to do** or **on doing sth** désirer vivement faire qch, tenir beaucoup à faire qch; **to be ~ on sth/sb** aimer beaucoup qch/qn

**keep** [ki:p] (*pt, pp* **kept**) *vt* (retain, preserve) garder; (detain) retenir; (shop, accounts, diary, promise) tenir; (house) avoir; (support) entretenir; (chickens, bees etc) élever ♦ *vi* (remain) rester; (food) se conserver ♦ *n* (of castle) donjon *m*; (food etc): **enough for his** ~ assez pour (assurer) sa subsistance; (inf): **for ~s** pour de bon, pour toujours; **to ~ doing sth** ne pas arrêter de faire qch; **to ~ sb from doing** empêcher qn de faire or que qn ne fasse qch; **to ~ sb happy/a place tidy** faire que qn soit content/qu'un endroit reste propre; **to ~ sth to o.s.** garder qch pour soi, tenir qch secret; **to ~ sth (back) from sb** cacher qch à qn; **to ~ time** (clock) être à l'heure, ne pas retarder; **well kept** bien entretenu(e); ~ **on** *vi*: **to ~ on doing** continuer à faire; **don't ~ on about it!** arrête (d'en parler)!; ~ **out** *vt* empêcher d'entrer; "~ **out**" "défense d'entrer"; ~ **up** *vt* continuer, maintenir ♦ *vi*: **to ~ up with sb** (in race etc) aller aussi vite que qn; (in work etc) se maintenir au niveau de qn; ~**er** *n* gardien(ne); ~**ing** *n* (care) garde *f*; **in ~ing with** en accord avec; ~**sake** *n* souvenir *m*

**kennel** ['kɛnl] *n* niche *f*; ~**s** *npl* (boarding ~s) chenil *m*

**kerb** [kə:b] (BRIT) *n* bordure *f* du trottoir

**kernel** ['kə:nl] *n* (of nut) amande *f*; (fig) noyau *m*

**kettle** ['kɛtl] *n* bouilloire *f*; ~**drum** *n* timbale *f*

**key** [ki:] *n* (gen, MUS) clé *f*; (of piano, typewriter) touche *f* ♦ cpd clé ♦ *vt* (also: ~ **in**) saisir; ~**board** *n* clavier *m*; ~ **card** *n* (at hotel etc) carte *f* magnétique; ~**ed up** *adj* (person) surexcité(e); ~**hole** *n* trou *m* de la serrure; ~**hole surgery** *n* chirurgie *f* endoscopique; ~**note** *n* (of speech) note dominante; (MUS) tonique *f*; ~ **ring** *n* porte-clés *m*

**khaki** ['kɑ:ki] *n* kaki *m*

**kick** [kik] *vt* donner un coup de pied à ♦ *vi* (horse) ruer ♦ *n* coup *m* de pied; (thrill): **he does it for ~s** il le fait parce que ça l'excite, il le fait pour le plaisir; **to ~ the habit** (inf) arrêter; ~ **off** *vi* (SPORT) donner le coup d'envoi

**kid** [kid] *n* (inf: child) gamin(e), gosse *m/f*; (animal, leather) chevreau *m* ♦ *vi* (inf) plaisanter, blaguer

**kidnap** ['kidnæp] *vt* enlever, kidnapper; ~**per** *n* ravisseur(-euse); ~**ping** *n* enlèvement *m*

**kidney** ['kidni] *n* (ANAT) rein *m*; (CULIN) rognon *m*

**kill** [kil] *vt* tuer ♦ *n* mise *f* à mort; ~**er** *n* tueur(-euse); meurtrier(-ère); ~**ing** *n* meurtre *m*; (of group of people) tuerie *f*, massacre *m*; **to make a ~ing** (inf) réussir un beau coup (de filet); ~**joy** *n* rabat-joie *m/f*

**kiln** [kiln] *n* four *m*

**kilo** ['ki:ləu] *n* kilo *m*; ~**byte** *n* (COMPUT) kilo-octet *m*; ~**gram(me)** *n* kilogramme *m*; ~**metre** (US **kilometer**) *n* kilomètre *m*; ~**watt** *n* kilowatt *m*

**kilt** [kilt] *n* kilt *m*

**kin** [kin] *n* see **next**

**kind** [kaind] *adj* gentil(le), aimable ♦ *n* sorte *f*, espèce *f*, genre *m*; **to be two of a ~** se ressembler; **in ~** (COMM) en nature

**kindergarten** ['kindəgɑ:tn] *n* jardin *m* d'enfants

**kind-hearted** [kaind'hɑ:tid] *adj* bon (bonne)

**kindle** ['kindl] *vt* allumer, enflammer

**kindly** ['kaindli] *adj* bienveillant(e), plein(e) de gentillesse ♦ *adv* avec bonté; **will you ~ ...!** auriez-vous la bonté or l'obligeance de ...?

**kindness** ['kaindnis] *n* bonté *f*, gentillesse *f*

**king** [kiŋ] *n* roi *m*; ~**dom** *n* royaume *m*; ~**fisher** *n* martin-pêcheur *m*; ~**-size bed** *n* grand lit (de 1,95 m de large); ~**-size(d)** *adj* format géant *inv*; (cigarettes) long (longue)

**kiosk** ['ki:ɔsk] n kiosque m; (BRIT: TEL) cabine f (téléphonique)

**kipper** ['kɪpə'] n hareng fumé et salé

**kiss** [kɪs] n baiser m ♦ vt embrasser; **to ~ (each other)** s'embrasser; **~ of life** (BRIT) n bouche à bouche m

**kit** [kɪt] n équipement m, matériel m; (set of tools etc) trousse f; (for assembly) kit m

**kitchen** ['kɪtʃɪn] n cuisine f; **~ sink** n évier m

**kite** [kaɪt] n (toy) cerf-volant m

**kitten** ['kɪtn] n chaton m, petit chat

**kitty** ['kɪtɪ] n (money) cagnotte f

**km** abbr = **kilometre**

**knack** [næk] n: **to have the ~ of doing** avoir le coup pour faire

**knapsack** ['næpsæk] n musette f

**knead** [ni:d] vt pétrir

**knee** [ni:] n genou m; **~cap** n rotule f

**kneel** [ni:l] (pt, pp **knelt**) vi (also: **~ down**) s'agenouiller

**knew** [nju:] pt of **know**

**knickers** ['nɪkəz] (BRIT) npl culotte f (de femme)

**knife** [naɪf] (pl **knives**) n couteau m ♦ vt poignarder, frapper d'un coup de couteau

**knight** [naɪt] n chevalier m; (CHESS) cavalier m; **~hood** (BRIT) n (title): **to get a ~hood** être fait chevalier

**knit** [nɪt] n tricoter ♦ vi tricoter; (broken bones) se ressouder; **to ~ one's brows** froncer les sourcils; **~ting** n tricot m; **~ting needle** n aiguille f à tricoter; **~wear** n tricots mpl, lainages mpl

**knives** [naɪvz] npl of **knife**

**knob** [nɔb] n bouton m

**knock** [nɔk] n frapper m; (bump into) heurter; (inf) dénigrer ♦ vi (at door etc): **to ~ at** or **on** frapper à; **~ down** vt renverser; **~ off** vi (inf: finish) s'arrêter (de travailler) ♦ vt (from price) faire un rabais de; (inf: steal) piquer; **~ out** vt assommer; (BOXING) mettre k.-o.; (defeat) éliminer; **~ over** vt renverser, faire tomber; **~er** n (on door) heurtoir

m; **~out** n (BOXING) knock-out m, K.-O. m; **~out competition** compétition f avec épreuves éliminatoires

**knot** [nɔt] n (gen) nœud m ♦ vt nouer

**know** [nəu] (pt **knew**, pp **known**) vt savoir; (person, place) connaître; **to ~ how to do** savoir (comment) faire; **to ~ how to swim** savoir nager; **to ~ about** or **of sth** être au courant de qch; **to ~ about** or **of sb** avoir entendu parler de qn; **~-all** (pej) n je-sais-tout m/f; **~-how** n savoir-faire m; **~ing** adj (look etc) entendu(e); **~ingly** adv sciemment; (smile, look) d'un air entendu

**knowledge** ['nɔlɪdʒ] n connaissance f; (learning) connaissances, savoir m; **~able** adj bien informé(e)

**knuckle** ['nʌkl] n articulation f (des doigts), jointure f

**Koran** [kɔ'rɑ:n] n Coran m

**Korea** [kə'rɪə] n Corée f

**kosher** ['kəuʃə'] adj kascher inv

**Kosovo** ['kɔsɔvəu] n Kosovo m

## L, l

**L** abbr (= lake, large) L; (= left) g; (BRIT: AUT: learner) signale un conducteur débutant

**lab** [læb] n abbr (= laboratory) labo m

**label** ['leɪbl] n étiquette f ♦ vt étiqueter

**labor** etc ['leɪbə'] (US) = **labour**

**laboratory** [lə'bɔrətəri] n laboratoire m

**labour** ['leɪbə'] (US **labor**) n (work) travail m; (workforce) main-d'œuvre f ♦ vi: **to ~ (at)** travailler dur (à), peiner (sur) ♦ vt: **to ~ a point** insister sur un point; **in ~** (MED) en travail, en train d'accoucher; **L~, the L~ party** (BRIT) le parti travailliste, les travaillistes mpl; **~ed** ['leɪbəd] adj (breathing) pénible, difficile; **~er** n manœuvre m; **farm ~er** n ouvrier m agricole

**lace** [leɪs] n dentelle f; (of shoe etc) lacet m ♦ vt (shoe: also: **~ up**) lacer

**lack** [læk] n manque m ♦ vt manquer

de; **through** or **for ~** faute de, par manque de; **to be ~ing** manquer, faire défaut; **to be ~ing in** manquer de

**lacquer** ['lækə*] n laque f

**lad** [læd] n garçon m, gars m

**ladder** ['lædə*] n échelle f; (BRIT: in tights) maille filée

**laden** ['leɪdn] adj: **~ (with)** chargé(e) (de)

**ladle** ['leɪdl] n louche f

**lady** ['leɪdɪ] n dame f; (in address): **ladies and gentlemen** Mesdames (et) Messieurs; **young ~** jeune fille f; (married) jeune femme f; **the ladies' (room)** les toilettes fpl (pour dames); **~bird** (US **ladybug**) n coccinelle f; **~like** adj distingué(e); **~ship** n: **your ~ship** Madame la comtesse/la baronne etc

**lag** [læg] n retard m ♦ vi (also: **~ behind**) rester en arrière, traîner; (fig) rester en traîne ♦ vt (pipes) calorifuger

**lager** ['lɑːgə*] n bière blonde

**lagoon** [lə'guːn] n lagune f

**laid** [leɪd] pt, pp of **lay**; **~-back** (inf) adj relaxe, décontracté(e); **~ up** adj alité(e)

**lain** [leɪn] pp of **lie**

**lake** [leɪk] n lac m

**lamb** [læm] n agneau m; **~ chop** n côtelette f d'agneau

**lame** [leɪm] adj boiteux(-euse)

**lament** [lə'ment] n lamentation f ♦ vt pleurer, se lamenter sur

**laminated** ['læmɪneɪtɪd] adj laminé(e); (windscreen) (en verre) feuilleté

**lamp** [læmp] n lampe f; **~post** (BRIT) n réverbère m; **~shade** n abat-jour m inv

**lance** [lɑːns] vt (MED) inciser

**land** [lænd] n (as opposed to sea) terre f (ferme); (soil) terre; terrain m; (estate) terre(s), domaine(s) m(pl); (country) pays m ♦ vi (AVIAT) atterrir; (fig) (re)tomber ♦ vt (passengers, goods) débarquer; **to ~ sb with sth** (inf) coller qch à qn; **~ up** vi atterrir, (finir par) se retrouver; **~fill site** n décharge f; **~ing** n (AVIAT) atterrissage m; (of staircase)

palier m; (of troops) débarquement m; **~ing strip** n piste f d'atterrissage; **~lady** n propriétaire f, logeuse f; (of pub) patronne f; **~locked** adj sans littoral; **~lord** n propriétaire m, logeur m; (of pub etc) patron m; **~mark** (point m de) repère m; **to be a ~mark** (fig) faire date or époque; **~owner** n propriétaire foncier or terrien; **~scape** n paysage m; **~scape gardener** n jardinier(-ère) paysagiste; **~slide** n (GEO) glissement m (de terrain); (fig: POL) raz-de-marée (électoral)

**lane** [leɪn] n (in country) chemin m; (AUT) voie f; file f; (in race) couloir m; **"get in ~"** (AUT) "mettez-vous dans or sur la bonne file"

**language** ['læŋgwɪdʒ] n langue f; (way one speaks) langage m; **bad ~** grossièretés fpl, langage grossier; **~ laboratory** n laboratoire m de langues; **~ school** n école f de langues

**lank** [læŋk] adj (hair) raide et terne

**lanky** ['læŋkɪ] adj grand(e) et maigre, efflanqué(e)

**lantern** ['læntən] n lanterne f

**lap** [læp] n (of track) tour m (de piste); (of body): **in** or **on one's ~** sur les genoux ♦ vt (also: **~ up**) laper ♦ vi (waves) clapoter; **~ up** vt (fig) avaler, gober

**lapel** [lə'pel] n revers m

**Lapland** ['læplænd] n Laponie f

**lapse** [læps] n défaillance f; (in behaviour) écart m de conduite ♦ vi (LAW) cesser d'être en vigueur; (contract) expirer; **to ~ into bad habits** prendre de mauvaises habitudes; **~ of time** laps m de temps, intervalle m

**laptop (computer)** ['læptɒp(-)] n portable m

**larceny** ['lɑːsənɪ] n vol m

**larch** [lɑːtʃ] n mélèze m

**lard** [lɑːd] n saindoux m

**larder** ['lɑːdə*] n garde-manger m inv

**large** [lɑːdʒ] adj grand(e); (person, animal) gros(se); **at ~** (free) en liberté; (generally) en général; see also **by**; **~ly**

*adv* en grande partie; (*principally*) surtout; **~-scale** *adj* (*action*) d'envergure; (*map*) à grande échelle

**lark** [lɑːk] *n* (*bird*) alouette *f*; (*joke*) blague *f*, farce *f*

**laryngitis** [lærɪnˈdʒaɪtɪs] *n* laryngite *f*

**laser** [ˈleɪzəʳ] *n* laser *m*; **~ printer** *n* imprimante *f* laser

**lash** [læʃ] *n* coup *m* de fouet; (*also*: **eyelash**) cil *m* ♦ *vt* fouetter; (*tie*) attacher; **~ out** *vi*: to **~ out at** *or* **against** attaquer violemment

**lass** [læs] (*BRIT*) *n* (jeune) fille *f*

**lasso** [læˈsuː] *n* lasso *m*

**last** [lɑːst] *adj* dernier(-ère) ♦ *adv* en dernier; (*finally*) finalement ♦ *vi* durer; **~ week** la semaine dernière; **~ night** (*evening*) hier soir; (*night*) la nuit dernière; **at ~** enfin; **~ but one** avant-dernier(-ère); **~-ditch** *adj* (*attempt*) ultime, désespéré(e); **~ing** *adj* durable; **~ly** *adv* en dernier lieu, pour finir; **~-minute** *adj* de dernière minute

**latch** [lætʃ] *n* loquet *m*

**late** [leɪt] *adj* (*not on time*) en retard; (*far on in the day etc*) tardif(-ive); (*edition*, *delivery*) dernier(-ère); (*former*) ancien(ne) ♦ *adv* tard; (*behind time*, *schedule*) en retard; **of ~** dernièrement; **in ~ May** vers la fin (du mois) de mai, fin mai; **the ~ Mr X** feu M. X; **~comer** *n* retardataire *m/f*; **~ly** *adv* récemment; **~r** *adj* (*date etc*) ultérieur(e); (*version etc*) plus récent(e) ♦ *adv* plus tard; **~r on** plus tard; **~st** *adj* tout(e) dernier(-ère); **at the ~st** au plus tard

**lathe** [leɪð] *n* tour *m*

**lather** [ˈlɑːðəʳ] *n* mousse *f* (de savon) ♦ *vt* savonner

**Latin** [ˈlætɪn] *n* latin *m* ♦ *adj* latin(e); **~ America** *n* Amérique latine; **~ American** *adj* latino-américain(e)

**latitude** [ˈlætɪtjuːd] *n* latitude *f*

**latter** [ˈlætəʳ] *adj* deuxième, dernier (-ère) ♦ *n*: **the ~** ce dernier, celui-ci; **~ly** *adv* dernièrement, récemment

**laudable** [ˈlɔːdəbl] *adj* louable

**laugh** [lɑːf] *n* rire *m* ♦ *vi* rire; **~ at** *vt fus* se moquer de; rire de; **~ off** *vt* écarter par une plaisanterie or par une boutade; **~able** *adj* risible, ridicule; **~ing stock** *n*: the **~ing stock of** la risée de; **~ter** *n* rire *m*; rires *mpl*

**launch** [lɔːntʃ] *n* lancement *m*; (*motorboat*) vedette *f* ♦ *vt* lancer; **~ into** *vt fus* se lancer dans

**Launderette** ® [lɔːnˈdrɛt] (*BRIT*), **Laundromat** ® [ˈlɔːndrəmæt] (*US*) *n* laverie *f* (automatique)

**laundry** [ˈlɔːndrɪ] *n* (*clothes*) linge *m*; (*business*) blanchisserie *f*; (*room*) buanderie *f*

**laurel** [ˈlɔrl] *n* laurier *m*

**lava** [ˈlɑːvə] *n* lave *f*

**lavatory** [ˈlævətərɪ] *n* toilettes *fpl*

**lavender** [ˈlævəndəʳ] *n* lavande *f*

**lavish** [ˈlævɪʃ] *adj* (*amount*) copieux (-euse); (*person*): **~ with** prodigue de ♦ *vt*: to **~ sth on sb** prodiguer qch à qn; (*money*) dépenser qch sans compter pour qn/qch

**law** [lɔː] *n* loi *f*; (*science*) droit *m*; **~-abiding** *adj* respectueux(-euse) des lois; **~ and order** *n* l'ordre public; **~ court** *n* tribunal *m*, cour *f* de justice; **~ful** *adj* légal(e); **~less** *adj* (*action*) illégal(e)

**lawn** [lɔːn] *n* pelouse *f*; **~mower** *n* tondeuse *f* à gazon; **~ tennis** *n* tennis *m*

**law school** (*US*) *n* faculté *f* de droit

**lawsuit** [ˈlɔːsuːt] *n* procès *m*

**lawyer** [ˈlɔːjəʳ] *n* (*consultant, with company*) juriste *m*; (*for sales, wills etc*) notaire *m*; (*partner, in court*) avocat *m*

**lax** [læks] *adj* relâché(e)

**laxative** [ˈlæksətɪv] *n* laxatif *m*

**lay** [leɪ] (*pt, pp* **laid**) *pt of* **lie** ♦ *adj* laïque; (*not expert*) profane ♦ *vt* poser, mettre; (*eggs*) pondre; to **~ the table** mettre la table; **~ aside** *vt* mettre de côté; **~ by** *vt* = **lay aside**; **~ down** *vt* poser; to **~ down the law** faire la loi; to **~ down one's life** sacrifier sa vie;

**off** vt (workers) licencier; **~ on** vt (provide) fournir; **~ out** vt (display) disposer, étaler; abandon (inf) n fainéant(e); **~by** (BRIT) n aire f de stationnement (sur le bas-côté)

**layer** ['leɪə'] n couche f

**layman** ['leɪmən] n profane m

**layout** ['leɪaʊt] n disposition f, plan m, agencement m; (PRESS) mise f en page

**laze** [leɪz] vi (also: **~ about**) paresser

**lazy** ['leɪzɪ] adj paresseux(-euse)

**lb** abbr = **pound** (weight)

**lead¹** [liːd] (pt, pp led) n (distance, time ahead) avance f; (clue) piste f; (ELEC) fil m; (for dog) laisse f ♦ vt mener, conduire; (be ~er of) être à la tête de ♦ vi (street etc) mener, conduire; (SPORT) mener, être en tête; **in the ~** en tête; **to ~ the way** montrer le chemin; **~ away** vt emmener; **~ back** vt: **to ~ back to** ramener à; **~ on** vt (tease) faire marcher; **to ~ to** vt fus mener à; conduire à; **~ up to** vt fus conduire à

**lead²** [lɛd] n (metal) plomb m; (in pencil) mine f; **~-free petrol** n essence f au plomb; **~en** adj (sky, seq) de plomb

**leader** ['liːdə'] n chef m; dirigeant(e), leader m; (SPORT: in league) leader m; (: in race) coureur m de tête; **~ship** n direction f; (quality) qualités fpl de chef

**lead-free** ['lɛdfriː] adj (petrol) sans plomb

**leading** ['liːdɪŋ] adj principal(e); de premier plan; (in race) de tête; **~ lady** n (THEATRE) vedette (féminine); **~ light** n (person) vedette f, sommité f; **~ man** (irreg) n vedette (masculine)

**lead singer** [liːd-] n (in pop group) (chanteur m) vedette f

**leaf** [liːf] (pl **leaves**) n feuille f ♦ vi: **to ~ through** feuilleter; **to turn over a new ~** changer de conduite or d'existence

**leaflet** ['liːflɪt] n prospectus m, brochure f; (POL, REL) tract m

**league** [liːg] n ligue f; (FOOTBALL) cham-

pionnat m; **to be in ~ with** avoir partie liée avec, être de mèche avec

**leak** [liːk] n fuite f; (pipe, liquid etc) fuir; (shoes) prendre l'eau; (ship) faire eau ♦ vt (information) divulguer

**lean** [liːn] (pt, pp leaned or leant) adj maigre ♦ vt: **to ~ sth on sth** appuyer qch sur qch ♦ vi (slope) pencher; (rest): **to ~ against** s'appuyer contre; être appuyé(e) contre; **to ~ on** s'appuyer sur; **to ~ back/forward** se pencher en arrière/avant; **~ out** vi se pencher au dehors; **~ over** vi se pencher; **~ing** n: **~ing (towards)** tendance f (à), penchant m (pour); **~t** [lɛnt] pt, pp of **lean**

**leap** [liːp] (pt, pp leaped or leapt) n bond m, saut m ♦ vi bondir, sauter; **~frog** n saute-mouton m; **~t** [lɛpt] pt, pp of **leap**; **~ year** n année f bissextile

**learn** [ləːn] (pt, pp learned or learnt) vt, vi apprendre; **to ~ to do sth** apprendre à faire qch; **to ~ about or of sth** (hear, read) apprendre qch; **~ed** ['ləːnɪd] adj érudit(e), savant(e); **~er** (BRIT) n (also: **~er driver**) (conducteur (-trice)) débutant(e); **~ing** n (knowledge) savoir m; **~t** pt, pp of **learn**

**lease** [liːs] n bail m ♦ vt louer à bail

**leash** [liːʃ] n laisse f

**least** [liːst] adj: **the ~** (+noun) le (la) plus petit(e), le (la) moindre; (: smallest amount of) le moins de ♦ adv (+verb) le moins; (+adj): **the ~** le (la) moins; **at ~** au moins; (or rather) du moins; **not in the ~** pas le moins du monde

**leather** ['lɛðə'] n cuir m

**leave** [liːv] (pt, pp left) vt laisser; (go away from) quitter; (forget) oublier ♦ vi partir, s'en aller ♦ n (time off) congé m; (MIL also: consent) permission f; **to be left** rester; **there's some milk left over** il reste du lait; **on ~** en permission; **~ behind** vt (person, object) laisser; (forget) oublier; **~ out** vt oublier, omettre; **~ of absence** n congé exceptionnel; (MIL) permission spéciale

**leaves** [liːvz] npl of **leaf**

**Lebanon** ['lebənən] n Liban m

**lecherous** ['letʃərəs] (pej) adj lubrique

**lecture** ['lektʃər] n conférence f; (SCOL) cours m ♦ vi donner des cours; enseigner ♦ vt (scold) sermonner, réprimander; **to give a ~ on** faire une conférence sur; donner un cours sur; **~r** (BRIT) n (at university) professeur m (d'université)

**led** [led] pt, pp of **lead¹**

**ledge** [ledʒ] n (of window, on wall) rebord m; (of mountain) saillie f, corniche f

**ledger** ['ledʒər] n (COMM) registre m, grand livre

**leech** [liːtʃ] n (also fig) sangsue f

**leek** [liːk] n poireau m

**leer** [lɪər] vi: **to ~ at sb** regarder qn d'un air mauvais or concupiscent

**leeway** ['liːweɪ] n (fig): **to have some ~** avoir une certaine liberté d'action

**left** [left] pt, pp of **leave** ♦ adj (not right) gauche ♦ adv à gauche; **on the ~, to the ~** à gauche; **the L~** (POL) la gauche; **~-handed** adj gaucher(-ère); **~-hand side** n gauche f; **~-luggage locker** n (casier m à) consigne f automatique; **~-luggage (office)** (BRIT) n consigne f; **~overs** npl restes mpl; **~-wing** adj (POL) de gauche

**leg** [leg] n jambe f; (of animal) patte f; (of furniture) pied m; (CULIN: of chicken, pork) cuisse f; (: of lamb) gigot m; (of journey) étape f; **1st/2nd ~** (SPORT) match m aller/retour

**legacy** ['legəsɪ] n héritage m, legs m

**legal** ['liːgl] adj légal(e); **~ holiday** (US) n jour férié; **~ tender** n monnaie légale

**legend** ['ledʒənd] n légende f

**leggings** ['legɪŋz] npl caleçon m

**legible** ['ledʒəbl] adj lisible

**legislation** [ledʒɪs'leɪʃən] n législation f; **legislature** ['ledʒɪslətʃər] n (corps m) législatif

**legitimate** [lɪ'dʒɪtɪmət] adj légitime

**leg-room** ['legruːm] n place f pour les jambes

**leisure** ['leʒər] n loisir m, temps m libre; loisirs mpl; **at ~** (tout) à loisir; à tête reposée; **~ centre** n centre m de loisirs; **~ly** adj tranquille; fait(e) sans se presser

**lemon** ['lemən] n citron m; **~ade** [lemə'neɪd] n limonade f; **~ tea** n thé au citron

**lend** [lend] (pt, pp **lent**) vt: **to ~ sth (to sb)** prêter qch (à qn)

**length** [leŋθ] n longueur f; (section: of road, pipe etc) morceau m, bout m; (of time) durée f; **at ~** (at last) enfin, à la fin; (~ily) longuement; **~en** vt allonger, prolonger ♦ vi s'allonger; **~ways** adv dans le sens de la longueur, en long; **~y** adj (très) long (longue)

**lenient** ['liːnɪənt] adj indulgent(e), clément(e)

**lens** [lenz] n lentille f; (of spectacles) verre m; (of camera) objectif m

**Lent** [lent] n carême m

**lent** [lent] pt, pp of **lend**

**lentil** ['lentɪl] n lentille f

**Leo** ['liːəu] n le Lion

**leotard** ['liːətɑːd] n maillot m (de danseur etc), collant m

**leprosy** ['leprəsɪ] n lèpre f

**lesbian** ['lezbɪən] n lesbienne f

**less** [les] adj moins de ♦ pron, adv moins ♦ prep moins; **~ than that/you** moins que cela/vous; **~ than half** moins de la moitié; **~ than ever** moins que jamais; **~ and ~** de moins en moins; **the ~ he works ...** moins il travaille ...; **~en** vi diminuer, s'atténuer ♦ vt diminuer, réduire, atténuer; **~er** adj moindre; **to a ~er extent** à un degré moindre

**lesson** ['lesn] n leçon f; **to teach sb a ~** (fig) donner une bonne leçon à qn

**let** [let] (pt, pp **let**) vt laisser; (BRIT: lease) louer; **to ~ sb do sth** laisser qn faire qch; **to ~ sb know sth** faire savoir qch à qn, prévenir qn de qch; **~'s go** allons-y; **~ him come** qu'il vienne; **"to ~"** "à louer"; **~ down** vt (tyre) dégonfler; (person) décevoir, faire faux bond à; **~ go** vi lâcher prise ♦ vt lâcher; **~ in**

*vt* laisser entrer; (*visitor etc*) faire entrer; **~ off** *vt* (*culprit*) ne pas punir; (*firework etc*) faire partir; **~ on** (*inf*) *vi* dire; **~ out** *vt* laisser sortir; (*scream*) laisser échapper; **~ up** *vi* diminuer; (*cease*) s'arrêter

**lethal** ['liː·θl] *adj* mortel(le), fatal(e)

**letter** ['lɛtə*] *n* lettre *f*; **~ bomb** *n* lettre piégée; **~box** (*BRIT*) *n* boîte *f* aux or à lettres; **~ing** *n* lettres *fpl*; caractères *mpl*

**lettuce** ['lɛtɪs] *n* laitue *f*, salade *f*

**let-up** ['lɛtʌp] *n* répit *m*, arrêt *m*

**leukaemia** [luː'kiːmɪə] (*US* **leukemia**) *n* leucémie *f*

**level** ['lɛvl] *adj* plat(e), plan(e), uni(e); horizontal(e) ♦ *n* niveau *m* ♦ *vt* niveler, aplanir; **to be ~ with** être au même niveau que; **to draw ~ with** (*person, vehicle*) arriver à la hauteur de; **"A" ~s** (*BRIT*) ≈ baccalauréat *m*; **"O" ~s** ≈ B.E.P.C.; **on the ~** (*fig: honest*) régulier(-ère); **~ off** *vi* (*prices etc*) se stabiliser; **~ out** *vi* = **level off**; **~ crossing** (*BRIT*) *n* passage *m* à niveau; **~-headed** *adj* équilibré(e)

**lever** ['liːvə*] *n* levier *m*; **~age** *n*: **~age (on or with)** prise *f* (sur)

**levy** ['lɛvɪ] *n* taxe *f*, impôt *m* ♦ *vt* prélever, imposer; percevoir

**lewd** [luːd] *adj* obscène, lubrique

**liability** [laɪə'bɪlɪtɪ] *n* responsabilité *f*; (*handicap*) handicap *m*; **liabilities** *npl* (*on balance sheet*) passif *m*

**liable** ['laɪəbl] *adj* (*subject*): **~ to** sujet(te) à; passible de; (*responsible*): **~ (for)** responsable de(); (*likely*): **~ to do** susceptible de faire

**liaise** [liː'eɪz] *vi*: **to ~ (with)** assurer la liaison avec; **liaison** *n* liaison *f*

**liar** ['laɪə*] *n* menteur(-euse)

**libel** ['laɪbl] *n* diffamation *f*; (*document*) écrit *m* diffamatoire ♦ *vt* diffamer

**liberal** ['lɪbərl] *adj* libéral(e); (*generous*): **~ with** prodigue de, généreux(-euse) avec; **the L~ Democrats** le parti libéral-démocrate

**liberation** [lɪbə'reɪʃən] *n* libération *f*

**liberty** ['lɪbətɪ] *n* liberté *f*; **to be at ~ to do** être libre de faire

**Libra** ['liːbrə] *n* la Balance

**librarian** [laɪ'brɛərɪən] *n* bibliothécaire *m/f*

**library** ['laɪbrərɪ] *n* bibliothèque *f*

**libretto** [lɪ'brɛtəu] *n* livret *m*

**Libya** ['lɪbɪə] *n* Libye *f*

**lice** [laɪs] *npl of* **louse**

**licence** ['laɪsns] (*US* **license**) *n* autorisation *f*, permis *m*; (*RADIO, TV*) redevance *f*; **driving ~**, (*US*) **driver's license** permis *m* (de conduire); **~ number** *n* numéro *m* d'immatriculation; **~ plate** *n* plaque *f* minéralogique

**license** ['laɪsns] (*US*) *n* = **licence** ♦ *vt* donner une licence à; **~d** *adj* (*car*) muni(e) de la vignette; (*to sell alcohol*) patenté(e) pour la vente des spiritueux, qui a une licence de débit de boissons

**lick** [lɪk] *vt* lécher; (*inf: defeat*) écraser; **to ~ one's lips** (*fig*) se frotter les mains

**licorice** ['lɪkərɪs] (*US*) *n* = **liquorice**

**lid** [lɪd] *n* couvercle *m*; (*eyelid*) paupière *f*

**lie** [laɪ] (*pt* **lay**, *pp* **lain**) *vi* (*rest*) être étendu(e) or allongé(e) or couché(e); (*in grave*) être enterré(e), reposer; (*be situated*) se trouver, être; (*be untruthful: pt, pp* **~d**) mentir ♦ *n* mensonge *m*; **to ~ low** (*fig*) se cacher; **~ about** *vi* traîner; **~ around** *vi* = **lie about**; **~-down** (*BRIT*) *n*: **to have a ~-down** s'allonger, se reposer; **~-in** (*BRIT*) *n*: **to have a ~-in** faire la grasse matinée

**lieutenant** [lɛf'tɛnənt, (*US*) luː'tɛnənt] *n* lieutenant *m*

**life** [laɪf] (*pl* **lives**) *n* vie *f*; **to come to ~** (*fig*) s'animer; **~ assurance** (*BRIT*) *n* = **life insurance**; **~belt** (*BRIT*) *n* bouée *f* de sauvetage; **~boat** *n* canot *m* or chaloupe *f* de sauvetage; **~buoy** *n* bouée *f* de sauvetage; **~guard** *n* surveillant *m* de baignade; **~ insurance** *n* assurance-vie *f*; **~ jacket** *n* gilet *m* or ceinture *f* de sauvetage; **~less** *adj* sans vie, inanimé(e); (*dull*) qui manque de vie or de vigueur; **~like** adj qui semble vrai(e) or vivant(e); (painting) réaliste; **~long** adj de toute une vie, de toujours; **~ preserver** (US) n = **lifebelt**; **life jacket** n sauvetage m; **~-saving** n sauvetage m; **~-size(d)** adj grandeur nature inv; **~ span** n (durée f de) vie f; **~style** n style m or mode m de vie; **~-support system** n (MED) respirateur artificiel; **~time** n vie f; **in his ~time** de son vivant

**lift** [lɪft] vt soulever, lever; (end) supprimer, lever ♦ vi (fog) se lever ♦ n (BRIT: elevator) ascenseur m; **to give sb a ~** (BRIT: AUT) emmener or prendre qn en voiture; **~-off** n décollage m

**light** [laɪt] (pt, pp **lit**) n lumière f; (lamp) lampe f; (AUT: rear ~) feu m; (: headlight) phare m; (for cigarette etc): **have you got a ~?** avez-vous du feu?; **to ~** (candle, cigarette, fire) allumer; (room) éclairer ♦ adj (room, colour) clair(e); (not heavy) léger(-ère); (not strenuous) peu fatigant(e); **~s** npl (AUT: traffic ~s) feux mpl; **to come to ~** être dévoilé(e) or découvert(e); **~ up** vi (face) s'éclairer ♦ vt (illuminate) éclairer, illuminer; **~ bulb** n ampoule f; **~en** vt (make less heavy) alléger; **~er** n (also: **cigarette ~er**) briquet m; **~-headed** adj étourdi(e); (excited) grisé(e); **~-hearted** adj gai(e), joyeux(-euse), enjoué(e); **~house** n phare m; **~ing** n (on road) éclairage m; (in theatre) éclairages; **~ly** adv légèrement; **to get off ~ly** s'en tirer à bon compte; **~ness** n (in weight) légèreté f

**lightning** [ˈlaɪtnɪŋ] n éclair m, foudre f; **~ conductor** (US **lightning rod**) n paratonnerre m

**light pen** n crayon m optique

**lightweight** [ˈlaɪtweɪt] adj (suit) léger(-ère) n (BOXING) poids léger

**like** [laɪk] vt aimer (bien) ♦ prep comme ♦ adj semblable, pareil(le) ♦ n: **and the ~** et d'autres du même genre; **his ~s** 

and dislikes ses goûts mpl or préférences fpl; **I would ~, I'd ~** je voudrais, j'aimerais; **would you ~ a coffee?** voulez-vous du café?; **to be/look ~ sb/sth** ressembler à qn/qch; **what does it look ~?** de quoi est-ce que ça a l'air?; **what does it taste ~?** quel goût est-ce que ça a?; **that's just ~ him** c'est bien de lui, ça lui ressemble; **do it ~ this** fais-le comme ceci; **it's nothing ~ ...** ce n'est pas du tout comme ...; **~able** adj sympathique, agréable

**likelihood** [ˈlaɪklɪhʊd] n probabilité f

**likely** [ˈlaɪklɪ] adj probable; plausible; **he's ~ to leave** il va sûrement partir, il risque fort de partir; **not ~!** (inf) pas de danger!

**likeness** [ˈlaɪknɪs] n ressemblance f; **that's a good ~** c'est très ressemblant

**likewise** [ˈlaɪkwaɪz] adv de même, pareillement

**liking** [ˈlaɪkɪŋ] n (for person) affection f; (for thing) penchant m, goût m

**lilac** [ˈlaɪlək] n lilas m

**lily** [ˈlɪlɪ] n lis m; **~ of the valley** n muguet m

**limb** [lɪm] n membre m

**limber up** [ˈlɪmbəʳ-] vi se dégourdir, faire des exercices d'assouplissement

**limbo** [ˈlɪmbəʊ] n: **to be in ~** (fig) être tombé(e) dans l'oubli

**lime** [laɪm] n (tree) tilleul m; (fruit) lime f, citron vert; (GEO) chaux f

**limelight** [ˈlaɪmlaɪt] n: **in the ~** (fig) en vedette, au premier plan

**limerick** [ˈlɪmərɪk] n poème m humoristique (de 5 vers)

**limestone** [ˈlaɪmstəʊn] n pierre f à chaux; (GEO) calcaire m

**limit** [ˈlɪmɪt] n limite f ♦ vt limiter; **~ed** adj limité(e), restreint(e); **to be ~ed to** se limiter à, ne concerner que; **~ed (liability) company** (BRIT) n ≈ société f anonyme

**limousine** [ˈlɪməziːn] n limousine f

**limp** [lɪmp] n: **to have a ~** boiter ♦ vi

boiter ♦ adj mou (molle)

**limpet** ['lɪmpɪt] n patelle f

**line** [laɪn] n ligne f; (stroke) trait m; (wrinkle) ride f; (rope) corde f; (wire) fil m; (of poem) vers m; (row, series) rangée f; (of people) file f, queue f; (railway track) voie f; (COMM: series of goods) article(s) m(pl); (work) métier m, type m d'activité; (attitude, policy) position f ♦ vt (subj: trees, crowd) border; **in a ~** aligné(e); **in his ~ of business** dans sa partie, dans son rayon; **in ~ with** en accord avec; **to ~ (with)** (clothes) doubler (de); (box) garnir ou tapisser (de); **~ up** vi s'aligner, se mettre en rang(s) ♦ vt aligner; (event) prévoir, préparer; **~d** adj (face) ridé(e), marqué(e); (paper) réglé(e)

**linen** ['lɪnɪn] n linge m (de maison); (cloth) lin m

**liner** ['laɪnəʳ] n paquebot m (de ligne); (for bin) sac m à poubelle

**linesman** ['laɪnzmən] (irreg) n juge m de touche; (TENNIS) juge m de ligne

**line-up** ['laɪnʌp] n (US: queue) file f; (SPORT) composition f de l'équipe f

**linger** ['lɪŋgəʳ] vi s'attarder; traîner; (smell, tradition) persister

**linguist** ['lɪŋgwɪst] n: **to be a good ~** être doué(e) par les langues; **~ics** [lɪŋ'gwɪstɪks] n linguistique f

**lining** ['laɪnɪŋ] n doublure f

**link** [lɪŋk] n lien m, rapport m; (of a chain) maillon m ♦ vt relier, lier, unir; **~s** npl (GOLF) (terrain m de) golf m; **~ up** vt relier ♦ vi se rejoindre; s'associer

**lino** ['laɪnəu] n = **linoleum**

**linoleum** [lɪ'nəulɪəm] n linoléum m

**lion** ['laɪən] n lion m; **~ess** n lionne f

**lip** [lɪp] n lèvre f

**liposuction** ['lɪpəusʌkʃən] n liposuction f

**lip:** **~-read** vi lire sur les lèvres; **~ salve** n pommade f rosat ou pour les lèvres; **~ service** n: **to pay ~ service to sth** ne reconnaître le mérite de qch que pour la forme; **~stick** n rouge m à lèvres

**liqueur** [lɪ'kjuəʳ] n liqueur f

**liquid** ['lɪkwɪd] adj liquide ♦ n liquide m; **~ize** vt (CULIN) passer au mixer; **~izer** n mixer m

**liquor** ['lɪkəʳ] (US) n spiritueux m, alcool m

**liquorice** ['lɪkərɪs] (BRIT) n réglisse f

**liquor store** (US) n magasin m de vins et spiritueux

**lisp** [lɪsp] vi zézayer

**list** [lɪst] n liste f ♦ vt (write down) faire une ou la liste de; (mention) énumérer; **~ed building** (BRIT) n monument classé

**listen** ['lɪsn] vi écouter; **to ~ to** écouter; **~er** n auditeur(-trice)

**listless** ['lɪstlɪs] adj indolent(e), apathique

**lit** [lɪt] pt, pp of **light**

**liter** ['liːtəʳ] (US) n = **litre**

**literacy** ['lɪtərəsɪ] n degré m d'alphabétisation, fait m de savoir lire et écrire

**literal** ['lɪtərəl] adj littéral(e); **~ly** adv littéralement; (really) réellement

**literary** ['lɪtərərɪ] adj littéraire

**literate** ['lɪtərət] adj qui sait lire et écrire, instruit(e)

**literature** ['lɪtrɪtʃəʳ] n littérature f; (brochures etc) documentation f

**lithe** [laɪð] adj agile, souple

**litigation** [lɪtɪ'geɪʃən] n litige m; contentieux m

**litre** ['liːtəʳ] (US **liter**) n litre m

**litter** ['lɪtəʳ] n (rubbish) détritus mpl, ordures fpl; (young animals) portée f; **~ bin** (BRIT) n boîte f à ordures, poubelle f; **~ed** adj: **~ed with** jonché(e) de, couvert(e) de

**little** ['lɪtl] adj (small) petit(e) ♦ adv: **~ milk/time** peu de lait/temps; **a ~** un peu (de); **a ~ bit** un peu; **~ by ~** petit à petit, peu à peu

**live**[1] [laɪv] adj (animal) vivant(e), en vie; (wire) sous tension; (bullet, bomb) non explosé(e); (broadcast) en direct; (performance) en public

**live**[2] [lɪv] vi vivre; (reside) vivre, habiter; **~ down** vt faire oublier (avec le temps); **~ on** vt fus (food, salary) vivre de; **~ together** vi vivre ensemble, cohabiter; **~ up to** vt fus se montrer à la hauteur de

**livelihood** ['laɪvlɪhud] n moyens mpl d'existence

**lively** ['laɪvlɪ] adj vif (vive), plein(e) d'entrain; (place, book) vivant(e)

**liven up** ['laɪvn-] vt animer ♦ vi s'animer

**liver** ['lɪvər] n foie m

**lives** [laɪvz] npl of **life**

**livestock** ['laɪvstɔk] n bétail m, cheptel m

**livid** ['lɪvɪd] adj livide, blafard(e); (inf: furious) furieux(-euse), furibond(e)

**living** ['lɪvɪŋ] adj vivant(e), en vie ♦ n: **to earn** or **make a ~** gagner sa vie; **~ conditions** npl conditions fpl de vie; **~ room** n salle f de séjour; **~ standards** npl niveau m de vie; **~ wage** n salaire m permettant de vivre (décemment)

**lizard** ['lɪzəd] n lézard m

**load** [ləud] n (weight) poids m; (thing carried) chargement m, charge f ♦ vt (also: **~ up**): **to ~ (with)** charger (de); (gun, camera) charger (avec); (COMPUT) charger; **a ~ of**, **~s of** (fig) un or des tas de, des masses de; **to talk a ~ of rubbish** dire des bêtises; **~ed** adj (question) insidieux(-euse); (inf: rich) bourré(e) de fric

**loaf** [ləuf] (pl **loaves**) n pain m, miche f

**loan** [ləun] n prêt m ♦ vt prêter; **on ~** prêté(e), en prêt

**loath** [ləuθ] adj: **to be ~ to do** répugner à faire

**loathe** [ləuð] vt détester, avoir en horreur

**loaves** [ləuvz] npl of **loaf**

**lobby** ['lɔbɪ] n hall m, entrée f; (POL) groupe m de pression, lobby m ♦ vt faire pression sur

**lobster** ['lɔbstər] n homard m

**local** ['ləukl] adj local(e) ♦ n (BRIT: pub) pub m or café m du coin; **the ~s** npl (in-

habitants) les gens mpl du pays or du coin; **~ anaesthetic** n anesthésie locale; **~ authority** n collectivité locale, municipalité f; **~ call** n communication urbaine; **~ government** n administration locale or municipale; **~ity** [ləu'kælɪtɪ] n région f, environs mpl; (position) lieu m

**locate** [ləu'keɪt] vt (find) trouver, repérer; (situate): **to be ~d in** être situé(e) à or en; **location** n emplacement m; **on location** (CINEMA) en extérieur

**loch** [lɔx] n lac m, loch m

**lock** [lɔk] n (of door, box) serrure f; (of canal) écluse f; (of hair) mèche f, boucle f ♦ vt (with key) fermer à clé ♦ vi (door etc) fermer à clé; (wheels) se bloquer; **~ in** vt enfermer; **~ out** vt enfermer dehors; (deliberately) mettre à la porte; **~ up** vt (person) enfermer; (house) fermer à clé ♦ vi tout fermer (à clé)

**locker** ['lɔkər] n casier m; (in station) consigne f automatique

**locket** ['lɔkɪt] n médaillon m

**locksmith** ['lɔksmɪθ] n serrurier m

**lockup** ['lɔkʌp] n (prison) prison f

**locum** ['ləukəm] n (MED) suppléant(e) (de médecin)

**lodge** [lɔdʒ] n pavillon m (de gardien); (hunting ~) pavillon de chasse ♦ vi (person): **to ~ (with)** être logé(e) (chez), être en pension (chez); (bullet) se loger ♦ vt: **to ~ a complaint** porter plainte; **~r** n locataire m/f; (with meals) pensionnaire m/f; **lodgings** npl chambre f; meublé m

**loft** [lɔft] n grenier m

**lofty** ['lɔftɪ] adj (noble) noble, élevé(e); (haughty) hautain(e)

**log** [lɔg] n (of wood) bûche f; (book) = **logbook** ♦ vt (record) noter; **~book** n (NAUT) livre m or journal m de bord; (AVIAT) carnet m de vol; (of car) = carte grise

**loggerheads** ['lɔgəhedz] npl: **at ~ (with)** à couteaux tirés (avec)

**logic** ['lɔdʒɪk] n logique f; **~al** adj logique

**loin** [lwɛ̃] n (CULIN) filet m, longe f

**loiter** ['lɔɪtər] vi traîner

**loll** [lɔl] vi (also: ~ **about**) se prélasser, fainéanter

**lollipop** ['lɔlɪpɔp] n sucette f; ~ **man/lady** (BRIT: inf) n contractuel qui fait traverser la rue aux enfants

___

lollipop men/ladies

Les lollipop men/ladies sont employés pour aider les enfants à traverser la rue à proximité des écoles et à l'heure où ils entrent en classe et à la sortie. On les repère facilement à cause de leur long ciré blanc et ils portent une pancarte ronde pour faire signe aux automobilistes de s'arrêter. On les appelle ainsi car la forme circulaire de cette pancarte rappelle une sucette.

___

**lolly** ['lɔlɪ] (inf) n (lollipop) sucette f; (money) fric m

**London** ['lʌndən] n Londres m; **~er** n Londonien(ne)

**lone** [ləun] adj solitaire

**loneliness** ['ləunlɪnɪs] n solitude f, isolement m

**lonely** ['ləunlɪ] adj seul(e), isolé(e)

**long** [lɔŋ] adj (longue (longue)) ♦ adv longtemps ♦ vi: **to ~ for sth** avoir très envie de qch; attendre qch avec impatience; **so** or **as ~ as** pourvu que; **don't be ~!** dépêchez-vous!; **how ~ is this river/course?** quelle est la longueur de ce fleuve/la durée de ce cours?; **6 metres ~** (long) de 6 mètres; **6 months ~** qui dure 6 mois, de 6 mois; **all night ~** toute la nuit; **he no ~er comes** il ne vient plus; **they're no ~er going out together** ils ne sortent plus ensemble; **I can't stand it any ~er** je ne peux plus le supporter; **~ before/after** longtemps avant/après; **before ~** (+future) avant

peu, dans peu de temps; (+past) peu (de temps) après; **at ~ last** enfin; **~-distance** adj (call) interurbain(e); **~er** ['lɔŋgər] adv see **long**; **~hand** n écriture normale or courante; **~ing** n désir m, envie f, nostalgie f

**longitude** ['lɔŋgɪtjuːd] n longitude f

**long**: **~ jump** n saut m en longueur; **~-life** adj (batteries etc) longue durée inv; (milk) longue conservation; **~-lost** adj (person) perdu(e) de vue depuis longtemps; **~-range** adj à longue portée; **~-sighted** adj (MED) presbyte; **~-standing** adj de longue date; **~-suffering** adj empreint(e) d'une patience résignée; extrêmement patient(e); **~-term** adj à long terme; **~ wave** n grandes ondes; **~-winded** adj intarissable, interminable

**loo** [luː] (BRIT: inf) n W.-C. mpl, petit coin

**look** [luk] vi regarder; (seem) sembler, paraître, avoir l'air; (building etc): **to ~ south/(out) onto the sea** donner au sud/sur la mer ♦ n regard m; (appearance) air m, allure f, aspect m; **~s** npl (good ~s) physique m, beauté f; **to have a ~** regarder; **~! regardez!; ~ (here)!** (annoyance) écoutez!; **~ after** vt fus (care for, deal with) s'occuper de; **~ at** vt fus regarder; (problem etc) examiner; **~ back** vi: **to ~ back on** (event etc) évoquer, repenser à; **~ down on** vt fus (fig) regarder de haut, dédaigner; **~ for** vt fus chercher; **~ forward to** vt fus attendre avec impatience; **we ~ forward to hearing from you** (in letter) dans l'attente de vous lire; **~ into** vt fus examiner, étudier; **~ on** vi regarder (en spectateur); **~ out** vi (beware): **to ~ out (for)** prendre garde (à), faire attention (à); **~ out for** vt fus être à la recherche de; guetter; **~ round** vi regarder derrière soi, se retourner; **~ to** vt fus (rely on) compter sur; **~ up** vi lever les yeux; (improve) s'améliorer ♦ vt (word, name) chercher; **~ up to** vt fus

**loom** [luːm] vi (also: ~ up) surgir; (approach: event etc) être imminent(e); (threaten) menacer ♦ n (for weaving) métier m à tisser

**loony** ['luːnɪ] (inf) adj, n timbré(e), cinglé(e)

**loop** [luːp] n boucle f; ~hole n (fig) porte f de sortie; échappatoire f

**loose** [luːs] adj (knot, screw) desserré(e); (clothes) ample, lâche; (hair) dénoué(e), épars(e); (morals, discipline) relâché(e) ♦ n: **on the ~** en liberté; ~ **change** n petite monnaie; ~ **chippings** npl (on road) gravillons mpl; ~ **end** n: **to be at a ~ end** or (US) **at ~ ends** ne pas trop savoir quoi faire; ~**ly** adv sans serrer; (imprecisely) approximativement; ~**n** vt desserrer

**loot** [luːt] n (inf: money) pognon m, fric m ♦ vt piller

**lopsided** ['lɔp'saɪdɪd] adj de travers, asymétrique

**lord** [lɔːd] n seigneur m; **L~ Smith** lord Smith; **the L~** le Seigneur; **good L~!** mon Dieu!; **the (House of) L~s** (BRIT) la Chambre des lords; **my L~** or **your Lordship**; **L~ship** n: **your L~ship** Monsieur le comte/le baron/le juge; (to bishop) Monseigneur

**lore** [lɔː<sup>r</sup>] n tradition(s) f(pl)

**lorry** ['lɔrɪ] (BRIT) n camion m; ~ **driver** (BRIT) n camionneur m, routier m

**lose** [luːz] (pt, pp **lost**) vt, vi perdre; **to ~ (time)** (clock) retarder; **to get lost** ♦ vi se perdre; ~**r** n perdant(e)

**loss** [lɔs] n perte f; **to be at a ~** être perplexe or embarrassé(e)

**lost** [lɔst] pt, pp of **lose** ♦ adj perdu(e); ~ **and found** (US), ~ **property** n objets trouvés

**lot** [lɔt] n (set) lot m; **the ~** le tout; **a ~ (of)** beaucoup (de); ~**s of** des tas de; **to draw ~s (for sth)** tirer (qch) au sort

**lotion** ['ləuʃən] n lotion f

**lottery** ['lɔtərɪ] n loterie f

**loud** [laud] adj bruyant(e), sonore; (voice) fort(e); (support, condemnation) vigoureux(-euse); (gaudy) voyant(e), tapageur(-euse) ♦ adv (speak etc) fort; **out ~** tout haut; ~**hailer** n (BRIT) porte-voix m inv; ~**ly** adv fort, bruyamment; ~**speaker** n haut-parleur m

**lounge** [laundʒ] n salon m; (at airport) salle f; (BRIT: also: ~ **bar**) (salle de) café m or bar m ♦ vi (also: ~ **about** or **around**) se prélasser, paresser; ~ **suit** (BRIT) n complet m; (on invitation) "tenue de ville"

**louse** [laus] (pl **lice**) n pou m

**lousy** ['lauzɪ] (inf) adj infect(e), moche; **I feel ~** je suis mal fichu(e)

**lout** [laut] n rustre m, butor m

**lovable** ['lʌvəbl] adj adorable; très sympathique

**love** [lʌv] n amour m ♦ vt aimer; (caringly, kindly) aimer beaucoup; "~ (from) Anne" "affectueusement, Anne"; **I ~ chocolate** j'aime le chocolat; **to be/fall in ~ with** être/tomber amoureux(-euse) de; **to make ~** faire l'amour; **"15 ~"** (TENNIS) "15 à rien or zéro"; ~ **affair** n liaison (amoureuse); ~ **life** n vie sentimentale

**lovely** ['lʌvlɪ] adj (très) joli(e), ravissant(e); (delightful: person) charmant(e); (holiday etc) (très) agréable

**lover** ['lʌvə<sup>r</sup>] n amant m; (person in love) amoureux(-euse); (amateur): **a ~ of** un amateur de; une(e) amoureux (-euse) de

**loving** ['lʌvɪŋ] adj affectueux(-euse), tendre

**low** [lau] adj bas (basse); (quality) mauvais(e), inférieur(e); (person: depressed) déprimé(e); (: ill) bas (basse), affaibli(e) ♦ adv bas ♦ n (METEOROLOGY) dépression f; **to be ~ on** être à court de; **to feel ~** se sentir déprimé(e); **to reach an all-time ~** être au plus bas; ~**-alcohol** adj peu alcoolisé(e); ~**-calorie** adj hypoca-

lorique; **~-cut** adj (dress) décolleté(e);
**~er** adj inférieur(e) ♦ vt abaisser, baisser; **~er sixth** (BRIT) n (SCOL) première f; **~-fat** adj maigre; **~lands** npl (GEO) plaines fpl; **~ly** adj humble, modeste

**loyal** ['lɔɪəl] adj loyal(e), fidèle; **~ty** n loyauté f, fidélité f; **~ty card** n carte f de fidélité

**lozenge** ['lɔzɪndʒ] n (MED) pastille f

**LP** n abbr = **long-playing record**

**LPG** n abbr (AUT = liquefied petroleum gas) GPL m

**L-plates** ['elpleɪts] (BRIT) npl plaques fpl d'apprenti conducteur

---

**L-plates**

Les **L-plates** sont des carrés blancs portant un "L" rouge que l'on met à l'avant et à l'arrière de sa voiture pour montrer qu'on n'a pas encore son permis de conduire. Jusqu'à l'obtention du permis, l'apprenti conducteur a un permis provisoire et n'a le droit de conduire que si un conducteur qualifié est assis à côté de lui. Il est interdit aux apprentis conducteurs de circuler sur les autoroutes, même s'ils sont accompagnés.

---

**LRP** n abbr (AUT = lead replacement petrol) super m

**Ltd** abbr (= limited) ≈ S.A.

**lubricant** ['luːbrɪkənt] n lubrifiant m

**lubricate** ['luːbrɪkeɪt] vt lubrifier, graisser

**luck** [lʌk] n chance f; **bad ~** malchance f, malheur m; **bad** or **hard** or **tough ~!** pas de chance!; **good ~!** bonne chance!; **~ily** adv heureusement, par bonheur; **~y** adj (person) qui a de la chance; (coincidence, event) heureux(-euse); (object) porte-bonheur inv

**ludicrous** ['luːdɪkrəs] adj ridicule, absurde

**lug** [lʌg] (inf) vt traîner, tirer

**luggage** ['lʌgɪdʒ] n bagages mpl; **~ rack** n (on car) galerie f

**lukewarm** ['luːkwɔːm] adj tiède

**lull** [lʌl] n accalmie f; (in conversation) pause f ♦ vt: **to ~ sb to sleep** bercer qn pour qu'il s'endorme; **to be ~ed into a false sense of security** s'endormir dans une fausse sécurité

**lullaby** ['lʌləbaɪ] n berceuse f

**lumbago** [lʌm'beɪgəu] n lumbago m

**lumber** ['lʌmbər] n (wood) bois m de charpente; (junk) bric-à-brac m inv; **~jack** n bûcheron m

**luminous** ['luːmɪnəs] adj lumineux (-euse)

**lump** [lʌmp] n morceau m; (swelling) grosseur f ♦ vt: **to ~ together** réunir, mettre en tas; **~ sum** n somme globale ou forfaitaire; **~y** adj (sauce) avec des grumeaux; (bed) défoncé(e), peu confortable

**lunar** ['luːnər] adj lunaire

**lunatic** ['luːnətɪk] adj fou (folle), cinglé(e) (inf)

**lunch** [lʌntʃ] n déjeuner m

**luncheon** ['lʌntʃən] n déjeuner m (chic); **~ meat** n sorte de mortadelle; **~ voucher** (BRIT) n chèque-repas m

**lung** [lʌŋ] n poumon m

**lunge** [lʌndʒ] vi (also: **~ forward**) faire un mouvement brusque en avant; **to ~ at** envoyer ou assener un coup à

**lurch** [lɜːtʃ] vi vaciller, tituber ♦ n écart m brusque; **to leave sb in the ~** laisser qn en plan (inf)

**lure** [luər] n (attraction) attrait m, charme m ♦ vt attirer ou persuader par la ruse

**lurid** ['luərɪd] adj affreux(-euse), atroce; (pej: colour, dress) criard(e)

**lurk** [lɜːk] vi se tapir, se cacher

**luscious** ['lʌʃəs] adj succulent(e); appétissant(e)

**lush** [lʌʃ] adj luxuriant(e)

**lust** [lʌst] n (sexual) désir m; (fig): **~ for** soif f de; **~y** adj vigoureux(-euse), robuste

**Luxembourg** ['lʌksəmbəːg] n Luxembourg m

**luxurious** [lʌgˈzjuəriəs] *adj* luxueux (-euse)

**luxury** [ˈlʌkʃəri] *n* luxe *m* ♦ *cpd* de luxe

**lying** [ˈlaɪɪŋ] *n* mensonge(s) *m(pl)* ♦ *vb see* lie

**lyrical** [ˈlɪrɪkl] *adj* lyrique

**lyrics** [ˈlɪrɪks] *npl* (of song) paroles *fpl*

## M, m

**m.** *abbr* = **metre; mile; million**

**M.A.** *abbr* = **Master of Arts**

**mac** [mæk] (BRIT) *n* imper(méable) *m*

**macaroni** [mækəˈrəuni] *n* macaroni *mpl*

**machine** [məˈʃiːn] *n* machine *f* ♦ *vt* (TECH) façonner à la machine; (dress etc) coudre à la machine; **~ gun** *n* mitrailleuse *f*; **~ language** *n* (COMPUT) langage-machine *m*; **~ry** *n* machinerie *f*, machines *fpl*; (fig) mécanisme(s) *m(pl)*

**mackerel** [ˈmækrl] *n inv* maquereau *m*

**mackintosh** [ˈmækɪntɔʃ] (BRIT) *n* imperméable *m*

**mad** [mæd] *adj* fou (folle); (foolish) insensé(e); (angry) furieux(-euse); (keen): **to be ~ about** être fou (folle) de

**madam** [ˈmædəm] *n* madame *f*

**madden** [ˈmædn] *vt* exaspérer

**made** [meɪd] *pt, pp of* **make**

**Madeira** [məˈdɪərə] *n* (GEO) Madère *f*; (wine) madère *m*

**made-to-measure** [ˈmeɪdtəˈmeʒəʳ] (BRIT) *adj* fait(e) sur mesure

**madly** [ˈmædli] *adv* follement; **~ in love** éperdument amoureux(-euse)

**madman** [ˈmædmən] (irreg) *n* fou *m*

**madness** [ˈmædnɪs] *n* folie *f*

**magazine** [mægəˈziːn] *n* (PRESS) magazine *m*, revue *f*; (RADIO, TV: also: **~ programme**) magazine

**maggot** [ˈmægət] *n* ver *m*, asticot *m*

**magic** [ˈmædʒɪk] *n* magie *f* ♦ *adj* magique; **~al** *adj* magique; (experience, evening) merveilleux(-euse); **~ian** [məˈdʒɪʃən] *n* magicien(ne)

**magistrate** [ˈmædʒɪstreɪt] *n* magistrat *m*; juge *m*

**magnet** [ˈmægnɪt] *n* aimant *m*; **~ic** [mægˈnetɪk] *adj* magnétique

**magnificent** [mægˈnɪfɪsnt] *adj* superbe, magnifique; (splendid: robe, building) somptueux(-euse), magnifique

**magnify** [ˈmægnɪfaɪ] *vt* grossir; (sound) amplifier; **~ing glass** *n* loupe *f*

**magnitude** [ˈmægnɪtjuːd] *n* ampleur *f*

**magpie** [ˈmægpaɪ] *n* pie *f*

**mahogany** [məˈhɔgəni] *n* acajou *m*

**maid** [meɪd] *n* bonne *f*

**maiden** [ˈmeɪdn] *n(pl)* jeune fille *f* ♦ *adj* (aunt etc) non mariée; (speech, voyage) inaugural(e); **~ name** *n* nom *m* de jeune fille

**mail** [meɪl] *n* poste *f*; (letters) courrier *m* ♦ *vt* envoyer (par la poste); **~box** (US) *n* boîte *f* aux lettres; **~ing list** *n* liste *f* d'adresses; **~-order** *n* vente *f* or achat *m* par correspondance

**maim** [meɪm] *vt* mutiler

**main** [meɪn] *adj* principal(e) ♦ *n*: **the ~(s)** *n(pl)* (gas, water) conduite principale, canalisation *f*; **the ~s** *npl* (ELEC) le secteur; **the ~ thing** l'essentiel; **in the ~** dans l'ensemble; **~frame** *n* (COMPUT) unité centrale; **~land** *n* continent *m*; **~ly** *adv* principalement, surtout; **~ road** *n* grand-route *f*; **~stay** *n* (fig) pilier *m*; **~stream** *n* courant principal

**maintain** [meɪnˈteɪn] *vt* entretenir; (continue) maintenir; (affirm) soutenir; **maintenance** [ˈmeɪntənəns] *n* entretien *m*; (alimony) pension *f* alimentaire

**maize** [meɪz] *n* maïs *m*

**majestic** [məˈdʒestɪk] *adj* majestueux (-euse)

**majesty** [ˈmædʒɪsti] *n* majesté *f*

**major** [ˈmeɪdʒəʳ] *n* (MIL) commandant *m* ♦ *adj* (important) important(e); (most important) majeur(e); (MUS) majeur(e)

**Majorca** [məˈjɔːkə] *n* Majorque *f*

**majority** [məˈdʒɔrɪti] *n* majorité *f*

**make** [meɪk] (pt, pp **made**) *vt* faire; (manufacture) faire, fabriquer; (earn) gagner; (cause to be): to ~ sb sad etc rendre qn triste etc; (force): to ~ sb do sth obliger qn à faire qch, faire faire qch à qn; (equal): 2 and 2 ~ 4 2 et 2 font 4 ♦ n fabrication f; (brand) marque f; to ~ a fool of sb (ridicule) ridiculiser qn; (trick) duper qn; to ~ a profit faire un or des bénéfice(s); to ~ a loss essuyer une perte; to ~ it (arrive) arriver; (achieve sth) parvenir à qch, réussir; what time do you ~ it? quelle heure avez-vous?; to ~ do with se contenter de; se débrouiller avec; ~ for vt fus (place) se diriger vers; ~ out vt (write out: cheque) faire; (decipher) déchiffrer; (understand) comprendre; (see) distinguer; ~ up vt (constitute) constituer; (invent) inventer, imaginer; (parcel, bed) faire ♦ vi se réconcilier; (with cosmetics) se maquiller; ~ up for vt fus compenser; ~-believe n: it's just ~-believe (game) c'est pour faire semblant; (invention) c'est de l'invention pure; ~r n fabricant m; ~shift adj provisoire, improvisé(e); ~-up n maquillage m

**making** ['meɪkɪŋ] n (fig): in the ~ in formation or gestation; to have the ~s of (actor, athlete etc) avoir l'étoffe de

**malaria** [mə'leərɪə] n malaria f

**Malaysia** [mə'leɪzɪə] n Malaisie f

**male** [meɪl] n (BIO) mâle m ♦ adj mâle; (sex, attitude) masculin(e); (child etc) du sexe masculin

**malevolent** [mə'levələnt] adj malveillant(e)

**malfunction** [mæl'fʌŋkʃən] n fonctionnement défectueux

**malice** ['mælɪs] n méchanceté f, malveillance f; **malicious** [mə'lɪʃəs] adj méchant(e), malveillant(e)

**malignant** [mə'lɪgnənt] adj (MED) malin(-igne)

**mall** [mɔːl] n (also: **shopping ~**) centre commercial

**mallet** ['mælɪt] n maillet m

**malpractice** [mæl'præktɪs] n faute pro-

fessionnelle; négligence f

**malt** [mɔːlt] n malt m ♦ cpd (also: ~ whisky) pur malt

**Malta** ['mɔːltə] n Malte f

**mammal** ['mæml] n mammifère m

**mammoth** ['mæməθ] n mammouth m ♦ adj géant(e), monstre

**man** [mæn] (pl **men**) n homme m ♦ vt (NAUT: ship) garnir d'hommes; (MIL: gun) servir; (: post) être de service à; (machine) assurer le fonctionnement de; **an old** ~ un vieillard; ~ **and wife** mari et femme

**manage** ['mænɪdʒ] vi se débrouiller ♦ vt (be in charge of) s'occuper de; (: business etc) gérer; (control: ship) manier, manœuvrer; (: person) savoir s'y prendre avec; to ~ to do réussir à faire; ~**able** adj (task) faisable; (number) raisonnable; ~**ment** n gestion f, administration f, direction f; ~**r** n directeur m; administrateur m; (SPORT) manager m; (of artist) impresario m; ~**ress** [mænɪdʒə'res] n directrice f; gérante f; ~**rial** [mænɪ'dʒɪərɪəl] adj directorial(e); (skills) de cadre, de gestion; **managing director** n directeur général

**mandarin** ['mændərɪn] n (also: ~ **orange**) mandarine f; (person) mandarin m

**mandatory** ['mændətərɪ] adj obligatoire

**mane** [meɪn] n crinière f

**maneuver** [mə'nuːvə(r)] (US) vt, vi, n = **manoeuvre**

**manfully** ['mænfʊlɪ] adv vaillamment

**mangle** ['mæŋgl] vt déchiqueter; mutiler

**mango** ['mæŋgəʊ] (pl ~**es**) n mangue f

**mangy** ['meɪndʒɪ] adj galeux(-euse)

**man:** ~**handle** vt malmener; ~**hole** n trou m d'homme; ~**hood** n âge m d'homme, virilité f; ~**hour** n heure f de main-d'œuvre; ~**hunt** n (POLICE) chasse f à l'homme

**mania** ['meɪnɪə] n manie f; ~**c** ['meɪnɪæk] n maniaque m/f; (fig) fou (folle) m/f; **manic** ['mænɪk] adj maniaque

**manicure** ['mænɪkjuɐʳ] n manucure f

**manifest** ['mænɪfest] vt manifester ♦ adj manifeste, évident(e); **~o** [mænɪ'festəu] n manifeste m

**manipulate** [mə'nɪpjuleɪt] vt manipuler; (system, situation) exploiter

**man**: **~kind** [mæn'kaɪnd] n humanité f, genre humain; **~ly** adj viril(e); **~made** adj artificiel(le); (fibre) synthétique

**manner** ['mænəʳ] n manière f, façon f; (behaviour) attitude f, comportement m; (sort): **all ~ of** toutes sortes de; **~s** npl (behaviour) manières; **~ism** n particularité f de langage (or de comportement), tic m

**manoeuvre** [mə'nu:vəʳ] (US **maneuver**) vt (move) manœuvrer; (manipulate: person) manipuler; (: situation) exploiter ♦ vi manœuvrer ♦ n manœuvre f

**manor** ['mænəʳ] n (also: **~ house**) manoir m

**manpower** ['mænpauəʳ] n main-d'œuvre f

**mansion** ['mænʃən] n château m, manoir m

**manslaughter** ['mænslɔ:təʳ] n homicide m involontaire

**mantelpiece** ['mæntlpi:s] n cheminée f

**manual** ['mænjuəl] adj manuel(le) ♦ n manuel m

**manufacture** [mænju'fæktʃəʳ] vt fabriquer ♦ n fabrication f; **~r** n fabricant m

**manure** [mə'njuəʳ] n fumier m

**manuscript** ['mænjuskrɪpt] n manuscrit m

**many** ['mɛnɪ] adj beaucoup de, de nombreux(-euses) ♦ pron beaucoup, un grand nombre; **a great ~** un grand nombre (de); **~ a ...** bien des ..., plus d'un(e) ...

**map** [mæp] n carte f; (of town) plan m; **~ out** vt tracer; (task) planifier

**maple** ['meɪpl] n érable m

**mar** [mɑːʳ] vt gâcher, gâter

**marathon** ['mærəθən] n marathon m

**marble** ['mɑ:bl] n marbre m; (toy) bille f

**March** [mɑ:tʃ] n mars m

**march** [mɑ:tʃ] vi marcher au pas; (fig: protesters) défiler ♦ n marche f; (demonstration) manifestation f

**mare** [mɛəʳ] n jument f

**margarine** [mɑ:dʒə'ri:n] n margarine f

**margin** ['mɑ:dʒɪn] n marge f; **~al (seat)** n (POL) siège disputé

**marigold** ['mærɪgəuld] n souci m

**marijuana** [mærɪ'wɑ:nə] n marijuana f

**marina** [mə'ri:nə] n (harbour) marina f

**marine** [mə'ri:n] adj marin(e) ♦ n fusilier marin; (US) marine m

**marital** ['mærɪtl] adj matrimonial(e); **~ status** situation f de famille

**marjoram** ['mɑ:dʒərəm] n marjolaine f

**mark** [mɑ:k] n marque f; (of skid etc) trace f; (BRIT: SCOL) note f; (currency) mark m ♦ vt marquer; (stain) tacher; (BRIT: SCOL) noter; corriger; **to ~ time** marquer le pas; **~er** n (sign) jalon m; (bookmark) signet m

**market** ['mɑ:kɪt] n marché m ♦ vt (COMM) commercialiser; **~ garden** (BRIT) n jardin maraîcher; **~ing** n marketing m; **~place** n place f du marché; (COMM) marché m; **~ research** n étude f de marché

**marksman** ['mɑ:ksmən] (irreg) n tireur m d'élite

**marmalade** ['mɑ:məleɪd] n confiture f d'oranges

**maroon** [mə'ru:n] vt: **to be ~ed** être abandonné(e); (fig) être bloqué(e) ♦ adj bordeaux inv

**marquee** [mɑ:'ki:] n chapiteau m

**marriage** ['mærɪdʒ] n mariage m; **~ certificate** n extrait m d'acte de mariage

**married** ['mærɪd] adj marié(e); (life, love) conjugal(e)

**marrow** ['mærəu] n moelle f; (vegetable) courge f

**marry** ['mærɪ] vt épouser, se marier

avec; (*subj: father, priest etc*) marier ♦ *vi*
(*also:* **get married**) se marier
**Mars** [mɑːz] *n* (*planet*) Mars *f*
**marsh** [mɑːʃ] *n* marais *m*, marécage *m*
**marshal** ['mɑːʃl] *n* maréchal *m*; (*US: fire, police*) ≈ capitaine *m*; (*SPORT*) membre *m* du service d'ordre ♦ *vt* rassembler
**marshy** ['mɑːʃɪ] *adj* marécageux(-euse)
**martyr** ['mɑːtəʳ] *n* martyr(e); **~dom** *n* martyre *m*
**marvel** ['mɑːvl] *n* merveille *f* ♦ *vi:* to ~ (**at**) s'émerveiller (de); **~lous** (*US* **marvelous**) *adj* merveilleux(-euse)
**Marxist** ['mɑːksɪst] *adj* marxiste ♦ *n* marxiste *m/f*
**marzipan** ['mɑːzɪpæn] *n* pâte *f* d'amandes
**mascara** [mæs'kɑːrə] *n* mascara *m*
**masculine** ['mæskjulɪn] *adj* masculin(e)
**mash** [mæʃ] *vt* écraser, réduire en purée; **~ed potatoes** *npl* purée *f* de pommes de terre
**mask** [mɑːsk] *n* masque *m* ♦ *vt* masquer
**mason** ['meɪsn] *n* (*also:* **stonemason**) maçon *m*; (*also:* **freemason**) franc-maçon *m*; **~ry** *n* maçonnerie *f*
**masquerade** [mæskə'reɪd] *vi:* to ~ as se faire passer pour
**mass** [mæs] *n* multitude *f*, masse *f*; (*PHYSICS*) masse; (*REL*) messe *f* ♦ *cpd* (*communication*) de masse; (*unemployment*) massif(-ive) ♦ *vi* se masser; **the ~es** les masses; **~es of** des tas de
**massacre** ['mæsəkəʳ] *n* massacre *m*
**massage** ['mæsɑːʒ] *n* massage *m* ♦ *vt* masser
**massive** ['mæsɪv] *adj* énorme, massif (-ive)
**mass media** *n inv* mass-media *mpl*
**mass production** *n* fabrication *f* en série
**mast** [mɑːst] *n* mât *m*; (*RADIO*) pylône *m*
**master** ['mɑːstəʳ] *n* maître *m*; (*in secondary school*) professeur *m*; (*title for*

*boys*): **M~ X** Monsieur X ♦ *vt* maîtriser; (*learn*) apprendre à fond; **~ly** *adj* magistral(e); **~mind** *n* esprit supérieur ♦ *vt* diriger, être le cerveau de; **M~ of Arts/Science** *n* ≈ maîtrise *f* (en lettres/sciences); **~piece** *n* chef-d'œuvre *m*; **~plan** *n* stratégie *f* d'ensemble; **~y** *n* maîtrise *f*; connaissance parfaite
**mat** [mæt] *n* petit tapis; (*also:* **doormat**) paillasson *m*; (*also:* **tablemat**) napperon *m* ♦ *adj* = **matt**
**match** [mætʃ] *n* allumette *f*; (*game*) match *m*, partie *f*; (*fig*) égal(e) ♦ *vt* (*also:* ~ **up**) assortir; (*go well with*) aller bien avec, s'assortir à; (*equal*) égaler, valoir ♦ *vi* être assorti(e); **to be a good ~** être bien assorti(e); **~box** *n* boîte *f* d'allumettes; **~ing** *adj* assorti(e)
**mate** [meɪt] *n* (*inf*) copain (copine); (*animal*) partenaire *m/f*, mâle/femelle; (*in merchant navy*) second *m* ♦ *vi* s'accoupler
**material** [mə'tɪərɪəl] *n* (*substance*) matière *f*, matériau *m*; (*cloth*) tissu *m*, étoffe *f*; (*information, data*) données *fpl* ♦ *adj* matériel(le); (*relevant: evidence*) pertinent(e); **~s** *npl* (*equipment*) matériaux *mpl*
**maternal** [mə'tɜːnl] *adj* maternel(le)
**maternity** [mə'tɜːnɪtɪ] *n* maternité *f*; **~ dress** *n* robe *f* de grossesse; **~ hospital** *n* maternité *f*
**mathematical** [mæθə'mætɪkl] *adj* mathématique
**mathematics** [mæθə'mætɪks] *n* mathématiques *fpl*
**maths** [mæθs] (*US* **math**) *n* math(s) *fpl*
**matinée** ['mætɪneɪ] *n* matinée *f*
**mating call** *n* appel *m* du mâle
**matrices** ['meɪtrɪsiːz] *npl of* **matrix**
**matriculation** [mətrɪkju'leɪʃən] *n* inscription *f*
**matrimonial** [mætrɪ'məunɪəl] *adj* matrimonial(e), conjugal(e)
**matrimony** ['mætrɪmənɪ] *n* mariage *m*
**matrix** ['meɪtrɪks] (*pl* **matrices**) *n* ma-

trice f

**matron** ['meɪtrən] n (in hospital) infirmière-chef f; (in school) infirmière f

**mat(t)** [mæt] adj mat(e)

**matted** ['mætɪd] adj emmêlé(e)

**matter** ['mætər] n question f; (PHYSICS) matière f; (content) contenu m, fond m; (MED: pus) pus m ♦ vi importer; ~s npl (affairs, situation) la situation; **it doesn't ~** cela n'a pas d'importance; (I don't mind) cela ne fait rien; **what's the ~?** qu'est-ce qu'il y a?, qu'est-ce qui ne va pas?; **no ~ what** quoiqu'il arrive; **as a ~ of course** tout naturellement; **as a ~ of fact** en fait; **~-of-fact** adj (person, voice) neutre

**mattress** ['mætrɪs] n matelas m

**mature** [mə'tjuər] adj mûr(e); (wine) arrivé(e) à maturité ♦ vi (person) mûrir; (wine, cheese) se faire

**maul** [mɔːl] vt lacérer

**mauve** [məuv] adj mauve

**maximum** ['mæksɪməm] (pl **maxima**) adj maximum ♦ n maximum m

**May** [meɪ] n mai m; **~ Day** n le Premier Mai; see also **mayday**

**may** [meɪ] (conditional **might**) vi (indicating possibility): **he ~ come** il se peut qu'il vienne; (be allowed to): **~ I smoke?** puis-je fumer?; (wishes): **~ God bless you!** (que) Dieu vous bénisse!; **you ~ as well go** à votre place, je partirais

**maybe** ['meɪbiː] adv peut-être; **~ he'll ...** peut-être qu'il ...

**mayday** ['meɪdeɪ] n SOS m

**mayhem** ['meɪhem] n grabuge m

**mayonnaise** [meɪə'neɪz] n mayonnaise f

**mayor** [meər] n maire m; **~ess** n épouse f du maire

**maze** [meɪz] n labyrinthe m, dédale m

**M.D.** n abbr (= Doctor of Medicine) titre universitaire; = **managing director**

**me** [miː] pron me, m' +vowel; (stressed, after prep) moi; **he heard ~** il m'a entendu(e); **give ~ a book** donnez-moi

un livre; **after ~** après moi

**meadow** ['medəu] n prairie f, pré m

**meagre** ['miːgər] (US **meager**) adj maigre

**meal** [miːl] n repas m; (flour) farine f; **~time** n l'heure f du repas

**mean** [miːn] (pt, pp **meant**) adj (with money) avare, radin(e); (unkind) méchant(e); (shabby) misérable; (average) moyen(ne) ♦ vt signifier, vouloir dire; (refer to) faire allusion à, parler de; (intend): **to ~ to do** avoir l'intention de faire ♦ n moyenne f; **~s** npl (way, money) moyens mpl; **by ~s of** par l'intermédiaire de; au moyen de; **by all ~s!** je vous en prie!; **to be ~t for sb/sth** être destiné(e) à qn/qch; **do you ~ it?** vous êtes sérieux?; **what do you ~?** que voulez-vous dire?

**meander** [mɪ'ændər] vi faire des méandres

**meaning** ['miːnɪŋ] n signification f, sens m; **~ful** adj significatif(-ive); (relationship, occasion) important(e); **~less** adj dénué(e) de sens

**meanness** ['miːnnɪs] n (with money) avarice f; (unkindness) méchanceté f; (shabbiness) médiocrité f

**meant** [ment] pt, pp of **mean**

**meantime** ['miːntaɪm] adv (also: **in the ~**) pendant ce temps

**meanwhile** ['miːnwaɪl] adv = **meantime**

**measles** ['miːzlz] n rougeole f

**measure** ['meʒər] vt, vi mesurer ♦ n mesure f; (ruler) règle (graduée); **~ments** npl mesures fpl; **chest/hip ~ment(s)** tour m de poitrine/hanches

**meat** [miːt] n viande f; **~ball** n boulette f de viande

**Mecca** ['mekə] n La Mecque

**mechanic** [mɪ'kænɪk] n mécanicien m; **~al** adj mécanique ♦ **~s** n (PHYSICS) mécanique f ♦ npl (of reading, government etc) mécanisme m

**mechanism** ['mekənɪzəm] n mécanisme m

**medal** ['medl] n médaille f; **~lion** [mɪ'dælɪən] n médaillon m; **~list** n (SPORT) médaillé(e)

**meddle** ['medl] vi: **to ~ in** se mêler de, s'occuper de; **to ~ with** toucher à

**media** ['miːdɪə] npl media mpl

**mediaeval** [medɪ'iːvl] adj = **medieval**

**median** ['miːdɪən] (US) n (also: **~ strip**) bande médiane

**mediate** ['miːdɪeɪt] vi servir d'intermédiaire

**Medicaid** ® ['medɪkeɪd] (US) n assistance médicale aux indigents

**medical** ['medɪkl] adj médical(e) ♦ n visite médicale

**Medicare** ® ['medɪkɛəʳ] (US) n assistance médicale aux personnes âgées

**medication** [medɪ'keɪʃən] n (drugs) médicaments mpl

**medicine** ['medsɪn] n médecine f; (drug) médicament m

**medieval** [medɪ'iːvl] adj médiéval(e)

**mediocre** [miːdɪ'əʊkəʳ] adj médiocre

**meditate** ['medɪteɪt] vi méditer

**Mediterranean** [medɪtə'reɪnɪən] adj méditerranéen(ne); **the ~ (Sea)** la (mer) Méditerranée

**medium** ['miːdɪəm] (pl **media**) adj moyen(ne) ♦ n (means) moyen m; (pl **~s: person**) médium m; **the happy ~** le juste milieu; **~-sized** adj de taille moyenne; **~ wave** n ondes moyennes

**medley** ['medlɪ] n mélange m; (MUS) pot-pourri m

**meek** [miːk] adj doux (douce), humble

**meet** [miːt] (pt, pp **met**) vt rencontrer; (by arrangement) retrouver, rejoindre; (for the first time) faire la connaissance de; (go and fetch): **I'll ~ you at the station** j'irai te chercher à la gare; (opponent, danger) faire face à; (obligations) satisfaire à ♦ vi (friends) se rencontrer, se retrouver; (in session) se réunir; (join: lines, roads) se rejoindre; **~ with** vt fus rencontrer; **~ing** n rencontre f; (session: of club etc) réunion f; (POL) meeting m; **she's at a ~ing**

(COMM) elle est en conférence

**mega** ['mega] (inf) adv: **he's ~ rich** il est hyper-riche; **~byte** n (COMPUT) méga-octet m; **~phone** n porte-voix m inv

**melancholy** ['melənkəlɪ] n mélancolie f ♦ adj mélancolique

**mellow** ['meləʊ] adj velouté(e); doux (douce); (sound) mélodieux(-euse) ♦ vi (person) s'adoucir

**melody** ['melədɪ] n mélodie f

**melon** ['melən] n melon m

**melt** [melt] vi fondre ♦ vt faire fondre; (metal) fondre; **~ away** vi fondre complètement; **~ down** vt fondre; **~down** n fusion f (du cœur d'un réacteur nucléaire); **~ing pot** n (fig) creuset m

**member** ['membəʳ] n membre m; **M~ of Parliament** (BRIT) député m; **M~ of the European Parliament** Eurodéputé m; **~ship** n adhésion f; statut m de membre; (members) membres mpl, adhérents mpl; **~ship card** n carte f de membre

**memento** [mə'mentəʊ] n souvenir m

**memo** ['meməʊ] n note f (de service)

**memoirs** ['memwɑːz] npl mémoires mpl

**memorandum** [memə'rændəm] (pl **memoranda**) n note f (de service)

**memorial** [mɪ'mɔːrɪəl] n mémorial m ♦ adj commémoratif(-ive)

**memorize** ['meməraɪz] vt apprendre par cœur; retenir

**memory** ['memərɪ] n mémoire f; (recollection) souvenir m

**men** [mɛn] npl of **man**

**menace** ['menɪs] n menace f; (nuisance) plaie f ♦ vt menacer; **menacing** adj menaçant(e)

**mend** [mend] vt réparer; (darn) raccommoder, repriser ♦ n: **on the ~** en voie de guérison; **to ~ one's ways** s'amender; **~ing** n réparation f; (clothes) raccommodage m

**menial** ['miːnɪəl] adj subalterne

**meningitis** [menɪnˈdʒaɪtɪs] *n* méningite *f*

**menopause** [ˈmenəupɔːz] *n* ménopause *f*

**menstruation** [menstruˈeɪʃən] *n* menstruation *f*

**mental** [ˈmentl] *adj* mental(e); **~ity** [menˈtælɪtɪ] *n* mentalité *f*

**mention** [ˈmenʃən] *n* mention *f* ♦ *vt* mentionner, faire mention de; **don't ~ it!** je vous en prie, il n'y a pas de quoi!

**menu** [ˈmenjuː] *n* (*set ~, COMPUT*) menu *m*; (*list of dishes*) carte *f*

**MEP** *n abbr* = **Member of the European Parliament**

**mercenary** [ˈmɜːsɪnərɪ] *adj* intéressé(e), mercenaire ♦ *n* mercenaire *m*

**merchandise** [ˈmɜːtʃəndaɪz] *n* marchandises *fpl*

**merchant** [ˈmɜːtʃənt] *n* négociant *m*, marchand *m*; **~ bank** (*BRIT*) *n* banque *f* d'affaires; **~ navy** (*US* **merchant marine**) *n* marine marchande

**merciful** [ˈmɜːsɪful] *adj* miséricordieux(-euse), clément(e); **a ~ release** une délivrance

**merciless** [ˈmɜːsɪlɪs] *adj* impitoyable, sans pitié

**mercury** [ˈmɜːkjurɪ] *n* mercure *m*

**mercy** [ˈmɜːsɪ] *n* pitié *f*, indulgence *f*; (*REL*) miséricorde *f*; **at the ~ of** à la merci de

**mere** [mɪəʳ] *adj* simple; (*chance*) pur(e); **a ~ two hours** seulement deux heures; **~ly** *adv* simplement, purement

**merge** [mɜːdʒ] *vt* unir ♦ *vi* (*colours, shapes, sounds*) se mêler; (*roads*) se joindre; (*COMM*) fusionner; **~r** *n* (*COMM*) fusion *f*

**meringue** [məˈræŋ] *n* meringue *f*

**merit** [ˈmerɪt] *n* mérite *m*, valeur *f*

**mermaid** [ˈmɜːmeɪd] *n* sirène *f*

**merry** [ˈmerɪ] *adj* gai(e); **M~ Christmas!** Joyeux Noël!; **~-go-round** *n* manège *m*

**mesh** [meʃ] *n* maille *f*

**mesmerize** [ˈmezməraɪz] *vt* hypnoti-

ser; fasciner

**mess** [mes] *n* désordre *m*, fouillis *m*, pagaille *f*; (*muddle: of situation*) gâchis *m*; (*dirt*) saleté *f*; (*MIL*) mess *m*, cantine *f*; **~ about** (*inf*) *vi* perdre son temps; **~ about with** (*inf*) *vt* tripoter; **~ around** (*inf*) *vi* = **mess about**; **~ around with** *vt fus* = **mess about with**; **~ up** *vt* (*dirty*) salir; (*spoil*) gâcher

**message** [ˈmesɪdʒ] *n* message *m*; **messenger** [ˈmesɪndʒəʳ] *n* messager *m*

**Messrs** [ˈmesəz] *abbr* (*on letters*) MM

**messy** [ˈmesɪ] *adj* sale; en désordre

**met** [met] *pt, pp of* **meet**

**metal** [ˈmetl] *n* métal *m*; **~lic** [mɪˈtælɪk] *adj* métallique

**meteorology** [miːtɪəˈrɔlədʒɪ] *n* météorologie *f*

**meter** [ˈmiːtəʳ] *n* (*instrument*) compteur *m*; (*also:* **parking ~**) parcomètre *m*; (*US: unit*) = **metre**

**method** [ˈmeθəd] *n* méthode *f*; **~ical** [mɪˈθɔdɪkl] *adj* méthodique; **M~ist** *n* méthodiste *m/f*

**meths** [meθs] (*BRIT*), **methylated spirit** [ˈmeθɪleɪtɪd-] (*BRIT*) *n* alcool *m* à brûler

**metre** [ˈmiːtəʳ] (*US* **meter**) *n* mètre *m*; **metric** [ˈmetrɪk] *adj* métrique

**metropolitan** [metrəˈpɔlɪtn] *adj* métropolitain(e); **the M~ Police** (*BRIT*) la police londonienne

**mettle** [ˈmetl] *n*: **to be on one's ~** être d'attaque

**mew** [mjuː] *vi* (*cat*) miauler

**mews** [mjuːz] (*BRIT*) *n*: **~ cottage** *cottage aménagé dans une ancienne écurie*

**Mexico** [ˈmeksɪkəu] *n* Mexique *m*

**miaow** [miːˈau] *vi* miauler

**mice** [maɪs] *npl of* **mouse**

**micro** [ˈmaɪkrəu] *n* (*also:* **~computer**) micro-ordinateur *m*; **~chip** *n* puce *f*; **~phone** *n* microphone *m*; **~scope** *n* microscope *m*; **~wave** *n* (*also:* **~wave oven**) four *m* à micro-ondes

**mid** [mɪd] *adj*: **in ~ May** à la mi-mai; **in ~ afternoon** le milieu de l'après-midi; **in**

**~ air** en plein ciel; **~day** n midi m

**middle** ['mɪdl] n milieu m; (waist) taille f ♦ adj du milieu; (average) moyen(ne); **in the ~ of the night** au milieu de la nuit; **~-aged** adj d'un certain âge; **M~ Ages** npl: **the M~ Ages** le moyen âge; **~-class** adj ≃ bourgeois(e); **~ class(es)** n(pl): **the ~ class(es)** ≃ les classes moyennes; **M~ East** n Proche-Orient m, Moyen-Orient m; **~man** (irreg) n intermédiaire m; **~ name** n deuxième nom m; **~-of-the-road** adj (politician) modéré(e); (music) neutre; **~weight** n (BOXING) poids moyen; **middling** adj moyen(ne)

**midge** [mɪdʒ] n moucheron m

**midget** ['mɪdʒɪt] n nain(e)

**Midlands** ['mɪdləndz] npl comtés du centre de l'Angleterre

**midnight** ['mɪdnaɪt] n minuit m

**midriff** ['mɪdrɪf] n estomac m, taille f

**midst** [mɪdst] n: **in the ~ of** au milieu de

**mid** [mɪd-]: **~summer** [mɪd'sʌmər] n milieu m de l'été; **~way** [mɪd'weɪ] adj, adv: **~way (between)** à mi-chemin (entre); **~way through** ... au milieu de ..., en plein(e) ...; **~week** [mɪd'wiːk] adj au milieu de la semaine

**midwife** ['mɪdwaɪf] (pl **midwives**) n sage-femme f

**might** [maɪt] vb see **may** ♦ n puissance f, force f; **~y** adj puissant(e)

**migraine** ['miːgreɪn] n migraine f

**migrant** ['maɪgrənt] adj (bird) migrateur(-trice); (worker) saisonnier (-ère)

**migrate** [maɪ'greɪt] vi émigrer

**mike** [maɪk] n abbr (= microphone) micro m

**mild** [maɪld] adj doux (douce); (reproach, infection) léger(-ère); (illness) bénin(-igne); (interest) modéré(e); (taste) peu relevé(e) ♦ n (beer) bière légère; **~ly** adv doucement; légèrement; **to put it ~ly** c'est le moins qu'on puisse dire

**mile** [maɪl] n mi(l)le m (= 1609 m); **~age** n distance f en milles; ≃ kilométrage m; **~ometer** [maɪ'lɔmɪtər] n compteur m (kilométrique); **~stone** n borne f; (fig) jalon m

**militant** ['mɪlɪtnt] adj militant(e)

**military** ['mɪlɪtərɪ] adj militaire

**militia** [mɪ'lɪʃə] n milice(s) f(pl)

**milk** [mɪlk] n lait m ♦ vt (cow) traire; (fig: person) dépouiller, plumer; (: situation) exploiter à fond; **~ chocolate** n chocolat m au lait; **~man** (irreg) n laitier m; **~ shake** n milk-shake m; **~y** adj (drink) au lait; (colour) laiteux(-euse); **M~y Way** n voie lactée

**mill** [mɪl] n moulin m; (steel ~) aciérie f; (spinning ~) filature f; (flour ~) minoterie f ♦ vt moudre, broyer ♦ vi (also: **~ about**) grouiller; **~er** n meunier m

**millennium bug** [mɪ'lenɪəm-] n bogue m or bug m de l'an 2000

**milligram(me)** ['mɪlɪgræm] n milligramme m

**millimetre** ['mɪlɪmiːtər] (us **millimeter**) n millimètre m

**million** ['mɪljən] n million m; **~aire** n millionnaire m

**milometer** [maɪ'lɔmɪtər] n ≃ compteur m kilométrique

**mime** [maɪm] n mime m ♦ vt, vi mimer;

**mimic** ['mɪmɪk] n imitateur(-trice) ♦ vt imiter, contrefaire

**min.** abbr = **minute(s)**; **minimum**

**mince** [mɪns] vt hacher ♦ n (BRIT: CULIN) viande hachée, hachis m; **~meat** n (fruit) hachis de fruits secs utilisé en pâtisserie; (US: meat) viande hachée, hachis; **~ pie** n (sweet) sorte de tarte aux fruits secs; **~r** n hachoir m

**mind** [maɪnd] n esprit m ♦ vt (attend to, look after) s'occuper de; (be careful) faire attention à; (object to): **I don't ~ the noise** le bruit ne me dérange pas; **I don't ~** cela ne me dérange pas; **it is on my ~** cela me préoccupe; **to my ~** à mon avis or sens; **to be out of one's ~** ne plus avoir toute sa raison; **to**

keep or bear sth in ~ tenir compte de qch; **to make up one's ~** se décider; **~ you, ...** remarquez ...; **never ~** ça ne fait rien; (don't worry) ne vous en faites pas; **"~ the step"** "attention à la marche"; **~er** n (child-minder) gardienne f; (inf: baby-sitter) ange gardien (fig); **~ful** adj: **~ful of** attentif(-ive) à, soucieux(-euse) de; **~less** adj irréfléchi(e); (boring: job) idiot(e)

**mine¹** [maɪn] pron le (la) mien(ne), les miens (miennes) ♦ adj: **this book is ~** ce livre est à moi

**mine²** [maɪn] n mine f ♦ vt (coal) extraire; (ship, beach) miner; **~field** n champ m de mines; (fig) situation (très délicate); **~r** n mineur m

**mineral** ['mɪnərəl] adj minéral(e) ♦ n minéral m; **~s** npl (BRIT: soft drinks) boissons gazeuses; **~ water** n eau minérale

**mingle** ['mɪŋɡl] vi: **to ~ with** se mêler à

**miniature** ['mɪnɪtʃər] adj (en) miniature ♦ n miniature f

**minibus** ['mɪnɪbʌs] n minibus m

**minimal** ['mɪnɪml] adj minime

**minimize** ['mɪnɪmaɪz] vt (reduce) réduire au minimum; (play down) minimiser

**minimum** ['mɪnɪməm] (pl minima) adj, n minimum m

**mining** ['maɪnɪŋ] n exploitation minière

**miniskirt** ['mɪnɪskɜːt] n mini-jupe f

**minister** ['mɪnɪstər] n (BRIT: POL) ministre m; (REL) pasteur m ♦ vi: **to ~ to sb('s needs)** pourvoir aux besoins de qn; **~ial** [mɪnɪs'tɪərɪəl] (BRIT) adj (POL) ministériel(le); **ministry** n (BRIT: POL) ministère m; (REL): **to go into the ministry** devenir pasteur

**mink** [mɪŋk] n vison m

**minor** ['maɪnər] adj petit(e), de peu d'importance; (MUS, poet, problem) mineur(e) ♦ n (LAW) mineur/e

**minority** [maɪ'nɔrɪtɪ] n minorité f

**mint** [mɪnt] n (plant) menthe f; (sweet) bonbon m à la menthe ♦ vt (coins) bat-

tre; **the (Royal) M~,** (US) **the (US) M~** ≈ l'Hôtel m de la Monnaie; **in ~ condition** à l'état de neuf

**minus** ['maɪnəs] n (also: **~ sign**) signe m moins ♦ prep moins

**minute¹** [maɪ'njuːt] adj minuscule; (detail, search) minutieux(-euse)

**minute²** ['mɪnɪt] n minute f; **~s** npl (official record) procès-verbal, compte rendu

**miracle** ['mɪrəkl] n miracle m

**mirage** ['mɪrɑːʒ] n mirage m

**mirror** ['mɪrər] n miroir m, glace f; (in car) rétroviseur m

**mirth** [mɜːθ] n gaieté f

**misadventure** [mɪsəd'ventʃər] n mésaventure f

**misapprehension** ['mɪsæprɪ'henʃən] n malentendu m, méprise f

**misappropriate** [mɪsə'prəuprɪeɪt] vt détourner

**misbehave** [mɪsbɪ'heɪv] vi mal se conduire

**miscalculate** [mɪs'kælkjuleɪt] vt mal calculer

**miscarriage** ['mɪskærɪdʒ] n (MED) fausse couche f; **~ of justice** erreur f judiciaire

**miscellaneous** [mɪsɪ'leɪnɪəs] adj (items) divers(es); (selection) varié(e)

**mischief** ['mɪstʃɪf] n (naughtiness) sottises fpl; (fun) farce f; (playfulness) espièglerie f; (maliciousness) méchanceté f; **mischievous** ['mɪstʃɪvəs] adj (playful, naughty) coquin(e), espiègle

**misconception** ['mɪskən'sepʃən] n idée fausse

**misconduct** [mɪs'kɔndʌkt] n inconduite f; **professional ~** faute professionnelle

**misdemeanour** [mɪsdɪ'miːnər] (US **misdemeanor**) n écart m de conduite; infraction f

**miser** ['maɪzər] n avare m/f

**miserable** ['mɪzərəbl] adj (person, expression) malheureux(-euse); (conditions) misérable; (weather) maussade;

(offer, donation) minable; (failure) pitoyable

**miserly** ['maɪzəlɪ] adj avare

**misery** ['mɪzərɪ] n (unhappiness) tristesse f; (pain) souffrances fpl; (wretchedness) misère f

**misfire** [mɪs'faɪə˧] vi rater

**misfit** ['mɪsfɪt] n (person) inadapté(e)

**misfortune** [mɪs'fɔːtʃən] n malchance f, malheur m

**misgiving** [mɪs'gɪvɪŋ] n (apprehension) craintes fpl; **to have ~s about** avoir des doutes quant à

**misguided** [mɪs'gaɪdɪd] adj malavisé(e)

**mishandle** [mɪs'hændl] vt (mismanage) mal s'y prendre pour faire or résoudre etc

**mishap** ['mɪshæp] n mésaventure f

**misinform** [mɪsɪn'fɔːm] vt mal renseigner

**misinterpret** [mɪsɪn'təːprɪt] vt mal interpréter

**misjudge** [mɪs'dʒʌdʒ] vt méjuger

**mislay** [mɪs'leɪ] (irreg: like **lay**) vt égarer

**mislead** [mɪs'liːd] (irreg: like **lead**) vt induire en erreur; **~ing** adj trompeur(-euse)

**mismanage** [mɪs'mænɪdʒ] vt mal gérer

**misplace** [mɪs'pleɪs] vt égarer

**misprint** ['mɪsprɪnt] n faute f d'impression

**Miss** [mɪs] n Mademoiselle

**miss** [mɪs] vt (fail to get, attend, see) manquer, rater; (regret absence of): **I ~ him/it** il/cela me manque ♦ vi manquer ♦ n (shot) coup manqué; **~ out** (BRIT) vt oublier

**misshapen** [mɪs'ʃeɪpən] adj difforme

**missile** ['mɪsaɪl] n (MIL) missile m; (object thrown) projectile m

**missing** ['mɪsɪŋ] adj manquant(e); (after escape, disaster: person) disparu(e); **to go ~** disparaître; **to be ~** avoir disparu

**mission** ['mɪʃən] n mission f; **~ary** ['mɪʃənrɪ] n missionnaire m/f; **~ statement** n déclaration f d'intention

**mist** [mɪst] n brume f ♦ vi (also: **~ over**: eyes) s'embuer; **~ up** vi = **mist over**

**mistake** [mɪs'teɪk] (irreg: like **take**) n erreur f, faute f ♦ vt (meaning, remark) mal comprendre; se méprendre sur; **to make a ~** se tromper, faire une erreur; **by ~** par erreur, par inadvertance; **to ~ for** prendre pour; **~n** pp of **mistake** ♦ adj (idea etc) erroné(e); **to be ~n** faire erreur, se tromper

**mister** ['mɪstə˧] (inf) n Monsieur m; see also **Mr**

**mistletoe** ['mɪsltəʊ] n gui m

**mistook** [mɪs'tʊk] pt of **mistake**

**mistress** ['mɪstrɪs] n maîtresse f; (BRIT: in primary school) institutrice f; (: in secondary school) professeur m

**mistrust** [mɪs'trʌst] vt se méfier de

**misty** ['mɪstɪ] adj brumeux(-euse); (glasses, window) embué(e)

**misunderstand** [mɪsʌndə'stænd] (irreg) vt, vi mal comprendre; **~ing** n méprise f, malentendu m

**misuse** [n mɪs'juːs, vb mɪs'juːz] n mauvais emploi; (of power) abus m ♦ vt mal employer; abuser de; **~ of funds** détournement m de fonds

**mitigate** ['mɪtɪgeɪt] vt atténuer

**mitt(en)** ['mɪt(n)] n mitaine f; moufle f

**mix** [mɪks] vt (sauce, drink etc) préparer ♦ vi se mélanger; (socialize): **he doesn't ~ well** il est peu sociable ♦ n mélange m; **to ~ with** (people) fréquenter; **~ up** vt mélanger; (confuse) confondre; **~ed** adj (feelings, reactions) contradictoire; (salad) mélangé(e); (school, marriage) mixte; **~ed grill** n assortiment m de grillades; **~ed-up** adj (confused) désorienté(e), embrouillé(e); **~er** n (for food) batteur m, mixer m; (person): **he is a good ~er** il est très liant; **~ture** n assortiment m, mélange m; (MED) préparation f; **~-up** n confusion f

**MLA** (BRIT) n abbr (= Member of the Legislative Assembly) député m

**mm** abbr (= millimetre) mm

**moan** [məun] n gémissement m ♦ vi gémir; (inf: complain): **to ~ (about)** se plaindre (de)

**moat** [məut] n fossé m, douves fpl

**mob** [mɔb] n foule f; (disorderly) cohue f ♦ vt assaillir

**mobile** ['məubaɪl] adj mobile ♦ n mobile m; **~ home** n (grande) caravane; **~ phone** n téléphone portatif

**mock** [mɔk] vt ridiculiser; (laugh at) se moquer de ♦ adj faux (fausse); **~ exam** n examen blanc; **~ery** n moquerie f, raillerie f; **to make a ~ery of** tourner en dérision; **~-up** n maquette f

**mod** [mɔd] adj see **convenience**

**mode** [məud] n mode m

**model** ['mɔdl] n modèle m; (person: for fashion) mannequin m; (: for artist) modèle m ♦ vt (with clay etc) modeler ♦ vi travailler comme mannequin ♦ adj (railway: toy) modèle réduit inv; (child, factory) modèle; **to ~ clothes** présenter des vêtements; **to ~ o.s. on** imiter

**modem** ['məudem] n (COMPUT) modem m

**moderate** [adj 'mɔdərət, vb 'mɔdəreɪt] adj modéré(e); (amount, change) peu important(e) ♦ vi se calmer ♦ vt modérer

**modern** ['mɔdən] adj moderne; **~ize** vt moderniser

**modest** ['mɔdɪst] adj modeste; **~y** n modestie f

**modify** ['mɔdɪfaɪ] vt modifier

**mogul** ['məugl] n (fig) nabab m

**mohair** ['məuhɛər] n mohair m

**moist** [mɔɪst] adj humide, moite; **~en** vt humecter, mouiller légèrement; **~ure** n humidité f; **~urizer** n produit hydratant

**molar** ['məulər] n molaire f

**molasses** [mə'læsɪz] n mélasse f

**mold** [məuld] (US) n, vt = **mould**

**mole** [məul] n (animal, fig: spy) taupe f; (spot) grain m de beauté

**molest** [mə'lest] vt (harass) molester; (LAW: sexually) attenter à la pudeur de

**mollycoddle** ['mɔlɪkɔdl] vt chouchouter, couver

**molt** [məult] (US) vi = **moult**

**molten** ['məultən] adj fondu(e); (rock) en fusion

**mom** [mɔm] (US) n = **mum**

**moment** ['məumənt] n moment m, instant m; **at the ~** en ce moment; **at that ~** à ce moment-là; **~ary** adj momentané(e), passager(-ère); **~ous** [məu'mentəs] adj important(e), capital(e)

**momentum** [məu'mentəm] n élan m, vitesse acquise; (fig) dynamique f; **to gather ~** prendre de la vitesse

**mommy** ['mɔmɪ] (US) n maman f

**Monaco** ['mɔnəkəu] n Monaco m

**monarch** ['mɔnək] n monarque m; **~y** n monarchie f

**monastery** ['mɔnəstərɪ] n monastère m

**Monday** ['mʌndɪ] n lundi m

**monetary** ['mʌnɪtərɪ] adj monétaire

**money** ['mʌnɪ] n argent m; **to make ~** gagner de l'argent; **~ belt** n ceinture-portefeuille f; **~ order** n mandat m; **~-spinner** (inf) n mine f d'or (fig)

**mongrel** ['mʌŋɡrəl] n (dog) bâtard m

**monitor** ['mɔnɪtər] n (TV, COMPUT) moniteur m ♦ vt contrôler; (broadcast) être à l'écoute de; (progress) suivre (de près)

**monk** [mʌŋk] n moine m

**monkey** ['mʌŋkɪ] n singe m; **~ nut** (BRIT) n cacahuète f

**monopoly** [mə'nɔpəlɪ] n monopole m

**monotone** ['mɔnətəun] n ton m (or voix f) monocorde; **monotonous** [mə'nɔtənəs] adj monotone

**monsoon** [mɔn'suːn] n mousson f

**monster** ['mɔnstər] n monstre m; **monstrous** ['mɔnstrəs] adj monstrueux(-euse); (huge) gigantesque

**month** [mʌnθ] n mois m; **~ly** adj mensuel(le) ♦ adv mensuellement

**monument** ['mɔnjumənt] n monument m

**moo** [muː] vi meugler, beugler

**mood** [muːd] n humeur f, disposition f; **to be in a good/bad ~** être de bonne/mauvaise humeur; **~y** adj (variable) d'humeur changeante, lunatique; (sullen) morose, maussade

**moon** [muːn] n lune f; **~light** n clair m de lune; **~lighting** n travail m au noir; **~lit** adj: **a ~lit night** une nuit de lune

**moor** [muər] n lande f ♦ vt (ship) amarrer ♦ vi mouiller; **~land** n lande f

**moose** [muːs] n inv élan m

**mop** [mɔp] n balai m à laver; (for dishes) lavette f (à vaisselle) ♦ vt essuyer; **~ of hair** tignasse f; **~ up** vt éponger

**mope** [məup] vi avoir le cafard, se morfondre

**moped** ['məuped] n cyclomoteur m

**moral** ['mɔrl] adj moral(e) ♦ n morale f; **~s** npl (attitude, behaviour) moralité f

**morale** [mɔ'rɑːl] n moral m

**morality** [mə'ræliti] n moralité f

**morass** [mə'ræs] n marais m, marécage m

**more** [mɔːr] adj **1** (greater in number etc) plus (de), davantage; **more people/work (than)** plus de gens/de travail (que)

**2** (additional) encore (de); **do you want (some) more tea?** voulez-vous encore du thé?; **I have no or don't have any more money** je n'ai plus d'argent; **it'll take a few more weeks** ça prendra encore quelques semaines ♦ pron plus, davantage; **more than 10** plus de 10; **it cost more than we expected** cela a coûté plus que prévu; **I want more** j'en veux plus or davantage; **is there any more?** est-ce qu'il en reste?; **there's no more** il n'y en a plus; **a little more** un peu plus; **many/much more** beaucoup plus, bien davantage

♦ adv: **more dangerous/easily (than)** plus dangereux/facilement (que); **more and more expensive** de plus en plus

cher; **more or less** plus ou moins; **more than ever** plus que jamais

**moreover** [mɔː'rəuvər] adv de plus

**morning** ['mɔːnɪŋ] n matin m; matinée f ♦ cpd matinal(e); (paper) du matin; **in the ~** le matin; **7 o'clock in the ~** 7 heures du matin; **~ sickness** n nausées matinales

**Morocco** [mə'rɔkəu] n Maroc m

**moron** ['mɔːrɔn] n (inf) idiot(e)

**Morse** [mɔːs] n: **~ code** morse m

**morsel** ['mɔːsl] n bouchée f

**mortar** ['mɔːtər] n mortier m

**mortgage** ['mɔːɡɪdʒ] n hypothèque f; (loan) prêt m (or crédit m) hypothécaire ♦ vt hypothéquer; **~ company** (US) n société f de crédit immobilier

**mortuary** ['mɔːtjuərɪ] n morgue f

**mosaic** [məu'zeɪɪk] n mosaïque f

**Moscow** ['mɔskəu] n Moscou

**Moslem** ['mɔzləm] adj, n = **Muslim**

**mosque** [mɔsk] n mosquée f

**mosquito** [mɔs'kiːtəu] (pl **~es**) n moustique m

**moss** [mɔs] n mousse f

**most** [məust] adj la plupart de; le plus de ♦ pron la plupart ♦ adv le plus; (very) très, extrêmement; **the ~** (also: **+ adjective**) le plus; **~ of** la plus grande partie de; **~ of them** la plupart d'entre eux; **I saw (the) ~** j'en ai vu la plupart; c'est moi qui en ai vu le plus; **at the (very) ~** au plus; **to make the ~ of** profiter au maximum de; **~ly** adv (chiefly) surtout; (usually) généralement

**MOT** n abbr (BRIT: Ministry of Transport): **the MOT (test)** la visite technique (annuelle) obligatoire des véhicules à moteur

**motel** [məu'tel] n motel m

**moth** [mɔθ] n papillon m de nuit; (in clothes) mite f

**mother** ['mʌðər] n mère f ♦ vt (act as ~ to) servir de mère à; (pamper, protect) materner; **~ country** mère patrie; **~hood** n maternité f; **~-in-law** n belle-mère f; **~ly** adj maternel(le);

**of-pearl** n nacre f; **M~'s Day** n fête f des Mères; **~to-be** n future maman; **~ tongue** n langue maternelle

**motion** ['məʊʃən] n mouvement m; (gesture) geste m; (at meeting) motion f ♦ vt, vi: **to ~ (to) sb to do** faire signe à qn de faire; **~less** adj immobile, sans mouvement; **~ picture** n film m

**motivated** ['məʊtɪveɪtɪd] adj motivé(e); **motivation** [məʊtɪ'veɪʃən] n motivation f

**motive** ['məʊtɪv] n motif m, mobile m

**motley** ['mɒtlɪ] adj hétéroclite

**motor** ['məʊtər] n moteur m; (BRIT: inf: vehicle) auto f ♦ cpd (industry, vehicle) automobile; **~bike** n moto f; **~boat** n bateau m à moteur; **~car** (BRIT) n automobile f; **~cycle** n vélomoteur m; **~cycle racing** n course f de motos; **~cyclist** n motocycliste m/f; **~ing** (BRIT) n tourisme m automobile; **~ist** n automobiliste m/f; **~ mechanic** n mécanicien m garagiste; **~ racing** (BRIT) n course f automobile; **~way** (BRIT) n autoroute f

**mottled** ['mɒtld] adj tacheté(e), marbré(e)

**motto** ['mɒtəʊ] (pl **~es**) n devise f

**mould** [məʊld] (US **mold**) n moule m; (mildew) moisissure f ♦ vt mouler, modeler; (fig) façonner; **mo(u)ldy** adj moisi(e); (smell) de moisi

**moult** [məʊlt] (US **molt**) vi muer

**mound** [maʊnd] n monticule m, tertre m; (heap) monceau m, tas m

**mount** [maʊnt] n mont m, montagne f ♦ vt monter ♦ vi (inflation, tension) augmenter; (also: **~ up**: problems etc) s'accumuler; **~ up** vi (bills, costs, savings) s'accumuler

**mountain** ['maʊntɪn] n montagne f ♦ cpd de montagne; **~ bike** n VTT m, vélo tout-terrain; **~eer** [maʊntɪ'nɪər] n alpiniste m/f; **~eering** n alpinisme m; **~ous** adj montagneux(-euse); **~ rescue team** n équipe f de secours en montagne; **~side** n flanc m or versant

m de la montagne

**mourn** [mɔːn] vt pleurer ♦ vi: **to ~ (for)** (person) pleurer (la mort de); **~er** n parent(e) or ami(e) du défunt; personne f en deuil; **~ing** n deuil m; **in ~ing** en deuil

**mouse** [maʊs] (pl **mice**) n (also COMPUT) souris f; **~ mat** (COMPUT) tapis m de souris; **~trap** n souricière f

**mousse** [muːs] n mousse f

**moustache** [məs'tɑːʃ] (US **mustache**) n moustache(s) f(pl)

**mousy** ['maʊsɪ] adj (hair) d'un châtain terne

**mouth** [maʊθ] (pl **~s**) n bouche f; (of dog, cat) gueule f; (of river) embouchure f; (of hole, cave) ouverture f; **~ful** n bouchée f; **~ organ** n harmonica m; **~piece** n (of musical instrument) embouchure f; (spokesman) porte-parole m inv; **~wash** n eau f dentifrice; **~watering** adj qui met l'eau à la bouche

**movable** ['muːvəbl] adj mobile

**move** [muːv] n (~ment) mouvement m; (in game) coup m; (: turn to play) tour m; (change: of house) déménagement m; (: of job) changement m d'emploi ♦ vt déplacer, bouger; (emotionally) émouvoir; (POL: resolution etc) proposer; (in game) jouer ♦ vi (gen) bouger, remuer; (traffic) circuler; (also: **~ house**) déménager; (situation) progresser; **that was a good ~** bien joué; **to get a ~ on** se dépêcher, se remuer; **to ~ sb to do sth** pousser or inciter qn à faire qch; **~ about** vi (fidget) remuer; (travel) voyager, se déplacer; (change residence, job) ne pas rester au même endroit; **~ along** vi se pousser; **~ around** vi = **move about**; **~ away** vi s'en aller; **~ back** vi revenir, retourner; **~ forward** vi avancer; **~ in** vi (to a house) emménager; (police, soldiers) intervenir; **~ on** vi se remettre en route; **~ out** vi (of house) déménager; **~ over** vi se pousser, se déplacer; **~ up** vi (pupil) passer dans la classe supérieure; (*employee*) avoir de l'avancement; **~able** *adj* = **movable**

**movement** ['muːvmənt] *n* mouvement *m*

**movie** ['muːvɪ] *n* film *m*; **the ~s** le cinéma

**moving** ['muːvɪŋ] *adj* en mouvement; (*emotional*) émouvant(e)

**mow** [məʊ] (*pt* mowed, *pp* mowed *or* mown) *vt* faucher; (*lawn*) tondre; **~ down** *vt* faucher; **~er** *n* (*also:* **lawn-mower**) tondeuse *f* à gazon

**MP** *n abbr* = **Member of Parliament**

**mph** *abbr* = **miles per hour**

**Mr** ['mɪstə*] *n*: **~ Smith** Monsieur Smith, M. Smith

**Mrs** ['mɪsɪz] *n*: **~ Smith** Madame Smith, Mme Smith

**Ms** [mɪz] *n* (= **Miss** *or* **Mrs**): **~ Smith** Madame Smith, Mme Smith

**MSc** *abbr* = **Master of Science**

**MSP** [ɛmɛs'piː] *n abbr* = **Member of the Scottish Parliament**

**much** [mʌtʃ] *adj* beaucoup de ♦ *adv*, *n*, *pron* beaucoup; **how ~ is it?** combien est-ce que ça coûte?; **too ~** trop (de); **as ~ as** autant de

**muck** [mʌk] *n* (*dirt*) saleté *f*; **~ about** *or* **around** (*inf*) *vi* faire l'imbécile; **~ up** (*inf*) *vt* (*exam, interview*) se planter à (*fam*); **~y** *adj* (*very*) sale

**mud** [mʌd] *n* boue *f*

**muddle** ['mʌdl] *n* (*mess*) pagaille *f*, désordre *m*; (*mix-up*) confusion *f* ♦ *vt* (*also:* **~ up**) embrouiller; **~ through** *vi* se débrouiller

**muddy** ['mʌdɪ] *adj* boueux(-euse)

**mudguard** ['mʌdgɑːd] *n* garde-boue *m inv*

**muesli** ['mjuːzlɪ] *n* muesli *m*

**muffin** ['mʌfɪn] *n* muffin *m*

**muffle** ['mʌfl] *vt* (*sound*) assourdir, étouffer; (*against cold*) emmitoufler; **~d** *adj* (*sound*) étouffé(e); **~r** *n* (*US*) (*AUT*) silencieux *m*

**mug** [mʌg] *n* (*cup*) grande tasse (*sans*

soucoupe); (: *for beer*) chope *f*; (*inf*: *face*) bouille *f*; (: *fool*) poire *f* ♦ *vt* (*assault*) agresser; **~ger** *n* agresseur *m*, **~ging** *n* agression *f*

**muggy** ['mʌgɪ] *adj* lourd(e), moite

**mule** [mjuːl] *n* mule *f*

**multi-level** ['mʌltɪlɛvl] (*US*) *adj* = **multistorey**

**multiple** ['mʌltɪpl] *adj* multiple ♦ *n* multiple *m*; **~ sclerosis** [-sklɪ'rəʊsɪs] *n* sclérose *f* en plaques

**multiplex cinema** [mʌltɪplɛks-] *n* cinéma *m* multisalles

**multiplication** [mʌltɪplɪ'keɪʃən] *n* multiplication *f*; **multiply** ['mʌltɪplaɪ] *vt* multiplier ♦ *vi* se multiplier

**multistorey** ['mʌltɪ'stɔːrɪ] (*BRIT*) *adj* (*building*) à étages; (*car park*) à étages *or* niveaux multiples ♦ *n* (*car park*) parking *m* à plusieurs étages

**mum** [mʌm] (*BRIT*: *inf*) *n* maman *f* ♦ *adj*: **to keep ~** ne pas souffler mot

**mumble** ['mʌmbl] *vt, vi* marmotter, marmonner

**mummy** ['mʌmɪ] *n* (*BRIT*: *mother*) maman *f*; (*embalmed*) momie *f*

**mumps** [mʌmps] *n* oreillons *mpl*

**munch** [mʌntʃ] *vt, vi* mâcher

**mundane** [mʌn'deɪn] *adj* banal(e), terre à terre *inv*

**municipal** [mjuː'nɪsɪpl] *adj* municipal(e)

**murder** ['mɜːdə*] *n* meurtre *m*, assassinat *m* ♦ *vt* assassiner; **~er** *n* meurtrier *m*, assassin *m*; **~ous** ['mɜːdərəs] *adj* meurtrier(-ère)

**murky** ['mɜːkɪ] *adj* sombre, ténébreux(-euse); (*water*) trouble

**murmur** ['mɜːmə*] *n* murmure *m* ♦ *vt, vi* murmurer

**muscle** ['mʌsl] *n* muscle *m*; (*fig*) force *f*; **~ in** *vi* (*on territory*) envahir; (*on success*) exploiter; **muscular** ['mʌskjulə*] *adj* musculaire; (*person, arm*) musclé(e)

**muse** [mjuːz] *vi* méditer, songer

**museum** [mjuː'zɪəm] *n* musée *m*

**mushroom** ['mʌʃrum] *n* champignon *m* ♦ *vi* pousser comme un champignon

**music** ['mjuːzɪk] n musique f; **~al** adj musical(e); (person) musicien(ne) ♦ n (show) comédie musicale; **~al instrument** n instrument m de musique; **~centre** n chaîne compacte; **~ian** [mjuːˈzɪʃən] n musicien(ne)

**Muslim** ['mʌzlɪm] adj, n musulman(e)

**muslin** ['mʌzlɪn] n mousseline f

**mussel** ['mʌsl] n moule f

**must** [mʌst] aux vb (obligation): **I ~ do it** je dois le faire, il faut que je le fasse; (probability): **he ~ be there by now** il doit y être maintenant, il est probablement maintenant; (suggestion, invitation): **you ~ come and see me** il faut que vous veniez me voir; (indicating sth unwelcome): **why ~ he behave so badly?** qu'est-ce qui le pousse à se conduire si mal? ♦ n nécessité f, impératif m; **it's a ~** c'est indispensable

**mustache** ['mʌstæʃ] (US) n = **moustache**

**mustard** ['mʌstəd] n moutarde f

**muster** ['mʌstə*] vt rassembler

**mustn't** ['mʌsnt] = **must not**

**mute** [mjuːt] adj muet(te); **~d** adj (colour) sourd(e); (reaction) voilé(e)

**mutiny** ['mjuːtɪnɪ] n mutinerie f ♦ vi se mutiner

**mutter** ['mʌtə*] vt, vi marmonner, marmotter

**mutton** ['mʌtn] n mouton m

**mutual** ['mjuːtʃuəl] adj mutuel(le), réciproque; (benefit, interest) commun(e); **~ly** adv mutuellement

**muzzle** ['mʌzl] n museau m; (protective device) muselière f; (of gun) gueule f ♦ vt museler

**my** [maɪ] adj mon(ma), mes pl; **~ house/car/gloves** ma maison/mon auto/mes gants; **I've washed ~ hair/cut ~ finger** je me suis lavé les cheveux/coupé le doigt; **~self** [maɪˈself] pron (reflexive) me; (emphatic) moi-même; (after prep) moi; see also **oneself**

**mysterious** [mɪsˈtɪərɪəs] adj mysté-

rieux(-euse)

**mystery** ['mɪstərɪ] n mystère m

**mystify** ['mɪstɪfaɪ] vt mystifier; (puzzle) ébahir

**myth** [mɪθ] n mythe m; **~ology** [mɪˈθɒlədʒɪ] n mythologie f

# N, n

**n/a** abbr = **not applicable**

**naff** [næf] (BRIT: inf) adj nul(le)

**nag** [næg] vt (scold) être toujours après, reprendre sans arrêt; **~ging** adj (doubt, pain) persistant(e)

**nail** [neɪl] n (human) ongle m; (metal) clou m ♦ vt clouer; **to ~ sb down to a date/price** contraindre qn à accepter or donner une date/un prix; **~brush** n brosse f à ongles; **~file** n lime f à ongles; **~ polish** n vernis m à ongles; **~ polish remover** n dissolvant m; **~ scissors** npl ciseaux mpl à ongles; **~ varnish** (BRIT) n = **nail polish**

**naïve** [naɪˈiːv] adj naïf(-ive)

**naked** ['neɪkɪd] adj nu(e)

**name** [neɪm] n nom m; (reputation) réputation f ♦ vt nommer; (identify: accomplice etc) citer; (price, date) fixer, donner; **by ~** par son nom; **in the ~ of** au nom de; **what's your ~?** comment vous appelez-vous?; **~less** adj sans nom; (witness, contributor) anonyme; **~ly** adv à savoir; **~sake** n homonyme

**nanny** ['nænɪ] n bonne f d'enfants

**nap** [næp] n (sleep) (petit) somme ♦ vi: **to be caught ~ping** être pris à l'improviste or en défaut

**nape** [neɪp] n: **~ of the neck** nuque f

**napkin** ['næpkɪn] n serviette f (de table)

**nappy** ['næpɪ] (BRIT) n couche f (gen pl); **~ rash** n: **to have ~ rash** avoir les fesses rouges

**narcissus** [naːˈsɪsəs] (pl **narcissi**) n narcisse m

**narcotic** ['nɑ:'kɔtɪk] n (drug) stupéfiant m; (MED) narcotique m

**narrative** ['nærətɪv] n récit m

**narrow** ['nærəʊ] adj étroit(e); (fig) restreint(e), limité(e) ♦ vi (road) devenir plus étroit, se rétrécir; (gap, difference) se réduire; **to have a ~ escape** l'échapper belle; **to ~ sth down to** réduire qch à; **~ly** adv: **he ~ly missed injury/the tree** il a failli se blesser/rentrer dans l'arbre; **~-minded** adj à l'esprit étroit, borné(e); (attitude) borné(e)

**nasty** ['nɑ:stɪ] adj (person: malicious) méchant(e); (: rude) très désagréable; (smell) dégoûtant(e); (wound, situation, disease) mauvais(e)

**nation** ['neɪʃən] n nation f

**national** ['næʃənl] adj national(e) ♦ n (abroad) ressortissant(e); (when home) national(e); **~ anthem** n hymne national; **~ dress** n costume national; **N~ Health Service** (BRIT) n service national de santé; ≈ Sécurité Sociale; **N~ Insurance** (BRIT) n ≈ Sécurité Sociale; **~ism** n nationalisme m; **~ist** adj nationaliste ♦ n nationaliste m/f; **~ity** [næʃə'nælɪtɪ] n nationalité f; **~ize** vt nationaliser; **~ly** adv (as a nation) du point de vue national; (nationwide) dans le pays entier; **~ park** n parc national

---

**National Trust**

Le **National Trust** est un organisme indépendant, à but non lucratif, dont la mission est de protéger et de mettre en valeur les monuments et les sites britanniques en raison de leur intérêt historique ou de leur beauté naturelle.

---

**nationwide** ['neɪʃənwaɪd] adj s'étendant à l'ensemble du pays; (problem) à l'échelle du pays entier ♦ adv à travers or dans tout le pays

**native** ['neɪtɪv] n autochtone m/f, habitant(e) du pays ♦ adj du pays, indigène; (country) natal(e); (ability) inné(e); **a ~**

**of Russia** une personne originaire de Russie; **a ~ speaker of French** une personne de langue maternelle française; **N~ American** n Indien(ne) d'Amérique; **~ language** n langue maternelle

**NATO** ['neɪtəʊ] n abbr (= North Atlantic Treaty Organization) OTAN f

**natural** ['nætʃrəl] adj naturel(le); **~ gas** n gaz naturel; **~ist** n naturaliste m/f; **~ly** adv naturellement

**nature** ['neɪtʃəʳ] n nature f; **by ~** par tempérament, de nature

**naught** [nɔ:t] n = **nought**

**naughty** ['nɔ:tɪ] adj (child) vilain(e), pas sage

**nausea** ['nɔ:sɪə] n nausée f

**naval** ['neɪvl] adj naval(e); **~ officer** n officier m de marine

**nave** [neɪv] n nef f

**navel** ['neɪvl] n nombril m

**navigate** ['nævɪgeɪt] vt (steer) diriger; (plot course) naviguer ♦ vi naviguer; **navigation** [nævɪ'geɪʃən] n navigation f

**navvy** ['nævɪ] (BRIT) n terrassier m

**navy** ['neɪvɪ] n marine f; **~(-blue)** adj bleu marine inv

**Nazi** ['nɑ:tsɪ] n Nazi(e)

**NB** abbr (= nota bene) NB

**near** [nɪəʳ] adj proche ♦ adv près ♦ prep (also: **~ to**) près de ♦ vt approcher de; **~by** [nɪə'baɪ] adj proche ♦ adv tout près, à proximité; **~ly** adv presque; **I ~ly fell** j'ai failli tomber; **~ miss** n (AVIAT) quasi-collision f; **that was a ~ miss** (gen) on s'en est fallu de peu; (of shot) c'est passé très près; **~side** n (AUT: in Britain) côté m gauche; (: in US, Europe etc) côté droit; **~-sighted** adj myope

**neat** [ni:t] adj (person, work) soigné(e); (room etc) bien tenu(e) or rangé(e); (skilful) habile; (spirits) pur(e); **~ly** adv avec soin or ordre; habilement

**necessarily** ['nesɪsrɪlɪ] adv nécessairement

**necessary** ['nesɪsrɪ] adj nécessaire; **ne-**

**cessity** [nɪˈsesɪtɪ] n nécessité f; (*thing needed*) chose nécessaire or essentielle; **necessities** npl nécessaire m

**neck** [nek] n cou m; (*of animal, garment*) encolure f; (*of bottle*) goulot m ♦ vi (*inf*) se peloter; **~ and ~** à égalité; **~lace** n collier m; **~line** n encolure f; **~tie** n cravate f

**need** [ni:d] n besoin m ♦ vt avoir besoin de; **to ~** to devoir faire; avoir besoin de faire; **you don't ~ to go** vous n'avez pas besoin or vous n'êtes pas obligé de partir

**needle** [ni:dl] n aiguille f ♦ vt asticoter, tourmenter

**needless** [ni:dlɪs] adj inutile

**needlework** [ni:dlwə:k] n (*activity*) travaux mpl d'aiguille; (*object(s)*) ouvrage m

**needn't** [ni:dnt] = **need not**

**needy** [ni:dɪ] adj nécessiteux(-euse)

**negative** [negətɪv] n (PHOT, ELEC) négatif m; (LING) terme m de négation ♦ adj négatif(-ive); **~ equity** situation dans laquelle la valeur d'une maison est inférieure à celle de l'emprunt-logement contracté pour la payer

**neglect** [nɪˈɡlekt] vt négliger ♦ n le fait de négliger; (*state of ~*) abandon m; **~ed** adj négligé(e), à l'abandon

**negligee** [negliʒeɪ] n déshabillé m

**negotiate** [nɪˈɡəʊʃɪeɪt] vi, vt négocier; **negotiation** [nɪɡəʊʃɪˈeɪʃən] n négociation f, pourparlers mpl

**neigh** [neɪ] vi hennir

**neighbour** [ˈneɪbəʳ] (US **neighbor**) n voisin(e); **~hood** n (*place*) quartier m; (*people*) voisinage m; **~ing** adj voisin(e), avoisinant(e); **~ly** adj obligeant(e); (*action etc*) amical(e)

**neither** [ˈnaɪðəʳ] adj, pron aucun(e) (des deux), ni l'un(e) ni l'autre ♦ conj: **I didn't move and ~ did Claude** je n'ai pas bougé, (et) Claude non plus ♦ adv: **~ good nor bad** ni bon ni mauvais; ... **~ did I refuse ...**, (et or mais) je n'ai pas non plus refusé ...

**neon** [ˈniːɔn] n néon m; **~ light** n lampe f au néon

**nephew** [ˈnevjuː] n neveu m

**nerve** [nɜːv] n nerf m; (*fig: courage*) sang-froid m, courage m; (: *impudence*) aplomb m, toupet m; **to have a fit of ~s** avoir le trac; **~-racking** adj angoissant(e)

**nervous** [ˈnɜːvəs] adj nerveux(-euse); (*anxious*) inquiet(-ète), plein(e) d'appréhension; (*timid*) intimidé(e); **~ breakdown** n dépression nerveuse

**nest** [nest] n nid m ♦ vi (se) nicher, faire son nid; **~ egg** n (*fig*) bas m de laine, magot m

**nestle** [ˈnesl] vi se blottir

**net** [net] n filet m; **the N~** (*Internet*) le Net ♦ adj net(te) ♦ vt (*fish etc*) prendre au filet; (*profit*) rapporter; **~ball** n netball m

**Netherlands** [ˈneðələndz] npl: **the ~** les Pays-Bas mpl

**nett** [net] adj = **net**

**netting** [ˈnetɪŋ] n (*for fence etc*) treillis m, grillage m

**nettle** [ˈnetl] n ortie f

**network** [ˈnetwɜːk] n réseau m

**neurotic** [njuəˈrɒtɪk] adj névrosé(e)

**neuter** [ˈnjuːtəʳ] adj neutre ♦ vt (*cat etc*) châtrer, couper

**neutral** [ˈnjuːtrəl] adj neutre ♦ n (AUT) point mort; **~ize** vt neutraliser

**never** [ˈnevəʳ] adv (ne ...) jamais; **~ again** plus jamais; **~ in my life** jamais de ma vie; *see also* **mind**; **~-ending** adj interminable; **~theless** adv néanmoins, malgré tout

**new** [njuː] adj nouveau (nouvelle); (*brand ~*) neuf (neuve); **N~ Age** n New Age m; **~born** adj nouveau-né(e); **~comer** n nouveau venu/nouvelle venue; **~fangled** [ˈnjuːfæŋɡld] (*pej*) adj ultramoderne (et farfelu(e)); **~found** adj (*enthusiasm*) de fraîche date; (*friend*) nouveau (nouvelle); **~ly** adv nouvellement, récemment; **~ly-weds** npl jeunes mariés mpl

**news** [nju:z] n nouvelle(s) f(pl); (RADIO, TV) informations fpl, actualités fpl; **a piece of ~** une nouvelle; **~ agency** n agence f de presse; **~agent** (BRIT) n marchand m de journaux; **~caster** n présentateur(-trice); **~flash** n flash m d'information; **~letter** n bulletin m; **~paper** n journal m; **~print** n papier m (de) journal; **~reader** n = newscaster; **~reel** n actualités (filmées) fpl; **~ stand** n kiosque m à journaux

**newt** [nju:t] n triton m

**New Year** n Nouvel An; **~'s Day** n le jour de l'An; **~'s Eve** n la Saint-Sylvestre

**New Zealand** [-'zi:lənd] n la Nouvelle-Zélande; **~er** n Néo-zélandais(e)

**next** [nekst] adj (seat, room) voisin(e), d'à côté; (meeting, bus stop) suivant(e); (in time) prochain(e) ♦ adv (place) à côté; (time) la fois suivante, la prochaine fois; (afterwards) ensuite; **the ~ day** le lendemain, le jour suivant or d'après; **~ year** l'année prochaine; **~ time** la prochaine fois; **~ to** à côté de; **~ to nothing** presque rien; **~, please!** (at doctor's etc) au suivant!; **~ door** adv à côté ♦ adj d'à côté; **~-of-kin** n parent m le plus proche

**NHS** n abbr = **National Health Service**

**nib** [nɪb] n (bec m de) plume f

**nibble** ['nɪbl] vt grignoter

**nice** [naɪs] adj (pleasant, likeable) agréable; (pretty) joli(e); (kind) gentil(le); **~ly** adv agréablement; joliment; gentiment

**niceties** ['naɪsɪtɪz] npl subtilités fpl

**nick** [nɪk] n (indentation) encoche f; (wound) entaille f ♦ vt (BRIT: inf) faucher, piquer; **in the ~ of time** juste à temps

**nickel** ['nɪkl] n nickel m; (US) pièce f de 5 cents

**nickname** ['nɪkneɪm] n surnom m ♦ vt surnommer

**nicotine patch** ['nɪkəti:n-] n timbre m anti-tabac, patch m

**niece** [ni:s] n nièce f

**Nigeria** [naɪ'dʒɪərɪə] n Nigéria m or f

**niggling** ['nɪglɪŋ] adj (person) tatillon(ne); (detail) insignifiant(e); (doubts, injury) persistant(e)

**night** [naɪt] n nuit f; (evening) soir m; **at ~** la nuit; **by ~** de nuit; **the ~ before last** avant-hier soir; **~cap** n boisson prise avant le coucher; **~ club** n boîte f de nuit; **~dress** n chemise f de nuit; **~fall** n tombée f de la nuit; **~gown** n, **~ie** ['naɪtɪ] n chemise f de nuit; **~ingale** ['naɪtɪŋgeɪl] n rossignol m; **~life** n vie f nocturne; **~ly** adj de chaque nuit or soir; (by night) nocturne ♦ adv chaque nuit or soir; **~mare** n cauchemar m; **~ porter** n gardien m de nuit, concierge m de service la nuit; **~ school** n cours mpl du soir; **~ shift** n équipe f de nuit; **~-time** n nuit f; **~ watchman** n veilleur m or gardien m de nuit

**nil** [nɪl] n rien m; (BRIT: SPORT) zéro m

**Nile** [naɪl] n: **the ~** le Nil

**nimble** ['nɪmbl] adj agile

**nine** [naɪn] num neuf m; **to call 999** (BRIT) or **911** (US) appeler les urgences; **~teen** ['naɪn'ti:n] num dix-neuf; **~ty** ['naɪntɪ] num quatre-vingt-dix; **ninth** [naɪnθ] num neuvième

**nip** [nɪp] vt pincer

**nipple** ['nɪpl] n (ANAT) mamelon m, bout m du sein

**nitrogen** ['naɪtrədʒən] n azote m

---

**KEYWORD**

---

**no** [nəʊ] (pl **noes**) adv (opposite of "yes") non; **are you coming? - no (I'm not)** est-ce que vous venez? - non; **would you like some more? - no thank you** vous en voulez encore? - non merci

♦ adj (not any) pas de, aucun(e) (used with "ne"); **I have no money/books** je n'ai pas d'argent/de livres; **no student would have done it** aucun étudiant ne l'aurait fait; **"no smoking"** "défense de fumer"; **"no dogs"** "les

chiens ne sont pas admis"
♦ *n* non *m*

**nobility** [nəʊ'bɪlɪtɪ] *n* noblesse *f*
**noble** ['nəʊbl] *adj* noble
**nobody** ['nəʊbədɪ] *pron* personne
**nod** [nɒd] *vi* faire un signe de tête (*affirmatif ou amical*); (*sleep*) somnoler ♦ *vt*:
**to ~ one's head** faire un signe de (la)
tête; (*in agreement*) faire signe que oui
♦ *n* signe *m* de (la) tête; **~ off** *vi* s'assoupir
**noise** [nɔɪz] *n* bruit *m*; **noisy** *adj*
bruyant(e)
**nominal** ['nɒmɪnl] *adj* symbolique
**nominate** ['nɒmɪneɪt] *vt* (*propose*) proposer; (*appoint*) nommer; **nominee**
[nɒmɪ'niː] *n* candidat agréé; personne
nommée
**non...** [nɒn] *prefix* non-; **~-alcoholic**
*adj* non-alcoolisé(e); **~committal** *adj*
évasif(-ive); **~descript** *adj* quelconque,
indéfinissable
**none** [nʌn] *pron* aucun(e); **~ of** you
aucun d'entre vous, personne parmi
vous; **I've ~ left** je n'en ai plus; **he's
the worse for it** il ne s'en porte pas
plus mal
**nonentity** [nɒ'nentɪtɪ] *n* personne insignifiante
**nonetheless** ['nʌnðə'les] *adv* néanmoins
**non-existent** [nɒnɪg'zɪstənt] *adj*
inexistant(e)
**non-fiction** [nɒn'fɪkʃən] *n* littérature *f*
non-romanesque
**nonplussed** [nɒn'plʌst] *adj* perplexe
**nonsense** ['nɒnsəns] *n* absurdités *fpl*,
idioties *fpl*; **~!** ne dites pas d'idioties!
**non:** **~-smoker** *n* non-fumeur *m*; **~-
smoking** *adj* non-fumeur; **~-stick** *adj*
qui n'attache pas; **~-stop** *adj* direct(e),
sans arrêt (*or escale*) ♦ *adv* sans arrêt
**noodles** ['nuːdlz] *npl* nouilles *fpl*
**nook** [nʊk] *n*: **~s and crannies** recoins
*mpl*
**noon** [nuːn] *n* midi *m*

**no one** ['nəʊwʌn] *pron* = **nobody**
**noose** [nuːs] *n* nœud coulant; (*hangman's*) corde *f*
**nor** [nɔːr] *conj* = **neither** ♦ *adv* see
**neither**
**norm** [nɔːm] *n* norme *f*
**normal** *adj* normal(e); **~ly** ['nɔːməlɪ]
*adv* normalement
**Normandy** ['nɔːməndɪ] *n* Normandie *f*
**north** [nɔːθ] *n* nord *m* ♦ *adj* du nord,
nord *inv* ♦ *adv* au *or* vers le nord; **N~
America** *n* Amérique *f* du Nord; **~
east** *n* nord-est *m*; **~erly** ['nɔːðəlɪ] *adj*
du nord; **~ern** ['nɔːðən] *adj* du nord,
septentrional(e); **N~ern Ireland** *n* Irlande *f* du Nord; **N~ Pole** *n* pôle *m*
Nord; **N~ Sea** *n* mer *f* du Nord;
**~ward(s)** *adv* vers le nord; **~-west** *n*
nord-ouest *m*
**Norway** ['nɔːweɪ] *n* Norvège *f*; **Norwegian** [nɔː'wiːdʒən] *adj* norvégien(ne) ♦ *n* Norvégien(ne); (*LING*) norvégien *m*
**nose** [nəʊz] *n* nez *m*; **~ about,
around** *vi* fureter *or* fureter (partout);
**~bleed** *n* saignement *m* du nez; **~
dive** *n* (descente *f* en) piqué *m*; **~y**
(*inf*) *adj* = **nosy**
**nostalgia** [nɒs'tældʒɪə] *n* nostalgie *f*
**nostril** ['nɒstrɪl] *n* narine *f*; (*of horse*)
naseau *m*
**nosy** ['nəʊzɪ] (*inf*) *adj* curieux(-euse)
**not** [nɒt] *adv* (ne ...) pas; **he is ~ or
isn't here** il n'est pas ici; **you must ~
or you mustn't do that** tu ne dois pas
faire ça; **it's too late, isn't it** *or* **is it ~?**
c'est trop tard, n'est-ce pas?; **~ yet/
now** pas encore/maintenant; **~ at all**
pas du tout; *see also* **all**; **only**
**notably** ['nəʊtəblɪ] *adv* (*particularly*) en
particulier; (*markedly*) spécialement
**notary** ['nəʊtərɪ] *n* notaire *m*
**notch** [nɒtʃ] *n* encoche *f*
**note** [nəʊt] *n* note *f*; (*letter*) mot *m*;
(*banknote*) billet *m* ♦ *vt* (*also:* **~ down**)
noter; (*observe*) constater; **~book** *n*
carnet *m*; **~d** *adj* réputé(e); **~pad** *n*

bloc-notes *m*; **~paper** *n* papier *m* à lettres

**nothing** ['nʌθɪŋ] *n* rien *m*; **he does ~** il ne fait rien; **~ new** rien de nouveau; **for ~** pour rien

**notice** ['nəʊtɪs] *n* (*announcement, warning*) avis *m*; (*period of time*) délai *m*; (*resignation*) démission *f*; (*dismissal*) congé *m* ♦ *vt* remarquer, s'apercevoir de; **to take ~ of** prêter attention à; **to bring sth to sb's ~** porter qch à la connaissance de qn; **at short ~** dans un délai très court; **until further ~** jusqu'à nouvel ordre; **to hand in one's ~** donner sa démission, démissionner; **~able** *adj* visible; **~ board** (BRIT) *n* panneau *m* d'affichage

**notify** ['nəʊtɪfaɪ] *vt*: **to ~ sth to sb** notifier qch à qn; **to ~ sb (of sth)** avertir qn (de qch)

**notion** ['nəʊʃən] *n* idée *f*; (*concept*) notion *f*

**notorious** [nəʊ'tɔːrɪəs] *adj* notoire (*souvent en mal*)

**nought** [nɔːt] *n* zéro *m*

**noun** [naʊn] *n* nom *m*

**nourish** ['nʌrɪʃ] *vt* nourrir; **~ing** *adj* nourrissant(e); **~ment** *n* nourriture *f*

**novel** ['nɒvl] *n* roman *m* ♦ *adj* nouveau (nouvelle), original(e); **~ist** *n* romancier *m*; **~ty** *n* nouveauté *f*

**November** [nəʊ'vembər] *n* novembre *m*

**now** [naʊ] *adv* maintenant ♦ *conj*: **~ (that)** maintenant que; **right ~** tout de suite; **by ~** à l'heure qu'il est; **just ~**: **that's the fashion just ~** c'est la mode en ce moment; **~ and then**, **~ and again** de temps en temps; **from ~ on** dorénavant; **~adays** *adv* de nos jours

**nowhere** ['nəʊweər] *adv* nulle part

**nozzle** ['nɒzl] *n* (*of hose etc*) ajutage *m*; (*of vacuum cleaner*) suceur *m*

**nuclear** ['njuːklɪər] *adj* nucléaire

**nucleus** ['njuːklɪəs] (*pl* **nuclei**) *n* noyau *m*

**nude** [njuːd] *adj* nu(e) ♦ *n* nu *m*; **in the ~** (tout(e)) nu(e)

**nudge** [nʌdʒ] *vt* donner un (petit) coup de coude à

**nudist** ['njuːdɪst] *n* nudiste *m/f*

**nuisance** ['njuːsns] *n*: **it's a ~** c'est (très) embêtant; **he's a ~** il est assommant or casse-pieds; **what a ~!** quelle barbe!

**null** [nʌl] *adj*: **~ and void** nul(le) et non avenu(e)

**numb** [nʌm] *adj* engourdi(e); (*with fear*) paralysé(e)

**number** ['nʌmbər] *n* nombre *m*; (*numeral*) chiffre *m*; (*of house, bank account etc*) numéro *m* ♦ *vt* numéroter (*amount to*) compter; **a ~ of** un certain nombre de; **they were seven in ~** ils étaient (au nombre de) sept; **to be ~ed among** compter parmi; **~ plate** (AUT) plaque *f* minéralogique or d'immatriculation

**numeral** ['njuːmərəl] *n* chiffre *m*

**numerate** ['njuːmərɪt] (BRIT) *adj*: **to be ~** avoir des notions d'arithmétique

**numerical** [njuːˈmerɪkl] *adj* numérique

**numerous** ['njuːmərəs] *adj* nombreux(-euse)

**nun** [nʌn] *n* religieuse *f*, sœur *f*

**nurse** [nɜːs] *n* infirmière *f* ♦ *vt* (*patient, cold*) soigner

**nursery** ['nɜːsərɪ] *n* (*room*) nursery *f*; (*institution*) crèche *f*; (*for plants*) pépinière *f*; **~ rhyme** *n* comptine *f*, chansonnette *f* pour enfants; **~ school** *n* école maternelle; **~ slope** *n* (SKI) piste *f* pour débutants

**nursing** ['nɜːsɪŋ] *n* (*profession*) profession *f* d'infirmière; (*care*) soins *mpl*; **~ home** *n* clinique *f*, maison *f* de convalescence

**nut** [nʌt] *n* (*of metal*) écrou *m*; (*fruit*) noix *f*, noisette *f*; cacahuète *f*; **~crackers** *npl* casse-noix *m inv*, casse-noisette(s) *m*

**nutmeg** ['nʌtmeg] *n* (noix *f*) muscade *f*

**nutritious** [njuːˈtrɪʃəs] *adj* nutritif(-ive)

nourrissant(e)

**nuts** [nʌts] (inf) adj dingue

**nutshell** ['nʌtʃel] n: **in a ~** en un mot

**nutter** ['nʌtə*] (BRIT: inf) n: **he's a complete ~** il est complètement cinglé

**nylon** ['naɪlɔn] n nylon m ♦ adj de or en nylon

## O, o

**oak** [əuk] n chêne m ♦ adj de or en (bois de) chêne

**OAP** (BRIT) n abbr = **old-age pensioner**

**oar** [ɔ:*] n aviron m, rame f

**oasis** [au'eɪsɪs] (pl **oases**) n oasis f

**oath** [əuθ] n serment m; (swear word) juron m; **under ~**, (BRIT) **on ~** sous serment

**oatmeal** ['əutmi:l] n flocons mpl d'avoine

**oats** [əuts] n avoine f

**obedience** [ə'bi:dɪəns] n obéissance f; **obedient** adj obéissant(e)

**obey** [ə'beɪ] vt obéir à; (instructions) se conformer à

**obituary** [ə'bɪtjuərɪ] n nécrologie f

**object** [n 'ɔbdʒɪkt, vb əb'dʒekt] n objet m; (purpose) but m, objet; (LING) complément m d'objet ♦ vi: **to ~ to** (attitude) désapprouver; (proposal) protester contre; **expense is no ~** l'argent n'est pas un problème; **he ~ed that ...** il a fait valoir or a objecté que ...; **I ~!** je proteste!; **~ion** [əb'dʒekʃən] n objection f; **~ionable** adj très désagréable; (language) choquant(e); **~ive** n objectif m ♦ adj objectif(-ive)

**obligation** [ɔblɪ'geɪʃən] n obligation f, devoir m; **without ~** sans engagement; **obligatory** [ə'blɪgətərɪ] adj obligatoire

**oblige** [ə'blaɪdʒ] vt (force): **to ~ sb to do** obliger or forcer qn à faire; (do a favour) rendre service à, obliger; **to be ~d to sb for sth** être obligé(e) à qn de qch; **obliging** adj obligeant(e), serviable

**oblique** [ə'bli:k] adj oblique; (allusion) indirect(e)

**obliterate** [ə'blɪtəreɪt] vt effacer

**oblivion** [ə'blɪvɪən] n oubli m; **oblivious** adj: **oblivious of** oublieux (-euse) de

**oblong** ['ɔblɔŋ] adj oblong (oblongue) ♦ n rectangle m

**obnoxious** [əb'nɔkʃəs] adj odieux (-euse); (smell) nauséabond(e)

**oboe** ['əubəu] n hautbois m

**obscene** [əb'si:n] adj obscène

**obscure** [əb'skjuə*] adj obscur(e) ♦ vt obscurcir; (hide: sun) cacher

**observant** [əb'zə:vənt] adj observateur(-trice)

**observation** [ɔbzə'veɪʃən] n (remark) observation f; (watching) surveillance f

**observatory** [əb'zə:vətrɪ] n observatoire m

**observe** [əb'zə:v] vt observer; (remark) faire observer or remarquer; **~r** n observateur(-trice)

**obsess** [əb'ses] vt obséder; **~ive** adj obsédant(e)

**obsolete** ['ɔbsəli:t] adj dépassé(e); démodé(e)

**obstacle** ['ɔbstəkl] n obstacle m; **~ race** n course f d'obstacles

**obstinate** ['ɔbstɪnɪt] adj obstiné(e)

**obstruct** [əb'strʌkt] vt (block) boucher, obstruer; (hinder) entraver

**obtain** [əb'teɪn] vt obtenir

**obvious** ['ɔbvɪəs] adj évident(e), manifeste; **~ly** adv manifestement; **~ly not!** bien sûr que non!

**occasion** [ə'keɪʒən] n occasion f; (event) événement m; **~al** adj pris(e) or fait(e) de temps en temps; occasionnel(le); **~ally** adv de temps en temps, quelquefois

**occupation** [ɔkju'peɪʃən] n occupation f; (job) métier m, profession f; **~al hazard** n risque m du métier

**occupier** ['ɔkjupaɪə*] n occupant(e)

**occupy** ['ɔkjupaɪ] vt occuper; **to ~ o.s.**

**in** *or* **with doing** s'occuper à faire

**occur** [ə'kɜːʳ] *vi* (*event*) se produire; (*phenomenon, error*) se rencontrer; **to ~ to sb** venir à l'esprit de qn; **~rence** *f* (*existence*) existence *f*, existence *f*; (*event*) cas *m*, fait *m*

**ocean** ['əʊʃən] *n* océan *m*

**o'clock** [ə'klɒk] *adv*: **it is 5 ~** il est 5 heures

**OCR** *n abbr* = **optical character reader; optical character recognition**

**October** [ɒk'təʊbəʳ] *n* octobre *m*

**octopus** ['ɒktəpəs] *n* pieuvre *f*

**odd** [ɒd] *adj* (*strange*) bizarre, curieux (-euse); (*number*) impair(e); (*not of a set*) dépareillé(e); **60~** 60 et quelques; **at ~ times** de temps en temps; **the ~ one out** l'exception *f*; **~ity** *n* (*person*) excentrique *m/f*; (*thing*) curiosité *f*; **~job man** *n* homme *m* à tout faire; **~jobs** *npl* petits travaux divers; **~ly** *adv* bizarrement, curieusement; **~ments** *npl* (*COMM*) fins *fpl* de série; **~s** *npl* (*in betting*) cote *f*; **it makes no ~s** cela n'a pas d'importance; **at ~s** en désaccord; **~s and ends** de petites choses

**odour** ['əʊdəʳ] (*US* **odor**) *n* odeur *f*

*KEYWORD*

**of** [ɒv, əv] *prep* 1 (*gen*) de; **a friend of ours** un de nos amis; **a boy of 10** un garçon de 10 ans; **that was kind of you** c'était gentil de votre part

2 (*expressing quantity, amount, dates etc*) de; **a kilo of flour** un kilo de farine; **how much of this do you need?** combien vous en faut-il?; **there were 3 of them** (*people*) ils étaient 3; (*objects*) il y en avait 3; **3 of us went** 3 d'entre nous y sont allé(e)s; **the 5th of July** le 5 juillet

3 (*from, out of*) en, de; **a statue of marble** une statue de *or* en marbre; **made of wood** (fait) en bois

**off** [ɒf] *adj, adv* (*engine*) coupé(e); (*tap*) fermé(e); (*BRIT: food: bad*) mauvais(e); (:

**milk: bad**) tourné(e); (*absent*) absent(e); (*cancelled*) annulé(e) ♦ *prep* de; sur; **t be ~** (*to leave*) partir, s'en aller; **to b die**; **a day ~** un jour de congé; **t have an ~ day** n'être pas en forme; **h had his coat ~** il avait enlevé so manteau; **10% ~** (*COMM*) 10% de ra bais; **~ the coast** au large de la côte **I'm ~ meat** je ne mange plus de vian de, je n'aime plus la viande; **on th ~ chance** à tout hasard

**offal** ['ɒfl] *n* (*CULIN*) abats *mpl*

**off-colour** ['ɒf'kʌləʳ] (*BRIT*) *adj* (*ill*) mala de, mal fichu(e)

**offence** [ə'fɛns] (*US* **offense**) *n* (*crime délit *m*, infraction *f*; **to take ~ at s vexer de, s'offenser de

**offend** [ə'fɛnd] *vt* (*person*) offense blesser; **~er** *n* délinquant(e)

**offense** [ə'fɛns] (*US*) *n* = **offence**

**offensive** [ə'fɛnsɪv] *adj* offensant(e choquant(e), (*smell etc*) très déplais sant(e), (*weapon*) offensif(-ive) ♦ *n* (*MIL* offensive *f*

**offer** ['ɒfəʳ] *n* offre *f*, proposition *f* ♦ *offrir, proposer; "on ~"** (*COMM*) "e promotion"; **~ing** *n* offrande *f*

**offhand** [ɒf'hænd] *adj* désinvolte ♦ *ac* spontanément

**office** ['ɒfɪs] *n* (*place, room*) bureau *m* (*position*) charge *f*, fonction *f*; **doctor's ~** (*US*) cabinet (médical); **to take ~** entrer en fonctions; **~ automation** *bureautique *f*; **~ block** (*US* **office buil ding**) *n* immeuble *m* de bureaux; **~ hours** *npl* heures *fpl* de bureau; (*US MED*) heures de consultation

**officer** ['ɒfɪsəʳ] *n* (*MIL etc*) officier *m* (*also*: **police ~**) agent *m* (de police); (*c organization*) membre *m* du bureau d recteur

**office worker** *n* employé(e) de bureau

**official** [ə'fɪʃl] *adj* officiel(le) ♦ *n* offici m; (*civil servant*) fonctionnaire *m/f*; em ployé(e)

**officiate** [ə'fɪʃɪeɪt] *vi* (*REL*) officier; **to**

**at a marriage** célébrer un mariage

**officious** [əˈfɪʃəs] *adj* trop empressé(e)

**offing** [ˈɒfɪŋ] *n*: **in the** ~ (*fig*) en perspective

**off:** ~**-licence** (BRIT) *n* (*shop*) débit *m* de vins et de spiritueux; ~**-line** *adj, adv* (COMPUT) (en mode) autonome; (*: switched off*) non connecté(e); ~**-peak** *adj* aux heures creuses; (*electricity, heating, ticket*) aux heures creuses; ~**-putting** (BRIT) *adj* (*remark*) rébarbatif (-ive); (*person*) rebutant(e), peu engageant(e); ~**-road vehicle** *n* véhicule *m* tout-terrain; ~**-season** *adj, adv* hors-saison *inv*; ~**-set** (*irreg*) *vt* (*counteract*) contrebalancer, compenser; ~**-shoot** *n* (*fig*) ramification *f*, antenne *f*; ~**-shore** *adj* (*breeze*) de terre; (*fishing*) côtier (-ère); ~**-side** *adj* (SPORT) hors jeu; (AUT: *in Britain*) de droite; (*: in US, Europe*) de gauche; ~**-spring** *n inv* progéniture *f*; ~**-stage** *adv* dans les coulisses; ~**-the-peg** (US **off-the-rack**) *adv* en prêt-à-porter; ~**-white** *adj* blanc cassé *inv*

---
**off-licence**

*Un* **off-licence** *est un magasin où l'on vend de l'alcool (à emporter) aux heures où les pubs sont fermés. On peut également y acheter des boissons non alcoolisées, des cigarettes, des chips, des bonbons, des chocolats etc.*

---

**Oftel** [ˈɒftel] *n* organisme qui supervise les télécommunications

**often** [ˈɒfn] *adv* souvent; **how ~ do you go?** vous y allez tous les combien?; **how ~ have you gone there?** vous y êtes allé combien de fois?

**Ofwat** [ˈɒfwɒt] *n* organisme qui surveille les activités des compagnies des eaux

**oh** [əu] *excl* ô! oh!

**oil** [ɔɪl] *n* huile *f*; (*petroleum*) pétrole *m*; (*for central heating*) mazout *m* ♦ *vt* (*machine*) graisser; (*for storing*) bidon *m* à huile;

~**field** *n* gisement *m* de pétrole; ~ **filter** *n* (AUT) filtre *m* à huile; ~ **painting** *n* peinture *f* à l'huile; ~ **refinery** *n* raffinerie *f*; ~ **rig** *n* derrick *m*; (*at sea*) plate-forme pétrolière; ~ **slick** *n* nappe *f* de mazout; ~ **tanker** *n* (*ship*) pétrolier *m*; (*truck*) camion-citerne *m*; ~ **well** *n* puits *m* de pétrole; ~**y** *adj* huileux (-euse); (*food*) gras(se)

**ointment** [ˈɔɪntmənt] *n* onguent *m*

**O.K., okay** [ˈəuˈkeɪ] *excl* d'accord! ♦ *adj* (*average*) pas mal ♦ *vt* approuver; **is it ~?, are you ~?** ça va?

**old** [əuld] *adj* vieux (vieille); (*person*) âgé(e); (*former*) ancien(ne), vieux, vieux?; **how ~ are you?** quel âge avez-vous?; **he's 10 years ~** il a 10 ans, il est âgé de 10 ans; ~**er brother/sister** frère/sœur aîné(e); ~ **age** vieillesse *f*; ~ **age pensioner** (BRIT) *n* retraité(e); ~**-fashioned** *adj* démodé(e); (*person*) vieux jeu *inv*; ~ **people's home** *n* maison *f* de retraite

**olive** [ˈɒlɪv] *n* (*fruit*) olive *f*; (*tree*) olivier *m* ♦ *adj* (*also*: ~**-green**) (vert) olive *inv*; ~ **oil** *n* huile *f* d'olive

**Olympic** [əuˈlɪmpɪk] *adj* olympique; **the ~ Games, the ~s** les Jeux *mpl* olympiques

**omelet(te)** [ˈɒmlɪt] *n* omelette *f*

**omen** [ˈəumən] *n* présage *m*

**ominous** [ˈɒmɪnəs] *adj* menaçant(e), inquiétant(e); (*event*) de mauvais augure

**omit** [əuˈmɪt] *vt* omettre; **to ~ to do** omettre de faire

---
*KEYWORD*

**on** [ɒn] *prep* **1** (*indicating position*) sur; **on the table** sur la table; **on the wall** sur le *or* au mur; **on the left** à gauche **2** (*indicating means, method, device etc*): **on foot** à pied; **on the train/plane** (*be*) dans le train/l'avion; (*go*) en train/avion; **on the telephone/radio/television** au téléphone/à la radio/à la télévision; **to be on drugs** se droguer;

on holiday en vacances

**3** (*referring to time*): **on Friday** vendredi; **on Fridays** le vendredi; **on June 20th** le 20 juin; **a week on Friday** vendredi en huit; **on seeing this** en voyant cela

**4** (*about, concerning*) sur, de; **a book on Balzac/physics** un livre sur Balzac/de physique

♦ *adv* **1** (*referring to dress, covering*): **to have one's coat on** avoir (mis) son manteau; **to put one's coat on** mettre son manteau; **what's she got on?** qu'est-ce qu'elle porte?; **screw the lid on tightly** vissez bien le couvercle

**2** (*further, continuously*): **to walk etc on** continuer à marcher etc; **on and off de** temps à autre

♦ *adv* **1** (*in operation: machine*) en marche; (*: radio, TV, light*) allumé(e); (*: tap, gas*) ouvert(e); (*: brakes*) mis(e); **is the meeting still on?** (*not cancelled*) est-ce que la réunion a bien lieu?; (*in progress*) la réunion dure-t-elle encore?; **when is this film on?** quand passe ce film?

**2** (*inf*): **that's not on!** (*not acceptable*) cela ne se fait pas!; (*not possible*) pas question!

**once** [wʌns] *adv* une fois; (*formerly*) autrefois ♦ *conj* une fois que; **~ he had left/it was done** une fois qu'il fut parti/que ce fut terminé; **at ~** tout de suite, immédiatement; (*simultaneously*) à la fois; **a week ~** une fois par semaine; **~ more** encore une fois; **~ and for all** une fois pour toutes; **~ upon a time** il y avait une fois, il était une fois

**oncoming** [ˈɔnkʌmɪŋ] *adj* (*traffic*) venant en sens inverse

┌─────────────────┐
│ KEYWORD │
└─────────────────┘

**one** [wʌn] *num* un(e); **one hundred and fifty** cent cinquante; **one day un** jour

♦ *adj* **1** (*sole*) seul(e), unique; **the one**

book which l'unique *or* le seul livre qui; **the one man who** le seul (homme) qui

**2** (*same*) même; **they came in the one car** ils sont venus dans la même voiture

♦ *pron* **1**: **this one** celui-ci (celle-ci); **that one** celui-là (celle-là); **I've already got one/a red one** j'en ai déjà un(e)/un(e) rouge; **one by one** un(e) à *or* par un(e)

**2**: **one another** l'un(e) l'autre; **to look at one another** se regarder

**3** (*impersonal*) on, nous; **one never knows** on ne sait jamais; **to cut one's finger** se couper le doigt

**one:** **~-day excursion** (*US*) *n* billet *m* d'aller-retour (valable pour la journée); **~-man** *adj* (*business*) dirigé(e) *etc* par un seul homme; **~-man band** *n* homme-orchestre *m*; **~-off** (*BRIT: inf*) *n* exemplaire *m* unique

**oneself** [wʌnˈself] *pron* (*reflexive*) se; (*after prep*) soi(-même); (*emphatic*) soi-même; **to hurt ~** se faire mal; **to keep sth for ~** garder qch pour soi; **to talk to ~** se parler à soi-même

**one:** **~-sided** *adj* (*argument*) unilatéral; **~-to-~** *adj* (*relationship*) univoque; **~-way** *adj* (*street, traffic*) à sens unique

**ongoing** [ˈɔngəʊɪŋ] *adj* en cours; (*relationship*) suivi(e)

**onion** [ˈʌnjən] *n* oignon *m*

**on-line** [ˈɔnlaɪn] *adj, adv* (*COMPUT*) en ligne; (*: switched on*) connecté(e); **to go ~** se mettre en mode interactif

**onlooker** [ˈɔnlʊkəʳ] *n* spectateur(-trice)

**only** [ˈəʊnlɪ] *adv* seulement ♦ *adj* seul(e), unique ♦ *conj* seulement, mais; **an ~ child** un enfant unique; **not ~... but also** non seulement... mais aussi

**onset** [ˈɔnset] *n* début *m*; (*of winter, old age*) approche *f*

**onshore** [ˈɔnʃɔːʳ] *adj* (*wind*) du large

**onslaught** [ˈɔnslɔːt] *n* attaque *f*, assaut

**onto** [ˈɔntu] *prep* = **on to**

**onward(s)** ['ɒnwəd(z)] *adv* (*move*) en avant; **from that time ~** à partir de ce moment

**ooze** [uːz] *vi* suinter

**opaque** [əu'peɪk] *adj* opaque

**OPEC** ['əupɛk] *n abbr* (= *Organization of Petroleum-Exporting Countries*) O.P.E.P. *f*

**open** ['əupn] *adj* (*window etc*) découvert(e); (*car*) découvert(e); (*road, view*) dégagé(e); (*meeting*) public(-ique); (*admiration*) manifeste ♦ *vt* ouvrir ♦ *vi* (*flower, eyes, door, debate*) s'ouvrir; (*shop, bank, museum*) ouvrir; (*book etc*) commencer, débuter ♦ **in the ~** (*air*) en plein air; **~ on to** *vt fus* (*subj: room, door*) donner sur; **~ up** *vt* ouvrir; (*blocked road*) dégager ♦ *vi* s'ouvrir; **~ing** *n* ouverture *f*; (*opportunity*) occasion *f* ♦ *adj* (*remarks*) préliminaire; **~ing hours** *npl* heures *fpl* d'ouverture; **~ly** *adv* ouvertement; **~-minded** *adj* à l'esprit ouvert; **~-necked** *adj* à col ouvert; **~-plan** *adj* sans cloisons

---

**Open University**

L'**Open University** a été fondée en 1969. Ce type d'enseignement comprend des cours (certaines plages horaires sont réservées à cet effet à la télévision et à la radio), des devoirs qui sont envoyés par l'étudiant à son directeur ou sa directrice d'études, et un séjour obligatoire en université d'été. Il faut couvrir un certain nombre d'unités de valeur pendant une période de temps déterminée et obtenir la moyenne à un certain nombre d'entre elles pour recevoir le diplôme visé.

---

**opera** ['ɒpərə] *n* opéra *m*; **~ singer** *n* chanteur(-euse) d'opéra

**operate** ['ɒpəreɪt] *vt* (*machine*) faire marcher, faire fonctionner ♦ *vi* fonctionner; (*MED*) opérer; **to ~ on (sb)** opérer (qn)

**operatic** [ɒpə'rætɪk] *adj* d'opéra

**operating table** *n* table *f* d'opération

**operating theatre** *n* salle *f* d'opération

**operation** [ɒpə'reɪʃən] *n* opération *f*; (*of machine*) fonctionnement *m*; **to be in ~** (*system, law*) être en vigueur; **to have an ~** (MED) se faire opérer

**operative** ['ɒpərətɪv] *adj* (*measure*) en vigueur

**operator** ['ɒpəreɪtə*r*] *n* (*of machine*) opérateur(-trice); (TEL) téléphoniste *m/f*

**opinion** [ə'pɪnjən] *n* opinion *f*, avis *m*; **in my ~** à mon avis; **~ated** *adj* aux idées bien arrêtées; **~ poll** *n* sondage *m* (d'opinion)

**opponent** [ə'pəunənt] *n* adversaire *m/f*

**opportunity** [ɒpə'tjuːnɪtɪ] *n* occasion *f*; **to take the ~ of doing** profiter de l'occasion pour faire; en profiter pour faire

**oppose** [ə'pəuz] *vt* s'opposer à; **~d to** opposé(e) à; **as ~d to** par opposition à; **opposing** *adj* (*side*) opposé(e)

**opposite** ['ɒpəzɪt] *adj* opposé(e); (*house etc*) d'en face ♦ *adv* en face ♦ *prep* en face de ♦ *n* opposé *m*, contraire *m*; **the ~ sex** l'autre sexe, le sexe opposé; **opposition** [ɒpə'zɪʃən] *n* opposition *f*

**oppressive** [ə'prɛsɪv] *adj* (*political regime*) oppressif(-ive); (*weather*) lourd(e); (*heat*) accablant(e)

**opt** [ɒpt] *vi*: **to ~ for** opter pour; **to ~ to do** choisir de faire; **~ out** *vi*: **to ~ out of** choisir de ne pas participer à *or* de ne pas faire

**optical** ['ɒptɪkl] *adj* optique; (*instrument*) d'optique; **~ character recognition/reader** *n* lecture *f*/ lecteur *m* optique

**optician** [ɒp'tɪʃən] *n* opticien(ne)

**optimist** ['ɒptɪmɪst] *n* optimiste *m/f*; **~ic** [ɒptɪ'mɪstɪk] *adj* optimiste

**option** ['ɒpʃən] *n* choix *m*, option *f*; (SCOL) matière *f* à option; (COMM) option; **~al** *adj* facultatif(-ive); (COMM) en option

**or** [ɔː*r*] *conj* ou; (*with negative*): **he hasn't seen ~ heard anything** il n'a

## oral

rien vu ni entendu; ~ else sinon; ou bien

**oral** ['ɔːrəl] adj oral(e) ♦ n oral m

**orange** ['ɔrɪndʒ] n (fruit) orange f ♦ adj orange inv

**orbit** ['ɔːbɪt] n orbite f ♦ vt graviter autour de; ~al (motorway) n périphérique m

**orchard** ['ɔːtʃəd] n verger m

**orchestra** ['ɔːkɪstrə] n orchestre m; (US: seating) (fauteuils mpl d')orchestre

**orchid** ['ɔːkɪd] n orchidée f

**ordain** [ɔː'deɪn] vt (REL) ordonner

**ordeal** [ɔː'diːl] n épreuve f

**order** ['ɔːdər] n ordre m; (COMM) commande f ♦ vt ordonner; (COMM) commander; in ~ en ordre; (document) en règle; in (working) ~ en état de marche; out of ~ (not in correct ~) en désordre; (not working) en dérangement; in ~ to do/that pour faire/que +sub; en ~ to (COMM) en commande; to ~ sb to do ordonner à qn de faire; ~ form n bon m de commande; ~ly n (MIL) ordonnance f; (MED) garçon m de salle ♦ adj (room) en ordre; (person) qui a de l'ordre

**ordinary** ['ɔːdnrɪ] adj ordinaire, normal(e); (pej) ordinaire, quelconque; out of the ~ exceptionnel(le)

**Ordnance Survey map** ['ɔːdnəns-] n ≈ carte f d'État-Major

**ore** [ɔːr] n minerai m

**organ** ['ɔːgən] n organe m; (MUS) orgue m, orgues fpl; ~ic [ɔː'gænɪk] adj organique; (food) biologique

**organization** [ɔːgənaɪ'zeɪʃən] n organisation f

**organize** ['ɔːgənaɪz] vt organiser; ~r n organisateur(-trice)

**orgasm** ['ɔːgæzəm] n orgasme m

**Orient** ['ɔːrɪənt] n: the ~ l'Orient m; **o~al** [ɔːrɪ'entl] adj oriental(e)

**origin** ['ɔrɪdʒɪn] n origine f

**original** [ə'rɪdʒɪnl] adj original(e); (earliest) originel(le) ♦ n original m; ~ly adv (at first) à l'origine

## out

**originate** [ə'rɪdʒɪneɪt] vi: to ~ from (person) être originaire de; (suggestion) provenir de; to ~ in prendre naissance dans; avoir son origine dans

**Orkney** ['ɔːknɪ] n (also: the ~ Islands) les Orcades fpl

**ornament** ['ɔːnəmənt] n ornement m; (trinket) bibelot m; ~al [ɔːnə'mentl] adj décoratif(-ive); (garden) d'agrément

**ornate** [ɔː'neɪt] adj très orné(e)

**orphan** ['ɔːfn] n orphelin(e)

**orthopaedic** [ɔːθə'piːdɪk] (US orthopedic) adj orthopédique

**ostensibly** [ɔs'tensɪblɪ] adv en apparence

**ostentatious** [ɔsten'teɪʃəs] adj prétentieux(-euse)

**ostracize** ['ɔstrəsaɪz] vt frapper d'ostracisme

**ostrich** ['ɔstrɪtʃ] n autruche f

**other** ['ʌðər] adj autre ♦ pron: the ~ (one) l'autre; ~s (~ people) d'autres; ~ than autrement que; à part; ~wise adv, conj autrement

**otter** ['ɔtər] n loutre f

**ouch** [autʃ] excl aïe!

**ought** [ɔːt] (pt ought) aux vb: I ~ to do it je devrais le faire, il faudrait que je le fasse; this ~ to have been corrected cela aurait dû être corrigé; he ~ to win il devrait gagner

**ounce** [auns] n once f (= 28.35g; 16 in a pound)

**our** ['auər] adj notre, nos pl; see also my; ~s pron le (la) nôtre, les nôtres; see also mine[1]; ~selves [auə'selvz] pron pl (reflexive, after preposition) nous; (emphatic) nous-mêmes; see also oneself

**oust** [aust] vt évincer

**out** [aut] adv dehors; (published, not at home etc) sorti(e); (light, fire) éteint(e); ~ here ici; ~ there là-bas; he's ~ (absent) il est sorti; (unconscious) il est sans connaissance; to be ~ in one's calculations s'être trompé dans ses calculs; to run/back etc ~ sortir en courant/en reculant etc; ~ loud à haute voix; ~ of

(~*side*) en dehors de; (*because of: anger etc*) par; (*from among*): ~ **of 10** sur 10; (*without*): ~ **of petrol** sans essence, à court d'essence; ~ **of order** (*machine*) en panne; (*TEL: line*) en dérangement; **~and–** *adj* (*liar, thief etc*) véritable; **~back** *n* (*in Australia*): **the ~back** l'intérieur *m*; **~board** *n* (*also:* **~board motor**) (moteur *m*) hors-bord *m*; **~break** *n* (*of war, disease*) début *m*; (*of violence*) éruption *f*; **~burst** *n* explosion *f*, accès *m*; **~cast** *n* exilé(e); (*socially*) paria *m*; **~come** *n* issue *f*, résultat *m*; **~crop** *n* (*of rock*) affleurement *m*; **~cry** *n* tollé (général); **~dated** *adj* démodé(e); **~do** (*irreg*) *vt* surpasser; **~door** *adj* de or en plein air; **~doors** *adv* dehors; au grand air

**outer** ['autəʳ] *adj* extérieur(e); ~ **space** *n* espace *m* cosmique

**outfit** ['autfɪt] *n* (*clothes*) tenue *f*

**out:** **~going** *n* (*character*) ouvert(e), extraverti(e); (*departing*) sortant(e); **~goings** (*BRIT*) *npl* (*expenses*) dépenses *fpl*; **~grow** (*irreg*) *vt* (*clothes*) devenir trop grand(e) pour; **~house** *n* appentis *m*, remise *f*

**outing** ['autɪŋ] *n* sortie *f*, excursion *f*

**out:** **~law** *n* hors-la-loi *m inv* ♦ *vt* mettre hors-la-loi; **~lay** *n* dépenses *fpl*; (*investment*) mise *f* de fonds; **~let** *n* (*for liquid etc*) issue *f*, sortie *f*; (*US: ELEC*) prise *f* de courant; (*also:* **retail ~let**) point *m* de vente; **~line** *n* (*shape*) contour *m*; (*summary*) esquisse *f*, grandes lignes ♦ *vt* (*fig: theory, plan*) exposer à grands traits; **~live** *vt* survivre à; **~look** *n* perspective *f*; **~lying** *adj* écarté(e); **~moded** *adj* démodé(e); dépassé(e); **~number** *vt* surpasser en nombre; **~of-date** *adj* (*passport*) périmé(e); (*theory etc*) dépassé(e); (*clothes etc*) démodé(e); **~of-the-way** *adj* (*place*) loin de tout; **~patient** *n* malade *m/f* en consultation externe; **~post** *n* avant-poste *m*; **~put** *n* rendement *m*, production *f*; (*COMPUT*) sortie *f*

**outrage** ['autreɪdʒ] *n* (*anger*) indignation *f*; (*violent act*) atrocité *f*; (*scandal*) scandale *m* ♦ *vt* outrager; **~ous** [aut'reɪdʒəs] *adj* atroce; scandaleux(-euse)

**outright** [*adv* aut'raɪt, *adj* 'autraɪt] *adv* complètement; (*deny, refuse*) catégoriquement; (*ask*) carrément; (*kill*) sur le coup ♦ *adj* complet(-ète); catégorique

**outset** ['autset] *n* début *m*

**outside** [aut'saɪd] *n* extérieur *m* ♦ *adj* extérieur(e) ♦ *adv* (au) dehors, à l'extérieur ♦ *prep* hors de, à l'extérieur de; **at the ~** (*fig*) au plus or maximum; ~ **lane** *n* (*AUT: in Britain*) voie *f* de droite; (*: in US, Europe*) voie de gauche; ~ **line** *n* (*TEL*) ligne extérieure; **~r** *n* (*stranger*) étranger(-ère)

**out:** **~size** ['autsaɪz] *adj* énorme; (*clothes*) grande taille *inv*; **~skirts** *npl* faubourgs *mpl*; **~spoken** *adj* très franc (franche); **~standing** *adj* remarquable, exceptionnel(le); (*unfinished*) en suspens; (*debt*) impayé(e); (*problem*) non réglé(e); **~stay** *vt*: **to ~stay one's welcome** abuser de l'hospitalité de son hôte; **~stretched** [aut'stretʃt] *adj* (*hand*) tendu(e); **~strip** [aut'strɪp] *vt* (*competitors, demand*) dépasser; **~tray** *n* courrier *m* "départ"

**outward** ['autwəd] *adj* (*sign, appearances*) extérieur(e); (*journey*) (d')aller

**outweigh** [aut'weɪ] *vt* l'emporter sur

**outwit** [aut'wɪt] *vt* se montrer plus malin que

**oval** ['əuvl] *adj* ovale ♦ *n* ovale *m*

Oval Office

*L'Oval Office est le bureau personnel du président des États-Unis à la Maison-Blanche, ainsi appelé du fait de sa forme ovale. Par extension, ce terme désigne la présidence elle-même.*

**ovary** ['əuvərɪ] *n* ovaire *m*

**oven** ['ʌvn] *n* four *m*; **~proof** *adj* allant au four

**over** ['əuvə<sup>r</sup>] adv (par-)dessus ♦ adj (finished) fini(e), terminé(e); (too much) en plus ♦ prep sur; par-dessus; (above) au-dessus de; (on the other side of) de l'autre côté de; (more than) plus de; (during) pendant; ~ **here** ici; ~ **there** là-bas; **all** ~ (everywhere) partout, fini(e); ~ **and** ~ **(again)** à plusieurs reprises; ~ **and above** en plus de; **to ask sb** ~ inviter qn (à passer)

**overall** [adj, n 'əuvərɔːl, adv əuvər'ɔːl] adj (length, cost etc) total(e); (study) d'ensemble ♦ n (BRIT) blouse f ♦ adv dans l'ensemble, en général; ~**s** npl bleus mpl (de travail)

**over**: ~**awe** vt impressionner; ~**balance** vi basculer; (NAUT) par-dessus bord; ~**book** vt faire du surbooking; ~**cast** adj couvert(e)

**overcharge** [əuvə'tʃɑːdʒ] vt: **to** ~ **sb for sth** faire payer qch trop cher à qn

**overcoat** ['əuvəkəut] n pardessus m

**overcome** [əuvə'kʌm] (irreg) vt (defeat) triompher de; (difficulty) surmonter

**over**: ~**crowded** adj bondé(e); ~**do** (irreg) vt exagérer; (overcook) trop cuire; **to** ~**do it** (work etc) se surmener; ~**dose** n dose excessive; ~**draft** n découvert m; ~**drawn** adj (account) à découvert; (person) dont le compte est à découvert; ~**due** adj en retard; (change, reform) qui tarde; ~**estimate** vt surestimer

**overflow** [vi əuvə'fləu, n 'əuvəfləu] vi déborder ♦ n (also: ~ **pipe**) tuyau m d'écoulement, trop-plein m

**overgrown** [əuvə'grəun] adj (garden) envahi(e) par la végétation

**overhaul** [vb əuvə'hɔːl, n 'əuvəhɔːl] vt réviser ♦ n révision f

**overhead** [adv əuvə'hed, adj, n 'əuvəhed] adv au-dessus ♦ adj aérien(ne); (lighting) vertical(e) ♦ n (US) ~**s**; ~**s** npl (expenses) frais généraux; ~ **projector** n rétroprojecteur m

**over**: ~**hear** (irreg) vt entendre (par

hasard); ~**heat** vi (engine) chauffe ~**joyed** adj: ~**joyed (at)** ravi(e) (de enchanté(e) (de)

**overland** ['əuvəlænd] adj, adv par vo de terre

**overlap** [əuvə'læp] vi se chevaucher

**over**: ~**leaf** adv au verso; ~**load** vt su charger; ~**look** vt (have view of) donn sur; (miss: by mistake) oublier; (forgiv fermer les yeux sur

**overnight** [adv əuvə'nait, 'əuvənait] adv (happen) durant la nu (fig) soudain ♦ adj d'une (or de) nu **he stayed there** ~ il y a passé la nui

**overpass** ['əuvəpɑːs] n pont autoro tier

**overpower** [əuvə'pauə<sup>r</sup>] vt vaincr (fig) accabler; ~**ing** adj (heat, stenc suffocant(e)

**over**: ~**rate** vt surestimer; ~**ride** (irre like ride) vt (order, objection) passer o tre à; ~**riding** adj prépondérant(e ~**rule** vt (decision) annuler; (claim) rej ter; (person) rejeter l'avis de; ~**run** (ir reg: like run) vt (country) occuper; (tin limit) dépasser

**overseas** [əuvə'siːz] adv outre-me (abroad) à l'étranger ♦ adj (trade) ext rieur(e); (visitor) étranger(-ère)

**overshadow** [əuvə'ʃædəu] vt (fi éclipser

**oversight** ['əuvəsait] n omission f, o bli m

**oversleep** [əuvə'sliːp] (irreg) vi se r veiller (trop) tard

**overstep** [əuvə'step] vt: **to** ~ **the mar** dépasser la mesure

**overt** [əu'vəːt] adj non dissimulé(e)

**overtake** [əuvə'teik] (irreg) vt (AUT) d passer, doubler

**over**: ~**throw** (irreg) vt (governmer renverser; ~**time** n heures fpl suppl mentaires; ~**tone** n (also: ~**tones**) no f, sous-entendus mpl

**overture** ['əuvətʃuə<sup>r</sup>] n (MUS, fig) ouve ture f

**over**: ~**turn** vt renverser ♦ vi se retou

ner; **~weight** adj (person) trop gros(se); **~whelm** vt (subj: emotion) accabler; (enemy, opponent) écraser; **~whelming** adj (victory, defeat) écrasant(e); (desire) irrésistible

**verwrought** [əuvə'rɔːt] adj excédé(e)

**we** [au] vt: **to ~ sb sth, to ~ sth to sb** devoir qch à qn; **owing to** prep à cause de, en raison de

**wl** [aul] n hibou m

**wn** [əun] vt posséder ♦ adj propre; **a room of my ~** une chambre à moi, ma propre chambre; **to get one's ~ back** prendre sa revanche; **on one's ~** tout(e) seul(e); **~ up** vi avouer; **~er** n propriétaire m/f; **~ership** n possession f

**x** [ɔks] (pl **~en**) n bœuf m; **~tail** n: **~tail soup** soupe f à la queue de bœuf

**xygen** ['ɔksidʒən] n oxygène m

**yster** ['ɔistə'] n huître f

**z.** abbr = **ounce(s)**

**zone** ['əuzəun]: **~friendly** adj qui n'attaque pas or qui préserve la couche d'ozone; **~ hole** n trou m d'ozone; **~ layer** n couche f d'ozone

# P, p

**a** [pa:] (inf) n papa m

**A** n abbr = **personal assistant; public address system**

**a.** abbr = **per annum**

**ace** [peis] n pas m; (speed) allure f; vitesse f ♦ vi: **to ~ up and down** faire les cent pas; **to keep ~ with** aller à la même vitesse que; **~maker** n (MED) stimulateur m cardiaque; (SPORT: also: **~setter**) meneur(-euse) de train

**acific** [pə'sifik] n: **the ~ (Ocean)** le Pacifique, l'océan m Pacifique

**ack** [pæk] n (~et, US: of cigarettes) paquet m; (of hounds) meute f; (of cards) band e f; (back ~) sac m à dos; (of cards) jeu m ♦ vt (goods) empaqueter, emballer; (box) remplir; (cram) entasser;

**to ~ one's suitcase** faire sa valise; **to ~ (one's bags)** faire ses bagages; **to ~ sb off** to expédier qn à; **~ it in!** laisse tomber!, écrase!

**package** ['pækidʒ] n paquet m; (also: **~ deal**) forfait m; **~ tour** n voyage organisé

**packed** adj (crowded) bondé(e); **~ lunch** (BRIT) n repas froid

**packet** ['pækɪt] n paquet m

**packing** ['pækɪŋ] n emballage m; **~ case** n caisse f (d'emballage)

**pact** [pækt] n pacte m; traité m

**pad** [pæd] n bloc-notes m; (to prevent friction) tampon m; (inf: home) piaule f ♦ vt rembourrer; **~ding** n rembourrage m

**paddle** ['pædl] n (oar) pagaie f; (US: for table tennis) raquette f de ping-pong ♦ vt: **to ~ a canoe** etc pagayer ♦ vi barboter, faire trempette; **paddling pool** (BRIT) n petit bassin

**paddock** ['pædək] n enclos m; (RACING) paddock m

**padlock** ['pædlɔk] n cadenas m

**paediatrics** [pi:dɪ'ætrɪks] (US **pediatrics**) n pédiatrie f

**pagan** ['peɪgən] adj, n païen(ne)

**page** [peɪdʒ] n (of book) page f; (also: ~ **boy**) garçon m, chasseur m; (at wedding) garçon m d'honneur ♦ vt (in hotel etc) (faire) appeler

**pageant** ['pædʒənt] n spectacle m historique; **~ry** n apparat m, pompe f

**pager** ['peɪdʒə'], **paging device** (TEL) n récepteur m d'appels

**paid** [peɪd] pt, pp of **pay** ♦ adj (work, official) rémunéré(e); (holiday) payé(e); **to put ~ to** (BRIT) mettre fin à, régler

**pail** [peɪl] n seau m

**pain** [peɪn] n douleur f; **to be in ~** souffrir, avoir mal; **to take ~s to** do se donner du mal pour faire; **~ed** adj peiné(e), chagrin(e); **~ful** adj douloureux(-euse); (fig) difficile, pénible; **~fully** adv (fig: very) terriblement; **~killer** n analgésique m; **~less** adj indo-

# paint

**paint**

lore; **~staking** ['peɪnzteɪkɪŋ] adj (person) soigneux(-euse); (work) soigné(e)

**paint** [peɪnt] n peinture f ♦ vt peindre; **to ~ the door blue** peindre la porte en bleu; **~brush** n pinceau m; **~er** n peintre m; **~ing** n peinture f; (picture) tableau m; **~work** n peinture f

**pair** [pɛər] n (of shoes, gloves etc) paire f; (of people) couple m; **~ of scissors** (paire de) ciseaux mpl; **~ of trousers** pantalon m

**pajamas** [pə'dʒɑːməz] (US) npl pyjama(s) m(pl)

**Pakistan** [pɑːkɪ'stɑːn] n Pakistan m; **~i** adj pakistanais(e) ♦ n Pakistanais(e)

**pal** [pæl] (inf) n copain (copine)

**palace** ['pæləs] n palais m

**palatable** ['pælɪtəbl] adj bon (bonne), agréable au goût

**palate** ['pælɪt] n palais m (ANAT)

**pale** [peɪl] adj pâle ♦ n: **beyond the ~** (behaviour) inacceptable; **to grow ~** pâlir

**Palestine** ['pælɪstaɪn] n Palestine f; **Palestinian** [pælɪs'tɪnɪən] adj palestinien(ne) ♦ n Palestinien(ne)

**palette** ['pælɪt] n palette f

**pall** [pɔːl] n (of smoke) voile m ♦ vi devenir lassant(e)

**pallet** ['pælɪt] n (for goods) palette f

**pallid** ['pælɪd] adj blême

**palm** [pɑːm] n (of hand) paume f; (also: **~ tree**) palmier m ♦ vt: **to ~ sth off on sb** (inf) refiler qch à qn; **P~ Sunday** n le dimanche des Rameaux

**paltry** ['pɔːltrɪ] adj dérisoire

**pamper** ['pæmpər] vt gâter, dorloter

**pamphlet** ['pæmflət] n brochure f

**pan** [pæn] n (also: **saucepan**) casserole f; (also: **frying ~**) poêle f; **~cake** n crêpe f

**panda** ['pændə] n panda m

**pandemonium** [pændɪ'məʊnɪəm] n tohu-bohu m

**pander** ['pændər] vi: **to ~** flatter bassement; obéir servilement à

**pane** [peɪn] n carreau m, vitre f

**panel** ['pænl] n (of wood, cloth etc) panneau m; (RADIO, TV) experts mpl; (for interview, exams) jury m; **~ling** (US **paneling**) n boiseries fpl

**pang** [pæŋ] n: **~s of remorse** jealousy affres mpl du remords/de jalousie; **~s of hunger/conscience** raillements mpl d'estomac/de conscience

**panic** ['pænɪk] n panique f, affolement m ♦ vi s'affoler, paniquer; **~ky** adj (person) qui panique or s'affole facilement; **~-stricken** adj affolé(e)

**pansy** ['pænzɪ] n (BOT) pensée f; (inf: pej) tapette f, pédé m

**pant** [pænt] vi haleter

**panther** ['pænθər] n panthère f

**panties** ['pæntɪz] npl slip m

**pantomime** ['pæntəmaɪm] (BRIT) n spectacle m de Noël

___

| pantomime |

Une **pantomime**, que l'on appelle également de façon familière "panto", est un genre de farce où le personnage principal est souvent un jeune garçon et où il y a toujours une **dame**, c'est-à-dire une vieille femme jouée par un homme, et un méchant. La plupart du temps, l'histoire est basée sur un conte de fées comme Cendrillon ou Le Chat botté, et le public est encouragé à participer en prévenant le héros d'un danger imminent. Ce genre de spectacle, qui s'adresse surtout aux enfants, vise également un public d'adultes au travers des nombreuses plaisanteries faisant allusion à des faits d'actualité.

___

**pantry** ['pæntrɪ] n garde-manger m inv

**pants** [pænts] npl (BRIT: woman's) slip m; (: man's) slip, caleçon m; (US: trousers) pantalon m

**pantyhose** ['pæntɪhəʊz] (US) npl collant m

**paper** ['peɪpər] n papier m; (also: **wallpaper**) papier peint; (also: **newspaper**

journal m; (academic essay) article m; (exam) épreuve écrite ♦ adj en or de papier ♦ vt tapisser (de papier peint); ~s npl (also: identity ~s) papiers (d'identité); ~back n livre m de poche; livre broché or non relié; ~ bag n sac m en papier; ~ clip n trombone m; ~weight n presse-papiers m inv; ~work n papiers mpl; (pej) paperasserie f

**ar** [paːʳ] n pair m, (GOLF) normale f du parcours; **on a ~ with** à égalité avec, au même niveau que

**arachute** ['pærəʃuːt] n parachute m

**arade** [pə'reɪd] n défilé m ♦ vt (fig) faire étalage de ♦ vi défiler

**aradise** ['pærədaɪs] n paradis m

**aradox** ['pærədɒks] n paradoxe m; ~**ically** [pærə'dɒksɪklɪ] adv paradoxalement

**araffin** ['pærəfɪn] (BRIT) n (also: ~ oil) pétrole (lampant)

**aragon** ['pærəgən] n modèle m

**aragraph** ['pærəgrɑːf] n paragraphe m

**arallel** ['pærəlɛl] adj parallèle; (fig) semblable ♦ n (line) parallèle f; (fig, GEO) parallèle m

**aralyse** ['pærəlaɪz] (BRIT) vt paralyser; **paralysis** [pə'rælɪsɪs] n paralysie f; **paralyze** (US) vt = **paralyse**

**aramount** ['pærəmaunt] adj: **of ~ importance** de la plus haute or grande importance

**aranoid** ['pærənɔɪd] adj (PSYCH) paranoïaque

**araphernalia** [pærəfə'neɪlɪə] n attirail m

**arasol** ['pærəsɔl] n ombrelle f; (over table) parasol m

**aratrooper** ['pærətruːpəʳ] n parachutiste m (soldat)

**arcel** ['paːsl] n paquet m, colis m ♦ vt (also: ~ **up**) empaqueter

**archment** ['paːtʃmənt] n parchemin m

**ardon** ['paːdn] n pardon m; grâce f

♦ vt pardonner à; ~ **me!, I beg your** ~! pardon!, je suis désolé!; **(I beg your)** ~?, (US) ~ **me?** pardon?

**parent** ['pɛərənt] n père m or mère f; ~**s** npl parents mpl

**Paris** ['pærɪs] n Paris

**parish** ['pærɪʃ] n paroisse f; (BRIT: civil) ≃ commune f

**Parisian** [pə'rɪzɪən] adj parisien(ne) ♦ n Parisien(ne)

**park** [paːk] n parc m, jardin public ♦ vt garer ♦ vi se garer

**parking** ['paːkɪŋ] n stationnement m; **"no ~"** "stationnement interdit"; ~ **lot** (US) n parking m, parc m de stationnement; ~ **meter** n parcomètre m; ~ **ticket** n P.V. m

**parliament** ['paːləmənt] n parlement m; ~**ary** [paːlə'mɛntərɪ] adj parlementaire

**parlour** ['paːləʳ] (US **parlor**) n salon m

**parochial** [pə'rəukɪəl] (pej) adj s'esprit de clocher

**parole** [pə'rəul] n: **on ~** en liberté conditionnelle

**parrot** ['pærət] n perroquet m

**parry** ['pærɪ] vt (blow) esquiver

**parsley** ['paːslɪ] n persil m

**parsnip** ['paːsnɪp] n panais m

**parson** ['paːsn] n ecclésiastique m; (Church of England) pasteur m

**part** [paːt] n partie f; (of machine) pièce f; (THEATRE etc) rôle m; (of serial) épisode m; (US: in hair) raie f ♦ adv = **partly** ♦ vt séparer ♦ vi (people) se séparer; (crowd) s'ouvrir; **to take ~ in** participer à, prendre part à; **to take sth in good ~** prendre qch du bon côté; **to take sb's ~** prendre la partie de qn, prendre parti pour qn; **for my ~** en ce qui me concerne; **for the most ~** dans la plupart des cas; ~ **with** vt fus se séparer de; ~ **exchange** (BRIT) n: **in ~ exchange** en reprise

**partial** ['paːʃl] adj (not complete) partiel(le); **to be ~ to** avoir un faible pour

**participate** [paː'tɪsɪpeɪt] vi: **to ~ (in)**

participer (à), prendre part (à); **participation** [pɑːtɪsɪ'peɪʃən] n participation f

**participle** ['pɑːtɪsɪpl] n participe m

**particle** ['pɑːtɪkl] n particule f

**particular** [pə'tɪkjʊlər] adj particulier (-ère); (special) spécial(e); (fussy) difficile; méticuleux(-euse); **~s** npl (details) détails mpl; (personal) nom, adresse etc; **in ~** en particulier; **~ly** adv particulièrement

**parting** ['pɑːtɪŋ] n séparation f; (BRIT: in hair) raie f ♦ adj d'adieu

**partisan** [pɑːtɪ'zæn] n partisan(e) f ♦ adj partisan(e); de parti

**partition** [pɑː'tɪʃən] n (wall) cloison f; (POL) partition f, division f

**partly** ['pɑːtlɪ] adv en partie, partiellement

**partner** ['pɑːtnər] n partenaire m/f; (in marriage) conjoint(e); (boyfriend, girlfriend) ami(e); (COMM) associé(e); (at dance) cavalier(-ère); **~ship** n association f

**partridge** ['pɑːtrɪdʒ] n perdrix f

**part-time** ['pɑːt'taɪm] adj, adv à mi-temps, à temps partiel

**party** ['pɑːtɪ] n (POL) parti m; (group) groupe m; (LAW) partie f; (celebration) réception f, soirée f, fête f ♦ cpd (POL) de or du parti; (LAW) en cause; **~ dress** n robe habillée

**pass** [pɑːs] vt passer devant; (friend) croiser; (overtake) dépasser; (exam) être reçu(e) à, réussir; (approve) approuver, accepter ♦ vi passer; (SCOL) être reçu(e) or admis(e), réussir ♦ n (permit) laissez-passer m inv; carte f d'accès or d'abonnement; (in mountains) col m; (SPORT) passe f; (SCOL: also: **~ mark**): **to get a ~** être reçu(e) (sans mention); **to make a ~ at sb** (inf) faire des avances à qn; **~ away** vi mourir; **~ by** vi passer ♦ vt négliger; **~ on** vt (news, object) transmettre; (illness) passer; **~ out** vi s'évanouir; **~ up** vt (opportunity) laisser passer; **~able** adj (road) praticable; (work) acceptable

**passage** ['pæsɪdʒ] n (also: **~way**) couloir m; (gen, in book) passage m; (by boat) traversée f

**passbook** ['pɑːsbʊk] n livret m

**passenger** ['pæsɪndʒər] n passager (-ère)

**passer-by** [pɑːsə'baɪ] (pl **~s~**) n passant(e)

**passing** ['pɑːsɪŋ] adj (fig) passager (-ère); **in ~** en passant; **~ place** n (AUT) aire f de croisement

**passion** ['pæʃən] n passion f; **~ate** adj passionné(e)

**passive** ['pæsɪv] adj (also LING) passif (-ive); **~ smoking** n tabagisme m passif

**Passover** ['pɑːsəʊvər] n Pâque f (juive)

**passport** ['pɑːspɔːt] n passeport m; **~ control** n contrôle m des passeports; **~ office** n bureau m de délivrance des passeports

**password** ['pɑːswɜːd] n mot m de passe

**past** [pɑːst] prep (in front of) devant; (further than) au delà de, plus loin que; (later than) après ♦ adj passé(e), (president etc) ancien(ne) ♦ n passé m; **he's ~ forty** il a dépassé la quarantaine, il a plus de or passé quarante ans, **for the ~ few/3 days** depuis quelques/3 jours; ces derniers/3 derniers jours; **ten/quarter ~ eight** huit heures dix/un or et quart

**pasta** ['pæstə] n pâtes fpl

**paste** [peɪst] n pâte f; (meat ~) pâté m (à tartiner); (tomato ~) purée f, concentré m; (glue) colle f (de pâte) ♦ vt coller

**pasteurized** ['pæstʃəraɪzd] adj pasteurisé(e)

**pastille** ['pæstɪl] n pastille f

**pastime** ['pɑːstaɪm] n passe-temps m inv

**pastry** ['peɪstrɪ] n pâte f; (cake) pâtisserie f

**pasture** ['pɑːstʃər] n pâturage m

**pasty** [n 'pæstɪ, adj 'peɪstɪ] n petit pâté (en croûte) ♦ adj (complexion) terreux (-euse)

**pat** [pæt] vt tapoter; (dog) caresser

**patch** [pætʃ] n (of material) pièce f; (eye

~) cache m; (spot) tache f; (on tyre) rustine f ♦ vt (clothes) rapiécer; **(to go through) a bad** ~ (passer par) une période difficile; ~ **up** vt réparer (grossièrement); **to** ~ **up a quarrel** se raccommoder; **~y** adj inégal(e); (incomplete) fragmentaire

**pâté** ['pæteɪ] n pâté m, terrine f

**patent** ['peɪtnt] n brevet m (d'invention) ♦ vt faire breveter ♦ adj patent(e), manifeste; ~ **leather** n cuir verni

**paternal** [pə'tɜːnl] adj paternel(le)

**path** [pɑːθ] n chemin m, sentier m; (in garden) allée f; (trajectory) trajectoire f

**pathetic** [pə'θetɪk] adj (pitiful) pitoyable; (very bad) lamentable, minable

**pathological** [pæθə'lɒdʒɪkl] adj pathologique

**pathway** ['pɑːθweɪ] n sentier m, passage m

**patience** ['peɪʃns] n patience f; (BRIT: CARDS) réussite f

**patient** ['peɪʃnt] n malade m/f; (of dentist etc) patient(e) ♦ adj patient(e)

**patio** ['pætɪəu] n patio m

**patriotic** [pætrɪ'ɒtɪk] adj patriotique; (person) patriote

**patrol** [pə'trəul] n patrouille f ♦ vt patrouiller dans; ~ **car** n voiture f de police; **~man** (irreg) (US) n agent m de police

**patron** ['peɪtrən] n (in shop) client(e); (of charity) patron(ne); ~ **of the arts** mécène m; **~ize** ['pætrənaɪz] vt (pej) traiter avec condescendance; (shop, club) être (un) client or un habitué de

**patter** ['pætər] n crépitement m, tapotement m; (sales talk) boniment m

**pattern** ['pætən] n (design) motif m; (SEWING) patron m

**pauper** ['pɔːpər] n indigent(e)

**pause** [pɔːz] n pause f, arrêt m ♦ vi faire une pause, s'arrêter

**pave** [peɪv] vt paver, daller; **to** ~ **the way for** ouvrir la voie à

**pavement** ['peɪvmənt] (BRIT) n trottoir m

**pavilion** [pə'vɪlɪən] n pavillon m; tente f

**paving** ['peɪvɪŋ] n (material) pavé m, dalle f; ~ **stone** n pavé m

**paw** [pɔː] n patte f

**pawn** [pɔːn] n (CHESS, also fig) pion m ♦ vt mettre en gage; **~broker** n prêteur m sur gages; **~shop** n mont-de-piété m

**pay** [peɪ] (pt, pp **paid**) n salaire m; paie f ♦ vt payer ♦ vi payer; (be profitable) être rentable; **to** ~ **attention (to)** prêter attention (à); **to** ~ **sb a visit** rendre visite à qn; **to** ~ **one's respects to sb** présenter ses respects à qn; ~ **back** vt rembourser; ~ **for** vt fus payer; ~ **in** vt verser; ~ **off** vt régler, acquitter; (person) rembourser ♦ vi (scheme, decision) se révéler payant(e); ~ **up** vt (money) payer; **~able** adj: **~able to sb** (cheque) à l'ordre de qn; **~ee** [peɪ'iː] n bénéficiaire m/f; ~ **envelope** (US) n = **pay packet**; **~ment** n paiement m; règlement m; **monthly ~ment** mensualité f; ~ **packet** (BRIT) n paie f; ~ **phone** n cabine f téléphonique, téléphone public; **~roll** n registre m du personnel; ~ **slip** (BRIT) n bulletin m de paie; ~ **television** n chaînes fpl payantes

**PC** n abbr = **personal computer**

**p.c.** abbr = **per cent**

**pea** [piː] n (petit) pois

**peace** [piːs] n paix f; (calm) calme m, tranquillité f; **~ful** adj paisible, calme

**peach** [piːtʃ] n pêche f

**peacock** ['piːkɒk] n paon m

**peak** [piːk] n (mountain) pic m, cime f; (of cap) visière f; (fig: highest level) maximum m; (: of career, fame) apogée m; ~ **hours** npl heures fpl de pointe

**peal** [piːl] n (of bells) carillon m; ~ **of laughter** éclat m de rire

**peanut** ['piːnʌt] n arachide f, cacahuète f; ~ **butter** n beurre m de cacahuète

**pear** [pɛər] n poire f

**pearl** [pɜːl] n perle f

**peasant** ['peznt] n paysan(ne)

**peat** [pi:t] n tourbe f

**pebble** ['pebl] n caillou m, galet m

**peck** [pek] vt (also: ~ at) donner un coup de bec à ♦ n coup m de bec; (kiss) bise f; **~ing order** n ordre m des préséances; **~ish** (BRIT: inf) adj: **I feel ~ish** je mangerais bien quelque chose

**peculiar** [pɪ'kju:lɪə] adj étrange, bizarre, curieux(-euse); **~ to** particulier(-ère) à

**pedal** ['pedl] n pédale f ♦ vi pédaler

**pedantic** [pɪ'dæntɪk] adj pédant(e)

**peddler** ['pedlə] n (of drugs) revendeur(-euse)

**pedestal** ['pedəstl] n piédestal m

**pedestrian** [pɪ'destrɪən] n piéton m; **~ crossing** (BRIT) n passage clouté; **~ized** adj: **a ~ized street** une rue piétonne

**pediatrics** [pi:dɪ'ætrɪks] (US) n = **paediatrics**

**pedigree** ['pedɪgri:] n ascendance f; (of animal) pedigree m ♦ cpd (animal) de race

**pee** [pi:] (inf) vi faire pipi, pisser

**peek** [pi:k] vi jeter un coup d'œil (furtif)

**peel** [pi:l] n pelure f, épluchure f; (of orange, lemon) écorce f ♦ vt peler, éplucher ♦ vi (paint etc) s'écailler; (wallpaper) se décoller; (skin) peler

**peep** [pi:p] n (BRIT: look) coup d'œil furtif; (sound) pépiement m ♦ vi (BRIT) jeter un coup d'œil (furtif); **~ out** (BRIT) vi se montrer (furtivement); **~hole** n judas m

**peer** [pɪə] vi: **~ at** regarder attentivement, scruter ♦ n (noble) pair m; (equal) pair, égal(e); **~age** ['pɪərɪdʒ] n pairie f

**peeved** [pi:vd] adj irrité(e), fâché(e)

**peg** [peg] n (for coat etc) patère f; (BRIT: also: **clothes ~**) pince f à linge

**Pekin(g)ese** [pi:kɪ'ni:z] n (dog) pékinois m

**pelican** ['pelɪkən] n pélican m; **~ crossing** (BRIT) n (AUT) feu m à

commande manuelle

**pellet** ['pelɪt] n boulette f; (of lead) plomb m

**pelt** [pelt] vt: **to ~ sb (with)** bombarder qn (de) ♦ vi (rain) tomber à seau; (inf: run) courir à toutes jambes ♦ n peau f

**pelvis** ['pelvɪs] n bassin m

**pen** [pen] n (for writing) stylo m; (for sheep) parc m

**penal** ['pi:nl] adj pénal(e); (system, colony) pénitentiaire; **~ize** [pi:nəlaɪz] vt pénaliser

**penalty** ['penltɪ] n pénalité f; sanction f; (fine) amende f; (SPORT) pénalisation f; (FOOTBALL) penalty m; (RUGBY) pénalité

**penance** ['penəns] n pénitence f

**pence** [pens] (BRIT) npl of **penny**

**pencil** ['pensl] n crayon m; **~ case** trousse f (d'écolier); **~ sharpener** n taille-crayon(s) m inv

**pendant** ['pendnt] n pendentif m

**pending** ['pendɪŋ] prep en attendant ♦ adj en suspens

**pendulum** ['pendjuləm] n (of clock) balancier m

**penetrate** ['penɪtreɪt] vt pénétrer dans; pénétrer

**penfriend** ['penfrend] (BRIT) n correspondant(e)

**penguin** ['pengwɪn] n pingouin m

**penicillin** [penɪ'sɪlɪn] n pénicilline f

**peninsula** [pə'nɪnsjulə] n péninsule f

**penis** ['pi:nɪs] n pénis m, verge f

**penitentiary** [penɪ'tenʃərɪ] n prison f

**penknife** ['pennaɪf] n canif m

**pen name** n nom m de plume, pseudonyme m

**penniless** ['penɪlɪs] adj sans le sou

**penny** ['penɪ] (pl **pennies** or (BRIT) **pence**) n penny m

**penpal** ['penpæl] n correspondant(e)

**pension** ['penʃən] n pension f; (from company) retraite f; **~er** (BRIT) n retraité(e); **~ fund** n caisse f de pension; **plan** n plan m de retraite

**Pentagon**

*e* **Pentagon** *est le nom donné aux ureaux du ministère de la Défense mericain, situés à Arlington en Virginie, à cause de la forme pentagonale lu bâtiment dans lequel ils se trouvent. Par extension, ce terme est également utilisé en parlant du ministère lui-même.*

**entathlon** [pen'tæθlən] *n* pentathlon *m*

**entecost** ['pentikɔst] *n* Pentecôte *f*

**enthouse** ['penthaus] *n* appartement *n* (de luxe) (en attique)

**ent-up** ['pentʌp] *adj* (*feelings*) refoulé(e)

**enultimate** [pe'nʌltimət] *adj* avant-ernier(-ère)

**ople** ['pi:pl] *npl* gens *mpl*; personnes *ol*; (*inhabitants*) population *f*; (POL) euple *m* ♦ *n* (*nation*, *race*) peuple *m*; **everal ~ came** plusieurs personnes ont venues; ~ **say that ...** on dit que

**ep up** ['pep-] (*inf*) *vt* remonter

**epper** ['pepər] *n* poivre *m*; (*vegetable*) oivron *m* ♦ *vt* (*fig*): **to ~ with** bombarder de; ~ **mill** *n* moulin *m* à poivre; ~**mint** (*sweet*) pastille *f* de menthe

**eptalk** ['peptɔ:k] (*inf*) *n* (petit) discours d'encouragement

**er** [pə:r] *prep* par; ~ **hour** (*miles* etc) à l'heure; (*fee*) de l'heure; ~ **kilo** etc le kilo etc; ~ **annum** par an; ~ **capita** par personne, par habitant

**erceive** [pə'si:v] *vt* percevoir; (*notice*) emarquer, s'apercevoir de

**er cent** *adv* pour cent; **percentage** *n* ourcentage *m*

**erception** [pə'sepʃən] *n* perception *f*; *insight*) perspicacité *f*

**erceptive** [pə'septiv] *adj* pénétrant(e); *person*) perspicace

**erch** [pə:tʃ] *n* (*fish*) perche *f*; (*for bird*) erchoir *m* ♦ *vi*: **to ~ on** se percher sur

**percolator** ['pə:kəleitər] *n* cafetière *f* (électrique)

**percussion** [pə'kʌʃən] *n* percussion *f*

**perennial** [pə'reniəl] *adj* perpétuel(le); (BOT) vivace

**perfect** [*adj*, *n* 'pə:fikt, *vb* pə'fekt] *adj* parfait(e) ♦ *n* (*also*: ~ **tense**) parfait *m* ♦ *vt* parfaire; mettre au point; ~**ly** *adv* parfaitement

**perforate** ['pə:fəreit] *vt* perforer, percer; **perforation** [pə:fə'reiʃən] *n* perforation *f*

**perform** [pə'fɔ:m] *vt* (*carry out*) exécuter; (*concert* etc) jouer, donner ♦ *vi* jouer; ~**ance** *n* représentation *f*, spectacle *m*; (*of an artist*) interprétation *f*; (SPORT) performance *f*; (*of car*, *engine*) fonctionnement *m*; (*of company*, *economy*) résultats *mpl*; ~**er** *n* artiste *m/f*, interprète *m/f*

**perfume** ['pə:fju:m] *n* parfum *m*

**perhaps** [pə'hæps] *adv* peut-être

**peril** ['peril] *n* péril *m*

**perimeter** [pə'rimitər] *n* périmètre *m*

**period** ['piəriəd] *n* période *f*; (*of history*) époque *f*; (SCOL) cours *m*; (*full stop*) point *m*; (MED) règles *fpl* ♦ *adj* (*costume*, *furniture*) d'époque; ~**ic(al)** [piəri'ɔd-ik(l)] *adj* périodique; ~**ical** [piəri'ɔdikl] *n* périodique *m*

**peripheral** [pə'rifərəl] *adj* périphérique ♦ *n* (COMPUT) périphérique *m*

**perish** ['periʃ] *vi* périr; (*decay*) se détériorer; ~**able** *adj* périssable

**perjury** ['pə:dʒəri] *n* parjure *m*, faux serment

**perk** [pə:k] *n* avantage *m* accessoire, à-côté *m*; ~ **up** *vi* (*cheer up*) se ragaillardir; ~**y** *adj* (*cheerful*) guilleret(te)

**perm** [pə:m] *n* (*for hair*) permanente *f*

**permanent** ['pə:mənənt] *adj* permanent(e)

**permeate** ['pə:mieit] *vi* s'infiltrer ♦ *vt* s'infiltrer dans; pénétrer

**permissible** [pə'misibl] *adj* permis(e), acceptable

**permission** [pə'miʃən] *n* permission *f*,

autorisation f

**permissive** [pə'mɪsɪv] adj tolérant(e), permissif(-ive)

**permit** [n 'pɜːmɪt, vb pə'mɪt] n permis m ♦ vt permettre

**perpendicular** [pɜːpən'dɪkjulə*] adj perpendiculaire

**perplex** [pə'pleks] vt (person) rendre perplexe

**persecute** ['pɜːsɪkjuːt] vt persécuter

**persevere** [pɜːsɪ'vɪə*] vi persévérer

**Persian** ['pɜːʃən] adj persan(e) ♦ n (LING) persan m; **the ~ Gulf** le golfe Persique

**persist** [pə'sɪst] vi: **to ~ (in doing)** persister or s'obstiner (à faire); **~ent** [pə'sɪstənt] adj persistant(e), tenace; **~ent vegetative state** état m végétatif persistant

**person** ['pɜːsn] n personne f; **in ~** en personne; **~al** adj personnel(le); **~al assistant** n secrétaire privé(e); **~al column** n annonces personnelles; **~al computer** n ordinateur personnel; **~ality** [pɜːsə'nælɪtɪ] n personnalité f; **~ally** adv personnellement; **to take sth ~ally** se sentir visé(e) (par qch); **~al organizer** n filofax m ®; **~al stereo** n Walkman ® m, baladeur m

**personnel** [pɜːsə'nel] n personnel m

**perspective** [pə'spektɪv] n perspective f; **to get things into ~** faire la part des choses

**Perspex** ['pɜːspeks] ® n plexiglas ® m

**perspiration** [pɜːspɪ'reɪʃən] n transpiration f

**persuade** [pə'sweɪd] vt: **to ~ sb to do sth** persuader qn de faire qch; **persuasion** [pə'sweɪʒən] n persuasion f; (creed) religion f

**perverse** [pə'vɜːs] adj pervers(e); (contrary) contrariant(e); **pervert** [n 'pɜːvɜːt, vb pə'vɜːt] n perverti(e) ♦ vt pervertir; (words) déformer

**pessimist** ['pesɪmɪst] n pessimiste m/f; **~ic** [pesɪ'mɪstɪk] adj pessimiste

**pest** [pest] n animal m (or insecte) nuisible; (fig) fléau m

**pester** ['pestə*] vt importuner, harcel

**pet** [pet] n animal familier ♦ cpd (favo ite) favori(te) ♦ vt (stroke) caress câliner; **teacher's ~** chouchou m professeur; **~ hate** bête noire

**petal** ['petl] n pétale m

**peter out** ['piːtə-] vi (stream, conver tion) tarir; (meeting) tourner cou (road) se perdre

**petite** [pə'tiːt] adj menu(e)

**petition** [pə'tɪʃən] n pétition f

**petrified** ['petrɪfaɪd] adj (fig) mort de peur

**petrol** ['petrəl] (BRIT) n essence f; fo **star** ~ super m; ~ **can** n bidon m à sence

**petroleum** [pə'trəʊlɪəm] n pétrole m

**petrol:** ~ **pump** (BRIT) n pompe f à sence; ~ **station** (BRIT) n station-serv f; ~ **tank** (BRIT) n réservoir m d'essenc

**petticoat** ['petɪkəʊt] n combinaison

**petty** ['petɪ] adj (mean) mesquin (unimportant) insignifiant(e), sans i portance; ~ **cash** n caisse f des dépe ses courantes; ~ **officer** n secon maître m

**petulant** ['petjulənt] adj boude (-euse), irritable

**pew** [pjuː] n banc m (d'église)

**pewter** ['pjuːtə*] n étain m

**phantom** ['fæntəm] n fantôme m

**pharmacy** ['fɑːməsɪ] n pharmacie f

**phase** [feɪz] n phase f ♦ vt: ~ **to ~ in/out** introduire/supprimer qch p gressivement

**PhD** abbr = **Doctor of Philosophy** ♦ abbr (title) = docteur m (en droit or l tres etc), = doctorat m; (person) titula m/f d'un doctorat

**pheasant** ['feznt] n faisan m

**phenomenon** [fə'nɔmɪnən] (pl ph nomena) n phénomène m

**philosophical** [fɪlə'sɔfɪkl] adj philos phique

**philosophy** [fɪ'lɔsəfɪ] n philosophie f

**obia** ['fəubjə] n phobie f

**one** [fəun] n téléphone m ♦ vt téléphoner; **to be on the ~** avoir le téléphone; *(be calling)* être au téléphone;
**~ack** vi vt se rappeler; **~ up** vt téléphoner ♦ vi téléphoner; **~ bill** n facture f de
téléphone; **~ book** n annuaire m; **~**
**ooth, ~ box** (BRIT) n cabine f télépho-
ique; **~ call** n coup m de fil or de télé-
hone; **~card** n carte f de téléphone;
**~-in** (BRIT) n (RADIO, TV) programme m à
igne ouverte; **~ number** n numéro m
e téléphone

**onetics** [fə'nɛtɪks] n phonétique f

**oney** ['fəunɪ] adj faux (fausse), facti-
e; *(person)* pas franc (franche),
oseur(-euse)

**oto** ['fəutəu] n photo f; **~copier** n
hotocopieuse f; **~copy** n photocopie f
vt photocopier; **~graph** n photogra-
hie f ♦ vt photographier; **~grapher**
[fə'tɔgrəfə*] n photographe m/f; **~gra-**
**hy** [fə'tɔgrəfɪ] n photographie f

**rase** [freɪz] n expression f; (LING) lo-
ution f ♦ vt exprimer; **~ book** n re-
ueil m d'expressions (pour touristes)

**ysical** ['fɪzɪkl] adj physique; **~ edu-**
**ation** n éducation f physique; **~ly** adv
hysiquement

**ysician** [fɪ'zɪʃən] n médecin m

**ysicist** ['fɪzɪsɪst] n physicien(ne)

**ysics** ['fɪzɪks] n physique f

**ysiotherapist** [fɪzɪəu'θerəpɪst] n ki-
ésithérapeute m/f

**ysiotherapy** [fɪzɪəu'θerəpɪ] n kinési-
hérapie f

**ysique** [fɪ'ziːk] n physique m; consti-
ution f

**anist** ['pɪənɪst] n pianiste m/f

**ano** [pɪ'ænəu] n piano m

**ck** [pɪk] n (tool: also: **~axe**) pic m, pio-
he f ♦ vt choisir; *(fruit etc)* cueillir; *(re-*
*ove)* prendre; *(lock)* forcer; **take your**
~ faites votre choix; **the ~ of** (la) (la
eilleur(e) de; **to ~ one's nose** se
ettre les doigts dans le nez; **to ~**
ne's teeth se curer les dents; **to ~ a**

quarrel with sb chercher noise à qn;
**~ at** vt fus: **to ~ at one's food** manger
du bout des dents, chipoter; **~ on** vt
fus *(person)* harceler; **~ out** vt choisir;
*(distinguish)* distinguer; **~ up** vi *(im-*
*prove)* s'améliorer ♦ vt ramasser; *(col-*
*lect)* passer prendre; (AUT: *give lift to)*
prendre, emmener; *(learn)* apprendre;
(RADIO) capter; **to ~ up speed** prendre
de la vitesse; **to o.s. up** se relever

**picket** ['pɪkɪt] n (in strike) piquet m de
grève ♦ vt mettre un piquet de grève
devant

**pickle** ['pɪkl] n (also: **~s**: as condiment)
pickles mpl; *petits légumes macérés dans du*
vinaigre ♦ vt conserver dans du vinaigre
or dans de la saumure; **to be in a ~**
*(mess)* être dans le pétrin

**pickpocket** ['pɪkpɔkɪt] n pickpocket m

**pick-up** ['pɪkʌp] n (small truck) pick-up
m inv

**picnic** ['pɪknɪk] n pique-nique m

**picture** ['pɪktʃə*] n image f; (painting)
peinture f, tableau m; (etching) gravure
f; (photograph) photo(graphie) f; (drawing) dessin m; (film) film m; (fig) description f; tableau m ♦ vt se représenter;
**the ~s** (BRIT: inf) le cinéma; **~ book** n
livre m d'images

**picturesque** [pɪktʃə'resk] adj pittoresque

**pie** [paɪ] n tourte f; (of fruit) tarte f; (of
meat) pâté m en croûte

**piece** [piːs] n morceau m; (item): **a ~ of**
**furniture/advice** un meuble/conseil ♦
vt: **to ~ together** rassembler; **to take**
**to ~s** démonter; **~meal** adv (irregular)
(by) au coup par coup; (bit by bit) petit à
bouts; **~work** n travail aux pièces

**pie chart** n graphique m circulaire, ca-
membert m

**pier** [pɪə*] n jetée f

**pierce** [pɪəs] vt percer, transpercer; **~d**
adj (ears etc) percé(e)

**pig** [pɪg] n cochon m, porc m

**pigeon** ['pɪdʒən] n pigeon m; **~hole** n
casier m

**piggy bank** ['pɪgɪ-] n tirelire f

**pig**: ~**headed** adj entêté(e), têtu(e); ~**let** n porcelet m, petit cochon; ~**skin** n peau de porc; ~**sty** n porcherie f; ~**tail** n natte f, tresse f

**pike** [paɪk] n (fish) brochet m

**pilchard** ['pɪltʃəd] n pilchard m (sorte de sardine)

**pile** [paɪl] n (pillar, of books) pile f; (heap) tas m, monceau m; (of carpet) poils mpl ♦ vt (also: ~ **up**) empiler, entasser ♦ vi (also: ~ **up**) s'entasser, s'accumuler; **to ~ into** (car) s'entasser dans; ~**s** npl hémorroïdes fpl; ~**-up** n (AUT) télescopage m, collision f en série

**pilfering** ['pɪlfərɪŋ] n chapardage m

**pilgrim** ['pɪlgrɪm] n pèlerin m

**pill** [pɪl] n pilule f

**pillage** ['pɪlɪdʒ] vt piller

**pillar** ['pɪlər] n pilier m; ~ **box** (BRIT) n boîte f aux lettres (publique)

**pillion** ['pɪljən] n: **to ride ~** (on motorcycle) monter derrière

**pillow** ['pɪləʊ] n oreiller m; ~**case** n taie f d'oreiller

**pilot** ['paɪlət] n pilote m ♦ cpd (scheme etc) pilote, expérimental(e) ♦ vt piloter; ~ **light** n veilleuse f

**pimp** [pɪmp] n souteneur m, maquereau m

**pimple** ['pɪmpl] n bouton m

**pin** [pɪn] n épingle f; (TECH) cheville f ♦ vt épingler; ~**s and needles** fourmis fpl; **to ~ sb down** (fig) obliger qn à répondre; **to ~ sth on sb** (fig) mettre qch sur le dos de qn

**PIN** [pɪn] n abbr (= personal identification number) numéro m d'identification personnel

**pinafore** ['pɪnəfɔːr] n tablier m

**pinball** ['pɪnbɔːl] n flipper m

**pincers** ['pɪnsəz] npl tenailles fpl; (of crab etc) pinces fpl

**pinch** [pɪntʃ] n (of salt etc) pincée f ♦ vt pincer; (inf: steal) piquer, chiper; **at a ~** à la rigueur

**pincushion** ['pɪnkuʃən] n pelote f à

épingles

**pine** [paɪn] n (also: ~ **tree**) pin m ♦ vi: **to ~ for** s'ennuyer de, désirer ardemment; ~ **away** vi dépérir

**pineapple** ['paɪnæpl] n ananas m

**ping** [pɪŋ] n (noise) tintement m; **pong** ® n ping-pong ® m

**pink** [pɪŋk] adj rose ♦ n (colour) rose (BOT) œillet m, mignardise f

**PIN (number)** ['pɪn(-)] n code m confidentiel

**pinpoint** ['pɪnpɔɪnt] vt indiquer or localiser (avec précision); (problem) mettre le doigt sur

**pint** [paɪnt] n pinte f (BRIT = 0.57l; US = 0.47l); (BRIT: inf) ≈ demi m

**pioneer** [paɪə'nɪər] n pionnier m

**pious** ['paɪəs] adj pieux(-euse)

**pip** [pɪp] n (seed) pépin m; **the ~s** (BRIT: time signal on radio) le(s) top(s) sonore(s)

**pipe** [paɪp] n tuyau m, conduite f; (for smoking) pipe f ♦ vt amener par tuyau; ~**s** npl (also: **bagpipes**) cornemuse f; ~ **cleaner** n cure-pipe m; ~ **dream** n chimère f, château m en Espagne; ~**line** n pipe-line m; ~**r** n joueur(-euse) de cornemuse

**piping** ['paɪpɪŋ] adv: ~ **hot** très chaud(e)

**pique** [piːk] n dépit m

**pirate** ['paɪərət] n pirate m; ~**d** adj pirate

**Pisces** ['paɪsiːz] n les Poissons mpl

**piss** [pɪs] (inf!) vi pisser; ~**ed** (inf!) adj (drunk) bourré(e)

**pistol** ['pɪstl] n pistolet m

**piston** ['pɪstən] n piston m

**pit** [pɪt] n trou m, fosse f; (also: **coal** **pit**) puits m de mine; (quarry) carrière f ♦ vt: **to ~ one's wits against sb** se mesurer à qn; ~**s** npl (AUT) aire f de service

**pitch** [pɪtʃ] n (MUS) ton m; (BRIT: SPORT) terrain m; (tar) poix f; (fig) degré m; point m ♦ vt (throw) lancer ♦ vi (fall) tomber; **to ~ a tent** dresser une tente; ~**-black** adj noir(e) (comme le cirage)

**~ed battle** n bataille rangée

**pitfall** ['pitfɔ:l] n piège m

**pith** [piθ] n (of orange etc) intérieur m de l'écorce; **~y** adj piquant(e)

**pitiful** ['pitiful] adj (touching) pitoyable

**pitiless** ['pitilis] adj impitoyable

**pittance** ['pitns] n salaire m de misère

**pity** ['piti] n pitié f ♦ vt plaindre; **what a ~!** quel dommage!

**pizza** ['pi:tsə] n pizza f

**placard** ['plækɑːd] n affiche f; (in march) pancarte f

**placate** [plə'keit] vt apaiser, calmer

**place** [pleis] n endroit m, lieu m; (proper position, job, rank, seat) place f; (home): **at/to his ~** chez lui ♦ vt (object) placer, mettre; (identify) situer; reconnaître; **to take ~** avoir lieu; **out of ~** (not suitable) déplacé(e), inopportun(e); **to change ~s with sb** changer de place avec qn; **in the first ~** d'abord, en premier

**plague** [pleig] n fléau m; (MED) peste f ♦ vt tourmenter

**plaice** [pleis] n inv carrelet m

**plaid** [plæd] n tissu écossais

**plain** [plein] adj (in one colour) uni(e); (simple) simple; (clear) clair(e), évident(e); (not handsome) quelconque, ordinaire ♦ adv franchement, carrément ♦ n plaine f; **~ chocolate** n chocolat m à croquer; **~ clothes** adj (police officer) en civil; **~ly** adv clairement; (frankly) carrément, sans détours

**plaintiff** ['pleintif] n plaignant(e)

**plait** [plæt] n tresse f, natte f

**plan** [plæn] n plan m; (scheme) projet m ♦ vt (think in advance) projeter; (prepare) organiser; (house) dresser les plans de, concevoir ♦ vi faire des projets; **to ~ to do** prévoir de faire

**plane** [plein] n (AVIAT) avion m; (ART, MATH etc) plan m; (fig) niveau m, plan; (tool) rabot m; (also: ~ **tree**) platane m ♦ vt raboter

**planet** ['plænit] n planète f

**plank** [plæŋk] n planche f

**planner** ['plænər] n planificateur(-trice); (town ~) urbaniste m/f

**planning** ['plæniŋ] n planification f; **family ~** planning familial; **~ permission** n permis m de construire

**plant** [plɑːnt] n plante f; (machinery) matériel m; (factory) usine f ♦ vt planter; (bomb) poser; (microphone, incriminating evidence) cacher

**plaster** ['plɑːstər] n plâtre m; (also: ~ **of Paris**) plâtre à mouler; (BRIT: also: **sticking ~**) pansement adhésif ♦ vt plâtrer; (cover): **to ~ with** couvrir de; **~ed** (inf) adj soûl(e)

**plastic** ['plæstik] n plastique m ♦ adj (made of ~) en plastique; **~ bag** n sac m en plastique

**Plasticine** ® ['plæstisi:n] n pâte f à modeler

**plastic surgery** n chirurgie f esthétique

**plate** [pleit] n (dish) assiette f; (in book) gravure f, planche f; (dental ~) dentier m

**plateau** ['plætəu] (pl ~s or ~x) n plateau m

**plate glass** n verre m (de vitrine)

**platform** ['plætfɔːm] n plate-forme f; (at meeting) tribune f; (stage) estrade f; (RAIL) quai m

**platinum** ['plætinəm] n platine m

**platter** ['plætər] n plat m

**plausible** ['plɔːzibl] adj plausible; (person) convaincant(e)

**play** [plei] n (THEATRE) pièce f (de théâtre) ♦ vt (game) jouer à; (team, opponent) jouer contre; (instrument) jouer de; (part, piece of music, note) jouer; (record etc) passer ♦ vi jouer; **to ~ safe** ne prendre aucun risque; **~ down** vt minimiser; **~ up** vi (cause trouble) faire des siennes; **~boy** n playboy m; **~er** n joueur(-euse); (THEATRE) acteur(-trice); (MUS) musicien(ne); **~ful** adj enjoué(e); **~ground** n cour f de récréation; (in park) aire f de jeux; **~group** n garderie f; **~ing card** n carte f à jouer; **~ing**

**field** *n* terrain *m* de sport; **~mate** *n* camarade *m/f*, copain (copine); **~off** *n* (SPORT) belle *f*; **~ park** *n* terrain *m* de jeu; **~pen** *n* parc *m* (pour bébé); **~thing** *n* jouet *m*; **~time** *n* récréation *f*; **~wright** *n* dramaturge *m*

**plc** *abbr* (= public limited company) SARL

**plea** [pli:] *n* (request) appel *m*; (LAW) défense *f*

**plead** [pli:d] *vt* plaider; (give as excuse) invoquer ♦ *vi* (LAW) plaider; (beg): **to ~ with sb** implorer qn

**pleasant** ['plɛznt] *adj* agréable; **~ries** *npl* (polite remarks) civilités *fpl*

**please** [pli:z] *excl* s'il te (or vous) plaît ♦ *vt* plaire à ♦ *vi* plaire; (think fit): **do as you ~** faites comme il vous plaira; **~ yourself!** à ta (or votre) guise!; **~d** *adj*: **~d (with)** content(e) (de); **~d to meet you** enchanté (de faire votre connaissance); **pleasing** *adj* plaisant(e), qui fait plaisir

**pleasure** ['plɛʒər] *n* plaisir *m*; **"it's a ~"** "je vous en prie"

**pleat** [pli:t] *n* pli *m*

**pledge** [plɛdʒ] *n* (promise) promesse *f* ♦ *vt* engager; promettre

**plentiful** ['plɛntɪful] *adj* abondant(e), copieux(-euse)

**plenty** ['plɛntɪ] *n*: **~ of** beaucoup de; (bien) assez de

**pliable** ['plaɪəbl] *adj* flexible; (person) malléable

**pliers** ['plaɪəz] *npl* pinces *fpl*

**plight** [plaɪt] *n* situation *f* critique

**plimsolls** ['plɪmsəlz] (BRIT) *npl* chaussures *fpl* de tennis, tennis *mpl*

**plinth** [plɪnθ] *n* (of statue) socle *m*

**P.L.O.** *n abbr* (= Palestine Liberation Organization) OLP *f*

**plod** [plɔd] *vi* avancer péniblement; (fig) peiner

**plonk** [plɔŋk] (inf) *n* (BRIT: wine) pinard *m*, piquette *f* ♦ *vt*: **to ~ sth down** poser brusquement qch

**plot** [plɔt] *n* complot *m*, conspiration *f*;

(of story, play) intrigue *f*; (of land) lot *m* de terrain, lopin *m* ♦ *vt* (sb's downfall) comploter; (mark out) pointer; relever, déterminer ♦ *vi* comploter

**plough** [plaʊ] (US **plow**) *n* charrue *f* ♦ *vt* (earth) labourer; **to ~ money into** investir dans; **~ through** *vt fus* (snow etc) avancer péniblement dans; **~man's lunch** (BRIT) *n* assiette froide avec du pain, du fromage et des pickles

**ploy** [plɔɪ] *n* stratagème *m*

**pluck** [plʌk] *vt* (fruit) cueillir; (musical instrument) pincer; (bird) plumer; (eyebrow) épiler ♦ *n* courage *m*, cran *m*; **to ~ up courage** prendre son courage à deux mains

**plug** [plʌg] *n* (ELEC) prise *f* de courant; (stopper) bouchon *m*, bonde *f*; (AUT: also: **spark(ing) ~**) bougie *f* ♦ *vt* (hole) boucher; (inf: advertise) faire de la battage pour; **~ in** *vt* (ELEC) brancher

**plum** [plʌm] *n* (fruit) prune *f* ♦ *cpd*: **~ job** (inf) travail *m* en or

**plumb** [plʌm] *vt*: **to ~ the depths** (fig) toucher le fond (du désespoir)

**plumber** ['plʌmər] *n* plombier *m*

**plumbing** ['plʌmɪŋ] *n* (trade) plomberie *f*; (piping) tuyauterie *f*

**plummet** ['plʌmɪt] *vi*: **to ~ (down)** plonger, dégringoler

**plump** [plʌmp] *adj* rondelet(te), dodu(e), bien en chair ♦ *vi*: **to ~ for** (inf: choose) se décider pour

**plunder** ['plʌndər] *n* pillage *m*; (loot) butin *m* ♦ *vt* piller

**plunge** [plʌndʒ] *n* plongeon *m*; (fig) chute *f* ♦ *vt* plonger ♦ *vi* (dive) plonger; (fall) tomber, dégringoler; **to take the ~** se jeter à l'eau; **plunging** ['plʌndʒɪŋ] *adj*: **plunging neckline** décolleté plongeant

**pluperfect** [plu:'pə:fɪkt] *n* plus-que-parfait *m*

**plural** ['pluərl] *adj* pluriel(le) ♦ *n* pluriel *m*

**plus** [plʌs] *n* (also: **~ sign**) signe *m* plus ♦ *prep* plus; **ten/twenty ~** plus de dix/vingt

**plush** [plʌʃ] *adj* somptueux(-euse)

**ply** [plaɪ] *vt* (*a trade*) exercer ♦ *vi* (*ship*) faire la navette ♦ *n* (*of wool, rope*) fil *m*, brin *m*; **to ~ sb with drink** donner continuellement à boire à qn; **to ~ sb with questions** presser qn de questions; **~wood** *n* contre-plaqué *m*

**PM** *abbr* = **Prime Minister**

**p.m.** *adv abbr* (= *post meridiem*) de l'après-midi

**pneumatic drill** [nju:'mætɪk-] *n* marteau-piqueur *m*

**pneumonia** [nju:'məunɪə] *n* pneumonie *f*

**poach** [pəutʃ] *vt* (*cook*) pocher; (*steal*) pêcher (*or* chasser) sans permis ♦ *vi* braconner; **~ed egg** *n* œuf poché; **~er** *n* braconnier *m*

**P.O. box** *n abbr* = **post office box**

**pocket** ['pɔkɪt] *n* poche *f* ♦ *vt* empocher; **to be out of ~** (*BRIT*) en être de sa poche; **~book** (*US*) *n* (*wallet*) portefeuille *m*; **~ calculator** *n* calculette *f*; **~ knife** *n* canif *m*; **~ money** *n* argent *m* de poche

**pod** [pɔd] *n* cosse *f*

**podgy** ['pɔdʒɪ] *adj* rondelet(te)

**podiatrist** [pɔ'di:ətrɪst] (*US*) *n* pédicure *m/f*, podologue *m/f*

**poem** ['pəuɪm] *n* poème *m*

**poet** ['pəuɪt] *n* poète *m*; **~ic** [pəu'ɛtɪk] *adj* poétique; **~ry** ['pəuɪtrɪ] *n* poésie *f*

**poignant** ['pɔɪnjənt] *adj* poignant(e); (*sharp*) vif (vive)

**point** [pɔɪnt] *n* point *m*; (*tip*) pointe *f*; (*in time*) moment *m*; (*in space*) endroit *m*; (*subject, idea*) point, sujet *m*; (*purpose*) sens *m*; (*ELEC*) prise *f*; (*also:* **decimal ~**): **2 ~ 3 (2.3)** 2 virgule 3 (2,3) ♦ *vt* (*show*) indiquer; (*gun etc*): **to ~ sth at** braquer *or* diriger qch sur ♦ *vi*: **to ~ at** montrer du doigt; **~s** *npl* (*AUT*) vis platinées; (*RAIL*) aiguillage *m*; **to be on the ~ of doing sth** être sur le point de faire qch; **to make a ~ of doing** ne pas manquer de faire; **to get the ~** comprendre, saisir; **to miss the ~** ne pas comprendre; **to come to the ~** en venir au fait; **there's no ~ (in doing)** cela ne sert à rien (de faire); **~ out** *vt* faire remarquer, souligner; **~ to** *vt fus* (*fig*) indiquer; **~-blank** *adv* (*fig*) catégoriquement; (*also:* **at ~-blank range**) à bout portant; **~ed** *adj* (*shape*) pointu(e); (*remark*) plein(e) de sous-entendus; **~er** *n* (*needle*) aiguille *f*; (*piece of advice*) conseil *m*; (*clue*) indice *m*; **~less** *adj* inutile, vain(e); **~ of view** *n* point *m* de vue

**poise** [pɔɪz] *n* (*composure*) calme *m*

**poison** ['pɔɪzn] *n* poison *m* ♦ *vt* empoisonner; **~ous** *adj* (*snake*) venimeux(-euse); (*plant*) vénéneux(-euse); (*fumes etc*) toxique

**poke** [pəuk] *vt* (*fire*) tisonner; (*jab with finger, stick etc*) piquer; pousser du doigt; (*put*): **to ~ sth in(to)** fourrer *or* enfoncer qch dans; **~ about** *vi* fureter; **~r** *n* tisonnier *m*; (*CARDS*) poker *m*

**poky** ['pəukɪ] *adj* exigu(ë)

**Poland** ['pəulənd] *n* Pologne *f*

**polar** ['pəuləʳ] *adj* polaire; **~ bear** *n* ours blanc

**Pole** [pəul] *n* Polonais(e)

**pole** [pəul] *n* poteau *m*; (*of wood*) mât *m*, perche *f*; (*GEO*) pôle *m*; **~ bean** (*US*) *n* haricot *m* (à rames); **~ vault** *n* saut *m* à la perche

**police** [pə'li:s] *npl* police *f* ♦ *vt* maintenir l'ordre dans; **~ car** *n* voiture *f* de police; **~man** (*irreg*) *n* agent *m* de police, policier *m*; **~ station** *n* commissariat *m* de police; **~woman** (*irreg*) *n* femme-agent *f*

**policy** ['pɔlɪsɪ] *n* politique *f*; (*also:* **insurance ~**) police *f* (d'assurance)

**polio** ['pəulɪəu] *n* polio *f*

**Polish** ['pəulɪʃ] *adj* polonais(e) ♦ *n* (*LING*) polonais *m*

**polish** ['pɔlɪʃ] *n* (*for shoes*) cirage *m*; (*for floor*) cire *f*, encaustique *f*; (*shine*) éclat *m*, poli *m*; (*fig: refinement*) raffinement *m* ♦ *vt* (*put ~ on shoes, wood*) cirer; (*make shiny*) astiquer, faire briller; ~

**off** (inf) vt (food) liquider; **~ed** adj (fig) raffiné(e)

**polite** [pə'laɪt] adj poli(e); **in ~ society** dans la bonne société; **~ly** adv poliment; **~ness** n politesse f

**political** [pə'lɪtɪkl] adj politique; **~ly correct** adj politiquement correct(e)

**politician** [pɒlɪ'tɪʃən] n homme m/ femme f politique

**politics** ['pɒlɪtɪks] npl politique f

**poll** [pəul] n scrutin m, vote m; (also: **opinion ~**) sondage m (d'opinion) ♦ vt obtenir

**pollen** ['pɒlən] n pollen m

**polling day** ['pəulɪŋ-] (BRIT) n jour m des élections

**polling station** (BRIT) n bureau m de vote

**pollute** [pə'luːt] vt polluer; **pollution** [pə'luːʃən] n pollution f

**polo** ['pəuləu] n polo m; **~-necked** adj à col roulé; **~ shirt** n polo m

**polyester** [pɒlɪ'estər] n polyester m

**polystyrene** [pɒlɪ'staɪriːn] n polystyrène m

**polythene** ['pɒlɪθiːn] n polyéthylène m; **~ bag** n sac m en plastique

**pomegranate** ['pɒmɪɡrænɪt] n grenade f

**pomp** [pɒmp] n (of ceremony) pompe f, faste m, apparat m; **~ous** adj pompeux(-euse)

**pond** [pɒnd] n étang m; mare f

**ponder** ['pɒndər] vt considérer, peser; **~ous** adj pesant(e), lourd(e)

**pong** [pɒŋ] (BRIT: inf) n puanteur f

**pony** ['pəunɪ] n poney m; **~tail** n queue f de cheval; **~ trekking** (BRIT) n randonnée f à cheval

**poodle** ['puːdl] n caniche m

**pool** [puːl] n (of rain) flaque f; (pond) mare f; (also: **swimming ~**) piscine f; (billiards) pool ♦ vt mettre en commun; **~s** npl (football ~s) ≈ loto sportif

**poor** [puər] adj pauvre; (mediocre) médiocre, faible, mauvais(e) ♦ npl: **the ~** les pauvres mpl; **~ly** adj souffrant(e),

malade ♦ adv mal; médiocrement

**pop** [pɒp] n (MUS) musique f pop; (drink) boisson gazeuse; (US: inf: father) papa m; (noise) bruit sec ♦ vt (put) mettre (rapidement) ♦ vi éclater; (cork) sauter; **~ in** vi entrer en passant; **~ out** vi sortir (brièvement); **~ up** vi apparaître, surgir; **~corn** n pop-corn m

**pope** [pəup] n pape m

**poplar** ['pɒplər] n peuplier m

**popper** ['pɒpər] (BRIT: inf) n bouton-pression m

**poppy** ['pɒpɪ] n coquelicot m; pavot m

**Popsicle** ® ['pɒpsɪkl] (US) n esquimau m (glace)

**popular** ['pɒpjulər] adj populaire; (fashionable) à la mode

**population** [pɒpju'leɪʃən] n population f

**porcelain** ['pɔːslɪn] n porcelaine f

**porch** [pɔːtʃ] n porche m; (US) véranda f

**porcupine** ['pɔːkjupaɪn] n porc-épic m

**pore** [pɔːr] n pore m ♦ vi: **to ~ over** s'absorber dans, être plongé(e) dans

**pork** [pɔːk] n porc m

**porn** [pɔːn] (inf) adj, n porno m

**pornographic** [pɔːnə'ɡræfɪk] adj pornographique

**pornography** [pɔː'nɔɡrəfɪ] n pornographie f

**porpoise** ['pɔːpəs] n marsouin m

**porridge** ['pɒrɪdʒ] n porridge m

**port** [pɔːt] n (harbour) port m; (NAUT: left side) bâbord m; (wine) porto m; **~ of call** escale f

**portable** ['pɔːtəbl] adj portatif(-ive)

**porter** ['pɔːtər] n (for luggage) porteur m; (doorkeeper) gardien(ne); portier m

**portfolio** [pɔːt'fəuliəu] n portefeuille m; (of artist) portfolio m

**porthole** ['pɔːthəul] n hublot m

**portion** ['pɔːʃən] n portion f, part f

**portrait** ['pɔːtreɪt] n portrait m

**portray** [pɔː'treɪ] vt faire le portrait de; (in writing) dépeindre, représenter; (subj: actor) jouer

**Portugal** ['pɔːtjugl] n Portugal m; Por-

**tuguese** [pɔːtjuˈgiːz] *adj* portugais(e)
♦ *n inv* Portugais(e); (LING) portugais *m*

**pose** [pəuz] *n* pose *f* (*pretend*): **to ~
as** se poser en ♦ *vt* poser; (*problem*)
créer

**posh** [pɔʃ] (*inf*) *adj* chic *inv*

**position** [pəˈzɪʃən] *n* position *f*; (*job*) situation *f* ♦ *vt* placer

**positive** [ˈpɔzɪtɪv] *adj* positif(-ive); (*certain*) sûr(e), certain(e); (*definite*) for-
mel(le), catégorique

**possess** [pəˈzes] *vt* posséder; **~ion** *n*
possession *f*

**possibility** [pɔsɪˈbɪlɪtɪ] *n* possibilité *f*;
éventualité *f*

**possible** [ˈpɔsɪbl] *adj* possible; **as big
as ~** aussi gros que possible; **possibly**
*adv* (*perhaps*) peut-être; **if you possibly can** si cela vous est possible; **I
cannot possibly come** il m'est impossible de venir

**post** [pəust] *n* poste *f*, (BRIT: *letters,
delivery*) courrier *m*; (*job, situation,* MIL)
poste *m*; (*pole*) poteau *m* ♦ *vt* (BRIT: *send
by ~*) poster; (: *appoint*): **to ~ to** affecter à; **~age** *n* tarifs *mpl* d'affranchissement; **~al order** *n* mandat(-poste) *m*;
**~box** (BRIT) *n* boîte *f* aux lettres; **~card**
*n* carte postale; **~code** (BRIT) *n* code
postal

**poster** [ˈpəustər] *n* affiche *f*

**poste restante** [pəustˈrestɑ̃nt] (BRIT)
*n* poste restante

**postgraduate** [ˈpəustˈgrædjuət] *n* ≈
étudiant(e) de troisième cycle

**posthumous** [ˈpɔstjuməs] *adj* posthume

**postman** [ˈpəustmən] (*irreg*) *n* facteur
*m*

**postmark** [ˈpəustmɑːk] *n* cachet *m* (de
la poste)

**postmortem** [pəustˈmɔːtəm] *n* autopsie *f*

**post office** *n* (*building*) poste *f*; (*organization*): **the P~ O~** les Postes; **~ ~
box** *n* boîte postale

**postpone** [pəusˈpəun] *vt* remettre (à

plus tard)

**posture** [ˈpɔstʃər] *n* posture *f*; (*fig*) attitude *f*

**postwar** [pəustˈwɔːr] *adj* d'après-guerre

**postwoman** *n* factrice *f*

**posy** [ˈpəuzi] *n* petit bouquet

**pot** [pɔt] *n* pot *m*; (*for cooking*) marmite
*f*, casserole *f*; (*teapot*) théière *f*; (*coffee-
pot*) cafetière *f*; (*inf: marijuana*) herbe
*f* ♦ *vt* (*plant*) mettre en pot; **to go to ~**
(*inf: work, performance*) aller à vau-l'eau

**potato** [pəˈteɪtəu] (*pl* **~es**) *n* pomme *f*
de terre; **~ peeler** *n* épluche-légumes
*m inv*

**potent** [ˈpəutnt] *adj* puissant(e); (*drink*)
fort(e), très alcoolisé(e); (*man*) viril

**potential** [pəˈtenʃl] *adj* potentiel(le) ♦ *n*
potentiel *m*

**pothole** [ˈpɔthəul] *n* (*in road*) nid *m* de
poule; (BRIT: *underground*) gouffre *m*,
caverne *f*; **potholing** (BRIT) *n*: **to go
potholing** faire de la spéléologie

**potluck** [pɔtˈlʌk] *n*: **to take ~** tenter
sa chance

**pot plant** *n* plante *f* d'appartement

**potted** [ˈpɔtɪd] *adj* (*food*) en conserve;
(*plant*) en pot; (*abbreviated*) abrégé(e)

**potter** [ˈpɔtər] *n* potier *m* ♦ *vi*: **to ~
around, ~ about** (BRIT) bricoler; **~y** *n*
poterie *f*

**potty** [ˈpɔti] *adj* (*inf: mad*) dingue ♦ *n*
(*child's*) pot *m*

**pouch** [pautʃ] *n* (ZOOL) poche *f*; (*for tobacco*) blague *f*; (*for money*) bourse *f*

**poultry** [ˈpəultri] *n* volaille *f*

**pounce** [pauns] *vi*: **to ~ (on)** bondir
(sur), sauter (sur)

**pound** [paund] *n* (*unit of money*) livre *f*;
(*unit of weight*) livre ♦ *vt* (*beat*) bourrer
de coups, marteler; (*crush*) piler, pulvériser ♦ *vi* (*heart*) battre violemment, taper

**pour** [pɔːr] *vt* verser ♦ *vi* couler à flots;
**to ~ (with rain)** pleuvoir à verse; **to ~
sb a drink** verser or servir à boire à qn;
**~ away** *vt* vider; **~ in** *vi* (*people*) affluer, se précipiter; (*news, letters etc*) ar-

river en masse; ~ **off** vt = **pour away**; ~ **out** vi (people) sortir en masse ♦ vt vider; (fig) déverser; (serve: a drink) verser; ~**ing** ['pɔːrɪŋ] adj: ~**ing rain** pluie torrentielle

**pout** [paut] vi faire la moue

**poverty** ['pɔvətɪ] n pauvreté f, misère f; ~**-stricken** adj pauvre, déshérité(e)

**powder** ['paudə<sup>r</sup>] n poudre f ♦ vt: **to ~ one's face** se poudrer; ~ **compact** n poudrier m; ~**ed milk** n lait m en poudre; ~ **room** n toilettes fpl (pour dames)

**power** ['pauə<sup>r</sup>] n (strength) puissance f, force f; (ability, authority) pouvoir m; (of speech, thought) faculté f; (ELEC) courant m; **to be in ~** (POL etc) être au pouvoir; ~ **cut** (BRIT) n coupure f de courant; ~**ed** adj: ~**ed by** actionné(e) par, fonctionnant à; ~ **failure** n panne f de courant; ~**ful** adj puissant(e); ~**less** adj impuissant(e); ~ **point** (BRIT) n prise f de courant; ~ **station** n centrale f électrique; ~ **struggle** n lutte f pour le pouvoir

**p.p.** abbr (= per procurationem): **p.p. J. Smith** pour M. J. Smith

**PR** n abbr = **public relations**

**practical** ['præktɪkl] adj pratique; ~**ity** [præktɪ'kælɪtɪ] (no pl) n (of person) sens m pratique; ~**ities** npl (of situation) aspect m pratique; ~ **joke** n farce f; ~**ly** adv (almost) pratiquement

**practice** ['præktɪs] n pratique f; (of profession) exercice m; (at football etc) entraînement m; (business) cabinet m ♦ vt, vi (US) = **practise**; **in ~** (in reality) en pratique; **out of ~** rouillé(e)

**practise** ['præktɪs] (US **practice**) vt (musical instrument) travailler; (train for: sport) s'entraîner à; (a sport, religion) pratiquer; (profession) exercer ♦ vi s'exercer, travailler; (train) s'entraîner; (lawyer, doctor) exercer; **practising** adj (Christian etc) pratiquant(e); (lawyer) en exercice

**practitioner** [præk'tɪʃənə<sup>r</sup>] n praticien(ne)

**prairie** ['prɛərɪ] n steppe f, prairie f

**praise** [preɪz] n éloge(s) m(pl), louange(s) f(pl) ♦ vt louer, faire l'éloge de; ~**worthy** adj digne d'éloges

**pram** [præm] (BRIT) n landau m, voiture f d'enfant

**prance** [prɑːns] vi (also: ~ **about**: person) se pavaner

**prank** [præŋk] n farce f

**prawn** [prɔːn] n crevette f (rose); ~ **cocktail** n cocktail m de crevettes

**pray** [preɪ] vi prier; ~**er** [prɛə<sup>r</sup>] n prière f

**preach** [priːtʃ] vt, vi prêcher

**precaution** [prɪ'kɔːʃən] n précaution f

**precede** [prɪ'siːd] vt précéder

**precedent** ['prɛsɪdənt] n précédent m

**preceding** adj qui précède/précédait etc

**precinct** ['priːsɪŋkt] n (US) circonscription f, arrondissement m; ~**s** npl (neighbourhood) alentours mpl, environs mpl; **pedestrian ~** (BRIT) zone piétonnière or piétonne; **shopping ~** (BRIT) centre commercial

**precious** ['prɛʃəs] adj précieux(-euse)

**precipitate** [prɪ'sɪpɪteɪt] vt précipiter

**precise** [prɪ'saɪs] adj précis(e); ~**ly** adv précisément

**precocious** [prɪ'kəuʃəs] adj précoce

**precondition** [priːkən'dɪʃən] n condition f nécessaire

**predecessor** ['priːdɪsesə<sup>r</sup>] n prédécesseur m

**predicament** [prɪ'dɪkəmənt] n situation f difficile

**predict** [prɪ'dɪkt] vt prédire; ~**able** adj prévisible

**predominantly** [prɪ'dɔmɪnəntlɪ] adv en majeure partie; surtout

**pre-empt** [priː'emt] vt anticiper, devancer

**preen** [priːn] vt: **to ~ itself** (bird) se lisser les plumes; **to ~ o.s.** s'admirer

**prefab** ['priːfæb] n bâtiment m préfabriqué

**preface** ['prefəs] n préface f

**prefect** ['priːfɛkt] (BRIT) n (in school) élève chargé(e) de certaines fonctions de discipline

**prefer** [prɪ'fɜː] vt préférer; **~ably** ['prɛfrəblɪ] adv de préférence; **~ence** ['prɛfrəns] n préférence f; **~ential** [prɛfə'rɛnʃəl] adj: **~ential treatment** traitement m de faveur or préférentiel

**prefix** ['priːfɪks] n préfixe m

**pregnancy** ['prɛgnənsɪ] n grossesse f

**pregnant** ['prɛgnənt] adj enceinte; (animal) pleine

**prehistoric** ['priːhɪs'tɔrɪk] adj préhistorique

**prejudice** ['prɛdʒʊdɪs] n préjugé m; **~d** adj (person) plein(e) de préjugés; (in a matter) partial(e)

**premarital** ['priː'mærɪtl] adj avant le mariage

**premature** ['prɛmətʃuə'] adj prématuré(e)

**premenstrual syndrome** [priː'mɛnstruəl-] n syndrome prémenstruel

**premier** ['prɛmɪə'] adj premier(-ère), principal(e) ♦ n (POL) Premier ministre

**première** ['prɛmɪɛə'] n première f

**Premier League** n première division

**premise** ['prɛmɪs] n prémisse f; **~s** npl (building) locaux mpl; **on the ~s** sur les lieux; sur place

**premium** ['priːmɪəm] n prime f; **to be at a ~** faire prime; **~ bond** (BRIT) n bon m à lot, obligation f à prime

**premonition** [prɛmə'nɪʃən] n prémonition f

**preoccupied** [priː'ɔkjupaɪd] adj préoccupé(e)

**prep** [prɛp] n (SCOL) étude f

**prepaid** [priː'peɪd] adj payé(e) d'avance

**preparation** [prɛpə'reɪʃən] n préparation f; **~s** npl (for trip, war) préparatifs mpl

**preparatory** [prɪ'pærətərɪ] adj préliminaire; **~ school** (BRIT) n école primaire privée

**prepare** [prɪ'pɛə'] vt préparer ♦ vi: **to ~ for** se préparer à; **~d to** prêt(e) à

**preposition** [prɛpə'zɪʃən] n préposition f

**preposterous** [prɪ'pɔstərəs] adj absurde

**prep school** n = preparatory school

**prerequisite** [priː'rɛkwɪzɪt] n condition f préalable

**Presbyterian** [prɛzbɪ'tɪərɪən] adj, n presbytérien(ne) m/f

**prescribe** [prɪ'skraɪb] vt prescrire; **prescription** [prɪ'skrɪpʃən] n (MED) ordonnance f; (: medicine) médicament (obtenu sur ordonnance)

**presence** ['prɛzns] n présence f; **~ of mind** présence d'esprit

**present** [adj, n 'prɛznt, vb prɪ'zɛnt] adj présent(e) ♦ n (gift) cadeau m; (actuality) présent m ♦ vt présenter; (prize, medal) remettre; (give): **to ~ sb with sth** or **sth to sb** offrir qch à qn; **to give sb a ~** offrir un cadeau à qn; **at ~** en ce moment; **~ation** [prɛzn'teɪʃən] n présentation f; (ceremony) remise f du cadeau (or de la médaille etc); **~-day** adj contemporain(e), actuel(le); **~er** n (RADIO, TV) présentateur(-trice); **~ly** adv (with verb in past) peu après; (soon) tout à l'heure, bientôt; (at present) en ce moment

**preservative** [prɪ'zɜːvətɪv] n agent m de conservation

**preserve** [prɪ'zɜːv] vt (keep safe) préserver, protéger; (maintain) conserver, garder; (food) mettre en conserve ♦ n (often pl: jam) confiture f

**president** ['prɛzɪdənt] n président(e); **~ial** [prɛzɪ'dɛnʃl] adj présidentiel(le)

**press** [prɛs] n presse f; (for wine) pressoir m ♦ vt (squeeze) presser, serrer; (push) appuyer sur; (clothes: iron) repasser; (put ~ure on) faire pression sur; (insist): **to ~ sth on sb** presser qn d'accepter qch ♦ vi appuyer, peser; **to ~ for sth** faire pression pour obtenir qch; **we are ~ed for time/money** le temps/l'argent nous manque; **~ on** vi continuer; **~ conference** n conférence f de presse; **~ing** adj urgent(e), pressant(e); **~ stud** (BRIT) n bouton-pression m; **~-up** (BRIT) n traction f

**pressure** ['prɛʃər] n pression f; (stress) tension f; **to put ~ on sb (to do)** faire pression sur qn (pour qu'il/elle fasse); **~ cooker** n cocotte-minute f; **~ gauge** n manomètre m; **~ group** n groupe m de pression

**prestige** [prɛs'tiːʒ] n prestige m; **prestigious** [prɛs'tɪdʒəs] adj prestigieux(-euse)

**presumably** [prɪ'zjuːməblɪ] adv vraisemblablement

**presume** [prɪ'zjuːm] vt présumer, supposer

**pretence** [prɪ'tɛns] (US **pretense**) n (claim) prétention f; **under false ~s** sous des prétextes fallacieux

**pretend** [prɪ'tɛnd] vt (feign) feindre, simuler ♦ vi faire semblant

**pretext** ['priːtɛkst] n prétexte m

**pretty** ['prɪtɪ] adj joli(e) ♦ adv assez

**prevail** [prɪ'veɪl] vi (be usual) avoir cours; (win) l'emporter, prévaloir; **~ing** adj dominant(e); **prevalent** ['prɛvələnt] adj répandu(e), courant(e)

**prevent** [prɪ'vɛnt] vt: **to ~ (from doing)** empêcher (de faire); **~ative** [prɪ'vɛntətɪv], **~ive** [prɪ'vɛntɪv] adj préventif(-ive)

**preview** ['priːvjuː] n (of film etc) avant-première f

**previous** ['priːvɪəs] adj précédent(e); antérieur(e); **~ly** adv précédemment, auparavant

**prewar** [priː'wɔːr] adj d'avant-guerre

**prey** [preɪ] n proie f ♦ vi: **to ~** s'attaquer à; **it was ~ing on his mind** cela le travaillait

**price** [praɪs] n prix m ♦ vt (goods) fixer le prix de; **~less** adj sans prix, inestimable; **~ list** n liste f des prix, tarif m

**prick** [prɪk] n piqûre f ♦ vt piquer; **to ~ up one's ears** dresser or tendre l'oreille

**prickle** ['prɪkl] n (of plant) épine f; (sensation) picotement m; **prickly** adj piquant(e), épineux(-euse); **prickly heat** n fièvre f miliaire

**pride** [praɪd] n orgueil m, fierté f ♦ vt: **to ~ o.s. on** se flatter de; s'enorgueillir de

**priest** [priːst] n prêtre m; **~hood** n prêtrise f, sacerdoce m

**prim** [prɪm] adj collet monté inv, guindé(e)

**primarily** ['praɪmərɪlɪ] adv principalement, essentiellement

**primary** ['praɪmərɪ] adj (first in importance) premier(-ère), primordial(e), principal(e) ♦ n (US: election) (élection f) primaire f; **~ school** (BRIT) n école primaire f

**prime** [praɪm] adj primordial(e), fondamental(e); (excellent) excellent(e) ♦ n: **in the ~ of life** dans la fleur de l'âge ♦ vt (wood) apprêter; (fig) mettre au courant; **P~ Minister** n Premier ministre m

**primeval** adj primitif(-ive); **~ forest** forêt f vierge

**primitive** ['prɪmɪtɪv] adj primitif(-ive)

**primrose** ['prɪmrəʊz] n primevère f

**primus (stove)** ® ['praɪməs-] (BRIT) n réchaud m de camping

**prince** [prɪns] n prince m

**princess** [prɪn'sɛs] n princesse f

**principal** ['prɪnsɪpl] adj principal(e) ♦ n (headmaster) directeur(-trice), principal m

**principle** ['prɪnsɪpl] n principe m; **in/on ~** en/par principe

**print** [prɪnt] n (mark) empreinte f; (letters) caractères mpl; (ART) gravure f, estampe f; (: photograph) photo f ♦ vt imprimer; (publish) publier; (write in block letters) écrire en caractères d'imprimerie; **out of ~** épuisé(e); **~ed matter** n imprimé(s) m(pl); **~er** n imprimeur m; (machine) imprimante f; **~ing** n impression f; **~-out** n copie f papier

**prior** ['praɪər] adj antérieur(e), précédent(e); (more important) prioritaire ♦ adv: ~ **to doing** avant de faire; **~ity** ['praɪˈɔrɪti] n priorité f

**prise** [praɪz] vt: **to ~ open** forcer

**prison** ['prɪzn] n prison f ♦ cpd pénitentiaire; **~er** n prisonnier(-ère)

**pristine** ['prɪstiːn] adj parfait(e)

**privacy** ['prɪvəsɪ] n intimité f, solitude f

**private** ['praɪvɪt] adj privé(e); (personal) personnel(le); (house, lesson) particulier(-ère); (quiet: place) tranquille; (reserved: person) secret(-ète) ♦ n soldat m de deuxième classe; **"~"** (on envelope) "personnelle"; **in ~** en privé; **~ detective** n détective privé; **~ enterprise** n l'entreprise privée; **~ property** n propriété privée; **privatize** vt privatiser

**privet** ['prɪvɪt] n troène m

**privilege** ['prɪvɪlɪdʒ] n privilège m

**privy** ['prɪvɪ] adj: **to be ~ to** être au courant de

**prize** [praɪz] n prix m ♦ adj (example, idiot) parfait(e); (bull, novel) primé(e) ♦ vt priser, faire grand cas de; **~-giving** n distribution f des prix; **~winner** n gagnant(e)

**pro** [prəu] n (SPORT) professionnel(le) ♦ n: **the ~s and cons** le pour et le contre

**probability** [prɔbəˈbɪlɪti] n probabilité f

**probable** ['prɔbəbl] adj probable; **probably** adv probablement

**probation** [prəˈbeɪʃən] n: **on ~** (LAW) en liberté surveillée, en sursis; (employee) à l'essai

**probe** [prəub] n (MED, SPACE) sonde f; (enquiry) enquête f, investigation f ♦ vt sonder, explorer

**problem** ['prɔbləm] n problème m

**procedure** [prəˈsiːdʒər] n (ADMIN, LAW) procédure f; (method) marche f à suivre, façon f de procéder

**proceed** [prəˈsiːd] vi continuer; (go forward) avancer; **to ~ (with)** continuer, poursuivre; **to ~ to do** se mettre à faire; **~ings** npl (LAW) poursuites fpl; (meeting) réunion f, séance f; **~s**

['prəusiːdz] npl produit m, recette f

**process** ['prəuses] n processus m; (method) procédé m ♦ vt traiter; **~ing** n (PHOT) développement m; **~ion** [prəˈseʃən] n défilé m, cortège m; (REL) procession f; **funeral ~ion** (on foot) cortège m funèbre; (in cars) convoi m mortuaire

**proclaim** [prəˈkleɪm] vt déclarer, proclamer

**procrastinate** [prəuˈkræstɪneɪt] vi faire traîner les choses, vouloir tout remettre au lendemain

**procure** [prəˈkjuər] vt obtenir

**prod** [prɔd] vt pousser

**prodigal** ['prɔdɪgl] adj prodigue

**prodigy** ['prɔdɪdʒɪ] n prodige m

**produce** [n 'prɔdjuːs, vb prəˈdjuːs] n (AGR) produits mpl ♦ vt (show) présenter; (cause) provoquer, causer; (THEATRE) monter, mettre en scène; **~r** n producteur m; (THEATRE) metteur m en scène

**product** ['prɔdʌkt] n produit m

**production** [prəˈdʌkʃən] n production f; (THEATRE) mise f en scène; **~ line** n chaîne f (de fabrication)

**productivity** [prɔdʌkˈtɪvɪti] n productivité f

**profession** [prəˈfeʃən] n profession f; **~al** n professionnel(le) ♦ adj professionnel(le); (work) de professionnel; **~ally** adv professionnellement; (SPORT: play) en professionnel; **she sings ~ally** c'est une chanteuse professionnelle; **I only know him ~ally** je n'ai avec lui que des relations de travail

**professor** [prəˈfesər] n professeur m (titulaire d'une chaire)

**proficiency** [prəˈfɪʃənsi] n compétence f, aptitude f

**profile** ['prəufaɪl] n profil m

**profit** ['prɔfɪt] n bénéfice m; profit m ♦ vi: **to ~ (by or from)** profiter (de); **~able** adj lucratif(-ive), rentable

**profound** [prəˈfaund] adj profond(e)

**profusely** [prəˈfjuːsli] adv abondam-

**prognosis** ['prɒgnəusɪs] (*pl* **prognoses**) *n* pronostic *m*

**programme** ['prəugræm] (*US* **program**) *n* programme *m*; (*RADIO, TV*) émission *f* ♦ *vt* programmer; **~r** (*US* **programer**) *n* programmeur(-euse) *f*; **programming** (*US* **programing**) *n* programmation *f*

**progress** [*n* 'prəugres, *vb* prə'gres] *n* progrès *m*(*pl*) ♦ *vi* progresser, avancer; **in ~** en cours; **~ive** [prə'gresɪv] *adj* progressif(-ive); (*person*) progressiste

**prohibit** [prə'hɪbɪt] *vt* interdire, défendre

**project** [*n* 'prɒdʒekt, *vb* prə'dʒekt] *n* (*plan*) projet *m*, plan *m*; (*venture*) opération *f*, entreprise *f*; (*research*) étude *f*, dossier *m* ♦ *vt* projeter ♦ *vi* faire saillie, s'avancer; **~ion** *n* projection *f*; (*overhang*) saillie *f*; **~or** *n* projecteur *m*

**prolong** [prə'lɒŋ] *vt* prolonger

**prom** [prɒm] *n abbr* = **promenade**; (*US: ball*) bal *m* d'étudiants

**promenade** [prɒmə'nɑːd] *n* (*by sea*) esplanade *f*, promenade *f*; **~ concert** (*BRIT*) *n* concert *m* populaire (de musique classique)

promenade concert

En Grande-Bretagne, un *promenade concert* (ou *prom*) est un concert de musique classique, ainsi appelé car, à l'origine, le public restait debout et se promenait au lieu de rester assis. De nos jours, une partie du public reste debout, mais il y a également des places assises (plus chères). Les *Proms* les plus connus sont les *Proms* londoniens. La dernière séance (the *Last Night of the Proms*) est un grand événement médiatique où se jouent des airs traditionnels et patriotiques. Aux États-Unis et au Canada, le *prom* ou *promenade* est un bal organisé par le lycée.

**prominent** ['prɒmɪnənt] *adj* (*standing out*) proéminent(e); (*important*) important(e)

**promiscuous** [prə'mɪskjuəs] *adj* (*sexually*) de mœurs légères

**promise** ['prɒmɪs] *n* promesse *f* ♦ *vt, vi* promettre; **promising** *adj* prometteur(-euse)

**promote** [prə'məut] *vt* promouvoir; (*new product*) faire la promotion de; **~r** *n* (*of event*) organisateur(-trice), (*of cause, idea*) promoteur(-trice); **promotion** *n* promotion *f*

**prompt** [prɒmpt] *adj* rapide ♦ *adv* (*punctually*) à l'heure ♦ *n* (*COMPUT*) message *m* (de guidage) ♦ *vt* provoquer; (*person*) inciter, pousser; (*THEATRE*) souffler (son rôle * or* ses répliques) à; **~ly** *adv* rapidement, sans délai; ponctuellement

**prone** [prəun] *adj* (*lying*) couché(e) (face contre terre); **~ to** enclin(e) à

**prong** [prɒŋ] *n* (*of fork*) dent *f*

**pronoun** ['prəunaun] *n* pronom *m*

**pronounce** [prə'nauns] *vt* prononcer; **pronunciation** [prənʌnsɪ'eɪʃən] *n* prononciation *f*

**proof** [pruːf] *n* preuve *f*; (*TYP*) épreuve *f* ♦ *adj*: **~ against** à l'épreuve de

**prop** [prɒp] *n* support *m*, étai *m*; (*fig*) soutien *m* ♦ *vt* (*also:* **~ up**) étayer, soutenir; (*lean*): **to ~ sth against** appuyer qch contre *or* à

**propaganda** [prɒpə'gændə] *n* propagande *f*

**propel** [prə'pel] *vt* propulser, faire avancer; **~ler** *n* hélice *f*

**propensity** [prə'pensɪtɪ] *n*: **a ~ for** or **to/to do** une propension à faire

**proper** ['prɒpəʳ] *adj* (*suited, right*) approprié(e), bon (bonne); (*seemly*) correct(e), convenable; (*authentic*) vrai(e), véritable; (*referring to place*): **the village ~** le village proprement dit; **~ly** *adv* correctement, convenablement; **~ noun** *n* nom *m* propre

**property** ['prɒpətɪ] *n* propriété *f*;

**prophecy** ['prɒfɪsɪ] *n* prophétie *f*

**prophesy** ['prɒfɪsaɪ] *vt* prédire

**prophet** ['prɒfɪt] *n* prophète *m*

**proportion** [prə'pɔːʃən] *n* proportion *f*; (*share*) part *f*; partie *f*; **~al, ~ate** *adj* proportionnel(le)

**proposal** [prə'pəuzl] *n* proposition *f*, offre *f*; (*plan*) projet *m*; (*of marriage*) demande *f* en mariage

**propose** [prə'pəuz] *vt* proposer, suggérer ♦ *vi* faire sa demande en mariage; **to ~ to do** avoir l'intention de faire; **proposition** [prɒpə'zɪʃən] *n* proposition *f*

**proprietor** [prə'praɪətə*r*] *n* propriétaire *m/f*

**propriety** [prə'praɪətɪ] *n* (*seemliness*) bienséance *f*, convenance *f*

**prose** [prəuz] *n* (*not poetry*) prose *f*

**prosecute** ['prɒsɪkjuːt] *vt* poursuivre; **prosecution** [prɒsɪ'kjuːʃən] *n* poursuites *fpl* judiciaires; (*accusing side*) partie plaignante; **prosecutor** *n* (*also:* **public prosecutor**) procureur *m*, ministère public

**prospect** [*n* 'prɒspekt, *vb* prə'spekt] *n* perspective *f* ♦ *vt, vi* prospecter; **~s** *npl* (*for work etc*) possibilités *fpl* d'avenir, débouchés *mpl*; **~ing** *n* (*for gold, oil etc*) prospection *f*; **~ive** *adj* (*possible*) éventuel(le); (*future*) futur(e)

**prospectus** [prə'spektəs] *n* prospectus *m*

**prosperity** [prɒ'spɛrɪtɪ] *n* prospérité *f*

**prostitute** ['prɒstɪtjuːt] *n* prostitué(e)

**protect** [prə'tɛkt] *vt* protéger; **~ion** *n* protection *f*; **~ive** *adj* protecteur(-trice); (*clothing*) de protection

**protein** ['prəutiːn] *n* protéine *f*

**protest** [*n* 'prəutest, *vb* prə'test] *n* protestation *f* ♦ *vi, vt:* **to ~ (that)** protester (que)

**Protestant** ['prɒtɪstənt] *adj, n* protestant(e)

**protester** [prə'testə*r*] *n* manifestant(e)

**protracted** [prə'træktɪd] *adj* prolongé(e)

**protrude** [prə'truːd] *vi* avancer, dépasser

**proud** [praud] *adj* fier(-ère); (*pej*) orgueilleux(-euse)

**prove** [pruːv] *vt* prouver, démontrer ♦ *vi:* **to ~ (to be) correct** *etc* s'avérer juste *etc*; **to ~ o.s.** montrer ce dont on est capable

**proverb** ['prɒvəːb] *n* proverbe *m*

**provide** [prə'vaɪd] *vt* fournir; **to ~ sb with sth** fournir qch à qn; **~ for** *vt fus* (*person*) subvenir aux besoins de; (*future event*) prévoir; **~d (that)** *conj* à condition que +*sub*; **providing** *conj:* **providing (that)** à condition que +*sub*

**province** ['prɒvɪns] *n* province *f*; (*fig*) domaine *m*; **provincial** [prə'vɪnʃəl] *adj* provincial(e)

**provision** [prə'vɪʒən] *n* (*supplying*) fourniture *f*; approvisionnement *m*; (*stipulation*) disposition *f*; **~s** *npl* (*food*) provisions *fpl*; **~al** *adj* provisoire

**proviso** [prə'vaɪzəu] *n* condition *f*

**provocative** [prə'vɒkətɪv] *adj* provocateur(-trice), provocant(e)

**provoke** [prə'vəuk] *vt* provoquer

**prowess** ['prauɪs] *n* prouesse *f*

**prowl** [praul] *vi* (*also:* **~ about, ~ around**) rôder ♦ *n:* **on the ~** à l'affût; **~er** *n* rôdeur(-euse)

**proxy** ['prɒksɪ] *n* procuration *f*

**prudent** ['pruːdnt] *adj* prudent(e)

**prune** [pruːn] *n* pruneau *m* ♦ *vt* élaguer

**pry** [praɪ] *vi:* **to ~ into** fourrer son nez dans

**PS** *n abbr* (= *postscript*) p.s.

**psalm** [sɑːm] *n* psaume *m*

**pseudonym** ['sjuːdənɪm] *n* pseudonyme *m*

**psyche** ['saɪkɪ] *n* psychisme *m*

**psychiatrist** [saɪ'kaɪətrɪst] *n* psychiatre *m/f*

**psychic** ['saɪkɪk] *adj* (*also:* **~al**) (*méta*)psychique; (*person*) doué(e) d'un sixième sens

**psychoanalyst** [saɪkəʊˈænəlɪst] *n* psychanalyste *m/f*

**psychological** [saɪkəˈlɒdʒɪkl] *adj* psychologique

**psychologist** [saɪˈkɒlədʒɪst] *n* psychologue *m/f*

**psychology** [saɪˈkɒlədʒɪ] *n* psychologie *f*

**PTO** *abbr* (= please turn over) T.S.V.P.

**pub** [pʌb] *n* (*public house*) pub *m*

---

**pub**

*Un pub comprend en général deux salles: l'une ("the lounge") est plutôt confortable, avec des fauteuils et des bancs capitonnés, tandis que l'autre ("the public bar") est simplement un bar où les consommations sont en général moins chères. Cette dernière est souvent aussi une salle de jeux, les jeux les plus courants étant les fléchettes, les dominos et le billard. Il y a parfois aussi une petite arrière-salle douillette appelée "the snug". Beaucoup de pubs servent maintenant des repas, surtout à l'heure du déjeuner, et c'est alors le seul moment où les enfants sont acceptés, à condition d'être accompagnés. Les pubs sont en général ouverts de 11 h à 23 h, mais cela peut varier selon leur licence; certains pubs ferment l'après-midi.*

---

**public** [ˈpʌblɪk] *adj* public(-ique) ♦ *n* public *m*; **in ~** en public; **to make ~** rendre public; **~ address system** *n* (système *m* de) sonorisation *f*; haut-parleurs *mpl*

**publican** [ˈpʌblɪkən] *n* patron *m* de pub

**public: ~ company** *n* société *f* anonyme (cotée en Bourse); **~ convenience** (BRIT) *n* toilettes *fpl*; **~ holiday** *n* jour férié; **~ house** (BRIT) *n* pub *m*

**publicity** [pʌbˈlɪsɪtɪ] *n* publicité *f*

**publicize** [ˈpʌblɪsaɪz] *vt* faire connaître, rendre public(-ique)

**public: ~ opinion** *n* opinion publique; **~ relations** *n* relations publiques; **~ school** *n* (BRIT) école (secondaire) privée; (US) école publique; **~-spirited** *adj* qui fait preuve de civisme; **~ transport** *n* transports *mpl* en commun

**publish** [ˈpʌblɪʃ] *vt* publier; **~er** *n* éditeur *m*; **~ing** *n* édition *f*

**pub lunch** *n* repas *m* de bistrot

**pucker** [ˈpʌkəʳ] *vt* plisser

**pudding** [ˈpʊdɪŋ] *n* pudding *m*; (BRIT: sweet) dessert *m*, entremets *m*; **black ~**, (US) **blood ~** *n* boudin (noir)

**puddle** [ˈpʌdl] *n* flaque *f* (d'eau)

**puff** [pʌf] *n* bouffée *f* ♦ *vt*: **to ~ one's pipe** tirer sur sa pipe ♦ *vi* (pant) haleter; **~ out** *vt* (fill with air) gonfler; **~ pastry** (US **puff paste**) *n* pâte feuilletée; **~y** *adj* bouffi(e), boursouflé(e)

**pull** [pʊl] *n* (tug): **to give sth a ~** tirer sur qch ♦ *vt* tirer; (trigger) presser ♦ *vi* tirer; **to ~ to pieces** mettre en morceaux; **to ~ one's punches** ménager son adversaire; **to ~ one's weight** faire sa part (du travail); **to ~ o.s. together** se ressaisir; **to ~ sb's leg** (fig) faire marcher qn; **~ apart** *vt* (break) mettre en pièces, démantibuler; **~ down** *vt* (house) démolir; **~ in** *vi* (AUT) entrer; (RAIL) entrer en gare; **~ off** *vt* enlever, ôter; (deal etc) mener à bien, conclure; **~ out** *vi* démarrer, partir ♦ *vt* sortir; arracher; **~ over** *vi* (AUT) se ranger; **~ through** *vi* s'en sortir; **~ up** *vi* (stop) s'arrêter ♦ *vt* remonter; (uproot) déraciner, arracher

**pulley** [ˈpʊlɪ] *n* poulie *f*

**pullover** [ˈpʊləʊvəʳ] *n* pull(-over) *m*, tricot *m*

**pulp** [pʌlp] *n* (of fruit) pulpe *f*

**pulpit** [ˈpʊlpɪt] *n* chaire *f*

**pulsate** [pʌlˈseɪt] *vi* battre, palpiter; (music) vibrer

**pulse** [pʌls] *n* (of blood) pouls *m*; (of heart) battement *m*; (of music, engine) vibrations *fpl*; (BOT, CULIN) légume sec

**pump** [pʌmp] *n* pompe *f*; (shoe) escar-

**pin** *m* ♦ *vt* pomper; **~ up** *vt* gonfler

**pumpkin** ['pʌmpkɪn] *n* potiron *m*, citrouille *f*

**pun** [pʌn] *n* jeu *m* de mots, calembour *m*

**punch** [pʌntʃ] *n* (*blow*) coup *m* de poing; (*tool*) poinçon *m*; (*drink*) punch *m* ♦ *vt* (*hit*): **to ~ sb/sth** donner un coup de poing à qn/sur qch; **~line** *n* (*of joke*) conclusion *f*; **~-up** (*BRIT: inf*) *n* bagarre *f*

**punctual** ['pʌŋktjuəl] *adj* ponctuel(le)

**punctuation** [pʌŋktju'eɪʃən] *n* ponctuation *f*

**puncture** ['pʌŋktʃər] *n* crevaison *f*

**pundit** ['pʌndɪt] *n* individu *m* qui pontifie, pontife *m*

**pungent** ['pʌndʒənt] *adj* piquant(e), âcre

**punish** ['pʌnɪʃ] *vt* punir; **~ment** *n* punition *f*, châtiment *m*

**punk** [pʌŋk] *n* (*also:* **~ rocker**) punk *m/f*; (*also:* **~ rock**) le punk rock; (*US: inf: hoodlum*) voyou *m*

**punt** [pʌnt] *n* (*boat*) bachot *m*

**punter** ['pʌntər] *n* (*BRIT: gambler*) parieur(-euse); (*inf*): **the ~s** le public

**puny** ['pju:nɪ] *adj* chétif(-ive); (*effort*) piteux(-euse)

**pup** [pʌp] *n* chiot *m*

**pupil** ['pju:pl] *n* (*SCOL*) élève *m/f*; (*of eye*) pupille *f*

**puppet** ['pʌpɪt] *n* marionnette *f*, pantin *m*

**puppy** ['pʌpɪ] *n* chiot *m*, jeune chien(ne)

**purchase** ['pə:tʃɪs] *n* achat *m* ♦ *vt* acheter; **~r** *n* acheteur(-euse)

**pure** [pjuər] *adj* pur(e); **~ly** *adv* purement

**purge** [pə:dʒ] *n* purge *f* ♦ *vt* purger

**purple** ['pə:pl] *adj* violet(te); (*face*) cramoisi(e)

**purpose** ['pə:pəs] *n* intention *f*, but *m*; **on ~** exprès; **~ful** *adj* déterminé(e), résolu(e)

**purr** [pə:r] *vi* ronronner

**purse** [pə:s] *n* (*BRIT: for money*) portemonnaie *m inv*; (*US: handbag*) sac *m* à main ♦ *vt* serrer, pincer

**purser** *n* (*NAUT*) commissaire *m* du bord

**pursue** [pə'sju:] *vt* poursuivre; **pursuit** [pə'sju:t] *n* poursuite *f*; (*occupation*) occupation *f*, activité *f*

**push** [puʃ] *n* poussée *f* ♦ *vt* pousser; (*button*) appuyer sur; (*product*) faire de la publicité pour; (*thrust*): **to ~ sth (into)** enfoncer qch (dans) ♦ *vi* pousser; (*demand*): **to ~ for** exiger, demander avec insistance; **~ aside** *vt* écarter; **~ off** (*inf*) *vi* filer, ficher le camp; **~ on** *vi* (*continue*) continuer; **~ through** *vi* se frayer un chemin ♦ *vt* (*measure*) faire accepter; **~ up** *vt* (*total, prices*) faire monter; **~chair** (*BRIT*) *n* poussette *f*; **~er** *n* (*drug pusher*) revendeur(-euse) (de drogue); ravitailleur(-euse) (en drogue); **~over** (*inf*) *n*: **it's a ~over** c'est un jeu d'enfant; **~-up** (*US*) *n* traction *f*; **~y** (*pej*) *adj* arriviste

**puss** [pus], **pussy** (*cat*) ['pusɪkæt] (*inf*) *n* minet *m*

**put** [put] (*pt, pp put*) *vt* mettre, poser, placer; (*say*) dire, exprimer; (*a question*) poser; (*case, view*) exposer, présenter; (*estimate*) estimer; **~ about** (*rumour*) faire courir; **~ across** *vt* (*ideas etc*) communiquer; **~ away** *vt* (*store*) ranger; **~ back** *vt* (*replace*) remettre, replacer; (*postpone*) remettre; (*delay*) retarder; **~ by** *vt* (*money*) mettre de côté, économiser; **~ down** *vt* (*parcel etc*) poser, déposer; (*in writing*) mettre par écrit, inscrire; (*suppress: revolt etc*) réprimer, faire cesser; (*animal*) abattre; (*dog, cat*) faire piquer; (*attribute*) attribuer; **~ forward** *vt* (*ideas*) avancer; **~ in** *vt* (*gas, electricity*) installer; (*application, complaint*) soumettre; (*time, effort*) consacrer; **~ off** *vt* (*light etc*) éteindre; (*postpone*) remettre à plus tard, ajourner; (*discourage*) dissuader; **~ on** *vt* (*clothes, lipstick, record*) mettre; (*light etc*) allumer; (*play etc*) monter; (*food:*

*cook)* mettre à cuire *or* à chauffer; *(gain):* **to ~ on weight** prendre du poids, grossir; **to ~ the brakes on** freiner; **to ~ the kettle on** mettre l'eau à chauffer; **~ out** *vt (take out)* mettre dehors; *(one's hand)* tendre; *(light etc)* éteindre; *(person: inconvenience)* déranger, gêner; **~ through** *vt (TEL: call)* passer; *(: person)* mettre en communication; *(plan)* faire accepter; **~ up** *vt (raise)* lever, relever, remonter; *(pin up)* afficher; *(hang)* accrocher; *(build)* construire, ériger; *(tent)* monter; *(umbrella)* ouvrir; *(increase)* augmenter; *(accommodate)* loger; **~ up with** *vt fus* supporter

**putt** [pʌt] *n* coup roulé; **~ing green** *n* green *m*

**putty** [ˈpʌti] *n* mastic *m*

**put-up** [ˈputʌp] *(BRIT) adj:* **~~ job** coup monté

**puzzle** [ˈpʌzl] *n* énigme *f*, mystère *m*; *(jigsaw)* puzzle *m* ♦ *vt* intriguer, rendre perplexe ♦ *vi* se creuser la tête; **~d** *adj* perplexe; **puzzling** *adj* déconcertant(e)

**pyjamas** [pəˈdʒɑːməz] *(BRIT) npl* pyjama(s) *m(pl)*

**pylon** [ˈpaɪlən] *n* pylône *m*

**pyramid** [ˈpɪrəmɪd] *n* pyramide *f*

**Pyrenees** [pɪrəˈniːz] *npl:* **the ~** les Pyrénées *fpl*

# Q, q

**quack** [kwæk] *n (of duck)* coin-coin *m inv*; *(pej: doctor)* charlatan *m*

**quad** [kwɔd] *n abbr* = **quadrangle; quadruplet**

**quadrangle** [ˈkwɔdræŋgl] *n (courtyard)* cour *f*

**quadruple** [kwɔˈdruːpl] *vt, vi* quadrupler; **~ts** *npl* quadruplés

**quail** [kweɪl] *n (ZOOL)* caille *f* ♦ *vi:* **to ~ at** *or* **before** reculer devant

**quaint** [kweɪnt] *adj* bizarre; *(house, village)* au charme vieillot, pittoresque

**quake** [kweɪk] *vi* trembler

**qualification** [kwɔlɪfɪˈkeɪʃən] *n (often pl: degree etc)* diplôme *m*; *(training)* qualification(s) *f(pl)*, expérience *f*; *(ability)* compétence(s) *f(pl)*; *(limitation)* réserve *f*, restriction *f*

**qualified** [ˈkwɔlɪfaɪd] *adj (trained)* qualifié(e); *(professionally)* diplômé(e); *(fit, competent)* compétent(e), qualifié(e); *(limited)* conditionnel(le)

**qualify** [ˈkwɔlɪfaɪ] *vt* qualifier; *(modify)* atténuer, nuancer ♦ *vi:* **to ~ (as)** obtenir son diplôme (de); **to ~ (for)** remplir les conditions requises (pour); *(SPORT)* se qualifier (pour)

**quality** [ˈkwɔlɪti] *n* qualité *f*; **~ time** *n* moments privilégiés

---

quality (news)papers

*Les* **quality (news)papers** *(ou la* **quality press)** *englobent les journaux sérieux, quotidiens ou hebdomadaires, par opposition aux journaux populaires (*tabloid press). *Ces journaux visent un public qui souhaite des informations détaillées sur un éventail très vaste de sujets et qui est prêt à consacrer beaucoup de temps à leur lecture. Les* quality newspapers *sont en général de grand format.*

---

**qualm** [kwɑːm] *n* doute *m*; scrupule *m*

**quandary** [ˈkwɔndrɪ] *n:* **in a ~** devant un dilemme, dans l'embarras

**quantity** [ˈkwɔntɪti] *n* quantité *f*; **~ surveyor** *n* métreur *m* vérificateur

**quarantine** [ˈkwɔrntiːn] *n* quarantaine *f*

**quarrel** [ˈkwɔrl] *n* querelle *f*, dispute *f* ♦ *vi* se disputer, se quereller

**quarry** [ˈkwɔrɪ] *n (for stone)* carrière *f*; *(animal)* proie *f*, gibier *m*

**quart** [kwɔːt] *n* ≈ litre *m*

**quarter** [ˈkwɔːtə[r]] *n* quart *m*; *(US: coin: 25 cents)* quart de dollar; *(of year)* trimestre *m*; *(district)* quartier *m* ♦ *vt (divide)* partager en quartiers *or* en quatre

**~s** npl (living ~) logement m; (MIL) quartiers mpl, cantonnement m; **a ~ of an hour** un quart d'heure; **~ final** n quart m de finale; **~ly** adj trimestriel(le) ♦ adv tous les trois mois

**quartet(te)** [kwɔːˈtɛt] n quatuor m; (jazz players) quartette m

**quartz** [kwɔːts] n quartz m

**quash** [kwɔʃ] vt (verdict) annuler

**quaver** ['kweɪvə'] vi trembler

**quay** [kiː] n (also: **~side**) quai m

**queasy** ['kwiːzɪ] adj: **to feel ~** avoir mal au cœur

**queen** [kwiːn] n reine f; (CARDS etc) dame f; **~ mother** n reine mère f

**queer** [kwɪə'] adj étrange, curieux (-euse); (suspicious) louche ♦ n (inf!) homosexuel m

**quell** [kwɛl] vt réprimer, étouffer

**quench** [kwɛntʃ] vt: **to ~ one's thirst** se désaltérer

**query** ['kwɪərɪ] n question f ♦ vt remettre en question, mettre en doute

**quest** [kwɛst] n recherche f, quête f

**question** ['kwɛstʃən] n question f ♦ vt (person) interroger; (plan, idea) remettre en question, mettre en doute; **beyond** ~ sans aucun doute; **out of the ~** hors de question; **~able** adj discutable; **~ mark** n point m d'interrogation; **~naire** [kwɛstʃəˈnɛə'] n questionnaire m

**queue** [kjuː] (BRIT) n queue f, file f ♦ vi (also: **~ up**) faire la queue

**quibble** ['kwɪbl] vi: **to ~ (about** or **over)** or **(with sth)** ergoter (sur qch)

**quick** [kwɪk] adj rapide; (reply) agile, vive) ♦ n: **cut to the ~** (fig) touché(e) au vif; **be ~!** dépêche-toi!; **~en** vi accélérer, presser ♦ vi s'accélérer, devenir plus rapide; **~ly** adv vite, rapidement; **~sand** n sables mouvants; **~-witted** adj à l'esprit vif

**quid** [kwɪd] (BRIT: inf) n, pl inv livre f

**quiet** ['kwaɪət] adj tranquille, calme; (voice) bas(se); (ceremony, colour) discret(-ète) ♦ n tranquillité f, calme m

(silence) silence m ♦ vt, vi (US) = **quieten**; **keep ~!** tais-toi!; **~en** vi (also: **~en down**) se calmer, s'apaiser ♦ vt calmer, apaiser; **~ly** adv tranquillement, calmement; (silently) silencieusement; **~ness** n tranquillité f, calme m; (silence) silence m

**quilt** [kwɪlt] n édredon m; (continental ~) couette f

**quin** [kwɪn] n abbr = **quintuplet**

**quintuplets** [kwɪnˈtjuːplɪts] npl quintuplé(e)s

**quip** [kwɪp] n remarque piquante or spirituelle, pointe f

**quirk** [kwəːk] n bizarrerie f

**quit** [kwɪt] (pt, pp quit or quitted) vt quitter; (smoking, grumbling) arrêter de ♦ vi (give up) abandonner, renoncer; (resign) démissionner

**quite** [kwaɪt] adv (rather) assez, plutôt; (entirely) complètement, tout à fait; (following a negative = almost): **that's not ~ big enough** ce n'est pas tout à fait assez grand; **I ~ understand** je comprends très bien; **~ a few of them** un assez grand nombre d'entre eux; **~ (so)!** exactement!

**quits** [kwɪts] adj: **~ (with)** quitte (envers); **let's call it ~** restons-en là

**quiver** ['kwɪvə'] vi trembler, frémir

**quiz** [kwɪz] n (game) jeu-concours m ♦ vt interroger; **~zical** adj narquois(e)

**quota** ['kwəʊtə] n quota m

**quotation** [kwəʊˈteɪʃən] n citation f; (estimate) devis m; **~ marks** npl guillemets mpl

**quote** [kwəʊt] n citation f; (estimate) devis m ♦ vt citer; (price) indiquer; **~s** npl guillemets mpl

# R, r

**rabbi** ['ræbaɪ] n rabbin m

**rabbit** ['ræbɪt] n lapin m; **~ hutch** n clapier m

**rabble** ['ræbl] (pej) n populace f

**rabies** ['reɪbiːz] n rage f

**RAC** n abbr (BRIT) = Royal Automobile Club

**rac(c)oon** [rə'kuːn] n raton laveur

**race** [reɪs] n (species) race f; (competition, rush) course f ♦ vt (horse) faire courir ♦ vi (compete) faire la course, courir; (hurry) aller à toute vitesse, courir; (engine) s'emballer; (pulse) augmenter; ~ **car** (US) n = **racing car**; ~ **car driver** (US) n = **racing driver**; **~course** n champ m de courses; **~horse** n cheval m de course; **~r** n (bike) vélo m de course; **~track** n piste f

**racial** ['reɪʃl] adj racial(e)

**racing** ['reɪsɪŋ] n courses fpl; ~ **car** (BRIT) n voiture f de course; ~ **driver** (BRIT) n pilote m de course

**racism** ['reɪsɪzəm] n racisme m; **racist** adj raciste ♦ n raciste m/f

**rack** [ræk] n (for guns, tools) râtelier m; (also: **luggage ~**) porte-bagages m inv, filet m à bagages; (also: **roof ~**) galerie f; (dish ~) égouttoir m ♦ vt tourmenter; **to ~ one's brains** se creuser la cervelle

**racket** ['rækɪt] n (for tennis) raquette f; (noise) tapage m; vacarme m; (swindle) escroquerie f

**racquet** ['rækɪt] n raquette f

**racy** ['reɪsɪ] adj plein(e) de verve; (slightly indecent) osé(e)

**radar** ['reɪdɑːʳ] n radar m

**radial** ['reɪdɪəl] adj (also: **~-ply**) à carcasse radiale

**radiant** ['reɪdɪənt] adj rayonnant(e)

**radiate** ['reɪdɪeɪt] vt (heat) émettre, dégager; (emotion) rayonner de ♦ vi (lines) rayonner; **radiation** [reɪdɪ'eɪʃən] n rayonnement m; (radioactive) radia-

tion f; **radiator** ['reɪdɪeɪtəʳ] n radiateur m

**radical** ['rædɪkl] adj radical(e)

**radii** ['reɪdɪaɪ] npl of **radius**

**radio** ['reɪdɪəu] n radio f ♦ vt appeler par radio; **on the ~** à la radio; **~active** ['reɪdɪəu'æktɪv] adj radioactif(-ive); ~ **cassette** n radiocassette m; **~-controlled** adj téléguidé(e); ~ **station** n station f de radio

**radish** ['rædɪʃ] n radis m

**radius** ['reɪdɪəs] (pl **radii**) n rayon m

**RAF** n abbr = **Royal Air Force**

**raffle** ['ræfl] n tombola f

**raft** [rɑːft] n (craft; also: **life ~**) radeau m

**rafter** ['rɑːftəʳ] n chevron m

**rag** [ræg] n chiffon m; (pej: newspaper) feuille f de chou, torchon m; (student ~) attractions organisées au profit d'œuvres de charité; **~s** npl (torn clothes) haillons mpl; **~ doll** n poupée f de chiffon

**rage** [reɪdʒ] n (fury) rage f, fureur f ♦ vi (person) être fou (folle) de rage; (storm) faire rage, être déchaîné(e); **it's all the ~** cela fait fureur

**ragged** ['rægɪd] adj (edge) inégal(e); (clothes) en loques; (appearance) déguenillé(e)

**raid** [reɪd] n (attack, also: MIL) raid m; (criminal) hold-up m inv; (by police) descente f, rafle f ♦ vt faire un raid sur ou un hold-up ou une descente dans

**rail** [reɪl] n (on stairs) rampe f; (on bridge, balcony) balustrade f; (of ship) bastingage m; **~s** npl (track) rails mpl, voie ferrée; **by ~** par chemin de fer, en train; **~ing(s)** n(pl) grille f; **~road** (US), **~way** (BRIT) n voie ferrée; (company) chemin m de fer; **~way line** (BRIT) n ligne f de chemin de fer; **~wayman** (BRIT) (irreg) n cheminot m; **~way station** n gare f

**rain** [reɪn] n pluie f ♦ vi pleuvoir; **in the ~** sous la pluie; **it's ~ing** il pleut; **~bow** n arc-en-ciel m; **~coat** n imperméable m; **~drop** n goutte f de pluie; **~fall** n chute f de pluie; (measurement) hauteur f des précipitations; **~forest** n forêt f tropicale humide; **~y** adj pluvieux(-euse)

**raise** [reɪz] n augmentation f ♦ vt (lift) lever; hausser; (increase) augmenter; (morale) remonter; (standards) améliorer; (question, doubt) provoquer, soulever; (cattle, family) élever; (crop) faire pousser; (funds) rassembler; (loan) obtenir; (army) lever; **to ~ one's voice** élever la voix

**raisin** ['reɪzn] n raisin sec

**rake** [reɪk] n (tool) râteau m ♦ vt (garden, leaves) ratisser

**rally** ['rælɪ] n (POL etc) meeting m, rassemblement m; (AUT) rallye m; (TENNIS) échange m ♦ vt (support) gagner à ♦ vi (sick person) aller mieux; (Stock Exchange) reprendre; **~ round** vt fus venir en aide à

**RAM** [ræm] n abbr (= random access memory) mémoire vive

**ram** [ræm] n bélier m ♦ vt enfoncer; (crash into) emboutir; percuter

**ramble** ['ræmbl] n randonnée f ♦ vi (walk) se promener, faire une randonnée; (talk: also: **~ on**) discourir, pérorer; **~r** n promeneur(-euse), randonneur (-euse); (BOT) rosier grimpant; **rambling** adj (speech) décousu(e); (house) plein(e) de coins et de recoins; (BOT) grimpant(e)

**ramp** [ræmp] n (incline) rampe f; dénivellation f; **on ~, off ~** (US: AUT) bretelle f d'accès

**rampage** [ræm'peɪdʒ] n: **to be on the ~** se déchaîner

**rampant** ['ræmpənt] adj (disease etc) qui sévit

**ram raiding** [-reɪdɪŋ] n pillage d'un magasin en enfonçant la vitrine avec une voiture

**ramshackle** ['ræmʃækl] adj (house) délabré(e); (car etc) déglingué(e)

**ran** [ræn] pt of **run**

**ranch** [rɑːntʃ] n ranch m; **~er** n propriétaire m de ranch

**rancid** ['rænsɪd] adj rance

**rancour** ['ræŋkəʳ] (US **rancor**) n rancune f

**random** ['rændəm] adj fait(e) or établi(e) au hasard; (MATH) aléatoire ♦ n: **at ~** au hasard; **~ access** (COMPUT) accès sélectif

**randy** ['rændɪ] (BRIT: inf) adj excité(e); lubrique

**rang** [ræŋ] pt of **ring**

**range** [reɪndʒ] n (of mountains) chaîne f; (of missile, voice) portée f; (of products) choix m, gamme f; (MIL: also: **shooting ~**) champ m de tir; (indoor) stand m de tir; (also: **kitchen ~**) fourneau m (de cuisine) ♦ vt (place in a line) mettre en rang, ranger ♦ vi: **to ~ over** (extend) couvrir; **to ~ from ... to** aller de ... à; **a ~ of** (series: of proposals etc) divers(es)

**ranger** ['reɪndʒəʳ] n garde forestier

**rank** [ræŋk] n rang m; (MIL) grade m; (BRIT: also: **taxi ~**) station f de taxis ♦ vi: **to ~ among** compter or se classer parmi ♦ adj (stinking) fétide, puant(e); **the ~ and file** (fig) la masse, la base

**ransack** ['rænsæk] vt fouiller (à fond); (plunder) piller

**ransom** ['rænsəm] n rançon f; **to hold sb to ~** (fig) exercer un chantage sur qn

**rant** [rænt] vi fulminer

**rap** [ræp] vt frapper sur or à; taper sur ♦ n: **~ music** rap m

**rape** [reɪp] n viol m; (BOT) colza m ♦ vt violer; **~(seed) oil** n huile f de colza

**rapid** ['ræpɪd] adj rapide; **~s** npl (GEO) rapides mpl

**rapist** ['reɪpɪst] n violeur m

**rapport** [ræ'pɔːʳ] n entente f

**rapturous** ['ræptʃərəs] adj enthousiaste, frénétique

**rare** [rɛəʳ] adj rare; (CULIN: steak) saignant(e)

**raring** ['rɛərɪŋ] adj: **~ to go** (inf) très impatient(e) de commencer

**rascal** ['rɑːskl] n vaurien m

**rash** [ræʃ] adj imprudent(e), irréfléchi(e)

**♦** n (MED) rougeur f, éruption f; (spate: of events) série (noire)

**rasher** ['ræʃər] n fine tranche (de lard)

**raspberry** ['rɑːzbərɪ] n framboise f; ~ **bush** n framboisier m

**rasping** ['rɑːspɪŋ] adj: ~ **noise** grincement m

**rat** [ræt] n rat m

**rate** [reɪt] n taux m; (speed) vitesse f, rythme m; (price) tarif m **♦** vt classer; évaluer; ~**s** npl (BRIT: tax) impôts locaux; (fees) tarifs mpl; **to ~ sb/sth as** considérer qn/qch comme; ~**able value** (BRIT) n valeur locative imposable; ~**payer** ['reɪtpeɪər] (BRIT) n contribuable m/f (payant les impôts locaux)

**rather** ['rɑːðər] adv plutôt; **it's ~ expensive** c'est assez cher; (too much) c'est un peu trop; **there's ~ a lot** il y en a beaucoup; **I would** or **I'd ~ go** j'aimerais mieux or je préférerais m'en aller

**rating** ['reɪtɪŋ] n (assessment) évaluation f; (score) classement m; ~**s** npl (RADIO, TV) indice m d'écoute

**ratio** ['reɪʃɪəʊ] n proportion f

**ration** ['ræʃən] n (gen pl) ration(s) f(pl)

**rational** ['ræʃənl] adj raisonnable, sensé(e); (solution, reasoning) logique; ~**e** [ræʃə'nɑːl] n raisonnement m; ~**ize** vt rationaliser; (conduct) essayer d'expliquer or de motiver

**rat race** n foire f d'empoigne

**rattle** ['rætl] n (of door, window) battement m; (of coins, chain) cliquetis m; (of train, engine) bruit m de ferraille; (object: for baby) hochet m **♦** vi cliqueter; (car, bus): **to ~ along** rouler dans un bruit de ferraille **♦** vt agiter (bruyamment); (unnerve) décontenancer; ~**snake** n serpent m à sonnettes

**raucous** ['rɔːkəs] adj rauque; (noisy) bruyant(e), tapageur(-euse)

**rave** [reɪv] vi (in anger) s'emporter; (with enthusiasm) s'extasier; (MED) délirer **♦** n (BRIT: inf: party) rave, soirée f techno

**raven** ['reɪvən] n corbeau m

**ravenous** ['rævənəs] adj affamé(e)

**ravine** [rə'viːn] n ravin m

**raving** ['reɪvɪŋ] adj: ~ **lunatic ♦** n fou (folle) furieux(-euse)

**ravishing** ['rævɪʃɪŋ] adj enchanteur(-eresse)

**raw** [rɔː] adj (uncooked) cru(e); (not processed) brut(e); (sore) à vif, irrité(e); (inexperienced) inexpérimenté(e); (weather, day) froid(e) et humide; ~ **deal** (inf) n sale coup m; ~ **material** n matière première

**ray** [reɪ] n rayon m; ~ **of hope** lueur f d'espoir

**raze** [reɪz] vt (also: ~ **to the ground**) raser, détruire

**razor** ['reɪzər] n rasoir m; ~ **blade** n lame f de rasoir

**Rd** abbr = **road**

**RE** n abbr = **religious education**

**re** [riː] prep concernant

**reach** [riːtʃ] n portée f, atteinte f; (of river etc) étendue f **♦** vt atteindre; (conclusion, decision) parvenir à **♦** vi s'étendre, étendre le bras; **out of/within ~** hors de/à portée; **within ~ of the shops** pas trop loin des or à proximité des magasins; ~ **out** vt tendre **♦** vi: **to ~ out (for)** allonger le bras (pour prendre)

**react** [riː'ækt] vi réagir; ~**ion** n réaction f

**reactor** [riː'æktər] n réacteur m

**read** [riːd, pt, pp red] (pt, pp **read**) vi lire **♦** vt lire; (understand) comprendre, interpréter; (study) étudier; (meter) relever; ~ **out** vt lire à haute voix; ~**able** adj facile or agréable à lire; (writing) lisible; ~**er** n lecteur(-trice); (BRIT: at university) chargé(e) d'enseignement; ~**ership** n (of paper etc) (nombre m de) lecteurs mpl

**readily** ['redɪlɪ] adv volontiers, avec empressement; (easily) facilement

**readiness** ['redɪnɪs] n empressement m; **in ~** (prepared) prêt(e)

**reading** ['riːdɪŋ] n lecture f; (understanding) interprétation f; (on instrument) indications fpl

**ready** ['rɛdɪ] adj prêt(e); (willing) prêt, disposé(e); (available) disponible ♦ n: **at the ~** (MIL) prêt à faire feu; **to get ~** se préparer ♦ vt préparer; **~-made** adj tout(e) fait(e); **~-to-wear** adj prêt(e) à porter

**real** [rɪəl] adj véritable, réel(le); **in ~ terms** dans la réalité; **~ estate** n biens fonciers or immobiliers; **~istic** [rɪə'lɪstɪk] adj réaliste; **~ity** [rɪ:'ælɪtɪ] n réalité f

**realization** [rɪəlaɪ'zeɪʃən] n (awareness) prise f de conscience; (fulfilment; also: of asset) réalisation f

**realize** ['rɪəlaɪz] vt (understand) se rendre compte de; (a project, COMM: asset) réaliser

**really** ['rɪəlɪ] adv vraiment; **~?** vraiment?, c'est vrai?

**realm** [rɛlm] n royaume m; (fig) domaine m

**realtor** ® ['rɪəltɔːr] (US) n agent immobilier

**reap** [rɪːp] vt moissonner; (fig) récolter

**reappear** [rɪːə'pɪər] vi réapparaître, reparaître

**rear** [rɪər] adj de derrière, arrière inv; (AUT: wheel etc) arrière n arrière m ♦ vt (cattle, family) élever ♦ vi (also: **~ up**: animal) se cabrer; **~guard** n (MIL) arrière-garde f; **~-view mirror** n (AUT) rétroviseur m

**reason** ['rɪːzn] n raison f ♦ vi: **to ~ with sb** raisonner qn, faire entendre raison à qn; **to have ~ to think** avoir lieu de penser; **it stands to ~ that** il va sans dire que; **~able** adj raisonnable; (not bad) acceptable; **~ably** adv raisonnablement; **~ing** n raisonnement m

**reassurance** [rɪːə'ʃuərəns] n réconfort m; (factual) assurance f, garantie f

**reassure** [rɪːə'ʃuər] vt rassurer

**rebate** ['rɪːbeɪt] n (on tax etc) dégrèvement m

**rebel** [n 'rɛbl, vb rɪ'bɛl] n rebelle m/f ♦ vi se rebeller, se révolter; **~lious** [rɪ'bɛljəs] adj rebelle

**rebound** [vb rɪ'baund, n 'rɪːbaund] vi (ball) rebondir ♦ n rebond m; **to marry on the ~** se marier immédiatement après une déception amoureuse

**rebuff** [rɪ'bʌf] n rebuffade f

**rebuke** [rɪ'bjuːk] vt réprimander

**rebut** [rɪ'bʌt] vt réfuter

**recall** [vb rɪ'kɔːl, n 'rɪːkɔːl] vt rappeler; (remember) se rappeler, se souvenir de ♦ n rappel m; (ability to remember) mémoire f

**recant** [rɪ'kænt] vi se rétracter; (REL) abjurer

**recap** ['rɪːkæp], **recapitulate** [rɪ:kə'pɪtjuleɪt] vt, vi récapituler

**rec'd** abbr = **received**

**recede** [rɪ'sɪːd] vi (tide) descendre; (disappear) disparaître peu à peu; (memory, hope) s'estomper; **receding** adj (chin) fuyant(e); **receding hairline** front dégarni

**receipt** [rɪ'sɪːt] n (document) reçu m; (for parcel etc) accusé m de réception; (act of receiving) réception f; **~s** npl (COMM) recettes fpl

**receive** [rɪ'sɪːv] vt recevoir; **~r** n (TEL) récepteur m, combiné m; (RADIO) récepteur m; (of stolen goods) receleur m; (LAW) administrateur m judiciaire

**recent** ['rɪːsnt] adj récent(e); **~ly** adv récemment

**receptacle** [rɪ'sɛptɪkl] n récipient m

**reception** [rɪ'sɛpʃən] n réception f; (welcome) accueil m, réception; **~ desk** n réception f; **~ist** n réceptionniste m/f

**recess** [rɪ'sɛs] n (in room) renfoncement m, alcôve f; (secret place) recoin m; (POL etc: holiday) vacances fpl

**recession** [rɪ'sɛʃən] n récession f

**recipe** ['rɛsɪpɪ] n recette f

**recipient** [rɪ'sɪpɪənt] n (of payment) bénéficiaire m/f; (of letter) destinataire m/f

**recital** [rɪ'saɪtl] n récital m

**recite** [rɪ'saɪt] vt (poem) réciter

**reckless** ['rekləs] adj (driver etc) imprudent(e)

**reckon** ['rekən] vt (count) calculer, compter; (think): **I ~ that ...** je pense que ...; **~ on** vt fus compter sur, s'attendre à; **~ing** n compte m, calcul m, estimation f

**reclaim** [rɪ'kleɪm] vt (demand back) réclamer (le restitution or la restitution de); (land: from sea) assécher; (waste materials) récupérer

**recline** [rɪ'klaɪn] vi être allongé(e) or étendu(e); **reclining** adj (seat) à dossier réglable

**recluse** [rɪ'klu:s] n reclus(e), ermite m

**recognition** [rekəg'nɪʃən] n reconnaissance f; **to gain ~** être reconnu(e); **transformed beyond ~** méconnaissable

**recognizable** ['rekəgnaɪzəbl] adj: **~ (by)** reconnaissable (à)

**recognize** ['rekəgnaɪz] vt: **to ~ (by/as)** reconnaître (à/comme étant)

**recoil** [vb rɪ'kɔɪl, n 'ri:kɔɪl] vi (person): **to ~ (from sth/doing sth)** reculer (devant qch/l'idée de faire qch) ♦ n (of gun) recul m

**recollect** [rekə'lekt] vt se rappeler, se souvenir de; **~ion** n souvenir m

**recommend** [rekə'mend] vt recommander

**reconcile** ['rekənsaɪl] vt (two people) réconcilier; (two facts) concilier, accorder; **to ~ o.s.** se résigner à

**recondition** [ri:kən'dɪʃən] vt remettre à neuf; réviser entièrement

**reconnoitre** [rekə'nɔɪtə'] (US **reconnoiter**) vt (MIL) reconnaître

**reconsider** [ri:kən'sɪdə'] vt reconsidérer

**reconstruct** [ri:kən'strʌkt] vt (building) reconstruire; (crime, policy, system) reconstituer

**record** [n 'rekɔːd, vb rɪ'kɔːd] n rapport m, récit m; (of meeting etc) procès-verbal m; (register) registre m; (file) dossier m; (also: **criminal ~**) casier m judiciaire; (MUS: disc) disque m; (SPORT) record m ♦ vt (set down) noter; (MUS: song etc) enregistrer; **in ~ time** en un temps record inv; **off the ~** ♦ adj officieux(-euse) ♦ adv officieusement; **~ card** n (in file) fiche f; **~ed delivery** n (BRIT: POST): **~ed delivery letter** etc lettre etc recommandée; **~er** n (MUS) flûte f à bec; **~ holder** n (SPORT) détenteur(-trice) du record; **~ing** n (MUS) enregistrement m; **~ player** n tourne-disque m

**recount** [rɪ'kaʊnt] vt raconter

**re-count** ['ri:kaʊnt] n (POL: of votes) deuxième compte m

**recoup** [rɪ'ku:p] vt: **to ~ one's losses** récupérer ce qu'on a perdu, se refaire

**recourse** [rɪ'kɔːs] n: **to have ~ to** avoir recours à

**recover** [rɪ'kʌvə'] vt récupérer ♦ vi: **to ~ (from)** (illness) se rétablir (de); (from shock) se remettre (de); **~y** n récupération f; rétablissement m; (ECON) redressement m

**recreation** [rekrɪ'eɪʃən] n récréation f, détente f; **~al** adj pour se détendre, récréatif(-ive)

**recruit** [rɪ'kru:t] n recrue f ♦ vt recruter

**rectangle** ['rektæŋgl] n rectangle m; **rectangular** [rek'tæŋgjulə'] adj rectangulaire

**rectify** ['rektɪfaɪ] vt (error) rectifier, corriger

**rector** ['rektə'] n (REL) pasteur m

**recuperate** [rɪ'kju:pəreɪt] vi récupérer; (from illness) se rétablir

**recur** [rɪ'kɜː'] vi se reproduire; (symptoms) réapparaître; **~rence** n répétition f; réapparition f; **~rent** adj périodique, fréquent(e)

**recycle** [ri:'saɪkl] vt recycler; **recycling** n recyclage m

**red** [red] n rouge m; (POL: pej) rouge m/f ♦ adj rouge; (hair) roux (rousse); **in the ~** (account) à découvert; (business) en déficit; **~ carpet treatment** n réception f en grande pompe; **R~ Cross** n

Croix-Rouge f; **~currant** n groseille f (rouge); **~den** vt, vi rougir

**redecorate** [riː'dekəreɪt] vi (with wallpaper) retapisser; (with paint) refaire les peintures

**redeem** [rɪ'diːm] vt (debt) rembourser; (sth in pawn) dégager; (fig, also REL) racheter; **~ing** adj (feature) qui sauve, qui rachète (le reste)

**redeploy** [riːdɪ'plɔɪ] vt (resources) réorganiser

**red**: **~-haired** adj roux (rousse); **~-handed** adj: **to be caught ~-handed** être pris(e) en flagrant délit or la main dans le sac; **~head** n roux (rousse); **~ herring** n (fig) diversion f, fausse piste; **~-hot** adj chauffé(e) au rouge, brûlant(e)

**redirect** [riːdaɪ'rekt] vt (mail) faire suivre

**red light** n: **to go through a ~** (AUT) brûler un feu rouge; **red-light district** n quartier m des prostituées

**redo** [riː'duː] (irreg) vt refaire

**redress** [rɪ'dres] n réparation f ♦ vt redresser

**red**: **R~ Sea** n mer Rouge f; **~skin** n Peau-Rouge m/f; **~ tape** n (fig) paperasserie (administrative)

**reduce** [rɪ'djuːs] vt réduire, (lower) abaisser; **"~ speed now"** (AUT) "ralentir"; **reduction** [rɪ'dʌkʃən] n réduction f; (discount) rabais m

**redundancy** [rɪ'dʌndənsɪ] (BRIT) n licenciement m, mise f au chômage

**redundant** [rɪ'dʌndnt] adj (BRIT: worker) mis(e) au chômage, licencié(e); (detail, object) superflu(e); **to be made ~** être licencié(e), être mis(e) au chômage

**reed** [riːd] n (BOT) roseau m; (MUS: of clarinet etc) anche f

**reef** [riːf] n (at sea) récif m, écueil m

**reek** [riːk] vi: **to ~ (of)** puer, empester

**reel** [riːl] n bobine f; (FISHING) moulinet m; (CINEMA) bande f; (dance) quadrille écossais ♦ vi (sway) chanceler; **~ in** vt

(fish, line) ramener

**ref** [ref] (inf) n abbr (= referee) arbitre m

**refectory** [rɪ'fektərɪ] n réfectoire m

**refer** [rɪ'fəː] vt: **to ~ sb to** (inquirer: for information, patient: to specialist) adresser qn à; (reader: to text) renvoyer qn à; (dispute, decision): **to ~ sth to** soumettre qch à ♦ vi: **to ~** (allude to) parler de, faire allusion à; (consult) se reporter à

**referee** [refə'riː] n arbitre m; (BRIT: for job application) répondant(e)

**reference** ['refrəns] n référence f, renvoi m; (mention) allusion f, mention f; (for job application: letter) références, lettre f de recommandation; **with ~ to** (COMM: in letter) me référant à, suite à; **~ book** n ouvrage m de référence

**refill** [vb rɪː'fɪl, n 'rɪːfɪl] vt remplir à nouveau; (pen, lighter etc) recharger ♦ n (for pen etc) recharge f

**refine** [rɪ'faɪn] vt (sugar, oil) raffiner; (taste) affiner; (theory, idea) fignoler (inf); **~d** adj (person, taste) raffiné(e); **~ry** n raffinerie f

**reflect** [rɪ'flekt] vt (light, image) réfléchir, refléter; (fig) refléter ♦ vi (think) réfléchir, méditer; **it ~s badly on him** cela le discrédite; **it ~s well on him** c'est tout à son honneur; **~ion** n réflexion f; (image) reflet m; (criticism): **~ion** on critique f de; atteinte f à; **on ~ion** réflexion faite

**reflex** ['riːfleks] adj réflexe ♦ n réflexe m; **~ive** [rɪ'fleksɪv] adj (LING) réfléchi(e)

**reform** [rɪ'fɔːm] n réforme f ♦ vt réformer; **~atory** [rɪ'fɔːmətərɪ] (US) n ≈ centre m d'éducation surveillée

**refrain** [rɪ'freɪn] vi: **to ~ from doing** s'abstenir de faire ♦ n refrain m

**refresh** [rɪ'freʃ] vt rafraîchir; (subj: sleep) reposer; **~er course** (BRIT) n cours m de recyclage; **~ing** adj (drink) rafraîchissant(e); (sleep) réparateur(-trice); **~ments** npl rafraîchissements mpl

**refrigerator** [rɪ'frɪdʒəreɪtə] n réfrigérateur m, frigidaire m ®

**refuel** [riːˈfjʊəl] vi se ravitailler en carburant

**refuge** [ˈrɛfjuːdʒ] n refuge m; **to take ~ in** se réfugier dans; **~e** [rɛfjuːˈdʒiː] n réfugié(e)

**refund** [n ˈriːfʌnd, vb rɪˈfʌnd] n remboursement m ♦ vt rembourser

**refurbish** [riːˈfɜːbɪʃ] vt remettre à neuf

**refusal** [rɪˈfjuːzəl] n refus m; **to have first ~ on** avoir droit de préemption sur

**refuse¹** [rɪˈfjuːz] vt, vi refuser

**refuse²** [ˈrɛfjuːs] n ordures fpl, détritus mpl; **~ collection** n ramassage m d'ordures

**regain** [rɪˈgeɪn] vt regagner; retrouver

**regal** [ˈriːgl] adj royal(e)

**regard** [rɪˈgɑːd] n respect m, estime f, considération f ♦ vt considérer; **to give one's ~s to** faire ses amitiés à; **"with kindest ~s"** "bien amicalement"; **as ~s, with ~ to** = regarding; **~ing** prep en ce qui concerne; **~less** adv quand même; **~less of** sans se soucier de

**régime** [reɪˈʒiːm] n régime m

**regiment** [ˈrɛdʒɪmənt] n régiment m; **~al** [rɛdʒɪˈmɛntl] adj d'un ou du régiment

**region** [ˈriːdʒən] n région f; **in the ~ of** (fig) aux alentours de; **~al** adj régional(e)

**register** [ˈrɛdʒɪstəʳ] n registre m; (also: **electoral ~**) liste électorale ♦ vt enregistrer; (birth, death) déclarer; (vehicle) immatriculer; (POST: letter) envoyer en recommandé; (subj: instrument) marquer ♦ vi s'inscrire; (at hotel) signer le registre; (make impression) être (bien) compris(e); **~ed** adj (letter, parcel) recommandé(e); **~ed trademark** n marque déposée; **registrar** [ˈrɛdʒɪstrɑːʳ] n officier m de l'état civil; **registration** [rɛdʒɪsˈtreɪʃən] n enregistrement m; (BRIT: AUT: also: **registration number**) numéro m d'immatriculation

**registry** [ˈrɛdʒɪstrɪ] n bureau m de l'enregistrement; **~ office** (BRIT) n bureau

m de l'état civil; **to get married in a ~ office** ≈ se marier à la mairie

**regret** [rɪˈgrɛt] n regret m ♦ vt regretter; **~fully** adv à ou avec regret

**regular** [ˈrɛgjʊləʳ] adj régulier(-ère); (usual) habituel(le); (soldier) de métier ♦ n (client etc) habitué(e); **~ly** adv régulièrement

**regulate** [ˈrɛgjʊleɪt] vt régler; **regulation** [rɛgjʊˈleɪʃən] n (rule) règlement m; (adjustment) réglage m

**rehabilitation** [riːəˌbɪlɪˈteɪʃən] n (of offender) réinsertion f; (of addict) réadaptation f

**rehearsal** [rɪˈhɜːsəl] n répétition f

**rehearse** [rɪˈhɜːs] vt répéter

**reign** [reɪn] n règne m ♦ vi régner

**reimburse** [riːɪmˈbɜːs] vt rembourser

**rein** [reɪn] n (for horse) rêne f

**reindeer** [ˈreɪndɪəʳ] n, pl inv renne m

**reinforce** [riːɪnˈfɔːs] vt renforcer; **~d concrete** n béton armé; **~ments** npl (MIL) renfort(s) m(pl)

**reinstate** [riːɪnˈsteɪt] vt rétablir, réintégrer

**reject** [n ˈriːdʒɛkt, vb rɪˈdʒɛkt] n (COMM) article m de rebut ♦ vt refuser; (idea) rejeter; **~ion** n rejet m, refus m

**rejoice** [rɪˈdʒɔɪs] vi: **to ~ (at** or **over)** se réjouir de)

**rejuvenate** [rɪˈdʒuːvəneɪt] vt rajeunir

**relapse** [rɪˈlæps] n (MED) rechute f

**relate** [rɪˈleɪt] vt (tell) raconter; (connect) établir un rapport entre ♦ vi: **this ~s to** cela se rapporte à; **to ~ to sb** entretenir des rapports avec qn; **~d** adj apparenté(e); **relating to** prep concernant

**relation** [rɪˈleɪʃən] n (person) parent(e); (link) rapport m, lien m; **~ship** n rapport m, lien m; (personal ties) relations fpl, rapports mpl; (also: **family ~ship**) lien de parenté

**relative** [ˈrɛlətɪv] n parent(e) ♦ adj relatif(-ive); **all her ~s** toute sa famille; **~ly** adv relativement

**relax** [rɪˈlæks] vi (muscle) se relâcher;

**relay** [*n* 'ri:leɪ, *vb* rɪ'leɪ] *n* (SPORT) course *f* de relais ♦ *vt* (*message*) retransmettre, relayer

**release** [rɪ'li:s] *n* (*from prison, obligation*) libération *f*; (*of gas etc*) émission *f*; (*of film etc*) sortie *f*; (*new recording*) disque *m* ♦ *vt* (*prisoner*) libérer; (*gas etc*) émettre, dégager; (*free: from wreckage etc*) dégager; (TECH: *catch, spring etc*) faire jouer; (*book, film*) sortir; (*report, news*) rendre public, publier

**relegate** ['relɪgeɪt] *vt* reléguer; (BRIT: SPORT): **to be ~d** descendre dans une division inférieure

**relent** [rɪ'lent] *vi* se laisser fléchir; **~less** *adj* implacable; (*unceasing*) continuel(le)

**relevant** ['reləvənt] *adj* (*question*) pertinent(e); (*fact*) significatif(-ive); (*information*) utile; **~ to** ayant rapport à, approprié à

**reliable** [rɪ'laɪəbl] *adj* (*person, firm*) sérieux(-euse), fiable; (*method, machine*) fiable; (*news, information*) sûr(e); **reliably** *adv*: **to be reliably informed** savoir de source sûre

**reliance** [rɪ'laɪəns] *n*: **~ (on)** (*person*) confiance *f* (en); (*drugs, promises*) besoin *m* (de), dépendance *f* (de)

**relic** ['relɪk] *n* (REL) relique *f*; (*of the past*) vestige *m*

**relief** [rɪ'li:f] *n* (*from pain, anxiety etc*) soulagement *m*; (*help, supplies*) secours *m(pl)*; (ART, GEO) relief *m*

**relieve** [rɪ'li:v] *vt* (*pain, patient*) soulager; (*fear, worry*) dissiper; (*bring help*) secourir; (*take over from: gen*) relayer; (: *guard*) relever; **to ~ sb of sth** débarrasser qn de qch; **to ~ o.s.** se soulager

**religion** [rɪ'lɪdʒən] *n* religion *f*; **religious** *adj* religieux(-euse); (*book*) de piété

**relinquish** [rɪ'lɪŋkwɪʃ] *vt* abandonner; (*plan, habit*) renoncer à

**relish** ['relɪʃ] *n* (CULIN) condiment *m*; (*enjoyment*) délectation *f* ♦ *vt* (*food etc*) savourer; **to ~ doing** se délecter à faire

**relocate** [ri:ləu'keɪt] *vt* installer ailleurs ♦ *vi* déménager, s'installer ailleurs

**reluctance** [rɪ'lʌktəns] *n* répugnance *f*

**reluctant** [rɪ'lʌktənt] *adj* peu disposé(e), qui hésite; **~ly** *adv* à contrecœur

**rely on** [rɪ'laɪ-] *vt fus* (*be dependent*) dépendre de; (*trust*) compter sur

**remain** [rɪ'meɪn] *vi* rester; **~der** *n* reste *m*; **~ing** *adj* qui reste; **~s** *npl* restes *mpl*

**remake** ['ri:meɪk] *n* (CINEMA) remake *m*

**remand** [rɪ'mɑ:nd] *n*: **on ~** en détention préventive ♦ *vt*: **to be ~ed in custody** être placé(e) en détention préventive

**remark** [rɪ'mɑ:k] *n* remarque *f*, observation *f* ♦ *vt* (*faire*) remarquer, dire; **~able** *adj* remarquable; **~ably** *adv* remarquablement

**remarry** [ri:'mærɪ] *vi* se remarier

**remedial** [rɪ'mi:dɪəl] *adj* (*tuition, classes*) de rattrapage; **~ exercises** gymnastique corrective

**remedy** ['remədɪ] *n*: **~ (for)** remède *m* (contre *or* à) ♦ *vt* remédier à

**remember** [rɪ'membə*r*] *vt* se rappeler, se souvenir de; (*send greetings*): **~ me to him** saluez-le de ma part; **remembrance** *n* souvenir *m*; mémoire *f*; **Remembrance Day** *n* le jour de l'Armistice

> **Remembrance Sunday**
>
> Remembrance Sunday *ou* Remembrance Day *est le dimanche le plus proche du 11 novembre, jour où la Première Guerre mondiale a officiellement pris fin, et rend hommage aux victimes des deux guerres mondiales. À cette occasion, un silence de deux minutes est observé à 11 h, heure de la signature de l'armistice avec l'Alle-*

magne en 1918; certains membres de la famille royale et du gouvernement déposent des gerbes de coquelicots au cénotaphe de Whitehall, et des couronnes sont placées sur les monuments aux morts dans toute la Grande-Bretagne; par ailleurs, les gens portent des coquelicots artificiels fabriqués et vendus par des membres de la légion britannique blessés au combat, au profit des blessés de guerre et de leur famille.

**remind** [rɪ'maɪnd] vt: **to ~ sb of** rappeler à qn; **to ~ sb to do** faire penser à qn à faire, rappeler à qn qu'il doit faire; **~er** n (souvenir) souvenir m; (letter) rappel m

**reminisce** [remɪ'nɪs] vi: **to ~** (about) évoquer ses souvenirs (de); **~nt** adj: **to be ~nt of** rappeler, faire penser à

**remiss** [rɪ'mɪs] adj négligent(e); **~ion** n (of illness, sins) rémission f; (of debt, prison sentence) remise f

**remit** [rɪ'mɪt] vt (send: money) envoyer; **~tance** n paiement m

**remnant** ['remnənt] n reste m, restant m; (of cloth) coupon m; **~s** npl (COMM) fins fpl de série

**remorse** [rɪ'mɔːs] n remords m; **~ful** adj plein(e) de remords; **~less** adj (fig) impitoyable

**remote** [rɪ'məʊt] adj éloigné(e), lointain(e); (person) distant(e); (possibility) vague; **~ control** n télécommande f; **~ly** adv au loin; (slightly) très vaguement

**remould** ['riːməʊld] (BRIT) n (tyre) pneu rechapé

**removable** [rɪ'muːvəbl] adj (detachable) amovible

**removal** [rɪ'muːvəl] n (taking away) enlèvement m; suppression f; (BRIT: from house) déménagement m; (from office: dismissal) renvoi m; (of stain) nettoyage m; (MED) ablation f; **~ van** (BRIT) n camion m de déménagement

**remove** [rɪ'muːv] vt enlever, retirer; (employee) renvoyer; (stain) faire partir; (abuse) supprimer; (doubt) chasser

**render** ['rendə*] vt rendre; **~ing** n (MUS etc) interprétation f

**rendezvous** ['rɒndɪvuː] n rendez-vous m inv

**renew** [rɪ'njuː] vt renouveler; (negotiations) reprendre; (acquaintance) renouer; **~able** adj (energy) renouvelable; **~al** n renouvellement m; reprise f

**renounce** [rɪ'naʊns] vt renoncer à

**renovate** ['renəveɪt] vt rénover; (art work) restaurer

**renown** [rɪ'naʊn] n renommée f; **~ed** adj renommé(e)

**rent** [rent] n loyer m ♦ vt louer; **~al** n (for television, car) (prix m de) location f

**reorganize** [riː'ɔːgənaɪz] vt réorganiser

**rep** [rep] n abbr = **representative**; **repertory**

**repair** [rɪ'pɛə*] n réparation f ♦ vt réparer; **in good/bad ~** en bon/mauvais état; **~ kit** n trousse f de réparation

**repatriate** [riː'pætrieit] vt rapatrier

**repay** [riː'peɪ] (irreg) vt (money, creditor) rembourser; (sb's efforts) récompenser; **~ment** n remboursement m

**repeal** [rɪ'piːl] n (of law) abrogation f ♦ vt (law) abroger

**repeat** [rɪ'piːt] n (RADIO, TV) reprise f ♦ vt répéter; (COMM: order) renouveler; (SCOL: a class) redoubler ♦ vi répéter; **~edly** adv souvent, à plusieurs reprises

**repel** [rɪ'pel] vt repousser; **~lent** adj repoussant(e) ♦ n: **insect ~lent** insectifuge m

**repent** [rɪ'pent] vi: **to ~ (of)** se repentir (de); **~ance** n repentir m

**repertory** ['repətərɪ] n (also: **~ theatre**) théâtre m de répertoire

**repetition** [repɪ'tɪʃən] n répétition f

**repetitive** [rɪ'petɪtɪv] adj (movement, work) répétitif(-ive); (speech) plein(e) de redites

**replace** [rɪ'pleɪs] vt (put back) remettre, replacer; (take the place of) remplacer;

**~ment** n (substitution) remplacement m; (person) remplaçant(e)

**replay** ['ri:pleɪ] vt (of match) match rejoué; (of tape, film) répétition f

**replenish** [rɪ'plenɪʃ] vt (glass) remplir (de nouveau); (stock etc) réapprovisionner

**replica** ['replɪkə] n réplique f, copie exacte

**reply** [rɪ'plaɪ] n réponse f ♦ vi répondre

**report** [rɪ'pɔ:t] n rapport m; (PRESS etc) reportage m; (BRIT: also: **school ~**) bulletin m (scolaire); (of gun) détonation f ♦ vt rapporter, faire un compte rendu de; (PRESS etc) faire un reportage sur; (bring to notice: occurrence) signaler ♦ vi (make a ~) faire un rapport (or un reportage); (present o.s.): **to ~ (to sb)** se présenter (chez qn); (be responsible to): **to ~ to sb** être sous les ordres de qn; **~ card** (US, SCOTTISH) n bulletin m scolaire; **~edly** adv: **she is ~edly living in ...** elle habiterait ...; **he ~edly told them to ...** il leur aurait ordonné de ...; **~er** n reporter m

**repose** [rɪ'pəʊz] n: **in ~** en ou au repos

**represent** [reprɪ'zent] vt représenter; (view, belief) présenter, expliquer; (describe): **to ~ sth as** présenter ou décrire qch comme; **~ation** [-'teɪʃən] n représentation f; **~ations** npl (protest) démarche f; **~ative** [reprɪ'zentətɪv] n représentant(e); (US: POL) député m ♦ adj représentatif(-ive), caractéristique

**repress** [rɪ'pres] vt réprimer; **~ion** n répression f

**reprieve** [rɪ'pri:v] n (LAW) grâce f; (fig) sursis m, délai m

**reprisal** [rɪ'praɪzl] n: **~s** npl représailles fpl

**reproach** [rɪ'prəʊtʃ] vt: **to ~ sb with sth** reprocher qch à qn; **~ful** adj de reproche

**reproduce** [ri:prə'dju:s] vt reproduire ♦ vi se reproduire; **reproduction** [ri:prə'dʌkʃən] n reproduction f

**reproof** [rɪ'pru:f] n reproche m

**reptile** ['reptaɪl] n reptile m

**republic** [rɪ'pʌblɪk] n république f; **~an** adj républicain(e)

**repudiate** [rɪ'pju:dɪeɪt] vt répudier, rejeter

**repulsive** [rɪ'pʌlsɪv] adj repoussant(e), répulsif(-ive)

**reputable** ['repjʊtəbl] adj de bonne réputation; (occupation) honorable

**reputation** [repjʊ'teɪʃən] n réputation f

**reputed** [rɪ'pju:tɪd] adj (supposed) supposé(e); **~ly** adv d'après ce qu'on dit

**request** [rɪ'kwest] n demande f; (formal) requête f ♦ vt: **to ~ (of ou from sb)** demander (à qn); **~ stop** (BRIT) n (for bus) arrêt facultatif

**require** [rɪ'kwaɪə*] vt (need: subj: person) avoir besoin de; (: thing, situation) demander; (want) exiger; (order): **to ~ sb to do sth/sth of sb** exiger que qn fasse qch/qch de qn; **~ment** n exigence f; besoin m; condition requise

**requisition** [rekwɪ'zɪʃən] n: **~ (for)** demande f (de) ♦ vt (MIL) réquisitionner

**rescue** ['reskju:] n (from accident) sauvetage m; (help) secours mpl ♦ vt sauver; **~ party** n équipe f de sauvetage; **~r** n sauveteur m

**research** [rɪ'sɜ:tʃ] n recherche f(pl) ♦ vt faire des recherches sur

**resemblance** [rɪ'zembləns] n ressemblance f

**resemble** [rɪ'zembl] vt ressembler à

**resent** [rɪ'zent] vt être contrarié(e) par; **~ful** adj irrité(e), plein(e) de ressentiment; **~ment** n ressentiment m

**reservation** [rezə'veɪʃən] n (booking) réservation f; (doubt) réserve f; (for tribe) réserve f; **to make a ~ (in a hotel/a restaurant/on a plane)** réserver ou retenir une chambre/une table/une place

**reserve** [rɪ'zɜ:v] n réserve f; (SPORT) remplaçant(e) ♦ vt (seats etc) réserver, retenir; **~s** npl (MIL) réservistes mpl; **in ~** en réserve; **~d** adj réservé(e)

**reshuffle** [riː'ʃʌfl] n: Cabinet ~ (POL) remaniement ministériel

**residence** ['rezidəns] n résidence f; ~ **permit** (BRIT) n permis m de séjour

**resident** ['rezidənt] n résident(e) ♦ adj résidant(e); **~ial** [rezi'denʃəl] adj résidentiel(le); (course) avec hébergement sur place; **~ial school** n internat m

**residue** ['rezidjuː] n reste m; (CHEM, PHYSICS) résidu m

**resign** [ri'zain] vt (one's post) démissionner de ♦ vi démissionner; **to ~ o.s. to** se résigner à; **~ation** [rezig'neiʃən] n (of post) démission f; (state of mind) résignation f; **~ed** adj résigné(e)

**resilient** [ri'ziliənt] adj (material) élastique; (person) qui réagit, qui a du ressort

**resist** [ri'zist] vt résister à; **~ance** n résistance f

**resit** [riː'sit] vt (exam) repasser ♦ n deuxième session f (d'un examen)

**resolution** [rezə'luːʃən] n résolution f

**resolve** [ri'zɔlv] n résolution f ♦ vi: **to ~ to do** (problem) résoudre ♦ vi: **to ~ to do** se résoudre or décider de faire

**resort** [ri'zɔːt] n (seaside town) station f balnéaire; (ski ~) station de ski; (recourse) recours m ♦ vi: **to ~ to** avoir recours à; **in the last ~** en dernier ressort

**resounding** [ri'zaundiŋ] adj retentissant(e)

**resource** [ri'sɔːs] n ressource f; **~s** npl (supplies, wealth etc) ressources; **~ful** adj ingénieux(-euse), débrouillard(e)

**respect** [ris'pekt] n respect m ♦ vt respecter; **~s** npl (compliments) respects, hommages mpl; **with ~ to** en ce qui concerne; **in this ~** à cet égard; **~able** adj respectable; **~ful** adj respectueux(-euse); **~ively** adv respectivement

**respite** ['respait] n répit m

**respond** [ris'pɔnd] vi répondre; (react) réagir; **response** n réponse f; réaction f

**responsibility** [rispɔnsi'biliti] n responsabilité f

**responsible** [ris'pɔnsibl] adj (liable): ~ **(for)** responsable (de); (person) digne de confiance; (job) qui comporte des responsabilités

**responsive** [ris'pɔnsiv] adj qui réagit; (person) qui n'est pas réservé(e) or indifférent(e)

**rest** [rest] n repos m; (stop) arrêt m, pause f; (MUS) silence m; (support) support m, appui m; (remainder) reste m, restant m ♦ vi se reposer; (be supported): **to ~ on** s'appuyer or reposer sur; (remain) rester ♦ vt (lean): **to ~ sth on/against** appuyer qch sur/contre; **the ~ of them** les autres; **it ~s with him to ...** c'est à lui de ...

**restaurant** ['restərɔ̃] n restaurant m; **~ car** (BRIT) n wagon-restaurant m

**restful** ['restful] adj reposant(e)

**restive** ['restiv] adj agité(e), impatient(e); (horse) rétif(-ive)

**restless** ['restlis] adj agité(e)

**restoration** [restə'reiʃən] n restauration f; restitution f; rétablissement m

**restore** [ri'stɔː] vt (building) restaurer; (sth stolen) restituer; (peace, health) rétablir; **to ~ to** (former state) ramener à

**restrain** [ris'trein] vt contenir; (person): **to ~ (from doing)** retenir (de faire); **~ed** adj (style) sobre; (manner) mesuré(e); **~t** n (restriction) contrainte f; (moderation) retenue f

**restrict** [ris'trikt] vt restreindre, limiter; **~ion** n restriction f, limitation f

**rest room** (US) n toilettes fpl

**result** [ri'zʌlt] n résultat m ♦ vi: **to ~ in** aboutir à, se terminer par; **as a ~ of** à la suite de

**resume** [ri'zjuːm] vt, vi (work, journey) reprendre

**résumé** ['reizjuːmei] n résumé m; (US) curriculum vitae m

**resumption** [ri'zʌmpʃən] n reprise f

**resurgence** [ri'səːdʒəns] n (of energy, activity) regain m

**resurrection** [rezə'rekʃən] n résurrection f

**resuscitate** [rɪ'sʌsɪteɪt] vt (MED) réanimer

**retail** ['ri:teɪl] adj de or au détail ♦ adv au détail; **~er** n détaillant m, e m; **~ price** n prix m de détail

**retain** [rɪ'teɪn] vt (keep) garder, conserver; **~er** n (fee) acompte m, provision f

**retaliate** [rɪ'tælɪeɪt] vi: to ~ (against) se venger (de); **retaliation** [rɪtælɪ'eɪʃən] n représailles fpl, vengeance f

**retarded** [rɪ'tɑːdɪd] adj retardé(e)

**retch** [retʃ] vi avoir des haut-le-cœur

**retentive** [rɪ'tentɪv] adj: **~ memory** excellente mémoire

**retina** ['retɪnə] n rétine f

**retire** [rɪ'taɪə*] vi (give up work) prendre sa retraite; (withdraw) se retirer, partir; (go to bed) (aller) se coucher; **~d** adj (person) retraité(e); **~ment** n retraite f; **retiring** adj (shy) réservé(e); (leaving) sortant(e)

**retort** [rɪ'tɔːt] vi riposter

**retrace** [ri:'treɪs] vt: **to ~ one's steps** revenir sur ses pas

**retract** [rɪ'trækt] vt (statement, claws) rétracter; (undercarriage, aerial) rentrer, escamoter

**retrain** [ri:'treɪn] vt (worker) recycler

**retread** [rɪ'tred] n (tyre) pneu rechapé

**retreat** [rɪ'triːt] n retraite f ♦ vi battre en retraite

**retribution** [retrɪ'bjuːʃən] n châtiment m

**retrieval** [rɪ'triːvəl] n (see vb) récupération f; réparation f

**retrieve** [rɪ'triːv] vt (sth lost) récupérer; (situation, honour) sauver; (error, loss) réparer; **~r** n chien m d'arrêt

**retrospect** ['retrəspekt] n: **in ~** rétrospectivement, après coup; **~ive** [retrə'spektɪv] adj rétrospectif(-ive); (law) rétroactif(-ive)

**return** [rɪ'tɜːn] n (going or coming back) retour m; (of sth stolen back, shares) restitution f; (FINANCE: from land, shares) rendement m, rapport m ♦ cpd (journey) de retour; (BRIT: ticket) aller et retour; (match) retour ♦ vi (come back) revenir; (go back) retourner ♦ vt rendre; (bring back) rapporter; (send back: also: ball) renvoyer; (put back) remettre; (POL: candidate) élire; **~s** npl (COMM) recettes fpl; (FINANCE) bénéfices mpl; **in ~** (for) en échange (de); **by ~ (of post)** par retour (du courrier); **many happy ~s (of the day)!** bon anniversaire!

**reunion** [riː'juːnɪən] n réunion f

**reunite** [riːju:'naɪt] vt réunir

**reuse** [riː'juːz] vt réutiliser

**rev** [rev] n abbr (AUT: = revolution) tour m ♦ vt (also: **rev up**) emballer

**revamp** [riː'væmp] vt (firm, system etc) réorganiser

**reveal** [rɪ'viːl] vt (make known) révéler; (display) laisser voir; **~ing** adj révélateur(-trice); (dress) au décolleté généreux or suggestif

**revel** ['revl] vi: **to ~ in sth/in doing** se délecter de qch/à faire

**revenge** [rɪ'vendʒ] n vengeance f; **to take ~ on** (enemy) se venger sur

**revenue** ['revənjuː] n revenu m

**reverberate** [rɪ'vɜːbəreɪt] vi (sound) retentir, se répercuter; (fig: shock etc) se propager

**reverence** ['revərəns] n vénération f, révérence f

**Reverend** ['revərənd] adj (in titles): **the ~ John Smith** (Anglican) le révérend John Smith; (Catholic) l'abbé (John) Smith; (Protestant) le pasteur (John) Smith

**reversal** [rɪ'vɜːsl] n (of opinion) revirement m; (of order) renversement m; (of direction) changement m

**reverse** [rɪ'vɜːs] n contraire m, opposé m; (back) dos m, envers m; (of paper) verso m; (of coin; also: setback) revers m; (AUT: also: **~ gear**) marche f arrière ♦ adj (order, direction) opposé(e), inverse ♦ vt (order, position) changer, inverser; (direction, policy) changer complètement de; (decision) annuler; (roles) renverser; (car) faire marche arrière avec ♦ vt (BRIT: AUT) faire marche arrière; **he ~d (the car) into a wall** il a embouti un mur en marche arrière; **~d charge call** (BRIT) (TEL) communication f en PCV; **reversing lights** (BRIT) npl feux mpl de marche arrière or de recul

**revert** [rɪˈvəːt] vi: **to ~** revenir à, retourner à

**review** [rɪˈvjuː] n revue f; (of book, film) critique f, compte rendu; (of situation, policy) examen m, bilan m ♦ vt passer en revue; faire la critique de; examiner; **~er** n critique m

**revise** [rɪˈvaɪz] vt réviser, modifier; (manuscript) revoir, corriger ♦ vi (study) réviser; **revision** [rɪˈvɪʒən] n révision f

**revival** [rɪˈvaɪvəl] n reprise f; (recovery) rétablissement m; (of faith) renouveau m

**revive** [rɪˈvaɪv] vt (person) ranimer; (custom) rétablir; (economy) relancer; (hope, courage) raviver, faire renaître; (play) reprendre ♦ vi (person) reprendre connaissance; (: from ill health) se rétablir; (hope etc) renaître; (activity) reprendre

**revoke** [rɪˈvəuk] vt révoquer; (law) abroger

**revolt** [rɪˈvəult] n révolte f ♦ vi se révolter, se rebeller ♦ vt révolter, dégoûter; **~ing** adj dégoûtant(e)

**revolution** [revəˈluːʃən] n révolution f; (of wheel, engine) tour m, révolution; **~ary** adj révolutionnaire ♦ n révolutionnaire m/f

**revolve** [rɪˈvɔlv] vi tourner

**revolver** [rɪˈvɔlvəʳ] n revolver m

**revolving** [rɪˈvɔlvɪŋ] adj tournant(e); (chair) pivotant(e); **~ door** n (porte f à) tambour m

**revulsion** [rɪˈvʌlʃən] n dégoût m, répugnance f

**reward** [rɪˈwɔːd] n récompense f ♦ vt: **to ~ (for)** récompenser (de); **~ing** adj (fig) qui en vaut la peine, gratifiant(e)

**rewind** [riːˈwaɪnd] (irreg) vt (tape) rembobiner

**rewire** [riːˈwaɪəʳ] vt (house) refaire l'installation électrique de

**rheumatism** [ˈruːmətɪzəm] n rhumatisme m

**Rhine** [raɪn] n Rhin m

**rhinoceros** [raɪˈnɔsərəs] n rhinocéros m

**Rhone** [rəun] n Rhône m

**rhubarb** [ˈruːbɑːb] n rhubarbe f

**rhyme** [raɪm] n rime f; (verse) vers mpl

**rhythm** [ˈrɪðm] n rythme m

**rib** [rɪb] n (ANAT) côte f

**ribbon** [ˈrɪbən] n ruban m; **in ~s** (torn) en lambeaux

**rice** [raɪs] n riz m; **~ pudding** n riz au lait

**rich** [rɪtʃ] adj riche; (gift, clothes) somptueux(-euse) ♦ npl: **the ~** les riches mpl; **~es** npl richesses fpl; **~ly** adv richement; (deserved, earned) largement

**rickets** [ˈrɪkɪts] n rachitisme m

**rid** [rɪd] (pt, pp rid) vt: **to ~ sb of** débarrasser qn de; **to get ~ of** se débarrasser de

**riddle** [ˈrɪdl] n (puzzle) énigme f ♦ vt: **to be ~d with** être criblé(e) de; (fig: guilt, corruption, doubts) être en proie à

**ride** [raɪd] (pt rode, pp ridden) n promenade f, tour m; (distance covered) trajet m ♦ vi (as sport) monter (à cheval), faire du cheval; (go somewhere: on horse, bicycle) aller (à cheval or bicyclette etc); (journey: on bus, motorcycle, bus) rouler ♦ vt (a certain horse) monter; (distance) parcourir, faire; **to take sb for a ~** (fig) faire marcher qn; **to ~ a horse/bicycle** monter à cheval/à bicyclette; **~r** n cavalier(-ère); (in race) jockey m; (on bicycle) cycliste m/f; (on motorcycle) motocycliste m/f

**ridge** [rɪdʒ] n (of roof, mountain) arête f; (of hill) faîte m; (on object) strie f

**ridicule** [ˈrɪdɪkjuːl] n ridicule m; dérision f

**ridiculous** [rɪˈdɪkjuləs] adj ridicule

**riding** [ˈraɪdɪŋ] n équitation f;

**school** n manège m, école f d'équitation

**rife** [raɪf] adj répandu(e); ~ **with** abondant(e) en, plein(e) de

**riffraff** ['rɪfræf] n racaille f

**rifle** ['raɪfl] n fusil m (à canon rayé) ♦ vt vider, dévaliser; ~ **through** vt (belongings) fouiller; (papers) feuilleter; ~ **range** n champ m de tir; (at fair) stand m de tir

**rift** [rɪft] n fente f, fissure f; (fig: disagreement) désaccord m

**rig** [rɪg] n (also: oil ~: at sea) plateforme pétrolière ♦ vt (election etc) truquer; ~ **out** (BRIT) vt: **to ~ out as/in** habiller en/de; ~ **up** vt arranger, faire avec des moyens de fortune; ~**ging** n (NAUT) gréement m

**right** [raɪt] adj (correctly chosen: answer, road etc) bon (bonne); (true) juste, exact(e); (suitable) approprié(e), convenable; (just) juste, équitable; (morally good) bien inv; (not left) droit(e) ♦ n (what is morally) ~ bien m; (title, claim) droit m; (not left) droite f ♦ adv (answer) correctement, juste; (treat) bien, comme il faut; (not on the left) à droite ♦ vt redresser ♦ excl bon!; **to be** ~ (person) avoir raison; (answer) être juste ou correct(e); (clock) à l'heure (juste); **by** ~**s** en toute justice; **on the** ~ à droite; **to be in the** ~ avoir raison; ~ **now** en ce moment même; tout de suite; ~ **in the middle** en plein milieu; ~ **away** immédiatement; ~ **angle** n (MATH) angle droit; ~**eous** ['raɪtʃəs] adj droit(e), vertueux(-euse); (anger) justifié(e); ~**ful** adj légitime; ~-**handed** adj (person) droitier(-ère); ~-**hand man** n bras droit (fig); ~-**hand side** n-la droite; ~**ly** adv (with reason) à juste titre; ~ **of way** n droit m de passage; (AUT) priorité f; ~-**wing** adj (POL) de droite

**rigid** ['rɪdʒɪd] adj rigide; (principle, control) strict(e)

**rigmarole** ['rɪgmərəʊl] n comédie f

**rigorous** ['rɪgərəs] adj rigoureux(-euse)

**rile** [raɪl] vt agacer

**rim** [rɪm] n bord m; (of spectacles) monture f; (of wheel) jante f

**rind** [raɪnd] n (of bacon) couenne f; (of lemon etc) écorce f, zeste m; (of cheese) croûte f

**ring** [rɪŋ] (pt rang, pp rung) n anneau m; (on finger) bague f; (also: **wedding** ~) alliance f; (of people, objects) cercle m; (of spies) réseau m; (of smoke etc) rond m; (arena) piste f, arène f; (for boxing) ring m; (sound of bell) sonnerie f ♦ vi (telephone, bell) sonner; (person: by telephone) téléphoner; (also: ~ **out**: voice, words) retentir; (ears) bourdonner ♦ vt (BRIT: TEL: also: ~ **up**) téléphoner à, appeler; (bell) faire sonner; **to** ~ **the bell** sonner; **to give sb a** ~ (BRIT: TEL) appeler qn; ~ **back** (BRIT) vt, vi (TEL) rappeler; ~ **off** (BRIT) vi (TEL) raccrocher; ~ **up** (BRIT) vt (TEL) appeler; ~ **binder** n classeur m à anneaux; ~**ing** ['rɪŋɪŋ] n (of telephone) sonnerie f; (of bell) tintement m; (in ears) bourdonnement m; ~**ing tone** n (BRIT) (TEL) sonnerie f; ~**leader** n (of gang) chef m, meneur m; ~**lets** npl anglaises fpl; ~ **road** (BRIT) n route f de ceinture; (motorway) périphérique m

**rink** [rɪŋk] n (also: **ice** ~) patinoire f

**rinse** [rɪns] vt rincer

**riot** ['raɪət] n émeute f; (of flowers, colour) profusion f ♦ vi faire une émeute, manifester avec violence; **to run** ~ se déchaîner; ~**ous** adj (mob, assembly) séditieux(-euse), déchaîné(e); (living, behaviour) débauché(e); (party) très animé(e); (welcome) délirant(e)

**rip** [rɪp] n déchirure f ♦ vt déchirer ♦ vi se déchirer; ~**cord** n poignée f d'ouverture

**ripe** [raɪp] adj (fruit) mûr(e); (cheese) fait(e); ~**n** vt mûrir ♦ vi mûrir

**rip-off** (inf) n: **it's a** ~~! c'est de l'arnaque!

**ripple** ['rɪpl] n ondulation f; (of applause, laughter) cascade f ♦ vi onduler

**rise** [raɪz] (pt **rose**, pp **risen**) n (slope) côte f, pente f; (hill) hauteur f; (increase: in wages: BRIT) augmentation f; (: in prices, temperature) hausse f, augmentation; (fig: to power etc) ascension f ♦ vi s'élever, monter; (prices, numbers) augmenter; (waters) monter; (sun; person: from chair, bed) se lever; (also: ~ **up**: tower, building) s'élever; (: rebel) se révolter; (in rank) s'élever; **to give ~ to** donner lieu à; **to ~ to the occasion** se montrer à la hauteur; **~r** n: **to be an early ~r** être matinal(e); **rising** adj (number, prices) en hausse; (tide) montant(e); (sun, moon) levant(e)

**risk** [rɪsk] n risque m ♦ vt risquer; **at ~** en danger; **at one's own ~** à ses risques et périls; **~y** adj risqué(e)

**rissole** ['rɪsəʊl] n croquette f

**rite** [raɪt] n rite m; **last ~s** derniers sacrements

**ritual** ['rɪtjuəl] adj rituel(le) ♦ n rituel m

**rival** ['raɪvl] adj, n rival(e); (in business) concurrent(e) ♦ vt (match) égaler; **~ry** ['raɪvlrɪ] n rivalité f, concurrence f

**river** ['rɪvə'] n rivière f; (major, also fig) fleuve m ♦ cpd (port, traffic) fluvial(e); **up/down ~** en amont/aval; **~bank** n rive f, berge f; **~bed** n lit m de rivière or de fleuve)

**rivet** ['rɪvɪt] n rivet m ♦ vt (fig) river, fixer

**Riviera** [rɪvɪ'eərə] n: **the (French) ~** la Côte d'Azur; **the Italian ~** la Riviera (italienne)

**road** [rəʊd] n route f; (in town) rue f; (fig) chemin, voie f; **major/minor ~** route principale or à priorité/voie secondaire; **~ accident** n accident m de la circulation; **~block** n barrage routier; **~hog** n chauffard m; **~ map** n carte routière; **~ rage** n comportement très agressif de certains usagers de la route; **~ safety** n sécurité routière; **~side** n bord m de la route, bas-côté m; **~ sign** n panneau m de signalisation; **~way** n chaussée f; **~ works** npl travaux mpl

(de réfection des routes); **~worthy** adj en bon état de marche

**roam** [rəʊm] vi errer, vagabonder

**roar** [rɔːʳ] n rugissement m; (of crowd) hurlements mpl; (of vehicle, thunder, storm) grondement m ♦ vi rugir; hurler; gronder; **to ~** with laughter éclater de rire; **to do a ~ing trade** faire des affaires d'or

**roast** [rəʊst] n rôti m ♦ vt (faire) rôtir; (coffee) griller, torréfier; **~ beef** n rôti m de bœuf, rosbif m

**rob** [rɒb] vt (person) voler; (bank) dévaliser; **to ~ sb of sth** voler or dérober qch à qn; (fig: deprive) priver qn de qch; **~ber** n bandit m, voleur m; **~bery** n vol m

**robe** [rəʊb] n (for ceremony etc) robe f; (also: **bathrobe**) peignoir m; (US) couverture f

**robin** ['rɒbɪn] n rouge-gorge m

**robot** ['rəʊbɒt] n robot m

**robust** [rəʊ'bʌst] adj robuste; (material, appetite) solide

**rock** [rɒk] n (substance) roche f, roc m; (boulder) rocher m; (US: small stone) caillou m; (BRIT: sweet) ≃ sucre m d'orge ♦ vt (swing gently: cradle) balancer; (: child) bercer; (shake) ébranler, secouer ♦ vi (se) balancer; être ébranlé(e) or secoué(e); **on the ~s** (drink) avec des glaçons; (marriage etc) en train de craquer; **~ and roll** n rock (and roll) m, rock'n'roll m; **~-bottom** adj (fig: prices) sacrifié(e); **~ery** n (jardin m de) rocaille f

**rocket** ['rɒkɪt] n fusée f; (MIL) fusée, roquette f; (CULIN) roquette f

**rocking chair** n fauteuil m à bascule

**rocking horse** n cheval m à bascule

**rocky** ['rɒkɪ] adj (hill) rocheux(-euse); (path) rocailleux(-euse)

**rod** [rɒd] n (wooden) baguette f; (metallic) tringle f; (TECH) tige f; (also: **fishing ~**) canne f à pêche

**rode** [rəʊd] pt of **ride**

**rodent** ['rəʊdnt] n rongeur m

**rodeo** ['rəʊdɪəʊ] (US) n rodéo m

**roe** [rəʊ] n (species: also: ~ **deer**) chevreuil m; (of fish: also: **hard** ~) œufs mpl de poisson; **soft** ~ laitance f

**rogue** [rəʊg] n coquin m

**role** [rəʊl] n rôle m; ~ **play** n jeu de rôle

**roll** [rəʊl] n rouleau m; (of banknotes) liasse f; (also: **bread** ~) petit pain; (register) liste f; (sound: of drums etc) roulement m ♦ vt rouler; (also: ~ **up**: string) enrouler; (: sleeves) retrousser; (also: ~ **out**: pastry) étendre au rouleau, abaisser ♦ vi rouler; ~ **about** vi rouler çà et là; (person) se rouler par terre; ~ **around** vi = **roll about**; ~ **by** vi (time) s'écouler, passer; ~ **over** vi se retourner; ~ **up** vi (inf: arrive) s'amener ♦ vt rouler; ~ **call** n appel m; ~**er** n rouleau m; (wheel) roulette f; (for road) rouleau compresseur; ~**er blade** n patin m en ligne; ~**er coaster** n montagnes fpl russes; ~**er skates** npl patins mpl à roulettes; ~**er skating** n patin m à roulettes; ~**ing** adj (landscape) onduleux(-euse); ~**ing pin** n rouleau m à pâtisserie; ~**ing stock** n (RAIL) matériel roulant

**ROM** [rɔm] n abbr (= read only memory) mémoire morte

**Roman** ['rəʊmən] adj romain(e); ~ **Catholic** adj, n catholique m/f

**romance** [rə'mæns] n (love affair) idylle f; (charm) poésie f; (novel) roman m à l'eau de rose

**Romania** [rəʊ'meɪnɪə] n Roumanie f; ~**n** adj roumain(e) ♦ n Roumain(e); (LING) roumain m

**Roman numeral** n chiffre romain

**romantic** [rə'mæntɪk] adj romantique; sentimental(e)

**Rome** [rəʊm] n Rome

**romp** [rɔmp] n jeux bruyants ♦ vi (also: ~ **about**) s'ébattre, jouer bruyamment; ~**ers** npl barboteuse f

**roof** [ruːf] (pl ~**s**) n toit m ♦ vt couvrir (d'un toit); **the ~ of the mouth** la

voûte du palais; ~**ing** n toiture f; ~ **rack** n (AUT) galerie f

**rook** [rʊk] n (bird) freux m; (CHESS) tour f

**room** [ruːm] n (in house) pièce f; (also: **bedroom**) chambre f (à coucher); (in school etc) salle f; (space) place f; ~**s** npl (lodging) meublé m; "~**s to let**" (BRIT) or "~**s for rent**" (US) "chambres à louer"; **single/double** chambre pour une personne/deux personnes; **there is ~ for improvement** cela laisse à désirer; ~**ing house** n (US) maison f ou immeuble m de rapport; ~**mate** n camarade m/f de chambre; ~ **service** n service m des chambres (dans un hôtel); ~**y** adj spacieux(-euse); (garment) ample

**roost** [ruːst] vi se jucher

**rooster** ['ruːstər] n (esp US) coq m

**root** [ruːt] n (BOT, MATH) racine f; (fig: of problem) origine f, fond m ♦ vi (plant) s'enraciner; ~ **about** vi (fig) fouiller; ~ **for** fus encourager, applaudir; ~ **out** vt (find) dénicher

**rope** [rəʊp] n corde f; (NAUT) cordage m ♦ vt (tie up or secure) attacher; (climbers: also: ~ **together**) encorder; (area: ~ **off**) interdire l'accès de; (: divide off) séparer; **to know the ~s** (fig) être au courant, connaître les ficelles; ~ **in** vt (fig: person) embringuer

**rosary** ['rəʊzərɪ] n chapelet m

**rose** [rəʊz] pt of **rise** ♦ n rose f; (also: ~**bush**) rosier m; (on watering can) pomme f

**rosebud** ['rəʊzbʌd] n bouton m de rose

**rosemary** ['rəʊzmərɪ] n romarin m

**roster** ['rɔstər] n: **duty** ~ tableau m de service

**rostrum** ['rɔstrəm] n tribune f (pour un orateur etc)

**rosy** ['rəʊzɪ] adj rose; **a ~ future** un bel avenir

**rot** [rɔt] n (decay) pourriture f; (fig: pej)

idioties *fpl* ♦ *vt, vi* pourrir

**rota** ['rəutə] *n* liste *f*, tableau *m* de service; **on a ~ basis** par roulement

**rotary** ['rəutəri] *adj* rotatif(-ive)

**rotate** [rəu'teit] *vt* (*revolve*) faire tourner; (*change round: jobs*) faire à tour de rôle ♦ *vi* (*revolve*) tourner; **rotating** *adj* (*movement*) tournant(e).

**rotten** ['rɔtn] *adj* (*decayed*) pourri(e); (*dishonest*) corrompu(e); (*inf: bad*) mauvais(e), moche; **to feel ~** (*ill*) être mal fichu(e)

**rotund** [rəu'tʌnd] *adj* (*person*) rondelet(te)

**rough** [rʌf] *adj* (*cloth, skin*) rêche, rugueux(-euse); (*terrain*) accidenté(e); (*path*) rocailleux(-euse); (*voice*) rauque, rude; (*person, manner: coarse*) rude, fruste; (: *violent*) brutal(e); (*district, weather*) mauvais(e); (*sea*) houleux(-euse); (*plan etc*) ébauché(e); (*guess*) approximatif(-ive) ♦ *n* (GOLF) rough *m* ♦ *vt*: **to ~ it** vivre à la dure; **to sleep ~** (BRIT) coucher à la dure; **~age** *n* fibres *fpl* alimentaires; **~-and-ready** *adj* rudimentaire; **~ copy, ~ draft** *n* brouillon *m*; **~ly** *adv* (*handle*) rudement, brutalement; (*speak*) avec brusquerie; (*make*) grossièrement; (*approximately*) à peu près, en gros

**roulette** [ru:'let] *n* roulette *f*

**Roumania** [ru:'meiniə] *n* = **Romania**

**round** [raund] *adj* rond(e) ♦ *n* (BRIT: *of toast*) tranche *f*; (*duty: of policeman, milkman etc*) tournée *f*; (: *of doctor*) visites *fpl*; (*game: of cards, in competition*) partie *f*; (BOXING) round *m*; (*of talks*) série *f* ♦ *vt* (*corner*) tourner ♦ *prep* autour de ♦ *adv*: **all ~** tout autour; **the long way ~** (par) le chemin le plus long; **all the year ~** toute l'année; **it's just ~ the corner** (*fig*) c'est tout près; **~ the clock** 24 heures sur 24; **to go ~ to sb's (house)** aller chez qn; **go ~ the back** passez par derrière; **enough to go ~** assez pour tout le monde; **~ of ammunition** cartouche *f*; **~ of ap-**

**plause** ban *m*, applaudissements *mpl*; **~ of drinks** tournée *f*; **~ of sandwiches** sandwich *m*; **~ off** *vt* (*speech etc*) terminer; **~ up** *vt* rassembler; (*criminals*) effectuer une rafle de; (*price, figure*) arrondir (au chiffre supérieur); **~about** *n* (BRIT: AUT) rond-point *m* (à sens giratoire); (: *at fair*) manège *m* (de chevaux de bois) ♦ *adj* (*route, means*) détourné(e); **~ers** *n* (*game*) sorte de baseball; **~ly** *adv* (*fig*) tout net, carrément; **~ trip** *n* (*voyage m*) aller et retour *m*; **~up** *n* rassemblement *m*; (*of criminals*) rafle *f*

**rouse** [rauz] *vt* (*wake up*) réveiller; (*stir up*) susciter; provoquer; **rousing** *adj* (*welcome*) enthousiaste

**route** [ru:t] *n* itinéraire *m*; (*of bus*) parcours *m*; (*of trade, shipping*) route *f*

**routine** [ru:'ti:n] *adj* (*work*) ordinaire, courant(e); (*procedure*) d'usage ♦ *n* (*habits*) habitudes *fpl*; (*pej*) train-train *m*; (THEATRE) numéro *m*

**rove** [rəuv] *vt* (*area, streets*) errer dans

**row¹** [rəu] *n* (*line*) rangée *f*; (*of people, seats,* KNITTING) rang *m*; (*behind one another: of cars, people*) file *f* ♦ *vi* (*in boat*) ramer; (*as sport*) faire de l'aviron ♦ *vt* (*boat*) faire aller à la rame ou à l'aviron; **in a ~** (*fig*) d'affilée

**row²** [rau] *n* (*noise*) vacarme *m*; (*dispute*) dispute *f*, querelle *f*; (*scolding*) réprimande *f*, savon *m* ♦ *vi* se disputer, se quereller

**rowboat** ['rəubəut] (US) *n* canot *m* (à rames)

**rowdy** ['raudi] *adj* chahuteur(-euse); (*occasion*) tapageur(-euse)

**rowing** ['rəuiŋ] *n* canotage *m*; (*as sport*) aviron *m*; **~ boat** (BRIT) *n* canot *m* (à rames)

**royal** ['rɔiəl] *adj* royal(e); **R~ Air Force** (BRIT) *n* armée de l'air britannique; **~ty** *n* (*royal persons*) (membres *mpl* de la) famille royale; (*payment: to author*) droits *mpl* d'auteur; (: *to inventor*) royalties *mpl*

**rpm** *abbr* (AUT) (= *revolutions per minute*)

tr/mn

**RSVP** abbr (= répondez s'il vous plaît) R.S.V.P.

**Rt Hon.** abbr (BRIT: Right Honourable) titre donné aux députés de la Chambre des communes

**rub** [rʌb] vt frotter; frictionner; (hands) se frotter ♦ n (with cloth) coup m chiffon or de torchon; **to give sth a ~** donner un coup de chiffon or de torchon à; **to ~ sb up** (BRIT) or **to ~ sb** (US) **the wrong way** prendre qn à rebrousse-poil; **~ off** vi partir; **~ off on** vt fus déteindre sur; **~ out** vt effacer

**rubber** [ˈrʌbəʳ] n caoutchouc m; (BRIT: eraser) gomme f (à effacer); **~ band** n élastique m; **~ plant** n caoutchouc m (plante verte)

**rubbish** [ˈrʌbɪʃ] n (from household) ordures fpl; (fig: pej) camelote f; (: nonsense) bêtises fpl, idioties fpl; **~ bin** n (BRIT) poubelle f; **~ dump** n décharge publique, dépotoir m

**rubble** [ˈrʌbl] n décombres mpl; (smaller) gravats mpl; (CONSTR) blocage m

**ruby** [ˈruːbɪ] n rubis m

**rucksack** [ˈrʌksæk] n sac m à dos

**rudder** [ˈrʌdəʳ] n gouvernail m

**ruddy** [ˈrʌdɪ] adj (face) coloré(e); (inf: damned) sacré(e), fichu(e)

**rude** [ruːd] adj (impolite) impoli(e); (coarse) grossier(-ère); (shocking) indécent(e), inconvenant(e)

**ruffle** [ˈrʌfl] vt (hair) ébouriffer; (clothes) chiffonner; (fig: person): **to get ~d** s'énerver

**rug** [rʌg] n petit tapis; (BRIT: blanket) couverture f

**rugby** [ˈrʌgbɪ] n (also: ~ football) rugby m

**rugged** [ˈrʌgɪd] adj (landscape) accidenté(e); (features, character) rude

**ruin** [ˈruːɪn] n ruine f ♦ vt ruiner; (spoil: clothes) abîmer; (event) gâcher; **~s** npl (of building) ruine(s)

**rule** [ruːl] n règle f; (regulation) règlement m; (government) autorité f,

gouvernement m ♦ vt (country) gouverner; (person) dominer ♦ vi commander; (LAW) statuer; **as a ~** normalement, en règle générale; **~ out** vt exclure; **~d** adj (paper) réglé(e); **~r** n (sovereign) souverain(e); (for measuring) règle f; **ruling** adj (party) au pouvoir; (class) dirigeant(e) ♦ n (LAW) décision f

**rum** [rʌm] n rhum m

**Rumania** [ruːˈmeɪnɪə] n = **Romania**

**rumble** [ˈrʌmbl] vi gronder; (stomach, pipe) gargouiller

**rummage** [ˈrʌmɪdʒ] vi fouiller

**rumour** [ˈruːməʳ] (US **rumor**) n rumeur f, bruit m (qui court) ♦ vt: **it is ~d that** le bruit court que

**rump** [rʌmp] n (of animal) croupe f; (inf: of person) postérieur m; **~ steak** n rumsteck m

**rumpus** [ˈrʌmpəs] (inf) n tapage m, chahut m

**run** [rʌn] (pt **ran**, pp **run**) n (fast pace) (pas m de) course f; (outing) tour m or promenade f (en voiture); (distance travelled) parcours m, trajet m; (series) suite f, série f; (THEATRE) série de représentations; (SKI) piste f; (CRICKET, BASEBALL) point m; (in tights, stockings) maille filée, échelle f ♦ vt (operate: business) diriger; (: competition, course) organiser; (: hotel, house) tenir; (race) participer à; (COMPUT) exécuter; (to pass: hand, finger) passer; (water, bath) faire couler; (PRESS: feature) publier ♦ vi courir; (flee) s'enfuir; (work: machine, factory) marcher; (bus, train) circuler; (continue: play) se jouer; (: contract) être valide; (flow: river, bath; nose) couler; (colours, washing) déteindre; (in election) être candidat, se présenter; **to go for a ~** faire un peu de course à pied; there was a ~ on ... (meat, tickets) les gens se sont rués sur ...; **in the long ~** à longue échéance; à la longue; en fin de compte; **on the ~** en fuite; **I'll ~ you to the station** je vais vous emmener or conduire à la gare; **to ~ a risk** courir un risque; **~ about** vi (children) courir çà et là; **~ across** vt fus (find) trouver par hasard; (person) rencontrer par hasard; **~ around** vi = **run about**; **~ away** vi s'enfuir; **~ down** vt (production) réduire progressivement; (factory) réduire progressivement la production de; (AUT) renverser; (criticize) critiquer, dénigrer; **to be ~ down** (person: tired) être épuisé(e) or à plat; **~ in** (BRIT) vt (car) roder; **~ into** vt fus (meet: person) rencontrer par hasard; (trouble) se heurter à; (collide with) heurter; **~ off** vi s'enfuir ♦ vt (water) laisser s'écouler; (copies) tirer; **~ out** vi (person) sortir en courant; (liquid) couler; (lease) expirer; (money) être épuisé(e); **~ out of** vt fus se trouver à court de; **~ over** vt (AUT) écraser ♦ vt fus (revise) revoir, reprendre; **~ through** vt fus (recapitulate) reprendre; (play) répéter; **~ up** vt: **to ~ up against** (difficulties) se heurter à; **to ~ up a debt** s'endetter; **~away** adj qui roule

**rung** [rʌŋ] pp of **ring** ♦ n (of ladder) barreau m

**runner** ['rʌnəʳ] n (in race: person) coureur(-euse) m/f; (: horse) partant m; (on sledge) patin m; (for drawer etc) coulisseau m; **~ bean** (BRIT) n haricot m (à rames); **~-up** n second(e)

**running** ['rʌnɪŋ] n course f; (of business, organization) gestion f, direction f ♦ adj (water) courant(e); **to be in/out of the ~** for sth être/ne pas être sur les rangs pour qch; **6 days ~** 6 jours de suite; **~ commentary** n commentaire détaillé; **~ costs** npl frais mpl d'exploitation

**runny** ['rʌnɪ] adj qui coule

**run-of-the-mill** ['rʌnəvðə'mɪl] adj ordinaire, banal(e)

**runt** [rʌnt] n avorton m

**run-up** ['rʌnʌp] n: **~~ to sth** (election etc) période f précédant qch

**runway** ['rʌnweɪ] n (AVIAT) piste f

**rupture** ['rʌptʃəʳ] n (MED) hernie f

**rural** ['rʊərl] adj rural(e)

**rush** [rʌʃ] n (hurry) hâte f, précipitation f; (of crowd, COMM: sudden demand) ruée f; (current) flot m; (of emotion) vague f; (BOT) jonc m ♦ vt (hurry) transporter or envoyer d'urgence ♦ vi se précipiter; **~ hour** n heures fpl de pointe

**rusk** [rʌsk] n biscotte f

**Russia** ['rʌʃə] n Russie f; **~n** adj russe ♦ n Russe m/f; (LING) russe m

**rust** [rʌst] n rouille f ♦ vi rouiller

**rustic** ['rʌstɪk] adj rustique

**rustle** ['rʌsl] vi bruire, produire un bruissement ♦ vt froisser

**rustproof** ['rʌstpru:f] adj inoxydable

**rusty** ['rʌstɪ] adj rouillé(e)

**rut** [rʌt] n ornière f; (ZOOL) rut m; **to be in a ~** suivre l'ornière, s'encroûter

**ruthless** ['ru:θlɪs] adj sans pitié, impitoyable

**rye** [raɪ] n seigle m

# S, s

**Sabbath** ['sæbəθ] n (Jewish) sabbat m; (Christian) dimanche m

**sabotage** ['sæbətɑːʒ] n sabotage m ♦ vt saboter

**saccharin(e)** ['sækərɪn] n saccharine f

**sachet** ['sæʃeɪ] n sachet m

**sack** [sæk] n (bag) sac m ♦ vt (dismiss) renvoyer, mettre à la porte; (plunder) piller, mettre à sac; **to get the ~** être renvoyé(e), être mis(e) à la porte; **~ing** n (material) toile f à sac; (dismissal) renvoi m

**sacrament** ['sækrəmənt] n sacrement m

**sacred** ['seɪkrɪd] adj sacré(e)

**sacrifice** ['sækrɪfaɪs] n sacrifice m ♦ vt sacrifier

**sad** [sæd] adj triste; (deplorable) triste, fâcheux(-euse)

**saddle** ['sædl] n selle f ♦ vt (horse) seller; **to be ~d with sth** (inf) avoir qch sur les bras; **~bag** n sacoche f

**sadistic** [sə'dıstık] adj sadique

**sadly** ['sædlı] adv tristement; (unfortunately) malheureusement; (seriously) fort

**sadness** ['sædnıs] n tristesse f

**s.a.e.** n abbr = stamped addressed envelope

**safe** [seıf] adj (out of danger) hors de danger, en sécurité; (not dangerous) sans danger; (cautious) prudent(e); (sure: bet etc) assuré(e) ♦ n coffre-fort m; **~ from** à l'abri de; **~ and sound** sain(e) et sauf (sauve); **(just) to be on the ~ side** pour plus de sûreté, par précaution; **~ journey!** bon voyage!; **~-conduct** n sauf-conduit m; **~ deposit** n (vault) dépôt m de coffres-forts; (box) coffre-fort m; **~guard** n sauvegarde f, protection ♦ vt sauvegarder, protéger; **~keeping** n bonne garde f; **~ly** adv (assume, say) sans risque d'erreur; (drive, arrive) sans accident; **~ sex** n rapports mpl sexuels sans risque

**safety** ['seıftı] n sécurité f; **~ belt** n ceinture f de sécurité; **~ pin** n épingle f de sûreté or de nourrice; **~ valve** n soupape f de sûreté

**sag** [sæg] vi s'affaisser; (hem, breasts) pendre

**sage** [seıdʒ] n (herb) sauge f; (person) sage m

**Sagittarius** [sædʒı'tεərıəs] n le Sagittaire

**Sahara** [sə'hɑːrə] n: **the ~ (Desert)** (désert du) Sahara

**said** [sεd] pt, pp of **say**

**sail** [seıl] n (on boat) voile f; (trip): **to go for a ~** faire un tour en bateau ♦ vt (boat) manœuvrer, piloter ♦ vi (travel: ship) avancer, naviguer; (set off) partir, prendre la mer; (SPORT) faire de la voile; **they ~ed into Le Havre** ils sont entrés dans le port du Havre; **~ through** vi, vt fus (fig) réussir haut la main; **~boat** (US) n bateau m à voiles, voilier m; **~ing** n (SPORT) voile f; **to go ~ing** faire de la

voile; **~ing boat** n bateau m à voiles, voilier m; **~ing ship** n grand voilier m; **~or** n marin m, matelot m

**saint** [seınt] n saint(e)

**sake** [seık] n: **for the ~ of** pour (l'amour de), dans l'intérêt de; **par** égard pour

**salad** ['sæləd] n salade f; **~ bowl** n saladier m; **~ cream** (BRIT) n (sorte f de) mayonnaise f; **~ dressing** n vinaigrette f

**salami** [sə'lɑːmı] n salami m

**salary** ['sælərı] n salaire m

**sale** [seıl] n vente f; (at reduced prices) soldes mpl; **"for ~"** "à vendre"; **on ~** en vente; **on ~ or return** vendu(e) avec faculté de retour; **~room** n salle f des ventes; **~s assistant** (US sales clerk) n vendeur(-euse); **~sman** (irreg) n vendeur m; (representative) représentant m; **~s rep** n (COMM) représentant(e) m/f; **~swoman** (irreg) n vendeuse f; (representative) représentante f

**salmon** ['sæmən] n inv saumon m

**salon** ['sælɔn] n salon m

**saloon** [sə'luːn] n (US) bar m; (BRIT: AUT) berline f; (ship's lounge) salon m

**salt** [sɔːlt] n sel m ♦ vt saler; **~ cellar** n salière f; **~water** adj de mer; **~y** adj salé(e)

**salute** [sə'luːt] n salut m ♦ vt saluer

**salvage** ['sælvıdʒ] n (saving) sauvetage m; (things saved) biens sauvés or récupérés ♦ vt sauver, récupérer

**salvation** [sæl'veıʃən] n salut m; **S~ Army** n armée f du Salut

**same** [seım] adj même ♦ pron: **the ~** (la) même, les mêmes; **the ~ book as** le même livre que; **at the ~ time** en même temps; **all** or **just the ~** tout de même, quand même; **to do the ~** faire de même; **to do the ~ as sb** faire comme qn; **the ~ to you!** à vous de même!; (after insult) toi-même!

**sample** ['sɑːmpl] n échantillon m; (blood) prélèvement m ♦ vt (food, wine) goûter

**sanction** ['sæŋkʃən] n approbation f, sanction f

**sanctity** ['sæŋktɪtɪ] n sainteté f, caractère sacré

**sanctuary** ['sæŋktjuərɪ] n (holy place) sanctuaire m; (refuge) asile m; (for wild life) réserve f

**sand** [sænd] n sable m ♦ vt (furniture: also: ~ **down**) poncer

**sandal** ['sændl] n sandale f

**sand: ~box** (US) n tas de sable; **~castle** n château m de sable; **~paper** n papier m de verre; **~pit** (BRIT) n (for children) tas m de sable; **~stone** n grès m

**sandwich** ['sændwɪtʃ] n sandwich m; **cheese/ham ~** n sandwich au fromage/jambon; **~ course** (BRIT) n cours m de formation professionnelle

**sandy** ['sændɪ] adj sablonneux(-euse); (colour) sable inv, blond roux inv

**sane** [seɪn] adj (person) sain(e) d'esprit; (outlook) sensé(e), sain(e)

**sang** [sæŋ] pt of **sing**

**sanitary** ['sænɪtərɪ] adj (system, arrangements) sanitaire; (clean) hygiénique; **~ towel** (US **sanitary napkin**) n serviette f hygiénique

**sanitation** [sænɪ'teɪʃən] n (in house) installations fpl sanitaires; (in town) système m sanitaire; **~ department** (US) n service m de voirie

**sanity** ['sænɪtɪ] n santé mentale; (common sense) bon sens

**sank** [sæŋk] pt of **sink**

**Santa Claus** [sæntə'klɔːz] n le père Noël

**sap** [sæp] n (of plants) sève f ♦ vt (strength) saper, miner

**sapling** ['sæplɪŋ] n jeune arbre m

**sapphire** ['sæfaɪə*] n saphir m

**sarcasm** ['sɑːkæzm] n sarcasme m, raillerie f; **sarcastic** [sɑː'kæstɪk] adj sarcastique

**sardine** [sɑː'diːn] n sardine f

**Sardinia** [sɑː'dɪnɪə] n Sardaigne f

**sash** [sæʃ] n écharpe f

**sat** [sæt] pt, pp of **sit**

**satchel** ['sætʃl] n cartable m

**satellite** ['sætəlaɪt] n satellite m; **~ dish** n antenne f parabolique; **~ television** n télévision f par câble

**satin** ['sætɪn] n satin m ♦ adj en or de satin, satiné(e)

**satire** ['sætaɪə*] n satire f

**satisfaction** [sætɪs'fækʃən] n satisfaction f

**satisfactory** [sætɪs'fæktərɪ] adj satisfaisant(e)

**satisfied** ['sætɪsfaɪd] adj satisfait(e)

**satisfy** ['sætɪsfaɪ] vt satisfaire, contenter; (convince) convaincre, persuader; **~ing** adj satisfaisant(e)

**Saturday** ['sætədɪ] n samedi m

**sauce** [sɔːs] n sauce f; **~pan** n casserole f

**saucer** ['sɔːsə*] n soucoupe f

**Saudi** ['saudi-]: **~ Arabia** n Arabie Saoudite; **~ (Arabian)** adj saoudien(ne)

**sauna** ['sɔːnə] n sauna m

**saunter** ['sɔːntə*] vi: **to ~ along/in/out** etc marcher/entrer/sortir etc d'un pas nonchalant

**sausage** ['sɔsɪdʒ] n saucisse f; (cold meat) saucisson m; **~ roll** n ≈ friand m

**savage** ['sævɪdʒ] adj (cruel, fierce) brutal(e), féroce; (primitive) primitif(-ive), sauvage ♦ n sauvage m/f

**save** [seɪv] vt (person, belongings) sauver; (money) mettre de côté, économiser; (time) (faire) gagner; (keep) garder; (COMPUT) sauvegarder; (SPORT: stop) arrêter; (avoid: trouble) éviter ♦ vi (also: ~ up) mettre de l'argent de côté ♦ n (SPORT) arrêt m (du ballon) ♦ prep sauf, à l'exception de

**saving** ['seɪvɪŋ] n économie f; **the ~ grace of sth** ce qui rachète qch; **~s** npl (money saved) économies fpl; **~s account** n compte m d'épargne; **~s bank** n caisse f d'épargne

**saviour** ['seɪvjə*] (US **savior**) n sauveur m

**savour** ['seɪvə'] (*US* **savor**) *vt* savourer; **~y** (*US* **savory**) *adj* (*dish: not sweet*) salé(e)

**saw** [sɔː] (*pt* **sawed**, *pp* **sawed** *or* **sawn**) *vt* scier ♦ *n* (*tool*) scie *f* ♦ *pt of* **see**; **~dust** *n* sciure *f*; **~mill** *n* scierie *f*; **~-off** *adj*: **~n-off shotgun** carabine *f* à canon scié

**sax** [sæks] (*inf*) *n* saxo *m*

**saxophone** ['sæksəfəun] *n* saxophone *m*

**say** [seɪ] (*pt, pp* **said**) *n*: **to have one's ~** dire ce qu'on a à dire ♦ *vt* dire; **to have a** *or* **some ~ in sth** avoir voix au chapitre; **could you ~ that again?** pourriez-vous répéter ce que vous venez de dire?; **that goes without ~ing** cela va sans dire, cela va de soi; **~ing** *n* dicton *m*, proverbe *m*

**scab** [skæb] *n* croûte *f*; (*pej*) jaune *m*

**scaffold** ['skæfəld] *n* échafaud *m*; **~ing** *n* échafaudage *m*

**scald** [skɔːld] *n* brûlure *f* ♦ *vt* ébouillanter

**scale** [skeɪl] *n* (*of fish*) écaille *f*; (*MUS*) gamme *f*; (*of ruler, thermometer etc*) graduation *f*, échelle *f* (graduée); (*of salaries, fees etc*) barème *m* *f* (*of map, also size, extent*) échelle *f* ♦ *vt* (*mountain*) escalader; **~s** *npl* (*for weighing*) balance *f*; (*also*: **bathroom ~**) pèse-personne *m inv*; **on a large ~** sur une grande échelle, en grand; **~ of charges** tableau *m* des tarifs; **~ down** *vt* réduire

**scallop** ['skɔləp] *n* coquille *f* Saint-Jacques; (*SEWING*) feston *m*

**scalp** [skælp] *n* cuir chevelu ♦ *vt* scalper

**scampi** ['skæmpɪ] *npl* langoustines (frites)

**scan** [skæn] *vt* scruter, examiner; (*glance at quickly*) parcourir; (*TV, RADAR*) balayer ♦ *n* (*MED*) scanographie *f*

**scandal** ['skændl] *n* scandale *m*; (*gossip*) ragots *mpl*

**Scandinavia** [skændɪ'neɪvɪə] *n* Scandinavie *f*; **~n** *adj* scandinave

**scant** [skænt] *adj* insuffisant(e); **~y** ['skæntɪ] *adj* peu abondant(e), insuffisant(e); (*underwear*) minuscule

**scapegoat** ['skeɪpgəut] *n* bouc *m* émissaire

**scar** [skɑː] *n* cicatrice *f* ♦ *vt* marquer (d'une cicatrice)

**scarce** [skɛəs] *adj* rare, peu abondant(e); **to make o.s. ~** (*inf*) se sauver; **~ly** *adv* à peine; **scarcity** *n* manque *m*, pénurie *f*

**scare** [skɛə'] *n* peur *f*, panique *f* ♦ *vt* effrayer, faire peur à; **to ~ sb stiff** faire une peur bleue à qn; **bomb ~** alerte *f* à la bombe; **~ away** *vt* faire fuir; **~ off** *vt* = **scare away**; **~crow** *n* épouvantail *m*; **~d** *adj*: **to be ~d** avoir peur

**scarf** [skɑːf] (*pl* **~s** *or* **scarves**) *n* (*long*) écharpe *f*; (*square*) foulard *m*

**scarlet** ['skɑːlɪt] *adj* écarlate; **~ fever** *n* scarlatine *f*

**scary** ['skɛərɪ] (*inf*) *adj* effrayant(e)

**scathing** ['skeɪðɪŋ] *adj* cinglant(e), acerbe

**scatter** ['skætə'] *vt* éparpiller, répandre; (*crowd*) disperser ♦ *vi* se disperser; **~brained** *adj* écervelé(e), étourdi(e)

**scavenger** ['skævəndʒə'] *n* (*person: in bins etc*) pilleur *m* de poubelles

**scene** [siːn] *n* scène *f*; (*of crime, accident*) lieu(x) *m(pl)*; (*sight, view*) spectacle *m*, vue *f*; **~ry** ['siːnərɪ] *n* (*THEATRE*) décor(s) *m(pl)*; (*landscape*) paysage *m*; **scenic** *adj* (*picturesque*) offrant de beaux paysages *or* panoramas

**scent** [sɛnt] *n* parfum *m*, odeur *f*; (*track*) piste *f*

**sceptical** ['skɛptɪkl] (*US* **skeptical**) *adj* sceptique

**schedule** ['ʃedjuːl, (*US*) 'skedjuːl] *n* programme *m*, plan *m*; (*of trains*) horaire *m*; (*of prices etc*) barème *m*, tarif *m* ♦ *vt* prévoir; **on ~** à l'heure (prévue); à la date prévue; **to be ahead of/behind ~** avoir de l'avance/du retard; **~d flight** *n* vol régulier

**scheme** [skiːm] *n* plan *m*, projet *m*;

(dishonest plan, plot) complot m, combine f; (arrangement) arrangement m, classification f; (pension ~ etc) régime m ♦ vi comploter, manigancer; **scheming** adj rusé(e), intrigant(e) ♦ n manigances fpl, intrigues fpl

**scholar** ['skɔləʳ] n érudit(e); (pupil) boursier(-ère); **~ship** n (knowledge) érudition f; (grant) bourse f (d'études)

**school** [skuːl] n école f; (secondary ~) collège m, lycée m; (US: university) université f; (in university) faculté f ♦ cpd scolaire; **~book** n livre m scolaire or de classe; **~boy** n écolier m; collégien m, lycéen m; **~children** npl écoliers mpl; collégiens mpl, lycéens mpl; **~girl** n écolière f; collégienne f, lycéenne f; **~ing** n instruction f, études fpl; **~master** n professeur m; **~mistress** n professeur m; **~teacher** n instituteur(-trice); professeur m

**science** ['saɪəns] n science f; ~ **fiction** n science-fiction f; **scientific** [saɪən'tɪfɪk] adj scientifique; **scientist** n scientifique m/f; (eminent) savant m

**scissors** ['sɪzəz] npl ciseaux mpl

**scoff** [skɔf] vt (BRIT: inf: eat) avaler, bouffer ♦ vi: **to ~ (at)** (mock) se moquer (de)

**scold** [skəuld] vt gronder

**scone** [skɔn] n sorte de petit pain rond au lait

**scoop** [skuːp] n pelle f (à main); (for ice cream) boule f à glace; (PRESS) scoop m; **~ out** vt évider, creuser; **~ up** vt ramasser

**scooter** ['skuːtəʳ] n (also: motor ~) scooter m; (toy) trottinette f

**scope** [skəup] n (capacity: of plan, undertaking) portée f, envergure f; (: of person) compétence f, capacités fpl; (opportunity) possibilités fpl; **within the ~ of** dans les limites de

**scorch** [skɔːtʃ] vt (clothes) brûler (légèrement), roussir; (earth, grass) dessécher, brûler

**score** [skɔːʳ] n score m, décompte m

des points; (MUS) partition f; (twenty) vingt ♦ vt (goal, point) marquer; (success) remporter ♦ vi marquer des points; (FOOTBALL) marquer un but; (keep ~) compter les points; **~s of** (very many) beaucoup de, un tas de (fam); **on that ~** sur ce chapitre, à cet égard; **to ~ 6 out of 10** obtenir 6 sur 10; **~ out** vt rayer, barrer, biffer; **~board** n tableau m

**scorn** [skɔːn] n mépris m, dédain m

**Scorpio** ['skɔːpɪəu] n le Scorpion

**Scot** [skɔt] n Écossais(e)

**Scotch** [skɔtʃ] n whisky m, scotch m

**scot-free** ['skɔt'friː] adv: **to get off ~~** s'en tirer sans être puni(e)

**Scotland** ['skɔtlənd] n Écosse f; **Scots** adj écossais(e); **Scotsman** (irreg) m Écossais; **Scotswoman** (irreg) f Écossaise f; **Scottish** adj écossais(e); **Scottish Parliament** n Parlement m écossais

**scoundrel** ['skaundrl] n vaurien m

**scour** ['skauəʳ] vt (search) battre, parcourir

**scout** [skaut] n (MIL) éclaireur m; (also: boy ~) scout m; girl ~ (US) guide f; **~ around** vi explorer, chercher

**scowl** [skaul] vi avoir l'air maussade; **to ~ at** regarder de travers

**scrabble** ['skræbl] vi (also: ~ around: search) chercher à tâtons; (claw): **to ~ (at)** gratter; n: **S~** ® Scrabble ® m

**scram** [skræm] (inf) vi ficher le camp

**scramble** ['skræmbl] n (rush) bousculade f, ruée f ♦ vi: **to ~ up/down** grimper/descendre tant bien que mal; **to ~ out** sortir or descendre à toute vitesse; **to ~ through** se frayer un passage (à travers); **to ~ for** se bousculer or se disputer pour (avoir); **~d eggs** npl œufs brouillés

**scrap** [skræp] n bout m, morceau m; (fight) bagarre f; (also: ~ iron) ferraille f ♦ vt jeter, mettre au rebut; (fig) abandonner, laisser tomber ♦ vi (fight) se bagarrer; **~s** npl (waste) déchets mpl;

~**book** n album m; ~ **dealer** n marchand m de ferraille

**scrape** [skreɪp] vt, vi gratter, racler ♦ n: **to get into a** ~ s'attirer des ennuis; **to** ~ **through** vi réussir de justesse; ~ **together** vt (money) racler ses fonds de tiroir pour réunir

**scrap**: ~ **heap** n: **on the** ~ **heap** (fig) au rancart or rebut; ~ **merchant** (BRIT) n marchand m de ferraille; ~ **paper** n papier m brouillon

**scratch** [skrætʃ] n égratignure f, rayure f; éraflure f; (from claw) coup m de griffe ♦ cpd: ~ **team** équipe de fortune or improvisée ♦ vt (rub) (se) gratter; (record) rayer; (paint etc) érafler; (with claw, nail) griffer ♦ vt vi (se) gratter; **to start from** ~ partir de zéro; **to be up to** ~ être à la hauteur

**scrawl** [skrɔːl] vi gribouiller

**scrawny** ['skrɔːni] adj décharné(e)

**scream** [skriːm] n cri perçant, hurlement m ♦ vi crier, hurler

**screech** [skriːtʃ] vi hurler; (tyres) crisser; (brakes) grincer

**screen** [skriːn] n écran m; (in room) paravent m; (fig) écran, rideau m ♦ vt (conceal) masquer, cacher; (from the wind etc) abriter, protéger; (film) projeter; (candidates etc) filtrer; ~**ing** n (MED) test m (or tests) de dépistage; ~**play** n scénario m; ~ **saver** n (COMPUT) économiseur m d'écran

**screw** [skruː] n vis f ♦ vt (also: ~ **up**) visser; ~ **up** vt (paper etc) froisser; **to** ~ **up one's eyes** plisser les yeux; ~**driver** n tournevis m

**scribble** ['skrɪbl] vt, vi gribouiller, griffonner

**script** [skrɪpt] n (CINEMA etc) scénario m, texte m; (writing) écriture f; script m

**Scripture(s)** ['skrɪptʃə(-əz)] n(pl) (Christian) Écriture sainte; (other religions) écritures saintes

**scroll** [skrəul] n rouleau m

**scrounge** [skraundʒ] (inf) vt: **to** ~ **sth off** or **from sb** taper qn de qch; ~**r**

(inf) n parasite m

**scrub** [skrʌb] n (land) broussailles fpl ♦ vt (floor) nettoyer à la brosse; (pan) récurer; (washing) frotter; (inf: cancel) annuler

**scruff** [skrʌf] n: **by the** ~ **of the neck** par la peau du cou

**scruffy** ['skrʌfi] adj débraillé(e)

**scrum(mage)** ['skrʌm(ɪdʒ)] n (RUGBY) mêlée f

**scruple** ['skruːpl] n scrupule m

**scrutiny** ['skruːtɪni] n examen minutieux

**scuff** [skʌf] vt érafler

**scuffle** ['skʌfl] n échauffourée f, rixe f

**sculptor** ['skʌlptə*] n sculpteur m

**sculpture** ['skʌlptʃə*] n sculpture f

**scum** [skʌm] n écume f, mousse f; (pej: people) rebut m, lie f

**scurry** ['skʌri] vi filer à toute allure; ~ **off** détaler, se sauver

**scuttle** ['skʌtl] n (also: **coal** ~) seau m (à charbon) ♦ vt (ship) saborder ♦ vi (scamper): **to** ~ **away** or **off** détaler

**scythe** [saɪð] n faux f

**SDP** n abbr (= Social Democratic Party)

**sea** [siː] n mer f ♦ cpd marin(e), de (la) mer; **by** ~ (travel) par mer, en bateau; **on the** ~ (boat) en mer; (town) au bord de la mer; **to be all at** ~ (fig) nager complètement; **out to** ~ au large; (out) **at** ~ en mer; ~**board** n côte f; ~**food** n fruits mpl de mer; ~**front** n bord m de mer; ~**going** adj (ship) de mer; ~**gull** n mouette f

**seal** [siːl] n (animal) phoque m; (stamp) sceau m, cachet m ♦ vt sceller; (envelope) coller; (: with ~) cacheter; ~ **off** vt (forbid entry to) interdire l'accès de

**sea level** n niveau m de la mer

**sea lion** n otarie f

**seam** [siːm] n couture f; (of coal) veine f, filon m

**seaman** ['siːmən] (irreg) n marin m

**seance** ['seɪɔns] n séance f de spiritisme

**seaplane** ['si:plein] n hydravion m

**search** [sə:tʃ] n (for person, thing, COMPUT) recherche(s) f(pl); (LAW: at sb's home) perquisition f ♦ vt fouiller; (examine) examiner minutieusement; scruter ♦ vi: **to ~ for** chercher; **in ~ of** à la recherche de; **~ through** vt fus fouiller; **~ing** adj pénétrant(e); **~light** n projecteur m; **~ party** expédition f de secours; **~ warrant** n mandat m de perquisition

**sea**: **~shore** n rivage m, plage f, bord m de (la) mer; **~sick** adj: **to be ~sick** avoir le mal de mer; **~side** n bord m de la mer; **~side resort** n station f balnéaire

**season** ['si:zn] n saison f ♦ vt assaisonner, relever; **to be in/out of ~** être/ne pas être de saison; **~al** adj (work) saisonnier(-ère); **~ed** adj (fig) expérimenté(e); **~ ticket** n carte f d'abonnement

**seat** [si:t] n siège m; (in bus, train: place) place f; (buttocks) postérieur m; (of trousers) fond m ♦ vt faire asseoir, placer; (have room for) avoir des places assises pour, pouvoir accueillir; **~ belt** n ceinture f de sécurité

**sea**: **~ water** n eau f de mer; **~weed** n algues fpl; **~worthy** adj en état de naviguer

**sec.** abbr = **second(s)**

**secluded** [sɪ'klu:dɪd] adj retiré(e), à l'écart

**seclusion** [sɪ'klu:ʒən] n solitude f

**second1** ['sɛkənd] (BRIT) vt (employee) affecter provisoirement

**second2** ['sɛkənd] adj deuxième, second(e) ♦ adv (in race etc) en seconde position ♦ n (unit of time) seconde f; (AUT: ~ gear) seconde; (COMM: imperfect) article m de second choix; (BRIT: UNIV) licence f avec mention ♦ vt (motion) appuyer; **~ary** adj secondaire; **~ary school** n collège m, lycée m; **~class** adj de deuxième classe; (RAIL) de seconde (classe); (POST) au tarif réduit;

(pej) de qualité inférieure ♦ adv (RAIL) en seconde; (POST) au tarif réduit; **~hand** adj d'occasion; de seconde main; **~ hand** n (on clock) trotteuse f; **~ly** adv deuxièmement; **~ment** [sɪ'kɔndmənt] (BRIT) n détachement m; **~rate** adj de deuxième ordre, de qualité inférieure; **~ thoughts** npl doutes mpl; **on ~ thoughts** or (US) **thought** à la réflexion

**secrecy** ['si:krəsɪ] n secret m

**secret** ['si:krɪt] adj secret(-ète) ♦ n secret m; **in ~** en secret, secrètement, en cachette

**secretary** ['sɛkrətərɪ] n secrétaire m/f; (COMM) secrétaire général; **S~ of State (for)** (BRIT: POL) ministre m (de)

**secretive** ['si:krətɪv] adj dissimulé(e)

**secretly** ['si:krɪtlɪ] adv en secret, secrètement

**sectarian** [sɛk'tɛərɪən] adj sectaire

**section** ['sɛkʃən] n section f; (of document) section, article m, paragraphe m; (cut) coupe f

**sector** ['sɛktər] n secteur m

**secular** ['sɛkjuər] adj profane; laïque; séculier(-ère)

**secure** [sɪ'kjuər] adj (free from anxiety) sans inquiétude, sécurisé(e); (firmly fixed) solide, bien attaché(e) or fermé(e) etc); (in safe place) en lieu sûr, en sûreté ♦ vt (fix) fixer, attacher; (get) obtenir, se procurer

**security** [sɪ'kjuərɪtɪ] n sécurité f, mesures fpl de sécurité; (for loan) caution f, garantie f; **~ guard** n garde chargé de la sécurité; (when transporting money) convoyeur m de fonds

**sedate** [sɪ'deɪt] adj calme; posé(e) ♦ vt (MED) donner des sédatifs à

**sedative** ['sɛdɪtɪv] n calmant m, sédatif m

**seduce** [sɪ'dju:s] vt séduire; **seduction** [sɪ'dʌkʃən] n séduction f; **seductive** [sɪ'dʌktɪv] adj séduisant(e); (smile) séducteur(-trice); (fig: offer) alléchant(e)

**see** [si:] (pt **saw**, pp **seen**) vt voir; (accompany): **to ~ sb to the door** reconduire or raccompagner qn jusqu'à la porte ♦ vi voir ♦ n évêché m; **to ~ that** (ensure) veiller à ce que +sub, faire en sorte que +sub; **s'assurer que; ~ you soon!** à bientôt!; **~ about** vt fus s'occuper de; **~ off** vt accompagner (à la gare or à l'aéroport etc); **~ through** vt mener à bonne fin ♦ vt fus voir clair dans; **~ to** vt fus s'occuper de, se charger de

**seed** [siːd] n graine f; (sperm) semence f; (fig) germe m; (TENNIS etc) tête f de série; **to go to ~** monter en graine; (fig) se laisser aller; **~ling** n jeune plant m, semis m; **~y** adj (shabby) minable, miteux(-euse)

**seeing** ['siːɪŋ] conj: **~ (that)** vu que, étant donné que

**seek** [siːk] (pt, pp **sought**) vt chercher, rechercher

**seem** [siːm] vi sembler, paraître; **there ~s to be ...** il semble qu'il y a ...; on dirait qu'il y a ...; **~ingly** adv apparemment

**seen** [siːn] pp of **see**

**seep** [siːp] vi suinter, filtrer

**seesaw** ['siːsɔː] n (jeu m de) bascule f

**seethe** [siːð] vi être en effervescence; **to ~ with anger** bouillir de colère

**see-through** ['siːθruː] adj transparent(e)

**segment** ['sɛgmənt] n segment m; (of orange) quartier m

**segregate** ['sɛgrɪgeɪt] vt séparer, isoler

**seize** [siːz] vt saisir, attraper; (take possession of) s'emparer de; (opportunity) saisir; **~ up** vi (TECH) se gripper; **~ (up)on** vt fus saisir, sauter sur

**seizure** ['siːʒəʳ] n (MED) crise f, attaque f; (of power) prise f

**seldom** ['sɛldəm] adv rarement

**select** [sɪ'lɛkt] adj choisi(e), d'élite ♦ vt sélectionner, choisir; **~ion** n sélection f, choix m

**self** [sɛlf] (pl **selves**) n: **the ~** le moi inv ♦ prefix auto-; **~-assured** adj sûr(e) de soi; **~-catering** (BRIT) adj avec cui-

ne, où l'on peut faire sa cuisine; **~-centred** (US **self-centered**) adj égocentrique; **~-confidence** n confiance f en soi; **~-conscious** adj timide, qui manque d'assurance; **~-contained** (BRIT) adj (flat) avec entrée particulière, indépendant(e); **~-control** n maîtrise f de soi; **~-defence** (US **self-defense**) n autodéfense f; (LAW) légitime défense f; **~-discipline** n discipline personnelle; **~-employed** adj qui travaille à son compte; **~-evident** adj: **to be ~-evident** être évident(e), aller de soi; **~-governing** adj autonome; **~-indulgent** adj qui ne se refuse rien; **~-interest** n intérêt personnel; **~-ish** adj égoïste; **~-ishness** n égoïsme m; **~-less** adj désintéressé(e); **~-pity** n apitoiement m sur soi-même; **~-possessed** adj assuré(e); **~-preservation** n instinct m de conservation; **~-respect** n respect m de soi, amour-propre m; **~-righteous** adj satisfait(e); **~-sacrifice** n abnégation f; **~-satisfied** adj content(e) de soi, suffisant(e); **~-service** n libre-service, self-service; **~-sufficient** adj autosuffisant(e); (person: independent) indépendant(e); **~-taught** adj (artist, pianist) qui a appris par lui-même

**sell** [sɛl] (pt, pp **sold**) vt vendre ♦ vi se vendre; **to ~ at or for 10 F** se vendre 10 F; **~ off** vt liquider; **~ out** vi: **to ~ out (of sth)** (use up stock) vendre tout son stock (de qch); **the tickets are all sold out** il ne reste plus de billets; **~by date** n date f limite de vente; **~er** n vendeur(-euse), marchand(e); **~ing price** n prix m de vente

**Sellotape** ® ['sɛləʊteɪp] (BRIT) n papier m collant, scotch ® m

**selves** [sɛlvz] npl of **self**

**semblance** ['sɛmbləns] n semblant m

**semen** ['siːmən] n sperme m

**semester** [sɪ'mɛstəʳ] (esp US) n semestre m

**semi** ['sɛmɪ] prefix semi-, demi-; à demi,

à moitié; **~circle** n demi-cercle m; **~co-lon** n point-virgule m; **~detached (house)** (BRIT) n maison jumelée or jumelle; **~final** n demi-finale f

**seminar** ['semɪnɑːʳ] n séminaire m; **~y** n (REL: for priests) séminaire m

**semiskilled** ['semɪ'skɪld] adj: **~ worker** ouvrier(-ère) spécialisé(e)

**semi-skimmed milk** [semɪ'skɪmd-] n lait m demi-écrémé

**senate** ['senɪt] n sénat m; **senator** n sénateur m

**send** [send] (pt, pp **sent**) vt envoyer; **~away** vt (letter, goods) envoyer; **~away for** vt fus commander par correspondance, se faire envoyer; **~back** vt renvoyer; **~for** vt fus envoyer chercher; faire venir; **~off** vt (goods) envoyer, expédier; (BRIT: SPORT: player) expulser ou renvoyer du terrain; **~out** vt (invitation) envoyer (par la poste); (light, heat, signal) émettre; **~up** vt faire monter; (BRIT: parody) mettre en boîte, parodier; **~er** n expéditeur (-trice); **~off** n: **a good ~off** des adieux chaleureux

**senior** ['siːnɪəʳ] adj (high-ranking) de haut niveau; (of higher rank): **to be ~ to sb** être le supérieur de qn ♦ n (older): **she is 15 years his ~** elle est son aînée de 15 ans, elle est plus âgée que lui de 15 ans; **~ citizen** n personne âgée; **~ity** [siːnɪ'ɔrɪtɪ] n (in service) ancienneté f

**sensation** [sen'seɪʃən] n sensation f; **~al** adj qui fait sensation; (marvellous) sensationnel(le)

**sense** [sens] n sens m; (feeling) sentiment m; (meaning) sens, signification f; (wisdom) bon sens ♦ vt sentir, pressentir; **it makes ~** c'est logique; **~less** adj insensé(e), stupide; (unconscious) sans connaissance

**sensible** ['sensɪbl] adj sensé(e), raisonnable; sage

**sensitive** ['sensɪtɪv] adj sensible

**sensual** ['sensjuəl] adj sensuel(le)

**sensuous** ['sensjuəs] adj voluptueux (-euse), sensuel(le)

**sent** [sent] pt, pp of **send**

**sentence** ['sentns] n (LING) phrase f; (LAW: judgment) condamnation f, sentence f; (: punishment) peine f ♦ vt: **to ~ sb to death/to 5 years in prison** condamner qn à mort/à 5 ans de prison

**sentiment** ['sentɪmənt] n sentiment m; (opinion) opinion f, avis m; **~al** [sentɪ'mentl] adj sentimental(e)

**sentry** ['sentrɪ] n sentinelle f

**separate** [adj 'seprɪt, vb 'sepəreɪt] adj séparé(e), indépendant(e), différent(e) ♦ vt séparer; (make a distinction between) distinguer ♦ vi se séparer; **~ly** adv séparément; **~s** npl (clothes) coordonnés mpl; **separation** [sepə'reɪʃən] n séparation f

**September** [sep'tembəʳ] n septembre m

**septic** ['septɪk] adj (wound) infecté(e); **~ tank** n fosse f septique

**sequel** ['siːkwl] n conséquence f; séquelles fpl; (of story) suite f

**sequence** ['siːkwəns] n ordre m, suite f; (film ~) séquence f; (dance ~) numéro m

**sequin** ['siːkwɪn] n paillette f

**Serbia** ['sɜːbɪə] n Serbie f

**serene** [sɪ'riːn] adj serein(e), calme, paisible

**sergeant** ['sɑːdʒənt] n sergent m; (PO-LICE) brigadier m

**serial** ['sɪərɪəl] n feuilleton m; **~ killer** n meurtrier m tuant en série; **~ number** n numéro m de série

**series** ['sɪərɪz] n inv série f; (PUBLISHING) collection f

**serious** ['sɪərɪəs] adj sérieux(-euse); (illness) grave; **~ly** adv sérieusement; (hurt) gravement

**sermon** ['sɜːmən] n sermon m

**serrated** [sɪ'reɪtɪd] adj en dents de scie

**servant** ['sɜːvənt] n domestique m/f;

(fig) serviteur/servante

**serve** [səːv] vt (employer etc) servir, être au service de; (purpose) servir à; (customer, food, meal) servir; (subj: train) desservir; (apprenticeship) faire, accomplir; (prison term) purger ♦ vi servir; (be useful): to ~ as/for/to do servir de/à/à faire ♦ n (TENNIS) service m; **it ~s him right** c'est bien fait pour lui; ~ **out**, ~ **up** vt (food) servir

**service** ['səːvɪs] n service m; (AUT: maintenance) révision f ♦ vt (car, washing machine) réviser; **the S~s** les forces armées; **to be of ~ to sb** rendre service à qn; **15% ~ included** service 15% compris; ~ **not included** service non compris; ~**able** adj pratique, commode; ~ **area** n (on motorway) aire f de services; ~ **charge** (BRIT) n service m à qn; ~**man** (irreg) n militaire m; ~ **station** n station-service f

**serviette** [səːvɪ'et] (BRIT) n serviette f (de table)

**session** ['seʃən] n séance f

**set** [set] (pt, pp set) n série f, assortiment m; (of tools etc) jeu m; (RADIO, TV) poste m; (TENNIS) set m; (group of people) cercle m, milieu m; (THEATRE: stage) scène f; (scenery) décor m; (MATH) ensemble m; (HAIRDRESSING) mise f en plis ♦ adj (fixed) fixe, déterminé(e); (ready) prêt(e) ♦ vt (place) poser, placer; (fix, establish) fixer; (: record) établir; (adjust) régler; (decide: rules etc) fixer, choisir; (task) donner; (exam) composer ♦ vi (sun) se coucher; (jam, jelly, concrete) prendre; (bone) se ressouder; **to be ~ on doing** être résolu à faire; **to ~ the table** mettre le couvert; **to ~ (to music)** mettre en musique; **to ~ on fire** mettre le feu à; **to ~ free** libérer; **to ~ going** déclencher qqch; **to ~ sail** prendre la mer; ~ **about** vt fus (task) entreprendre, se mettre à; ~ **aside** vt mettre de côté; (time) garder; ~ **back** vt (in time): **to ~ back (by)** retarder (de); (cost): **to ~ sb back £5** coûter 5 livres

à qn; ~ **off** vi se mettre en route, partir ♦ vt (bomb) faire exploser; (cause to start) déclencher; (show up well) mettre en valeur, faire valoir; ~ **out** vi se mettre en route, partir ♦ vt (arrange) disposer; (arguments) présenter, exposer; **to ~ out to do** entreprendre de faire, avoir pour but or intention de faire; ~ **up** vt (organization) fonder, créer; ~**back** n (hitch) revers m, contretemps m; ~ **menu** n menu m

**settee** [se'tiː] n canapé m

**setting** ['setɪŋ] n cadre m; (of jewel) monture f; (position: of controls) réglage m

**settle** ['setl] vt (argument, matter, account) régler; (problem) résoudre; (MED: calm) calmer ♦ vi (bird, dust etc) se poser; (also: ~ **down**) s'installer, se fixer; (calm down) se calmer; **to ~ for sth** accepter qch, se contenter de qch; **to ~ on sth** opter or se décider pour qch; ~ **in** vi s'installer; ~ **up** vi: **to ~ up with sb** régler (ce que l'on doit à) qn; ~**ment** n (payment) règlement m; (agreement) accord m; (village etc) établissement m; hameau m; ~**r** n colon m

**setup** ['setʌp] n (arrangement) manière f dont les choses sont organisées; (situation) situation f

**seven** ['sevn] num sept; ~**teen** num dix-sept; ~**th** num septième; ~**ty** num soixante-dix

**sever** ['sevə*] vt couper, trancher; (relations) rompre

**several** ['sevrəl] adj, pron plusieurs m/ fpl; ~ **of us** plusieurs d'entre nous

**severance** ['sevərəns] n (of relations) rupture f; ~ **pay** n indemnité f de licenciement

**severe** [sɪ'vɪə*] adj (stern) sévère, strict(e); (serious) grave, sérieux(-euse); (plain) sévère, austère; **severity** [sɪ'verɪtɪ] n sévérité f; gravité f; rigueur f

**sew** [səu] (pt sewed, pp sewn) vt, vi coudre; ~ **up** vt (re)coudre

**sewage** ['su:ɪdʒ] n vidange/s f(pl)

**sewer** ['su:əʳ] n égout m

**sewing** ['səuɪŋ] n couture f; (item(s)) ouvrage m; **~ machine** n machine f à coudre

**sewn** [səun] pp of **sew**

**sex** [sɛks] n sexe m; **to have ~ with** avoir des rapports (sexuels) avec; **~ism** n sexisme m; **~ist** adj sexiste; **~ual** ['sɛksjuəl] adj sexuel(le); **~uality** [sɛksjuˈælɪtɪ] n sexualité f; **~y** adj sexy inv

**shabby** ['ʃæbɪ] adj miteux(-euse) (behaviour): mesquin(e), méprisable

**shack** [ʃæk] n cabane f, hutte f

**shackles** ['ʃæklz] npl chaînes fpl, entraves fpl

**shade** [ʃeɪd] n ombre f; (for lamp) abat-jour m inv; (of colour) nuance f, ton m ♦ vt abriter du soleil, ombrager; **in the ~** à l'ombre; **a ~ too large/more** un tout petit peu trop grand(e)/plus

**shadow** ['ʃædəu] n ombre f ♦ vt (follow) filer; **~ cabinet** (BRIT) n (POL) cabinet parallèle formé par l'Opposition; **~y** adj ombragé(e); (dim) vague, indistinct(e)

**shady** ['ʃeɪdɪ] adj ombragé(e); (fig: dishonest) louche, véreux(-euse)

**shaft** [ʃɑːft] n (of arrow, spear) hampe f; (AUT, TECH) arbre m; (of mine) puits m; (of lift) cage f; (of light) rayon m, trait m

**shaggy** ['ʃægɪ] adj hirsute; en broussaille

**shake** [ʃeɪk] (pt **shook**, pp **shaken**) vt secouer; (bottle, cocktail) agiter; (house, confidence) ébranler ♦ vi trembler; **to ~ one's head** (in refusal) dire or faire non de la tête; (in dismay) secouer la tête; **to ~ hands with sb** serrer la main à qn; **~ off** vt secouer; (pursuer) débarrasser de; **~ up** vt secouer; **~n** cp of **shake**; **shaky** adj (hand, voice) tremblant(e); (building) branlant(e), peu solide

**shall** [ʃæl] aux vb: **I ~** go j'irai; **~ I open the door?** j'ouvre la porte?; **I'll get**

the coffee, ~ **I?** je vais chercher le café, d'accord?

**shallow** ['ʃæləu] adj peu profond(e); (fig) superficiel(le)

**sham** [ʃæm] n frime f ♦ vt simuler

**shambles** ['ʃæmblz] n (muddle) confusion f, pagaïe f, fouillis m

**shame** [ʃeɪm] n honte f ♦ vt faire honte à; **it is a ~ (that/to do)** c'est dommage (que +sub/de faire); **what a ~!** quel dommage!; **~ful** adj honteux(-euse), scandaleux(-euse); **~less** adj éhonté(e), effronté(e)

**shampoo** [ʃæmˈpuː] n shampooing m ♦ vt faire un shampooing à; **~ and set** n shampooing m (et) mise f en plis

**shamrock** ['ʃæmrɔk] n trèfle m (emblème de l'Irlande)

**shandy** ['ʃændɪ] n bière panachée

**shan't** [ʃɑːnt] = **shall not**

**shanty town** ['ʃæntɪ-] n bidonville m

**shape** [ʃeɪp] n forme f ♦ vt façonner, modeler; (sb's ideas) former; (sb's life) déterminer ♦ vi (also: **~ up**: events) prendre tournure; (: person) faire des progrès, s'en sortir; **to take ~** prendre forme or tournure; **~d** suffix: **heart~ed** en forme de cœur; **~less** adj informe, sans forme; **~ly** adj bien proportionné(e), beau (belle)

**share** [ʃɛəʳ] n part f; (COMM) action f ♦ vt partager; (have in common) avoir en commun; **~ out** vi partager; **~holder** n actionnaire m/f

**shark** [ʃɑːk] n requin m

**sharp** [ʃɑːp] adj (razor, knife) tranchant(e), bien aiguisé(e); (point, voice) aigu(-guë); (nose, chin) pointu(e); (outline, increase) net(te); (cold, pain) vif (vive); (taste) piquant(e), âcre; (MUS) dièse; (person: quick-witted) vif (vive) éveillé(e); (: unscrupulous) malhonnête ♦ n (MUS) dièse m ♦ adv (precisely): **at 2 o'clock ~** à 2 heures pile or précises; **~en** vt aiguiser; (pencil) tailler; **~ener** n (also: **pencil ~ener**) taille-crayon(s) m inv; **~-eyed** adj à qui rien n'échappe

**~ly** adv (turn, stop) brusquement; (stand out) nettement; (criticize, retort) sèchement, vertement

**hatter** ['ʃætə'] vt briser; (fig: upset) bouleverser; (: ruin) briser, ruiner ♦ vi voler en éclats, se briser

**have** [ʃeɪv] vt raser ♦ vi se raser ♦ n: to **have a ~** se raser; **~r** n (also: **electric ~r**) rasoir m électrique

**having** ['ʃeɪvɪŋ] n (action) rasage m; **~s** npl (of wood etc) copeaux mpl; **~ brush** n blaireau m; **~ cream** n crème f à raser; **~ foam** n mousse f à raser

**he** [ʃiː] pron elle ♦ prefix: **~-cat** chatte f; **~-elephant** éléphant m femelle

**heaf** [ʃiːf] (pl **sheaves**) n gerbe f; (of papers) liasse f

**hear** [ʃɪə'] (pt **sheared**, pp **shorn**) vt (sheep) tondre; **~s** npl (for hedge) cisaille(s) f(pl)

**heath** [ʃiːθ] n gaine f, fourreau m, étui m; (contraceptive) préservatif m

**hed** [ʃed] (pt, pp **shed**) n remise f, resserre f ♦ vt perdre; (tears) verser, répandre; (workers) congédier

**he'd** [ʃiːd] = **she had; she would**

**heen** [ʃiːn] n lustre m

**heep** [ʃiːp] n inv mouton m; **~dog** n chien m de berger; **~skin** n peau f de mouton

**heer** [ʃɪə'] adj (utter) pur(e), simple; (steep) à pic, abrupt(e); (almost transparent) extrêmement fin(e) ♦ adv à pic, abruptement

**heet** [ʃiːt] n (on bed) drap m; (of paper) feuille f; (of glass, metal etc) feuille, plaque f

**heik(h)** [ʃeɪk] n cheik m

**helf** [ʃelf] (pl **shelves**) n étagère f, rayon m

**hell** [ʃel] n (on beach) coquillage m; (of egg, nut etc) coquille f; (explosive) obus m; (of building) carcasse f ♦ vt (peas) écosser; (MIL) bombarder (d'obus)

**he'll** [ʃiːl] = **she will; she shall**

**hellfish** ['ʃelfɪʃ] n inv (crab etc) crusta-

cé m; (scallop etc) coquillage m ♦ npl (as food) fruits mpl de mer

**shell suit** n survêtement m (en synthétique froissé)

**shelter** ['ʃeltə'] n abri m, refuge m ♦ vt abriter, protéger; (give lodging to) donner asile à ♦ vi s'abriter, se mettre à l'abri; **~ed housing** n foyers mpl (pour personnes âgées ou handicapées)

**shelve** [ʃelv] vt (fig) mettre en suspens or en sommeil; **~s** npl of **shelf**

**shepherd** ['ʃepəd] n berger m ♦ vt (guide) guider, escorter; **~'s pie** (BRIT) n ≈ hachis m Parmentier

**sheriff** ['ʃerɪf] (US) n shérif m

**sherry** ['ʃerɪ] n xérès m, sherry m

**she's** [ʃiːz] = **she is; she has**

**Shetland** ['ʃetlənd] n (also: **the ~ Islands**) les îles fpl Shetland

**shield** [ʃiːld] n bouclier m; (protection) écran m de protection ♦ vt: to **~ (from)** protéger (de or contre)

**shift** [ʃɪft] n (change) changement m, (work period) période f de travail; (of workers) équipe f, poste m ♦ vt déplacer, changer de place; (remove) enlever ♦ vi changer de place, bouger; **~ work** n travail m en équipe or par relais or par roulement; **~y** adj sournois(e); (eyes) fuyant(e)

**shimmer** ['ʃɪmə'] vi miroiter, chatoyer

**shin** [ʃɪn] n tibia m

**shine** [ʃaɪn] (pt, pp **shone**) n éclat m, brillant m ♦ vi briller ♦ vt (torch etc): to **~ on** braquer sur; (polish: pt, pp **~d**) faire briller or reluire

**shingle** ['ʃɪŋgl] n (on beach) galets mpl; **~s** n (MED) zona m

**shiny** ['ʃaɪnɪ] adj brillant(e)

**ship** [ʃɪp] n bateau m; (large) navire m ♦ vt transporter (par mer); (send) expédier (par mer); **~building** n construction navale; **~ment** n cargaison f; **~ping** n (ships) navires mpl; (the industry) industrie navale; (transport) transport m; **~wreck** n (ship) épave f; (event) naufrage m ♦ vt: to **be**

**~wrecked** faire naufrage; **~yard** n chantier naval

**shire** ['ʃaɪə] (BRIT) n comté m

**shirt** [ʃəːt] n (man's) chemise f; (woman's) chemisier m; **in (one's) ~sleeves** en bras de chemise

**shit** [ʃɪt] (infl) n, excl merde f (!)

**shiver** ['ʃɪvə] n frisson m ♦ vi frissonner

**shoal** [ʃəul] n (of fish) banc m; (fig: also: **~s**) masse f, foule f

**shock** [ʃɔk] n (impact) choc m; (ELEC) secousse f, (MED) commotion f, choc ♦ vt (offend) choquer, scandaliser; (upset) bouleverser; **~ absorber** n amortisseur m; **~ing** adj (scandalizing) choquant(e), scandaleux(-euse); (appalling) épouvantable

**shoddy** ['ʃɔdɪ] adj de mauvaise qualité, mal fait(e)

**shoe** [ʃuː] (pt, pp shod) n chaussure f, soulier m; (also: **horseshoe**) fer m à cheval ♦ vt (horse) ferrer; **~lace** n lacet m (de soulier); **~ polish** n cirage m; **~ shop** n magasin m de chaussures; **~string** n (fig): **on a ~string** avec un budget dérisoire

**shone** [ʃɔn] pt, pp of **shine**

**shook** [ʃuk] pt of **shake**

**shoot** [ʃuːt] (pt, pp shot) n (on branch, seedling) pousse f ♦ vt (game) chasser; tirer; abattre; (person) blesser (or tuer) d'un coup de fusil (or de revolver); (execute) fusiller; (arrow) tirer; (gun) tirer un coup de; (film) tourner ♦ vi (with gun, bow): to **~ (at)** tirer (sur); (FOOTBALL) shooter, tirer; **~ down** vt (plane) abattre; **~ in** vi entrer comme une flèche; **~ out** vi sortir comme une flèche; **~ up** vi (fig) monter en flèche; **~ing** n (shots) coups mpl de feu, fusillade f; (HUNTING) chasse f; **~ing star** n étoile filante

**shop** [ʃɔp] n magasin m; (workshop) atelier m ♦ vi (also: **go ~ping**) faire ses courses or ses achats; **~ assistant** (BRIT) n vendeur(-euse); **~ floor** (BRIT) n (INDUSTRY: fig) ouvriers mpl; **~keeper** n

commerçant(e); **~lifting** n vol m à l'étalage; **~per** n personne f qui fait ses courses, acheteur(-euse); **~ping** n (goods) achats mpl, provisions fpl; **~ping bag** n sac m (à provisions or à commissions); **~ping centre** (US **shopping center**) n centre commercial; **~-soiled** adj défraîchi(e), qui a fait la vitrine; **~ steward** (BRIT) n (INDUSTRY) délégué(e) syndical(e); **~ window** n vitrine f

**shore** [ʃɔːʳ] n (of sea, lake) rivage m, rive f ♦ vt: to **~ (up)** étayer; **on ~** à terre

**shorn** [ʃɔːn] pp of **shear**

**short** [ʃɔːt] adj (not long) court(e); (soon finished) court, bref (brève); (person, step) petit(e); (curt) brusque, sec (sèche); (insufficient) insuffisant(e); be/run **~ of sth** être à court de or manquer de qch; **in ~** bref; en bref; **of doing** ... à moins de faire ...; **everything ~ of** tout sauf; **it is ~ for** c'est l'abréviation or le diminutif de; **to cut ~** (speech, visit) abréger, écourter; to fall **~ of** ne pas être à la hauteur de; to **run ~ of** arriver à court de, venir à manquer de; to **stop ~** s'arrêter net; to **stop ~ of** ne pas aller jusqu'à; **~age** n manque m, pénurie f; **~bread** n sablé m; **~change** vt ne pas rendre assez à; **~circuit** n court-circuit m; **~coming** n défaut m; **~(crust) pastry** (BRIT) n pâte brisée; **~cut** n raccourci m; **~en** vt raccourcir; (text, visit) abréger; **~fall** n déficit m; **~hand** (BRIT) n sténo(graphie) f; **~hand typist** (BRIT) n sténodactylo m/f; **~list** (BRIT) n (for job) liste f des candidats sélectionnés; **~ly** adv bientôt, sous peu; **~ notice** n: at notice au dernier moment; **~s** npl: (a **pair of) ~s** un short; **~-sighted** adj (BRIT) myope; (fig) qui manque de clairvoyance; **~-staffed** adj à court de personnel; **~-stay** adj (car park) de courte durée; **~ story** n nouvelle f; **~-tempered** adj qui s'emporte facilement; **~-term** adj (effect) à court terme; **~-wave** n (RADIO) ondes courtes

**ot** [ʃɔt] pt, pp of **shoot** ♦ n coup m
de feu; (try) coup, essai m; (injection)
iqûre f; (PHOT) photo f; **he's a good/
oor ~** il tire bien/mal; **like a ~**
omme une flèche; (very readily) sans
ésiter; **~gun** n fusil m de chasse

**ould** [ʃud] aux vb: **I ~ go now je de-
rais partir maintenant; he ~ be there
now** il devrait être arrivé maintenant;
**I ~ go if I were you** si j'étais vous,
irais; **I ~ like to** j'aimerais bien, volon-
iers

**oulder** [ˈʃəuldəʳ] n épaule f ♦ vt (fig)
ndosser, se charger de; **~ bag** n sac m
bandoulière; **~ blade** n omoplate f

**ouldn't** [ˈʃudnt] = **should not**

**out** [ʃaut] n cri m ♦ vt crier ♦ vi (also:
**~ out**) crier, pousser des cris; **~ down**
t huer; **~ing** n cris mpl

**ove** [ʃʌv] vt pousser; (inf: put): **to ~
sth in** fourrer ou ficher qch dans; **~ off**
(inf) vi ficher le camp

**ovel** [ˈʃʌvl] n pelle f

**ow** [ʃəu] (pt **showed**, pp **shown**) n
(of emotion) manifestation f, démons-
ration f; (semblance) semblant m, ap-
arence f; (exhibition) exposition f, sa-
on m; (THEATRE, TV) spectacle m ♦ vt
montrer; (film) donner; (courage etc)
aire preuve de, manifester; (exhibit) ex-
oser ♦ vi se voir, être visible; **for ~**
our l'effet; **on ~** (exhibits etc) expo-
é(e); **~ in** vt (person) faire entrer; **~
out** vt (person) reconduire (jusqu'à la
orte); **~ up** vi (stand out) ressortir;
(inf: turn up) se montrer ♦ vt (flaw) faire
essortir; **~ business** n le monde du
spectacle; **~down** n épreuve f de force

**ower** [ˈʃauəʳ] n (rain) averse f, (of
ctones etc) pluie f, grêle f; (~bath) douche f ♦ vi prendre une douche, se doucher ♦ vt: **to ~ sb with** (gifts etc)
combler qn de; **to have** ou **take a ~**
srendre une douche; **~ gel** n gel m
douche; **~proof** adj imperméabilisé(e)

**nowing** [ˈʃəuɪŋ] n (of film) projection f

**show jumping** n concours m hippique
**shown** [ʃəun] pp of **show**
**show:** **~-off** (inf) n (person) crâneur
(-euse), m'as-tu-vu(e); **~piece** n (of exhibition) trésor m; **~room** n magasin m
ou salle f d'exposition

**shrank** [ʃræŋk] pt of **shrink**
**shrapnel** [ˈʃræpnl] n éclats mpl d'obus
**shred** [ʃred] n (gen pl) lambeau m, petit
morceau f ♦ vt mettre en lambeaux, déchirer; (CULIN: grate) râper; (: lettuce etc)
couper en lanières; **~der** n (for vegetables) râpeur m/f; (for documents) déchi-
queteuse f

**shrewd** [ʃru:d] adj astucieux(-euse),
perspicace; (businessman) habile
**shriek** [ʃri:k] n hurler, crier
**shrill** [ʃrɪl] adj perçant(e), aigu(-guë),
strident(e)

**shrimp** [ʃrɪmp] n crevette f
**shrine** [ʃraɪn] n (place) lieu m de
pèlerinage

**shrink** [ʃrɪŋk] (pt **shrank**, pp **shrunk**) vi
rétrécir; (fig) se réduire, diminuer;
(move: also: **~ away**) reculer ♦ vt (wool)
(faire) rétrécir ♦ n (inf: pej) psychiatre
m/f, psy m/f; **to ~ from (doing) sth** reculer devant (la pensée de faire) qch;
**~wrap** vt emballer sous film plastique

**shrivel** [ˈʃrɪvl] vt (also: **~ up**) ratatiner,
flétrir ♦ vi se ratatiner, se flétrir
**shroud** [ʃraud] n linceul m ♦ vt: **~ed in
mystery** enveloppé(e) de mystère
**Shrove Tuesday** [ˈʃrəuv-] n (le) Mardi
gras

**shrub** n arbuste m; **~bery** n massif m
d'arbustes
**shrug** [ʃrʌg] vt, vi: **to ~ (one's shoulders)** hausser les épaules; **~ off** vt faire
fi de

**shrunk** [ʃrʌŋk] pp of **shrink**
**shudder** [ˈʃʌdəʳ] vi frissonner, frémir
**shuffle** [ˈʃʌfl] vt (cards) battre; **to ~
(one's feet)** traîner les pieds
**shun** [ʃʌn] vt éviter, fuir
**shunt** [ʃʌnt] vt (RAIL) aiguiller
**shut** [ʃʌt] (pt, pp **shut**) vt fermer ♦ vi

(se) fermer; **~ down** vt, vi fermer définitivement; **~ off** vt couper, arrêter; **~ up** vi (inf: keep quiet) se taire ♦ vt (close) (silence) faire taire; **~ter** n volet m; (PHOT) obturateur m

**shuttle** ['ʃʌtl] n navette f; (also: **~ service**) (service m de) navette f; **~cock** n volant m (de badminton); **~ diplomacy** n navettes fpl diplomatiques

**shy** [ʃaɪ] adj timide

**Siberia** [saɪ'bɪərɪə] n Sibérie f

**Sicily** ['sɪsɪlɪ] n Sicile f

**sick** [sɪk] adj (ill) malade; (vomiting): **to be ~** vomir; (humour) noir(e), macabre; **to feel ~** avoir envie de vomir, avoir mal au cœur; **to be ~ of** (fig) en avoir assez de; **~ bay** n infirmerie f; **~en** vt écœurer; **~ening** adj (fig) écœurant(e), dégoûtant(e)

**sickle** ['sɪkl] n faucille f

**sick: ~ leave** n congé m de maladie; **~ly** adj maladif(-ive), souffreteux(-euse); (causing nausea) écœurant(e); **~ness** n maladie f; (vomiting) vomissement(s) m(pl); **~ note** n (from parents) mot m d'absence; (from doctor) certificat médical; **~ pay** n indemnité f de maladie

**side** [saɪd] n côté m; (of lake, road) bord m; (team) camp m, équipe f ♦ adj (door, entrance) latéral(e) ♦ vi: **to ~ with sb** prendre le parti de qn, se ranger du côté de qn; **by the ~ of** au bord de; **by ~** côte à côte; **from ~ to ~** d'un côté à l'autre; **to take ~s (with)** prendre parti (pour); **~board** n buffet m; **~boards** (BRIT), **~burns** npl (whiskers) pattes fpl; **~ drum** n tambour plat; **~ effect** n effet m secondaire; **~light** n (AUT) veilleuse f; **~line** n (SPORT) (ligne f de) touche f; (fig) travail m secondaire; **~long** adj oblique; **~show** n attraction f; **~step** vt (fig) éluder; éviter; **~ street** n (petite) rue transversale; **~track** vt (fig) faire dévier de son sujet; **~walk** n (US) trottoir m; **~ways** adv de côté

**siding** ['saɪdɪŋ] n (RAIL) voie f de garage

**siege** [siːdʒ] n siège m

**sieve** [sɪv] n tamis m, passoire f

**sift** [sɪft] vt (fig: also: **~ through**) passer en revue; (lit: flour etc) passer au tamis

**sigh** [saɪ] n soupir m ♦ vi soupirer, pousser un soupir

**sight** [saɪt] n (faculty) vue f; (spectacle) spectacle m; (on gun) mire f ♦ vt apercevoir; **in ~** visible; **out of ~** hors de vue; **~seeing** n tourisme m; **to go ~seeing** faire du tourisme

**sign** [saɪn] n signe m; (with hand etc) signe, geste m; (notice) panneau m, écriteau m ♦ vt signer; **~ on** vi (as unemployed) s'inscrire au chômage; (for course) s'inscrire ♦ vt (employee) embaucher; **~ over** vt: **to ~ sth over to sb** céder qch par écrit à qn; **~ up** vi (MIL) s'engager; (for course) s'inscrire

**signal** ['sɪɡnl] n signal m ♦ vi (AUT) mettre son clignotant ♦ vt (person) faire signe à; (message) communiquer par signaux; **~man** (irreg) n (RAIL) aiguilleur m

**signature** ['sɪɡnətʃər] n signature f; **~ tune** n indicatif musical

**signet ring** ['sɪɡnæt-] n chevalière f

**significance** [sɪɡ'nɪfɪkəns] n signification f; importance f

**significant** [sɪɡ'nɪfɪkənt] adj significatif(-ive); (important) important(e), considérable

**sign language** n langage m per signes

**signpost** n poteau indicateur

**silence** ['saɪləns] n silence m ♦ vt faire taire, réduire au silence; **~r** n (on gun, BRIT: AUT) silencieux m

**silent** ['saɪlənt] adj silencieux(-euse), (film) muet(te); **to remain ~** garder le silence, ne rien dire; **~ partner** n (COMM) bailleur m de fonds, commanditaire m

**silhouette** [sɪluː'et] n silhouette f

**silicon chip** ['sɪlɪkən-] n puce f électronique

**silk** [sɪlk] n soie f ♦ cpd de or en soie; **~y**

*adj* soyeux(-euse)

**illy** ['sɪlɪ] *adj* stupide, sot(te), bête

**ilt** [sɪlt] *n* vase *f*; limon *m*

**ilver** ['sɪlvə<sup>r</sup>] *n* argent *m*; (*money*) monnaie *f* (en pièces d'argent); (*also*: **~ware**) argenterie *f* ♦ *adj* d'argent, en argent; **~ paper** *n* papier *m* d'argent ou d'étain; **~-plated** *adj* plaqué(e) argent *inv*; **~smith** *n* orfèvre *m/f*; **~y** *adj* argenté(e)

**imilar** ['sɪmɪlə<sup>r</sup>] *adj*: **~ (to)** semblable (à); **~ly** *adv* de la même façon, de même

**immer** ['sɪmə<sup>r</sup>] *vi* cuire à feu doux, mijoter

**imple** ['sɪmpl] *adj* simple; **simplicity** [sɪm'plɪsɪtɪ] *n* simplicité *f*; **simply** *adv* (*without fuss*) avec simplicité

**imultaneous** [sɪməl'teɪnɪəs] *adj* simultané(e)

**in** [sɪn] *n* péché *m* ♦ *vi* pécher

**ince** [sɪns] *adv*, *prep* depuis ♦ *conj* (*time*) depuis que; (*because*) puisque, étant donné que, comme; **~ then**, **ever ~** depuis ce moment-là

**incere** [sɪn'sɪə<sup>r</sup>] *adj* sincère; **~ly** *adv see* **yours**; **sincerity** [sɪn'serɪtɪ] *n* sincérité *f*

**inew** ['sɪnjuː] *n* tendon *m*

**ing** [sɪŋ] (*pt* **sang**, *pp* **sung**) *vt*, *vi* chanter

**ingapore** [sɪŋɡə'pɔː] *n* Singapour *m*

**inge** [sɪndʒ] *vt* brûler légèrement; (*clothes*) roussir

**inger** ['sɪŋə<sup>r</sup>] *n* chanteur(-euse)

**inging** ['sɪŋɪŋ] *n* chant *m*

**ingle** ['sɪŋɡl] *adj* seul(e), unique; (*unmarried*) célibataire; (*not double*) simple ♦ *n* (*BRIT*: *also*: **~ ticket**) aller *m* (simple); (*record*) 45 tours *m*; **~ out** *vt* choisir; (*distinguish*) distinguer; **~ bed** *n* lit *m* d'une personne; **~-breasted** *adj* droit(e); **~ file** *n*: **in ~ file** en file indienne; **~-handed** *adv* tout(e) seul(e), sans (aucune) aide; **~-minded** *adj* résolu(e), tenace; **~ parent** *n* parent *m* unique; **~ room** *n* chambre *f* à un lit ou

pour une personne; **~s** *n* (*TENNIS*) simple *m*; **~-track road** *n* route *f* à voie unique; **singly** *adv* séparément

**singular** ['sɪŋɡjulə<sup>r</sup>] *adj* singulier(-ère), étrange; (*outstanding*) remarquable; (*LING*) (au) singulier, du singulier ♦ *n* singulier *m*

**sinister** ['sɪnɪstə<sup>r</sup>] *adj* sinistre

**sink** [sɪŋk] (*pt* **sank**, *pp* **sunk**) *n* évier *m* ♦ *vt* (*ship*) (faire) couler, faire sombrer; (*foundations*) creuser ♦ *vi* couler, sombrer; (*ground etc*) s'affaisser; (*also*: **~ back**, **~ down**) s'affaisser, se laisser retomber; **to ~ sth into** enfoncer qch dans; **my heart sank** j'ai complètement perdu courage; **~ in** *vi* (*fig*) pénétrer, être compris(e)

**sinner** ['sɪnə<sup>r</sup>] *n* pécheur(-eresse)

**sinus** ['saɪnəs] *n* sinus *m inv*

**sip** [sɪp] *n* gorgée *f* ♦ *vt* boire à petites gorgées

**siphon** ['saɪfən] *n* siphon *m*; **~ off** *vt* siphonner; (*illegally*) détourner

**sir** [sɜː<sup>r</sup>] *n* monsieur *m*; **S~ John Smith** sir John Smith; **yes ~** oui, Monsieur

**siren** ['saɪərn] *n* sirène *f*

**sirloin** ['sɜːlɔɪn] *n* (*also*: **~ steak**) aloyau *m*

**sissy** ['sɪsɪ] (*inf*) *n* (*coward*) poule mouillée

**sister** ['sɪstə<sup>r</sup>] *n* sœur *f*; (*nun*) religieuse *f*, sœur; (*BRIT*: *nurse*) infirmière *f* en chef; **~-in-law** *n* belle-sœur *f*

**sit** [sɪt] (*pt*, *pp* **sat**) *vi* s'asseoir; (*be ~ting*) être assis(e); (*assembly*) être en séance, siéger; (*for painter*) poser ♦ *vt* (*exam*) passer, se présenter à; **~ down** *vi* s'asseoir; **~ in on** *vt fus* assister à; **~ up** *vi* s'asseoir; (*straight*) se redresser; (*not go to bed*) rester debout, ne pas se coucher

**sitcom** ['sɪtkɔm] *n abbr* (= *situation comedy*) comédie *f* de situation

**site** [saɪt] *n* emplacement *m*, site *m*; (*also*: **building ~**) chantier *m* ♦ *vt* placer

**sit-in** ['sɪtɪn] *n* (*demonstration*) sit-in *m inv*, occupation *f* (de locaux)

**sitting** ['sɪtɪŋ] n (of assembly etc) séance f; (in canteen) service m; ~ **room** n salon m

**situated** ['sɪtjʊeɪtɪd] adj situé(e)

**situation** [sɪtjʊ'eɪʃən] n situation f; "~s **vacant**" (BRIT) "offres d'emploi"

**six** [sɪks] num six; ~**teen** num seize; ~**th** num sixième; ~**ty** num soixante

**size** [saɪz] n taille f; dimensions fpl; (of clothing) taille; (of shoes) pointure f; (fig) ampleur f; (glue) colle f; ~ **up** vt juger, jauger; ~**able** adj assez grand(e); assez important(e)

**sizzle** ['sɪzl] vi grésiller

**skate** [skeɪt] n patin m; (fish: pl inv) raie f ♦ vi patiner; ~**board** n skateboard m, planche f à roulettes; ~**boarding** n skateboard m; ~**r** n patineur(-euse); **skating** n patinage m; **skating rink** n patinoire f

**skeleton** ['skelɪtn] n squelette m; (outline) schéma m; ~ **staff** n effectifs réduits

**skeptical** ['skeptɪkl] (US) adj = **sceptical**

**sketch** [sketʃ] n (drawing) croquis m, esquisse f; (THEATRE) sketch m, saynète f ♦ vt esquisser, faire un croquis or une esquisse de; ~ **book** n carnet m à dessin; ~**y** adj incomplet(-ète), fragmentaire

**skewer** ['skju:ə<sup>r</sup>] n brochette f

**ski** [ski:] n ski m ♦ vi skier, faire du ski; ~ **boot** n chaussure f de ski

**skid** [skɪd] vi déraper

**ski:** ~**er** n skieur(-euse); ~**ing** n ski m; ~ **jump** n saut m à skis

**skilful** ['skɪlful] (US **skillful**) adj habile, adroit(e)

**ski lift** n remonte-pente m inv

**skill** [skɪl] n habileté f, adresse f, talent m; (requiring training: gen pl) compétences fpl; ~**ed** adj habile, adroit(e); (worker) qualifié(e)

**skim** [skɪm] vt (milk) écrémer; (glide over) raser, effleurer ♦ vi: to ~ **through** (fig) parcourir; ~**med milk** n lait écré-

mé

**skimp** [skɪmp] vt (also: ~ **on**: work) bâcler, faire à la va-vite; (: cloth etc) lésiner sur; ~**y** adj (skirt) étriqué(e)

**skin** [skɪn] n peau f ♦ vt (fruit etc) éplucher; (animal) écorcher; ~ **cancer** n cancer m de la peau; ~-**deep** adj superficiel(le); ~-**diving** n plongée sous-marine; ~**head** n skinhead m/f; ~**ny** adj maigre, maigrichon(ne); ~**tight** adj (jeans etc) moulant(e), ajusté(e)

**skip** [skɪp] n petit bond or saut; (BRIT: container) benne f ♦ vi gambader, sautiller; (with rope) sauter à la corde ♦ vt sauter

**ski pass** n forfait-skieur(s) m

**ski pole** n bâton m de ski

**skipper** ['skɪpə<sup>r</sup>] n capitaine m; (in race) skipper m

**skipping rope** ['skɪpɪŋ-] (BRIT) n corde f à sauter

**skirmish** ['skə:mɪʃ] n escarmouche f, accrochage m

**skirt** [skə:t] n jupe f ♦ vt longer, contourner; ~**ing board** (BRIT) n plinthe f

**ski:** ~ **slope** n piste f de ski; ~ **suit** n combinaison f (de ski); ~ **tow** n remonte-pente m inv

**skittle** ['skɪtl] n quille f; ~**s** n (game) (jeu m de) quilles fpl

**skive** [skaɪv] (BRIT: inf) vi tirer au flanc

**skull** [skʌl] n crâne m

**skunk** [skʌŋk] n mouffette f

**sky** [skaɪ] n ciel m; ~**light** n lucarne f; ~**scraper** n gratte-ciel m inv

**slab** [slæb] n (of stone) dalle f; (of cake) grosse tranche

**slack** [slæk] adj (loose) lâche, desserré(e); (slow) stagnant(e); (careless) négligent(e), peu sérieux(-euse); ~**s** npl (trousers) pantalon m; ~**en** vi ralentir, diminuer ♦ vt (speed) réduire; (grip) relâcher; (clothing) desserrer

**slag heap** [slæg-] n crassier m

**slag off** (BRIT: inf) vt dire du mal de

**lam** [slæm] vt (door) (faire) claquer; (throw) jeter violemment, flanquer (fam); (criticize) démolir ♦ vi claquer

**lander** ['slɑ:ndər] n calomnie f; diffamation f

**lang** [slæŋ] n argot m

**lant** [slɑ:nt] n inclinaison f; (fig) angle m, point de vue; **~ed** adj = **slanting**; **~ing** adj en pente, incliné(e); **~ing eyes** yeux bridés

**lap** [slæp] n claque f, gifle f; tape f ♦ vt donner une claque ou une gifle ou une tape à; (paint) appliquer rapidement ♦ adv (directly) tout droit, en plein; **~dash** adj fait(e) sans soin ou à la va-vite; (person) insouciant(e), négligent(e); **~stick** n (comedy) grosse farce, style m tarte à la crème; **~up** (BRIT) adj: a **~up meal** un repas extra ou fameux

**lash** [slæʃ] vt entailler, taillader; (fig: prices) casser

**lat** [slæt] n latte f, lame f

**late** [sleɪt] n ardoise f ♦ vt (fig: criticize) éreinter, démolir

**laughter** ['slɔ:tər] n carnage m, massacre m ♦ vt (animal) abattre; (people) massacrer; **~house** n abattoir m

**lave** [sleɪv] n esclave m/f ♦ vi (also: **~ away**) trimer, travailler comme un forçat; **~ry** n esclavage m

**lay** [sleɪ] (pt **slew**, pp **slain**) vt tuer

**leazy** ['sli:zɪ] adj miteux(-euse), minable

**ledge** [sledʒ] n luge f ♦ vi: **to go sledging** faire de la luge

**ledgehammer** n marteau m de forgeron

**leek** [sli:k] adj (hair, fur etc) brillant(e), lisse; (car, boat etc) aux lignes pures et élégantes

**leep** [sli:p] (pt, pp **slept**) n sommeil m ♦ vi dormir; (spend night) dormir, coucher; **to go to ~** s'endormir; **~ around** vi coucher à droite et à gauche; **~ in** vi (oversleep) se réveiller trop tard; **~er** (BRIT) n (RAIL: train) train-

couchettes m; (: berth) couchette f; **~ing bag** n sac m de couchage; **~ing car** n (RAIL) wagon-lit m, voiture-lit f; **~ing partner** (BRIT) n = **silent partner**; **~ing pill** n somnifère m; **~less** adj: a **~less night** une nuit blanche; **~walker** n somnambule m/f; **~y** adj qui a sommeil; (fig) endormi(e)

**sleet** [sli:t] n neige fondue

**sleeve** [sli:v] n manche f; (of record) pochette f

**sleigh** [sleɪ] n traîneau m

**sleight** [slaɪt] n: **~ of hand** tour m de passe-passe

**slender** ['slendər] adj svelte, mince; (fig) faible, ténu(e)

**slept** [slept] pt, pp of **sleep**

**slew** [slu:] vi (also: **~ around**) virer, pivoter ♦ pt of **slay**

**slice** [slaɪs] n tranche f; (round) rondelle f; (utensil) spatule f, truelle f ♦ vt couper en tranches (or en rondelles)

**slick** [slɪk] adj (skilful) brillant(e) (en apparence); (salesman) qui a du bagout ♦ n (also: **oil ~**) nappe f de pétrole, marée noire

**slide** [slaɪd] (pt, pp **slid**) n (in playground) toboggan m; (PHOT) diapositive f; (BRIT: also: **hair ~**) barrette f; (in prices) chute f, baisse f ♦ vt faire glisser ♦ vi glisser; **sliding** adj (door) coulissant(e); **sliding scale** n échelle f mobile

**slight** [slaɪt] adj (slim) mince, menu(e); (frail) frêle; (trivial) faible, insignifiant(e); (small) petit(e), léger(-ère) (before n) ♦ n offense f, affront m; **not in the ~est** pas le moins du monde, pas du tout; **~ly** adv légèrement, un peu

**slim** [slɪm] adj mince ♦ vi maigrir; (diet) suivre un régime amaigrissant

**slime** [slaɪm] n (mud) vase f; (other substance) substance visqueuse

**slimming** ['slɪmɪŋ] adj (diet, pills) amaigrissant(e); (foodstuff) qui ne fait pas grossir

**sling** [slɪŋ] (pt, pp **slung**) n (MED) écharpe f; (for baby) porte-bébé m; (weapon) fronde f, lance-pierre m ♦ vt lancer, jeter

**slip** [slɪp] n faux pas; (mistake) erreur f, étourderie f; (underskirt) combinaison f; (of paper) petite feuille, fiche f ♦ vt (slide) glisser ♦ vi glisser; (decline) baisser; (move smoothly): **to ~ into/out** se glisser ou se faufiler dans/hors de; **to ~ sth on/off** enfiler/enlever qch; **to give sb the ~** fausser compagnie à qn; **a ~ of the tongue** un lapsus; **~ away** vi s'esquiver; **~ in** vt glisser ♦ vi (errors) s'y glisser; **~ out** vi sortir; **~ up** vi faire une erreur, gaffer; **~ped disc** n déplacement m de vertèbre

**slipper** ['slɪpəʳ] n pantoufle f

**slippery** ['slɪpərɪ] adj glissant(e)

**slip:** **~ road** (BRIT) n (to motorway) bretelle f d'accès; **~-up** n bévue f; **~way** n cale f (de construction ou de lancement)

**slit** [slɪt] (pt, pp **slit**) n fente f; (cut) incision f ♦ vt fendre; couper; inciser

**slither** ['slɪðəʳ] vi glisser; (snake) onduler

**sliver** ['slɪvəʳ] n (of glass, wood) éclat m; (of cheese etc) petit morceau, fine tranche

**slob** [slɔb] (inf) n rustaud(e)

**slog** [slɔg] (BRIT) vi travailler très dur ♦ n gros effort; tâche fastidieuse

**slogan** ['sləugən] n slogan m

**slope** [sləup] n pente f, côte f; (side of mountain) versant m; (slant) inclinaison f ♦ vi: **to ~ down** être ou descendre en pente; **to ~ up** monter; **sloping** adj en pente; (writing) penché(e)

**sloppy** ['slɔpɪ] adj (work) peu soigné(e), bâclé(e); (appearance) négligé(e), débraillé(e)

**slot** [slɔt] n fente f ♦ vt: **to ~ sth into** encastrer ou insérer qch dans

**sloth** [sləuθ] n (laziness) paresse f

**slouch** [slautʃ] vi avoir le dos rond, être voûté(e)

**slovenly** ['slʌvənlɪ] adj sale, débrail-

lé(e); (work) négligé(e)

**slow** [sləu] adj lent(e); (watch): **to be ~** retarder ♦ adv lentement ♦ vt, vi (also ~ **down**, ~ **up**) ralentir; **"~"** (road sign) "ralentir"; **~ly** adv lentement; **~ motion** n: **in ~ motion** au ralenti

**sludge** [slʌdʒ] n boue f

**slug** [slʌg] n limace f; (bullet) balle f

**sluggish** ['slʌgɪʃ] adj (person) mou (molle), lent(e); (stream, engine, trade) lent

**sluice** [sluːs] n (also: ~ **gate**) vanne f

**slum** [slʌm] n (house) taudis m

**slump** [slʌmp] n baisse soudaine, effondrement m; (ECON) crise f ♦ vi s'effondrer, s'affaisser

**slung** [slʌŋ] pt, pp of **sling**

**slur** [sləːʳ] n (fig: smear): ~ (**on**) atteinte f(à); insinuation f (contre) ♦ vt mal articuler

**slush** [slʌʃ] n neige fondue

**slut** [slʌt] (pej) n souillon f

**sly** [slaɪ] adj (person) rusé(e); (smile, expression, remark) sournois(e)

**smack** [smæk] n (slap) tape f; (on face) gifle f ♦ vt donner une tape à; (on face) gifler; (on bottom) donner la fessée à ♦ vi: **to ~ of** avoir des relents de, sentir

**small** [smɔːl] adj petit(e); **~ ads** (BRIT) npl petites annonces; **~ change** n petite ou menue monnaie; **~holder** (BRIT) n petit cultivateur; **~ hours** npl: **in the ~ hours** au petit matin; **~pox** n variole f; **~ talk** n menus propos

**smart** [smɑːt] adj (neat, fashionable) élégant(e), chic inv; (clever) intelligent(e), astucieux(-euse), futé(e); (quick) rapide, vif (vive), prompt(e) ♦ vi faire mal, brûler; (fig) être piqué(e) au vif; **~ card** n carte f à puce; **~en up** vi devenir plus élégant(e), se faire beau (belle) ♦ vt rendre plus élégant(e)

**smash** [smæʃ] n (also: **~-up**) collision f, accident m; (also: ~ **hit**) succès foudroyant ♦ vt casser, briser, fracasser; (opponent) écraser; (SPORT: record) pulvériser ♦ vi se briser, se fracasser; s'écraer; **~ing** (inf) adj formidable

**mattering** ['smætərɪŋ] n: **a ~ of** quelques notions de

**near** [smɪəʳ] n tache f, salissure f; trace f; (MED) frottis m ♦ vt enduire; (make dirty) salir; **~ campaign** n campagne f de diffamation

**mell** [smel] (pt, pp **smelt** or **smelled**) n odeur f; (sense) odorat m ♦ vt sentir ♦ vi (food etc): **to ~ (of)** sentir (de); (pej) sentir mauvais; **~y** adj qui sent mauvais; malodorant(e)

**mile** [smaɪl] n sourire m ♦ vi sourire

**mirk** [smɜːk] n petit sourire suffisant or affecté

**mock** [smɒk] n blouse f

**mog** [smɒg] n brouillard mêlé de fumée, smog m

**moke** [sməʊk] n fumée f ♦ vt, vi fumer; **~d** adj (bacon, glass) fumé(e); **~r** n (person) fumeur(-euse); (RAIL) wagon m fumeurs; **~ screen** n rideau m or écran m de fumée; (fig) paravent m; **smoking** n tabagisme m; **"no smoking"** (sign) "défense de fumer"; **to give up smoking** arrêter de fumer; **smoking compartment** (US **smoking car**) n wagon m fumeurs; **smoky** adj enfumé(e); (taste) fumé(e)

**smolder** ['sməʊldəʳ] (US) vi = **smoulder**

**mooth** [smuːð] adj lisse; (sauce) onctueux(-euse); (flavour, whisky) moelleux(-euse); (movement) régulier (-ère), sans à-coups or heurts; (pej: person) doucereux(-euse), mielleux(-euse) ♦ vt (also: **~ out**: skirt, paper) lisser, défroisser; (: creases, difficulties) faire disparaître

**smother** ['smʌðəʳ] vt étouffer

**smoulder** ['sməʊldəʳ] (US **smolder**) vi couver

**smudge** [smʌdʒ] n tache f, bavure f ♦ vt salir, maculer

**smug** [smʌg] adj suffisant(e)

**smuggle** ['smʌgl] vt passer en contrebande en fraude; **~r** n

**contrebandier(-ère)**; **smuggling** n contrebande f

**smutty** ['smʌtɪ] adj (fig) grossier(-ère), obscène

**snack** [snæk] n casse-croûte m inv; **~ bar** n snack(-bar) m

**snag** [snæg] n inconvénient m, difficulté f

**snail** [sneɪl] n escargot m

**snake** [sneɪk] n serpent m

**snap** [snæp] n (sound) claquement m, bruit sec; (photograph) photo f, instantané m ♦ adj subit(e); fait(e) sans réfléchir ♦ vt (break) casser net; (fingers) faire claquer ♦ vi se casser net or avec un bruit sec; (speak sharply) parler d'un ton brusque; **to ~ shut** se refermer brusquement; **~ at** vt fus (subj: dog) essayer de mordre; **~ off** vi (break) casser net; **~ up** vt sauter sur, saisir; **~py** (inf) adj prompt(e); (slogan) qui a du punch; **make it ~py!** grouille-toi, et que ça saute!; **~shot** n photo f, instantané m

**snare** [snɛəʳ] n piège m

**snarl** [snɑːl] vi gronder

**snatch** [snætʃ] n (small amount): **~es of** des fragments mpl or bribes fpl de ♦ vt saisir (d'un geste vif); (steal) voler

**sneak** [sniːk] vi: **to ~ in/out** entrer/sortir furtivement or à la dérobée ♦ n (inf: pej: informer) faux jeton; **to ~ up on sb** s'approcher de qn sans faire de bruit; **~ers** npl tennis mpl, baskets mpl

**sneer** [snɪəʳ] vi ricaner; **to ~ at** traiter avec mépris

**sneeze** [sniːz] vi éternuer

**sniff** [snɪf] vi renifler ♦ vt renifler, flairer; (glue, drugs) sniffer, respirer

**snigger** ['snɪgəʳ] vi ricaner; pouffer de rire

**snip** [snɪp] n (cut) petit coup; (BRIT: inf: bargain) (bonne) occasion or affaire f ♦ vt couper

**sniper** ['snaɪpəʳ] n tireur embusqué

**snippet** ['snɪpɪt] n bribe(s) f(pl)

**snob** [snɒb] n snob m/f; **~bish** adj snob inv

**snooker** ['snu:kər] *n* sorte de jeu de billard

**snoop** [snu:p] *vi*: **to ~ about** fureter

**snooze** [snu:z] *n* petit somme ♦ *vi* faire un petit somme

**snore** [snɔ:ʳ] *vi* ronfler

**snorkel** ['snɔ:kl] *n (of swimmer)* tuba *m*

**snort** [snɔ:t] *vi* grogner, *(horse)* renâcler

**snout** [snaut] *n* museau *m*

**snow** [snəu] *n* neige *f* ♦ *vi* neiger; **~ball** *n* boule *f* de neige; **~bound** *adj* enneigé(e), bloqué(e) par la neige; **~drift** *n* congère *f*; **~drop** *n* perceneige *m or f*; **~fall** *n* chute *f* de neige; **~flake** *n* flocon *m* de neige; **~man** *(irreg) n* bonhomme *m* de neige; **~plough** *(US* **snowplow)** *n* chasseneige *m inv*; **~shoe** *n* raquette *f (pour la neige)*; **~storm** *n* tempête *f* de neige

**snub** [snʌb] *vt* repousser, snober ♦ *n* rebuffade *f*; **~-nosed** *adj* au nez retroussé

**snuff** [snʌf] *n* tabac *m* à priser

**snug** [snʌg] *adj* douillet(te), confortable; *(person)* bien au chaud

**snuggle** ['snʌgl] *vi*: **to ~ up to sb** se serrer *or* se blottir contre qn

---

KEYWORD

**so** [səu] *adv* **1** *(thus, likewise)* ainsi; **if so** si oui; **so do** *or* **have I** moi aussi; **it's 5 o'clock – so it is!** il est 5 heures – en effet! *or* c'est vrai!; **I hope/think so** je l'espère/le crois; **so far** jusqu'ici, jusqu'à maintenant; *(in past)* jusque-là

**2** *(in comparisons etc: to such a degree)* si, tellement; **so big (that)** si *or* tellement grand (que); **she's not so clever as her brother** elle n'est pas aussi intelligente que son frère

**3: so much**

♦ *adj, adv* tant (de); **I've got so much work** j'ai tant de travail; **I love you so much** je vous aime tant; **so many** tant (de)

**4** *(phrases)*: **10 or so** à peu près *or* environ 10; **so long!** *(inf: goodbye)* au re-

voir!, à un de ces jours!

♦ *conj* **1** *(expressing purpose)*: **so as t_** do *or* faire, afin de faire; **so (tha_** pour que *or* afin que +*sub*

**2** *(expressing result)* donc, par consé quent; **so that** si bien que, *(telle_* sorte que

---

**soak** [səuk] *vt* faire tremper; *(drench_* tremper ♦ *vi* tremper; **~ in** *vi* être ab sorbé(e) *or* ~ **up** *vt* absorber; **~ing** *ad_* trempé(e)

**soap** [səup] *n* savon *m*; **~flakes** *fpl* paillettes *fpl* de savon; **~ opera** *n* feui leton télévisé; **~ powder** *n* lessive *f*; **~** *adj* savonneux(-euse)

**soar** [sɔ:ʳ] *vi* monter (en flèche), s'éla_ cer; *(building)* s'élancer

**sob** [sɔb] *n* sanglot *m* ♦ *vi* sangloter

**sober** ['səubəʳ] *adj* qui n'est pas (_ plus) ivre; *(serious)* sérieux(-euse), se_ sé(e); *(colour, style)* sobre, discret(-ète_ ~ **up** *vt* dessoûler *(inf)* ♦ *vi* dessoûle_ *(inf)*

**so-called** ['səu'kɔ:ld] *adj* soi-disant *inv*

**soccer** ['sɔkəʳ] *n* football *m*

**social** ['səuʃl] *adj* social(e); *(sociable)* so ciable ♦ *n* (petite) fête; **~ club** *n* amica le *f*, foyer *m*; **~ism** *n* socialisme *m*; *~* *adj* socialiste *n* socialiste *m/f*; **~ize** *vi_* **to ~ize (with)** lier connaissance (avec_ parler (avec); **~ security** *(BRIT)* *n* aide sociale; **~ work** *n* assistance sociale travail social; **~ worker** *n* assistant(_ social(e)

**society** [sə'saɪətɪ] *n* société *f*; *(club)* so ciété, association *f*; *(also:* **high ~)** *(hau_* te) société, grand monde

**sociology** [səusɪ'ɔlədʒɪ] *n* sociologie *f*

**sock** [sɔk] *n* chaussette *f*

**socket** ['sɔkɪt] *n* cavité *f*; *(BRIT: ELEC: also_* **wall ~)** prise *f* de courant

**sod** [sɔd] *n (of earth)* motte *f*; *(BRIT: infl_* con *m (!)*; salaud *m (!)*

**soda** ['səudə] *n (CHEM)* soude *f*; *(also:* **~ water)** eau *f* de Seltz; *(US: also:* **~ pop)** soda *m*

**ofa** ['saufa] n sofa m, canapé m

**ft** [sɔft] adj (not rough) doux (douce); (not hard) doux; mou (molle); (not loud) doux, léger(-ère); (kind) doux, tendre; ~ **drink** n boisson non alcoolisée; ~**en** vt (r)amollir; (fig) adoucir; atténuer ♦ vi se ramollir; s'adoucir; s'atténuer; ~**ly** adv doucement; gentiment; ~**ness** n douceur f; ~**ware** n (COMPUT) logiciel m, software m

**ggy** ['sɔgɪ] adj trempé(e); détrempé(e)

**il** [sɔɪl] n (earth) sol m, terre f ♦ vt salir; (fig) souiller

**olar** ['saula'] adj solaire; ~ **panel** n panneau m solaire; ~ **power** n énergie f solaire

**ld** [sauld] pt, pp of **sell**

**lder** ['sauldə'] vt souder (au fil à souder) ♦ n soudure f

**ldier** ['sauldʒə'] n soldat m, militaire m

**le** [saul] n (of foot) plante f; (of shoe) semelle f; (fish: pl inv) sole f ♦ adj seul(e), unique

**lemn** ['sɔləm] adj solennel(le); (person) sérieux(-euse), grave

**le trader** n (COMM) chef m d'entreprise individuelle

**licit** [sə'lɪsɪt] vt (request) solliciter ♦ vi (prostitute) racoler

**licitor** [sə'lɪsɪtə'] n (for wills etc) ≈ notaire m; (in court) ≈ avocat m

**lid** ['sɔlɪd] adj solide; (not hollow) plein(e), compact(e), massif(-ive); (entire): **3 ~ hours** 3 heures entières ♦ n solide m

**lidarity** [sɔlɪ'dærɪtɪ] n solidarité f

**litary** ['sɔlɪtərɪ] adj solitaire; ~ **confinement** n (LAW) isolement m

**lo** ['saulau] n solo m ♦ adv (fly) en solitaire; ~**ist** n soliste m/f

**luble** ['sɔljubl] adj soluble

**lution** [sə'lu:ʃən] n solution f

**lve** [sɔlv] vt résoudre

**lvent** ['sɔlvənt] adj (COMM) solvable ♦ n (CHEM) (dis)solvant m

**some** [sʌm] adj 1 (a certain amount or number of): **some tea/water/ice cream** du thé/de l'eau/de la glace; **some children/apples** des enfants/pommes

2 (certain: in contrasts): **some people say that ...** il y a des gens qui disent que ...; **some films were excellent, but most ...** certains films étaient excellents, mais la plupart ...

3 (unspecified): **some woman was asking for you** il y avait une dame qui vous demandait; **he was asking for some book (or other)** il demandait un livre quelconque; **some day** un de ces jours; **some day next week** un jour la semaine prochaine

♦ pron 1 (a certain number) quelques-un(e)s, certain(e)s; **I've got some (books etc)** j'en ai (quelques-uns); **some (of them) have been sold** certains ont été vendus

2 (a certain amount) un peu; **I've got some (money, milk)** j'en ai (un peu)

♦ adv: **some 10 people** quelque 10 personnes, 10 personnes environ

**some:** ~**body** ['sʌmbədɪ] pron = **someone**; ~**how** adv d'une façon ou d'une autre; (for some reason) pour une raison ou une autre; ~**one** pron quelqu'un; ~**place** (US) adv = **somewhere**

**somersault** ['sʌməsɔ:lt] n culbute f, saut périlleux ♦ vi faire la culbute or un saut périlleux; (car) faire un tonneau

**some:** ~**thing** pron quelque chose; ~**thing interesting** quelque chose d'intéressant; ~**time** adv (in future) un de ces jours, un jour ou l'autre; (in past): ~**time last month** au cours du mois dernier; ~**times** adv quelquefois, parfois; ~**what** adv quelque peu, un peu; ~**where** adv quelque part

**son** [sʌn] n fils m

**song** [sɔŋ] n chanson f; (of bird) chant

*m*

**son-in-law** *n* gendre *m*, beau-fils *m*

**soon** [su:n] *adv* bientôt; (early) tôt; **~er** *adv* (rather) plus tôt; (preference): **I would ~er do** j'aimerais autant *or* je préférerais faire; **~er or later** tôt ou tard

**soot** [sut] *n* suie *f*

**soothe** [su:ð] *vt* calmer, apaiser

**sophisticated** [sə'fɪstɪkeɪtɪd] *adj* raffiné(e); sophistiqué(e); (machinery): hautement perfectionné(e), très complexe

**sophomore** ['sɔfəmɔ:r] *n* (US) étudiant(e) de seconde année

**sopping** ['sɔpɪŋ] *adj* (also: **~ wet**) complètement trempé(e)

**soppy** ['sɔpɪ] (pej) *adj* sentimental(e)

**soprano** [sə'prɑːnəu] *n* (singer) soprano *m/f*

**sorcerer** ['sɔːsərər] *n* sorcier *m*

**sore** [sɔːr] *adj* (painful) douloureux (-euse), sensible ♦ *n* plaie *f*; **~ly** ['sɔːlɪ] *adv* (tempted) fortement

**sorrow** ['sɔrəu] *n* peine *f*, chagrin *m*

**sorry** ['sɔrɪ] *adj* désolé(e); (condition, excuse) triste, déplorable; **~!** pardon!, excusez-moi!; **~?** pardon?; **to feel ~ for sb** plaindre qn

**sort** [sɔːt] *n* genre *m*, espèce *f*, sorte *f* ♦ *vt* (also: **~ out**) trier; classer; ranger; (: problems) résoudre, régler; **~ing office** ['sɔːtɪŋ-] *n* bureau *m* de tri

**SOS** *n* S.O.S. *m*

**so-so** ['səusəu] *adv* comme ci comme ça

**sought** [sɔːt] *pt, pp of* **seek**

**soul** [səul] *n* âme *f*; **~ful** ['səulful] *adj* sentimental(e); (eyes) expressif(-ive)

**sound** [saund] *adj* (healthy) en bonne santé, sain(e); (safe, not damaged) solide, en bon état; (reliable, not superficial) sérieux(-euse), solide; (sensible) sensé(e) ♦ *adv*: **~ asleep** profondément endormi(e) ♦ *n* son *m*; bruit *m*; (GEO) détroit *m*, bras *m* de mer ♦ *vt* (alarm) sonner ♦ *vi* sonner, retentir; (fig: seem) sembler

(être); **to ~ like** ressembler à; **~ out** *vt* sonder; **~ barrier** *n* mur *m* du son; **bite** *n* phrase *f* toute faite (pour être citée dans les médias); **~ effects** *npl* bruitage *m*; **~ly** *adv* (sleep) profondément; (beat) complètement, à plate coutu **~proof** *adj* insonorisé(e); **~track** *n* (film) bande *f* sonore

**soup** [su:p] *n* soupe *f*, potage *m*; **plate** *n* assiette creuse *or* à soup **~spoon** *n* cuiller *f* à soupe

**sour** ['sauər] *adj* aigre; **it's ~ grap** (fig) c'est du dépit

**source** [sɔːs] *n* source *f*

**south** [sauθ] *n* sud *m* ♦ *adj* sud *inv*, d sud ♦ *adv* au sud, vers le sud; **S~ Afr ca** *n* Afrique *f* du Sud; **S~ African** *a* sud-africain(e) ♦ *n* Sud-Africain(e); **S America** *n* Amérique *f* du Sud; **S American** *adj* sud-américain(e) ♦ Sud-Américain(e); **~-east** *n* sud-est *n* **~erly** ['sʌðəlɪ] *adj* du sud; au sud **~ern** ['sʌðən] *adj* (du) sud; méridional(e); **S~ Pole** *n* Pôle *m* Sud; **S Wales** *n* sud *m* du Pays de Galle **~ward(s)** *adv* vers le sud; **~-west** sud-ouest *m*

**souvenir** [su:və'nɪər] *n* (objet) souvenir *m*

**sovereign** ['sɔvrɪn] *n* souverain(e)

**soviet** ['səuvɪət] *adj* soviétique; **the S Union** l'Union *f* soviétique

**sow**[1] [sau] *n* truie *f*

**sow**[2] [səu] (pt sowed, pp sown) *vt* se mer

**sown** [səun] *pp of* **sow**[2]

**soya** ['sɔɪə] (US **soy**) *n*: **~ bean** graine de soja; **soy(a) sauce** sauce *f* au soja

**spa** [spɑː] *n* (town) station thermale (US: also: **health ~**) établissement *m* d cure de rajeunissement *etc*

**space** [speɪs] *n* espace *m*; (room) plac espace; (length of time) laps *m* de temps ♦ *cpd* spatial(e) ♦ *vt* (also: **~ out** espacer; **~craft** *n* engin spatial; **~ma** (irreg) *n* astronaute *m*, cosmonaute *m* **~ship** *n* = **spacecraft**; **spacing** *n* es

●acement m; **spacious** ['speɪʃəs] adj spacieux(-euse), grand(e)

●ade [speɪd] n (tool) bêche f, pelle f; (child's) pelle f; ~s npl (CARDS) pique m

●an [spæn] n Espagne f

●an [spæn] n (of bird, plane) envergure f; (of arch) portée f; (in time) espace m de temps, durée f ♦ vt enjamber, franchir; (fig) couvrir, embrasser

●aniard ['spænjəd] n Espagnol m

●aniel ['spænjəl] n épagneul m

●anish ['spænɪʃ] adj espagnol(e) ♦ n (LING) espagnol m; **the** ~ npl les Espagnols mpl

●ank [spæŋk] vt donner une fessée à

●anner ['spænər] (BRIT) n clé f (de mécanicien)

●are [speər] adj de réserve, de rechange; (surplus) de or en trop, de reste ♦ n (part) pièce f de rechange, pièce détachée ♦ vt (do without) se passer de; (afford to give) donner, accorder; (refrain from hurting) épargner; to ~ (surplus) en surplus, de trop; ~ **part** n pièce f de rechange, pièce détachée; ~ **time** n moments mpl de loisir, temps m libre; ~ **wheel** n (AUT) roue f de secours; **sparingly** adv avec modération

●ark [spɑːk] n étincelle f; ~(**ing**) **plug** n bougie f

●arkle ['spɑːkl] n scintillement m, éclat m ♦ vi étinceler, scintiller; **sparkling** adj (wine) mousseux(-euse), pétillant(e); (water) pétillant(e); (fig: conversation, performance) étincelant(e), pétillant(e)

●arrow ['spærəu] n moineau m

●arse [spɑːs] adj clairsemé(e)

●artan ['spɑːtən] adj (fig) spartiate

●asm ['spæzəm] n (MED) spasme m; ~**odic** [spæz'mɔdɪk] adj (fig) intermittent(e)

●astic ['spæstɪk] n handicapé(e) moteur

●at [spæt] pt, pp of **spit**

●ate [speɪt] n (fig): **a ~ of** une avalanche or un torrent de

**spawn** [spɔːn] vi frayer ♦ n frai m

**speak** [spiːk] (pt **spoke**, pp **spoken**) vt parler; (truth) dire ♦ vi parler; (make a speech) prendre la parole; **to ~ to sb/ of** or **about sth** parler à qn/de qch; ~ **up!** parle plus fort!; ~**er** n (in public) orateur m; (also: **loudspeaker**) hautparleur m; **the S~er** (BRIT: POL) le président de la chambre des Communes; (US: POL) le président de la chambre des Représentants

**spear** [spɪər] n lance f ♦ vt transpercer; ~**head** vt (attack etc) mener

**spec** [spek] (inf) n: **on** ~ à tout hasard

**special** ['speʃl] adj spécial(e); ~**ist** n spécialiste m/f; ~**ity** [speʃɪ'ælɪtɪ] n spécialité f; ~**ize** vi: **to** ~**ize (in)** se spécialiser (dans); ~**ly** adv spécialement, particulièrement; ~**ty** (esp US) n = **speciality**

**species** ['spiːʃiːz] n inv espèce f

**specific** [spə'sɪfɪk] adj précis(e); particulier(-ère); (BOT, CHEM etc) spécifique; ~**ally** adv expressément, explicitement; ~**ation** [spesɪfɪ'keɪʃən] n (TECH) spécification f; (requirement) stipulation f

**specimen** ['spesɪmən] n spécimen m, échantillon m; (of blood) prélèvement m

**speck** [spek] n petite tache, petit point; (particle) grain m

**speckled** ['spekld] adj tacheté(e), moucheté(e)

**specs** [speks] (inf) npl lunettes fpl

**spectacle** ['spektəkl] n spectacle m; ~**s** npl (glasses) lunettes fpl; **spectacular** [spek'tækjulər] adj spectaculaire

**spectator** [spek'teɪtər] n spectateur (-trice)

**spectrum** ['spektrəm] (pl **spectra**) n spectre m

**speculation** [spekju'leɪʃən] n spéculation f

**speech** [spiːtʃ] n (faculty) parole f; (talk) discours m, allocution f; (manner of speaking) façon f de parler, langage m; (enunciation) élocution f; ~**less** adj muet(te)

**speed** [spiːd] ♦ vi: **to ~ along/past** etc
aller/passer etc à toute vitesse or allure;
**at full** or **top ~** à toute vitesse or allure; **~ up** vi aller plus vite, accélérer ♦ vt
accélérer; **~boat** n vedette f, hors-bord
m inv; **~ily** adv rapidement, prompte-
ment; **~ing** n (AUT) excès m de vitesse;
**~ limit** n limitation f de vitesse, vitesse
maximale permise; **~ometer** [spɪˈdɒm-
ɪtəʳ] n compteur m (de vitesse); **~way**
n (SPORT: also: **~way racing**) épreuve(s)
f(pl) de vitesse de motos; **~y** adj rapide,
prompt(e)

**spell** [spɛl] (pt, pp **spelt** or **spelled**) n
(also: **magic ~**) sortilège m, charme m;
(period of time) (courte) période ♦ vt (in
writing) écrire, orthographier; (aloud)
épeler; (fig) signifier; **to cast a ~ on sb**
jeter un sort à qn; **he can't ~** il fait
des fautes d'orthographe; **~bound** adj
envoûté(e), subjugué(e); **~ing** n orthographe f

**spend** [spɛnd] (pt, pp **spent**) vt (money)
dépenser; (time, life) passer, consacrer;
**~thrift** n dépensier(-ère)

**sperm** [spəːm] n sperme m

**sphere** [sfɪəʳ] n sphère f

**spice** [spaɪs] n épice f; **spicy** adj épi-
cé(e), relevé(e); (fig) piquant(e)

**spider** [ˈspaɪdəʳ] n araignée f

**spike** [spaɪk] n pointe f; (BOT) épi m

**spill** [spɪl] (pt, pp **spilt** or **spilled**) vt renverser; répandre ♦ vi se répandre; **~
over** vi déborder

**spin** [spɪn] (pt **span** or **span**, pp **span**) n
(revolution of wheel) tour m; (AVIAT)
(chute f en) vrille f; (trip in car) petit
tour, balade f ♦ vt (wool etc) filer;
(wheel) faire tourner ♦ vi filer; (turn)
tourner, tournoyer

**spinach** [ˈspɪnɪtʃ] n épinard m; (as
food) épinards

**spinal** [ˈspaɪnl] adj vertébral(e), spi-
nal(e); **~ cord** n moelle épinière

**spin doctor** n personne employée pour pré-

senter un parti politique sous un jour fa-
rable

**spin-dryer** [spɪnˈdraɪəʳ] (BRIT) n ess
reuse f

**spine** [spaɪn] n colonne vertébrale
(thorn) épine f; **~less** adj (fig) mo
(molle)

**spinning** [ˈspɪnɪŋ] n (of thread) filatu
f; **~ top** n toupie f

**spin-off** [ˈspɪnɔf] n avantage inattend
sous-produit m

**spinster** [ˈspɪnstəʳ] n célibataire f; vie
le fille (péj)

**spiral** [ˈspaɪərl] n spirale f ♦ vi (fi
monter en flèche; **~ staircase** n esca
lier m en colimaçon

**spire** [ˈspaɪəʳ] n flèche f, aiguille f

**spirit** [ˈspɪrɪt] n esprit m; (mood) état
d'esprit; (courage) courage m, énergie
**~s** npl (drink) spiritueux mpl, alcool n
**in good ~s** de bonne humeur; **~ed a**
vif (vive), fougueux(-euse), plein(e
d'allant; **~ual** adj spirituel(le); (religiou
religieux(-euse)

**spit** [spɪt] (pt, pp **spat**) n (for roasting
broche f; (saliva) salive f ♦ vi crache
(sound) crépiter

**spite** [spaɪt] n rancune f, dépit m ♦ 
contrarier, vexer; **in ~ of** en dépit de
malgré; **~ful** adj méchant(e), malvei
lant(e)

**spittle** [ˈspɪtl] n salive f; (of anima
bave f; (spat out) crachat m

**splash** [splæʃ] n (sound) plouf m; (c
colour) tache f ♦ vt éclabousser ♦ 
(also: **~ about**) barboter, patauger

**spleen** [spliːn] n (ANAT) rate f

**splendid** [ˈsplɛndɪd] adj splendide, su
perbe, magnifique

**splint** [splɪnt] n attelle f, éclisse f

**splinter** [ˈsplɪntəʳ] n (wood) écharde f
(glass) éclat m ♦ vi se briser, se fendre

**split** [splɪt] (pt, pp **split**) n fente f, déchi
rure f; (fig: POL) scission f ♦ vt (divide
(work, profits) partager, répartir ♦ vi (di
vide) se diviser; **~ up** vi (couple) se sé
parer, rompre; (meeting) se disperser

**oil** [spɔɪl] (*pt, pp* **spoilt** *or* **spoiled**) *vt* (*damage*) abîmer; (*mar*) gâcher; (*child*) gâter; **~s** *npl* butin *m*; (*fig: profits*) bénéfices *npl*; **~sport** *n* trouble-fête *m*, gâbat-joie *m*

**oke** [spəʊk] *pt of* speak ♦ *n* (*of wheel*) rayon *m*

**oken** ['spəʊkn] *pp of* speak

**okesman** ['spəʊksmən], **spokesroman** ['spəʊkswʊmən] (*irreg*) *n* porte-parole *m inv*

**onge** [spʌndʒ] *n* éponge *f*; (*also:* **~ake**) ≈ biscuit *m* de Savoie ♦ *vt* éponger ♦ *vi*: **to ~ off** *or* **on** vivre aux crochets de; **~ bag** (BRIT) *n* trousse *f* de oilette

**onsor** ['spɒnsər] *n* (RADIO, TV, SPORT) onsor *m*, (*for application*) parrain *m*, arraine *f*; (BRIT: *for fund-raising event*) onateur(-trice) ♦ *vt* sponsoriser; parrainer; faire un don à; **~ship** *n* sponsoring *m*; parrainage *m*; dons *mpl*

**ontaneous** [spɒnˈteɪnɪəs] *adj* spontané(e)

**ooky** ['spuːkɪ] (*inf*) *adj* qui donne la hair de poule

**ool** [spuːl] *n* bobine *f*

**oon** [spuːn] *n* cuiller *f*, **~-feed** *vt* ourrir à la cuiller; (*fig*) mâcher le travail; **~ful** *n* cuillerée *f*

**ort** [spɔːt] *n* sport *m*; (*person*) chic pe (*fille*) ♦ *vt* arborer; **~ing** *adj* portif(-ive); **to give sb a ~ing chance** onner sa chance à qn; **~ jacket** (US) *n* = **~s jacket**; **~s car** *n* voiture *f* de port; **~s jacket** (BRIT) *n* veste *f* de port; **~sman** (*irreg*) *n* sportif *m*; **~smanship** *n* esprit sportif, sportivité *f*; **~swear** *n* vêtements *mpl* de sport; **~swoman** (*irreg*) *n* sportive *f*; **~y** *adj* portif(-ive)

**ot** [spɒt] *n* tache *f*; (*dot: on pattern*) ois *m*; (*pimple*) bouton *m*; (*place*) enroit *m*, coin *m*; (RADIO, TV: *in programme: for person*) numéro *m*; (*: for tivity*) rubrique *f*; (*small amount*): **a ~** un peu de ♦ *vt* (*notice*) apercevoir;

repérer; **on the ~** sur place, sur les lieux; (*immediately*) sur-le-champ; (*in difficulty*) dans l'embarras; **~ check** *n* sondage *m*, vérification ponctuelle; **~less** *adj* immaculé(e); **~light** *n* projecteur *m*; **~ted** *adj* (*fabric*) à pois; **~ty** *adj* (*face, person*) boutonneux(-euse)

**spouse** [spaʊs] *n* époux (épouse)

**spout** [spaʊt] *n* (*of jug*) bec *m*; (*of pipe*) orifice *m* ♦ *vi* jaillir

**sprain** [spreɪn] *n* entorse *f*, foulure *f* ♦ *vt*: **to ~ one's ankle** *etc* se fouler *or* se tordre la cheville *etc*

**sprang** [spræŋ] *pt of* spring

**sprawl** [sprɔːl] *vi* s'étaler

**spray** [spreɪ] *n* (*in fine gouttelettes*); (*from sea*) embruns *mpl*, vaporisateur *m*; (*for garden*) pulvérisateur *m*; (*aerosol*) bombe *f*; (*of flowers*) petit bouquet ♦ *vt* vaporiser, pulvériser; (*crops*) traiter

**spread** [spred] (*pt, pp* **spread**) *n* (*distribution*) répartition *f*; (CULIN) pâte *f* à tartiner; (*inf: meal*) festin *m* ♦ *vt* étendre, étaler; répandre; (*wealth, workload*) distribuer ♦ *vi* (*disease, news*) se propager; (*also:* **~ out**: *stain*) s'étaler; **~ out** *vi* (*people*) se disperser; **~-eagled** *adj* étendu(e) bras et jambes écartés; **~sheet** *n* (COMPUT) tableur *m*

**spree** [spriː] *n*: **to go on a ~** faire la fête

**sprightly** ['spraɪtlɪ] *adj* alerte

**spring** [sprɪŋ] (*pt* **sprang**, *pp* **sprung**) *n* (*leap*) bond *m*, saut *m*; (*coiled metal*) ressort *m*; (*season*) printemps *m*; (*of water*) source *f* ♦ *vi* (*leap*) bondir, sauter; **in ~** au printemps; **to ~ from** provenir de; **~ up** *vi* (*problem*) se présenter, surgir; (*plant, buildings*) surgir de terre; **~board** *n* tremplin *m*; **~-clean(ing)** *n* grand nettoyage de printemps; **~time** *n* printemps *m*

**sprinkle** ['sprɪŋkl] *vt*: **to ~ water** *etc* **on,** **~ with water** *etc* asperger d'eau *etc*; **to ~ sugar** *etc* **on,** **~ with sugar** *etc* saupoudrer de sucre *etc*; **~r** *n* (*for*

**sprint** [sprɪnt] n sprint m ♦ vi courir à
toute vitesse; (SPORT) sprinter; **~er** n
sprinteur(-euse)

**sprout** [spraʊt] vi germer, pousser; **~s**
npl (also: **Brussels ~s**) choux mpl de
Bruxelles

**spruce** [spru:s] n inv épicéa m ♦ adj
net(te), pimpant(e)

**sprung** [sprʌŋ] pp of **spring**

**spun** [spʌn] pt, pp of **spin**

**spur** [spə:ʳ] n éperon m; (fig) aiguillon
m ♦ vt (also: **~ on**) éperonner; aiguillonner; **on the ~ of the moment** sous
l'impulsion du moment

**spurious** ['spjʊərɪəs] adj faux (fausse)

**spurn** [spə:n] vt repousser avec mépris

**spurt** [spə:t] n (of blood) jaillissement m;
(of energy) regain m, sursaut m ♦ vi jaillir, gicler

**spy** [spaɪ] n espion(ne) ♦ vi: **to ~ on** espionner, épier; (see) apercevoir; **~ing** n
espionnage m

**sq.** abbr = **square**

**squabble** ['skwɒbl] vi se chamailler

**squad** [skwɒd] n (MIL, POLICE) escouade
f, groupe m; (FOOTBALL) contingent m

**squadron** ['skwɒdrn] n (MIL) escadron
m; (AVIAT, NAUT) escadrille f

**squalid** ['skwɒlɪd] adj sordide

**squall** [skwɔ:l] n rafale f, bourrasque f

**squalor** ['skwɒləʳ] n conditions fpl sor-
dides

**squander** ['skwɒndəʳ] vt gaspiller, dilapider

**square** [skwɛəʳ] n carré m; (in town)
place f ♦ adj carré(e); (inf: ideas, tastes)
vieux jeu inv ♦ vt (arrange) régler; arranger; (MATH) élever au carré ♦ vi (reconcile) concilier; **all ~** quitte; à égalité;
**a ~ meal** un repas convenable; **2
metres ~** de 2 mètres sur 2; **2
metres** 2 mètres carrés; **~ly** adv carrément

**squash** [skwɒʃ] n (BRIT: drink): **lemon/**
**orange ~** citronnade f/orangeade f;
(US: marrow) courge f; (SPORT) squash m
♦ vt écraser

**squat** [skwɒt] adj petit(e) et épais(se),
ramassé(e) ♦ vi (also: **~ down**) s'accroupir; **~ter** n squatter m

**squeak** [skwi:k] vi grincer, crier;
(mouse) pousser un petit cri

**squeal** [skwi:l] vi pousser un or des
cri(s) aigu(s) or perçant(s); (brakes)
grincer

**squeamish** ['skwi:mɪʃ] adj facilement
dégoûté(e)

**squeeze** [skwi:z] n pression f; (ECON)
restrictions fpl de crédit ♦ vt presser;
(hand, arm) serrer; **~ out** vt exprimer

**squelch** [skweltʃ] vi faire un bruit de
succion

**squid** [skwɪd] n calmar m

**squiggle** ['skwɪgl] n gribouillis m

**squint** [skwɪnt] vi loucher ♦ n: **he has
a ~** il louche, il souffre de strabisme

**squirm** [skwə:m] vi se tortiller

**squirrel** ['skwɪrəl] n écureuil m

**squirt** [skwə:t] vi jaillir, gicler

**Sr** abbr = **senior**

**St** abbr = **saint; street**

**stab** [stæb] n (with knife etc) coup m (de
couteau etc); (of pain) lancée f; (inf: try)
**to have a ~ at (doing) sth** s'essayer à
(faire) qch ♦ vt poignarder

**stable** ['steɪbl] n écurie f ♦ adj stable

**stack** [stæk] n tas m, pile f ♦ vt (also:
**~ up**) empiler, entasser

**stadium** ['steɪdɪəm] (pl **stadia** or **~s**) n
stade m

**staff** [stɑ:f] n (workforce) personnel m;
(BRIT: SCOL) professeurs mpl ♦ vt pourvoir
en personnel

**stag** [stæg] n cerf m

**stage** [steɪdʒ] n scène f; (platform) estrade f ♦ n (point) étape f, stade m;
(profession): **the ~** le théâtre ♦ vt (play)
monter, mettre en scène; (demonstration) organiser; **in ~s** par étapes,
par degrés; **~coach** n diligence f;
**manager** n régisseur m

**agger** ['stægə'] vi chanceler, tituber

**vt** (person: amaze) stupéfier; (hours, lidays) étaler, échelonner; **~ing** adj mazing) stupéfiant(e), renversant(e)

**gnate** [stæg'neɪt] vi stagner, croupir

**g party** n enterrement m de vie de rçon

**id** [steɪd] adj posé(e), rassis(e)

**in** [steɪn] n tache f; (colouring) colo nt m ♦ vt tacher; (wood) teindre; **~ed ass window** n vitrail m; **~less eel** n acier m inoxydable, inox m; **~ mover** n détachant m

**ir** [steə'] n (step) marche f; **~s** npl ight of steps) escalier m; **~case**, **way** n escalier m

**ake** [steɪk] n pieu m, poteau m; (ST NG) enjeu m; (COMM: interest) intérêts nl ♦ vt risquer, jouer; **to be at ~** a jeu; **to ~ one's claim (to)** revendi uer

**ale** [steɪl] adj (bread) rassis(e); (food) s frais (fraîche); (beer) éventé(e); mell) de renfermé; (air) confiné(e)

**alemate** ['steɪlmeɪt] n (CHESS) pat m; ig) impasse f

**alk** [stɔ:k] n tige f ♦ vt traquer ♦ vi: **to out/off** sortir/partir d'un air digne

**all** [stɔ:l] n (BRIT: in street, market etc) ventaire m, étal m; (in stable) stalle f ♦ vt (AUT) caler; (delay) retarder ♦ vi (AUT) caler; (fig) essayer de gagner du emps; **~s** npl (BRIT: in cinema, theatre) rchestre m

**allion** ['stæljən] n étalon m (cheval)

**amina** ['stæmɪnə] n résistance f, en urance f

**ammer** ['stæmə'] n bégaiement m ♦ vi bégayer

**amp** [stæmp] n timbre m; (rubber ~) ampon m; (mark, also fig) empreinte f ♦ vi (also: **~ one's foot**) taper du pied ♦ vt (letter) timbrer; (with rubber ~) amponner; **~ album** n album m de imbres(-poste); **~ collecting** n phila élie f

**ampede** [stæm'piːd] n ruée f

**stance** [stæns] n position f

**stand** [stænd] (pt, pp **stood**) n (position) position f; (for taxis) station f (de taxis); (music ~) pupitre m à musique; (COMM) étalage m, stand m; (SPORT: also: **~s**) tri bune f ♦ vi être or se tenir (debout); (be placed) se trouver; (remain: offer etc) rester valable; (BRIT: in election) être candidat(e), se présenter ♦ vt (place) mettre, poser; (tolerate, withstand) sup porter; (treat, invite to) offrir, payer; **to make** or **take a ~** prendre position; **to ~ at** (score, value etc) être de; **to ~ for parliament** (BRIT) se présenter aux élec tions législatives; **~ by** vi (be ready) se tenir prêt(e) ♦ vt fus (opinion) s'en tenir à; (person) ne pas abandonner, soute nir; **~ down** vi (withdraw) se retirer; **~ for** vt fus (signify) représenter, signifier; (tolerate) supporter, tolérer; **~ in for** vt fus remplacer; **~ out** vi (be prominent) ressortir; **~ up** vi (rise) se lever, se met tre debout; **~ up for** vt fus défendre; **~ up to** vt fus tenir tête à, résister à

**standard** ['stændəd] n (level) niveau m (voulu); (norm) norme f, étalon m; (cri terion) critère m; (flag) étendard m ♦ adj (size etc) ordinaire, normal(e); cou rant(e); (text) de base; **~s** npl (morals) morale f, principes mpl; **~ lamp** n (BRIT) lampadaire m; **~ of living** n niveau m de vie

**stand-by** ['stændbaɪ] n remplaçant(e); **to be on ~~** se tenir prêt(e) à (inter venir); être de garde; **~~ ticket** n (AVIAT) billet m stand-by

**stand-in** ['stændɪn] n remplaçant(e)

**standing** ['stændɪŋ] adj debout inv, (permanent) permanent(e) ♦ n réputa tion f, rang m, standing m; **of many years'** ~ qui dure or existe depuis longtemps; **~ joke** n vieux sujet de plaisanterie; **~ order** n (BRIT: at bank) virement m automatique, prélèvement m bancaire; **~ room** n places fpl de bout

**standpoint** ['stændpɔint] n point m de vue

**standstill** ['stændstɪl] n: **at a ~** paralysé(e); **to come to a ~** s'immobiliser, s'arrêter

**stank** [stæŋk] pt of **stink**

**staple** ['steɪpl] n (for papers) agrafe f
♦ adj (food etc) de base ♦ vt agrafer; **~r**
n agrafeuse f

**star** [stɑː<sup>r</sup>] n étoile f; (celebrity) vedette f
♦ vi: **to ~ (in)** être la vedette (de) ♦ vt
(CINEMA etc) avoir pour vedette; **the ~s**
npl l'horoscope m

**starboard** ['stɑːbɔːd] n tribord m

**starch** [stɑːtʃ] n amidon m; (in food) fécule f

**stardom** ['stɑːdəm] n célébrité f

**stare** [stɛə<sup>r</sup>] n regard m fixe ♦ vi: **to ~**
**at** regarder fixement

**starfish** ['stɑːfɪʃ] n étoile f de mer

**stark** [stɑːk] adj (bleak) désolé(e), morne ♦ adv: **~ naked** complètement nu(e)

**starling** ['stɑːlɪŋ] n étourneau m

**starry** ['stɑːrɪ] adj étoilé(e); **~-eyed** adj
(innocent) ingénu(e)

**start** [stɑːt] n commencement m, début
m; (of race) départ m; (sudden movement) sursaut m; (advantage) avance f,
avantage m ♦ vt commencer; (found)
créer; (engine) mettre en marche ♦ vi
partir, se mettre en route; (jump) sursauter; **to ~ doing** or **to do sth** se
mettre à faire qch; **~ off** vi commencer; (leave) partir; **~ up** vi commencer;
(car) démarrer ♦ vt (business) créer;
(car) mettre en marche; **~er** n (AUT) démarreur m; (SPORT: official) starter m;
(BRIT: CULIN) entrée f; **~ing point** n
point m de départ

**startle** ['stɑːtl] vt faire sursauter; donner un choc à; **startling** adj (news)
surprenant(e)

**starvation** [stɑː'veɪʃən] n faim f, famine f

**starve** [stɑːv] vi mourir de faim; être affamé(e) ♦ vt affamer

**state** [steɪt] n état m; (POL) État ♦ vt dé-

clarer, affirmer; **the S~s** npl (Amer
les États-Unis mpl; **to be in a ~**
dans tous ses états; **~(ly)**
majestueux(-euse), imposant(e)

**home** n château m; **~ment** n décla
tion f; **~sman** (irreg) n homme m d'É

**static** ['stætɪk] n (RADIO, TV) parasites
♦ adj statique

**station** ['steɪʃən] n gare f; (police
poste m de police ♦ vt placer, poster
majestueux(-euse), imposant(e)

**stationary** ['steɪʃnərɪ] adj à l'arrêt,
mobile

**stationer** ['steɪʃənə<sup>r</sup>] n papetier(-è
**~'s (shop)** n papeterie f; **~y** n pap
m à lettres, petit matériel de bureau

**stationmaster** ['steɪʃənmɑːstə<sup>r</sup>]
(RAIL) chef m de gare

**station wagon** (US) n break m

**statistic** n statistique f; **~s** ['stɪstɪ
n (science) statistique f

**statue** ['stætjuː] n statue f

**status** ['steɪtəs] n position f, situatio
(official) statut m; (prestige) prestige
**~ symbol** n signe extérieur de riches

**statute** ['stætjuːt] n loi f, statut m; **st**
**tutory** adj statutaire, prévu(e) par
article de loi

**staunch** [stɔːntʃ] adj sûr(e), loyal(e)

**stay** [steɪ] n (period of time) séjour
♦ vi rester; (reside) loger; (spend son
time) séjourner; **to ~ put** ne pas bo
ger; **to ~ with friends** loger chez c
amis; **to ~ the night** passer la nuit;
**behind** vi rester en arrière; **~ in** vi
home) rester à la maison; **~ on** vi re
ter; **~ out** vi (of house) ne pas rentre
**~ up** vi (at night) ne pas se couche
**~ing power** n endurance f

**stead** [stɛd] n: **in sb's ~** à la place c
qn; **to stand sb in good ~** être tr
utile à qn

**steadfast** ['stɛdfɑːst] adj ferme, rés
lu(e)

**steadily** ['stɛdɪlɪ] adv (regularly) pr
gressivement; (firmly) fermement; (
walk) d'un pas ferme; (fixedly: loo
sans détourner les yeux

**dy** ['stedɪ] *adj* stable, solide; ferme; *ular*) constant(e), régulier(-ère); *n*) calme, pondéré(e) ♦ *vt* stabili- *(nerves)* calmer; **a ~ boyfriend** un *t* ami

**k** [steɪk] *n (beef)* bifteck *m*, steak *m*; *n, pork)* tranche *f*

**l** [stiːl] *(pt* **stole***, pp* **stolen***) vt* voler; *(move secretly)* se faufiler; *lacer furtivement

**lth** [stelθ] *n:* **by ~** furtivement

**am** [stiːm] *n* vapeur *f* ♦ *vt (CULIN)* *e* à la vapeur ♦ *vi* fumer; **~ engine** *ocomotive* f à vapeur; **~er** *n (bateau* *)* vapeur *m;* **~ship** *n* = **steamer**; **~y** embué(e), humide

**l** [stiːl] *n* acier *m* ♦ *adj* d'acier; *orks n* aciérie *f*

**ep** [stiːp] *adj* raide, escarpé(e); *ice)* excessif(-ive)

**ple** ['stiːpl] *n* clocher *m*

**er** [stɪəˈ] *vt* diriger; *(boat)* gouverner; *rson)* guider, conduire ♦ *vi* tenir le *vernail;* **~ing** *n (AUT)* conduite *f;* **ng wheel** *n* volant *m*

**m** [stem] *n (of plant)* tige *f; (of glass)* *d n* jambe *f* ♦ *vt* contenir, arrêter, juguler; **~ m** *vt fus* provenir de, découler de

**ch** [stentʃ] *n* puanteur *f*

**ncil** ['stensl] *n* stencil *m; (pattern ed)* pochoir *m* ♦ *vt* polycopier

**nographer** [steˈnɔɡrəfəˈ] *(US) n* sté- *graphe m/f*

**p** [step] *n* pas *m; (stair)* marche *f; *ction)* mesure *f,* disposition *f* ♦ *vi:* **to forward/back** faire un pas en *ant/arrière,* avancer/reculer; **~s** *npl RIT)* = **stepladder**; **to be in/out of ~ with)** *(fig)* aller dans le sens (de)/être *ephasé(e)* (par rapport à); **~ down** *vi* *g)* se retirer, se désister; **~ up** *vi* aug- *enter;* intensifier; **~brother** *n* demi- *ère m;* **~daughter** *n* belle-fille *f;* *ather n* beau-père *m;* **~ladder** *(BRIT)* *escabeau m;* **~mother** *n* belle- *ing stone n* pierre *f* de gué; *(fig)* *emplin m;* **~sister** *n* demi-sœur *f;*

**~son** *n* beau-fils *m*

**stereo** ['stɪərɪəʊ] *n (sound)* stéréo *f; (hi-fi)* chaîne *f* stéréo *inv* ♦ *adj (also:* **~phonic)** stéréo(phonique)

**sterile** ['steraɪl] *adj* stérile; **sterilize** ['steraɪlaɪz] *vt* stériliser

**sterling** ['stɜːlɪŋ] *adj (silver)* de bon aloi, fin(e) ♦ *n (ECON)* livres *fpl* sterling *inv;* **a pound ~** une livre sterling

**stern** [stɜːn] *adj* sévère ♦ *n (NAUT)* ar- rière *m,* poupe *f*

**stew** [stjuː] *n* ragoût *m* ♦ *vt, vi* cuire (à la casserole)

**steward** ['stjuːəd] *n (on ship, plane, train)* steward *m;* **~ess** *n* hôtesse *f* (de l'air)

**stick** [stɪk] *(pt, pp* **stuck***) n* bâton *m; (walking ~)* canne *f* ♦ *vt (glue)* coller; *(inf: put)* mettre, fourrer; (: *tolerate)* supporter; *(thrust):* **to ~ sth into** plan- ter *or* enfoncer qch dans ♦ *vi (become attached)* rester collé(e) *or* fixé(e); (be *unmoveable: wheels etc)* se bloquer; (re- *main)* rester; **~ out** *vi* dépasser, sortir; **~ up** *vi* = **stick out**; **~ up for** *vt fus* défendre; **~er** *n* auto-collant *m;* **~ing plaster** *n* sparadrap *m,* pansement ad- hésif

**stick-up** ['stɪkʌp] *(inf) n* braquage *m,* hold-up *m inv*

**sticky** ['stɪkɪ] *adj* poisseux(-euse); *(label)* adhésif(-ive); *(situation)* délicat(e)

**stiff** [stɪf] *adj* raide; rigide; dur(e); *(diffi- cult)* difficile, ardu(e); *(cold)* froid(e), distant(e); *(strong, high)* fort(e), éle- vé(e) ♦ *adv:* **to be bored/scared/ frozen ~** s'ennuyer à mort/être mort(e) de peur/froid; **~en** *vi* se raidir; **~ neck** *n* torticolis *m*

**stifle** ['staɪfl] *vt* étouffer, réprimer

**stigma** ['stɪɡmə] *n* stigmate *m*

**stile** [staɪl] *n* échalier *m*

**stiletto** [stɪˈletəʊ] *(BRIT) n (also:* **~ heel)** talon *m* aiguille

**still** [stɪl] *adj* immobile ♦ *adv (up to this time)* encore, toujours; *(even)* encore; *(nonetheless)* quand même, tout de même; **~born** adj mort-né(e); **~ life** n nature morte

**stilt** [stɪlt] n (for walking on) échasse f; (pile) pilotis m

**stilted** ['stɪltɪd] adj guindé(e), emprunté(e)

**stimulate** ['stɪmjuleɪt] vt stimuler

**stimuli** ['stɪmjulaɪ] npl of **stimulus**

**stimulus** ['stɪmjuləs] (pl **stimuli**) n stimulant m; (BIOL, PSYCH) stimulus m

**sting** [stɪŋ] (pt, pp **stung**) n piqûre f; (organ) dard m ♦ vt, vi piquer

**stingy** ['stɪndʒɪ] adj avare, pingre

**stink** [stɪŋk] (pt **stank**, pp **stunk**) n puanteur f ♦ vi puer, empester; **~ing** (inf) adj (fig) infect(e), vache; **a ~ing** ... un(e) foutu(e) ...

**stint** [stɪnt] n part f de travail ♦ vi: **to ~ on** lésiner sur, être chiche de

**stir** [stə:r] n agitation f, sensation f ♦ vt remuer ♦ vi remuer, bouger; **~ up** vt (trouble) fomenter, provoquer

**stirrup** ['stɪrəp] n étrier m

**stitch** [stɪtʃ] n (SEWING) point m; (KNITTING) maille f; (MED) point de suture; (pain) point de côté ♦ vt coudre, piquer; (MED) suturer

**stoat** [stəut] n hermine f (avec son pelage d'été)

**stock** [stɔk] n réserve f, provision f; (COMM) stock m; (AGR) cheptel m, bétail m; (CULIN) bouillon m; (descent, origin) souche f; (FINANCE) valeurs fpl, titres mpl ♦ adj (fig: reply etc) classique (to have in ~) avoir, vendre; **~s and shares** valeurs (mobilières); titres; **in/out of ~** en stock ou en magasin/épuisé(e); **to take ~ of** (fig) faire le point de; **~ up** vi: **to ~ up (with)** s'approvisionner (en); **~broker** n agent de change; **~ cube** n bouillon-cube m; **~ exchange** n Bourse f

**stocking** ['stɔkɪŋ] n bas m

**stock:** **~ market** n Bourse f, marché financier; **~pile** n stock m, réserve f ♦ vt stocker, accumuler; **~taking** (BRIT) n (COMM) inventaire m

**stocky** ['stɔkɪ] adj trapu(e), râblé(e)

**stodgy** ['stɔdʒɪ] adj bourratif(ive), lourd(e)

**stoke** [stəuk] vt (fire) garnir, entretenir; (boiler) chauffer

**stole** [stəul] pt of **steal** ♦ n étole f

**stolen** ['stəuln] pp of **steal**

**stomach** ['stʌmək] n estomac m; (abdomen) ventre m ♦ vt digérer, supporter; **~ache** n mal m à l'estomac ou au ventre

**stone** [stəun] n pierre f; (pebble) caillou m, galet m; (in fruit) noyau m; (MED) calcul m; (BRIT: weight) 6,348 kg ♦ adj (wall) en pierre ♦ vt (person) lancer des pierres sur, lapider; **~cold** adj complètement froid(e); **~deaf** adj sourd(e) comme un pot; **~work** n maçonnerie f

**stood** [stud] pt, pp of **stand**

**stool** [stu:l] n tabouret m

**stoop** [stu:p] vi (also: **have a ~**) avoir le dos voûté(e); (also: **~ down**: bend) se baisser

**stop** [stɔp] n arrêt m; halte f; (in punctuation: also: **full ~**) point m ♦ vt arrêter; bloquer; (break off) interrompre; (also: **put a ~ to**) mettre fin à ♦ vi s'arrêter; (rain, noise etc) cesser, s'arrêter; **to ~ doing sth** cesser ou arrêter de faire qch; **~ dead** vi s'arrêter net; **~ off** vi faire une courte halte; **~ up** vt (hole) boucher; **~gap** n (person) bouche-trou m; (measure) mesure f intérimaire; **~over** n halte f; (AVIAT) escale f; **~page** n (strike) arrêt de travail; (blockage) obstruction f; **~per** n bouchon m; **~ press** n nouvelles fpl de dernière heure; **~watch** n chronomètre m

**storage** ['stɔ:rɪdʒ] n entreposage m; **~ heater** n radiateur m électrique par accumulation

**store** [stɔ:r] n (stock) provision f, réserve f; (depot) entrepôt m; (BRIT: large shop) grand magasin; (US) magasin m ♦ vt emmagasiner; (information) enregistrer; **~s** npl (food) provisions; **in ~** en réserve ve; **~ up** vt mettre en réserve; accumuler; **~room** n réserve f, magasin m

**torey** ['stɔːrɪ] (US **story**) n étage m

**tork** [stɔːk] n cigogne f

**torm** [stɔːm] n tempête f; (thunderstorm) orage m ♦ vi (fig) fulminer ♦ vt prendre d'assaut; **~y** adj orageux(-euse)

**tory** ['stɔːrɪ] n histoire f; récit m; (US) = **storey**; **~book** n livre m d'histoires or de contes

**tout** [staut] adj solide; (fat) gros(se), corpulent(e) ♦ n bière brune

**tove** [stauv] n (for cooking) fourneau m; (: small) réchaud m; (for heating) poêle m

**tow** [stau] vt (also: **~ away**) ranger; **~away** n passager(-ère) clandestin(e)

**traddle** ['strædl] vt enjamber, être à cheval sur

**traggle** ['strægl] vi être (or marcher) en désordre

**traight** [streɪt] adj droit(e); (hair) raide; (frank) honnête, franc (franche); (simple) simple ♦ adv (tout) droit; (drink) sec, sans eau; **to put** or **get** (fig) mettre au clair; **~ away**, **~ off** (at once) tout de suite; **~en** vt ajuster; (bed) arranger; **~en out** vt (fig) débrouiller; **~-faced** adj impassible; **~forward** adj simple; (honest) honnête, direct(e)

**train** [streɪn] n tension f; pression f; (physical) effort m; (mental) tension (nerveuse); (breed) race f ♦ vt (hurt: resources etc) mettre à rude épreuve; grever; (hurt: back etc) se faire mal à; (vegetables) égoutter; **~s** npl (MUS) accords mpl, accents mpl; **back ~** tour m de rein; **~ed** adj (muscle) froissé(e); (laugh etc) forcé(e), contraint(e); (relations) tendu(e); **~er** n passoire f

**trait** [streɪt] n (GEO) détroit m; **~s** npl: **to be in dire ~s** avoir de sérieux ennuis (financiers); **~-jacket** n camisole f de force; **~-laced** adj collet monté inv

**trand** [strænd] n (of thread) fil m, brin m; (of rope) toron m; (of hair) mèche f;

**~ed** adj en rade, en plan

**strange** [streɪndʒ] adj (not known) inconnu(e); (odd) étrange, bizarre; **~ly** adv étrangement, bizarrement; see also **enough**; **~r** n inconnu(e); (from another area) étranger(-ère)

**strangle** ['stræŋgl] vt étrangler; **~hold** n (fig) emprise totale, mainmise f

**strap** [stræp] n lanière f, courroie f, sangle f; (of slip, dress) bretelle f; **~py** adj (dress) à bretelles; (sandals) à lanières

**strategy** ['strætɪdʒɪ] n stratégie f

**straw** [strɔː] n paille f; **that's the last ~!** ça, c'est le comble!

**strawberry** ['strɔːbərɪ] n fraise f

**stray** [streɪ] adj (animal) perdu(e), errant(e); (scattered) isolé(e) ♦ vi s'égarer; **~ bullet** n balle perdue

**streak** [striːk] n bande f, filet m; (in hair) raie f ♦ vt zébrer, strier ♦ vi: **to ~ past** passer à toute allure

**stream** [striːm] n (brook) ruisseau m; (current) courant m, flot m; (of people) défilé ininterrompu, flot m ♦ vi (SCOL) répartir par niveau ♦ vi ruisseler; **to ~ in/out** entrer/sortir à flots

**streamer** ['striːmə*] n serpentin m; (banner) banderole f

**streamlined** ['striːmlaɪnd] adj aérodynamique; (fig) rationalisé(e)

**street** [striːt] n rue f; **~car** (US) n tramway m; **~ lamp** n réverbère m; **~ plan** n plan m (des rues); **~wise** (inf) adj futé(e), réaliste

**strength** [streŋθ] n force f; (of girder, knife etc) solidité f; **~en** vt (muscle etc) fortifier; (nation, case etc) renforcer; (building, ECON) consolider

**strenuous** ['strenjuəs] adj vigoureux(-euse), énergique

**stress** [stres] n (force, pressure) pression f; (mental strain) tension (nerveuse), stress m; (accent) accent m ♦ vt insister sur, souligner

**stretch** [stretʃ] n (of sand etc) étendue f ♦ vi s'étirer; (extend): **to ~ to** or **as far**

**stretcher** ['stretʃər] n brancard m, civière f

**stretchy** ['stretʃɪ] adj élastique

**strewn** [struːn] adj: ~ **with** jonché(e) de

**stricken** ['strɪkən] adj (person) très éprouvé(e); (city, industry etc) dévasté(e); ~ **with** (disease etc) frappé(e) or atteint(e) de

**strict** [strɪkt] adj strict(e)

**stride** [straɪd] (pt **strode**, pp **stridden**) n grand pas, enjambée fretar ♦ vi marcher à grands pas

**strife** [straɪf] n conflit m, dissensions fpl

**strike** [straɪk] (pt, pp **struck**) n grève f; (of oil field etc) découverte f; (attack) raid m ♦ vt frapper; (oil etc) trouver, découvrir; (deal) conclure ♦ vi faire grève; (attack) attaquer; (clock) sonner; on ~ (workers) en grève; **to ~ a match** frotter une allumette; ~ **down** vt terrasser; ~ **up** vt (MUS) se mettre à jouer; **to ~ up a friendship** se lier d'amitié avec; **to ~ up a conversation (with)** engager une conversation (avec); ~**r** n gréviste m/f; (SPORT) buteur m; **striking** adj frappant(e), saisissant(e); (attractive) éblouissant(e)

**string** [strɪŋ] (pt, pp **strung**) n ficelle f; (row: of beads) rang m; (: of onions) chapelet m; (MUS) corde f; **to ~ out** échelonner; **the ~s** npl (MUS) les instruments mpl à cordes; **to ~ together** enchaîner; **to pull ~s** (fig) faire jouer le piston; ~**(ed) instrument** n (MUS) instrument m à cordes

**stringent** ['strɪndʒənt] adj rigoureux (-euse)

**strip** [strɪp] n bande f ♦ vt (undress) déshabiller; (paint) décaper; (also: ~ **down:** machine) démonter ♦ vi se déshabiller; ~ **cartoon** n bande dessinée

**stripe** [straɪp] n raie f, rayure f; (MIL) ga-

lon m; ~**d** adj rayé(e), à rayures

**strip:** ~ **lighting** (BRIT) n éclairage m à néon or fluorescent; ~**per** n strip-teaseur(-euse) f; ~ **search** n fouille corporelle (en faisant se déshabiller la personne) ♦ vt: **he was ~ searched** on l'a fait se déshabiller et soumis à une fouille corporelle

**stripy** ['straɪpɪ] adj rayé(e)

**strive** [straɪv] (pt **strove**, pp **striven**) vi **to ~ to do/for sth** s'efforcer de faire/d'obtenir qch

**strode** [strəʊd] pt of **stride**

**stroke** [strəʊk] n coup m; (SWIMMING: nage f; (MED) attaque f ♦ vt caresser; **a ~** a ~ d'un (seul) coup

**stroll** [strəʊl] n petite promenade ♦ vi flâner, se promener nonchalamment; ~**er** (US) n (pushchair) poussette f

**strong** [strɒŋ] adj fort(e); vigoureux (-euse); (heart, nerves) solide; **they are 50 ~** ils sont au nombre de 50; ~**hold** n bastion m; ~**ly** adv fortement, avec force; vigoureusement, solidement; ~**room** n chambre forte

**strove** [strəʊv] pt of **strive**

**struck** [strʌk] pt, pp of **strike**

**structural** ['strʌktʃrəl] adj structural(e); (CONSTR: defect) de construction; (damage) affectant les parties portantes

**structure** ['strʌktʃər] n structure f; (building) construction f

**struggle** ['strʌgl] n lutte f ♦ vi lutter, se battre

**strum** [strʌm] vt (guitar) jouer (en sourdine) de

**strung** [strʌŋ] pt, pp of **string**

**strut** [strʌt] n étai m, support m ♦ vi se pavaner

**stub** [stʌb] n (of cigarette) bout m, mégot m; (of cheque etc) talon m ♦ vt: **to ~ one's toe** se cogner le doigt de pied; ~ **out** vt écraser

**stubble** ['stʌbl] n (on chin) chaume m; barbe f de plusieurs jours

**stubborn** ['stʌbən] adj têtu(e), obstiné(e), opiniâtre

**stuck** [stʌk] pt, pp of **stick ♦** adj (jammed) bloqué(e), coincé(e); **~-up** adj (inf) prétentieux(-euse)

**stud** [stʌd] n (on boots etc) clou m; (on collar) bouton m de col; (earring) boucle d'oreille; (of horses: also: **~ farm**) écurie f, haras m; (also: **~ horse**) étalon m ♦ vt (fig): **~ded with** parsemé(e) or criblé(e) de

**student** ['stju:dənt] n étudiant(e) ♦ adj estudiantin(e); d'étudiant; **~ driver** (US) n (conducteur(-trice)) débutant(e)

**studio** ['stju:dɪəʊ] n studio m, atelier m; (TV etc) studio

**studious** ['stju:dɪəs] adj studieux (-euse), appliqué(e); (attention) soutenu(e); **~ly** adv (carefully) soigneusement

**study** ['stʌdɪ] n étude f; (room) bureau m ♦ vt étudier; (examine) examiner ♦ vi étudier, faire ses études

**stuff** [stʌf] n chose(s) f(pl); affaires fpl, trucs mpl; (substance) substance f ♦ vt rembourrer; (CULIN) farcir; (inf: push) fourrer; **~ing** n bourre f, rembourrage m; (CULIN) farce f; **~y** adj (room) mal ventilé(e) or aéré(e); (ideas) vieux jeu inv

**stumble** ['stʌmbl] vi trébucher; **to ~ across** or **on** (fig) tomber sur; **stumbling block** n pierre f d'achoppement

**stump** [stʌmp] n souche f; (of limb) moignon m ♦ vt: **to be ~ed** sécher, ne pas savoir que répondre

**stun** [stʌn] vt étourdir; (fig) abasourdir

**stung** [stʌŋ] pt, pp of **sting**

**stunk** [stʌŋk] pp of **stink**

**stunned** [stʌnd] adj sidéré(e)

**stunning** ['stʌnɪŋ] adj (news etc) stupéfiant(e); (girl etc) éblouissant(e)

**stunt** [stʌnt] n (in film) cascade f, acrobatie f; (publicity) **~** truc m publicitaire ♦ vt retarder, arrêter; **~man** ['stʌntmæn] (irreg) n cascadeur m

**stupendous** [stju:'pendəs] adj prodigieux(-euse), fantastique

**stupid** ['stju:pɪd] adj stupide, bête; **~ity** [stju:'pɪdɪtɪ] n stupidité f, bêtise f

**sturdy** ['stɜ:dɪ] adj robuste; solide

**stutter** ['stʌtə] vi bégayer

**sty** [staɪ] n (for pigs) porcherie f

**stye** [staɪ] n (MED) orgelet m

**style** [staɪl] n style m; (distinction) allure f, cachet m, style; **stylish** adj élégant(e), chic inv

**stylus** ['staɪləs] (pl **styli** or **~es**) n (of record player) pointe f de lecture

**suave** [swɑːv] adj doucereux(-euse), onctueux(-euse)

**sub...** [sʌb] prefix sub..., sous-; **~conscious** adj subconscient(e); **~contract** vt sous-traiter

**subdue** [səb'djuː] vt subjuguer, soumettre; **~d** adj (light) tamisé(e); (person) qui a perdu de son entrain

**subject** [n 'sʌbdʒɪkt, vb səb'dʒekt] n sujet m; (SCOL) matière f ♦ vt: **to ~ to** soumettre à; exposer à; **to be ~ to** (law) être soumis(e) à; (disease) être sujet(te) à; **~ive** [səb'dʒektɪv] adj subjectif(-ive); **~ matter** n (content) contenu m

**sublet** [sʌb'let] vt sous-louer

**submarine** [sʌbmə'riːn] n sous-marin m

**submerge** [səb'mɜːdʒ] vt submerger ♦ vi plonger

**submission** [səb'mɪʃən] n soumission f; **submissive** adj soumis(e)

**submit** [səb'mɪt] vt soumettre ♦ vi se soumettre

**subnormal** [sʌb'nɔːml] adj au-dessous de la normale

**subordinate** [sə'bɔːdɪnət] adj subalterne ♦ n subordonné(e)

**subpoena** [səb'piːnə] n (LAW) citation f, assignation f

**subscribe** [səb'skraɪb] vi cotiser; **to ~ to** (opinion, fund) souscrire à; (newspaper) s'abonner à; être abonné(e) à; **~r** n (to periodical, telephone) abonné(e); **subscription** [səb'skrɪpʃən] n (to magazine etc) abonnement m

**subsequent** ['sʌbsɪkwənt] adj ultérieur(e), suivant(e); consécutif(-ive); **~ly**

*adv* par la suite

**subside** [səb'saɪd] *vi* (*flood*) baisser; (*wind*, *feelings*) tomber; **~nce** [səb'saɪdns] *n* affaissement *m*

**subsidiary** [səb'sɪdɪərɪ] *adj* subsidiaire; accessoire ♦ *n* filiale *f*

**subsidize** ['sʌbsɪdaɪz] *vt* subventionner; **subsidy** ['sʌbsɪdɪ] *n* subvention *f*

**substance** ['sʌbstəns] *n* substance *f*

**substantial** [səb'stænʃl] *adj* substantiel(le); (*fig*) important(e); **~ly** *adv* considérablement; (*in essence*) en grande partie

**substantiate** [səb'stænʃɪeɪt] *vt* étayer, fournir des preuves à l'appui de

**substitute** ['sʌbstɪtjuːt] *n* (*person*) remplaçant(e); (*thing*) succédané *m* ♦ *vt*: to **~ sth/sb for** substituer qch/qn à, remplacer par qch/qn

**subterranean** [sʌbtə'reɪnɪən] *adj* souterrain(e)

**subtitle** ['sʌbtaɪtl] *n* (*CINEMA*, *TV*) sous-titre *m*; **~d** *adj* sous-titré(e)

**subtle** ['sʌtl] *adj* subtil(e)

**subtotal** [sʌb'təʊtl] *n* total partiel

**subtract** [səb'trækt] *vt* soustraire, retrancher; **~ion** *n* soustraction *f*

**suburb** ['sʌbəːb] *n* faubourg *m*; the **~s** *npl* la banlieue; **~an** [sə'bəːbən] *adj* de banlieue, suburbain(e); **~ia** [sə'bəːbɪə] *n* la banlieue

**subway** ['sʌbweɪ] *n* (*US: railway*) métro *m*; (*BRIT: underpass*) passage souterrain

**succeed** [sək'siːd] *vi* réussir ♦ *vt* succéder à; to **~ in** doing réussir à faire; **~ing** *adj* (*following*) suivant(e)

**success** [sək'ses] *n* succès *m*; réussite *f*; **~ful** *adj* (*venture*) couronné(e) de succès; to be **~ful (in doing)** réussir (à faire); **~fully** *adv* avec succès

**succession** [sək'seʃən] *n* succession *f*; **3 days in ~** 3 jours de suite

**successive** [sək'sesɪv] *adj* successif (-ive); consécutif(-ive)

**such** [sʌtʃ] *adj* tel (telle); (*of that kind*): **~ a book** un livre de ce genre, un livre pareil, un tel livre; (*so much*): **~ cour-**

**age** un tel courage ♦ *adv* si; **~ book**s des livres de ce genre, des livres pareils or de tels livres; **~ a long trip** un si long voyage; **~ a lot of** tellement or tant de; **~ as** (*like*) tel que, comme; **as ~** en tant que tel, à proprement parler; **and-~** *adj* tel ou tel

**suck** [sʌk] *vt* sucer; (*breast*, *bottle*) téter; **~er** *n* ventouse *f*; (*inf*) poire *f*

**suction** ['sʌkʃən] *n* succion *f*

**sudden** ['sʌdn] *adj* soudain(e), subit(e); **all of a ~** soudain, tout à coup; **~ly** *adv* brusquement, tout à coup, soudain

**suds** [sʌdz] *npl* eau savonneuse

**sue** [su:] *vt* poursuivre en justice, intenter un procès à

**suede** [sweɪd] *n* daim *m*

**suet** ['sʊɪt] *n* graisse *f* de rognon

**suffer** ['sʌfər] *vt* souffrir, subir; (*bear*) tolérer, supporter ♦ *vi* souffrir; **~er** *n* (*MED*) malade *m/f*; **~ing** *n* souffrance(s) *f(pl)*

**sufficient** [sə'fɪʃənt] *adj* suffisant(e); **~ money** suffisamment d'argent; **~ly** *adv* suffisamment, assez

**suffocate** ['sʌfəkeɪt] *vi* suffoquer, étouffer

**sugar** ['ʃʊgər] *n* sucre *m* ♦ *vt* sucrer; **~ beet** *n* betterave sucrière; **~ cane** *n* canne *f* à sucre

**suggest** [sə'dʒest] *vt* suggérer, proposer; (*indicate*) dénoter; **~ion** *n* suggestion *f*

**suicide** ['sʊɪsaɪd] *n* suicide *m*; *see also* **commit**

**suit** [su:t] *n* (*man's*) costume *m*, complet *m*; (*woman's*) tailleur *m*, ensemble *m*; (*LAW*) poursuite(s) *f(pl)*, procès *m*; (*CARDS*) couleur *f* ♦ *vt* aller à; convenir à; (*adapt*): to **~ sth to** adapter or approprier qch à; **well ~ed** (*well matched*) faits l'un pour l'autre, très bien assortis; **~able** *adj* qui convient; approprié(e); **~ably** *adv* comme il se doit (*or* se devait *etc*), convenablement

**suitcase** ['su:tkeɪs] *n* valise *f*

**suite** [swi:t] *n* (*of rooms*, *also MUS*) suite

f; (furniture): **bedroom/dining room ~**
(ensemble m de) chambre f à coucher/
salle f à manger

**suitor** ['su:tər] n soupirant m, prétendant m

**sulfur** ['sʌlfər] (US) n = **sulphur**

**sulk** [sʌlk] vi bouder; **~y** adj boudeur
(-euse), maussade

**sullen** ['sʌlən] adj renfrogné(e), maussade

**sulphur** ['sʌlfər] (US **sulfur**) n soufre m

**sultana** [sʌl'tɑːnə] n (CULIN) raisin (sec)
de Smyrne

**sultry** ['sʌltrɪ] adj étouffant(e)

**sum** [sʌm] n somme f; (SCOL etc) calcul
m; **~ up** vt, vi résumer

**summarize** ['sʌməraɪz] vt résumer

**summary** ['sʌmərɪ] n résumé m

**summer** ['sʌmər] n été m ♦ adj d'été,
estival(e); **~house** n (in garden) pavillon m; **~time** n été m; **~ time** n (by
clock) heure f d'été

**summit** ['sʌmɪt] n sommet m

**summon** ['sʌmən] vt appeler, convoquer; **~ up** vt rassembler, faire appel à;
**~s** n citation f, assignation f

**sun** [sʌn] n soleil m; **in the ~** au soleil;
**~bathe** vi prendre un bain de soleil;
**~block** n écran m total; **~burn** n coup
m de soleil; **~burned**, **~burnt** adj
(tanned) bronzé(e)

**Sunday** ['sʌndɪ] n dimanche m; **~
school** n ≈ catéchisme m

**sundial** ['sʌndaɪəl] n cadran m solaire

**sundown** ['sʌndaun] n coucher m du
(or de) soleil

**sundries** ['sʌndrɪz] npl articles divers

**sundry** ['sʌndrɪ] adj divers(e), différent(e) ♦ n: **all and ~** tout le monde,
n'importe qui

**sunflower** ['sʌnflauər] n tournesol m

**sung** [sʌŋ] pp of **sing**

**sunglasses** ['sʌnglɑːsɪz] npl lunettes
fpl de soleil

**sunk** [sʌŋk] pp of **sink**

**sun**: **~light** n (lumière f du) soleil m;
**~lit** adj ensoleillé(e); **~ny** adj ensoleil-

lé(e); **~rise** n lever m du (or de) soleil;
**~ roof** n (AUT) toit ouvrant; **~screen** n
crème f solaire; **~set** n coucher m du
(or de) soleil; **~shade** n (over table) parasol m; **~shine** n (lumière f du) soleil
m; **~stroke** n insolation f; **~tan** n
bronzage m; **~tan lotion** n lotion f or
lait m solaire; **~tan oil** n huile f solaire

**super** ['su:pər] (inf) adj formidable

**superannuation** [su:pəræŋju'eɪʃən] n
(contribution) cotisations fpl pour la
pension

**superb** [su:'pə:b] adj superbe, magnifique

**supercilious** [su:pə'sɪlɪəs] adj hautain(e), dédaigneux(-euse)

**superficial** [su:pə'fɪʃl] adj superficiel(le)

**superimpose** ['su:pərɪm'pəuz] vt superposer

**superintendent** [su:pərɪn'tendənt] n
directeur(-trice); (POLICE) ≈ commissaire
m

**superior** [su'pɪərɪər] adj, n supérieur(e);
**~ity** [supɪərɪ'ɔrɪtɪ] n supériorité f

**superlative** [su'pə:lətɪv] adj, n (LING) superlatif m

**superman** ['su:pəmæn] (irreg) n surhomme m

**supermarket** ['su:pəmɑ:kɪt] n supermarché m

**supernatural** [su:pə'nætʃərəl] adj surnaturel(le)

**superpower** ['su:pəpauər] n (POL) superpuissance f

**supersede** [su:pə'si:d] vt remplacer,
supplanter

**superstitious** [su:pə'stɪʃəs] adj
superstitieux(-euse)

**supervise** ['su:pəvaɪz] vt surveiller; diriger; **supervision** [su:pə'vɪʒən] n surveillance f; contrôle m; **supervisor** n
surveillant(e); (in shop) chef m de rayon

**supper** ['sʌpər] n dîner m; (late) souper
m

**supple** ['sʌpl] adj souple

**supplement** [n 'sʌplɪmənt, vb

**supplier** [sʌplɪ'mənt] *n* supplément *m* ♦ *vt* compléter; **~ary** [sʌplɪ'mentərɪ] *adj* supplémentaire; **~ary benefit** (BRIT) allocation *f* (supplémentaire) d'aide sociale

**supplier** [sə'plaɪə*r*] *n* fournisseur *m*

**supply** [sə'plaɪ] *vt* (*provide*) fournir; (*equip*): **to ~ (with)** approvisionner or ravitailler (en); (*furnish*) fournir ♦ *n* provision *f*, réserve *f*; (~*ing*) approvisionnement *m*; **supplies** *npl* (*food*) vivres *mpl*; (MIL) subsistances *fpl*; **~ teacher** (BRIT) *n* suppléant(e)

**support** [sə'pɔːt] *n* (*moral, financial etc*) soutien *m*, appui *m*; (TECH) support *m*, soutien ♦ *vt* soutenir, supporter; (*financially*) subvenir aux besoins de; (*uphold*) être pour, être partisan de, appuyer; **~er** *n* (POL *etc*) partisan(e); (SPORT) supporter *m*

**suppose** [sə'pəuz] *vt* supposer; imaginer; **to be ~d to do** être censé(e) faire; **~dly** [sə'pəuzɪdlɪ] *adv* soi-disant; **supposing** *conj* si, à supposer que +*sub*

**suppress** [sə'pres] *vt* (*revolt*) réprimer; (*information*) supprimer; (*yawn*) étouffer; (*feelings*) refouler

**supreme** [su'priːm] *adj* suprême

**surcharge** [sə'tʃɑːdʒ] *n* surcharge *f*

**sure** [ʃuə*r*] *adj* sûr(e); (*definite, convinced*) sûr, certain(e); **~!** (*of course*) bien sûr!; **~ enough** effectivement; **to make ~ of sth** s'assurer de or vérifier qch; **to make ~ that** s'assurer or vérifier que; **~ly** *adv* sûrement; certainement

**surf** [sə:f] *n* (*waves*) ressac *m*

**surface** ['sə:fɪs] *n* surface *f* ♦ *vt* (*road*) poser un revêtement sur ♦ *vi* remonter à la surface; faire surface; **~ mail** *n* courrier *m* par voie de terre (or maritime)

**surfboard** ['sə:fbɔːd] *n* planche *f* de surf

**surfeit** ['sə:fɪt] *n*: **a ~ of** un excès de; une indigestion de

**surfing** ['sə:fɪŋ] *n* surf *m*

**surge** [sə:dʒ] *n* vague *f*, montée *f* ♦ *vi*

déferler

**surgeon** ['sə:dʒən] *n* chirurgien *m*

**surgery** ['sə:dʒərɪ] *n* chirurgie *f*; (BRIT: *room*) cabinet *m* (de consultation); (: *also*: **~ hours**) heures *fpl* de consultation

**surgical** ['sə:dʒɪkl] *adj* chirurgical(e); **~ spirit** (BRIT) *n* alcool *m* à 90°

**surname** ['sə:neɪm] *n* nom *m* de famille

**surplus** ['sə:pləs] *n* surplus *m*, excédent *m* ♦ *adj* en surplus, de trop; (COMM) excédentaire

**surprise** [sə'praɪz] *n* surprise *f*; (*astonishment*) étonnement *m* ♦ *vt* surprendre; (*astonish*) étonner; **surprising** *adj* surprenant(e), étonnant(e); **surprisingly** *adv* (*easy, helpful*) étonnamment

**surrender** [sə'rendə*r*] *n* reddition *f*, capitulation *f* ♦ *vi* se rendre, capituler

**surreptitious** [sʌrəp'tɪʃəs] *adj* subreptice, furtif(-ive)

**surrogate** ['sʌrəgɪt] *n* substitut *m*; **~ mother** *n* mère porteuse or de substitution

**surround** [sə'raund] *vt* entourer; (MIL *etc*) encercler; **~ing** *adj* environnant(e); **~ings** *npl* environs *mpl*, alentours *mpl*

**surveillance** [sə:'veɪləns] *n* surveillance *f*

**survey** [*n* 'sə:veɪ, *vb* sə:'veɪ] *n* enquête *f*, étude *f*; (*in housebuying etc*) inspection *f*, (rapport *m* d')expertise *f*; (*of land*) levé *m* ♦ *vt* enquêter sur; inspecter; (*look at*) embrasser du regard; **~or** *n* (*of house*) expert *m*; (*of land*) (arpenteur *m*) géomètre *m*

**survival** [sə'vaɪvl] *n* survie *f*; (*relic*) vestige *m*

**survive** [sə'vaɪv] *vi* survivre; (*custom etc*) subsister ♦ *vt* survivre à; **survivor** *n* survivant(e); (*fig*) battant(e)

**susceptible** [sə'septəbl] *adj*: **~ (to)** sensible (à); (*disease*) prédisposé(e) à

**suspect** [*adj, n* 'sʌspekt, *vb* səs'pekt] *adj, n* suspect(e) ♦ *vt* soupçonner, suspecter

**suspend** [səs'pɛnd] vt suspendre; **~ed sentence** n condamnation f avec sursis; **~er belt** n porte-jarretelles m inv; **~ers** npl (BRIT) jarretelles fpl; (US) bretelles fpl

**suspense** [sas'pɛns] n attente f, incertitude f; (in film etc) suspense m

**suspension** [sas'pɛnʃən] n suspension f; (of driving licence) retrait m provisoire; **~ bridge** n pont suspendu

**suspicion** [sas'pɪʃən] n soupçon(s) m(pl); **suspicious** adj (suspecting) soupçonneux(-euse), méfiant(e); (causing suspicion) suspect(e)

**sustain** [sas'teɪn] vt soutenir; (food etc) nourrir, donner des forces à; (suffer) subir; recevoir; **~able** adj (development, growth etc) viable; **~ed** adj (effort) soutenu(e), prolongé(e); **sustenance** ['sʌstɪnəns] n nourriture f; (money) moyens mpl de subsistance

**swab** [swɔb] n (MED) tampon m

**swagger** ['swægər] vi plastronner

**swallow** ['swɔləu] n (bird) hirondelle f ♦ vt avaler; **~ up** vt engloutir

**swam** [swæm] pt of **swim**

**swamp** [swɔmp] n marais m, marécage m ♦ vt submerger

**swan** [swɔn] n cygne m

**swap** [swɔp] vt: **to ~ (for)** échanger (contre), troquer (contre)

**swarm** [swɔːm] n essaim m ♦ vi fourmiller, grouiller

**swastika** ['swɔstɪkə] n croix gammée

**swat** [swɔt] vt écraser

**sway** [sweɪ] vi se balancer, osciller ♦ vt (influence) influencer

**swear** [sweər] (pt **swore**, pp **sworn**) vt, vi jurer; **~word** n juron m, gros mot

**sweat** [swet] n sueur f, transpiration f ♦ vi suer

**sweater** ['swetər] n tricot m, pull m

**sweaty** ['swetɪ] adj en sueur, moite ou mouillé(e) de sueur

**Swede** [swiːd] n Suédois(e)

**swede** [swiːd] (BRIT) n rutabaga m

**Sweden** ['swiːdn] n Suède f; **Swedish**
adj suédois(e) ♦ n (LING) suédois m

**sweep** [swiːp] (pt, pp **swept**) n (also: **chimney ~**) ramoneur m ♦ vt balayer; (subj: current) emporter; **~ away** vt balayer; entraîner; emporter; **~ past** vi passer majestueusement ou rapidement; **~ up** vt, vi balayer; **~ing** adj (gesture) large; circulaire; **a ~ing statement** une généralisation hâtive

**sweet** [swiːt] n (candy) bonbon m; (BRIT: pudding) dessert m ♦ adj doux (douce); (not savoury) sucré(e); (fig: kind) gentil(le); (baby) mignon(ne); **~corn** ['swiːtkɔːn] n maïs m; **~en** vt adoucir; (with sugar) sucrer; **~heart** n amoureux(-euse); **~ness** n goût sucré; douceur f; **~ pea** n pois m de senteur

**swell** [swel] (pt **swelled**, pp **swollen** ou **swelled**) n (of sea) houle f ♦ adj (US: inf: excellent) chouette ♦ vi grossir, augmenter; (sound) s'enfler; (MED) enfler; **~ing** n (MED) enflure f; (lump) grosseur f

**sweltering** ['sweltərɪŋ] adj étouffant(e), oppressant(e)

**swept** [swept] pt, pp of **sweep**

**swerve** [swəːv] vi faire une embardée ou un écart; dévier

**swift** [swɪft] n (bird) martinet m ♦ adj rapide, prompt(e)

**swig** [swɪg] (inf) n (drink) lampée f

**swill** [swɪl] vt (also: **~ out, ~ down**) laver à grande eau

**swim** [swɪm] (pt **swam**, pp **swum**) n: **to go for a ~** aller nager ou se baigner ♦ vi nager; (SPORT) faire de la natation; (head, room) tourner ♦ vt traverser (à la nage); (a length) faire (à la nage); **~mer** n nageur(-euse); **~ming** n natation f; **~ming cap** n bonnet m de bain; **~ming costume** (BRIT) n maillot m (de bain); **~ming pool** n piscine f; **~ming trunks** npl caleçon m ou slip m de bain; **~suit** n maillot m (de bain)

**swindle** ['swɪndl] n escroquerie f

**swine** [swaɪn] (inf!) n inv salaud m (!)

**swing** [swɪŋ] (pt, pp **swung**) n balan-

**swingeing** coire f; (movement) balancement m, oscillations fpl; (change: in opinion etc) revirement m ♦ vt balancer, faire osciller; (also: ~ round) tourner, faire virer ♦ vi se balancer, osciller; (also: ~ round) virer, tourner; (also: ~ round) vi-rer, tourner; **to be in full ~** battre son plein; **~ bridge** n pont tournant; **~ door** (US **swinging door**) n porte battante

**swingeing** ['swɪndʒɪŋ] (BRIT) adj écrasant(e); (cuts etc) considérable

**swipe** [swaɪp] (inf) vt (steal) piquer

**swirl** [swəːl] vi tourbillonner, tournoyer

**Swiss** [swɪs] adj suisse ♦ n inv Suisse m/f

**switch** [swɪtʃ] n (for light, radio etc) bouton m; (change) changement m, revirement m ♦ vt changer; **~ off** vt éteindre; (engine) arrêter; **~ on** vt allumer; (engine, machine) mettre en marche; **~board** n (TEL) standard m

**Switzerland** ['swɪtsələnd] n Suisse f

**swivel** ['swɪvl] vi (also: ~ round) pivoter, tourner

**swollen** ['swəulən] pp of swell

**swoon** [swuːn] vi se pâmer

**swoop** [swuːp] n (by police) descente f ♦ vi (also: ~ down) descendre en piqué, piquer

**swop** [swɔp] vt = swap

**sword** [sɔːd] n épée f; **~fish** n espadon m

**swore** [swɔːr] pt of swear

**sworn** [swɔːn] pp of swear ♦ adj (statement, evidence) donné(e) sous serment

**swot** [swɔt] vi bûcher, potasser

**swum** [swʌm] pp of swim

**swung** [swʌŋ] pt, pp of swing

**syllable** ['sɪləbl] n syllabe f

**syllabus** ['sɪləbəs] n programme m

**symbol** ['sɪmbl] n symbole m

**symmetry** ['sɪmɪtrɪ] n symétrie f

**sympathetic** [sɪmpə'θetɪk] adj compatissant(e); bienveillant(e), compréhensif(-ive); (likeable) sympathique; **~ towards** bien disposé(e) envers

**sympathize** ['sɪmpəθaɪz] vi: **to ~ with sb** plaindre qn; (in grief) s'associer à la douleur de qn; **to ~ with sth** comprendre qch; **~r** n (POL) sympathisant(e)

**sympathy** ['sɪmpəθɪ] n (pity) compassion f; **sympathies** npl (support) soutien m; **left-wing** etc **sympathies** penchants mpl à gauche etc; **in ~ with** (strike) en or par solidarité avec; **with our deepest ~** en vous priant d'accepter nos sincères condoléances

**symphony** ['sɪmfənɪ] n symphonie f

**symptom** ['sɪmptəm] n symptôme m; indice m

**syndicate** ['sɪndɪkɪt] n syndicat m, coopérative f

**synopsis** [sɪ'nɔpsɪs] (pl **synopses**) n résumé m

**synthetic** [sɪn'θetɪk] adj synthétique

**syphon** ['saɪfən] n, vb = siphon

**Syria** ['sɪrɪə] n Syrie f

**syringe** [sɪ'rɪndʒ] n seringue f

**syrup** ['sɪrəp] n sirop m; (also: **golden ~**) mélasse raffinée

**system** ['sɪstəm] n système m; (ANAT) organisme m; **~atic** [sɪstə'mætɪk] adj systématique; méthodique; **~ disk** n (COMPUT) disque m système; **~s analyst** n analyste fonctionnel(le)

# T, t

**ta** [taː] (BRIT: inf) excl merci!

**tab** [tæb] n (label) étiquette f; (on drinks can etc) languette f; **to keep ~s on** (fig) surveiller

**tabby** ['tæbɪ] n (also: ~ **cat**) chat(te) tigré(e)

**table** ['teɪbl] n table f ♦ vt (BRIT: motion etc) présenter; **to lay** or **set the ~** mettre le couvert or la table; **~cloth** n nappe f; **~ d'hôte** [taːbl'dəut] adj (meal) à prix fixe; **~ lamp** n lampe f de table; **~mat** n (for plate) napperon m, set m; (for hot dish) dessous-de-plat m inv; **~ of contents** n table f des matières; **~spoon** n cuiller f de service;

**~spoonful** *(also:* as measurement) cuillerée f à soupe

**ablet** ['tæblɪt] n (MED) comprimé m

**able tennis** n ping-pong ® m, tennis m de table

**able wine** n vin m de table

**abloid** ['tæblɔɪd] n quotidien m populaire

tabloid press

Le terme tabloid press désigne les journaux populaires de demi-format où l'on trouve beaucoup de photos et qui adoptent un style très concis. Ce type de journaux vise des lecteurs s'intéressant aux faits divers ayant un parfum de scandale; voir quality (news)papers.

**ack** [tæk] n (nail) petit clou ♦ vt clouer; (fig) direction f; (BRIT: stitch) faufiler ♦ vi tirer un ou des bord(s)

**ackle** ['tækl] n matériel m, équipement m; (for lifting) appareil m de levage; (RUGBY) plaquage m ♦ vt (difficulty, animal, burglar etc) s'attaquer à; (person: challenge) s'expliquer avec; (RUGBY) plaquer

**acky** ['tækɪ] adj collant(e); (pej: poor quality) miteux(-euse)

**act** [tækt] n tact m; **~ful** adj plein(e) de tact

**actical** ['tæktɪkl] adj tactique

**actics** ['tæktɪks] npl tactique f

**actless** ['tæktlɪs] adj qui manque de tact

**adpole** ['tædpəul] n têtard m

**ag** [tæg] n étiquette f; **~ along** vi suivre

**tail** [teɪl] n queue f; (of shirt) pan m ♦ vt (follow) suivre, filer; **~s** npl habit m; **~ away, ~ off** vi (in size, quality etc) baisser peu à peu; **~back** n (AUT) bouchon m; **~ end** n bout m, fin f; **~gate** n (AUT) hayon m arrière

**tailor** ['teɪlə*] n tailleur m; **~ing** n (cut) coupe f; **~-made** adj fait(e) sur mesure;

(fig) conçu(e) spécialement

**tailwind** ['teɪlwɪnd] n vent m arrière inv

**tainted** ['teɪntɪd] adj (food) gâté(e); (water, air) infecté(e); (fig) souillé(e)

**take** [teɪk] (pt took, pp taken) vt prendre; (gain: prize) remporter; (require: effort, courage) demander; (tolerate) accepter, supporter; (hold: passengers etc) contenir; (accompany) emmener, accompagner; (bring, carry) apporter, emporter; (exam) passer, se présenter à; **to ~ sth from** (drawer etc) prendre qch dans; (person) prendre qch à; **I ~ it that ...** je suppose que ...; **~ after** vt fus ressembler à; **~ apart** vt démonter; **~ away** vt enlever; (carry off) emporter; **~ back** vt (return) rendre, rapporter; (one's words) retirer; **~ down** vt (building) démolir; (letter etc) prendre, écrire; **~ in** vt (deceive) tromper, rouler; (understand) comprendre, saisir; (include) comprendre, inclure; (lodger) prendre; **~ off** vi (AVIAT) décoller ♦ vt (go away) s'en aller; (remove) enlever; **~ on** vt (work) accepter, se charger de; (employee) prendre, embaucher; (opponent) accepter de se battre contre; **~ out** vt (invite) emmener, sortir; (remove) enlever; **to ~ sth out of** (drawer, pocket etc) prendre qch dans qch; **~ over** vt (business) reprendre ♦ vi: **to ~ over from sb** prendre la relève de qn; **~ to** vt fus (person) se prendre d'amitié pour; (thing) prendre goût à; **~ up** vt (activity) se mettre à; (dress) raccourcir; (occupy: time, space) prendre, occuper; **to ~ sb up on an offer** accepter la proposition de qn; **~away** (BRIT) adj (food) à emporter ♦ n (shop, restaurant) café m qui vend des plats à emporter; **~off** n (AVIAT) décollage m; **~over** n (COMM) rachat m; **takings** npl (COMM) recette f

**talc** [tælk] n (also: **~um powder**) talc m

**tale** [teɪl] n (story) conte m, histoire f; (account) récit m; **to tell ~s** (fig) rapporter

**talent** ['tælnt] n talent m, don m; **~ed**

*adj* doué(e), plein(e) de talent

**talk** [tɔːk] *n* (*a speech*) causerie *f*, exposé *m*; (*conversation*) discussion *f*, entretien *m*; (*gossip*) racontars *mpl* ♦ *vi* parler; **~s** *npl* (POL *etc*) entretiens *mpl*; **to ~ about** parler de; **to ~ into/out of doing** persuader qn de faire/ne pas faire; **to ~ shop** parler métier *or* affaires; **~ over** *vt* discuter (de); **~ative** *adj* bavard(e); **~ show** *n* causerie (télévisée *or* radiodiffusée

**tall** [tɔːl] *adj* (*person*) grand(e); (*building, tree*) haut(e); **to be 6 feet ~** = mesurer 1 mètre 80; **~ story** *n* histoire *f* invraisemblable

**tally** ['tælɪ] *n* compte *m* ♦ *vi*: **to ~ (with)** correspondre (à)

**talon** ['tælən] *n* griffe *f*; (*of eagle*) serre *f*

**tame** [teɪm] *adj* apprivoisé(e); (*fig: story, style*) insipide

**tamper** ['tæmpər] *vi*: **to ~ with** toucher à

**tampon** ['tæmpən] *n* tampon *m* (hygiénique *or* périodique)

**tan** [tæn] *n* (*also*: **suntan**) bronzage *m* ♦ *vt*, *vi* bronzer ♦ *adj* (*colour*) brun clair

**tang** [tæŋ] *n* odeur (*or* saveur) piquante

**tangent** ['tændʒənt] *n* (MATH) tangente *f*; **to go off at a ~** (*fig*) changer de sujet

**tangerine** [tændʒə'riːn] *n* mandarine *f*

**tangle** ['tæŋgl] *n* enchevêtrement *m*; **to get in(to) a ~** s'embrouiller

**tank** [tæŋk] *n* (*water* ~) réservoir *m*; (*for fish*) aquarium *m*; (MIL) char *m* d'assaut

**tanker** ['tæŋkər] *n* (*ship*) pétrolier *m*, tanker *m*; (*truck*) camion-citerne *m*

**tantalizing** ['tæntəlaɪzɪŋ] *adj* (*smell*) extrêmement appétissant(e); (*offer*) terriblement tentant(e)

**tantamount** ['tæntəmaunt] *adj*: **~ to** qui équivaut à

**tantrum** ['tæntrəm] *n* accès *m* de colère

**Taoiseach** ['tiːʃəx] *n* Premier ministre *m* irlandais

**tap** [tæp] *n* (*on sink etc*) robinet *r* (*gentle blow*) petite tape ♦ *vt* frapper taper légèrement; (*resources*) exploite utiliser; (*telephone*) mettre sur écout **on ~** (*fig: resources*) disponible; **~ dancing** *n* claquettes *fpl*

**tape** [teɪp] *n* ruban *m*; (*also*: **magneti ~**) bande *f* (magnétique); (*cassette*) ca sette *f*; (*sticky*) scotch *m* ♦ *vt* (*recorc* enregistrer; (*stick with* ~) coller avec d scotch; **~ deck** *n* platine *f* d'enregistre ment; **~ measure** *n* mètre *m* à ruban

**taper** ['teɪpər] *vi* s'effiler

**tape recorder** *n* magnétophone *m*

**tapestry** ['tæpɪstrɪ] *n* tapisserie *f*

**tar** [tɑː] *n* goudron *m*

**target** ['tɑːgɪt] *n* cible *f*; (*fig*) objectif *m*

**tariff** ['tærɪf] *n* (COMM) tarif *m*; (*taxes* tarif douanier

**tarmac** ['tɑːmæk] *n* (BRIT: *on road*) ma cadam *m*; (AVIAT) piste *f*

**tarnish** ['tɑːnɪʃ] *vt* ternir

**tarpaulin** [tɑː'pɔːlɪn] *n* bâche (gou dronnée)

**tarragon** ['tærəgən] *n* estragon *m*

**tart** [tɑːt] *n* (CULIN) tarte *f*; (BRIT: *inf prostitute*) putain *f* ♦ *adj* (*flavour*) âpre aigrelet(te); **~ up** (BRIT: *inf*) *vt* (*object* retaper; **to ~ o.s. up** se faire beau (bel le), s'attifer (*pej*)

**tartan** ['tɑːtn] *n* tartan *m* ♦ *adj* écos sais(e)

**tartar** ['tɑːtər] *n* (*on teeth*) tartre *m*; **~(e) sauce** *n* sauce *f* tartare

**task** [tɑːsk] *n* tâche *f*; **to take sb to ~** prendre qn à partie; **~ force** *n* (MIL, PO LICE) détachement spécial

**tassel** ['tæsl] *n* gland *m*; pompon *m*

**taste** [teɪst] *n* goût *m*; (*fig: glimpse, idea*) idée *f*, aperçu *m* ♦ *vt* goûter ♦ *vi*: **to ~ of** *or* **like** (*food etc*) avoir le *or* una goût de; **you can ~ the garlic (in it)** on sent bien l'ail; **can I have a ~ of this wine?** puis-je goûter un peu de ce vin?; **in good/bad ~** de bon/mauvais goût; **~ful** *adj* de bon goût; **~less** *adj* (*food*) fade; (*remark*) de mauvais goût;

**tasty** adj savoureux(-euse), délicieux (-euse)

**atters** ['tætəz] npl: **in ~** en lambeaux

**attoo** [tə'tu:] n tatouage m; (spectacle) parade f militaire ♦ vt tatouer

**atty** ['tætɪ] (BRIT: inf) adj (clothes) frippé(e); (shop, area) délabré(e)

**aught** [tɔ:t] pt, pp of **teach**

**aunt** [tɔ:nt] n raillerie f ♦ vt railler

**aurus** ['tɔ:rəs] n le Taureau

**aut** [tɔ:t] adj tendu(e)

**ax** [tæks] n (on goods etc) taxe f; (on income) impôts mpl, contributions fpl ♦ vt taxer; imposer; (fig: patience etc) mettre à l'épreuve; **~able** adj (income) imposable; **~ation** [tæk'seɪʃən] n taxation f; impôts mpl, contributions fpl; **~ avoidance** n dégrèvement fiscal; **~ disc** (BRIT) n (AUT) vignette f (automobile); **~ evasion** n fraude fiscale; **~-free** adj exempt(e) d'impôts

**axi** ['tæksɪ] n taxi m ♦ vi (AVIAT) rouler (lentement) au sol; **~ driver** n chauffeur m de taxi; **~ rank** (BRIT) n station f de taxis; **~ stand** n = **taxi rank**

**ax**: **~ payer** n contribuable m/f; **~ relief** n dégrèvement fiscal; **~ return** n déclaration f d'impôts or de revenus

**B** n abbr = **tuberculosis**

**ea** [ti:] n thé m; (BRIT: snack: for children) goûter m; **high ~** collation combinant goûter et dîner; **~ bag** n sachet m de thé; **~ break** (BRIT) n pause-thé f

**each** [ti:tʃ] (pt, pp **taught**) vt: **to ~ sb sth, ~ sth to sb** apprendre qch à qn; (in school etc) enseigner qch à qn ♦ vi enseigner; **~er** n (in secondary school) professeur m; (in primary school) instituteur(-trice); **~ing** n enseignement m

**ea**: **~ cloth** n torchon m; **~ cosy** n cloche f à thé; **~cup** n tasse f à thé

**eak** [ti:k] n teck m

**ea leaves** npl feuilles fpl de thé

**eam** [ti:m] n équipe f; (of animals) attelage m; **~work** n travail m d'équipe

**eapot** ['ti:pɒt] n théière f

**tear**[1] [tɛəʳ] (pt **tore**, pp **torn**) n déchirure f ♦ vt déchirer; vi se déchirer; **~ along** vi (rush) aller à toute vitesse; **~ up** vt (sheet of paper etc) déchirer, mettre en morceaux or pièces

**tear**[2] [tɪəʳ] n larme f; **in ~s** en larmes; **~ful** adj larmoyant(e); **~ gas** n gaz m lacrymogène

**tearoom** ['tɪ:ru:m] n salon m de thé

**tease** [ti:z] vt taquiner; (unkindly) tourmenter

**tea set** n service m à thé

**teaspoon** ['ti:spu:n] n petite cuiller; (also: **~ful**: as measurement) ≈ cuillerée f à café

**teat** [ti:t] n tétine f

**teatime** ['ti:taɪm] n l'heure f du thé

**tea towel** (BRIT) n torchon m (à vaisselle)

**technical** ['teknɪkl] adj technique; **~ity** [teknɪ'kælɪtɪ] n (detail) détail m technique; (point of law) vice m de forme; **~ly** adv techniquement; (strictly speaking) en théorie

**technician** [tek'nɪʃən] n technicien(ne)

**technique** [tek'ni:k] n technique f

**techno** ['teknəu] n (music) techno f

**technological** [teknə'lɔdʒɪkl] adj technologique

**technology** [tek'nɔlədʒɪ] n technologie f

**teddy (bear)** ['tedɪ(-)] n ours m en peluche

**tedious** ['ti:dɪəs] adj fastidieux(-euse)

**tee** [ti:] n (GOLF) tee m

**teem** [ti:m] vi: **to ~ (with)** grouiller (de); **it is ~ing (with rain)** il pleut à torrents

**teenage** ['ti:neɪdʒ] adj (fashions etc) pour jeunes, pour adolescents; (children) adolescent(e); **~r** n adolescent(e)

**teens** [ti:nz] npl: **to be in one's ~** être adolescent(e)

**tee-shirt** ['ti:ʃə:t] n = **T-shirt**

**teeter** ['ti:təʳ] vi chanceler, vaciller

**teeth** [ti:θ] npl of **tooth**

**teethe** [ti:ð] vi percer ses dents

**teething troubles** *npl* (fig) difficultés initiales

**teetotal** ['tiː'təʊtl] *adj* (person) qui ne boit jamais d'alcool

**tele**: **~communications** *npl* télécommunications *fpl*; **~conferencing** *n* téléconférence(s) *f(pl)*; **~gram** *n* télégramme *m*; **~graph** *n* télégraphe *m*; **~graph pole** *n* poteau *m* télégraphique

**telephone** ['telɪfəʊn] *n* téléphone *m* ♦ *vt* (person) téléphoner à; (message) téléphoner; **on the ~** au téléphone; **to be on the ~** (BRIT: have a ~) avoir le téléphone; **~ booth**, **~ box** (BRIT) *n* cabine *f* téléphonique; **~ call** *n* coup *m* de téléphone, appel *m* téléphonique; **~ directory** *n* annuaire *m* (du téléphone); **~ number** *n* numéro *m* de téléphone; **telephonist** [tə'lefənɪst] (BRIT) *n* téléphoniste *m/f*

**telesales** ['telɪseɪlz] *n* télévente *f*

**telescope** ['telɪskəʊp] *n* télescope *m*

**television** ['telɪvɪʒən] *n* télévision *f*; **on ~** à la télévision; **~ set** *n* (poste *f* de) télévision *m*

**telex** ['teleks] *n* télex *m* ♦ *vt*

**tell** [tel] (*pt, pp* **told**) *vt* dire; (relate: story) raconter; (distinguish): **to ~ sth from** distinguer qch de ♦ *vi* (talk): **to ~ (of)** parler (de); (have effect): se faire sentir, se voir; **to ~ sb to do** dire à qn de faire; **~ off** *vt* réprimander, gronder; **~er** *n* (in bank) caissier(-ère); **~ing** *adj* (remark, detail) révélateur(-trice); **~tale** *adj* (sign) éloquent(e), révélateur(-trice)

**telly** ['telɪ] (BRIT: inf) *n abbr* (= television) télé *f*

**temp** [temp] *n abbr* (= temporary) (secrétaire *f*) intérimaire *f*

**temper** ['tempəʳ] *n* (nature) caractère *m*; (mood) humeur *f*; (fit of anger) colère *f* ♦ *vt* (moderate) tempérer, adoucir; **to be in a ~** être en colère; **to lose one's ~** se mettre en colère

**temperament** ['temprəmənt] *n* (nature) tempérament *m*; **~al** [temprə'mentl] *adj* capricieux(-euse)

**temperate** ['temprət] *adj* (climate, country) tempéré(e)

**temperature** ['temprətʃəʳ] *n* température *f*; **to have** *or* **run a ~** avoir de l fièvre

**temple** ['templ] *n* (building) temple *n* (ANAT) tempe *f*

**temporary** ['tempərərɪ] *adj* temporaire provisoire; (job, worker) temporaire

**tempt** [tempt] *vt* tenter; **to ~ sb int** **doing** persuader qn de faire; **~atior** [temp'teɪʃən] *n* tentation *f*; **~ing** *adj* tentant(e)

**ten** [ten] *num* dix

**tenacity** [tə'næsɪtɪ] *n* ténacité *f*

**tenancy** ['tenənsɪ] *n* location *f*; état *n* de locataire

**tenant** ['tenənt] *n* locataire *m/f*

**tend** [tend] *vt* s'occuper de ♦ *vi*: **to ~** **to do** avoir tendance à faire; **~ency** ['tendənsɪ] *n* tendance *f*

**tender** ['tendəʳ] *adj* tendre; (delicate) délicat(e); (sore) sensible ♦ *n* (COMM: offer) soumission *f* ♦ *vt* offrir

**tenement** ['tenəmənt] *n* immeuble *m*

**tennis** ['tenɪs] *n* tennis *m*; **~ ball** *n* bal le *f* de tennis; **~ court** *n* (court *m* de) tennis; **~ player** *n* joueur(-euse) de tennis; **~ racket** *n* raquette *f* de tennis; **~ shoes** *npl* (chaussures *fpl* de) tennis *mpl*

**tenor** ['tenəʳ] *n* (MUS) ténor *m*

**tenpin bowling** ['tenpɪn-] (BRIT) *n* bowling *m* (à dix quilles)

**tense** [tens] *adj* tendu(e) ♦ *n* (LING) temps *m*

**tension** ['tenʃən] *n* tension *f*

**tent** [tent] *n* tente *f*

**tentative** ['tentətɪv] *adj* timide, hésitant(e); (conclusion) provisoire

**tenterhooks** ['tentəhʊks] *npl*: **on ~** sur des charbons ardents

**tenth** [tenθ] *num* dixième

**tent peg** *n* piquet *m* de tente

**tent pole** *n* montant *m* de tente

**tenuous** ['tenjʊəs] *adj* ténu(e)

**tenure** ['tenjʊəʳ] *n* (of property) bail *m*;

**tepid** ['tepɪd] adj tiède

**term** [tɜːm] n terme m; (SCOL) trimestre m ♦ vt appeler; **~s** npl (conditions) conditions fpl; (COMM) tarif m; **in the short/long ~** à court/long terme; **to come to ~s** with (problem) faire face à

**terminal** ['tɜːmɪnl] adj (disease) dans sa phase terminale; (patient) incurable ♦ n (ELEC) borne f; (for oil, ore etc, COMPUT) terminal m; (also: **air ~**) aérogare f; (BRIT: also: **coach ~**) gare routière; **~ly** adv: **to be ~ly ill** être condamné(e)

**terminate** ['tɜːmɪneɪt] vt mettre fin à; (pregnancy) interrompre

**terminus** ['tɜːmɪnəs] (pl termini) n terminus m inv

**terrace** ['terəs] n terrasse f; (BRIT: row of houses) rangée f de maisons (attenantes); **the ~s** npl (BRIT: SPORT) les gradins mpl; **~d** adj (garden) en terrasses

**terracotta** ['terə'kɔtə] n terre cuite

**terrain** [te'reɪn] n terrain m (sol)

**terrible** ['terɪbl] adj terrible, atroce; (weather, conditions) affreux(-euse), épouvantable; (very badly) affreusement; **terribly** adv terriblement; (very badly) affreusement mal

**terrier** ['terɪə*] n terrier m (chien)

**terrific** [tə'rɪfɪk] adj fantastique, incroyable, terrible; (wonderful) formidable, sensationnel(le)

**terrify** ['terɪfaɪ] vt terrifier

**territory** ['terɪtəri] n territoire m

**terror** ['terə*] n terreur f; **~ism** n terrorisme m; **~ist** n terroriste m/f

**test** [test] n (trial, check) essai m; (of courage etc) épreuve f; (MED) examen m; (CHEM) analyse f; (SCOL) interrogation f; (also: **driving ~**) (examen du) permis m de conduire ♦ vt essayer; mettre à l'épreuve; examiner; analyser; faire subir une interrogation à

**testament** ['testəmənt] n testament m; **the Old/New T~** l'Ancien/le Nouveau Testament

**testicle** ['testɪkl] n testicule m

**testify** ['testɪfaɪ] vi (LAW) témoigner, déposer; **to ~ to sth** attester qch

**testimony** ['testɪmənɪ] n témoignage m; (clear proof): **to be (a) ~** to être la preuve de

**test match** n (CRICKET, RUGBY) match international

**test tube** n éprouvette f

**tetanus** ['tetənəs] n tétanos m

**tether** ['teðə*] vt attacher ♦ n: **at the end of one's ~** à bout (de patience)

**text** [tekst] n texte m ♦ vt envoyer un texto à; **~book** n manuel m; **~ message** n texto m

**textile** ['tekstaɪl] n textile m

**texture** ['tekstʃə*] n texture f; (of skin, paper etc) grain m

**Thailand** ['taɪlænd] n Thaïlande f

**Thames** [temz] n: **the ~** la Tamise

**than** [ðæn, ðən] conj que; (with numerals): **more ~ 10/once** plus de 10/d'une fois; **I have more/less ~ you** j'en ai plus/moins que toi; **she has more apples ~ pears** elle a plus de pommes que de poires

**thank** [θæŋk] vt remercier, dire merci à; **~s** npl (gratitude) remerciements mpl ♦ excl merci; **~ you (very much)** merci (beaucoup); **~s to** grâce à; **~ God!** Dieu merci; **~ful** adj: **~ful (for)** reconnaissant(e) (de); **~less** adj ingrat(e); **T~sgiving (Day)** n jour m d'action de grâce (fête américaine)

---

**Thanksgiving Day**

Thanksgiving Day est un jour de congé aux États-Unis, le quatrième jeudi du mois de novembre, commémorant la bonne récolte que les Pèlerins venus de Grande-Bretagne ont eue en 1621; traditionnellement, c'est un jour où l'on remerciait Dieu et où l'on organisait un grand festin. Une fête semblable a lieu au Canada le deuxième lundi d'octobre.

# that

**that** [ðæt] *adj* (*demonstrative: pl those*) ce, cet +*vowel or* h *mute*, cette f; that man/woman/book cet homme/cette femme/ce livre; (*not "this"*) cet homme-là/cette femme-là/ce livre-là; that one celui-là (celle-là)

♦ *pron* **1** (*demonstrative: pl those*) ce; (*not "this one"*) cela, ça; who's that? qui est-ce?; what's that? qu'est-ce que c'est?; is that you? c'est toi?; I prefer this to that je préfère ceci à cela *or* ça; that's what he said c'est or voilà ce qu'il a dit; that is (to say) c'est-à-dire, à savoir

**2** (*relative: subject*) qui; (*: object*) que; (*: indirect object*) lequel (laquelle), lesquels (lesquelles) *pl*; the book that I read ce livre que j'ai lu; the books that are in the library les livres qui sont dans la bibliothèque; all that I have tout ce que j'ai; the box that I put it in la boîte dans laquelle je l'ai mis; the people that I spoke to les gens auxquels *or* à qui j'ai parlé

**3** (*relative: of time*) où; the day that he came le jour où il est venu

♦ *conj* que; he thought that I was ill il pensait que j'étais malade

♦ *adv* (*demonstrative*): I can't work that much je ne peux pas travailler autant que cela; I didn't know it was that bad je ne savais pas que c'était si *or* aussi mauvais; it's about that high c'est à peu près de cette hauteur

**thatched** [θætʃt] *adj* (*roof*) de chaume; ~ cottage chaumière f

**thaw** [θɔː] *n* dégel *m* ♦ *vi* (*ice*) fondre; (*food*) dégeler ♦ *vt* (*food: also:* ~ out) (faire) dégeler

**the** [ðiː, ðə] *def art* **1** (*gen*) le, f, l' +*vowel or* h *mute*, *les pl*; the boy/girl/ink le garçon/la fille/l'encre; the child-

---

ren les enfants; the history of the world l'histoire du monde; give it to the postman donne-le au facteur; to play the piano/flute jouer du piano/ de la flûte; the rich and the poor les riches et les pauvres

**2** (*in titles*): Elizabeth the First Elisabeth première; Peter the Great Pierre le Grand

**3** (*in comparisons*): the more he works, the more he earns plus il travaille, plus il gagne de l'argent

**theatre** [ˈθɪətəʳ] *n* théâtre *m*; (*also:* lecture ~) amphi(théâtre) *m*; (MED: *also:* operating ~) salle f d'opération; ~goer *n* habitué(e) du théâtre; **theatrical** [θɪˈætrɪkl] *adj* théâtral(e)

**theft** [θɛft] *n* vol *m* (*larcin*)

**their** [ðɛəʳ] *adj* leur; (*pl*) leurs; *see also* **my**; ~s *pron* le (la) leur; (*pl*) les leurs; *see also* **mine**[1]

**them** [ðɛm, ðəm] *pron* (*direct*) les; (*indirect*) leur; (*stressed, after prep*) eux (elles); *see also* **me**

**theme** [θiːm] *n* thème *m*; ~ park *n* parc *m* (d'attraction) à thème; ~ song *n* chanson principale

**themselves** [ðəmˈselvz] *pl pron* (*reflexive*) se; (*emphatic, after prep*) eux mêmes (elles-mêmes); *see also* **oneself**

**then** [ðɛn] *adv* (*at that time*) alors, à ce moment-là; (*next*) puis, ensuite; (*and also*) et puis ♦ *conj* (*therefore*) alors, dans ce cas ♦ *adj*: the ~ president le président d'alors *or* de l'époque; by ~ (*past*) à ce moment-là; (*future*) d'ici là; from ~ on dès lors

**theology** [θɪˈɒlədʒɪ] *n* théologie f

**theoretical** [θɪəˈretɪkl] *adj* théorique

**theory** [ˈθɪərɪ] *n* théorie f

**therapy** [ˈθerəpɪ] *n* thérapie f

---

# there

**there** [ðɛəʳ] *adv* **1**: there is, there are il y a; there are 3 of them (*people, things*) il y en a 3; there has been an

accident il y a eu un accident
**2** (referring to place) là, là-bas; **it's there** c'est là-bas!; **in/on/up/down there** là-dedans/là-dessus/là-haut/en bas; **he went there on Friday** il y est allé vendredi; **I want that book there** je veux ce livre-là; **there he is!** le voilà!
**3: there, there** (esp to child) allons, allons!

**there:** **~abouts** adv (place) par là, près de là; (amount) environ, à peu près; **~after** adv par la suite; **~by** adv ainsi; **~fore** adv donc, par conséquent; **~'s** = there is; there has

**thermal** [ˈθəːml] adj (springs) thermal(e); (underwear) en thermolactyl ®; (COMPUT: paper) thermosensible; (: printer) thermique

**thermometer** [θəˈmɔmɪtəʳ] n thermomètre m

**Thermos** ® [ˈθəːməs] n (also: **~ flask**) thermos ® m or f inv

**thermostat** [ˈθəːməustæt] n thermostat m

**thesaurus** [θɪˈsɔːrəs] n dictionnaire m des synonymes

**these** [ðiːz] pl adj ces; (not "those"): **~ books** ces livres-ci ♦ pl pron ceux-ci (celles-ci)

**thesis** [ˈθiːsɪs] (pl **theses**) n thèse f

**they** [ðeɪ] pl pron ils (elles); (stressed) eux (elles); ... (it is said that) on dit que ...; **~'d** = they had; they would; **~'ll** = they shall; they will; **~'re** = they are; **~'ve** = they have

**thick** [θɪk] adj épais(se); (stupid) bête, borné(e) ♦ n: **in the ~ of** au plus milieu de, en plein cœur de; **it's 20 cm ~** il/elle a 20 cm d'épaisseur); **~en** vi s'épaissir ♦ vt (sauce etc) épaissir; **~ness** n épaisseur f; **~set** adj trapu(e), costaud(e)

**thief** [θiːf] (pl **thieves**) n voleur(-euse)

**thigh** [θaɪ] n cuisse f

**thimble** [ˈθɪmbl] n dé m (à coudre)

**thin** [θɪn] adj mince; (skinny) maigre;

(soup, sauce) peu épais(se), clair(e); (hair, crowd) clairsemé(e) ♦ vt: **to ~ (down)** (sauce, paint) délayer

**thing** [θɪŋ] n chose f; (object) objet m; (contraption) truc m; (mania): **to have a ~ about** être obsédé(e) par; **~s** npl (belongings) affaires fpl; **poor ~!** le (la) pauvre!; **the best ~ would be to** le mieux serait de; **how are ~s?** comment ça va?

**think** [θɪŋk] (pt, pp **thought**) vi penser, réfléchir; (believe) penser ♦ vt (imagine) imaginer; **what did you ~ of them?** qu'avez-vous pensé d'eux?; **to ~ about sth/sb** penser à qch/qn; **I'll ~ about it** je vais y réfléchir; **to ~ of doing** avoir l'idée de faire; **I ~ so/not** je crois or pense que oui/non; **to ~ well of** avoir une haute opinion de; **~ over** vt bien réfléchir à; **~ up** vt inventer, trouver; **~ tank** n groupe m de réflexion

**thinly** [ˈθɪnlɪ] adv (cut) en fines tranches; (spread) en une couche mince

**third** [θəːd] num troisième ♦ n (fraction) tiers m; (AUT) troisième (vitesse) f; (BRIT: SCOL: degree) ≈ licence f sans mention; **~ly** adv troisièmement; **~ party insurance** (BRIT) n assurance f au tiers; **~-rate** adj de qualité médiocre; **the T~ World** n le tiers monde

**thirst** [θəːst] n soif f; **~y** adj (person) qui a soif, assoiffé(e); (work) qui donne soif; **to be ~y** avoir soif

**thirteen** [ˈθəːˈtiːn] num treize

**thirty** [ˈθəːtɪ] num trente

**KEYWORD**

**this** [ðɪs] adj (demonstrative: pl **these**) ce, cet +vowel or h mute, cette f; **this man/woman/book** cet homme/cette femme/ce livre; (not "that") ce homme-ci/cette femme-ci/ce livre-ci; **this one** celui-ci (celle-ci)

♦ pron (demonstrative: pl **these**) ce; (not "that one") celui-ci (celle-ci), ceci; **who's this?** qui est-ce?; **what's this?** qu'est-ce que c'est?; **I prefer this to** that je préfère ceci à cela; **this is what he said** voici ce qu'il a dit; **this is Mr Brown** (in introductions) je vous présente Mr Brown; (on telephone) c'est Mr Brown; (on telephone) ici Mr Brown ♦ adv (demonstrative): **it was about this big** c'était à peu près de cette grandeur or grand comme ça; **I didn't know it was this bad** je ne savais pas que c'était si or aussi mauvais

**thistle** ['θɪsl] n chardon m

**thorn** [θɔ:n] n épine f

**thorough** ['θʌrə] adj (search) minutieux(-euse); (knowledge, research) approfondi(e); (work, person) consciencieux(-euse); (cleaning) à fond; ~**bred** n (horse) pur-sang m inv; ~**fare** n route f; **"no "fare"** "passage interdit"; ~**ly** adv minutieusement; (in depth) en profondeur; à fond; (very) tout à fait

**those** [ðəʊz] adj ces; (not "these"): ~ **books** ces livres-là ♦ pl pron ceux-là (celles-là)

**though** [ðəʊ] conj bien que +sub, quoique +sub ♦ adv pourtant

**thought** [θɔ:t] pt, pp of **think** ♦ n pensée f; (idea) idée f; (opinion) avis m; ~**ful** adj (deep in thought) pensif(-ive); (serious) réfléchi(e); (considerate) prévenant(e); ~**less** adj étourdi(e); qui manque de considération

**thousand** ['θaʊznd] num mille; **two ~** deux mille; **~s of** des milliers de; **~th** num millième

**thrash** [θræʃ] vt rouer de coups; (defeat) battre à plate couture; ~ **about**, ~ **around** vi se débattre; ~ **out** vt débattre de

**thread** [θred] n fil m; (TECH) pas m, filetage m ♦ vt (needle) enfiler; **~bare** adj râpé(e), élimé(e)

**threat** [θret] n menace f; **~en** vi menacer ♦ vt: **to ~en sb with sth/to do** menacer qn de qch/de faire

**three** [θri:] num trois; **~-dimensional** adj à trois dimensions; **~-piece suit** n

complet m (avec gilet); **~-piece suite** n salon m comprenant un canapé et deux fauteuils assortis; **~-ply** adj (wool) trois fils inv

**threshold** ['θreʃhəʊld] n seuil m

**threw** [θru:] pt of **throw**

**thrifty** ['θrɪftɪ] adj économe

**thrill** [θrɪl] n (excitement) émotion f, sensation forte; (shudder) frisson m ♦ vt (audience) électriser; **to be ~ed** (with gift etc) être ravi(e); ~**er** n film m (or roman m or pièce f) à suspense; ~**ing** adj saisissant(e), palpitant(e)

**thrive** [θraɪv] (pt, pp **thrived**) vi pousser, se développer; (business) prospérer; **he ~s on it** cela lui réussit; **thriving** adj (business, community) prospère

**throat** [θrəʊt] n gorge f; **to have a sore ~** avoir mal à la gorge

**throb** [θrɒb] vi (heart) palpiter; (engine) vibrer; **my head is ~bing** j'ai des élancements dans la tête

**throes** [θrəʊz] npl: **in the ~ of** au beau milieu de

**throne** [θrəʊn] n trône m

**throng** ['θrɒŋ] n foule f ♦ vt se presser dans

**throttle** ['θrɒtl] n (AUT) accélérateur m ♦ vt étrangler

**through** [θru:] prep à travers; (time) pendant, durant; (by means of) par, par l'intermédiaire de; (owing to) à cause de ♦ adj (ticket, train, passage) direct(e) ♦ adv à travers; **to put sb ~ to sb** (BRIT: TEL) passer qn à qn; **to be ~** (BRIT: TEL) avoir la communication; (esp US: have finished) avoir fini; **to be ~ with sb** (relationship) avoir rompu avec qn; **"no ~ road"** (BRIT) "impasse"; **~out** prep (place) partout dans; (time) durant tout(e) le (la) ♦ adv partout

**throw** [θrəʊ] (pt **threw**, pp **thrown**) n jet m; (SPORT) lancer m ♦ vt jeter, lancer; (SPORT) lancer; (rider) désarçonner; (fig) déconcerter; **to ~ a party** donner une réception; ~ **away** vt jeter; ~ **out** vt jeter; (reject) rejeter; (*person*) mettre à la porte; ~ **up** vi vomir; **~away** adj à jeter; (*remark*) fait(e) en passant; **~in** n (SPORT) remise f en jeu

**hru** [θru:] (*US*) = **through**

**hrush** [θrʌʃ] n (*bird*) grive f

**hrust** [θrʌst] (*pt, pp* **thrust**) n (TECH) poussée f ♦ vt pousser brusquement; (*push in*) enfoncer

**hud** [θʌd] n bruit sourd

**hug** [θʌg] n voyou m

**humb** [θʌm] n (ANAT) pouce m ♦ vt: to ~ **a lift** faire de l'auto-stop, arrêter une voiture; **~through** vt (*book*) feuilleter; **~tack** (*US*) n punaise f (*clou*)

**hump** [θʌmp] n grand coup; (*sound*) bruit sourd ♦ vt cogner sur ♦ vi cogner, battre fort

**hunder** [ˈθʌndər] n tonnerre m ♦ vi tonner; (*train etc*): to ~ **past** passer dans un grondement ou un bruit de tonnerre; **~bolt** n foudre f; **~clap** n coup m de tonnerre; **~storm** n orage m; **~y** adj orageux(-euse)

**hursday** [ˈθɜːzdɪ] n jeudi m

**hus** [ðʌs] adv ainsi

**hwart** [θwɔːt] vt contrecarrer

**hyme** [taɪm] n thym m

**iara** [tɪˈɑːrə] n diadème m

**ick** [tɪk] n (*sound: of clock*) tic-tac m; (*mark*) coche f; (ZOOL) tique f; (BRIT: *inf*): **in a** ~ dans une seconde ♦ vi faire tic-tac ♦ vt (*item on list*) cocher; **~ off** vt (*item on list*) cocher; (*person*) réprimander, attraper; **~ over** vt (*engine*) tourner au ralenti; (*fig*) aller ou marcher doucettement

**icket** [ˈtɪkɪt] n billet m; (*for bus, tube*) ticket m; (*in shop: on goods*) étiquette f; (*for library*) carte f; (*parking* ~) papillon m, p.-v. m; **~ collector** n inspector n contrôleur(-euse); **~ office** n guichet m, bureau m de vente des billets

**ickle** [ˈtɪkl] vt, vi chatouiller; **ticklish** adj (*person*) chatouilleux(-euse); (*problem*) épineux(-euse)

**tidal** [ˈtaɪdl] adj (*force*) de la marée; (*estuary*) à marée; ~ **wave** n raz-de-marée m inv

**tidbit** [ˈtɪdbɪt] (*US*) n = **titbit**

**tiddlywinks** [ˈtɪdlɪwɪŋks] n jeu m de puce

**tide** [taɪd] n marée f; (*fig: of events*) cours m ♦ vt: to ~ **sb over** dépanner qn; **high/low** ~ marée haute/basse

**tidy** [ˈtaɪdɪ] adj (*room*) bien rangé(e); (*dress, work*) net(te), soigné(e); (*person*) ordonné(e), qui a de l'ordre ♦ vt (*also: ~ up*) ranger

**tie** [taɪ] n (*string etc*) cordon m; (BRIT: *also:* **necktie**) cravate f; (*fig: link*) lien m; (SPORT: *draw*) égalité f de points; match nul ♦ vt (*parcel*) attacher; (*ribbon, shoelaces*) nouer ♦ vi (SPORT) faire match nul; finir à égalité de points; to ~ **sth in a bow** faire un nœud à ou avec qch; to ~ **a knot in sth** faire un nœud à qch; **~ down** vt (*fig*): to ~ **sb down (to)** contraindre qn (à accepter); to **be ~d down** (*by relationship*) se fixer; **~ up** vt (*parcel*) ficeler; (*dog, boat*) attacher; (*prisoner*) ligoter; (*arrangements*) conclure; to **be ~d up** (*busy*) être pris(e) ou occupé(e)

**tier** [tɪər] n gradin m; (*of cake*) étage m

**tiger** [ˈtaɪɡər] n tigre m

**tight** [taɪt] adj (*rope*) tendu(e), raide; (*clothes*) étroit(e), très juste; (*budget, programme, bend*) serré(e); (*control*) strict(e), sévère; (*inf: drunk*) ivre, rond(e) ♦ adv (*squeeze*) très fort; (*shut*) hermétiquement, bien; **~en** vt (*rope*) tendre; (*screw*) resserrer; (*control*) renforcer ♦ vi se tendre, se resserrer; **~fisted** adj avare; **~ly** adv (*grasp*) très fort; **~rope** n corde f raide; **~s** (BRIT) npl collant m

**tile** [taɪl] n (*on roof*) tuile f; (*on wall or floor*) carreau m; **~d** adj en tuiles; carrelé(e)

**till** [tɪl] n caisse (enregistreuse) ♦ vt (*land*) cultiver ♦ prep, conj = **until**

**tiller** [ˈtɪlər] n (NAUT) barre f (du gouvernail)

**tilt** [tɪlt] *vt* pencher, incliner ♦ *vi* pencher, être incliné(e)

**timber** ['tɪmbə<sup>r</sup>] *n* (*material*) bois *m* (de construction); (*trees*) arbres *mpl*

**time** [taɪm] *n* temps *m*; (*epoch: often pl*) époque *f*, temps; (*by clock*) heure *f*; (*moment*) moment *m*; (*occasion, also MATH*) fois *f*; (*MUS*) mesure *f* ♦ *vt* (*race*) chronométrer; (*programme*) minuter; (*visit*) fixer; (*remark etc*) choisir le moment; **a long ~** un long moment, longtemps; **for the ~ being** pour le moment; **4 at a ~** 4 à la fois; **from ~ to ~** de temps en temps; **at ~s** parfois; **in ~** (*soon enough*) à temps; (*after some ~*) avec le temps, à la longue; (*MUS*) en mesure; **in a week's ~** dans une semaine; **in no ~** en un rien de temps; **any ~** n'importe quand; **on ~** à l'heure; **5 ~s 5** 5 fois 5; **what ~ is it?** quelle heure est-il?; **to have a good ~** bien s'amuser; **~ bomb** *n* bombe *f* à retardement; **~ lag** (*BRIT*) *n* décalage *m*; (*in travel*) décalage horaire; **~less** *adj* éternel(le); **~ly** *adj* opportun(e); **~ off** *n* temps *m* libre; **~r** *n* (*TECH*) minuteur *m*; (*in kitchen*) compte-minutes *m inv*; **~scale** *n* délais *mpl*; **~share** *n* maison *f*/appartement *m* en multipropriété; **~ switch** (*BRIT*) *n* minuteur *m*; (*for lighting, heating*) minuterie *f*; **~table** *n* (*RAIL*) (indicateur *m*) horaire *m*; (*SCOL*) emploi *m* du temps; **~ zone** *n* fuseau *m* horaire

**timid** ['tɪmɪd] *adj* timide; (*easily scared*) peureux(-euse)

**timing** ['taɪmɪŋ] *n* minutage *m*; chronométrage *m*; **the ~ of his resignation** le moment choisi pour sa démission

**timpani** ['tɪmpənɪ] *npl* timbales *fpl*

**tin** [tɪn] *n* étain *m*; (*also: ~ plate*) ferblanc *m*; (*BRIT: can*) boîte *f* (de conserve); (*for storage*) boîte *f*; **~foil** *n* papier *m* d'étain *or* aluminium

**tinge** [tɪndʒ] *n* nuance *f* ♦ *vt*: **~d with** teinté(e) de

**tingle** ['tɪŋgl] *vi* picoter; (*person*) avoir des picotements

**tinker** ['tɪŋkə<sup>r</sup>] *n* (*gipsy*) romanichel *m*; **~ with** *vt fus* bricoler, rafistoler

**tinkle** ['tɪŋkl] *vi* tinter

**tinned** [tɪnd] (*BRIT*) *adj* (*food*) en boîte, en conserve

**tin opener** (*BRIT*) *n* ouvre-boîte(s) *m*

**tinsel** ['tɪnsl] *n* guirlandes *fpl* de Noël (argentées)

**tint** [tɪnt] *n* teinte *f*; (*for hair*) shampooing colorant; **~ed** *adj* (*hair*) teinté(e); (*spectacles, glass*) teinté(e)

**tiny** ['taɪnɪ] *adj* minuscule

**tip** [tɪp] *n* (*end*) bout *m*; (*gratuity*) pourboire *m*; (*BRIT: for rubbish*) décharge *f*; (*advice*) tuyau *m* ♦ *vt* (*waiter*) donner un pourboire à; (*tilt*) incliner; (*overturn, also: ~ over*) renverser; (*empty: also: ~ out*) déverser; **~-off** *n* (*hint*) tuyau *m*; **~ped** (*BRIT*) *adj* (*cigarette*) (à bout) filtre *inv*

**tipsy** ['tɪpsɪ] (*inf*) *adj* un peu ivre, éméché(e)

**tiptoe** ['tɪptəu] *n*: **on ~** sur la pointe des pieds

**tiptop** ['tɪp'tɔp] *adj*: **in ~ condition** en excellent état

**tire** ['taɪə<sup>r</sup>] *n* (*US*) = **tyre** ♦ *vt* fatiguer ♦ *vi* se fatiguer; **~d** *adj* fatigué(e); **to be ~d of** en avoir assez de, être las (lasse) de; **~less** *adj* (*person*) infatigable; (*efforts*) inlassable; **~some** *adj* ennuyeux(-euse); **tiring** *adj* fatigant(e)

**tissue** ['tɪʃuː] *n* tissu *m*; (*paper handkerchief*) mouchoir *m* en papier, kleenex ® *m*; **~ paper** *n* papier *m* de soie

**tit** [tɪt] *n* (*bird*) mésange *f*; **to give ~ for tat** rendre la pareille

**titbit** ['tɪtbɪt] *n* (*food*) friandise *f*; (*news*) potin *m*

**title** ['taɪtl] *n* titre *m*; **~ deed** *n* (*LAW*) titre (constitutif) de propriété; **~ role** *n* rôle principal

**TM** *abbr* = **trademark**

KEYWORD

**to** [tuː, tə] *prep* **1** (*direction*) à; **to go**

France/Portugal/London/school aller en France/au Portugal/à Londres/à l'école; **to go to Claude's/the doctor's** aller chez Claude/le docteur; **the road to Edinburgh** la route d'Édimbourg

**2** (as far as) (jusqu')à; **to count to 10** compter jusqu'à 10; **from 40 to 50 people** de 40 à 50 personnes

**3** (with expressions of time): **a quarter to 5** 5 heures moins le quart; **it's twenty to 3** il est 3 heures moins vingt

**4** (for, of) de; **the key to the front door** la clé de la porte d'entrée; **a letter to his wife** une lettre (adressée) à sa femme

**5** (expressing indirect object) à; **to give sth to sb** donner qch à qn; **to talk to sb** parler à qn

**6** (in relation to) à; **3 goals to 2** 3 (buts) à 2; **30 miles to the gallon** 9,4 litres aux cent (km)

**7** (purpose, result): **to come to sb's aid** venir au secours de qn, porter secours à qn; **to sentence sb to death** condamner qn à mort; **to my surprise** à ma grande surprise

♦ with vb **1** (simple infinitive): **to go/eat** aller/manger

**2** (following another vb): **to want/try/start to do** vouloir/essayer de/commencer à faire

**3** (with vb omitted): **I don't want to** je ne veux pas

**4** (purpose, result) pour; **I did it to help you** je l'ai fait pour vous aider

**5** (equivalent to relative clause): **I have things to do** j'ai des choses à faire; **the main thing is to try** l'important est d'essayer

**6** (after adjective etc): **ready to go** prêt(e) à partir; **too old/young to ...** trop vieux/jeune pour ...

♦ adv: **push/pull the door to** tirez/poussez la porte

**toad** [təud] n crapaud m

**toadstool** ['təudstu:l] n champignon (vénéneux)

**toast** [təust] n (CULIN) pain grillé, toast m; (drink, speech) toast m ♦ vt (CULIN) faire griller; (drink) to porter un toast à; **~er** n grille-pain m inv

**tobacco** [tə'bækəu] n tabac m; **~nist's** marchand(e) de tabac; **~nist's (shop)** n (bureau m de) tabac m

**toboggan** [tə'bɔgən] n toboggan m; (child's) luge f ♦ vi: **to go ~ing** faire de la luge

**today** [tə'deɪ] adv (also fig) aujourd'hui ♦ n aujourd'hui m

**toddler** ['tɔdlə*] n enfant m/f qui commence à marcher, bambin m

**toe** [təu] n doigt m de pied, orteil m; (of shoe) bout m ♦ vt: **to ~ the line** (fig) obéir, se conformer; **~nail** n ongle m du pied

**toffee** ['tɔfɪ] n caramel m; **~ apple** n (BRIT) pomme caramélisée

**together** [tə'geðə*] adv ensemble; (at same time) en même temps; **~ with** avec

**toil** [tɔɪl] n dur travail, labeur m ♦ vi peiner

**toilet** ['tɔɪlət] n (BRIT: lavatory) toilettes fpl ♦ cpd (accessories etc) de toilette; **~ bag** n nécessaire m de toilette; **~ paper** n papier m hygiénique; **~ries** npl articles mpl de toilette; **~ roll** n rouleau m de papier hygiénique

**token** ['təukən] n (sign) marque f, témoignage m; (metal disc) jeton m ♦ adj (strike, payment etc) symbolique; **book/record ~** n (BRIT) chèque-livre/-disque m; **gift ~** n bon-cadeau m

**told** [təuld] pt, pp of **tell**

**tolerable** ['tɔlərəbl] adj (bearable) tolérable; (fairly good) passable

**tolerant** ['tɔlərnt] adj: **~ (of)** tolérant(e) (à l'égard de)

**tolerate** ['tɔləreɪt] vt supporter, tolérer

**toll** [təul] n (tax, charge) péage m ♦ vi (bell) sonner; **the accident ~ on the**

**roads** le nombre des victimes de la route

**tomato** [təˈmɑːtəu] (*pl* **~es**) *n* tomate *f*

**tomb** [tuːm] *n* tombe *f*

**tomboy** [ˈtɒmbɔɪ] *n* garçon manqué

**tombstone** [ˈtuːmstəun] *n* pierre tombale

**tomcat** [ˈtɒmkæt] *n* matou *m*

**tomorrow** [təˈmɒrəu] *adv* (*also* big) demain ♦ *n* demain *m*; **the day after ~** après-demain; **~ morning** demain matin

**ton** [tʌn] *n* tonne *f* (*BRIT* = 1016kg; *US* = 907kg); (*metric*) tonne (= 1000 kg); **~s of** (*inf*) des tas de

**tone** [təun] *n* ton *m* ♦ *vi* (*also:* **~ in**) s'harmoniser; **~ down** *vt* (*colour, criticism*) adoucir; (*sound*) baisser; **~ up** *vt* (*muscles*) tonifier; **~-deaf** *adj* qui n'a pas d'oreille

**tongs** [tɒŋz] *npl* (*for coal*) pincettes *fpl*; (*for hair*) fer m à friser

**tongue** [tʌŋ] *n* langue *f*; **~ in cheek** ironiquement; **~-tied** *adj* (*fig*) muet(te); **~ twister** *n* phrase *f* très difficile à prononcer

**tonic** [ˈtɒnɪk] *n* (*MED*) tonique *m*; (*also:* **~ water**) tonic *m*, Schweppes ® *m*

**tonight** [təˈnaɪt] *adv, n* cette nuit; (*this evening*) ce soir

**tonsil** [ˈtɒnsl] *n* amygdale *f*; **~litis** [tɒnsɪˈlaɪtɪs] *n* angine *f*

**too** [tuː] *adv* (*excessively*) trop; (*also*) aussi; **~ much** *adv* trop ♦ *adj* trop de; **~ many** trop de; **~ bad!** tant pis!

**took** [tuk] *pt of* **take**

**tool** [tuːl] *n* outil *m*; **~ box** *n* boîte à outils

**toot** [tuːt] *n* (*of car horn*) coup *m* de klaxon; (*of whistle*) coup *m* de sifflet ♦ *vi* (*with car horn*) klaxonner

**tooth** [tuːθ] (*pl* **teeth**) *n* (*ANAT, TECH*) dent *f*; **~ache** *n* mal *m* de dents; **~brush** *n* brosse *f* à dents; **~paste** *n* (*pâte f*) dentifrice *m*; **~pick** *n* cure-dent *m*

**top** [tɒp] *n* (*of mountain, head*) sommet

*m*; (*of page, ladder, garment*) haut *m* (*of box, cupboard, table*) dessus *m*; (*lid: of box, jar*) couvercle *m*; (*of bottle*) bouchon *m*; (*toy*) toupie *f* ♦ *adj* de haut; (*in rank*) premier(-ère); (*best*) meilleur(e) ♦ *vt* (*exceed*) dépasser; (*be first in*) être en tête de; **on ~ of** sur; (*in addition to*) en plus de; **from ~ to bottom** de fond en comble; **~ up** (*US* **~ off**) *vt* (*bottle*) remplir; (*salary*) compléter; **~ floor** *n* dernier étage; **~ hat** *n* haut-de-forme *m*; **~-heavy** *adj* (*object*) trop lourd(e) du haut

**topic** [ˈtɒpɪk] *n* sujet *m*, thème *m*; **~al** *adj* d'actualité

**top: ~less** *adj* (*bather etc*) aux seins nus; **~-level** *adj* (*talks*) au plus haut niveau; **~most** *adj* le (la) plus haut(e)

**topple** [ˈtɒpl] *vt* renverser, faire tomber ♦ *vi* basculer, tomber

**top-secret** [ˈtɒpˈsiːkrɪt] *adj* top secret (-ète)

**topsy-turvy** [ˈtɒpsɪˈtɜːvɪ] *adj, adv* sens dessus dessous

**torch** [tɔːtʃ] *n* torche *f*; (*BRIT: electric*) lampe *f* de poche

**tore** [tɔː*] *pt of* **tear**[1]

**torment** [*n* ˈtɔːment, *vb* tɔːˈment] *n* tourment *m* ♦ *vt* tourmenter; (*fig: annoy*) harceler

**torn** [tɔːn] *pp of* **tear**[1]

**tornado** [tɔːˈneɪdəu] (*pl* **~es**) *n* tornade *f*

**torpedo** [tɔːˈpiːdəu] (*pl* **~es**) *n* torpille *f*

**torrent** [ˈtɒrnt] *n* torrent *m*; **~ial** [tɔːˈrenʃl] *adj* torrentiel(le)

**tortoise** [ˈtɔːtəs] *n* tortue *f*; **~shell** *adj* en écaille

**torture** [ˈtɔːtʃə*] *n* torture *f* ♦ *vt* torturer

**Tory** [ˈtɔːrɪ] (*BRIT: POL*) *adj, n* tory (*m/f*), conservateur(-trice)

**toss** [tɒs] *vt* lancer, jeter; (*pancake*) faire sauter; (*head*) rejeter en arrière; **to ~ a coin** jouer à pile ou face; **to ~ up for sth** jouer qch à pile ou face; **to ~ and turn** (*in bed*) se tourner et se retourner

**tot** [tɒt] *n* (*BRIT: drink*) petit verre; (*child*)

bambin m

**total** ['təutl] adj total(e) ♦ n total m ♦ vt (add up) faire le total de, additionner; (amount to) s'élever à; **~ly** adv totalement

**totter** ['tɒtə'] vi chanceler

**touch** [tʌtʃ] n contact m, toucher m; (sense, also skill: of pianist etc) toucher ♦ vt toucher; (tamper with) toucher à; ~ of (fig) un petit peu de; une touche de; **to get in ~ with** prendre contact avec; **to lose ~** (friends) se perdre de vue; ~ **on** vt fus (topic) effleurer, aborder; ~ **up** vt (paint) retoucher; **~-and-go** adj incertain(e); **~down** n atterrissage m; (on sea) amerrissage m; (US: FOOTBALL) touché-en-but m; **~ed** adj (moved) touché(e); **~ing** adj touchant(e), attendrissant(e); **~line** n (SPORT) (ligne f de) touche f; **~y** adj (person) susceptible

**tough** [tʌf] adj dur(e); (resistant) résistant(e), solide; (meat) dur, coriace; (firm) inflexible; (task) dur, pénible; **~en** vt (character) endurcir; (glass etc) renforcer

**toupee** ['tuːpeɪ] n postiche m

**tour** ['tuə'] n voyage m; (also: package ~) voyage organisé; (of town, museum) tour m, visite f; (by artist) tournée f ♦ vt visiter; **~ guide** n (person) guide m/f

**tourism** ['tuərɪzm] n tourisme m

**tourist** ['tuərɪst] n touriste m/f ♦ cpd touristique; ~ **office** n syndicat m d'initiative

**tournament** ['tuənəmənt] n tournoi m

**tousled** ['tauzld] adj (hair) ébouriffé(e)

**tout** [taut] vi: **to ~ for** essayer de racoler, racoler ♦ n (also: **ticket ~**) revendeur m de billets

**tow** [təu] vt remorquer; (caravan, trailer) tracter; **"on ~"** (BRIT) or **"in ~"** (US) (AUT) "véhicule en remorque"

**towel** ['tauəl] n serviette f (de toilette);

**~ling** n (fabric) tissu éponge m; ~ **rail** (US **towel rack**) n porte-serviettes m inv

**tower** ['tauə'] n tour f; ~ **block** (BRIT) n tour f (d'habitation); **~ing** adj très haut(e), imposant(e)

**town** [taun] n ville f; **to go to ~** aller en ville; (fig) y mettre le paquet; ~ **centre** n centre m de la ville, centre-ville m; ~ **council** n conseil municipal; ~ **hall** n ≈ mairie f; ~ **plan** n plan m de ville; ~ **planning** n urbanisme m

**towrope** ['təurəup] n (câble m de) remorque f

**tow truck** (US) n dépanneuse f

**toy** [tɔɪ] n jouet m; ~ **with** vt fus jouer avec; (idea) caresser

**trace** [treɪs] n trace f ♦ vt (draw) tracer, dessiner; (follow) suivre la trace de; (locate) retrouver; **tracing paper** n papier-calque m

**track** [træk] n (mark) trace f; (path: gen) chemin m, piste f; (: of bullet etc) trajectoire f; (: of suspect, animal) piste f; (RAIL) voie ferrée, rails mpl; (on tape, SPORT) piste; (on record) plage f ♦ vt suivre la trace or la piste de; **to keep ~ of** suivre; ~ **down** vt (prey) trouver et capturer; (sth lost) finir par retrouver; **~suit** n survêtement m

**tract** [trækt] n (of land) étendue f

**traction** ['trækʃən] n traction f; (MED): **in ~** en extension

**tractor** ['træktə'] n tracteur m

**trade** [treɪd] n commerce m; (skill, job) métier m ♦ vi faire du commerce ♦ vt (exchange): **to ~ sth (for sth)** échanger qch (contre qch); ~ **in** vt (old car etc) faire reprendre; ~ **fair** n foire(-exposition) commerciale; **~-in price** n prix m à la reprise; **~mark** n marque f de fabrique; **~ name** n nom m de marque; **~r** n commerçant(e), négociant(e); **~sman** (irreg) n (shopkeeper) commerçant; ~ **union** n syndicat m; **~ unionist** n syndicaliste m/f

**tradition** [trə'dɪʃən] n tradition f; **~al** adj traditionnel(le)

**traffic** ['træfɪk] n trafic m; (cars) circulation f ♦ vi: **to ~ in** (pej: liquor, drugs) faire le trafic de; **~ calming** n ralentissement m de la circulation; **~ circle** (US) n rond-point m; **~ jam** n embouteillage m; **~ lights** npl feux mpl (de signalisation); **~ warden** n contractuel(le)

**tragedy** ['trædʒədɪ] n tragédie f

**tragic** ['trædʒɪk] adj tragique

**trail** [treɪl] n (tracks) trace f, piste f; (path) chemin m, piste; (of smoke etc) traînée f ♦ vt traîner, tirer; (follow) suivre ♦ vi traîner; (in game, contest) être en retard; **~ behind** vi traîner, être à la traîne; **~er** n (AUT) remorque f; (US) caravane f; (CINEMA) bande-annonce f; **~er truck** (US) n (camion m à) semi-remorque m

**train** [treɪn] n train m; (in underground) rame f; (of dress) traîne f ♦ vt (apprentice, doctor etc) former; (sportsman) entraîner; (dog) dresser; (memory) exercer; (point: gun etc): **to ~ sth on** braquer qch sur ♦ vi suivre une formation; (SPORT) s'entraîner; **one's ~ of thought** le fil de sa pensée; **~ed** adj qualifié(e), qui a reçu une formation; (animal) dressé(e); **~ee** [treɪ'niː] n stagiaire m/f; (in trade) apprenti(e); **~er** n (SPORT: coach) entraîneur(-euse); (: shoe) chaussure f de sport; (of dogs etc) dresseur (-euse); **~ing** n formation f; entraînement m; **in ~ing** (SPORT) à l'entraînement; (fit) en forme; **~ing college** n école professionnelle; (for teachers) ≈ école normale; **~ing shoes** npl chaussures fpl de sport

**trait** [treɪt] n trait m (de caractère)

**traitor** ['treɪtər] n traître m

**tram** [træm] (BRIT) n (also: **~car**) tram(way) m

**tramp** [træmp] n (person) vagabond(e), clochard(e); (inf: pej: woman): **to be a ~** être coureuse ♦ vi marcher d'un pas lourd

**trample** ['træmpl] vt: **to ~ (underfoot)**

piétiner

**trampoline** ['træmpəliːn] n trampoline m

**tranquil** ['træŋkwɪl] adj tranquille; **~lizer** (US **tranquilizer**) n (MED) tranquillisant m

**transact** [træn'zækt] vt (business) traiter; **~ion** n transaction f

**transatlantic** ['trænzət'læntɪk] adj transatlantique

**transfer** [n 'trænsfər, vb træns'fɜːr] n (gen, also SPORT) transfert m; (POL: of power) passation f; (picture, design) décalcomanie f; (: stick-on) autocollant m ♦ vt transférer; passer; **to ~ the charges** (BRIT: TEL) téléphoner en P.C.V.; **~ desk** n (AVIAT) guichet m de transit

**transform** [træns'fɔːm] vt transformer; **~ation** n transformation f

**transfusion** [træns'fjuːʒən] n transfusion f

**transient** ['trænzɪənt] adj transitoire, éphémère

**transistor** [træn'zɪstər] n (~ radio) transistor m

**transit** ['trænzɪt] n: **in ~** en transit

**transitive** ['trænzɪtɪv] adj (LING) transitif(-ive)

**transit lounge** n salle f de transit

**translate** [trænz'leɪt] vt traduire; **translation** n traduction f; **translator** n traducteur(-trice)

**transmission** [trænz'mɪʃən] n transmission f

**transmit** [trænz'mɪt] vt transmettre; (RADIO, TV) émettre

**transparency** [træns'pɛərnsɪ] n (of glass etc) transparence f; (BRIT: PHOT) diapositive f

**transparent** [træns'pærnt] adj transparent(e)

**transpire** [træns'paɪər] vi (turn out): **it ~d that ...** on a appris que ...; (happen) arriver

**transplant** [vb træns'plɑːnt, n 'trænsplɑːnt] vt transplanter; (seedlings) repiquer ♦ n (MED) transplantation f

**transport** [n 'trænspɔːt, vb træns'pɔːt]

*n* transport *m*; (car) moyen *m* de transport, voiture ♦ *vt* transporter; **~ation** ['trænspɔː'teɪʃən] *n* transport *m* (means of transportation) moyen *m* de transport; **~ café** (BRIT) *n* ≃ restaurant *m* de routiers

**trap** [træp] *n* (snare, trick) piège *m*; (carriage) cabriolet *m* ♦ *vt* prendre au piège; (confine) coincer; **~ door** *n* trappe *f*

**trapeze** [trə'piːz] *n* trapèze *m*

**trappings** ['træpɪŋz] *npl* ornements *mpl*; attributs *mpl*

**trash** [træʃ] (pej) *n* (goods) camelote *f*; (nonsense) sottises *fpl*; **~ can** (US) *n* poubelle *f*; **~y** (inf) adj de camelote; (novel) de quatre sous

**trauma** ['trɔːmə] *n* traumatisme *m*; **~tic** [trɔː'mætɪk] adj traumatisant(e)

**travel** ['trævl] *n* voyage(s) *m(pl)* ♦ *vi* voyager; (news, sound) circuler, se propager ♦ *vt* (distance) parcourir; **~ agency** *n* agence *f* de voyages; **~ agent** *n* agent *m* de voyages; **~ler** (US **traveler**) *n* voyageur(-euse); **~ler's cheque** (US **traveler's check**) *n* chèque *m* de voyage; **~ling** (US **traveling**) *n* voyage(s) *m(pl)*; **~ sickness** *n* mal *m* de la route (or de mer or de l'air)

**trawler** ['trɔːləʳ] *n* chalutier *m*

**tray** [treɪ] *n* (for carrying) plateau *m*; (on desk) corbeille *f*

**treacherous** ['tretʃərəs] adj (person, look) traître(-esse); (ground, tide) dont il faut se méfier

**treacle** ['triːkl] *n* mélasse *f*

**tread** [tred] (pt **trod**, pp **trodden**) *n* pas *m*; (sound) bruit *m* de pas; (of tyre) chape *f*, bande *f* de roulement ♦ *vi* marcher; **~ on** *vt* fus marcher sur

**treason** ['triːzn] *n* trahison *f*

**treasure** ['treʒəʳ] *n* trésor *m* ♦ *vt* (value) tenir beaucoup à; **~r** *n* trésorier(-ère); **treasury** *n*: **the Treasury**, (US) **the Treasury Department** le ministère des Finances

**treat** [triːt] *n* petit cadeau, petite surpri-

se ♦ *vt* traiter; **to ~ sb to sth** offrir qch à qn

**treatment** *n* traitement *m*

**treaty** ['triːtɪ] *n* traité *m*

**treble** ['trebl] adj triple ♦ *vt*, *vi* tripler; **~ clef** *n* (MUS) clé *f* de sol

**tree** [triː] *n* arbre *m*

**trek** [trek] *n* (long) voyage; (on foot) (longue) marche, tirée *f*

**tremble** ['trembl] *vi* trembler

**tremendous** [trɪ'mendəs] adj (enormous) énorme, fantastique; (excellent) formidable

**tremor** ['tremɔʳ] *n* tremblement *m*; (also: **earth ~**) secousse *f* sismique

**trench** [trentʃ] *n* tranchée *f*

**trend** [trend] *n* (tendency) tendance *f*; (of events) cours *m*; (fashion) mode *f*; **~y** adj (idea, person) dans le vent; (clothes) dernier cri *inv*

**trespass** ['trespəs] *vi*: **to ~ on** s'introduire sans permission dans; **"no ~ing"** "propriété privée", "défense d'entrer"

**trestle** ['tresl] *n* tréteau *m*

**trial** ['traɪəl] *n* (LAW) procès *m*, jugement *m*; (test of machine etc) essai *m*; **~s** *npl* (unpleasant experiences) épreuves *fpl*; **to be on ~** (LAW) passer en jugement; **by ~ and error** par tâtonnements; **~ period** *n* période d'essai

**triangle** ['traɪæŋgl] *n* (MATH, MUS) triangle *m*; **triangular** [traɪ'æŋgjuləʳ] adj triangulaire

**tribe** [traɪb] *n* tribu *f*; **~sman** (irreg) *n* membre *m* d'une tribu

**tribunal** [traɪ'bjuːnl] *n* tribunal *m*

**tributary** ['trɪbjutərɪ] *n* (river) affluent *m*

**tribute** ['trɪbjuːt] *n* tribut *m*, hommage *m*; **to pay ~ to** rendre hommage à

**trick** [trɪk] *n* (magic ~) tour *m*; (joke, prank) tour, farce *f*; (skill, knack) astuce *f*, truc *m*; (CARDS) levée *f* ♦ *vt* attraper, rouler; **to play a ~ on sb** jouer un tour à qn; **that should do the ~** ça devrait faire l'affaire; **~ery** *n* ruse *f*

**trickle** ['trɪkl] *n* (of water etc) filet *m*

♦ vi couler en un filet or goutte à goutte

**tricky** ['trɪkɪ] adj difficile, délicat(e)

**tricycle** ['traɪsɪkl] n tricycle m

**trifle** ['traɪfl] n bagatelle f; (CULIN) ≃ diplomate m ♦ adv: **a ~ long** un peu long; **trifling** adj insignifiant(e)

**trigger** ['trɪɡə*] n (of gun) gâchette f; ~ **off** vt déclencher

**trim** [trɪm] adj (house, garden) bien tenu(e); (figure) svelte ♦ n (haircut etc) légère coupe; (on car) garnitures fpl ♦ vt (cut) couper légèrement; (NAUT: a sail) gréer; (decorate): **to ~ (with)** décorer (de); **~mings** npl (CULIN) garniture f

**trinket** ['trɪŋkɪt] n bibelot m; (piece of jewellery) colifichet m

**trip** [trɪp] n voyage m; (excursion) excursion f; (stumble) faux pas ♦ vi faire un faux pas, trébucher; **on a ~** en voyage; ~ **up** vi trébucher ♦ vt faire un croc-en-jambe à

**tripe** [traɪp] n (CULIN) tripes fpl; (pej: rubbish) idioties fpl

**triple** ['trɪpl] adj triple; **~ts** npl triplés (-ées); **triplicate** ['trɪplɪkət] n: **in triplicate** en trois exemplaires

**tripod** ['traɪpɒd] n trépied m

**trite** [traɪt] (pej) adj banal(e)

**triumph** ['traɪʌmf] n triomphe m ♦ vi: **to ~ (over)** triompher (de)

**trivia** ['trɪvɪə] (pej) npl futilités fpl; **~l** adj insignifiant(e); (commonplace) banal(e)

**trod** [trɒd] pt of **tread**; **~den** pp of **tread**

**trolley** ['trɒlɪ] n chariot m

**trombone** [trɒm'bəun] n trombone m

**troop** [tru:p] n bande f, groupe m ♦ vi: ~ **in/out** entrer/sortir en groupe; **~s** npl (MIL) troupes fpl; (: men) hommes mpl, soldats mpl; **~ing the colour** (BRIT) n (ceremony) le salut au drapeau

**trophy** ['trəufɪ] n trophée m

**tropic** ['trɒpɪk] n tropique m; **~al** adj tropical(e)

**trot** [trɒt] n trot m ♦ vi trotter; **on the ~** (BRIT: fig) d'affilée

**trouble** ['trʌbl] n difficulté(s) f(pl), problème(s) m(pl); (worry) ennuis mpl, soucis mpl; (bother, effort) peine f; (POL) troubles mpl; (MED): **stomach etc ~** troubles gastriques etc ♦ vt (disturb) déranger, gêner; (worry) inquiéter ♦ vi: **to ~ to do** prendre la peine de faire; **~s** npl (POL etc) troubles mpl; (personal) ennuis, soucis; **to be in ~** avoir des ennuis; (ship, climber etc) être en difficulté; **what's the ~?** qu'est-ce qui ne va pas?; **~d** adj (person) inquiet(-ète); (epoch, life) agité(e); **~maker** n élément perturbateur, fauteur de troubles; **~shooter** n (POL etc) médiateur m; **~some** adj (child) fatigant(e), difficile; (cough etc) gênant(e)

**trough** [trɒf] n (also: **drinking ~**) abreuvoir m; (also: **feeding ~**) auge f; (depression) creux m

**trousers** ['trauzəz] npl pantalon m; **short ~** culottes courtes

**trout** [traut] n inv truite f

**trowel** ['trauəl] n truelle f; (garden tool) déplantoir m

**truant** ['truənt] (BRIT) n: **to play ~** faire l'école buissonnière

**truce** [tru:s] n trêve f

**truck** [trʌk] n camion m; (RAIL) wagon m à plate-forme; ~ **driver** n camionneur m; ~ **farm** (US) n jardin maraîcher m

**true** [tru:] adj (accurate) exact(e); (genuine) vrai, véritable; (faithful) fidèle; **to come ~** se réaliser

**truffle** ['trʌfl] n truffe f

**truly** ['tru:lɪ] adv vraiment, réellement; (truthfully) sans mentir; see also **yours**

**trump** [trʌmp] n (also: ~ **card**) atout m

**trumpet** ['trʌmpɪt] n trompette f

**truncheon** ['trʌntʃən] (BRIT) n bâton m (d'agent de police); matraque f

**trundle** ['trʌndl] vt, vi: **to ~ along** rouler lentement et bruyamment

**trunk** [trʌŋk] n (of tree, person) tronc m; (of elephant) trompe f; (case) malle f; (US: AUT) coffre m; **~s** npl (also: **swimming ~s**) maillot m or slip m de bain

**truss** [trʌs] vt: **to ~ (up)** ligoter

**trust** [trʌst] n confiance f; (LAW) fidéicommis m ♦ vt (rely on) avoir confiance en; (hope) espérer; (entrust): **to ~ sth to sb** confier qch à qn; **to take sth on ~** accepter qch les yeux fermés; **~ed** adj en qui l'on a confiance; **~ee** [trʌs'ti:] n (LAW) fidéicommissaire m/f; (of school etc) administrateur(-trice); **~ful, ~ing** adj confiant(e); **~worthy** adj digne de confiance

**truth** [tru:θ] n vérité f; **~ful** adj (person) qui dit la vérité; (answer) sincère

**try** [traɪ] n essai m, tentative f; (RUGBY) essai ♦ vt (attempt) essayer, tenter; (test: sth new: also: ~ out) essayer, tester; (LAW: person) juger; (strain) éprouver ♦ vi essayer; **to have a ~** essayer; **to ~ to do** essayer de faire; (seek) chercher à faire; **~ on** vt (clothes) essayer; **~ing** adj pénible

**T-shirt** ['ti:ʃə:t] n tee-shirt m

**T-square** ['ti:skwɛə'] n équerre f en T, té m

**tub** [tʌb] n cuve f; (for washing clothes) baquet m; (bath) baignoire f

**tuba** ['tju:bə] n tuba m

**tubby** ['tʌbɪ] adj rondelet(te)

**tube** [tju:b] n tube m; (BRIT: underground) métro m; (for tyre) chambre f à air

**tuberculosis** [tjubə:kju'ləusɪs] n tuberculose f

**TUC** n abbr (BRIT: Trades Union Congress) confédération des syndicats britanniques

**tuck** [tʌk] vt (put) mettre; **~ away** vt cacher, ranger; **~ in** vt rentrer; (BRIT) border ♦ vi (eat) manger de (bon appétit); **~ up** vt (child) border; **~ shop** (BRIT) n boutique f à provisions (dans une école)

**Tuesday** ['tju:zdɪ] n mardi m

**tuft** [tʌft] n touffe f

**tug** [tʌg] n (ship) remorqueur m ♦ vt tirer (sur); **~-of-war** n lutte f à la corde; (fig) lutte acharnée

**tuition** [tju:'ɪʃən] n (BRIT) leçons fpl; (: private ~) cours particuliers; (US: school fees) frais mpl de scolarité

**tulip** ['tju:lɪp] n tulipe f

**tumble** ['tʌmbl] n (fall) chute f, culbute f ♦ vi tomber, dégringoler; **to ~ to sth** (inf) réaliser qch; **~down** adj délabré(e); **~ dryer** (BRIT) n séchoir m à air chaud

**tumbler** ['tʌmblə'] n (glass) verre (droit), gobelet m

**tummy** ['tʌmɪ] (inf) n ventre m; **~ upset** n maux mpl de ventre

**tumour** ['tju:mə'] (US **tumor**) n tumeur f

**tuna** ['tju:nə] n inv (also: **~ fish**) thon m

**tune** [tju:n] n (melody) air m ♦ vt (MUS) accorder; (RADIO, TV, AUT) régler; **to be in/out of ~** (instrument) être accordé/désaccordé; (singer) chanter juste/faux; **to be in/out of ~ with** (fig) être en accord/désaccord avec; **~ in** vi (RADIO, TV): **to ~ in (to)** se mettre à l'écoute (de); **~ up** vi (musician) accorder son instrument; **~ful** adj mélodieux(-euse); **~r** n: **piano ~r** accordeur m (de pianos)

**tunic** ['tju:nɪk] n tunique f

**Tunisia** [tju:'nɪzɪə] n Tunisie f

**tunnel** ['tʌnl] n tunnel m; (in mine) galerie f ♦ vi percer un tunnel

**turbulence** ['tə:bjuləns] n (AVIAT) turbulence f

**tureen** [tə'ri:n] n (for soup) soupière f; (for vegetables) légumier m

**turf** [tə:f] n gazon m; (clod) motte f (de gazon) ♦ vt gazonner; **~ out** (inf) vt (person) jeter dehors

**Turk** [tə:k] n Turc (Turque)

**Turkey** ['tə:kɪ] n Turquie f

**turkey** ['tə:kɪ] n dindon m, dinde f

**Turkish** ['tə:kɪʃ] adj turc (turque) ♦ n (LING) turc m

**turmoil** ['tə:mɔɪl] n trouble m, bouleversement m; **in ~** en émoi, en effervescence

**turn** [tə:n] n tour m; (in road) tournant m; (of mind, events) tournure f; (performance) numéro m; (MED) crise f, attaque f ♦ vt tourner; (collar, steak) retourner; (change): to ~ sth into changer qch en ♦ vi (object, wind, milk) tourner; (person: look back) se (re)tourner; (reverse direction) faire demi-tour; (become) devenir; (age) atteindre; to ~ into se changer en; a good ~ un service; it gave me quite a ~ ça m'a fait un coup; "no left ~" (AUT) "défense de tourner à gauche"; it's your ~ c'est (à) votre tour; in ~ à son tour; à tour de rôle; to take ~s (at) se relayer (pour or à); ~ away vi se détourner ♦ vt (applicants) refuser; ~ back vi revenir, faire demi-tour ♦ vt (person, vehicle) faire faire demi-tour à; (clock) reculer; ~ down vt (refuse) rejeter, refuser; (reduce) baisser; (fold) rabattre; ~ in vi (inf: go to bed) aller se coucher ♦ vt (fold) rentrer; ~ off vi (from road) tourner ♦ vt (light, radio etc) éteindre; (tap) fermer; (engine) arrêter; ~ on vt (light, radio etc) allumer; (tap) ouvrir; (engine) mettre en marche; ~ out vt (light, gas) éteindre; (produce) produire ♦ vi (voters, troops etc) se présenter; to ~ out to be ... s'avérer ..., se révéler ...; ~ over vi (person) se retourner ♦ vt (object) retourner; (page) tourner; ~ round vi faire demi-tour; (rotate) tourner; ~ up (person) arriver, se pointer (inf); (lost object) être retrouvé(e) ♦ vt (collar) remonter; (radio, heater) mettre plus fort; ~ing n (in road) tournant m; ~ing point n (fig) tournant m, moment décisif

**turnip** ['tə:nɪp] n navet m

**turn**: ~out n (of voters) taux m de participation; ~over n (COMM: amount of money) chiffre m d'affaires; (: of goods) roulement m; (of staff) renouvellement m, changement m; ~pike (US) n autoroute f à péage; ~stile n tourniquet m (d'entrée); ~table n (on record player) platine f; ~up (BRIT) n (on trousers) revers m

**turpentine** ['tə:pəntɪn] n (also: turps)

(essence f de) térébenthine f

**turquoise** ['tə:kwɔɪz] n (stone) turquoise f ♦ adj turquoise inv

**turret** ['tʌrɪt] n tourelle f

**turtle** ['tə:tl] n tortue marine or d'eau douce; ~neck (sweater) n (BRIT) pullover m à col montant; (US) pullover m col roulé

**tusk** [tʌsk] n défense f

**tutor** ['tju:tə*] n (in college) directeur (-trice) d'études; (private teacher) précepteur(-trice); ~ial [tju:'tɔ:rɪəl] (SCOL) (séance f de) travaux mpl pratiques

**tuxedo** [tʌk'si:dəu] (US) n smoking m

**TV** n abbr (= television) télé f

**twang** [twæŋ] n (of instrument) son vibrant; (of voice) ton nasillard

**tweed** [twi:d] n tweed m

**tweezers** ['twi:zəz] npl pince f à épiler

**twelfth** [twelfθ] num douzième

**twelve** [twelv] num douze; at ~ (o'clock) à midi; (midnight) à minuit

**twentieth** ['twentiθ] num vingtième

**twenty** ['twentɪ] num vingt

**twice** [twaɪs] adv deux fois; ~ as much deux fois plus

**twiddle** ['twɪdl] vt, vi: to ~ (with) sth tripoter qch; to ~ one's thumbs (fig) se tourner les pouces

**twig** [twɪg] n brindille f ♦ vi (inf) piger

**twilight** ['twaɪlaɪt] n crépuscule m

**twin** [twɪn] adj, n jumeau(-elle) ♦ vt jumeler; ~-(bedded) room n chambre f à deux lits; ~ beds npl lits jumeaux

**twine** [twaɪn] n ficelle f ♦ vi (plant) s'enrouler

**twinge** [twɪndʒ] n (of pain) élancement m; a ~ of conscience un certain remords; a ~ of regret un pincement au cœur

**twinkle** ['twɪŋkl] vi scintiller; (eyes) pétiller

**twirl** [twə:l] vt faire tournoyer ♦ vi tournoyer

**twist** [twɪst] n torsion f, tour m; (in road) virage m; (in wire, flex) tortilla *m*; (*in story*) coup *m* de théâtre ♦ *vt* tordre; (*weave*) entortiller; (*roll around*) enrouler; (*fig*) déformer ♦ *vi* (*road, river*) serpenter

**twit** [twɪt] (*inf*) *n* crétin(e)

**twitch** [twɪtʃ] *n* (*pull*) coup sec, saccade *f*; (*nervous*) tic *m* ♦ *vi* se convulser; avoir un tic

**two** [tu:] *num* deux; **to put ~ and ~ together** (*fig*) faire le rapprochement; **~-door** *adj* (AUT) à deux portes; **~-faced** (*pej*) *adj* (*person*) faux (fausse); **~fold** *adv*: **to increase ~fold** doubler; **~piece (suit)** *n* (*man's*) costume *m* (deux-pièces); (*woman's*) deux-pièces *m inv*; **~-piece (swimsuit)** *n* (maillot *m* de bain) deux-pièces *m inv*; **~some** *n* (*people*) couple *m*; **~way** *adj* (*traffic*) dans les deux sens

**tycoon** [taɪˈku:n] *n*: (**business**) **~** gros homme d'affaires

**type** [taɪp] *n* (*category*) type *m*, genre *m*, espèce *f*; (*model, example*) type *m*, modèle *m*; (TYP) type, caractère *m* ♦ *vt* (*letter etc*) taper (à la machine); **~cast** *adj* (*actor*) condamné(e) à toujours jouer le même rôle; **~face** (TYP) *n* œil *m* de caractère; **~script** *n* texte dactylographié; **~writer** *n* machine *f* à écrire; **~written** *adj* dactylographié(e)

**typhoid** [ˈtaɪfɔɪd] *n* typhoïde *f*

**typical** [ˈtɪpɪkl] *adj* typique, caractéristique

**typing** [ˈtaɪpɪŋ] *n* dactylo(graphie) *f*

**typist** [ˈtaɪpɪst] *n* dactylo *m/f*

**tyrant** [ˈtaɪərnt] *n* tyran *m*

**tyre** [ˈtaɪəʳ] (*US* **tire**) *n* pneu *m*; **~ pressure** *n* pression *f* (de gonflage)

# U, u

**U-bend** [ˈju:bend] *n* (*in pipe*) coude *m*

**ubiquitous** [ju:ˈbɪkwɪtəs] *adj* omniprésent(e)

**udder** [ˈʌdəʳ] *n* pis *m*, mamelle *f*

**UFO** [ˈju:fəʊ] *n abbr* (= unidentified

flying object) OVNI *m*

**Uganda** [ju:ˈgændə] *n* Ouganda *m*

**ugh** [əːh] *excl* pouah!

**ugly** [ˈʌglɪ] *adj* laid(e), vilain(e); (*situation*) inquiétant(e)

**UHT** *abbr* (= ultra heat treated): **UHT milk** lait *m* UHT *or* longue conservation

**UK** *n abbr* = **United Kingdom**

**ulcer** [ˈʌlsəʳ] *n* ulcère *m*; (*also*: **mouth ~**) aphte *m*

**Ulster** [ˈʌlstəʳ] *n* Ulster *m*; (*inf*: *Northern Ireland*) Irlande *f* du Nord

**ulterior** [ʌlˈtɪərɪəʳ] *adj*: **~ motive** arrière-pensée *f*

**ultimate** [ˈʌltɪmət] *adj* ultime, final(e); (*authority*) suprême; **~ly** *adv* (*at last*) en fin de compte; (*fundamentally*) finalement

**ultrasound** [ˈʌltrəsaʊnd] *n* ultrason *m*

**umbilical cord** [ʌmˈbɪlɪkl-] *n* cordon ombilical

**umbrella** [ʌmˈbrelə] *n* parapluie *m*; (*for sun*) parasol *m*

**umpire** [ˈʌmpaɪəʳ] *n* arbitre *m*

**umpteen** [ʌmpˈti:n] *adj* je ne sais combien de; **~th** *adj*: **for the ~th time** pour la nième fois

**UN** *n abbr* = **United Nations**

**unable** [ʌnˈeɪbl] *adj*: **to be ~ to** ne pas pouvoir, être dans l'impossibilité de; (*incapable*) être incapable de

**unacceptable** [ʌnəkˈseptəbl] *adj* (*behaviour*) inadmissible; (*price, proposal*) inacceptable

**unaccompanied** [ʌnəˈkʌmpənɪd] *adj* (*child, lady*) non accompagné(e); (*song*) sans accompagnement

**unaccustomed** [ʌnəˈkʌstəmd] *adj*: **to be ~ to sth** ne pas avoir l'habitude de qch

**unanimous** [ju:ˈnænɪməs] *adj* unanime; **~ly** *adv* à l'unanimité

**unarmed** [ʌnˈɑ:md] *adj* (*without a weapon*) non armé(e); (*combat*) sans armes

**unattached** [ʌnəˈtætʃt] *adj* libre, sans attaches; (*part*) non attaché(e), indépendant(e)

**unattended** [ʌnə'tɛndɪd] adj (car, child, luggage) sans surveillance

**unattractive** [ʌnə'træktɪv] adj peu attrayant(e); (character) peu sympathique

**unauthorized** [ʌn'ɔ:θəraɪzd] adj non autorisé(e), sans autorisation

**unavoidable** [ʌnə'vɔɪdəbl] adj inévitable

**unaware** [ʌnə'wɛəʳ] adj: **to be ~ of** ignorer, être inconscient(e) de; **~s** adv à l'improviste, au dépourvu

**unbalanced** [ʌn'bælənst] adj déséquilibré(e); (report) peu objectif(-ive)

**unbearable** [ʌn'bɛərəbl] adj insupportable

**unbeatable** [ʌn'bi:təbl] adj imbattable

**unbeknown(st)** [ʌnbɪ'nəun(st)] adv: **~ to me/Peter** à mon insu/l'insu de Peter

**unbelievable** [ʌnbɪ'li:vəbl] adj incroyable

**unbend** [ʌn'bɛnd] (irreg) vi se détendre ♦ vt (wire) redresser, détordre

**unbiased** [ʌn'baɪəst] adj impartial(e)

**unborn** [ʌn'bɔ:n] adj à naître, qui n'est pas encore né(e)

**unbreakable** [ʌn'breɪkəbl] adj incassable

**unbroken** [ʌn'brəukən] adj intact(e); (fig) continu(e), ininterrompu(e)

**unbutton** [ʌn'bʌtn] vt déboutonner

**uncalled-for** [ʌn'kɔ:ldfɔ:ʳ] adj déplacé(e), injustifié(e)

**uncanny** [ʌn'kænɪ] adj étrange, troublant(e)

**unceremonious** [ʌnsɛrɪ'məunɪəs] adj (abrupt, rude) brusque

**uncertain** [ʌn'sɜ:tn] adj incertain(e); (hesitant) hésitant(e); **in no ~ terms** sans équivoque possible; **~ty** n incertitude f, doute(s) m(pl)

**uncivilized** [ʌn'sɪvɪlaɪzd] adj (gen) non civilisé(e); (fig: behaviour etc) barbare; (hour) indue(e)

**uncle** ['ʌŋkl] n oncle m

**uncomfortable** [ʌn'kʌmfətəbl] adj inconfortable, peu confortable; (uneasy) mal à l'aise, gêné(e); (situation) désagréable

**uncommon** [ʌn'kɔmən] adj rare singulier(-ère), peu commun(e)

**uncompromising** [ʌn'kɔmprəmaɪzɪŋ] adj intransigeant(e), inflexible

**unconcerned** [ʌnkən'sɜ:nd] adj: **to be ~ (about)** ne pas s'inquiéter (de)

**unconditional** [ʌnkən'dɪʃənl] adj sans conditions

**unconscious** [ʌn'kɔnʃəs] adj sans connaissance, évanoui(e); (unaware): **~ of** inconscient(e) de ♦ n: **the ~** l'inconscient m; **~ly** adv inconsciemment

**uncontrollable** [ʌnkən'trəuləbl] adj indiscipliné(e); (temper, laughter) irrépressible

**unconventional** [ʌnkən'vɛnʃənl] adj peu conventionnel(le)

**uncouth** [ʌn'ku:θ] adj grossier(-ère), fruste

**uncover** [ʌn'kʌvəʳ] vt découvrir

**undecided** [ʌndɪ'saɪdɪd] adj indécis(e), irrésolu(e)

**under** [ʌndəʳ] prep sous; (less than) (de) moins de; au-dessous de; (according to) selon, en vertu de ♦ adv au-dessous; en dessous; **~ there** là-dessous; **~ repair** (en cours de réparation; **~age** adj (person) qui n'a pas l'âge réglementaire; **~carriage** n (AVIAT) train m d'atterrissage; **~charge** vt ne pas faire payer assez à; **~coat** n (paint) couche f de fond; **~cover** adj secret(-ète), clandestin(e); **~current** n courant m ou sentiment sous-jacent; **~cut** (irreg) vt vendre moins cher que; **~dog** n opprimé m; **~done** adj (CULIN) saignant(e); (pej) pas assez cuit(e); **~estimate** vt sous-estimer; **~fed** adj sous-alimenté(e); **~foot** adv sous les pieds; **~go** (irreg) vt subir; (treatment) suivre; **~graduate** n étudiant(e) (qui prépare la licence); **~ground** n (BRIT: railway) métro m; (POL) clandestinité f ♦ adj clandestin(e); (fig) clandestin ♦ adv dans la clandestinité, clandestinement; **~growth** n broussailles fpl, sous-bois m; **~hand(ed)** adj (fig: behaviour, method etc) en dessous; **~lie** (irreg) vt être à la base de; **~line** vt souligner; **~mine** vt saper, miner; **~neath** adv (en) dessous ♦ prep sous, au-dessous de; **~paid** adj sous-payé(e); **~pants** npl caleçon m, slip m; **~pass** (BRIT) n passage souterrain; (on motorway) passage inférieur; **~privileged** adj défavorisé(e), économiquement faible; **~rate** vt sous-estimer; **~shirt** (US) n tricot de corps; **~shorts** (US) npl caleçon m, slip m; **~side** n dessous m; **~skirt** (BRIT) n jupon m

**understand** [ʌndəˈstænd] (irreg: like stand) vt, vi comprendre; **I ~ that ...** je me suis laissé dire que ...; je crois comprendre que ...; **~able** adj compréhensible; **~ing** adj compréhensif(-ive) ♦ n compréhension f; (agreement) accord m

**understatement** [ˈʌndəsteitmənt] n: **that's an ~** c'est (bien) peu dire, le terme est faible

**understood** [ʌndəˈstud] pt, pp of **understand** ♦ adj entendu(e); (implied) sous-entendu(e)

**understudy** [ˈʌndəstʌdɪ] n doublure f

**undertake** [ʌndəˈteik] (irreg) vt entreprendre; se charger de; **to ~ to do sth** s'engager à faire qch

**undertaker** [ˈʌndəteikəʳ] n entrepreneur m des pompes funèbres, croquemort m

**undertaking** [ˈʌndəteikɪŋ] n entreprise f; (promise) promesse f

**under-**: **~tone** n: **in an ~tone** à mi-voix; **~water** adv sous l'eau ♦ adj sous-marin(e); **~wear** n sous-vêtements mpl; (women's only) dessous mpl; **~world** n (of crime) milieu m, pègre f; **~write** vt (INSURANCE) assureur m

**undies** [ˈʌndɪz] (inf) npl dessous mpl, lingerie f

**undiplomatic** [ˈʌndɪpləˈmætɪk] adj peu diplomatique

**undo** [ʌnˈduː] (irreg) vt défaire; **~ing** n ruine f, perte f

**undoubted** [ʌnˈdautɪd] adj indubitable, certain(e); **~ly** adv sans aucun doute

**undress** [ʌnˈdres] vi se déshabiller

**undue** [ʌnˈdjuː] adj indu(e), excessif(-ive)

**undulating** [ˈʌndjuleitɪŋ] adj ondoyant(e), onduleux(-euse)

**unduly** [ʌnˈdjuːlɪ] adv trop, excessivement

**unearth** [ʌnˈɜːθ] vt déterrer; (fig) dénicher

**unearthly** [ʌnˈɜːθlɪ] adj (hour) indu(e), impossible

**uneasy** [ʌnˈiːzɪ] adj mal à l'aise, gêné(e); (worried) inquiet(-ète); (feeling) désagréable; (peace, truce) fragile

**uneconomic(al)** [ˈʌnɪkəˈnɔmɪk(l)] adj peu économique

**uneducated** [ʌnˈedjukeitɪd] adj (person) sans instruction

**unemployed** [ʌnɪmˈplɔid] adj sans travail, en or au chômage ♦ n: **the ~** les chômeurs mpl; **unemployment** n chômage m

**unending** [ʌnˈendɪŋ] adj interminable, sans fin

**unerring** [ʌnˈɜːrɪŋ] adj infaillible, sûr(e)

**uneven** [ʌnˈiːvn] adj inégal(e); (quality, work) irrégulier(-ère)

**unexpected** [ʌnɪksˈpektɪd] adj inattendu(e), imprévu(e); **~ly** [ʌnɪksˈpektɪdlɪ] adv (arrive) à l'improviste; (succeed) contre toute attente

**unfailing** [ʌnˈfeiliŋ] adj inépuisable; (remedy) infaillible

**unfair** [ʌnˈfeəʳ] adj: **~ (to)** injuste (envers)

**unfaithful** [ʌnˈfeiθful] adj infidèle

**unfamiliar** [ʌnfəˈmiliəʳ] adj étrange, inconnu(e); **to be ~ with** mal connaître

**unfashionable** [ʌnˈfæʃnəbl] adj

(clothes) démodé(e); (place) peu chic inv

**unfasten** [ʌn'fɑːsn] vt défaire; détacher; (open) ouvrir

**unfavourable** [ʌn'feivrəbl] (US **unfavorable**) adj défavorable

**unfeeling** [ʌn'fiːlɪŋ] adj insensible, dur(e)

**unfinished** [ʌn'fɪnɪʃt] adj inachevé(e)

**unfit** [ʌn'fɪt] adj en mauvaise santé; pas en forme; (incompetent): ~ **(for)** impropre (à); (work, service) inapte (à)

**unfold** [ʌn'fəuld] vt déplier ♦ vi se dérouler

**unforeseen** [ʌnfɔː'siːn] adj imprévu(e)

**unforgettable** [ʌnfə'getəbl] adj inoubliable

**unfortunate** [ʌn'fɔːtʃnət] adj malheureux(-euse); (event, remark) malencontreux(-euse); **~ly** adv malheureusement

**unfounded** [ʌn'faundɪd] adj sans fondement

**unfriendly** [ʌn'frendlɪ] adj inamical(e), peu aimable

**ungainly** [ʌn'geinlɪ] adj gauche, dégingandé(e)

**ungodly** [ʌn'gɔdlɪ] adj (hour) indu(e)

**ungrateful** [ʌn'greitful] adj ingrat(e)

**unhappiness** [ʌn'hæpɪnɪs] n tristesse f, peine f

**unhappy** [ʌn'hæpɪ] adj triste, malheureux(-euse); ~ **about** or **with** (arrangements etc) mécontent(e) de, peu satisfait(e) de

**unharmed** [ʌn'hɑːmd] adj indemne, sain(e) et sauf (sauve)

**UNHCR** n abbr (= United Nations High Commission for refugees) HCR m

**unhealthy** [ʌn'helθɪ] adj malsain(e); (person) maladif(-ive)

**unheard-of** [ʌn'həːdɔv] adj inouï(e), sans précédent

**unhurt** [ʌn'həːt] adj indemne

**unidentified** [ʌnai'dentifaid] adj non identifié(e); see also **UFO**

**uniform** ['juːnifɔːm] n uniforme m ♦ adj uniforme

**uninhabited** [ʌnin'hæbitid] adj inhabité(e)

**unintentional** [ʌnin'tenʃənəl] adj involontaire

**union** ['juːnjən] n union f; (also: **trade ~**) syndicat m ♦ cpd du syndicat, syndical(e): **U~ Jack** n drapeau du Royaume-Uni

**unique** [juː'niːk] adj unique

**UNISON** ['juːnisn] n grand syndicat des services publics en Grande-Bretagne

**unison** ['juːnisn] n: **in ~** (sing) à l'unisson; (say) en chœur

**unit** ['juːnit] n unité f; (section: of furniture etc) élément m, bloc m; **kitchen ~** élément de cuisine

**unite** [juː'nait] vt unir ♦ vi s'unir; **~d** adj uni(e); unifié(e); (effort) conjugué(e); **U~d Kingdom** n Royaume-Uni m; **U~d Nations (Organization)** n Organisation f des Nations Unies; **U~d States (of America)** n États-Unis mpl

**unit trust** (BRIT) n fonds commun de placement

**unity** ['juːniti] n unité f

**universal** [juːni'vəːsl] adj universel(le)

**universe** ['juːnivəːs] n univers m

**university** [juːni'vəːsiti] n université f

**unjust** [ʌn'dʒʌst] adj injuste

**unkempt** [ʌn'kempt] adj négligé(e), débraillé(e); (hair) mal peigné(e)

**unkind** [ʌn'kaind] adj peu gentil(le), méchant(e)

**unknown** [ʌn'nəun] adj inconnu(e)

**unlawful** [ʌn'lɔːful] adj illégal(e)

**unleaded** [ʌn'ledid] adj (petrol, fuel) sans plomb

**unleash** [ʌn'liːʃ] vt (fig) déchaîner, déclencher

**unless** [ʌn'les] conj: ~ **he leaves** à moins qu'il ne parte

**unlike** [ʌn'laik] adj dissemblable, différent(e) ♦ prep contrairement à

**unlikely** [ʌn'laikli] adj (happening) improbable; (explanation) invraisemblable

**unlimited** [ʌn'limitid] adj illimité(e)

**unlisted** ['ʌn'listid] (US) adj (TEL) sur la

liste rouge

**unload** [ʌnˈləud] vt décharger

**unlock** [ʌnˈlɔk] vt ouvrir

**unlucky** [ʌnˈlʌkɪ] adj (person) malchanceux(-euse); (object, number) qui porte malheur; **to be ~** (person) ne pas avoir de chance

**unmarried** [ʌnˈmærɪd] adj célibataire

**unmistak(e)able** [ʌnmɪsˈteɪkəbl] adj indubitable; qu'on ne peut pas ne pas reconnaître

**unmitigated** [ʌnˈmɪtɪɡeɪtɪd] adj non mitigé(e), absolu(e), pur(e)

**unnatural** [ʌnˈnætʃrəl] adj non naturel(le); (habit) contre nature

**unnecessary** [ʌnˈnesəsərɪ] adj inutile, superflu(e)

**unnoticed** [ʌnˈnəutɪst] adj: **(to go or pass) ~** (passer) inaperçu(e)

**UNO** n abbr = United Nations Organization

**unobtainable** [ʌnəbˈteɪnəbl] adj impossible à obtenir

**unobtrusive** [ʌnəbˈtruːsɪv] adj discret(-ète)

**unofficial** [ʌnəˈfɪʃl] adj (news) officieux(-euse); (REL) hétérodoxe

**unorthodox** [ʌnˈɔːθədɔks] adj peu orthodoxe; (REL) hétérodoxe

**unpack** [ʌnˈpæk] vi défaire sa valise ♦ vt (suitcase) défaire; (belongings) déballer

**unpalatable** [ʌnˈpælətəbl] adj (meal) mauvais(e); (truth) désagréable (à entendre)

**unparalleled** [ʌnˈpærəleld] adj incomparable, sans égal

**unpleasant** [ʌnˈpleznt] adj déplaisant(e), désagréable

**unplug** [ʌnˈplʌɡ] vt débrancher

**unpopular** [ʌnˈpɔpjulər] adj impopulaire

**unprecedented** [ʌnˈpresɪdentɪd] adj sans précédent

**unpredictable** [ʌnprɪˈdɪktəbl] adj imprévisible

**unprofessional** [ʌnprəˈfeʃənl] adj: ~

**conduct** manquement m aux devoirs de la profession

**UNPROFOR** n abbr (= United Nations Protection Force) FORPRONU f

**unqualified** [ʌnˈkwɔlɪfaɪd] adj (teacher) non diplômé(e), sans titres; (success, disaster) sans réserve, total(e)

**unquestionably** [ʌnˈkwestʃənəblɪ] adv incontestablement

**unravel** [ʌnˈrævl] vt démêler

**unreal** [ʌnˈrɪəl] adj irréel(le); (extraordinary) incroyable

**unrealistic** [ʌnrɪəˈlɪstɪk] adj irréaliste; peu réaliste

**unreasonable** [ʌnˈriːznəbl] adj qui n'est pas raisonnable

**unrelated** [ʌnrɪˈleɪtɪd] adj sans rapport; sans lien de parenté

**unreliable** [ʌnrɪˈlaɪəbl] adj sur qui (or quoi) on ne peut pas compter, peu fiable

**unremitting** [ʌnrɪˈmɪtɪŋ] adj inlassable, infatigable, acharné(e)

**unreservedly** [ʌnrɪˈzəːvɪdlɪ] adv sans réserve

**unrest** [ʌnˈrest] n agitation f, troubles mpl

**unroll** [ʌnˈrəul] vt dérouler

**unruly** [ʌnˈruːlɪ] adj indiscipliné(e)

**unsafe** [ʌnˈseɪf] adj (in danger) en danger; (journey, car) dangereux(-euse)

**unsaid** [ʌnˈsed] adj: **to leave sth ~** passer qch sous silence

**unsatisfactory** [ˈʌnsætɪsˈfæktərɪ] adj peu satisfaisant(e)

**unsavoury** [ʌnˈseɪvərɪ] (US **unsavory**) adj (fig) peu recommandable

**unscathed** [ʌnˈskeɪðd] adj indemne

**unscrew** [ʌnˈskruː] vt dévisser

**unscrupulous** [ʌnˈskruːpjuləs] adj sans scrupules

**unsettled** [ʌnˈsetld] adj perturbé(e); instable

**unshaven** [ʌnˈʃeɪvn] adj non or mal rasé(e)

**unsightly** [ʌnˈsaɪtlɪ] adj disgracieux(-euse), laid(e)

**unskilled** [ʌnˈskɪld] *adj*: ~ **worker** manœuvre *m*

**unspeakable** [ʌnˈspiːkəbl] *adj* indicible; *(awful)* innommable

**unstable** [ʌnˈsteɪbl] *adj* instable

**unsteady** [ʌnˈstedɪ] *adj* mal assuré(e), chancelant(e), instable

**unstuck** [ʌnˈstʌk] *adj*: **to come** ~ se décoller; *(plan)* tomber à l'eau

**unsuccessful** [ʌnsəkˈsesful] *adj (attempt)* infructueux(-euse), vain(e); *(writer, proposal)* qui n'a pas de succès; **to be** ~ *(in attempting sth)* ne pas réussir; ne pas avoir de succès; *(application)* ne pas être retenu(e)

**unsuitable** [ʌnˈsuːtəbl] *adj* qui ne convient pas, peu approprié(e); inopportun(e)

**unsure** [ʌnˈʃuəʳ] *adj* pas sûr(e); **to be** ~ **of o.s.** manquer de confiance en soi

**unsuspecting** [ʌnsəˈspektɪŋ] *adj* qui ne se doute de rien

**unsympathetic** [ˈʌnsɪmpəˈθetɪk] *adj (person)* antipathique; *(attitude)* peu compatissant(e)

**untapped** [ʌnˈtæpt] *adj (resources)* inexploité(e)

**unthinkable** [ʌnˈθɪŋkəbl] *adj* impensable, inconcevable

**untidy** [ʌnˈtaɪdɪ] *adj (room)* en désordre; *(appearance, person)* débraillé(e); *(person: in character)* sans ordre, désordonné

**untie** [ʌnˈtaɪ] *vt (knot, parcel)* défaire; *(prisoner, dog)* détacher

**until** [ʌnˈtɪl] *prep* jusqu'à; *(after negative)* avant ♦ *conj* jusqu'à ce que +*sub*; *(in past, after negative)* avant que +*sub*; ~ **he comes** jusqu'à ce qu'il vienne, jusqu'à son arrivée; ~ **now** jusqu'à présent, jusqu'ici; ~ **then** jusque-là

**untimely** [ʌnˈtaɪmlɪ] *adj* inopportun(e); *(death)* prématuré(e)

**untold** [ʌnˈtəʊld] *adj (story)* jamais raconté(e); *(wealth)* incalculable; *(joy, suffering)* indescriptible

**untoward** [ʌntəˈwɔːd] *adj* fâcheux

(-euse), malencontreux(-euse)

**unused¹** [ʌnˈjuːzd] *adj (clothes)* neuf (neuve)

**unused²** [ʌnˈjuːst] *adj*: **to be** ~ **to sth/to doing sth** ne pas avoir l'habitude de qch/de faire qch

**unusual** [ʌnˈjuːʒuəl] *adj* insolite, exceptionnel(le), rare

**unveil** [ʌnˈveɪl] *vt* dévoiler

**unwanted** [ʌnˈwɒntɪd] *adj (child, pregnancy)* non désiré(e); *(clothes etc)* à donner

**unwelcome** [ʌnˈwelkəm] *adj* importun(e); *(news)* fâcheux(-euse)

**unwell** [ʌnˈwel] *adj* souffrant(e); **to feel** ~ ne pas se sentir bien

**unwieldy** [ʌnˈwiːldɪ] *adj (object)* difficile à manier; *(system)* lourd(e)

**unwilling** [ʌnˈwɪlɪŋ] *adj*: **to be** ~ **to do** ne pas vouloir faire; ~**ly** *adv* à contrecœur, contre son gré

**unwind** [ʌnˈwaɪnd] *(irreg) vt* dérouler ♦ *vi (relax)* se détendre

**unwise** [ʌnˈwaɪz] *adj* irréfléchi(e), imprudent(e)

**unwitting** [ʌnˈwɪtɪŋ] *adj* involontaire

**unworkable** [ʌnˈwəːkəbl] *adj (plan)* impraticable

**unworthy** [ʌnˈwəːðɪ] *adj* indigne

**unwrap** [ʌnˈræp] *vt* défaire; ouvrir

**unwritten** [ʌnˈrɪtn] *adj (agreement)* tacite

---

KEYWORD

**up** [ʌp] *prep*: **he went up the stairs/the hill** il a monté l'escalier/la colline; **the cat was up a tree** le chat était dans un arbre; **they live further up the street** ils habitent plus haut dans la rue

♦ *adv* 1 *(upwards, higher)*: **up in the sky/the mountains** (là-haut) dans le ciel/les montagnes; **put it a bit higher up** mettez-le un peu plus haut; **up there** là-haut; **up above** au-dessus

2: **to be up** *(out of bed)* être levé(e); *(prices)* avoir augmenté *or* monté

3: up to (as far as) jusqu'à; up to now jusqu'à présent

4: to be up to (depending on): it's up to you c'est à vous de décider; (equal to): he's not up to it (job, task etc) il n'en est pas capable; (inf: be doing): what is he up to? qu'est-ce qu'il fait bien faire

♦ n: ups and downs hauts et bas mpl

up-and-coming [ʌpandˈkʌmɪŋ] adj plein(e) d'avenir or de promesses

upbringing [ˈʌpbrɪŋɪŋ] n éducation f

update [ʌpˈdeɪt] vt mettre à jour

upgrade [ʌpˈgreɪd] vt (house) moderniser; (job) revaloriser; (employee) promouvoir

upheaval [ʌpˈhiːvl] n bouleversement m; branle-bas m

uphill [ˈʌpˈhɪl] adj qui monte; (fig: task) difficile, pénible ♦ adv (face, look) en amont; to go ~ monter

uphold [ʌpˈhəuld] (irreg) vt (law, decision) maintenir

upholstery [ʌpˈhəulstərɪ] n rembourrage m; (cover) tissu m d'ameublement; (of car) garniture f

upkeep [ˈʌpkiːp] n entretien m

upon [əˈpɔn] prep sur

upper [ˈʌpəʳ] adj supérieur(e); du dessus ♦ n (of shoe) empeigne f; ~-class adj de la haute société, aristocratique; ~ hand n: to have the ~ hand avoir le dessus; ~most adj le (la) plus haut(e); what was ~most in my mind ce à quoi je pensais surtout; ~ sixth n terminale f

upright [ˈʌpraɪt] adj droit(e); vertical(e); (fig) droit, honnête

uprising [ˈʌpraɪzɪŋ] n soulèvement m, insurrection f

uproar [ˈʌprɔːʳ] n tumulte m; (protests) tempête f de protestations

uproot [ʌpˈruːt] vt déraciner

upset [n ˈʌpset, vb, adj ʌpˈset] (irreg: like set) n bouleversement m; (stomach ~) indigestion f ♦ vt (glass etc) renverser;

(plan) déranger; (person: offend) contrarier; (: grieve) faire de la peine à ♦ adj contrarié(e); peiné(e); (stomach) dérangé(e)

upshot [ˈʌpʃɔt] n résultat m

upside-down [ˈʌpsaɪdˈdaun] adv à l'envers; to turn ~ ~ mettre sens dessus dessous

upstairs [ʌpˈstɛəz] adv en haut ♦ adj (room) du dessus, d'en haut ♦ n: the ~ l'étage m

upstart [ˈʌpstɑːt] (pej) n parvenu(e)

upstream [ʌpˈstriːm] adv en amont

uptake [ˈʌpteɪk] n: to be quick/slow on the ~ comprendre vite/être lent à comprendre

uptight [ʌpˈtaɪt] (inf) adj très tendu(e), crispé(e)

up-to-date [ˈʌptəˈdeɪt] adj moderne; (information) très récent(e)

upturn [ˈʌptəːn] n (in luck) retournement m; (COMM: in market) hausse f

upward [ˈʌpwəd] adj ascendant(e); vers le haut; ~(s) adv vers le haut; ~(s) of 200 200 et plus

urban [ˈəːbən] adj urbain(e); ~ clearway n rue f à stationnement einterdit

urbane [əːˈbeɪn] adj urbain(e), courtois(e)

urchin [ˈəːtʃɪn] n polisson m

urge [əːdʒ] n besoin m; envie f; forte envie, désir m ♦ vt: to ~ sb to do exhorter qn à faire, pousser qn à faire; recommander vivement à qn de faire

urgency [ˈəːdʒənsɪ] n urgence f; (of tone) insistance f

urgent [ˈəːdʒənt] adj urgent(e); (tone) insistant(e), pressant(e)

urinal [ˈjuərɪnl] n urinoir m

urine [ˈjuərɪn] n urine f

urn [əːn] n urne f; (also: tea ~) fontaine f à thé

US n abbr = United States

us [ʌs] pron nous; see also me

USA n abbr = United States of America

use [n juːs, vb juːz] n emploi m, utilisa-

tion f; usage m; (~fulness) utilité f ♦ vt
se servir de, utiliser, employer; **in ~** en
usage; **out of ~** hors d'usage; **to be**
**of ~** servir, être utile; **it's no ~** ça ne
sert à rien; **she ~d to do it** elle le faisait (autrefois), elle avait coutume de le
faire; **~d: to be ~d to** avoir l'habitude de, être habitué(e) à; **~ up** vt finir,
épuiser; consommer; **~d** [ju:zd] adj
(car) d'occasion; **~ful** [ju:sful] adj utile; **~fulness** ut utilité f; **~less** [ju:slɪs]
adj inutile; (person: hopeless) nul(le); **~r**
[ju:zə⁎] n utilisateur(-trice), usager m;
**~r-friendly** (computer) convivial(e),
facile d'emploi

**usher** [ˈʌʃə⁎] n (at wedding ceremony)
placeur m; **~ette** [ʌʃəˈrɛt] n (in cinema)
ouvreuse f

**usual** [ˈju:ʒuəl] adj habituel(le); **as ~**
comme d'habitude; **~ly** [ˈju:ʒuəlɪ] adv
d'habitude, d'ordinaire

**utensil** [ju:ˈtɛnsl] n ustensile m

**uterus** [ˈju:tərəs] n utérus m

**utility** [ju:ˈtɪlɪtɪ] n utilité f; (also: **public**
**~**) service public; **~ room** n buanderie
f

**utmost** [ˈʌtməust] adj extrême, le (la)
plus grand(e) ♦ n: **to do one's ~** faire
tout son possible

**utter** [ˈʌtə⁎] adj total(e), complet(-ète)
♦ vt (words) prononcer, proférer;
(sounds) émettre; **~ance** n paroles fpl;
**~ly** adv complètement, totalement

**U-turn** [ˈju:ˈtɜ:n] n demi-tour m

# V, v

**v.** abbr = **verse**; **versus**; **volt**; (= vide)
voir

**vacancy** [ˈveɪkənsɪ] n (BRIT: job) poste
vacant; (room) chambre f disponible;
**"no vacancies"** "complet"

**vacant** [ˈveɪkənt] adj (seat etc) libre,
disponible; (expression) distrait(e)

**vacate** [vəˈkeɪt] vt quitter

**vacation** [vəˈkeɪʃən] n vacances fpl

**vaccinate** [ˈvæksɪneɪt] vt vacciner

**vacuum** [ˈvækjum] n vide m; **~ clean-**
**er** n aspirateur m; **~-packed** adj em-
ballé(e) sous vide

**vagina** [vəˈdʒaɪnə] n vagin m

**vagrant** [ˈveɪgrənt] n vagabond(e)

**vague** [veɪg] adj vague, imprécis(e);
(blurred: photo, outline) flou(e); **~ly** ad
vaguement

**vain** [veɪn] adj (useless) vain(e); (con
ceited) vaniteux(-euse); **in ~** en vain

**valentine** [ˈvæləntaɪn] n (also: **~ care**
carte f de la Saint-Valentin; (person
bien-aimé(e) (le jour de la Sain
Valentin); **V~'s day** n Saint-Valentin f

**valiant** [ˈvælɪənt] adj vaillant(e)

**valid** [ˈvælɪd] adj valable; (documen
valable, valide

**valley** [ˈvælɪ] n vallée f

**valour** [ˈvælə⁎] (US **valor**) n courage m

**valuable** [ˈvæljuəbl] adj (jewel) de v
leur; (time, help) précieux(-euse); **~s** n
objets mpl de valeur

**valuation** [væljuˈeɪʃən] n (price) est
mation f; (quality) appréciation f

**value** [ˈvæljuː] n valeur f ♦ vt (fix pric
évaluer, expertiser; (appreciate) appre
cier; **~ added tax** (BRIT) n taxe f à
valeur ajoutée; **~d** adj (person) esti
mé(e); (advice) précieux(-euse)

**valve** [vælv] n (in machine) soupape
valve f; (MED) valve, valvule f

**van** [væn] n (AUT) camionnette f

**vandal** [ˈvændl] n vandale m/f; **~ism**
vandalisme m; **~ize** vt saccager

**vanguard** [ˈvængɑːd] n (fig): **in the ~**
de à l'avant-garde de

**vanilla** [vəˈnɪlə] n vanille f

**vanish** [ˈvænɪʃ] vi disparaître

**vanity** [ˈvænɪtɪ] n vanité f

**vantage point** [ˈvɑːntɪdʒ-] n bonn
position

**vapour** [ˈveɪpə⁎] (US **vapor**) n vapeur
(on window) buée f

**variable** [ˈvɛərɪəbl] adj variable; (moo
changeant(e)

**variance** [ˈvɛərɪəns] n: **to be at**

**(with)** être en désaccord (avec); (facts) être en contradiction (avec)

**varicose** ['værɪkəus] adj: ~ **veins** varices fpl

**varied** ['veərɪd] adj varié(e), divers(e)

**variety** [və'raɪətɪ] n variété f; (quantity) nombre m, quantité f; ~ **show** n (spectacle m de) variétés fpl

**various** ['veərɪəs] adj divers(e), différent(e); (several) divers, plusieurs

**varnish** ['vɑːnɪʃ] n vernis m ♦ vt vernir

**vary** ['veərɪ] vt, vi varier, changer

**vase** [vɑːz] n vase m

**Vaseline** ® ['væsɪliːn] n vaseline f

**vast** [vɑːst] adj vaste, immense; (amount, success) énorme

**VAT** [væt] n abbr (= value added tax) TVA f

**vat** [væt] n cuve f

**vault** [vɔːlt] n (of roof) voûte f; (tomb) caveau m; (in bank) salle f des coffres; chambre forte ♦ vt (also: ~ **over**) sauter (d'un bond)

**vaunted** ['vɔːntɪd] adj: **much-~** tant vanté(e)

**VCR** n abbr = **video cassette recorder**

**VD** n abbr = **venereal disease**

**VDU** n abbr = **visual display unit**

**veal** [viːl] n veau m

**vegan** ['viːgən] n végétalien(ne)

**vegeburger** ['vedʒɪbəːgər] n burger végétarien

**vegetable** ['vedʒtəbl] n légume m ♦ adj végétal(e)

**vegetarian** [vedʒɪ'teərɪən] adj, n végétarien(ne)

**vehement** ['viːɪmənt] adj violent(e), impétueux(-euse); (impassioned) ardent(e)

**vehicle** ['viːɪkl] n véhicule m

**veil** [veɪl] n voile m

**vein** [veɪn] n veine f; (on leaf) nervure f

**velocity** [vɪ'lɔsɪtɪ] n vitesse f

**velvet** ['velvɪt] n velours m

**vending machine** ['vendɪŋ-] n distributeur m automatique

**veneer** [və'nɪər] n (on furniture) placage m; (fig) vernis m

**venereal** [vɪ'nɪərɪəl] adj: ~ **disease** maladie vénérienne

**Venetian blind** [vɪ'niːʃən-] n store vénitien

**vengeance** ['vendʒəns] n vengeance f; **with a ~** (fig) vraiment, pour de bon

**venison** ['venɪsn] n venaison f

**venom** ['venəm] n venin m

**vent** [vent] n conduit m d'aération; (in dress, jacket) fente f ♦ vt (fig: one's feelings) donner libre cours à

**ventilator** ['ventɪleɪtər] n ventilateur m

**ventriloquist** [ven'trɪləkwɪst] n ventriloque m/f

**venture** ['ventʃər] n entreprise f ♦ vt risquer, hasarder ♦ vi s'aventurer, se risquer

**venue** ['venjuː] n lieu m

**verb** [vɜːb] n verbe m; ~**al** adj verbal(e); (translation) littéral(e)

**verbatim** [vɜː'beɪtɪm] adj, adv mot pour mot

**verdict** ['vɜːdɪkt] n verdict m

**verge** [vɜːdʒ] n (BRIT) bord m, bas-côté m; "**soft ~s**" (BRIT: AUT) "accotement non stabilisé"; **on the ~ of doing** sur le point de faire; ~ **on** vt fus approcher de

**verify** ['verɪfaɪ] vt vérifier; (confirm) confirmer

**vermin** ['vɜːmɪn] npl animaux mpl nuisibles; (insects) vermine f

**vermouth** ['vɜːməθ] n vermouth m

**versatile** ['vɜːsətaɪl] adj polyvalent(e)

**verse** [vɜːs] n (poetry) vers mpl; (stanza) strophe f; (in Bible) verset m

**version** ['vɜːʃən] n version f

**versus** ['vɜːsəs] prep contre

**vertical** ['vɜːtɪkl] adj vertical(e) ♦ n verticale f

**vertigo** ['vɜːtɪgəu] n vertige m

**verve** [vɜːv] n brio m, enthousiasme m

**very** ['verɪ] adv très ♦ adj: **the ~ book which** le livre même que; **the ~ last** tout dernier; **at the ~ least** tout au moins; ~ **much** beaucoup

**vessel** ['vesl] n (ANAT, NAUT) vaisseau m; (container) récipient m

**vest** [vest] n (BRIT) tricot m de corps; (US: waistcoat) gilet m

**vested interest** n (COMM) droits acquis

**vet** [vet] n abbr (BRIT: veterinary surgeon) vétérinaire m/f ♦ vt examiner soigneusement

**veteran** ['vetərn] n vétéran m; (also: ~ **war** ~) ancien combattant

**veterinary surgeon** ['vetrɪnərɪ-] (BRIT), **veterinarian** [vetrɪˈneərɪən] (US) n vétérinaire m/f

**veto** ['viːtəu] (pl ~**es**) n veto m ♦ vt opposer son veto à

**vex** [veks] vt fâcher, contrarier; ~**ed** adj (question) controversé(e)

**via** ['vaɪə] prep par, via

**viable** ['vaɪəbl] adj viable

**vibrate** [vaɪˈbreɪt] vi vibrer

**vicar** ['vɪkə*] n pasteur m (de l'Église anglicane); ~**age** n presbytère m

**vicarious** [vɪˈkeərɪəs] adj indirect(e)

**vice** [vaɪs] n (evil) vice m; (TECH) étau m

**vice-** [vaɪs] prefix vice-

**vice squad** n ≈ brigade mondaine

**vice versa** ['vaɪsɪ'vɜːsə] adv vice versa

**vicinity** [vɪˈsɪnɪtɪ] n environs mpl, alentours mpl

**vicious** ['vɪʃəs] adj (remark) cruel(le), méchant(e); (blow) brutal(e); (dog) méchant(e), dangereux(-euse); (horse) vicieux(-euse); ~ **circle** n cercle vicieux

**victim** ['vɪktɪm] n victime f

**victor** ['vɪktə*] n vainqueur m

**Victorian** [vɪkˈtɔːrɪən] adj victorien(ne)

**victory** ['vɪktərɪ] n victoire f

**video** ['vɪdɪəu] cpd vidéo inv ♦ n (~ film) vidéo f; (also: ~ **cassette**) vidéocassette f; (also: ~ **cassette recorder**) magnétoscope m; ~ **tape** n bande f vidéo inv; (cassette) vidéocassette f; ~ **wall** n mur m d'images vidéo

**vie** [vaɪ] vi: to ~ with rivaliser avec

**Vienna** [vɪˈenə] n Vienne

**Vietnam** ['vjet'næm] n Viêt-Nam m,

Vietnam m; ~**ese** [vjetnə'miːz] adj vietnamien(ne) ♦ n inv Vietnamien(ne); (LING) vietnamien m

**view** [vjuː] n vue f; (opinion) avis m, vue f ♦ vt voir, regarder; (situation) considérer; (house) visiter; **in full ~ of** sous les yeux de; **in the weather/the fact that** étant donné le temps/que; **my ~** à mon avis; ~**er** n (TV) téléspectateur(-trice); ~**finder** n viseur m; ~**point** n point m de vue

**vigorous** ['vɪgərəs] adj vigoureux(-euse)

**vile** [vaɪl] adj (action) vil(e); (smell, food) abominable; (temper) massacrant(e)

**villa** ['vɪlə] n villa f

**village** ['vɪlɪdʒ] n village m; ~**r** n villageois(e)

**villain** ['vɪlən] n (scoundrel) scélérat m; (BRIT: criminal) bandit m; (in novel etc) traître m

**vindicate** ['vɪndɪkeɪt] vt (person) innocenter; (action) justifier

**vindictive** [vɪnˈdɪktɪv] adj vindicatif(-ive), rancunier(-ère)

**vine** [vaɪn] n vigne f; (climbing plant) plante grimpante

**vinegar** ['vɪnɪgə*] n vinaigre m

**vineyard** ['vɪnjɑːd] n vignoble m

**vintage** ['vɪntɪdʒ] n (year) année f, millésime m; ~ **car** n voiture f d'époque; ~ **wine** n vin m de grand cru

**viola** [vɪˈəulə] n (MUS) alto m

**violate** ['vaɪəleɪt] vt violer

**violence** ['vaɪələns] n violence f

**violent** ['vaɪələnt] adj violent(e)

**violet** ['vaɪələt] adj violet(te) ♦ n (colour) violet m; (plant) violette f

**violin** [vaɪə'lɪn] n violon m; ~**ist** [vaɪə'lɪnɪst] n violoniste m/f

**VIP** n abbr (= very important person) V.I.P. f

**virgin** ['vɜːdʒɪn] n vierge f ♦ adj vierge

**Virgo** ['vɜːgəu] n la Vierge

**virile** ['vɪraɪl] adj viril(e)

**virtually** ['vɜːtjuəlɪ] adv (almost) pratiquement

**virtual reality** ['vəːtjuəl-] n (COMPUT) réalité virtuelle

**virtue** ['vəːtjuː] n vertu f; (advantage) mérite m, avantage m; **by ~ of** en vertu or en raison de; **virtuous** (-euse)

**virus** ['vaɪərəs] n (COMPUT) virus m

**visa** ['viːzə] n visa m

**visibility** [vɪzɪ'bɪlɪtɪ] n visibilité f

**visible** ['vɪzəbl] adj visible

**vision** ['vɪʒən] n (sight) vue f, vision f (foresight, in dream) vision f

**visit** ['vɪzɪt] n visite f; (stay) séjour m ♦ vt (person) rendre visite à; (place) visiter; **~ing hours** npl (in hospital etc) heures fpl de visite; **~or** n visiteur(-euse); (to one's house) visite f, invité(e); **~or centre** n hall m or centre m d'accueil

**visor** ['vaɪzə] n visière f

**vista** ['vɪstə] n vue f

**visual** ['vɪzjuəl] adj visuel(le); **~ aid** n support visuel; **~ display unit** n console f de visualisation, visuel m; **~ize** vt se représenter, s'imaginer; **~ly-impaired** adj malvoyant(e)

**vital** ['vaɪtl] adj vital(e); (person) plein(e) d'entrain; **~ly** adv (important) absolument; **~ statistics** npl (fig) mensurations fpl

**vitamin** ['vɪtəmɪn] n vitamine f

**vivacious** [vɪ'veɪʃəs] adj animé(e), qui a de la vivacité

**vivid** ['vɪvɪd] adj (account) vivant(e); (light, imagination) vif (vive); **~ly** adv (describe) d'une manière vivante; (remember) de façon précise

**V-neck** ['viːnek] n décolleté m en V

**vocabulary** [vəu'kæbjuləri] n vocabulaire m

**vocal** ['vəukl] adj vocal(e); (articulate) qui sait s'exprimer; **~ cords** npl cordes vocales

**vocation** [vəu'keɪʃən] n vocation f; **~al** adj professionnel(le)

**vociferous** [və'sɪfərəs] adj bruyant(e)

**vodka** ['vɔdkə] n vodka f

**vogue** [vəug] n: **in ~** en vogue f

**voice** [vɔɪs] n voix f ♦ vt (opinion) exprimer, formuler; **~ mail** n (system) messagerie f vocale; (device) boîte f vocale

**void** [vɔɪd] n vide m ♦ adj nul(le); **~ of** vide de, dépourvu(e) de

**volatile** ['vɔlətaɪl] adj volatil(e); (person) versatile; (situation) explosif(-ive)

**volcano** [vɔl'keɪnəu] (pl **~es**) n volcan m

**volition** [və'lɪʃən] n: **of one's own ~** de son propre gré

**volley** ['vɔlɪ] n (of gunfire) salve f; (of stones etc) grêle f, volée f; (of questions) multitude f, série f; (TENNIS etc) volée f; **~ball** n volley(-ball) m

**volt** [vəult] n volt m; **~age** n tension f, voltage m

**volume** ['vɔljuːm] n volume m

**voluntarily** ['vɔləntrɪlɪ] adv volontairement

**voluntary** ['vɔləntərɪ] adj volontaire; (unpaid) bénévole

**volunteer** [vɔlən'tɪə] n volontaire m/f ♦ vi (MIL) s'engager comme volontaire; **to ~ to do** se proposer pour faire

**vomit** ['vɔmɪt] n, vi vomir

**vote** [vəut] n vote m, suffrage m; (cast) voix f, vote; (franchise) droit m de vote ♦ vt (elect): **to be ~d chairman** etc être élu président etc; (propose): **to ~ that** proposer que ♦ vi voter; **~ of thanks** discours m de remerciement; **~r** n électeur(-trice); **voting** n scrutin m, vote m

**voucher** ['vautʃə] n (for meal, petrol, gift) bon m

**vouch for** ['vautʃ-] vt fus se porter garant de

**vow** [vau] n vœu m, serment m ♦ vi jurer

**vowel** ['vauəl] n voyelle f

**voyage** ['vɔɪɪdʒ] n voyage m par mer, traversée f; (by spacecraft) voyage

**vulgar** ['vʌlgə] adj vulgaire

**vulnerable** ['vʌlnərəbl] adj vulnérable

**vulture** ['vʌltʃə] n vautour m

# W, w

**wad** [wɔd] *n* (of cotton wool, paper) tampon *m*; (of banknotes) liasse *f*

**waddle** ['wɔdl] *vi* se dandiner

**wade** [weɪd] *vi*: **to ~ through** marcher dans, patauger dans; (fig: book) s'évertuer à lire

**wafer** ['weɪfəʳ] *n* (CULIN) gaufrette *f*

**waffle** ['wɔfl] *n* (CULIN) gaufre *f*; (inf) verbiage *m*, remplissage *m* ♦ *vi* parler pour ne rien dire, faire du remplissage

**waft** [wɔft] *vt* porter ♦ *vi* flotter

**wag** [wæg] *vt* agiter, remuer ♦ *vi* remuer

**wage** [weɪdʒ] *n* (also: **~s**) salaire *m*, paye *f* ♦ *vt*: **to ~ war** faire la guerre; **~ earner** *n* salarié(e); **~ packet** *n* (enveloppe *f* de) paye *f*

**wager** ['weɪdʒəʳ] *n* pari *m*

**wag(g)on** ['wægən] *n* (horse-drawn) chariot *m*; (BRIT: RAIL) wagon *m* (de marchandises)

**wail** [weɪl] *vi* gémir; (siren) hurler

**waist** [weɪst] *n* taille *f*; **~coat** (BRIT) *n* gilet *m*; **~line** *n* (tour *m* de) taille *f*

**wait** [weɪt] *n* attente *f* ♦ *vi* attendre; **to keep sb ~ing** faire attendre qn; **to ~ for** attendre; **I can't ~ to ...** (fig) je meurs d'envie de ...; **~ behind** *vi* rester (à attendre); **~ on** *vt fus* servir; **~er** *n* garçon *m* (de café), serveur *m*; **~ing** *n*: **"no ~ing"** (BRIT: AUT) "stationnement interdit"; **~ing list** *n* liste *f* d'attente; **~ing room** *n* salle *f* d'attente; **~ress** *n* serveuse *f*

**waive** [weɪv] *vt* renoncer à, abandonner

**wake** [weɪk] (*pt* **woke**, **waked**, *pp* **woken**, **waked**) *vt* (also: **~ up**) réveiller ♦ *vi* (also: **~ up**) se réveiller ♦ *n* (for dead person) veillée *f* mortuaire; (NAUT) sillage *m*

**Wales** [weɪlz] *n* pays *m* de Galles; **the Prince of ~** le prince de Galles

**walk** [wɔ:k] *n* promenade *f*; (short) petit tour; (gait) démarche *f*; (path) chemin *m*; (in park etc) allée ♦ *vi* marcher; (for pleasure, exercise) se promener ♦ *vt* (distance) faire à pied; (dog) promener; **10 minutes' ~ from** à 10 minutes pied de; **from all ~s of life** de toutes conditions sociales; **~ out** *vi* (audience) sortir, quitter la salle; (workers) se mettre en grève; **~ out on** (inf) *vt fus* quitter, plaquer; **~er** *n* (person) marcheur (-euse); **~ie-talkie** *n* talkie-walkie *m*; **~ing** *n* marche *f* à pied; **~ing shoes** *npl* chaussures *fpl* de marche; **~ing stick** *n* canne *f*; **W~man** ® *n* Walkman ® *m*; **~out** *n* (of workers) grève surprise *f*; **~over** (inf) *n* victoire *f* *ou* examen *etc* facile; **~way** *n* promenade *f*

**wall** [wɔ:l] *n* mur *m*; (of tunnel, cave etc) paroi *f*; **~ed** *adj* (city) fortifié(e); (garden) entouré(e) d'un mur, clos(e)

**wallet** ['wɔlɪt] *n* portefeuille *m*

**wallflower** ['wɔ:lflauəʳ] *n* giroflée *f*; **to be a ~** (fig) faire tapisserie

**wallow** ['wɔləu] *vi* se vautrer

**wallpaper** ['wɔ:lpeɪpəʳ] *n* papier peint ♦ *vt* tapisser

**walnut** ['wɔ:lnʌt] *n* noix *f*; (tree, wood) noyer *m*

**walrus** ['wɔ:lrəs] (*pl* **~** *or* **~es**) *n* morse *m*

**waltz** [wɔ:lts] *n* valse *f* ♦ *vi* valser

**wand** [wɔnd] *n* (also: **magic ~**) baguette *f* (magique)

**wander** ['wɔndəʳ] *vi* (person) errer; (thoughts) vagabonder, errer ♦ *vt* errer dans

**wane** [weɪn] *vi* (moon) décroître; (reputation) décliner

**wangle** ['wæŋgl] (BRIT: inf) *vt* se débrouiller pour avoir; carotter

**want** [wɔnt] *vt* vouloir; (need) avoir besoin de ♦ *n*: **for ~ of** par manque de, faute de; **~s** *npl* (needs) besoins *mpl*; **to ~ to do** vouloir faire; **to ~ sb to do** vouloir que qn fasse; **~ed** *adj* (criminal) recherché(e) par la police; **"cook ~ed"** "on recherche un cuisinier"; **~ing** adj: **to be found ~ing** ne pas être à la hauteur

**var** [wɑːʳ] n guerre f; **to make ~ (on)** faire la guerre (à)

**ward** [wɔːd] n (in hospital) salle f; (POL) canton m; (LAW: child) pupille m/f; **~ off** vt (attack, enemy) repousser, éviter

**warden** [ˈwɔːdn] n gardien(ne); (BRIT: of institution) directeur(-trice); (: of: traffic ~) contractuel(le); (of youth hostel) père m or mère f aubergiste

**warder** [ˈwɔːdəʳ] n (BRIT) gardien m de prison

**wardrobe** [ˈwɔːdrəub] n (cupboard) armoire f; (clothes) garde-robe f; (THEATRE) costumes mpl

**warehouse** [ˈwɛəhaus] n entrepôt m

**wares** [wɛəz] npl marchandises fpl

**warfare** [ˈwɔːfɛəʳ] n guerre f

**warhead** [ˈwɔːhɛd] n (MIL) ogive f

**warily** [ˈwɛərɪlɪ] adv avec prudence

**warm** [wɔːm] adj chaud(e); (thanks, welcome, applause, person) chaleureux(-euse); **it's ~** il fait chaud; **I'm ~** j'ai chaud; **~ up** vi (person, room) se réchauffer; (water) chauffer; (athlete) s'échauffer ♦ vt (food) (faire) réchauffer; (faire) chauffer; (engine) faire chauffer; **~-hearted** adj affectueux(-euse); **~ly** adv chaudement; chaleureusement; **~th** n chaleur f

**warn** [wɔːn] vt avertir, prévenir; **to ~ sb (not) to do** conseiller à qn de (ne pas) faire; **~ing** n avertissement m; (notice) avis m; (signal) avertissement m; **~ing light** n avertisseur lumineux; **~ing triangle** n (AUT) triangle m de présignalisation

**warp** [wɔːp] vi (wood) travailler, se déformer ♦ vt (fig: character) pervertir

**warrant** [ˈwɔrənt] n (guarantee) garantie f; (LAW: to arrest) mandat d'arrêt; (: to search) mandat de perquisition; **~y** n garantie f

**warren** [ˈwɔrən] n (of rabbits) terrier m;

(fig: of streets etc) dédale m

**warrior** [ˈwɔrɪəʳ] n guerrier(-ère)

**Warsaw** [ˈwɔːsɔː] n Varsovie f

**warship** [ˈwɔːʃɪp] n navire m de guerre

**wart** [wɔːt] n verrue f

**wartime** [ˈwɔːtaɪm] n: **in ~** en temps de guerre

**wary** [ˈwɛərɪ] adj prudent(e)

**was** [wɔz] pt of **be**

**wash** [wɔʃ] vt laver ♦ vi se laver; (sea): **to ~ over/against sth** innonder/baigner qch ♦ n (clothes) lessive f; (~ing programme) lavage m; (of ship) sillage m; **to have a ~** se laver, faire sa toilette; **to give sth a ~** laver qch; **~ away** vt (stain) enlever au lavage; (subj: river etc) emporter; **~ off** vi partir au lavage; **~ up** vi (BRIT) faire la vaisselle; (US) se débarbouiller; **~able** adj lavable; **~-basin** (US **washbowl**) n lavabo m; **~cloth** (US) n gant m de toilette; **~er** n (TECH) rondelle f, joint m; **~ing** n linge m; (clean) lessive f; **~ing machine** n machine f à laver; **~ing powder** (BRIT) n lessive f (en poudre); **~ing-up** n vaisselle f; **~ing-up liquid** n produit m pour la vaisselle; **~-out** (inf) n désastre m; **~room** (US) n toilettes fpl

**wasn't** [ˈwɔznt] = **was not**

**wasp** [wɔsp] n guêpe f

**wastage** [ˈweɪstɪdʒ] n gaspillage m; (in manufacturing, transport etc) pertes fpl, déchets mpl; **natural ~** départs naturels

**waste** [weɪst] n gaspillage m; (of time) perte f; (rubbish) déchets mpl; (also: household ~) ordures fpl ♦ adj (land, ground: in city) à l'abandon; (leftover): **~ material** déchets mpl ♦ vt gaspiller; (time, opportunity) perdre; **~s** npl (area) étendue f désertique; **~ away** vi dépérir; **~ disposal unit** (BRIT) n broyeur m d'ordures; **~ful** adj gaspilleur(-euse); (process) peu économique; **~ ground** (BRIT) n terrain m vague; **~paper basket** n corbeille f à papier

**watch** [wɔtʃ] n montre f; (act of ~ing)

surveillance f; guet m; (MIL: guards) garde f; (NAUT: guards, spell of duty) quart m ♦ vt (look at) observer; (: match, programme, TV) regarder; (spy on, guard) surveiller; (be careful of) faire attention à ♦ vi regarder; (keep guard) monter la garde; ~ **out** vi faire attention; ~**dog** n chien m de garde; (fig) gardien(ne); ~**ful** adj attentif(-ive), vigilant(e); ~**maker** n horloger(-ère); ~**man** (irreg) n see **night**; ~**strap** n bracelet m de montre

**water** ['wɔːtəʳ] n eau f ♦ vt (plant, garden) arroser ♦ vi (eyes) larmoyer; (mouth): **it makes my mouth ~** j'en ai l'eau à la bouche; **in British ~s** dans les eaux territoriales britanniques; ~ **down** vt (milk) couper d'eau; (fig: story) édulcorer; ~**colour** (US **watercolor**) n aquarelle f; ~**cress** n cresson m (de fontaine); ~**fall** n chute f d'eau; ~ **heater** n chauffe-eau m; ~**ing can** n arrosoir m; ~ **lily** n nénuphar m; ~**line** n (NAUT) ligne f de flottaison; ~**logged** adj (ground) détrempé(e); ~ **main** n canalisation f d'eau; ~**melon** n pastèque f; ~**proof** adj imperméable; ~**shed** n (GEO) ligne f de partage des eaux; (fig) moment m critique, point décisif; ~**skiing** n ski m nautique; ~**tight** adj étanche; ~**works** n (building) station f hydraulique; ~**y** adj (coffee, soup) trop faible; (eyes) humide, larmoyant(e)

**watt** [wɔt] n watt m

**wave** [weɪv] n vague f; (of hand) geste m, signe m; (RADIO) onde f; (in hair) ondulation f ♦ vi faire signe de la main; (flag) flotter au vent; (grass) ondoyer ♦ vt (handkerchief) agiter; (stick) brandir; ~**length** n longueur f d'ondes

**waver** ['weɪvəʳ] vi vaciller; (voice) trembler; (person) hésiter

**wavy** ['weɪvɪ] adj (hair, surface) ondulé(e); (line) onduleux(-euse)

**wax** [wæks] n cire f; (for skis) fart m ♦ vt cirer; (car) lustrer; (skis) farter ♦ vi (moon) croître; ~**works** npl personnages mpl de cire ♦ n musée m de cire

**way** [weɪ] n chemin m, voie f; (distance) distance f; (direction) chemin, direction f; (manner) façon f, manière f; (habit) habitude f, façon; **which ~? - this ~** par où? - par ici; **on the ~** (en route) en route; **to be on one's ~** être en route; **to go out of one's ~ to do** (fig) se donner du mal pour faire; **to be in the ~** bloquer le passage; (fig) gêner; **to lose one's ~** perdre son chemin; **under ~** en cours; **in a ~** dans un sens; **in some ~s** à certains égards; **no ~!** (inf) pas question!; **by the ~ ...** à propos ...; "**~ in**" (BRIT) "entrée"; "**~ out**" (BRIT) "sortie"; **the ~ back** chemin du retour; "**give ~**" (BRIT: AUT) "cédez le passage"; ~**lay** (irreg) vt attaquer

**wayward** ['weɪwəd] adj capricieux(-euse), entêté(e)

**W.C.** n abbr w.c. mpl, waters mpl

**we** [wiː] pl pron nous

**weak** [wiːk] adj faible; (health) fragile; (beam etc) peu solide; ~**en** vi faiblir, décliner ♦ vt affaiblir; ~**ling** n (physically) gringalet m; (morally etc) faible m/f; ~**ness** n faiblesse f; (fault) point m faible; **to have a ~ness for** avoir un faible pour

**wealth** [welθ] n (money, resources) richesse f(pl); (of details) profusion f; ~**y** adj riche

**wean** [wiːn] vt sevrer

**weapon** ['wepən] n arme f

**wear** [weəʳ] (pt **wore**, pp **worn**) n (use) usage m; (deterioration through use) usure f; (clothing): **sports/babywear** vêtements mpl de sport/pour bébés ♦ vt (clothes) porter; (put on) mettre; (damage: through use) user ♦ vi (last) faire de l'usage; (rub etc through) s'user; ~ **town/evening** ~ tenue f de ville/de soirée; ~ **away** vt user, ronger ♦ vi s'effacer; ~ **down** vt (strength, person) épuiser; ~ **off** vi disparaître; ~ **out** vt user; (person, strength) épuiser; ~ **and tear** n usure f

**eary** ['wɪərɪ] adj (tired) épuisé(e); (dispirited) (en la lasse), abattu(e) ♦ vi: **to ~ of** se lasser de

**easel** ['wi:zl] n (ZOOL) belette f

**eather** ['weðəᵊ] n temps m ♦ vt (tempest, crisis) essuyer, réchapper à, survivre à; **under the ~** (fig: ill) mal fichu(e); **~-beaten** adj (person) hâlé(e); (building) dégradé(e) par les intempéries; **~cock** n girouette f; **~ forecast** n prévisions fpl météorologiques, météo f; **~ man** (irreg) (inf) météorologue m; **~ vane** n weathercock

**eave** [wi:v] (pt **wove**, pp **woven**) vt (cloth) tisser; (basket) tresser; **~r** n tisserand(e)

**eb** [web] n (of spider) toile f; (on foot) palmure f; (fabric, also fig) tissu m; **the (World Wide) W~** le Web

**ebsite** ['websaɪt] n (COMPUT) site m Web

**ed** [wed] (pt, pp **wedded**) vt épouser ♦ vi se marier

**e'd** [wi:d] = **we had; we would**

**edding** ['wedɪŋ] n mariage m; **silver/ golden ~ (anniversary)** noces fpl d'argent/d'or; **~ day** n jour m du mariage; **~ dress** n robe f de mariée; **~ ring** n alliance f

**edge** [wedʒ] n (of wood etc) coin m, cale f; (of cake) part f ♦ vt (fix) caler; (pack tightly) enfoncer

**Wednesday** ['wednzdɪ] n mercredi m

**ee** [wi:] (SCOTTISH) adj (tout(e)) petit(e)

**eed** [wi:d] n mauvaise herbe ♦ vt désherber; **~killer** n désherbant m; **~y** adj (man) gringalet

**eek** [wi:k] n semaine f; **a ~ today/on Friday** aujourd'hui/vendredi en huit; **~day** n jour m de semaine; (COMM) jour ouvrable; **~end** n week-end m; **~ly** adv une fois par semaine, chaque semaine ♦ adj hebdomadaire

**eep** [wi:p] (pt, pp **wept**) vi (person) pleurer; **~ing willow** n saule pleureur

**eigh** [weɪ] vt, vi peser; **to ~ anchor** lever l'ancre; **~ down** vt (person, ani-

mal) écraser; (fig: with worry) accabler; **~ up** vt examiner

**weight** [weɪt] n poids m; **to lose/put on ~** maigrir/grossir; **~ing** (allowance) indemnité f, allocation f; **~lifter** n haltérophile m; **~lifting** n haltérophilie f; **~y** adj lourd(e); (important) de poids, important(e)

**weir** [wɪəᵊ] n barrage m

**weird** [wɪəd] adj bizarre

**welcome** ['welkəm] adj bienvenu(e) ♦ n accueil m ♦ vt accueillir; (also: **bid ~**) souhaiter la bienvenue à; (be glad of) se réjouir de; **thank you - you're ~!** merci - de rien or il n'y a pas de quoi!

**welder** [weldəᵊ] n soudeur(-euse)

**welfare** ['welfɛəᵊ] n (wellbeing) bienêtre m; (social aid) assistance sociale; **~ state** n État-providence m

**well** [wel] n puits m ♦ adv bien ♦ adj: **to be ~** aller bien ♦ excl eh bien!; (relief also) bon!; (resignation) enfin!; **as ~** aussi, également; **as ~ as** en plus de; **~ done!** bravo!; **get ~ soon** remets-toi vite!; **to do ~** bien réussir; (business) prospérer; **~ up** vi monter

**we'll** [wi:l] = **we will; we shall**

**well: ~-behaved** adj sage, obéissant(e); **~-being** n bien-être m; **~-built** adj (person) bien bâti(e); **~-deserved** adj (bien) mérité(e); **~-dressed** adj bien habillé(e); **~-heeled** (inf) adj (wealthy) nanti(e)

**wellingtons** ['welɪŋtənz] npl (also: **wellington boots**) bottes fpl de caoutchouc

**well: ~-known** adj (person) bien connu(e); **~-mannered** adj bien élevé(e); **~-meaning** adj bien intentionné(e); **~-off** adj aisé(e); **~-read** adj cultivé(e); **~-to-do** adj aisé(e); **~-wishers** npl amis mpl et admirateurs mpl; (friends) amis mpl

**Welsh** [welʃ] adj gallois(e) ♦ n (LING) gallois m; **the ~** npl (people) les Gallois mpl; **~ Assembly** n Parlement m gallois; **~man** (irreg) n Gallois m;

**~woman** *(irreg)* *n* Galloise *f*
**went** [wɛnt] *pt of* **go**
**wept** [wɛpt] *pt, pp of* **weep**
**were** [wəːʳ] *pt of* **be**
**we're** [wɪəʳ] = **we are**
**weren't** [wəːnt] = **were not**

**west** [wɛst] *n* ouest *m* ♦ *adj* ouest *inv*,
de *or* à l'ouest ♦ *adv* à *or* vers l'ouest;
**the W~** l'Occident *m*, l'Ouest; **the W~**
**Country** *(BRIT)* ♦ *n* le sud-ouest de l'Angleterre; **~erly** *adj (wind)* d'ouest;
*(point)* à l'ouest; **~ern** *adj* occidental(e),
de *or* à l'ouest ♦ *n (CINEMA)* western *m*;
**W~ Indian** *adj* antillais(e) ♦ *n* An-
tillais(e); **W~ Indies** *npl* Antilles *fpl*;
**~ward(s)** *adv* vers l'ouest

**wet** [wɛt] *adj* mouillé(e); *(damp)* humide; *(soaked)* trempé(e); *(rainy)*
pluvieux(-euse) ♦ *n (BRIT: POL)* modéré
*m* du parti conservateur; **to get ~** se
mouiller; **"~ paint"** "attention peinture fraîche"; **~ suit** *n* combinaison *f* de
plongée

**we've** [wiːv] = **we have**

**whack** [wæk] *vt* donner un grand coup
à

**whale** [weɪl] *n (ZOOL)* baleine *f*

**wharf** [wɔːf] *(pl* **wharves**) *n* quai *m*

KEYWORD

**what** [wɔt] *adj* quel(le); **what size is**
**he?** quelle taille fait-il?; **what colour is**
**it?** de quelle couleur est-ce?; **what**
**books do you need?** quels livres vous
faut-il?; **what a mess!** quel désordre!
♦ *pron* 1 *(interrogative)* que, prep +quoi;
**what are you doing?** que faites-
vous?, qu'est-ce que vous faites?; **what**
**is happening?** qu'est-ce qui se passe?,
que se passe-t-il?; **what are you talk-**
**ing about?** de quoi parlez-vous?;
**what is it called?** comment est-ce
que ça s'appelle?; **what about me?** et
moi?; **what about doing ...?** et si on
faisait ...?

2 *(relative: subject)* ce qui; *(: direct object)* ce que; *(: indirect object)* ce +prep

+quoi, ce dont; **I saw what you di**
**was on the table** j'ai vu ce que vo
avez fait/ce qui était sur la table; t
me **what you remember** dites-moi
dont vous vous souveniez

♦ *excl (disbelieving)* quoi!, comment!

**whatever** [wɔtˈɛvəʳ] *adj:* **~ book** qu
que soit le livre qu'il *(ou* qu'i) +subr; n'i
porte quel livre ♦ *pron:* **do ~ is nece**
**sary** faites *(tout)* ce qui est nécessair
**~ happens** quoi qu'il arrive; **no re**
**son ~** pas la moindre raison; **nothin**
**~** rien du tout

**whatsoever** [wɔtsəʊˈɛvəʳ] *adj =* **what**
**ever**

**wheat** [wiːt] *n* blé *m*, froment *m*

**wheedle** [ˈwiːdl] *vt:* **to ~ sb into**
**doing sth** cajoler *or* enjôler qn pou
qu'il fasse qch; **to ~ sth out of sb** o
tenir qch de qn par des cajoleries

**wheel** [wiːl] *n* roue *f*; *(also:* **steering** ·
volant *m*; *(NAUT)* gouvernail *m* ♦ *v*
*(pram etc)* pousser ♦ *vi (birds)* tou
noyer; *(also:* **~ round:** *person)* virevol
ter; **~barrow** *n* brouette *f*; **~chair**
fauteuil roulant; **~ clamp** *n (AUT)* sabo
*m* (de Denver)

**wheeze** [wiːz] *vi* respirer bruyamment

KEYWORD

**when** [wɛn] *adv* quand; **when did h**
**go?** quand est-ce qu'il est parti?

♦ *conj* 1 *(at, during, after the time tha*
quand, lorsque; **she was readin**
**when I came in** elle lisait quand *ou*
lorsque je suis entré

2 *(on, at which)* où; **on the day when**
**met him** le jour où je l'ai rencontré

3 *(whereas)* alors que; **I thought I wa**
**wrong when in fact I was right** j'a
cru que j'avais tort alors qu'en fait
j'avais raison

**whenever** [wɛnˈɛvəʳ] *adv* quand donc
♦ *conj* quand; *(every time that)* chaque
fois que

**here** [weə<sup>r</sup>] *adv, conj* où; **this is ~**
'est là que; **~abouts** ['weərəbauts]
*adv* où donc ♦ *n*: **nobody knows his
~abouts** personne ne sait où il se trou-
e; **~as** [weər'æz] *conj* alors que; **~by**
du par lequel (or laquelle *etc*); **~ver**
weər'evə<sup>r</sup>] *adv* où donc ♦ *conj* où
sub; **~withal** ['weəwiðɔ:l] *n* moyens
pl

**hich** [witʃ] *adj* (*interrogative: direct, indirect*) quel(le); **which picture do you
want?** quel tableau voulez-vous?;
**which one?** lequel (laquelle)?; **in
which case** auquel cas
♦ *pron* **1** (*interrogative*) lequel (laquelle),
esquels (lesquelles) *pl*; **I don't mind
which** peu importe lequel; **which (of
these) are yours?** lesquels sont à
ous?; **tell me which you want** dites-
dites-moi lesquels or ceux que vous
oulez
**2** (*relative: subject*) qui; (: *object*) que,
rep +lequel (laquelle); **the apple
which you ate/which is on the table
** la pomme que vous avez mangée/qui
est sur la table; **the chair on which
you are sitting** la chaise sur laquelle
vous êtes assis; **the book of which
you spoke** le livre dont vous avez par-
é; **he knew, which is true/I feared it
** he savait, ce qui est vrai/ce que je crai-
gnais; **after which** après quoi

**hichever** [witʃ'evə<sup>r</sup>] *adj*: **take ~
book you prefer** prenez le livre que
vous préférez, peu importe lequel; **~
book you take** quel que soit le livre
que vous prenez

**hile** [wail] *n* moment *m* ♦ *conj* pendant que; (*as long as*) tant que;

(*whereas*) alors que; bien que +*sub*; **for
a ~** pendant quelque temps; **~ away**
*vt* (*time*) (faire) passer
**whim** [wim] *n* caprice *m*
**whimper** ['wimpə<sup>r</sup>] *vi* geindre
**whimsical** ['wimzikəl] *adj* (*person*)
capricieux(-euse); (*look, story*) étrange
**whine** [wain] *vi* gémir, geindre
**whip** [wip] *n* fouet *m*; (*for riding*) cravache *f*; (POL: *person*) chef *m* de file assurant la
discipline dans son groupe parlementaire
♦ *vt* fouetter; (*eggs*) battre; **~ped
cream** *n* crème fouettée; **~round**
(BRIT) *n* collecte *f*
**whirl** [wə:l] *vt* tourbillonner; (*dancers*)
tournoyer ♦ *vi* faire tourbillonner; faire
tournoyer; **~pool** *n* tourbillon *m*;
**~wind** *n* tornade *f*
**whirr** [wə:<sup>r</sup>] *vi* (*motor etc*) ronronner;
(: *insect*) vrombir
**whisk** [wisk] *n* (CULIN) fouet *m* ♦ *vt*
fouetter; (*eggs*) battre; **to ~ sb away** or
**off** emmener qn rapidement
**whiskers** ['wiskəz] *npl* (*of animal*)
moustaches *fpl*; (*of man*) favoris *mpl*
**whisky** (IRELAND, US **whiskey**) [wiski] *npl*
whisky *m*
**whisper** ['wispə<sup>r</sup>] *vt, vi* chuchoter
**whistle** ['wisl] *n* (*sound*) sifflement *m*;
(*object*) sifflet *m* ♦ *vi* siffler
**white** [wait] *adj* blanc (blanche); (*with
fear*) blême ♦ *n* blanc *m*; (*person*) blanc
(blanche); **~ coffee** (BRIT) *n* café *m* au
lait, (café) crème *m*; **~collar worker**
*n* employé(e) de bureau; **~ elephant**
*n* (*fig*) objet dispendieux et superflu; **~
lie** *n* pieux mensonge; **W~ Pages** (US)
*npl* (TEL) pages *fpl* blanches; **~ paper** *n*
(POL) livre blanc; **~wash** *vt* blanchir à
la chaux; (*fig*) blanchir ♦ *n* (*paint*) blanc
*m* de chaux
**whiting** ['waitiŋ] *n inv* (*fish*) merlan *m*
**Whitsun** ['witsn] *n* la Pentecôte
**whizz** [wiz] *vi*: **to ~ past** or **by** passer à
toute vitesse; **~ kid** (*inf*) *n* petit prodige
**who** [hu:] *pron* qui; **~dunit** [hu:'dʌnit]
(*inf*) *n* roman policier

**whoever** [huːˈɛvəʳ] *pron:* ~ **finds it** celui (celle) qui le trouve, (qui que ce soit), quiconque le trouve; **ask ~ you like** demandez à qui vous voulez; ~ **he marries** quelle que soit la personne qu'il épouse; ~ **told you that?** qui a bien pu vous dire ça?

**whole** [həʊl] *adj* (complete) entier(-ère), tout(e); (not broken) intact(e), complet(-ète) ♦ *n* (all): **the ~ of** la totalité de, tout(e) le (la); (entire unit) tout *m*; **the ~ of the town** la ville tout entière; **on the ~, as a ~** dans l'ensemble; ~**food:s** *n(pl)* aliments complets; ~**hearted** *adj* sans réserve(s); ~**meal** (BRIT) *adj* (bread, flour) complet(-ète); ~**sale** *n* (vente *f* en): gros *m* ♦ *adj* (price) de gros; (destruction) systématique ♦ *adv* en gros; ~**saler** *n* grossiste *m/f*; ~**some** *adj* sain(e); ~**wheat** *adj* = **wholemeal**; **wholly** [ˈhəʊlɪ] *adv* entièrement, tout à fait

KEYWORD

**whom** [huːm] *pron* **1** (interrogative) qui; **whom did you see?** qui avez-vous vu?; **to whom did you give it?** à qui l'avez-vous donné?

**2** (relative) que, qui; **the man whom I saw/to whom I spoke** l'homme que j'ai vu/à qui j'ai parlé

**whooping cough** [ˈhuːpɪŋ-] *n* coqueluche *f*

**whore** [hɔːʳ] (inf: pej) *n* putain *f*

KEYWORD

**whose** [huːz] *adj* **1** (possessive: interrogative): **whose book is this?** à qui est ce livre?; **whose pencil have you taken?** à qui est le crayon que vous avez pris?, c'est le crayon de qui que vous avez pris?; **whose daughter are you?** de qui êtes-vous la fille?

**2** (possessive: relative): **the man whose son you rescued** l'homme dont or de qui vous avez sauvé le fils; **the girl**

**whose sister you were speaking** la fille à la sœur de qui or de laquelle vous parliez; **the woman whose ⊂ was stolen** la femme dont la voiture ⊂ été volée

♦ *pron* à qui; **whose is this?** à qui ceci?; **I know whose it is** je sais à ⊂ c'est

**why** [waɪ] *adv* pourquoi ♦ *excl* eh bie tiens!; **the reason ~** la raison pour quelle; **tell me ~** dites-moi pourqu ~ **not?** pourquoi pas?

**wicked** [ˈwɪkɪd] *adj* mauvais(e), m chant(e); (crime) pervers(e); (mischi vous) malicieux(-euse)

**wicket** [ˈwɪkɪt] *n* (CRICKET) guichet terrain *m* (entre les deux guichets)

**wide** [waɪd] *adj* large; (area, knowledg vaste, très étendu(e); (choice) grand( ♦ *adv*: **to open** ~ ouvrir tout grand; shoot ~ tirer à côté; ~**awake** *adj* bien éveillé(e); ~**ly** *adv* (differing) rac calement; (spaced) sur une gran étendue; (believed) généralement; (tra el) beaucoup; ~**n** *vt* élargir ♦ *vi* s'éla gir; ~ **open** *adj* grand(e) ouvert(e ~**spread** *adj* (belief etc) très répandu(e

**widow** [ˈwɪdəʊ] *n* veuve *f*; ~**ed** *adj* ve (veuve); ~**er** *n* veuf *m*

**width** [wɪdθ] *n* largeur *f*

**wield** [wiːld] *vt* (power) exercer

**wife** [waɪf] (pl **wives**) *n* femme *f*, épou se *f*

**wig** [wɪg] *n* perruque *f*

**wiggle** [ˈwɪgl] *vt* agiter, remuer

**wild** [waɪld] *adj* sauvage; (sea) de chaîné(e); (idea, life) fou (folle); (b haviour) extravagant(e), déchaîné(e); t **make a ~ guess** émettre une hypo thèse à tout hasard; ~**card** *n* (COMPU (caractère *m*) joker *m*; ~**ernes** [ˈwɪldənɪs] *n* désert *m*, région *f* sauva ge; ~**life** *n* (animals) faune *f*; ~**ly** *adv* (behave) de manière déchaînée; (ap plaud) frénétiquement; (hit, guess) a hasard; (happy) follement; ~**s** *npl* (re

*note area)* régions fpl sauvages
**ostiné(e);** *(action)* délibéré(e)

**ill** [wɪl] *(vt: pt, pp* **willed** *) aux vb* 1
*(forming future tense)*: **I will finish it
omorrow** je le finirai demain; **I will
have finished it by tomorrow** j'au-
ai fini d'ici demain; **will you do it? -
 will/no I won't** le ferez-vous? -
ui/non

2 *(in conjectures, predictions)*: **he'll
e'll be there by now** il doit être arri-
é à l'heure qu'il est; **that will be the
ostman** ça doit être le facteur

3 *(in commands, requests, offers)*: **will
ou be quiet!** voulez-vous bien vous
aire!; **will you help me?** est-ce que
ous pouvez m'aider?; **will you have a
up of tea?** voulez-vous une tasse de
hé?; **I won't put up with it!** je ne le
olérerai pas!

♦ *vt:* **to will sb to do** souhaiter ardem-
nent que qn fasse; **he willed himself
o go on** par un suprême effort de vo-
onté, il continua

♦ *n* volonté f; testament m

**illing** ['wɪlɪŋ] *adj* de bonne volonté,
erviable; **he's ~ to do it** il est disposé
 le faire, il veut bien le faire; **~ly** *adv*
olontiers; **~ness** *n* bonne volonté
**illow** ['wɪləu] *n* saule m
**ilpower** ['wɪl'pauə] *n* volonté f
**illy-nilly** ['wɪlɪ'nɪlɪ] *adv* bon gré mal
ré
**ilt** [wɪlt] *vi* dépérir; *(flower)* se faner
**in** [wɪn] *(pt, pp* **won***) n (in sports etc)*
ictoire f ♦ *vt* gagner; *(prize)* remporter;
*popularity)* acquérir ♦ *vi* gagner; **~
ver** *vt* convaincre; **~ round** *(BRIT) vt* =
**win over**
**ince** [wɪns] *vi* tressaillir
**inch** [wɪntʃ] *n* treuil m
**ind**[1] [wɪnd] *n (also MED)* vent *m; (breath)* souffle *m* ♦ *vt (take breath)*

couper le souffle à
**wind**[2] [waɪnd] *(pt, pp* **wound***) vt* enrouler; *(wrap)* envelopper; *(clock, toy)*
remonter ♦ *vi (road, river)* serpenter; **~
up** *vt (clock)* remonter; *(debate)* terminer, clôturer
**windfall** ['wɪndfɔ:l] *n* coup m de chance
**winding** ['waɪndɪŋ] *adj (road)*
sinueux(-euse); *(staircase)* tournant(e)
**wind instrument** ['wɪnd-] *n (MUS)* instrument m à vent
**windmill** ['wɪndmɪl] *n* moulin m à vent
**window** ['wɪndəu] *n* fenêtre *f; (in car,
train, also: ~ pane)* vitre *f; (in shop etc)*
vitrine *f;* **~ box** *n* jardinière *f;* **~ cleaner** *n* (person) laveur(-euse) de vitres; **~
ledge** *n* rebord m de la fenêtre; **~
pane** *n* vitre *f,* carreau *m;* **~-shopping**
*n:* **to go ~-shopping** faire du lèche-
vitrines; **~sill** ['wɪndəusɪl] *n (inside)* appui m de la fenêtre; *(outside)* rebord m
de la fenêtre
**windpipe** ['wɪndpaɪp] *n* trachée f
**wind power** ['wɪnd-] *n* énergie éolien-
ne
**windscreen** ['wɪndskri:n] *n* pare-brise
*m inv;* **~ washer** *n* lave-glace *m inv;* **~
wiper** *n* essuie-glace *m inv*
**windshield** ['wɪndʃi:ld] *(US) n =* **windscreen**
**windswept** ['wɪndswept] *adj* balayé(e)
par le vent; *(person)* ébouriffé(e)
**windy** ['wɪndɪ] *adj* venteux(-euse); **it's
~** il y a du vent
**wine** [waɪn] *n* vin *m;* **~ bar** *n* bar *m* à
vin; **~ cellar** *n* cave *f* à vin; **~ glass** *n*
verre *m* à vin; **~ list** *n* carte *f* des vins;
**~ waiter** *n* sommelier *m*
**wing** [wɪŋ] *n* aile *f;* **~s** *npl (THEATRE)* coulisses *fpl;* **~er** *n (SPORT)* ailier m
**wink** [wɪŋk] *n* clin m d'œil ♦ *vi* faire un
clin d'œil; *(blink)* cligner des yeux
**winner** ['wɪnə] *n* gagnant(e)
**winning** ['wɪnɪŋ] *adj (team)* ga-
gnant(e); *(goal)* décisif(-ive); **~s** *npl*
gains mpl

**winter** ['wɪntə*] n hiver m; **in ~** en hiver; **~ sports** npl sports mpl d'hiver; **wintry** adj hivernal(e)

**wipe** [waɪp] n: to give sth a ~ donner un coup de torchon/de chiffon/ d'éponge à qch ♦ vt essuyer; (erase: tape) effacer; **~ off** vt enlever; **~ out** vt (debt) éteindre, amortir; (memory) effacer; (destroy) anéantir; **~ up** vt essuyer

**wire** ['waɪə*] n fil m (de fer); (ELEC) fil électrique; (TEL) télégramme m ♦ vt (house) faire l'installation électrique de; (also: ~ **up**) brancher; (person: send telegram to) télégraphier à; **~less** (BRIT) n poste m de radio; **wiring** n installation f électrique; **wiry** adj noueux(-euse), nerveux(-euse); (hair) dru(e)

**wisdom** ['wɪzdəm] n sagesse f; (of action) prudence f; **~ tooth** n dent f de sagesse

**wise** [waɪz] adj sage, prudent(e); (remark) judicieux(-euse) ♦ suffix: **...wise: timewise** etc en ce qui concerne le temps etc

**wish** [wɪʃ] n (desire) désir m; (specific desire) souhait m, vœu m ♦ vt souhaiter, désirer, vouloir; **best ~es** (on birthday etc) meilleurs vœux; **with best ~es** (in letter) bien amicalement; **to ~ sb goodbye** dire au revoir à qn; **he ~ed me well** il m'a souhaité bonne chance; **to ~ to do/sb to do** désirer or vouloir faire/que qn fasse; **to ~ for** souhaiter; **~ful** adj: **it's ~ful thinking** c'est prendre ses désirs pour des réalités

**wistful** ['wɪstful] adj mélancolique

**wit** [wɪt] n (gen pl) intelligence f, esprit m; (presence of mind) présence f d'esprit; (wittiness) esprit; (person) homme/femme d'esprit

**witch** [wɪtʃ] n sorcière f; **~craft** n sorcellerie f

─────────────
KEYWORD
─────────────

**with** [wɪð, wɪθ] prep **1** (in the company of) avec; (at the home of) chez; **we stayed with friends** nous avons logé

chez des amis; **I'll be with you in** minute je suis à vous dans un instan **2** (descriptive): **a room with a vi** une chambre avec vue; **the man w the grey hair/blue eyes** l'homme chapeau gris/aux yeux bleus

**3** (indicating manner, means, cau **with tears in my eyes** les larmes yeux; **to walk with a stick** marc avec une canne; **red with anger** ro de colère; **to shake with fear** tremb de peur; **to fill sth with water** rem qch d'eau

**4: I'm with you** (I understand) je v suis; **to be with it** (inf: up-to-date) dans le vent

**withdraw** [wɪθ'drɔː] (irreg) vt ret ♦ vi se retirer; **~al** n retrait m; **symptoms** npl (MED): **to have symptoms** être en état de manq **~n** adj (person) renfermé(e)

**wither** ['wɪðə*] vi (plant) se faner

**withhold** [wɪθ'həuld] (irreg) vt (mon retenir); **to ~ from** (information) cher (à); (permission) refuser (à)

**within** [wɪð'ɪn] prep à l'intérieur ♦ adv à l'intérieur; **~ his reach** à portée; **~ sight of** en vue de; **~ a k metre of** à moins d'un kilomètre de; **the week** avant la fin de la semaine

**without** [wɪð'aut] prep sans; **~ a c** sans manteau; **~ speaking** sans par **to go ~ sth** se passer de qch

**withstand** [wɪθ'stænd] (irreg) vt rési à

**witness** ['wɪtnɪs] n (person) témoi ♦ vt (event) être témoin de; (docume attester l'authenticité de; **to bear (to)** (fig) attester; **~ box** (US witn stand) n barre f des témoins

**witty** ['wɪtɪ] adj spirituel(le), plein(e d'esprit

**wives** [waɪvz] npl of **wife**

**wizard** ['wɪzəd] n magicien m

**wk** abbr = week

**wobble** ['wɔbl] vi trembler; (ch

ranler

**woe** [wəu] n malheur m

**woke** [wəuk] pt of **wake**; **~n** pp of **wake**

**wolf** [wulf] (pl **wolves**) n loup m

**woman** ['wumən] (pl **women**) n femme f; **~ doctor** n femme f médecin; **~ly** adj féminin(e)

**womb** [wu:m] n (ANAT) utérus m

**women** ['wimin] npl of **woman**; **~'s lib** (inf) n MLF m; **W~'s (Liberation) Movement** n mouvement m de libération de la femme

**won** [wʌn] pt, pp of **win**

**wonder** ['wʌndə'] n merveille f, miracle m; (feeling) émerveillement m ♦ vi: **to ~ whether/why** se demander si/pourquoi; **to ~ at** (marvel) s'émerveiller de; **to ~ about** songer à; **it's no ~ that** il n'est pas étonnant que (+sub); **~ful** adj merveilleux(-euse)

**won't** [wəunt] = **will not**

**wood** [wud] n (timber, forest) bois m; **~ed** adj boisé(e); **~en** adj en bois; (fig) raide, inexpressif(-ive); **~pecker** n pic m (oiseau); **~wind** n (MUS): **the ~wind** les bois mpl; **~work** n menuiserie f; **~worm** n ver m du bois

**wool** [wul] n laine f; **to pull the ~ over sb's eyes** (fig) en faire accroire à qn; **~len** (US **woolen**) adj en laine; (industry) lainier(-ère); **~lens** npl (clothes) lainages mpl; **~ly** (US **wooly**) adj laineux(-euse); (fig: ideas) confus(e)

**word** [wə:d] n mot m; (promise) parole f; (news) nouvelles fpl ♦ vt rédiger, formuler; **in other ~s** d'autres termes; **to break/keep one's ~** manquer à sa parole/tenir parole; **~ing** n termes mpl; libellé m; **~ processing** n traitement m de texte; **~ processor** n machine f de traitement de texte

**wore** [wɔ:'] pt of **wear**

**work** [wə:k] n travail m; (ART, LITERATURE) œuvre f ♦ vi travailler; (mechanism) marcher, fonctionner; (plan etc) marcher; (medicine) agir ♦ vt (clay, wood

etc) travailler; (mine etc) exploiter; (machine) faire marcher ou fonctionner; (miracles, wonders etc) faire; **to be out of ~** être sans emploi; **to ~ loose** se défaire, se desserrer; **~ on** vt fus travailler à; (influence) (essayer d')influencer; **~ out** vi (plans etc) marcher ♦ vt (problem) résoudre; (plan) élaborer; **it ~s out at £100** ça fait 100 livres; **~ up** vt: **to get ~ed up** se mettre dans tous ses états; **~able** adj (solution) réalisable; **~aholic** [wə:kə'hɔlik] n bourreau m de travail; **~er** n travailleur(-euse), ouvrier(-ère); **~ experience** n stage m; **~force** n main-d'œuvre f; **~ing class** n classe ouvrière; **~ing-class** adj ouvrier(-ère); **~ing order** n: **in ~ing order** en état de marche; **~man** (irreg) n ouvrier m; **~manship** (skill) n métier m, habileté f; **~s** n (BRIT: factory) usine f ♦ npl (of clock, machine) mécanisme m; **~ sheet** n (for pupil) fiche f d'exercices; (COMPUT) feuille f de programmation; **~shop** n atelier m; **~ station** n poste de travail; **~-to-rule** (BRIT) n grève f du zèle

**world** [wə:ld] n monde m ♦ cpd (champion) du monde; (power, war) mondial(e); **to think the ~ of sb** (fig) ne jurer que par qn; **~ly** adj de ce monde; (knowledgeable) qui a l'expérience du monde; **~-wide** adj universel(le); **W~-Wide Web** n Web m

**worm** [wə:m] n ver m

**worn** [wɔ:n] pp of **wear** ♦ adj usé(e); **~-out** adj (object) complètement usé(e); (person) épuisé(-ète)

**worried** ['wʌrid] adj inquiet(-ète)

**worry** ['wʌri] n souci m ♦ vt inquiéter ♦ vi s'inquiéter, se faire du souci

**worse** [wə:s] adj pire, plus mauvais(e) ♦ adv plus mal ♦ n pire m; **a change for the ~** une détérioration; **~n** vt, vi empirer; **~ off** adj moins à l'aise financièrement; (fig): **you'll be ~ off this way** ça ira moins bien de cette façon

**worship** ['wə:ʃip] n culte m ♦ vt (God

**worst** rendre un culte à; (person) adorer; **Your W~** (BRIT: to mayor) Monsieur le maire; (: to judge) Monsieur le juge

**worst** [wɜːst] adj le (la) pire, le (la) plus mauvais(e) ♦ adv le plus mal ♦ n pire m; **at ~** au pis aller

**worth** [wɜːθ] n valeur f ♦ adj: **to be ~** valoir; **it's ~ it** cela en vaut la peine, ça vaut la peine; **it is ~ one's while (to do)** on gagne (à faire); **~less** adj qui ne vaut rien; **~while** adj (activity, cause) utile, louable

**worthy** [wɜːðɪ] adj (person) digne; (motive) louable; **~ of** digne de

---

KEYWORD

**would** [wʊd] aux vb 1 (conditional tense): **if you asked him he would do it** si vous le lui demandiez, il le ferait; **if you had asked him he would have done it** si vous le lui aviez demandé, il l'aurait fait

2 (in offers, invitations, requests): **would you like a biscuit?** voulez-vous un biscuit?; **would you close the door please?** voulez-vous fermer la porte, s'il vous plaît?

3 (in indirect speech): **I said I would do it** j'ai dit que je le ferais

4 (emphatic): **it WOULD have to snow today!** naturellement il a fallu qu'il neige aujourd'hui! or il fallait qu'il neige aujourd'hui!

5 (insistence): **she wouldn't do it** elle n'a pas voulu or elle a refusé de le faire

6 (conjecture): **it would have been midnight** il devait être minuit

7 (indicating habit): **he would go there on Mondays** il y allait le lundi

**would-be** [wʊdbɪ] (pej) adj soi-disant

**wouldn't** [wʊdnt] = **would not**

**wound**¹ [waʊnd] n blessure f ♦ vt blesser

**wound**² [waʊnd] pt, pp of **wind**²

**wove** [wəʊv] pt of **weave**; **~n** pp of **weave**

**wrap** [ræp] vt (also: ~ **up**) envelopp emballer; (wind) enrouler; **~per** n (B of book) couverture f; (on chocola emballage m, papier m; **~ping pap** (for gift) papier cadeau

**wreak** [riːk] vt: **to ~ havoc (on)** av un effet désastreux (sur)

**wreath** [riːθ] (pl **~s**) n couronne f

**wreck** [rek] n (ship) épave f; (vehic véhicule accidenté; (pej: person) loqu humaine ♦ vt démolir; (fig) briser, r ner; **~age** n débris mpl; (of buildir décombres mpl; (of ship) épave f

**wren** [ren] n (ZOOL) roitelet m

**wrench** [rentʃ] n (TECH) clé f (à écrou (tug) violent mouvement de torsio (fig) déchirement m ♦ vt tirer violen ment sur, tordre; **to ~ sth from** s cher qch à or de

**wrestle** [resl] vi: **to ~ (with sb)** lutt (avec qn); **~r** n lutteur(-euse); **wres ling** n lutte f; (also: **all-in wrestlin** catch m, lutte f libre

**wretched** [retʃɪd] adj misérable; (in maudit(e)

**wriggle** [rɪgl] vi (also: ~ **about**) se to tiller

**wring** [rɪŋ] (pt, pp **wrung**) vt tordr (wet clothes) essorer; (fig): **to ~ sth ou of sb** arracher qch à qn

**wrinkle** [rɪŋkl] n (on skin) ride f; (o paper etc) pli m ♦ vt plisser ♦ vi se pliss ser; **~d** adj (skin, face) ridé(e)

**wrist** [rɪst] n poignet m; **~watch** montre-bracelet f

**writ** [rɪt] n acte m judiciaire

**write** [raɪt] (pt **wrote**, pp **written**) vt, écrire; (prescription) rédiger; **~ down** noter; (put in writing) mettre par écrit; **~ off** (debt) passer aux profits et perte tes; (project) mettre une croix sur; **~ out** vt écrire; ~ **up** vt rédiger; **~-off** perte totale; **~r** n auteur m, écrivain m

**writhe** [raɪð] vi se tordre

**writing** [raɪtɪŋ] n écriture f; (of autho œuvres fpl; **in ~** par écrit; **~ paper**

apier m à lettres

**rong** [rɒŋ] adj (incorrect) faux (fausse); (morally) mauvais(e); (wicked) mal; (unfair) injuste ♦ adv mal ♦ n tort m ♦ vt faire du tort à, léser; **you are ~ to do** tu as tort de le faire; **you are ~ about that, you've got it ~** tu te trompes; **what's ~?** qu'est-ce que ne va pas?; **you've got the ~ number** vous vous êtes trompé de numéro; **to go ~** (person) se tromper; (plan) mal tourner; (machine) tomber en panne; **to be in the ~** avoir tort; **~ful** adj injustifié(e); **~ly** adv mal, incorrectement; **~ side** n (of material) envers m

**rote** [rəut] pt of **write**

**rought iron** [rɔːt-] n fer forgé

**rung** [rʌŋ] pt, pp of **wring**

**t.** abbr = **weight**

**WW** n abbr (= World Wide Web): **the** ~ le Web

# X, x

**mas** ['eksməs] n abbr = **Christmas**
**~ray** ['eksreɪ] n (ray) rayon m X; (photo) radio(graphie) f
**ylophone** ['zaɪləfəun] n xylophone m

# Y, y

**2K** abbr (= year 2000) l'an m 2000
**acht** [jɒt] n yacht m; voilier m; **~ing** n, navigation f de plaisance; **~sman** (irreg) n plaisancier m
**ank** [jæŋk], **Yankee** ['jæŋkɪ] (pej) n Amerloque m/f
**ap** [jæp] vi (dog) japper
**ard** [jɑːd] n (of house etc) cour f; (measure) yard m (= 91,4 cm); **~stick** n (fig) mesure f, critères mpl
**arn** [jɑːn] n fil m; (tale) longue histoire
**awn** [jɔːn] n bâillement m ♦ vi bâiller; **~ing** adj (gap) béant(e)
**d.** abbr = **yard(s)**

**yeah** [jeə] (inf) adv ouais
**year** [jɪəʳ] n an m, année f; **to be 8 ~s old** avoir 8 ans; **an eight-~-old child** un enfant de huit ans; **~ly** adj annuel(le) ♦ adv annuellement
**yearn** [jɜːn] vi: **to ~ for sth** aspirer à qch, languir après qch
**yeast** [jiːst] n levure f
**yell** [jel] vi hurler
**yellow** ['jeləu] adj jaune; **Y~ Pages ®** (BRIT) npl (TEL) pages fpl jaunes
**yelp** [jelp] vi japper, glapir
**yes** [jes] adv oui; (answering negative question) si ♦ n oui m; **to say/answer ~** dire/répondre oui
**yesterday** ['jestədɪ] adv hier ♦ n hier m; **~ morning/evening** hier matin/soir; **all day ~** toute la journée d'hier
**yet** [jet] adv encore; déjà ♦ conj pourtant, néanmoins; **it is not finished ~** ce n'est pas encore fini or toujours pas fini; **the best ~** le meilleur jusqu'ici or jusque-là; **as ~** jusqu'ici, encore
**yew** [juː] n if m
**yield** [jiːld] n production f, rendement m; rapport m ♦ vt produire, rendre, rapporter; (surrender) céder ♦ vi céder; (US: AUT) céder la priorité
**YMCA** n abbr (= Young Men's Christian Association) YMCA m
**yob** [jɔb] (BRIT: inf) n loubar(d) m
**yog(h)urt** ['jəugət] n yaourt m
**yoke** [jəuk] n joug m
**yolk** [jəuk] n jaune m (d'œuf)

KEYWORD

**you** [juː] pron 1 (subject) tu; (polite form) vous; (plural) vous; **you French enjoy your food** vous autres Français, vous aimez bien manger; **you and I will go** toi et moi or vous et moi, nous irons
2 (object: direct, indirect) te, t' +vowel, vous; **I know you** je te or vous connais; **I gave it to you** je vous l'ai donné, je te l'ai donné
3 (stressed) toi; vous; **I told YOU to do it** c'est à toi or vous que j'ai dit de le faire

**4** (after prep, in comparisons) toi; vous; **it's for you** c'est pour toi or vous; **she's younger than you** elle est plus jeune que toi or vous

**5** (impersonal: one) on; **fresh air does you good** l'air frais fait du bien; **you never know** on ne sait jamais

**you'd** [juːd] = you had; you would

**you'll** [juːl] = you will; you shall

**young** [jʌŋ] adj jeune ♦ npl (of animal) petits mpl; (people): **the ~** les jeunes, la jeunesse; **~er** [jʌŋgəʳ] adj (brother etc) cadet(te); **~ster** n jeune m (garçon m); (child) enfant m/f

**your** [jɔːʳ] adj ton (ta), tes pl; (polite form, pl) votre, vos pl; see also **my**

**you're** [juəʳ] = you are

**yours** [jɔːz] pron le (la) tien(ne), les tiens (tiennes); (polite form, pl) le (la) vôtre, les vôtres; **~ sincerely/faithfully/truly** veuillez agréer l'expression de mes sentiments les meilleurs; see also **mine**[1]

**yourself** [jɔːˈsɛlf] pron (reflexive) te; (: polite form) vous; (after prep) toi; vous; (emphatic) toi-même; vous-même; see also **oneself**; **yourselves** pl pron vous; (emphatic) vous-mêmes

**youth** [juːθ] n jeunesse f; (young man: pl ~s) jeune homme m; **~ club** n centre m de jeunes; **~ful** adj jeune; (enthusiasm) de jeunesse, juvénile; **~ hostel** n auberge f de jeunesse

**you've** [juːv] = you have

**YTS** n abbr (BRIT: Youth Training Scheme) ≈ TUC m

**Yugoslav** ['juːgəʊslɑːv] adj yougoslave ♦ n Yougoslave m/f

**Yugoslavia** ['juːgəʊ'slɑːvɪə] n Yougoslavie f

**yuppie** ['jʌpɪ] (inf) n yuppie m/f

**YWCA** n abbr (= Young Women's Christian Association) YWCA m

# Z, z

**zany** ['zeɪnɪ] adj farfelu(e), loufoque

**zap** [zæp] vt (COMPUT) effacer

**zeal** [ziːl] n zèle m, ferveur f; empressement m

**zebra** ['ziːbrə] n zèbre m; **~ crossing** (BRIT) n passage clouté or pour piétons

**zero** ['zɪərəʊ] n zéro m

**zest** [zɛst] n entrain m, élan m; (of orange) zeste m

**zigzag** ['zɪgzæg] n zigzag m

**Zimbabwe** [zɪm'bɑːbwɪ] n Zimbabwe

**Zimmer frame** ['zɪmə-] n déambulateur m

**zinc** [zɪŋk] n zinc m

**zip** [zɪp] n fermeture f éclair ® ♦ vt (also: **~ up**) fermer avec une fermeture éclair ®; **~ code** (US) n code postal; **~per** (US) n = zip

**zit** [zɪt] (inf) n bouton m

**zodiac** ['zəʊdɪæk] n zodiaque m

**zone** [zəʊn] n zone f

**zoo** [zuː] n zoo m

**zoom** [zuːm] vi: **to ~ past** passer en trombe; **~ lens** n zoom m

**zucchini** [zuːˈkiːnɪ] (US) n(pl) courgette(s) f(pl)

# VERB TABLES

*1* Participe présent *2* Participe passé *3* Présent *4* Imparfait *5* Futu Conditionnel *7* Subjonctif présent

**acquérir** *1* acquérant *2* acquis *3* acquiers, acquérons, acquièrent *4* acquérais *5* acquerrai *7* acquière

**ALLER** *1* allant *2* allé *3* vais, vas, va, allons, allez, vont *4* allais *5* irai *6* irais *7* aille

**asseoir** *1* asseyant *2* assis *3* assieds, asseyons, asseyez, asseyent *4* asseyais *5* assiérai *7* asseye

**atteindre** *1* atteignant *2* atteint *3* atteins, atteignons, atteignais *7* atteigne

**AVOIR** *1* ayant *2* eu *3* ai, as, a, avons, avez, ont *4* avais *5* aurai *6* aurais *7* aie, aies, ait, ayons, ayez, aient

**battre** *1* battant *2* battu *3* bats, bat, battons *4* battais *7* batte

**boire** *1* buvant *2* bu *3* bois, buvons, boivent *4* buvais *7* boive

**bouillir** *1* bouillant *2* bouilli *3* bous, bouillons *4* bouillais *7* bouille

**conclure** *1* concluant *2* conclu *3* conclus, concluons *4* concluais *7* conclue

**conduire** *1* conduisant *2* conduit *3* conduis, conduisons *4* conduisais *7* conduise

**connaître** *1* connaissant *2* connu *3* connais, connaît, connaissons *4* connaissais *7* connaisse

**coudre** *1* cousant *2* cousu *3* couds, cousons, cousez, cousent *4* cousais *7* couse

**courir** *1* courant *2* couru *3* cours, courons *4* courais *5* courrai *7* coure

**couvrir** *1* couvrant *2* couvert *3* couvre, couvrons *4* couvrais *7* couvre

**craindre** *1* craignant *2* craint *3*

crains, craignons *4* craignai *7* craigne

**croire** *1* croyant *2* cru *3* croyons, croient *4* croyais *7* cro

**croître** *1* croissant *2* crû, crue, crues *3* croîs, croissons *4* crois *7* croisse

**cueillir** *1* cueillant *2* cueill cueille, cueillons *4* cueillai cueillerai *7* cueille

**devoir** *1* devant *2* dû, due, dues *3* dois, devons, doivent *4* vais *5* devrai *7* doive

**dire** *1* disant *2* dit *3* dis, disons, disent, disait *7* dise

**dormir** *1* dormant *2* dormi *3* d dormons *4* dormais *7* dorme

**écrire** *1* écrivant *2* écrit *3* é écrivons *4* écrivais *7* écrive

**ÊTRE** *1* étant *2* été *3* suis, es, sommes, êtes, sont *4* étais *5* s *6* serais *7* sois, sois, soit, soyez, soient

**FAIRE** *1* faisant *2* fait *3* fais, f fait, faisons, faites, font *4* faisa ferai *6* ferais *7* fasse

**falloir** *2* fallu *3* faut *4* fallait *5* dra *7* faille

**FINIR** *1* finissant *2* fini *3* finis, finit, finissons, finissez, finisser finissais *5* finirai *6* finirai finisse

**fuir** *1* fuyant *2* fui *3* fuis, fuy fuient *4* fuyais *7* fuie

**joindre** *1* joignant *2* joint *3* joignons *4* joignais *7* joigne

**lire** *1* lisant *2* lu *3* lis, lisons *4* l *7* lise

**luire** *1* luisant *2* lui *3* luis, luison luisais *7* luise

**maudire** *1* maudissant *2* maudi

612

audis, maudissons *4* maudissait
maudisse

ntir *1* mentant *2* menti *3* mens,
entons *4* mentais *7* mente

ttre *1* mettant *2* mis *3* mets,
ettons *4* mettais *7* mette

urir *1* mourant *2* mort *3* meurs,
ourons, meurent *4* mourais *5*
ourrai *7* meure

vir *1* naissant *2* né *3* nais, naît,
aissons *4* naissais *7* naisse

rir *1* offrant *2* offert *3* offre, of-
ons *4* offrais *7* offre

RLER *1* parlant *2* parlé *3* parle,
arles, parle, parlons, parlez,
arlent *4* parlais, parlais, parlait,
arlions, parliez, parlaient *5*
arlerai, parleras, parlera, parle-
ons, parlerez, parleront *6* parle-
ais, parlerais, parlerait, parle-
ons, parleriez, parleraient *7*
arle, parles, parle, parlons,
arliez, parlent *impératif* parle!
arlez!

tir *1* partant *2* parti *3* pars,
artons *4* partais *7* parte

ire *1* plaisant *2* plu *3* plais, plaît,
aisons *4* plaisais *7* plaise

uvoir *1* pleuvant *2* plu *3* pleut,
euvent *4* pleuvait *5* pleuvra *7*
euve

urvoir *1* pourvoyant *2* pourvu *3*
ourvois, pourvoyons, pourvoient
pourvoyais *7* pourvoie

uvoir *1* pouvant *2* pu *3* peux,
eut, pouvons, peuvent *4* pouvais *5*
pourrai *7* puisse

endre *1* prenant *2* pris *3* prends,
renons, prennent *4* prenais *7*
renne

évoir *like voir* *5* prévoirai

CEVOIR *1* recevant *2* reçu *3* re-
ois, reçois, reçoit, recevons, rece-
ez, reçoivent *4* recevais *5* rece-
rai *6* recevrais *7* reçoive

RENDRE *1* rendant *2* rendu *3*
rends, rends, rend, rendons,
rendez, rendent *4* rendais *5* ren-
drai *6* rendrais *7* rende

résoudre *1* résolvant *2* résolu *3* ré-
sous, résolvons *4* résolvais *7* résolve

rire *1* riant *2* ri *3* ris, rions *4* riais *7*
rie

savoir *1* sachant *2* su *3* sais, savons, savent *4* savais *5* saurai *7*
sache *impératif* sache, sachons, sa-
chez

servir *1* servant *2* servi *3* sers,
servons *4* servais *7* serve

sortir *1* sortant *2* sorti *3* sors,
sortons *4* sortais *7* sorte

souffrir *1* souffrant *2* souffert *3*
souffre, souffrons *4* souffrais *7*
souffre

suffire *1* suffisant *2* suffi *3* suffis,
suffisons *4* suffisais *7* suffise

suivre *1* suivant *2* suivi *3* suis, sui-
vons *4* suivais *7* suive

taire *1* taisant *2* tu *3* tais, taisons *4*
taisais *7* taise

tenir *1* tenant *2* tenu *3* tiens, te-
nons, tiennent *4* tenais *5* tiendrai
*7* tienne

vaincre *1* vainquant *2* vaincu *3*
vaincs, vainc, vainquons *4*
vainquais *7* vainque

valoir *1* valant *2* valu *3* vaux, vaut,
valons *4* valais *5* vaudrai *7* vaille

venir *1* venant *2* venu *3* viens, ve-
nons, viennent *4* venais *5* viendrai *7* vienne

vivre *1* vivant *2* vécu *3* vis, vivons
*4* vivais *7* vive

voir *1* voyant *2* vu *3* vois, voyons,
voient *4* voyais *5* verrai *7* voie

vouloir *1* voulant *2* voulu *3* veux,
veut, voulons, veulent *4* voulais *5*
voudrai *7* veuille *impératif* veuillez

# VERBES IRRÉGULIERS

| present | pt | pp | present | pt | pp |
|---------|-----|-----|---------|-----|-----|
| arise | arose | arisen | draw | drew | drawn |
| awake | awoke | awaked | dream | dreamed, | dreamed, |
| be (am, is, | was, were | been | | dreamt | dreamt |
| are; being) | | | drink | drank | drunk |
| bear | bore | born(e) | drive | drove | driven |
| beat | beat | beaten | dwell | dwelt | dwelt |
| become | became | become | eat | ate | eaten |
| begin | began | begun | fall | fell | fallen |
| behold | beheld | beheld | feed | fed | fed |
| bend | bent | bent | feel | felt | felt |
| beset | beset | beset | fight | fought | fought |
| bet | bet, | bet, | find | found | found |
| | betted | betted | flee | fled | fled |
| bid | bid, bade | bid, | fling | flung | flung |
| | | bidden | fly (flies) | flew | flown |
| bind | bound | bound | forbid | forbade | for- |
| bite | bit | bitten | | | bidden |
| bleed | bled | bled | forecast | forecast | forecast |
| blow | blew | blown | forget | forgot | forgotten |
| break | broke | broken | forgive | forgave | forgiven |
| breed | bred | bred | forsake | forsook | forsaken |
| bring | brought | brought | freeze | froze | frozen |
| build | built | built | get | got | got, (US) |
| burn | burnt, | burnt, | | | gotten |
| | burned | burned | give | gave | given |
| burst | burst | burst | go (goes) | went | gone |
| buy | bought | bought | grind | ground | ground |
| can | could | (been | grow | grew | grown |
| | | able) | hang | hung, | hung, |
| cast | cast | cast | | hanged | hanged |
| catch | caught | caught | have (has; | had | had |
| choose | chose | chosen | having) | | |
| cling | clung | clung | hear | heard | heard |
| come | came | come | hide | hid | hidden |
| cost | cost | cost | hit | hit | hit |
| creep | crept | crept | hold | held | held |
| cut | cut | cut | hurt | hurt | hurt |
| deal | dealt | dealt | keep | kept | kept |
| dig | dug | dug | kneel | knelt, | knelt, |
| do (3rd | did | done | | kneeled | kneeled |
| person; | | | know | knew | known |
| he/she/it/ | | | lay | laid | laid |
| does) | | | lead | led | led |

614

| present | pt | pp | present | pt | pp |
|---|---|---|---|---|---|
| …n | leant, leaned | leant, leaned | shine | shone | shone |
| …p | leapt, leaped | leapt, leaped | shoot | shot | shot |
| …rn | learnt, learned | learnt, learned | show | showed | shown |
| …ve | left | left | shrink | shrank | shrunk |
| …d | lent | lent | shut | shut | shut |
| … | let | let | sing | sang | sung |
| …(lying) | lay | lain | sink | sank | sunk |
| …ht | lit, lighted | lit, lighted | sit | sat | sat |
| …e | lost | lost | slay | slew | slain |
| …ke | made | made | sleep | slept | slept |
| …y | might | — | slide | slid | slid |
| …ean | meant | meant | sling | slung | slung |
| …eet | met | met | slit | slit | slit |
| …stake | mistook | mistaken | smell | smelt, smelled | smelt, smelled |
| …ow | mowed | mown, mowed | sow | sowed | sown, sowed |
| …ust | (had to) | (had to) | speak | spoke | spoken |
| …y | paid | paid | speed | sped, speeded | sped, speeded |
| …t | put | put | spell | spelt, spelled | spelt, spelled |
| …it | quit, quitted | quit, quitted | spend | spent | spent |
| …ad | read | read | spill | spilt, spilled | spilt, spilled |
| … | rid | rid | spin | spun | spun |
| …de | rode | ridden | spit | spat | spat |
| …ng | rang | rung | split | split | split |
| …e | rose | risen | spoil | spoiled, spoilt | spoiled, spoilt |
| …n | ran | run | spread | spread | spread |
| …w | sawed | sawn | spring | sprang | sprung |
| …y | said | said | stand | stood | stood |
| …e | saw | seen | steal | stole | stolen |
| …ek | sought | sought | stick | stuck | stuck |
| …ll | sold | sold | sting | stung | stung |
| …nd | sent | sent | stink | stank | stunk |
| …t | set | set | stride | strode | stridden |
| …ake | shook | shaken | strike | struck | struck, stricken |
| …all | should | — | strive | strove | striven |
| …ear | sheared | shorn, sheared | swear | swore | sworn |
| …hed | shed | shed | sweep | swept | swept |

| present | pt | pp | present | pt | pp |
|---|---|---|---|---|---|
| swell | swelled | swollen, swelled | wake | woke, waked | woken, waked |
| swim | swam | swum | wear | wore | worn |
| swing | swung | swung | weave | wove, weaved | woven, weaved |
| take | took | taken | | | |
| teach | taught | taught | wed | wedded, wed | wedded, wed |
| tear | tore | torn | | | |
| tell | told | told | weep | wept | wept |
| think | thought | thought | win | won | won |
| throw | threw | thrown | wind | wound | wound |
| thrust | thrust | thrust | wring | wrung | wrung |
| tread | trod | trodden | write | wrote | written |

| NOMBRES | | NUMBERS |
|---|---|---|
| (une) | 1 | one |
| x | 2 | two |
| s | 3 | three |
| tre | 4 | four |
| d | 5 | five |
| | 6 | six |
| t | 7 | seven |
| f | 8 | eight |
| | 9 | nine |
| | 10 | ten |
| e | 11 | eleven |
| ze | 12 | twelve |
| ze | 13 | thirteen |
| torze | 14 | fourteen |
| nze | 15 | fifteen |
| e | 16 | sixteen |
| -sept | 17 | seventeen |
| -huit | 18 | eighteen |
| -neuf | 19 | nineteen |
| gt | 20 | twenty |
| gt et un(une) | 21 | twenty-one |
| gt-deux | 22 | twenty-two |
| nte | 30 | thirty |
| arante | 40 | forty |
| quante | 50 | fifty |
| xante | 60 | sixty |
| xante-dix | 70 | seventy |
| xante et onze | 71 | seventy-one |
| xante-douze | 72 | seventy-two |
| atre-vingts | 80 | eighty |
| atre-vingt-un(-une) | 81 | eighty-one |
| atre-vingt-dix | 90 | ninety |
| atre-vingt-onze | 91 | ninety-one |
| nt | 100 | a hundred |
| nt un(une) | 101 | a hundred and one |
| is cents | 300 | three hundred |
| is cent un(une) | 301 | three hundred and one |
| lle | 1 000 | a thousand |
| million | 1 000 000 | a million |

| | |
|---|---|
| emier(première), 1er | first, 1st |
| uxième, 2e or 2ème | second, 2nd |
| oisième, 3e or 3ème | third, 3rd |
| atrième | fourth, 4th |
| nquième | fifth, 5th |
| xième | sixth, 6th |

# LES NOMBRES

# NUMBERS

| | |
|---|---|
| septième | seventh |
| huitième | eighth |
| neuvième | ninth |
| dixième | tenth |
| onzième | eleventh |
| douzième | twelfth |
| treizième | thirteenth |
| quatorzième | fourteenth |
| quinzième | fifteenth |
| seizième | sixteenth |
| dix-septième | seventeenth |
| dix-huitième | eighteenth |
| dix-neuvième | nineteenth |
| vingtième | twentieth |
| vingt-et-unième | twenty-first |
| vingt-deuxième | twenty-second |
| trentième | thirtieth |
| centième | hundredth |
| cent-unième | hundred-and-first |
| millième | thousandth |

## Les Fractions etc

## Fractions etc

| | |
|---|---|
| un demi | a half |
| un tiers | a third |
| deux tiers | two thirds |
| un quart | a quarter |
| un cinquième | a fifth |
| zéro virgule cinq, 0,5 | (nought) point five, 0.5 |
| trois virgule quatre, 3,4 | three point four, 3.4 |
| dix pour cent | ten per cent |
| cent pour cent | a hundred per cent |

## Exemples

## Examples

| | |
|---|---|
| il habite au dix | he lives at number 10 |
| c'est au chapitre sept | it's in chapter 7 |
| à la page sept | on page 7 |
| il habite au septième (étage) | he lives on the 7th floor |
| il est arrivé (le) septième | he came in 7th |
| une part d'un septième | a share of one seventh |
| échelle au vingt-cinq millième | scale one to twenty-five thousand |

618

| French | English |
|---|---|
| *e heure est-il?* | *what time is it?* |
| *… | *it's …* |
| uit | midnight, twelve p.m. |
| heure (du matin) | one o'clock (in the morning), one (a.m.) |
| heure cinq | five past one |
| heure dix | ten past one |
| heure et quart | a quarter past one, one fifteen |
| heure vingt-cinq | twenty-five past one, one twenty-five |
| heure et demie, une heure nte | half past one, one thirty |
| e heure trente-cinq, deux heu-s moins vingt-cinq | twenty-five to two, one thirty-five |
| x heures moins vingt, une eure quarante | twenty to two, one forty |
| x heures moins le quart, une eure quarante-cinq | a quarter to two, one forty-five |
| ax heures moins dix, une heu-cinquante | ten to two, one fifty |
| di | twelve o'clock, midday, noon |
| x heures (de l'après-midi) | two o'clock (in the afternoon), two (p.m.) |
| t heures (du soir) | seven o'clock (in the evening), seven (p.m.) |
| *uelle heure?* | *at what time?* |
| ninuit | at midnight |
| ept heures | at seven o'clock |
| ns vingt minutes | in twenty minutes |
| y a quinze minutes | fifteen minutes ago |